T0396152

THE OXFORD ENCYCLOPEDIA OF QUEER STUDIES AND COMMUNICATION

EDITORIAL BOARD

Editor in Chief
Isaac West
VANDERBILT UNIVERSITY

Associate Editors
E Cram
UNIVERSITY OF IOWA

Frederik Dhaenens
GHENT UNIVERSITY

Pamela J. Lannutti
WIDENER UNIVERSITY

Gust A. Yep
SAN FRANCISCO STATE UNIVERSITY

THE OXFORD ENCYCLOPEDIA OF QUEER STUDIES AND COMMUNICATION

Isaac West
EDITOR IN CHIEF

VOLUME 2

OXFORD
UNIVERSITY PRESS

OXFORD
UNIVERSITY PRESS

Oxford University Press is a department of the University of Oxford.
It furthers the University's objective of excellence in research, scholarship,
and education by publishing worldwide. Oxford is a registered trade mark of
Oxford University Press in the UK and in certain other countries.

Published in the United States of America by Oxford University Press
198 Madison Avenue, New York, NY 10016, United States of America.

© Oxford University Press 2024

All rights reserved. No part of this publication may be reproduced, stored in a retrieval system, or transmitted, in any form or by any means, without the prior permission in writing of Oxford University Press, or as expressly permitted by law, by license or under terms agreed with the appropriate reprographics rights organization. Inquiries concerning reproduction outside the scope of the above should be sent to the Rights Department, Oxford University Press, at the address above.

You must not circulate this work in any other form and you must impose this same condition on any acquirer

Library of Congress Cataloging-in-Publication Data
Names: West, Isaac, editor.
Title: The Oxford encyclopedia of queer studies and communication /
Isaac West, editor in chief.
Description: New York, NY : Oxford University Press, [2023] |
Series: Oxford research encyclopedia of communication |
Includes bibliographical references and index.
Identifiers: LCCN 2023026346 (print) | LCCN 2023026347 (ebook) |
ISBN 9780190099671 (2 vol. set; hardback) | ISBN 9780190099695 (vol. 1 ; hardback) |
ISBN 9780190099701 (vol. 2 ; hardback) | ISBN 9780190099688 (ebk)
Subjects: LCSH: Gay and lesbian studies. | Queer theory. |
Mass media and gays. | Communication—Study and teaching.
Classification: LCC HQ75.I15 O94 2023 (print) | LCC HQ75.I15 (ebook) |
DDC 306.7601—dc23/eng/20230830
LC record available at https://lccn.loc.gov/2023026346
LC ebook record available at https://lccn.loc.gov/2023026347

Integrated Books International, United States of America

About the *Oxford Research Encyclopedia of Communication*

The *Oxford Encyclopedia of Queer Studies and Communication* is published as part of the *Oxford Research Encyclopedia of Communication*, a dynamic and scholarly digital resource. This online collection of overview articles provides in-depth, foundational essays on both core and emerging topics in communication. All articles are commissioned under the editorial leadership of international experts of the highest caliber and are vetted through rigorous peer review. A living reference work, the online publication is updatable and enriched with crosslinking and multimedia features. The essays are intended for scholars, practitioners, and university-level readers, including advanced undergraduates, graduate students, and researchers.

Oxford Research Encyclopedia of Communication
Editor in Chief: Matthew Powers

Selected print titles from the *Oxford Research Encyclopedia of Communication*:

The Oxford Encyclopedia of Health and Risk Message Design and Processing
Edited by Roxanne L. Parrott

The Oxford Encyclopedia of Intergroup Communication
Edited by Howard Giles and Jake Harwood

The Oxford Encyclopedia of Journalism Studies
Edited by Henrik Örnebring

The Oxford Encyclopedia of Communication and Critical Cultural Studies
Edited by Dana L. Cloud

Contents

List of Articles   ix

Preface (vol. 1)   xv

Acknowledgments (vol. 1)   xix

THE OXFORD ENCYCLOPEDIA OF
QUEER STUDIES AND COMMUNICATION

Directory of Contributors   1263

Index   1269

List of Articles

VOLUME 1

GLOBAL QUEER STUDIES

1. Brazilian Queer Cinema   3
   JOÃO NEMI NETO
2. Chinese Pink Markets   25
   TERRIE SIANG-TING WONG
3. Cultural Productions of Queer Asia   44
   SHINSUKE EGUCHI
4. Queer Migration and Digital Media   64
   ANDREW DJ SHIELD
5. Queer Sexualities in Latin America   76
   HÉCTOR DOMÍNGUEZ-RUVALCABA
6. Spanish Queer Cinema   91
   SANTIAGO FOUZ HERNÁNDEZ
7. Transnational and Queer Diasporic Sexualities   105
   FATIMA ZAHRAE CHRIFI ALAOUI
8. Transnational Queer Translations   117
   AHMET ATAY

KEY TERMS

9. Disidentification — 135
   MEGAN ELIZABETH MORRISSEY
10. Homonormativity — 152
    DAWN MARIE D. MCINTOSH
11. Queer Memory — 168
    THOMAS R. DUNN
12. Queer Perspectives in Communication Studies — 187
    ISAAC WEST
13. Queer Temporalities — 209
    DUSTIN GOLTZ

QUEER HEALTH

14. Crip Theory — 229
    JEFFREY BENNETT
15. HIV/AIDS: The Queer Communication of HIV in the LGBTQ Community — 243
    ANDREW R. SPIELDENNER AND BOLIVAR X. NIETO
16. Queer Healthcare Communication — 259
    NICOLE HUDAK
17. Queer Safer Sex Communication — 276
    KAMI KOSENKO
18. Sexual Orientation and Gender Identity Disclosure in the Medical Context — 295
    L. BROOKE FRILEY AND MARIA K. VENETIS
19. Stress and Coping in Sexual and Gender Minority Relationships — 321
    STEVEN SAMROCK, KAI KLINE, AND ASHLEY K. RANDALL

QUEER IDENTITIES

20. Alternatives to Coming-Out Discourses — 341
    SHUZHEN HUANG
21. Coming Out in Interpersonal and Relational Perspectives — 353
    YACHAO LI
22. Coming Out Narratives in Audiovisual Culture — 366
    PARIS S. CAMERON-GARDOS
23. Gay Aging and Discourses of Future — 385
    DUSTIN GOLTZ
24. Jotería Studies and/in Communication — 400
    LUIS M. ANDRADE
25. Kuaer Theory — 417
    RYAN M. LESCURE
26. LGBTQ+ Workers — 424
    ELIZABETH K. EGER, MORGAN L. LITRENTA,
    SIERRA R. KANE, AND LACE D. SENEGAL

27. Performance of Brown Sexualities ... 457
    SHANE MOREMAN
28. Queer Intercultural Communication: Sexuality and Intercultural Communication ... 471
    TAISHA MCMICKENS, MIRANDA DOTTIE OLZMAN, AND BERNADETTE MARIE CALAFELL
29. Queer Men's Bodies and Digital Media ... 483
    JAMIE HAKIM
30. Transfeminisms ... 496
    DANIEL COLEMAN

QUEER INTIMACIES

31. LGBTQ+ Marriage: Relational Communication Perspectives ... 521
    PAMELA J. LANNUTTI AND HILARY WERMERS
32. Molecular Images, Leaky Masculinities: Pain, Photography, and Queer Desire ... 534
    KATRIN KÖPPERT
33. Relational Communication and Consensual Non-Monogamy ... 552
    VALERIE RUBINSKY AND LUCY C. NIESS
34. Sex Work, Queer Economic Justice, and Communicative Ethics ... 568
    CARLY LEILANI FABIAN
35. Sexual Pleasure in Queer Communication Studies ... 582
    MICHAELA FRISCHHERZ

VOLUME 2

QUEER KINSHIP

36. Divorce and Relational Termination ... 599
    MADELEINE REDLICK HOLLAND AND PAMELA J. LANNUTTI
37. Minority Stress and Relationships ... 613
    ROBERT CARROLL
38. Parenting of Queer Offspring ... 627
    PAMELA J. LANNUTTI AND MARIA BUTAUSKI
39. Queer African Studies ... 637
    GODFRIED ASANTE
40. Queer People's Communication with Families of Origin ... 656
    CIMMIARON ALVAREZ AND KRISTINA M. SCHARP
41. Queer Safe Spaces and Communication ... 674
    LITAL PASCAR, YOSSI DAVID, GILLY HARTAL, AND BRANDON WILLIAM EPSTEIN
42. Queer Worldmaking ... 686
    HAILEY N. OTIS AND THOMAS R. DUNN
43. Queer(ing) Reproductive Justice ... 705
    NATALIE FIXMER-ORAIZ AND SHUI-YIN SHARON YAM

44. Queering the Study of U.S. Military Family Communication — 723
    ERIN SAHLSTEIN PARCELL AND DANIELLE C. ROMO
45. Same-Sex Couple Relationship Maintenance — 734
    STEPHEN M. HAAS
46. Sexual Communication Between Queer Partners — 750
    BRANDON T. PARRILLO AND RANDAL D. BROWN
47. Sexual Satisfaction in LGB Relationships — 756
    MADELEINE REDLICK HOLLAND
48. Social Support and LGBTQ+ Individuals and Communities — 767
    ÁINE M. HUMBLE

QUEER MEDIA

49. African American Queer Cinema — 791
    VICTOR EVANS
50. Agonistic Queer TV Studies for Western Europe — 810
    FLORIAN VANLEE
51. Black Gay Men in Television Comedy — 831
    CAMERON LYNN BROWN AND ALFRED L. MARTIN
52. Gay Pornography — 847
    JOSEPH BRENNAN
53. Homonationalism and Media — 874
    ALEXANDER DHOEST
54. Homonationalism's Viral Travels — 889
    HANA MASRI
55. LGBTQ Youth Cultures and Social Media — 906
    OLU JENZEN
56. LGBTQ+ Epistolary Rhetoric/Letter Writing — 934
    PAMELA VANHAITSMA
57. Media Depictions of Sexual Attitudes — 952
    KEREN EYAL
58. Queer Chinese Media and Pop Culture — 969
    JAMIE J. ZHAO
59. Queer Comics — 991
    KC COUNCILOR
60. Queer Melodrama — 1011
    CORA BUTCHER-SPELLMAN
61. Queer Memory and Film — 1027
    ANAMARIJA HORVAT
62. Queer Music Practices in the Digital Realm — 1042
    BEN DE SMET
63. Queer Production Studies — 1062
    EVE NG

64. Queer(ing) Popular Music Culture — 1075
DORIS LEIBETSEDER
65. Representations of Drag Culture — 1089
NIALL BRENNAN
66. Speculative Fiction and Queer Theory — 1112
WENDY GAY PEARSON

QUEER METHODS

67. Arts-based Queer Communication Studies — 1145
SANDRA L. FAULKNER AND MADISON A. POLLINO
68. Methodological and Statistical Considerations in Studying Sexual Minority and Gender Diverse Relationships — 1162
GABRIEL A. LEÓN AND ASHLEY K. RANDALL
69. Queer Communication Pedagogy — 1185
LORE/TTA LEMASTER
70. Queer Studies and Organizational Communication — 1207
JAMIE MCDONALD AND SEAN C. KENNEY
71. Queer/ing Archives — 1224
MORGAN DICESARE AND CHARLES E. MORRIS
72. Queering Colonialisms and Empire — 1242
ROBERTA CHEVRETTE

Queer Kinship

DIVORCE AND RELATIONAL TERMINATION

INTRODUCTION

As same-gender and queer relationships have become increasingly visible and socially accepted in many cultures around the globe (Pfefffer & Castañeda, 2019; Poushter & Kent, 2020), it has been encouraging to see the flourishing of the discourse devoted to developing a deeper understanding of these relationships in the communication literature. While the growth of knowledge in this field is admirable, it must also be noted that this growth has been uneven, with most scholarly attention focused on the differences between intact relationships involving LGBTQ+ individuals and relationships involving heterosexual individuals (Redlick & Lannutti, 2021). Significantly less attention has been paid to the phenomenon of LGBTQ+ relational dissolution, and, with the legalization of same-gender marriage via *Obergefell v. Hodges* (2015), to LGBTQ+ divorce. While dissolution and divorce exist as possible outcomes of both LGBTQ+ and seemingly heterosexual relationships, there are likely important nuances in these experiences for LGBTQ+ people occasioned by their continued marginalization and stigmatization as sexual minority individuals. This marginalization and stigmatization may be further compounded by the stigma that is applied to unpartnered and divorced individuals (Day, 2013; Day et al., 2011; DePaulo & Morris, 2005; Fisher & Sakaluk, 2020).

As such, the goal of this article is to review the literature that does exist addressing relationship termination and divorce for LGBTQ+ relationships, with special attention given to unique aspects that may arise for LGBTQ+ individuals. The article will begin by reviewing unique factors that may place LGBTQ+ relationships at increased risk of dissolution. Then, attention will be given to experiences of dissolution for LGBTQ+ people and the relationships that ex-partners may develop after romantic relationship dissolution. The article concludes by offering some suggestions for continued growth of this field.

TERMINOLOGY AND SCOPE

This article uses the acronym LGBTQ+ as a shorter version of LGBTQQIPAA, which is used to represent people who identify as lesbian, gay, bisexual, transgender, queer, questioning, intersex, pansexual, asexual, and ally. The article uses LGBTQ+ marriage to indicate legally recognized marriage between two members of the LGBTQ+ community and to distinguish these relationships from legally recognized marriage between two people who are generally assumed to be a heterosexual cisgender man and a heterosexual cisgender woman. Most of the research on LGBTQ+ marriage uses the term "same-sex marriage" to refer to these relationships and in doing so either assumes or assesses that the partners are both cisgender. Therefore, this article indicates when a study had significant participation from transgender or gender nonbinary participants. Most research on LGBTQ+ relationships focuses on couples rather than people in a polyamorous relationship; therefore, the content of this article does so as well.

RISK FACTORS FOR RELATIONSHIP DISSOLUTION

While it would be impossible to comprehensively specify all of the factors that place romantic relationships at risk of dissolution or divorce, there are some factors that may deserve specific attention in LGBTQ+ relationship dissolution. The article begins a review of the existing literature on this topic with the question of who might be at greater or lesser risk for dissolution and/or divorce. It then specifies some specific resource-related factors within LGBTQ+ relationships that may contribute to dissolution and/or divorce, and finally it engages an organizing theory, minority stress, to help understand more about these factors.

GENDER COMPOSITION

One question that research studies have taken up is a question of comparative couple stability: whether some couple types are more or less likely to end in dissolution/divorce. Often, when focusing on LGBTQ+ relationships, researchers have sought to make this assessment of relative risk as determined by the gender composition of individuals in a dyadic romantic relationship. Studies have made comparisons both between cisgender male–cisgender female couples and cisgender same-gender couples, and between cisgender male–male and cisgender female–female couples of different gender compositions (e.g., Allen & Price, 2020; Chen & van Ours, 2020). However, consensus has yet to be reached as to whether the gender composition of a couple (be it composed of cisgender male–cisgender female individuals or cisgender same-gender individuals) plays a consistent role in the likelihood of relational dissolution and/or divorce, with findings oftentimes being heavily influenced by the nature of the sample used in each study (Manning & Joyner, 2019; Reczek, 2020). For example, research has found that the influence of gender composition fluctuates over time, with cisgender male–male couples being more likely to dissolve prior to cohabitation, but cisgender female–female couples being at an elevated risk of dissolution following cohabitation (DeLecce & Wiesfeld, 2016; Joyner et al., 2017). Indeed, in their review of the literature surrounding LGBTQ+ families and relationships, Reczek (2020) suggests that integrating a life-course approach to future studies may help researchers to better understand phenomena such as relational dissolution. A life-course approach recognizes that dissolution/divorce is more than just a moment in time, but rather is the culmination of many experiences and many factors that may be more or less important given individuals' unique histories (Reczek, 2020).

Other studies take a more concrete stance on the role gender composition plays in relationship stability, finding that cisgender same-gender relationships composed of two women are more likely to terminate than those composed of two men (Manning & Joyner, 2019; Petruzzella et al., 2019). However, other reviews of the literature surrounding gender composition suggest that relationships composed of two cisgender women are more protected from dissolution than those between two cisgender men due to greater levels of commitment to establishing emotional intimacy (Allen, 2019), and that higher termination rates of relationships composed of two cisgender women is artifactual of these women formalizing their relationship more frequently than two cisgender men formalize their relationships (Badgett & Mallory, 2014). The question of how gender composition affects the relationships of transgender individuals remains similarly unsettled because of a lack of research on these relationships (Pfeffer & Castañeda, 2019). Thus, while the exact role that gender composition may play in placing relationships at greater or lesser risk for dissolution is still to be determined, there is ample evidence that gender composition does foreground other known risk factors for relationship dissolution, which are reviewed next.

RELATIONAL ARRANGEMENTS: CONSENSUAL NONMONOGAMY AND MARRIAGE

While there are myriad relational arrangements that individuals can choose from for their romantic partnerships, monogamous relationships have long been held up as a heteronormative standard against which all other relationships are judged (also see Day, 2013; Day et al., 2011). Failure to comply with this standard of mononormativity (Pieper & Bauer, 2005) leads individuals to see nonmonogamous relationships as inferior to their monogamous counterparts (Hutzler et al., 2016). However, very little research supports the notion that maintaining monogamy is more beneficial to relationships than engaging in nonmonogamous relationships (Conley et al., 2012). Perhaps in light of this, some LGBTQ+ individuals have rejected mononormativity (Grov et al., 2014; Whitton et al., 2015). As it relates to rejecting mononormativity, this seems to be particularly common in male–male relationships, though women in relationships with women, and individuals in male–female relationships certainly participate as well (Grov et al., 2014; Haupert et al., 2017; Parsons et al., 2012).

Incorporating consensual nonmonogamy into a relationship involves the establishment of rules and boundaries for extradyadic sexual activity, which serve the purpose of clarifying who can be involved in these encounters, and what can be done under what circumstances (Grov et al., 2014; Perry et al., 2015; Van Eeden-Moorefield et al., 2016; Wosick-Correa, 2010). These rules may act as a protective factor for couples integrating consensual nonmonogamy into their relationships, as research finds that those in male–male relationships with consensual nonmonogamy are just as committed and satisfied as their monogamous counterparts (Bonello, 2009; Parsons et al., 2012; Stults, 2019; Whitton et al., 2015). Still, even in the presence of such rules, agreements can be violated, which may lead to relational dissatisfaction, and potentially relational dissolution (Perry et al., 2015).

In addition to the unspoken assumption that monogamous relationships are more successful and stable than those involving consensual nonmonogamy, there is also an assumption that all individuals should and will seek marriage as the end goal of romantic partnerships (DePaulo & Morris, 2005), and that being married is a key to relational longevity. However, this is not necessarily the case for all couples, and once again, the role of gender composition complicates this assumption. While LGBTQ+ people who marry do generally have greater stability than those couples who do not marry, this effect is stronger for cisgender male–male couples than cisgender female–female couples (Chen & van Ours, 2020; Lev, 2004).

Additionally, other studies have found that cisgender female–female couples who formalize their relationships are in fact elevating their risk of dissolution (Ketcham & Bennett, 2019). Still complicating the myth of marriage as an essential stabilizing force is the finding that formalizing relationships plays less of a role in determining relational stability in LGBTQ+ relationships than it does in cisgender male–female relationships (Marteau & Dutreuilh, 2019). Again, there is conflicting evidence about the role that marriage plays in contributing to or protecting against dissolution and/or divorce, given that a different study found that legally recognized LGBTQ+ couples were no more likely than legally recognized cisgender male–female couples to dissolve (Joyner et al., 2017). Thus, while the existing body of knowledge suggests that different relational arrangements (i.e., marriage and consensual nonmonogamy) do have a role to play in understanding LGBTQ+ relational dissolution and divorce, the nature of that role is not yet clear.

RESOURCES

Regardless of the relational arrangement that LGBTQ+ individuals choose, there are additional risk factors that arise from the material resources available to the couple and how those resources are spent within the relationship. Some studies have suggested that cisgender same-gender couples may enjoy elevated levels of relational satisfaction when compared to cisgender male–female couples as a result of a more equitable division of labor, both related to emotional and physical tasks (Carlson et al., 2016; Cooke, 2006; Kim & Stein, 2019 for a comprehensive review; Umberson et al., 2015). This increased relational satisfaction may well contribute to relational stability. However, this commitment to egalitarianism may not translate outside the home, in that gender-based disparities in wages may introduce a unique and meaningful amount of financial strain and stress into cisgender female–female relationships (Goldberg et al., 2015; Ketcham & Bennett, 2019). Indeed, data from the 2016 US Census confirms that couples who identified as male–male are, on average, better off economically than couples who identified as female–female. Adding this layer of economic stress into female–female relationships may be a contributing factor to an observed elevated rate of dissolution in female–female relationships (Allen & Goldberg, 2020; Balsam et al., 2017). Economic stress may also affect partnerships of transgender people in the form of discrimination in employment directed toward trans individuals, as evidenced by the disproportionate rates of un(der)employment and homelessness in this population (Bethea & McCollum, 2013; Lenning & Buist, 2013; Pyne et al., 2015). Furthermore, the cost of hormonal therapies or other gender affirming medical interventions may drain the financial resources of transgender people, introducing another form of stress unique to their relationships. The process of transitioning may also bring about stress associated with the need to renegotiate sexual intimacy as body parts and preferences change and couples find themselves unable to rely on the resource of knowledge gained from previous sexual encounters (Pfeffer & Castañeda, 2019). Individuals in trans partnerships also frequently face a loss of emotional and material resources connected to rejection from their own families (Bethea & McCollum, 2013; Devor, 2004; Lev, 2004; Riggs et al., 2015).

Another place in which resources coming from outside of the couple may be lacking is in regard to support for LGBTQ+ parents. Reczek's (2020) review of LGBTQ+ families highlighted the general consensus among researchers that these families involving children (biological or otherwise) consistently receive less institutional and social support than the families of cisgender male–female couples with children. Again, this lack of resources, both formal and social, may contribute to elevated levels of stress that place LGBTQ+ families, and specifically families with children, at a greater risk for instability and potentially dissolution (Allen & Price, 2020).

MINORITY STRESS

In reviewing the aforementioned literature, one might note that there are multiple sources of stress that uniquely impact those in LGBTQ+ relationships (e.g., mononormativity, wage discrimination, lack of social support). The role that stresses unique to sexual minorities (as well as other minority populations) plays in relationships was articulated by Meyer (2003), in minority stress theory, which is the dominant theory that has been used to examine LGBTQ+ relational dissolution (Farr et al., 2020). This theory suggests that individuals in LGBTQ+ relationships may come to experience heightened levels of stress as a result of (1) objectively stressful external events; (2) expectations that these aforementioned events may occur, and a vigilance toward detecting them; and (3) internalized homophobia, which is the personal endorsement of negative attitudes toward LGBTQ+ people by a member of that population (Meyer, 2003). While the overall experience of minority stress has been related to decrements in relationship length and quality (Doyle & Molix, 2015, 2014a, 2014b, 2014c), internalized homophobia may be of particular importance when considering relational dissolution risk factors. Individuals who have higher degrees of internalized homophobia tend to evince lower levels of "outness," or disclosiveness about their sexual orientation (Vale & Bisconti, 2021a). This lower level of "outness" has in turn been linked to lower levels of relational satisfaction (Ballester et al., 2021; Vale & Bisconti, 2021b), which may also contribute to increased risk of relational dissolution. Higher levels of internalized homophobia have also been associated with reports of increased conflict severity and decreased relationship quality (Totenhagen et al., 2018). Managing internalized homophobia and its impact within couples has been identified as an integral part of developing resilience to stress in LGBTQ+ couples (Song et al., 2021).

Beyond individual experiences, individuals in LGBTQ+ relationships may also experience couple-level stressors, which are events that couple experiences together, rather than events that an individual in a relationship may experience on their own (Frost et al., 2017). One example of a couple-level stressor was the previous unequal recognition of LGBTQ+ marriages across different states, and indeed, even in different counties within states. Research found that exposure to discourse about state-level bans on same-gender marriages was associated with decreased mental health (Fingerhut et al., 2011; Frost & Fingerhut, 2016; Maisel & Fingerhut, 2011). More recently, Frost and LeBlanc (2019) have suggested that these couple-level stressors may place same-gender relationships at a greater risk of dissolution. Recent research has suggested that this couple-level stress affects individuals in trans partnerships as well (Dierckx et al., 2016; Gamarel et al., 2014; Schilt & Westbrook, 2009; Westbrook & Schilt, 2014).

Another pertinent stressor for sexual minority couples is related to the phenomenon of the "model minority," which suggests that individuals of a given minority group must present themselves as "perfect" or "poster children" in order to gain acceptance from dominant groups. Studies have suggested that individuals in LGBTQ+ relationships feel this demand for perfection, and that this makes experiences of dissolution more painful and harder to cope with if it does occur (Allen, 2019; Allen & Goldberg, 2021; Lavner, 2017). Taken as a whole, research suggests that the experiences associated with sexual minority stress, both at the individual and couple level may place relationships at a higher risk of dissolution (Frost & LeBlanc, 2019; Otis et al., 2006). Having now reviewed many of the factors that may lead individuals in LGBTQ+ relationships to be more likely to experience dissolution, we turn to reviewing literature examining experiences during and after dissolutions of relationships.

EXPERIENCES OF RELATIONSHIP DISSOLUTION

When considering the experiences of relationship dissolution for LGBTQ+ people, it is important to consider the degree to which couples formalized their relationship. The institutionalization of same-sex relationships involves both legalization (e.g., marriage certificates, licenses) and ritualization (e.g., ceremonies, family traditions, rings), and the level of institutionalization for a given relationship may vary (Oswald & Clausell, 2006). It is important to understand that even when legally married, an LGBTQ+ couple may not be institutionalized to the same degree as their heterosexual counterparts because legal marriage does not automatically equate to the support and acceptance needed for many forms of ritualization. Further, legal LGBTQ+ marriage may not include important rights such as parental protections (Lannutti, 2014; Oswald & Clausell, 2006) and laws protecting LGBTQ+ marriage are often contested or in flux. Individuals in same-sex relationships have reported that navigating evolving and shifting laws regarding dissolving a civil union constitute a "legal nightmare" (Balsam et al., 2017, p. 12). Thus, legal marriage may be an important factor when considering the dissolution of same-sex relationships, and research supports this notion.

Hoy (2018) interviewed a small sample of LGBTQ+ individuals who divorced after being legally married to a same-sex partner and found that those who divorced a same-sex partner felt there was a lack of awareness of same-sex divorce within the LGBTQ+ community and beyond. This lack of awareness translated to divorced individuals feeling unsupported because the seriousness of divorce was not widely understood or recognized (Balsam et al., 2017; Hoy, 2018). Those experiencing same-sex divorce often had to explain and justify their divorce to others during uncomfortable interactions, which led to divorced individuals withdrawing from social interactions (Hoy, 2018). These uncomfortable experiences have been reported on in detail by women. Balsam et al. (2017) found that women reported experiencing shame and guilt after a same-sex divorce because they felt they had to overcome many challenges to get married in the first place and now were voluntarily exiting their relationships (Balsam et al., 2017). Further, Allen and Goldberg (2020) found that divorced lesbian mothers had to contend with gendered heteronormative expectations, including the ideas that couples should stay together for the sake of children and that divorce is bad for children even when they ultimately believed that their divorce was better for them and their children.

Hoy (2019) also examined the explanations, or accounts, that LGBTQ+ people shared when discussing their divorce. LGBTQ+ divorced individuals used two kinds of accounts: (1) Relationship-focused accounts, which explained how the relationship failed; and (2) self-focused accounts, which explained that the marriage had a negative effect on the divorced person (Hoy, 2019). Hoy (2019) argued that by using both relationship-focused and self-focused accounts of divorce, LGBTQ+ divorced individuals showed that they endorsed two common ways of framing marriage: (1) the individualized model of marriage (associated with self-focused accounts) and (2) the companionate model of marriage (associated with relationship-focused accounts). Hoy (2019) showed not only that LGBTQ+ divorced individuals understood marriage and its dissolution in ways consistent with existing models of the meaning of marriage, but that the understanding of a marriage, and subsequently a divorce, may significantly differ from the understanding of a non-marital same-sex relationship and dissolution. Said another way, this study established that the dissolution of a same-sex marriage may differ meaningfully from a break-up, the dissolution of a civil union, or other ritualized but not legalized partnership. Relationship-focused themes of divorce accounts identified by Hoy (2019) are similar to those found by Bacon (2012), who examined lesbians' accounts of their divorce. Bacon (2012) found that lesbian divorce stories were characterized by favoring supportive language over adversarial language, using vocabulary of family to describe ex-spouses, and using a language of fairness to describe their divorce.

RELATIONSHIPS AFTER ROMANTIC RELATIONSHIP DISSOLUTION

Just because a relationship goes through a divorce does not mean that relationship is "over." Indeed, research suggests that a social norm to remain connected to a former partner after a romantic relationship ends may be particularly salient for LGBTQ+ people (Lannutti & Cameron, 2002; Weston, 1991). In support of this notion, Allen and Goldberg (2020) interviewed divorced lesbian mothers and identified the idea that lesbian ex-lovers should be lifelong friends as a key cultural discourse. This social norm may result in LGBTQ+ individuals continuing to be friends with their ex-partners following dissolution, therefore turning their social circles into an "army of ex-lovers" (Allen & Goldberg, 2020; Hoffman, 2007). Harkless and Fower (2005) found that lesbians and gay men were significantly more likely to maintain a close relationship with an ex-partner than were heterosexual men and women, yet they point out that the specific behaviors that maintain these relationships may be different for lesbians and gay men. Ex-partners are frequently identified as members of LGBTQ+ people's "chosen family," a group that are not biologically or legally related but serve as a family group, often functioning in place of biological and legal relations who are not supportive of the LGBTQ+ person's sexual and/or gender minority identity (Bacon, 2012; Blair & Pukall, 2014; Duran & Perez, 2019; Lannutti & Cameron, 2002; Weston, 1991). There may be more than social norms driving the postdissolutional relationships for LGBTQ+ people. For example, Lannutti and Cameron (2002) found that personal variables, such as liking for the ex-partner, had a stronger influence on the quality of the same-sex postdissolutional relationship than did structural variables, such as social network norms.

Another important aspect of relationships formed by LGBTQ+ people after romantic dissolution is continued coparenting. While there is conflicting data on whether same-sex couples with children are more likely to dissolve their relationships than those without children (Allen & Price, 2020; Farr & Goldberg, 2018; Wiik et al., 2014), those couples who do have children together must negotiate how they will relate to each other, their children, and possible new partners in the forming of stepfamilies. Negotiating coparenting relationships post–same sex divorce may be complicated by the type of parenting arrangement that the couple had predivorce. For example, a nonbiological lesbian mother may not have legal protection for her relationship with her child unless she legally adopted her wife's biological child. Additionally, Gartrell et al. (2011) found that divorced lesbians were more likely to continue to coparent their children if the nonbiological mother had legally adopted the child than if she had not. LGBTQ+ coparents who terminate their romantic relationship often go on to form new romantic partnerships and create stepfamily relationships. Connected to this, Bergeson et al. (2020) found that successful negotiation of LGBTQ+ stepfamily roles often involved a combination of intentional planning and redefinition of relationships. Bermea et al. (2020) discussed in detail one aspect of intentional planning for queer stepfamilies: Boundary management. This work found that many of the boundary management strategies employed by queer families, such as keeping a normal schedule, were similar to those found in research on heterosexual stepfamilies. However, there were unique experiences of heteronormativity and homophobia (e.g., a new stepfamily member made denigrating comments related to a household formally headed by a same-gender couple; Bermea et al., 2020). Further, multiple separations from multiple types of coparenting relationships over time may result in postdissolutional coparenting relationships among groups of lesbian and gay adults described by Gahan (2019) as "guild parented families." Gahan (2019) describes how guild-parented families face challenges from a heteronormative culture that protects only biological parents and recognizes only two parents for a child. In response to this, guild-parented families often must develop creative ways to manage their complex kinship arrangements (Gahan, 2019).

FUTURE DIRECTIONS

While any attempt to review the entire corpus of literature on a given subject will certainly fall short of absolute comprehensiveness, this article has striven to cover the major themes and findings related to the dissolution of LGBTQ+ relationships that have been produced up to this point. As such, attention can now be turned to the future of this field. As researchers continue to investigate the termination of LGBTQ+ relationships, there are at least three suggestions that can be made to productively shape the next wave of research: (1) avoid generalizations, (2) avoid unproductive comparisons, and (3) diversify methodological and theoretical perspectives.

While respecting the fact that research into LGBTQ+ relationship termination is both a relatively small and young field that has not reached full maturity, the research produced thus far is limited by its reliance on overly general characterizations of LGBTQ+ relationships. At the most basic level, researchers have yet to investigate how a vast array of sociodemographic variables might be associated with rates of dissolution in LGBTQ+ relationships, which is somewhat surprising given the known associations between these variables and dissolution in heterosexual mixed-gender relationships (Manning & Joyner, 2019). Beyond simple bivariate correlations between these variables and dissolution, there must also be a recognition of the intersectionality of those variables and how the unique combinations of identities that individuals bring to their relationships may be at play in LGBTQ+ relationship dissolution as well (Fish & Russell, 2018; Reczek, 2020).

Beyond recognizing sociodemographic diversity, researchers should also take care to be sensitive to diversity in the types of partnerships that LGBTQ+ people may take part in. For example, there are likely different factors at hand and outcomes to be explored when considering legally formalized versus nonformalized relationships (Manning & Joyner, 2019), whether a couple is cohabitating or not (Manning & Joyner, 2019), whether a couple is encountering their first break up or if they're in a cycling relationship (Monk et al., 2018), if a couple has children, and if they do, how they came to have those children (e.g., via adoption, surrogacy, from a previous relationship; Manning & Joyner, 2019). Additionally, and with specific respect to trans individuals, there must also be a consideration of the timing of coming to identify as trans and the transition process (if it occurs), as there are likely important differences associated with identification and transition taking place before a couple was formed, once a couple had already been established, or if the relationship is formed wholly after transition (Farr et al., 2020).

Finally, researchers should avoid generalizing findings from samples that fail to adequately represent individuals of all gender identities and sexual orientations. For example, much research conducted in this field draws from cisgender individuals and ignores or fails to explicitly include gender nonbinary or gender-fluid individuals (Pfeffer & Castañeda, 2019). Again, with specific reference to trans individuals, most research has been focused on individuals in heterosexual relationships (e.g., trans men in relationships with women) and very little focused on other sexual orientations (e.g., trans women in relationships with women). This lack of granularity is likely an artifact of the relative lack of research on LGBTQ+ relationships more generally and will almost certainly improve over time as the field matures.

Another note of caution for researchers to attend to is to avoid comparing the dissolution of LGBTQ+ relationships to relationships that conform to hegemonic narratives and ideals such as the Standard North American Family, mononormativity, motherhood, and parenthood mandates (Allen, 2019; Fish & Russell, 2018). When these conceptualizations of what relationships "should be" are held as the standard against which all other types of relationships are compared against, this can lead to suggestions that other relationships are somehow inferior to these archetypes. This type of perspective has been characterized as a "deficit comparison" approach (e.g., Van Eeden-Moorefield et al., 2011), which researchers should be careful not to reify.

Finally, as the body of literature related to this topic grows, the field would certainly benefit from an increase in the diversity of both the methodological and theoretical approaches used to generate knowledge. Research on LGBTQ+ relationships, and specifically relationship termination, is heavily dominated by minority stress theory, as mentioned earlier (Farr et al., 2020). However, there are many other perspectives on relationship dissolution that could be profitably applied to this same topic. Some examples might include the relational turbulence model (Solomon & Knobloch, 2004) and uncertainty management theory (Brashers, 2001). An increase in the diversity of theories applied to this field could also result in a concomitant rise in the diversity of methods present in the literature. For example, there is a striking lack of mixed-methods research present in LGBTQ+ dissolution literature, as well as in the study of the relational lives of LGBTQ+ people more generally (Fish & Russell, 2018). Research on trans individuals also evinces a lack of methodological diversity, with almost all research coming from a qualitative standpoint (Pfeffer & Castañeda, 2019). Additionally, given the difficulty associated with generating a large and representative sample of LGBTQ+ individuals, many studies have relied on convenience or snowball sampling techniques (Manning & Joyner, 2019). As large and publicly available data sets become increasingly common and available, researchers should aim to make use of this "big data" to improve the validity of their findings.

The hope of this final portion is not to place a focus on shortcomings, but rather to encourage growth in the next phase of research, with the end result of generating more knowledge that can be used to understand and support LGBTQ+ people as they experience and endure relational dissolution.

FURTHER READING

Allen, K. R., & Lavender-Stott, E. S. (2020). The families of LGBTQ older adults: Theoretical approaches to creative family connections in the context of marginalization, social-historical change, and resilience. *Journal of Family Theory & Review, 12*, 200–219. https://doi.org/10.1111/jftr.12370

Haas, S. M., & Lannutti, P. J. (2021). The impact of minority stress and social support on positive relationship functioning in same-sex relationships. *Health Communication, 36*, 315–323. https://doi.org/10.1080/10410236.2019.1687130

Lannutti, P. J., Butauski, M., Rubinsky, V., & Hudak, N. (2021). Setting the agenda: LGBTQ+ and SGM family communication. *Journal of Family Communication, 21*, 1–6. https://doi.org/10.1080/15267431.2021.1912048

LeBlanc, A. J., & Frost, D. M. (2020). Couple-level minority stress and mental health among people in same-sex relationships: Extending minority stress theory. *Society and Mental Health, 10*, 276–290. https://doi.org/10.1177/2156869319884724

REFERENCES

Allen, D., & Price, J. (2020). Stability rates of same-sex couples: With and without children. *Marriage and Family Review, 56*, 51–71. https://doi.org/10.1080/01494929.2019.1630048

Allen, K. R. (2019). Family, loss, and change: Navigating family breakup before the advent of legal marriage and divorce. In A. E. Goldberg & A. P. Romero (Eds.), *LGBTQ divorce and relationship dissolution: Psychological and legal perspectives and implications for practice* (pp. 221–232). Oxford University Press.

Allen, K. R., & Goldberg, A. E. (2020). Lesbian women disrupting gendered, heteronormative discourses of motherhood, marriage, and divorce. *Journal of Lesbian Studies, 24*, 12–24. https://doi.org/10.1080/10894160.2019.1615356

Allen, K. R., & Goldberg, A. E. (2021). Lesbian adoptive mothers' emotional responses and adaptation in the wake of relational dissolution. *Journal of Women & Aging, 33*, 184–200. https://doi.org/10.1080/08952841.2020.1826623

Bacon, J. (2012). Until death do us part: Lesbian rhetorics of relational divorce. *Women's Studies in Communication, 35*, 158–177. https://doi.org/10.1080/07491409.2012.724523

Badgett, M. V. L., & Mallory, C. (2014). *Relationship recognition patterns of same-sex couples by gender.* Williams Institute, UCLA. https://williamsinstitute.law.ucla.edu/publications/relation-recog-ss-couples-gender/

Ballester, E., Cornish, M. A., & Hanks, M. A. (2021). Predicting relationship satisfaction in LGBQ+ people using internalized stigma, outness, and concealment. *Journal of GLBT Family Studies, 17*, 1–16.

Balsam, K. F., Rostosky, S. S., & Riggle, E. D. (2017). Breaking up is hard to do: Women's experience of dissolving their same-sex relationship. *Journal of Lesbian Studies, 21*, 30–46. https://doi.org/10.1080/10894160.2016.1165561

Bergeson, C., Bermeia, A., Bible, J., Matera, K., Van Eeden-Moorefield, B., & Jushak, M. (2020). Pathways to successful queer stepfamily formation. *Journal of GLBT Family Studies, 16*(4), 368–384. https://doi.org/10.1080/1550428X.2019.1673866

Bermea, A. M., Van Eeden-Moorefield, B., & Bible, J. (2020). Perceived boundary negotiations with former partners among queer stepfamilies. *Psychology of Sexual Orientation and Gender Diversity, 7*, 162–175. https://doi.org/10.1037/sgd0000370

Bethea, M. S., & McCollum, E. E. (2013). The disclosure experiences of male-to-female transgender individuals: A systems theory perspective. *Journal of Couple & Relationship Therapy, 12*, 89–112.

Blair, K. L., & Pukall, C. F. (2014). Family matters, but sometimes chosen family matters more: Perceived social network influence in the dating decisions of same- and mixed-sex couples. *The Canadian Journal of Human Sexuality, 24*, 257–270.

Bonello, K. (2009). Gay monogamy and extra-dyadic sex: A critical review of the theoretical and empirical literature. *Counselling Psychology Review, 24*, 51–65.

Brashers, D. E. (2001). Communication and uncertainty management. *Journal of Communication, 51*, 477–497. https://doi.org/10.1111/j.1460-2466.2001.tb02892.x

Carlson, D. L., Miller, A. J., Sassler, S., & Hanson, S. (2016). The gendered division of housework and couples' sexual relationships: A reexamination. *Journal of Marriage and Family, 78*, 975–995.

Chen, S., & van Ours, J. C. (2020). Symbolism matters: The effect of same-sex marriage legalization on partnership stability. *Journal of Economic Behavior & Organization, 178*, 44–58.

Conley, T. D., Ziegler, A., Moors, A. C., Matsick, J. L., & Valentine, B. (2012). A critical examination of popular assumptions about the benefits and outcomes of monogamous relationships. *Personality and Social Psychology Review, 17*, 124–141. https://doi.org/10.1177/1088868312467087

Cooke, L. P. (2006). "Doing" gender in context: Household bargaining and risk of divorce in Germany and the United States. *American Journal of Sociology, 112*, 442–472.

Day, M. V. (2013). Stigma, halo effects, and threats to ideology: Comment on the fewer the merrier? *Analyses of Social Issues and Public Policy, 13*, 49–51.

Day, M. V., Kay, A. C., Holmes, J. G., & Napier, J. L. (2011). System justification and the defense of committed relationship ideology. *Journal of Personality and Social Psychology, 101*, 291–306.

DeLecce, T., & Weisfeld, G. (2016). An evolutionary explanation for sex differences in nonmarital breakup experiences. *Adaptive Human Behavior and Physiology, 2*, 234–251.

DePaulo, B. M., & Morris, W. L. (2005). Singles in society and in science. *Psychological Inquiry, 16*, 57–83.

Devor, A. H. (2004). Witnessing and mirroring: A fourteen stage model of transsexual identity formation. *Journal of Gay & Lesbian Psychotherapy, 8*, 41–67.

Dierckx, M., Motmans, J., Mortelmans, D., & T'sjoen, G. (2016). Families in transition: A literature review. *International Review of Psychiatry, 28*, 36–43.

Doyle, D. M., & Molix, L. (2014a). Love on the margins: The effects of social stigma and relationship length on romantic relationship quality. *Social Psychological and Personality Science, 5*, 102–110.

Doyle, D. M., & Molix, L. (2014b). How does stigma spoil relationships? Evidence that perceived discrimination harms romantic relationship quality through impaired self-image. *Journal of Applied Social Psychology, 44*, 600–610.

Doyle, D. M., & Molix, L. (2014c). Perceived discrimination as a stressor for close relationships: Identifying psychological and physiological pathways. *Journal of Behavioral Medicine, 37*, 1134–1144.

Doyle, D. M., & Molix, L. (2015). Perceived discrimination and social relationship functioning among sexual minorities: Structural stigma as a moderating factor. *Analyses of Social Issues and Public Policy, 15*, 357–381.

Duran, A., & Perez, D. (2019). The multiple roles of chosen familia: Exploring the interconnections of queer Latino men's community cultural wealth. *International Journal of Qualitative Studies in Education, 32*, 67–84.

Farr, R. H., & Goldberg, A. E. (2018). Same-sex relationship dissolution and divorce. In A. E. Goldberg & A. P. Romero (Eds.), *LGBTQ divorce and relationship dissolution: Psychological and legal perspectives and implications for practice* (pp. 151–172). Oxford University Press.

Farr, R. H., Simon, K. A., & Goldberg, A. E. (2020). Separation and divorce among LGBTQ-parent families. In *LGBTQ-Parent Families* (pp. 337–348). Springer.

Fingerhut, A. W., Riggle, E. D., & Rostosky, S. S. (2011). Same-sex marriage: The social and psychological implications of policy and debates. *Journal of Social Issues, 67*, 225–241.

Fish, J. N., & Russell, S. T. (2018). Queering methodologies to understand queer families. *Family Relations, 67*, 12–25.

Fisher, A. N., & Sakaluk, J. K. (2020). Are single people a stigmatized "group"? Evidence from examinations of social identity, entitativity, and perceived responsibility. *Journal of Experimental Social Psychology, 86*, 1–15, 103,844.

Frost, D. M., & Fingerhut, A. W. (2016). Daily exposure to negative campaign messages decreases same-sex couples' psychological and relational well-being. *Group Processes & Intergroup Relations, 19*, 477–492.

Frost, D. M., & Leblanc, A. J. (2019). Stress in the lives of same-sex couples: Implications for relationship dissolution and divorce. In A. E. Goldberg & A. P. Romero (Eds.), *LGBTQ divorce and relationship dissolution: Psychological and legal perspectives and implications for practice* (pp. 70–86). Oxford University Press.

Frost, D. M., LeBlanc, A. J., de Vries, B., Alston-Stepnitz, E., Stephenson, R., & Woodyatt, C. (2017). Couple-level minority stress: An examination of same-sex couples' unique experiences. *Journal of Health and Social Behavior, 58*, 455–472.

Gahan, L. (2019). Separation and post-separation parenting within lesbian and gay co-parenting (guile parented) families. *Australian and New Zealand Journal of Family Therapy, 40*, 98–113. https://doi.org/10.1002/anzf.1343

Gamarel, K. E., Reisner, S. L., Laurenceau, J. P., Nemoto, T., & Operario, D. (2014). Gender minority stress, mental health, and relationship quality: A dyadic investigation of transgender women and their cisgender male partners. *Journal of Family Psychology, 28*, 437–447.

Gartrell, N., Bos, H., Peyser, H., Deck, A., & Rodas, C. (2011). Family characteristics, custody arrangements and adolescent psychological well-being after lesbian mothers break-up. *Family Relations, 60,* 572–585.

Goldberg, A. E., Moyer, A. M., Black, K., & Henry, A. (2015). Lesbian and heterosexual adoptive mothers' experiences of relationship dissolution. *Sex Roles, 73,* 141–156. https://doi.org/10.1007/s11199-014-0432-2

Grov, C., Starks, T. J., Rendina, H. J., & Parsons, J. (2014). Rules about casual sex partners, relationship satisfaction, and HIV risk in partnered gay and bisexual men. *Journal of Sex and Marital Therapy, 40,* 105–122. https://doi.org/10.1080/0092623X.2012.691948

Haas, S. M., & Lannutti, P. J. (2021). The impact of minority stress and social support on positive relationship functioning in same-sex relationships. *Health Communication, 36,* 315–323. https://doi.org/10.1080/10410236.2019.1687130

Harkless, L. E., & Fower, B. J. (2005). Similarities and differences in relational boundaries among heterosexuals, gay men, and lesbians. *Psychology of Women Quarterly, 29,* 167–176.

Haupert, M. L., Gesselman, A. N., Moors, A. C., Fisher, H. E., & Garcia, J. R. (2017). Prevalence of experiences with consensual nonmonogamous relationships: Findings from two national samples of single Americans. *Journal of Sex & Marital Therapy, 43,* 424–440. https://doi.org/10.1080/0092623X.2016.1178675

Hoffman, A. (2007). *An army of ex-lovers: My life at the Gay Community News.* University of Massachusetts Press.

Hoy, A. (2018). Invisibility, illegibility, and stigma: The citizenship experiences of divorced gays and lesbians. *Journal of Divorce & Remarriage, 59,* 69–91.

Hoy, A. (2019). Accounting for same-sex divorce: Relationship- vs. self-focused divorce accounts and the meanings of marriage among gays and lesbians. *Journal of Divorce & Remarriage, 61,* 320–343.

Hutzler, K. T., Giuliano, T. A., Herselman, J. R., & Johnson, S. M. (2016). Three's a crowd: Public awareness and (mis)perceptions of polyamory. *Psychology & Sexuality, 7,* 69–87.

Joyner, K., Manning, W., & Bogle, R. (2017). Gender and the stability of same-sex and different-sex relationships among young adults. *Demography, 54,* 2351–2374.

Ketcham, E., & Bennett, N. G. (2019). Comparative couple stability: Same-sex and male-female unions in the United States. *Socius, 5,* 2378023119829312.

Kim, S. A., & Stein, E. (2019). The role of gender and gender dynamics in same-sex divorce and dissolution. In A. E. Goldberg & A. P. Romero (Eds.), *LGBTQ divorce and relationship dissolution: Psychological and legal perspectives and implications for practice* (pp. 353–382). Oxford University Press.

Lannutti, P. J. (2014). *Experiencing same-sex marriage. Individuals, couples, and social networks.* Peter Lang.

Lannutti, P. J., Butauski, M., Rubinsky, V., & Hudak, N. (2021). Setting the agenda: LGBTQ+ and SGM family communication. *Journal of Family Communication,* 1–6. https://doi.org/10.1080/15267431.2021.1912048

Lannutti, P. J., & Cameron, K. A. (2002). Beyond the breakup: Heterosexual and homosexual postdissolutional relationships. *Communication Quarterly, 50,* 153–170.

Lavner, J. A. (2017). Relationship satisfaction in lesbian couples: Review, methodological critique, and research agenda. *Journal of Lesbian Studies, 21,* 7–29.

LeBlanc, A. J., & Frost, D. M. (2020). Couple-level minority stress and mental health among people in same-sex relationships: Extending minority stress theory. *Society and Mental Health, 10,* 276–290. https://doi.org/10.1177/2156869319884724

Lenning, E., & Buist, C. L. (2013). Social, psychological and economic challenges faced by transgender individuals and their significant others: Gaining insight through personal narratives. *Culture, Health & Sexuality, 15,* 44–57.

Lev, A. I. (2004). *Transgender emergence: Therapeutic guidelines for working with gender-variant people and their families*. The Haworth Clinical Practice Press.

Maisel, N. C., & Fingerhut, A. W. (2011). California's ban on same-sex marriage: The campaign and its effects on gay, lesbian, and bisexual individuals. *Journal of Social Issues, 67*, 242–263.

Manning, W. D., & Joyner, K. (2019). Demographic approaches to same-sex relationship dissolution and divorce: Research findings, data challenges, and implications for future research. In A. E. Goldberg & A. P. Romero (Eds.), *LGBTQ divorce and relationship dissolution: Psychological and legal perspectives and implications for practice* (pp. 35–48). Oxford University Press.

Marteau, B., & Dutreuilh, C. (2019). Separation among cohabiting same-sex and different-sex couples. *Population, 74*(4), 483–506.

Meyer, I. H. (2003). Prejudice, social stress, and mental health in lesbian, gay, and bisexual populations: Conceptual issues and research evidence. *Psychological Bulletin, 129*, 674–697.

Monk, J. K., Ogolsky, B. G., & Oswald, R. F. (2018). Coming out and getting back in: Relationship cycling and distress in same-and different-sex relationships. *Family Relations, 67*, 523–538.

Oswald, R. F., & Clausell, E. (2006). Same-sex relationships and their dissolution. In M. A. Fine & J. H. Harvey (Eds.), *Handbook of divorce and relationship dissolution* (pp. 499–513). Lawrence Erlbaum Associates.

Otis, M. D., Rostosky, S. S., Riggle, E. D., & Hamrin, R. (2006). Stress and relationship quality in same-sex couples. *Journal of social and Personal Relationships, 23*, 81–99.

Parsons, J. T., Starks, T. J., Gamarel, K. E., & Grov, C. (2012). Non-monogamy and sexual relationships quality among same-sex male couples. *Journal of Family Psychology, 26*, 669–677. https://doi.org/10.1037/a0029561

Perry, N. S., Huebner, D. M., Baucom, B. R., & Hoff, C. C. (2015). Relationship power, sociodemographics, and their relative influence on sexual agreements among gay male couples. *AIDS Behavior, 20*, 1302–1314. https://doi.org/10.1007/s10461-015-1196-6

Petruzzella, A., Feinstein, B. A., & Lavner, J. A. (2019). Sexual orientation-related stigma and relationship functioning among female same-sex couples. *Journal of Lesbian Studies, 23*, 439–450.

Pfeffer, C. A., & Castañeda, N. N. (2019). Trans partnership and marriage: Risk factors for conflict, dissolution, and divorce. In A. E. Goldberg & A. P. Romero (Eds.), *LGBTQ divorce and relationship dissolution: Psychological and legal perspectives and implications for practice* (pp. 287–311). Oxford University Press.

Pieper, M., & Bauer, R. (2005). Call for papers: International conference on polyamory and mononormativity. *University of Hamburg, 5*(6.11), 2005.

Poushter, J., & Kent, N. (2020, June 25). *The global divide on homosexuality persists*. Pew Research Center. https://www.pewresearch.org/global/2020/06/25/global-divide-on-homosexuality-persists/

Pyne, J., Bauer, G., & Bradley, K. (2015). Transphobia and other stressors impacting trans parents. *Journal of GLBT Family Studies, 11*, 107–126.

Reczek, C. (2020). Sexual- and gender-minority families: A 2010 to 2020 decade in review. *Journal of Marriage and Family, 82*, 300–325.

Redlick, M. H., & Lannutti, P. J. (2021). LGBTQ communication. In T. A. Cofflet (Ed.), *Interpersonal Sexual Communication Across the Lifespan*.

Riggs, D. W., von Doussa, H., & Power, J. (2015). The family and romantic relationships of trans and gender diverse Australians: An exploratory survey. *Sexual and Relationship Therapy, 30*, 243–255.

Schilt, K., & Westbrook, L. (2009). Doing gender, doing heteronormativity: "Gender normals," transgender people, and the social maintenance of heterosexuality. *Gender & Society, 23*, 440–464.

Solomon, D. H., & Knobloch, L. K. (2004). A model of relational turbulence: The role of intimacy, relational uncertainty, and interference from partners in appraisals of irritations. *Journal of Social and Personal Relationships, 21*, 795–816. https://doi.org/10.1177/0265407504047838

Song, C., Buysse, A., Zhang, W. H., Lasser, J., & Dewaele, A. (2021). Sex differences in the romantic relationships of same-gender couples: The role of visibility management. *Psychological Reports*, 0033294120988134.

Stults, C. B. (2019). Relationship quality among young gay and bisexual men in consensual nonmonogamous relationships. *Journal of Social and Personal Relationships, 36*, 3037–3056. https://doi.org/10.1177/0265407518809530

Totenhagen, C. J., Randall, A. K., & Lloyd, K. (2018). Stress and relationship functioning in same-sex couples: The vulnerabilities of internalized homophobia and outness. *Family Relations, 67*, 399–413.

Umberson, D., Thomeer, M. B., & Lodge, A. C. (2015). Intimacy and emotion work in lesbian, gay, and heterosexual relationships. *Journal of Marriage and Family, 77*, 542–556.

US Census Bureau. (2016). Characteristics of same-sex couple households: 2015. https://www.census.gov/data/tables/time-series/demo/same-sex-couples/ssc-house-characteristics.html

Vale, M. T., & Bisconti, T. L. (2021a). Age differences in sexual minority stress and the importance of friendship in later life. *Clinical Gerontologist, 44*, 235–248.

Vale, M. T., & Bisconti, T. L. (2021b). Minority stress and relationship well-being in sexual minorities: The varying role of outness on relationship and sexual satisfaction. *International Journal of Sexual Health*, 1–15.

Van Eeden-Moorefield, B., Malloy, K., & Benson, K. (2016). Gay men's (non)monogamy ideal and lived experiences. *Sex Roles, 75*, 43–55. https://doi.org/10.1007/s11199-015-0566-x

Van Eeden-Moorefield, B., Martell, C. R., Williams, M., & Preston, M. (2011). Same-sex relationships and dissolution: The connection between heteronormativity and homonormativity. *Family Relations, 60*, 562–571.

Westbrook, L., & Schilt, K. (2014). Doing gender, determining gender: Transgender people, gender panics, and the maintenance of the sex/gender/sexuality system. *Gender & Society, 28*, 32–57.

Weston, K. (1991). *Families we choose: Lesbians, gays, kinship*. Columbia University Press.

Whitton, S. A., Weitbrecht, E. M., & Kuryluk, A. D. (2015). Monogamy agreements in male same-sex couples: Associations with relationship quality and individual well-being. *Journal of Couple & Relationship Therapy, 14*, 39–63. https://doi.org/10.1080/15332691.2014.953649

Wiik, K. A., Seierstad, A., & Noack, T. (2014). Divorce in Norwegian same-sex marriages and registerd partnerships: The role of children. *Journal of Marriage and Family, 76*, 919–929.

Wosick-Correa, K. (2010). Agreements, rules and agentic fidelity in polyamorous relationships. *Psychology & Sexuality, 1*, 44–61.

Madeleine Redlick Holland and Pamela J. Lannutti

MINORITY STRESS AND RELATIONSHIPS

INTRODUCTION

At its core, minority stress is about the relationship between an individual and society. Drawn heavily from sociological and social psychological theories, the concept of minority stress provides researchers a lens with which to better understand how minorities, such as the lesbian, gay, bisexual, transgender, and queer (LGBTQ+) and African American communities, are affected by homophobia, prejudice, and racism.

In crafting his argument for exploring minority stress within lesbian, gay, and bisexual (LGB) individuals, Meyer (2003, p. 674) posited that if they are "indeed at risk for excess mental distress and disorders due to social stress, it is important to understand this risk, as well as factors that ameliorate stress and contribute to mental health." As research on this subject has grown in recent years, the minority stress model has shown "that circumstances in the environment, especially related to stigma and prejudice, may bring about stressors that LGBT experience their entire lives" (Meyer, 2015, p. 209).

Yet much of the research that will be discussed here is limited in scope, often failing to include meaningful aspects of society. Thus, this article addresses four key pieces. The first section, "Defining Minority Stress," speaks to prior research on minority stress and its limitations. Next, to move understanding forward, "Calls for Change" discusses the growing pains of our research community in regards to minority stress and inclusive research. "Social Identities in Context" then speaks to the current political and social climate that should be recognized in this work. Finally, "Conclusions and Future Directions" are discussed.

Before moving forward, it is important to acknowledge the growth and changes associated with the LGBTQ+ community and acronym. In Meyer's (2003) original article, he spoke about the lesbian, gay, and bisexual (LGB) community, but then in a 2015 update, he refers to the LGBT community. Between those articles and now, the LGBTQ+ acronym has grown in meaningful and inclusive ways. This article references the original language used by the authors to maintain fidelity of their works. When speaking about future directions or the community in general, LGBTQ+ is used to celebrate and acknowledge diversity.

DEFINING MINORITY STRESS

Importantly, minority stress research has documented the high levels of stress experienced by members of stigmatized identities such as the LGBTQ+ community and African Americans. Generally speaking, "minority populations are exposed to unique stressors, including stigma or expectations of rejection, experiences of discrimination, internalization of negative social beliefs about one's social group or social identity, and stressors related to the concealment or management of a stigmatized identity" (LeBlanc et al., 2015, p. 4).

Compared to other constructions of stress, which often focus on personal rather than social issues (Hobfoll, 2004; Lazarus & Folkman, 1984), minority stress speaks more to the environmental stressors, social conditions, and conflicts that exist between the minority and majority groups (Meyer, 2003). Within these conceptualizations, researchers speak about the distal-proximal nature of stress (Meyer, 2003) as well as inter- and intragroup stressors (Clark et al., 1999) that may negatively affect members of minority groups.

Consequently, it is known that being a member of a stigmatized community can lead to alienation from social structures, norms, and institutions, all of which can have negative implications for mental health, well-being, and relationships (Casey et al., 2019; Mays & Cochran, 2001; Meyer, 2003). Although the term "minority stress" is often most closely associated with Meyer's (2003) work on prejudice, social stress, and the LGB community, extensive research has shown that African Americans and other racial minorities experience similar negative health outcomes.

However, as this article discusses, current research and conceptualizations of minority identities are both limited in their operationalization yet broad in areas of exploration, often with mixed findings. To explore how the field of research can be strengthened in order to better respond to the evolving social environment, it is important to review the work that has been done thus far, outline limitations, and develop opportunities for growth.

Minority Stress and the LGBTQ+ Community. First, and perhaps most notably, minority stress is closely associated with Meyer's (2003) foundational piece on LGB identities. Here, Meyer (2003) argued for an expansion of social stress theory to include stigmatized identities in order to better understand the association between hostile and stressful social environments and mental health problems. It is helpful to visualize Meyer's (2003, 2015) work as a model that identifies processes through which (1) prejudice and stigma directed toward the LGBT community bring about unique stressors, and (2) the stressors cause adverse health outcomes.

Using this lens, research has explored how prejudice events, expectations of rejection or discrimination, concealment of one's sexual orientation, internalized homophobia, and other societal issues such as a lack of legal relationship recognition may increase feelings of rejection and suicidal ideation, and lower levels of well-being for the LGBTQ+ community (Braams et al., 2015; Cochran et al., 2003; Fulginiti et al., 2020; Lick et al., 2013; Meyer, 2003; Riggle et al., 2010, Rosario et al., 1996).

Minority Stress and Relationship Quality. When speaking about LGB relationships, fears of prejudice or discrimination may lead LGB individuals to hide their romantic relationship status, which can negatively affect relationship quality because of a lack of social support, or create an inability to commit to a romantic partner (Green & Mitchell, 2002). Rostosky et al. (2007, p. 1) further note that LGB couples "experience minority stress as they interact with their family members, coworkers, and communities." Although research on same-sex relationships and minority stress is limited (Mohr & Daly, 2008), a few key themes can be discussed.

First, clinical research has shown that internalized homonegativity and sexual orientation concealment can have extremely negative effects on same-sex relationships (Mohr & Daly, 2008), especially for LGB youth (Toomey et al., 2018). Further, negative correlations between internalized homonegativity and relationship quality (Balsam & Szymanski, 2005; Mohr & Fassinger, 2006; Otis et al., 2006) have been found at both the individual and couple levels. Both Rostosky et al. (2007) and Frost (2013) found that, to cope with these stressors, same-sex couples try to use coping strategies that may include reframing the experiences, concealing their relationships, and using stigma as an opportunity to strengthen their relationship. Additionally, Doyle and Molix (2015) note a small but significant inverse association between social stigma and relationship functioning for sexual minority couples.

Next, Balsam and Szymanski (2005) found that minority stress variables (including internalized homophobia and discrimination) were associated with lower relationship quality and both domestic violence perpetration and victimization. Similarly, Edwards and Sylaska's (2013) research discovered that intimate partner violence was tied to minority stress concerns. Specifically, physical perpetration (toward one's partner) was related to identity concealment and internalized homonegativity, with sexual perpetration related to internalized homonegativity as well.

Additionally, LGB individuals in committed relationships, compared to legally recognized relationships, experienced significantly more psychological distress and found less meaning in their relationship (Riggle et al., 2010). Wight et al. (2013) echoed these findings and added that LGB individuals who were not in legalized relationships had the highest psychological distress compared to both heterosexual and LGB individuals within legalized relationships.

Complicating these findings, though, Kamen et al. (2011) found that although minority stress was not directly related to relationship satisfaction in same-sex male relationships, internalized homonegativity is. In fact, they continue, "for individuals high in internalized heterosexism (homonegativity)...a less committed relationship may be seen as more comfortable or more satisfying (Kamen et al., 2011, p. 1385).

Outside of romantic relationships, research is further limited. Diamond and Lucas (2004) found that younger sexual-minority male adolescents had smaller overall peer networks and lost or drifted away from more friends than did heterosexuals. Yet those who were "out" to their peers experienced larger friend networks but greater worries over friendship loss (Diamond & Lucas, 2004).

Counterpoints. LGBTQ+ minority stress research is important and heuristic, but it is imperfect. Speaking generally about same-sex research, Savin-Williams (2008, p. 137) argues that "attention to the healthy lives of same-sex attracted populations as a counterweight to the usual doom-and-gloom fare is long overdue." And as we've seen, minority stress research typically only focuses on the negative aspects, but there are a few studies that seeks to highlight the unique coping skills and resilient nature of LGBTQ+ individuals.

Both Meyer (2003) and Szymanski (2009) found that LGB individuals are resilient and that positive coping skills and self-esteem may moderate the relationship between perceived minority stress and mental health (Chen & Tyron, 2012). Similarly, research has shown that LGB relationship satisfaction and quality can remain high despite negative, heterosexist contexts and minority stress, in part because of the protective factor of the relationship itself (Blair & Holmberg, 2008; Connolly, 2005; Frost, 2013; Graham & Barnow, 2013; Puckett et al., 2017). For LGB youth, coping strategies such as seeking support and problem-solving are generally associated with positive adjustment (Toomey et al., 2018). Additionally, Heck (2015) has begun exploring the impacts of gay–straight alliances (GSA) and their effect on disrupting the minority stress–psychiatric distress relationship.

While there is a strong need to explore positive health outcomes using minority stress, the theory has been critiqued due to many studies that use limited and homogenous sample sizes. Noted earlier, the term "LGBTQ+" is meant to be inclusive of all identities and genders, but it is often erroneously connoted in research with White middle-class and urban LGBTQ+ people (Meyer, 2015). Parra and Hastings (2018, p. 1) specifically note that current minority stress models "predominantly focus on single categorical social identities and do not account for interlocking systems and processes of oppression based on" intersectional frameworks.

Because of this, there is an opportunity to expand understanding of what it means to identify as LGBTQ+. Similar to research on minority stress and non-romantic relationships, research on trans, queer, and other LGBTQ+ relationships is extremely limited. And, as Cyrus (2017) notes, although there is mounting evidence confirming that living as an LGBTQ person of color (POC) can lead to worse physical or mental health outcomes, the extent to which membership in multiple minority groups affects these individuals is unclear. She continues by arguing that many of the theoretical concepts, such as minority stress theory, risk, and resilience, do not "capture the complete story of how being the 'other' in multiple contexts relates" (Cyrus, 2017, p. 200) to these issues.

Speaking about transgender romantic relationships, Gamarel et al. (2014) found that transgender-related discrimination and relationship stigma were associated with both partners' relationship quality. And similar to other minority stress findings, social support and resiliency may buffer the negative effects of discrimination for trans and gender-nonconforming individuals, including suicidal ideation (Bockting et al., 2016; Hendricks & Testa, 2012).

Lastly, as noted by Correro and Nielson (2020), there is a need to research the effects of minority stress as a risk factor for cognitive decline in LGB individuals. In their work, these authors note that chronic minority stress (CMS) contributes to negative health outcomes, such as cardiovascular disease and depression, which may lead to premature cognitive decline (Correro & Nielson, 2020).

African American and Racial Minority Stress. In addition to an LGBTQ+ focus, considerable research has explored minority stress from a racial minority perspective. Here, the landmark article by Clark et al. (1999) outlined many tenets that are still used in racial minority stress research today.

Unsurprisingly, Clark et al.'s (1999) meta-analysis found that the perception of racism, whether intergroup or intragroup, usually resulted in psychological and physiological stress responses, including coping strategies and negative health outcomes (Clark et al., 1999). A 2012 meta-analysis found similar positive associations between perceived racism and negative mental health outcomes among Black American adults (Pieterse et al., 2012).

Similar to findings on LGBTQ+ minority stress and mental health, when racial minorities know they are being devalued and excluded from society, an increase in distress can be seen, as well as poorer mental and physical health (Hughes et al., 2015; Meyer, 2003; Stuber et al., 2008). Similarly, as Hughes et al. (2015) note, simply having an awareness or acceptance of a negative stereotype can undermine well-being. While some of these negative outcomes can be offset with positive group identification and evaluation (Hughes et al., 2015), minority status groups are still affected by majority group perceptions and prejudice (Tropp & Pettigrew, 2005).

Regarding coping skills and racial minority status, Meyer et al. (2008, p. 12) found that "black and Latino LGBs (who) were exposed to more stress...had fewer available coping resources than whites (both heterosexual and LGB)." Furthermore, their findings showed that racial identity was linked to an increase in overall external stressors, including prejudiced (or discriminatory) events (Meyer et al., 2008).

Double Jeopardy, Additive Minority Stress, and LGBTQ+ POC. Over time, minority stress research has shifted toward the double jeopardy hypothesis (Ferraro & Farmer, 1996), additive notions of minority stress (Hayes et al., 2011), and even triple jeopardy (Bowleg et al., 2003). Through these lenses, it is hypothesized that members of multiple minority groups would experience additional psychological distress beyond that experienced by members of a single minority group (Hayes et al., 2011).

As an example, Zamboni and Crawford (2007) found that racial discrimination, gay bashing, and male gender role stress may increase the chances that sexual problems develop among

African American gay or bisexual men. Additionally, perceived experiences with discrimination based on race or ethnicity and sexual orientation can create stress and adversely affect sexual functioning (Zamboni & Crawford, 2007).

Other studies have shown mixed results when exploring whether a racial or ethnic minority identity or sexual minority status is associated with more negative health outcomes (Chen & Tyron, 2012; Hayes et al., 2011; LeBlanc et al., 2015), suicidal ideation (Sutter & Perrin, 2016), and illicit drug use (Drazdowski et al., 2016). Regardless, these studies represent a shift toward incorporating intersectional identities into minority stress research.

CALLS FOR CHANGE

Many authors referenced here note the extensive research on minority stress, compared to many other topics with the field of interpersonal communication; nevertheless, the body of work is quite small and limited in scope. Although discussions about minority stress have been around for over 30 years (Clark et al., 1999; Meyer, 2003), there is a need for minority stress research that captures present-day intersectional identities and the societal movements that shape them. As McConnell et al. (2018, p. 2) note, "social identities are understood in the context of their relationships to power, which are shaped by systems of privilege and oppression." And as the late 2010s demonstrated, there are many inadequacies in the research; political systems; and diversity, inclusion, and equity initiatives. In exploring LGB minority stress since the 2016 election, Gonzalez et al. (2018) found that since Trump's inauguration, there have been significant increases in stress related to sexual orientation rumination and daily experiences of harassment or discrimination, as well as more symptoms of depression and anxiety post-election.

Specifically, within the field of interpersonal communication, researchers continue to see calls for "making our research matter" (Afifi, 2017; Goodwin & Pillay, 2006). The transformation needed within the field of interpersonal communication can, and should, inform conceptualizations of minority stress. Presently, there is an opportunity to move beyond lip service (Savin-Williams, 2008) and conduct ethical, inclusive, and representative research.

In their chapter on "Relationships, Culture, and Social Change," Goodwin and Pillay (2006) argue researchers have largely ignored the role of social change and its implications for the way in which people interrelate with one another. In their discussion, they challenge us to examine the ways in which we "might expect significant economic and political transitions to influence our personal relationships" (p. 702).

And while this field has grown significantly since Goodwin and Pillay's (2006) chapter, there is still a need to support minority communities with further work, through advocacy, and dialogue. In a direct but supportive editorial about how to grow LGBTQ+ research, the former editor of *Communication Monographs*, Tamara Afifi (2017, p. 3) put forth another call to improve our disciplinary approach by "giving more attention to the role of culture in communication." Although many scholars give a "head nod" to the homogenous nature of their research samples, there is a need to study culture in an authentic and meaningful manner (Afifi, 2017). For the concept of minority stress, Afifi's charge carries greater weight and is one that must be answered soon and in full.

Minority Stress Limitations. Since the publication of Meyer's (2003) landmark piece, concepts such as critical race theory, intersectionality, and inclusive research have become meaningful aspects of the work, and this article looks to those concepts to move understanding of minority stress forward.

Historically, minority stress research has focused on the White LGBTQ+ community. The term "LGBTQ+" is meant to be inclusive of all identities and genders, but it is often erroneously connotated in research with White middle-class and urban LGBTQ+ people (Meyer, 2015); yet 22% of the all individuals involved in same-sex relationships in the United States identify as LGBT people of color (Balsam et al., 2011).

Although the literature presented up to this point is both heuristic and fruitful, much work remains. Discussed here, minority stress conceptualizations and limitations include a research agenda predominately focused on negative health outcomes rather than coping skills or positive outcomes (e.g., Mohr & Daly, 2008; Savin-Williams, 2008); small correlational or narrative data sets (e.g., Balsam & Szymanski, 2005; Frost, 2014); and a homogenous, White research sample (e.g., Bowleg, 2008; Frost et al., 2015).

Additionally, as noted in the work on racial minority stress, findings have been mixed. Researchers have had trouble identifying which minority identity (sexual or racial) is the cause of greater stress (i.e., Chen & Tyron, 2012). Speaking to intersectional research, Bowleg (2008) argues that methodological limitations are limited, creating unmeasurable and unanalyzable data.

Similarly, Balsam et al. (2011, p. 3) argue that "while there has been much recent research on LGBT minority stress, fewer studies have examined within-group variation, and very few have had large enough samples of LGBT participations who are also people of color (LGBT POC) to examine the unique issues facing this group." As noted by Kamen et al. (2011), same-sex couples are an invisible minority among American family structures. Other minorities do not have the privilege of blending in with society.

Speaking to areas of growth, Frost et al. (2015, p. 2) noted that "existing research on the effects of minority stress on the physical health of sexual minorities is limited by cross-sectional data, and an exclusive focus on subjectively reported stressors." Similarly, there have been calls for more inclusive research that better defines and explores intersectional identities to strengthen our understanding of stressors and their effects (Mohr & Daly, 2008). Additionally, there is an opportunity to research concepts of resilience (Meyer, 2003, 2015) and adaptive coping skills (Szymanski, 2009).

Simply put, minority stress as a concept has proven useful in understanding how individuals with a stigmatized identity may be affected by their environment. To move forward, though, research surrounding minority stress and relationships must evolve. Critically speaking, Meyer's (2003) call to explore greater societal issues that could affect minority stress has gone, in part, unanswered. Yet interpersonal communication scholars are primed to continue this work as their field is in the midst of an evolution as well.

SOCIAL IDENTITIES IN CONTEXT

To enrich both the field of interpersonal communication and concept of minority stress, the social change and unrest that is rightfully calling attention to the systemic racism and inequalities that have existed for minorities in the United States for hundreds of years must be acknowledged. Again, as McConnell et al. (2018, p. 2) note, "social identities are understood in the context of their relationships to power, which are shaped by systems of privilege and oppression." Thus, researchers can begin to strengthen minority stress by grounding it in the meaningful contexts that presently exist.

In 2015, the Pew Research Center found that 50% of Americans believe racism is a significant problem and 59% believe the country needs to continue making changes in order to give Blacks equal rights with White (Pew Research Center, 2015). In 2020, these issues carry more weight than ever. The Black Lives Matter group and movement, which the *New York Times* (Buchanan et al., 2020) suggested may be the largest protests in U.S. history, with over 15 million participants, seeks to bring justice, healing, and freedom to Black people across the globe (BlackLivesMatter.com, 2020) in response to the murders of Trayvon Martin, George Floyd, Breonna Taylor, and others.

Further adding pain, sorrow, and urgency to the Black Lives Matter movement are "at least 44 transgender or gender non-conforming people fatally shot or killed, the majority of which were Black and Latinx transgender women" (Human Rights Campaign, 2020). The Human Rights Campaign (HRC), a leading advocate for LGBTQ+ rights, noted:

> While the details of these cases differ, it is clear that fatal violence disproportionately affects transgender women of color—particularly Black transgender women—and that the intersections of racism, sexism, homophobia, biphobia, transphobia and unchecked access to guns conspire to deprive them of employment, housing, healthcare and other necessities (Human Rights Campaign, 2020).

According to HRC research, there is a climate of anti-transgender stigma, denial of opportunity, and increased risk factors that have led to a culture of violence (Human Rights Campaign, 2020).

Similarly, the Women's March of 2017 saw over 1 million participants protest the inauguration of President Donald Trump (Stein et al., 2017). In a *Washington Post* article discussing the march, protestors noted they were "inspired to join because of Trump's divisive campaign and his disparagement of women, minorities, and immigrants" (Stein et al., 2017).

Globally, there are have been momentous social movements focused on inequality and freedom as well. According to the BBC (2019a), there have been protests in Ecuador over a change in fuel subsidies that could affect indigenous and rural communities' access to food and public transport. Similarly, in Hong Kong, protesters are fighting an extradition bill that could put Hongkongers at risk for unfair treatment and trials by the Chinese government (BBC, 2019b).

As noted earlier, discussions of minority stress have typically centered around the LGBTQ+ community (Meyer, 2003) and African Americans (Clark et al., 1999); however, thanks to discussions of intersectionality and increased opportunities for visibility, there is an opportunity to expand our conceptualization of what it means to be a minority in today's world.

CONCLUSIONS AND FUTURE DIRECTIONS

At the heart of each of these movements, is a minority group who is fighting to have its peoples' voices heard and lives valued. Although there is a lot of negativity in these discussions, there is also hope. There has been tremendous positive growth in many areas, including those who support an LGBTQ identity (Pew Research Center, 2015), and there is opportunity.

The purpose of this article was to review the literature on minority stress and provide heuristic ways to move the concept forward. The social world is changing rapidly, and while academic research typically moves a bit more slowly, this should not be an impetus to crafting inclusive and meaningful work. In addition to calling for a stronger cultural lens in researchers' work, Afifi (2017) also argues for a greater interdisciplinary approach. The majority of work cited in this article does not come from the field of communication. Instead, understanding of minority stress is drawn heavily from the fields of psychology, sociology, and others. As communication experts with a wealth of theories, methodologies, and skills, researchers are uniquely positioned to grow conceptualizations of minority stress. To close, the author of this article offers three specific suggestions for scholars who seek to continue this work, though this list is not exhaustive.

Intersectionality. First, as noted repeatedly throughout the minority stress research, compared to White LGBs, Black and Latino LGB individuals experience higher levels of minority stressors regardless of the type of measure used (Meyer et al., 2008). Yet many measures do not capture the nuances of intersectional identities, so "researchers interested in examining the differential impact of minority stressors stemming from different stigmatized social statuses (e.g., sexual minority vs. racial/ethnic minority status) should incorporate measures that allow for such distinctions (Frost et al., 2015, p. 8).

Here, an intersectional approach (Bowleg, 2008; Stewart & McDermott, 2004) would argue that lived experience of sexual identity is not separable from other identities (e.g., race or ethnicity, gender) (Frost et al., 2015). And as Bowleg (2008, p. 322) argues, researchers can craft meaningful constructs that measure intersectionality rather than "relying instead on the erroneous assumptions that variables such as race, sex, sexual orientation, class, and disability are explanatory constructs in and of themselves."

Much of the research on racial minority stress is drawn from cross-sectional research and is highly correlational in nature. Using Bowleg (2008) and others as guides, minority stress can enrich understanding of the intersectional nature of identities through intentional and inclusive research.

Critical and Queer Theory. Next, researchers can turn to critical and queer theories, which allow them to better analyze everyday identity work and understand the complicated relationship between minority stress and relationships. For many researchers, interpersonal communication practices are inseparable from cultural systems (Moore, 2017). Thankfully there are a few theories and lenses with which to explore how "identity work relates to broad materializations of power" (Moore, 2017, p. 259).

In a recent article, Moore (2017, p. 258) noted that critical theories "have the potential to provide insight into interpersonal communication practices, especially about identities." Specifically, critical theories such as intersectionality, narrative performance theory, and feminist ideologies, can "provide multiple lenses with which to identify, critique, and transform power relations" (p. 258).

Further, with the incorporation of queer and critical lenses in this work, researchers can better understand the greater political forces at work besides perceived stigma that affect LGBTQ+ and racial minority identities. Queer theory (Butler 1990, 2010) argues that sexual identity is socially constructed, constituted through language, and enacted through performances that are situated within the body itself. Thus, an LGBTQ+ identity can be seen as performance, one that is fluid, changing, and socially constructed in certain contexts.

Queering Notions of Relationships. Finally, researchers can queer their notions of relationships and look beyond the traditional structures that have been represented in research. In a searing editorial, Elia (2003 p. 1) critiqued the "blatant and insidious ways in which a specific brand of heterosexual relationship has been promoted as the ultimate relational form at the expense of others who neither believe in nor practice such idealized relationships." To understand his point, we can look at prior minority stress research and the numerous ways in which it compares same-sex relationships to heterosexual ones. Here, Elia (2003) argues that researchers should instead queer their notion of relationships so that they can liberate individuals from the constraints of heteronormativity, address inequalities, contest the status quo, redress social injustices, and ultimately allow for more creativity in relationship construction.

As an example, Better (2014) explored relationship and identity choices some American women are making today around their sexuality, including the desire to identify as queer and break from traditional definitions of gender. Continuing, Better (2014, p. 36) notes that moving "towards queerness or sexual fluidity is often erased in American society today due to a lack of language with which to define and explain our understandings of sexuality."

Author's Note (January 2021). 2020 was a terrible year for people of color and so far, 2021 has been no better. The protests at the U.S. Capitol highlight grave inequalities in policing for White versus African American bodies. Additionally, when this article was begun, its author was saddened and enraged by the news that no one has been charged or held responsible for the murder of Breonna Taylor. The grand jury charges fell short of the justice that is needed. As a scholar, ally, and human, the author of this article feels it is so important to pause and say her name.

Whereas here Breonna and others are spoken about, the recent news and unrest in the United States highlight just how important this work is. Within the field of interpersonal communication, minority stress is a relatively new concept, but one that carries so much weight and history. Researchers must do better in their work. The author here cannot imagine the fear that Black Americans felt in 2020 and for decades before.

Researchers must vow to do better and work for change. It is one thing to acknowledge what is happening right now and another to do what it takes to move forward. This article encourages everyone who sees it to do the same. Please pick up the charge outlined here and work to create research that is diverse, equitable, and inclusive: Black Lives Matter.

FURTHER READING

Fingerhut, A. W., Riggle, E. D., & Rostosky, S. S. (2011). Same-sex marriage: The social and psychological implications of policy and debates. *Journal of Social Issues, 67*(2), 225–241.

Graham, J. M., & Barnow, Z. B. (2013). Stress and social support in gay, lesbian, and heterosexual couples: Direct effects and buffering models. *Journal of Family Psychology, 27*(4), 569.

Griffin, K. W., Scheier, L. M., Botvin, G. J., Diaz, T., & Miller, N. (1999). Interpersonal aggression in urban minority youth: Mediators of perceived neighborhood, peer, and parental influences. *Journal of Community Psychology, 27*(3), 281–298.

Lindahl, K. M., & Wigderson, S. (2020). Cultural considerations in the context of romantic relationships. In L. Benuto, F. Gonzalez, & J. Singer (Eds.), *Handbook of cultural factors in behavioral health* (pp. 431–446). Springer, Cham.

Riggle, E. D., Whitman, J. S., Olson, A., Rostosky, S. S., & Strong, S. (2008). The positive aspects of being a lesbian or gay man. *Professional Psychology: Research and Practice, 39*(2), 210–217.

Wei, M., Ku, T. Y., & Liao, K. Y. H. (2011). Minority stress and college persistence attitudes among African American, Asian American, and Latino students: Perception of university environment as a mediator. *Cultural Diversity and Ethnic Minority Psychology, 17*(2), 195–203.

Wei, M., Liao, K. Y. H., Chao, R. C. L., Mallinckrodt, B., Tsai, P. C., & Botello-Zamarron, R. (2010). Minority stress, perceived bicultural competence, and depressive symptoms among ethnic minority college students. *Journal of Counseling Psychology, 57*(4), 411.

REFERENCES

Afifi, T. D. (2017). Making our research matter. *Communication Monographs, 84*(1), 1–4. https://doi.org/10.1080/03637751.2017.1273645

Baams, L., Grossman, A. H., & Russell, S. T. (2015). Minority stress and mechanisms of risk for depression and suicidal ideation among lesbian, gay, and bisexual youth. *Developmental Psychology, 51*(5), 688–696. https://doi.org/10.1037/a0038994

Balsam, K. F., Molina, Y., Beadnell, B., Simoni, J., & Walters, K. (2011). Measuring multiple minority stress: The LGBT people of color Microaggressions scale. *Cultural Diversity and Ethnic Minority Psychology, 17*(2), 163–174.

Balsam, K. F., & Szymanski, D. M. (2005). Relationship quality and domestic violence in women's same-sex relationships: The role of minority stress. *Psychology of Women Quarterly, 29*(3), 258–269.

BBC News. (2019a, November 11). Do today's global protests have anything in common?, https://www.bbc.com/news/world-50123743

BBC News. (2019b, November 28). The Hong Kong protests explained in 100 and 500 words. https://www.bbc.com/news/world-asia-china-49317695

Better, A. (2014). Redefining queer: Women's relationships and identity in an age of sexual fluidity. *Sexuality & Culture, 18*(1), 16–38.

Black Lives Matter. (2020, September 22). About Black Lives Matter. http://www.blacklivesmatter.com/about

Blair, K. L., & Holmberg, D. (2008). Perceived social network support and well-being in same-sex versus mixed-sex romantic relationships. *Journal of Social and Personal Relationships, 25*(5), 769–791. https://doi.org/10.1177/0265407508096695

Bockting, W., Coleman, E., Deutsch, M. B., Guillamon, A., Meyer, I., Meyer, W., III, Reisner, S., Sevelius, J., & Ettner, R. (2016). Adult development and quality of life of transgender and gender nonconforming people. *Current Opinion in Endocrinology, Diabetes, and Obesity, 23*(2), 188–197.

Bowleg, L. (2008). When Black+ lesbian+ woman≠ Black lesbian woman: The methodological challenges of qualitative and quantitative intersectionality research. *Sex Roles, 59*(5–6), 312–325.

Bowleg, L., Huang, J., Brooks, K., Black, A., & Burkholder, G. (2003). Triple jeopardy and beyond: Multiple minority stress and resilience among Black lesbians. *Journal of Lesbian Studies*, 7(4), 87–108.

Braams, B. R., van Duijvenvoorde, A. C., Peper, J. S., & Crone, E. A. (2015). Longitudinal changes in adolescent risk-taking: A comprehensive study of neural responses to rewards, pubertal development, and risk-taking behavior. *Journal of Neuroscience*, 35(18), 7226–7238.

Buchanan, L., Bui, Q., & Patel, J. (2020, July 3). Black Lives Matter may be the largest movement in U.S. history. https://www.nytimes.com/interactive/2020/07/03/us/george-floyd-protests-crowd-size.html

Butler, J. (1990). *Gender trouble: Feminism and the subversion of identity*. Routledge.

Butler, J. (2010). Performative agency. *Journal of Cultural Economy*, 3(2), 147–161. https://doi.org/10.1080/17530350.2010.494117

Casey, L. S., Reisner, S. L., Findling, M. G., Blendon, R. J., Benson, J. M., Sayde, J. M., & Miller, C. (2019). Discrimination in the United States: Experiences of lesbian, gay, bisexual, transgender, and queer Americans. *Health Services Research*, 54(Suppl. 2), 1454–1466.

Chen, Y. C., & Tyron, G. S. (2012). Dual minority stress and Asian American gay men's psychological distress. *Journal of Community Psychology*, 40(5), 539–544.

Clark, R., Anderson, N. B., Clark, V. R., & Williams, D. R. (1999). Racism as a stressor for African Americans: A biopsychosocial model. *American Psychologist*, 54(10), 805–816.

Cochran, S. D., Sullivan, J. G., & Mays, V. M. (2003). Prevalence of mental disorders, psychological distress, and mental health services use among lesbian, gay, and bisexual adults in the United States. *Journal of Consulting and Clinical Psychology*, 71(1), 53–61. http://dx.doi.org/10.1037/0022-006X.71.1.53

Connolly, C. M. (2005). A qualitative exploration of resilience in long-term lesbian couples. *The Family Journal*, 13(3), 266–280. https://doi.org/10.1177/1066480704273681

Correro, A. N., & Nielson, K. A. (2020). A review of minority stress as a risk factor for cognitive decline in lesbian, gay, bisexual, and transgender (LGBT) elders. *Journal of Gay & Lesbian Mental Health*, 24(1), 2–19.

Cyrus, K. (2017). Multiple minorities as multiply marginalized: Applying the minority stress theory to LGBTQ people of color. *Journal of Gay & Lesbian Mental Health*, 21(3), 194–202.

Diamond, L. M., & Lucas, S. (2004). Sexual-minority and heterosexual youths' peer relationships: Experiences, expectations, and implications for well-being. *Journal of Research on Adolescence*, 14(3), 313–340.

Doyle, D. M., & Molix, L. (2015). Social stigma and sexual minorities' romantic relationship functioning: A meta-analytic review. *Personality and Social Psychology Bulletin*, 41(10), 1363–1381.

Drazdowski, T. K., Perrin, P. B., Trujillo, M., Sutter, M., Benotsch, E. G., & Snipes, D. J. (2016). Structural equation modeling of the effects of racism, LGBTQ discrimination, and internalized oppression on illicit drug use in LGBTQ people of color. *Drug and Alcohol Dependence*, 159, 255–262.

Edwards, K. M., & Sylaska, K. M. (2013). The perpetration of intimate partner violence among LGBTQ college youth: The role of minority stress. *Journal of Youth and Adolescence*, 42(11), 1721–1731.

Elia, J. P. (2003). Queering relationships: Toward a paradigmatic shift. *Journal of Homosexuality*, 45(2–4), 61–86.

Ferraro, K. F., & Farmer, M. M. (1996). Double jeopardy to health hypothesis for African Americans: Analysis and critique. *Journal of Health and Social Behavior*, 37, 27–43.

Frost, D. M. (2013). Stigma and intimacy in same-sex relationships: A narrative approach. *Qualitative Psychology*, 1(S), 49–61. https://doi.org/10.1037/2326-3598.1.S.49

Frost, D. M. (2014). Redemptive framings of minority stress and their association with closeness in same-sex relationships. *Journal of Couple & Relationship Therapy*, 13(3), 219–239.

Frost, D. M., Lehavot, K., & Meyer, I. H. (2015). Minority stress and physical health among sexual minority individuals. *Journal of Behavioral Medicine*, 38(1), 1–8. https://doi.org/10.1007/s10865-013-9523-8

Fulginiti, A., Rhoades, H., Mamey, M. R., Klemmer, C., Srivastava, A., Weskamp, G., & Goldbach, J. T. (2020, November 17). Sexual minority stress, mental health symptoms, and suicidality among LGBTQ youth accessing crisis services. *Journal of Youth and Adolescence*, 1–13. https://doi.org/10.1007/s10964-020-01354-3

Gamarel, K. E., Reisner, S. L., Laurenceau, J. P., Nemoto, T., & Operario, D. (2014). Gender minority stress, mental health, and relationship quality: A dyadic investigation of transgender women and their cisgender male partners. *Journal of Family Psychology, 28*(4), 437–447.

Gonzalez, K. A., Ramirez, J. L., & Galupo, M. P. (2018). Increase in GLBTQ minority stress following the 2016 US presidential election. *Journal of GLBT Family Studies, 14*(1–2), 130–151.

Goodwin, R., & Pillay, U. (2006). Relationship, culture, and social change. In A. L. Vangelisti & D. Perlman (Eds.), *The Cambridge handbook of personal relationships* (pp. 695–708). Cambridge University Press.

Graham, J. M., & Barnow, Z. B. (2013). Stress and social support in gay, lesbian, and heterosexual couples: Direct effects and buffering models. *Journal of Family Psychology, 27*(4), 569–578. https://doi.org/10.1037/a0033420

Green, R. J., & Mitchell, V. (2002). Gay and lesbian couples in therapy: Homophobia, relational ambiguity, and social support. In A. S. Gurman & N. S. Jacobson (Eds.), *Clinical handbook of couple therapy* (pp. 546–568). Guilford Press.

Hayes, J. A., Chun-Kennedy, C., Edens, A., & Locke, B. D. (2011). Do double minority students face double jeopardy? Testing minority stress theory. *Journal of College Counseling, 14*(2), 117–126.

Heck, N. C. (2015). The potential to promote resilience: Piloting a minority stress-informed, GSA-based, mental health promotion program for LGBTQ youth. *Psychology of Sexual Orientation and Gender Diversity, 2*(3), 225–231.

Hendricks, M. L., & Testa, R. J. (2012). A conceptual framework for clinical work with transgender and gender nonconforming clients: An adaptation of the Minority Stress Model. *Professional Psychology: Research and Practice, 43*(5), 460–467.

Hobfoll, S. E. (2004). *Stress, culture, and community: The psychology and philosophy of stress*. Springer Science & Business Media.

Hughes, M., Kiecolt, K. J., Keith, V. M., & Demo, D. H. (2015). Racial identity and well-being among African Americans. *Social Psychology Quarterly, 78*(1), 25–48.

Human Rights Campaign. (2020). *Fatal violence against the transgender and gender non-conforming community in 2020*. https://www.hrc.org/resources/violence-against-the-trans-and-gender-non-conforming-community-in-2020

Kamen, C., Burns, M., & Beach, S. R. (2011). Minority stress in same-sex male relationships: When does it impact relationship satisfaction? *Journal of Homosexuality, 58*(10), 1372–1390.

Lazarus, R. S., & Folkman, S. (1984). *Stress, appraisal, and coping*. Springer.

LeBlanc, A. J., Frost, D. M., & Wight, R. G. (2015). Minority stress and stress proliferation among same-sex and other marginalized couples. *Journal of Marriage and Family, 77*(1), 40–59.

Lick, D. J., Durso, L. E., & Johnson, K. L. (2013). Minority stress and physical health among sexual minorities. *Perspectives on Psychological Science, 8*(5), 521–548.

Mays, V. M., & Cochran, S. D. (2001). Mental health correlates of perceived discrimination among lesbian, gay, and bisexual adults in the United States. *American Journal of Public Health, 91*(11), 1869–1876.

McConnell, E. A., Janulis, P., Phillips, G., II, Truong, R., & Birkett, M. (2018). Multiple minority stress and LGBT community resilience among sexual minority men. *Psychology of Sexual Orientation and Gender Diversity, 5*(1), 1–12. https://doi.org/10.1037/sgd0000265

Meyer, I. H. (2003). Prejudice, social stress, and mental health in lesbian, gay, and bisexual populations: Conceptual issues and research evidence. *Psychological Bulletin, 129*(5), 674–697.

Meyer, I. H. (2014). Minority stress and positive psychology: Convergences and divergences to understanding LGBT health. *Psychology of Sexual Orientation and Gender Diversity, 1*(4), 348–349.

Meyer, I. H. (2015). Resilience in the study of minority stress and health of sexual and gender minorities. *Psychology of Sexual Orientation and Gender Diversity, 2*(3), 209.

Meyer, I. H., Schwartz, S., & Frost, D. M. (2008). Social patterning of stress and coping: Does disadvantaged social statuses confer more stress and fewer coping resources? *Social Science & Medicine, 67*(3), 368–379.

Mohr, J. J., & Daly, C. A. (2008). Sexual minority stress and changes in relationship quality in same-sex couples. *Journal of Social and Personal Relationships, 25*(6), 989–1007.

Mohr, J. J., & Fassinger, R. E. (2006). Sexual orientation identity and romantic relationship quality in same-sex couples. *Personality and Social Psychology Bulletin, 32*(8), 1085–1099.

Moore, J. (2017). Performative face theory: A critical perspective on interpersonal identity work. *Communication Monographs, 84*(2), 258–276. https://doi.org/10.1080/03637751.2017.1315891

Otis, M. D., Rostosky, S. S., Riggle, E. D. B., & Hamrin, R. (2006). Stress and relationship quality in same-sex couples. *Journal of Social and Personal Relationships, 23*(1), 81–99.

Parra, L. A., & Hastings, P. D. (2018). Integrating the neurobiology of minority stress with an intersectionality framework for LGBTQ-Latinx populations. *New Directions for Child and Adolescent Development, 2018*(161), 91–108.

Pascoe, E. A., & Smart Richman, L. (2009). Perceived discrimination and health: A meta-analytic review. *Psychological Bulletin, 135*(4), 531–554.

Pew Research. (2015, August 5). Across racial lines, more say nation needs to make changes to achieve racial equality. https://www.pewresearch.org/politics/2015/08/05/across-racial-lines-more-say-nation-needs-to-make-changes-to-achieve-racial-equality/

Pieterse, A. L., Todd, N. R., Neville, H. A., & Carter, R. T. (2012). Perceived racism and mental health among Black American adults: A meta-analytic review. *Journal of Counseling Psychology, 59*(1), 1–9.

Puckett, J. A., Horne, S. G., Herbitter, C., Maroney, M. R., & Levitt, H. M. (2017). Differences across contexts: Minority stress and interpersonal relationships for lesbian, gay, and bisexual women. *Psychology of Women Quarterly, 41*(1), 8–19.

Riggle, E. D., Rostosky, S. S., & Horne, S. G. (2010). Psychological distress, well-being, and legal recognition in same-sex couple relationships. *Journal of Family Psychology, 24*(1), 82–86.

Rosario, M., Rotheram-Borus, M. J., & Reid, H. (1996). Gay-related stress and its correlates among gay and bisexual male adolescents of predominantly Black and Hispanic background. *Journal of Community Psychology, 24*(2), 136–159.

Rostosky, S. S., Riggle, E. D., Gray, B. E., & Hatton, R. L. (2007). Minority stress experiences in committed same-sex couple relationships. *Professional Psychology: Research and Practice, 38*(4), 392–400.

Savin-Williams, R. C. (2008). Then and now: Recruitment, definition, diversity, and positive attributes of same-sex populations. *Developmental Psychology, 44*(1), 135.

Stein, P., Hendrix, S., & Hauslohner, A. (2017, January 22). Women's marches: More than one million protesters vow to resist President Trump. *Washington Post.*

Stewart, A. J., & McDermott, C. (2004). Gender in psychology. *Annual Review of Psychology, 55,* 519–544.

Stuber, J., Meyer, I., & Link, B. (2008). Stigma, prejudice, discrimination and health. *Social Science & Medicine (1982), 67*(3), 351–357.

Sutter, M., & Perrin, P. B. (2016). Discrimination, mental health, and suicidal ideation among LGBTQ people of color. *Journal of Counseling Psychology, 63*(1), 98–105.

Szymanski, D. M. (2009). Examining potential moderators of the link between heterosexist events and gay and bisexual men's psychological distress. *Journal of Counseling Psychology, 56,* 142–151.

Toomey, R. B., Ryan, C., Diaz, R. M., & Russell, S. T. (2018). Coping with sexual orientation–related minority stress. *Journal of Homosexuality, 65*(4), 484–500.

Tropp, L. R., & Pettigrew, T. F. (2005). Relationships between intergroup contact and prejudice among minority and majority status groups. *Psychological Science, 16*(12), 951–957.

Wight, R. G., LeBlanc, A. J., & Lee Badgett, M. V. (2013). Same-sex legal marriage and psychological well-being: Findings from the California Health Interview Survey. *American Journal of Public Health, 103*(2), 339–346.

Zamboni, B. D., & Crawford, I. (2007). Minority stress and sexual problems among African-American gay and bisexual men. *Archives of Sexual Behavior, 36*(4), 569–578.

Robert Carroll

PARENTING OF QUEER OFFSPRING

The parent–child relationships of queer (lesbian, gay, bisexual, transgender, etc.) offspring have generated a growing body of scholarly inquiry in various fields, including communication, psychology, social work, and sociology, largely focused on how a child's coming out (i.e., disclosure of their queer identity) impacts the family (Grafsky et al., 2018; Heatherington & Lavner, 2008; Jhang, 2018; Mena & Vaccaro, 2013; Norwood & Lannutti, 2015; Reeves et al., 2010) and the parent–child relationship (e.g., Saltzburg, 2004; Savin-Williams, 2001; Tyler, 2015), with particular attention to perspectives of queer offspring (Baiocco et al., 2015; Potoczniak et al., 2009; Ryan et al., 2009; Savin-Williams, 1989; Savin-Williams & Dubè, 1998; Savin-Williams & Ream, 2003; Willoughby et al., 2006). Researchers have also attended to the experiences of parents of queer offspring regarding their child's coming out (Butauski & Horstman, 2020; Gonzalez et al., 2013; Grafsky, 2014;). Although scholars have recently begun investigating experiences of parents of queer offspring, decades of research shows consistent evidence of the importance of parent–child relationships, and specifically parents' communication, to the well-being of queer offspring (e.g., Baiocco et al., 2015; Ryan et al., 2009; Savin-Williams, 1989). Parental rejection or lack of support is damaging to queer offspring's concepts of self (Savin-Williams, 1989), and those who experience memorable rejections are at higher risk for suicide, depression, and substance abuse (Ryan et al., 2009; Willoughby et al., 2006). On the other hand, reliable, supportive parents function as a protective factor contributing to better health outcomes for queer offspring (Mena & Vaccaro, 2013; Ryan et al., 2009). Beginning with a discussion of parents' perspectives of their children coming out and the importance of parental reactions, this article reviews extant literature and identifies directions for future communication research on the parents of queer offspring.

PARENTAL REACTIONS TO CHILDREN COMING OUT

Parental reactions to a child's coming out are highly variable, ranging from responding with shock, denial, and anger to more positive responses illustrating support or casual acceptance (i.e., treating it as a non-issue; Butauski & Horstman, 2020; Savin-Williams & Dubè, 1998; Savin-Williams & Ream, 2003). Although some parents may react to a child's coming out with extremely negative responses, many are supportive and express concern for their child's well-being (Butauski & Horstman, 2020; Grafsky, 2014; Savin-Williams & Ream, 2003). Positive responses foster more positive senses of self among queer offspring (Kwon, 2013; Savin-Williams,

1989). Parental support upon a child's coming out fosters queer offspring's resilience and contributes to more positive mental health outcomes (Mena & Vaccaro, 2013; Ryan et al., 2009). After a child comes out, parents have described their own resilience as being a result of focusing on their child's needs through emphasizing love and support, learning how to best support their child, and acknowledging concerns they may have for their child's well-being due to heterosexist stigmas and discrimination (Butauski & Horstman, 2020).

The initial parental reactions to one's coming out are memorable and consequential for queer individuals, but they also have a lasting impact on parents. Upon a child's coming out, parents may progress through a series of stages like those faced by individuals nearing the end of life (Savin-Williams & Dubè, 1998). Tyler and Abetz (2019) found that parents of a LGBTQ child struggled with navigating the expectations they had for their child before the child came out while still trying to communicate support for their child. Parents of transgender individuals likely additionally mourn expectations related to their child's identity based on the gender their child assigned at birth. As such, family members of transgender individuals experience ambiguous loss describing a "phenomenon like a 'living death' of their TG [transgender] family member" (Norwood, 2012, p. 88). Overall, a child's coming out is often described as a significant family stressor (Heatherington & Lavner, 2008; Norwood, 2012). This stressor often requires adjustment from parents, and these adjustments may involve questioning deeply held values and beliefs about sexuality and gender (Gonzalez et al., 2013; Norwood, 2013a, 2013b).

Savin-Williams and Dubè (1998) outlined a developmental model of parental reactions to their child's coming out, starting with a state of shock that leads to feelings of denial and isolation. At this stage, parents grapple with refusing to believe their child's disclosure and thinking their child is going through a phase or experimenting. Some may refuse to acknowledge the disclosure and ignore that aspect of their child's identity in hopes that it will disappear. This leaves parents feeling isolated, which then leads to a stage of anger characterized by frustration with and consternation and rage toward their child and sometimes resulting in rejecting or physically abusing the child. During this stage, parents may search for reasons their child is queer in the hope of projecting blame elsewhere. Failing to find a scapegoat, parents progress to the bargaining stage. Parents may attempt to bargain with their child and say they will act as though their child never came out or will not stop providing financial support or housing if the child recants. After bargaining, the following stage is "characterized by depression and, in some cases, resigned tolerance" (Savin-Williams & Dubè, 1998, p. 8). At this point, parents may feel shame and humiliation if or when others learn about their child's identity, so they may isolate themselves. Parents may also feel depressed due to worries about discrimination their child might endure. Parents may reach the next stage, acceptance, but often need help reaching this stage through learning about their child's queer identity and seeking support groups (Saltzburg, 2009; Savin-Williams & Dubè, 1998). Of those who reach the stage of acceptance, some may grow to become proud and open about their child's queer identity.

PARENTS' JOURNEYS TO ACCEPTANCE

Queer children have indicated a desire to be accepted by their parents but at the same time wish to be their authentic selves (Tyler & Abetz, 2019). Research on parents' experiences with their child's coming out shows evidence of parents' journeys to acceptance of and pride for their child's queer identity (Gonzalez et al., 2013; Grafsky, 2014). Their journeys typically start with grief and concern over disclosing to other family members and their social networks, leaving parents feeling isolated and yearning for support (Saltzburg, 2009). To overcome negative feelings and learn how to best support their child, parents rely on "gaining information through exposure" (Saltzburg, 2004, p. 114) by talking to friends in the queer community and other parents of queer children and reading books (Butauski & Horstman, 2020; Saltzburg, 2009). Parents describe challenging themselves to be more open-minded and adopt new perspectives and, through this, becoming more compassionate and understanding of queer experiences (Gonzalez et al., 2013). Tyler and Abetz (2019) found that parents of a GLBTQ child often moved from concerns of improving their relationship with their child after the child came out to contentment with that relationship after comparing their family's experiences to those of other families with queer children. For some, this leads to engaging in activism and helping other parents accept their queer children (Gonzalez et al., 2013).

Notably, the research on parents' experiences with their child's coming out showcased instances in which parents responded to their child's coming out disclosure with *casual acceptance* marked by little or no emotion (Butauski & Horstman, 2020). In other words, these parents did not have significant feelings toward or need to make major adjustments in response to their child's coming out. Parents described having diverse social networks and valuing queer identities, making their child's disclosure a nonissue, whereas others described having an inkling that their child was queer, so their child's disclosure was essentially a nonevent. These findings indicate cultural shifts toward greater acceptance of the queer community over recent years and support the notion that coming out may be easier for younger generations in comparison to their elder counterparts (Dunlap, 2014).

Although studies challenge the pervasive negative rhetoric surrounding parental reactions to children coming out (Butauski & Horstman, 2020; Gonzalez et al., 2013; Grafsky, 2014), parents' reactions and adjustments are still highly variable and nuanced. The history of each parent–child relationship will play a significant role in parent–child relationship adjustment after a child's coming out. Those with stronger, healthier relational histories have a stronger likelihood of overcoming the relationship stressor (e.g., the child's coming out) and strengthening the parent–child bond (Savin-Williams, 2001). For some parents, this leads to engaging in activism for the queer community by starting Parents and Friends of Lesbians and Gays (PFLAG) chapters, educating others about the queer community, and helping other parents adjust to their child's coming out (Gonzalez et al., 2013). These findings are hopeful, but instances in which parents do not reach acceptance cannot be overlooked.

When parents do not reach the stage of acceptance of their child's queer identity, it can have serious deleterious effects on their child's well-being. Katz-Wise et al. (2016) presented a case describing the experience of a transgender teen that demonstrates how integral parental acceptance is to the well-being of queer youth. The case details the complexities of a teen who was referred to psychotherapy for clinical depression and, after seven months of treatment and building a relationship with her doctor, discloses "I'm a girl. I don't feel like I'm a girl, I *am* a girl" (Katz-Wise et al., 2016, p. 1022. After coming out to her doctor, she came out to her parents, who were very avoidant and reluctant to acknowledge or support her disclosure. On the other hand, she was met with support when she came out to people in her school community. She was adamantly focused on gender affirmation (i.e., working to enact gender identity through appearance, name, and pronoun changes; colloquially known as "transitioning"), so her doctor referred her to a gender management service, but her parents rejected the request. They would not agree to seeking such services while the teen, to whom the parents referred to using a masculine pronoun, was still a minor. The teen's depression persisted. She would experience improvements in mood with each supportive encounter as she continued coming out to her social community, but depression always recurred. Eventually, the teen gave up on trying to gain support and acceptance from her parents and chose to stop pursuing gender affirmation completely, including no longer being addressed by feminine name and pronoun, until she could pursue it independently. Ultimately, "without the support of the parents, the patient regressed and acquiesced to the sex assigned at birth, followed by depression that required pharmacological treatment" (Katz-Wise et al., 2016, p. 1024). This case illuminates the importance of parental acceptance and support to queer offspring. In addition to coming out, parent–child relationships such as the one presented in the case are often riddled with communication challenges that likely have significant impacts on the parent–child relationships as well as both parents' and children's well-being.

From the child's initial disclosure of a queer identity and beyond, it is imperative that communication scholars work to examine parents' relationships with their queer children. In doing so, it is important for researchers to interrogate differences between parents who do and those who do not reach acceptance of their child's queer identity and the implications of not reaching acceptance on parent–child communication and both parents' and children's well-being. Finally, researchers should aim to create and test interventions to help parents reach acceptance and learn how to best support their child.

CENTERING COMMUNICATION

Despite the centrality of communication behaviors such as disclosure (e.g., coming out) and reactions to such disclosures to research on the parent–child relationships of queer offspring, the research has been generated primarily outside of the communication discipline. Communication scholars are well-suited to advance scholarly and practical understanding of the experiences of parents of queer offspring. In doing so, scholars can (re)center a communication perspective to parents' relationships with their queer children by using communication theory as a guide. The following sections provide avenues for future research guided by communicated narrative sense-making (CNSM) theory, communication accommodation theory (CAT), communication privacy management (CPM) theory, relational dialectics theory (RDT), and the theory of resilience and relational load.

Communicated Narrative Sense-Making Theory. Communicated narrative sense-making theory (Koenig Kellas, 2018) serves as a guide to research examining the content, process, and functions of storytelling as it relates to individual and relational well-being through analyses of retrospective (i.e., storytelling of past interactions), interactional (i.e., storytelling together with one or more relational partners), and translational (i.e., applying CNSM theory to test and carry out narrative-based interventions) storytelling. From this perspective, storytelling is "the communicative manifestation of narrative sense-making" (Koenig Kellas, 2018, p. 63). More positive sense-making in the process of storytelling contributes to better personal and relational well-being (Butauski & Horstman, 2020; Koenig Kellas, 2018).

Using CNSM theory as a guide, Butauski and Horstman's (2020) examination of parents' retrospective storytelling of their child's coming out suggests that children's communication behaviors when coming out to their parents may foster parents' understanding and acceptance of their child. Findings showed that parents' perceptions of their child's communicated perspective-taking (CPT) behaviors (i.e., communicating attention to and validation of another's ideas) during the child's coming out were related to higher levels of relational satisfaction and positive affect toward their child's coming out. When parents believed their child engaged in CPT when coming out, they were also more likely to express love and support for their child in their storytelling of their child's coming out.

Centering communication theory, such as CNSM theory, in guiding investigations of parents' relationships with their queer children will provide a deeper understanding of parent–child relationship dynamics and opportunity to create and test interventions to foster effective, healthy parent–child communication and parental adjustment after a child comes out. For example, narrative interventions have been found to reduce political polarization by decreasing negative feelings toward out-group members and malevolent out-group attributions (Warner et al., 2020). Similar interventions could be created and tested to foster more positive feelings toward the queer community. Such programming could be implemented through schools and community organizations to educate parents on queer identities and better prepare them to respond and adjust if their child were to come out.

CNSM theory also provides an excellent framework for analyzing parent–child interactions through investigations of interactional storytelling. For example, future researchers could bring parents and their queer offspring together to tell the child's coming out story interactively. This would allow for investigation of interactional sense-making behaviors such as engagement, turn-taking, perspective-taking, and coherence (Koenig Kellas, 2018). Higher levels of interactional sense-making behaviors during such interactions would indicate higher levels of narrative sense-making and positively contribute to personal and relational well-being in the parent–child relationship.

In addition, researchers should seek to uncover the stories less heard. For example, little is known about how parents navigate their relationship with their child if they never come to accept their child's identity. This undoubtedly has important implications for the health of queer individuals but also for the well-being of parents. Parents are known to feel shame and fault for their child's queer identity. Reaching acceptance can be particularly difficult when it involves questioning deeply held values and beliefs about religion, gender, and sexuality (Gonzalez et al., 2013). If parents can never reach the stage of acceptance for their child's queer identity, they are likely left feeling shameful, at fault, and worried for their child. Researchers should seek to purposefully sample parents who have not grown to accept their child's queer identity and examine their retrospective storytelling of their child's coming out to highlight the meanings, values, and beliefs evidenced in their stories (Koenig Kellas, 2018). Gaining an understanding of these parents' sense-making of their child's identity may be the first step in identifying pathways to reaching acceptance of their child.

Communication Accommodation Theory. It is clear that intergroup dynamics may be at play in many parents' relationships with their queer children. Intergroup communication occurs when interlocutors communicate based on divergent social identities or group differences. Intergroup theorizing asserts that communication is influenced by the social identities of interlocutors, even between those with a common group identity, such as a shared family identity (Soliz & Rittenour, 2012). In the context of parents' relationships with their queer children, group differences based on gender and sexuality, as well as religion/religiosity and age, may contribute to group salience, or the degree to which the group memberships and social identities of interlocutors impact the interaction. Although many parents reach acceptance and grow to embrace their child's queer identity (Gonzalez et al., 2013; Grafsky, 2014), some have difficulty coming to accept their child's queer identity because of their deeply held religious and traditional family values (Baiocco et al., 2015; Gonzalez et al., 2013). Likewise, older generations may struggle to accept queer identities (Dunlap, 2014). Group salience is likely at work in these parent–child interactions because the beliefs and values of parents and queer offspring may diverge based on social identities related to religion, age, gender, and sexual orientation. As such, CAT serves as a useful guiding framework for investigating communication in these parent–child relationships as it relates to both parents' and queer offspring's personal and relational well-being (Butauski, 2018).

Guided by intergroup theorizing, CAT focuses on the extent to which communication may enhance, ameliorate, or sustain group salience during intergroup interactions (Harwood et al., 2006). Accommodative communication can help increase interpersonal connection and diminish group salience, whereas non-accommodative communication can maintain or amplify group salience. Accommodative communication involves showing acknowledgment of and respect for others' personal and group characteristics (Gallois et al., 2018) through supportive communication (Soliz et al., 2009), illustrating respect for divergent values, and showing support for another's social identity (Butauski, 2018). Future research should investigate how parents' and queer offspring's communication accommodation, or lack thereof, impacts the parent–child relationship and their personal well-being, as well as what motivates them to be accommodating—or non-accommodating—in their interactions with one another.

Communication Privacy Management Theory. Communication privacy management theory provides a framework for understanding how people manage and negotiate ownership of their private information or anything they might feel vulnerable to disclose (Petronio, 2002). CPM theory posits that individuals feel ownership over their private information and thus work to manage their privacy through the use of privacy rules that guide their decisions to disclose or conceal information as well as their decisions to engage in boundary coordination or communicate privacy expectations to co-owners (i.e., confidants) of their private information. In doing so, CPM theory outlines various factors influencing privacy rules ranging from gender and culture to considerations of context, motivations, and potential risks and benefits associated with sharing private information. In the context of parents' relationships with their queer offspring, parents may feel a right to ownership over their child's private information (Petronio, 2002, 2010).

Beyond the initial coming out event, CPM theory would be useful for investigating how parents make decisions to disclose or conceal their child's queer identity (Petronio, 2002, 2010) because parents often grapple with how others will react (Saltzburg, 2009). Investigations from this perspective could reveal how parents manage privacy on their children's behalf as information guardians (Hays & Butauski, 2017; Petronio, 2010), as well as how parents and children may come to CPM decisions together regarding disclosing the child's identity to other family members and outsiders. As information guardians, parents may want control over how, when, and if their child's queer identity is disclosed to other family members and outsiders in the same way their child might desire control over these decisions. How parents communicatively navigate these CPM decisions with, or perhaps without, their children will further reveal the complexities of coming out and how the disclosure is made across the family system and beyond (Grafsky et al., 2018; Jhang, 2018).

Relational Dialectics Theory. Relational dialectics theory (Baxter, 2006, 2011) would be useful in helping scholars further understand how parents of queer offspring communicate about queer identities and the systems of meaning that shape this communication (Norwood, 2012). RDT assumes that "relating is a complex process of meaning-making" (Baxter, 2006, p. 130). Scholars using RDT as a guide focus on uncovering the discursive struggles of competing meanings. Such work would build upon Norwood's (2012) work uncovering discursive tensions surrounding discussions and sense-making of transgender identity.

First, Norwood (2012) found that the family members (partners, parents, and siblings) were grappling with the "presence and absence" of their transgender family member that made them feel as if they were grieving the loss of someone who was not actually gone. This feeling was particularly salient upon and during the transgender person's transition or journey toward gender affirmation. Second, family members struggled with the tensions between sameness and difference. Norwood (2012) explained, "This struggle for meaning was related to two issues: sameness–difference of the transgender person throughout the transition process and sameness–difference of the relationship between a transgender person and his or her partner" (p. 84). Finally, a struggle between self and other was uncovered. This tension illustrated how family members desired to be supportive of the transgender person, but because of a lack of understanding, deeply held beliefs, or their own emotional struggles, they had difficulty being supportive. In other words, they wanted to support their transgender family member but were also focused on their own needs, thus illustrating the tension between self and other.

Future work guided by RDT could further investigate discursive tensions surrounding transgender identity. Norwood (2013a) has employed RDT to show how cultural discourses about gender influence not only a person's understanding of a family member's transition but also their understanding of their relationship with that person and of themselves. Norwood (2012) suggests further investigation of the contradiction between presence and absence to better "understand the complexities of transition as an experience of death and rebirth of the (transgender) individual" (p. 88). Future research employing RDT in this area would allow for greater understanding of what they are grieving (e.g., the physical appearance or communication behaviors of the person pretransition, the nature of their relationship pretransition, or the person's family role, such as being a husband or wife). Identifying how parents make meaning surrounding this tension of presence and absence at a deeper level could provide information crucial to helping parents reach acceptance of their transgender child. In addition, research guided by RDT should also investigate discursive tensions surrounding lesbian, gay, bisexual, and nonbinary identities. Tyler and Abetz (2018, 2019) used RDT in their study of interactions between parents and an GLBTQ child and discovered competing cultural discourses in their communication. For example, these competing discourses included invisible versus common, which showed how views on GLBTQ identities have changed over the past decades; tradition versus equality, which centered on marriage equality; and choice versus innate, which focused on the centrality of GLBTQ identity to a person (Tyler & Abetz, 2018). Research such as that by Tyler and Abetz (2018) shows the discursive tensions surrounding some queer identities, but further work focusing on the intersection of these identities and other aspects of identity will lead to increased understanding of the experiences of queer people and their relationships. Although an umbrella of queer identities are often included in many research endeavors, it is possible that focusing on each identity as unique (e.g., lesbian) may lead to increased understanding of the discursive tensions experienced by different members of the queer community and shed light on the nuances in meaning-making within the larger community.

CONCLUSION

Although researchers emphasize the importance of parents' responses to their children coming out, as well as the importance of how people communicate and make sense of queer identities, the nature of parent–child communication *beyond* the initial coming out event is also central to the personal and relational well-being of parents and their queer children. Future research should shift attention to this relational context beyond a child's coming out and parents' sense-making of that disclosure. Outside of adjusting to and discussing queer identities, parents of queer offspring face the same challenges as parents of children who are not queer. For example, parents of queer offspring also become grandparents. Future research could examine the communication between parents and their queer offspring's children (i.e., queer parents' grandchildren), as well as their communication about their offspring's children and family planning because there are unique challenges involved with queer family planning. Scholars of interpersonal and family communication should also be sure to include more diverse samples across race, gender, and sexuality, with attention to parents of queer offspring. Doing so will provide a more accurate picture of the wide diversity of parents and how parents communicate with their children.

FURTHER READING

Lannutti, P. J., Butauski, M., Rubinsky, V., & Hudak, N. (2021). Setting the agenda: LGBTQ+ and SGM family communication. *Journal of Family Communication, 21*(2), 138–143. https://doi.org/10.1080/15267431.2021.1912048

Pollitt, A. M., Blair, K., & Lannutti, P. J. (2022). A review of two decades of LGBTQ-inclusive research in JSPR and PR. *Personal Relationships.* https://doi.org/10.1111/pere.12432

Soliz, J., & Harwood, J. (2006). Shared family identity, age salience, and intergroup contact: Investigation of the grandparent–grandchild relationship. *Communication Monographs, 73*, 87–107. https://doi.org/10.1080/03637750500534388

Tyler, R. T., Huddleston, B. S., Barnett, F. A., Kohring, C. L., & Spaeth, C. M. (2020). Parents learning about their children's TGNC identities. *Journal of Gay & Lesbian Social Services, 32*(4), 393–420. https://doi.org/10.1080/10538720.2020.1763224

Tyler, R. T., Huddleston, B. S., Barnett, F. A., Kohring, C. L., & Spaeth, C. M. (2021). Parents of TGNC children interfacing with their social networks. *Journal of LGBT Youth, 18*(2), 211–232. https://doi.org/10.1080/19361653.2020.1714527

REFERENCES

Baiocco, R., Fontanesi, L., Santamaria, F., Ioverno, S., Marasco, B., Baumgartner, E., Willoughby, B. L. B., & Laghi, F. (2015). Negative parental responses to coming out and family functioning in a sample of lesbian and gay young adults. *Journal of Child and Family Studies, 24*, 1490–1500. https://doi.org/10.1007/s10826-014-9954-z

Baxter, L. A. (2006). Relational dialectics theory. In D. O. Braithwaite & L. A. Baxter (Eds.), *Engaging theories in family communication: Multiple perspectives* (pp. 130–145). SAGE.

Baxter, L. A. (2011). *Voicing relationships*. SAGE.

Butauski, M. (2018). *Assessing perceptions of parents' communication accommodation in relation to sexual and gender minority adult children's communication apprehension and mental health* [Unpublished doctoral dissertation]. University of Missouri.

Butauski, M., & Horstman, H. K. (2020). Parents' retrospective storytelling of their child's coming out: Investigating contributions of communicated perspective-taking in relation to well-being. *Journal of Family Communication, 20*(4), 345–359. https://doi.org/10.1080/15267431.2020.1794872

Dunlap, A. (2014). Coming-out narratives across generations. *Journal of Gay & Lesbian Social Services, 26*, 318–335. https://doi.org/10.1080/10538720.2014.924460

Gallois, C., Watson, B. M., & Giles, H. (2018). Intergroup communication: Identities and effective interactions. *Journal of Communication, 68*, 309–317. https://doi.org/10.1093/joc/jqx016

Gonzalez, K., Rostosky, S., Odom, R., & Riggle, E. (2013). The positive aspects of being the parent of an LGBTQ child. *Family Process, 52*, 325–337. https://doi.org/10.1111/famp.12009

Grafsky, E. L. (2014). Becoming the parent of a GLB son or daughter. *Journal of GLBT Family Studies, 10*, 36–57. https://doi.org/10.1080/1550428X.2014.857240

Grafsky, E. L., Hickey, K., Nguyen, H. N., & Wall, J. D. (2018). Youth disclosure of sexual orientation to siblings and extended family. *Family Relations, 67*, 147–160. https://doi.org/10.1111/fare.12299

Harwood, J., Soliz, J., & Mei-Chen, L. (2006). Communication accommodation theory: An intergroup approach to family relationships. In D. O. Braithwaite & L. Baxter (Eds.), *Engaging theories in family communication: Multiple perspectives* (pp. 19–34). SAGE.

Hays, A., & Butauski, M. (2017). Privacy, disability, and family: Exploring the privacy management behaviors of parents with a child with autism. *Western Journal of Communication, 3*, 376–391. https://doi.org/10.1080/10570314.2017.1398834

Heatherington, L., & Lavner, J. A. (2008). Coming to terms with coming out: Review and recommendations for family systems-focused research. *Journal of Family Psychology, 22*, 329–343. https://doi.org/10.1037/0893-3200.22.3.329

Jhang, J. (2018). Scaffolding in family relationships: A grounded theory of coming out to family. *Family Relations, 67*(1), 161–175. https://doi.org/10.1111/fare.12302

Katz-Wise, S. L., Rosario, M., & Tsappis, M. (2016). LGBT youth and family acceptance. *Pediatric Clinics of North America, 63*(6), 1011–1025. https://doi.org/10.1016/j.pcl.2016.07.005

Koenig Kellas, J. (2018). Communicated narrative sense-making theory: Linking storytelling and well-being. In D. O. Braithwaite, E. A. Suter, & K. Floyd (Eds.), *Engaging theories and family communication* (2nd ed., pp. 62–74). Routledge.

Kwon, P. (2013). Resilience in lesbian, gay, and bisexual individuals. *Personality and Social Psychology Review, 17*, 371–383. https://doi.org/10.1177/1088868313490248

Mena, J. A., & Vaccaro, A. (2013). Tell me you love me no matter what: Relationships and self-esteem. *Journal of GLBT Family Studies, 9*, 2–23. https://doi.org/10.1080/1550428X.2013.746052

Norwood, K. M. (2012). Transitioning meanings? Family members' communicative struggles surrounding transgender identity. *Journal of Family Communication, 12*, 75–92. https://doi.org/10.1080/15267431.2010.509283

Norwood, K. M. (2013a). Grieving gender: Trans-identities, transition, and ambiguous loss. *Communication Monographs, 80*, 24–45. https://doi.org/10.1080/03637751.2012.739705

Norwood, K. M. (2013b). Meaning matters: Framing trans identity in the context of family relationships. *Journal of GLBT Family Studies, 9*, 152–178. https://doi.org/10.1080/1550428X.2013.765262

Norwood, K. M., & Lannutti, P. J. (2015). Families' experiences with transgender identity and transition: A family stress perspective. In L. Spencer & J. Capuzza (Eds.), *Transgender communication: Histories, trends, and trajectories* (pp. 51–68). Lexington.

Petronio, S. (2002). *Boundaries of privacy: Dialectics of disclosure*. State University of New York Press.

Petronio, S. (2010). Communication privacy management theory: What do we know about family privacy regulation? *Journal of Family Theory & Review, 2*, 175–196.

Potoczniak, D., Crosbie-Burnett, M., & Saltzburg, N. (2009). Experiences regarding coming out to parents among African American, Hispanic, and White gay, lesbian, bisexual, transgender, and questioning adolescents. *Journal of Gay & Lesbian Social Services, 21*, 189–205. https://doi.org/10.1080/10538720902772063

Ryan, C., Hueber, D., Diaz, R. M., & Sanchez, J. (2009). Family rejection as a predictor of negative health outcomes in White and Latino lesbian, gay, and bisexual young adults. *Pediatrics, 123*(1), 346–352. https://doi.org/10.1542/peds.2007-3524

Reeves, T., Horne, S. G., Rostosky, S. S., Riggle, E. D. B., Baggett, L. R., & Aycock, R. A. (2010). Family members' support for GLBT issues: The role of family adaptability and cohesion. *Journal of GLBT Family Studies, 6*, 80–97. https://doi.org/10.1080/15504280903472857

Saltzburg, S. (2004). Learning that an adolescent is gay or lesbian: The parent experience. *Social Work, 49*, 109–118.

Saltzburg, S. (2009). Parents' experience of feeling socially supported as adolescents come out as lesbian and gay: A phenomenological study. *Journal of Family Social Work, 12*, 340–358. https://doi.org/10.1080/10522150903261932

Savin-Williams, R. C. (1989). Coming out to parents and self-esteem among gay and lesbian youths. *Journal of Homosexuality, 18*, 35.

Savin-Williams, R. C. (2001). *Mom, Dad. I'm gay: How families negotiate coming out*. American Psychological Association.

Savin-Williams, R. C., & Dubè, E. M. (1998). Parental reactions to their child's disclosure of a gay/lesbian identity. *Family Relations, 47*, 7–13.

Savin-Williams, R. C., & Ream, G. L. (2003). Sex variations in the disclosure to parents of same-sex attraction. *Journal of Family Psychology, 17*, 429–438. https://doi.org/10.1037/0893-3200.17.3.429

Soliz, J., & Rittenour, C. E. (2012). Family as an intergroup arena. In H. Giles (Ed.), *The handbook of intergroup communication* (pp. 331–343). Routledge.

Soliz, J., Thorson, A. R., & Rittenour, C. E. (2009). Communicative correlates of satisfaction, family identity, and group salience in multiracial/ethnic families. *Journal of Marriage and Family, 71*, 819–832. https://doi.org/10.1111/j.1741-3737.2009.00637.x

Tyler, T. R. (2015). Our story: The parent and LGBTQ child relational process. *Journal of Gay & Lesbian Social Services, 27*, 17–45. https://doi.org/10.1080/10538720.2015.988313

Tyler, T. R., & Abetz, J. S. (2018). A contrapuntal analysis of cultural discourses between parent and GLBTQ child. *Journal of GLBT Family Studies, 14*(3), 467–487. https://doi.org/10.1080/1550428X.2017.1393784

Tyler, T. R., & Abetz, J. S. (2019). Interpersonal discourses between parent and LGBTQ child. *Journal of Gay & Lesbian Social Services, 31*(3), 267–289. https://doi.org/10.1080/10538720.2019.1596859

Warner, B. R., Horstman, H. K., & Kearney, C. C. (2020). Reducing political polarization through narrative writing. *Journal of Applied Communication Research, 48*(4), 459–477. https://doi.org/10.1080.00909882.2020.1789195

Willoughby, B. L. B., Malik, N. M., & Lindahl, K. M. (2006). Parental reactions to their sons' sexual orientation disclosures: The roles of family cohesion, adaptability, and parenting style. *Psychology of Men & Masculinity, 7*(1), 14–26. https://doi.org/10.1037/1524-9220.7.1.14

Pamela J. Lannutti and Maria Butauski

QUEER AFRICAN STUDIES

INTRODUCTION

Queer African studies (QAS) has emerged as a growing interdisciplinary field of studies that draws on scholarship from legal studies, postcolonial studies, African studies, cultural studies, development studies, health, communication studies, sociology, history, anthropology, and queer theory. On the one hand, queer African scholarship seeks to disrupt the colonial reification of "African culture" currently being used to debase and criminalize the lives of queer, trans, nonbinary, same-gender-loving Africans. On the other hand, scholars who center their work in QAS have resisted the contemporary refrain that sutures "homophobia" to "Africa" without attending to the needed cultural meanings, historical context, neocolonial reifications, transnational geopolitical relations, and local sociocultural complexities that are creating the anti-Lesbian Gay Bisexual Transgender hysteria and anti-queer animus in parts of Africa. Notably, queer African scholars reveal the ongoing (re)negotiations of the erotic, desire, care, and love by harnessing the theoretical foundations of queerness embedded in customary laws, and cultural traditions within the postcolonial national context that is as dynamic and shifting as its precolonial precedent. Given this broad overview, this article will detail the emergent theoretical concerns in QAS and how it can be taken up within queer communication studies. The article begins by discussing the tensions surrounding the use of "queer"—a Western-based concept in Africa—and how queer African scholars have reconciled its use in the African context. An outline is then presented of the sociohistorical contexts that produced what is now known as QAS in the discipline of African studies, followed by an exploration of the theoretical intersections between African studies and queer studies by outlining where they intersect and where tensions still exist. Finally, a discussion thematically organizes how QAS can reinvigorate and work toward what is concurrently a move toward de-Westernization in queer communication studies.

DEFINING "QUEER" IN QUEER AFRICAN STUDIES?

Queer often connotes an idea that can be used to challenge and destabilize rigid sex/gender categories. Queering is often referenced as an umbrella term to describe the active process of making normative and taken-for-granted social relations look strange. In doing so, queering is a trenchant process of exposing underlying power relations and, importantly, offers possibilities of resistance (Eguchi & Asante, 2016; Jagose, 1996; Yep, 2013). However, deliberations about the meaning and utility of the term in the African context also exist. For one, scholars such as Nyanzi (2014) have critiqued the uncritical deployment of the term in African contexts as a neo-imperial project. Additionally, Matebeni (2014) notes that the term can occlude diversities within groups of people or within Africans themselves (also see a forum in Chevrette & Eguchi, 2020). Regardless of the possibility of cooptation, some scholars have largely embraced the critical impulse embedded in the idea of "queer" and "queering" while regionalizing its analytical and theoretical tools (among several others, see Adjepong, 2021; Camminga, 2020; Livermon, 2020; Nyeck and Epprecht, 2013; Tamale, 2011). Matebeni et al. (2018) note that "African non-heterosexual sexualities and gender diversities are, in our view neither static nor uniform; rather they are dynamic, multifarious, and resilient" (p. 1). As such, it is important to note that other non-heterosexual or nonbinaried identities coexist alongside globalized terms such as queer at a local country-specific level. Examples include Sassoi in Ghana (Otu, 2019), Hungochani in Zimbabwe (Epprecht, 2013), Yan Daudo in northern Nigeria (Gaudio, 2011), Magai on the East African Coast (Amory, 1998), and Khuntha in North Africa (Almarri, 2018). The experiential realities of these terms sometimes conflict with the normative constructions of queerness, particularly in Western academic milieus. Similarly, such local terms are themselves not immutable but are equally contestable as bodies cross borders, and economic and familial conditions change. In this vein, queer African scholarship has provided varying definitions of queerness in the African context. Central to their definitions are questions on the political utility of queerness, as a tool to critique heteronormativity, its intersections to geopolitical imbalances, and neocolonial economic realities. Here, the larger contention is whether queer studies and its theoretical commitments, sutured to the identity polities of the United States, may limit the radical imagination of freedom and liberation on the African continent (Macharia, 2016; Matebeni, 2014).

In one of her ardent critiques of how the emerging scholarship called "queer African studies (QAS)" has attended to the idea of "queering Africa," Nyanzi (2014) unsettles normative ideas of the queer subject in Africa. Mainly, how can queer African scholars identify whom to study when examining the material existence and identity performance of nonnormative embodiment in a continent with diverse and complex social systems and cultural practices? Nyanzi warns against evaluating queerness through a Western frame of reference where the subject is identified by their sexual object choice. It is important to note that the critique of what is queerness in QAS is much less about the policing of the definitional boundaries of "queerness" in Africa. There are concerns about how the uncritical application of queer theory as it is done in the United States may occlude the conditions and possibilities that give rise to being queer in current African contexts. Her critique reveals how queer studies, with its beginnings in U.S. academic circles, may overlook cultural nuances that may not always be about same-sex desire. In her essay "Queering Queer Africa," Nyanzi (2014) poses a question to her queer colleagues who are unable to read her as queer: "if queer is indeed an open invitation to all of us opposed to essentialized patriarchal, heterosexist, heteronormative binary configurations of sexual orientations and gender identities, why do I repel queers…is it my Africanness or queerness that is lacking?" (p. 61). Nyanzi, a feminist, heterosexual-identified cis woman, is one of the fiercest critics of anti-LGBT laws in Uganda. However, her depiction of queerness seems elusive to some queer Ugandans. In fact, she has been charged by some queer Ugandans as occupying "queer African spaces." Her question is an invitation to queer scholars in general to reconceptualize their definition of queerness on the African continent. The contentions around definitional boundaries, embodiment, and limitations of the potentiality of U.S.-based queer studies in QAS is connected to ongoing criticisms of queer studies to fully capture the intersectional material realities of people of color in the United States and Europe (Haritaworn et al., 2008; Johnson, 2001; Puar, 2007). Even though the genesis of queer of color critique is the United States and Europe, its analytical tools have been harnessed to explicate the limitations of queer studies and queer of color itself on the African continent.

Traditional queer studies seek to destabilize heteronormativity by acutely occupying the site of anti-normativity as the site for critiquing normativity. However, some queer African scholars have consistently shown that such reductive binaries (normativity and anti-normativity) pose analytical limitation in exploring how queer Africans negotiate their identities (Asante, 2019; Hoad, 2007). Notably, some key communal identities, traditional customs, and religious institutions that can be overlooked as an "oppressive cultural heterosexual institution" can be reworked and may appear as an integral aspect of queer African subjectivities. A key example of an area that can be an integral aspect of queer African subjectivities is religion. Given that much of the resistance to queerness has emanated from religious institutions, queer is seen as frequently antagonistic to religion and spirituality. Van Klinken (2019) writes that "while religious studies has overlooked queer theory's potential insights to challenge religion's control over 'public morality' and 'purity of the nation,' queer theory has also neglected to engage with religion" (p. 12). The resulting impasse is that queer studies fails to "grasp the potential of religious traditions to not only reinforce but subvert heteronormativity" (p. 14). In this vein, a question that Van Klinken's work unravels is whether Christian religious beliefs and practices can serve even as a source of queer creativity and its implication for theorizing queer African subjectivity. In a continent where several people identify with a religious institution, queer worldmaking is not always outside of, but is enacted in relation to traditional customs, religious beliefs, and globalized LGBTQI+ identities. Thus, African sexual subjects remake themselves in ways that hold onto certain African customs, religions, and traditions but also find ways that undermine its totalizing heterosexist power structure (e.g., see Mbasalaki, 2019).

Defining Queerness. Overall, queer has largely been defined as a political framework and not as a form of identity in queer African scholarship. Ekine and Abbas, in their seminal anthology *Queer African Reader*, take a careful approach to their definition of queerness in Africa by emphasizing its political utility rather than as a form of gender identity or sexual behavior. They emphasize that attention to how Africanness and queerness intersect could be productive to the political work of queer African studies. They wrote:

> We define "queer" here and in the title to denote a political frame rather than a gender identity or sexual behavior. We use queer to underscore a perspective that embraces gender and sexual plurality and seeks to transform, overhaul, and revolutionize African order rather than seek to assimilate into oppressive hetero-patriarchal-capitalist framework. Queer is our dissidence stance, but we use it here knowing the limitations of the terminology in relation to our African neocolonial realities. (Ekine & Abbas, 2013, p. 4)

In her introduction to the *Handbook on Queer African Studies*, S. N. Nyeck (2019) similarly utilizes "queer" as a political frame rather than as a gender or sexual identity. She notes that queer in Africa is a "non-exhaustive umbrella for non-heteronormative sexualities and gender identities" (p. 3). Here, adopting queerness as a political frame and a dissidence stance means that the politics of sexuality is hardly taken up alone; it appears always in tandem with a dynamic sociopolitical and postcolonial material reality.

The scholarly conversations in the nascent field of queer African studies about defining queerness as a political dissidence has implications in the ways queer African communicative practices are researched and archived. It is important to note that the point of this debate is not to assert a unique kind of "queerness" as distinctly "African" or "Western." Instead, Matebeni et al. (2018) assert that the knowledge of being queer in Africa "mediates southern and northern queer scholarship, directing attention towards African-centered understandings accessible to a wider audience" (p. 7). The emphasis on African-centered framings and enactments of queerness is crucial because, as Asante (2019) contends, nonnormativity could appear in unlikely modalities in different regions of the African continent. Reflecting on his experience while presenting at an academic conference on how Black figures encounter each other to revamp oppressive gendered systems, Keguro Macharia (2015) writes,

> When I examine, say, how wearing trousers was an important moment in Gikuyu colonial modernity when gender and sexuality shifted in radical ways, or how shifting practices of labor and punishment in pre- and postemancipation Jamaica remade notions of gender and sexuality, I see yawns lining up in mainstream queer studies. Where are the "queers"? Sometimes, the question is, where are the white people we care about and at other times, "where are the Europeans and U.S. inhabitants we can care about?" (p. 186)

In summary, Macharia suggests that how queerness is defined in the African context is a shifting and unstable endeavor. Ultimately, though there are disagreements on what constitutes queerness on the African continent, QAS scholarship is united around its potentiality to challenge (hetero)normative institutions and structures that sustain oppressive and essentialized gendered and sexual identities.

HISTORICAL BEGINNINGS AND POLITICAL CONTEXTS OF QUEER AFRICAN STUDIES

While queer African studies (QAS) is a relatively recent area of inquiry in communication studies, it began as a subfield of study in African studies in the 1990s (see Amory, 1997). Parallel to the absorption of queer theory in numerous university departments in the United States, queer scholars in African studies also began to resist the studied avoidance of research on "homosexuality." Mirroring the ongoing debasement of same-sex sexuality on the African continent by political leaders such as the former president of Zimbabwe, Robert Mugabe, and the former president of Namibia, Sam Nujoma, Amory (1997) notes that some scholars in African studies were also reproducing the insidious accusation that "homosexuality" is a Western import and an immoral residue of European colonization of Africa (Amory, 1997; Currier & Migraine-George, 2016). This charge meant that Western scholars did most of the research on gender and sexuality in Africa, some of whom wanted to prove a distinct "African sexuality" often represented in pathological ways (e.g., Caldwell et al., 1989).

Since colonization, European colonialists have been preoccupied with the morality of African sexuality, especially with regards to behaviors they deemed as sinful and uncivilized, such as clitoridectomy, polygyny, and woman-to-woman marriages, among others. In fact, much of what has been written about precolonial African sexualities can be found in the colonial archive (Hoad, 2007; Macharia, 2015; Tamale, 2011). Drawing on postcolonial scholars such as Edward Said and V. Y. Mudimbe, Desiree Lewis (2011) explains how the linguistic, visual, scholarly, and popular interpretation of African bodies relied on a false notion of perceived sexual depravity to serve as a "polemical argument for the West's desperate desire to assert its difference from the rest of the world" (Mbembe, 2001, p. 2). In another example, McClintock (1995) examined the connections between imperial sexuality and colonial conquest and settlement. She showed how eroticism was central to the narratives of the sexual superiority of European colonialists. Murray and Roscoe (1998) make a similar argument that the overemphasis on Africans' "primitive" stature formed the bases for European colonialists to "highlight that which distinguishes Western cultures by describing that which is not Western" (p. xi). Thus, the promulgation of myths about "African sexualities" has partially contributed to the belief that same-sex desires were imported to the continent through colonialism.

One such myth is the belief that because Africans epitomized primitiveness and, thus, closeness to nature, they could not exhibit homoerotic desires. In this regard, Dlamini (2006) explained, "since primitive man was perceived to be close to nature, ruled by instincts, and culturally unsophisticated, he had to be heterosexual; his sexual energies and outlets devoted exclusively to their 'natural' purpose" (p. 132). The myth of primitive Africans and their inherent heterosexuality can be traced to anthropologist Edward Gibbon's work in sub-Saharan Africa. Gibbons is quoted by Murray and Roscoe (1998) to have written: "I believe and hope the negros, in their own country, were exempt from this moral pestilence [i.e. homosexual vice]." The pervasiveness of the narrative that same-sex desires are absent on the African continent prompted other influential anthropologists who witnessed same-sex sexual intimacies and activities to exclude such findings in their ethnographic reports. Murray and Roscoe (1998) wrote that anthropologists such as Richard Burton (1893), and Evans Pritchard & Gillies (1937), evaded recording their observations about same-sex sexual activities. The consequences of such intended absences have concretized the now-proselytized mantra that homosexuality is not innate to Africans but a Western import. The effect of false narratives and myths about the absence of same-sex sexuality through European colonialists' reports has been exacerbated by the proliferation of Pentecostalist Charismatic churches across sub-Saharan Africa (Kaoma, 2012), some of whom have connections to the Catholic Church and U.S. conservative evangelical Churches, losing a cultural war in the United States.

Kaoma (2012) wrote that Christian conservatives have found a growing acceptance of their ideologies in African countries due to their declining popularity in the United States. With an emphasis on abstinence-only education, faithfulness within heterosexual marriage, and anti-abortion, groups such as Family Watch International have lobbied African governments and traditional African churches to adopt U.S. conservative-right ideologies as "African culture." With already a Christianity saturated with identified demons and the prosperity gospel, which claims that simple faith in Jesus Christ will bring financial wealth and well-being, Kaoma

(2012) explains that Africa provides a receptive home for U.S. Christian right movements that may be a minority in the United States. Similarly, the embrace of reproduction as a virtue and childlessness as a tragedy in some African communities provide an opening for the U.S. Christian right's promotion of "family values." The claim to a particular "African family values" reproduces essentialized gendered binaries that leave no room for the expression of nonnormative genders and sexualities.

The influx of international funding from the Joint United Nations Program on AIDS (UNAIDS) and the U.S. President's Emergency Plan for AIDS Relief (PEPFAR), among others, to expand resources toward HIV infections in many parts of Africa has opened the door for the emergence of sexual and reproductive health rights discourse. Marc Epprecht (2012) stated that the "strategic embrace of health discourses is one 'cloaking' mechanisms to slip sexual minority rights onto the local agenda." This shows that there is some progress toward the attainment of sexual rights for LGBT people across West Africa through the strategic use of HIV/AIDS relief funds. However, Sylvia Tamale (2011) argues that the proliferation of policies focusing on HIV/AIDS, in connections with the World Health Organization, civil societies, bilateral partners, pharmaceutical corporations, and Western medical and health professionals, has largely been advanced using quantitative biomedical tools which "ignores the qualitative socio-economic aspects of the epidemic" (p. 17). The consequence is that research that centers on queer pleasure, desire, and sexual agency is deprioritized. As such, sex is approached only as a problem to be fixed, which ultimately reinforces the colonial-era myths and stereotypes of a specific "African sexuality" that is deviant, insatiable, morally corrupt, and dangerous.

In an often-critiqued example of the essentialist approach to representing "African sexuality," demographers Caldwell et al. (1989) developed a theory about African sexuality (a problematic framework) to understand the social context of HIV/AIDS in sub-Saharan Africa. In their influential text, Caldwell et al. claimed that one could explain the apparent differences of African AIDS by paying attention to the specifics of a particular "African sexuality" as a distinct and coherent system (Caldwell et al., 1989). The authors created seven recognizable traits that distinguished African sexuality from so-called Eurasian sexuality. African sexuality thereby: (1) does not occupy a central position in African moralities; (2) allows for general "sexual permissiveness"; (3) accords low value to female chastity because of the reproduction focus of African lineage ideologies; (4) is based on a dual sex system that separates a female sphere from a male sphere; (5) produces loose and emotionally weak conjugal bonds; (6) does not recognize female pleasure; and (7) is characterized by a high occurrence of transactional sex. Caldwell's conceptual framework and assertions have been subjected to rigorous critique, setting up a barrage of criticism in contemporary sexuality scholarship (Ahlberg, 1994; Le blanc et al., 1991; Tamale, 2011). In her trenchant critique of Caldwell's "African sexuality" thesis, Beth Maina Ahlberg (1994) counterargued that Caldwell et al.'s conceptualization of African sexuality "ignores and suppresses patterns of change that would undermine their thesis of permissive African sexuality" (p. 25). For instance, Ahlberg notes that by assuming that African sexuality has

> no religious moral value and that the forces of change (including European colonization and urbanization) had no impact or that early anthropologists reached wrong conclusions

about change, Caldwell et al. have few options but to see change only in terms of expanded permissiveness. (p. 25, my emphasis)

Exploring how knowledge about sexuality has been developed across the African region, Undie and Benaya (2006) write that Caldwell et al.'s conceptualization of African sexuality made clear the limitations of addressing research on African sexuality through colonial lenses and methodologies even if the motive is prudent.

From a focus on sexuality as a moral question to the study of sexuality as a problem and the production of African sexuality as exclusively heterosexual, these historical trends form part of the historical and political context that drives QAS research. For centuries, gender and sexuality in parts of Africa have been resignified as sites of perversion, morality, incivility, and irrationality. These views continue to influence contemporary knowledge about gender and sexuality in Africa. It is within these historical developments that QAS has emerged as a necessary interdisciplinary field of study within African studies. Nonetheless, since QAS is largely composed of scholars based in the United States and Europe, scholarly disagreements have emerged on how the interdisciplinary endeavor between queer studies and African studies could be deployed productively. The productive tensions between African studies and queer studies are necessary to explore, as they re-ignite discussions about the need for decolonization.

BRIDGING TWO WORLDVIEWS: QUEER STUDIES, AFRICAN STUDIES, AND THEIR IMPLICATIONS FOR QUEER COMMUNICATION STUDIES

Unequivocally, both queer studies and African studies have political goals that align more than they diverge, even though they tend to be represented as two seemingly incommensurable sites of study. Still, it would be naïve to not acknowledge the divergent historiographies of the fields of African studies and queer studies. More importantly, the theoretical goals of African studies and queer studies can be aligned with each other while maintaining a productive tension between the two areas of study. In a long-overdue essay that charts the intersectional theoretical possibilities between African studies and queer studies despite their divergent historical beginnings and political interests, Currier and Migraine-George (2016) note that African studies scholars have decidedly avoided developing theoretical insights into queer theory. Simultaneously, they claim that some queer studies scholars have primarily overlooked gender and sexual plurality in different African societies. Epprecht (2008) notes that queer studies scholars who invariably include Africa "cherry-pick obscure references" to bolster arguments (particularly in the Global North) that queerness is indeed everywhere. Currier and Migraine-George conclude that the lack of engagement between African studies and queer theory is a missed opportunity for both to enrich each other's disciplinary circumference. An examination of the intersections between queer studies and African studies shows that they can used together to leverage a more robust critique of cisheteronormativity on the African continent and beyond. And aligning both can generate productive tensions that has implications for how queer communication studies is theorized.

Queer studies and African studies can complement each other and, as such, can build on each other's theoretical limitations if utilized sufficiently. While queer studies has produced several insights into the working of heteronormativity, it has been critiqued as unable to adequately capture the material realities of people who are non-Western, white, able-bodied queer subjects. In response to such critiques, several adjustments to queer theory have been made (e.g., Quare studies, Kaur Studies, Crip studies, etc.). Transnational queer scholars have also argued that the breadth of queer studies has been uncritically used preemptively to define and explore sexual politics in non-Western contexts without first grounding it in the cultural and material context of that location (Moussawi, 2020). This critique is particularly relevant in the African context. As Neville Hoad reminds us, Africanness is an "intimate structure" that cannot be excised from the continent's histories of colonialism and current postcolonial and geopolitical formations. Additionally, the continent has a wealth of knowledge that is typically unacknowledged or overlooked because of its demarcation as "customary" or "cultural," and, thus, theoretically unusable even though several studies suggest that queer Africans adapt traditional and cultural norms for alternative purposes. In a recently published special issue in GLQ titled: *Time of Out Joint: The Queer and the Customary in Africa*, Fiereck et al. (2020) drew attention to the African queer customary as a possible space of political pragmatism. Here, the customary is not the same as the hegemonic realm of customary law. Customary practices and discourses are used in ways that produce unexpected outcomes, or they rearticulate the terms of their use. This is what Xavier Livermon (2015) referred to as "usable traditions." Exploring same-sex marriages in South Africa, Yarbrough (2018) asserted that the transaction between civil and customary law, embedded in same-sex marriage ideals, opens the possibilities to reform personhood, intimacy, and social relation. For instance, Mbasalaki (2019, 2020) essay shows how Black lesbians who wish to engage in traditional marriage ceremonies engage in a kind of cultural labor that enables the reproduction of spaces of belonging in their communities, "therefore contributing, not only to the township but also to African cultural capital, thus underwriting the very culture that often rejects and expels them" (p.38). Thus, as Fiereck et al. (2020) note, "there is an archive of the customary that may provide intellectual and affective resources to reimagine African sexual sovereignty." (p. 2). As has been shown, some queer, gender-nonconforming, same-gender-loving Africans may use indigenous traditions and customs to redefine and refashion themselves. As such, an examination of their embodied experiences demand that the scholar understand the cultural nuances of traditions and customs and how they intersect with gender and sexuality.

Integrating queer studies and African studies has some implications for global queer communication studies. For one, it enriches the theoretical debates around intersectionality so central to queer and trans of color criticism. Although queer of color theorists have revealed limitations of using singular frameworks for understanding social phenomena, Arondekar (2005) notes that these fields of studies remain sutured to their U.S. academic origins despite their efforts to criticize the epidemic violence involved in the "provincial conflation of race and sex." As such, Black queer studies and queer of color critique remain oriented to a particular geopolitical horizon of queer critique that produces other illegibilities of bodies outside of the United States. Such illegibilities have implications on how intersectionality is theorized within queer communication studies. In particular, Currier and Migraine-George (2016) assert that the interdisciplinary theorization of intersectionality largely produced by queer of color scholars in the United States remains embedded in cultural norms, that have sometimes "resolidified the Other—that is 'ethnic' and 'queer'—identities as necessarily 'intersectional' in contrast to white, heterosexual identities assumed to be central and homogenous" (p. 285).

Currier and Migraine-George also point out that the deployment of intersectional analysis tends to centralize the United States as the "primary matrix," which, in turn, privileges a "grid-like model" that fails to capture the shifting dynamics of identity formation over a period of time. The consequences of such dichotomizing are that queerness in African contexts tends to be "read" through U.S.-based queer identity politics of race, gender, class, and nationality that may or may not resonate with queer African subjects. In summary, drawing from the works of African/ist scholars may intervene in such oversight and hold queer communication studies accountable to its political commitments beyond the United States (Huang, 2021; Lee, 2014).

INCORPORATING QUEER AFRICAN STUDIES IN QUEER COMMUNICATION STUDIES

Some scholars have productively and provocatively taken up gender and sexuality studies in Africa in communication studies by focusing on various themes. The various scholarship can be divided into subthemes: (1) colonial, postcolonial, and neoliberal entanglements of anti-LGBT violence in Africa; (2) discursive negotiations of identity; (3) coalition building and political activism; and (4) media presentation and queer African diasporic connections on social media.

Colonial, Postcolonial, and Neoliberal Entanglements of Anti-LGBT Violence in Africa. Several scholars outside of communication studies have argued against the simplification of episodes of anti-queer violence in parts of Africa, noting that the recent emergence of "homosexuality" as a public debate has encouraged a stereotypical view of Africa as an excessively homophobic space in relation to a tolerant and moral West (Ndashe, 2013). One such important critique is presented by Awondo et al. (2012), who contend that there are several and different trajectories in the formation of views on "homosexuality" across the African continent. Comparing the multiple ways that homosexuality became politicized in Senegal, Cameroun, Uganda, and South Africa, they found out, for example, in Senegal and Cameroon, that the "homosexual" is represented as a rich and powerful "Big Man" who utilizes anal sex as a form of the subjection of his victims to be rich. Such views connect homosexuality to occultism, wealth, and power, thus producing a particular reaction to "homosexuality" in a region with vast fundamentalist religious influence. They conclude that more studies are needed to shed light on the "variations that are loosely labeled homophobia in Africa because the homosexual figure can take on such different contours" (p. 160).

In another essay, Awondo et al. (2012) maintains that the persistent African newspaper publications of anti-LGBT rhetoric from religious leaders and politicians should instead be read as the result of fierce rivalry between emerging news media companies in such countries as such anti-queer discourses do not always mirror the general public's sentiments around nonnormative sexuality. In fact, sprouting progressive voices are hardly mentioned in such reports. Ndashe (2013) avers that while there have been progressive voices against homophobic attacks, such voices are drowned in the global search for homophobes in Africa. Also, several local activists and community-based organizations are speaking out against homophobic attacks. Activists such as Alice Nkom, a lawyer in Doula, Cameroon, are among the few lawyers who defend those accused of homosexual acts. She is the founder of the Defense of Homosexuals in Cameroon in Cameroon. In Uganda, Stella Nyanzi is a fierce critic of President Yoweri Museveni, who has been in power for more than 30 years and recently signed the infamous Uganda anti-homosexuality bill into law. Leila Slimani has denounced the humiliation of gay people in Morocco. Lastly, musicians such as Wanlov Kubolo Efya and C-Real have taken to social media to condemn homophobic attacks in Ghana. However, such progressive voices hardly make it into local and Western media narratives of homophobic violence, laws, and attacks, which reproduce homonationalist frames that establish Western Europe and the United States as exceptional and Africa as backward and uncivilized (Ndashe, 2013). These scholars resist the single story of Africa's homophobia and call for more nuanced intersectional analysis of anti-LGBT violence by emphasizing queer studies, African studies, and postcolonial theory to highlight the historicity of the recent explosions of anti-queer violence in Africa (Thoreson, 2014).

In communication studies, Asante's (2020) essay, "Anti-LGBT Violence and the Ambivalence (Colonial) Discourses of Ghanaian Pentecostalist Charismatic Church Leaders," examined the rhetoric used by Ghanaian Pentecostalist Charismatic church leaders to rationalize the continuation of criminalization of same-sex desires and non-heterosexual relations without being held accountable for how such discourses influence the normalization of anti-LGBT violence. Drawing from critical discourse analysis, (queer) postcolonial studies, and critical intercultural communication, Asante examined the relationship between institutionally produced discourses and the material conditions of anti-LGBT violence in Ghana. Largely centralizing the fabricated notion of the "African family" and heterosexuality as "natural," some GPCC church leaders have argued that nonnormative sexuality is unnatural and, therefore, "unAfrican." Furthermore, most of these pastors have contended that decriminalization of homosexuality will bring God's wrath to the nation. The false claim that same-sex sexual relations are "unnatural" and thus "unAfrican" is also made by other Christian religious groups in other African countries, such as Pastor Martin Ssempe in Uganda and Bishop Joseph Akonga Essomba from Cameroon, exposing a concerted continental effort to delegitimize queer sexuality in Africa.

Asante's critical discourses analysis of GPCC's anti-LGBT rhetoric similarly revealed that while resistance to such rhetoric exists, they are hardly reported by private and public news organizations and thus create the view that most Ghanaians support anti-LGBT views (Tettey, 2016). GPCC's rhetoric is pervasive and persuasive because it draws on anticolonial rhetoric to argue that they are protecting Africans from being colonized. In short, although Christianity is a colonial institution in Africa, GPCCs are currently portraying it as innately an "African institution," protecting the interest of all Africans (except queers, lesbians, and sex workers). Asante's research questions the very notion of the "post" in postcolonial theory by asking scholars to "queer" the postcolonial by paying attention to the marginalized voices that are left out in the (re)production of "Africa" as homophobic or the unholy defense of Africa as exclusively heterosexual (Epprecht, 2008).

Discursive Negotiations of Identity. In his essay, "Queering/Quaring/Kuaring/Crippin'/Transing 'Other Bodies' in Intercultural Communication," Gust Yep (2013) called attention to the potential misreading of Other bodies when researchers ignore the multiple contexts that produces particular meaning in other places. As an example, using Donham's (1998) case study of Linda, a gender and sexual nonnormative Black man who lived in post-apartheid South Africa, Yep (2013) critiques Donham's characterization of Linda as a gay man by noting that Linda was not always gay. In response, he opines that what Donham (1998) needed to do was examine "how the larger political, cultural and historical forces, attitudes and relationships between social and cultural groups, and interactions between individuals in various communities operated simultaneously in and through Linda's body to produce an international and Westernized conception of gay identity" (p. 121). In short, the proliferation of LGBT identities across the world as they are defined and enacted in the West does not mirror how gender and sexuality are lived in non-Western contexts.

While LGBT identities have become a site for political activism in many parts of Africa, the "LGBT acronym" does not fully capture the nuances and multilevel interplay that produces specific sexual behaviors in many parts of Africa. In other words, the language that is used to describe same-sex sexual relations (especially in academic circles) developed in a specific history pertaining to scientific inquiry, social relations, and political struggles that did not exist in Africa (Epprecht, 2008). As such, while African women or men may engage in same-sex eroticism, simply calling them "lesbian" or "gay" is incomplete. For instance, Broqua (2013) revealed that while some Malian men may engage in same-sex sexual behaviors, they do not identify as "gay" or "homosexual." In fact, some men who engage in same-sex sexuality may resist LGBT rights altogether while still engaging in same-sex erotics. Other men also believe that heterosexuality and homosexuality are not incompatible (Broqua, 2013). What is largely understood to be at play is the glocalization of discourses around sexuality—an interplay between local discourses around sexuality and global discourses of sexual identity. This interplay is captured by the essay, "'Queerly Ambivalent': Navigating Global and Local Normativities in Postcolonial Ghana." In this essay, Asante (2019) highlights how some Sasso (a Ghanaian colloquial term for same-gender-loving people in Ghana) navigate both the local sexual politics that enforce silence around sexualities and the visibility politics of transnational LGBT organizations by being queerly ambivalent. Drawing from the works of Muñoz (1999) and Bhabha (2012), according to Asante (2019), "queerly ambivalent captures the tensed space between the desire for same-sex pleasure, the need to maintain familial relationships and the material context of anti-LGBT violence" (p. 166). Asante asserts that ambivalence offers the theoretical energy to describe how queer Africans deploy and resist the suffocating constraints of LGBT identities and the restrictive boundaries of Ghanaian sexual citizenship simultaneously. For instance, he uses an emergent sexual culture called "classy" to describe "queerly ambivalent" by showing how being "classy" inflects a class positioning that makes one's sexual identity ambiguous and irrelevant in certain situations. As such, "classy" is an expression and performance of class positioning that intersects with existing social hierarchies around gender and sexuality. In this vein, "classy" also reproduces a gendered hierarchy that debases queer femininity. However, Asante explains that although certain performances of "classy" debase male effeminacy in order to maintain a sense of ambiguity around sexual identity, queer scholars should not assume it is similar to the debasement of queer femininity in the United States and Western Europe. He explicates, "In the context of anti-LGBT violence, transnational LGBT visibility politics and the cultural silences around sexuality in Ghana, effeminate queer men (read as gay) by other queer Ghanaian men disrupt ambivalent meanings, which some Sasso deploy to navigate their same-sex desires and familial relationships" (Asante, 2019, p. 171).

In another study, Goltz et al. (2016), identified and analyzed sites of discursive negotiations among sexual and gender minorities in Kenya. First, they examined cultural myths or master narratives about LGBTI identities in Kenya and how LGBT Kenyans navigate such myths. Secondly, they explored the tension between mainstream understandings of homosexuality as an imported influence and the arising resistant articulations of LGBT identities as innate or natural; therefore, they should be granted the right to privacy. This discursive site revealed the tensions between individual sexual identity and the need to engage in sexual identity politics. Lastly, the authors analyzed how a glocal queer frame constitutes gay and lesbian identities in contemporary Kenya. They stated:

> In a globalized world, where films, texts, meanings images, and representations of Western gay and lesbian culture circulate broadly and regularly, the criticism of the Western import is both a homophobic tool of the Kenyan master narrative and a necessary site of resistance for queer persons in Kenya. (p. 114)

Both studies by Asante and Goltz et al. point out how identity negotiation strategies among LGBT, queer, same-gender-loving, and gender-nonbinary individuals used in many parts of Africa defy simplistic categorizations such as local–global, normative–transgressive, and how such identities deploy glocal and disidentificatory identity negotiation practices that do not neatly follow similar rubrics of identity politics used in the West. To resist the simplistic reading of queer identity negotiation strategies in parts of Africa, Goltz et al. (2016) advise scholars doing research in African contexts to exercise caution in using a normative lens that may be complicit in the recentralizing Western conceptualization of gender and sexual identity. They advise scholars trained in Western traditions and universities to engage in cultural humility because it "requires acknowledging how researchers and the research process itself can function to falsely universalize Western knowledge" (Goltz et al., 2016, p. 118). Asante (2019) equally states that scholars who engage in research in Africa should centralize African material lived experiences and how they re-articulate queer theory altogether, and not only how queer theory is taken up in Africa.

Coalition Building and Political Activism. While numerous studies have emerged in African feminist studies and queer African studies, there is a lack of theoretical and political fluidity. These charges were quite evident at a U.N. Fourth World Conference on Women in Beijing in 1995, where many African women's activists flagrantly explicated that matters relating to the sexual were not of priority to African women (Jolly, 2000; Okech, 2013). Awino Okech (2013) writes that the lack of cross engagement is quite ironic since LGBTI organizing and feminist/women's rights draw from the intellectual history that is collectively called feminist theory and politics. Queer African studies and African feminist theorizing in parts of Africa typically converge on their critique of what Jacqui Alexander terms

> heteropatriarchal recolonization—the similar use of militarized masculinities as a foundation for liberation and postcolonial nation-building—however, Jackson notes that

because feminists are usually concerned with the ways heteronormativity depends on gender division, they are far less interested in the everyday practices of heterosexual relations. (as cited in Okech, 2013, p. 2)

Even though these troubling precepts exist, some African feminists such as Amina Mama, Sylvia Tamale, and Stella Nyanzi, among many others across the continent, are finding creative ways to develop spaces of solidarity with the emerging queer African movement. Awino Okech (2013) advises that the fundamental theories that structure such spaces need to shift for such emergent spaces to be effective. She writes, "the solidarity offered toward the growing queer movement in Africa cannot be seen as one that is simply building bridges across movements but as one that destabilizes heteronormativity by dismantling how the family, the state, the economy reproduces normative heterosexuality" (p. 26).

In a special forum titled "Queer African and African Feminist Coalitional Possibilities," published in 2020 in the journal *Women's Studies in Communication*, Godfried Asante, Jenna Hanchey, Joelle Cruz, Gloria Pindi, and Consolata Mutua-Mambo explored the intricate and nuanced ways queer Africans and African feminists/womanists based in and outside continental Africa enact their alliances and (dis)connections across transnational borders. In doing so, they discussed the transformative possibilities that can emerge when queer Africans and African feminists/womanists provocatively and publicly show solidarity against heteropatriarchal structures that seek to regulate queer Africans, women, and gender-nonconforming folks across Africa. Drawing largely on African studies, queer theory, queer of color critique, and transnational feminism, these scholars examined what such coalitions could reveal about social justice and feminist alliances on the continent. Introducing the forum, Cruz (2020) lamented the lack of scholarship about Africa in general in the field of communication, noting that such absences reproduce "Africa" as a theoretical vacuum even though American Western feminist communication scholars can learn much about thriving through crises by closely paying attention to three key ideas in African feminist and queer perspectives—material conditions, holism, and situationality (Cruz, 2015).

Mutua-Mambo's (2020) and Gloria Pindi's (2020) essays critiqued the consequential and reactionary standpoint from many women political activists in Africa that African feminism and queer studies are a Western import. They argue that feminist sensibilities and political organizing around the need to provide better living and working conditions for all African women (irrespective of one's sexual proclivity) are indeed not alien to African culture. As such, they both lament the lack of attention to sexuality and sex in African feminist theorizing. For Pindi, queer and feminist solidarity means having a conversation that ruptures the seams of heteronormativity by advancing an African feminist queer agenda that seeks to decolonize African consciousness through the stronghold of Christianity-imposed religious practices that have been weaponized to perpetrate hate crimes against sexual minorities in Africa (see Pindi & De la Garza, 2018).

Focusing on erotic belongings as a site of coalitional building, Asante (2020) examines how to reimagine African feminist and queer African solidarity by focusing on both queer Africans and African feminists' shared material concerns. Expanding Cruz's (2015) African feminists' theoretical framework, Asante contends that sexuality should also be explored as a concern of the everyday, which is often overlooked by feminist scholars who emphasize the need to pay attention to the materiality/material conditions for African feminists (such as food, shelter, and water). Through what he terms "queer African eros," Asante (2020) highlights the way that the needs of queer Africans and African feminists collide in fruitful, albeit creative ways when both explore the erotic as a site of both oppression and political resistance. The essays from the special issue gesture toward a kind of "Africanfuturism" where creative imaginations and disruptive possibilities intertwine that are often overlooked in U.S. feminist theorizing or diasporic theorizing of Afrofuturism (Hanchey, 2020).

Media Representation and Queer African Diasporic Connections on Social Media. While the production and circulations of queer African media texts are sparse in general, an analysis of queer African representations in communication studies is surprisingly quite few. On the one hand, several studies examine media representations of queer African subjects (e.g., Sloop, 2012; Winslow, 2012). However, studies that examine queer African subjects from an Africanist perspective are almost nonexistent in communication studies. One of the few studies in communication studies that takes an Africanist perspective to the study of media representations of queerness in Africa is Asante et al.'s (2019) essay "Depoliticized Pleasures and the Construction of (White) Queer Utopia in Netflix's *Sense8*." In this essay, the authors examine the representation of desire and pleasure as a site of racial transgression where the non-Western body can be desired and consumed outside of its geopolitical, sociohistorical, and material contexts. Drawing on Hooks's (2015) influential essay, "Eating the Other: Desire and Resistance," the authors advance an argument that the non-Western, non-white sensates, Kala's, Capheus's, and Sun's bodies are visually consumed through a depoliticized gaze that perceives sexually desiring the Other as an outlet for recuperating the humanity of a global heteronormative (white) politic. Although being sensate is already a queer position, the queers of color in the TV series lack a thorough examination of the geopolitical productions of their identities. Of particular importance to this entry is the character Capheus, the Kenyan sensate. The authors contend that although being a sensate is a queer position that is not constrained by any normative position, such as racial identity or cultural tradition, this transgressive position is, in fact, built on a particular kind of experience and geography. In other words, the sensates' seemingly transgressive position seems to apply only when one is white, and U.S. American. In the case of Capheus, Western viewers are not able to see him beyond the normative representation of Africa (mother dying of AIDS, warlords, poor, etc.), which African viewers are encouraged to leave behind through the borrowing of the bodies of other sensates. The issue that the authors take with such constructions of queerness is that African cultural identities are represented as oppressive identities rather than as avenues to critique other forms of oppression besides sexual identity.

Besides media representation, some scholars have focused on how queer Africans in the diaspora use social media as safe spaces to speak back to national discussions on LGBT issues (e.g., see Camminga, 2020). Social media sites such as Facebook and Twitter have opened the door for sexual subjects to find safe spaces to connect and seek reaffirmation of their identities (Cooper & Dzara, 2010). In this regard, many queer Africans have shifted to social media to seek safe spaces. Using one of such spaces as an example, Asante (2018) examined the (im)possibilities of creating a diasporic home in a queer African migrant virtual community on Facebook. Asante found out that while virtual communities offer the space for the imaginations of "home" for queer African subjects in the diaspora, these spaces are not without contentions and as such, virtual safe spaces should be understood as riddled with power relations even though they provide opportunities for the re-imagination of home.

FUTURE DIRECTIONS IN QUEER AFRICAN STUDIES IN COMMUNICATION STUDIES

As this article has shown, queer African studies (QAS) as a subfield of queer studies in communication is still in nascent growth as an area of research. In spite of this, more studies are needed to show how queer studies, African studies, and communication studies could intimately have productive conversations. Cruz (2020) incisively asserts that "to think that African contexts can teach us something is provocative on many levels" (p. 102). QAS can expand communication studies in various ways.

First, queer African perspectives on kinship and family can influence the way queer relationalities are theorized in communication studies. In his initial conceptualization of queer relationalities, Gust Yep (2017) explains

> Queer relationality entails modes of recognition, systems of intelligibility, cultural expressions, affective articulations, encrypted sociality, embodied relations, forms of belonging, community formations, and collective histories of oppression that circulate outside of regimes of heteronormativity- but frequently in relation to it –characterized by potentiality and becoming as individuals inhabiting intersectional cultural nonnormativities negotiate and navigate social worlds. (p. 120)

QAS could expand the theorization for queer relationalities by centralizing queer African forms of sociality, embodied relations, and forms of belonging that circulate parallel to heteronormative institutions. For instance, how do sexual relationships among women in Ghana, commonly known as "Supi," contribute to the ways we theorize relationships in interpersonal communication? (see Dankwa, 2009). Furthermore, it would be beneficial to explore the transactional role of money, gifts, and love, and how they influence the formations of intimate relationships across different parts of Africa (e.g., Spronk, 2019). Lastly, various forms of families exist in Africa, such as polygyny, the extended family system, and women-to-women marriages (for a critique of the nuclear family system in Africa, see Macharia, 2016). How can the social relations established in these kinds of family systems expand how we theorize family communication in the West?

Second, the study of sexual pleasure and desire can reinvigorate various conversations in health communication research besides the unholy emphasis on risk and diseases. Sylvia Tamale (2011) notes that the overemphasis on HIV/AIDS and health when studying LGBT Africans has narrowed what scholars know about desire and sexual pleasure, especially since same-sex sexual desire is criminalized in most African countries. African men, in particular, have received less attention. Spronk and Hendriks (2020) explain that instead of taking patriarchal ideologies and their obsession with male libido at face value, how African men experience pleasure and how they discursively construct sex and sexuality should be studied. In this way, how African men experience sexual pleasure can be rigorously analyzed in its complexities and ambiguities rather than assumed to be complicit or complacent with patriarchy.

Lastly, there are very limited studies on trans and gender-nonconforming Africans from communication scholars even though trans scholarship is gaining relative popularity in queer studies within communication studies. (see LeMaster, 2017; Yep et al., 2015). This is especially crucial because while there is a rejection of "homosexuality," "gays," and "lesbians," trans people in certain parts of Africa have received relative acceptance. In a recent publication, Camminga (2020) explained that transgender is a term that is catching up in most parts of Africa. In this vein, queer communication scholars should examine how transness is being enacted, represented, coopted, and resisted on the African continent.

CONCLUSION

Mainly drawing from the field of African studies, postcolonial studies, and queer theory, queer African studies (QAS) is an interdisciplinary area of study that can expand and reinvigorate queer studies in communication. Researchers in communication studies should see the robust contributions that QAS can make to our field when fully incorporated into queer studies in communication. Integrating QAS works to decenter the assumed Western orientation of queer theorizing and encourages queer scholars to fully center the voices of queers from marginalized spaces instead of just selectively adopting same-sex sexual behaviors from queers in the Global South to bolster arguments in the Global North that queerness is everywhere. In other words, Africanizing queer studies in communication provides another layer of support to Yep's (2013) call to attend to the "complex particularities of individuals' lives and identities with their race, gender, sexuality, and national locations by understanding their history and personhood in concrete time and space" (p. 173). Africanizing is to attend to the historical, mythical creation of an entity called "African," and the contemporary ways Africanness is being produced and resisted.

QAS not only holds the potential for thinking of communication as an emancipatory and decolonial process, but it is fundamentally premised on taking Africa as a starting point for theorizing queerness where communication may constitute and promote empowerment possibilities. QAS add to critical discussions on decentering heteronormativity, cisgenderism, and whiteness in communication studies already begun by queers of color. To continually decenter the whiteness and U.S. Western-centeredness of queer theorizing, queer communication research should continually have productive and critical engagements with queer African scholarship.

FURTHER READING

Amory, D. P. (1997). "Homosexuality" in Africa: Issues and debates. *Issue: A Journal of Opinion*, 25(1), 5–10.
Camminga, B. (2019). *Transgender refugees and the imagined South Africa*. Springer International.
Ekine, S., & Abbas, H. (Eds.). (2013). *Queer African reader*. Pambazuka Press.
Epprecht, M. (2008). *Heterosexual Africa? The history of an idea from the age of exploration to the age of AIDS*. Ohio University Press.
Fiereck, K., Hoad, N., & Mupotsa, D. S. (2020). A queering-to-come. *GLQ: A Journal of Lesbian and Gay Studies*, 26(3), 363–376.

Gaudio, R. P. (2011). *Allah made us: Sexual outlaws in an Islamic African city* (Vol. 5). John Wiley & Sons.
Hoad, N. W. (2007). *African intimacies: Race, homosexuality, and globalization.* University of Minnesota Press.
Macharia, K. (2016). On being area-studied: A litany of complaint. *GLQ: A Journal of Lesbian and Gay Studies, 22*(2), 183–190.
Matebeni, Z. (Ed.). (2014). *Reclaiming Afrikan: Queer perspectives on sexual and gender identities.* Modjaji Books.
McClintock, A. (1995). *Imperial leather: Race, gender, and sexuality in the colonial contest.* Routledge.
Nyeck, S. N. (Ed.). (2019). *Routledge handbook of queer African studies.* Routledge.
Nyeck, S. N., & Epprecht, M. (Eds.). (2013). *Sexual diversity in Africa: Politics, theory, and citizenship.* McGill-Queen's University Press.
Spronk, R., & Hendriks, T. (Eds.). (2020). *Readings in sexualities from Africa.* Indiana University Press.
Tamale, S. (2011). *African sexualities: A reader.* Pambazuka Press.

REFERENCES

Adjepong, A. (2021). *Afropolitan projects: Redefining blackness, sexualities, and culture from Houston to Accra.* UNC Press Books.
Ahlberg, B. M. (1994). Is there a distinct African sexuality? A critical response to Caldwell. *Africa, 64*(2), 220–242.
Almarri, S. (2018). Identities of a single root: The triad of the khuntha, mukhannath, and khanith. *Women & Language, 41*(1), 97–109.
Amory, D. P. (1997). "Homosexuality" in Africa: Issues and debates. *African Issues, 25*(1), 5–10.
Amory, D. P. (1998). Mashoga, mabasha, and magai: 'Homosexuality' on the East African Coast. *Boy-wives and female husbands: Studies of African homosexualities* (pp. 67–87).
Arondekar, A. (2005). Border/line sex: Queer postcolonialities, or how race matters outside the United States. *Interventions, 7*(2), 236–250.
Asante, G. (2019). "Queerly ambivalent": Navigating global and local normativities in postcolonial Ghana. In S. Eguchi & B. M. Calafell (Eds.), *Queer intercultural communication: The intersectional politics of belonging in and across difference* (pp. 157–176). Rowman & Littlefield.
Asante, G. A. (2020). Anti-LGBT violence and the ambivalent (colonial) discourses of Ghanaian Pentecostalist-Charismatic church leaders. *Howard Journal of Communications, 31*(1), 20–34.
Asante, G. (2018). "Where is home?" Negotiating comm (unity) and un/belonging among queer African migrants on Facebook. *Borderlands, 17*(1), 1–22.
Asante, G., Baig, N., & Huang, S. (2019). (De)politicized pleasures and the construction of (white) queer utopia in Netflix's *Sense8*. *Queer Studies in Media & Popular Culture, 4*(3), 319–334. https://doi.org/10.1386/qsmpc_00015_1
Awondo, P., Geschiere, P., & Reid, G. (2012). Homophobic Africa? Toward a more nuanced view. *African Studies Review, 55*(3), 145–168.
Bhabha, H. K. (2012). *The location of culture.* Routledge.
Broqua, C. (2013). Male homosexuality in Bamako: A cross-cultural and cross historical comparative perspective. In S. N. Nyeck & M. Epprecht (Eds.), *Sexual diversity in Africa: Politics, theory, and citizenship.* McGill-Queen's University Press.
Burton, R. F. (1893). *A mission to Gelele, King of Dahome: with notices of the so called "Amazons," the grand customs, the yearly customs, the human sacrifices, the present state of the slave trade, and the Negro's place in nature* (Vol. 1). Tylston and Edwards.
Camminga, B. (2020). Digital borders, diasporic flows and the Nigerian transgender beauty queen who would not be denied. *Gender Questions, 8*(1), 1–15.

Caldwell, J. C., Caldwell, P., & Quiggin, P. (1989). The social context of AIDS in sub-Saharan Africa. *Population and Development Review, 15*(2), 185–234.

Chevrette, R., & Eguchi, S. (2020). "We don't see LGBTQ differences": Cisheteronormativity and concealing phobias and irrational fears behind rhetorics of acceptance. *QED: A Journal in GLBTQ Worldmaking, 7*(1), 55–59.

Cooper, M., & Dzara, K. (2010). The Facebook revolution: LGBT identity and activism. In C. Pullen & M. Cooper (Eds.), *LGBT identity and online new media* (pp. 114–126). Routledge.

Cruz, J. (2015). Reimagining feminist organizing in global times: Lessons from African feminist communication. *Women & Language, 38*(1), 23–41.

Cruz, J. M. (2020). Introduction: African feminist and queer coalitions. *Women's Studies in Communication, 43*(2), 101–105.

Currier, A., & Migraine-George, T. (2016). Queer studies/African studies: An (im)possible transaction? *GLQ: A Journal of Lesbian and Gay Studies, 22*(2), 281–305.

Dankwa, S. O. (2009). "It's a silent trade": Female same-sex intimacies in post-colonial Ghana. *NORA—Nordic Journal of Feminist and Gender Research, 17*(3), 192–205. https://doi.org/10.1080/08038740903117208

Dlamini, B. (2006). Homosexuality in the African context. *Agenda, 20*(67), 128–136.

Donham, D. L. (1998). Freeing South Africa: The "modernization" of male–male sexuality in Soweto. *Cultural Anthropology, 13*(1), 3–21.

Eguchi, S., & Asante, G. (2016). Disidentifications revisited: Queer(y)ing intercultural communication theory. *Communication Theory, 26*(2), 171–189.

Eguchi, S. (2009). Negotiating hegemonic masculinity: The rhetorical strategy of "straight-acting" among gay men. *Journal of Intercultural Communication Research, 38*(3), 193–209.

Ekine, S., & Abbas, H. (Eds.). (2013). *Queer African reader*. Pambazuka Press.

Epprecht, M. (2008). *Heterosexual Africa? The history of an idea from the age of exploration to the age of AIDS*. Ohio University Press.

Epprecht, M. (2012). Sexual minorities, human rights and public health strategies in Africa. *African Affairs, 111*(443), 223–243.

Epprecht, M. (2013). *Hungochani: The history of a dissident sexuality in southern Africa*. McGill-Queen's Press.

Evans-Pritchard, E. E., & Gillies, E. (1937). *Witchcraft, oracles and magic among the Azande* (Vol. 12). Clarendon Press.

Fiereck, K., Hoad, N., & Mupotsa, D. S. (2020). A queering-to-come. *GLQ: A Journal of Lesbian and Gay Studies, 26*(3), 363–376.

Gaudio, R. P. (2011). *Allah made us: Sexual outlaws in an Islamic African city*. John Wiley & Sons.

Goltz, D. B., Zingsheim, J., Mastin, T., & Murphy, A. G. (2016). Discursive negotiations of Kenyan LGBTI identities: Cautions in cultural humility. *Journal of International and Intercultural Communication, 9*(2), 104–121.

Hanchey, J. N. (2020). Desire and the politics of Africanfuturism. *Women's Studies in Communication, 43*(2), 119–124.

Hanchey, J. N. (2016). Agency beyond agents: Aid campaigns in sub-Saharan Africa and collective representations of agency. *Communication, Culture & Critique, 9*(1), 11–29.

Haritaworn, J., Tauqir, T., & Erdem, E. (2008). Gay imperialism: Gender and sexuality discourse in the "War on Terror." In A. Kuntsman & E. Miyake (Eds.), *Out of place: Interrogating silences in queerness/raciality* (pp. 71–95). Raw Nerve Books.

Hooks, B. (2015). Eating the other: Desire and resistance. In M. G. Durham &. D. M. Kellner (Eds.), *Media and cultural studies: Keyworks* (pp. 366–380). John Wiley and Sons.

Huang, S. (2021). Why does communication need transnational queer studies? *Communication and Critical/Cultural Studies, 18*(2), 204–211.

Jagose, A. (1996). *Queer theory: An introduction.* NYU Press.

Johnson, E. P. (2001). "Quare" studies or (almost) everything I know about queer studies I learned from my grandmother. *Text and Performance Quarterly, 21*(1), 1–25.

Jolly, S. (2000). 'Queering' development: Exploring the links between same-sex sexualities, gender, and development. *Gender & Development, 8*(1), 78–88.

LeMaster, B. (2017). Notes on trans relationality. *QED: A Journal in GLBTQ Worldmaking, 4*(2), 84–92.

Kaoma, K. (2012). *Colonizing African values: How the U.S right is transforming sexual politics in Africa.* Political Research Associates.

Le Blanc, M. N., Meintel, D., & Piché, V. (1991). The African sexual system: Comment on Caldwell et al. *Population and Development Review, 17*(3), 497–505.

Lee, W. (2014). Kuaering queer theory: My autocritography and a race-conscious, womanist, transnational turn. In G. A. Yep, K. E. Lovaas, and J. Elia (Eds.), *Queer Theory and Communication: From Disciplining Queers to Queer the Disciplines* (pp. 147–170). Routledge.

Lewis, D. (2011). Representing African sexualities. *African Sexualities: A Reader,* 199–205.

Livermon, X. (2015). Usable traditions: Creating sexual autonomy in postapartheid South Africa. *Feminist Studies, 41*(1), 14–41.

Livermon, X. (2020). *Kwaito bodies: Remastering space and subjectivity in post-apartheid South Africa.* Duke University Press.

Macharia, K. (2015). Archive and method in queer African studies. *Agenda, 29*(1), 140–146.

Macharia, K. (2016). On being area-studied: A litany of complaint. *GLQ: A Journal of Lesbian and Gay Studies, 22*(2), 183–190.

Matebeni, Z., Monro, S., & Reddy, V. (2018). *Queer in Africa: LGBTQI identities, citizenship, and activism* (p. 222). Taylor & Francis.

Mbasalaki, P. K. (2019). Women who love women. In S. N. Nyeck (Ed.), *Routledge handbook of queer African studies.* Routledge.

Mbasalaki, P. K. (2020). Through the lens of modernity: Reflections on the (colonial) cultural archive of sexuality and gender in South Africa. *GLQ: A Journal of Lesbian and Gay Studies, 26*(3), 455–475.

Mbembe, A. (2001). *On the postcolony* (Vol. 41). University of California Press.

McClintock, A. (1995). *Imperial leather: Race, gender, and sexuality in the colonial contest.* Routledge.

Moussawi, G. (2020). *Disruptive situations: Fractal orientalism and queer strategies in Beirut.* Temple University Press.

Muñoz, J. E. (1999). *Disidentifications: Queers of color and the performance of politics.* University of Minnesota Press.

Murray, S. O., & Roscoe, W. (1998). *Boy-wives and female husbands: Studies of African homosexualities.* State University of New York Press.

Mutua-Mambo, C. N. (2020). Living in a liminal space: Feminist and LGBT alliances in Kenya. *Women's Studies in Communication, 43*(2), 125–130.

Ndashe, S. (2013). The single story of "African homophobia" is dangerous for LGBTI activism. In S. Ekine & H. Abbas (Eds.), *Queer African reader* (pp. 155–164). Pambazuka Press.

Nyanzi, S. (2014). Queering queer Africa. In Z. Matebeni (Ed.), *Reclaiming Afrikan: Queer perspectives on sexual and gender identities* (pp. 61–66). Modjaji Books.

Nyeck, S. N. (Ed.). (2019). *Routledge handbook of queer African studies.* Routledge.

Nyeck, S. N., & Epprecht, M. (Eds.). (2013). *Sexual diversity in Africa: Politics, theory, and citizenship.* McGill-Queen's University Press.

Okech, A. (2013). "In sisterhood and solidarity": Queering African feminist spaces. In S. Ekine & H. Abbas (Eds.), *Queer African reader*. Pambazuka Press.
Otu, K. E. (2019). Normative collusions and amphibious evasions. In S. N. Nyeck (Ed.), *Routledge handbook of queer African studies* (pp. 213–224). Routledge.
Pindi, G. N., & De La Garza, A. T. (2018). "The colonial Jesus": Deconstructing White Christianity. In D. M. D. McIntosh, D. G. Moon, & T. K. Nakayama (Eds.), *Interrogating the communicative power of whiteness* (pp. 218–238). Routledge.
Pindi, G. N. (2020). Beyond labels: envisioning an alliance between African feminism and queer theory for the empowerment of African sexual minorities within and beyond Africa. *Women's Studies in Communication, 43*(2), 106–112.
Puar, J. K. (2007). *Terrorist assemblages: Homonationalism in queer times*. Duke University Press.
Tamale, S. (2011). *African sexualities: A reader*. Pambazuka Press.
Thoreson, R. R. (2014). Troubling the waters of a "wave of homophobia": Political economies of anti-queer animus in sub-Saharan Africa. *Sexualities, 17*(1–2), 23–42.
Sloop, J. M. (2012). "This is not natural:" Caster Semenya's gender threats. *Critical Studies in Media Communication, 29*(2), 81–96.
Spronk, R. (2019). Queering love: Sex, care, capital, and academic prejudices. In *Routledge handbook of queer African studies* (pp. 25–36). Routledge.
Spronk, R., & Hendriks, T. (Eds.). (2020). *Readings in sexualities from Africa*. Indiana University Press.
Tettey, W. J. (2016). Homosexuality, moral panic, and politicized homophobia in Ghana: Interrogating discourses of moral entrepreneurship in Ghanaian media. *Communication, Culture & Critique, 9*(1), 86–106. https://doi.org/10.1111/cccr.12132
Undie, C. C., & Benaya, K. (2006). The state of knowledge on sexuality in sub-Saharan Africa: A synthesis of literature. *JENDA: A Journal of Culture and African Women's Studies, 8*(119).
Van Klinken, A. (2019). *Kenyan, Christian, Queer*. Penn State University Press.
Winslow, L. (2012). Colonizing Caster Semenya: Gender transformation and the makeover genre. *Western Journal of Communication, 76*(3), 298–313.
Yarbrough, M. W. (2018). Something old, something new: Historicizing same-sex marriage within ongoing struggles over African marriage in South Africa. *Sexualities, 21*(7), 1092–1108.
Yep, G. A. (2013). Queering/quaring/kuaring/crippin'/transing "other bodies" in intercultural communication. *Journal of International and Intercultural Communication, 6*(2), 118–126.
Yep, G. A., Russo, S. E., & Allen, J. (2015). Pushing boundaries: Toward the development of a model for transing communication in (inter)cultural contexts. In L. G. Spencer & J. C. Capuzza (Eds.), *Transgender communication studies: Histories, trends, and trajectories* (pp. 69–89). Lexington Books.
Yep, G. A. (2017). Further notes on healing from "The violence of heteronormativity in communication studies". *QED: A Journal in GLBTQ Worldmaking, 4*(2), 115–122.

Godfried Asante

QUEER PEOPLE'S COMMUNICATION WITH FAMILIES OF ORIGIN

DISCLOSING TO HETEROSEXUAL FAMILIES OF ORIGIN

Disclosing a queer identity, which may include a sexual and/or gender identity, can often be difficult given societal expectations and prejudices (Adams, 2011). Thus, before queer people communicate about this aspect of their identities, scholars and lay people alike use the metaphor of the "closet" to suggest this information is private or a secret. Indeed, this metaphor illustrates the general cultural assumption of cis heteronormativity and its power to silence alternative gender and sexual identities (Adams, 2011). When a queer person decides to disclose their queer identity and "come out" of the closet, family members are often at the center of those disclosures. These family members may serve to support their queer family member or hinder them, and some members' actions can accomplish both simultaneously (Valentine et al., 2003). In this section on disclosure, we begin by addressing disclosure considerations (i.e., whether people will disclose their sexual and/or gender identities) before turning to a discussion of disclosure recipients and disclosure practices. While the disclosure experiences differ between sexual and gender identities for a variety of reasons (see Zimman, 2009), disclosure considerations, recipients, and practices do not differ between the sexual or gender identities of queer individuals.

Disclosure Considerations. Given the stigma the LGBTQ+ community faces, queer people must first decide whether or not they want to disclose or "come out." Research suggests that queer people base this decision on a variety of factors. For example, some queer people anticipated reactions from family members that played an important role in whether or not they chose to disclose. Indeed, queer people report considering not only family reactions but also their family's general reputation (Valentine et al., 2003). Deciding to disclose to family members or even at all is also contingent on cultural factors. Merighi and Grimes (2000) examined sexual orientation disclosures from young gay men (ages 18 to 24) of African, European, Mexican, and Vietnamese descent. For these queer men, they were less inclined to disclose if they came from a culture where that disclosure would negatively affect the perceptions of the entire family. For example, Latinx queer individuals reported being afraid to express any gender nonconformity because of the hegemonic masculinity and homophobia that are present in their communities (Pollitt et al., 2021). Meanwhile, men felt encouraged to disclose their queer identity when family unity and unconditional love pervaded the values of their culture (Merighi & Grimes, 2000). In a U.S. context, Grafsky (2018) found four factors that created a pressure, or lack thereof, for nonheterosexual youth (gay, lesbian, bisexual, queer, and pansexual) to disclose to their families: (1) comfortability, (2) closeness, (3) prior messages, and (4) expected outcomes. In other words, these youth were more comfortable disclosing their sexual identity to their families if they were close and comfortable with their family members. In addition, the findings from this study suggested that nonheterosexual youth disclosed in different ways depending on how their family members communicated about same-sex attraction in the past. For example, if family members spoke poorly about queer people in the past (i.e., prior messages), then youth were less likely to disclose. Finally, youth also took into consideration how their family members might react to their disclosure by anticipating potential responses (i.e., expected outcomes). Taken together, this research suggests that the decision to disclose is fraught with complex considerations about how that disclosure may reflect on their family of origin more broadly.

Disclosure Recipients. In addition to concerns about how disclosing sexual and gender identities may reflect on their family, queer people must also decide to whom they want to disclose. Adams (2011) suggests that queer individuals often include their family in the coming out process. Yet disclosing a queer identity does not only occur between parents and children. Indeed, families are interdependent, meaning that information shared with one member may quickly proliferate throughout the entire family system. Grafsky et al. (2018) differentiate between horizontal relationships, between siblings and cousins, and vertical relationships, between parents and children. Vertical relationships involve guidance, boundaries, and hierarchy, while horizontal relationships are egalitarian and marked by reciprocity. When choosing to disclose, regardless of the relationship they were disclosing to, 75% of queer individuals disclosed face to face, while 25% disclosed used a mediated form of communication (Manning, 2014; Savin-Williams & Ream, 2003). Savin-Williams (2001) found that 38% of queer individuals in their study disclosed to their siblings, a horizontal relationship, before any other family member. Based on their sample, Grafsky (2018) found that often this initial disclosure occurred at the age of 16. In Savin-Williams and Ream's (2003) sample of young men and women who had same-sex attractions, 46% of males and 44% of females had disclosed their identities to both parents. Meanwhile, 81% of all queer youth in Grafsky's (2018) study had disclosed to at least one parent. Of those queer youth who had disclosed, 10 engaged in planned conversations with their mothers, and seven with their fathers. Unplanned disclosures happened for seven individuals to their mothers and six to their fathers (Grafsky, 2018). Queer youth disclosed to mothers more than fathers, and of the queer youth who were out to both parents, 35% came out to both parents together; 54% came out to mothers first, and only 12% came out to fathers first (Savin-Williams & Ream, 2003). In sum, this research suggests that regardless of timing, queer people find it important to disclose their sexual and/or gender identities to at least some of their immediate family members.

Disclosure Practices. Once queer individuals decide they will disclose and to whom, they must then contend with how to share this information. Manning (2014) specifically explored the ways gay, lesbian, and bisexual individuals disclosed their sexual identity and developed a typology of seven types of disclosures: (1) preplanned conversations, (2) emergent conversations, (3) coaxed conversations, (4) confrontational conversations, (5) mediated conversations, (6) romantic conversations, and (7) activist conversations. In accordance with Adams (2011), the most common type of disclosure was preplanned conversations. During disclosures that were preplanned, the queer person decided they were going to disclose and then initiated the conversation. Emergent conversations, though not planned, occurred when the queer person chose to disclose because the conversation naturally led to an established trust between the communicators. Queer men who utilized preplanned and emergent disclosures likely communicated in a direct style in which they clearly stated their LGBTQ identity (Merighi & Grimes, 2000). Meanwhile, some queer individuals reported that their communication partners coaxed them to disclosure through nudges, hints, or questions (Manning, 2014). Although queer people did not initiate these conversations, they reported feeling as if they had the power to disclose or not. Individuals did not necessarily have to be direct, however, in their disclosure because they could assume that their family member knew their sexuality (Merighi & Grimes, 2000). As a result, queer individuals within coaxed conversations could integrate their identities into the discourse indirectly. Similarly, a Native American, gay, and queer participant in Pollitt et al.'s (2021) study stated:

> Oh, I never really had to come out.... From a young age, my mom said she knew when I was little. I just wanted to be a ballerina and all this stuff and she just knew. I never really had to say "I'm gay!" or anything like that. (p. 11)

For those with similar experiences, Pollitt et al. (2021) argue that some queer individuals who expressed gender nonconforming behavior, such as an individual assigned male at birth wanting to be a ballerina, did not feel the need to directly disclose their queer identities because their behavior made this aspect of their identity clear to family members. Although coaxed conversations were voluntary disclosures, a level of force characterized confrontational conversations (Manning, 2014). Confrontational conversations included evidence, confrontation, and chaotic communication. Moreover, most face-to-face confrontations occurred after the parent looked through the child's bedroom, came upon notes or letters, or overheard phone conversations. Recounts of these experiences were overwhelmingly negative. The LGB individuals described their parents as angry while they described themselves as feeling betrayed, scared, or confused. Through confrontation, queer individuals reported being punished, censored, accused of being insane, or banished. Although preplanned, emergent, coaxed, and confrontational conversations all occurred face to face, mediated disclosures also occurred through the use of emails, letters, texts, or phone calls. As it happens, LGB individuals also disclosed their same-sex attraction through implicit conversations about attraction or as a way to advocate for LGBTQ rights. Thus, this research suggests that the disclosure itself may take many forms based on a variety of factors and in anticipation of a variety of responses. Similarly, McDonald et al. (2020) argue that disclosure, or coming out of the closet, "is constituted in communication and is not merely the outcome of an individual's internal decisions and intentions" (p. 87). In the next section, we will address how queer people perceive that their family members receive their disclosures.

(PERCEIVED) FAMILY OF ORIGIN INITIAL AND COMMUNICATIVE REACTIONS

Adams (2011) reports that the immediate reactions to disclosure—the seconds, minutes, hours, and days that follow—are so significant that people will remember and incorporate these reactions into the stories they tell about coming out. Because family members are often the recipients of these disclosures, how family members react can become an integral part of a queer person's story and experience. Disclosure can have both extreme negative consequences and positive impacts (McDonald et al., 2020). Further, these reactions may be complicated by the fact that many families do not have family traditions or rituals to help guide them through this familial transition (Valentine et al., 2003). Other heteronormative familial transitions, such as births of children and weddings, although sometimes difficult, have coalesced into a familial script over generations. Because of the nonheteronormative transition that the family experiences after a queer individual discloses their identity, the family often does not have a script to follow. As a result of a lack of scripts, Valentine et al. (2003) note that several of their lesbian and gay participants reported that their families appeared to be in a state of denial by never acknowledging the disclosure. Adams (2011) clarifies that coming out is an ongoing process. Even after an LGBTQ individual discloses to one family member, they may disclose, or not, to every other family member. Adams (2014) even reports that there are some individuals who have to come out to their parents several times for various reasons, such as if the parent has Alzheimer's or refuses to accept the queer identity.

Yet not all families react this way. In their study of 516 gay, lesbian, and bisexual youth, D'Augelli et al. (2008) found that in single-parent families, reactions were equally positive and negative. Meanwhile, in two-parent families where the LGB individual had disclosed to both parents, one-third of parents reacted positively, one-third negatively, and one-third of parental dyads had one parent who reacted positively while the other parent reacted negatively. In D'Augelli et al.'s (2008) study, mothers and fathers did not differ in their likelihood to react positively or negatively. Furthermore, Ben-Ari (1995) found that the most important postdisclosure factor that impacted family dynamics was how the parents reacted to the disclosure of same-sex attraction. By including parents and their gay or lesbian child in the sample, Ben-Ari found that after disclosure, the family experienced increased honesty while also struggling to maintain the parent–child relationship. The disclosure of a queer identity can be a shock to some family members, resulting in one of the initial perceived reactions of family support or rejection. Next, we describe what family support and rejection may look like for queer individuals.

(Perceived) Family Support. Even though coming out can be an arduous process, family support can play an integral role. Queer people may perceive family support and acceptance of an individual's queer identity to take several forms. In their study on sexual orientation disclosures of males during emerging adulthood, Merighi and Grimes (2000) found two types of support: (1) support through action and (2) support that preserves the kinship bond. Some family members showed these men support by taking action to advocate for and support the queer community. Other family members showed their support of the men's sexual identity by preserving a kinship bond. Because their family members did not treat them differently, these men perceived support; their disclosure did not change the family dynamics. Meanwhile, Reczek (2014), studying gay men and lesbian women in midlife long-term intimate partnerships, characterizes family support (including in-laws) into four types: (1) integration, (2) inclusion through language, (3) social support, and (4) words of affirmation. Queer individuals perceived support through integration when their families incorporated them into everyday life. Families showed support through their language use by using familial language such as son, daughter, or in-law. When parents or in-laws relied on the queer person for social support, they perceived this as familial acceptance. Finally, queer individuals perceived acceptance when their family used words of affirmation about them and their identities.

Acceptance in Context. Families that are perceived as accepting and supportive of queer identities often have certain qualities or characteristics. For example, some research suggests that White family members of queer young adults are more likely to accept their queer family member than other ethnicities (Snapp et al., 2015). Queer youth who lived with their parents at the time of the study reported more familial support and experienced less parental verbal harassment (D'Augelli et al., 2008). Gay, lesbian, and bisexual youth who reported higher parental acceptance and lower parental rejection during childhood disclosed at an earlier age with more parental acceptance (D'Amico & Julien, 2012). Fuller and Riggs (2018) studied transgender individuals and found that those who rated their family as emotionally close perceived their family as supportive of their gender. Although transgender individuals reported moderate to high levels of gender-related support from their families, nonbinary individuals received less support than their transitioned male or female counterparts. Meanwhile, transwomen of color reported that their female family members were more accepting than their male family members (Koken et al., 2009). Youth who reported feeling supported by their families were less likely to fear rejection at a later date (D'Augelli et al., 2008). Similarly, gay, lesbian, bisexual, transgender, and questioning youth who reported that their family would consider counseling also reported that they did not fear expulsion from their home because of their queer identity and had a fairly good relationship with their parents (Potoczniak et al., 2009).

Each and every family member has their own reaction to a queer identity disclosure, but most GLB youth reported that their siblings were accepting of their identity (D'Augelli et al., 2008). In their study of lesbian, gay, and bisexual individuals between the ages of 14 and 21, D'Augelli et al. (1998) found that 51% of mothers, 27% of fathers, and 57% of siblings accepted their sexual identities. Watson (2014) studied bisexual adults and found that half of the 47 individuals they interviewed experienced comfort, solace, encouragement, and support from their families. Half of the transwomen of color in Koken et al.'s (2009) study described verbal, physical, and symbolic affection from their parents and close family members. Gay and lesbian adolescents with a queer family member (a sibling, cousin, aunt, or uncle) reported that this individual often played a supportive familial role (Roe, 2017).

Acceptance Outcomes. Queer individuals who experience familial acceptance experience a myriad of better psychological and health outcomes. Following disclosure and acceptance, 56% of gay and lesbian individuals perceived an improved relationship within their family unit, 66% in their relationship with their mother and 44% in their relationship with their father (Ben-Ari, 1995). Meanwhile, 84% of mothers and 63% of fathers thought their parent–child relationship improved. Family acceptance predicted higher self-esteem and well-being for gay, lesbian, bisexual, and transgender youth (Snapp et al., 2015). Furthermore, gay and lesbian individuals with accepting parents experienced less minority stress, fewer depressive symptoms, and more family support (Feinstein et al., 2014). Lesbian youth reported that they were more comfortable being queer when their mothers and fathers accepted their identity (Savin-Williams, 1989). Gay youth were more comfortable being gay when their parents accepted them, and they had better self-esteem. In their study of gay males, Elizur and Ziv (2001) found that family acceptance was correlated with the individual's gay identity, mental health, self-esteem, and family support. In addition, gay, lesbian, and bisexual adolescents who reported higher acceptance by their mothers had lower levels of psychological and identity maladjustments (D'Amico & Julien, 2012). Transgender individuals who reported being accepted by their family experienced lower levels of psychological distress and perceived more gender-related support (Fuller & Riggs, 2018). Finally, transwomen of color described familial acceptance as an essential part of transitioning during adolescence and early adulthood (Koken et al., 2009). Needless to say, family acceptance is an optimal response.

Family Responses. Studying parents of lesbian, gay, bisexual, transgender, or queer children, Gonzalez et al. (2013) found that 95% of the parents reported at least one positive aspect of having a queer child. The positive aspects of being a parent of a queer child resulted in five themes: (1) personal growth, (2) positive emotions, (3) activism, (4) social connection, and (5) closer relationships. Fifty-six percent of parents reported that they experienced personal growth. As a result of this growth, parents were more openminded because their queer children challenged them to step out of their comfort zone. Other parents adopted new perspectives because they had to reconsider and reevaluate their previously held beliefs. Being open to new perspectives increased parents' awareness of discrimination and prejudice toward all minority groups. As parents became more aware of discrimination, they expressed a deeper compassion and empathy for others. Forty-one percent of parents expressed enhanced feelings for their queer child. Some parents reported feeling pride because they were a parent of a queer child; feelings of pride included being proud of their child and proud of themselves. Parents also reported that unconditional love transcends sexual or gender identity. Some parents (33%) increased their activism as a result of having a queer child. Thirty-one percent of parents explained that their queer child led them to make social connections they would not have established otherwise. Having a queer child established closer family relationships for 20% of parents, both with their child and with the family unit as a whole. Lee and Lee (2006) interviewed 14 parents of gay sons who were members of a chapter of Parents and Friends of Lesbians and Gays. These parents reported that they wanted to show their sons that their disclosure would not disturb the parent–child relationship by demonstrating verbal support, inclusion in family events, acceptance of significant others, and unconditional love.

Family Rejection. Although some parents were quite supportive, others were not. Most siblings accepted an individual's queer identities, but male siblings, compared with female siblings, were more likely to respond poorly to a sexual orientation disclosure (D'Augelli et al., 2008). Overall, D'Augelli et al. (1998) reported that 10% of mothers, 27% of fathers, and 15% of siblings reacted negatively to disclosure. Mothers attacked lesbian women the most, while brothers of gay men were most likely to turn to physical violence. Very few family members stepped in to protect the queer individual from violence, although 43% of men reported being protected by their mothers.

Thus, same-sex attraction or a queer identity can be contentious and stigmatized; as a result, disclosing a queer identity can be dangerous for the individual (Adams, 2011). A queer individual can experience hostility, rejection, or even violence from their family members after disclosure. Adams points out that family rejection can occur for three reasons: (1) the family member may consider same-sex attraction or a queer identity as inappropriate or immoral; (2) the queer individual may reveal and then be held accountable for hiding, lying, or omitting information; or (3) the disclosure may not have happened at the appropriate time because the individual hid their identity for too long or they disclosed in an inappropriate context. Thus, a family member may draw upon any of these reasons not to support their queer children.

Rejection in Context. Familial reactions may also be subject to cultural contexts. African American gay, lesbian, bisexual, transgender, and questioning adolescents often experience initial rejection from their parents after disclosure; however, some familial relationships do heal over time (Potoczniak et al., 2009). Of the 30% of adolescents who were expelled from their homes in the Potoczniak et al. (2009) study, all were African American. In the Siconolfi et al. (2020) study on youth experiencing homelessness in Los Angeles, California, 70.3% of the queer youth identified as nonwhite, 38.2% of whom were Black. Similarly, adolescents who described their family as religious felt that religion was related to their family's negative reactions. Religion was even used against queer youth to condemn their relationships (Roe, 2017). The adolescents who feared family rejection doubted that their family would attend counseling because family problems are private and not to be shared with outsiders (Potoczniak et al., 2009). In sum, these studies suggest that particular communities may have norms that enable and constrain some families from accepting queer identities.

Forms of Rejection. Of note, the experience of rejection may take a variety of forms, including minor hostilities. Roe (2017) reports that for the gay and bisexual adolescents in the study, initial parental reactions to queer identity disclosure were not supportive. Unsupportive parental reactions included disappointment and anger; some parents even chose to ignore the disclosure. Of the lesbian, gay, and bisexual youth who lived at home in the D'Augelli et al. (1998) study, 25% of males and one-third of female queer individuals reported verbal abuse. In their ethnically diverse study of gay males, Merighi and Grimes (2000) found that some men reported that their family members used distancing and disengagement strategies. Meanwhile, other men were not outright rejected by their families, but the family would avoid the topic of same-sex attraction and assume heterosexuality, a tactic that was also found in Watson's (2014) study. Of the queer individuals who had disclosed to at least one parent during adolescence in the Ryan et al. (2020) study, 21.22% experienced a parent or caregiver attempting to change their sexual orientation, and 31.84% experienced an attempted change with the addition of external conversion efforts, such as therapy.

Forms of rejection also varied by identity. For example, Todd et al. (2016) found that family members often engaged in microaggressions in which they would use passive-aggressive tactics to invalidate bisexual identities. Although sometimes manifesting in microaggressions, some family members were more overtly hostile. In these cases, family members would call bisexual kin names or isolate the individual. Furthermore, bisexual individuals reported that after disclosing to their families, their families used language that suggested they now thought of them as permanently lesbian, gay, or heterosexual (Scherrer et al., 2015). These family members also fetishized bisexual women for the pleasure of heterosexual men. Further, queer homeless youth in Los Angeles were more likely to be bisexual rather than gay or lesbian (Siconolfi et al., 2020). In Reczek's (2014) study, midlife gay men and lesbian women experienced rejection in three ways: (1) rejection in everyday life through negative or limited interactions; (2) traumatic events and statements; and (3) the threat of being usurped in which parents would not honor their wishes in the case of death or illness. Transwomen of color experienced indifference/neglect, in which their families would withhold emotional or material support without engaging in overt hostility (Koken et al., 2009). Meanwhile, 55% of these women reported that their family utilized undifferentiated rejection when the family failed to relate to them. In their study of young gay and bisexual men, Bird et al. (2017) found that parents communicated rejection through negative messages about being gay, such as an HIV infection being inevitable for the queer men.

Rejection could also be violent for queer individuals. Forty percent of the transwomen of color in Koken et al.'s (2009) study reported that they experienced hostile and aggressive rejection from their family including physical violence and being forced out of their home.

Classified as overt hostility, bisexual individuals reported experiencing threats of physical violence (Todd et al., 2016). More than their gay male counterparts, lesbian women were threatened with physical violence, often by their mothers (D'Augelli et al., 1998). Meanwhile, two men in the Bird et al. (2017) study reported experiencing physical abuse after disclosing to their families. Indeed, queer people may experience a range of rejection behaviors and messages to varying degrees and with a multitude of outcomes.

Rejection Outcomes. Similar to queer individuals having positive outcomes as a result of family acceptance, queer individuals experienced negative outcomes as a result of familial rejection. Lesbian and gay youth who experienced negative family reactions conformed to heteronormativity to get along with their family members (Waldner & Magruder, 1999). When gay, lesbian, and bisexual youth were rejected by their families, they had higher levels of identity and psychological maladjustment (D'Amico & Julien, 2012). Higher levels of current rejection by family members were associated with a higher prevalence of the GLB youth consuming drugs and alcohol. Transgender individuals who experienced gender-related discrimination from their families had higher levels of psychological distress. As a result of familial rejection, young gay and bisexual men engaged in risky sexual behaviors to fill the void left by familial emotional and tangible support (Bird et al., 2017). Of the eight men who were expelled from their homes, five engaged in sexual acts to survive, by trading sex for a place to stay, food, or money. Nine men sought out older partners who they believed could provide emotional and instrumental support. The average duration of the homelessness episode for queer homeless youth in Los Angeles was 1.3 years (Siconolfi et al., 2020). Similarly, 89% of homeless queer youth reported that they engaged in tobacco use through cigarette smoking, 87% smoked while 43% vaped marijuana, and 52.4% reported binge drinking. Of the LGB adolescents who had disclosed to their parents in the D'Augelli et al. (1998) study, 51% had attempted suicide. Bisexual individuals had lower self-esteem, more mental health issues, and less family cohesion after familial rejection (Todd et al., 2016). Of the 60 gay and lesbian individuals who experienced familial rejection in Reczek's (2016) study, 44 experienced parental disapproval of their romantic relationship. Once the family has reacted to the disclosure of a member's queer identity, they must make sense of the disclosure and establish a new family identity.

FAMILY OF ORIGIN ADJUSTMENT: SENSE-MAKING AND IDENTITY WORK

After family members initially react to a queer individual's disclosure, they continue to engage in sense-making to establish their own identity as a family member of a queer person. Adams (2014) explains that disclosure may perpetually complicate relationships with family members. A family member can be supportive immediately following the disclosure and then engage in rejection behaviors over time. Other family members may need to adjust to the disclosure but, over time, may come to be accepting of the individual's queer identity (Beeler & DiProva, 1999). For example, in Grossman et al.'s (in press) study on transgender and gender-nonconforming youth, 42% of transfeminine youth experienced initial positive responses from their mothers, while 45.3% were positive at the time of the study; 30% of fathers had initial positive reactions and 36% were currently positive. For transmasculine youth, mothers were initially positive for 26% of individuals, but 53.3% were currently positive, while 24% of fathers were initially positive and 44.6% were currently positive. Beeler and DiProva (1999) interviewed entire families and found that family members had to develop a narrative coherency that linked the past behaviors of the queer individual to the disclosure event. Though some family members felt sadness that their queer family member would have a difficult life, over time, as the queer individual lived their everyday life, these families added queer individuals into their social networks.

Norwood (2012, 2013) studied how a variety of family members made sense of a family member being transgender. Her study revealed three sites of dialectical tension in the online posts of partners, parents, and siblings of transgender individuals: (1) presence versus absence, (2) sameness versus difference, and (3) self versus other (Norwood, 2012). Family members described the tension of presence versus absence when they acknowledged the transgender individual being physically present while they still grieved the loss of the individual's former identity. This ambiguous loss, which occurs when an individual is physically present but mentally gone or mentally present but physically gone, was dominant in the experience of family members during the transitioning process because of a perceived sex/gender binary (Norwood, 2013). Families also viewed the transgender individual as the same, yet different (Norwood, 2012). Family members described the self in one of two ways: sovereign or social (Norwood, 2013). A sovereign identity is an inborn combination of mind and soul that is independent of the physical body and therefore remains intact through transition; meanwhile, a social identity views the transitioned person as different because of a change in body and behaviors. As a result of their understanding of the self, family members made sense of their kin's transition in one of four ways: (1) replacement, (2) revision, (3) evolution, or (4) removal. Regardless of whether the family member viewed the self as sovereign or social, they engaged in replacement when the family member discussed their transgender relative as a different person because of the transition. Family members engaged in revision when they viewed transition as a change of the outward identity, while the individual was still the same person they had always been. When family members gave voice to a revision discourse, they did not need to grieve the individual because the change was superficial and localized to outward appearances and behavior, not inborn identity. Meanwhile, for families that viewed transition as an evolution, the transition created an updated version of the same self. When families viewed transition as an evolution, they created a hybrid discourse in which the self was both sovereign and social at the same time. Removal, on the other hand, was an aesthetic moment in which family members made the intersection of sex and gender irrelevant to personhood, completely erasing the competition between the sovereign and social origin of identity. Finally, family members experienced a tension of the self versus other where they wanted to be unconditionally supportive of their transgender kin but also struggled with their own conceptions (Norwood, 2012). In addition to this overarching picture of family sense-making, researchers have also illuminated patterns among parent and sibling responses respectively.

Parents. Overall, research suggests that parents have a myriad of reactions and sense-make in a multitude of ways that reflect various levels of support for their children. For example, after the initial disclosure, some parents constructed their identity as a parent of a queer child (1) cognitively, (2) emotionally, and/or (3) behaviorally (Goodrich, 2009). Parents engaged in cognitive action when they would make a shift, utilizing higher-order thinking, to be more open to change. Alternatively, when outsiders responded negatively to their queer child, or to queerness in general, parents experienced an emotional response. Finally, parents took behavioral action when they educated themselves about queerness, advocated for queer rights, and renegotiated their relationship with their child.

Although some parents engaged in these prosocial identity constructions, other parents were subject to institutionalized heterosexuality (Fields, 2001). "Institutionalized heterosexuality organized the parents' identity work strategies, offering them a language of heterosexual rituals, gender norms, and parenting models" (pp. 174–175). Parents often have heteronormative ideas for their children's future that revolve around the nuclear family (Beeler & DiProva, 1999; Goodrich, 2009). After the disclosures, parents must develop alternative visions for their children's future. Adams (2014) argues that parents may mourn the loss of future biological grandchildren. When studying parents of transgender individuals, Whitley (2013) found that parents had to change their gendered expectations and dreams for their child, such as biological grandchildren and wedding customs. While observing parents who attended a Parents and Allies for Gay Empowerment meeting, Fields (2001) found that the heteronormative culture led parents at the group to search for a script that would make both them and their child normal. In keeping with heteronormative understandings of family, some parents, prior to the legalization of same-sex marriage across the entire United States, would rely on a legal perspective of family in order to exclude their queer child's partner (Adams, 2014). For example, Adams explains in his autoethnography how his mother would schedule family photos that included his siblings' partners. When Adams would confront his mother about this, her reasoning was that Adams's partner was not his husband, something that was impossible in the state in which they lived. Throughout this identity work, parents often engaged in sense-making, looking back in time and then coming to a conclusion about their role in the process. Yet other parents were concerned with the safety of their child because of institutionalized heteronormativity. In Hill and Menvielle's (2009) study of parents with gender-variant children, 60% of parents reported that they feared that others would hurt their children through teasing or violence because of their gender nonconformity. Many parents worried for their children's physical safety and especially their well-being and treatment by others. They ultimately concluded that the world wasn't safe for their children.

Parental Suspicion. Part of the sense-making process for parents included sharing their retrospective account of their suspicions about their children's queer identities. Most parents suspected that their child was queer around the age of 15; however, average disclosure for these parents occurred when the child was 22 (Aveline, 2006). Although some parents were relieved that their son finally disclosed, others described the disclosure as emotional, stressful, or shocking. Although parents may have known about their child's queer identity, the suspicion must have remained at a subliminal level (Aveline, 2006). In their retroactive sense-making, parents described indicators and counter indicators to their child's queerness that centered around three topics: (1) gender traits, (2) relationships, and (3) sports. Some parents described their child as having personality traits, talents, or interests that were different than other boys of the same age; however, parents attributed this to less rigid gender roles among this generation. Meanwhile, other parents described their son as fitting the expected gender roles. Parents described their son's relationships as expected or too close to girls during childhood, yet not close enough during the teenage years. Parents considered participation in sports as a counter indicator while the lack of interest was either considered an indicator or as the child just having different interests. When parents reflected on the indicators and counter indicators, they used one of three reflective actions: (1) revelations, (2) confirmations, or (3) justifications. Parents cited that disclosure was a revelation when they did not understand an indicator's meaning or when they attributed a different meaning to an indicator. Parents engaged in confirmation when they solidified their interpretations based on what they considered indicators. Justifications occurred when parents relayed an event then gave a reason as to why they had not seen the incident as an indicator or used a counter indicator.

Perceived Blame. After the initial disclosure, regardless of their suspicions, parents typically reacted either by blaming themselves for their children's queer identity or by expressing pride in their children. While studying the attendants of the support group, Fields (2001) found that parents feared they were to blame for their child's queer identity. The parents, specifically mothers, that attended the support group were working to overcome the idea that they were the cause of their child's sexuality; these individuals needed help understanding queerness as nature versus nurture. Freud's conceptualization that parents perpetuate masculine and feminine traits in their children exacerbated parental fears. More than fathers, mothers felt blamed for their child's sexuality; fathers typically attended the group only to support their wives. In Whitley's (2013) study of family members of trans individuals, all nine parents feared they were the cause of their child's gender. As a result, their own identity shifted based on their children's transition. The fact that parents perceived their child's sexual orientation to change as they went through the transition process further complicated their sense-making around their children's queer identity.

Parental Pride. Although some parents blamed themselves for their child's queer identity, others felt that being the parent of a queer child was a point of pride (Fields, 2001). Parents who felt pride about raising a queer child felt they were good parents because they were the parents of a queer individual. These prideful parents did not engage in the nature versus nurture debate on sexuality and gender identity because this was irrelevant to their queer child. The expectation of the Parents and Allies for Gay Empowerment group was that parents who did blame themselves would over time transition their identity work from caring about the cause of their child's queerness and striving to be normal to embracing their child's queerness (Fields, 2001). Parents of transgender children struggled to figure out how they could maintain their religious identity while being supportive of their transgender children (Whitley, 2013). Identity conflicts led some parents to leave the Catholic Church to support their transgender child. For these parents, their identity was not tied to how their child came to be queer but rather how good they were as parents following the disclosure of a queer identity. For some parents several identities were considered incompatible, and as a result, being a good parent was the more important identity to enact.

Siblings. Similar to parents, siblings engaged in a variety of sense-making behaviors, albeit arguably less negative. Despite having closer relationships, some siblings described shock after an individual disclosed their queer identity (Hilton & Szymanski, 2011). Siblings thought they knew their sibling and the disclosure changed that. Yet disclosure often brought the siblings closer together (Toomey & Richardson, 2009). When siblings described a closer relationship with their queer kin, they cited the fact that their queer sibling now shared more of their life with them (Hilton & Szymanski, 2011). Many siblings expressed that they felt protective and concerned for their queer sibling because they belonged to a sexual minority group. As such, siblings reported that having a queer sibling brought queer issues to their attention and normalized queerness, bringing the sibling more comfort. These siblings were more aware of heterosexism in their own life and even expressed disappointment for how their parents reacted to their sibling's disclosure.

FAMILIES OF ORIGIN AND COMMUNICATING WITH THE OUTSIDE WORLD

Following disclosure, initial reactions, and sense-making, families must figure out how and when to come out to extended family and friends (Beeler & DiProva, 1999). Once parents and siblings came to terms with their identities as family members of a queer individual, they had to go through their own disclosure, or "coming out," process (Whitley, 2013). Goodrich (2009) found that all the parents interviewed reported that they discussed as a family who they should tell, who was responsible for the disclosure to extended family, and when it was appropriate to disclose. For some families, the queer individual wanted to disclose for themselves; for other families the queer individual disclosed with the support of their immediate family. In their case study, Baptist and Allen (2008) describe the family "coming out" process as involving three stages. The familial "coming out" started in the personal and private realms, spread to relational and social realms, and finally the family embraced the political realm as an altruistic need to educate others. The initial stage of the personal and private has already been discussed as the family making sense of the disclosure and their new identities.

All the families in Goodrich's (2009) study kept the disclosure a secret for a period of time. Queer individuals who were planning to share the news about their same-sex marriage or engagement consulted family members before making a public announcement (Lannutti, 2013). Yet family members who had not accepted their new identity as a family member of a queer individual continued to practice secrecy when communicating with the outside world. For example, one parent of a transgender male told Whitley (2013) that they used female pronouns when their child was not around and male pronouns when they were. Indeed, parents and children experienced conflict when parents attempted to keep their same-sex marriage a secret when the couple wished to publicly announce their news (Lannutti, 2013). Because disclosure of same-sex marriage is a kind of "coming out" for the family, these couples experienced privacy dilemmas regarding the fact that some family members were uncomfortable with their identity as an individual with a queer family member. Sometimes this uncomfortableness was because the family member associated their identity as having a queer family member as also carrying a stigma. Some couples felt betrayed when their family reacted negatively or discouraged the disclosure of their same-sex marriage to outsiders. Although many families engaged in secrecy in regard to sharing their child's queer identity with the outside world, parents of transgender individuals in Whitley's (2013) study described feeling guilty when they did not explain their child's transgender status to the outside world. For some families, secrecy was a result of not yet coming to terms with their new identities; for other families, disclosure was selective, with members only disclosing to those they thought would react positively to the information (Baptist & Allen, 2008; Hilton & Szymanski, 2011). Yet Tyler and Abetz (2020) found that parents and queer children differed on inclusion versus privacy, with parents wanting to keep the disclosure private while the child wanted to be open about their identity. Over time, often after receiving support and acceptance from their social networks, parents came to find that secrecy was a mistake.

In the second stage, relational and social realms of familial disclosure, family members shared their identities with their social systems outside the family. Parents who suspected their child's queer identity prior to disclosure were less guarded about communicating their new identity with the outside world and were more likely to seek resources following disclosure compared with those who had no preconceived notions (Goodrich, 2009). Siblings reported that as they became more comfortable with their siblings, they were more likely to disclose their siblings' queer identity to the outside world (Hilton & Szymanski, 2011). When taking the step to share their identity as a parent of a queer child, parents reported a competing discourse of hope for acceptance versus fear of rejection or a loss of friendship (Tyler & Abetz, in press). In Baptist and Allen's (2008) case study, they found that once the family had built relationships within the queer community and became comfortable in these relationships, they started disclosing their identities to their own individual communities at home, work, and school. Yet if a family member was disclosing to a familial acquaintance, they sought permission from their queer family member first.

Finally, families enter the political realm when they accept themselves as a queer family and therefore as marginalized (Baptist & Allen, 2008). Once the family in the case study identified as a marginal group, they were more attuned to and started taking a stand on social issues. Similarly, in Tyler and Abetz's (in press) study, parents reported that as they heard or received homophobic messages, they became more and more outspoken about queer rights. For family members in Baptist and Allen's (2008) and Tyler and Abetz's (2020) studies, having a queer family member allowed them to enter the political realm and advocate for queer acceptance.

CONCLUSION

Communication plays an essential role as queer people disclose their identities to their families, their families react to those disclosures, and they all collectively make sense of their family identity. Indeed, how people react may even be a driving force in whether a queer person perceives another person to even be a family member. For example, Carpineto et al. (2008) asked men who have sex with men who they consider their family. Regardless of whether the men upheld a biogenetic or choice perspective on family, they expected a certain level of support from these individuals. In fact, the men described "family as a supportive group of people, those who provide love and support," and who will always be there (p. 60). Consequently, communication in queer people's family of origin has the power not only to change the lives of queer people but also to both construct and deconstruct what it means to be a family.

FURTHER READING

Acosta, K. (2010). "How could you do this to me?": How lesbian, bisexual, and queer Latinas negotiate sexual identity with their families. *Black Women, Gender & Families, 4*, 63–85. http://dx.doi.org/10.5406/blacwomegendfami.4.1.0063

Almack, K. (2008). Display work: Lesbian parent couples and their families of origin negotiating new kin relationships. *Sociology, 42,* 1183–1199. http://dx.doi.org/10.1177/0038038508096940

Brainer, A. (2017). Mothering gender and sexual nonconforming children in Taiwan. *Journal of Family Issues, 38,* 921–927. http://dx.doi.org/10.1177/0192513X15598549

Brumbaugh-Johnson, S. M., & Hull, K. E. (2019). Coming out as transgender: Navigating the social implications of transgender identity. *Journal of Homosexuality, 66*(8), 1148–1177. http://dx.doi.org/10.1080/00918369.2018.1493253

Chung, G., Oswald, R. F., & Wiley, A. (2006). Good daughters: Three different ways of being Korean American queer women. *Journal of GLBT Family Studies, 2,* 101–124. http://dx.doi.org/10.1300/J461v02n02_05

Costa, P. A., Tasker, F., Carneiro, F. A., Pereira, H., & Leal, I. (2020). Reactions from family of origin to the disclosure of lesbian motherhood via donor insemination. *Journal of Lesbian Studies, 24,* 1–11. http://dx.doi.org/10.1080/10894160.2019.1614378

Figueroa, V., & Tasker, F. (2014). "I always have the idea of sin in my mind....": Family of origin, religion, and Chilean young gay men. *Journal of GLBT Family Studies, 10,* 269–297. http://dx.doi.org/10.1080/1550428X.2013.834424

Friedman, C. K., & Morgan, E. M. (2009). Comparing sexual-minority and heterosexual young women's friends and parents as sources of support for sexual issues. *Journal of Youth and Adolescence, 38,* 920–936. http://dx.doi.org/10.1007/s10964-008-9361-0

Goldberg, A. E., Allen, K. R., Ellawala, T., & Ross, L. E. (2018). Male-partnered bisexual women's perceptions of disclosing sexual orientation to family across the transition to parenthood: Intensifying heteronormativity or queering family? *Journal of Marital & Family Therapy, 44,* 150–164. http://dx.doi.org/10.1111/jmft.12242

Kuvalanka, K. A., Allen S. H., Munroe, C., Goldberg, A. E., & Weiner, J. L. (2018). The experiences of sexual minority mothers with trans children. *Family Relations, 67,* 70–87. http://dx.doi.org/10.1111/fare.12226

Lazarevic, V., Holman, E., Oswald, R., & Kramer, K. (2016). Relations between economic well-being, family support, community attachment, and life satisfaction among LGBQ adults. *Journal of Family & Economic Issues, 37,* 594–606. http://dx.doi.org/10.1007/s10834-015-9464-1

McConnell, E. A., Birkett, M., & Mustanski, B. (2016). Families matter: Social support and mental health trajectories among lesbian, gay, bisexual, and transgender youth. *Journal of Adolescent Health, 59,* 674–680. http://dx.doi.org/10.1016/j.jadohealth.2016.07.026

Mehus, C. J., Watson, R. J., Eisenberg, M. E., Corliss, H. L., & Porta, C. M. (2017). Living as an LGBT adolescent and a parent's child: Overlapping or separate experiences. *Journal of Family Nursing, 23,* 175–200. http://dx.doi.org/10.1177/1074840717696924

Oswald, R. F. (2002a). Inclusion and belonging in the family rituals of gay and lesbian people. *Journal of Family Psychology, 16,* 428–436. http://dx.doi.org/10.1037/0893-3200.16.4.428

Reczek, C. (2016a). Ambivalence in gay and lesbian family relationships. *Journal of Marriage & Family, 78,* 644–659. http://dx.doi.org/10.1111/jomf.12308

Rostosky, S. S., Korfhage, B. A., Duhigg, J. M., Stern, A. J., Bennett, L., & Riggle, E. D. B. (2004). Same-sex couple perceptions of family support: A consensual qualitative study. *Family Process, 43,* 43–57.

Rothberg, B., & Weinstein, D. L. (1996). A primer on lesbian and gay families. *Journal of Gay & Lesbian Social Services, 4,* 55–68. http://dx.doi.org/10.1300/J041v04n02_05

Sellnow-Richmond, S., Bolen, D., Maguire, K. C., Hartshorn, L., & Millard, M. (2015). A qualitative examination of family communication patterns and lesbian, gay, and bisexual gender identity development. *Iowa Journal of Communication, 47,* 50–72.

Sheets, R. L., & Mohr, J. J. (2009). Perceived social support from friends and family and psychosocial functioning in bisexual young adult college students. *Journal of Counseling Psychology, 56,* 152–163. http://dx.doi.org/10.1037/0022-0167.56.1.152

Soler, J. H., Caldwell, C. H., Córdova, D., Harper, G., & Bauermeister, J. A. (2017). Who counts as family? Family typologies, family support, and family undermining among young adult gay and bisexual men. *Sexuality Research and Social Policy, 15*, 123–138. http://dx.doi.org/10.1007/s13178-017-0288-7

Soliz, J., Ribarsky, E., Harrigan, M. M., & Tye-Williams, S. (2010). Perceptions of communication with gay and lesbian family members: Predictors of relational satisfaction and implications for outgroup attitudes. *Communication Quarterly, 58*, 77–95. http://dx.doi.org/10.1080/01463370903538622

Švab, A., & Kuhar, R. (2014). The transparent and family closets: Gay men and lesbians and their families of origin. *Journal of GLBT Family Studies, 10*, 15–35. http://dx.doi.org/10.1080/1550428X.2014.857553

Wisniewski, T. J., Robinson, T. N., & Deluty, R. H. (2010). An evolutionary psychological investigation of parental distress and reproductive coercion during the "coming out" of gay sons. *Journal of Homosexuality, 57*, 163–190. http://dx.doi.org/10.1080/00918360903446077

REFERENCES

Adams, T. E. (2011). *Narrating the closet: An autoethnography of same-sex attraction.* Left Coast Press.

Adams, T. E. (2014). Post-coming out complications. In R. M. Boylorn & M. P. Orbe (Eds.), *Critical autoethnography: Intersecting cultural identities in everyday life* (pp. 62–72). Routledge.

Aveline, D. (2006). "Did I have blinders on or what?": Retrospective sense making by parents of gay sons recalling their sons' earlier years. *Journal of Family Issues, 27*, 777–802. http://dx.doi.org/10.1177/0192513X05285613

Baptist, J. A., & Allen, K. R. (2008). A family's coming out process: Systematic change and multiple realities. *Contemporary Family Therapy, 30*, 92–110. https://doi.org/10.1007/s10591-008-9057-3

Beeler, J., & DiProva, V. (1999). Family adjustment following disclosure of homosexuality by a member: Themes discerned in narrative accounts. *Journal of Marital & Family Therapy, 25*, 443–459. http://dx.doi.org/10.1111/j.1752-0606.1999.tb00261.x

Ben-Ari, A. (1995). The discovery that an offspring is gay: Parents', gay men's, and lesbians' perspectives. *Journal of Homosexuality, 30*, 89–112. http://dx.doi.org/10.1300/J082v30n01_05

Bird, J. D. P., LaSala, M. C., Hidalgo, M. A., Kuhns, L. M., & Garofalo, R. (2017). "I had to go to the streets to get love": Pathways from parental rejection to HIV risk among young gay and bisexual men. *Journal of Homosexuality, 64*, 321–342. http://dx.doi.org/10.1080/00918369.2016.1179039

Carpineto, J., Kubicek, K., Wiss, G., Iverson, E., & Kipke, M. D. (2008). Young men's perspectives on family support and disclosure of same-sex attraction. *Journal of LGBT Issues in Counseling, 2*, 53–80. http://dx.doi.org/10.1080/15538600802077533

D'Amico, E., & Julien, D. (2012). Disclosure of sexual orientation and gay, lesbian, and bisexual youths' adjustment: Associations with past and current parental acceptance and rejection. *Journal of GLBT Family Studies, 8*, 215–242. http://dx.doi.org/10.1080/1550428X.2012.677232

D'Augelli, A. R., Grossman, A. H., & Starks, M. T. (2008). Families of gay, lesbian, and bisexual youth: What do parents and siblings know and how do they react? *Journal of GLBT Family Studies, 4*, 95–115. http://dx.doi.org/10.1080/15504280802084506

D'Augelli, A. R., Hershberger, S. L., & Pilkington, N. W. (1998). Lesbian, gay, and bisexual youth and their families: Disclosure of sexual orientation and its consequences. *American Journal of Orthopsychiatry, 68*, 361–371. http://dx.doi.org/10.1037/h0080345

Elizur, Y., & Ziv, M. (2001). Family support and acceptance, gay male identity, and psychological adjustment: A path model. *Family Process, 40*, 125–144. http://dx.doi.org/10.1111/j.1545-5300.2001.4020100125.x

Feinstein, B. A., Wadsworth, L. P., Davila, J., & Goldfried, M. R. (2014). Do parental acceptance and family support moderate associations between dimensions of minority stress and depressive symptoms among lesbians and gay men? *Professional Psychology: Research and Practice, 45*, 239–246. http://dx.doi.org/10.1037/a0035393

Fields, J. (2001). Normal queers: Straight parents respond to their children's "coming out". *Symbolic Interaction, 24*, 165–187. http://dx.doi.org/10.1525/si.2001.24.2.165

Fuller, K. A., & Riggs, D. W. (2018). Family support and discrimination and their relationship to psychological distress and resilience amongst transgender people. *International Journal of Transgenderism, 19*, 379–388. http://dx.doi.org/10.1080/15532739.2018.1500966

Gonzalez, K. A., Rostosky, S. S., Odom, R. D., & Riggle, E. D. B. (2013). The positive aspects of being the parent of an LGBTQ child. *Family Process, 52*, 325–337. http://dx.doi.org/10.1111/famp.12009

Goodrich, K. M. (2009). Mom and dad come out: The process of identifying as a heterosexual parent with a lesbian, gay, or bisexual child. *Journal of LGBT Issues in Counseling, 3*, 37–61. http://dx.doi.org/10.1080/15538600902754478

Grafsky, E. L. (2018). Deciding to come out to parents: Toward a model of sexual orientation disclosure decisions. *Family Process, 57*, 783–799. http://dx.doi.org/10.1111/famp.12313

Grafsky, E. L., Hickey, K., Nguyen, H. N., & Wall, J. D. (2018). Youth disclosure of sexual orientation to siblings and extended family. *Family Relations, 67*, 147–160. http://dx.doi.org/10.1111/fare.12299

Grossman, A. H., Park, J. Y., Frank, J. A., & Russell, S. T. (in press). Parental responses to transgender and gender nonconforming youth: Associations with parent support, parental abuse, and youths' psychological adjustment. *Journal of Homosexuality*. http://dx.doi.org/10.1080/00918369.2019.1696103

Hill, D. B., & Menvielle, E. (2009). "You have to give them a place where they feel protected and safe and loved": The views of parents who have gender-variant children and adolescents. *Journal of LGBT Youth, 6*, 243–271. http://dx.doi.org/10.1080/19361650903013527

Hilton, A., & Szymanski, D. (2011). Family dynamics and change in sibling of origin relationship after lesbian and gay sexual orientation disclosure. *Contemporary Family Therapy: An International Journal, 33*, 291–309. http://dx.doi.org/10.1007/s10591-011-9157-3

Koken, J. A., Bimbi, A. D., & Parsons, J. T. (2009). Experiences of familial acceptance–rejection among transwomen of color. *Journal of Family Psychology, 23*, 853–860. http://dx.doi.org/10.1037/a0017198

Lannutti, P. J. (2013). Same-sex marriage and privacy management: Examining couples' communication with family members. *Journal of Family Communication, 13*, 60–75. http://dx.doi.org/10.1080/15267431.2012.742088

Lee, M. M., & Lee, R. E. (2006). The voices of accepting and supportive parents of gay sons: Towards an ecosystemic strengths model. *Journal of GLBT Family Studies, 2*, 1–27. http://dx.doi.org/10.1300/J461v02n02_01

Manning, J. (2014). Communicating sexual identities: A typology of coming out. *Sexuality & Culture, 19*, 122–138. http://dx.doi.org/10.1007/s12119-014-9251-4

McDonald, J., Harris, K. L., & Ramirez, J. (2020). Revealing and concealing difference: A critical approach to disclosure and an intersectional theory of "closeting". *Communication Theory, 30*, 84–104. http://dx.doi.org/10.1093/ct/qtz017

Merighi, J. R., & Grimes, M. D. (2000). Coming out to families in a multicultural context. *Families in Society, 81*, 32–41. http://dx.doi.org/10.1606/1044-3894.1090

Norwood, K. (2012). Transitioning meanings? Family members' communicative struggles surrounding transgender identity. *Journal of Family Communication, 12*, 79–92. http://dx.doi.org/10.1080/15267431.2010.509283

Norwood, K. (2013). Grieving gender: Trans-identities, transition, and ambiguous loss. *Communication Monographs, 80*, 24–45. http://dx.doi.org/10.1080/03637751.2012.739705

Pollitt, A. M., Mernitz, S. E., Russell, S. T., Curran, M. A., & Toomey, R. B. (2021). Heteronormativity in the lives of lesbian, gay, bisexual, and queer young people. *Journal of Homosexuality, 68*(3), 522–544. http://dx.doi.org/10.1080/00918369.2019.1656032

Potoczniak, D., Crosbie-Burnett, M., & Saltzburg, N. (2009). Experiences regarding coming out to parents among African American, Hispanic, and white gay, lesbian, bisexual, transgender, and questioning adolescents. *Journal of Gay & Lesbian Social Services, 21*, 189–205. http://dx.doi.org/10.1080/10538720902772063

Reczek, C. (2014). The intergenerational relationships of gay men and lesbian women. *Journals of Gerontology, Series B: Psychological Sciences and Social Sciences, 69*, 909–919. http://dx.doi.org/10.1093/geronb/gbu042

Reczek, C. (2016). Parental disapproval and gay and lesbian relationship quality. *Journal of Family Issues, 37*, 2189–2212. http://dx.doi.org/10.1177/0192513X14566638

Roe, S. (2017). "Family support would have been like amazing": LGBTQ youth experiences with parental and family support. *The Family Journal: Counseling and Therapy for Couples and Families, 25*, 55–62. http://dx.doi.org/10.1177/1066480716679651

Ryan, C., Toomey, R. B., Diaz, R. M., & Russel, S. T. (2020). Parent-initiated sexual orientation change efforts with LGBT adolescents: Implications for young adult mental health and adjustment. *Journal of Homosexuality, 67*(2), 159–173. http://dx.doi.org/10.1080/00918369.2018.1538407

Savin-Williams, R. C. (1989). Parental influences on the self-esteem of gay and lesbian youths: A reflected appraisals model. *Journal of Homosexuality, 17*, 93–110. http://dx.doi.org/10.1300/J082v17n01_04

Savin-Williams, R. C. (2001). *Mom, dad, I'm gay*. American Psychological Association.

Savin-Williams, R. C., & Ream, G. L. (2003). Sex variation in the disclosure to parents of same-sex attractions. *Journal of Family Psychology, 17*, 429–438. http://dx.doi.org/10.1037/0893-3200.17.3.429

Scherrer, K. S., Kazyak, E., & Schmitz, R. (2015). Getting "bi" in the family: Bisexual people's disclosure experiences. *Journal of Marriage & Family, 77*, 680–696. http://dx.doi.org/10.1111/jomf.12190

Siconolfi, D., Tucker, J. S., Shadel, W. G., Seelam, R., & Golinelli, D. (2020). Health, homelessness severity, and substance use among sexual minority youth experiencing homelessness: A comparison of bisexual versus gay and lesbian youth. *Journal of Sex Research, 57*(7), 933–942. http://dx.doi.org/10.1080/00224499.2019.1695723

Snapp, S. D., Watson, R. J., Russel, S. T., Diaz, R. M., & Ryan, C. (2015). Social support networks for LGBT young adults: Low cost strategies for positive adjustment. *Family Relations, 64*, 420–430. http://dx.doi.org/10.1111/fare.12124

Todd, M. E., Oravecz, L., & Vejar, C. (2016). Biphobia in the family context: Experiences and perceptions of bisexual individuals. *Journal of Bisexuality, 16*, 144–162. http://dx.doi.org/10.1080/15299716.2016.1165781

Toomey, R. B., & Richardson, R. A. (2009). Perceived sibling relationships of sexual minority youth. *Journal of Homosexuality, 56*, 849–860. http://dx.doi.org/10.1080/00918360903187812

Tyler, T. R., & Abetz, J. S. (2020). Parent–LGBTQ child communication about disclosure to their social networks. *Journal of LGBT Youth*. http://dx.doi.org/10.1080/19361653.2020.1731400

Valentine, G., Skelton, T., & Butler, R. (2003). Coming out and outcomes: Negotiating lesbian and gay identities with, and in, the family. *Environment and Planning: Society and Space, 21*, 479–499. http://dx.doi.org/10.1068/d277t

Waldner, L. K., & Magruder, B. (1999). Coming out to parents: Perceptions of family relations, perceived resources, and identity expression as predictors of identity disclosure for gay and lesbian adolescents. *Journal of Homosexuality, 37*, 83–100.

Watson, J. B. (2014). Bisexuality and family: Narratives of silence, solace, and strength. *Journal of GLBT Family Studies, 10*, 101–123. http://dx.doi.org/10.1080/1550428X.2014.857497

Whitley, C. T. (2013). Tran-kin undoing and redoing gender: Negotiating relational identity among friends and family of transgender persons. *Sociological Perspectives, 56*(4), 597–621. https://doi.org/10.1525/sop.2013.56.4.597

Zimman, L. (2009). "The other kind of coming out": Transgender people and the coming out narrative genre. *Gender and Language, 3*(1), 53–80. http://dx.doi.org/10.1558/genl.v3i1.53

Cimmiaron Alvarez and Kristina M. Scharp

QUEER SAFE SPACES AND COMMUNICATION

INTRODUCTION

Safe spaces generally aim to protect marginalized groups and individuals providing their participants refuge in/from an unsafe environment; these practices can be temporal, spatial, or even a combination thereof depending on the approach and abilities of the marginalized group(s) and the power relations between them. Queer safe spaces, therefore, are produced specifically for queer[1] and LGBT+ people and thus the practices they use to construct safety are focused on sexuality and gender issues. However, Barrett (2010) shows that queer safe space as a term is an "overused but undertheorized metaphor" (p. 1). An amalgam of safety and queerness, the term queer safe spaces suggests that queers and LGBT+ people need safety in space and that a given space may offer queer and LGBT+ individuals a sense of safety (Asante, 2018; Hartal, 2017; Mishali, 2018; Pascar et al., 2018; Thajib, 2018). Consequently, the term "queer safe spaces" encompasses diverse understandings regarding the meaning of queerness, safety, and specifically queer safety. Thus, the fluidity embedded in "queer safe spaces" as a concept is based on its different usage across disciplines; its genealogy, originating from both feminist theory and LGBTQ+ activism; and its frequently changing form depending on time and place.

Queer safe spaces, then, usually refer to spaces that allow members of the queer and LGBT+ communities to be protected for purposes such as being and learning, performing and producing queer identifications. Although the term has been used within queer and LGBT+ communities for several decades, there is neither a clear definition of queer safe spaces nor of how they should operate. This article then locates queer safe spaces within a wider genealogy of safe spaces having grown out of feminist safe spaces. Moreover, it explores how dynamics common to general safe spaces are translated and manifested within queer safe spaces in particular; this focus on the specificities of queer safe spaces foregrounds their qualities, difficulties, dilemmas, contradictions, and fallacies. Finally, drawing on a wider body of rhetorical studies, communication and education research, and geographic literature, this article shows how issues around queer safe spaces are replicated across different contexts such as LGBTQ events, online communities, and classroom discussions. This focus on queer safe spaces informs the broader term and highlights the need for further contextualization and specificity within safe space(s) research.

SAFE SPACES

A growing number of communication studies use the term safe spaces to describe spaces dedicated to marginalized group members (McAlister, 2019, p. 3). For instance, Workman and Coleman (2014) explored a Reddit group dedicated to women suggesting that the group fulfills women and girls' need for a safe place. Cole et al. (2011) offer a reflective narrative inquiry into an online group of women with disabilities asking how these women actively created a safe and open space for like-minded individuals. Similarly, Nuru and Arendt (2019) analyzed Facebook posts and chats to understand how women of color navigated racial microaggressions in online support groups designated as feminist-ally safe spaces. Whereas these and other communication studies used the term safe space to describe and examine certain spaces, they often fail to offer a clear definition thereof (see, for example, Lee, 2016).

Examining the commonalities across the spaces such studies define as "safe," one could loosely define safe spaces as spaces (either virtual or physical) open exclusively to members of a specific marginalized group that seemingly offer their participants some form of safety. Such uses of the term fail, however, to identify and problematize the assumptions underlying constructions and uses of safe spaces. For instance, what kind of safety do safe spaces offer? Which kinds of safety are understood to be lacking in other spaces? What makes safe spaces safe and for whom? Identifying these issues, Clark-Parsons (2018) stated that the ambiguity of the term in question has made it both overused and undertheorized while allowing it to be used by different communities. She suggested that, in both theory and praxis, the term "has been treated as a closed concept, erasing the context-specific relational work required to construct and maintain its material and symbolic boundaries" (p. 2125).

Therefore, coding safe spaces as a physical location across contexts and uses obscures the ways in which individuals interpret and inhabit them. In such a way, several researchers have suggested that the safety promised within the framings of a safe space might not and does not apply equally to all of its participants. Focusing on public high school classroom discourses of safe spaces and non-White, nonheterosexual, and gender nonconforming identities, Woolley (2013) suggested that safe spaces are often used to protect White people who need to engage with race. Thus, safe spaces can be created at the expense of the safety and comfort of people of color and can censor critical thinking. Moreover, she suggests that discourses of safe space and diversity may actually reinforce *unequal* power structures and lead to the silencing of some marginalized voices.

Several scholars even view safe spaces in academic contexts as being at odds with and even as threatening educational aims. Hill (2020) discussed the controversies over safe spaces in university settings detailing how they were inconsistent with freedom of speech while naturalizing the dominance of privileged voices. In addition, Barrett (2010) examined the effectiveness of safe spaces in classrooms by deconstructing the common meaning of safety in learning environments. She argued that for marginalized or oppressed populations, safety was even less conceivable. Ziv (2018) similarly questioned the feasibility and desirability of safe spaces in an academic course on pornography. Whereas the classes allowed for a reexamination of the meanings of trauma and agency by foregrounding new forms of feminist and queer subjectivities, she showed how critical discourses on sexuality were used to legitimize protectionist approaches to students. Ultimately, Ziv concluded that safe spaces had the potential to (re)produce exclusion from and inclusion in diverse power structures and contexts.

Furthermore, Karolak and Maier (2015) claimed that the growing focus on safe spaces in academia has led such spaces to focus on protecting students' psychological and emotional needs hindering the process of learning and students' intellectual growth. Slater (2016) continues that academic safe spaces aim to eliminate offensive words or upsetting ideas and therefore as threatening to curtail free speech on campuses. Like Woolley, Slater, as well as Karolak and Maier, view academic safe spaces as a potentially conflicting enmeshment of sheltering and learning thus suggesting that the use of safe spaces to protect students' emotions could hinder their intellectual development. Both Slater and Karolak and Maier, however, dichotomize safe spaces and learning—separating them into pathos and logos, emotion and reason.

Safe spaces are therefore understood in communication research as open exclusively to marginalized group members offering their participants some form of "safety." At the same time, discussions of safe spaces often fail to contextualize how ideas and practices of "safety" are articulated within a specific safe space. Nuru and Arendt (2019) similarly suggested that online safe spaces could lead to further marginalization of some of their more vulnerable members. In sum, when contextualizing safe spaces, their practices might operate as a continued mechanism of and for marginalization limiting opportunities for critical dialogue and activism.

QUEER SAFE SPACES

Within the wider context of safe spaces, queer safe spaces aim to offer safety to queer and LGBT+ participants. Despite the significant legal and political achievements of the queer and LGBT+ community in the US and other Western (Chéry, 2017) and non-Western countries (Cooney, 2018), it seems that queer and LGBT+ bodies are at high risk for violation of their safety (Edgecomb, 2017). As a result, queer safe spaces—both physical and virtual—remain relevant and popular. At the same time, however, queer safe spaces seem to reproduce safe spaces' tendencies toward inclusion and exclusion within different power structures and spaces.

Thus, Pascar et al. (2018) argue that queer space spaces are characterized by the following: (1) underscoring resistance and subversion as significant capacities required in the queer space's construction; (2) formulating a space for the community and its culture; (3) constructing subjective boundaries that are known to the members of the marginalized group, but do not have to be known to outsiders; and finally (4) establishing a new organization of temporality, which creates continuous subjective gender experiences and performances rather than producing dissociations.

Queer Safe Spaces From a Spatial Perspective.
Historically, exclusion and discrimination against queers and LGBT+ in various cities have led to their concentration in specific neighborhoods and areas. This serves two main purposes: avoiding hegemonic heterosexuality, hostile attitudes, oppression, and discrimination by the environment (Myslik, 1996); and developing a unique culture by socializing individuals in the community and providing them with unique services. The "gayborhoods" created by this segregation (Bitterman & Hess, 2021; Doan, 2015; Ghaziani, 2014; Wimark & Östh, 2014) have played an important role in shaping discussions on homonormativity (Brown, 2009, 2012) and in shaping the notion of what queer safe space is. Attractive for young queers and LGBT+s looking for spaces to negotiate and establish their identities, gayborhoods foreground debates about gentrification (Curran, 2017; Doan, 2015) and their emancipatory role for LGBT+s (D'Emilio, 1983; Knopp, 2004) and for the city in general. The formation of enclaves that provide spaces safe from homophobia and discrimination (Ghaziani, 2014) is a tactic that provides physical security, community consciousness, and collective identity producing a wide base for LGBT+ activism and mobilization (G. Brown, 2015; M. Brown, 2008; Castells, 1983; Shepard & Hyduk, 2002). These circumstances, specifically in the West, have served as the background for creating physical (ontological) queer safe spaces and for (epistemologically) advancing the notion of queer safety.

Geographies of sexualities offer a queer approach to spatial constructions anchored in feminist and postcolonial theories (Oswin, 2008). Investigating diverse relationships to power and intersectional identities reveals how privileges produce different needs for safety. From this perspective, the discourse on queer safe spaces is preoccupied with paradoxes that are the result of specific intersections, such as gender, race, and class (Browne, 2009; Cisneros & Bracho, 2019; Guha, 2019; Hanhardt, 2013; Hartal, 2017). Thus, the need for safety is frequently grounded in a liberal or neoliberal logic manifested in practices such as fortifying the space; using anonymity as a tool for alienation so that people are not publicly identified as queers or LGBT+ people and outed; constructing an inclusive space respectful of diverse positionalities; separatism and the formation of social boundaries; and establishing a controlled environment that prevents exposure to outsiders' gaze (Hartal, 2017). Such practices reveal that while discourses of queer safe spaces are designed to counteract unsafety, they (re)produce modes of surveillance and exclusion of particular queer and LGBT+ groups (David et al., 2018).

Designated spaces for queers are generally perceived as sites of resistance. Oswin (2008), however, argues that such spaces, although they can serve as safe spaces, simultaneously operate to reinforce normativity, constructing assimilationist politics in which gays and lesbians demonstrate that they are just like heterosexuals. Hence, such politics reproduces heteronormativity rather than queer spaces that are autonomous from heteronormative logics. In addition, Bain and Podmore (2021) contend that safe spaces are perceived through heteronormative lenses highlighting the need for a queer conceptualization. They show how suburban areas entail more difficulties for queer youth revealing multiple social and spatial exclusions by reinforcing an urban bias that regulates compulsory heteronormativity. From a geographical perspective, queer safe spaces are thus dynamic constructions of space, aiming to accomplish temporary safety for diverse groups. The dynamics between identity groups, normative and queer politics, the geopolitical context, and various affectivities produce the specific formation of safe spaces in different places. The only constant in this ongoing project is that producing queer safety is always contingent, negotiated, and fragile. It is therefore important to keep in mind the ever-changing form of queer safe spaces, which are intertwined with larger spatial and social discourses of normativity and axes of repression. Safe spaces are not universal constructs, and the feeling of safety is always contingent (Bain & Podmore, 2021). Rather they are constructed as performative spaces directly linked to place and identity (Cisneros & Bracho, 2019) but also practiced in different ways by their inhabitants.

Offline Contexts. The safety of queer safe spaces often aims to allow their participants the safety to *be* but additionally affords them the safety to explore and perhaps *become* who they inherently are. These additional expectations and understandings of the safety inherent to queer safe spaces, as opposed to other safe spaces, adds a level of complexity to the meaning of safety. Therefore, participants in queer safe spaces might hold different and even conflicting expectations and understandings of what safety is. Drawing on their experiences with queer and LGBT+ communities in West Jerusalem, David et al. (2018) discussed how these spaces remained shaped by Israel's continuous state of unsafety and militaristic culture. They concluded that queer safe spaces embodied the unsafety, nonbelonging, and alienation of their surroundings.

Similarly, writing about the 2016 Orlando nightclub shooting, Hanhardt (2016) reminded readers that while LGBTQ bars and clubs have played an important role in many individuals' lives, they have never been fully inclusive. Examining how discussions of the attack framed the Pulse nightclub, whose patrons were mostly people of color, Hanhardt suggested that the idea of safety-in-place remained bound up in the spatial production of racial and economic hierarchy. We agree then with Pascar et al. (2018) in arguing that the "room for error" (p. 2) vision of safe space encourages the participants to engage with and practice new ideas and behaviors functioning as spaces of tolerance for social mistakes. In contrast, the "room for difference" (pp. 2–3) vision of safety focuses on creating differentiation and separation from the violent surroundings of hegemonic space, a space as welcoming as possible to nonnormative identities and practices.

Likewise, writers in the field of education have similarly indicated the potential of queer safe spaces to offer LGBTQ individuals both safety and exclusion. The term safe spaces has both political and pedagogical value and has been effectively utilized in queer and LGBT+ education politics to make significant gains for some students in specific spaces. Discussing LGBTQ safe spaces in educational settings, Sadowski (2016) mapped the development of the Gay, Lesbian, and Straight Education Network (GLSEN) in Massachusetts in the late 1980s and early 1990s. He claimed that schools should be constructed as affirming spaces, where queer students and educators not only survive but also develop and flourish. Therefore, safety should be considered as a form of *livability* (Browne et al., 2019; Butler, 2004). Sadowski (2016) proposed approaches and strategies for constructing affirming school environments for LGBTQ students through the integration of affirming practices and respect. Bain and Podmore (2021) looked specifically at suburban areas in North America where LGBTQ2S (two spirit) youth are in large proportions compared to central city areas. They argued that queer youth cocreated spatialities, using more-than-safety processes (J. C. Bowstead, 2019; Peters, 2003) such as resourcefulness and conviviality. In doing so, they achieved more than safety in fostering opportunities for meaningful social interactions and collaborations. Bain and Podmore (2021) also argued that queer spaces in suburban areas were not unified but rather constructed via local adult responses to "perceived suburban hetero- and cis-normativities resulting in weak integration, a lack of collaboration, and the rebounding of identity parcels across an extensive geography" (p. 3).

Moreover, teacher-researchers such as Britzman (1995), Nelson (2006), Sauntson (2018), Paiz (2020), and Paiz and Coda (2021) argued for not just the place to add more queer inclusivity but also the pedagogical space. Nelson (2006) continued that "classroom cohorts and curricula tend to be constructed as domains in which straight people are interacting exclusively with other straight people" (p. 1; see also Sauntson, 2012). Thus, classrooms—albeit physical or online—tend to reinforce heteronormativity under the guise of basic curricular needs and requirements. Paiz (2020), using his own teaching contexts both in the United States and in China, calls for not just the inclusion of queer bodies, voices, and agents within curricular materials, but he also furthers what Nelson argues for, queer inclusion within a local context. Thus, both Nelson and Paiz agree that it is not enough just to include queer contexts to be a queer safe space, but we must also refine and relocate such bodies, content, and more within a localized context.

However, queer pedagogies such as the ones the aforementioned teacher-scholars call for are not singular, nor are they formalized. Queer pedagogies then are queer in that there is no one unifying pedagogical strategy or tool for teachers to use. Furthermore, were the classroom to be a safe space, then teachers need no longer be the only ones to foster such an environment; we must now also call upon the students to help teachers understand contemporary queerness. Students, then, must be afforded opportunities to become experts, both about themselves and about their local environments. Not much has changed, apparently, since Luhmann (1998) argued that "when posed as pedagogy, beyond suggesting the limitations of transformation of content, of queering curriculum, [we must] render suspect the very basics of pedagogy and its appeal to rational subjects capable of toleration or consolation through accurate representation" (p. 124).

Thus, we argue that to become a queer safe space, it is not enough that pedagogy be just inclusive of queer content. Classrooms, formal or otherwise, must instead become the active production, analysis, and deconstruction of normative ways of teaching, knowing, and seeing. Queer pedagogies as a queer safe space must allow for a critical discourse and dialogue engaging with identity and power necessitating queer culture exists both in and out of the classroom walls thereof. This further implies that a pedagogical and/or educative queer safe space must exemplify the fluidity between education, knowledge, and the larger societal context. Students then become the arbiters of their own learning and knowledge allowing their voices volume rather than a more traditional, heteronormative, top-down approach to education.

Constructing Queer Safe Spaces Within Online Contexts. Traditional media outlets—such as newspapers, television, and radio—are usually perceived and performed as a platform of mainstream groups and ideologies, and, as such, do not aspire to be nor are able to provide a safe space for marginalized groups, among them gendered and sexual minorities. In contrast, researchers have found that the patterns of inclusion and exclusion within queer safe spaces persist within digital queer safe spaces (Boyd & Ellison, 2007; Nash & Gorman-Murray, 2019, pp. 32–33; Papacharissi, 2002). In recent decades, the development of digital media technologies and social networks have provided safe spaces for marginalized groups and ideas, especially for sectoral, local, ideological, and alternative media platforms (J. Bowstead, 2019; Cranston & Lloyd, 2019; David & Baden, 2020; Light & Cassidy, 2014). These spaces have been specifically discussed in communication research (Manning et al., 2020) with the focus on queer and LGBT+ individuals in particular (Asante, 2018; Scheuerman et al., 2018) and have played a central role in producing and practicing safe spaces for marginalized groups and ideas (Asante, 2018; Scheuerman et al., 2018).

Moreover, digital spaces have also offered new opportunities and challenges. For example, Cavalcante (2019, pp. 1719–1720) argued that queer safe spaces such as social media have become the new gayborhoods and gay bars for youth. As a result, he argued that youth come together via social media to perform various sociopolitical and cultural functions such as educating themselves about LGBTQ issues and use them for tools of self-expression and exploration; to foster sexual networks and encounters; to digitally narrate intimate storytelling practices for likeminded communities; and to establish repositories for collective memory. In addition, Asante (2018) explored perceptions of belonging and the dynamics within queer safe space among queer African men in closed Facebook groups. He suggested that social media enabled queer Africans in continental Africa and in diaspora to create transnational diasporic relations in a virtual space. Such research provides insight into how safe spaces translate into digital media in which content is less controlled by hegemony and where less privileged groups can create their own spaces. Despite the desire to create alternative and safe spaces for marginalized groups online, however, these spaces can rapidly transform into threatening spaces of harassment and bullying similar to their offline counterparts.

These processes of communication through digital channels have become significantly intensified since 2020 with the outbreak of the COVID-19 crisis. Following the restrictions on freedom of movement and the call for social distancing (Browne et al., 2020; David & Sommerlad, 2021; Kay, 2020), numerous public and private institutions worldwide have switched to digital communication as a substitute for face-to-face communication. The rapid transition to digital communication platforms and live-stream technologies (e.g., Skype, Zoom) resulted in increased cyberbullying, including the specific type of "zoom bombing" (Sommerlad & David, 2022) defined as disrupting communication by hijacking a virtual meeting for targeted reasons such as promoting racist or sexist agenda but also just for fun.

Lectures, academic conferences, and meetings of organizations dealing with issues of gender, race, and sexuality have been the focus of these attacks led mainly by racists, sexists, and White supremacists. Among the attacked groups, we can find a high percentage of LGBT+ and queer organizations and meetings (Coughlan, 2020). Thus, the desire to create a safe digital space in order to maintain the role and function of offline spaces ended in unsafety and in the intrusion of racists, sexists, and White supremacist groups into the participants' homes. The practices through which safe spaces are structured also reveal the failures in the production of such spaces, specifically in the digital sphere, where online communication has a central role in providing and denying safety to queer and LGBT+ individuals.

To some extent, the online arena is similar to the offline one, in that inequalities and power relations are reproduced in different ways. However, due to their structure and features that enable various groups to express their voice(s), digital spaces have a unique potential to provide safe space for marginalized groups and ideas. At the same time, their use as such should be managed and regulated in order to protect the participants from vicious attacks due to their marginalized identities.

CONCLUSION

Queer safe spaces seem to reproduce the tendencies of safe spaces toward inclusion and exclusion within different power structures and spaces. At the same time, a focus on the rhetoric of queer safe spaces offers an essential contextualization of safe spaces. Such contextualization reveals how the understanding of safety vis a vis practices that construct safe spaces are shaped and reimagined according to the needs and specificities of different communities. Therefore, queer safety is often imagined as the spaces in which diversity may be explored and practiced. This imagery leads to different expectations around the notion of queer safety. Various unacknowledged assumptions regarding the meaning and practices of safety may combine with the general tendency of safe spaces toward dynamics of inclusion and exclusion. This in turn may result in tensions or even collusion between diverse participants. Thus, queer safe spaces are shaped by wider cultural, political, and economic inequalities, as highlighted by discussions of the surveillance state, homonationalism (Puar, 2007, 2017), and the construction of queer safe spaces within current regimes of (un)safety (Pascar et al., 2018). This dynamic can lead to the exclusion of those whose experiences and performances fail to match the safe space norms resulting in limited access to the symbolic power and resources offered by that space. Exclusions in queer safe spaces could also result from aspects unique to queer safe spaces.

Queer safe spaces consequently remain convenient spaces without judgment by allowing for various manifestations and diverse performances and identifications, even ones that will be considered nonnormative outside of that space. These different expectations can collide as participants enter the same queer safe space with different expectations and assumptions about the "correct" ways to act in it. Similar to physical spaces, then, queer safe spaces might become unsafe due to threats coming from both within and without (Hartal, 2017; Pascar et al., 2018; Scheuerman et al., 2018). Thus, in order to develop a holistic and relational approach to queer safe spaces, we argue that queer safe spaces serve as an intersection of its physical, discursive, rhetoric, virtual, material, emotional, and imagined capacities (Clark-Parsons, 2018; Cranston & Lloyd, 2019; Djohari et al., 2018; Lewis et al., 2015; Nash et al., 2019; Roestone Collective, 2014).

Queer safe spaces also reinforce the potential to limit such dialogue and growth. For instance, participants who fail to follow the dominant understanding of "safety" within a specific queer safe space might find themselves excluded; and one participant's interest in exploration and dialogue might be curbed in order to avoid denying other participants' expectations of safety within the queer safe space. Similarly, within educational settings, queer safe spaces have a constructive task to improve students' progress and enforce liberal values. Nonetheless, their limits are palpable due to the specific contexts and identities in which educational spaces are enacted. This too indicates that safety is ambiguous and that creating a queer safe space has to always take into consideration multiple specific aspects such as where the space is and who is it for.

Essentially, queer safe spaces are negotiated spatial constructions. Whether discursive, online, physical, or within an educational setting, they reveal an emotional politics that is contradictory and contested. These negotiated spaces have inherent difficulties. Thus, in order to produce a personal or collective sense of safety, careful attention is required from both participants and producers of these spaces. This attention is needed for both the practices of producing safe spaces and for the way queer safe spaces are implemented. Moreover, the understanding of safety varies for different identity groups and changes over time and between places. This multiplicity of discourses on safety constructs queer safe spaces as a temporal concept and leads to diverse situations of exclusion or marginalization.

Following the outbreak of COVID-19, the year 2021 highlighted the importance of creating safe spaces for marginalized groups. The pandemic also revealed the importance of virtual platforms as spaces for social negotiations. The transition from physical to virtual spaces involves multiple risks. Specifically, since online spaces very quickly became nearly exclusive sites for social interactions due to social distancing restrictions, they lacked adequate protection for the participants due to the almost total neglecting of the complex discourse that had previously shaped the production of offline queer safe spaces. Far-right groups and individuals attacked organizations and events that critically engaged with issues of race, gender, and sexuality highlighting not only the importance of online queer safe spaces but also the temporality and the lack of security inherent to them. Thus, creating a working definition for queer safe spaces both online and off can help scholars as well as activists better understand the negotiations that shape these spaces and help protect participants from potential harm.

Similar to other safe spaces, queer safe spaces often lead to exclusion of some members and further marginalization of others within different power structures and spaces. At the same time, a focus on the rhetoric of queer safe spaces reveals how notions and practices of safety are shaped and reimagined according to the specific needs and specificities of queer and LGBT+ communities. First, queer and LGBT+ communities' need to explore and practice a marginalized existence could lead to different expectations of queer safety. When this tension is unacknowledged, it may produce divergent assumptions regarding the meaning of safety.

Second, like other safe spaces, queer safe spaces at times protect their members against specific kinds of discourse framed as provocative or offensive. This tendency could limit dialogue and growth as well as silence some of the participants. As argued by Monk (2011) and others (Guha, 2019; Hartal, 2017), protection camouflaged as safety does not prevent bullying and victimization discourses (Ringrose & Renold, 2010) but rather maintains the binary discourse of "safety from" and "safety to" and reproduces modes of (adult) surveillance and exclusions of marginalized queer and LGBT+ identities. Accordingly, a relational and holistic approach to queer safe spaces needs to take into consideration multiple aspects of safe-unsafe dynamics that are ever-changing within spaces of queer activism albeit offline or online.

FURTHER READING

Boklage, E. (2016). Safe space, dangerous space: Counterpublic discourses in the Russian LGBT blogging community. In A. Dhoest, L. Szulc, & B. Eeckhout (Eds.), *LGBTQs, media and culture in Europe* (pp. 119–134). Routledge.

Bramberger, A., & Winter, K. (Eds.). (2021). *Re-conceptualizing safe spaces*. Emerald Publishing Limited.

Campbell, B., & Manning, J. (2018). *The rise of victimhood culture: Microaggressions, safe spaces, and the new culture wars*. Palgrave Macmillan.

Cram, E. (2019). Queer geographies and the rhetoric of orientation. *Quarterly Journal of Speech*, 105(1), 98–115.

Du Preez, P. (2012). The human right to education, the ethical responsibility of curriculum, and the irony in "safe spaces." In C. Roux (Ed.), *Safe spaces: Human rights education in diverse contexts* (pp. 51–62). Sense Publishers.

Hanhardt, C. B. (2020). Safe. In B. Burgett & G. Hendler (Eds.), *Keywords in American cultural studies* (3rd ed., pp. 213–216). NYU Press.

Lucero, L. (2017). Safe spaces in online places: Social media and LGBTQ youth. *Multicultural Education Review*, 9(2), 117–128.

Usher, N., & Morrison, E. (2010). The demise of the gay enclave, communication infrastructure theory, and the transformation of gay public space. In C. Pullen & M. Cooper (Eds.), *LGBT identity and online new media* (pp. 271–287). Routledge.

Yep, G. A. (2003). The violence of heteronormativity in Communication Studies: Notes on injury, healing, and queer world-making. *Journal of Homosexuality*, 45(2–4), 11–59.

REFERENCES

Asante, G. (2018). "Where is home?" Negotiating comm(unity) and un/belonging among queer African men on Facebook. *Borderlands*, 17(1), 1–26.

Bain, A. L., & Podmore, J. A. (2021). More-than-safety: Co-creating resourcefulness and conviviality in suburban LGBTQ2S youth out-of-school spaces. *Children's Geographies*, 19(2), 131–144. https://doi.org/10.1080/14733285.2020.1745755

Barrett, B. J. (2010). Is "safety" dangerous? A critical examination of the classroom as safe space. *Canadian Journal for the Scholarship of Teaching and Learning, 1*, 1–12. https://doi.org/10.5206/cjsotl-rcacea.2010.1.9

Bitterman, A., & Hess, D. B. (Eds.). (2021). *The life and afterlife of gay neighborhoods: Renaissance and resurgence*. Springer.

Bowstead, J. (2019). Safe spaces of refuge, shelter and contact: Introduction. *Gender, Place & Culture, 26*, 52–58. https://doi.org/10.1080/0966369X.2019.1573808

Bowstead, J. C. (2019). Spaces of safety and more-than-safety in women's refuges in England. *Gender, Place & Culture, 26*(1), 75–90.

Boyd, D. M., & Ellison, N. B. (2007). Social network sites: Definition, history, and scholarship. *Journal of Computer-Mediated Communication, 13*(1), 210–230.

Britzman, D. P. (1995). Is there a queer pedagogy? Or, stop reading straight. *Educational Theory, 45*(2), 151–165.

Brown, G. (2009). Thinking beyond homonormativity: Performative explorations of diverse gay economies. *Environment and Planning A, 41*(6), 1496–1510. https://doi.org/10.1068/a4162

Brown, G. (2012). Homonormativity: A metropolitan concept that denigrates "ordinary" gay lives. *Journal of Homosexuality, 59*(7), 1065–1072. https://doi.org/10.1080/00918369.2012.699851

Brown, G. (2015). Queer movements. In D. Paternotte & M. Tremblay (Eds.), *The Ashgate Research Companion to Lesbian and Gay Activism* (pp. 73–88). Ashgate.

Brown, M. (2008). Working political geography through social movements theory: The case of gay and lesbian Seattle. In K. Cox, M. Low, & J. Robinson (Eds.), *The Sage handbook of political geography* (pp. 285–304). SAGE.

Browne, K. (2009). Womyn's separatist spaces: Rethinking spaces of difference and exclusion. *Transactions of the Institute of British Geographers, 34*(4), 541–556.

Browne, K., Banerjea, N., & Bakshi, L. (2020). Survival and livability in #COVIDtimes: Queer women's transnational witnessing of COVID-19. *Dialogues in Human Geography, 10*(2), 128–131. https://doi.org/10.1177/2043820620930833

Browne, K., Banerjea, N., McGlynn, N., Bakshi, L., Beethi, S., & Biswas, R. (2019). The limits of legislative change: Moving beyond inclusion/exclusion to create "a life worth living." *Environment and Planning C: Politics and Space, 39*(1), 30–52. https://doi.org/10.1177/2399654419845910

Butler, J. (2004). *Undoing gender*. Psychology Press.

Castells, M. (1983). *The city and the grassroots*. University of California Press.

Cavalcante, A. (2019). Tumbling into queer utopias and vortexes: Experiences of LGBTQ social media users on Tumblr. *Journal of Homosexuality, 66*(12), 1715–1735.

Chéry, T. M. (2017). "No one shakes me": Rejected queer identities and the creation of sacred Ugandan spaces in honor of the Orlando massacre. *Qualitative Inquiry, 23*(7), 550–556.

Cisneros, J., & Bracho, C. (2019). Undocuqueer stress: How safe are "safe" spaces, and for whom? *Journal of Homosexuality, 67*(11), 1491–1511.

Clark-Parsons, R. (2018). Building a digital girl army: The cultivation of feminist safe spaces online. *New Media & Society, 20*(6), 2125–2144.

Cole, J., Nolan, J., Seko, Y., Mancuso, K., & Ospina, A. (2011). GimpGirl grows up: Women with disabilities rethinking, redefining, and reclaiming community. *New Media & Society, 13*(7), 1161–1179.

Cooney, E. (2018). *Art in Tunisian LGBTQI++ NGOs*. SIT Digital Collections. https://digitalcollections.sit.edu/cgi/viewcontent.cgi?article=3866&context=isp_collection

Coughlan, S. (2020, October 22). LGBT students attacked in University Zoom meeting. *BBC News*. https://www.bbc.com/news/education-54648103

Cranston, S., & Lloyd, J. (2019). Bursting the bubble: Spatialising safety for privileged migrant women in Singapore. *Antipode, 51*, 478–496. https://doi.org/10.1111/anti.12433

Curran, W. (2017). *Gender and gentrification*. Routledge.

D'Emilio, J. (1983). *Sexual politics, sexual communities: The making of a homosexual minority in the United States, 1940–1970*. University of Chicago Press.

David, Y., & Baden, C. (2020). Reframing community boundaries: The erosive power of new media spaces in authoritarian societies. *Information, Communication and Society*, 23(1), 110–127.

David, Y., & Sommerlad, E. (2021). Media and information in times of crisis: The case of the coronavirus (COVID-19) infodemic. In G. Andrews, V. Crooks, J. Pearce, & J. Messina (Eds.), *COVID-19 and similar futures: Geographical perspectives, issues and agendas*. Springer.

David, Y., Hartal, G., & Pascar, L. (2018). The right to Jerusalem: The danger of queer safe spaces. *Borderlands*, 17(1), 1–26.

Djohari, N., Pyndiah, G., & Arnone, A. (2018). Rethinking "safe spaces" in children's geographies. *Children's Geographies*, 16(4), 351–355. https://doi.org/10.1080/14733285.2018.1487032

Doan, P. (Ed.). (2015). *Planning and LGBTQ communities: The need for inclusive queer spaces*. Routledge.

Edgecomb, S. (2017). Architecting queer space: Charles Ludlam's Bluebeard in the West Village. In K. Landis & S. Macaulay (Eds.), *Cultural performance: Ethnographic approaches to performance studies* (pp. 88–100). Red Globe Press.

Ghaziani, A. (2014). *There goes the gayborhood?* Princeton University Press.

Guha, M. (2019). "Safe spaces" and "bad" girls: "Child marriage victims'" experiences from a shelter in Eastern India. *Gender, Place & Culture*, 26(1), 128–144. https://doi.org/10.1080/0966369X.2019.1574720

Hanhardt, C. B. (2013). *Safe space: Gay neighborhood history and the politics of violence*. Duke University Press.

Hanhardt, C. B. (2016). Safe space out of place. *QED: A Journal in GLBTQ Worldmaking*, 3(3), 121–125.

Hartal, G. (2017). Fragile subjectivities: Constructing queer safe spaces. *Social & Cultural Geography*, 19(8), 1053–1072. https://doi.org/10.1080/14649365.2017.1335877

Hill, D. W. (2020). Communication as a moral vocation: Safe space and freedom of speech. *The Sociological Review*, 68(1), 3–16.

Karolak, H., & Maier, C. T. (2015). From "safe spaces" to "communicative spaces": Semiotic labor, authentic civility and the basic communication course. *Journal of the Association for Communication Administration*, 34(2), 88–101.

Kay, J. B. (2020). "Stay the fuck at home!": Feminism, family and the private home in a time of coronavirus. *Feminist Media Studies*, 20(6), 883–888. https://doi.org/10.1080/14680777.2020.1765293

Knopp, L. (2004). Ontologies of place, placelessness, and movement: Queer quests for identity and their impacts on contemporary geographic thought. *Gender, Place, and Culture*, 11(1), 121–134.

Lee, E. Y. (2016). Looking forward: Decentering and reorienting Communication Studies in the spatial turn. *Women's Studies in Communication*, 39(2), 132–136.

Lewis, R., Sharp, E., Remnant, J., & Redpath, R. (2015). "Safe spaces": Experiences of feminist women-only space. *Sociological Research Online*, 20(4), 1–14. https://doi.org/10.5153/sro.3781

Light, B., & Cassidy, E. (2014). Strategies for the suspension and prevention of connection: Rendering disconnection as socioeconomic lubricant with Facebook. *New Media & Society*, 16(7), 1169–1184.

Luhmann, S. (1998). Queering/querying pedagogy? Or, pedagogy is a pretty queer thing. In W. F. Pinar (Ed.), *Queer theory in education* (pp. 120–132). Routledge.

Manning, J., Asante, G., Huerta Moreno, L., Johnson, R., LeMaster, B., Li, Y., Rudnik, J. J., Stern, D. M., & Young, S. (2020). Queering communication studies: A Journal of Applied Communication Research forum. *Journal of Applied Communication Research*, 48(4), 413–437.

MacAlister, J. F. (2019). Space in rhetorical theory. In *Oxford research encyclopedia of communication*. Oxford University Press. https://doi.org/10.1093/acrefore/9780190228613.013.123

Mishali, Y. (2018). (In)visibly unsafe: Passing under the radar and the limits of queer space. *Borderlands, 17*(1), 1–31.

Monk, D. (2011). Challenging homophobic bullying in schools: The politics of progress. *International Journal of Law in Context, 7*, 181–207. https://doi.org/10.1017/S1744552311000061

Myslik, W. D. (1996). Gay communities as safe havens or sites of resistance. In N. Duncan (Ed.), *BodySpace: Destabilising geographies of gender and sexuality* (pp. 155–169). Routledge.

Nash, C. J., & Gorman-Murray, A. (2019). Queer mobilities and new spatial media. In C. J. Nash & A. Gorman-Murray (Eds.), *The geographies of digital sexuality* (pp. 29–47). Oxford University Press.

Nash, C. J., Gorman-Murray, A., & Browne, K. (2019). Geographies of intransigence: Freedom of speech and heteroactivist resistances in Canada, Great Britain and Australia. *Social & Cultural Geography, 22*(7), 979–999. https://doi.org/10.1080/14649365.2019.1652929

Nelson, C. D. (2006). Queer inquiry in language education. *Journal of Language, Identity & Education, 5*(1), 1–9.

Nuru, A. K., & Arendt, C. E. (2019). Not so safe a space: Women activists of color's responses to racial microaggressions by White women allies. *Southern Communication Journal, 84*(2), 85–98.

Oswin, N. (2008). Critical geographies and the uses of sexuality: Deconstructing queer space. *Progress in Human Geography, 32*(1), 89–103.

Paiz, J. M. (2020). *Queering the English language classroom: A practical guide for teachers*. Equinox Publishing.

Paiz, J. M., & Coda, J. E. (Eds.). (2021). *International perspectives on LGBTQ+ issues in modern language teaching and learning*. Palgrave Macmillan.

Papacharissi, Z. (2002). The virtual sphere: The internet as a public sphere. *New Media & Society, 4*(1), 9–27.

Pascar, L., Hartal, G., & David, Y. (2018). Queering safety? An introduction. *Borderlands, 17*(1), 1–11.

Peters, A. J. (2003). Isolation or inclusion: Creating safe spaces for lesbian and gay youth. *Families in Society, 84*(3), 331–337.

Puar, J. K. (2007). *Terrorist assemblages: Homonationalism in queer times*. Duke University Press.

Puar, J. K. (2017). *The right to maim: Debility, capacity, disability*. Duke University Press.

Ringrose, J., & Renold, E. (2010). Normative cruelties and gender deviants: The performative effects of bully discourses for girls and boys in school. *British Educational Research Journal, 36*, 573–596. https://doi.org/10.1080/01411920903018117

Roestone Collective. (2014). Safe space: Towards a reconceptualization. *Antipode, 46*, 1346–1365. https://doi.org/10.1111/anti.12089

Sadowski, M. (2016). *Safe is not enough: Better schools for LGBTQ students*. Cambridge Education Press.

Sauntson, H. (2012). *Approaches to gender and spoken classroom discourse*. Palgrave Macmillan.

Sauntson, H. (2018). Language, sexuality and inclusive pedagogy. *International Journal of Applied Linguistics*, 1–19.

Scheuerman, M. K., Branham, S. M., & Hamidi, F. (2018). Safe spaces and safe places: Unpacking technology-mediated experiences of safety and harm with transgender people. *Proceedings of the ACM on Human-Computer Interaction, 2*(CSCW), 1–27. https://doi.org/10.1145/3274424

Shepard, B., & Hayduk, R. (Eds.). (2002). *From ACT UP to the WTO: Urban protest and community building in the era of globalization*. Verso.

Slater, T. (2016). Conclusion: How to make your university and unsafe space. In T. Slater (Ed.), *Unsafe space: The crisis of free speech on campus* (pp. 129–131). Palgrave Macmillan.

Sommerlad, E., & David, Y. (2022). Digital inequalities in times of the COVID-19 pandemic in Israel and Germany. In S. Brunn & D. Gilbreath (Eds.), *COVID-19 and an emerging world of ad hoc geographies*. Springer.

Thajib, F. (2018). The making and breaking of Indonesian Muslim queer safe spaces. *Borderlands, 17*(1), 1–24.

Wimark, T., & Östh, J. (2014). The city as a single gay male magnet? Gay and lesbian geographical concentration in Sweden. *Population Space and Place, 20*(8), 739–752.

Woolley, S. W. (2013). Speech that silences, silences that speak: "That's so gay," "that's so ghetto," and safe space in high school. *Journal of Language and Sexuality, 2*(2), 292–319.

Workman, H., & Coleman, C. A. (2014). "The front page of the Internet": Safe spaces and hyperpersonal communication among females in an online community. *Southwestern Mass Communication Journal, 29*(2), 1–21.

Ziv, A. (2018). Questioning safe space in the classroom: Reflections on pedagogy, vulnerability, and sexual explicitness. *Borderlands, 17*(1), 1–16.

NOTE

1. Since its emergence as a term that refers to specific kinds of sexuality at the end of 20th century, various terminologies take shelter under the umbrella of the term *queer*. For example, it is commonly used when the terms LGBT or LGBTQ+ fail to represent the full ideological meaning under discussion. In this article, the term "queer" refers to a diverse range of sexual identities, such as gay, bisexual, lesbian, or transgender. By using the term queer rather than LGBTQ+, we aim to highlight queerness as potentially replacing identity politics with the politics of identification as an alternative to the bankrupt notion of an essentialist identity.

Lital Pascar, Yossi David, Gilly Hartal, and Brandon William Epstein

QUEER WORLDMAKING

ORIGINS OF QUEER WORLDMAKING

Queer worldmaking—the project of building affirming queer life worlds within, among, and between persistently heteronormative and anti-queer societies—is an exercise in *praxis*, a synthesis of theory and practice. In this way, queer worldmaking emulates other strands of the wider 1990s queer theory project—an exciting new academic framework (i.e., theory) informed and invigorated by the acts, activism, and artistry of people on the margins of society (i.e., practice). Of the two, the practice of queer worldmaking surely predates its academic theorization. Indeed, evidence of the *doing* of queer worldmaking is scattered across LGBT+ and queer cultures of the past and present—hidden beneath the surface or between the cracks of dominant publics and practiced and performed in ephemera of queer life. Thus, "*doing* queerness" and "*making* queer worlds" have been central to understanding queer worldmaking from the earliest theorizations of the term (Muñoz, 1996, p. 12). But while individual and collective acts of making queer worlds have been essential to the queer worldmaking project, the elaboration and refinement of the project's conceptualization at the end of the 20th century vastly multiplied the dynamism of this practice, extending its scope and reach to make possible kinds of queer worlds previously unimaginable.

Theorizing queer worldmaking relied on a canon of liberal, Western thought that was decidedly un-queer, namely: theories of the "public sphere" or "public realm." While notions of "the public" have deep roots in academia and civil discourse, the theoretical traditions connecting the public sphere to queer worldmaking are notably 20th century. One might begin with the idea of the "phantom public" (Lippman, 1925), *The Public and Its Problems* (Dewey, 1927), or the theorization of the "public realm" (Arendt, 1958, p. 29). However, by most accounts, the notion of "public sphere" most directly links to queer worldmaking by way of Jürgen Habermas (1989) in his *Structural Transformation of the Public Sphere*, though primarily via later scholars' robust critiques of his work.

Although Habermas first published *Structural Transformation* in German in 1962, it would not appear in English until 1989. In the book, Habermas (1989) theorized the public sphere—or more specifically, the "bourgeois public sphere"—as "the sphere of private people [who] come together" to claim "the public sphere regulated from above against the public authorities themselves" and "to engage them in a debate over the general rules governing relations in the basically privatized but publicly relevant sphere of commodity exchange and social labor" (p. 27). Explicit in this definition is Habermas's concern with how individuals formed a social space for criticism and debate in opposition to authorities of the time, an idea that, for Habermas, was foundational to modern civil society. In Habermas's view, such a sphere of human life was ideal largely because this public was, in theory, open and accessible to all people.

While Habermas's theory of an ideal public sphere was both appealing and influential, an assortment of critics quickly challenged his notion of a single, all-inclusive public sphere. Some critics, like Michel Foucault, Jean-François Lyotard, and Jean Baudrillard, "question[ed] the basic suppositions of public realm theory" altogether (Villa, 1992, p. 712). Meanwhile, other critics repudiated Habermas's account of the actually existing public sphere while also innovating upon his ideas. Among the most vociferous critics of Habermas's public sphere were scholars from minoritized and marginalized communities who found his ideal both ahistorical and unhelpful for empowering people like themselves. Indeed, for many critics, the universal public imagined by Habermas and rooted in the limited experiences of White male heterosexuals in 18th-century Europe seemed wholly inadequate for theorizing "the real social experiences" (Negt et al., 1988, p. 60) of living people at the end of the 20th century. In Germany, interests of the proletariat exemplify this point in the work of Oskar Negt and Alexander Kluge, who as early as 1972 bemoaned theories of "the bourgeois public sphere" that exclude "substantial life-interests and nevertheless claims to represent society as a whole" (Negt et al., 1988, p. 63). Upon *Structural Transformation*'s publication in English, feminist scholars Rita Felski (1989) and Nancy Fraser (1992) further repudiated Habermas's public sphere as equitable and called for the theorization of "counterpublics" that could make space for "subaltern" communities to debate and formulate contrary ideas, stand in opposition to the public, and expand the notion of democratic democracy. In a similar vein, the Black Public Sphere Collective (1995) sought to resituate the ideas of multiple, co-existing publics within the Black experience, calling for a radical rethinking of the relationships laid out in Habermas's text—an idea elaborated on later by Catherine Squires (2002) in *Communication Theory*.

Similar critiques of Habermas were forwarded at this time by queer scholars, who made revising public sphere theory with an emphasis on counterpublics foundational to their elaborations of queer worldmaking. One such scholar was Michael Warner (1992) in his essay "The Mass Public and the Mass Subject," which he presented for the first time at the conference inaugurating the English translation of Habermas's *Structural Transformations* alongside Fraser. Drawing on notorious queer artists like John Waters, Warner both builds upon and critiques Habermas's public sphere and its modern instantiations for their "double movement of identification and alienation," which have the effect of presuming a mass subject that simultaneously soothes the need for a united *we* while exposing the implicit assumptions of embodiment and identity that render so many members of this mass public a minoritized *they* (Warner, 1992, p. 397). Such thinking previews more foundational work that Warner would do with co-author Lauren Berlant in their essay "Sex in Public" a few years later. Both "Sex in Public" and "The Mass Public" would later be published as part of an influential manuscript on worldmaking, *Publics and Counterpublics* (Warner, 2002a), an abbreviated and apportioned version of which would appear in both *Public Culture* and the *Quarterly Journal of Speech*. Meanwhile, in his examination of Pedro Zamora's ethics of self as counterpublicity on the MTV television series *The Real World*, José Esteban Muñoz (1999) worked to theorize queer worldmaking in a "post-Habermasian" field (p. 148). Muñoz began this project in earnest several years earlier but does not link his ideas of worldmaking to the Habermas tradition in full until the appearance of this chapter in Muñoz's book *Disidentifications*. Heralding the queer potential within innovations of the public sphere by the likes of Negt, Kluge, and Fraser, Muñoz (1999) shared his "misgiving" about Habermas, particularly his "use of and investment in communicative reason" (p. 148) that presupposes a general notion of "good" seen as unproblematically valid across all degrees of social difference. Nonetheless, while both Warner and Muñoz take Habermas's public sphere to task from a queer vantage point, the public sphere tradition remains an essential gateway to the theorizing of queer worldmaking.

DEFINING QUEER WORLDMAKING

Although some scholars of queer theory often point to "Sex in Public" (Berlant & Warner, 1998) as the first appearance of the actual term "queer worldmaking," the phrase can be traced farther back to Muñoz (1996), "Ephemera as Evidence: Introductory Notes to Queer Acts." Although Muñoz (1999) would elaborate on the concept in much more depth in his influential text, *Disidentifications: Queers of Color and the Performance of Politics*, in this early essay, he had gestured to the "worldmaking capabilities" of the performative, broadly, and of live, public performances enacted by minoritarian subjects, specifically (Muñoz, 1996, p. 11).

In *Disidentifications*, Muñoz (1999) developed the relationship between performance and worldmaking, arguing that through disidentificatory performances—those that work "on, with, and against a cultural form" (p. 12) rather than attempting to totally assimilate within a structure or completely oppose it—minoritarian subjects can disidentify with the current world and perform a new one. Queer worldmaking, thus:

> delineates the ways in which performances—theatrical and everyday rituals—have the ability to establish alternate views of the world.... Oppositional counterpublics are enabled by visions, "worldviews," that reshape as they deconstruct reality. Such counterpublics are the aftermath of minoritarian performance. Such performances *transport* the performer *and* the spectator to advantage point where transformation and politics are imaginable. Worldmaking performances produce these vantage points by slicing into

the facade of the real that is the majoritarian public sphere. Disidentificatory performances opt to do more than simply tear down the majoritarian public sphere. They disassemble that sphere of publicity and use its parts to build an alternative reality. Disidentification uses the majoritarian culture as raw material to make a new world. (Muñoz, 1999, pp. 195–196)

According to Muñoz (1999), queer worldmaking requires "an active kernel of utopian possibility" (p. 25) and can be found in the moments in which minoritarian subjects refuse to simply survive but, instead, opt to fashion a new world via "spectacles, performances, and willful enactments of the self for others" (p. 200).

Although Muñoz was the first to mobilize the term "queer worldmaking," Berlant and Warner's definition of the concept reigns as the dominant "origin story" in much queer theory—including queer communication scholarship—illustrating how logics of whiteness and the colonization of knowledge production remain imbedded throughout the academy. These citational politics, however, do not minimize the significant contributions of Berlant and Warner to deepening and circulating queer worldmaking alongside Muñoz in the realms of both academic thought and community practice.

For Berlant and Warner, queer worldmaking is less about performance and utopia and more concerned with the topic of "intimacy." In "Sex in Public," Berlant and Warner (1998) highlighted the ways in which U.S. society's commitment to ideas of intimacy is essentially a commitment to the creation and maintenance of heteronormativity, which they defined as "the institutions, structures of understanding, and practical orientations that make heterosexuality seem not only coherent...but also privileged" (p. 548). It is the need to disrupt heteronormativity, undergirded by certain notions of intimacy, privacy, and publicness that led them to queer worldmaking.

Berlant and Warner (1998) made clear that they are not so much interested in describing sex as an "act" per se, but rather the (counter-)publics "organized around sex" (p. 547) and these (counter-)publics' ability to engage in radical "queer culture building" by imagining and bringing into reality something other than the heteronormative (p. 548). Their vision of what a queer world is, means, or could look like is ultimately now rehearsed with regularity within contemporary queer communication scholarship and other worldmaking scholarship alike:

By queer culture we mean a world-making project, where "world," like "public," differs from community or group because it necessarily includes more people than can be identified, more spaces than can mapped beyond a few reference points, modes of feeling that can learned rather than experienced as a birthright. The queer world is space of entrances, exits, unsystematized lines of acquaintance, projected horizons, typifying examples, alternate routes, blockages, incommensurate geographies. World making, as much in the mode of dirty talk of print-mediated representation, is dispersed through incommensurate registers, by definition *unrealizable* as community or identity. (Berlant & Warner, 1998, p. 558)

For Berlant and Warner (1998), then, queer worldmaking is a "project" (p. 558)—one they intend to promote as a counterstrategy to the notions of intimacy and publicity that "prevent the recognition, memory, elaboration, or institutionalization of all the nonstandard intimacies that people have in everyday life" (p. 560). In this way, queer worldmaking's aim is:

> not just to destigmatize those average intimacies, not just to give access to the sentimentality of the couple to persons of the same sex, and definitely not to certify as properly private the personal lives of gays and lesbians. Rather, it is to support forms of affective, erotic, and personal living that are public in the sense of accessible, available to memory, and sustained through collective activity. (Berlant & Warner, 1998, p. 562)

Both Berlant and Warner's as well as Muñoz's early theorizations of queer worldmaking have proven deeply resonant with queer communication scholars. On the one hand, Berlant and Warner (1998) offered communication scholars a useful *theoretical* contribution through defining publics, counterpublics, and their worldmaking capacities as not simply representative but, in fact, inherently rhetorical—that is, constructed and reconstructed through the circulation of texts among people practicing what Warner would later call a "stranger sociability" (Warner, 2002b, p. 75). Said otherwise, Berlant and Warner theorized worldmaking as a profoundly communicative phenomenon from which scholars might critique and build alternative visions of society beyond the heteronormative. Muñoz (1996), on the other hand, presented a useful *practical* starting point for worldmaking by directing communication scholars' attention to minoritarian subjects that engage the labor of worldmaking through performance, while casting a critical eye on a certain strain of "communicative rationality" with longstanding cache within the history of the discipline.

QUEER WORLDMAKING IN COMMUNICATION STUDIES

In his germinal essay, "The Violence of Heteronormativity in Communication Studies," Gust Yep (2003) brought the concept of "queer worldmaking" to bear on the contours and commitments of queer communication studies. Yep (2003) drew on Berlant and Warner's conceptualization to define queer worldmaking as "the opening and creation of spaces without a map, the invention and proliferation of ideas without an unchanging and predetermined goal, and the expansion of individual freedom and collective possibilities without the constraints of suffocating identities and restrictive membership" (p. 35). Yep offered a set of procedures for moving away from the violence(s) of heteronormativity toward more livable queer worlds, both within communication scholarship, specifically, as well as within broader areas of public life. He offered the process of moving through injury (being negatively affected by the violences of heteronormativity) to healing (unpacking and critiquing heteronormativity) to finally making queer worlds, wherein such worldmaking includes living and embodying queer theory, confronting the challenges posed by queer theory, and embracing a *communicative ethic* (as opposed to a *normalizing ethic*) that "asserts that sex acts are given moral meaning by their communication context... [and] shifts moral judgements about the character of sexual desires and acts to the qualities of the social exchange and communication encounter, such as mutual consent, responsibility, respect, and reciprocity" (Yep, 2003, p. 48).

Yep's early work on queer worldmaking set the stage for much of the contemporary work in this area of scholarship first by providing an accessible and adaptable definition of heteronormativity and tracing out its nuances (both within communication as a field of study and more broadly in the lives of queer people) and then, more importantly, by proffering a process for healing from anti-queer violences that can be taken up by both queer people and communication scholars of all genders, sexualities, identities, and embodiments. He also identified and addressed challenges that are likely to emerge, and his anticipation of such challenges related to race, gender, and class—inspired by Muñoz's work on disidentification—is still being productively grappled with today. Certainly, Yep's invitation to communication scholars to participate in diverse worldmaking projects resonates louder and clearer today than ever:

> I invite communication scholars across the spectrum of social locations to join these theorists and practitioners in this radical project to expand, stretch, reorient, and re-map the conceptual landscape of the field of communication. I urge communication teachers and scholars to interrogate and unpack the homo/heterosexual binary, disentangle and demystify the power of heteronormativity in our scholarship, pedagogy, and cultural politics, and to create and produce historically specific and embodied racialized knowledges of the human sexual subject. (Yep, 2003, p. 48)

Moreover, in his concluding thoughts, Yep (2003) identified queer communication scholarship at the time as having "race problems" (p. 41) as he called out queer theory for putting on a misleading "façade" of racial inclusivity, employing the language found in Muñoz (1999), that race is a "queer blind spot" (p. 10). This acknowledgement is followed by the recommendation that disidentifications and quare theory are "productive points of engagement with mainstream queer theory about racialized knowledges and experiences" (Yep, 2003, p. 42)—both of which have been taken up by many queer scholars of color in recent queer communication scholarship.

QUEER WORLDS, QUEER THEMES

Although it feels contrary to the goals of any queer project to try to organize the path that worldmaking has taken into neat boxes, scholarship in this area of communication has tended toward certain discernible themes and patterns. First, many queer worldmaking pursuits in the discipline of communication take as their foundation—or at least draw upon—queer of color theories, particularly Muñoz's theories of disidentification(s) and queer futurity. A second theme is the notion that academia, scholarship, and academic pursuits serve as productive sites for envisioning and creating queer worlds. Finally, a growing body of scholarship tending to the worldmaking potentialities of queer memories, monuments, and archives deserves special attention. These intellectual themes and patterns overlap, interweave, and split off into unpredictable rhizomatic directions, paving the way for scholarship that converses with, diverges from, and pushes forward queer worldmaking in communication studies in curiously queer directions.

Queer of Color Worlds and Theories. Many queer scholars within the discipline, particularly queer scholars of color, have adopted Yep's invitation to demonstrate what queer of color/ quare theories can offer understandings of queer worldmaking. Building on Muñoz's labor, E. Patrick Johnson's "quare studies" (2001), and Roderick Ferguson's (2013) "queer of color critique," theories of disidentification(s), queer futurity, queer utopias, hope, queer relationality, and belonging thread through today's disciplinary conversations on queer worldmaking.

Disidentifications. The concept of disidentification and the "worldmaking power of disidentificatory performances" (Muñoz, 1999, p. ix) have found particular resonance with queer worldmakers and queer scholars of worldmaking in communication. Through the concept of disidentification, Muñoz (1999) advocated for minoritarian subjects to disidentify with one world and perform a new one as a practice of survival. It can be understood as a third response to interpellation that refuses to play by the binary rules set forth by either identification or resistance and counteridentification. Said otherwise: disidentification is a refusal to either totally assimilate within a structure or completely oppose it; rather, to disidentify is to work "on, with, and against a cultural form" (Muñoz, 1999, p. 12).

Queer work in communication studies suggests that disidentification can function as a process of worldmaking and coalition-building for minoritarian subjects from different social locations (Eguchi & Asante, 2016; Eguchi & Long, 2018). By bringing a theory of disidentification together with performative methodologies, intercultural communication scholars, specifically, have carved out ways to "look at, critique, and shift embodied performances of minoritarian identities and subjectivities that reveal nuanced forms of neither assimilation nor resistance," offering a form of intercultural praxis that questions "the epistemological assumptions through which we must analyze and understand complex, contingent, and contradictory renegotiations of identity and practices of belonging" (Eguchi & Asante, 2016, p. 183). This sub-area of study has also revealed the possibilities of taking an anti-anti-relational approach to queerness and worldmaking in ways that reimagine queer relationality as a "political and intellectual moving toward the future" (Eguchi & Long, 2018, p. 1603).

Indeed, the theme of futurity—a distinct category discussed in the section "Queer Futurity, Futures, and Utopias"—animates significant queer worldmaking work on disidentification as a way of enacting "a futurity of self-empowerment in the present" (Gutierrez-Perez & Andrade, 2018, p. 5). For example, in their work on marriage as an "embodied ideograph" Robert Gutierrez-Perez and Luis Andrade (2018) suggested that queers of color can resist the dominant oppressive structures written into the archive of marriage through embodied repertoires that remake and reimagine marriage queerly. In doing so, queers of color imagine the queer futurity of marriage differently while negotiating its varied meanings in the present. This same notion of the "embodied ideograph" and of making efforts in the present to work toward better queer futures animates Andrade's whose work on migrant/queer worldmaking examines how migrant/queers have (re)drawn and (re)articulated border signs to "enact new world-making tactics and to formulate new possibilities for who we are and what we can be" (Andrade, 2019, p. 222). Rather than eschew the border sign—a symbol of violence, death, and dehumanization—queers and migrants disidentify with and invigorate the border sign with new life and meaning in the present with the vision of a queerer future in mind.

Queer communication scholarship on disidentification also illuminates the possibilities and potentialities of disidentifying with(in) particular cultural texts. For example, Shinsuke Eguchi and Myra N. Roberts (2015) wrote about gay rapper Fly Young Red's rehearsal of new and alternative possibilities for Black masculinity that resists dominant norms through his controversial single "Throw That Boy Pussy." Rooted in Quare studies, Eguchi and Roberts brought questions of identification and counteridentification to bear on the Black queer world (re)made through Fly Young Red's music, revealing how such embodied texts can work on and against norms and offer new possibilities for performing Black masculine identities. In a similar vein, Kimberlee Pérez (2019) wrote about the stage performance, "Ramble-Ations: A One D'Lo Show," wherein D'Lo invites his audience to disidentify with his narratives and family storytelling, "extending out from and through the performance the worldmaking potential of a proximate and familiar elation from which to view both the performance and potentially the audience's own viewing selves as already within it" (p. 378). Through this invitation to disidentify, D'Lo reveals how cultural forms such as stage performance can foster queer intimacy between audience and performer.

This scholarship highlights how disidentification becomes an enactment of queer worldmaking that refuses to abide by the procedures set forth by heteronormativity, illuminating how queer worldmakers play with cultural codes in ways that service their visions. In doing so, they create and affirm new possibilities for meaning-making across cultural venues.

Queer Futurity, Futures, and Utopias. With Muñoz's theory of disidentification driving much contemporary communication scholarship on worldmaking, it is inevitable that such scholarship looks toward queer futures and utopias in the pursuit of more livable queer worlds. If the "worldmaking power of disidentificatory performances" (Muñoz, 1999, p. xi) lies in disidentifying with one world and performing a new one, the temporality of a queer world tends toward a utopian future. Muñoz (1999) elaborated:

> Disidentificatory performances and readings require an active kernel of utopian possibility. Although utopianism has become the bad object of much contemporary political thinking, we nonetheless need to hold to and even *risk* utopianism to engage in the labor of making a queerworld. (p. 25)

Not all work on queer futures and utopias in communication draws specifically on Muñoz; however, significant enough portions of it does to make citing his work again an important maneuver in citational politics. Indeed, even if this area of queer scholarship does not always mention Muñoz, much of the queer investment in the future emerges against—or at least in response to—anti-social and anti-relational queer theories that posit the future as futile. Dustin Bradley Goltz (2009, 2013; Goltz & Zingsheim, 2015) contributed much to the work on queer futures. Goltz (2013) suggested that reclaiming the futurity of queerness is a generative space for queer scholars and that anti-social approaches foreclose "queer hope, queer potential, and the project of queer worldmaking" (p. 136). Sisco King and West (2014, pp. 62–63) built on this critique of the anti-social thesis, suggesting that an investment in futurity, utopia, and the "not yet" paves the path to livable queer worlds. Their examination of the film *Lars and the Real Girl* (Gillespie, 2007) reveals that "the process of queering demands vigilance to strive for the "not yet" and to maintain a reflexive awareness of the constitutive exclusions that make the social possible in the here and now" (Sisco King & West, 2014, p. 62), pointing to *Lars and the Real Girl* as "a utopian allegory told through the everyday lived relations of a community brought together by a sex doll... [that] models forms of sociality that remind us that the gaps between the here and there may not be as great as we imagine them to be" (Sisco King & West, 2014, p. 79).

Another explanation for the aversion to anti-social approaches within queer worldmaking scholarship could be the investment in queer of color theories that tend to value lived, embodied experiences of survival within racist and heteronormative cultures (Eguchi & Spieldenner, 2015). By investing in queerness as a "structuring and educated mode of desiring that allows us to see and feel beyond the quagmire of the present" (Muñoz, 2009, p. 1), queer worldmaking becomes a way of seeing and feeling the world differently, utopically. That fact may explain why Nakayama and Morris (2015) drew on this Muñoz quote to articulate the aims of *QED: A Journal in GLBTQ Worldmaking*: "We are driven by our commitment to another world, despite how fleeting and dynamic the images of that other world might be" (p. vii).

To glance toward queer futures, invest in queer futurity, and envision queer utopias often entails looking to unexpected sites and spaces for kernels of radical queer futures, including legal settings (Campbell, 2012) and the labor movement (Tiffe, 2015). Scholarship that harnesses the power of worldmaking is also instructive on *how* to imagine queer futures, whether that be through remembering and honoring past collective trauma (Eguchi, 2016), practicing (specifically queer and trans relational) liberatory pedagogies that retheorize liberation, embracing the "criminal," and working toward prison abolition (LeMaster et al., 2019), or through various experiments in research methodology and praxis. For example, Gutierrez-Perez and Andrade (2019) offered *Joteria* as both a game and a form of research praxis, which rejects the here and now and insists on the possibility of another world, a utopian world for queer intercultural communication scholarship. Petermon and Spencer (2019), harnessing a similar impulse, made the case that queer Black feminist critiques and lenses for research can function as a tool of queer Black feminist worldmaking—"a tool for hope, possibility, and survival—one that never only tears down the forces of oppression, but that also imagines and contributes to the construction of better, more just worlds" (p. 353).

Indeed, fostering a sense of critical hope may be one of the most productive offerings to emerge from work on queer futures and utopias, for although "we are not queer yet... we have hope" (Gutierrez-Perez & Andrade, 2019, p. 190). Both the future in general and certain subfields of communication scholarship such as intercultural communication can be thought of as spaces to nourish a sense of critical hope that works in the domain of "unexhausted potentials" (Goltz, 2009, p. 565) to envision queer worlds and futures.

Queer Relationality. Another response to the anti-relational turn in queer theory could be labeled the "anti-anti-relational turn," or the turn to queer relationality. Queer relationality has become a popular mode of queer worldmaking in queer communication scholarship. Gust Yep (2017) foreshadowed this turn in the sequel to his essay on the violence of heteronormativity in communication studies, wherein he argued that "queer relationality has become an increasingly important area of investigation" that works toward "maintaining wholeness in a heteronormative world" (p. 116), healing "from the symbolic and material violences of heteronormativity (p. 120), and embodying "nonheteronormative relations and social arrangements...to explore the possibilities of queer worldmaking" (p. 119). Yep (2017) provided a way of conceptualizing queer relationality that honors its temporality, roots in the body, and sense of possibility:

> Queer relationality involves spheres of intimacy, such as closeness, deep knowing, mutual attunement, sensuality, and eroticism that could range from fleeting to enduring, and spheres of desire, such as wishes, longings, needs, affinities, and yearnings that could range from internally held to externally articulated. (p. 120)

Much of Benny LeMaster's body of work is instructive when it comes to understanding the connections between queer relationality and queer worldmaking. Their work on trans relationality (LeMaster, 2017) is particularly telling. Trans relationality "emerges as mundane, embodied, and subversive mode of resistance" (LeMaster, 2017, p. 86) and a mode of queer worldmaking that is particular to the context of existing in the midst of an alt-right presidency. It results from "transing" queer bonds and carves out the possibility for queer worlds by "exploring the dialectic tension between the individual and the institutional" (LeMaster, 2017, p. 86). LeMaster's work not only offers a conception of queer relational formations based on the notion of inventing resistant modes of belonging, it also reminds us that the queer worlds one makes are both born of one's own creation but also "shaped by institutional expectancies" (p. 86). Drawing on Yep's notion of healing from systemic injury in pursuit of worldmaking, LeMaster (2017) offered myth-making—constructing personal/ized mythic entities "set in opposition to culturally imposed religious forms" (p. 90)—as an arts-based project that allows queer folks to create and discover their own mythologies while engaging the dialectic tension between individual and institutional, thus processing systemic injuries, beginning the work of healing, and ultimately enacting alternative queer worlds. LeMaster's various methods and approaches to healing and worldmaking animate much of the section on "Academia as Site for Queer Worldmaking," especially when discussing various forms of relational performance as methodologies for making queer worlds and worldmaking scholarship.

The ways in which cultural texts enact and represent queer forms of relationality has begun to take hold as a productive field of inquiry. Sisco King and West (2014) examined the film, *Lars and the Real Girl*, finding queer forms of relationality within and between Lars, his sex doll girlfriend, and their community—a set of lived relations that "models forms of sociality that remind us that the gaps between the here and there may not be as great as we imagine them to be" (p. 79). The beauty of this relational formation emerges in representations of "secular modalities of acceptance that engender openness to being undone by others and commitment to making our ways through the world together" (Sisco King & West, 2014, p. 80). In a similar way, Pérez (2019) investigated "Ramble-Ations: A One D'Lo Show" to illustrate how personal narrative and family storytelling can come together in stage performance to produce a "family unfamiliar" (the stage/staging where performer and audience collectively and relationally negotiate *the* family) that queers intimacy and audience-performer relationality (p. 373).

Considering various types and forms of relational performance as a methodology for scholarship emerges as a useful outcome of the scholarly work on queer relationality. Examples of this kind of work abound, including the queer of color performance and performative writing in response to the Pulse nightclub shooting (Andrade & Gutierrez-Perez, 2017), the method of collaborative autoethnography (Eguchi & Spieldenner, 2015), the blending of autoethnography and intersectional reflexivity (Eguchi & Long, 2018), and endeavors in collaged relational autoethnography (LeMaster et al., 2019). These experiments in method reveal that queer worldmaking could, might, or should entail a sense of "radical interconnectedness" (Andrade & Gutierrez-Perez, 2017), relational performance linked to the norm/ativies of the academy-governing queer racialized bodies (Eguchi & Spieldenner, 2015), embracing "queer family as a temporal and present mode of relational and political resistance" (Eguchi & Long, 2018, p. 1604), as well as a process of healing through coalition, love—"relationally derived self-love" (LeMaster et al., 2019, p. 364)—and collaborative unlearning of cisheteronormativity. Moreover, these scholarly endeavors are never solely scholarly in nature. They are personal, felt, and embodied, and such embodied methodologies highlight how queer and/or racialized bodies "become powerful and central sites of knowledge production" (Eguchi & Spieldenner, 2015, pp. 126–127) in the pursuit of better, more ethical understandings of the world—another key aspect of livable queer(er) worlds.

Academia as a Site for Queer Worldmaking. Although academia's often coercive and systemically oppressive tendencies provide numerous reasons to consider it both uninhabitable for queers and a space of impossibility for queer worldmaking, queer worldmaking can and does happen in unexpected spaces. Queer communication scholars, holding interest in matters such as space, pedagogy, performance, theory, and criticism, have developed and continue to cultivate a growing body of scholarship that recognizes academia, scholarship, and academic pursuits more broadly as productive sites for envisioning and creating queer worlds.

One of the first—and certainly most provocative—endeavors in carving out a space for queer worldmaking in academic work in communication can be traced back to "Sextext," an essay by Frederick Corey and Thomas Nakayama (1997) published in *Text and Performance Quarterly*. "Sextext" endures as an early example of what it looks like to write desire into academic pursuits, often eschewing accepted academic language in favor of more visceral and performative approaches to writing and theorizing. The essay announces its aim as such, claiming to "write aloud desire in an elaborate performance that indexes the fleeting nature of desire in the context of academic discourse that attempts (never successfully) to capture and ground that flight" (Corey & Nakayama, 1997, p. 59). Although "Sextext" emerged before the wide adoption of the language of queer worldmaking, it nonetheless set the stage for considering how to remake academic spaces—like academic journals—into worlds where queer desire might thrive.

It follows, then, that Nakayama makes up half the partnership with Charles E. Morris III that established *QED: A Journal in GLBTQ Worldmaking*, a journal whose main purpose is to provide a space to both participate in and publish on instances of queer worldmaking across diverse domains of scholarship; for, even though Nakayama and Morris are both scholars of communication themselves, *QED* is highly interdisciplinary at heart. Morris and Nakayama (2013) "envision[ed] *QED* as a space of coalitional thinking, conversation, critique, debate, performance, review, and mobilization across boundaries of GLBTQ scholarship, activism, art, culture, and policy making" (p. v) and believed that, at its heart, *QED* asks: What potentialities might we foment, foster, and enact by bringing together GLBTQ worldmakers from multiple, intersectional domains? How we do so will be an ongoing inventive, material, and political challenge, reinforcing the imperative that queer must always be lived as a verb. (p. vi)

Drawing explicitly on Berlant and Warner's early formulation of queer worldmaking—and tuning into its "creative, performative, intimate, public, disruptive, utopian" energies (Morris and Nakayama, 2013 p. vi)—the authors have carved out a space for the performance and consideration of worldmaking to flourish, privileging traditional modes of intellectual inquiry alongside activist endeavors in the form of essays, commentaries, interviews, roundtable discussions, and book and event reviews.

Beyond establishing and contributing to a specific journal dedicated to interdisciplinary scholarly endeavors into worldmaking, queer communication scholars have also identified different ways in which queer worldmaking can be enacted in the space of the classroom through certain pedagogical maneuvers, choices, and forms of resistance. A particularly powerful example of how pedagogues can make queer worlds in the classroom can be found in Ragan Fox (2013). In his essay on "homo-work," queer pedagogy, and peri-performativity, Fox (2013) theorized peri-performativity as "performative discourse about performativity" (p. 68) that has the potential to disrupt performativity's habituated reiteration, specifically in academic spaces. Fox viewed peri-performativity as a form of queer pedagogy that exposes heteronormative epistemological frameworks, disrupts the heteronormative expectations of the classroom, and, in doing so, generates space for queer worlds to emerge in the hallowed spaces of academia. In a similar vein, Alyssa Samek and Theresa Donofrio (2013) theorized "academic drag" as a means of critiquing discourses of professionalism in academic spaces—particularly the graduate classroom—in ways that revive the transformative possibilities of queer rhetoric. Finally, Morris (2013) considered the possibilities of reimagining rhetorical education as queer rhetorical pedagogy in the K-12 classroom, pointing to the worldmaking potential of "disruptive undoings of historically leveraged 'truths' and normativities" (p. 397) while queering boundaries of remembering. Whether by queering one's pedagogy, one's sense of professionalism in the classroom, or one's ways of remembering and teaching about important historical figures, queer communication scholars have provided useful models for what it might look like to re-envision the classroom as a space of queer worldmaking.

Communication, broadly, and queer communication, specifically, are incredibly diverse bodies of academic inquiry that cannot be thought of as a monolith. Indeed, communication as a broad field of study is made up of several subdisciplines, many of which have begun to consider what possibilities for queer worldmaking exist within their specific subdisciplinary contexts. Many scholars of intercultural communication, after noticing that their subdisciplinary context was severely lacking in queer perspectives and approaches in general have, in the last 10 years, begun to explore intercultural communication as a site for resistive worldmaking (Johnson, 2013). Nowadays, it is not uncommon to see theories and analyses of queer worldmaking animate the pages of intercultural communication essays and journals, highlighting the potential for queer worlds themselves to emerge at the intersections of diverse fields of inquiry, especially those fields that have always prioritized the perspectives of minoritarian subjects (Chávez, 2013; Eguchi, 2015; Eguchi & Asante, 2016;

Eguchi & Calafell, 2019; Gutierrez-Perez & Andrade, 2019; LeMaster et al., 2019; Moreman & Briones, 2018).

Intercultural communication is not, however, the only subdisciplinary space identified as rich with worldmaking potential. Thomas Dunn (2016a), in evaluating the queer potential of Macklemore and Ryan Lewis's song, "Same Love," both warned of texts that impede the possibility of the very alternative worlds those texts supposedly promote and pointed to critical/cultural critique as having the capacity to work toward more radical anti-liberal visions of the world. In this way, critical/cultural scholars and scholarship are positioned on the frontline of the battle "against the neoliberal project" (Dunn, 2016a, p. 283). Anjali Vats (2020, p. 92) similarly positioned rhetoric and communication as playing a role in worldmaking, specifically in helping (or potentially hindering) the construction of worlds in which others can thrive.

Moreover, scholars of queer rhetoric have time and again articulated the role that rhetoric, rhetorical history, and rhetorical criticism play in cultivating inhabitable queer worlds. Isaac West (2013), for example, made the case that rhetorical criticism is generative of queer worldmaking by virtue of its focus on the contingent and the particular, in its capacity to privilege rhetors that do the work of queering and playing the norms against each other, and by its potential to harness a reparative or generous approach to evaluating texts. Morris (2015) extended this understanding of rhetoric-as-worldmaking by adding that the praxis of rhetorical history—doing, making, and (re)writing rhetorical history queerly—is included in what it means to enact queer worldmaking as a rhetorician. Finally, Dunn (2016b), in his work on queer monuments and memorials, distinguished the "world-changing" or worldmaking objectives of rhetoric, itself, defining rhetoric as "a highly communicative act; one which, at its heart, seeks to move audiences to see, act, and be in the world differently" (p. 9).

Indeed, the turn to reparative (rather than paranoid) criticism, in many ways ushered into the field of rhetoric by West, demonstrates a specific example of how academic work can "help us create the worlds we want to live in" (West, 2013, p. 540). We see this impulse animate the examination of the It Gets Better campaign by West et al. (2013), the investigation of Norman Rockwell's art by Sisco King (2016), the historical study of Robbie Rogers's coming out story by John Sloop and West (2016), and the analysis of plus-size model Tess Holliday's performance of fatness in the body positive movement by Hailey Nicole Otis (2020). This line of scholarship teaches us that textual productions and critical evaluations of those texts should eschew a binary conception of queerness (West, 2013; West et al., 2013), engender a queer politics of hope (King, 2016; West et al., 2013), consider rhetorical context (Sloop & West, 2016), as well as understand the limits of queer worlds in terms of who they are made for and who they make life livable for (Otis, 2020).

Scholarship, and its arrangement with other trajectories, participates in "the world's becoming," as Joshua Ewalt (2016, p. 140) argued. The scholarship traced out here illustrates the ways in which academic spaces and pursuits can facilitate the making of queer worlds—a conclusion that should urge queer communication scholars to continue to consider what queer worlds their work makes possible and what kinds of bodies, identities, or ways of being those queer worlds make life livable for.

Queer Memories, Monuments, and Archives. A growing body of scholarship on the queer worldmaking potential within public memories, histories, monuments, and archives is evident in the work of communication scholars—particularly in rhetoric and/or performance studies. Morris has, in many ways, laid the foundation for this work, having long advocated for the worldmaking power in queer(ing) our shared pasts. His work on Abraham Lincoln is perhaps most instructive here—work that considers the possibilities "for queer worldmaking through disruptive undoings of historically leveraged 'truths' and normativities, challenges to institutional and individual violences, and enticing invitations to rhetorical reconstitutions" (Morris, 2013, p. 397). What, Morris (2013) asked, might rhetorically reconstituting historical truths look like? Certainly, it involves the rhetorical critic and theorist taking a more active role in the praxis of rhetorical history or, as Morris (2015) argued, "thorough[ly] recounting… LGBTQ history while making it" (p. 238).

Queering public memory—both in terms of queering the memories themselves and the ways people think about writing, doing, and conceptualizing them—has surfaced as a provocative direction in the path toward discovering the worldmaking potentials of queer pasts. Morris's work is important here as well, both for his queering of public memories of historical figures like Lincoln (Morris, 2013) and J. Edgar Hoover (Morris, 2002), as well as his offering of the concept of the "archival queer"—those who "enact memory's political promise" (Morris, 2012, p. 51) by inventing, disrupting, and critically transforming GLBTQ pasts, using both those pasts and their presence in the present in service of new, queerer futurities.

Thomas R. Dunn's work on queer public memories, monuments, and monumentality is valuable in this endeavor as well. Like Morris, Dunn (2016b) found queer worldmaking value in memory, particularly LGBT+ and queer people's ability to turn to their shared memories of the past "to produce social, political, and cultural change in the minds of their audiences" (p. 9). He also drew attention to the more visual and material instantiations of memories and how they help (re)make possible queer worlds in physical spaces, often by "making do" with the detritus of heteronormative culture and historical practice, including the retrofitting of the discarded idea of monumentality for queer purposes.

Investigations of queer(ing) public memories are not the only worthwhile endeavors toward understanding and evaluating the queer worldmaking potentialities of LGBTQ histories and pasts. Indeed, queer approaches to archival research and materials serve an important role in working toward queer worlds as well. "Archival queers," argued Morris (2012), "are proponents and practitioners of mnemonic world making" (p. 51). They:

> individually and collectively perform inventive, disruptive, and critical accumulations, exhibitions, preservations, and transformations of GLBTQ pasts and their presence. Archival queers desire, deconstruct, and deploy copious and contradictory holdings and ostensible detritus—from official collections and privileged stacks to the undocumented archive, archive of feelings, talking archives, video remains, sweet tea, and ephemera—in pursuit and production of what José Muñoz's describes as "a temporal arrangement in which the past is a field of possibility in which subjects can act in the present in the service of a new futurity." (Morris, 2012, p. 51)

Queer(ing) archives involves taking queer approaches to researching and representing archival materials in scholarly publications as well as attending to the queer worlds made possible by queer archivists (and/or archivists of queer materials) themselves. Daniel Brouwer

(2014) proffered two key questions to those who do the latter work in his introduction to *QED*'s special issue and forum on GLBTQ worldmaking and archives: "How do you understand the relationship between your archival holdings and the project of GLBTQ worldmaking? What does your archive do in the world for GLBTQ people, and how does your archive accomplish that work?" (p. 184). Brouwer concluded with the affirmation that "we are all invited to archive—we are all potential participants in archiving—GLBTQ lives" (p. 184), which should encourage queer scholars from all corners of communication to consider what their work has to offer in terms of building queer worlds from and within archival materials.

Other approaches to queer worldmaking and archives/archiving abound, including those that attend specifically to the embodiment of archival practices. Lydia Nelson (2014) considered the ways that "constricted archiving bodies mirror conscripted archival bodies of knowledge" (p. 133). Nelson looked to the re-envisioning of archival materials as a way of imagining and enacting queer futures and expanding people's present–pasts for future–pasts to come. Pamela VanHaitsma (2019) brought other consideration of archival bodies and embodiment to the forefront of queer archival work, focusing on the inventive possibilities of archive stories, intimate relations in the archives, and the potential eroticism of passing or "straightening up" in relationship to doing archival labor. "As in other realms of GLBTQ worldmaking," VanHaitsma (2019, p. 19) claimed, "archival encounters may become ongoing archival relations"—pointing once again to the power of queer relationality in the pursuit of queer(er) worlds.

It may seem counterintuitive that work on LGBTQ pasts, histories, memories (and the archives that maintain and conscribe them) can work in service of queer worldmaking, for queer worlds are often framed in the future's domain. However, Muñoz (2009) argued that "queerness is always on the horizon" (p. 11); although "we have never been queer... queerness exists for us as an ideality that can be distilled from the past and used to imagine a future" (p. 1). The queer worlds of the future all but require queer scholars to glance in the direction of the past while firmly rooted in the present in order to envision future possibilities. Thus, the unearthing and examining of queer pasts, memories, and archives is key to generating the livable, inhabitable queer worlds in front of us.

LIMITATIONS AND FUTURE DIRECTIONS

Although the voices and perspectives on queer worldmaking in communication scholarship are diverse and varied, certain voices are foregrounded more often and more loudly than others. While there seems to be no shortage of scholarly perspectives on worldmaking written by gay men about issues and topics related to gay men (Dunn, 2011; Gutierrez-Perez & Andrade, 2018; McCune, 2008; Morris & Sloop, 2006; Sloop & West, 2016), there is a notable lack of lesbian voices and experiences reflected in the literature. This absence is not unique to communication scholarship and mirrors broader trends across interdisciplinary inquiry on queer worldmaking. Additionally, studies of queer worldmaking within communication also have yet to center the impulse toward decolonizing queer that is emerging in many spaces outside communication studies (Channell-Justice, 2020; Driskill, 2011; Morgensen, 2011; Spurlin, 2001), highlighting another limitation and potentially fruitful area for future scholarship.

Other future directions for scholarship on queer worldmaking include exploring queer worldmaking enacted by and for bodies not traditionally considered queer, such as fat-positive queer worldmaking (Otis, 2020) as well as investigating the spatiality of queer worldmaking (Clark, 2020; Ewalt, 2016). Intersectional dynamics of queerness as they relate to issues of gender (Dunn, 2017; Evans & Janish, 2015; LeMaster, 2017; LeMaster et al., 2019) and sexuality (Pérez, 2019; VanHaitsma, 2019), but also race (Eguchi & Roberts, 2015; Eguchi & Spieldenner, 2015; Gutierrez-Perez & Andrade, 2018, 2019; Petermon & Spencer, 2019), ethnicity (Eguchi & Asante, 2016; Morris & Sloop, 2017), ability (Moreman & Briones, 2018), body size (Eguchi & Long, 2018; Otis, 2020), and other dynamics of culture and embodiment highlight both a burgeoning area of research on queer worldmaking as well as a broad area for future study.

CONCLUSIONS

Queer worldmaking simultaneously exists as a set of practices, a fruitful area of scholarship, and a form of praxis at the nexus of lived experience and academic theory. Communication scholars have made a welcoming home for theorizations and analyses of queer worldmaking that take Muñoz's and Berlant and Warner's focus on questions of (dis)identification, public, potentiality, and culture and expand them into exciting endeavors that coalesce around topics such as queer of color theories, academia as a space for worldmaking, and queer memories, monuments, and archives. As this scholarship extends out into various rhizomatic directions, many other key patterns and tensions arise, including the existence of competing interests and different visions across worldmaking projects, building of queer coalitions across lines of differences, envisioning anti-neoliberal queer words, questions of queer intimacy and desire, and considering the efficacy of mundane versus activist approaches to worldmaking. Because each queer world imagined is unique as well as ephemeral, there are nearly endless possibilities for generative work at the intersection of communication studies and queer worldmaking.

FURTHER READING

Buckland, F. (2002). *Impossible dance: Club culture and queer world-making*. Wesleyan University Press.

Duggan, L., & Muñoz, J. E. (2009). Hope and hopelessness: A dialogue. *Women & Performance: A Journal of Feminist Theory, 19*(2), 275–283.

Johnson, A. L., & LeMaster, B. (Eds.). (2020). *Gender futurity, intersectional autoethnography: Embodied theorizing from the margins*. Routledge.

Martin, L. T., & Licona, A. C. (2018). Remix as unruly play and participatory method for im/possible queer world-making. In J. Alexander, S. C. Jarratt, & N. Welch (Eds.), *Unruly rhetorics: Protest, persuasion, and publics* (pp. 244–260). University of Pittsburgh Press.

Pearson, K., & Lozano-Reich, N. M. (2009). Cultivating queer publics with an uncivil tongue: *Queer Eye*'s critical performances of desire. *Text and Performance Quarterly, 29*(4), 383–402.

Rawson, K. J. (2014). Transgender worldmaking in cyberspace: Historical activism on the internet. *QED: A Journal in GLBTQ Worldmaking, 1*(2), 38–60. https://doi.org/10.14321/qed.1.2.0038

REFERENCES

Andrade, L. M. (2019). CAUTION: On the many, unpredictable iterations of a yellow border sign ideograph and migrant/queer world-making. *Text and Performance Quarterly, 39*(3), 203–228. https://doi.org/10.1080/10462937.2019.1595123

Andrade, L. M., & Gutierrez-Perez, R. (2017). Bailando Con Las Sombras: Spiritual activism and soul healing in the war years. *Qualitative Inquiry, 23*(7), 502–504. https://doi.org/10.1177/1077800417718287

Arendt, H. (1958). *The human condition.* University of Chicago Press.

Berlant, L., & Warner, M. (1998). Sex in public. *Critical Inquiry, 24*(2), 547–566.

Black Public Sphere Collective (Eds.). (1995). *The Black public sphere.* University of Chicago Press.

Brouwer, D. C. (2014). From vernacular to official—and the spaces in between. *QED: A Journal in GLBTQ Worldmaking, 1*(2), 181–185. https://doi.org/10.14321/qed.1.2.0181

Campbell, P. O. (2012). The procedural queer: Substantive due process, *Lawrence v. Texas*, and queer rhetorical futures. *Quarterly Journal of Speech, 98*(2), 203–229. https://doi.org/10.1080/00335630.2012.663923

Channell-Justice, E. (2020). *Decolonizing queer experience: LGBT+ narratives from eastern Europe and Eurasia.* Rowman & Littlefield.

Chávez, K. R. (2013). Pushing boundaries: Queer intercultural communication. *Journal of International & Intercultural Communication, 6*(2), 83–95. https://doi.org/10.1080/17513057.2013.777506

Clark, J. (2020). "Daddy Pence come dance": Queer(ing) space in the suburbs. *Western Journal of Communication, 85*(2), 168–187. https://doi.org/10.1080/10570314.2020.1762915

Corey, F. C., & Nakayama, T. K. (1997). Sextext. *Text and Performance Quarterly, 17*(1), 58–68. https://doi.org/10.1080/10462939709366169

Dewey, J. (1927) *The public and its problems.* Henry Holt.

Driskill, Q.-L. (2011). *Queer indigenous studies: Critical interventions in theory, politics, and literature.* University of Arizona Press.

Dunn, T. R. (2011). Remembering "a great fag": Visualizing public memory and the construction of queer space. *Quarterly Journal of Speech, 97*(4), 435–460. https://doi.org/10.1080/00335630.2011.585168

Dunn, T. R. (2016a). Playing neoliberal politics: Post-racial and post-racist strategies in "Same Love." *Communication and Critical/Cultural Studies, 13*(3), 269–286. https://doi.org/10.1080/14791420.2016.1149201

Dunn, T. R. (2016b). *Queerly remembered: Rhetorics for representing the GLBTQ past.* University of South Carolina Press.

Dunn, T. R. (2017). Whence the lesbian in queer monumentality? Intersections of gender and sexuality in public memory. *Southern Communication Journal, 82*(4), 203–215. https://doi.org/10.1080/1041794X.2017.1332090

Eguchi, S. (2015). Queer intercultural relationality: An autoethnography of Asian–Black (dis)connections in white gay America. *Journal of International & Intercultural Communication, 8*(1), 27–43. https://doi.org/10.1080/17513057.2015.991077

Eguchi, S. (2016). The Orlando Pulse massacre: A transnational Japanese queer response. *QED: A Journal in GLBTQ Worldmaking, 3*(3), 164–167. https://doi.org/10.14321/qed.3.3.0164

Eguchi, S., & Asante, G. (2016). Disidentifications revisited: Queer(y)ing intercultural communication theory. *Communication Theory, 26*(2), 171–189. https://doi.org/10.1111/comt.12086

Eguchi, S., & Calafell, B. (2019). *Queer intercultural communication: The intersectional politics of belonging in and across differences.* Rowman & Littlefield.

Eguchi, S., & Long, H. R. (2018). Queer relationality as family: Yas fats! Yas femmes! Yas Asians!. *Journal of Homosexuality, 66*(11), 1589–1608. https://doi.org/10.1080/00918369.2018.1505756

Eguchi, S., & Roberts, M. N. (2015). Gay rapping and possibilities: A quare reading of "Throw that Boy P***y." *Text and Performance Quarterly, 35*(2–3), 142–157. https://doi.org/10.1080/10462937.2015.1025820

Eguchi, S., & Spieldenner, A. (2015). Two "gaysian" junior faculty talking about experience: A collaborative autoethnography. *QED: A Journal in GLBTQ Worldmaking, 2*(3), 125–143. https://doi.org/10.14321/qed.2.3.0125

Evans, S. B., & Janish, E. (2015). #INeedDiverseGames: How the queer backlash to GamerGate enables nonbinary coalition. *QED: A Journal in GLBTQ Worldmaking, 2*(2), 125–150. https://doi.org/10.14321/qed.2.2.0125

Ewalt, J. P. (2016). The agency of the spatial. *Women's Studies in Communication, 39*(2), 137–140. https://doi.org/10.1080/07491409.2016.1176788

Felski, R. (1989). Feminist theory and social change. *Theory, Culture, and Society, 6*(2), 219–240. https://doi.org/10.1177/026327689006002003

Ferguson, R. A. (2013). Introduction: Queer of color critique, historical materialism, and canonical sociology. In D. E. Hall & A. Jagose (Eds.), *The Routledge queer studies reader* (pp. 119–133). Routledge.

Fox, R. (2013). "Homo"-work: Queering academic communication and communicating queer in academia. *Text and Performance Quarterly, 33*(1), 58–76. https://doi.org/10.1080/10462937.2012.744462

Fraser, N. (1992). Rethinking the public sphere: A contribution to the critique of actually existing democracy. In C. Calhoun (Ed.), *Habermas and the public sphere* (pp. 109–142). MIT Press.

Gillespie, C. (Director) (2007). *Lars and the real girl* [Film]. Metro-Goldwyn-Mayer.

Goltz, D. B. (2009). Investigating queer future meanings: Destructive perceptions of "the harder path." *Qualitative Inquiry, 15*(3), 561–586. https://doi.org/10.1177/1077800408329238

Goltz, D. B. (2013). It gets better: Queer futures, critical frustrations, and radical potentials. *Critical Studies in Media Communication, 30*(2), 135–151. https://doi.org/10.1080/15295036.2012.701012

Goltz, D. B., & Zingsheim, J. (2015). *Queer praxis: Questions for LGBTQ worldmaking.* Peter Lang.

Gutierrez-Perez, R., & Andrade, L. M. (2018). Queer of color worldmaking: In the rhetorical archive and the embodied repertoire. *Text and Performance Quarterly, 38*(1–2), 1–18. https://doi.org/10.1080/10462937.2018.1435130

Gutierrez-Perez, R., & Andrade, L. M. (2019). How queer (of color) is intercultural communication? Then and there, joteria the game as a praxis of queerness, advocacy, and utopian aesthetics. In S. Eguchi & B. Calafell (Eds.), *Queer intercultural communication: The intersectional politics of belonging in and across differences* (pp. 179–193). Rowman & Littlefield.

Habermas, J. (1989). *The structural transformation of the public sphere* (T. Burger & F. Lawrence, Trans.). MIT Press. (Original work published 1962.)

Johnson, E. P. (2001). "Quare" studies, or (almost) everything I know about queer studies I learned from my grandmother. *Text and Performance Quarterly, 21*(1), 1–25. https://doi.org/10.1080/10462930128119

Johnson, J. R. (2013). Cisgender privilege, intersectionality, and the criminalization of CeCe McDonald: Why intercultural communication needs transgender studies. *Journal of International & Intercultural Communication, 6*(2), 135–144. https://doi.org/10.1080/17513057.2013.776094

King, C. S. (2016). American queerer: Norman Rockwell and the art of queer feminist critique. *Women's Studies in Communication, 39*(2), 157–176. https://doi.org/10.1080/07491409.2016.1165778

LeMaster, B. (2017). Notes on trans relationality. *QED: A Journal in GLBTQ Worldmaking, 4*(2), 84–92.

LeMaster, B., & Mapes, M. (2019). Embracing the criminal: Queer and trans relational liberatory pedagogies. In S. Eguchi & B. Calafell (Eds.), *Queer intercultural communication: The intersectional politics of belonging in and across differences* (pp. 63–77). Rowman & Littlefield.

LeMaster, B., Shultz, D., McNeill, J., Bowers, G., & Rust, R. (2019). Unlearning cisheteronormativity at the intersections of difference: Performing queer worldmaking through collaged relational autoethnography. *Text and Performance Quarterly, 39*(4), 341–370. https://doi.org/10.1080/10462937.2019.1672885

Lippmann, W. (1925). *The phantom public.* Macmillan.

McCune, J. Q. (2008). "Out" in the club: The down low, hip-hop, and the architexture of black masculinity. *Text and Performance Quarterly, 28*(3), 298–314. https://doi.org/10.1080/10462930802107415

Moreman, S. T., & Briones, S. R. (2018). Deaf queer world-making: A thick intersectional analysis of the mediated cultural body. *Journal of International and Intercultural Communication, 11*(3), 216–232. https://doi.org/10.1080/17513057.2018.1456557

Morgensen, S. L. (2011). *Spaces between us: Queer settler colonialism and indigenous decolonization.* University of Minnesota Press.

Morris, C. E., III (2002). Pink herring & the fourth persona: J. Edgar Hoover's sex crime panic. *Quarterly Journal of Speech, 88*(2), 228–244. https://doi.org/10.1080/00335630209384372

Morris, C. E., III (2012). ACT UP 25: HIV/AIDS, archival queers, and mnemonic world making. *Quarterly Journal of Speech, 98*(1), 49–53. https://doi.org/10.1080/00335630.2011.638658

Morris, C. E., III (2013). Sunder the children: Abraham Lincoln's queer rhetorical pedagogy. *Quarterly Journal of Speech, 99*(4), 395–422. https://doi.org/10.1080/00335630.2013.836281

Morris, C. E., III (2015). Context's critic, invisible traditions, and queering rhetorical history. *Quarterly Journal of Speech, 101*(1), 225–243. https://doi.org/10.1080/00335630.2015.995926

Morris, C. E., III, & Nakayama, T. K. (2013). Queer editorial overture. *QED: A Journal in GLBTQ Worldmaking,* v–x. https://doi.org/10.14321/qed.000v

Morris, C. E., III, & Sloop, J. M. (2006). "What lips these lips have kissed": Refiguring the politics of queer public kissing. *Communication & Critical/Cultural Studies, 3*(1), 1–26. https://doi.org/10.1080/14791420500505585

Morris, C. E., III, & Sloop, J. M. (2017). Other lips, whither kisses? *Communication and Critical/Cultural Studies, 14*(2), 182–186. https://doi.org/10.1080/14791420.2017.1293953

Muñoz, J. E. (Ed.). (1999). *Disidentifications: Queers of color and the performance of politics.* University of Minnesota Press.

Muñoz, J. E. (1996). Ephemera as evidence: Introductory notes to queer acts. *Women & Performance: A Journal of Feminist Theory, 8*(2), 5–16. https://doi.org/10.1080/07407709608571228

Muñoz, J. E. (2009). *Cruising utopia: The then and there of queer futurity.* New York University Press.

Nakayama, T. K., & Morris, C. E. (2015). Worldmaking and everyday interventions. *QED: A Journal in GLBTQ Worldmaking, 2*(1), v–viii. https://doi.org/10.14321/qed.2.1.000v

Negt, O., Kluge, A., & Labanyi, P. (1988). "The public sphere and experience": Selections. *October, 46,* 60–82. https://doi.org/10.2307/778678

Nelson, L. (2014). Reanimating archiving/archival corporealities: Deploying "Big Ears" in *De Rigueur Mortis* intervention. *QED: A Journal in GLBTQ Worldmaking, 1*(2), 132–159. https://doi.org/10.14321/qed.1.2.0132

Otis, H. N. (2020). Tess Holliday's queering of body-positive activism: Disrupting fatphobic logics of health and resignifying fat as fit. *Women's Studies in Communication, 43*(2), 157–180. https://doi.org/10.1080/07491409.2020.1737287

Pérez, K. (2019). Staging the family unfamiliar: The queer intimacies in *Ramble-Ations: A One D'Lo Show. Text and Performance Quarterly, 39*(4), 371–387. https://doi.org/10.1080/10462937.2018.1457174

Petermon, J. D., & Spencer, L. G. (2019). Black queer womanhood matters: Searching for the queer herstory of Black Lives Matter in television dramas. *Critical Studies in Media Communication, 36*(4), 339–356. https://doi.org/10.1080/15295036.2019.1607518

Samek, A. A., & Donofrio, T. A. (2013). "Academic Drag" and the performance of the critical personae: An exchange on sexuality, politics, and identity in the academy. *Women's Studies in Communication, 36*(1), 28–55. https://doi.org/10.1080/07491409.2012.754388

Sisco King, C., & West, I. (2014). This could be the place: Queer acceptance in *Lars and the Real Girl. QED: A Journal in GLBTQ Worldmaking, 1*(3), 59–84. https://doi.org/10.14321/qed.1.3.0059

Sloop, J. M., & West, I. (2016). Heroism's contexts: Robbie Rogers and the ghost of Justin Fashanu. *QED: A Journal in GLBTQ Worldmaking, 3*(3), 1–28. https://doi.org/10.14321/qed.3.3.0001

Spurlin, W. J. (2001). Broadening postcolonial studies/decolonizing queer studies. In J. C. Hawley (Ed.), *Postcolonial, queer: Theoretical intersections* (pp. 185–205). SUNY Press.

Squires, C. R. (2002). Rethinking the black public sphere: An alternative vocabulary for multiple public spheres. *Communication Theory 12*(4), 446–468. https://doi.org/10.1111/j.1468-2885.2002.tb00278.x

Tiffe, R. (2015). Interrogating industries of violence: Queering the labor movement to challenge police brutality and the prison industrial complex. *QED: A Journal in GLBTQ Worldmaking, 2*(1), 1–21. https://doi.org/10.14321/qed.2.1.0001

VanHaitsma, P. (2019). Stories of straightening up: Reading femmes in the archives of romantic friendship. *QED: A Journal in GLBTQ Worldmaking, 6*(3), 1–24. https://doi.org/10.14321/qed.6.3.0001

Vats, A. (2020). Affecting white accountability: What Mr. Rogers can tell us about the (racial) futures of communication. *Communication and Critical/Cultural Studies, 17*(1), 88–94. https://doi.org/10.1080/14791420.2020.1723800

Villa, D. R. (1992). Postmodernism and the public sphere. *The American Political Science Review, 86*(3), 712–721. https://doi.org/10.2307/1964133

Warner, M. (1992). The mass public and the mass subject. In C. Calhoun (Ed.), *Habermas and the public sphere* (pp. 377–401). MIT Press.

Warner, M. (2002a). *Publics and counterpublics*. Zone Books.

Warner, M. (2002b). Publics and counterpublics. *Public Culture, 14*(1), 49–90. https://doi.org/10.1215/08992363-14-1-49

West, I. (2013). Queer generosities. *Western Journal of Communication, 77*(5), 538–541. https://doi.org/10.1080/10570314.2013.784351

West, I., Frischherz, M., Panther, A., & Brophy, R. (2013). Queer Worldmaking in the "It Gets Better" campaign. *QED: A Journal in GLBTQ Worldmaking, 1*, 49–85. https://doi.org/10.1353/qed.2013.0003

Yep, G. A. (2003). The violence of heteronormativity in communication studies. *Journal of Homosexuality, 45*(2–4), 11–59. https://doi.org/10.1300/J082v45n02_02

Yep, G. A. (2017). Further notes on healing from "The violence of heteronormativity in communication studies." *QED: A Journal in GLBTQ Worldmaking, 4*(2), 115–122.

Hailey N. Otis and Thomas R. Dunn

QUEER(ING) REPRODUCTIVE JUSTICE

INTRODUCTION

In June 2019, the National LGBTQ+ Taskforce published a tool kit entitled "Queering Reproductive Justice." In it, the Taskforce outlined the ways in which reproductive justice (RJ) connected intimately with LGBTQ+ liberation movements as the RJ framework acknowledged how queer people were "impacted by intersecting forms of oppression" in their daily lives (National LGBTQ Taskforce, 2019, p. 6). In addition to outlining the barriers queer people faced in accessing healthcare, the report also outlined the shared legal histories and oppressions between the reproductive rights and justice movements and LGBTQ+ rights.

The Taskforce is not alone nor is it the first in identifying the intersections and coalition potential between RJ and LGBTQ+ advocacy. Long-standing alliances between reproductive politics and LGBTQ+ struggles exist—these include, for example, shared resistance to state interference in sexual expression, reproduction, and family formation, and affirmations of kin outside of White middle-class heteronuclearity (Enke, 2007; Samek, 2016; Thomsen & Morrison, 2020). Explicit assertions of this alliance are increasingly commonplace. In 2007, Miriam Zoila Pérez, a queer Latinx reproductive justice activist and author of the groundbreaking *Radical Doula Guide*, penned an op-ed, also entitled "Queering Reproductive Justice," in which she criticized a gay male leader in LGBTQ+ rights after he argued that it would be counterproductive for gay rights activists to take a stance on the federal abortion ban (Pérez, 2007). Pérez argued against divisive, single-issue advocacy that frames movements against one another, advocating instead for queer alliances with RJ through "shared principles based in the human rights to health and a desire for real social change" (Pérez, 2007, para. 6).

Scholars across disciplines have taken up this call to cultivate coalitions across social movements by queering reproductive justice (Nixon, 2013; Price, 2017, 2018; Radi, 2020; Russell, 2018; Smietana et al., 2018; Stacey, 2018). This body of scholarship explores the following: how LGBTQ+ rights activists build political coalitions with other social movements and advocacy groups through the intersectional framework of RJ; how and whether activists can analyze and dismantle the legal, material, and sociocultural barriers queer people face in reproduction and family formation through RJ; and how researchers and activists can productively draw on the confluences of "stratified reproduction," "reproductive justice," and "queer reproductions" as three key theoretical frameworks with distinctive lineages. Scholars hold different perspectives on the queering of RJ: While some scholars advocate for applying "political intersectionality" to cultivate coalitions between RJ and the LGBTQ+ movements (Price, 2018, p. 596), others argue that not all queer reproduction and family-making fit within the RJ framework (Russell, 2018; Smietana, 2018) and critique the homonormative impulse entailed therein (Butler, 2002; Stacey, 2018). The conversation is broadly interdisciplinary, spanning fields such as anthropology, sociology, and increasingly communication studies in which scholars draw on critical frameworks that understand human communication as constitutive and world-making in the queering of RJ.

This article first provides a brief background and history of RJ before exploring existing tensions on queer(ing) RJ. Then the article traces two central tenets in queer(ing) RJ: first, how the RJ framework applies to the reproductive health and social lives of queer people in areas such as access to assisted reproductive technologies (ART), adoption, and gender-affirming healthcare; and second, how queer RJ opens up possibilities for coalitions among different forms of "disruptive families" that challenge the heteronuclear familial model (Smietana et al., 2018, p. 121).

THE REPRODUCTIVE JUSTICE FRAMEWORK

A term coined in 1994 by 12 U.S. Black feminists at a conference in Chicago, reproductive justice includes three pillars: "The right not to have a child; the right to have a child; and the right to parent children in safe and healthy environments" (Ross & Solinger, 2017, p. 9). Reproductive justice expands the scope and stakeholders of the dominant pro-choice movement, led primarily by White women, by addressing the multiple systems of oppression experienced by Black, Indigenous, and other women of color in their reproductive lives (Price, 2010). The reproductive justice framework, in other words, contextualizes reproductive politics and oppression in relation to other social justice issues such as racism and poverty. This alliance of

Black women drew on the "epistemic privilege of the oppressed," while also integrating the shared experiences among women of color organizers who were convening at international human rights gatherings, such as the International Conference of Population and Development in Cairo (Narayan, 1988, p. 34; Price, 2010). This collaboration marked the beginning of a broad and intersectional movement that would slowly transform reproductive rights politics in the United States and, increasingly, in global contexts as well. In recent years, scholars in feminist studies have examined and called for a transnational turn in reproductive justice (Bailey, 2011; Fixmer-Oraiz, 2013; Garita, 2015; Hernández & Upton, 2018; Jolly, 2016; Radi, 2020).

Working alongside other women of color in the United States through the SisterSong Women of Color Reproductive Health Collective, the first SisterSong national conference in 2003 featured reproductive justice prominently in its programming (Ross & Solinger, 2017, p. 66). The reproductive justice framework proved pivotal in assembling a broad-based coalition that drew over 1.15 million people to the 2004 March for Women's Lives and other grass-roots initiatives organized by women of color-led advocacy groups (Hayden, 2009; Silliman et al., 2016). Shortly thereafter in 2005, Asian Communities for Reproductive Justice (ACRJ) published a formative report that distinguished the reproductive justice (RJ) framework from those of reproductive health and reproductive rights. ACRJ clarified that while the reproductive health framework focused on enhancing access to reproductive healthcare, the reproductive rights framework "is a legal and advocacy model that serves to protect an individual woman's legal right to reproductive health care services," often with an emphasis on the individual's right to privacy and to choice (Asian Communities for Reproductive Justice, 2005, p. 2).

Distinct but connected to these two frameworks, RJ is based on an intersectional approach to social injustices and oppression. While reproductive health and rights, respectively, emphasize the access to healthcare and legal infrastructure, RJ focuses on grass-roots organizing and coalition-building across advocacy organizations because reproductive oppression is the outcome of interlocking systems of power (Asian Communities for Reproductive Justice, 2005). As one of the cofounders, Loretta Ross, put it: "Reproductive Justice posits that the ability of any woman to determine her own reproductive destiny is directly linked to the conditions in her community and these conditions are not just a matter of individual choice and access" (Ross, 2006, p. 2). Rather than focusing on singular reproductive issues, such as abortion rights that preoccupied many White feminist activists, RJ focuses on "reproductive oppression" writ large, which Ross defined as "the control and exploitation of women, girls, and individuals through our bodies, sexuality, labor, and reproduction" (Price, 2010; Ross, 2006, p. 2). Given the multi-issue coalitional approach of RJ, scholars and advocates from across disciplines have used the framework to explore issues such as environmental justice, disability justice, immigration, transphobia, and prison reform (de Onís, 2012, 2015; Gaard, 2010; If/When/How, 2017; Olivera, 2018; Piepmeier, 2013; Radi, 2020; Smith, 2019).

RJ's principles, approaches, and vision—including its focus on movement building across social causes—are shaped by intersectionality. A term coined by legal feminist scholar Kimberlé Crenshaw (1989), but with a rich lineage traceable throughout the history of U.S. Black feminist activism and thought (Collins, 2008; Nash, 2019), the theory of intersectionality clarifies how marginalized people are often oppressed by multiple interlocking systems of power. In the context of reproductive politics, the mainstream pro-choice narrative grounded in "privacy" and "choice" fails to address the complexities of reproductive oppression for women marginalized by class, race, nation, and immigration—women for whom the right to have a child (or to parent children) has been violently curtailed through various mechanisms (e.g., eugenic state policies that rendered poor women and women of color particularly vulnerable to forced sterilization throughout most of the 20th century). Thus, an intersectional account of oppression in the context of reproductive politics significantly broadens the scope and potential impact of the movement.

As RJ scholar Kimala Price pointed out, intersectionality highlights "structural and institutional aspects of oppression" and sees "oppressions as overlapping and co-constituting" (Price, 2018, p. 594). Acknowledging structural intersectionality provides fertile ground for the RJ movement to bring together different marginalized communities—including Black women, Indigenous women, and queer and trans people—to organize in solidarity with one another (Price, 2010). As a multi-issue advocacy and movement-building network, for example, SisterSong Women of Color Reproductive Collective encompasses organizations and groups that share common goals, albeit having their unique political concerns and emphasis; the organization also collaborates with other social justice and reproductive rights grass-roots advocacy groups, including Black Lives Matter, to address reproductive oppression at the nexus of gender, race, and class (Rankin, 2016).

While RJ is founded by Black women in the United States, the framework has transnational significance and relevance. In addition to RJ activists' involvement in the 1994 U.N. International Conference on Population and Development in Cairo and the founding of a U.S. Women of Color Coalition for Reproductive Rights at the 1995 Fourth World Conference on Women in Beijing (Carrión), SisterSong co-authored a shadow report in 2014 for the U.N. Committee on the Elimination of Racial Discrimination with the Center for Reproductive Rights and the National Latina Institute for Reproductive Health. Scholars have drawn on RJ frameworks to consider transnational women's rights organizing (Carrión; Garita, 2015) to interrogate requisite sterilization for legal gender recognition by numerous states (Radi, 2020) and to think through the ethical terrain of transnational gestational surrogacy (Bailey, 2011; Fixmer-Oraiz, 2013). However, despite RJ's transnational history and involvement, most existing scholarship and political agendas continue to center RJ in the U.S. context. Jallicia Jolly (2016) and Sharon Yam (2021) have called for more uptake of the RJ framework to interrogate transnational oppressions of multiply marginalized women and queer people of color and to cultivate coalitions across national contexts. While this article attempts to address this gap by exploring queer and reproductive justice outside of the United States, it is limited by the scope of existing scholarship and research.

In recent years, LGBTQ+ and RJ advocacy groups have been building coalitions to address shared concerns and intersecting structural oppressions. For example, SisterSong collaborated with the National LGBTQ Task Force and Ipas—an international organization on safe abortion rights and contraception—to put together an interactive online database that ranks different U.S. states based on their laws on reproductive and LGBTQ+ rights (National Organization for Women, 2006). In addition to queer reproductive justice activists like Miriam Zoila Pérez, who advocates for coalitions between the LGBTQ+ movement and RJ, a recent article in *Out* made the case that the two movements were interconnected, as queer people of color often face barriers in accessing inclusive and gender-affirming reproductive healthcare; LGBTQ+ people of color also face tremendous legal difficulties and prohibitive costs when they try to foster, adopt, or have biological children (Berg, 2019). Moreover, as Blas Radi (2020) explained, gender-affirming care is often pitted against reproductive rights: "For trans people in many countries, the resignation of their reproductive capacities has been, and still is, a condition to access the legal recognition of gender identity" (p. 398). Radi and others insisted that a reproductive justice framework was critical to addressing the complexity of reproductive oppression for queer people. Monica Simpson, the current executive director of SisterSong, explained that she came to RJ organizing after working, respectively, in prison reform and in an LGBTQ+ community center. She states:

> In doing LGBTQ+ work, it couldn't hold my Blackness. In doing work around the prison industrial complex, you couldn't talk about queerness. [With RJ,] you didn't have to check off the boxes at the door.... The Reproductive Justice Movement felt like my political homecoming. (Cited in Berg, 2019, para. 6)

The reproductive justice framework has proven itself both powerful and nimble—a theoretical framework capable of understanding oppression as complex and multifaceted and an organizing strategy poised for unprecedented coalition building. Leading RJ scholars and activists Loretta Ross and Rickie Solinger have referred to reproductive justice as "open-source code," encouraging others to draw on and expand its capacity, to use it well in order to build better worlds (Ross & Solinger, 2017, p. 71).

ART, QUEER FAMILY FORMATION, AND REPRODUCTIVE JUSTICE

Reproductive justice meets a critical edge in its consideration of LGBTQ+ lives: Individuals for whom the ability to decide when, whether, and with whom to create a family is less straightforward. First, for LGBTQ+ couples who are interested in biological reproduction, many lack the physiological capacity to do so without some form of fertility assistance. Additional barriers stem from homophobic and transphobic beliefs that queer people will make unfit parents. Significantly, similar arguments about "fitness" have long been used to curtail the reproduction of poor women, women of color, immigrant women, and women with disabilities (Roberts, 1997; Solinger, 2007). Thus, myriad questions related to reproductive rights and justice emerge as a result. The second and third pillars of reproductive justice—"the right to have a child" and "the right to parent children in safe and healthy environments" (Ross & Solinger, 2017, p. 9)—are most central to LGBTQ-specific reproductive justice (RJ) struggles and thus the focus of this section.

The Right to Have a Child. Because the family and the nation-state are figured through White heteronuclear ideals in Western imaginaries, LGBTQ+ people face immense sociopolitical barriers when trying to exercise their right to have children (Wingard, 2015). While the European Court of Human Rights ruled in 2017 that sterilization requirements for trans people who seek legal recognition constitutes a human rights violation, as of April 2018, 14 countries in Europe still either explicitly or implicitly required trans people to undergo sterilization before they could change their gender markers on legal documents (Transgender Europe, 2018). In addition, fertility preservation for trans people is widely misunderstood, costly, and unlikely to be covered by medical insurance, thus rendering it inaccessible to many (Cheng et al., 2019; Nixon, 2013). Thus, while basic human rights protections based on sexual orientation and gender identity have recently garnered greater international attention (Human Rights Watch, 2016), eugenic practices such as these have been largely ignored.

In addition to structural barriers that bar trans reproduction outright, some reproductive justice advocates focus on LGBTQ+ individuals' limited access to assisted reproduction, adoption, and surrogacy. For lesbians and other queer people who lack sperm but are able to carry a pregnancy, access to assisted reproductive technologies (ART) is a primary site of concern. The specific concerns regarding access vary based on locale, but include some combination of expense, legal barriers, clinic restrictions, and health care provider bias. For example, ART in the United States lacks federal regulation and oversight. As a result, accessibility is determined by a patchwork of state laws, uneven insurance coverage, and private fertility clinic policies—all of which are shaped by various biases that prioritize the reproduction of wealthy heteronuclear families. Assisted reproduction is expensive—one vial of donor sperm generally costs $800–$1,000 and a single round of in vitro fertilization averages $10,000–$15,000 in the United States. ART is not uniformly covered by insurance policies; even among states that mandate coverage, some deliberately exclude LBGTQ families by barring the use of donor gametes (Society for Assisted Reproductive Technology, 2020).

Trans and nonbinary people experience additional obstacles and discrimination in the context of assisted reproduction, pregnancy, childbirth, and postpartum care (e.g., Cheng et al., 2019; Darwin & Greenfield, 2019; Lee, 2019). While existing research on trans people's opinions on fertility and desires to reproduce remains scant, several studies have shown that many trans people would like to parent biological children, but their desires are often hampered by the lack of legal protections and gender-affirming treatments such as hormonal therapy and surgeries that include fertility preservation (Tornello & Bos, 2017; Wierckx et al., 2012). Recent research further demonstrated that when trans and nonbinary people obtained access to reproductive health and prenatal care, they faced "rampant discrimination, harassment, lack of provider knowledge, and even refusals of care" (National LGBTQ Task Force, p. 6). Overt hostilities were compounded by cis-sexist norms that structured patient encounters and the near-exclusive reliance on feminine vocabulary for prenatal and—case in point—"maternity" care. Thus, reproductive and birth justice includes significant changes in the material conditions of reproduction and childbirth, such as the provision of a culturally competent healthcare provision for trans and nonbinary birthers and addressing the forms of structural racism that disproportionately bar Black, Indigenous, and Latinx people from accessing health care (National LGBTQ Task Force). RJ also includes discursive shifts to encompass the diversity of gender experience and identity in the context of reproduction. Transmasculine advocates, scholars, and parents have directed necessary attention toward these matters (Aizura, 2019; Fixmer-Oraiz & Wehman-Brown, 2020; Pérez, 2012; Wehman-Brown, 2018).

Trans women are less visible in the cultural conversation around assisted reproduction for trans and nonbinary people, as Micha Cárdenas (2016) noted in her art installation, *Pregnancy*, which traces her experience as she temporarily suspended femininizing hormones in order to produce gametes. A queer reproductive justice framework demands attention to the fertility and reproductive desires and experiences of transfeminine individuals and trans women. Current medical research has shown conflicting results on the extent to which feminizing hormonal therapies might hinder fertility due to "impaired spermatogenesis" (Cheng et al., 2019, p. 209). While technologies of fertility preservations are available, trans people—especially trans women of color who are multiply marginalized—often lack the financial resources and social support to benefit from them (Mitu, 2016). Moreover, many medical experts and providers have questioned whether trans people are fit as parents and, in particular, whether trans parents negatively impact the psychological development and mental health of their children (Freedman et al., 2002; Gómez-Gil et al., 2008; Murphy, 2012). The Ethics Committee of the American Society for Reproductive Medicine (2015) has issued a statement refuting these concerns. Taking this refutation a step further, a queer reproductive justice framework would recognize these concerns as stemming from eugenics ideologies that deem any nonnormative bodies unfit for reproduction.

Some research demonstrated that many LGBTQ+ adults preferred adoption as a path to parenthood and that the number of lesbian and gay adoptive parents has doubled in recent years (Wrobel et al., 2020). Still, adoption by LGBTQ+ individuals and couples remains controversial in many places. Ample research and case studies have shown that cis-gay couples faced significant barriers in fostering and adopting children both domestically in the United States and abroad due to homophobic laws and policies (Baumle & Compton, 2017; Goodfellow, 2015; Mamo, 2007). Laws that govern adoption by LGBTQ+ couples in the European Union are inconsistent among member states and create legal precarity for transnational couples and families in particular. As scholars and activists have argued, because the barriers LGBTQ+ people face in adoption are structural in nature and disproportionately affect multiply marginalized communities, they are examples of reproductive injustices that fall within the purview of the RJ framework (National Women's Law Center & Law Students for Reproductive Justice, 2011; Nixon, 2013; Russell, 2018).

The right to have a child, however, is fraught when fertility and biogenetics are not in one's favor (e.g., LGBTQ+ people and straight people who cannot biologically reproduce). Moreover, the terrain itself is uneven—scholars have noted profound asymmetries in access to assisted reproduction between lesbians and gay male couples, asymmetries linked to gendered assumptions about parenting that privilege motherhood over fatherhood (Imaz, 2017). One common avenue for gay and lesbian parents to have a child is through foster care and adoption. However, a number of RJ scholars and activists have raised significant concerns regarding foster care and adoption as systems that profit from the destruction of families who lack social, political, or economic power. For instance, Laury Oaks (2015) argued that while baby safe haven laws allowed parents to relinquish a newborn anonymously to a specified institution, they did not help structurally marginalized people, such as poor women of color and others culturally labeled as "bad mothers," to raise their children. Laura Briggs (2020), Dorothy Roberts (2012), and Rickie Solinger (2007) have examined how the state has long used foster care and adoption systems to remove children of color from their parents in lieu of offering resources and support for these children to be raised in their families and communities of origin. The current foster and adoption systems also harmed LGBTQ+ people as they were often marked as undesirable parents and prohibited from having and raising children (Baumle & Compton, 2017). The second pillar of the RJ, hence, encompasses critiques of policies and systems that regulate parenthood and family formation outside of the White heteronuclear ideal. The right to have a child also entails advocacy for all forms of family formation, including those that are crafted outside of heteronuclear biogenetics that are not readily recognized by the state, such as LGBTQ+ chosen families, young ("teen") parents, and othermothering (Collins, 2008; Newman, 2019; Vinson, 2017).

Similar to the foster care system and the adoption industry, many scholars who study ART have demonstrated that the fertility industry many LGBTQ+ people rely on to form biological families often employs practices that perpetuate stratified reproduction and reproductive injustice. For example, studies of assisted reproduction in various locales underscored the structural privileging of lesbian motherhood over cis-gay and trans parenting; many noted this pattern as a residual effect of the deep-seated gendered ideologies undergirding heteronormativity and compulsory motherhood (Hašková & Sloboda, 2018; Imaz, 2017; Willems & Sosson, 2017). In short, for lesbians who do not struggle with fertility or finances, biological reproduction is increasingly accessible—a fact that other queer-identified people do not (yet) enjoy. Researchers have also called attention to the unjust conditions that shape commercial gestational surrogacy, particularly in the case of surrogates from developing countries who provide service to clients from wealthy countries like the United States (Bailey, 2011; Deomampo, 2013; Fixmer-Oraiz, 2013; Khader, 2013; Markens, 2007; Rudrappa, 2015). International labor markets facilitate exploitative and racialized reproductive relationships between brown women and wealthy White clients, including middle-upper-class gay men (Mamo, 2007; Mamo & Alston-Stepnitz, 2015; Pande, 2014). As a result, common practices of commercial surrogacy fuel stratified reproduction due to the expense of the process, power imbalances between clients and surrogates, and—in some cases—constraints that pivot on citizenship status (e.g., in the United Kingdom, only citizens and permanent residents can access surrogacy). As Judith Stacey pointed out, "reproductive justice discourse is primarily critical of the stratification of assisted reproductive technology" in which only those who fit in the normative model of ideal citizens are encouraged to reproduce, often by relying on the reproductive labor of low-waged, racialized subjects (Stacey, 2018, p. 5). As Stacey noted, "generally, the types of family created through transnational surrogacy are not queer families in the affirmative sense" because the technology and process tended to reify and reproduce the nuclear family ideal (Stacey, 2018, p. 6).

The vexations of adoption and surrogacy leave gay men (and all who struggle with infertility regardless of sexual orientation) in a web of contradictions within the RJ framework. Camisha Russell (2018) argued that the RJ framework did not apply to gay men who sought biological kinship, particularly if they were affluent enough to purchase the service of a gestational surrogate. Distinguishing *dysfertility* ("a relationship within which biological children cannot be reproduced without a third party") from *infertility*, Russell cautioned against using "justice" to discuss gay men perusing surrogacy as it problematically implied that someone, most likely a woman with limited financial resources, had a duty to serve as an egg donor and a gestational surrogate. She argued instead for a productive expansion of Roberts' concept of "procreative liberty" in order to "emphasize the creative nature of family formation, affective bonds and kinship, whether biological or not" (Roberts, 1997, p. 312; Russell, 2018, p. 138). This way of thinking encourages gay men who want biological children to form alliances with women of color fighting for RJ through their shared goal of reimagining forms of procreation and family that fall outside existing norms.

As Smietana, Thompson, and Twine summarized, queer reproduction is connected to RJ because "self-identifying as LGBTQ+ should not place exceptional demands or restrictions upon one's access to reproductive care and services, any more than one's class, race, gender, nation, disability, religion, infertility, or relationship status should"; at the same time, one cannot lose sight of the fact that the fertility industry many queer couples rely on to form biological families is deeply entrenched in "racial ideologies, heteronormativity, gender logics, and European neocolonial practices" (Smietana et al., 2018, p. 119). Queer reproductive justice, therefore, must take into account not only the structural barriers LGBTQ+ people face in family formation and reproductive health care, but it must also acknowledge the inequities in transnational bioeconomies and hold privileged stakeholders accountable for the material conditions transnational reproductive laborers like gestational surrogates and egg donors face (Mamo, 2018).

The Right to Parent Children in Safe and Healthy Environments. The third pillar of reproductive justice directs one to broader intersectional considerations. Barriers to safe and sustainable parenting are compounded for poor queer people of color who are multiply burdened by interlocking systems of oppression, with much overlap among LGBTQ+ communities and their straight and cis peers. Parenting in safety and dignity includes addressing environmental racism, police brutality against racialized minorities, mass incarceration in the United States in particular, poverty and housing insecurity, disparities in education and health care, and the abuse of migrants and refugees by the state.

Poverty, for example, limits one's ability to parent in a safe environment. As political science researcher Virginia Eubanks (2019) has noted, the government often equates parenting while poor with poor parenting: Children whose parents are in poverty are much more likely to be taken into the foster care system. Socioeconomic marginalization disproportionally affects LGBTQ+ people. According to recent research conducted on the poverty rate of LGBTQ+ people in the United States (Badgett et al., 2019), LGBTQ+ people have a poverty rate of 21.6%, much higher than the 15.7% among cisgender straight people (p. 2). Within the LGBTQ+ community, transgender people experience poverty at the highest rate of 29.4% (Badgett et al., 2019, p. 2). Queer people who are young, disabled, non-White, and live in rural areas are the most likely to be in poverty (Badgett et al., 2019, p. 3). These intersecting vectors of marginalization diminish LGBTQ+ people as parents and caregivers in the mainstream familial imaginary—limiting their right to have children and to parent in a secure and safe environment.

In addition to poverty, various forms of state and transphobic violence also create barriers for queer people, particularly trans people, to parent safely. For trans women who experience disproportionally high rates of violence, murder, and premature death, their opportunity to form families and parent children may be shortchanged or foreclosed entirely (Bailey, 2013). Because trans people are often barred from participating in formal economies due to transphobia and stigma, they are more likely to participate in underground economies in order to survive, including theft, drug sales, and sex work (Zavidow, 2016). Trans people are also more likely to be unjustly profiled by law enforcement and targeted by the criminal justice system (Strangio, 2014). Once incarcerated, trans men who can become pregnant suffer additional forms of reproductive injustices, such as the denial of prenatal treatment, shackling during birth, forced feminization, and coercive sterilization (Ross & Solinger, 2017). By incarcerating poor trans and gender nonconforming people during their most fertile reproductive years, the state is destroying the potential for queer people to reproduce and parent (Arkles, 2008). For queer and trans people who do become parents, they continue to face struggles due to social and legal transphobia—for instance, they are more likely that their cis peers to be embroiled in custody disputes over their children (Smietana et al., 2018). LGBTQ+ people who are constantly worried that their children will be taken away lack the reproductive right to feel safe while raising their children.

QUEER(ING) KINSHIP AND FAMILY

The framework of reproductive justice (RJ) acknowledges that the biogenetic heteronuclear familial ideal is often mobilized to oppress people and families who exist outside of it, such as the practice of "othermothering" by Black women (Collins, 2008, p. 13; Gumbs et al., 2016). Those barred from reproducing the heteronuclear norm will experience more reproductive freedom when various forms of families are recognized and accepted just as they are. Dismantling the heteronuclear family ideal, therefore, is a matter of reproductive justice (Fixmer-Oraiz, 2019). Sociologist Joshua Gamson (2018) observed that family justice, "self-determination in the making of our families and in the use of our bodies in the creation of kinship, free from coercion and stigma," was intimately connected to RJ because "unconventional family creation," which included families formed by LGBTQ+ people with their biological or nonbiological kin, often faced structural barriers that prevented such families from thriving (Gamson, 2018, pp. 1–2). For example, single parents and queer people both experienced frequent discrimination and stigma in their family structure (Baumle & Compton, 2017; Dowd, 1996; Palmer-Mehta, 2016; Suter et al., 2016); the prohibitive costs of ART in the United States barred poor people—both queer and straight—from accessing the technologies (Smietana, 2017; Thompson, 2016). The latter connected LGBTQ+ people who desired biological offspring with Black women as Black women were much more likely than their White counterparts to experience infertility and were less likely to seek medical help due in part to stigma and racism (Wellons et al., 2008).

This confluence of shared concerns has prompted scholars like Gamson (2018) and Luna (2018) to advocate for cultivating solidarities among people who form nonnormative families through the RJ framework. In particular, they have argued that while these families faced different forms of marginalization, they can form alliances by recognizing their shared struggles against the heteronormative nuclear familial ideal. Public intellectual Alexis Pauline Gumbs (2016) noted that queer Black feminists have long engaged in nonnormative mothering and family-building as a form of revolutionary resistance. For Gumbs, nonnormative families challenged the property model of patriarchal relationships, thus allowing parents and children who may or may not have biological and legal ties with one another to function as autonomous subjects. The intersectional and coalitional spirits of RJ provide an avenue for connection among families and kin ties that are not readily recognized by the state.

While there is coalitional potential between RJ and queer family formation, scholars have long debated whether all families that involve LGBTQ+ people are by default queer. As Luna wrote, the perennial question was whether queer was "a political stance that can include anyone of 'deviant' reproductive modes or [if it] only describes people engaging in particular sexual practices" (Luna, 2018, p. 97). Drawing on Lisa Duggan's oft-cited work on homonormativity, Lasio et al. (2019) noted that "equal rights politics under neoliberalism have resulted in a new gay normality that privileges the normative family model over radical social change or a critique of heteronormativity" (p. 1059). Similarly, Judith Stacey argued that as the mainstream movement focused increasingly on the legalization of gay and lesbian marriage and parenting rights for married couples, the families queer people formed "are decreasingly queer, and increasingly normative and exclusionary" (Stacey, 2018, p. 5). For Stacey and others, many families created through ART, from intrauterine insemination (IUI) to commercial surrogacy, were not queer by its political definition even when queer-identified people were involved.

Some ethnographic research bolsters this claim. Focusing on lesbian motherhood through the lens of reproductive justice, Sandra Patton-Imani's (2020) research found that, despite the legalization of same-sex marriage and adoption in the United States, poor women of color continued to experience structural barriers as they navigated family-making. Other scholars (Baumle & Compton, 2017; Mamo, 2007; Smietana, 2017) demonstrated that gay couples tended to reproduce the existing norm of nuclear families in order to minimize legal precarity and to be granted recognition by dominant publics and the state. Studying the relationships between gay men and their surrogates in the United States, Smietana (2017) observed that both parties tended to hold tight to the conventional ideal of family: Neither parties engaged in relationships that would form politically queer kin against the heteronuclear grain. Smietana attributed this to the financial contracts between the gay men and the surrogates, which de-kinned the surrogates' parental claim (Smietana, 2017, p. 9). This form of financial de-kinning also occurred in commercial gamete donation through donor anonymity as the dominant industry norm. As a result, commercial surrogacy rarely resulted in families that deviated from the nuclear model.

Outside of biogenetic reproduction through surrogacy, Alison Shonkwiler (2008) observed that gay parents who chose to adopt were also increasingly assimilated into hegemonic familialism. This is not surprising because, as David Eng pointed out, "the possession of a child, whether biological or adopted, has today become the sign of guarantee not only for family but also for full and robust citizenship—for being a fully realized political, economic, and social subject in American life" (Eng, 2003, p. 14). In order to gain state legibility and protections, in other words, queer people must reproduce the heteronuclear family structure.

Thus, the "ideology of familialism" compels LGBTQ+ conformity as a way to counter the exclusions they face (Shonkwiler, 2008, p. 19). These familial norms, ironically, reside at the heart of long-standing anti-LGBTQ sentiment, discrimination, and violence. In this way, there exists a deep coalition potential between queer family formation and RJ. In one example, historian Don Romesburg (2014) offered "queer transracial family" in order to attend to the "power constellations"—including racism and poverty—that make his family (and, of course, many other families) possible. He wrote: "By articulating the historical, structural, cultural, and political processes through which we constantly renegotiate belonging, it seeks to narrate where we come from in ways that make personal and social justice possible for more people" (2014, p. 3). For Romesburg and his partner, this meant defining their family—in name and in practice—to include not only himself, his partner, and their foster-adopted daughter, but also their daughter's family of origin. Nonnormative family formations enacted by differentially marginalized people, Romesburg argued, functioned as a praxis that "contests colorblindness, homonormativity, and the consumerist, privatized family" (Romesburg, 2014, p. 1). Other examples might include the building of donor sibling registries, the embrace of voluntary kin, and the uptick in people parenting solo by choice (Fixmer-Oraiz, 2019). The queering of family formation, hence, opens up coalition potential across axioms of marginalization, which is a main tenet of the RJ framework.

Indeed, scholars on queer reproduction and family formation have been interrogating the ways in which LGBTQ+ people can form alliances that help advance the RJ agenda. For example, Mamo and Alston-Stepnitz argued that as LGBTQ+ people "negotiate and, at times, reinforce these contours [of marketplaces, notions of belonging, and inequalities], they also participate in new kinship forms as they demand inclusion in one of the most durable and supported social practice: having children" (Mamo & Alston-Stepnitz, 2015, p. 521). Mamo and Alston-Stepnitz (2015) pointed out that by deviating from the opposite sex two-parent familial model, LGBTQ+ people were already reinventing family structures in a significant way. Mamo's earlier research (2007) showed that when selecting sperm donors, lesbians took into consideration not only physical resemblances, but also a sense of affinity through shared interests and values. Kinship and families, in other words, were not merely defined by biological ties, but were formed by a constellation of choice, biological, and social connections that Mamo called "affinity ties" (Mamo, 2007, p. 205). Hence, Mamo and Alston-Stepniz posited that rather than focusing solely on the ways in which LGBTQ+ people reinforced reproductive inequalities and heteronuclear family structures through ART, it was more productive to queer the RJ framework by interrogating how "queer bodies and lives participate in the global form of reproduction in ways that enhance *and* limit power imbalances" (Mamo & Alston-Stepnitz, 2015, p. 528). By paying attention to the "structural intimacies" in transnational queer reproduction, RJ activists and scholars can better understand how marginalized actors negotiate intersecting power dynamics and social structures in ways that simultaneously produce power and precariousness (Mackenzie, 2013, p. 7).

While LGBTQ+ people and communities have historically, out of necessity and commitment to justice, engaged in practices that most readily destabilize the heteronuclear family ideal, scholars such as Gamson (2018) and Anthony Kwame Appiah (2016) have argued that they should not be obligated to shoulder all the responsibilities in promoting family justice. Rather, a queer reproductive justice framework demands communities and advocates from different positionalities to collectively reimagine and expand family structures and formations while remaining in solidarity with LGBTQ+ families who continue to negotiate their precarity. In one example of this, some scholars in family communication have questioned the centering of biogenetics within dominant imaginings of kin and explored other ways that families narrate their sense of belonging to and with one another beyond shared genetic material (Baxter, 2015; Braithwaite et al., 2010; Suter et al., 2014, 2016).

In another example, activists in the RJ movement have been advocating for greater recognition and celebration of family diversity. Founded in 2005, the Strong Families Network challenges conservative heteronormative representations of families; their advocacy connects diverse families with immigration and queer politics, as immigrant and LGBTQ+ families are often not readily recognized by the state (Zavella, 2020). Emerged from the movement building group Expanding the Movement for Empowerment and Reproductive Justice (EMERJ), the

Strong Families Network "is committed to creating the culture and conditions necessary for all families to thrive," including families that are outside of the normative national imaginary (Zavella, 2020, p. 55). This initiative is an example in which the intersectional framework of RJ effectively bolsters and supports queer family justice.

CONCLUSION

As an expansive and intersectional framework that recognizes the experiences of differentially marginalized people, reproductive justice (RJ) highlights the coalition potential among queer people, women of color, and people who struggle with poverty—in fact, RJ reminds people that these marginalizing positionalities often overlap with one another through intersecting systems of oppression. As this article has illustrated, multiply marginalized queer people often face structural barriers when they try to build families outside of heteronuclear norms, whether through biological reproduction, adoption, or through a more expansive definition of kin. Chosen families face great precarity as they are largely illegible to the state; still, even the embrace of more familiar family formations (e.g., the use of assisted reproduction by an LGBTQ+ couple to reproduce biologically) often involves confronting various forms of discrimination, hostility, and legal challenge. Much of reproductive health care—whether in research or in the provision of care—neither understands nor accommodates gay, lesbian, bisexual, trans, and nonbinary people, and mainstream reproductive rights discourse often fails to consider the unique challenges trans and nonbinary pregnant people face.

Despite the promise of coalition potential between RJ activists and LGBTQ+ people advocating for reproductive freedom, tension remains. As noted, critics have questioned whether some families created by queer people are, by default, politically queer, or whether they partake in homonationalist ideologies in ways that bolster rather than subvert the existing paradigm (Puar, 2007). Citing geopolitical power imbalance in commercial surrogacy and gamete transactions, some remain concerned that LGBTQ+ people who want to form biological families perpetuate transnational power imbalances (Lewis, 2019; Smietana, 2018).

Queer(ing) reproductive justice sharpens the critical edge of RJ, prompting new horizons in research and activism. Queer sensibilities may facilitate an RJ-informed expansion of belonging and relationality in ways that challenge the primacy of biogenetics and, relatedly, the entanglement of family and neoliberal capital. Reproductive justice, in turn, provides a critical framework, organizing tool, and set of alliances through which to interrogate myriad reproductive oppressions experienced by LGBTQ+ communities. By attending more to transnational mobilities, circulations, and networks of reproductive politics, queer(ing) reproductive justice could disentangle competing interests and further identify grounds for solidarities across differences. This nexus, rich with possibility, fuels the capacity of researchers and activists alike to advance reproductive freedom, bodily autonomy, and expansive understandings of what it means to form family.

FURTHER READING

Baumle, A., & Compton, D. R. (2017). *Legalizing LGBT families: How the law shapes parenthood*. New York University Press.

Enke, A. (2007). *Finding the movement: Sexuality, contested space, and feminist activism*. Duke University Press.

Gumbs, A. P., Martens, C., & Williams, M. (Eds.). (2016). *Revolutionary mothering: Love on the front lines.* PM Press.

Mamo, L. (2007). *Queering reproduction: Achieving pregnancy in the age of technoscience.* Duke University Press.

Mamo, L., & Alston-Stepnitz, E. (2015). Queer intimacies and structural inequalities: New directions in stratified reproduction. *Journal of Family Issues, 36*(4), 519–540.

Nixon, L. (2013). The right to (trans) parent: A reproductive justice approach to reproductive rights, fertility, and family-building issues facing transgender people. *William & Mary Journal of Race, Gender, and Social Justice, 20*(1), 73.

Roberts, D. (1997). *Killing the black body: Race, reproduction, and the meaning of liberty.* Vintage.

Ross, L., & Solinger, R. (2017). *Reproductive justice: An introduction.* University of California Press.

Silliman, J., Fried, M. G., Ross, L., & Gutiérrez, E. (2016). *Undivided rights: Women of color organizing for reproductive justice* (2nd ed.). Haymarket Books.

Smietana, M., Thompson, C., & Twine, F. W. (2018). Making and breaking families—Reading queer reproductions, stratified reproduction and reproductive justice together. *Reproductive Biomedicine & Society Online, 7*, 112–130. https://doi.org/10.1016/j.rbms.2018.11.001

Thomsen, C., & Morrison, G. T. (2020). Abortion as gender transgression: Reproductive justice, queer theory, and anti-crisis pregnancy center activism. *Signs: Journal of Women in Culture and Society, 45*(3), 703–730. https://doi.org/10.1086/706487

REFERENCES

Aizura, A. (2019, January 30). Aren Aizura on chestfeeding. *Mutha Magazine.* http://www.muthamagazine.com/2019/01/aren-azuria-chestfeeding/

Appiah, K. A. (2016, February 10). Is it selfish for a gay couple to have kids via surrogacy? *The New York Times.* https://www.nytimes.com/2016/02/14/magazine/is-it-selfish-for-a-gay-couple-to-have-kids-via-surrogacy.html

Arkles, G. (2008, September 27). Prisons as a tool for reproductive oppression: Cross-movement strategies for gender justice. *Sylvia Rivera Law Project.* https://srlp.org/prisons-as-a-tool-for-reproductive-oppression-cross-movement-strategies-for-gender-justice/

Asian Communities for Reproductive Justice. (2005). *A new vision for advancing our movement for reproductive health, reproductive rights and reproductive justice.* https://forwardtogether.org/tools/a-new-vision/

Badgett, M. V. L., Choi, S. K., & Wilson, B. D. M. (2019). *LGBT poverty in the United States: A study of differences between sexual orientation and gender identity groups* (p. 47). UCLA School of Law, Williams Institute. https://williamsinstitute.law.ucla.edu/wp-content/uploads/National-LGBT-Poverty-Oct-2019.pdf

Bailey, A. (2011). Reconceiving surrogacy: Toward a reproductive justice account of Indian surrogacy. *Hypatia, 26*(4), 715–741. https://doi.org/10.1111/j.1527-2001.2011.01168.x

Bailey, M. M. (2013). *Butch queens up in pumps: Gender, performance, and ballroom culture in Detroit.* University of Michigan Press.

Baumle, A., & Compton, D. R. (2017). *Legalizing LGBT families: How the law shapes parenthood.* New York University Press.

Baxter, L. A. (Ed.). (2015). *Remaking family communicatively.* Peter Lang.

Berg, A. (2019, February 19). Why reproductive justice is an LGBTQ+ rights issue. *Out.* https://www.out.com/out-exclusives/2019/2/19/why-reproductive-justice-lgbtq-rights-issue

Braithwaite, D. O., Bach, B. W., Baxter, L. A., DiVerniero, R., Hammonds, J. R., Hosek, A. M., Willer, E. K., & Wolf, B. M. (2010). Constructing family: A typology of voluntary kin. *Journal of Social and Personal Relationships, 27*(3), 388–407. https://doi.org/10.1177/0265407510361615

Briggs, L. (2020). *Taking children: A history of American terror*. University of California Press.
Butler, J. (2002). Is kinship always already heterosexual? *Differences, 13*(1), 14–44. https://doi.org/10.1215/10407391-13-1-14
Cárdenas, M. (2016). Pregnancy: Reproductive futures in trans of color feminism. *TSQ: Transgender Studies Quarterly, 3*(1–2), 48–57. https://doi.org/10.1215/23289252-3334187
Cheng, P. J., Pastuszak, A. W., Myers, J. B., Goodwin, I. A., & Hotaling, J. M. (2019). Fertility concerns of the transgender patient. *Translational Andrology and Urology, 8*(3), 209–218. https://doi.org/10.21037/tau.2019.05.09
Collins, P. H. (2008). *Black feminist thought: Knowledge, consciousness, and the politics of empowerment*. Routledge.
Crenshaw, K. (1989). Demarginalizing the intersection of race and sex: A black feminist critique of antidiscrimination doctrine, feminist theory and antiracist politics. *University of Chicago Legal Forum, 1989*(1). https://chicagounbound.uchicago.edu/uclf/vol1989/iss1/8
Darwin, Z., & Greenfield, M. (2019). Mothers and others: The invisibility of LGBTQ people in reproductive and infant psychology. *Journal of Reproductive and Infant Psychology, 37*(4), 341–343. https://doi.org/10.1080/02646838.2019.1649919
de Onís, K. M. (2012). "Looking both ways": Metaphor and the rhetorical alignment of intersectional climate justice and reproductive justice concerns. *Environmental Communication, 6*(3), 308–327. https://doi.org/10.1080/17524032.2012.690092
de Onís, K. M. (2015). Lost in translation: Challenging (white, monolingual feminism's) with justicia reproductiva. *Women's Studies in Communication, 38*(1), 1–19.
Deomampo, D. (2013). Transnational surrogacy in India: Interrogating power and women's agency. *Frontiers: A Journal of Women Studies, 34*(3), 167. https://doi.org/10.5250/fronjwomestud.34.3.0167
Dowd, N. E. (1996). *In defense of single-parent families*. New York University Press.
Eng, D. L. (2003). Transnational adoption and queer diasporas. *Social Text, 21*(3), 1–37.
Enke, A. (2007). *Finding the movement: Sexuality, contested space, and feminist activism*. Duke University Press.
Ethics Committee of the American Society for Reproductive Medicine. (2015). Access to fertility services by transgender persons: An ethics committee opinion. *Fertility and Sterility, 104*(5), 1111–1115. https://doi.org/10.1016/j.fertnstert.2015.08.021
Eubanks, V. (2019). *Automating inequality*. Picador.
Fixmer-Oraiz, N. (2013). Speaking of solidarity: Transnational gestational surrogacy and the rhetorics of reproductive (in)justice. *Frontiers: A Journal of Women Studies, 34*(3), 126. https://doi.org/10.5250/fronjwomestud.34.3.0126
Fixmer-Oraiz, N. (2019). *Homeland maternity: US security culture and the new reproductive regime*. University of Illinois Press.
Fixmer-Oraiz, N., & Wehman-Brown, G. (2020). Called into the world by all of us: An interview with masculine birth ritual podcast creator and host Grover Wehman-Brown. *QED: A Journal in GLBTQ Worldmaking, 7*(2), 94–105.
Freedman, D., Tasker, F., & di Ceglie, D. (2002). Children and adolescents with transsexual parents referred to a specialist gender identity development service: A brief report of key developmental features. *Clinical Child Psychology and Psychiatry, 7*(3), 423–432. https://doi.org/10.1177/1359104502007003009
Gaard, G. (2010). Reproductive technology, or reproductive justice?: An ecofeminist, environmental justice perspective on the rhetoric of choice. *Ethics and the Environment, 15*(2), 103–129. https://doi.org/10.2979/ete.2010.15.2.103
Gamson, J. (2018). Kindred spirits? *Reproductive Biomedicine & Society Online, 7*, 1–3. https://doi.org/10.1016/j.rbms.2018.04.002

Garita, A. (2015). Moving toward sexual and reproductive justice. In R. Baksh-Soodeen & W. Harcourt (Eds.), *The Oxford handbook of transnational feminist movements* (pp. 271–294). Oxford University Press.

Gómez-Gil, E., Vidal-Hagemeijer, A., & Salamero, M. (2008). MMPI-2 characteristics of transsexuals requesting sex reassignment: Comparison of patients in prehormonal and presurgical phases. *Journal of Personality Assessment, 90*(4), 368–374. https://doi.org/10.1080/00223890802108022

Goodfellow, A. (2015). *Gay fathers, their children, and the making of kinship*. Fordham University Press.

Gumbs, A. P., Martens, C., & Williams, M. (Eds.). (2016). *Revolutionary mothering: Love on the front lines*. PM Press.

Hašková, H., & Sloboda, Z. (2018). Negotiating access to assisted reproduction technologies in a post-socialist heteronormative context. *Journal of International Women's Studies, 20*(1), 53–67.

Hayden, S. (2009). Revitalizing the debate between <Life> and <Choice>: The 2004 March for Women's Lives. *Communication and Critical/Cultural Studies, 6*(2), 111–131.

Hernández, L. H., & Upton, S. D. L. S. (2018). *Challenging reproductive control and gendered violence in the Americas: Intersectionality, power, and struggles for rights*. Lexington Books.

Human Rights Watch. (2016, June 30). UN makes history on sexual orientation, gender identity. *Human Rights Watch*. https://www.hrw.org/news/2016/06/30/un-makes-history-sexual-orientation-gender-identity

If/When/How. (2017). *Reproductive justice in the prison system: If/when/how issue brief* (pp. 1–14). https://www.ifwhenhow.org/resources/reproductive-justice-in-the-prison-system/

Imaz, E. (2017). Same-sex parenting, assisted reproduction and gender asymmetry: Reflecting on the differential effects of legislation on gay and lesbian family formation in Spain. *Reproductive Biomedicine & Society Online, 4*, 5–12. https://doi.org/10.1016/j.rbms.2017.01.002

Jolly, J. (2016). On forbidden wombs and transnational reproductive justice. *Meridians: Feminism, Race, Transnationalism, 15*(1), 166–188.

Khader, S. J. (2013). Intersectionality and the ethics of transnational commercial surrogacy. *IJFAB: International Journal of Feminist Approaches to Bioethics, 6*(1), 68. https://doi.org/10.3138/ijfab.6.1.68

Lasio, D., Serri, F., Ibba, I., & Manuel De Oliveira, J. (2019). Hegemony and heteronormativity: Homonormative discourses of LGBTQ activists about lesbian and gay parenting. *Journal of Homosexuality, 66*(8), 1058–1081. https://doi.org/10.1080/00918369.2018.1493252

Lee, R. (2019). Queering lactation: Contributions of queer theory to lactation support for LGBTQIA2S+ individuals and families. *Journal of Human Lactation, 35*(2), 233–238. https://doi.org/10.1177/0890334419830992

Lewis, S. (2019). *Full surrogacy now: Feminism against family*. Verso.

Luna, Z. (2018). Black celebrities, reproductive justice and queering family: An exploration. *Reproductive Biomedicine & Society Online, 7*, 91–100. https://doi.org/10.1016/j.rbms.2018.12.002

Mackenzie, S. (2013). *Structural intimacies: Sexual stories in the black AIDS epidemic*. Rutgers University Press.

Mamo, L. (2007). *Queering reproduction: Achieving pregnancy in the age of technoscience*. Duke University Press.

Mamo, L. (2018). Queering reproduction in transnational bio-economies. *Reproductive Biomedicine & Society Online, 7*, 24–32. https://doi.org/10.1016/j.rbms.2018.10.008

Mamo, L., & Alston-Stepnitz, E. (2015). Queer intimacies and structural inequalities: New directions in stratified reproduction. *Journal of Family Issues, 36*(4), 519–540.

Markens, S. (2007). *Surrogate motherhood and the politics of reproduction*. University of California Press.

Mitu, K. (2016). Transgender reproductive choice and fertility preservation. *AMA Journal of Ethics, 18*(11), 1119–1125. https://doi.org/10.1001/journalofethics.2016.18.11.pfor2-1611

Murphy, T. F. (2012). Commentary: Crossing cultural divides: Transgender people who want to have children. *Cambridge Quarterly of Healthcare Ethics, 21*(2), 284–286. https://doi.org/10.1017/S0963180111000806

Narayan, U. (1988). Working together across difference: Some considerations on emotions and political practice. *Hypatia, 3*(2), 31–47. https://doi.org/10.2307/3809950

Nash, J. C. (2019). *Black feminism reimagined: After intersectionality*. Duke University Press.

National LGBTQ Taskforce. (2019). *Queering reproductive justice: A toolkit* (p. 16). https://www.thetaskforce.org/wp-content/uploads/2019/06/Queering-Reproductive-Justice-Mini-Toolkit.pdf

National Organization for Women. (2006). *Advocacy groups rank states based on reproductive, sexual rights*. https://now.org/readthis/advocacy_groups_rank_states_based_on_rep/

National Women's Law Center, & Law Students for Reproductive Justice. (2011). *If you really care about LGBT rights, you should care about reproductive justice!*, https://www.nwlc.org/sites/default/files/pdfs/final_lgbt_fact_sheet_2_.pdf

Newman, C. E. (2019). Queer families: Valuing stories of adversity, diversity and belonging. *Culture, Health & Sexuality, 21*(3), 352–359. https://doi.org/10.1080/13691058.2018.1468032

Nixon, L. (2013). The right to (trans) parent: A reproductive justice approach to reproductive rights, fertility, and family-building issues facing transgender people. *William & Mary Journal of Race, Gender, and Social Justice, 20*(1), 73.

Oaks, L. (2015). *Giving up baby: Safe haven laws, motherhood, and reproductive justice*. New York University Press.

Olivera, K. (2018, August 3). *Immigration is a reproductive justice issue*. International Women's Health Coalition. https://iwhc.org/2018/08/immigration-is-a-reproductive-justice-issue/

Palmer-Mehta, V. (2016). Subversive maternities: Staceyann Chin's contemplative voice. *QED: A Journal in GLBTQ Worldmaking, 3*(1), 34–60. https://doi.org/10.14321/qed.3.1.0034

Pande, A. (2014). *Wombs in labor: Transnational commercial surrogacy in India*. Columbia University Press.

Patton-Imani, S. (2020). *Queering family trees: Race, reproductive justice, and lesbian motherhood*. New York University Press.

Pérez, M. Z. (2007, May 31). Queering reproductive justice. *Rewire.News*. https://rewire.news/article/2007/05/31/queering-reproductive-justice/

Pérez, M. Z. (2012). *The radical doula guide: A political primer*. Self-published. https://radicaldoula.com/the-radical-doula-guide/

Piepmeier, A. (2013). The inadequacy of "choice": Disability and what's wrong with feminist framings of reproduction. *Feminist Studies, 39*(1), 159–186.

Price, K. (2010). What is reproductive justice?: How women of color activists are redefining the pro-choice paradigm. *Meridians: Feminism, Race, Transnationalism, 10*(2), 42–65.

Price, K. (2017). Queering reproductive justice: Toward a theory and praxis for building intersectional political alliances. In M. Brettschneider, S. Burgess, & C. Keating (Eds.), *LGBTQ politics: A critical reader* (pp. 72–88). New York University Press.

Price, K. (2018). Queering reproductive justice in the Trump era: A note on political intersectionality. *Politics & Gender, 14*(4), 581–601. https://doi.org/10.1017/S1743923X18000776

Puar, J. K. (2007). *Terrorist assemblages: Homonationalism in queer times*. Duke University Press.

Radi, B. (2020). Reproductive injustice, trans rights, and eugenics. *Sexual and Reproductive Health Matters, 28*(1), 1824318. https://doi.org/10.1080/26410397.2020.1824318

Rankin, K. (2016, February 9). Black lives matter partners with reproductive justice groups to fight for black women. *Colorlines*. https://www.colorlines.com/articles/black-lives-matter-partners-reproductive-justice-groups-fight-black-women

Roberts, D. (1997). *Killing the black body: Race, reproduction, and the meaning of liberty*. Vintage.

Roberts, D. E. (2012). Prison, foster care, and the systemic punishment of black mothers. *UCLA Law Review, 59*, 1474–1500.

Romesburg, D. (2014). Where she comes from: Locating queer transracial adoption. *QED: A Journal in GLBTQ Worldmaking, 1*(3), 1. https://doi.org/10.14321/qed.1.3.0001

Ross, L., & Solinger, R. (2017). *Reproductive justice: An introduction*. University of California Press.

Ross, L. J. (2006). *Understanding reproductive justice* (pp. 1–12). SisterSong Women of Color Reproductive Health Collective.

Rudrappa, S. (2015). *Discounted life: The price of global surrogacy in India*. New York University Press.

Russell, C. (2018). Rights-holders or refugees? Do gay men need reproductive justice? *Reproductive Biomedicine & Society Online*, 7, 131–140. https://doi.org/10.1016/j.rbms.2018.07.001

Samek, A. A. (2016). Violence and identity politics: 1970s lesbian-feminist discourse and Robin Morgan's 1973 West Coast Lesbian Conference keynote address. *Communication and Critical/Cultural Studies*, 13(3), 232–249. https://doi.org/10.1080/14791420.2015.1127400

Shonkwiler, A. (2008). The selfish-enough fathergay adoption and the late-capitalist family. *GLQ: A Journal of Lesbian and Gay Studies*, 14(4), 537–567. https://doi.org/10.1215/10642684-2008-004

Silliman, J., Fried, M. G., Ross, L., & Gutiérrez, E. (2016). *Undivided rights: Women of color organizing for reproductive justice* (2nd ed.). Haymarket Books.

SisterSong Women of Color Reproductive Collective, National Latina Institute for Reproductive Health, & Center for Reproductive Rights. (2014). *Reproductive injustice: Racial and gender discrimination in U.S. health care: A shadow report for the UN Commission on Racial Discrimination* (pp. 1–22). https://tbinternet.ohchr.org/Treaties/CERD/Shared%20Documents/USA/INT_CERD_NGO_USA_17560_E.pdf

Smietana, M. (2017). Affective de-commodifying, economic de-kinning: Surrogates' and gay fathers' narratives in U.S. surrogacy. *Sociological Research Online*, 22(2), 5.

Smietana, M. (2018). Procreative consciousness in a global market: Gay men's paths to surrogacy in the USA. *Reproductive Biomedicine & Society Online*, 7, 101–111. https://doi.org/10.1016/j.rbms.2019.03.001

Smietana, M., Thompson, C., & Twine, F. W. (2018). Making and breaking families: Reading queer reproductions, stratified reproduction and reproductive justice together. *Reproductive Biomedicine & Society Online*, 7, 112–130. https://doi.org/10.1016/j.rbms.2018.11.001

Smith, s. e. (2019, March 1). Women are not the only ones who get abortions. *Rewire.News*. https://rewire.news/article/2019/03/01/women-are-not-the-only-ones-who-get-abortions/

Society for Assisted Reproductive Technology. (2020). *Frequently asked questions*.

Solinger, R. (2007). *Pregnancy and power: A short history of reproductive politics in America*. New York University Press.

Stacey, J. (2018). Queer reproductive justice? *Reproductive Biomedicine & Society Online*, 7, 4–7. https://doi.org/10.1016/j.rbms.2018.06.004

Strangio, C. (2014, April 2). Arrested for walking while trans: An interview with Monica Jones. *American Civil Liberties Union*. https://www.aclu.org/blog/criminal-law-reform/arrested-walking-while-trans-interview-monica-jones

Suter, E. A., Baxter, L. A., Seurer, L. M., & Thomas, L. J. (2014). Discursive constructions of the meaning of "family" in online narratives of foster adoptive parents. *Communication Monographs*, 81(1), 59–78. https://doi.org/10.1080/03637751.2014.880791

Suter, E. A., Kellas, J. K., Webb, S. K., & Allen, J. A. (2016). A tale of two mommies: (Re)storying family of origin narratives. *Journal of Family Communication*, 16(4), 303–317. https://doi.org/10.1080/15267431.2016.1184150

Thompson, C. (2016). IVF global histories, USA: Between rock and a marketplace. *Reproductive Biomedicine & Society Online*, 2, 128–135. https://doi.org/10.1016/j.rbms.2016.09.003

Thomsen, C., & Morrison, G. T. (2020). Abortion as gender transgression: Reproductive justice, queer theory, and anti-crisis pregnancy center activism. *Signs: Journal of Women in Culture and Society*, 45(3), 703–730. https://doi.org/10.1086/706487

Tornello, S. L., & Bos, H. (2017). Parenting intentions among transgender individuals. *LGBT Health*, 4(2), 115–120. https://doi.org/10.1089/lgbt.2016.0153

Transgender Europe. (2018). *Trans rights Europe map 2018: 14 countries require sterilisation in gender identity recognition* [Map]. https://tgeu.org/wp-content/uploads/2018/05/MapB_TGEU2018_Online.pdf

Vinson, J. (2017). *Embodying the problem: The persuasive power of the teen mother.* Rutgers University Press.

Wehman-Brown, G. (2018, November 19). Bearing life with and alongside: On masculinity, pregnancy, and medical trauma. *Autostraddle.* https://www.autostraddle.com/bearing-life-with-and-alongside-on-masculinity-pregnancy-and-medical-trauma-438219/

Wellons, M. F., Lewis, C. E., Schwartz, S. M., Gunderson, E. P., Schreiner, P. J., Sternfeld, B., Richman, J., Sites, C. K., & Siscovick, D. S. (2008). Racial differences in self-reported infertility and risk factors for infertility in a cohort of black and white women: The CARDIA Women's Study. *Fertility and Sterility,* 90(5), 1640–1648. https://doi.org/10.1016/j.fertnstert.2007.09.056

Wierckx, K., Van Caenegem, E., Pennings, G., Elaut, E., Dedecker, D., Van de Peer, F., Weyers, S., De Sutter, P., & T'Sjoen, G. (2012). Reproductive wish in transsexual men. *Human Reproduction (Oxford, England),* 27(2), 483–487. https://doi.org/10.1093/humrep/der406

Willems, G., & Sosson, J. (2017). Donor assisted reproduction and surrogacy in Belgium: Equal access to parenthood and policy coherence. *Rights and Remedies,* 2017, 54–68.

Wingard, J. (2015). *Branded bodies, rhetoric, and the neoliberal nation-state.* Lexington Books.

Wrobel, G. M., Helder, E., & Marr, E. (2020). *The Routledge handbook of adoption.* Routledge.

Yam, S. S. (2021). The city of tears: Reproductive justice and community resistance in Hong Kong's anti-ELAB movement. *Feminist Formations,* 33(2), 1–24.

Zavella, P. (2020). *The movement for reproductive justice: Empowering women of color through social activism.* New York University Press.

Zavidow, E. (2016, May 11). Transgender people at higher risk for justice system involvement. *Vera: Institute of Justice.* Text/html][https://www.vera.org/blog/gender-and-justice-in-america/transgender-people-at-higher-risk-for-justice-system-involvement

Natalie Fixmer-Oraiz and Shui-yin Sharon Yam

QUEERING THE STUDY OF U.S. MILITARY FAMILY COMMUNICATION

Since 9/11, over two million U.S. service members have deployed (in some cases multiple times) in support of U.S. engagements abroad. While military families are framed as strong and resilient, they face many challenges in practice. Research about the military within communication studies has spanned decades with rhetorical and media scholars leading the field (Sahlstein Parcell, 2015); however, social-scientific inquiry focused on military families and communication has, albeit relatively recently, increased in numbers (Wilson & Knobloch, 2016). This scholarship reflects "traditional" family configurations in sampling and primarily takes postpositivist and interpretivist approaches, trends that parallel interpersonal and family communication studies broadly speaking (Sahlstein Parcell & Baker, 2018). Given calls for new approaches within military family communication research, we argue scholars should consider queering the study of military family communication.

The social-scientific study of military family communication is dominated by studies of white, heterosexual, cisgender, different sexed, married couples who are able-bodied with biological children. While this pattern mirrors most U.S. military families, extant research fails to include and reflect the growing diversity of military families serving the country. Studies that bring attention to single service members, women service members, dual-career couples, service member mothers, single-parent service members, service members of color, cohabitating military service members (i.e., nonmarried couples), LGB service members, and transgender service members would make significant contributions to the scholarship and make these families as well as their unique experiences visible. Informed by calls for critical military family studies (Basham & Bulmer, 2017; Sahlstein Parcell & Baker, 2018; Wool, 2015) and critical interpersonal and family communication research (Moore & Manning, 2019; Suter, 2016), we offer recommendations for future military family communication inquiry focused on the increasing sexual and gender minority, or queer, military families (Dixon, 2019; Eran-Jona & Aviram, 2019). This chapter begins with a brief history of important moments in the U.S. military related to LGBT service members.

LGBT HISTORY IN THE U.S. MILITARY

While the outward facing image of military families has long been a traditional one, the U.S. military has always included a diversity of membership and family forms. There is evidence dating back to the Revolutionary War that individuals with different sexual and gender identities have served in the U.S. military (Frank, 2009). While the U.S. military has only recently embraced (to a degree) lesbian, gay, and bisexual (LGB) service members and their families, its policies and practices were inconsistent at best through the early 1980s and dependent on the country's wartime status (Korb & Rothman, 2013). In 1982 the Department of Defense formalized its ban on gays and lesbians serving in the military with a directive that called for mandatory discharges for engagement in past, present, or attempted homosexual behavior.

In 1994, after making a campaign promise to lift the ban on LGB military service, President William H. Clinton signed Don't Ask, Don't Tell (DADT), which required LGB service members to refrain from disclosing their sexual identities to others. Not only did DADT ban openly LGB individuals from joining the military, this policy was also used to investigate existing military service members who were suspected of expressing a LGB identity. These investigations led to the discharge of more than 14,000 service members over the course of DADT's implementation (Oswald & Sternberg, 2014, p. 133). LGB military families were unable to serve in the open and feared being outed and ultimately forced to leave the military. During DADT, some LGB service members chose to take certain actions. For example, some service members participated in cover marriages to maintain their military status and access to benefits only afforded to married couples (Lundquist & Zu, 2014). Ultimately, DADT would last for more than 16 years.

On September 20, 2011, President Barack Obama repealed DADT allowing LGB service members to openly serve in all branches of the U.S. military. While the repeal was a historic moment for the military, the country, and LGB service members, it was not a complete victory for military families. The U.S. Defense of Marriage Act (DOMA) defined marriage at the federal level as a legal union between one man and one woman, and it gave states the right to ignore marriage licenses of other states (Sahlstein Parcell, 2014a). In effect, DOMA allowed for the denial of benefits and access to resources to LGB military spouses and children; but, in 2013 a U.S. Supreme Court decision (*United States v. Windsor*) resulted in the repeal of the federal ban on same-sex marriage, which then allowed the military to offer spousal and family benefits to all legally married service members (Smith & De Angelis, 2017). However, not all states issued same-sex marriage licenses. In 2015 the U.S. Supreme Court issued a decision in *Obergefell v. Hodges* that instituted marriage equality across the country and thus made same-sex marriage legal regardless of residence. This decision has had significant and widespread effects on LGB military families. No longer does a LGB service member's state of residence impact the validity of their marital status.

Transgender service members and their families have also had a complicated history within the military (Rosenstein, 2017). The U.S. military did not implement an *explicit* ban on transgender individuals serving in the military until 1960, which remained in place for over 55 years. In 2016, President Barack Obama instituted a policy that allowed transgender individuals to serve as well as receive healthcare across their transition. However, in 2017 President Donald Trump announced via Twitter that his administration would be issuing a transgender ban across the U.S. military. The policy was implemented in 2019 and limited the service of transgender individuals in the military to those who were currently serving and fully transitioned, which meant that those without a formal diagnosis of gender dysphoria had to file for it before April 12, 2019. Those service members that did not seek or obtain a diagnosis by the deadline were left to either serve as their biological sex assigned at birth or separate from the military. During the 2020 presidential election, then-Democratic candidate, Joseph Biden, promised to overturn the current administration's ban. On January 25, 2021, President Biden issued an executive order making way for the reinstatement of transgender service members and their families into the military by repealing former President Trump's orders. This included banning future discharges or denials of reenlistment based on gender identity, overturning prior gender identity dismissals, and initiating a process for open military service for transgender individuals (Detrow, 2021). On April 30, 2021, new policies regarding transgender service members went into effect. They include "provid[ing] a path for those in service for medical treatment, gender transition, and recognition in one's self-identified gender" (Department of Defense, 2021, para. 2). Moving forward, service members may not be involuntarily discharged or denied reenlistment because of their gender identity, and clinical practice guidelines will be created for the medical support of service members with a gender dysphoria diagnosis.

QUEER U.S. MILITARY FAMILY COMMUNICATION RESEARCH

Research about queer military families within communication studies is relatively nonexistent, although scholars have made calls for such research (Knobloch & Wilson, 2014; Sahlstein & Maguire, 2013; Sahlstein Parcell & Baker, 2018). The limited body of research that does exist explores the experiences of gay, lesbian, bisexual, and transgender service members. For example, Van Gilder (2017, 2019a, 2019b) has studied sexual stigma in the U.S. military, and Sahlstein Parcell and Baker (2018) interviewed LGBT service members and spouses about their experiences within the military. Scholars who do study military families within and beyond communication studies have typically operationalized them as married straight couples with children and studied them primarily from postpositivist or interpretivist approaches. And while military families are considered nonnormative due to their distinct characteristics compared to civilian families (e.g., frequent moves, separations due to deployments, and unique cultural norms; Sahlstein Parcell & Baker, 2018), queer military families have additional discursive burdens within and outside of the military context. Queer military family communication research should take a critical approach, which is described in the next section.

CIFC Framework. Families wield significant influence over the trajectory of their members' lives, from the way children are socialized at a young age well into adulthood (Heywood, 2001). Although the word "family" has historically been synonymous with a traditional form, that of a heteronormative, cohabitating couple with children, often White and middle class, nontraditional families who do not meet these criteria are now the dominant family form (Baxter, 2014). Nontraditional, or nonnormative families are those whose status is often stigmatized and challenged by societal norms that prescribe the traditional, nuclear family as ideal. Galvin (2014) advances that the less traditional a family is (e.g., lack of genetic ties), the more dependent they are on discourse to create and maintain their familial identity. As such, these families are more at risk of being buffeted about by changing sociohistorical forces that constrain their development and maintenance. Nonnormative families have an additional discursive burden to rationalize, justify, and explain their family identity because, historically, prevailing culture and societal institutions often failed to recognize their legitimacy. That they are rising in numbers and are heavily impacted by changing social norms makes these families and their experiences rich sites of exploration, particularly when using a critical approach.

Suter (2018) contends that a critical interpersonal family communication (CIFC) framework is useful for exploring sociopolitical dimensions of power around family identity and communication. In her framework, Suter proposes that CIFC research should explicitly take up one or more of four dimensions—the situatedness of power, a collapse of the public/private binary, research that engages in critique and resistance, and research that foregrounds author reflexivity. From a CIFC framework, issues of power are centered and foundational, and in turn, power is conceptualized "in terms of larger sociocultural systems and discourses impacting individuals, relationships, and family" (p. 5). Interpersonal and family researchers typically frame power as an individual-level phenomenon that is "a characteristic, property, attribute, or resource (e.g., credibility) of the person" (Suter, 2018, p. 5), but a CIFC framework advocates decentering the individual "variable" of power that resides in specific actors within interpersonal and familial contexts. Rather, power is assumed to be located in either systemic influence or localized discursive interplay. Foregrounding issues of power in this way requires researchers to examine power inside the family dynamic and, perhaps more importantly, as external to the family and situated in sociocultural systems (Suter & Norwood, 2017). These issues of power can manifest unobtrusively through the performance of roles and routines that seem normal. Taking a critical approach has the potential to expose how these messages are taken for granted and how families may be unwittingly contributing to their marginalization (Baxter, 2014).

Interpersonal and family communication research often separates public and private domains of family by studying the family in isolation from its larger political, historical, and material surroundings. However, in CIFC research, the binary of public and private domains collapses to illuminate the family's inherent politicized status (Suter, 2018). As Suter (2018) argues, "CIFC advocates interpersonal and family research that examines public/private interpenetrations" (p. 7). Families influence and are influenced by public institutions, such as government and religion. Combining macrodiscourses with microlevel discourses further attunes researchers to those nontraditional family types that are underrepresented in interpersonal and family communication research (Suter & Norwood, 2017).

CIFC calls upon researchers to also recognize and pursue the critique, resistance, and transformation of the "status quo in service of social-justice ends" (Suter, 2018, p. 124). In this way, CIFC has the potential to move military family research from a consensus-orientation to a dissensus-orientation, where investigators could seek to move beyond traditional translational research to "encourag[ing] the questioning of larger structures and discourses creating conditions that necessitate coping" while "empower[ing] participants to critically reflect on the current conditions of their own lives" (Suter, 2018, p. 132). Employing a stance of resistance, critique, and transformation in CIFC aids in better understanding research projects that do not always fit or tie together neatly. Instead, a dissensus view of research is undertaken (Deetz, 2001), one that "encourages studies that embrace rather than minimize conflict, that presumes that struggle is the natural state" (Suter & Norwood, 2017, p. 4) and sees societal systems as contributors to unequal representation. An orientation toward critique, resistance, and transformation further displaces the consensus view of research by introducing a social justice element whereby researchers may call on their participants to question and examine the otherwise accepted social conditions surrounding them (Suter, 2018).

Lastly, Suter (2018) encourages authors to exercise reflexivity by questioning and assessing their own assumptions and biases throughout their research. Author reflexivity in CIFC extends these practices by asking researchers to consider which actors are being privileged or which dominant beliefs are crowding out other ways of making meaning (Suter, 2018). In doing so, authors heed this call by recognizing and embodying possibilities of social justice for families—the essence of CIFC.

Taken together, Suter's framework for CIFC sees the family as a political site whose microlevel and macrolevel interdependency is inextricably linked. By focusing on how power is manifested in families externally and internally. communication scholars can critically interrogate how these intersections make meaning for families. When interpersonal and family communication scholars are willing to trouble their own assumptions in addition to prevailing cultural hierarchies, the transformative change CIFC proposes can take place.

FUTURE QUEER MILITARY FAMILY COMMUNICATION RESEARCH

What pathways should queer military family communication research take in the future? Guided by the CIFC framework, there are at least four recommendations. First, military family researchers should (re)consider how they conceptualize power by decentering it from within individuals and identifying discourses of "family" and related concepts (e.g., fatherhood, caregiving) that are at play when queer military families are making sense of their experiences and/or other military families. For example, research outside the discipline has considered how discourses of "heteronormative relations of kinship and care" underwrite the experiences of service members with disabilities (Wool, 2021). A theory communication scholars could use to frame similar work is relational dialectics theory (RDT; Baxter, 2011; Sahlstein Parcell, 2018; Sahlstein Parcell & Baker, 2018). Second, the CIFC framework pushes scholars to question the binary often assumed between the public and private, where interpersonal and family interactions are considered almost exclusively as "private." The case of queer military families brings into bold relief how "the family" is simultaneously a site of public and private considerations. Queer military family communication scholars at minimum should situate the site and subjects of their studies within the ongoing history of the military and families within it. Third, in relation to CIFC's call for research that critiques, resists, and transforms the status quo, queer military family research arguably is best conducted under the domain of critical scholarship to identify ways that queer military families are marginalized within the military context and seek positive change for them. Given that families are where heteronormative ideologies are mobilized, queer interventions into interpersonal and family communication research are appropriate (Chevrette, 2013). Instead of (re)establishing patterns of behavior and experience, the research should challenge the military and the communication within and about it. Lastly, the CIFC framework encourages queer military family communication scholars to engage in reflexivity. As much of the existing military family communication research has been conducted not only about normative military families but by white, cisgender, heterosexual scholars (Sahlstein Parcell & Baker, 2018) coming from primarily postpositivist and interpretive intellectual traditions (Braithwaite, Schrodt, et al., 2018; Braithwaite, Suter, et al., 2018), reflexivity on both fronts would be beneficial for future inquiry.

Beyond recommending the CIFC framework, a topic for future research should be the military's culture with respect to queer military families. United States military culture has distinct qualities (Knobloch & Wehrman, 2014), and it has been labeled a "greedy institution" given the demands it places on service members and their families (Segal, 1986); but what are the implications specifically for queer military families? For example, how do queer military families manage their privacy concerns within the strong metaphor of "family" that exists in the military (Trivette, 2010)? There is evidence that queer service members have evoked "family" to manage such needs (Ramirez & Sterzing, 2017). Family communication scholars have identified post DADT as an important period to study same-sex military marriages given the uncertainties queer service members and their family members experience and negotiate with significant policy changes and subsequent shifts in military culture (Lannutti, 2014; McNamara et al., 2021; Westcott & Sawyer, 2007). While post-DADT is an important period for queer military families, military family scholars should reflect on specifically who they are studying within these units.

Centering three types of family members in future research would add considerably to the queer military family communication scholarship. One important subpopulation are queer veteran service members, and those with mental health issues are of particular concern. Those training military health care professionals should "be alert to the unique needs of this population amongst both active duty service members and [veterans]" (Wiskoff & Sammons, 2017, p. 557). Further, the military should consider how their offerings for family members are also attentive to such needs. For example, akin to the extant research within family communication about military families and mental health (e.g., Knobloch & Basinger, 2021; Peck & Sahlstein Parcell, 2021; Wilson et al., 2021), scholars should focus on how mental health is talked about within queer military families. Military researchers have recommended studies of trauma and mental health for queer veterans (Averill et al., 2015, p. 3) and including their family members is key for understanding their experiences, and in particular surrounding DADT and other policy changes that impact service members relationships with their families. For example, one study reported after DADT was repealed showed family readiness was "enhanced" along with trust and honesty among troops (Belkin et al., 2012, p. 591). To underscore previous calls within the military family research (Kauth & Shipherd, 2016; Laski & Albright, 2017; Sherman et al., 2014), family communication researchers should seek out queer veterans given the vast majority of research conducted has been about active duty service members and their families. It is important that research extend beyond active service as for most their connections to the military are lifelong.

A second family member group in need of attention are queer military spouses/parents. Most extant family communication research studies concerning military spouses/parents are either explicitly or assumed to be focused on heterosexual marriages. Family communication researchers have explored the experiences of (heterosexual) military wives within their family readiness groups (Sahlstein Parcell & Maguire, 2014) and (heterosexual) motherhood within the military (McFarlane, 2021) among others. Future research should recognize the unique experiences of spouses/parents within queer military families (e.g., how lesbian military spouses navigate spaces within and outside the military; Tannenbaum, 2019).

A third group that is understudied within military family communication research are military children; especially children who are members of queer military families as studies are virtually non-existent within the field. While there are studies and calls for this scholarship in the broader area of military family studies (e.g., DePedro & Shim-Pelayo, 2018; Gyura & McCauley, 2015) and within family communication (e.g., Knobloch et al., 2017; Sahlstein Parcell, 2014b, 2015), there is a strong need for understanding the experiences of children of queer military parents as well as queer military youth.

Military family communication researchers have much to offer the study of queer military families given the astonishingly small studies that even begin to address the unique experiences and concerns of these families relative to the abundance of studies produced about heterosexual military families. It is important that as the scholarship moves forward researchers consider diversity (Rohall et al., 2017a) and intersectionality (Rich et al., 2012; Rohall et al., 2017b) as central to their thinking as well as how to "queer" their methods (Fish & Russell, 2018). Given the evidence that additional support will benefit queer service members (Conway et al., 2021), the next decade of military family communication research should help these underserved members of U.S. military communities. The CIFC framework (Suter, 2018) and RDT (Baxter, 2011) are two approaches well-suited for this work.

ADDITIONAL RESOURCES

Modern Military Association of America. https://modernmilitary.org/
Sparta: A Transgender Military Advocacy Organization. https://spartapride.org/
Transgender American Veterans Association. http://transveteran.org/

FURTHER READING

Basham, V. M., & Bulmer, S. (2017). Critical military studies as method: An approach to studying gender and the military. In R. Woodward & C. Duncanson (Eds.), *The Palgrave international handbook* (pp. 59–71). Palgrave Macmillan. http://doi.org/10.1057/978-1-137-51677-0_4

Baxter, L. A. (2011). *Voicing relationships: A dialogic perspective*. SAGE.

Rohall, D. E., Ender, M. G., & Matthews, M. D. (2017a). Diversity in the military. In D. E. Rohall, M. G. Ender, & M. D. Matthews (Eds.), *Inclusion in the American military: A force for diversity* (pp. 1–15). Lexington.

Rohall, D. E., Ender, M. G., & Matthews, M. D. (2017b). The intersection of race, class, gender, and sexuality in the military. In D. E. Rohall, M. G. Ender, & M. D. Matthews (Eds.), *Inclusion in the American military: A force for diversity* (pp. 191–210). Lexington.

Rosenstein, J. E. (2017). The integration of the trans people into the military. In D. E. Rohall, M. G. Ender, & M. D. Matthews (Eds.), *Inclusion in the American military: A force for diversity* (pp. 149–168). Lexington.

Sahlstein Parcell, E. (2014b). Military families: Remaking shared residence, traditional marriage, and future communication research. In L. A. Baxter (Ed.), *Remaking family communicatively* (pp. 195–210). Peter Lang.

Sahlstein Parcell, E., & Baker, B. M. A. (2018). Relational Dialectics Theory: A new approach for military/veteran-connected family research. *Journal of Family Theory & Review*, 10(3), 672–685. https://doi.org/10.1111/jftr.12279

Smith, D. G., & De Angelis, K. (2017). Lesbian and gay service members and their families. In D. E. Rohall, M. G. Ender, & M. D. Matthews (Eds.), *Inclusion in the American military: A force for diversity* (pp. 129–148). Lexington.

Suter, E. A. (2018). The promise of contrapuntal and intersectional methods for advancing critical interpersonal and family communication research. *Communication Monographs*, 85(1), 123–139. https://doi.org/10.1080/03637751.2017.1375131

Van Gilder, B. J. (2017). Coping with sexual identity stigma in the U.S. military: An examination of identity management practices prior to and after the repeal of "Don't Ask, Don't Tell." *Identity*, 17(3), 156–175. https://doi.org/10.1080/15283488.2017.1340162

Van Gilder, B. J. (2019a). Femininity as perceived threat to military effectiveness: How military service members reinforce hegemonic masculinity in talk. *Western Journal of Communication*, 83(2), 151–171. https://doi.org/10.1080/10570314.2018.1502892

Van Gilder, B. J. (2019b). Sexual orientation stigmatization and identity work for gays, lesbians, and bisexuals in the U.S. military. *Journal of Homosexuality*, 66(14), 1949–1973. https://doi.org/10.1080/00918369.2018.1522812

REFERENCES

Averill, L. A., Eubanks Fleming, C. J., Holens, P. L., & Larsen, S. E. (2015). Research on PTSD prevalence in OEF/OIF veterans: Expanding investigation of demographic variables. *European Journal of Psychotraumatology*, 6, 1–5. http://dx.doi.org/10.3402/ejpt.v6.27322

Basham, V. M., & Bulmer, S. (2017). Critical military studies as method: An approach to studying gender and the military. In R. Woodward & C. Duncanson (Eds.), *The Palgrave international handbook* (pp. 59–71). Palgrave Macmillan. https://link.springer.com/chapter/10.1057/978-1-137-51677-0_4

Baxter, L. A. (2011). *Voicing relationships: A dialogic perspective*. SAGE.

Baxter, L. A. (2014). Theorizing the communicative construction of "family": The three R's. In L. A. Baxter (Ed.), *Remaking "family" communicatively* (pp. 33–47). Peter Lang.

Belkin, A., Ender, M. G., Frank, N., Furia, S. R., Lucas, G., Packard, G., Samuels, S. M., Schultz, T., & Segal, D. R. (2012). Readiness and DADT repeal: Has the new policy of open service undermined the military? *Armed Forces & Society*, 39(4), 587–601. http://doi.org/10.1177/0095327X12466248

Braithwaite, D. O., Schrodt, P., & Car, K. (2018). Introduction: Meta-theory and theory in interpersonal communication research. In D. O. Braithwaite & P. Schrodt (Eds.), *Engaging theories in interpersonal communication: Multiple perspectives* (2nd ed., pp. 1–20). SAGE.

Braithwaite, D. O., Suter, E. A., & Floyd, K. (2018). The landscape of meta-theory and theory in family communication research. In D. O. Braithwaite, E. A. Suter, & K. Floyd (Eds.), *Engaging theories in family communication: Multiple perspectives* (2nd ed., pp. 1–16). SAGE.

Chevrette, R. (2013). Outing heteronormativity in interpersonal and family communication: Feminist applications of queer theory "beyond the sexy streets." *Communication Theory, 23*, 170–180. http://doi.org/10.1111/comt.12009

Conway, M. A., Dretsch, M. N., Taylor, M. R., & Quartana, P. J. (2021). The role of perceived support and perceived prejudice in the health of LGBT soldiers. *Sexuality Research & Social Policy, 18*, 547–554. https://doi.org/10.1007/s13178-020-00479-1

Deetz, S. (2001). Conceptual foundations. In F. M. Jablin & L. L. Putnam (Eds.), *The new handbook of organizational communication: Advances in theory, research, and methods* (pp. 3–46). SAGE.

Department of Defense. (2021, March 30). DOD announces policy updates for transgender military service. https://www.defense.gov/News/Releases/Release/Article/2557220/dod-announces-policy-updates-for-transgender-military-service/

DePedro, K. T., & Shim-Pelayo, H. (2018). Prevalence of substance use among lesbian, gay, bisexual, and transgender youth in military families: Findings from the California Healthy Kids Survey. *Substance Use & Misuse, 53*(8), 1372–1376. http://doi.org/10.1080/10826084.2017.1409241

Detrow, S. (2021). *Biden repeals Trump-era ban on transgender troops*. NPR. https://www.npr.org/sections/president-biden-takes-office/2021/01/25/960338217/biden-repeals-trump-era-ban-on-transgender-soldiers

Dixon, E. (2019). Becoming whole: Balancing dual identities as a graduate student Marine wife. In L. H. Hernáandez & J. Belding (Eds.), *Military spouses with graduate degrees: Interdisciplinary approaches to thriving amidst uncertainty* (pp. 109–124). Lexington.

Eran-Jona, M., & Aviram, D. (2019). New families in the IDF: Toward diversity in family policies. In R. Moelker, M. Andres, & N. Rones (Eds.), *The politics of military families: State, work organizations, and the rise of the negotiation household* (pp. 70–83). Routledge.

Fish, J. N., & Russell, S. T. (2018). Queering methodologies to understand queer families. *Family Relations, 67*(1), 12–25. https://doi.org/10.1111/fare.12297

Frank, N. (2009). *Unfriendly fire: How the gay ban undermines the military and weakens America*. Thomas Dunne Books.

Galvin, K. (2014). Blood, law, and discourse: Constructing and managing family identity. In L. Baxter (Ed.), *Remaking "family" communicatively* (pp. 17–32). Peter Lang.

Gyura, A. N., & McCauley, S. O. (2015). The whole family serves: Supporting sexual minority youth in military families. *Journal of Pediatric Health Care, 30*(5), 414–423. http://dx.doi.org/10.1016/j.pedhc.2015.10.006

Heywood, C. (2001). *A history of childhood: Children and childhood in the West from medieval to modern times*. Blackwell.

Kauth, M. R., & Shipherd, J. C. (2016). Transforming a system: Improving patient-centered care for sex and gender minority veterans. *LGBT Health, 3*(3), 177–179. https://doi.org/10.1089/lgbt.2016.0047

Knobloch, L. K., & Basinger, E. D. (2021). Communication mediators of the link between depressive symptoms and relationship satisfaction among Army soldiers. *Family Relations, 70*, 422–436. http://doi.org/10.1111/fare.12447

Knobloch, L. K., Knobloch-Fedders, L. M., Yorgason, J. B., Ebata, A. T., & McGlaughlin, P. C. (2017). Military children's difficulty with reintegration after deployment: A relational turbulence model perspective. *Journal of Family Psychology, 31*(5), 542–552. https://doi.org/10.1037/fam0000299

Knobloch, L. K., & Wehrman, E. C. (2014). Family relationships embedded in United States military culture. In C. R. Agnew (Ed.), *Social influences on close relationships: Beyond the dyad* (pp. 58–82). Cambridge University Press.

Knobloch, L. K., & Wilson, S. R. (2014). Communication in military families across the deployment cycle. In L. H. Turner & R. West (Eds.), *The Sage handbook of family communication* (pp. 370–385). SAGE.

Korb, L. J., & Rothman, A. (2013). Formalizing the ban: My experience in the Reagan administration. *Journal of Homosexuality, 60*, 273–281. https://doi.org/10.1080/00918369.2013.744672

Lannutti, P. J. (2014). *Experiencing same-sex marriage: Individuals, couples, and social networks.* Peter Lang.

Laski, S., & Albright, D. L. (2017). Sexual and gender minority veterans. In J. Beder (Ed.), *Caring for the military: A guide for helping professionals* (pp. 143–153). Routledge.

Lundquist, J., & Zu, Z. (2014). Reinstitutionalizing families: Life course policy and marriage in the military. *Journal of Marriage and the Family, 76*, 1063–1081. http://doi.org/10.1111/jomf.12131

McFarlane, M. D. (2021). *Militarized maternity: Experiencing pregnancy in the U.S. Armed Forces.* University of California Press.

McNamara, K. A., Lucas, C. L., Goldbach, J. T., Holloway, I. W., & Castro, C. A. (2021). "You don't want to be a candidate for punishment": A qualitative analysis of LGBT service member "outnesss." *Sexuality Research & Social Policy, 18*, 144–159. https://doi.org/10.1007/s13178-020-00445-x

Moore, J., & Manning, J. (2019). What counts as critical interpersonal and family communication research? A review of an emerging field of inquiry. *Annals of the International Communication Association, 43*(1), 40–57. https://doi.org/10.1080/23808985.2019.1570825

Oswald, R., & Sternberg, M. (2014). Lesbian, gay, and bisexual military families: Visible but legally marginalized. In S. MacDermid-Wadsworth (Ed.), *Military deployment and its consequences for families: Risk and resilience in military and veteran families* (pp. 133–147). Springer.

Peck, B., & Sahlstein Parcell, E. (2021). Talking about mental health: Dilemmas U.S. military service members and spouses experience post deployment. *Journal of Family Communication, 21*(2), 90–106. https://doi.org/10.1080/15267431.2021.1887195

Ramirez, M. H., & Sterzing, P. R. (2017). Coming out in camouflage: A queer theory perspective on the strength, resilience, and resistance of lesbian, gay, bisexual, and transgender service members and veterans. *Journal of Gay & Lesbian Social Services, 29*(1), 68–86. https://doi.org/10.1080/10538720.2016.1263983

Rich, C., Schutten, J., & Rogers, R. (2012). "Don't drop the soap": Organizing sexualities in the repeal of the U.S. military's "Don't Ask, Don't Tell" policy. *Communication Monographs, 79*, 269–291. https://doi.org/10.1080/03637751.2012.697633

Rohall, D. E., Ender, M. G., & Matthews, M. D. (2017a). Diversity in the military. In D. E. Rohall, M. G. Ender, & M. D. Matthews (Eds.), *Inclusion in the American military: A force for diversity* (pp. 1–15). Lexington.

Rohall, D. E., Ender, M. G., & Matthews, M. D. (2017b). The intersection of race, class, gender, and sexuality in the military. In D. E. Rohall, M. G. Ender, & M. D. Matthews (Eds.), *Inclusion in the American military: A force for diversity* (pp. 191–210). Lexington.

Rosenstein, J. E. (2017). The integration of trans people into the military. In D. E. Rohall, M. G. Ender, & M. D. Matthews (Eds.), *Inclusion in the American military: A force for diversity* (pp. 149–168). Lexington.

Sahlstein, E., & Maguire, K. (2013). Family relationships as more than blood: Military families as dialectics and discourses. In S. Marrow & D. Leoutsakas (Eds.), *More than blood: Today's reality and tomorrow's vision of family* (pp. 174–182). Kendall-Hunt.

Sahlstein Parcell, E. (2014a). Military families. In L. Ganong, M. Coleman, & J. G. Golson (Eds.), *The social history of the American family* (pp. 884–890). SAGE.

Sahlstein Parcell, E. (2014b). Military families: Remaking shared residence, traditional marriage, and future communication research. In L. A. Baxter (Ed.), *Remaking family communicatively* (pp. 195–210). Peter Lang.

Sahlstein Parcell, E. (2015). Research at the intersections of military and communication: A preview and review. In E. Sahlstein Parcell & L. Webb (Eds.), *A communication perspective on the military: Interactions, messages, and discourses* (pp. 1–15). Peter Lang.

Sahlstein Parcell, E. (2018). The United States military: Sites of intergroup discourses. In H. Giles & J. Harwood (Eds.), *Oxford encyclopedia of intergroup communication* (pp. 421–434). Oxford University Press.

Sahlstein Parcell, E., & Baker, B. M. A. (2018). Relational dialectics theory: A new approach for military/veteran-connected family research. *Journal of Family Theory & Review, 10*(3), 672–685. https://doi.org/10.1111/jftr.12279

Sahlstein Parcell, E., & Maguire, K. C. (2014). Comfort, cliques, and clashes: Family readiness groups as dilemmatic sites of relating during wartime. *Journal of Social and Personal Relationships, 31,* 497–515. https://doi.org/10.1177/0265407514521766

Segal, M. W. (1986). The military and the family as greedy institutions. *Armed Forces & Society, 13*(1), 9–38. https://doi.org/10.1177/0095327X8601300101

Sherman, M. D., Kauth, M. R., Ridener, L., Shipherd, J. C., Bratkovich, K., & Beaulieu, G. (2014). An empirical investigation of challenges and recommendations for welcoming sexual and gender minority veterans into VA care. *Professional Psychology: Research and Practice, 45*(6), 433–442. http://dx.doi.org/10.1037/a0034826

Smith, D. G., & De Angelis, K. (2017). Lesbian and gay service members and their families. In D. E. Rohall, M. G. Ender, & M. D. Matthews (Eds.), *Inclusion in the American military: A force for diversity* (pp. 129–148). Lexington.

Suter, E. A. (2016). Introduction: Critical approaches to family communication research: Representation, critique, and praxis. *Journal of Family Communication, 16,* 1–8. https://doi.org/10.1080/15267431.2015.1111219

Suter, E. A. (2018). The promise of contrapuntal and intersectional methods for advancing critical interpersonal and family communication research. *Communication Monographs, 85*(1), 123–139. https://doi.org/10.1080/03637751.2017.1375131

Suter, E. A., & Norwood, K. M. (2017). Critical theorizing in family communication studies: (Re)reading relational dialectics theory 2.0. *Communication Theory, 27*(3), 290–308. https://doi.org/10.1111/comt.12117

Tannenbaum, K. (2019). Joining the ranks: Considering military spouse life as a lesbian graduate student. In L. H. Hernández & J. Belding (Eds.), *Military spouses with graduate degrees: Interdisciplinary approaches to thriving amidst uncertainty* (pp. 179–195). Lexington.

Trivette, S. A. (2010). Secret handshakes and decoder rings: The queer space of Don't Ask/Don't Tell. *Sexual Research and Social Policy, 7,* 214–228. http://doi.org/10.1007/s13178-010-0020-3

Van Gilder, B. J. (2017). Coping with sexual identity stigma in the U.S. military: An examination of identity management practices prior to and after the repeal of "Don't Ask, Don't Tell." *Identity, 17*(3), 156–175. https://doi.org/10.1080/15283488.2017.1340162

Van Gilder, B. J. (2019a). Femininity as perceived threat to military effectiveness: How military service members reinforce hegemonic masculinity in talk. *Western Journal of Communication, 83*(2), 151–171. https://doi.org/10.1080/10570314.2018.1502892

Van Gilder, B. J. (2019b). Sexual orientation stigmatization and identity work for gays, lesbians, and bisexuals in the U.S. military. *Journal of Homosexuality, 66*(14), 1949–1973. https://doi.org/10.1080/00918369.2018.1522812

West, I. N. (2018). Queer perspectives in communication studies. In J. Nussbaum (Ed.), *Oxford encyclopedia of communication* (pp. 1–29). Oxford University Press. http://doi.org/10.1093/acrefore/9780190228613.013.81

Westcott, K., & Sawyer, R. (2007). Silent sacrifices: The impact of "Don't Ask, Don't Tell" on lesbian and gay military families. *Duke Journal of Gender Law & Policy, 14,* 1121–1139.

Wilson, S. R., Hintz, E. A., MacDermid Wadsworth, S. M., Topp, D. B., Southwell, K. H., & Spoont, M. (2021). Female U.S. military veterans' (non)disclosure of mental health issues with family and friends:

Privacy rules and boundary management. *Health Communication, 36*(4), 412–423. http://doi.org/10.1080/10410236.2019.1693128

Wilson, S. R., & Knobloch, L. K. (2016). Military families and communication. In J. F. Nussbaum (Ed.), *Oxford research encyclopedia of communication* (pp. 1–19). Oxford University Press. http://doi.org/10.1093/acrefore/9780190228613.013.182

Wiskoff, M. F., & Sammons, M. T. (2017). Applying military psychology: Looking back, looking ahead. In S. V. Bowles & P. T. Bartone (Eds.), *Handbook of military psychology* (pp. 551–563). Springer. https://doi.org/10.1007/978-3-319-66192-6_20

Wool, Z. H. (2015). Critical military studies, queer theory, and the possibilities of critique: The case of suicide and family caregiving in the US military. *Critical Military Studies, 1*(1), 23–37. https://doi.org/10.1080/23337486.2014.964600

Wool, Z. H. (2021). Disability, straight time, and the American dream: Disabled US veterans and the desire for heteronormative futures. *American Ethnologist, 48*(3), 288–300. https://doi.org/10.1111/amet.13027

Erin Sahlstein Parcell and Danielle C. Romo

SAME-SEX COUPLE RELATIONSHIP MAINTENANCE

LGBTQ+ ROMANTIC RELATIONSHIP RESEARCH

LGBTQ+ romantic relationships have been recognized as understudied by researchers across academic disciplines (Afifi & Cornejo, 2020; Ossana, 2000). LGBTQ+ (lesbian, gay, bisexual, transgender, and queer+) is an umbrella term that describes individuals who self-identify as members of the sexual minority community. Within this community, the term *same-sex couple* refers to LGBTQ+ romantic relationships in which both partners identify as cisgender male or cisgender female. To date, the existing research on LGBTQ+ romantic relationships primarily has focused on same-sex couples, and investigation of other types of LGBTQ+ romantic relationships (e.g., transgender partners, gender-nonconforming partners) remains lacking. In a 2020 analysis of interpersonal communication social science studies in eight communication journals spanning six years (2013–2018), Afifi and Cornejo (2020, p. 249) found that an

> abject failure to even report sexual orientation (93% of participants in this sample [71,000 across the studies] did not include sexual orientation identities), let alone examine the experiences of the LGBTQ population, is highly problematic for what we can claim to know about interpersonal communication processes.

The same-sex couple relationship maintenance research that does exist explores the communication and relational behaviors that partners enact to sustain and grow their intimate romantic partnerships, and is the focus here. But first, this article provides an overview of the foundations of relationship maintenance research in the communication studies discipline.

COMMUNICATION AND RELATIONSHIP MAINTENANCE

In the early 1990s, after much scholarly attention on how romantic relationships are developed and dissolve, relational communication researchers turned their attention to the communicative behaviors and strategies that partners use to maintain their romantic relationships (e.g., Baxter & Dindia, 1990; Canary & Stafford, 1992; Dainton & Stafford, 1993; Dindia & Baxter, 1987; Stafford & Canary, 1991). Relationship maintenance behaviors (RMBs) are verbal/nonverbal expressions and relationship-oriented actions that sustain a relationship (Canary & Stafford, 1992; Dindia, 2000) and desired positive relationship outcomes such as commitment and satisfaction (Stafford & Canary, 1991, p. 220). Based in social exchange theory (Homans, 1950; Stafford & Canary, 1991, p. 219) and equity theory (Walster & Walster, 1975), RMB scholars proposed that relationship partners will engage in maintenance behaviors as long as relationship investments are perceived to be equitable and fulfilling to partners (Canary & Stafford, 1992; Stafford & Canary, 2006). Feelings of being over-benefited (receiving more benefits than one's partner) or under-benefited (receiving fewer) are associated with a decreased desire to maintain the relationship (Stafford & Canary, 2006). As partners invest in the relationship through engagement in communicative maintenance behaviors, as long as some degree of equity exists, partners are likely to engage in maintenance and avoid relationship termination (Rusbult et al., 1994).

Early on, using open-ended surveys from different-sex dating and married couples, Stafford and Canary's (1991) research resulted in development of a typology of five maintenance behaviors that partners reported enacting to maintain their relationships: (1) *assurances* are verbal expressions and behaviors that reaffirm commitment to the relationship; (2) *openness* refers to willingness to self-disclose personal information about one's goals, needs, and desires, and discussion of the nature of the relationship; (3) *positivity* involves interacting with a partner in an upbeat and cheerful way; (4) *social networks* involve interacting with family, friends, and mutual affiliations; and (5) *shared tasks* refer to division of common relational responsibilities (e.g., household chores, paying bills, picking up the kids, etc.).

Canary and Stafford (1992) then developed their Relational Maintenance Strategies Measure (RMSM) from the maintenance literature and romantic partner open-ended reports of communicative maintenance behaviors to assess maintenance in romantic relationships. Dainton and Stafford (1993) also established that maintenance behaviors can be enacted both routinely (i.e., through everyday behaviors) and strategically (e.g., an anniversary party). Later, through factor analysis, Stafford et al. (2000) revised and expanded the RMSM to seven maintenance behaviors and developed the RMSM-R measure of the five original maintenance behaviors with revised subscales and two new RMBs and subscales: (1) *advice*—providing advice or teaching to one's partner based in prior experience; and (2) *conflict management*—engaging in listening, cooperation, and empathetic behaviors during disagreements. Stafford (2011) also proposed a third version of the RMSM with her Relational Maintenance Behavior Measure (RMBM). A 2012 meta-analysis of 35 relationship maintenance studies ($N = 12{,}273$) found that all three versions, the RMSM, RMSM-R, and RMBM, were equally valid and reliable, and use is dependent on the range of maintenance behaviors that researchers seek to measure (see Olgosky & Bowers, 2012). Since the early 1990s, the original RMSM has been widely used in relational maintenance research on different-sex couples to explore influences on relationship maintenance, such as marital duration, relational quality, self and partner perceptions, and jealousy (Canary & Stafford, 1992; Guerrero & Afifi, 1998; Weigel & Ballard-Reisch, 1999a, 1999b). Since 2000, studies have employed the RMSM-R to assess the expanded seven maintenance behaviors (assurance, openness, conflict management, shared tasks, positivity, shared networks, and advice).

MAINTENANCE AND POSITIVE RELATIONSHIP FUNCTIONING

Various positive relationship characteristics (i.e., relational quality outcomes) have been examined in relationship maintenance studies. Relational outcomes are desirable characteristics that indicate positive relational functioning and have been found to be associated with RMBs. Several of the most commonly studied relationship outcomes are relational satisfaction, relational commitment, partner liking, and control mutuality (see Olgosky & Bowers, 2012, for a meta-analysis review). Relationship researchers have long been interested in the degree to which individuals feel committed to and satisfied with their romantic partners. Commitment and satisfaction have been considered the two most important indicators of positive relational functioning, and have been studied using a social exchange theoretical framework, including research informed by the investment model (Rusbult, 1983) and interdependence theory (Kelley & Thibault, 1978). In the 2010s, scholars have begun to explore relational closeness as a deeper level indicator of relationship intimacy than mere partner liking in assessing relationship functioning (Dibble et al., 2012). Another frequently considered relational characteristic is control mutuality, which is defined as partner agreement about relational decision-making around relationship goals and behavioral norms (Stafford & Canary, 1991, p. 224). The meta-analysis by Olgosky and Bowers (2012) found the five original RMBs (assurances, openness, positivity, social networks, and sharing tasks) were positively correlated with satisfaction, commitment, and control mutuality across 25 years of research, and that relational assurances (i.e., expressions of partners' desire to be in the relationship) were the primary predictor of positive relationship functioning (Olgosky & Bowers, 2012; Stafford et al., 2000).

In addition to a social exchange approach, Baxter and colleagues (Baxter, 1994; Baxter & Montgomery, 1996) proposed a dialectic perspective of relationship maintenance that has received less scholarly attention. Relational dialectics are "tensions" between polar opposites that are central and necessary within relationships. The three primary relational dialectics that are present both within and from outside relationships are: connection–autonomy, predictability–novelty, and openness–closedness. First, within relationships, the dialectic of connection–autonomy is a tension individuals feel to bond with a partner while also maintaining their own sense of identity. Outside the relationship, this connection–autonomy dialectic manifests as a conflicting pull to connect with social networks and also to build intimacy within the relationship. The second dialectic of predictability–novelty comes from a need for stability within the relationship, and yet also to avoid complacency that leads to boredom. Externally to the relationship, a predictability–novelty tension is felt when couples enact cultural norms, but also maintain a sense of uniqueness and relational identity. Third, openness–closedness manifests as a dialectic within relationships through the conflicting need for self-disclosure and the protective need to avoid being hurt by revealing one's self. Outside the relationship, openness–closedness involves managing couple privacy, while also connecting with social networks. Baxter and colleagues' (Baxter, 1994; Baxter & Montgomery, 1996) dialectic perspective has been applied in romantic relationship research to increase understanding of macro-relational tensions that impact relationship maintenance. With the foundations of relationship maintenance research in mind, this article turns next to understanding same-sex couple relationship maintenance.

SAME-SEX COUPLE MINORITY STRESS

Minority stress theory (Meyer, 1995, 2003) has become the predominant macro-societal frame applied by social science researchers to understand sexual minority romantic relationships that are established and maintained in cultures dominated by heterosexism, such as the United States. Minority stress theory posits that perceived stigma (e.g., fear of loss of employment or housing) and received stigma, prejudice, or discrimination (e.g., rejection by family of origin or coworkers; verbal or physical assault by strangers) overshadows and deeply impacts the lives of sexual minorities, resulting in chronic minority stress (Otis et al., 2006; Rostosky et al., 2016). Minority stress "is the chronic psychological stress that results from belonging to a stigmatized social category" (Rostosky & Riggle, 2017, p. 29), and chronic feelings of stigma negatively affect sexual minority relationship quality (Doyle & Molix, 2014).

Same-sex couples experience social stigma and discrimination throughout their lives (Cao et al., 2017). McWhirter and Mattison (1982) explained four forms of stigma that affect same-sex relationships: (1) ignorance, which is a lack of knowledge of LGBTQ+ lifestyles; (2) homophobia, which is a persistent fear of LGBTQ+ individuals based in ignorance; (3) prejudice, which is forming negative attitudes toward LGBTQ+ people as a group; and (4) oppression, legal and social actions that deny equal rights to LGBTQ+ individuals and their relationships. Stigma can be particularly damaging when it is internalized by LGBTQ+ people (Rostosky et al., 2016). Internalized homophobia can result in emotional effects that impact both individual and relational well-being, such as low self-esteem, psychological cognitive dissonance, social isolation, identity concealment, and discomfort in one's own romantic relationships (LeBlanc et al., 2015; Otis et al., 2006).

Multiple forms of stigma may create barriers to establishing and maintaining long-term same-sex relationships. Same-sex marriage has been legalized in 30 countries (Pew Research Center, 2019), and became available across the 50 U.S. states in 2015 (*Obergefell v. Hodges*, 2015). Same-sex couple validation, however, is still lacking from many who do not perceive same-sex marriages as equal in status to different-sex marriages (Perry, 2015; Perry et al., 2016; Rostosky et al., 2016), and same-sex marriage remains illegal in 75 sovereign nations (punishable by death in eight) (Pew Research Center, 2019). As a result, same-sex couples may have to overly rely on relational partners for social support in maintaining their romantic relationships (Haas, 2002; Haas & Lannutti, 2019). Moreover, LGBTQ+ individuals may refrain from disclosing their sexual orientation and romantic relationships to others for fear of rejection, prejudice, and discrimination (Haas, 2019). A lack of openness about one's sexual orientation and same-sex relationship can bring additional minority stress into same-sex couples (Patterson & Schwartz, 1994; Riggle & Rostosky, 2017). Thus, the macro-social context of discrimination and minority stress is foundational to understanding how same-sex couples must work to establish and maintain their romantic relationships. Understanding how communication and interaction between partners contributes to relationship maintenance in the face of chronic minority stress advances knowledge of sexual minority relationship functioning and resilience. In the following sections, foundational research from other disciplines on same-sex couple relational dynamics will be reviewed, and then studies on same-sex couple relationship maintenance in the communication discipline up to 2021 in more detail.

SAME-SEX COUPLE RELATIONAL DYNAMICS

Past same-sex couple relationship dynamics studies from other disciplines have found trends indicating relational norms of role equality and role flexibility, as well as equity in sharing relational tasks related to relationship maintenance (Kurdek, 2003, 2006). Overwhelmingly, there has been no evidence in the literature to support assumptions that same-sex couples model themselves after different-sex relationships (i.e., that one partner assumes a "masculine role" and the other a "feminine role") (Kurdek, 1993; Kurdek & Schmitt, 1986; Peplau & Fingerhut, 2007). In early research, Tuller (1978) found in his study that "all of the couples claimed that they did not have any butch-femme roles in their relationships, and that, in fact, they shared household tasks and definitely did not sexually imitate conventional heterosexual roles" (p. 340). Dailey (1979) and Peplau (1982) also found no evidence of cross-gender endorsement or conforming to male and female traditional sex roles. Instead, masculine and feminine sex roles have been found to be blended in same-sex relationships toward more androgyny and flexible relational roles (Schullo & Alperson, 1984). In one direct comparison, Kurdek (1987) found that lesbian women tended to be more instrumental (task-oriented) than heterosexual women in their sex-role orientation; whereas gay and heterosexual men were more equivalent. Gay men were more emotionally expressive than heterosexual men, but heterosexual and lesbian women were more equivalent. Also, Kurdek and Schmitt (1986) found a fairly random and equal distribution of pairings of same-sex and different-sex partners across Bem's Sex Role Inventory categories of masculine, feminine, undifferentiated, and androgynous orientations.

Kurdek and Schmitt (1986) and Jones and Cecco (1982) found that androgynous and feminine partners reported the highest levels of relationship functioning in same-sex couples. Reece and Segrist (1981) also found that more androgynous same-sex couples remained together longer than those scoring low on cooperation. Studies also indicate that gender roles (e.g., instrumental vs. expressive orientations) are likely not linked to biological sex, but rather lie on a continuum much like other personality traits (Marecek et al., 1983). In a similar vein, Schullo and Alperson (1984) proposed the need to relabel the poles of this continuum from sex-related terms (masculine/feminine) to more accurately reflect the instrumental and expressive characteristics and behaviors being enacted regardless of gender or sexual orientation.

Furthermore, most same-sex couples are in dual-earner relationships that influence greater power expectations of equality and reciprocity (Kurdek, 2006; Peplau & Fingerhut, 2007). Because same-sex relationships do not adhere to traditional sex roles, issues surrounding "power imbalances manifested in unequal influence in decision making, unfair division of household labor, or biased allotment of rights, resources, and privileges" are most often negotiated in same-sex couples (Huston & Schwartz, 1995, p. 108). Instead, roles and relational duties are often assigned based on: (1) individual interest; (2) personal skill; and (3) time or scheduling constraints (Kurdek, 1993, 2006). Same-sex couples also have expressed equity in power dynamics as a relational ideal (Reilly & Lynch, 1990, also see Patterson, 2013, for a review). The means of establishing equity, however, may differ slightly in cisgender male–male and cisgender female–female couples. For example, female same-sex couples have been found to rely more on equal sharing of power (Peplau & Fingerhut, 2007); yet differences across same-sex couples indicate that partners who earn more, have more education, and spend more time working outside the home may take on more dominance in the relationship (Sutphin, 2010). Female same-sex couples also have described more focus on emotional closeness, interdependence, and relational equity (Lynch & Reilly, 1985–1986; Patterson et al., 2013). Regarding household tasks, female same-sex couples tend more often to share in tasks together, whereas male same-sex partners have been found to divide up and specialize in specific relational tasks (Kurdek, 2006). Overall, research finds that same-sex couples work to communicate and negotiate some type of balance in relational contribution (Sutphin, 2010).

Finally, regarding relationship quality, in examining 10 years of his same-sex couple data, Kurdek (2003) found that female same-sex couples reported higher levels of relationship quality than male couples. Kurdek (2006) posited this may likely be due to females being socialized to be more relationship-oriented and males to be more competitive. And Patterson et al. (2013) found female couples to have fluid psychological gender role identities. These types of gender identity-related findings may indicate subtle differences due to gendered socialization in the maintenance of same-sex romantic relationships.

RMBS IN SAME-SEX COUPLES

While the vast majority of communication relationship maintenance research has focused on different-sex married and dating relationships, several early small-sample qualitative studies have explored maintenance behaviors in same-sex couples (Haas & Stafford, 1998, 2005). Relational communication scholars also have qualitatively explored obstacles, reasons, and meanings of marriage in same-sex relationships (Haas & Whitton, 2015; Lannutti, 2005, 2006, 2007, 2011, 2014). Haas and Stafford (1998) were among the first communication scholars to qualitatively explore RMBs in same-sex couples through open-ended surveys ($N = 30$) and found similar maintenance behaviors (assurances, openness, shared tasks, positivity, and shared networks) were reported as in different-sex couples. This was further supported in a follow-up study where Haas and Stafford (2005) performed a direct matched sample comparison between the 30 same-sex relational partners and 30 different-sex married partners. Participants were matched on age, sex, education level, and length of relationship within 2 months. Open-ended responses describing maintenance strategies and behaviors were compared for similarity, differences, and frequency reported. Results primarily indicated similar maintenance behaviors reported across the same-sex and different-sex relationships, which provides further evidence for the use of common RMBs across couple type. Both couple types mentioned shared tasks most frequently, and yet several differences did emerge in the frequency with which maintenance behaviors were mentioned; with same-sex partners reporting greater use of relational assurances. Haas and Stafford (2005) suggested more mention of reassuring commitment to one's partner was perhaps due to the lack of legal marriage availability to same-sex couples at the time.

Also, several same-sex couple specific maintenance behaviors have emerged as strategies in maintaining sexual minority relationships: (1) being "Out as a Couple" to social networks (i.e., revealing one's sexual orientation and same-sex relationship) (Haas, 2002; Haas & Stafford, 1998); and (2) seeking out LGBTQ+ supportive environments (e.g., LGBTQ+ bars, Pride events, LGBTQ+-friendly B&Bs, etc.). Early indications suggested that managing sexual minority identity and same-sex relationship disclosures may be important aspects of same-sex couple relationship maintenance (Haas, 2003).

In another qualitative study, Haas (1999) interviewed both partners in 20 male same-sex couples (N = 40) where one or both were HIV positive. The study resulted in a grounded theory of communicative normalization of illness to explain the process of maintaining same-sex relationships that are dealing with chronic illness. More specifically, normalization of illness was accomplished in these couples through managing communication around two relational dialectics: (1) HIV communication engagement/avoidance; and (2) negotiating partner autonomy/involvement in health-related issues. Managing HIV communication involves negotiating and balancing HIV-related discussions to reduce overburden from focusing too much on the illness in day-to-day communication, while also not avoiding important health issues. In these couples, there was a drive to normalize illness; frequently using a combination of "balance" and "alternation" dialectic management strategies through HIV-related openness/closedness (Baxter & Montgomery, 1996). Alternation was described more often so that couples could focus on HIV as health issues arose, but at other times, downplay its relational impact to avoid burnout. In general, couples managed their communication along a continuum of HIV engagement/avoidance.

Related, partners described communicatively managing the level of the HIV-negative partner's involvement in monitoring the health of their HIV-positive partner. It was important for HIV-positive partners to maintain a sense of autonomy, but still feel that their HIV-negative partner was concerned about their health. Partner health involvement also was on a continuum from quite uninvolved (e.g., not knowing medications prescribed or schedules) to very involved (e.g., helping to keep track of medication adherence). However, the drive for relational normalization meant that HIV-related issues remained the HIV-positive partner's primary domain. Overall, Haas (1999) found that little partner involvement indicated disinterest and over-involvement indicated distrust of the partner's self-care abilities. Communicative management of these HIV-related relational dialectic tensions were described as central to relationship maintenance in these male same-sex couples. In addition to dialectic tensions, Haas (1999) found initial qualitative evidence of Stafford and Canary's (1991) five maintenance behaviors (assurances, openness, positivity, shared networks, and shared tasks) being reported in the male same-sex couples. Also, role equity was described as being important and established through partner specialization of tasks based on partner skill. Couples also rejected establishment of caregiver/receiver relational roles that helped to establish role equity (Haas, 1999).

In 2009, Olgosky was one of the first to quantitatively assess RMBs in same-sex couples by employing a daily maintenance activity report (N = 196). He developed a new measure consisting of 15 RMSM scale items focusing on daily maintenance behaviors (e.g., "My partner asks how my day has gone") (Stafford & Canary, 1991) and excluded RMSM items that assess periodic maintenance behaviors (e.g., "My partner likes to have periodic talks about our relationship"). Fourteen additional daily behavior items were created (e.g., "My partner did 'little things' to make my life better"). Participants answered dichotomously for each item (0 = no, 1 = yes). Results indicated longer-lasting, more committed same-sex couples reported more daily maintenance (Olgosky, 2009), and in a follow-up analysis of the same data, Olgosky and Gray (2016) found that couples lower in conflict employed more daily maintenance behaviors.

Haas and Lannutti (2021) have undertaken a large national survey of RMBs associated with positive relational functioning and resilience in LGBTQ+ romantic relationships ($N = 1,303$; mean length of relationship = 9.6 years). Given that most of the research on same-sex couples in the field of communication has been small-sample qualitative studies, this is the first large-scale 5-year survey project in the discipline to recruit representation from all 50 U.S. states and DC. RMB results indicate that relational assurances were the primary predictor of commitment, satisfaction, control mutuality, closeness, and relational resilience in same-sex couples. This finding compares with previous different-sex couple maintenance research (e.g., Stafford et al., 2000), adding further evidence that relational assurances (i.e., communicating messages of love, affection, and a desire to continue in the relationship) are central to romantic relationship maintenance. In addition, concealment of a sexual minority identity and same-sex relationship status were found to be negatively associated with relationship commitment and satisfaction, indicating that not "being out" can negatively impact a couple's relationship maintenance. Importantly, the study is the first to find that six of the seven RMSM-R RMBs (assurances, openness, positivity, conflict management, advice, and shared networks) predicted couple resilience (i.e., working together as team in the face of stressful situations) in these same-sex couple relationships. The research on relational maintenance behaviors in same-sex couples has encouraged other maintenance research exploring the impact of social support, same-sex marriage, and sexual (non)monogamy in maintaining same-sex relationships and will be addressed next.

MAINTENANCE AND SAME-SEX RELATIONSHIP SOCIAL SUPPORT

A few studies also have highlighted an association of social support with relationship maintenance. For example, Haas (2002) found that social stigma related to both HIV and homosexuality were relational stressors that impeded external sources of social support (e.g., family of origin) and negatively impacted maintenance in same-sex relationships. Importantly, male same-sex couples reported that when HIV-related social support was received from family, friends, and others, it functioned both as illness-related support and relationship maintenance support (Haas, 2002). These qualitative findings highlight a need for social validation and social support as important factors in same-sex couple relationship maintenance.

Haas and Lannutti (2019) quantitatively measured minority stress and social support in same-sex couples in the maintenance of their relationships, predicting relationship quality outcomes (commitment, satisfaction, closeness, and relational resilience). They found relational partner social support to be the primary predictor of all four positive relational indicators of relational quality. Another important finding was that partner, friend, and family social support all contributed to couple resilience, as well the influence of negative minority experiences that can increase bonding to help build relational resilience. The fact that family support was associated with couple resilience may indicate a progressive societal shift as more same-sex couples legally marry (50% of this sample) and become more accepted by family of origin and others. In this study, depression also emerged as a secondary negative predictor of commitment, satisfaction, and relational resilience. On a positive note, the negative impact of depression was lessened (i.e., mediated) by partner social support. Overall, findings underscored the importance of relational partner social support in contributing to positive relationship maintenance.

MAINTENANCE AND SAME-SEX MARRIAGE

In addition, in the United States since the late 1990s, civil unions and legal marriage progressively became available to same-sex couples in 36 U.S. states and later in all 50 states (see *Obergefell v. Hodges*, 2015). Research has found legal marriage to have positive benefits for same-sex couples related to relationship maintenance, such as increased legal protections, increased social network support, and decreased psychological distress, and it also may create a greater sense of relational meaning, greater relational satisfaction, increased security in the relationship, and greater commitment to one's partner (Badgett, 2009, Haas & Whitton, 2015; Lannutti, 2014, Ogolsky et al., 2019; Riggle et al., 2010). Several studies have found that married same-sex couples report increased feelings of relational commitment and couple validation from social networks (e.g., family of origin) (Haas & Whitton, 2015; Ogolsky et al., 2019; Rostosky et al., 2016). Yet, some married same-sex couples have still reported increased negativity and rejection from their social networks as a result of getting married (Lannutti, 2007, 2014, and many religious conservatives remain opposed to same-sex relationships and same-sex marriage (Perry, 2015; Perry & Whitehead, 2016). Same-sex couples that do not marry also may experience pressure from their networks to marry, and may fear lack of relationship legitimacy if they do not (Lannutti, 2018).

Research remains sparse on the impact of marriage on maintenance in same-sex relationships. However, in one of the first examinations of RMBs in married and unmarried same-sex couples, Haas and Lannutti (2021) found only subtle differences in the association of RMBs with the positive relational outcomes of commitment and satisfaction. More specifically, assurances were found to be the primary predictor of relational commitment and satisfaction in both couple types, but married partners were statistically less likely to use assurances, and more likely to give advice in predicting commitment and satisfaction compared to unmarried partners. Overall, the study findings underscore the importance of an association of assurances with positive relational outcomes, regardless of marital status. Also, married partners were found to rely more on partner advice as a familial unit, whereas unmarried partners focused on keeping the relationship positive and connected to social networks. These patterns seem to indicate a positive impact of marriage on relational stability and bonding in same-sex relationships, yet requires further investigation.

MAINTENANCE AND (NON)MONOGAMY IN SAME-SEX COUPLES

Sexual monogamy has long been held up as the model for different-sex romantic relationships by church and state. Despite this relational ideal, estimates of marital infidelity in heterosexual relationships range between 26% and 70% for women, and 33% and 75% for men (Buss, 1994; Shackelford & Buss, 1997). Similar to different-sex relationships, research has found that many same-sex couples desire monogamy as a relational model (Bell & Weinberg, 1978; Berger, 1990; Blumstein & Schwartz, 1983; Haas & Lannutti, 2020; Mendola, 1980; Peplau, 1991). Same-sex couples also report fairly accurate perceptions of partner similarity, complementarity, and positive illusions about sexual satisfaction that contribute to the maintenance of the relationship (De Jong & Reis, 2015). Some monogamous same-sex couples are influenced by a heterosexual relationship model, some by religious beliefs, others may assume monogamy as a model but do not discuss it, and still others may negotiate a different sexual agreement in their relationship (Haas & Lannutti, 2020).

During the early AIDS epidemic, Berger (1990) and Carl (1986) found that male same-sex couple monogamy increased due to fear of HIV infection. Growing evidence, however, suggests an increase in consensual nonmonogamy (CNM) in male same-sex relationships. And nonmonogamy has been found to be more prevalent in cisgender male same-sex couples than cisgender female same-sex relationships (Haupert et al., 2017). Across qualitative studies, male same-sex partners have reported nonmonogamy at rates in the range of 30%–50%, and in national health surveys and U.S. Census data of adult romantic relationships in the range of 31%–37% (Haupert et al., 2017; Levine et al., 2018). In one qualitative study, Stults (2019) found that men in CNM relationships often view sexual activity outside their primary relationship as recreational, yet protect emotional commitment to their primary partner in monogamish (allowing outside sex with both partners present) and open relationships (allowing outside sex without both partners present). Polyamorous relationships are usually open and also allow an emotional connection with outside sexual partners (Bonello, 2009). Qualitative research suggests that male same-sex couples who negotiate CNM agreements can have increased levels of trust and relational satisfaction, and that such agreements reduce feelings of betrayal associated with infidelity (Lee, 1991; Stults, 2019). Limited studies also suggest that younger partners and partners who make less income may be less committed to following the established rules of a CNM agreement (Perry et al., 2016), but this needs further investigation. Overall, research suggests that "when relational expectations for sexual behavior are *shared* by partners, relationship quality and satisfaction are fairly equivalent across sexually-open and sexually-exclusive couples" (Haas, 2003, p. 216).

In 2020s research, Haas and Lannutti (2020) explored the prevalence of (non)monogamy in two years of their large national sample data ($N = 1,950$), and also were the first to examine LGBTQ+ romantic relationships in which one or both partners identify as non-cisgender. They found that a majority (60%–77%) of cisgender and non-cisgender LGBTQ+ partners reported being in a monogamous relationship. Cisgender female partners were most likely to describe their same-sex relationship as monogamous (77%), which aligns with previous research (Levine et al., 2018). Findings also indicated that non-cisgender relationships were similar to cisgender male same-sex relationships in reporting CNM agreements at 37% and 40%, respectively. It is possible that non-cisgender flexibility in gender identity extends to flexibility in sexual exclusivity in some LGBTQ+ romantic relationships. That a majority of the sample reported communicating to establish a monogamy agreement underscores the deeply enculturated ideal of monogamy as a preferred relational model, even in sexual minority relationships.

Additionally, this study is the first to explore (non)monogamy agreements in legally married and unmarried LGBTQ+ relationships. Results indicate that (non)monogamy agreements did not differ by marital status. The majority (72%) of married and unmarried partners reported communicating a monogamy agreement in their relationship. Importantly, though, over a quarter (27%) of the married LGBTQ+ spouses reported some type of nonmonogamy agreement that was similar to the unmarried relationships (27%). These findings support previous qualitative evidence that LGBTQ+ romantic partners may hold more pliable and varied conceptions of marriage than a purely mononormative model (Green et al., 2016).

Furthermore, regarding (non)monogamy and positive relational functioning, Haas and Lannutti's (2020) data offer a nuanced view of relational outcomes by examining four indicators of relational quality in LGBTQ+ relationships related to sexual agreements: relational commitment, relational satisfaction, closeness, and sexual satisfaction. Results indicated significant differences in relationship quality outcomes in those couples who had agreed to be monogamous and those who had not. Specifically, those who communicated a monogamy agreement reported significantly higher relational satisfaction, closeness, and sexual satisfaction with one's partner than did those who had not. However, there was no significant difference in relationship commitment between monogamous and nonmonogamous couples. These results suggest that, regardless of sexual agreement, LGBTQ+ relational partners can be equally committed to the relationship, and yet specific relational quality indicators may differ.

Finally, Haas and Lannutti (2020) also found when comparing relational quality outcomes between married and unmarried LGBTQ+ relationships from their 2 years of data, married participants reported statistically significantly higher relationship commitment, relational satisfaction, and closeness. Unmarried couples had significantly higher sexual satisfaction than married couples, which is in line with evidence that sexual satisfaction may decrease over time in marriages (McNulty & Windam, 2013). These results suggest that married LGBTQ+ spouses may have higher relationship quality and individual well-being compared to unmarried LGBTQ+ partners and individuals. Because there are so few studies on the influence of legal marriage on relational quality, quality of life, and well-being in LGBTQ+ romantic relationships (for an exception see Ogolsky et al., 2019), more research is required.

CONCLUSION

Research on communication and behaviors that same-sex couples use to maintain their relationships in the face of chronic minority stress continues to increase understanding of relational communication, in general, and importantly, in sexual minority relationships specifically. LGBTQ+ relationships remain understudied in communication studies (Afifi & Cornejo, 2020). This is partly due to academia being heterodominant, but also due to the challenge of accessing and recruiting study participants from community-based minority populations, and then subgroups within (i.e., committed couples). These factors contribute to the complexity of studying same-sex couple relationship maintenance. The existing research has found that being in a same-sex relationship strengthens partners' positive LGBTQ+ identity, increases self-concept over those not in a relationship, helps increase a belief in life control, and lowers anxiety and depression (Riggle & Rostosky, 2017). These types of relationship benefits underscore the need for further research to advance understanding of positive relationship functioning in the maintenance of sexual minority relationships.

Much remains to be learned about the maintenance of LGBTQ+ romantic relationships. It is important for researchers to continue to expand the diversity and inclusion of minority populations in communication studies. Early research from other disciplines illuminated relational dynamics, and studies have established evidence of types of RMBs enacted in same-sex couple relationships. Relational assurances have emerged as the primary maintenance predictor of positive relational functioning and resilience in same-sex couples, along with the use of other RMBs. Also, evidence of a positive impact of partner social support, multiple types of social support in resilience, benefits of same-sex marriage, and communicating to negotiate sexual agreements in LGBTQ+ relationships continue to emerge as important factors related to maintenance. More future research on same-sex couple relationship maintenance is needed to understand the evolving nature of maintenance and growth in LGBTQ+ romantic relationships and extend the communication studies literature.

LINKS TO DIGITAL RESOURCES

Pew Research Center: 5 Facts about Same-Sex Marriage, https://www.pewresearch.org/fact-tank/2019/06/24/same-sex-marriage/

UCLA Williams Institute: Same-Sex Couple US Data and Demographics, https://williamsinstitute.law.ucla.edu/visualization/lgbt-stats/?topic=SS#density

US Census Bureau: Same-Sex Couples Data, https://www.census.gov/topics/families/same-sex-couples/data.html

FURTHER READING

Haas, S. M., & Lannutti, P. J. (2019). The impact of minority stress and social support on positive relationship functioning in same-sex relationships. *Health Communication, 36*(3), 315–323. https://doi.org/10.1080/10410236.2019.1687130

Haas, S. M., & Lannutti, P. J. (2020). The influence of marriage and (non)monogamy agreements on relationship quality in LGBTQ+ relationships. Paper presented at the bi-annual national Kentucky Conference on Health Communication (KCHC) sponsored by the University of Kentucky, Lexington, KY, and partially funded by the National Institutes of Health National Cancer Institute and the Office of Behavioral and Social Sciences Research. In A. Hoy (Ed.), *The social science of same-sex marriage: LGBTQ people and their relationships in the era of marriage equality*. Routledge.

Haas, S. M., & Lannutti, P. J. (2021). Relationship maintenance behaviors, resilience, and relational quality in romantic relationships of LGBTQ+ people. *Couple & Family Psychology: Research & Practice*. Special volume: Risk and resilience in gender and sexual relationships. American Psychological Association Online First. https://doi.org/10.1037/cfp0000186

Haas, S. M., & Whitton, S. (2015). The significance of living together and importance of marriage in same-sex couples. *Journal of Homosexuality, 62*(9), 1241–1263. https://doi.org/10.1080/00918369.2015.1037137

Lannutti, P. J. (2014). *Experiencing same-sex marriage: Individuals, couples, and social networks*. Peter Lang.

Olgosky, B. G., & Bowers, J. R. (2012). A meta-analytic review of relationship maintenance and its correlates. *Journal of Social and Personal Relationships, 30*, 343–367. https://doi.org/10.1177/0265407512463338

Rostosky, S. S., & Riggle, E. D. B. (2017). Same-sex relationships and minority stress. *Current Opinion in Psychology, 13*, 29–38. https://doi.org/10.1016/j.copsyc.2016.04.011

REFERENCES

Afifi, W. A., & Cornejo, M. (2020). #CommSOWEIRD: The question of sample representativeness in interpersonal communication research. In M. Doerfel & J. Gibbs (Eds.), *Organizing inclusion: Moving diversity from demographics to communication processes* (pp. 238–259). Routledge.

Badgett, M. V. L. (2009). *When gay people get married: What happens when societies legalize same-sex marriage*. New York University Press.

Baxter, L. A. (1994). A dialogic approach to relationship maintenance. In D. J. Canary & L. Stafford (Eds.), *Communication and relationship maintenance* (pp. 233–254). Academic Press.

Baxter, L. A., & Dindia, K. (1990). Marital partners' perceptions of marital maintenance strategies. *Journal of Social and Personal Relationships, 7*, 187–208.

Baxter, L. A., & Montgomery, B. M. (1996). *Relating: Dialogues and dialectics*. Guilford Press.

Bell, A. P., & Weinberg, M. S. (1978). *Homosexualities: A study of diversity among men and women*. Simon & Schuster.

Berger, R. M. (1990). Men together: Understanding the gay couple. *Journal of Homosexuality, 19*, 31–49.

Blumstein, P., & Schwartz, P. (1983). *American couples*. William Morrow.

Bonello, K. (2009). Gay monogamy and extra-dyadic sex: A critical review of the theoretical and empirical literature. *Counselling Psychology Review, 24*(3–4), 51–65.

Buss, D. M. (1994). *The evolution of desire*. Basic Books.

Canary, D. J., & Stafford, L. (1992). Relational maintenance strategies and equity in marriage. *Communication Monographs, 59*, 243–267.

Cao, H., Zhou, N., Fine, M., Liang, Y., Li, J., & Mills-Koonce, W. R. (2017). Sexual minority stress and same-sex relationship well-being: A meta-analysis of research prior to the U.S. nationwide legalization of same-sex marriage. *Journal of Marriage and Family, 79*, 1258–1277. https://doi.org/10.1111/jomf.12415

Carl, D. (1986). Acquired immune deficiency syndrome: A preliminary examination of the effects on gay couples and coupling. *Journal of Marital and Family Therapy, 12*(3), 241–247. http://dx.doi.org.uc.idm.oclc.org/10.1111/j.1752-0606.1986.tb00650.x

Dailey, D. M. (1979). Adjustment of heterosexual and homosexual couples in pairing relationships: An exploratory study. *Journal of Sex Research, 15*, 143–157.

Dainton, M., & Stafford, L. (1993). Routine maintenance behaviors: A comparison of relationship type, partner similarity, and sex differences. *Journal of Social and Personal Relationships, 10*, 255–272.

De Jong, D. C., & Reis, H. T. (2015). Sexual similarity, complementarity, accuracy, and overperception in same-sex couples. *Personal Relationships, 22*, 647–665. https://doi.org/10.1111/pere.12101

Dibble, J. L., Levine, T. R., & Park, H. S. (2012). The Unidimensional Relationship Closeness Scale (URCS): Reliability and validity evidence for a new measure of relationship closeness. *Psychological Assessment, 24*(3), 565–572. https://doi.org/10.1037/a0026265

Dindia, K. (2000). Relational maintenance. In C. Hendrick & S. S. Hendrick (Eds.), *Close relationships: A sourcebook* (pp. 287–299). SAGE.

Dindia, K., & Baxter, L. A. (1987). Strategies for maintaining and repairing marital relationships. *Journal of Social and Personal Relationships, 4*, 143–158.

Doyle, D. M., & Molix, L. (2014). How does stigma spoil relationships? Evidence that perceived discrimination harms romantic relationship quality through impaired self-image. *Journal of Applied Social Psychology, 44*, 600–610. https://doi.org/10.1111/jasp.12252

Green, A. I., Valleriani, J., & Adam, B. (2016). Marital monogamy as ideal and practice: The detraditionalization thesis in contemporary marriages. *Journal of Marriage and Family, 78*(2), 416–430. https://doi.org/10.1111/jomf.12277

Guerrero, L. K., & Afifi, W. A. (1998). Communicative responses to jealousy as a function of self-esteem and relationship maintenance goals: A test of Bryson's motivation model. *Communication Reports, 11*, 111–122.

Haas, S. M. (1999). *Relationship maintenance in gay male couples coping with HIV/AIDS*. Ohio Link Electronic Theses & Dissertations Center. http://rave.ohiolink.edu/etdc/view?acc_num=osu1380547085

Haas, S. M. (2002). Social support as relationship maintenance in gay male couples coping with HIV. *Journal of Social and Personal Relationships, 19*(1), 87–111.

Haas, S. M. (2003). Relationship maintenance in same-sex couples. In D. Canary & M. Dainton (Eds.), *Maintaining relationships through communication: Relational, contextual, and cultural variations* (pp. 209–230). Lawrence Erlbaum.

Haas, S. M. (2019). Stigma, heteronormative passing with healthcare providers, and partner health involvement in male same-sex couples. In J. Theiss & K. Greene (Eds.), *Contemporary studies on relationships, health, and wellness* (pp. 30–48). Cambridge University Press.

Haas, S. M., & Lannutti, P. J. (2019). The impact of minority stress and social support on positive relationship functioning in same-sex relationships. *Health Communication, 36*(3), 315–323. https://doi.org/10.1080/10410236.2019.1687130

Haas, S. M., & Lannutti, P. J. (2020). The influence of marriage and (non)monogamy agreements on relationship quality in LGBTQ+ relationships. Paper presented at the Bi-Annual National Kentucky Conference on Health Communication (KCHC) sponsored by the University of Kentucky, Lexington, KY, and partially funded by the National Institutes of Health National Cancer Institute and the Office of Behavioral and Social Sciences Research. In A. Hoy (Ed.), *The social science of same-sex marriage: LGBTQ people and their relationships in the era of marriage equality*. Routledge.

Haas, S. M., & Lannutti, P. J. (2021). Relationship maintenance behaviors, resilience, and relational quality in romantic relationships of LGBTQ+ people. *Couple & Family Psychology: Research & Practice*. Special volume: Risk and resilience in gender and sexual relationships. American Psychological Association Online First. https://doi.org/10.1037/cfp0000186

Haas, S. M., & Stafford, L. (1998). An initial examination of maintenance behaviors in gay and lesbian relationships. *Journal of Social and Personal Relationships, 15*, 846–855.

Haas, S. M., & Stafford, L. (2005). Maintenance behaviors in same-sex and marital relationships: A matched sample comparison. *Journal of Family Communication, 5*(1), 43–60.

Haas, S. M., & Whitton, S. (2015). The significance of living together and importance of marriage in same-sex couples. *Journal of Homosexuality, 62*(9), 1241–1263. https://doi.org/10.1080/00918369.2015.1037137

Haupert, M. L., Gesselman, A. N., Moors, A. C., Fisher, H. E., & Garcia, J. R. (2017). Prevalence of experiences with consensual nonmonogamous relationships: Findings from two national samples of single Americans. *Journal of Sex & Marital Therapy, 43*(5), 424–440. https://doi.org/10.1080/0092623X.2016.1178675

Homans, G. C. (1950). *The human group*. Harcourt, Brace, & World.

Huston, M., & Schwartz, P. (1995). The relationships of lesbians and of gay men. In J. T. Wood & S. Duck (Eds.), *Under-studied relationships: Off the beaten track* (pp. 89–121). SAGE.

Jones, R. W., & Cecco, J. P. (1982). The femininity and masculinity of partners in heterosexual and homosexual relationships. *Journal of Homosexuality, 8*, 37–49.

Kelly, H. H., & Thibaut, J. W. (1978). *Interpersonal relations: A theory of interdependence*. John Wiley & Sons.

Kurdek, L. A. (1987). Sex role self-schema and psychological adjustment in coupled homosexual and heterosexual men and women. *Sex Roles, 17*, 549–562.

Kurdek, L. A. (1993). The allocation of household labor in gay, lesbian, and heterosexual married couples. *Journal of Social Issues, 49*, 127–139.

Kurdek, L. A. (2003). Differences between gay and lesbian cohabitating couples. *Journal of Social and Personal Relationships, 20*(4), 411–436.

Kurdek, L. A. (2006). Differences between partners from heterosexual, gay, and lesbian cohabiting couples. *Journal of Marriage and Family, 68*, 509–528. https://doi.org/10.1111/j.1741-3737.2006.00268.x

Kurdek, L. A., & Schmitt, J. P. (1986). Interaction of sex role self-concept with relationship quality and relationship beliefs in married, heterosexual cohabitating, gay, and lesbian couples. *Journal of Personality and Social Psychology, 51*, 365–370.

Lannutti, P. J. (2005). For better or worse: Exploring the meanings of same-sex marriage within the lesbian, gay, bisexual, and transgendered community. *Journal of Social and Personal Relationships, 22*, 5–18.

Lannutti, P. J. (2006). Attractions and obstacles while considering legally recognized same-sex marriage. *Journal of GLBT Family Studies, 4*, 244–264.

Lannutti, P. J. (2007). The influence of same-sex marriage on the understanding of same-sex relationships. *Journal of Homosexuality, 53*, 135–151.

Lannutti, P. J. (2011). Security, recognition, and misgivings: Exploring older same-sex couples' experiences of legally recognized same-sex marriage. *Journal of Social and Personal Relationships, 28*, 64–82.

Lannutti, P. J. (2014). *Experiencing same-sex marriage: Individuals, couples, and social networks.* Peter Lang.

Lannutti, P. J. (2018). Committed, unmarried same-sex couples and their social networks in the United States: Relationships and discursive strategies. *Journal of Homosexuality, 65*(9), 1232–1248. https://doi.org/10.1080/00918369.2017.1411690

Lee, J. A. (1991). Can we talk? Can we really talk? Communication as a key factor in the maturing homosexual couple. *Journal of Homosexuality, 17*(3–4), 143–168.

LeBlanc, A. J., Frost, D. M., & Wight, R. G. (2015). Minority stress and stress proliferation among same-sex and other marginalized couples. *Journal of Marriage and Family, 77*, 40–59. https://doi.org/10.1111/jomf.12160

Levine, E. C., Herbenick, D., Martinez, O., Fu, T. C. J., & Dodge, B. (2018). Open relationships, nonconsensual monogamy, and monogamy among U.S. adults: Findings from the 2012 National Survey of Sexual Health. *Archives of Sexual Behavior, 47*(5), 1439–1450. https://doi.org/10.1007/s10508-018-1178-7

Lynch, J. M., & Reilly, M. E. (1985–1986). Role relationships: Lesbian perspectives. *Journal of Homosexuality, 12*, 53–69.

Marecek, J., Finn, S. E., & Cardell, M. (1983). Gender roles in the relationships of lesbians and gay men. *Journal of Homosexuality, 8*, 45–50.

McNulty, J. K., & Widman, L. (2013). The implications of sexual narcissism for sexual and marital satisfaction. *Archives of Sexual Behavior, 42*(6), 1021–1032. https://doi.org/10.1007/s10508-012-0041-5

McWhirter, D. P., & Mattison, A. M. (1982). Psychotherapy for gay male couples. *Journal of Homosexuality, 8*, 79–91.

Mendola, M. (1980). *The Mendola report: A new look at gay couples.* Crown.

Meyer, I. H. (1995). Minority stress and mental health in gay men. *Journal of Health and Social Behavior, 36*, 38–56. http://dx.doi.org/10.2307/2137286

Meyer, I. H. (2003). Prejudice, social stress, and mental health in lesbian, gay, and bisexual populations: Conceptual issues and research evidence. *Psychological Bulletin, 129*, 674–697. http://dx.doi.org/10.1037/0033-2909.129.5.674

Obergefell v. Hodges, 14-556 U.S. (2015). Supreme Court. https://www.supremecourt.gov/opinions/14pdf/14-556_3204.pdf

Olgosky, B. G. (2009). Deconstructing the association of between relationship maintenance and commitment: Testing two competing models. *Personal Relationships, 16*, 99–115.

Olgosky, B. G., & Bowers, J. R. (2012). A meta-analytic review of relationship maintenance and its correlates. *Journal of Social and Personal Relationships, 30*, 343–367. https://doi.org/10.1177/0265407512463338

Olgosky, B. G., & Gray, C. R. (2016). Conflict, negative emotion, and reports of partners' relationship maintenance in same-sex couples. *Journal of Family Psychology, 30*, 171–180. https://doi.org/10.1037/fam0000148

Ogolsky, B. G., Monk, J. K., Rice, T. M., & Oswald, R. F. (2019). Personal well-being across the transition to marriage equality: A longitudinal analysis. *Journal of Family Psychology, 33*(4), 422–432. https://doi.org/https:/doi.org/10.1037/fam0000504

Ossana, S. M. (2000). Relationship and couples counseling. In R. M. Perez, K. A., DeBord, & K. J. Bieschke (Eds.), *Handbook of counseling and psychotherapy with lesbian, gay, and bisexual clients* (pp. 275–302). APA.

Otis, M. D., Rostosky, S. S., Riggle, E. D. B, & Harmin, R. (2006). Stress and relationship quality in same-sex couples. *Journal of Social and Personal Relationships, 23*(1), 81–99. https://doi.org/10.1177/0265407506060179

Patterson, C. J. (2013). Family lives of lesbian and gay adults. In G. W. Peterson & K. R. Bush (Eds.), *Handbook of marriage and the family* (pp. 659–681). Springer.

Patterson, D. G., & Schwartz, P. (1994). The social construction of conflict in intimate same-sex couples. In D. D. Cahn (Ed.), *Conflict in personal relationships* (pp. 3–26). Lawrence Erlbaum.

Patterson, G. E., Ward, D. B., & Brown, T. B. (2013). Relationship scripts: How young women develop and maintain same-sex relationships. *Journal of GLBT Family Studies, 9*, 179–201. https://doi.org/10.1080/1550428X.2013.765263

Peplau, L. A. (1982). Research on homosexual couples: An overview. *Journal of Homosexuality, 8*(2), 3–8.

Peplau, L. A. (1991). Lesbian and gay relationships. In J. C. Gonsiorek & J. D. Weinrich (Eds.), *Homosexuality: Research implications for public policy* (pp. 177–196). SAGE.

Peplau, L. A., & Fingerhut, A. W. (2007). The close relationships of lesbians and gay men. *Annual Review of Psychology, 58*, 405–424.

Perry, N. S., Huebner, D. M., Baucom, B. R., & Hoff, C. C. (2016). Relationship power, sociodemographics, and their relative influence on sexual agreements among gay male couples. *AIDS Behavior, 20*, 1302–1314. https://doi.org/10.1007/s10461-015-1196-6

Perry, S. L. (2015). Bible beliefs, conservative religious identity, and same-sex marriage support: Examining main and moderating effects. *Journal for the Scientific Study of Religion, 54*, 792–813.

Perry, S. L., & Whitehead, A. L. (2016). Religion and public opinion toward same-sex relations, marriage, and adoption: Does the type of practice matter? *Journal for the Scientific Study of Religion, 55*, 637–651.

Pew Research Center. (2019, October 28). *Same-sex marriage around the world* [Fact sheet]. https://www.pewforum.org/fact-sheet/gay-marriage-around-the-world/

Reece, R., & Segrist, A. E. (1981). The association of selected "masculine" sex-role variables with length of relationship in gay male couples. *Journal of Homosexuality, 7*, 33–47.

Reilly, M. E., & Lynch, J. M. (1990). Power-sharing in lesbian relationships. *Journal of Homosexuality, 19*, 1–30.

Riggle, E. D. B., Rostosky, S. S., & Horne, S. G. (2010). Psychological distress, well-being, and legal recognition in same-sex couples. *Journal of Family Psychology, 24*(1), 82–86. https://doi.org/10.1037/a0017942

Rostosky, S. S., & Riggle, E. D. B. (2017). Same-sex relationships and minority stress. *Current Opinion in Psychology, 13*, 29–38. https://doi.org/10.1016/j.copsyc.2016.04.011

Rostosky, S. S., Riggle, E. D. B., Rothblum, E. D., & Balsam, K. F. (2016). Same-sex couples' decisions and experiences of marriage in the context of minority stress: Interviews from a population-based longitudinal study. *Journal of Homosexuality, 63*, 1019–1040. https://doi.org/10.1080/00918369.2016.1191232

Rusbult, C. E. (1983). A longitudinal test of the investment model: The development (and deteriorations) of satisfaction and commitment in heterosexual involvements. *Journal of Personality and Social Psychology, 45*, 101–117.

Rusbult, C. E., Drigotas, S. M., & Verette, J. (1994). The investment model: An interdependence of commitment processes and relational maintenance phenomena. In D. J. Canary & L. Stafford (Eds.), *Communication and relational maintenance* (pp. 115–140). Academic Press.

Schullo, S. A., & Alperson, B. L. (1984). Interpersonal phenomenology as a function of sexual orientation, sex, sentiment, and trait categories in long-term dyadic relationships. *Journal of Personality and Social Psychology, 47*, 983–1002.

Shackelford, T. K., & Buss, D. M. (1997). Cues to infidelity. *Personality and Social Psychology Bulletin, 23*, 1034–1045.

Stafford, L. (2011). Measuring relationship maintenance behaviors: Critique and development of the revised relationship maintenance behaviors scale. *Journal of Social and Personal Relationships, 28*, 278–303. https://doi.org/10.1177/0265407510378125

Stafford, L., & Canary, D. J. (1991). Maintenance strategies and romantic relationship type, gender, and relational characteristics. *Journal of Social and Personal Relationships, 8*, 217–242.

Stafford, L., & Canary, D. J. (2006). Equity and interdependence as predictors of relational maintenance strategies. *Journal of Family Communication, 6*, 227–254.

Stafford, L., Dainton, M., & Haas, S. M. (2000). Measuring routine and strategic relational maintenance: Scale revision, sex versus gender roles, and the prediction of relational characteristics. *Communication Monographs, 67*(3), 306–323.

Stults, C. B. (2019). Relationship quality among young gay and bisexual men in consensual nonmonogamous relationships. *Journal of Social and Personal Relationships, 36*(10), 3037–3056. https://doi.org/10.1177/0265407518809530

Sutphin, S. T. (2010). Social exchange theory and the division of household labor in same-sex couples. *Marriage & Family Review, 46*, 191–206. https://doi.org/10.1080/01494929.2010.490102

Tuller, N. R. (1978). Couples: The hidden segment of the gay world. *Journal of Homosexuality, 3*(4), 331–343.

Walster, E., & Walster, G. W. (1975). Equity and social justice. *Journal of Social Issues, 31*(3), 21–43.

Weigel, D. J., & Ballard-Reisch, D. S. (1999a). All marriages are not maintained equally: Marital type, marital quality, and the use of maintenance behaviors. *Personal Relationships, 6*, 291–303.

Weigel, D. J., & Ballard-Reisch, D. S. (1999b). The influence of marital duration on the use of relationship maintenance behaviors. *Communication Reports, 12*, 291–303.

Stephen M. Haas

SEXUAL COMMUNICATION BETWEEN QUEER PARTNERS

INTRODUCTION

All relationships involve communication. Partners, friends, and family members communicate in order to understand one another's needs and wants. This can be as simple as asking a sibling to pass the salt, asking your friend where they want to go to hang out, asking your parent to bring home groceries, or negotiating with a relationship partner about what movie to watch together. Communicating basic needs and wants like these become second nature as life goes on, but what about needs on a more intimate level? Sexual communication can be an incredibly powerful force between partners, allowing them to build and enhance intimacy through vulnerability, yet sexual topics seem to be among the most difficult for partners to discuss. Given that these discussions are essential to happy, satisfactory relationships (Brown & Weigel, 2018; Frederick et al., 2017), it is important that romantic partners engage in such talks. For queer partners specifically, sexual communication provides additional opportunities to facilitate relationship and sexual happiness, such as through discussion of which sexual positions are enjoyable, the use or non-use of toys, fetishes, receiving or giving pleasure, and whether a partner or the relationship is openly queer, among others. This article begins with a definition of "Sexual Partner Communication," including "Queer Partner Studies," an overview of the research on sexual communication as it pertains to queer partners, and "Heterosexual Partner Studies." The "Conclusion" closes with a critique of the literature and calls for future sexual communication research centering queer partners.

SEXUAL PARTNER COMMUNICATION

What exactly is sexual communication? Much of the recent research on sexual communication focuses on partners and condom use (Jacobs et al., 2017; Li & Samp, 2019; Rubinsky & Hosek, 2019; Widman, Choukas-Bradley, et al., 2014; Xiao et al., 2013), which is ubiquitous among studies examining heterosexual and homosexual couples. Such research posits that sexual communication is centered on having conversations with a sexual partner about whether to use condoms, and considers whether having that conversation influences condom usage. Although this is an important facet of sexual communication, there is much more to sexual communication than just safe sex. La France (2019, p. 58) puts forth an encompassing definition: "an exchange of verbal and nonverbal cues that connotes attributes of human sexuality." This definition is less restrictive and places sexual communication outside of a narrow lens that only accounts for condom use. La France (2019) suggests that sexual communication goes beyond sexual health and includes topics such as sexual compatibility and sexual conflict. Although La France's definition is broader, there is room to further expand the definition of sexual communication. A more distinct definition of sexual communication would be any communication, verbal or nonverbal, that relates to any aspect of the sexual experience, including sexual identity, sexual relationships (e.g., sexual satisfaction, sexual positioning), and sexual orientation (e.g., straight, gay, bisexual, asexual, etc.).

Queer Partner Studies. Although it is clear that sexual communication covers a broad range of topics, research on sexual communication within queer partners is particularly focused on condom use (Crepaz & Marks, 2003; Eisenberg et al., 2011; Pantalone et al., 2019). Research on queer populations tends to focus on couples' or partners' use or non-use of condoms, or the disclosure or non-disclosure of HIV serostatus. For example, Eisenberg et al. (2011) found that condom use among young gay men was related to explicit conversations about engaging in safe sex, specific mention of condoms, and renegotiation when miscommunication about using condoms occurred. Another study conducted by Xiao et al. (2013) found that Chinese men who have sex with men communicate about condom use more often with casual partners than regular partners, and that those who communicated about condom use were more likely to use condoms than those who did not communicate about condom use.

It is also important to note that much of the literature on queer couples and condom use focuses on men who have sex with men, leaving out a broad range of queer partnerships. Moreover, these articles include cisgender men, broadly leaving out trans people. Yet, the scarce research centering on trans people is largely focused on condom use and HIV prevention (Konda et al., 2017; Kosenko, 2010, 2011). Using the condom-use or disuse definition of sexual communication willfully excludes queer partnerships that may never need to use condoms during sexual intercourse. This definition forces researchers into a narrow lens with which to explore sexual communication and leaves a large portion of the queer community unstudied. It is prudent to conduct more inclusive research, as sexual communication between men who have sex with men could look different from sexual communication between women who have sex with women, between partners where one partner is asexual and the other is pansexual, and queer partnerships where one or more partners do not identify as cisgender.

Another area of sexual communication among gay men deals with serostatus and serodisclosure. Crepaz and Marks (2003) surveyed HIV-positive men and learned that men who discussed their seropositive status and explicitly discussed safe sex had significantly higher prevalence of protected insertive intercourse than those who only disclosed their serostatus. They also found that those who disclosed their serostatus were more likely to discuss condom use, talk about sexual activities that would be safe, and to agree about safe sex practices than those who chose not to disclose serostatus (for further reading, see Kalichman & Nachimson, 1999; Prestage et al., 2006; Widman et al., 2013). This facet of sexual communication, though important, medicalizes gay men and may give the impression that sexual communication among gay men or men who have sex with men is only important because it may help stop the spread of disease. It may also imply that men who do not use condoms or who do not willfully disclose serostatus are intentionally spreading disease.

Much of the research focuses on gay men, but some studies focus on lesbian couples (Beals & Peplau, 2001; Scott et al., 2019). Whereas research on gay men seems to center heavily on disease prevention and serostatus, research on lesbian couples is directed toward communication dynamics between the couple and how it relates to relationship quality. Scott et al. (2019) found that in lesbian couples, positive partner communication was negatively associated with psychological aggression within the relationship, meaning that the more one partner engaged in positive communication, the more the other was less likely to report psychological aggression and less likely to report poor relationship quality. Beals and Peplau (2001) looked at the relationship between social involvement and disclosure of orientation on relationship quality and found that lesbian partners who were similar in levels of social involvement in the gay community were happier than mismatched couples. They also found that, despite literature documenting disclosure of orientation to family members, friends, and coworkers being associated with less anxiety, higher self-esteem, and more positive emotions, disclosure of orientation was not significantly associated with relationship quality.

Heterosexual Partner Studies. The findings reviewed above replicate research focused on heterosexual partners. Widman, Choukas-Bradley, et al. (2014) examined sexual communication between heterosexual adolescents and their dating partners and found that not much communication happens between them: over half of the participants reported that they did not have any kind of sexual discussion with their dating partners. Those who did communicate with their partners, however, were significantly more likely to use condoms than their counterparts. Similarly, a meta-analysis done by Widman, Noar, et al. (2014) studied 15,000 heterosexual adolescents and learned that adolescents who engaged in more sexual communication used condoms more frequently. These results again suggest that sexual communication is critical for safer sex behavior. Although such studies centered on heterosexual couples do focus on medicalization, research on heterosexual partners also encompasses a broader scope of topics, such as the link between sexual communication and sexual satisfaction (Byers & Demmons, 1999; Frederick et al., 2017; MacNeil & Byers, 2009; Rehman et al., 2011). This research suggests that higher levels of sexual communication in relationships lead to higher levels of sexual satisfaction within those relationships. In other words, the more that couples sexually self-disclose, the more satisfied they are in their relationship. Additionally, research on sexual communication between heterosexual partners has been examined in terms of closeness (Coffelt & Hess, 2014), orgasm frequency (Jones et al., 2017), and intimacy (MacNeil & Byers, 2005; for a review, see Brown & Orbuch, 2019). Such studies emphasize the importance of sexual communication to arenas beyond condom use and sexual health. These studies suggest sexual communication is important to relationship and sexual well-being in heterosexual couples, and researchers should lend the same lens to queer couples.

CONCLUSION

As much of the literature surrounding queer sexual partner communication is limited to condom use and prevention of communicable diseases, it is clear that the current field of research is underdeveloped and deserves much more attention and a greater range of study. The existing research medicalizes sexual communication among queer people, giving the appearance that it is only important as a function to stop the spread of sexually transmitted infections or HIV, and leads to the perception that those who engage in less safe sex practices are willfully spreading disease. Condom use, though very important and certainly not to be overlooked, is but one facet of a very broad definition.

The focus on medicalization ignores other realms of sexual communication between heterosexual partners, such as communication about sexual pleasure. There is a disparity in the sexual communication literature focused on queer couples compared to heterosexual couples. Whereas queer sexual communication research tends to focus on this medicalization, heterosexual sexual communication research has wider breadth and depth, also focusing on sexual satisfaction and intimacy processes. Queer partnerships exhibit many of the same risks and rewards as heterosexual partnerships, a reality the research should reflect.

Sexual communication research surrounding queer couples needs to be broadened to include more than condom use and HIV prevention as those topics alone are exclusionary and do not consider sexual acts that do not involve condom use. The limited body of literature concerning queer couples focuses on gay men and disease transmission, excluding partnership configurations such as lesbian couples and asexual people. It is important that future research fully encompasses all members of the queer community, not just gay men. Queer sexual communication research needs to focus on lesbian partners, asexual partners, and consensually non-monogamous configurations. Additionally, queer sexual communication research needs to focus on sexual communication topics that are unique to queer partners. For instance, position preference and negotiation is important for both gay and lesbian couples. Similarly, research on communicating sexual desire, including turn-ons, turn-offs, roughness, and kinks, is critical to ensuring the sexual satisfaction of queer partnerships. There is some research examining sexual communication and kink (Meyer & Chen, 2019; Rubinsky, 2018), but the majority of the participants were cisgender and heterosexual. This is not to take away from the fact that some participants were indeed queer or nonbinary, but it is imperative that including more queer people in sexual communication samples become commonplace. It is also important for researchers to study sexual and relational outness among queer partners and within queer relationships. All of these are crucial conversations occurring within queer partnerships and should be given attention by researchers in order to fully understand queer relationships.

Conversations about sex can serve to enhance the sexual and relational experience for queer partners. Broadening sexual communication research to focus on other topics will help de-medicalize sex and may even help destigmatize the field of human sexuality. Additional potential topics of future research include partner sexual communication in queer polyamorous relationships; sexual communication between queer partners who have dissimilar sexual interests; and a comparison between heterosexual partner sexual communication and queer partner sexual communication as it pertains to intimacy and sexual pleasure, specifically looking at rates of sexual communication between heterosexual versus queer partners. Additionally, researchers should include transgender individuals in studies examining sexual communication outside the bounds of safe sex and HIV prevention. Shifting the focus away from medicalized sexual communication research among queer partners and expanding the lens to include pleasure, intimacy, and other topics will help advance the field's knowledge of sexual communication between queer partners, as well as create a stream of research that can help queer partners romantically and sexually. Perhaps most importantly, transitioning sexual communication research on queer partnerships away from medicalization to focus on relational and sexual processes will help create a more equitable body of scholarship.

FURTHER READING

Cupach, W. R., & Metts, S. (1991). Sexuality and communication in close relationships. In K. McKinney & S. Sprecher (Eds.), *Sexuality in close relationships* (pp. 93–110). Lawrence Erlbaum.

Kattari, S. (2015). "Getting It": Identity and sexual communication for sexual and gender minorities with physical disabilities. *Sexuality & Culture, 19*(4), 882–899. https://doi.org/10.1007/s12119-015-9298-x

Leddy, A., Chakravarty, D., Dladla, S., de Bruyn, G., & Darbes, L. (2016). Sexual communication self-efficacy, hegemonic masculine norms and condom use among heterosexual couples in South Africa. *AIDS Care, 28*(2), 228–233. https://doi.org/10.1080/09540121.2015.1080792

Nagaraj, S., Segura, E. R., Peinado, J., Konda, K. A., Segura, P., Casapia, M., Ortiz, A., Montano, S. M., Clark, J. L., Sanchez, J., & Lama, J. R. (2013). A cross-sectional study of knowledge of sex partner serostatus among high-risk Peruvian men who have sex with men and transgender women: Implications for HIV prevention. *BMC Public Health, 13*, 181. https://doi.org/10.1186/1471-2458-13-181

REFERENCES

Beals, K. P., & Peplau, L. A. (2001). Social involvement, disclosure of sexual orientation, and the quality of lesbian relationships. *Psychology of Women Quarterly, 25*(1), 10–19. https://doi.org/10.1111/1471-6402.00002

Brown, R. D., & Orbuch, T. L. (2019). Sexual communication: Couple. In J. J. Ponzetti, M. Blankemeyer, S. M. Horan, H. A. Lyons, & A. Shigeto (Eds.), *Macmillan encyclopedia of families, marriages, and intimate relationships* (pp. 806–809). Macmillan.

Brown, R. D., & Weigel, D. J. (2018). Exploring a contextual model of sexual self-disclosure and sexual satisfaction. *Journal of Sex Research, 55*(2), 202–213. https://doi.org/10.1080/00224499.2017.1295299

Byers, E. S., & Demmons, S. (1999). Sexual satisfaction and sexual self-disclosure within dating relationships. *Journal of Sex Research, 36*(2), 180–189. https://doi.org/10.1080/00224499909551983

Coffelt, T. A., & Hess, J. A. (2014). Sexual disclosures: Connections to relational satisfaction and closeness. *Journal of Sex & Marital Therapy, 40*(6), 577–591. https://doi.org/10.1080/0092623X.2013.811449

Crepaz, N., & Marks, G. (2003). Serostatus disclosure, sexual communication and safer sex in HIV-positive men. *AIDS Care, 15*(3), 379–387. https://doi.org/10.1080/0954012031000105432

Eisenberg, A., Bauermeister, J. A., Pingel, E., Johns, M. M., & Santana, M. L. (2011). Achieving safety: Safer sex, communication, and desire among young gay men. *Journal of Adolescent Research, 26*(5), 645–669. https://doi.org/10.1177/0743558411402342

Frederick, D. A., Lever, J., Gillespie, B. J., & Garcia, J. R. (2017). What keeps passion alive? Sexual satisfaction is associated with sexual communication, mood setting, sexual variety, oral sex, orgasm, and sex frequency in a national US study. *Journal of Sex Research, 54*(2), 186–201. https://doi.org/10.1080/00224499.2015.1137854

Jacobs, R. J., Kane, M. N., & Sklar, E. M. (2017). Sexual communication and seroadaptation practices in HIV-negative midlife and older men who have sex with men. *Journal of Social Service Research, 43*(2), 193–204. https://doi.org/10.1080/01488376.2016.1248268

Jones, A. C., Robinson, W. D., & Seedall, R. B. (2017). The role of sexual communication in couples' sexual outcomes: A dyadic path analysis. *Journal of Marital and Family Therapy, 44*, 606–623. https://doi.org/10.1111/jmft.12282

Kalichman, S. C., & Nachimson, D. (1999). Self-efficacy and disclosure of HIV-positive serostatus to sex partners. *Health Psychology, 18*(3), 281–287. https://doi.org/10.1037/0278-6133.18.3.281

Konda, K. A., Castillo, R., Leon, S. R., Silva-santisteban, A., Salazar, X., Klausner, J. D., Coates, T. J., & Cáceres, C. F. (2017). HIV status communication with sex partners and associated factors among high-risk MSM and transgender women in Lima, Peru. *AIDS and Behavior, 21*(1), 152–162. https://doi.org/10.1007/s10461-016-1444-4

Kosenko, K. (2010). Meanings and dilemmas of sexual safety and communication for transgender individuals. *Health Communication, 25*(2), 131–141. https://doi.org/10.1080/10410230903544928

Kosenko, K. A. (2011). The safer sex communication of transgender adults: Processes and problems. *Journal of Communication, 61*(3), 476–495. https://doi.org/10.1111/j.1460-2466.2011.01556.x

La France, B. (2019). The impact of sexual self-disclosure, sexual compatibility, and sexual conflict on predicted outcome values in sexual relationships. *Canadian Journal of Human Sexuality, 28*(1), 57–67. https://doi.org/10.3138/cjhs.2018-0005

Li, Y., & Samp, J. A. (2019). Sexual relationship power, safer sexual communication, and condom use: A comparison of heterosexual young men and women. *Western Journal of Communication, 83*(1), 58–74. https://doi.org/10.1080/10570314.2017.1398835

MacNeil, S., & Byers, E. S. (2005). Dyadic assessment of sexual self-disclosure and sexual satisfaction in heterosexual dating couples. *Journal of Social and Personal Relationships, 22*(2), 169–181. https://doi.org/10.1177%2F0265407505050942

MacNeil, S., & Byers, E. S. (2009). Role of sexual self-disclosure in the sexual satisfaction of long-term heterosexual couples. *Journal of Sex Research, 46*(1), 3–14. https://doi.org/10.1080/00224490802398399

Meyer, C. G., & Chen, H.-M. (2019). Vanilla and kink: Power and communication in marriages with a BDSM-identifying partner. *Sexuality & Culture, 23*(3), 774–792. https://doi.org/10.1007/s12119-019-09590-x

Pantalone, D. W., Holloway, I. W., Goldblatt, A. E., Gorman, K. R., Herbitter, C., & Grov, C. (2019). The impact of pre-exposure prophylaxis on sexual communication and sexual behavior of urban gay and bisexual men. *Archives of Sexual Behavior, 49*(1), 147–160. https://doi.org/10.1007/s10508-019-01478-z

Prestage, G., Mao, L., McGuigan, D., Crawford, J., Kippax, S., Kaldor, J., & Grulich, A. E. (2006). HIV risk and communication between regular partners in a cohort of HIV-negative gay men. *AIDS Care, 18*(2), 166–172. https://doi.org/10.1080/09540120500358951

Rehman, U. S., Rellini, A. H., & Fallis, E. (2011). The importance of sexual self-disclosure to sexual satisfaction and functioning in committed relationships. *Journal of Sexual Medicine, 8*(11), 3108–3115. https://doi.org/10.1111/j.1743-6109.2011.02439.x

Rubinsky, V. (2018). "Sometimes it's easier to type things than to say them": Technology in BDSM Sexual Partner Communication. *Sexuality & Culture*, 22(4), 1412–1431. https://doi.org/10.1007/s12119-018-9534-2

Rubinsky, V., & Hosek, A. (2019). "We have to get over it": Navigating sex talk through the lens of sexual communication comfort and sexual self-disclosure in LGBTQ intimate partnerships. *Sexuality & Culture*, 24(3), 613–629. https://doi.org/10.1007/s12119-019-09652-0

Scott, S. B., Rhoades, G. K., & Markman, H. J. (2019). Observed communication and relationship quality in female same-gender couples. *Couple and Family Psychology: Research and Practice*, 8(3), 137–151. https://doi.org/10.1037/cfp0000121

Widman, L., Choukas-Bradley, S., Helms, S. W., Golin, C. E., & Prinstein, M. J. (2014). Sexual communication between early adolescents and their dating partners, parents, and best friends. *Journal of Sex Research*, 51(2), 731–741. https://doi.org/10.1080/00224499.2013.843148

Widman, L., Golin, C. E., & Noar, S. M. (2013). When do condom use intentions lead to actions? Examining the role of sexual communication on safer sexual behavior among people living with HIV. *Journal of Health Psychology*, 18(4), 507–517. https://doi.org/10.1177/1359105312446769

Widman, L., Noar, S. M., Choukas-Bradley, S., & Francis, D. B. (2014). Adolescent sexual health communication and condom use: A meta-analysis. *Health Psychology*, 33(10), 1113. https://doi.org/10.1037/hea0000112

Xiao, Z., Li, X., Liu, Y., Li, S., & Jiang, S. (2013). Sexual communication and condom use among Chinese men who have sex with men in Beijing. *Psychology, Health & Medicine*, 18(1), 98–106. https://doi.org/10.1080/13548506.2012.687826

Brandon T. Parrillo and Randal D. Brown

SEXUAL SATISFACTION IN LGB RELATIONSHIPS

INTRODUCTION

It is well documented at this point that sexual satisfaction plays an important role in the mental, physical, emotional, and relational lives of all individuals of all sexual orientations (Pascoal et al., 2019; World Health Organization, 2010). However, that does not mean that the experience and influence of sexual satisfaction operates in a universal manner across individuals and relationships. In fact, it is quite the opposite; recent research and theorizing on sexual satisfaction emphasizes that there are factors that are unique to individuals in LGB relationships that make both the antecedents and outcomes related to sexual satisfaction different from those that contribute to sexual satisfaction in mixed-gender relationships (Armstrong & Reissing, 2013; Baldwin et al., 2019; Blair et al., 2015; Calvillo, Sánchez-Fuentes, Parrón-Carreño, et al., 2020; Chatterji et al., 2017; Fleishman et al., 2019; Flynn et al., 2017; Paine et al., 2019; Shepler et al., 2018).

Additionally, there are specific reasons that make the study of sexual satisfaction as it relates to individuals in LGB relationships particularly important. The first reason is that generating empirically validated knowledge about sexual satisfaction in LGB relationships may be important to undoing damaging stereotypical discourses about LGB sexuality. These discourses may include ideas such as "lesbian bed death" (the notion that lesbians have very little or no sex as they age; Blumstein & Schwartz, 1983), hyperbolized media portrayals of gay men's sexuality (cruising culture), or stigmatizing attitudes toward consensual non-monogamy in

LGB relationships (Conley et al., 2013; Holmberg & Blair, 2009). Second, generating knowledge about the specific factors that are associated with sexual satisfaction among LGB individuals may help to combat the "cultures of silence" (Kosenko, 2010, p. 132) that surround sex and safer sex practices that exist in these communities (Elwood et al., 2003; Haig, 2006).

The task of this article is to document the current state of literature surrounding sexual satisfaction in LGB relationships. The first section, "What Is Sexual Satisfaction?," is devoted to the question of what is captured by the term "sexual satisfaction," as a clear consensus has not yet been reached. Following this, recent advances in research and theorizing on this topic are covered, supported by a review of the emerging "Key Findings" in research that have come from this scholarship. Finally, a few targeted areas for growth are outlined in "Conclusions and Future Directions."

Before moving forward, a brief note on language should be offered. In this article, the term "LGB relationships" is used to refer to individuals currently involved in a same-gender relationship. When possible, the type of same-gender relationship will be specified (i.e., lesbian, gay, bisexual). When the term "mixed-gender relationship" is used, it is used under the (often unspoken) assumption that individuals in this relationship are heterosexually identified, though that may not always be the case (Diamond, 2008).

WHAT IS SEXUAL SATISFACTION?

At a universal level, an organizing definition of sexual satisfaction has yet to be reached (Baldwin et al., 2019; Mark et al., 2014; McClelland, 2010). With specific reference to LGB relationships, however, defining sexual satisfaction carries additional and unique challenges. First, the idea of what constitutes "sex" in one population may not be what is thought of as "sex" in another. Said another way, "sex" is frequently heteronormatively operationalized (implicitly or otherwise) as penile–vaginal intercourse, when this is not the way that many individuals in LGB individuals have sex (Dyar et al., 2020; Scott et al., 2018). Second, sexual satisfaction may not be connected to having sex (under any definition) at all. Indeed, Carter et al. (2018) found that women may be highly sexually satisfied in the absence of having sex and may also be having sex while being highly unsatisfied. Yet sexual satisfaction is also not simply the opposite of sexual *dis*satisfaction (Bois et al., 2016; Lindley et al., 2020; Nimbi et al., 2018), which is a complex construct of its own (Staples et al., 2019; Stephenson & Meston, 2010). Further, sexual satisfaction, though related to the experience of orgasm or pleasure, is not the same thing. Relying on such physiological definitions of sex and satisfaction with sex produces an understanding of sexual satisfaction that is "narrow," "medicalized[,] and gendered" (Chatterji et al., 2017, p. 888).

Thus, perhaps unsurprisingly, out of this morass of complications, multiple measures of sexual satisfaction have emerged, though none has established a place as a centrally agreed-on definition. Some more common measures of sexual satisfaction include the Index of Sexual Satisfaction (Hudson, 2013), the Global Measure of Sexual Satisfaction (Lawrance & Byers, 1998), and the New Sexual Satisfaction Scale (Štulhofer et al., 2010). However, each of these measures relies on heteronormative understandings of sex, which make them potentially inappropriate and ineffective for use with LGB populations. These measures also share another common flaw, which is that they are all focused on sexual satisfaction as an individual-level construct. Thus, for researchers who are interested in LGB relationships, these measures may fall short once again, especially given research suggesting that sexual satisfaction is much more fully captured when considered from a dyadic lens (Chatterji et al., 2017; Paine et al., 2019; Scott et al., 2018).

One measure that seems to have overcome some of the challenges presented above is the Interpersonal Exchange Model of Sexual Satisfaction and its associated questionnaire (IEMSS; Lawrance & Byers, 1995, 1998). Drawing on exchange models of interpersonal communication and relationships (Thibaut & Kelley, 1952; Walster et al., 1978), the model posits that sexual satisfaction is the outcome of a combination of considerations, including individuals' perceptions of both the sexual rewards ("exchanges that are pleasurable and gratifying") and costs ("exchanges requiring physical or mental effort or those producing pain, embarrassment, or anxiety") (Lawrance & Byers, 1995, p. 268) in their current relationship. These perceptions are held up against individuals' expectations for costs and rewards in their relationship. Finally, individuals take into account the level of equality between their own perceived levels of costs and rewards and their perception of the costs and rewards that their partner experiences (Lawrance & Byers, 1995). For individuals to experience sexual satisfaction, a few conditions must be met simultaneously. The model posits that sexual satisfaction is likely to be experienced when rewards are equal to or greater than comparison level for rewards; costs are equal to or less than the comparison level for costs; rewards exceed costs; and there is relative equality of costs and rewards between partners. All of these components are meant to be captured not at a singular point in time, but rather over multiple time points so as to be able to better capture a more holistic view of the relationship (Lawrance & Byers, 1995). Flowing from this work, many researchers have taken up Lawrance and Byer's (1995) definition of sexual satisfaction as being "an affective response arising from one's subjective evaluation of the positive and negative dimensions associated with one's sexual relationship" (p. 268).

Although the IEMSS model, questionnaire, and definition draw strength from their strong theoretical background (Pascoal et al., 2019) and relational orientation, there are still some important shortcomings that must be noted. The first shortcoming is one that has already been pointed out above: the IEMSS is a theory and a measure that was originated and validated from research and participants who were heterosexual. Additionally, the theory and measure have relied almost exclusively (with notable exceptions detailed in Baldwin et al., 2019) on populations in committed, monogamous relationships, and so is affected by both heteronormativity and discourses that center and privilege monogamy (Baldwin et al., 2019; Barker & Langdridge, 2010).

Finally, and perhaps most importantly, though the IEMSS does account for the influence that the relational context has on sexual satisfaction, it continues to ignore the fact that relationships are embedded in broader social, political, and cultural structures and discourses, all of which act in concert to meaningfully alter the experience of sexual satisfaction, and in particular, for those in LGB relationships. To be specific, individuals in LGB relationships have an experience that is unique from individuals engaged in mixed-gender relationships as a result of "exist[ing] in a context of heterosexism, suppression, stigma, prejudice, discrimination, and violence" (Ritter et al., 2018, p. 1484). As suggested by minority stress theory (Meyer, 2003), existing in such a hostile environment may meaningfully impact the way that LGB individuals experience their relationships, among many other aspects of life. As Paine et al. (2019) eloquently point out, "people assign meaning to sex in light of social positions" (p. 9); thus to examine sexual satisfaction without incorporating the influence of the larger social context may meaningfully interfere with the validity of any associated findings. Often the forces that make up this larger social context go unnamed and thus disappear from our thinking and discourse. To crystallize some meaningful aspects of this larger social context, it should be pointed out that these aspects include things like whiteness, systemic racism, elevated rates of violence against LGB people of color, and many more contributing factors.

Activities that do (or don't) take place within a partnership are judged by sexual scripts, which carry gendered, racialized, and heteronormative expectations within them (Lindley et al., 2020; Simon & Gagnon, 1984, 1987, 2003). Sexual scripts dictate what type of sex, how much, and with whom individuals should be having sex (among many other things), and to the degree that they are internalized, affect how individuals judge their sexual lives (Chatterji et al., 2017; Paine et al., 2019; Redlick & Vangelisti, 2020). Research has found that individuals in LGB relationships conform to and (both consciously and unconsciously) deviate from heteronormative sexual scripts, and have also developed their own sexual scripts as well (Chatterji et al., 2017; Courtice & Shaughnessy, 2018; Klinkenberg & Rose, 1994; Pascoal et al., 2019).

The role that these scripts may play in contributing to the experience of sexual satisfaction can be seen in the IEMSS's notion of the importance of comparison levels. Sexual scripts may affect what individuals believe they should (or should not) be experiencing in their sexual lives, and thus influence what those same individuals judge as meeting, exceeding, or falling short of their expectations. Thus, individuals in LGB relationships may interact with larger social factors (such as scripts) in a way that is distinct from how individuals in mixed-gender relationships interact with these same cultural ideas and discourses. As a result, individuals in LGB relationships may find that different factors contribute to their experience of sexual satisfaction. They may also find that the factors that contribute to their sexual satisfaction have some overlap with the factors that contribute to sexual satisfaction in mixed-gender relationships (Holmberg & Blair, 2009; Holmberg et al., 2010; Shepler et al., 2018) but that those factors operate in a different form or fashion.

The points above represent challenges with using the IEMSS among LGB people, but researchers have attempted to validate the theory and measure in LGB populations with considerable success (Byers & Cohen, 2017; Calvillo, Sánchez-Fuentes, & Sierra, 2020; Cohen et al., 2008). In fact, a recent review of research on sexual satisfaction in LGB populations found that one in five studies utilized the IEMSS as a lens or measure (Calvillo, Sánchez-Fuentes, & Sierra, 2020). Outside of the IEMSS, other researchers have sought to move the study of sexual satisfaction forward by turning to different perspectives. For example, Paine et al. (2019) employed the gender-as-relational perspective (Springer et al., 2012; Umberson et al., 2015), which suggests that the gendered aspects of sexual scripts meaningfully influence how people make sense of their sexual lives. They applied this perspective to comparing accounts of women's sexual experiences in lesbian and heterosexual marriages. Others have turned to ecological models of relationships (Brofenbrenner, 1994), which stress the importance of considering individuals as interacting with their environments at a variety of levels, including with other individuals as well as other social forces and institutions (Calvillo, Sánchez-Fuentes, Parrón-Carreño, et al., 2020; Henderson et al., 2009).

The result of this push for perspectives and procedures for investigating sexual satisfaction that are tailored to the experiences of individuals in LGB relationships has been the growing generation of a base of literature regarding sexual satisfaction in these relationships. Though this body of literature is admittedly limited, researchers have been able to begin to map the complex constellation of variables to which it is connected. The next portion of this article details some of the emergent "Key Findings" from this literature.

KEY FINDINGS

Relationship Satisfaction. Sexual satisfaction's connection to levels of relationship satisfaction is one of the most thoroughly researched associations in the extant literature. These two variables have been found to be connected to each other in a positive manner in LGB relationships (Armstrong & Reissing, 2013; Byers, 2005; Calvillo, Sánchez-Fuentes, Parrón-Carreño, et al., 2020; Calvillo, Sánchez-Fuentes, & Sierra, 2020; Dyar et al., 2020; Fleishman et al., 2019; Holmberg et al., 2010; Rosser et al., 1997; Sánchez-Fuentes & Sierra, 2015) and also in mixed-gender relationships (Litzinger & Gordon, 2005; Mark & Jozkowski, 2013; Smith et al., 2011; Sprecher, 2002). In LGB couples, relationship satisfaction has been found to account for an impressive 44% of the variance in sexual satisfaction (Sánchez-Fuentes & Sierra, 2015). Although the two variables are connected with each other, there has not yet been consensus on whether one causally predicts the other. It is more likely that the two interact with each other bidirectionally (Byers, 2005) and that this relationship is also swayed by the presence of many other variables (e.g., age, gender composition of the couple, income) (Armstong & Reissing, 2013; Fleishman et al., 2019).

Internalized Homonegativity. One such important variable may be the level of internalized homonegativity that individuals each bring to the relationship. Internalized homonegativity refers to the phenomenon of LGB people possessing negative attitudes toward their own sexual identity (Meyer & Dean, 1998), and has frequently been found to be linked to lower levels of sexual satisfaction (Baldwin et al., 2019; Kuyper & Vanwesenbeeck, 2011; Rosser et al., 1997). The influence of internalized homonegativity on sexual satisfaction has been found to act over and above that of sociodemographic variables (Kuyper & Vanswansenbeeck, 2011). It may, however, be important to revisit this connection in future research projects, as some studies have not demonstrated this direct association (Biss & Horne, 2005; Shepler et al., 2018). This may be attributable to participants reporting low levels of internalized homonegativity (Biss & Horne, 2005) or to LGB participants more frequently reporting a positive appreciation of their sexual identity in the form of queer identity pride (Shepler et al., 2018).

Relationship Types and Arrangements. Another important variable that seems to play into levels of sexual satisfaction in LGB relationships is whether individuals are in committed relationships with their partners, and if they are, how they go about conducting that relationship. One fairly consistent finding related to sexual satisfaction for LGB individuals is that being in a committed and partnered relationship is associated with greater overall sexual satisfaction (Baldwin et al., 2019; Biss & Horne, 2005; Kuyper & Vanswansenbeeck, 2011; Ritter et al., 2018; Shepler et al., 2018; Tracy & Junginger, 2007). Additionally, individuals who live with their partners seem to evince greater levels of sexual satisfaction (Biss & Horne, 2005; Byers & Cohen, 2017).

As it relates to LGB relationships, the cultural stereotype that individuals in these relationships engage in consensual non-monogamy at higher rates than those in mixed-gender relationships seems to hold some truth when investigated empirically (Campbell, 2000; Haupert et al., 2017; Hickson et al., 1992; LaSala, 2004). However, it is important to note that the related idea that engaging in this type of relationship agreement harms sexual satisfaction is not similarly supported in samples of gay men or lesbian and bisexual women (Baldwin et al., 2019; Bricker & Horne, 2007; Carvalehira & Costa, 2015; LaSala, 2004; Parsons et al., 2012). Rather, it seems that the type of communication that takes places within these relationships, be it related to sex within the dyad or outside of the dyad, plays an important role.

Communication. According to Metts and Spitzberg (1996) sexual communication includes conversations with a partner about the meaning of sex, the function that sex plays in a relationship, and the outcomes of sex on the relationship. A direct and positive association between communication and sexual satisfaction has been found in heterosexual couples (Mark & Jozkowski, 2013), with communication explaining 46–49% of the variance in reported sexual satisfaction. Relatedly, in a sample of individuals in same-sex versus mixed-gender couples, the individuals in same-sex couples showed an inverse relationship between communication quality and experiences of sexual pain, which in turn were related to increased relationship functioning. Although this does not establish a direct link between communication and sexual satisfaction, given that relationship functioning and sexual satisfaction are closely linked, it is possible that this same association exists. Additionally, there is evidence to suggest that intimacy is closely related to sexual satisfaction in LGB relationships (Byers, 2005; Carvalheira & Costa, 2015; Scott et al., 2018). Communication is one route by which couple intimacy may be established, and so again it is quite likely that the frequency and type of communication, sexual and otherwise, that takes place within LGB couples plays an important role in determining levels of sexual satisfaction.

As is the case with many other constructs, there is likely a role for individual difference variables to play in determining sexual satisfaction. Some posit that age may play a role (Armstrong & Reissing, 2013; Paine et al., 2019; Sánchez-Fuentes & Sierra, 2015), with older individuals reporting less sexual satisfaction as a result of their generally decreased sexual frequency and functioning, as well as other life changes such as being asked to take on the caregiver role for aging parents or other aspects of physical decline. Socioeconomic status has also been posed as an important variable to consider, with higher status being linked to greater sexual satisfaction (Henderson et al., 2009; Ritter et al., 2018). Greater socioeconomic status may be associated with having access to a variety of resources (material, emotional, and otherwise) that might shield individuals in LGB relationships from some of the minority stressors that can hamper their relational and sexual satisfaction (Henderson et al., 2009).

Individual Difference Variables. Two other individual difference variables deserve mention here. Although some have questioned whether instances of childhood sexual abuse might be associated with an individuals' sexual satisfaction later in life, this was not found to be the case among all sexual minority women (Henderson et al., 2009). It appears that the presence of a history of attempted penetration does affect sexual satisfaction for some sexual minority women, but this effect does not extend to other domains of sexual well-being (Crump

& Byers, 2017). Additionally, some have proposed that spirituality or religious affiliation may be related to sexual satisfaction in LGB couples given that certain religions proscribe same-sex sexual activity (Armstrong & Reissing, 2013; Ritter et al., 2018; Smith & Horne, 2008). However, religious affiliation or spirituality has not been found to have a significant role in these studies, or when it did, the proportion of variance it accounted for in sexual satisfaction was very small (i.e., 3%; Ritter et al., 2018).

Sexual Orientation. The last key finding that should be raised regarding sexual satisfaction in LGB relationships is that the determinants of sexual satisfaction vary widely among each of the aforementioned identity categories (Biss & Horne, 2005; Cohen et al., 2008; Henderson et al., 2009; Kuyper & Vanwesenbeeck, 2011; Lindley et al., 2020). Individuals who identify as lesbian, gay, and bisexual each encounter different experiences of discrimination, marginalization, stereotyping, exclusion, and oppression, and bring these to their sexual experiences with others. These individuals also bring different corporeal realities to their sex lives. Thus, it should come as no surprise that their satisfaction with these experiences is not determined by a uniform set of variables.

CONCLUSIONS AND FUTURE DIRECTIONS

The purpose of this article has been to engage and review the literature on sexual satisfaction in LGB relationships. In doing so, questions of conceptualization and operationalization of this construct have been raised, and advances in both theoretical and empirical work have been highlighted as potential responses to these questions. This entry has also sought to highlight some key trends that are emerging from this knowledge base, with specific reference to the influences of relationship satisfaction, internalized homonegativity, relationship types and arrangements, individual difference variables related to sexual trauma, and sexual orientation. Much work has been done, but an even greater amount remains undone, so this article closes by offering a few considerations for scholars interested in continuing this line of inquiry.

The first suggestion is to encourage scholars to move beyond assessing simple mean differences between groups, whether those groups are LGB and mixed-gender relationships, or different identities within the LGB grouping. Although this type of research is important for creating a base of knowledge to operate from, eventually it reaches a point of diminishing returns (Cao et al., 2017). Research that considers mediating and moderating influences on the connection between sexual satisfaction and the previously reviewed variables will be important in assisting clinicians who wish to develop interventions for individuals or couples who might experience personal or relational distress resulting from lower than desired levels of sexual satisfaction (Byers & Cohen, 2017; Henderson et al., 2009). Some progress has been made on this front already (c.f., Calvillo, Sánchez-Fuentes, Parrón-Carreño, et al., 2020; Calvillo, Sánchez-Fuentes, & Sierra, 2020; Ritter et al., 2018).

A second suggestion relates to the lack of an organizing definition or measure for sexual satisfaction. It is possible that a single measure or definition that encompasses individuals of all sexual orientations is one that is not desirable, for reasons that were reviewed above. However, it may be that there are some core features of sexual satisfaction that are shared across orientations (as suggested by Shepler et al., 2018) and could prove useful if discovered and integrated into measurement. This is a task that is ripe for both quantitative and qualitative researchers, as there are aspects of sexual satisfaction that are likely not captured in current survey measures, and there will need to be refinement and validation of any findings derived from qualitative research (McClelland, 2014).

Finally, as efforts toward increased trans awareness and trans inclusivity gain strength in lay arenas (Gillig et al., 2018), the academy must not lag behind in this regard. Rather, researchers should seek to lead and be sure that their research respects, validates, and affirms the unique experience of trans individuals and their sex lives. As pointed out by Dyar et al. (2020), there is a relative dearth of sexual satisfaction and relationship research that includes trans individuals in its samples (notable exceptions to this include Shepler et al., 2018; and Staples et al., 2019). In order to truly move the field forward, researchers must be mindful to advance knowledge by recognizing the experiences of all individuals, not just those who have traditionally been seen.

REFERENCES

Armstrong, H. L., & Reissing, E. D. (2013). Women who have sex with women: A comprehensive review of the literature and conceptual model of sexual function. *Sexual and Relationship Therapy, 28*(4), 364–399.

Baldwin, A., Herbenick, D., Schick, V. R., Light, B., Dodge, B., Jackson, C. A., & Fortenberry, J. D. (2019). Sexual Satisfaction in monogamous, nonmonogamous, and unpartnered sexual minority women in the US. *Journal of Bisexuality, 19*(1), 103–119.

Barker, M., & Langdridge, D. (2010). Whatever happened to non-monogamies? Critical reflections on recent research and theory. *Sexualities, 13*(6), 748–772.

Biss, W. J., & Horne, S. G. (2005). Sexual satisfaction as more than a gendered concept: The roles of psychological well-being and sexual orientation. *Journal of Constructivist Psychology, 18*(1), 25–38.

Blair, K. L., Pukall, C. F., Smith, K. B., & Cappell, J. (2015). Differential associations of communication and love in heterosexual, lesbian, and bisexual women's perceptions and experiences of chronic vulvar and pelvic pain. *Journal of Sex & Marital Therapy, 41*(5), 498–524.

Blumstein, P., & Schwartz, P. (1983). *American couples: Money, work, and sex.* Morrow.

Bois, K., Bergeron, S., Rosen, N., Mayrand, M., Brassard, A., & Sadikaj, G. (2016). Intimacy, sexual satisfaction, and sexual distress in vulvodynia couples: An observational study. *Health Psychology, 35*(6), 531–540.

Bricker, M. E., & Horne, S. E. (2007). The impact of monogamy and non-monogamy on relational health. *Journal of Couple & Relationship Therapy, 6*, 27–47.

Brofenbrenner, U. (1994). Ecological models of human development. *International Encyclopedia of Education, 3*(2), 1643–1647.

Byers, E. S. (2005). Relationship satisfaction and sexual satisfaction: A longitudinal study of individuals in long-term relationships. *Journal of Sex Research, 42*, 113–118.

Byers, E. S., & Cohen, J. N. (2017). Validation of the interpersonal exchange model of sexual satisfaction with women in a same-sex relationship. *Psychology of Women Quarterly, 41*(1), 32–45.

Calvillo, C., Sánchez-Fuentes, M. D. M., Parrón-Carreño, T., & Sierra, J. C. (2020). Validation of the interpersonal exchange model of sexual satisfaction questionnaire in adults with a same-sex partner. *International Journal of Clinical and Health Psychology, 20*(2), 140–150.

Calvillo, C., Sánchez-Fuentes, M. D. M., & Sierra, J. C. (2020). An explanatory model of sexual satisfaction in adults with a same-sex partner: An analysis based on gender differences. *International Journal of Environmental Research and Public Health, 17*(10), 3393–3410.

Campbell, K. (2000). Relationship characteristics, social support, masculine ideologies and psychological functioning of gay men in couples (Unpublished doctoral dissertation). California School of Professional Psychology. http://www.drkevincampbell.net/DissertationKevinMCampbell.pdf

Cao, H., Zhou, N., Fine, M., Liang, Y., Li, J., & Mills-Koonce, W. R. (2017). Sexual minority stress and same-sex relationship well-being: A meta-analysis of research prior to the US Nationwide legalization of same-sex marriage. *Journal of Marriage and Family, 79*(5), 1258–1277.

Carter, A., Greene, S., Money, D., Sanchez, M., Webster, K., Nicholson, V., Brotto, L. A., Hankins, C., Kestler, M., Pick, N., & Salters, K. (2018). Supporting the sexual rights of women living with HIV: A critical analysis of sexual satisfaction and pleasure across five relationship types. *Journal of Sex Research, 55*(9), 1134–1154.

Carvalheira, A. A., & Costa, P. A. (2015). The impact of relational factors on sexual satisfaction among heterosexual and homosexual men. *Sexual and Relationship Therapy, 30*(3), 314–324.

Chatterji, S., Bay-Cheng, L. Y., Schick, V., Dodge, B., Baldwin, A., Van Der Pol, B., & Fortenberry, J. D. (2017). The year's best: Interpersonal elements of bisexual women's most satisfying sexual experiences in the past year. *Journal of Sex Research, 54*(7), 887–898.

Cohen, J. N., Byers, E. S., & Walsh, L. P. (2008). Factors influencing the sexual relationships of lesbians and gay men. *International Journal of Sexual Health, 20*(3), 162–176.

Conley, T. D., Moors, A. C., Matsick, J. L., & Ziegler, A. (2013). The fewer the merrier? Assessing stigma surrounding consensually non-monogamous romantic relationships. *Analyses of Social Issues and Public Policy, 13*(1), 1–30.

Courtice, E. L., & Shaughnessy, K. (2018). The partner context of sexual minority women's and men's cybersex experiences: Implications for the traditional sexual script. *Sex Roles, 78*(3–4), 272–285.

Crump, L., & Byers, E. S. (2017). Sexual well-being of sexual minority women in dating relationships who have experienced childhood sexual abuse and/or adolescent and adult sexual victimization. *Canadian Journal of Human Sexuality, 26*(2), 163–173.

Diamond, L. M. (2008). *Sexual fluidity: Understanding women's love and desire.* Harvard University Press.

Dyar, C., Newcomb, M. E., Mustanski, B., & Whitton, S. W. (2020). A structural equation model of sexual satisfaction and relationship functioning among sexual and gender minority individuals assigned female at birth in diverse relationships. *Archives of Sexual Behavior, 49*(2), 693–710.

Elwood, W. N., Greene, K., & Carter, K. K. (2003). Gentlemen don't speak: Communication norms and condom use in bathhouses. *Journal of Applied Communication Research, 31*(4), 277–297.

Fleishman, J. M., Crane, B., & Koch, P. B. (2019). Correlates and predictors of sexual satisfaction for older adults in same-sex relationships. *Journal of Homosexuality, 67*(14), 1–25.

Flynn, K. E., Lin, L., & Weinfurt, K. P. (2017). Sexual function and satisfaction among heterosexual and sexual minority US adults: A cross-sectional survey. *PloS One, 12*(4), e0174981.

Gillig, T. K., Rosenthal, E. L., Murphy, S. T., & Folb, K. L. (2018). More than a media moment: The influence of televised storylines on viewers' attitudes toward transgender people and policies. *Sex Roles, 78*(7–8), 515–527.

Haig, T. (2006). Bareback sex: Masculinity, silence, and the dilemmas of gay health. *Canadian Journal of Communication, 31*, 859–877.

Haupert, M. L., Moors, A. C., Gesselman, A. N., & Garcia, J. R. (2017). Estimates and correlates of engagement in consensually non-monogamous relationships. *Current Sexual Health Reports, 9*(2), 155–165.

Henderson, A. W., Lehavot, K., & Simoni, J. M. (2009). Ecological models of sexual satisfaction among lesbian/bisexual and heterosexual women. *Archives of Sexual Behavior, 38*(1), 50–65.

Hickson, F., Davies, P., Hunt, A., Weatherburn, P., McManus, T., & Coxon, A. (1992). Maintenance of open gay relationships: Some strategies for protection against HIV. *AIDS Care, 4*(4), 409–419.

Holmberg, D., & Blair, K. L. (2009). Sexual desire, communication, satisfaction, and preferences of men and women in same-sex versus mixed-sex relationships. *Journal of Sex Research, 46*(1), 57–66.

Holmberg, D., Blair, K. L., & Phillips, M. (2010). Women's sexual satisfaction as a predictor of well-being in same-sex versus mixed-sex relationships. *Journal of Sex Research, 47*(1), 1–11.

Hudson, W. W. (2013). Index of sexual satisfaction. In T. D. Fisher, C. M. Davis, & W. L. Yarber (Eds.), *Handbook of sexuality-related measures* (pp. 545–554). Routledge.

Klinkenberg, D., & Rose, S. (1994). Dating scripts of gay men and lesbians. *Journal of Homosexuality, 26*(4), 23–35.

Kosenko, K. A. (2010). Meanings and dilemmas of sexual safety and communication for transgender individuals. *Health Communication, 25*(2), 131–141.

Kuyper, L., & Vanwesenbeeck, I. (2011). Examining sexual health differences between lesbian, gay, bisexual, and heterosexual adults: The role of sociodemographics, sexual behavior characteristics, and minority stress. *Journal of Sex Research, 48*(2–3), 263–274.

LaSala, M. C. (2004). Extradyadic sex and gay male couples: Comparing monogamous and nonmonogamous relationships. *Families in Society, 85*(3), 405–412. https://doi.org/10.1177/104438940408500319

Lawrance, K. A., & Byers, E. S. (1995). Sexual satisfaction in long-term heterosexual relationships: The interpersonal exchange model of sexual satisfaction. *Personal Relationships, 2*(4), 267–285.

Lawrance, K., & Byers, E. S. (1998). Interpersonal exchange model of sexual satisfaction questionnaire. In C. M. Davis, W. L. Yarber, R. Bauserman, G. Schreer, & S. L. Davis (Eds.), *Sexuality-related measures: A compendium* (2nd ed., pp. 525–530). SAGE.

Lindley, L., Anzani, A., & Galupo, M. P. (2020). What constitutes sexual dissatisfaction for trans masculine and nonbinary individuals: A qualitative study. *Journal of Sex & Marital Therapy, 46*(7), 612–629.

Litzinger, S., & Gordon, K. C. (2005). Exploring relationships among communication, sexual satisfaction, and marital satisfaction. *Journal of Sex & Marital Therapy, 31*(5), 409–424.

Mark, K. P., & Jozkowski, K. N. (2013). The mediating role of sexual and nonsexual communication between relationship and sexual satisfaction in a sample of college-age heterosexual couples. *Journal of Sex & Marital Therapy, 39*(5), 410–427.

Mark, K. P., Herbenick, D., Fortenberry, J. D., Sanders, S., & Reece, M. (2014). A psychometric comparison of three scales and a single-item measure to assess sexual satisfaction. *Journal of Sex Research, 51*(2), 159–169.

McClelland, S. I. (2010). Intimate justice: A critical analysis of sexual satisfaction. *Social and Personality Psychology Compass, 4*(9), 663–680.

McClelland, S. I. (2014). "What do you mean when you say that you are sexually satisfied?" A mixed methods study. *Feminism & Psychology, 24*(1), 74–96.

Metts, S., & Spitzberg, B. H. (1996). Sexual communication in interpersonal contexts: A script-based approach. *Annals of the International Communication Association, 19*(1), 49–92.

Meyer, I. H. (2003). Prejudice, social stress, and mental health in lesbian, gay, and bisexual populations: Conceptual issues and research evidence. *Psychological Bulletin, 129*(5), 674–697.

Meyer, I. H., & Dean, L. (1998). Internalized homophobia, intimacy, and sexual behavior among gay and bisexual men. In G. M. Herek (Ed.), *Stigma and sexual orientation: Understanding prejudice against lesbians, gay men, and bisexuals* (pp. 160–186). SAGE.

Nimbi, F. M., Tripodi, F., Rossi, R., & Simonelli, C. (2018). Expanding the analysis of psychosocial factors of sexual desire in men. *Journal of Sexual Medicine, 15*(2), 230–244.

Paine, E. A., Umberson, D., & Reczek, C. (2019). Sex in midlife: Women's sexual experiences in lesbian and straight marriages. *Journal of Marriage and Family, 81*(1), 7–23.

Parsons, J. T., Starks, T. J., Gamarel, K. E., & Grov, C. (2012). Non-monogamy and sexual relationship quality among same-sex male couples. *Journal of Family Psychology, 26*(5), 669–677.

Pascoal, P. M., Narciso, I. D. S. B., & Pereira, N. M. (2014). What is sexual satisfaction? Thematic analysis of lay people's definitions. *Journal of Sex Research, 51*(1), 22–30.

Pascoal, P. M., Shaughnessy, K., & Almeida, M. J. (2019). A thematic analysis of a sample of partnered lesbian, gay, and bisexual people's concepts of sexual satisfaction. *Psychology & Sexuality, 10*(2), 101–118.

Redlick, M. H., & Vangelisti, A. L. (2020). The sexual double standard and topic avoidance in friendships. *Communication Quarterly, 68,* 306–330.

Ritter, L. J., Morris, H. R., & Knox, D. (2018). Who's getting the best sex? A comparison by sexual orientation. *Sexuality & Culture, 22*(4), 1466–1489.

Rosser, B. R., Metz, M. E., Bockting, W. O., & Buroker, T. (1997). Sexual difficulties, concerns, and satisfaction in homosexual men: An empirical study with implications for HIV prevention. *Journal of Sex & Marital Therapy, 23*(1), 61–73.

Sánchez-Fuentes, M. D. M., & Sierra, J. C. (2015). Sexual satisfaction in a heterosexual and homosexual Spanish sample: The role of socio-demographic characteristics, health indicators, and relational factors. *Sexual and Relationship Therapy, 30*(2), 226–242.

Scott, S. B., Ritchie, L., Knopp, K., Rhoades, G. K., & Markman, H. J. (2018). Sexuality within female same-gender couples: Definitions of sex, sexual frequency norms, and factors associated with sexual satisfaction. *Archives of Sexual Behavior, 47*(3), 681–692.

Shepler, D. K., Smendik, J. M., Cusick, K. M., & Tucker, D. R. (2018). Predictors of sexual satisfaction for partnered lesbian, gay, and bisexual adults. *Psychology of Sexual Orientation and Gender Diversity, 5*(1), 25–35.

Simon, W., & Gagnon, J. H. (1984). Sexual scripts. *Society, 22,* 52–60.

Simon, W., & Gagnon, J. H. (1987). A sexual scripts approach. In J. H. Greer & W. T. O'Donohue (Eds.), *Theories of human sexuality* (pp. 363–383). Plenum.

Simon, W., & Gagnon, J. H. (2003). Sexual scripts: Origins, influences and changes. *Qualitative Sociology, 26*(4), 491–497.

Smith, B. L., & Horne, S. G. (2008). What's faith got to do with it? *Women & Therapy, 31*(1), 73–87.

Smith, A., Lyons, A., Ferris, J., Richters, J., Pitts, M., Shelley, J., & Simpson, J. M. (2011). Sexual and relationship satisfaction among heterosexual men and women: The importance of desired frequency of sex. *Journal of Sex & Marital Therapy, 37*(2), 104–115.

Sprecher, S. (2002). Sexual satisfaction in premarital relationships: Associations with satisfaction, love, commitment, and stability. *Journal of Sex Research, 39*(3), 190–196

Springer, K. W., Hankivsky, O., & Bates, L. M. (2012). Gender and health: Relational, intersectional, and biosocial approaches. *Social Science and Medicine, 74*(11), 1661–1666.

Staples, J. M., Bird, E. R., Gregg, J. J., & George, W. (2019). Improving the gender-affirmation process for transgender and gender-nonconforming individuals: Associations among time since transition began, body satisfaction, and sexual distress. *Journal of Sex Research, 57*(3), 375–383.

Stephenson, K. R., & Meston, C. M. (2010). Differentiating components of sexual well-being in women: Are sexual satisfaction and sexual distress independent constructs? *The Journal of Sexual Medicine, 7*(7), 2458–2468.

Stulhofer, A., Busko, V., & Brouillard, P. (2010). Development and bicultural validation of the new sexual satisfaction scale. *Journal of Sex Research, 47*(4), 257–268.

Thibaut, J., & Kelley, H. H. (1952). *The social psychology of groups.* John Wiley & Sons.

Tracy, J. K., & Junginger, J. (2007). Correlates of lesbian sexual functioning. *Journal of Women's Health, 16*(4), 499–509.

Umberson, D., Thomeer, M. B., & Lodge, A. C. (2015). Intimacy and emotion work in lesbian, gay, and heterosexual relationships. *Journal of Marriage and Family, 77*(2), 542–556.

Walster, E., Walster, G. W., & Berscheid, E. (1978). *Equity: Theory and research.* Allyn & Bacon.

World Health Organization. (2010). Measuring sexual health: Conceptual and practical considerations and related indicators. http://whqlibdoc.who.int/hq/2010/who_rhr_10.12_eng.pdf

Madeleine Redlick Holland

SOCIAL SUPPORT AND LGBTQ+ INDIVIDUALS AND COMMUNITIES

INTRODUCTION

Exposure to stress differs based on factors such as gender, race, ethnicity, and income, which can create health-related inequalities at the societal level (Thoits, 2010). Stigmatization (Smith & Bishop, 2019) and discrimination can further harm the health of those who are members of minority groups (Thoits, 2010), such as individuals who identify as LGBTQ+ (lesbian, gay, bisexual, transgender, queer, plus).[1] LGBTQ+ individuals experience discrimination and prejudice related to homophobia, heterosexism, transphobia, and biphobia, and this additional burden is called *minority stress* (Meyer, 1995, 2003). Important assumptions of minority stress are that it is (1) experienced in addition to "regular" stresses and therefore requires additional adaptation, (2) chronic, and (3) based in social interactions (Meyer, 2003).

Minority stress processes related to LGBTQ+ individuals are threefold, consisting of: (1) objectively experienced events (*distal* sources); (2) subjective appraisals (*proximal* sources) and associated vigilance of anticipated or feared events; and (3) internalized homophobia (Meyer, 2003). Objectively experienced stressors can range from microaggressions, which are "behaviors and statements, often unconscious or unintentional, that communicate hostile or derogatory messages" (Nadal et al., 2016, p. 488), such as a person saying "that's so gay" to hostile and violent reactions from others. Some situations may involve negative *memorable messages* that impact individuals for years afterwards. Memorable messages are harmful messages communicated by significant others that individuals recall for a long time after they occur and which have a significant impact on their self-identities (Rubinsky & Cooke-Jackson, 2017). Stress can result from subjective appraisals such as worrying about whether co-workers will be friendly to a partner at a work-related function (LeBlanc et al., 2015). Internalized homophobia can result in negative self-perceptions and diminished psychological adjustment (Meyer, 2003). Stigmatization, thus, is experienced both externally and internally (Haas et al., 2020).

A list of sexuality-related stressors related to "family reactions, disclosure or visibility concerns, violence, harassment, societal misunderstanding, discrimination, HIV/AIDS, and sexual orientation conflict" (Doty et al., 2010, p. 1137) is found in the 52-item measure of gay-related stress (MOGS) (Lewis et al., 2003). These chronically experienced social situations can negatively affect both the mental and physical health of sexual- and gender-minority individuals (Haas & Lannutti, 2021; Meyer, 1995, 2003). Reactions to communicated stigma, however, may also include resistance and proactive responses such as advocacy (Smith & Bishop, 2019).

A key way in which stress can be reduced is through the communication of social support to those who identify as LGBTQ+ (Frost et al., 2016). Individuals typically expect to receive social support within close relationships (Goldsmith, 2004), and communities and other systems (e.g., institutions and government) also influence the well-being of LGBTQ+ individuals. Moreover, support comes not only from "outside" the LGBTQ+ community[2] but also from within it (Meyer, 2003). Being able to reach out to other sexuality minority youth for advice or to see them as role models, for example, can help youth who are in the process of coming out to others (Frost et al., 2016).

Social support may reduce the number of stressful events a person is experiencing, or it may help them to change their perceptions of how challenging a particular circumstance is (Brownell & Shumaker, 1984). For sexual- and gender-minority individuals, social support can reduce stress "by reducing isolation and offering resources, a sense of security, and a sense of identity" (Vyncke & Julien, 2007, p. 402). This article focuses solely on the positive effects of social support for LGBTQ+ individuals, while recognizing that social support can also be used in a controlling way (Nurullah, 2012; Vyncke & Julien, 2007).

Six sections are presented in this article. Social support is first defined and distinguished from the concept of tolerance, followed by a brief overview of factors influencing the effectiveness of communicated support efforts. The third section presents examples of changing attitudes around the world. Factors associated with acceptance are then briefly presented. The fifth section presents various examples of how social support has been operationalized in LGBTQ+ research. The final section notes the importance of a contextual approach to studying this topic: (1) different groups under the LGBTQ+ umbrella rather than as a group, including intersectional identities; (2) experiences across the lifespan; and (3) social support in formal environments.

DEFINING SOCIAL SUPPORT

Various definitions exist for social support (Dowers et al., 2020; Masini & Barrett, 2008; Williams et al., 2004), which was first studied as a "distinct construct" in the mid-1970s (Nurullah, 2012, p. 173). Cobb (1976) provided one of the earliest definitions in a Presidential Address to the American Psychosomatic Society: information leading a person to believe that they are "cared for and loved," "esteemed and valued," and "belongs to a network of communication and mutual obligation" (p. 300). In their review of social support in social science research, Williams et al. (2004) found 30 different definitions, with Cobb's definition used the most frequently. Cobb's definition is still used (e.g., Ingham et al., 2017). Many researchers (e.g., Hawthorne et al., 2020) also cite Peggy Thoits (2010, 2011), whose definition from research linked social support with health. Thoits (2010) defined social support as "emotional, informational, or practical assistance from significant others, such as family members, friends, or coworkers; support actually may be received from others or simply perceived to be available when needed" (p. S47). Definitions of each of these three types of assistance are also provided:

> Emotional support refers to demonstrations of love and caring, esteem and value, encouragement, and sympathy. Informational assistance is the provision of facts or advice that may help a person solve problems; this category of help can also include appraisal support—feedback about the person's interpretation of a situation and guidance regarding possible courses of action.... Instrumental support consists of offering or supplying behavioral or material assistance with practical tasks or problems. (Thoits, 2011, p. 146)

Applying Thoits's three types of assistance to LGBTQ+ individuals, one could look at what kind of responses others have when an LGBTQ+ person discloses harassment, whether they know of resources to refer an LGBTQ+ person to, and if they provide tangible assistance during times of need (e.g., finances to help with the purchase of a home or assist with a gender-affirming operation). Actions such as a heterosexual person marching in or attending a gay pride parade or posting signs of support on their social media site (Matsick et al., 2020) also communicate messages that LGBTQ+ individuals are accepted and valued (emotional support).

Major life events, such as the death of a partner or moving to a new country, represent opportunities for others to show their support. However, many daily, regular events also occur in which individuals hope to receive support from others (Thoits, 2011); this kind of support is less visible than support occurring in response to major events. Examples of daily support are (1) feeling heard after relaying a challenging work experience to a family member later in the day (e.g., completing a heterosexist-worded form); (2) chatting with neighbors about aggravating street construction; and (3) helping a same-sex couple prepare for a party.

> Routine or everyday emotional, informational, and instrumental acts are helpful in themselves and also may sustain self-esteem, a sense of mattering to others, and perceived control over minor or impending obstacles and thus indirectly maintain psychological well-being and (through positive affect) physical well-being as well. (Thoits, 2011, p. 150)

The previous examples are of informal social support, which comes from *primary groups* of people who are close to a person, such as family and friends (Thoits, 2010). Communities and religious organizations are also examples of informal social support (Glass & Few-Demo, 2013). Many researchers only focus their study of social support in this manner (e.g., Dowers et al., 2020) or emphasize that it is "informal" social support they are examining (e.g., Hawthorne et al., 2020; Ingham et al., 2017).

Social support is also demonstrated more broadly by *secondary groups* (Thoits, 2011), environments characterized by more formal and less personal interactions, compared to primary groups. Examples of secondary groups are workplaces, schools, healthcare settings, and organized athletics. Some researchers have examined the role that such support can play in the well-being of LGBTQ+ individuals, examining support in state, employment, educational, and sports contexts (Atteberry-Ash et al., 2018; Oswald et al., 2010; Pitcher et al., 2018; Woodford et al., 2015).

Social support is distinct from other concepts. For example, it is not the same as social integration, social capital, or a social network (Nurullah, 2012). A person may have social capital or a social network, but neither is a guarantee of receiving social support when it is needed. Additionally, social support is not the same as *tolerance*, which is defined in different ways in literature about LGBTQ+ individuals. Holman et al. (2019) suggested that tolerance consists of "a general source of support" at an institutional level, but with "very clear limitations to that support" (p. 554), whereas Twenge et al. (2015) defined tolerance as "agreeing that controversial outgroups should be allowed public expression" (p. 389). In general, tolerating differences is not the same as supporting them: "to support difference is to believe that individuals, families, and communities are better off when people are valued for their differences, rather than despite them" (Oswald et al., 2018, p. 42).

FACTORS INFLUENCING THE EFFECTIVENESS OF COMMUNICATED SOCIAL SUPPORT

Social support is typically viewed as a transaction occurring in everyday conversation (as cited in Haas, 2002) such as *troubles talk* (Goldsmith, 2004). It can be communicated in many other ways, however, such as through nonverbal actions (Burleson, 2003) (e.g., social media posts). A variety of factors interact to influence whether social support is effectively communicated (Burleson, 2009), and three factors are briefly described.

First, people vary in their ability to effectively communicate different types of support such as emotional support, which is communicated through both verbal and nonverbal means (Burleson, 2003). Support is not always provided when needed or effective when presented. People may be less likely to provide support when they do not feel confident that they will be effective in doing so (Rossetto et al., 2014). They may also be less likely to offer support when a situation feels emotionally challenging: "a lack of empathy acts as a barrier to offering support" (Rossetto et al., 2014, p. 51).

Second, the effectiveness of social support efforts is associated with the needs and perceptions of the recipient. That is, "the effects of received support do not come about mechanistically through the mere issuance of a supportive act (e.g., advice) but rather through participants' interpretations of acts and their implications" (Goldsmith & Fitch, 1997, p. 455). For example, a recipient may want emotional support but receive informational assistance (e.g., advice) instead, which is perceived as unhelpful. Feeling like one's identity is valued in a social support interaction (Goldsmith, 2004) may be particularly important for people who identify as LGBTQ+, and unwanted or ineffective advice can threaten a person's sense of self (MacGeorge et al., 2019).

Third, the effectiveness of communicated support is contextually bound, affected by many factors (Burleson, 2003; Goldsmith, 2004; Goldsmith & Fitch, 1997) such as the topic and level of stress being experienced. The characteristics of both the person attempting to provide the support and the recipient are key, as is their relationship to each other, which is an underexplored consideration in the study of advice (MacGeorge, 2020).

GLOBAL TRENDS IN ACCEPTANCE OF LGBTQ+ INDIVIDUALS

Research on trends related to acceptance of homosexuality and gay rights is limited (Smith et al., 2014). However, cross-sectional, cross-cultural research does show increased tolerance toward LGBTQ+ individuals since the early 21st century (Pew Research Center, 2020; Smith et al., 2014). The lives of sexual minorities—and to a lesser extent gender minorities—has improved in many countries since the first International Day Against Homophobia, Transphobia, and Biphobia (IDAHO) held on May 16, 2004 (Meyer, 2016). Positive attitudes are more likely found in individualistic countries (Twenge et al., 2015) such as in the Americas and Western European countries (Pew Research Center, 2020). Improvements have also occurred in South America (Meyer, 2016). Increasing acceptance is seen in other countries. For example, 14% of Kenyans said that homosexuality was acceptable in 2019, compared with 1% in 2002, and India increased in acceptance from 16% to 37% from 2014 to 2019 (Pew Research Center, 2020).

Support is also increasingly seen for same-sex marriage. From 2000 to 2020, 30 countries and territories legalized same-sex marriage, starting with the Netherlands in 2000 and more recently Costa Rica in 2020 (Pew Research Center, 2019).

Nevertheless, in some countries such as Russia and Uganda, LGBTQ+ individuals continue to face hostile and dangerous circumstances (Meyer, 2016). It is illegal to be gay in 32 African countries, and gay sex is criminalized in 67 countries (Greenhalgh, 2019). Moreover, even in countries in which support is more generally found, anti-gay political and institutional discourse and actions are found (see, e.g., Shear & Savage, 2017; Unger, 2020). Support, tolerance, and rejection can be communicated in the same country, and threats to LGBTQ+ protection cause concern and fear for LGBTQ+ individuals and their allies (Brown & Keller, 2018; Gonzalez et al., 2018).

Positive or negative attitudes toward LGBTQ+ individuals can also take many different forms. Negative attitudes about LGBTQ+ parenting exist (Weiner & Zinner, 2015), despite research showing that children raised in such families are as similarly well-adjusted as children raised by heterosexual parents (Patterson, 2017). Thus, a person might show support for homosexuality and same-sex intimate relationships, but not support parenting by LGBTQ+ individuals. Ambivalent attitudes (Costa & Salinas-Quiroz, 2019) about certain contexts can also exist.

FACTORS ASSOCIATED WITH ACCEPTANCE

A number of factors are related to acceptance of homosexuality, such as having interactions with LGBTQ+ individuals, age, education, religiosity, political ideology, and a country's wealth (Burgess & Baunach, 2014; Pew Research Center, 2020; Smith et al., 2014). These factors may also interact with other conditions. For instance, higher levels of education are less related to LGBTQ+ acceptance in countries in which sexual- and gender-minorities are still viewed very negatively (Smith et al., 2014).

Other research has examined factors related to acceptance of same-sex marriage and same-sex parenting (e.g., Costa & Salinas-Quiroz, 2019), finding similar results. In the United States, for example, interactions with LGBTQ+ individuals, higher educational levels, lower levels of religious intensity, younger ages, liberal ideology, and partisanship are positively related to acceptance of same-sex marriage (Daniels, 2019; Lee & Mutz, 2019). Women are also more supportive than men of same-sex marriage and parenting (Costa et al., 2018; Sloane & Robillard, 2018). Attitudes about same-sex parenting may depend on what parenting configurations are being assessed. Older Italians are more negative about gay parenting than they are about lesbian or heterosexual parenting (Baiocco et al., 2013). A study of attitudes about adoption by same-sex couples in 28 European countries found that both individual-level and country-level variables influence attitudes (Takács et al., 2016).

MEASURING SOCIAL SUPPORT FOR LGBTQ+ INDIVIDUALS

Most research is quantitative in design and uses social support as a predictor of health outcomes. Qualitative approaches to understanding social support for LGBTQ+ individuals also exist. This section provides some examples of the ways in which social support is operationalized and examined.

In quantitative research, social support is typically measured as an individual's *perception* of social support, rather than the actual receipt of social support (Frost et al., 2016; Goldsmith, 2004; Nurullah, 2012). Perceived social support is consistently shown to be related to better physical and mental well-being, but less is known about the actual receipt of support (Goldsmith, 2004; Nurullah, 2012).

Measures vary in their focus. They can focus on (1) general social support, (2) support within particular settings, or (3) very specific ways in which support is communicated. Previously existing measures (i.e., not developed specifically for LGBTQ+ populations) are used, as are scales created specifically for LGBTQ+ populations. Community-based measures distinguish between LGBTQ+ communities and general, broader communities. Some measures examine in more detail who provides social support (Goldsmith, 2004).

Doty et al. (2010) noted the importance of distinguishing between social support for general problems and those that are specifically related to one's sexuality, such as issues with disclosure, visibility, and family reactions. The authors used subscales from a previously existing general measure: the social support behaviors scale from Vaux et al. (1987). The emotional support and advice/guidance subscales were used twice: the first time to measure perceived support for general problems and the second time for problems related specifically to one's sexuality. Sample statements are "Listened when I needed to talk about my feelings," "Gave me a hug, or otherwise showed me I was cared about," and "Told me who to talk to for help" (Vaux et al., 1987, pp. 214–215). Results showed that sexual-minority friends provided higher levels of sexuality support than family members or heterosexual friends, and the authors noted the importance of connecting LGB (lesbian, gay, bisexual) youth with others. The scale items, however, are generally stated and make no reference to issues related to sexual orientation or gender identity.

In a review of research on trans, gender-diverse, and nonbinary (TGDNB) adults' experiences of social support, Dowers et al. (2020) raised concern about the application of cisnormative measures of social support to TGDNB individuals, for whom different forms of social support might exist outside typical family, friends, and/or partner configurations. The most commonly used measure of social support is the multidimensional scale of perceived social support (MSPSS) (Zimet et al., 1988). This measure includes a "significant other" subscale, which assumes a person has a monogamous relationship. Additionally, research on online forms of community support is needed.

Around 2010, studies with measures specifically designed to examine social support for LGBTQ+ individuals started appearing (e.g., Ryan et al., 2010; Shulman et al., 2012; Vyncke & Julien, 2007). These measures focus mainly on support communicated by family members (e.g., Ryan et al., 2010; Vyncke & Julien, 2007), and sometimes include other members of a person's network (e.g., Shulman et al., 2012).

The Measure of Family Acceptance (Ryan et al., 2010) focuses specifically on family and caregiver acceptance, and it was developed with a diverse sample of Latinx and non-Latinx White LGBT (lesbian, gay, bisexual, transgender) adolescents and their families. Participants indicate how often they experienced a positive reaction to 55 items, such as "How often did any of your parents/caregivers appreciate your clothing or hairstyle, even though it might not have been typical for your gender?" and "How often were your openly LGBT friends invited to join family activities?" (Ryan et al., 2010, p. 207). Overall scores are categorized into low, moderate, and high levels of family acceptance. This measure has been used numerous times by researchers, such as Snapp et al. (2015), who found that family acceptance had a strong influence on health outcomes for teenagers, even when accounting for friends and community support.

Vyncke and Julien (2007) also focused on family support, but studied support for same-sex couples as opposed to individuals. Their Social Support to the Couple measure consists of six items: five items measure support (e.g., "How often are you invited for a family dinner or reunion with your partner?"), and one item measures interference (e.g., "How often do members of your family criticize your partner?") (Vyncke & Julien, 2007, p. 409). Two items also examine support from heterosexual friends (e.g., "How often do you receive invitations from your heterosexual/GLB friends who assume that you will very probably come with your partner?") (Vyncke & Julien, 2007, p. 409). Vyncke and Julien found that social support helped strengthen the relationship as well as reduce stress.

In a study of social support and relationship satisfaction, Shulman et al. (2012) stated that no specific measures for social support related to LGBTQ+ identities existed. They created a measure called the Gay and Lesbian Acceptance and Support Index (GLASSI). This 22-item scale measures perceived support for being a sexuality minority (e.g., "How supportive is your mother of your gay/lesbian/bisexual identity?"; Shulman et al., 2012, p. 165) and for one's couple relationship. Three subscales measure support from different sources: (1) one's family of origin, (2) the larger heterosexual community, and (3) one's religious community. These researchers found that perceptions of support from one's family and the community were positively associated with relationship satisfaction.

In addition to what kind of support is perceived, research has examined *who* is perceived as providing support. Frost et al. (2016), for instance, used the Social Support Network measure from Martin and Dean (1987). Martin and Dean (1987) had modified the language from an earlier 1977 measure so that it could be used with gay and bisexual men. This measure asks lesbian, gay, and bisexual (LGB) individuals who they turned to for everyday support (e.g., being able to count on a person for small favors) and major support (e.g., borrowing money for a major purchase). After individuals are identified, additional questions are asked about them, such as their age, sexual orientation, and relationship to the LGB person. A summary is then generated regarding how many individuals provided daily or major support to an LGB person. In Frost et al. (2016), the results were also compared to heterosexual respondents. Results indicated that LGB individuals relied more on their friends than their families for major assistance, compared to heterosexual individuals.

Community connectedness and support measures started emerging around the same time as measures focusing on social support from significant others. Frost and Meyer (2012) noted that previously developed measures of community connectedness had limitations, such as not being originally developed for LGBTQ+ participants, lacking psychometric data, being too long, or only being tested with White participants. They therefore modified an earlier measure developed by Barrett and Pollack (2005) and tested it with a racially diverse population in the New York City area. Prior to completing the 8-item measure of Connectedness to the LGBT Community, individuals were instructed to think of community as not any "particular neighborhood or social group, but in general, groups of gay men, bisexual men and women, lesbians, and transgender individuals" (Barrett & Pollack, 2005, p. 40). Examples of items are "You feel a bond with the LGBT community" and "You really feel that any problems faced by NYC's LGBT community are also your own problems." This measure has been used in research looking at social support and the well-being of young bisexual people of color (Flanders et al., 2019), who found that connections to the LGBTQ+ community resulted in higher levels of binegativity for these individuals, despite broader levels of social support being related to lower levels of binegativity. These findings point to the ongoing issue of acceptance of bisexuality within the LGBTQ+ community.

A different line of research has looked more broadly at support in local and regional communities (Holman & Oswald, 2016; Oswald et al., 2010, 2018; Woodford et al., 2015), using the language of *community climate*. Community climate is "the level of community support for homosexuality, indicated by objectively measurable phenomenon such as religious and political affiliations, legal rights, workplace opportunities and policies, and the presence of GLBT [gay, lesbian, bisexual, transgender] community members and services" (Oswald et al., 2010, p. 215). Community climate influences the well-being of LGBTQ+ individuals by demonstrating support or rejection for them (Oswald et al., 2010). The research in this area has been both qualitative and mixed methods in design. Holman and Oswald (2016) qualitatively analyzed individuals' responses to open-ended questions about what were the best and worst aspects of living in their communities. Oswald et al. (2010) presented a list of specific municipal- and county-level tools to measure support for LGBTQ+ individuals, such as counting the number of businesses listed in local LGBTQ+ resources and examining county voting patterns. In contrast, Woodford et al. (2015) created two measures to focus specifically on lack of support in the form of microaggressions (Nadal et al., 2016) in distal and proximal environments. The first scale measures exposure to negative messages about LGBTQ+ people by media and politicians, (e.g., "I've heard politicians oppose equal rights and protections for LGBQ people"), and the second scale measures microaggressions happening in one's local community (e.g., "I saw people holding signs with religiously based anti-LGBQ messages [e.g., 'Faggots are going to hell']") (Woodford et al., 2015, pp. 124–125).[3] Exposure to these kinds of situations was related to higher levels of anxiety and perceived stress for LGBTQ+ individuals.

Some research has narrowed in on support within specific contexts (Holman et al., 2019) or very specific forms of support (Matsick et al., 2020). This is not surprising, as the developers of early definitions of social support recognized that the meaning of social support relates to the context in which it is being studied (Williams et al., 2004). As an example of specific context, the Lesbian, Gay, Bisexual, and Transgender Climate Inventory (LGBTCI) (Liddle et al., 2004) measures informal aspects of workplace environments that communicate supportiveness to LGBTQ+ employees. This measure consists of 20 items, such as "LGBT employees feel free to display pictures of same-sex partners" and "Employees are expected to not act 'too gay'" (Liddle et al., 2004, p. 551). This measure is typically used as a predictor of outcomes such as workplace satisfaction, but Holman et al. (2019) suggested that it measures two constructs rather than one. One subscale measures workplace support; the other measures workplace hostility. Operationalizing workplace climate in this manner allows for the fact that support and hostility can exist concurrently. They identified four types of workplaces climates: supportive, ambiguous, tolerant, and hostile. Tolerant work communities, for example, are those in which institutional support is provided yet not all employees agree with the institutional support (Holman et al., 2019).

Matsisk et al. (2020) provided an example of a very specific type of social support: the use of rainbow filters in women's Facebook profile photos. Rainbow filters are a type of "low-effort" pro-LGBTQ+ activism called "pictivism" (as cited in Matsick et al., 2020, p. 343). Although activist in nature, filters can be viewed as "empty gestures" of support (Matsick et al., 2020, p. 357) because they require little effort. Nevertheless, the authors argued that more research is needed in this area, given that approximately half of all Americans use social media to communicate political opinions (Pew Research Center, 2018). Using an experimental design, Matsick et al. (2020) examined how rainbow filters influenced viewers' perceptions, attitudes, and behaviors. Results indicated that the use of rainbow filters increased LGBTQ+ individuals' perceptions of acceptance within online communities, although this sense of acceptance was higher if the filter user was presented as queer rather than heterosexual. Moreover, heterosexual individuals were more impacted by pictivism if it was demonstrated by a queer user rather than another heterosexual user.

As the research field of social support for LGBTQ+ individuals develops, its study will need to become more focused on specific contexts, and researchers have argued that qualitative approaches are more amenable to understanding what social support means to people (Dowers et al., 2020; Williams et al., 2004). For example, Dowers et al. (2020) stated that "use of qualitative research methods, specifically phenomenology and grounded theory, would make it possible to develop a context-specific definition of what is social support from the perspectives of TGDNB adults" (p. 252). Additionally, qualitative methods are more appropriate for intersectional analysis (Shields, 2008), which examines how various social identities interact with each other. The following are a few examples of qualitative research on social support for LGBTQ+ individuals.

Price and Prosek (2020) used a phenomenological approach to examine the ways in which parents support their LGBTQ+ children in early adulthood. Instead of completing a battery of measures, participants were asked to discuss topics such as their experiences of disclosing their sexual orientation to their parents and their perceptions of their parents' support. Gay and lesbian participants perceived their parents to affirm their sexual identity during disclosure and after it in four ways: (1) "asking intentional questions about [LGBTQ+] community, (2) [having a] welcoming attitude toward child's potential partners, (3) providing encouragement during experiences of fear or discrimination, and (4) performing acts of service to promote child's expression of identity" (p. 89). The young adults described how such support helped them to feel more confident and authentic.

Two examples of intersectional approaches to studying social support are Glass and Few-Demo (2013) and Abelson (2016). In a study of Black lesbian couples, Glass and Few-Demo (2013) asked open-ended questions such as "(a) 'Tell me about your experiences with your extended families,' (b) 'When you have a challenge, as a couple, where do you turn?' and (c) 'Outside of your extended families, where do you get the most support? (What does that support look like?)'" (p. 716). Their richly detailed qualitative analysis revealed complex negotiations for the couples. Extended families supported them as parents (i.e., supported their children) but did not support them as a same-sex couple. Friends, churches, and lesbian and gay friends also supported them as sexual-minority individuals, but not as couples. This analysis raises interesting questions, such as "is it commonplace for Black lesbians to prioritize familial affinity and belonging over the need to be a part of LGBTQ communities?" (Glass & Few-Demo,

2013, p. 724). Another example of intersectional qualitative research is a study of trans men living in rural communities, which used a "modified life history approach" (Abelson, 2016, p. 1539) to explore the men's experiences. In Abelson (2016), trans men who carried out peaceful lives in rural areas made "claims to sameness" (p. 1539) in race and working-class masculinities in order to feel like they belonged. Abelson (2016) stated:

> An intersectional lens takes us beyond a binary understanding of acceptance and "othering" to a more finely shaded understanding or [sic] how race, gender, sexuality, and class work together to offer different possibilities for limited acceptance or exclusion in rural life for rural trans people.

In summary, various measures have been used to study social support for and within LGBTQ+ communities. Research tends to be quantitative in design, but qualitative research is also emerging. Scholars have commented on the importance of attending to context, studying different people represented in the LGBTQ+ community, such as gender-diverse and non-binary individuals, and acknowledging intersectionality in how social support is experienced. The final section explores some of the diverse ways in which support for LGBTQ+ individuals is studied.

CONTEXTUALIZING SUPPORT

Early research on this topic has been criticized for limitations such as focusing on LGBTQ+ individuals who are White (Dowers et al., 2020), middle class, and living in urban areas (Forstie, 2020). Additionally, some researchers have argued that more research needs to focus beyond family support in the adolescent years (Snapp et al., 2015) and beyond family responses to initial self-disclosure (Reeves et al., 2010). There are so many different contexts in which social support can be explored. LGBTQ+ individuals' needs for social support, and their perceptions and experiences of it differ depending on the context (Williams et al., 2004). Meyer (2016) noted the importance of intersectional research:

> Researchers have to be aware not only of generational and regional differences in the experiences of sexual- and gender-minorities, but also of differences related to race/ethnicity, gender and gender expression, socioeconomic status, and religiosity among people in any time and place. We can no longer portray LGBT people as one community, but need to recognize the multiple communities that LGBT people inhabit, and the multiple experiences they have in these varied environments. (p. 6)

This final section provides some examples of the study of social support (1) within different groups represented in the LGBTQ+ umbrella, (2) across the lifespan, and (3) during times of elevated anti-gay rhetoric. It concludes with some examples of social support in formal environments.

Moving Beyond Studying LGBTQ+ Individuals as a Group. Broad terms such as LGBTQ+ mask important differences among the many individuals represented by this umbrella acronym. Moreover, individuals' sexual and gender identities intersect with other social identities to create unique social support experiences and needs, which is referred to as "intersectionality" (APA, 2012). Some research has started focusing on these differences. The following are a few examples of findings representing this diversity.

Different patterns of social support exist for gay men, lesbians, bisexual individuals, and transgender individuals. For example, gay and bisexual men appear to rely more heavily on sexual-minority friends than family or heterosexual friends for major support (e.g., borrowing large amounts of money), compared to lesbian and heterosexual women (Frost et al., 2016). In lesbians' social support networks, ex-partners and lovers often play an important role in providing social support (Degges-White, 2012; Hawthorne et al., 2020; Ingham et al., 2017). Social support is particularly important for bisexual individuals because they can experience discrimination from both the heterosexual community and the LGBTQ+ community (Flanders et al., 2019; Pollitt et al., 2017). Close connections to each community can have conflicting results. Closer connections to the LGBTQ+ community result in higher levels of binegativity for bisexual individuals, but support from other people such as family members is related to more positive experiences with bisexuality (Flanders et al., 2019). Lastly, social support may be found in different sources for TGDNB adults beyond the normally considered "tripartite relations of family/friend/significant other" (Dowers et al., 2020, p. 243), such as online communities. Focusing on TGDNB individuals reveals that cisnormative ideals of social support may not apply to them (Dowers).

LGBTQ+ individuals who belong to ethnic and racial minority groups experience additional barriers when coming out, and research on this topic typically focuses on these intersectional challenges. Ideologies of collectivism and *familism*, for instance, complicate dynamics with families of origin, and LGBTQ+ individuals may be less likely to come out to their families (Price & Prosek, 2020). Racial and ethnic minority LGB individuals also report fewer ways in which everyday support is communicated to them than White LGBs (Frost et al., 2016). Yet not all families are unsupportive. An innovative special issue framed by intersectionality in the *Journal of GLBT Family Studies* challenges the notion that people of color and Indigenous people always invalidate their LGBTQ+ members (Abreu & Gonzalez, 2020). A range of reactions occur, and support and rejection can co-exist in Latinx families (Przeworski & Piedra, 2020). Moreover, older family members can be significant role models of resiliency for LGBTQ+ individuals through their overcoming of adversities such as racism and poverty (Stone et al., 2020).

Unique life circumstances related to immigration and health provide further opportunities to explore intersecting identities. LGBTQ+ individuals who emigrate from countries where their sexual or gender identities were not supported may be both surprised and disappointed to experience a lack of support in White-dominated LGBTQ+ communities in their new countries (Logie et al., 2016; Sadika et al., 2020). Perceptions of support can differ based on what kind of support is being sought, however (Gray et al., 2015). Undocumented immigrant trans Latinas are able to create "robust" social networks through a collection of informal and formal means (Hwahng et al., 2019).

Sexual- and gender-minority individuals with HIV/AIDS can experience additional strains such as (1) financial strains if a partner cannot maintain employment, (2) one partner is worried about infecting the other, and (3) the stigma associated with having this illness.

Haas (2002) found that support specific to HIV/AIDS helped gay men maintain their relationships, further noting that although support from close friends and family members was important and helpful, partners provided a unique form of daily social support that could not be replaced by others. However, HIV stereotypes and stigma can impede good sexual health conversations from occurring between sexual partners (Haas et al., 2020).

Life Course Approaches. Various experiences across the life course present opportunities to explore the social support needs of LGBTQ+ individuals. Family experiences and transitions are particularly key because family life habitually emphasizes *heteronormativity*, an ideology that "promotes gender conventionality, heterosexuality, and family traditionalism as the correct way for people to be" (as cited in Oswald et al., 2005, p. 143). Family traditions and roles can raise taken-for-granted ideologies to the surface and challenge the exchange of social support between individuals. Family transitions also create new role demands, which results in new needs or expectations for social support. Much diversity exists in sexual- and gender-minority families,[4] and research is lacking on marginalized families such as those with individuals who are transgender, asexual, or polyamorous (Reczek, 2020).

Individuals also experience sociohistorical events at different times in their lives that create or elevate minority stress, and such events can change support patterns (e.g., what support is needed, when it is sought, who it is sought from, who provides it, and so on). For example, as same-sex marriage becomes increasingly accepted by heteronormative individuals, individuals in same-sex relationships may be less likely to seek support from LGBTQ+ communities (Haas & Lannutti, 2021; Ogolsky et al., 2019). Formal support in organizations such as schools, the workforce, and athletic programs are also important as individuals move through the life course.

Intimate Relationships. Support can be demonstrated in many ways for individuals in intimate relationships, who experience not only individual-level minority stress but also couple-level minority stress (LeBlanc et al., 2015). Studies are more likely to examine the negative impacts of *lack* of social support rather than the positive impacts that social support can have on same-sex relationships (Haas & Lannutti, 2021).

Prior to being able to legally marry, commitment ceremonies were a way for friends and family members to show support for same-sex couples (Clarke et al., 2013; Haas, 2002). Weddings provide many ways for individuals, businesses, and organizations to show support for LGBTQ+ individuals (Humble, 2013, 2016; Lannutti, 2008, 2011, 2018; Ocobock, 2013), and in some cases are the first time a family member might actually show support for an LGBTQ+ relative (Ocobock, 2013). Yet American research shows that some LGBTQ+ individuals in committed relationships who chose not to marry report experiencing less support from others (Kennedy & Dalla, 2020; Lannutti, 2018; LeBlanc et al., 2015) because their cohabiting relationships are now viewed as inferior to married ones. Moreover, research examining broader societal contexts remains important. Unequal recognition at the state level has a negative impact on same-sex couples, regardless of whether they are married (LeBlanc et al., 2018).

Parenting. Research has started looking at the role that social support plays in a variety of LGBTQ+-parent families contexts (Patterson, 2017; Reczek, 2020), such as couples who plan parenthood through adoption or surrogacy. For instance, support from families, friends, and workplaces decreases depression and anxiety in the transition to adoptive parenting for lesbian and gay parents (Goldberg & Smith, 2011). Overall, the research to date indicates that social support is lacking for sexual- and gender-minority parents and their families (Reczek, 2020). An analysis of online communication about having a parent who had transitioned to their identified gender later in life found that younger family members often wrote about wanting to support their parents but struggling with doing so for various reasons (Norwood, 2012). More research is needed on TGDNB parenting (Abreu et al., 2019) and LGBTQ+-parent families outside Western and European countries (Costa & Salinas-Quiroz, 2019).

Older Adults. A life course approach is often used when studying LGBTQ+ older adults, which takes into account lifetime experiences of discrimination, historical timing, and linked lives (Fredriksen-Goldsen et al., 2019). Older individuals may have lost important sources of social support when they came out at younger ages (i.e., rejection from their families), which results in vulnerability in terms of social support later in life. They may rely more on friends than families and many report limited amounts of support (Hawthorne et al., 2020). For example, older men's reliance on other gay men for support is reduced due to AIDS mortality, which then results in increased reliance on formal supports (Jones et al., 2018). However, reaching out to formal support can be difficult for LGBTQ+ individuals who have experienced stigma throughout their lives—particularly in the healthcare system (Haas, 2019). Moreover, contemporary discrimination still exists.

Perceptions of support in later life differ based on age, gender, gender identity, and parental status; thus, an intersectional research approach is needed (Fredriksen-Goldsen et al., 2019). Moreover, LGBTQ+ older adults are resilient and demonstrate agency in the ways they have developed social supports throughout their lives, such as the creation of *chosen families*. Many gaps are found in the literature on social support for older individuals, such as research about caregiving (Fredriksen-Goldsen et al., 2019). Research participants also tend to be recruited through LGBTQ+ organizations and snowballing techniques. Individuals recruited in these ways often report good levels of social support, which raises issue around generalizability of results (Hawthorne et al., 2020).

Times of Elevated Anti-Gay Rhetoric. LGBTQ+ issues come to the forefront during times such as elections or when political initiatives are being considered. Such situations can result in elevated public displays of anti-gay rhetoric, which constitutes a minority stress factor for LGBTQ+ individuals (Verrelli et al., 2019) and can negatively impact their well-being (Frost & Fingerhut, 2016; Rostosky et al., 2010). Family members and friends play an important role in providing support during these times (Lannutti, 2011), and a limited amount of research has looked at this.

Verrelli et al. (2019) studied social support in Australia for LGB individuals during the Federal government's postal survey about the legalization of same-sex marriage. The Marriage Act was amended after the survey to include same-sex couples, but not without considerable public debate. Exposure to anti-gay messages in various forms such as online content, radio reports, and bumper stickers increased LGB individuals' psychological distress. However, perceived emotional support from one's social network (immediate and extended family, LGB and heterosexual friends, work colleagues, school peers, and neighbors) helped buffer this stress (Verrelli et al., 2019).

Several studies reported on experiences of social support in a special issue of the *Journal of GLBT Family Studies* (Lannutti & Galupo, 2018) about the 2016 U.S. election and LGBTQ+ communities. LGBTQ+ individuals with family members who chose to support political groups that were unsupportive of LGBTQ+ rights or threatening to take them away (i.e., the Republican Party) reported negative emotions and conflict with their family members (Brown & Keller, 2018; Gonzalez et al., 2018). In response, they sought out like-minded individuals for emotional support and also engaged in advocacy (Brown & Keller, 2018). In contrast, families who became closer after the 2016 U.S. election had non-LGBTQ+ family members who communicated support through becoming more educated about sexual- and gender-minority issues and shared their fears and concerns with the LGBTQ+ person (Gonzalez et al., 2018). Anti-gay administrations can actually result in stronger family relationships and greater awareness of marginalized individuals' experiences (Gonzalez et al., 2018).

Formal Support. Secondary groups need to use multifaceted approaches to not only effectively communicate support to LGBTQ+ individuals but also rectify longstanding systemic and structural histories of stigma and oppression. For example, in addition to creating more inclusive employment and patient settings, medical students need to be educated about LGBT healthcare *before* they enter their profession in order to help reduce homophobia and heterosexism perpetuated by physicians (Eliason et al., 2011). Sports coaches need guidelines on how to respond to microaggressions such as anti-gay LGBTQ+ language (NCAA, n.d.) often used in locker rooms. The longstanding binary-gendered structure of sport also creates specific challenges for trans athletes and needs rectifying (Atteberry-Ash et al., 2018). Inclusive services in agencies providing care to older LGBTQ+ adults include knowing correct terminology, examining intake forms for inclusive language, developing print and online materials that include same-sex couples and other diverse populations, and creating LGBT-specific support groups (National Resource Center on LGBT Aging, 2020). Aging service providers need to think carefully about misconceptions that they might hold, such as the assumption that their institution does not have any LGBTQ+ clients because nobody has openly identified as such. And in post-secondary campus athletics, the implementation of inclusive policies is not sufficient; educational campaigns to encourage support for such policies are also important, particularly ones geared toward male students (Atteberry-Ash et al., 2018). Secondary groups also consider intersectionality: guidelines for psychologists (APA, 2012, 2015) and sports coaches (NCAA, n.d.) note the importance of understanding how sexual orientation and gender identity interact with other cultural identities.

Many organizations have developed guidelines for developing more welcoming and inclusive environments, such as the National Collegiate Athletic Association and the Consortium of Higher Education LGBT Resource Professionals. Guidelines and policies are important in showing individuals how to communicate support to LGBTQ+ individuals. Research is needed to examine if and how guidelines are implemented at the interpersonal level, and how effective they are.

CONCLUSION

Social support is an important resource that helps prevent or ameliorate minority stress and other types of stress in LGBTQ+ individuals, couples, families, and communities. It is studied in many ways and contexts, and various operationalizations of social support for LGBTQ+ individuals emerged around the 2010s. Qualitative research also provides insight into complex dynamics and perceptions of social support. As the field grows, methodological reviews will be helpful to make sense of this burgeoning area of research. Researchers have also noted the need for contextualization and for intersectional research in this area. This type of research will likely increase in the future, with more research on specific life and family contexts. Research from underrepresented regions such as Africa will complement the current work being carried out in Western countries.

FURTHER READING

Abreu, R. L., & Gonzalez, K. A. (Eds.). (2020). Redefining collectivism: Family and community among sexual and gender diverse people of color and indigenous people [Special Issue]. *Journal of GLBT Family Studies, 16*(2), 107–110.

Abreu, R. L., Rosenkrantz, D. E., Ryser-Oatman, J. T., Rostosky, S. S., & Riggle, E. D. B. (2019). Parental reactions to transgender and gender diverse children: A literature review. *Journal of GLBT Family Studies, 15*(5), 461–485. https://doi.org/10.1080/1550428X.2019.1656132

APA (American Psychological Association). (2012). Guidelines for psychological practice with lesbian, gay, and bisexual clients. *American Psychologist, 67*(1), 10–42. https://doi.org/10.1037/a0024659

APA (American Psychological Association). (2015). Guidelines for psychological practice with transgender and gender nonconforming people. *American Psychologist, 70*(9), 832–864. https://doi.org/10.1037/a0039906

Burleson, B. R. (2003). Emotional support skill. In J. O. Greene & B. R. Burleson (Eds.), *Handbook of communication and social interaction skills* (pp. 551–591). Lawrence Erlbaum.

Burleson, B. R. (2009). Understanding the outcomes of supportive communication: A dual-process approach. *Journal of Social and Personal Relationships, 26*(1), 21–38. https://doi.org/10.1177/0265407509105519

Dowers, E., White, C., Cook, K., & Kingsley, J. (2020). Trans, gender diverse and non-binary adult experiences of social support: A systematic quantitative literature review. *International Journal of Transgender Health, 21*(3), 242–257. https://doi.org/10.1080/26895269.2020.1771805

FAP (Family Acceptance Project®). (n.d.). *Publications.* https://familyproject.sfsu.edu/publications

Forstie, C. (2020). Theory making from the middle: Researching LGBTQ communities in small cities. *City & Community, 19*(1), 153–168. https://doi.org/10.1111/cico.12446

Fredriksen-Goldsen, K. I., Hoy-Ellis, C. P., Goldsen, J., Emlet, C. A., & Hooyman, N. R. (2014). Creating a vision for the future: Key competencies and strategies for culturally competent practice with lesbian, gay, bisexual, and transgender (LGBT) older adults in the health and human services. *Journal of Gerontological Social Work, 57*(2–4), 80–107. https://doi.org/10.1080/01634372.2014.890690

Frost, D. M., & Meyer, I. H. (2012). Measuring community connectedness among diverse sexual minority populations. *Journal of Sex Research, 49*(1), 36–49. https://doi.org/10.1080/00224499.2011.565427

Goldberg, A. E., & Allen, K. R. (Eds.). (2020). *LGBTQ-parent families* (2nd ed.). Springer.

Goldsmith, D. J. (2004). *Advances in personal relationships: Communicating social support.* Cambridge University Press.

Haas, S. M., & Lannutti, P. J. (2021). The impact of minority stress and social support on positive relationship functioning in same-sex relationships. *Health Communication, 36*(3), 315–323. https://doi.org/10.1080/10410236.2019.1687130

Hawthorne, O., Camic, P. M., & Rimes, K. A. (2020). Understanding the structure, experiences and challenges of social support for older lesbian, gay and bisexual people: A systematic review. *Ageing & Society, 40*(2), 282–305. https://doi.org/10.1017/S0144686X18000910

Meyer, I. H. (2003). Prejudice, social stress, and mental health in lesbian, gay, and bisexual populations: Conceptual issues and research evidence. *Psychological Bulletin, 129*(5), 674–697. https://doi.org/10.1037/0033-2909.129.5.674

Norwood, K. (2012). Transitioning meanings? Family members' communicative struggles surrounding transgender identity. *Journal of Family Communication, 12*(1), 75–92. https://doi.org/10.1080/15267431.2010.509283

Oswald, R. F., Cuthbertson, C., Lazarevic, V., & Goldberg, A. E. (2010). New developments in the field: Measuring community climate. *Journal of GLBT Family Studies, 6*(2), 214–228. https://doi.org/10.1080/15504281003709230

Reczek, C. (2020). Sexual- and gender-minority families: A 2010 to 2020 decade in review. *Journal of Marriage and Family, 82*(1), 300–325. https://doi.org/10.1111/jomf.12607

Sadika, B., Wiebe, E., Morrison, M. A., & Morrison, T. G. (2020). Intersectional microaggressions and social support for LGBTQ persons of color: A systematic review of the Canadian-based empirical literature. *Journal of GLBT Family Studies, 16*(2), 111–147. https://doi.org/10.1080/1550428X.2020.1724125

Thoits, P. A. (2011). Mechanisms linking social ties and support to physical and mental health. *Journal of Health & Social Behavior, 52*(2), 145–161. https://doi.org/10.1177/0022146510395592

REFERENCES

Abelson, M. J. (2016). "You aren't from around here": Race, masculinity, and rural transgender men. *Gender, Place & Culture, 23*(11), 1535–1546. https://doi.org/10.1080/0966369X.2016.1219324

Abreu, R. L., & Gonzalez, K. A. (2020). Redefining collectivism: Family and community among sexual and gender diverse people of color and indigenous people: Introduction to the special issue. *Journal of GLBT Family Studies, 16*(2), 107–110. https://doi.org/10.1080/1550428X.2020.1736038

Abreu, R. L., Rosenkrantz, D. E., Ryser-Oatman, J. T., Rostosky, S. S., & Riggle, E. D. B. (2019). Parental reactions to transgender and gender diverse children: A literature review. *Journal of GLBT Family Studies, 15*(5), 461–485. https://doi.org/10.1080/1550428X.2019.1656132

APA (American Psychological Association). (2012). Guidelines for psychological practice with lesbian, gay, and bisexual clients. *American Psychologist, 67*(1), 10–42. https://doi.org/10.1037/a0024659

APA (American Psychological Association). (2015). Guidelines for psychological practice with transgender and gender nonconforming people. *American Psychologist, 70*(9), 832–864. https://doi.org/10.1037/a0039906

Atteberry-Ash, B., Woodford, M. R., & Spectrum Center. (2018). Support for policy protecting LGBT student athletes among heterosexual students participating in club and intercollegiate sports. *Sexuality Research and Social Policy, 15*(2), 151–162. https://doi.org/10.1007/s13178-017-0283-z

Baiocco, R., Nardelli, N., Pezzuti, L., & Lingiardi, V. (2013). Attitudes of Italian heterosexual older adults towards lesbian and gay parenting. *Sexuality Research and Social Policy, 10*(4), 285–292. https://doi.org/10.1007/s13178-013-0129-2

Barrett, D. C., & Pollack, L. M. (2005). Whose gay community? Social class, sexual self-expression, and gay community involvement. *Sociological Quarterly, 46*(3), 437–446. https://doi.org/10.1111/j.1533-8525.2005.00021.x

Brown, C., & Keller, C. J. (2018). The 2016 presidential election outcome: Fears, tension, and resiliency of GLBTQ communities. *Journal of GLBT Family Studies, 14*(1/2), 101–129. https://doi.org/10.1080/1550428X.2017.1420847

Brownell, A., & Shumaker, S. A. (1984). Social support: An introduction to a complex phenomenon. *Journal of Social Issues, 40*(4), 1–9. https://doi.org/10.1111/j.1540-4560.1984.tb01104.x

Burgess, E., & Baunach, D. (2014). Heterosexual allies? Understanding heterosexuals' alliance with the gay community. *Sexuality & Culture, 18*(4), 936–958. https://doi.org/10.1007/s12119-014-9230-9

Burleson, B. R. (2003). Emotional support skill. In J. O. Green & B. R. Burleson (Eds.), *Handbook of communication and social interaction skills* (pp. 551–594). Lawrence Erlbaum.

Burleson, B. R. (2009). Understanding the outcomes of supportive communication: A dual-process approach. *Journal of Social and Personal Relationships, 26*(1), 21–38. https://doi.org/10.1177/0265407509105519

Clarke, V., Burgoyne, C., & Burns, M. (2013). Unscripted and improvised: Public and private celebrations of same-sex relationships. *Journal of GLBT Family Studies, 9*(4), 393–418. https://doi.org/10.1080/1550428X.2013.808494

Cobb, S. (1976). Social support as a moderator of life stress. *Psychosomatic Medicine, 38*(5), 300–314. https://doi.org/10.1097/00006842-197609000-00003

Costa, P. A., Carneiro, F. A., Esposito, F., D'Amore, S., & Green, R.-J. (2018). Sexual prejudice in Portugal: Results from the first wave European study on heterosexual's attitudes toward same-gender marriage and parenting. *Sexuality Research and Social Policy, 15*(1), 99–110. https://doi.org/10.1007/s13178-017-0292-y

Costa, P. A., & Salinas-Quiroz, F. (2019). A comparative study of attitudes toward same-gender parenting and gay and lesbian rights in Portugal and in Mexico. *Journal of Homosexuality, 66*(13), 1909–1926. https://doi.org/10.1080/00918369.2018.1519303

Daniels, R. S. (2019). The evolution of attitudes on same-sex marriage in the United States, 1988–2014. *Social Science Quarterly, 100*(5), 1651–1663. https://doi.org/10.1111/ssqu.12673

Degges-White, S. (2012). Lesbian friendships: An exploration of lesbian social support networks. *Adultspan Journal, 11*(1), 16–26. https://doi.org/10.1002/j.2161-0029.2012.00002.x

Doty, N. D., Willoughby, B. L. B., Lindahl, K. M., & Malik, N. M. (2010). Sexuality related social support among lesbian, gay, and bisexual youth. *Journal of Youth and Adolescence, 39*(10), 1134–1147. https://doi.org/10.1007/s10964-010-9566-x

Dowers, E., White, C., Cook, K., & Kingsley, J. (2020). Trans, gender diverse and non-binary adult experiences of social support: A systematic quantitative literature review. *International Journal of Transgender Health, 21*(3), 242–257. https://doi.org/10.1080/26895269.2020.1771805

Eliason, M. J., Dibble, S. L., & Robertson, P. A. (2011). Lesbian, gay, bisexual, and transgender (LGBT) physicians' experiences in the workplace. *Journal of Homosexuality, 58*(10), 1355–1371. https://doi.org/10.1080/00918369.2011.614902

Flanders, C. E., Shuler, S. A., Desnoyers, S. A., & VanKim, N. A. (2019). Relationships between social support, identity, anxiety, and depression among young bisexual people of color. *Journal of Bisexuality, 19*(2), 253–275. https://doi.org/10.1080/15299716.2019.1617543

Forstie, C. (2020). Theory making from the middle: Researching LGBTQ communities in small cities. *City & Community, 19*(1), 153–168. https://doi.org/10.1111/cico.12446

Fredriksen-Goldsen, K. I., Jen, S., & Muraco, A. (2019). Iridescent life course: LGBTQ aging research and blueprint for the future: A systematic review. *Gerontology, 65*(3), 253–274. https://doi.org/10.1159/000493559

Frost, D. M., & Fingerhut, A. W. (2016). Daily exposure to negative campaign messages decreases same-sex couples' psychological and relational well-being. *Group Processes & Intergroup Relations, 19*(4), 477–492. https://doi.org/10.1177/1368430216642028

Frost, D. M., & Meyer, I. H. (2012). Measuring community connectedness among diverse sexual minority populations. *Journal of Sex Research, 49*(1), 36–49. https://doi.org/10.1080/00224499.2011.565427

Frost, D. M., Meyer, I. H., & Schwartz, S. (2016). Social support networks among diverse sexual minority populations. *American Journal of Orthopsychiatry, 86*(1), 91–102. https://doi.org/10.1037/ort0000117

Glass, V. Q., & Few-Demo, A. L. (2013). Complexities of informal social support arrangements for Black lesbian couples. *Family Relations, 62*(5), 714–726. https://doi.org/10.1111/fare.12036

Goldberg, A. E., & Smith, J. Z. (2011). Stigma, social context, and mental health: Lesbian and gay couples across the transition to adoptive parenthood. *Journal of Counseling Psychology*, 58(1), 139–150. https://doi.org/10.1037/a0021684

Goldsmith, D. J. (2004). *Advances in personal relationships: Communicating social support.* Cambridge University Press.

Goldsmith, D. J., & Fitch, K. (1997). The normative context of advice as social support. *Human Communication Research*, 23(4), 454–476. https://doi.org/10.1111/j.1468-2958.1997.tb00406.x

Gonzalez, K. A., Pulice-Farrow, L., & Galupo, M. P. (2018). "My aunt unfriended me:" Narratives of GLBTQ family relationships post 2016 presidential election. *Journal of GLBT Family Studies*, 14(1–2), 61–84. https://doi.org/10.1080/1550428X.2017.1420845

Gray, N. N., Mendelsohn, D. M., & Omoto, A. M. (2015). Community connectedness, challenges, and resilience among gay Latino immigrants. *American Journal of Community Psychology*, 55(1–2), 202–214. https://doi.org/10.1007/s10464-014-9697-4

Greenhalgh, H. (2019, June 28). *Stonewall 50. Where next for LGBT+ lives?*. World Economic Forum. https://www.weforum.org/agenda/2019/06/stonewall-50-where-next-for-lgbt-lives-by-thomson-reuters-foundation/

Haas, S. M. (2002). Social support as relationship maintenance in gay male couples coping with HIV or AIDS. *Journal of Social and Personal Relationships*, 19(1), 87–111. https://doi.org/10.1177/0265407502191005

Haas, S. M. (2019). Stigma, heteronormative passing with health-case providers, and partner health involvement in male same-sex couples. In J. A. Theiss & K. Greene (Eds.), *Contemporary studies on relationships, health, and wellness* (pp. 30–48). Cambridge University Press.

Haas, S. M., & Lannutti, P. J. (2021). The impact of minority stress and social support on positive relationship functioning in same-sex relationships. *Health Communication*, 36(3), 315–323. https://doi.org/10.1080/10410236.2019.1687130

Haas, S. M., Perazzo, J. D., Ruffner, A. H., & Lyons, M. S. (2020). Exploring current stereotypes and norms impacting sexual partner HIV-status communication. *Health Communication*, 35(11), 1376–1385. https://doi.org/10.1080/10410236.2019.1636340

Hawthorne, O., Camic, P. M., & Rimes, K. A. (2020). Understanding the structure, experiences and challenges of social support for older lesbian, gay and bisexual people: A systematic review. *Ageing & Society*, 40(2), 282–305. https://doi.org/10.1017/S0144686X18000910

Holman, E. G., Fish, J. N., Oswald, R. F., & Goldberg, A. (2019). Reconsidering the LGBT Climate Inventory: Understanding support and hostility for LGBTQ employees in the workplace. *Journal of Career Assessment*, 27(3), 544–559. https://doi.org/10.1177/1069072718788324

Holman, E. G., & Oswald, R. F. (2016). A decade of changes: Within-group analysis of LGBTQ individuals' perceptions of their community context and the relevance for social service providers. *Journal of Gay & Lesbian Social Services*, 28(3), 214–230. https://doi.org/10.1080/10538720.2016.1191406

Humble, A. M. (2013). Moving from ambivalence to certainty: Older same-sex couples marry in Canada. *Canadian Journal on Aging*, 32(2), 131–144. https://doi.org/10.1017/S0714980813000196

Humble, A. M. (2016). "She didn't bat an eye": Canadian same-sex wedding planning and support from the wedding industry. *Journal of GLBT Family Studies*, 12(3), 277–299. https://doi.org/10.1080/1550428X.2015.1065780

Hwahng, S. J., Allen, B., Zadoretzky, C., Barber, H., McKnight, C., & Des Jarlais, D. (2019). Alternative kinship structures, resilience and social support among immigrant trans Latinas in the USA. *Culture, Health & Sexuality*, 21(1), 1–15. https://doi.org/10.1080/13691058.2018.1440323

Ingham, C. F. A., Eccles, F. J. R., & Armitage, J. R. (2017). Non-heterosexual women's experiences of informal social support: A qualitative metasynthesis. *Journal of Gay & Lesbian Social Services*, 29(2), 109–143. https://doi.org/10.1080/10538720.2017.1295413

Jones, R. M., Simpson, G. M., & Stansbury, K. (2018). Informal support experiences of older African-American gay men living with HIV/AIDS. *Journal of Gay & Lesbian Social Services, 30*(3), 209–219. https://doi.org/10.1080/10538720.2018.1463886

Kennedy, H. R., & Dalla, R. L. (2020). "It may be legal, but it is not treated equally": Marriage equality and well-being implications for same-sex couples. *Journal of Gay & Lesbian Social Services, 32*(1), 67–98. https://doi.org/10.1080/10538720.2019.1681340

Kuvalanka, K. A., & Munroe, K. (2020). The "second generation": LGBTQ youth with LGBTQ parents. In A. E. Goldberg & K. R. Allen (Eds.), *LGBTQ-parent families* (2nd ed., pp. 241–256). Springer.

Lannutti, P. J. (2008). Attractions and obstacles while considering legally recognized same-sex marriage. *Journal of GLBT Family Studies, 4*(2), 245–264. https://doi.org/10.1080/15504280802096914

Lannutti, P. J. (2011). Examining communication about marriage amendments: Same-sex couples and their extended social networks. *Journal of Social Issues, 67*(2), 264–281. https://doi.org/10.1111/j.1540-4560.2011.01697.x

Lannutti, P. J. (2018). Committed, unmarried same-sex couples and their social networks in the United States: Relationships and discursive strategies. *Journal of Homosexuality, 65*(9), 1232–1248. https://doi.org/10.1080/00918369.2017.1411690

Lannutti, P., & Galupo, M. P. (2018). 2016 U.S. Presidential election and the LGBTQ community: Introduction to the special issue. *Journal of GLBT Family Studies, 14*(1–2), 1. https://doi.org/10.1080/1550428X.2017.1420857

LeBlanc, A. J., Frost, D. M., & Bowen, K. (2018). Legal marriage, unequal recognition, and mental health among same-sex couples. *Journal of Marriage and Family, 80*(2), 397–408. https://doi.org/10.1111/jomf.12460

LeBlanc, A. J., Frost, D. M., & Wight, R. G. (2015). Minority stress and stress proliferation among same-sex and other marginalized couples. *Journal of Marriage and Family, 77*(1), 40–59. https://doi.org/10.1111/jomf.12160

Lee, H.-Y., & Mutz, D. C. (2019). Changing attitudes toward same-sex marriage: A three-wave panel study. *Political Behavior, 41*(3), 701–722. https://doi.org/10.1007/s11109-018-9463-7

Lewis, R. J., Derlega, V. J., Griffin, J. L., & Krowinski, A. C. (2003). Stressors for gay men and lesbians: Life stress, gay-related stress, stigma consciousness, and depressive symptoms. *Journal of Social & Clinical Psychology, 22*(6), 716–729. https://doi.org/10.1521/jscp.22.6.716.22932

Liddle, B. J., Luzzo, D. A., Hauenstein, A. L., & Schuck, K. (2004). Construction and validation of the lesbian, gay, bisexual, and transgendered climate inventory. *Journal of Career Assessment, 12*(1), 33–50. https://doi.org/10.1177/1069072703257722

Logie, C. H., Lacombe-Duncan, A., Lee-Foon, N., Ryan, S., & Ramsay, H. (2016). "It's for us—Newcomers, LGBTQ persons, and HIV-positive persons. You feel free to be": A qualitative study exploring social support group participation among African and Caribbean lesbian, gay, bisexual and transgender newcomers and refugees in Toronto, Canada. *BMC International Health and Human Rights, 16*(1), Art 18. https://doi.org/10.1186/s12914-016-0092-0

Martin, J. L., & Dean, L. L. (1987). *Ego-dystonic homosexuality scale* [Unpublished manuscript]. Columbia University, New York, NY.

MacGeorge, E. L. (2020). Communicating advice: Introduction to the special issue. *Journal of Language and Social Psychology, 39*(3), 287–291. https://doi.org/10.1177/0261927X20912512

MacGeorge, E. L., Guntzviller, L. M., Branch, S. E., & Yakova, L. (2019). Advice in interaction: Quantity and placement of problem-solving behaviors. *Communication Research, 46*(6), 811–837. https://doi.org/10.1177/0093650215607612

Masini, B. E., & Barrett, H. A. (2008). Social support as a predictor of psychological and physical well-being and lifestyle in lesbian, gay, and bisexual adults aged 50 and over. *Journal of Gay & Lesbian Social Services, 20*(1–2), 91–110. https://doi.org/10.1080/10538720802179013

Matsick, J. L., Kim, L. M., & Kruk, M. (2020). Facebook LGBTQ pictivism: The effects of women's rainbow profile filters on sexual prejudice and online belonging. *Psychology of Women Quarterly, 44*(3), 342–361. https://doi.org/10.1177/0361684320930566

Meyer, I. H. (1995). Minority stress and mental health in gay men. *Journal of Health and Social Behavior, 36*(1), 38–56. https://doi.org/10.2307/2137286

Meyer, I. H. (2003). Prejudice, social stress, and mental health in lesbian, gay, and bisexual populations: Conceptual issues and research evidence. *Psychological Bulletin, 129*(5), 674–697. https://doi.org/10.1037/0033-2909.129.5.674

Meyer, I. H. (2016). Does an improved social environment for sexual and gender minorities have implications for a new minority stress research agenda? *Psychology of Sexualities Review, 7*(1), 81–90.

Nadal, K. L., Whitman, C. N., Davis, L. S., Erazo, T., & Davidoff, K. C. (2016). Microaggressions toward lesbian, gay, bisexual, transgender, queer, and genderqueer people: A review of the literature. *Journal of Sex Research, 53*(4–5), 488–508. https://doi.org/10.1080/00224499.2016.1142495

National Resource Center on LGBT Aging. (2020, May). *Inclusive services for LGBT older adults: A practical guide to creating welcoming agencies.* https://www.lgbtagingcenter.org/resources/resource.cfm?r=487

NCAA. (n.d.). *Champions of respect: Inclusion of LGBTQ student-athletes in NCAA® programs.* http://www.ncaapublications.com/p-4305-champions-of-respect-inclusion-of-lgbtq-student-athletes-and-staff-in-ncaa-programs.aspx

Norwood, K. (2012). Transitioning meanings? Family members' communicative struggles surrounding transgender identity. *Journal of Family Communication, 12*(1), 75–92. https://doi.org/10.1080/15267431.2010.509283

Nurullah, A. S. (2012). Received and provided social support: A review of current evidence and future directions. *American Journal of Health Studies, 27*(3), 173–188.

Ocobock, A. (2013). The power and limits of marriage: Married gay men's family relationships. *Journal of Marriage and Family, 75*(1), 191–205. https://doi.org/10.1111/j.1741-3737.2012.01032.x

Ogolsky, B. G., Monk, J. K., Rice, T. M., & Oswald, R. F. (2019). Personal well-being across the transition to marriage equality: A longitudinal analysis. *Journal of Family Psychology, 33*(4), 422–432. https://doi.org/10.1037/fam0000504

Oswald, R. F., Blume, L. B., & Marks, S. R. (2005). Decentering heteronormativity: A model for family studies. In V. L. Bengtson, A. C. Acock, K. R. Allen, P. Dilworth-Anderson, & D. M. Klein (Eds.), *Sourcebook of family theory and research* (pp. 143–165). SAGE.

Oswald, R. F., Cuthbertson, C., Lazarevic, V., & Goldberg, A. E. (2010). New developments in the field: Measuring community climate. *Journal of GLBT Family Studies, 6*(2), 214–228. https://doi.org/10.1080/15504281003709230

Oswald, R. F., Routon, J. M., McGuire, J. K., & Holman, E. G. (2018). Tolerance versus support: Perceptions of residential community climate among LGB parents. *Family Relations, 67*(1), 41–54. https://doi.org/10.1111/fare.12292

Patterson, C. J. (2017). Parents' sexual orientation and children's development. *Child Development Perspectives, 11*(1), 45–49. https://doi.org/10.1111/cdep.12207

Pew Research Center. (2018, July 11). *Activism in the social media age.* https://www.pewresearch.org/internet/2018/07/11/public-attitudes-toward-political-engagement-on-social-media/

Pew Research Center. (2019, October 28). *Same-sex marriage around the world.* https://www.pewforum.org/fact-sheet/gay-marriage-around-the-world/

Pew Research Center. (2020, June 25). *The global divide on homosexuality persists.* https://www.pewresearch.org/global/2020/06/25/global-divide-on-homosexuality-persists/

Pitcher, E. N., Camacho, T. P., Renn, K. A., & Woodford, M. R. (2018). Affirming policies, programs, and supportive services: Using an organizational perspective to understand LGBTQ+ college student success. *Journal of Diversity in Higher Education, 11*(2), 117–132. https://doi.org/10.1037/dhe0000048

Pollitt, A. M., Muraco, J. A., Grossman, A. H., & Russell, S. T. (2017). Disclosure stress, social support, and depressive symptoms among cisgender bisexual youth. *Journal of Marriage and Family, 79*(5), 1278–1294. https://doi.org/10.1111/jomf.12418

Price, E. W., & Prosek, E. A. (2020). The lived experiences of GLB college students who feel supported by their parents. *Journal of GLBT Family Studies, 16*(1), 83–102. https://doi.org/10.1080/1550428X.2019.1593278

Przeworski, A., & Piedra, A. (2020). The role of the family for sexual minority Latinx individuals: A systematic review and recommendations for clinical practice. *Journal of GLBT Family Studies, 16*(2), 211–240. https://doi.org/10.1080/1550428X.2020.1724109

Reczek, C. (2020). Sexual- and gender-minority families: A 2010 to 2020 decade in review. *Journal of Marriage and Family, 82*(1), 300–325. https://doi.org/10.1111/jomf.12607

Reeves, T., Horne, S. G., Rostosky, S., Riggle, E. D. B., Baggett, L. R., & Aycock, R. A. (2010). Family members' support for GLBT issues: The role of family adaptability and cohesion. *Journal of GLBT Family Studies, 6*(1), 80–97. https://doi.org/10.1080/15504280903472857

Rossetto, K. R., Lannutti, P. J., & Smith, R. A. (2014). Investigating self-efficacy and emotional challenge as contributors to willingness to provide emotional support. *Southern Communication Journal, 79*(1), 41–58. https://doi.org/10.1080/1041794X.2013.854404

Rostosky, S. S., Riggle, E. D. B., Horne, S. G., Denton, F. N., & Huellemeier, J. D. (2010). Lesbian, gay, and bisexual individuals' psychological reactions to amendments denying access to civil marriage. *American Journal of Orthopsychiatry, 80*(3), 302–310. https://doi.org/10.1111/j.1939-0025.2010.01033.x

Rubinsky, V., & Cooke-Jackson, A. (2017). "Where is the love?" Expanding and theorizing with LGBTQ memorable messages of sex and sexuality. *Health Communication, 32*(12), 1472–1480. https://doi.org/10.1080/10410236.2016.1230809

Ryan, C., Russell, S. T., Huebner, D., Diaz, R., & Sanchez, J. (2010). Family acceptance in adolescence and the health of LGBT young adults. *Journal of Child and Adolescent Psychiatric Nursing, 23*(4), 205–213. https://doi.org/10.1111/j.1744-6171.2010.00246.x

Sadika, B., Wiebe, E., Morrison, M. A., & Morrison, T. G. (2020). Intersectional microaggressions and social support for LGBTQ persons of color: A systematic review of the Canadian-based empirical literature. *Journal of GLBT Family Studies, 16*(2), 111–147. https://doi.org/10.1080/1550428X.2020.1724125

Shear, M. D., & Savage, C. (2017, July 27). In one day, Trump administration lands 3 punches against gay rights. *The New York Times*. https://www.nytimes.com/2017/07/27/us/politics/white-house-lgbt-rights-military-civil-rights-act.html

Shields, S. (2008). Gender: An intersectionality perspective. *Sex Roles, 59*(5–6), 301–311. https://doi.org/10.1007/s11199-008-9501-8

Shulman, J. L., Gotta, G., & Green, R.-J. (2012). Will marriage matter? Effects of marriage anticipated by same-sex couples. *Journal of Family Issues, 33*(2), 158–181. https://doi.org/10.1177/0192513X11406228

Sloane, J. L., & Robillard, L. M. (2018). Factors affecting heterosexual attitudes to same-sex marriage in Australia. *Sexuality Research and Social Policy, 15*(3), 290–301. https://doi.org/10.1007/s13178-017-0276-y

Smith, R. A., & Bishop, R. E. (2019). Insights into stigma management communication theory: Considering stigmatization as interpersonal influence. *Journal of Applied Communication Research, 47*(5), 571–590. https://doi.org/10.1080/00909882.2019.1675894

Smith, T. W., Son, J., & Kim, J. (2014, November). *Public attitudes toward homosexuality and gay rights across time and countries*. The Williams Institute. https://escholarship.org/uc/item/4p93w90c

Snapp, S. D., Watson, R. J., Russell, S. T., Diaz, R. M., & Ryan, C. (2015). Social support networks for LGBT young adults: Low cost strategies for positive adjustment. *Family Relations, 64*(3), 420–430. https://doi.org/10.1111/fare.12124

Stone, A. L., Nimmons, E. A., Salcido, R., & Schnarrs, P. (2020). "My Meemaw is a cool ass person": Family members as role models of resilience for sexual and gender diverse people of color. *Journal of GLBT Family Studies, 16*(2), 241–257. https://doi.org/10.1080/1550428X.2020.1724148

Takács, J., Szalma, I., & Bartus, T. (2016). Social attitudes toward adoption by same-sex couples in Europe. *Archives of Sexual Behavior, 45*(7), 1787–1798. https://doi.org/10.1007/s10508-016-0691-9

Thoits, P. A. (2010). Stress and health: Major findings and policy implications. *Journal of Health and Social Behavior, 51*(S), S41–S53. https://doi.org/10.1177/0022146510383499

Thoits, P. A. (2011). Mechanisms linking social ties and support to physical and mental health. *Journal of Health & Social Behavior, 52*(2), 145–161. https://doi.org/10.1177/0022146510395592

Twenge, J. M., Carter, N. T., & Campbell, W. K. (2015). Time period, generational, and age differences in tolerance for controversial beliefs and lifestyles in the United States, 1972–2012. *Social Forces, 94*(1), 379–399. https://doi.org/10.1093/sf/sov050

Unger, D. (2020, June 24). 'Just appalling': Pride Winnipeg cuts ties with human rights museum over LGBTQ2+ censorship. Winnipeg. CTV News. https://winnipeg.ctvnews.ca/just-appalling-pride-winnipeg-cuts-ties-with-human-rights-museum-over-lgbtq2-censorship-1.4998605

Vaux, A., Riedel, S., & Stewart, D. (1987). Modes of social support: The Social Support Behaviors (SS-B) Scale. *American Journal of Community Psychology, 15*(2), 209–237. https://doi.org/10.1007/BF00919279

Verrelli, S., White, F. A., Harvey, L. J., & Pulciani, M. R. (2019). Minority stress, social support, and the mental health of lesbian, gay, and bisexual Australians during the Australian Marriage Law Postal Survey. *Australian Psychologist, 54*(4), 336–346. https://doi.org/10.1111/ap.12380

Vyncke, J. D., & Julien, D. (2007). Social support, coming out, and adjustment of lesbian mothers in Canada and France: An exploratory study. *Journal of GLBT Family Studies, 3*(4), 397–424. https://doi.org/10.1300/J461v03n04_03

Weiner, B. A., & Zinner, L. (2015). Attitudes toward straight, gay male, and transsexual parenting. *Journal of Homosexuality, 62*(3), 327–339. https://doi.org/10.1080/00918369.2014.972800

Williams, P., Barclay, L., & Schmied, V. (2004). Defining social support in context: A necessary step in improving research, intervention, and practice. *Qualitative Health Research, 14*(7), 942–960. https://doi.org/10.1177/1049732304266997

Woodford, M. R., Paceley, M. S., Kulick, A., & Hong, J. S. (2015). The LGBQ social climate matters: Policies, protests, and placards and psychological well-being among LGBQ emerging adults. *Journal of Gay & Lesbian Social Services, 27*(1), 116–141. https://doi.org/10.1080/10538720.2015.990334

Zimet, G. D., Dahlem, N. W., Zimet, S. G., & Farley, G. K. (1988). The multidimensional scale of perceived social support. *Journal of Personality Assessment, 52*(1), 30–41. https://doi.org/10.1207/s15327752jpa5201_2

NOTES

1. In the acronym "LGBTQ+" the plus symbol refers to individuals who claim other identities, such as pansexual, non-binary, polyamorous, and questioning.
2. The term "community" is used at times in this article, with the caveat that it is a simplistic term that does not reflect the full diversity of LGBTQ+ individuals' experiences (Meyer, 2016). Some LGBTQ+ individuals do not feel connected to or represented by a broader queer community (Burgess & Baunach, 2014; Forstie, 2020; Frost & Meyer, 2012). Individuals may also differ in terms of how they define community or communities (Frost & Meyer, 2012).
3. "LGBQ" (lesbian, gay, bisexual, queer) was the acronym used by these researchers.
4. Research on sexual- and gender-minority families tends to focus on families in which children are LGBTQ+ or adults (e.g., partners or parents) are LGBTQ+. Less research is known about families in which multigenerations identify as sexual- or gender-minority individuals (see Kuvalanka & Munroe, 2020).

Áine M. Humble

Queer Media

Queer Media

AFRICAN AMERICAN QUEER CINEMA

INTRODUCTION

With the success of films like *Pariah* (Rees, 2011), *Moonlight* (Jenkins, 2016), and *The Death and Life of Marsha P. Johnson* (France, 2017), African American queer and lesbian, gay, bisexual, transgender, and queer (LGBTQ) stories have become more visible in the early 2000s, as bold, innovative Black LGBTQ producers, writers, and directors create unforgettable characters who are able to break through the White, heterosexual-dominated movie industry. From documentaries and biopics to romantic comedies and dramas, numerous films illustrate the beauty and complexity of the Black LGBTQ experience, all of which are considered a part of African American queer cinema. However, these films only make up a very small percentage of queer cinema as a whole.

This article will discuss the origins of African American queer cinema, including the films that preceded it, the films that fit squarely within the canon, and the ones that stretch beyond such arbitrary boundaries. Films that include LGBTQ content will also be discussed, noting the differences between mainstream films and "queer" films. Mainstream LGBT American blockbuster films will also be identified, particularly the very few that include Black characters. Lastly, the significance of documentary films within African American queer cinema is also evaluated before closing with the rising trend of video-on-demand and streaming services that offer the most diverse samplings of queer and LGBT cinema, specifically those featuring African Americans.

QUEER FILMS VS. LGBT FILMS

So what is queer cinema and how do films within this canon differ from other LGBT films? According to Griffin and Benshoff (2004), "queer cinema" has traditionally been relegated to the following three categories: (1) films that include LGBTQ themes, characters, references, and so on; (2) films that are directed by LGTBQ directors; and (3) films that have been appropriated by the gay community because the subject matter resonates with the queer audience, either via the plot or the icons featured within it, such as *The Wizard of Oz* with Judy Garland.

For the purposes of this article, the term "queer film" will prescribe to B. Ruby Rich's (1992) definition of the genre as outlined by her definition of the "New Queer Cinema" movement of the 1990s, which drew directly from queer theory perspectives, combining filmmaking with theoretical constructs whose sole purpose was to overtly disrupt heterosexual norms. "Consequently, many of the films during this era focused on polemical concerns of postmodernism and avant-garde queer theory" (Leung, 2008, p. 23). Therefore, many "queer" films include nonlinear narratives, incongruent visuals, overt political messages, theoretical complexity, pertinacious stylization, and implacable themes.

According to Wuest (2018), LGBT films, however, are defined as films that deal with or feature significant LGBT issues or characters, but don't overtly reject heteronormality, as is normally the case with a queer film, in an effort to appeal to a more mainstream audience. This new "LGBT film" category is creating new marketing venues for independent films, giving them a wider appeal, while also forcing these films (and their creators) to constantly balance the concepts of profit, mainstreaming, and queerness. Interestingly, Rich (2013), who established the groundwork for the distinction between "queer" and "LGBTQ" films, has noted the emergence of such LGBTQ-themed mainstream films, particularly in the early 2000s with films like *Brokeback Mountain* (Ang, 1995), as a key moment in the evolution of the genre.

History. Before the official establishment of an African American "queer cinema," there were a few U.S. "LGBT films" that contained images of African American LGBTQ characters. The first occurrence was featured in *Portrait of Jason* (Clarke, 1967), an independent, avant-garde *cinema vérité*-inspired film featuring a Black gay hustler and aspiring cabaret performer named Jason Holiday. In the documentary film, Holiday discusses the challenges he faced as a Black gay man when Oscar-nominated Shirley Clarke, her husband Carl Lee, and their crew turned a camera on him in a New York City apartment.

During the 1970s, numerous mainstream blaxploitation films included LGBTQ characters. Ed Guerrero (1993) defines blaxploitation films as the "production of the sixty or so Hollywood films that centered on black narratives, featured black casts playing out various action-adventures in the ghetto, and were released roughly between 1969 and 1974" (p. 69).

Just a few films in this genre with LGBTQ characters included *Sweet Sweetback's Baadasssss Song* (Van Peebles, 1971), *Women in Cages* (de Leon, 1971), *The Big Bird Cage* (Hill, 1972), *Black Mama/White Mama* (Romero, 1973), *Blacula* (Crain, 1972), *Super Fly* (Parks Jr., 1972), *Bucktown*

(Marks, 1975), *Cotton Comes to Harlem* (Davis, 1970), *Friday Foster* (Marks, 1975), *Sheba Baby* (Girdler, 1975), *Car Wash* (Schultz, 1976), and *Norman...Is That You?* (Schlatter, 1976). A common theme was pervasive in all of them. "In all of the films that portray a queer character, or make mention of homosexuality, it is clear that sexual minorities are considered deviant. Homosexuality is portrayed as abusive, blatantly offensive or humorous" (Harris, 2012, p. 220).

At the time, these films were considered Black nationalist texts: "Proof that blaxploitation harnessed Black Nationalist sentiment can be found in the films and in the pages of the community newsletters and magazines" (Mask, 2012, p. 8).

Other LGBT films in the 1970s and mid-1980s that included Black LGBTQ characters included *Boys in the Band* (Friedkin, 1970) and *The Color Purple* (Spielberg, 1985), which are both discussed in more detail in the "Mainstream African American LGBTQ Films" section.

Within most of these films, especially those that fall into the blaxploitation genre, Black is privileged above all other character demographics, and anything associated with not being Black is scorned, especially homosexuality. Such intra-racial homophobic mainstream media messages being sent to the Black community, along with the HIV/AIDS epidemic, which was ravaging the Black community, prompted three Black queer cinema directors in the late 1980s and early 1990s to turn to film to interrogate and dismantle the stringent boundaries of blackness and perpetuation of heteronormativity in Black communities. Those filmmakers were Marlon Riggs, Isaac Julien, and Cheryl Dunye.

Black activist and queer director Marlon Riggs's 1989 55-minute experimental documentary film, *Tongues Untied*, fractured the plague of silence around race and sexuality. In the author's own words, the film was created to "shatter the nation's brutalizing silence on matters of sexual and racial difference" (Riggs, 1996, p. 186). Given the political nature of the film, it fits right into queer cinema discourse as defined by Rich, which is why many scholars consider Riggs the pioneer of African American queer cinema.

The film combines documentary footage with personal testimonies and the poignant poetry of Essex Hemphill to depict the specificity of Black gay identity. At its core, it illustrates the silence thrust upon Black gay men who were unable to express themselves because of the prejudice of White and Black heterosexual society as well as within the White gay community. It was also the first film to show Black men intimately kissing, the first film to address HIV/AIDS within the Black gay community, and the first film to introduce voguing to mainstream audiences.

Tongues, which aired on the PBS television series *POV*, not only sparked controversy because of its frank betrayal of gay sexuality but it also triggered a national backlash to the National Endowment for the Arts grant funding when it was hurled into the spotlight by then-presidential candidate Pat Buchanan, who used it as an example to illustrate how President George H. W. Bush was using taxpayer dollars to fund "pornographic art" (Quinn, 1992).

Donald E. Wildmon, President of the American Family Association, also deemed the film offensive and spearheaded a censorship campaign. Riggs had used a $5,000 grant from the western state's regional arts fund, which is funded by the National Education Association (NEA). *POV* was also funded by the NEA to the amount of $250,000. Wildmon and several conservative US senators vehemently objected to using taxpayer money to fund what they considered were repulsive artistic works (Rosenberg, 1992).

Riggs and PBS executives vigorously defended the film, making it available to as many outlets and stations as wanted to air it. Riggs later stated that ironically the censorship campaign against *Tongues* actually brought more publicity to the film than it would have otherwise received and thus enhanced its effectiveness in challenging societal standards regarding depictions of race and sexuality (Riggs, 1996).

In May 2019, the Peabody Awards honored *Tongues*, and the same year *New York Times* critic-at-large Wesley Morris wrote, "*Tongues Untied* is Riggs' unclassifiable scrapbook of Black gay male sensibility (a hallucinatory whir of style, memory, psychology)... This is storytelling that arises from joy and pain and pride (Riggs' clearest emotional forbearer is James Baldwin)" (Morris, 2019, p. C4).

This proves that despite the film's condemnation by conservatives, *Tongues* is an undeniable love letter to gay Black men that went on to change the entire landscape of queer and trans people of color (QTPOC) representation in both television and film.

British Black queer filmmaker Isaac Julien artistically mixes archival newsreel footage with scripted scenes to recreate the essence of the Harlem Renaissance through the lens of Black gay men in his 1989 nonlinear impressionist film *Looking for Langston*. Even though Julien is a British filmmaker, his groundbreaking film made a significant impact in international queer cinema and in the United States with its release in 1990, which coincided with the beginning of a breakthrough cinematic era known as "New Queer Cinema," which is discussed in further detail later in this section.

The film is not a biography of the popular African American writer but instead is more of a commemorative portrait of Langston Hughes and how his works significantly contributed to the Harlem Renaissance in the 1920s as reconstructed from a Black gay male perspective. Using a similar experimental cinematic style as Riggs, *Looking* "appropriate[s] the forms of the avant-garde not for mere inclusion in the genre but in order to redefine it by changing its content and reordering its formal dispositions" (Diawara, 1996, p. 258). According to Manthia Diawara (1996), the genius of Julien's film is his ability to expertly interpenetrate two time periods and two sensibilities—one exemplified by the Cotton Club, the other reflecting contemporary Black gay expressiveness.

Unlike Riggs, Julien did not encounter challenges with funding when his film's Black queer content was realized by the National Endowment for the Arts; nonetheless *Looking for Langston* was not unmarked by criticism and backlash. Due to a copyright dispute between Julien and the Estate of Langston Hughes regarding a found footage scene of Hughes's poetry reading in a nightclub, the scene was required to be silenced during the film's premiere at the 1989 New York Film Festival.

Despite the controversy, *Looking* received the Teddy Award for Best Short Film at the 1989 Berlin International Film Festival, and to celebrate the 30th anniversary of the Teddy Awards, the film was selected to be shown at the 66th Berlin International Film Festival in February 2016.

Both Riggs and Julien's documentaries provided a counterpoint to the rising hip-hop movement of the 1990s, which was a conscious political statement by many Black artists to influence, empower, and educate Black communities on White supremacy and its prolific creation of numerous socioeconomic inequalities; however, the message in their music not only ignored the blackness of the Black queer community but often disavowed it.

Popular "gangsta rap" artists, like Ice Cube, included messages in their music that associated homosexuality with whiteness and labeled it as a subordinate status. In his song entitled "Horny Lil Devil," Cube spends most of the second verse asserting that queer Black people, because of their sexuality, could not assume an authentic role within the community. According to his lyrics, "true n—ain't gay." So while Cube's music exposes and examines the violent history of White supremacy, he also fuels homophobia and the exclusion of Black queer folks from the liberation that he argues that all (heterosexual) Black people deserve.

In response to these homophobic proclamations, Riggs continued making films into the 1990s, including his final 1994 film *Black is, Black Ain't* (1994), which he worked on before dying from AIDS-related complications that same year. Much like his previous films, *Black is, Black Ain't* directly addresses misogyny and homophobia within the Black community. The film specifically focuses on the misogynistic and anti-gay slurs found in popular hip-hop music during that time and includes interviews with African American intellectuals such as Cornell West, bell hooks, and Angela Davis.

Riggs also draws attention to Bayard Rustin, the civil rights leader responsible for the organization of the March on Washington in 1963. "Riggs uses Rustin's marginality in his area and his depression and popular memory as an indicator of how heteronormative Black political ideology preserved conservative construction to Blackness that helped to entrench white supremacy as well as sexism and heteronormativity" (Rutledge, 2020, p. 1).

Riggs was not alone in using film to comment on the perpetuation of monolithic understandings of blackness within Black communities. Cheryl Dunye's film *The Watermelon Woman* (1996) broke new ground by being the first feature film directed by a Black lesbian with a Black lesbian protagonist. *Watermelon* tells the story of Cheryl, a young Black lesbian who works at a video rental store while she is simultaneously trying to make a film about an obscure 1940s Black actress billed as a mammy-type figure called the Watermelon Woman. Like Riggs, Dunye uses the film to showcase a variance in embodied blackness by allowing some points of contention to manifest between characters, including the protagonist's choice to date White women. "Duyne's push back against the exclusion of Black warriors with white partners from Black and Black queer community is accompanied by the incorporation of Black lesbian acknowledgment and affirmation of Black women's beauty throughout the film" (Rutledge, 2020, p. 1).

Dunye was also not afraid to push boundaries by showing explicit lesbian sexuality within *Watermelon*. However, much like *Tongues* and *Looking*, the film was also fraught with controversy. Michigan Republican Pieter Hoekstra cited it as an inappropriate use of government funds. He tried unsuccessfully to get his colleagues in Congress to deduct Dunye's $31,500 grant from the NEA budget, citing NEA funding for a series of gay and lesbian films that "most Americans would find offensive" and referring to *The Watermelon Woman* specifically as "patently offensive and possibly pornographic" (Donegan, 2017).

Such a reaction was no surprise. The tenacity of both Dunye's vision and persistence and the NEA's recognition of the unique artistry that *Watermelon Woman* brought made the film all the more significant, particularly for its rare narrative on race, gender, and sexuality simultaneously.

Black lesbians exist at the crossroads of three of America's most persistent iniquities: they are Black, and women, and gay. Dunye's film is a monument to her own love of African American film history, but it is also a look into the ways that the histories of marginalized people are uncovered, people who were unable, because of access or because of taboo, to document themselves (Donegan, 2017).

Julien, Riggs, and Dunye paved the way for other Black queer filmmakers to make their mark in queer cinema, especially during the mid- to late 1990s and early 2000s when LGBT films were quite abundant and accessible, albeit mostly relegated to art houses. Dubbed by B. Ruby Rich in 1992 as the "New Queer Cinema," the movement was known for the proliferation of queer-themed independent filmmaking in which many LGBTQ directors found opportunities to showcase their work, including Gus Van Sant, Jennie Livingston, Greg Araki, and Angela Robinson.

"Historically, New Queer Cinema was inextricably tied to the AIDS crisis and the activism and community that formed out of it; its filmmaking made by and for people who were on the margins" (Jung, 2018, p. 1). While many of the films during that period would not be considered diverse, there were a few films that featured Black LGBTQ content. Julien's follow-up film in 1991, *Young Soul Rebels*, is part-thriller, part-love story, and is much more commercial than *Looking for Langston*. It follows the lives of two DJs in 1977 London who are thrust into a murder investigation when their close friend is murdered while cruising in a local park. The film highlights the racial and sexual tensions of 1970s Britain, portraying skinheads taunting the main characters and heterosexual Blacks who are unable to decide who they hated most: Whites, mixed-race people, or "batty boys."

One of the most well-known films during the new queer cinema that featured a Black character was the 1995 film *The Incredibly True Adventures of 2 Girls in Love*. The film is a classic indie success story: a teenage lesbian love story filmed in only 21 days (with most of the cast and crew working for free) that became a Sundance hit and later enjoyed modest commercial success. Written and directed by Maria Maggenti, the film follows the romance of boyish lesbian Randy Dean (played by Laurel Holloman) who falls in love with Evie (played by Nicole Ari Parker), a feminine, college-bound upper-class Black girl, who is way above Randy's high school social status. Evie's representation went against the type, specifically during the 1990s, when most films during that time focused on Blacks in lower socioeconomic settings surrounded by gangs, drugs, and violence (*Boyz n the Hood*, *Menace II Society*, and *South Central*). She was instead from an affluent family and, compared to Randy's unusual extended family situation, Evie's household was the most conventional.

Black lesbian director Angela Robinson's 2004 film *D.E.B.S.* was released at the tail end of the new queer film movement, but she is quick to point out that its success came about because of it: "Any movie being made is a miracle, and to make a queer movie is an extra miracle" (A. Robinson, personal communication, February 6, 2019). The action-comedy follows D.E.B.S. (Discipline, Energy, Beauty, Strength) clandestine paramilitary academy recruits who are in a cat-and-mouse game with supercriminal Lucy Diamond. The leader of the group is Max, played by African American actress Meagan Good. While the film was critically panned upon its initial release, it has since garnered success, with a pronounced cult following.

MAINSTREAM AFRICAN AMERICAN LGBTQ FILMS

There have been a few U.S. mainstream films that have included Black LGBTQ content in terms of themes and/or characters. One of the first was the 1970s film *Boys in the Band*, which was based on the 1968 off-Broadway play of the same name written by Mart Crowley. The film is considered controversial not only because it was among the first major American motion pictures to center exclusively on gay characters, but also because some film scholars see it as a progressive milestone in the history of queer cinema, while others see it as a commodification of sad, tragic images of gay sexuality used to provide a "comfortable" experience for straight viewers (Carrithers, 1995, p. 64).

At the time, many critics praised the film for its unapologetic look at the lives of gay men in the 1960s. "If the situation of the homosexual is ever to be understood by the public," a *TIME* film review stated in 1970, "it will be because of the breakthrough made by this humane, moving picture" (Cohen, 2015, p. 1).

Like the play, the entire film focused on a birthday party being held by group of seven New York City friends, one of them being African American. While this was one of the first portrayals of an openly Black gay man within a mainstream film, some scholars have also questioned this significance given that the Black character, Bernard, whose character is dealing with the complex issues of racism and homophobia, has only a peripheral role in the film. So, given there were those who agreed with most critics and believed *The Boys* was making great strides while others thought it portrayed a group of gay men wallowing in self-pity (Klemm, 2008), the film's place in queer cinema continues to be debated.

Another mainstream film, *The Color Purple* (Spielberg, 1982), based on Black bisexual author Alice Walker's bestselling Pulitzer Prize-winning novel, chronicles the life of an African American Southern woman, Celie, played by Whoopi Goldberg, who triumphantly overcomes racism, sexism, and mental and physical abuse while finding herself in the process. During the traumatic journey, the one thing that keeps her centered is her relationship with another woman, which was very explicit in the book, but the movie decided to downplay it into just one innocent kiss. Director Steven Spielberg expressed his regret about that decision:

> There were certain things in the [lesbian] relationship between Shug Avery and Celie that were very finely detailed in Alice's book, that I didn't feel we could get a [PG-13] rating... And I was shy about it. In that sense, perhaps I was the wrong director to acquit some of the more sexually honest encounters between Shug and Celie because I did soften those. I basically took something that was extremely erotic and very intentional, and I reduced it to a simple kiss. I got a lot of criticism for that. (Obenson, 2011)

F. Gary Gray did not gloss over the lesbian sexuality over 10 years later when he directed the crime action heist film *Set It Off* (1996), which includes an all-Black female lead cast, including Queen Latifah as Cleo, a butch Black lesbian. The film highlights the plight of working-class and blue-collar Black women, which was rarely done, especially within mainstream films. The film's theme was all about survival, which was personified in all the characters, including service worker Cleo whose own Black boss was constantly subjecting her to a combination of racism, misogyny, and homophobia. The lesbian sexuality portrayed in the film was not overly explicit but was less chaste than in *The Color Purple*.

NOTEWORTHY AFRICAN AMERICAN QUEER INDEPENDENT FILMS

Per B. Ruby Rich's definition, both *The Color Purple* and *Set It Off* cannot truly be classified as queer films, given their mainstream appeal and lack of overt rejection of heteronormativity, but they set the stage, along with Riggs's and Dunye's filmmaking, for future independent films in the 2000s to embrace African American queer content and finally place it front and center, one of those being Black queer director Patrik-Ian Polk's *Punks* (2000), which many critics likened to the TV show *Friends*, except everyone's Black and gay (Advocate, 2018, February). This was one of the first departures from the usual fare of all gay White films that cluttered the queer indie cinema during that time. *Punks* became the source material for his hit Logo series *Noah's Arc*. Polk went on to direct numerous queer films including *Noah's Arc: Jumping the Broom*, *The Skinny*, and *Blackbird*.

Like the TV show, the spin-off feature film, *Jumping the Broom*, continued to address issues relevant to the Black gay community, including HIV, same-sex marriage, racism, and even hyper-Black masculinity within the Black gay community. Following a similar format in his movie, *The Skinny*, Polk chronicles the romantic adventures of four Black graduates from Brown University who reunite for a weekend in New York City to celebrate gay pride. Polk has been questioned on his decision to exclude the familiar White gay characters that are so prevalent in most other queer films.

Polk answers the criticism by saying,

> That's not completely unrealistic. As adults, we set our social scenes, and a lot of gay people do self-segregate... You don't have a lot of films exploring Black LGBT experiences, so I make no apologies for setting these films in predominantly or all-Black gay worlds. (Thomas, 2012)

Featuring the star power of Mo'Nique and Isaiah Washington, Polk's latest project *Blackbird* (2014) is the adaptation of a novel by Black gay author Larry Duplechan about a boy from a small town in Mississippi trying to reconcile his religion with his sexuality while dealing with the disappearance of his younger sister.

Another trailblazer, albeit slightly after Polk, was openly gay Black filmmaker Rodney Evans whose *Brother to Brother* debuted at the 2004 Sundance Film Festival before playing the gay and lesbian film festival circuit with a limited theatrical release in late 2004. The film follows Black art student Perry, played by Anthony Mackie, who is thrown out of his house by his parents because of his sexuality, and they are even more perturbed by the fact he is engaged in a romantic entanglement with a White boy from his class. During his predicament, he befriends an elderly homeless man, Bruce, who turns out to have been an important figure in the Harlem Renaissance. Bruce recounts his friendships with important Harlem Renaissance figures and the challenges he faced while Perry realizes his obstacles in the early 21st century are almost identical. The film won the Miami, New York, Philadelphia film festival awards and Outfest jury awards as well as the Glitter Award for best feature indie gay film.

"*Brother to Brother* strives to acknowledge the diversity and complexity within the African American and gay and lesbian communities and to give voice to experiences that have been vastly underrepresented in cinema for far too long" (Evans, 2005).

Another noteworthy independent film that features one of the few lead LGBTQ teen characters of color is *Pariah* (Dee Rees, 2011). It premiered at the 2011 Sundance Film Festival and was awarded the Excellence in Cinematography Award. The film follows Alike (Adepero Oduye), a Black teenage lesbian in Brooklyn, who is dealing with her homophobic mother

(Kim Wayans). Fortunately, she is able to find solace in new crush Bina (Aasha Davis) and her poetry. While she has a positive relationship with her father, she realizes that she will never receive her mother's approval, so rather than running away, she chooses to move to Los Angeles, finding redemption by fully embracing her sexuality. Much like Polk's and Evans's films, *Pariah* includes characters that are fully realized as both LGBTQ and Black characters, surpassing the Ava DuVernay and Vito Russo representation tests. This makes sense considering the film is directed by out and proud Black lesbian Dee Rees, who even describes the film as semi-autobiographical.

Dee Rees has become quite the prolific Black queer director, putting Queen Latifah in yet another LGBTQ role, this time playing Bessie Smith in the biopic *Bessie*, an HBO Emmy-winning film made in 2015 that holds nothing back when it comes to the famous 1920s blues singer's bisexual life. The film was so successful that, as of 2016, *Bessie* remained the most-watched HBO original movie of all time with 1.34 million viewers (Patten, 2016).

Hailed as the first movie to be screened at the Sundance Film Festival shot almost entirely on an Apple iPhone, *Tangerine* (Baker) made history in 2015. It was also one of the first films to include transgender actresses as leads. The film follows a transgender sex worker, having just served a 28-day jail term, who discovers her boyfriend and pimp has been cheating on her with a cisgender woman. The film was well received by critics. According to Rotten Tomatoes, which reported a 96% rating in 2015, "*Tangerine* shatters casting conventions and its filmmaking techniques are up-to-the-minute, but it's an old-fashioned comedy at heart—and a pretty wonderful one at that." The film gave much-needed representation to Black, indigenous, and other people of color (BIPOC) transgender individuals and their real-world experiences.

No critically acclaimed Black queer cinema list is complete without the groundbreaking film *Moonlight* (Jenkins) in 2017, which began as an independent film and found its way into a wide-theatrical release. The coming-of-age drama focuses on three chapters in the life of a poor, gay Black boy, Chiron (aka Little and Black), living in the housing projects of Miami in the 1980s. Chiron must deal with his emerging sexual identity, violent bullying, and living with his emotionally abusive, drug-addicted mother. The film didn't include any A-list actors; however, Moonlight did something that previous queer films, even those with White protagonists like *Brokeback Mountain* didn't. It snagged the Best Picture Academy Award in 2018.

Moonlight received numerous accolades, particularly for being one of the first films to hit mainstream theaters, following in the footsteps of Riggs, that openly portrays the intersectionality of being gay and Black in America. Scholar Samantha Lauer (2017) talked about this in her journal article, "*Moonlight*: A Tale of Heartbreak, Brilliance, and Interhuman Artistry":

> In this film about growth, truth, and love, hardship is a great teacher. The protagonist, whether he goes by Little, Chiron, or Black, attempts to fit into a world where Black masculinity and gayness cancel each other out, and his struggles are powerful. Telling a big story like this doesn't necessarily mean a film full of spectacle, however, and director Barry Jenkins infuses this complex tale with artistry that's truly on another level. (Lauer, 2017, p. 1)

Moonlight is a powerful commentary on identity and the significance of making intimate connections throughout one's life that ultimately make a person who he or she is. Justin Chang (2016) of the *Los Angeles Times* wrote:

[Barry Jenkins] made a film that urges the viewer to look past Chiron's outward appearance and his superficial signifiers of identity, climbing inside familiar stereotypes in order to quietly dismantle them from within... [*Moonlight*] doesn't say much. It says everything.

Despite its critical acclaim and eventually wide release in theaters, *Moonlight* still only made a third of what a more mainstream movie featuring White gay male characters like *Brokeback Mountain* (Lee, 1995) made at the box office. Some scholars have postulated that because the film focuses on a Black gay lead character it could have alienated not only mainstream audiences but even the Black community, which is often thought to be more homophobic than other cultures due to their strong religious beliefs.

All of these films are integral components of not only Black queer cinema but also American cinema by shining a spotlight on individuals at poignant times in their lives and giving life to their stories, particularly when these voices have been muted or ignored by certain socioeconomic forces within the film industry as well as mainstream society.

LGBTQ BLOCKBUSTER FILMS

So has there ever been a high-grossing blockbuster LGBTQ film featuring a Black protagonist? The term "blockbuster" was first used to refer to films that brought in large amounts of box office revenue in the 1950s, but while its association continued in the following decades, it didn't reach mass appeal until the idea of a blockbuster movie became associated with summer action flicks, especially after Steven Spielberg's shark attack thriller *Jaws* (1975). However, it was when *Star Wars* came out two years later that the summer blockbuster genre was cemented, and its power has endured (Waxman, 2020).

For years, the mainstream film studios have cited lack of audience interest and fiscal profitability as the reasons for not making even general audience films with gay-themed content, so one can only imagine their reluctance to create films with queer people of color at the forefront. However, given the success of mainstream LGBTQ films in the early 2000s that garnered wide release, these excuses no longer ring true.

Thanks to lucrative films like *Bohemian Rhapsody* (Singer, 2018), *Rocketman* (Fletcher, 2019)—both films featuring prominent musical artists, which no doubt also factors into their popularity—and *Love, Simon* (Berlanti, 2018), studio executives are finally seeing there are audiences who are craving queer content and such films can be financially viable.

However, due to social pressures and financial risks, the major studios are still very slow to capitalize on this trend. According to the *2020 Studio Responsibility Report* by the Gay and Lesbian Alliance Against Defamation (GLAAD, 2020a), which indexed films released in 2019, the organization noted a concerning continuation of a downward trend in terms of racial diversity of LGBTQ characters: a significant decrease in racial diversity of LGBTQ characters for the third consecutive year. In 2019, just 34% of LGBTQ characters were people of color (POC) (17 of 50), down from 42% in the previous report and a decrease of 23 percentage points from the 57% of LGBTQ characters of color in 2017 (GLAAD, 2020a).

So to answer the question posed at the beginning of the section, when looking at the top 10 highest-grossing LGBT films, there has only been one film that has featured a Black protagonist, and that film is *The Crying Game* (Jordan, 1992), which comes in at the very bottom in the last spot in terms of revenue. According to Box Office Mojo (2020), the top films are as follows:

1. *Bohemian Rhapsody* (Singer, 2018)—$216,428,042
2. *The Birdcage* (Nichols, 1996)—$124,060,553
3. *Interview with a Vampire* (Jordan, 1994)—$105,264,608
4. *Rocketman* (Fletcher, 2019)—$96,368,160
5. *The Imitation Game* (Tyldum, 2014)—$91,125,683
6. *Brokeback Mountain* (Lee, 2005)—$83,043,761
7. *The Talented Mr. Ripley* (Minghella, 1999)—$81,298,265
8. *Philadelphia* (Demme, 1993)—$77,446,440
9. *In & Out* (Oz, 1997)—$63,856,929
10. *The Crying Game* (Jordan, 1992)—$62,548,947

Famous for its shocking twist, *The Crying Game* is the story of an unlikely friendship between Irish Republican Army member Fergus (Stephen Rea) and Jody (Forest Whitaker), a kidnapped British soldier in his custody. Fergus promises Jody that he'll visit his girlfriend, Dil (Jaye Davidson), in London. When he goes to the city and meets her, Fergus finds himself surprisingly drawn to her mysterious persona, which we learn in the end is because Dil is biologically a man. Many critics and viewers alike proclaim the theme of the film is love and that you can't help who you fall in love with and that love often transcends gender.

"In a style of agitated naturalism, [Neil] Jordan examines poignant matters of life and death, sex and friendship, duty and loyalty, freedom and bondage, manhood and womanhood and all the ambiguous areas in between" (Corliss, 1992, p. 14). *Crying Game* is the first film on the LGBTQ blockbuster list to include a person of color in a major role within the film (Davidson is biracial), as well as to truly shine a spotlight on the transgender community.

The list sheds quite a bit of light on which LGBT films have been more widely accepted by mainstream audiences as well as what type of queer-themed films studios feel more secure green-lighting in comparison to others, especially when looking at the diversity included, or rather not included, within them.

This is intriguing considering the 21st-century releases of *Love, Simon* (Berlanti, 2018), the first teen romance with a gay lead, and other critically acclaimed films that have come out in the 2010s: *Carol* (Haynes, 2015), *Una mujer fantástica* (Lelio, 2017), *Moonlight* (Jenkins, 2016), and *Call Me By Your Name* (Guadagnino, 2017), which all took the awards circuits by storm and almost all feature more diverse representations of the LGBTQ communities. However, the list also proves that adoration doesn't equate to box office sales. According to Box Office Mojo (2020, *Carol*, *Una mujer fantástica*, and *Call Me By Your Name* didn't even make the top 25 highest-grossing LGBT movies of all time. Despite winning the Academy Award for Best Picture at the Oscars in 2017, *Moonlight* isn't even in the top 20, earning just under $28 million. Even the groundbreaking and very well received *Love, Simon*, which also included biracial and Black gay characters, couldn't break into the top 10, and as of December 2020 is sitting at 13.

BLACK QUEER DOCUMENTARIES

Historically, beginning with *Portrait of Jason* in the 1960s (discussed in the "History" section), which the Library of Congress selected for preservation in the National Film Registry, finding it "culturally, historically or aesthetically significant" in 2015 (Anderson, 2019), and then later with Julien's *Looking for Langston* and Riggs's experimental projects, documentary films have been much more inclusive of the African American queer community than the majority of the scripted narrative independent and mainstream films.

Another groundbreaking film in this genre, also part of the New Queer Cinema movement, was Jennie Livingston's *Paris is Burning*. The 1991 documentary, filmed in the mid- to late 1980s, provides a candid exploration of the bar culture of New York City and the African American, Latino, gay, and transgender communities thriving within it. The film won numerous national and international awards and received countless positive reviews by critics.

Terrence Rafferty of the *New Yorker* said the film was

> a beautiful piece of work—lively, intelligent, exploratory.... Everything about "Paris is Burning" signifies so blatantly and so promiscuously that our formulations—our neatly paired theses and antitheses—multiply faster than we can keep track of them. What's wonderful about the picture is that Livingston is smart enough not to reduce her subjects to the sum of their possible meanings... (Rafferty, 1991)

The film introduced much of mainstream society to ball culture and more importantly to the challenges faced by gay and transgender people of color who were ostracized from "normal" society as well as from the predominantly White gay community.

In 1996, *All God's Children*, a documentary directed by Black LGBTQ activist Sylvia Rhue, along with Frances Reid and Dee Mosbacher, was the first film to analyze the relationship between Christianity and sexual orientation within the African American community. Documenting the experiences of LGBTQ congregates, it included testimonies from influential political and religious leaders. According to *Los Angeles Times* author Lynell George (1996), the goal of this film is to educate people about the troubles which gay and lesbian believers face when trying to find and be accepted into a church.

There have been few films of any kind that have specifically focused on the lives of Black trans men, but Kortney Ryan Ziegler's 2008 unconventional documentary *Still Black: A Portrait of Black Transmen* does just that when it challenges notions of Black masculinity, sexuality, and identity through a collection of six short black-and-white films. That same year visual artist, filmmaker, and curator Tiona McClodden released *Black./Womyn: Conversations with Lesbians of African Descent*. The documentary includes interviews with 49 out Black lesbians, including author Cheryl Clarke, filmmaker Aishah Shahidah Simmons, poet Staceyann Chin, artist Hanifah Walidah, and hip-hop duo KIN, among others. In the film, they discuss coming out, sexuality and religion, life and relationships, visibility in the media, discrimination and homophobia, and activism, and most importantly, what it means to call oneself a Black lesbian.

But then beginning in the 2010s, mostly due to increased distribution outlets and lower cost of production, there was a significant rise in the number of U.S. Black LGBTQ documentaries released. There are too many to mention, but a few should be highlighted. Filmmakers Katherine Fairfax Wright and Malika Zouhali-Worrall chronicle the last year of David Kato's life in their documentary *Call Me Kuchu* in 2012. Kato was Uganda's first openly gay man and one of the few who dared to publicly protest state-sanctioned homophobia. He was brutally murdered a year into filming. The film received the 2014 GLAAD Media Award for outstanding documentary. The 2013 documentary *The New Black* (Richen) analyzed homophobia within the Black community, including the Black church. The *Hollywood Reporter* called it a "thoughtful examination of socially conservative, church-based traditions responding to voice in several forms, many of them arising within churchgoing families" (Linden, 2013).

The year 2015 brought forth several queer-themed documentaries featuring Black people. One of those documentaries was *Treasure: From Tragedy to Trans Justice, Mapping a Detroit Story* (Hampton, 2015). The film explores the tragic murder of Shelly "Treasure" Hilliard, a young African American trans woman who died violently in 2011. The documentary highlights how the majority of the victims of violent hate-crime homicides in the United States are transgender women and how transgender people of color are six times more likely to experience physical violence from the police.

An updated follow-up to *All God's Children* is *Holler if You Hear Me: Black and Gay in the Church* (Cane, 2015), a documentary film produced and created by Clay Cane in conjunction with BET (Black Entertainment Television) in 2015. This documentary puts the narrative in the hands of Black LGBTQ people, all residing in Atlanta, who throughout the film discuss their struggle with the intersections of sexuality, faith, and race.

The following year, 2016, also brought some significant documentaries into the Black queer film canon. *Free CeCe* (Gares, 2016), executive produced by trans actress and activist Laverne Cox, follows the campaign to free Chrishaun Reed "CeCe" McDonald, a Black transwoman who, while being brutally attacked, killed a man in self-defense. After a coercive police interview, she was incarcerated in a Minnesota men's prison.

While *Paris is Burning* set the stage for the cinematic exploration of the LGBTQ "house" culture and the ball scene, *Kiki* (Jordenö, 2017) picks up where the previous film left off. The film serves as an update to the New York drag and voguing scenes. "Unlike the movie *Paris is Burning*, *Kiki* is more intertwined with activism and education as it focuses more so on people between the ages of 13 and 24 instead of older queer and transgender individuals" (Anderson, 2017). It won a Teddy Award as the best LGBT-related documentary film when it was screened at the 66th Berlin International Film Festival.

Jewel's Catch One is a legendary, queer, and Black-owned disco that closed its doors in 2015. The documentary of the same name directed by C. Fitz examines the life of its owner, entrepreneur and activist Jewel Thais-Williams, and the importance of the nightclub in the creation of safe spaces for queer, Black, and AIDS-impacted communities in Los Angeles for over 40 years. That same year Dana Flor and Toby Oppenheimer's film *Check It* was released, highlighting a Washington, DC gang formed by African American gay and transgender youth for their own protection.

In 2017, Netflix's documentary *The Death and Life of Marsha P. Johnson*, directed by Oscar-nominated David France, created quite the stir by detailing the life of the trans activist who played a pivotal role in the Stonewall riots in 1969. While the film celebrates her accomplishments and significant contributions to the LGBTQ movement via Johnson's former friend and fellow trans activist Victoria Cruz, it also focuses on the mystery surrounding her untimely death, as her body was found floating in the Hudson River. Another documentary released that year that highlights another innovative queer Black figure is *The Gospel According to Andre*. The film focuses on the life of Andre Leon Talley, a noted fashion journalist who broke racial barriers during his tenure at *Vogue*. Director Kate Novack explores his life and career, from growing up in the segregated South to his iconic career.

The 2020s have seen a continuation of documentaries featuring LGBTQ Black figures. One such film is *Neon*, a digital documentary series launched by GLAAD to highlight queer Black lives:

> "We hope to help shift the narratives of underrepresented communities in media, especially for the Black LGBTQ community and their allies," said DaShawn Usher, GLAAD's programs officer, communities of color, and producer of *Neon*. "With an increase in violence and murders of Black trans women, LGBTQ youth suicides, and a decrease in LGBTQ acceptance, *Neon* comes at a time when it's absolutely critical to showcase diverse, fair, and accurate representations of Black LGBTQ people within the media." (Gardner, 2020)

Netflix's documentary *Disclosure: Trans Lives on Screen* (Feder, 2020) takes a close look at the history of Hollywood's depiction of transgender people, specifically focusing on how these images, both past and present, have impacted the lives of transgender individuals as well as American culture.

So, in comparison, there have been more African American queer documentaries than scripted narrative films; therefore, such historical biopics tend to be one of the most pervasive genres to educate both American Black and non-Black heterosexual society about African American queer lives.

THE FUTURE

With the dearth of both African American queer and LGBT films in mainstream theaters and the national closure trend of independent art houses, audiences searching for such content are forced to turn to television or, more specifically, streaming and video-on-demand (SVOD) services, which offer a much larger array of diverse and inclusive content.

Some LGBTQ producers and creators feel that the rise of television led to the demise of the new queer cinema movement. Acclaimed LGBTQ director Angela Robinson of *D.E.B.S.* and *Professor Marston and the Wonder Women* fame said:

> During that time [the 1990s and early 2000s], you really felt like you were a part of the larger gay community, with each other and the world. It felt really dynamic and cutting edge, an exciting time to be making queer content.

But she went on to mention how the cable channel LOGO and TV in general in an unintentional way killed the queer cinema boom:

> LOGO launched and they had no money or no vision or commitment to pushing content. Before then, when there weren't TV queer outlets, the mini-majors felt a part of the mission and were pushing to put out queer films. But now we had LOGO, so they didn't feel the need to release them any more… The first wave of queer cinema died. (A. Robinson, personal communication, February 6, 2019)

While television can't completely fill the void left by the demise of the New Queer Cinema movement, SVOD platforms do offer viewers access to a myriad of LGBTQ content, including some of the radical, political, and esoteric queer films reminiscent of those in the 1990s. But more importantly, these platforms showcase the diversity of race, gender, class, and gender identity in the LGTBQ communities, much more than mainstream theaters, including most independent venues.

Streaming and on-demand services excel at providing content that showcases a larger spectrum of LGBTQ lifestyles and cultures with space for discussion and exploration that cannot be found on the traditional media outlets. SVOD platforms have created avenues for LGBTQ filmmakers, especially those with lower budgets, to connect their films with broader audiences.

In the history of independent LGBTQ filmmaking, distribution has often proved to be one of the most challenging hurdles to overcome. Failing to find a distributor meant your film would not play outside of local screenings or film festivals. Even films that did secure distribution were often limited to short runs in large cities with active art house theaters (McCracken, 2017).

SVOD services have changed this process by creating new possibilities for worldwide distribution. This change is quite different from the niche distribution that LGBTQ media was relegated to decades ago. These services include Netflix, HereTV, Revry, DEKKOO, YouTube, and a whole host of others, and they each have their specialties, giving LGBTQ audiences more choice in their entertainment options.

Since the early 2000s, Netflix's priority has changed from simply providing mainstream movies to the masses to producing more television shows and series, but despite the reduced number of feature films, U.S. Netflix still boasts close to 100 LGBTQ-themed films and, of those films, 63% of them feature diverse and inclusive content. The quality of the queer films are all over the map, ranging from the more renowned titles, like *Moonlight* (Jenkins, 2016) and LGBTQ classics such as *Paris is Burning* (Livingston, 1990) to more independent, low-budget films, like *The Half of It* (Wu, 2020), and an impressively large selection of their own original films and documentaries, like the revamped *Boys in the Band* (Johnson, 2018), the trans-focused documentary *Disclosure* (Feder, 2020), and *The Death and Life of Marsha P. Johnson* (France, 2017).

A true pioneer in LGBTQ-filmmaking, Wolfe Video began distributing gay-themed titles to the LGBTQ community in 1985. Distributing thousands of queer titles, even today, they are still the largest exclusive distributor of LGBT films. Wolfe debuted WolfeOnDemand, its global LGBTQ movie-watching platform, in June 2012, in collaboration with technology partner Distrify, an internet distribution service. As of 2020 their film library has just under 180 titles, which lands them ahead of Netflix in terms of inventory, but only 25% of their entire collection contains titles that feature POC, well below the diversity found at Netflix.

HereTV (http://www.heretv.com/), launched in 2004 by Paul Colichman and Stephen P. Jarchow, was the world's first SVOD LGBTQ+ video service. HereTV reaches millions of viewers each month and has produced Academy Award-winning films in addition to receiving three Daytime Emmy Award nominations. According to the HereTV website, "HereTV is the exclusive platform for LGBT filmmakers, artists and performers to showcase award-winning films and series in their original, uncensored form." The subscriber-based site proclaims to have the largest LGBT library, featuring over 300 hours of award-winning movies, series, documentaries, and short films, with new material being added every single week. Their video-on-demand section contains just under 200 titles, which is more than both Netflix and WolfeOnDemand. Although, much like Netflix, the majority of their titles feature gay men over lesbians, the platform does boast an impressive 42% of titles that are diverse and inclusive.

Operating under the tagline "Stream. Out. Loud." Revry (https://www.revry.tv/) is a queer-owned and operated subscriber-based, video-on-demand platform, offering "hours upon hours of queer movies and TV to viewers around the world—116 countries total, including China, where even Netflix can't get past censors." Created by Chief Business Officer Christopher Rodriguez and the company's CEO, Damian Pelliccione, Revry bills itself as the first global LGBTQ streaming service and has grown rapidly since its founding in 2015, hosting more than 4,000 hours of films, shows, podcasts, and music. Unlike the other LGBTQ on-demand platforms, Revry's mission is to highlight diverse content and spotlight voices and stories that have often been ignored by mainstream media: "Revry was founded to showcase the works that our community wants to see and to highlight stories that are still being overlooked by the mainstream."

Officially launching in 2016, DEKKOO is owned by media giant Gaius Media, an entertainment company that has multiple holdings, including their sister company, TLA Releasing, which has been the global leader in LGBT entertainment since its inception in 2001. The film distribution company has been devoted to providing the best in independent cinema for LGBT audiences. DEKKOO is no different, as of 2020 hosting over 600 hours of LGBTQ content, including a mix of feature films and episodic programming, outnumbering the combined LGBTQ content on Netflix and Amazon Video, with a specific focus on smaller lesser-known films. DEKKOO's COO Brian Sokel, who is a straight, cisgendered male, makes it very clear that they cater specifically to gay men: "We believe every letter of the LGBTQ+ acronym deserves attention. The 'G' just happens to be our specialty" (Amorosi, 2017, para. 7). With almost 50% of their titles featuring gay men of color, the platform is fulfilling their mission of giving voice to underrepresented populations:

> "We want to support queer cinema and give films that may not have a streaming home a place to live where fans can engage, interact and enjoy content that represents them," says Sokel. "We believe any content produced for diverse audiences deserves to be seen. We hope that we provide a unique and exclusive service for fans of queer cinema." (Schwartz & Hadley, 2017)

YouTube is another online destination where viewers can find LGBTQ content, including queer shorts and full-length feature films. Because the offerings on the site vary day to day, it is impossible to determine exactly how much content is available on the site, but just doing a cursory search for LGBT content brings up hundreds, if not thousands, of titles. Since the content is user-generated, the quality of the films varies from amateur to professional; however, the diversity offered is probably the most found at any one site. High-profile Black queer YouTubers such as Todrick Hall, Kat Blaque, Lasizwe Dambuza, and so many more, regularly produce content highlighting the experiences of LGBTQ Black people.

Television programming featuring Black queer characters is, in 2021, a stark contrast to the film industry where such images are few and far between. The CW shows, including *Black*

Lightning, Supergirl, Arrow, and *Flash,* all helmed by openly gay Executive Director Greg Berlanti, all include Black LGBTQ characters. This trend is happening throughout all television programming, including in all Shonda Rhimes creations, most notably *How to Get Away with Murder.*

According to GLAAD, LGBTQ representation on television hit a record high in 2019, with 8.8% out of 857 series regulars on broadcast TV openly identified as gay, lesbian, bisexual, trans, or queer. And for the second year in a row, LGBTQ characters of color outnumber White LGBTQ characters on broadcast television, 52% to 48%. Forty-seven percent of all series regulars on broadcast scripted television are POC, a 3% increase from the previous report and a record high. Ryan Murphy's series *Pose* on FX, which has eight LGBTQ characters, is a big contributor to this significant percentage progress. According to the study, Netflix is still the best streaming platform for diverse representation of LGBTQ characters, dominating outlets like Hulu and Amazon Prime. Their shows *Orange is the New Black, The Chilling Adventures of Sabrina, Dear White People,* and *Queer Eye* all feature Black queer characters.

Unfortunately, such Black queer representation has yet to be seen in the film industry. If anything, the opposite trend is occurring. Studios, filmmakers, and producers are failing to include Black LGBTQ characters in their work, and even when they do, the roles are minuscule and are more like afterthoughts.

The immense significance of having more POC and LGBTQ persons behind the scenes is evident when you look at successful TV show creators like Greg Berlanti and Shonda Rhimes, who are sexual and racial/gender minorities, respectively, and how they have each created financially viable, high-rated television shows, portraying multidimensional racial and sexual minorities who all have integral parts on their shows. Berlanti has ever crossed over into the film world by producing diverse queer films like *The Broken Hearts Club* and the 2018 blockbuster *Love, Simon,* which further proves that having more diverse directors equates to films with more diverse content.

There is a rising number of Black LGBTQ creators who are making their mark in queer cinema, including directors Angelica Robinson, Dee Rees, and Yance Ford, who made history by becoming the first out trans director nominated for an Academy Award in 2018 for his Netflix documentary *Strong Island.*

According to Darnell Hunt, Professor of Sociology and African American Studies at the University of California, Los Angeles (UCLA), and co-author of the annual *Hollywood Diversity Report,* movie studios are finally starting to take notice of their lack of diversity and inclusion in the majority of their offerings:

> Over time, as it became clear that audiences were becoming more diverse and that they were demanding diverse content, diversity itself was seen as a business imperative. Like, "We have to figure out ways to create more diverse products because that's what today's increasingly diverse audiences are demanding." That's a relatively new phenomenon that...most people would not have been talking about that, you know, five, 10 years ago. Today, everyone's talking about it. (Blair, 2019)

If movie studios, producers, and directors truly embrace this change and hire more Black LGBTQ creatives in front of the camera and behind the scenes, they could turn that talk into action, allowing more Black queer faces to grace the screen.

DIGITAL MATERIALS

Free CeCe (screenshot) (http://www.takepart.com/sites/default/files/styles/large/public/free-cece-2.jpg).
James Baldwin (screenshot).
Moonlight (screenshot 1) (https://film-grab.com/2019/03/15/moonlight/#bwg1954/121939).
Moonlight (screenshot 2) (https://film-grab.com/2019/03/15/moonlight/#bwg1954/121909).
One Iconic Look: *The Color Purple* (https://tomandlorenzo.com/wp-content/uploads/2020/06/One-Iconic-Look-The-Color-Purple-Margaret-Shug-Avery-Costumes-Movie-Tom-Lorenzo-Site-66.jpg).
Paris is Burning (screenshot) (https://iv1.lisimg.com/image/7452613/630full-paris-is-burning-screenshot.jpg).
Set It Off (screenshot).
Working in the Video Store (screenshot) (https://www.winnipegfilmgroup.com/wp-content/uploads/C-T-working-in-the-video-store.png).

FURTHER READING

Allen, S., & Miles, B. (2020). Unapologetic blackness in action: Embodied resistance and social movement scenes in Black celebrity activism. *Humanity & Society, 32*(3), 215–237.

Amorosi, A. D. (2017). Dekkoo, a new gay-focused TV/film streaming service, launches in Philly. *Metro.* https://www.metro.us/news/local-news/philadelphia/dekkoo-new-gay-focused-tvfilm-streaming-service-launches-philly

Anderst, L. (2019). Calling to witness: Complicating autobiography and narrative empathy in Marlon Riggs's *Tongues Untied. Studies in Documentary Film, 13*(1), 73–89. https://doi.org/10.1080/17503280.2019.1575567

Best, W. (2019). "Looking for Langston": Themes of religion, sexuality, and evasion in the life and work of Langston Hughes. *The Langston Hughes Review, 25*(1), 28–40. https://doi.org/10.5325/langhughrevi.25.1.0028

Ciasullo, A. (2001). Making her (in)visible: Cultural representations of lesbianism and the lesbian body in the 1990s. *Feminist Studies, 27*(3), 577–608. https://doi.org/10.2307/3178806

Copeland, K. J. (2018). *Moonlight*, directed by Barry Jenkins. *Journal of Homosexuality, 65*(5), 687–689. https://doi.org/10.1080/00918369.2017.1333815

Harper, P. (1994). "The subversive edge": *Paris is Burning*, social critique, and the limits of subjective agency. *Diacritics, 24*(2–3), 90–103. https://doi.org/10.2307/465166

Lewis, C. (2012). Cultivating Black lesbian shamelessness: Alice Walker's *The Color Purple. Rocky Mountain Review, 66*(2), 158–175. https://www.jstor.org/stable/41763555

Musanga, T., & Mukhuba, T. (2019). Toward the survival and wholeness of the African American community: A womanist reading of Alice Walker's *The Color Purple* (1982). *Journal of Black Studies, 50*(4), 388–400.

Riggs, M. (1991). Black macho revisited: Reflections of a snap! Queen. *Black American Literature Forum, 25*(2), 389–394.

Sullivan, L. L. (2004). Chasing fae: *The Watermelon Woman* and Black lesbian possibility. In J. Bobo, C. Hudley, & C. Michel (Eds.), *Black studies reader* (pp. 211–224). Routledge.

REFERENCES

Advocate. (2018, February). 17 essential Black queer films. https://www.advocate.com/film/2018/2/26/17-essential-black-queer-films

Anderson, T. (2017, February 24). At the movies: From "Paris" to an integral N.Y. circle. *Los Angeles Times.*

Anderson, T. (2019). 11 documentaries to celebrate Black LGBTQ+ history beyond February. *Out*. https://www.out.com/film/2019/2/28/11-documentaries-celebrate-black-lgbtq-history-beyond-february#media-gallery-media-1

Benshoff, H., & Griffin, S. (Eds.). (2004). *Queer cinema: The film reader*. Routledge.

Blair, E. (2019, February 21). Hollywood diversity report finds progress, but much left to gain. *NPR*. https://www.nprillinois.org/post/hollywood-diversity-report-finds-progress-much-left-gain#stream/0

Box Office Mojo. (2020. LGBTQ theme. *IMDbPro*.

Carrithers, J. (1995). The audiences of *The Boys in the Band*. *Journal of Popular Film & Television*, 23(2), 64–70.

Chang, J. (2016, September 11). Toronto 2016: Barry Jenkins' *Moonlight* makes the case for quiet eloquence. *Los Angeles Times*. https://www.latimes.com/entertainment/movies/la-et-mn-toronto-2016-barry-jenkins-moonlight-makes-the-case-for-quiet-eloquence-20160911-snap-story.html

Cohen, S. (2015, March 17). How one movie changed LGBTQ history. *TIME*.

Corliss, R. (1992, November 30). *The Crying Game*. *TIME*.

Diawara, M. (1996). The absent one: The avant-garde and the Black imaginary in *Looking for Langston*. In M. Blount & G. P. Cunningham (Eds.), *Representing Black men* (pp. 205–224). Routledge.

Donegan, M. (2017, July 5). *The Watermelon Woman* shows the power of gay history. *The New Republic*. https://newrepublic.com/article/143703/watermelon-woman-shows-power-gay-history

Evans, R. (2005). Filmmaker's statement. Independent Lens, PBS. http://www.pbs.org/independentlens/brothertobrother/statement.html

Gardner, C. (2020, February 6). GLAAD launches digital content series *Neon* to highlight Black LGBTQ people, stories. *Hollywood Reporter*.

George, L. (1996, April 15). Breaking the barriers that keep them from church. *Los Angeles Times*.

GLAAD (Gay and Lesbian Alliance Against Defamation). (2020a). Studio responsibility report: Overview of findings. https://www.glaad.org/sri/2019/overview

GLAAD (Gay and Lesbian Alliance Against Defamation). (2020b). Where we are on TV report—2019. https://www.glaad.org/whereweareontv19

Guerrero, E. (1993). *Framing blackness: The African American image in film*. Temple University Press. https://doi.org/10.2307/j.ctvrdf2mb

Harris, A. (2012). "I'm a militant queen": Queering blaxploitation films. In M. Mask (Ed.), *Contemporary Black American cinema: Race, gender and sexuality at the movies* (pp. 217–234). Routledge.

Jung, E. A. (2018, May 16). A beginner's guide to new queer cinema. *Vulture*.

Klemm, M. D. (2008, November). The boys are back in town. *CinemaQueer*.

Lauer, S. (2017). *Moonlight*: A tale of heartbreak, brilliance, and interhuman artistry. *Cinematic Codes Review*, 2(3), 28–58.

Leung, W. (2008). So queer yet so straight: Ang Lee's *The Wedding Banquet* and *Brokeback Mountain*. *Journal of Film and Video*, 60(1), 23–42.

Linden, S. (2013, October 28). The new Black: Film review. *The Hollywood Reporter*.

Mask, M. (2012). *Contemporary Black American cinema: Race, gender and sexuality at the movies*. Routledge.

McCracken, C. (2017, October 2). An LGBTQ Netflix: Productive? Restricting? Lasting? *Flow Journal*. https://www.flowjournal.org/2017/10/an-lgbtq-netflix

Morris, W. (2019, February 6). Blackness, gayness, representation: Marlon Riggs unpacks it all in his films. *New York Times*.

Obenson, T. (2011, November). Steven Spielberg admits that he softened lesbian sex in *The Color Purple*. *IndieWire*. https://www.indiewire.com/2011/12/steven-spielberg-admits-that-he-softened-lesbian-sex-in-the-color-purple-149521/

Patten, D. (2016, May 24). HBO's *All the Way* tops *Confirmation* in total viewers but not *Bessie*. *Deadline*. https://sports.yahoo.com/news/hbo-way-tops-confirmation-total-205927312.html

Quinn, M. (1992, February 29). Buchanan TV ad angers filmmaker. *Los Angeles Times*. http://articles.latimes.com/1992-02-29/entertainment/ca-2625_1_campaign-ad

Rafferty, T. (1991, September 16). *Paris is Burning*. *The New Yorker*.

Rich, B. R. (1992). New queer cinema. *Sight & Sound, 2*(5), 15–22.

Rich, B. R. (2013). *New queer cinema: The director's cut*. Duke University Press.

Riggs, M. (1996). Tongues re-tied. In M. Retina & R. Suderburg (Eds.), *Resolution: Contemporary video practices* (pp. 185–188). University of Minnesota Press.

Rosenberg, H. (1992, March 6). On the urge to purge public TV. *Los Angeles Times*.

Rutledge, E. (2020, October 28). The historical significance of Black queer films. *Black Perspectives*. https://www.aaihs.org/the-historical-significance-of-black-queer-films-2/

Schwartz, D. H., & Hadley, C. (2017, October 24). DEKKOO: Video entertainment for gay audiences. *Huffington Post*.

Thomas, J. (2012, July 6). Black, gay, and posh: Talking with Patrik-Ian Polk. *Slate*. https://slate.com/culture/2012/07/patrik-ian-polk-interview-making-movies-about-a-world-that-is-black-gay-and-middle-class.html

Travers, P. (2016, October 19). *Moonlight* review: Story of African-American boy growing up is a gamechanger. *Rolling Stone*. https://www.rollingstone.com/movies/movie-reviews/moonlight-review-story-of-african-american-boy-growing-up-is-a-gamechanger-122466/

Waxman, O. B. (2020, February 7). Why hit movies are called blockbusters. *TIME*.

Wuest, B. (2018). A shelf of one's own: A queer production studies approach to LGBT film distribution and categorization. *Journal of Film and Video, 70*(3–4), 24–43.

Victor Evans

AGONISTIC QUEER TV STUDIES FOR WESTERN EUROPE

INTRODUCTION

Queer-informed analyses of television—as individual text (Avila-Saavedra, 2009; Doran, 2013; Marshal, 2016; Munt, 2006), as a medium (Chambers, 2009; Ng, 2013; Villarejo, 2014), or as an industry (Aslinger, 2009; Becker, 2006)—have become a staple of queer studies. Since the first openly non-heterosexual characters surfaced in mainstream, prime time American TV series in the 1990s, a growing body of work has examined how they interlock with normative discourses on gender and sexuality (Avila-Saavedra, 2009; Doran, 2013; Dow, 2001; Fejes & Petrich, 1993; Kies, 2016; McCarthy, 2001), their subversion of commonplace assumptions about non-heterosexual lives (Chambers, 2009; Dhaenens, 2013, 2014; Munt, 2006), or the industrial mechanisms that underlie them (Aslinger, 2009; Martin, 2015, 2018; Ng, 2013). This demonstrable interest in television representation is unsurprising, of course. Queer thought concerns itself with the (re)production of commonplace constructions of gender and sexuality, the power relations they sustain, and the systems that naturalize them (Chambers, 2009; Seidman, 1995; Warner, 2000). Because television remains a formative medium to popular culture, albeit in changing forms, it presents a crucial site for queer analysis. Consequently, works of queer TV scholarship are as much academic contributions as they are political interventions, furnishing not just interpretative accounts of how LGBT+ people are and have been portrayed on television, but articulating critical assessments of their complicity in sustained social and cultural inequities related to sexuality and gender too (Chambers, 2009).

This expressively political dimension distinguishes "queer TV scholarship" from other studies of LGBT+ televisibility, which, apart from being scarcer, tend to be less overtly partisan in engaging the medium. Cultivation research like that of Larry Gross (2001), Amber Raley and Jennifer Lucas (2006), Sara Netzley (2010), Bradley Bond (2015), or Jamie Capuzza and Leland Spencer (2017) is more descriptive in outlook, employing quantitative methods to assess the type of stories and traits TV articulates to the LGBT+ community (Villarejo, 2008). Premised on the hypothesis that these images "cultivate" commonplace assumptions about sexual and gender diversity (Gross, 2001), these studies map prevalent representational practices and chart their temporal evolution (Netzley, 2010). Queer scholars of television tend to be quite critical of such approaches (Battles & Hilton-Morrow, 2002; Heller, 2011), attributing a degree of complacency to studies that allow "facile" celebrations of increased representation (Chambers, 2009). But these contestations tend to gloss over the valuable contributions such studies make. Descriptive research addresses LGBT+ televisibility in general terms and, in doing so, explicates the broader context queer analyses often gloss over (Vanlee, 2019a; Villarejo, 2008). In fact, the ability of queer TV scholarship to demarcate its disciplinary boundaries and dismiss the use of methods perceived as not critical enough (Villarejo, 2008) is at least partially supported by the scholarly and popular familiarity of the U.S. texts it discusses (Vanlee, 2019a). It is therefore important to recognize that any distinction between queer and non-queer approaches to TV depictions of sexual and gender diversity is relevant primarily in a U.S. context and is intimately related to the widespread familiarity with U.S. television culture (Vanlee, 2019a). Popular and scholarly knowledge of non-U.S. depictions of sexual and gender diversity on television is considerably more fragmented along linguistic lines, however. Studies on LGBT+ televisibility in Western European (Kerrigan, 2016; Malici, 2014; O'Brien & Kerrigan, 2020; Vanlee et al., 2018) television cultures are consequently a recent development—as are those discussing Asian (Bassi, 2016) or Latin American (RamíDrez, 2020) cases, for that matter.

Characterized mostly by an interest in domestic LGBT+ TV representations and queer-informed interpretative frameworks, these studies are not so much invested in the emancipation of a geographically defined subfield, but in the application of queer approaches in new contexts. Some reproduce the textual perspective dominant in U.S. scholarship (Horvat, 2020; Kerrigan, 2019; Vanlee et al., 2020a, 2020b), focusing on what televisual depictions reveal about "acceptable" and "unacceptable" ways of transgressing hetero- and cisnormativity (Chambers, 2009; Joyrich, 2014) in different contexts. Others interact directly with TV professionals (e.g., Dhoest, 2015; Kerrigan, 2016; Thorfinssdottir & Jensen, 2017; Vanlee, 2019b; O'Brien & Kerrigan, 2020) to gauge discursive processes that shape portrayals of sexual and gender diversity. Capitalizing on domestic industries' humble scale, they offer a depth and candor that proves difficult to pursue for U.S. queer production scholarship, which instead prioritizes secondary sources (Aslinger, 2009; Ng, 2013) or small respondent samples (Martin, 2015) to assess industrial logics of LGBT+ televisibility. While they do not necessarily constitute a conscious attempt to kickstart Western European queer TV scholarship as a distinct research practice, recent studies also demonstrate growing interest in historical trajectories of sexual and gender diversity on the domestic small screen (Horvat, 2020; Kerrigan & Vanlee, 2020; Vanlee, 2019a). Importantly, these studies point to the differences in how sexual and gender diversity have found their way to TV programming in Western Europe, explicating the crucial role of public service broadcasters (PSBs) in mainstreaming LGBT+ televisibility (Vanlee, 2019a), addressed passingly by earlier sources (Dhoest, 2015; Kerrigan, 2016; Thorfinssdottir & Jensen, 2017; Vanlee, 2019b).

Inasmuch as Western European queer television scholarship today does not quite constitute a distinct subfield, applications of queer thought to domestic TV cultures do share common traits. First—and perhaps unsurprisingly—U.S. LGBT+ televisibility and its critical (queer) analyses are the primary frame of reference for the studies concerned. The linguistic heterogeneity of Western Europe inhibits transnational popular circulation of domestic queer texts to the extent that scholars elect to address U.S. TV culture when partaking in scholarly debate (Dhaenens, 2014; Hess, 2017; Kooijman, 2005). In the face of this shared, transnational cultural affinity with U.S. programming, local forms of LGBT+ televisibility tend to be overlooked—notwithstanding their distinctive traits (Vanlee, 2019a). As a result, studies that do address domestic depictions of sexual and gender diversity (Dhoest, 2015; Kerrigan, 2016; O'Brien & Kerrigan, 2020; Thorfinssdottir & Jensen, 2017; Vanlee, 2019b) have little choice but to draw from empirical insights and theoretical perspectives derived from U.S. cases, which, among other things, has arguably resulted in an eschewal of descriptive methods suited to disclose and document local queer TV cultures (Vanlee, 2019a). Second, public service broadcasting punctuates each existing source on LGBT+ televisibility in Western Europe, and attention for commercial programming is marginal, especially in comparison to U.S.-focused scholarship (Avila-Saavedra, 2009; Becker, 2006). Historical accounts show how PSBs spearheaded popular attention for sexual and gender diversity since the 1960s (Horvat, 2020; Kerrigan, 2016; Kerrigan & Vanlee, 2020), and studies on contemporary LGBT+ depictions on Western European small screens point to the mainstreaming function of PSB fiction programming since the 1990s, naturalizing sexual and gender diversity across domestic productions (Kerrigan & Vanlee, 2020; Vanlee, 2019a).

In the face of these observations, it makes little sense to review Western European queer TV studies' state of the art; it is hardly an established field and has only recently acquired certain traction. Neither does a comprehensive account of queer TV in Western Europe seem desirable; LGBT+ televisibility on local small screens is discreet, and attempts to address it diachronically fall short due to the limited transnational circulation and recognition of domestic queer programming. But taking the growing emancipation of Western European queer TV studies as a premise (Horvat, 2020; Kerrigan, 2016; Malici, 2014) to reflect on existing U.S.-focused queer engagements with television programming (Avila-Saavedra, 2009; Battles & Hilton-Morrow, 2002; Joyrich, 2014; Munt, 2006) is today a desirable and necessary step to take. Particularly, the moment is opportune to explore what the distinct conditions of domestic TV cultures imply for future directions in the field and to reflect on its relation to commonplace assumptions in established queer TV scholarship. What follows is therefore not so much an encyclopedic account of the field, describing the historical development of its methods and theories and their recent application to Western European television cultures. Rather, this article commences by addressing the implications the institutional traits of U.S. TV production—such as deregulation and economic determination (Becker, 2006; Walters, 2003)—have had on queer television scholarship. Doing so illustrates how the field has few modalities to define itself as anything but an opponent of the TV industry (Chambers, 2009). This, in turn, dissuades scholars from complementing critical deconstructions of current, problematic configurations of LGBT+ televisibility with propositional, normative claims about alternative directions for the future. Subsequently pointing to the distinct context of PSB television production and its historical role in spearheading LGBT+ televisibility in Western Europe (Dupont, 2019; Kerrigan & Vanlee, 2020) demonstrates that the domestic small screen calls for a distinct approach in queer TV scholarship. Television professionals are not only more accessible to scholars in domestic industries (Dhoest, 2015), but PSBs often rely on scholars to address their democratic responsibilities of pluralism as well as diverse representation (Horsti & Hultén, 2011; Panis et al., 2019). This suggests that the representation of sexual and gender diversity can be conceived of as an agonistic process (Chouliaraki, 2011; Mouffe, 2013) wherein problematic depictions can be critiqued, contested, and ultimately amended through interaction and exchange (Mouffe, 2013). To capitalize on this potential, future queer engagements with TV in Western Europe will benefit from explicating not only what television does wrong, but how it also could do better.

OUTSIDER OUTLOOK: QUEER SCHOLARSHIP AND U.S. TELEVISION PRODUCTION

Like television, scholarship is a thoroughly globalized circuit of communication and exchange. When conducting research and reporting on inquiry in published form, academics rarely envision a regional or domestic audience as their preferred readership but address an international community of presumably interested peers. Theoretical ideas and empirical findings are discussed in English to facilitate an international uptake of knowledge, and authors carefully highlight why research is pertinent beyond an exclusively regional interest. Naturally, some fields are more attentive for the relevance of local phenomena than others, and distinctions between center and periphery are more explicit in some areas of study than others. Queer TV scholarship has predominantly focused on the United States and attention to domestic forms of LGBT+ televisibility has been modest to date (Bassi, 2016; Dhoest, 2015; Kerrigan, 2016; O'Brien & Kerrigan, 2020; RamíDrez, 2020; Thorfinssdottir & Jensen, 2017; Vanlee, 2019b). As such, local depictions of sexual and gender diversity have predominantly been understood through interpretative frameworks based on research into U.S. TV culture. This is neither surprising nor necessarily problematic. The global circulation of American TV culture ensures its relevance to scholarly debate elsewhere, and international lay and academic audiences tend to be familiar with its programming, organizational aspects, and broader sociocultural context (see Vanlee, 2019a). From the invisibility and demonization in the 1980s and early 1990s (Fejes & Petrich, 1993) and the sudden omnipresence of "sanitized" White, affluent gay men and lesbian women on network television at the turn of the century (Battles & Hilton-Morrow, 2002; Becker, 2006) to contemporary tensions between "normative" and "subversive" depictions of sexual and gender diversity (Cavalcante, 2015; Doran, 2013), the historical trajectory of U.S. LGBT+ televisibility has become common and useful knowledge in a popular and scholarly sense.

That European scholars examine American content like *Queer Eye* (Bravo, 2003–2007) (Kooijman, 2005), *True Blood* (HBO, 2008–2014) (e.g., Dhaenens, 2013), or *Transparent* (Amazon Prime Video, 2014–2019) (e.g., Hess, 2017) testifies to this, illustrating not only that non-American scholars value studying U.S. texts, but that they have the necessary contextual knowledge to comprehensively engage them too. Where Western European TV production tends to focus specifically on domestic markets and its international circulation is often hampered by language barriers, moreover, American programming provides a shared cultural frame of reference to queer scholars of television around the globe (Vanlee, 2019a). The rejection of methods considered "essentialist" or "positivist" in the field (e.g., Chambers, 2009, p. 93; Heller, 2011, p. 668)—which might offer tools to disclose and contextualize overlooked contexts to academic debate (see Shaw, 2017; Vanlee et al., 2020b; Villarejo, 2008)—further hinders broadening the scope of queer TV studies. In the face of these observations, further engagements with domestic LGBT+ televisibility in Western Europe must be predicated on methodological expansion. Peripheral queer TV scholarship should not simply transpose commonplace distinctions between queer and non-queer methods to new objects of study (Vanlee, 2019a), but carefully assess the tools needed to comprehensively address domestic TV culture. This need for openness and innovation extends to commonplace characterizations of the position that scholarship must assume vis-à-vis the industry it studies too, which may take various forms across different contexts.

Due to the U.S.-centric nature of queer scholarship in general (Amin, 2016) and queer TV scholarship in particular (Kerrigan & Vanlee, 2020), the position it assumes vis-à-vis its object of study is scarcely reflected upon; that is, the self-evidence of understanding the field on particularly U.S.-based terms largely remains unchallenged due to the lack of alternative modes of doing queer television studies. Consequently, few sources systematically explore queer television scholarship, as opposed to exploring television from a queer perspective. Approached as such, it is quite evident that the field conceives of its role as that of a critical watchdog, ready to identify, expose, and unpack the deficiencies in LGBT+ portrayals on TV (e.g., Cavalcante, 2015; Doran, 2013; Kies, 2016) or to single out those momentary instances television transcends normative traditionalism and offers a space for subversion (e.g., Chambers, 2009; Dhaenens, 2013; Joyrich, 2014; Munt, 2006). While legitimate and necessary, default analytics of queer TV studies therefore seem premised on an outsider perspective, disengaged from directly shaping television production. The subject of intended impact is rarely broached explicitly in the field, but it seems to mostly aim at contributing to public discourse about television. In other words, it operates on an implicit consensus that scholarship should popularize critical knowledge about television and its relation to the LGBT+ community (Chambers, 2009) but is less committed to explicitly address television production. Presumably, queer critiques of televisual depictions of sexual and gender diversity do trickle down to TV professionals, and works like Alfred Martin's production research certainly suggest as much (2015). But this is nevertheless distinct from engaging in research with the express intention of addressing TV professionals about the ramifications of their practices on the LGBT+ community and its role in society. Given queer television studies' vocal commitment to enacting sociocultural change through scholarly activities (Battles & Hilton-Morrow, 2002; Chambers, 2009; Heller, 2011; Joyrich, 2014), the scarcity of work explicitly addressing its position in relation to the TV industry might seem odd. This lack is not unique to queer approaches to television studies, of course, and popular critiques of the disjunction of the academy from everyday life are well-known. But at least in the context of queer TV studies, it is certainly wrong to perceive this limited commitment to exploring and understanding its particular relation to the industry it studies as disinterestedness or apathy. Rather, it is shaped by conditions characteristic of the American TV industry. Queer television studies have adapted to the expressively limited pathways offered by television production and its adjacent activities in the United States to the extent that it has become axiomatic to assume one particular positionality when engaging in queer scholarship on the subject.

Queer TV studies' perennial assumption of an outsider perspective in addressing issues of sexual and gender diversity in and on television is predicated on various elements. A first dimension to consider here is almost tangible in nature and pertains to the scale and operational logics of the U.S. television industry. The global reach of American TV is supported by extensive and continuous production (Straubhaar, 2007), ensuring a never-ending stream of new content—albeit in changing forms (Curtin & Shattuc, 2017, p. 116). Queer TV scholarship's recognition of the medium's fast-paced production cycles (Becker, 2006; Joyrich, 2014) leaves little to the imagination regarding the inclusion of or even attention for critical scholarly perspectives on the representation of sexual and gender diversity. Increasing competition between traditional and new, disruptive platforms (Curtin & Shattuc, 2017) further exasperates this. Steadfast constructions of television production as a mechanistic process, and of television professionals as under constant (commercial) pressure, foster a commonsensical disjunction of scholarship from the TV industry—naturalizing the assumption that pursuing direct interaction is altogether wasted. Matters of prestige and accessibility naturally play a role here as well. Expecting it to be difficult to reach key actors in TV production and adjacent activities due to their sociocultural status (see Caldwell, 2008) appears to be a very rational thought. Prolific producer and showrunner Ryan Murphy is an obvious case in point. His work—rife in materials explicitly addressing gender and sexuality—is amply discussed by queer TV scholarship (e.g., Joyrich, 2014; Meyer & Wood, 2013), garnering both praise (e.g., Geller & Banker, 2017; Sarkissian, 2014) and criticism (e.g., Cales, 2015; Jacobs, 2014). Apart from interviews in popular outlets cited as secondary sources, however, scholarly publications expanding on Murphy's work never engage him directly. Queer uses of approaches associated with production studies demonstrate the value of interaction between scholars and TV professionals (e.g., Kerrigan, 2016; Martin, 2015, 2018), and Murphy's absence from scholarly discourse on LGBT+ representation presumably does not result from an unwillingness on behalf of scholars to talk to TV professionals. More plausibly, it is a consequence of the disinterest queer critics ascribe to producers of television about their own activities.

CONSIDERING CONDITIONS: QUEER TV STUDIES FOR A DEREGULATED MARKET

Assuming that TV professionals as a rule do not prioritize interaction with queer television scholars—or even acknowledge their work—is not unwarranted in the context of the United States. Fully committing to the idea that the people and organizations responsible for prolific images of LGBT+ people and communities—ranging from the writers behind *The Wire*'s (HBO, 2002–2008), Omar Little (see Dhaenens & Van Bauwel, 2012), to the actors portraying Mitch and Cam in *Modern Family* (ABC, 2009–2020) (see Cavalcante, 2015)—are open to amend or even debate particular portrayals based on the input of queer TV scholars requires believing that the American television industry prioritizes social responsibilities over other motives. This is not at all the case, of course. It goes without saying that some TV professionals, teams, or organizations are committed to producing content having a beneficial role in society, and some authors have focused explicitly on these instances (e.g., Chambers, 2009; Dhaenens, 2013, 2014; Munt, 2006). They are generally emphasized as exceptions, however, and are often explicitly contrasted with "regular" (i.e., heteronormative and cisnormative) television content. Addressing *Six Feet Under*'s (HBO, 2001–2005) constant evocation of the epistemological function of "the closet" in heterosexist American society, for instance, Samuel Chambers (2003) asserts that this is a distinctive feature in the face of an increasing LGBT+ presence in series unwilling to tackle heteronormativity as such (p. 27). When Raffi Sarkissian (2014) discusses how *Glee* (Fox, 2009–2015) challenges representational tropes of young LGBT+ people (p. 154), the argument is, of course, predicated on the recognition that most other series portraying non-heterosexual youths *do* rely heavily on those conventions. Likewise, Frederik Dhaenens's (2014) conceptualization of TV's potential to resist and subvert heteronormative discourses (p. 521) assumes a heteronormative subtext in the majority of television productions, characterizing articulations of queer resistance as the exception rather than the rule (p. 529).

If conscious or unconscious productions of images and stories reflecting queer rather than hetero-, homo-, or cisnormative constructions of gender and sexuality are momentary exceptions, opportunistic and reductive portrayals of LGBT+ people and communities are the rule in the American TV industry. The term "opportunistic" here is deliberate, as it reflects the general assessment queer television scholarship offers about why and how non-heterosexual people are present in series. Work with an expressive interest in industrial logics shaping the entry of sexual and gender diversity to the small screen, like that of Suzanna Danuta Walters (2003) and Ron Becker (2006), points to generating advertising revenue by appealing to affluent, socially progressive audience segments as the primary motive to introduce lesbian and gay characters to mainstream television content. Obviously, primetime examples like Ellen Morgan in the eponymous sitcom (see Dow, 2001) or Will Truman in the semi-eponymous sitcom (see Avila-Saavedra, 2009) are not completely devoid of benevolence and do represent a distinct shift from earlier, outspokenly dismissive portrayals of same-sex desire (see Fejes & Petrich, 1993). Given that the existence of these characters—and others that resemble them—is not only predicated on their embrace by a body of valuable potential consumers, but that they also generally reflect the privileged sociocultural identity of these consumers (see Ng, 2013; Peters, 2011), it is nevertheless difficult to regard them as genuine attempts to benefit the LGBT+ community in its entirety. Here, it also pays to recognize that TV stories and characters often acknowledged as critical or even dismissive of hetero- and cisnormative constructions of LGBT+ identities (e.g., Chambers, 2003, 2009; Dhaenens, 2013, 2014; Munt, 2006) tend to be situated in American premium cable offerings, creating a paywall for portrayals that expand conventional views on gender and sexuality (see Becker, 2006, p. 175). While this argument is arguably losing its relevance in the face of piracy and streaming (Strangelove, 2015), it does illustrate that profitability is a core consideration in how various segments of the television industry in the United States engage with LGBT+ televisibility. The noted overrepresentation of White, affluent, gender-conforming gay and lesbian characters in mainstream network content (Avila-Saavedra, 2009; Doran, 2013; Heller, 2011) visually reflects this. But because more transgressive portrayals surface predominantly in subscription content, their formal and narrative qualities are predicated on the same logic.

If LGBT+ characters surface in TV content primarily because they are profitable and their endorsement or subversion of conventional constructions of LGBT+ people are dependent on business models, queer television scholarship's potential relations to the industry it studies are quite dramatically reduced. Television production and distribution in the United States is, like most of its economic sectors, comparatively deregulated (Nelson, 2007), and—contrasting historical conventions inhibiting the entry of queerness to the small screen (see Fejes & Petrich, 1993; Gross, 2001)—there are no formal expectations of the American TV industry to be attentive for diversity or sociocultural difference in whatever form. Lacking clear pathways to directly engage TV production and faced with the continuation of representational practices that reduce (see Avila-Saavedra, 2009; Doran, 2013; Kies, 2016) or even instrumentalize (see Cavalcante, 2015; Lovelock, 2017; Peters, 2011) LGBT+ people and communities, it is not surprising that queer TV scholarship's default position vis-à-vis the American television industry is mostly antagonistic. Generally, television has not presented itself as a cultural force recognizant of the validity of sexual and gender diversity, but has instead proved a hurdle to overcome (Fejes & Petrich, 1993; Gross, 2001). That queer TV scholars tend to caution against celebratory narratives of numerically increased LGBT+ representation (e.g., Battles & Hilton-Morrow, 2002; Beirne, 2008; Chambers, 2009; Heller, 2011) is illustrative of the suspicion and sometimes even hostility the field assumes to its object of study. The television industry is not so much seen as a potential partner to be engaged but as an opponent to be countered—and perhaps rightly so in the American context. It is nevertheless important to recognize that this construction is shaped by the conditions of television production and distribution in the United States and does not automatically apply everywhere, more so because there are particular ramifications to this antagonistic disposition in queer TV scholarship.

ANTAGONISTIC ADDRESSALS: CRYPTO-NORMATIVITY AND QUEER TV STUDIES

Normativity—related to constructions of gender or sexuality and their intersection with other identity axes—is a core business for queer studies (Chambers, 2009; Joyrich, 2014). Queer scholarship does not address physical phenomena associated with sexual and gendered difference, but the social and cultural conventions they instigate. Simultaneously shaping and reflecting uneven power relations, constructions of gender and sexuality are formative aspects to structural inequities between different groups of people. It is not hard to see, for instance, how the perennial portrayal of trans people as postoperative trans women (see Lovelock, 2017; Vipond, 2015) regulates how subjects may legitimately transgress conventional gender identities in society. These images and stories validate certain modes of being over others—in this particular case gender conformity in trans women—and reproduce normative frameworks discrediting other gendered subjectivities (see Vanlee et al., 2020a). Similar points could be made about other dimensions to LGBT+ televisibility, of course. Indeed, much of queer TV scholarship is concerned with understanding whether representations of sexual and gender diversity reproduce or subvert hetero- and cisnormative discourses (Chambers, 2003; Dhaenens, 2013, 2014; Peters, 2011), how these discourses interlock with organizational and commercial aspects of the television industry (Aslinger, 2009; Ng, 2013), or how individual TV professionals negotiate them in their craft (Martin, 2015; Thorfinssdottir & Jensen, 2017; Vanlee, 2019b). Arguably, such issues of normativity are the main interest of queer TV scholarship. Various dimensions of television are related to existing norms about "legitimate" modes of being—legitimate patterns of being LGBT+ included—and either critiqued for their complicity in (Doran, 2013; Joyrich, 2009; Kies, 2016; Kooijman, 2005) or praised for their subversion (Chambers, 2009; Dhaenens & Van Bauwel, 2012; Munt, 2006) of these conventional ways of constructing gender and sexuality. As is the case with other forms of queer inquiry (see Wiegman & Wilson, 2015), the application of queer perspectives to TV as industry and representation presents itself as a counter-normative activity; that is, critiquing the role television plays in upholding hegemonic norms on gender and sexuality is a predominant ambition in queer television scholarship, and even its alternative applications tend to celebrate programming that disrupts commonplace assumptions about LGBT+ lives and experiences.

But contesting norms or their reflection in representational regimes does not make queer TV scholarship non-normative. Critiquing the nefarious role LGBT+ portrayals play in upholding constrictive norms regulating legitimate embodiments of gender and sexuality pits queer TV scholarship against hegemonic frameworks of normativity (see Abbot, 2018; Vanlee et al., 2020a; Wiegman & Wilson, 2015). Devoting scholarly work to the deconstruction of hetero- and cisnormativity in and on television (Battles & Hilton-Morrow, 2002; Chambers, 2009; Joyrich, 2014), and the act of rejecting particular representations is predicated on a conviction that things *should* be different. Clearly, this is a normative stance. It builds on a negative evaluation of the status quo and a tacit validation of more desirable alternatives (Vanlee et al., 2020a). When Guillermo Avila-Saavedra (2009) demonstrates that *Will & Grace* (NBC, 1998–2006), *It's All Relative* (ABC, 2003–2006), and *Queer Eye* "not only reinforce patriarchal notions of masculinity but also traditional constructions of femininity" (p. 19), it clearly implies that these portrayals are to an extent reproachable. Insofar as the rejection of certain representational practices is clearly articulated by Avila-Saavedra (2009), however, the author does not explicate what a valid alternative would be. This example, and other queer scholarship discussing American TV (e.g., Beirne, 2008; Doran, 2013; Dow, 2001; Kies, 2016; Mitchell, 2005; Peters, 2011), demonstrates the discretion of the field's own normative orientations. Predicated mostly on critiquing television's reflection of existing sexual and gender norms, queer TV scholarship rarely disambiguates how the medium and the representations it circulates might address particular issues. Outspoken discussions of formal and narrative qualities that *do* correspond to queer convictions about sexuality and gender are indeed scarce. If and when they take place, they are not only furtive and underdeveloped, but happen at the fringes of queer TV studies. For instance, Jamie Capuzza and Leland Spencer (2017) conclude their detailed content analysis by hinting at the kind of narratives they envision for trans people (pp. 226–227), arguing for a recognition of difference while at the same time avoiding a collapse into identity categories. Their engagement with queer TV literature is limited, however, and corresponds more to cultivation theory-inspired approaches to television. Their use of descriptive methods further distances their work from queer TV studies, given that these approaches are generally dismissed by the field (see Vanlee, 2019a; Villarejo, 2008).

Generally speaking, queer TV scholarship is crypto-normative (see Abbott, 2018; Hesmondalgh & Toynbee, 2008; Vanlee, 2019b) in its addressal of various phenomena associated with LGBT+ televisibility. Problematizing representations and practices for their demonstrable refraction of normative identity frameworks is certainly warranted but obscures that it is also predicated on a set of beliefs and convictions about how sexual and gendered difference *should* be portrayed. This observation is hardly novel concerning queer theory and certain of its applications (Seidman, 1995; Wiegman & Wilson, 2015), but it pays to observe that the crypto-normativity of queer television scholarship is shaped by its antagonism vis-à-vis the TV industry, which itself is sustained by the latter's deregulation. If the existence of popular images and stories of LGBT+ people is demonstrably dependent on their profitability (Becker, 2006; Heller, 2011; Peters, 2011) and their compliance with or subversion of hetero- and cisnormative frameworks of sexuality and gender likewise hinge on commercial considerations, articulating scholarly insights in a prescriptive register appears ineffectual. And given that contemporary LGBT+ televisibility remains burdened by television's questionable history with the emancipation of sexual and gendered difference, treating the American TV industry as a well-meaning recipient of productive suggestions about LGBT+ representation may seem altogether delusional. Queer television scholarship's antagonistic mode of address has its practitioners approach its object of study as a powerful opponent. Consequently, prodding at its existing deficiencies seems to be prioritized over reflecting on the future steps LGBT+ televisibility might take for the better.

DIFFERENT DYNAMICS: QUEER TV STUDIES FOR WESTERN EUROPE

The antagonism and associated crypto-normativity of queer television scholarship are shaped by and continue to be tailored to the conditions of LGBT+ televisibility on the American small screen. Apart from notable exceptions—such as Páraic Kerrigan's (2016, 2019) work on LGBT+ televisibility in Ireland, Luca Malici's (2011, 2014) explorations of queerness on Italian television, or Peri Bradley's (2013) reading of gay romance on *EastEnders* (BBC1, 1985–)—Western European television cultures have received scarce attention in queer scholarship. Consequently, few sources comprehensively discuss comparable queer perspectives on other television industries. As noted, the limited traction contexts like Western Europe have in the field is at least partly brought by the international circulation of American content, on the one hand, and the national outlook and associated linguistic barriers of domestic TV production, on the other (see Vanlee, 2019a). That they are largely absent from queer scholarly discourse does not mean that LGBT+ characters and stories do not circulate in Western European television programming, however. *Skam* [Shame] (NRK, 2015–2017), a Norwegian web drama for adolescent and young adult audiences, for instance, prominently features same-sex desire with several characters (Sundet, 2020), which is furthermore reflected in remakes of the series in various other European countries. German soap operas like *Verbotene Liebe* [Forbidden love] (Das Erste, 1995–2015) or *Lindenstraße* [Linden street] (Das Erste, 1985–2020) have been attentive to issues of sexual and gender diversity since the 1990s (see Vanlee, 2019a), gaining international cult followings in online LGBT+ communities (Dhaenens, 2012). Western European LGBT+ televisibility is not confined to comparably recent fiction offerings either. In Flanders, same-sex desire was openly discussed by domestic informational programming in the 1960s (see Dupont, 2019), whereas Irish current affairs segments likewise offered visibility to homosexual couples in the 1970s and 1980s (see Kerrigan, 2016; Kerrigan & Vanlee, 2020).[1] Hence, queer TV scholarship is certainly not deprived of pertinent objects of study in Western Europe, and neither is it plausible that sexual and gender diversity are altogether invisible in other non-American television cultures around the world.

Critical queer perspectives could therefore certainly play an important role in TV cultures outside of the United States. Their deconstructive, interpretative approaches relate representations of sexual and gender diversity to the lived experiences and political fate of the LGBT+ community (Battles & Hilton-Morrow, 2002; Chambers, 2009; Doty, 1993) and offer pathways to address these topics in a variety of contexts. But the foregoing discussion of queer TV scholarship's relation to its object of study does caution against an all too comprehensive transposition of existing views to other television cultures' engagement with sexual and gender diversity. Valuing queer analytics must be distinct from simply reproducing them. Whether the antagonistic disposition fostered by U.S. queer scholarship is a suitable stance to reproduce in Western Europe is a particularly salient question here. Both historical developments in LGBT+ televisibility and contemporary organizational dimensions to Western European TV industries instead call for an agonistic mode of address. Such an agonistic approach is predicated on recognizing television production as a sector academics might productively interact with (Chouliaraki, 2011) to address hegemonic conceptions of gender and sexuality. Instead of the economic determinism that underpins most of U.S. queer TV scholarship, an agonistic approach to LGBT+ televisibility understands representations of sexual and gender diversity to result from a perpetual process of contestation and compromise (Mouffe, 2013). Crucially, this rearticulates the role of (queer) scholars from a critical outsider position whose function is defined in oppositional terms to a committed participant willing to substantively add to future forms of LGBT+ televisibility.

In clear juxtaposition to earlier observations made about the United States, the modest scale and prestige of Western European audiovisual industries is a first condition to consider. Certain exceptions notwithstanding, domestic television and film production proves relatively accessible to scholarship. This accessibility is demonstrated by various studies offering in-depth perspectives into Western European production cultures. Alexander Dhoest's (2015) study of how Flemish TV professionals give form and substance to demands for diversity in fiction programming is based on expert interviews rather than textual analysis, whereas Eduard Cuelenaere (2020) similarly employs direct interaction with Dutch and Flemish filmmakers to address monolingual remakes between the two regions. Discussing Danish children's television, Dia Thorfinnsdottir and Helle Jensen (2017) focus explicitly on how production discourses shape how gender and sexuality are addressed in this particular segment, directly engaging with relevant professionals to explore the issue. Clearly then, domestic TV industries in Western Europe at the very least accommodate directly addressing television professionals as participants and respondents (e.g., Horsti & Hultén, 2011; Klein, 2011; Vanlee, 2019b). The conviction that queer TV scholarship in Western Europe should define itself differently vis-à-vis the television industry is not merely predicated on the fact that the TV industry is accessible, however. Both historical trajectories of LGBT+ televisibility and current organizational dimensions to many TV industries in Western Europe substantiate this as well.

Here, public service broadcasters (PSBs) play a pivotal role and distinguish the mechanisms shaping the representation of sexual and gender diversity from the situation in the United States. Where public service broadcasting played—and plays—a comparatively marginal role in the United States (Pickard, 2017, p. 201), television landscapes in Western Europe are characterized by dominant PSBs, which often enjoyed monopolies well into the 1980s and 1990s (see Donders et al., 2016). Generally held to the threefold demand to "inform," "educate," and "entertain" the communities they serve (Horsti & Hultén, 2011; Kerrigan & Vanlee, 2020; Klein, 2011), these PSBs of course display national variations but are nevertheless comparable in their conceptualization as democratic institutions. Across its regions, PSBs are not only central actors in many Western European television markets, but fulfill a compensatory role as well (Klein, 2011). Where domestic commercial broadcasters are relatively free to ignore issues of sociocultural diversity (Donders et al., 2016), although they too tend to be attentive for societal heterogeneity, PSBs are formally expected to demonstrably reflect pluralism (see Bardoel & d'Haenens, 2008) and address demographic varieties in the national target audience. Crucially, PSBs cannot envision their viewership as an aggregate of consumers, of which particular segments can be targeted for profit maximization (Becker, 2006). Rather, media organizations like the UK's BBC, the Dutch NPO, DR in Denmark, or RTÉ in Ireland are supposed to define their practices—whether representational or otherwise—in a democratic framework predicated on attentiveness for sociocultural change and timely public debate (Vanlee et al., 2018).[2]

AGONISTIC ACADEMIA: LGBT+ EXPERTISE AND PUBLIC SERVICE BROADCASTING

Given that many public service broadcasters (PSBs) enjoyed monopolies in their domestic television markets until the end of the 20th century (see Kerrigan & Vanlee, 2020), it is unsurprising that the historical onset of LGBT+ televisibility in those contexts is situated in public service broadcasting. Early instances of televisual attention for same-sex desire and gender diversity documented by scholarly sources moreover do point to salient differences with contemporary American examples. At a time when Sid Davis's notorious short *Boys Beware* (1961) explicitly articulated homosexuality to child abuse, for instance, the Flemish VRT documentary *Diagnose van het Anders-Zijn* [Diagnosis of being different] (1966) featured progressive sexologists as well as testimonials of (anonymous) gay men to underscore undue stigmatization as the "problem" of same-sex desire (Dupont, 2019; Kerrigan & Vanlee, 2020).[3] In the Netherlands, gay and lesbian advocate and celebrated interior designer Benno Premsela openly addressed his homosexuality in an NPO current affairs show *Achter het Nieuws* (VARA, 1960–1992) on December 30, 1964 (Boelaars, 2008). German ARD-subsidiary WDR commissioned openly queer filmmaker Rosa Von Praunheim to direct a film on gay communities in Berlin.[4] The resulting feature—*Nicht der Homosexuelle ist pervers, sondern die Situation, in der er lebt* (1971)—and its circulation are considered a keystone to German-speaking LGBT+ advocacy (Holy, 2012). In Ireland, LGBT+ advocate David Lynch managed to pressure RTÉ producers into broadcasting an interview with gay marriage equality campaigner David Norris in 1975, explicitly citing the PSB remit as a supporting argument (see Kerrigan & Vanlee, 2020). What unites these early instances of LGBT+ televisibility in Western European TV cultures is not only that they are demonstrably less demonizing than contemporaneous—and even more recent—portrayals in American programming (Vanlee, 2019a), but more importantly, they resulted from direct interactions between LGBT+ advocacy and scholarship with TV production, bringing about representations that were not necessarily without their defaults (see Kerrigan, 2016, 2019), but nevertheless reflected a willingness to perceive attention for sexual and gender diversity as a social responsibility of PSB television content. Here, it also pays to recognize that Western European PSB programming tends to synergize with commercial domestic TV production and distribution (Raats & Pauwels, 2013). The initial introduction of LGBT+ characters and stories in PSB fiction and their subsequent diffusion over comparable domestic commercial programming was observed in various Western European contexts in the 1990s (see Kerrigan & Vanlee, 2020; Vanlee, 2019a) and illustrates how PSBs' engagement with sexual and gender diversity continues to impact regional markets.

In consonance with the expectation to address audiences as citizens rather than consumers (Bardoel & d'Haenens, 2008, p. 343), the documented receptiveness to expert perspectives in the representation of sexual and gender diversity and PSBs' wider impact on domestic programming problematizes the default antagonism of queer TV scholarship in Western Europe. To reproduce the assumption that TV production is generally disinterested in the contributions of (queer) scholars of television foregoes not only domestic histories of LGBT+ televisibility, but also glosses over existing mechanisms to mandate attention for sociocultural diversity with PSBs and the role academics play therein. Where stipulations requiring "fair and proportionate portrayals" of various groups are relatively common in the management agreements and remits of many Western European PSBs (see Cola et al., 2013; Harrison & Woods, 2001), many also actively monitor and amend their performance on such matters (Karppinen, 2006). More often than not, moreover, academics assist in shaping or directing strategic policy related to diversity and pluralism (Horsti & Hultén, 2011) and in empirical assessments thereof (e.g., Panis et al., 2019). At the very least, this invites conceiving of PSBs and the professionals they employ not as opponents to be combated, but as partners to be interacted with. The antagonism of American queer TV scholarship, predicated on the conviction that LGBT+ representations and programming result from exclusively commercial motives, is inconsiderate of the fact that "fair" portrayals of sexual and gender diversity are an inherent democratic responsibility of some of the most important actors in Western European television markets. Indeed, that management agreements and PSB remits have historically been employed to carve a space for LGBT+ representations (see Kerrigan & Vanlee, 2020) suggests that queer studies of television might envision an impact beyond vaguely defined "public discourse" about gender and sexuality (Chambers, 2009; Warner, 2000) and address TV professionals and organizations directly. While the structural conditions of the U.S. television industry both produce and legitimize an antagonistic approach, the existing pathways and mechanisms entrenched in Western European PSBs call for alternative, agonistic dispositions (see Chouliaraki, 2011).

Especially in the context of queer theories and convictions, the notion of agonism perhaps conjures misgivings about compliance or even complicity with the status quo. The profound differences between the deregulated television market of the United States and the hybrid systems of Western Europe do not exonerate the latter from disseminating images and stories that do the LGBT+ community a disservice, both in the past and today. Undoubtedly, some

PSB content refracts heterosexist family-based ideologies to make gay couples palatable to predominantly straight audiences, as Páraic Kerrigan (2016) notes on 1980s RTÉ programming. Conversely, other PSBs prioritize economic motives to schedule LGBT+- themed content, such as Italy's RAI, because it is expected to be more competitive than similar organizations in Western Europe (Malici, 2011). And the overall presence of LGBT+ characters in the fiction output of some PSBs display similar patterns as those found in the United States—only four out of 117 identifiably LGBT+ characters in Flemish TV fiction between 2001 and 2016 were non-White, for instance (see Vanlee et al., 2020b). Clearly, then, public service broadcasting does not guarantee equitable portrayals of sexual and gender diversity that do not reproduce detrimental modes of conceptualizing LGBT+ communities and people. If and when popular television representations of how people act on desire or embody gender serve to reinforce reductive hetero- and ciscentric norms, the articulation of stringent critiques by queer TV scholarship is a self-evidence (Chambers, 2009; Warner, 2000). But the existence of formal and informal pathways to address or even amend such images and stories reconfigures how disagreement and conflict between scholarship and industry can be mediated (Rohn & Evens, 2020). The "status quo" in such a context is not to be seen as the perennial victory of commerce over social responsibility (Warner, 2000), but as a compromise reflecting constant reconfiguration between opposing views (Mouffe, 2013). Vis-à-vis agonistic, dynamic conceptualizations of the status quo, or indeed, "the normal" (see Vanlee et al., 2018), established modes of queer TV scholarship fall short. TV production is not to be principally and diametrically *opposed*, but to be constantly and productively *altered*.

NECESSARILY NORMATIVE: QUEERNESS FOR TELEVISION IN WESTERN EUROPE

Evidently, committing to agonistic modes of queer television scholarship to more comprehensively answer the conditions offered by Western European TV cultures necessitates alternate engagements with normativity. Where antagonistic circumstances foster crypto-normativity in addressing deficiencies and inequities of LGBT+ televisibility, agonistic environments require a recognition of those normative convictions shaping how one evaluates representations of sexual and gender diversity. Doing so does not so much ask an explicit disjuncture from the realizations of queer scholarship on American TV programming as it supposes a search for complementary points of attention (Vanlee et al., 2020a). Because agonistic conditions are characterized by a structural instability of the status quo (see Mouffe, 2013) in that it is under constant reconfiguration by permanent negotiations between opposing views, pointing to its deficits is only half the equation. Deconstructions of existing representations may serve to accentuate what is objectionable in current televisual conceptions of sexual and gender diversity, but refuse to make a counteroffer. Steven Doran's (2013) reading of how *Modern Family* appropriates motives of homodomesticity to reproduce heteronormative frameworks of assimilation and depoliticization (pp. 96–97), for instance, offers a convincing account of the series' generally unquestioned but pervasive refraction of hegemonic beliefs about LGBT+ life. Beyond the problematization of these representational strategies, however, its propositional dimension remains callow. Doran's contribution is persuasive and poignant, and it is reasonable to assume that many of its readers will recognize that it justifiably rejects the idea that Mitch and Cam are "neutral" or "unassuming" portrayals of a same-sex couple. Admittedly, it is also attentive for the affordances offered by homodomesticity and its use by *Modern Family* (p. 102), refraining from a general disavowal of the representational framework. That this particular reflection of homodomesticity does not quite reflect the ideals of queer thought, then, seems crystal clear. But what would a queer mobilization of the homodomestic look like? One that does not equal assimilation with equity (p. 98) but capitalizes on the productive space offered by the familial home for queer politics (p. 103)? Doran's article is rife with discrete normative convictions on the subject, but does not explicate them.

If the status quo addressed by queer scholars of television is constantly reshaped (see Mouffe, 2013; Vanlee et al., 2018), it does not suffice to articulate only what is dissatisfactory about its current configuration. Taking seriously the generative productivity of agonistic conditions demands complementing deconstructions and critical readings of how TV currently engages with sexuality or gender with outspoken directives on what LGBT+ televisibility should look like in the future. If queer TV scholarship is to grasp the opportunity presented by PSB television production, and is committed to creating a space to weigh in on popular portrayals of same-sex desire and gender nonconformity, it must value affirmation and prospection alongside the established critical tools of rejection and disavowal (see Serrano, 2013; Vanlee et al., 2020). Conceived of as potential conversation partners, TV professionals and organizations benefit not only from queer scholarship attentive to the defaults and deficiencies in LGBT+ televisibility, but also from academic contributions willing to elucidate its ideals concerning representation. Shifting from crypt-normative registers whereby underlying convictions are left unaddressed to a mode of scholarship committed to formulating alternatives to limitations in existing representational paradigms is surely difficult. Crypto-normativity offers an opportunity to shape queer ideals for television after the facts—that is, queer-informed convictions of how sexual and gender diversity should be portrayed emerge exclusively from the rejection of existing texts (Felski, 2015; Sedgwick, 1997). The sustained traction of this implicit, ex-post queer normativity today logically dissuades an ex-ante model predicated on formulating ideal, utopian narratives on representation and its role on how individuals may legitimately act on desire and embody gender (Sedgwick, 1997, p. 20). But proposition and rebuttal are constitutive facets to agonistic conditions, and to omit either fundamentally disregards their potential to facilitate tangible impact through exchange.

Such a propositional, affirmative mode of queer TV scholarship will benefit from assessing the veiled normative orientations of existing works in the field. Literature that explores television's subversions of hegemonic conceptions of sexuality and gender (e.g., Chambers, 2009; Dhaenens, 2013, 2014; Munt, 2006) provides a point of departure here. Affirmatively discussing commendable aspects to LGBT+ televisibility, it hints at widely shared assumptions about queer scholarship's ideals for TV representation and its role in society (Dhaenens et al., 2008). But addressing representation from an outspokenly normative perspective intent on formulating ideal modes of television necessitates looking beyond queer TV scholarship as such. Proposing alterations to common practices shaping LGBT+ televisibility and the discourses it perpetuates supposes broader discussions on the ethics and ambitions of queer thought. If given the opportunity to change things around, would the field settle on amending the often reductive relation between particular LGBT+ subjects and their representation on television? Or would it prioritize contributing to a television culture that perpetuates norms that regulate respectful coexistence rather than legitimate existence? Both are valid considerations but represent distinct ethical interpretations queer theory may suggest about the role of TV (see Vanlee et al., 2020). The point here is not to obfuscate one perspective at the expense of the other or to (undoubtedly unsuccessfully) campaign for a universally applicable normative framework queer scholarship can simply impose on television. Rather, it argues for scholars to allow the normative subtext underlying and informing their work to take the front stage. It invites scholars to be concerned with exactly why and how they would argue for particular modes of representation, besides being attentive to the inadequacy of existing portrayals. Bruno Latour (2004) notes that the critic's role is not to "lift the rug from under the feet of naïve believers," but to "offer the participants arenas in which to gather" (p. 246). Instead of debunking, scholarship must concern itself with assembling (p. 246). To formulate in affirmative, normative terms what television should offer society and how it should do so is an act of assembly, of constructing an arena. Western European TV cultures offer queer scholars an opportunity to interact and collaborate instead of suspect and counteract. While this position holds no promise for perfection or even success, it nevertheless provides a space to think queer television beyond exclusively antagonistic frameworks.

CONCLUSION

Admittedly, this article offers a vague and perhaps abstract call, lacking the very clarity it desires of scholarly opinion. It could easily be caricatured as a suggestion to start drafting ideal queer stories and characters and pass them on to interested, committed TV professionals and organizations. Similarly, it might be brushed off as thinly veiled European exceptionalism intent on establishing the superiority of hybrid television industries in the face of the licentious capitalism in U.S. TV. Both accusations of naivety and ulterior motives might hold some truth, but neither detracts from the fact that TV production and programming in Western Europe have different characteristics than those shaping commonplace frames of understanding LGBT+ televisibility. It is perfectly possible that this article will prove too utopian in its belief that academics might interact meaningfully and productively with television organizations and professionals, having grossly overestimated either the accessibility of pathways to the industry or simply professional interest in what queer scholarship has to say. But seeing that the particularities offered by domestic Western European television cultures have scarcely been explored, one should at least aim to be a loser, not a quitter. Just as it is important to recognize that the overview of queer scholarship on American programming discussed here justifiably acts on the assumption that articulating alternatives is ineffectual, it is also crucial to acknowledge the fact that both historical trajectories and contemporary organizational patterns existing sources have observed in Western European television allow queer scholarship to openly reflect on the future of LGBT+ televisibility. And even though these ideals might sometimes be effaced by pragmatism or compromise, they nevertheless present an opportunity to explicate what the ambitions of queer thought stand for. In and of itself, this seems a valuable contribution to make at a time of unprecedented attention for representation in the public debate. After all, if those people who have made it their profession to study and understand the role of representation on the lives of marginalized groups in society refuse to explicate their view on what popular culture should contribute, how can they expect it to change?

FURTHER READING

Amin, K. (2016). Haunted by the 1990s: Queer theory's affective histories. *Women's Studies Quarterly*, 44(3–4), 173–189.

Capuzza, J. C., & Spencer, L. G. (2017). Regressing, progressing, or transgressing on the small screen? Transgender characters on U.S. scripted television series. *Communication Quarterly*, 65(2), 214–230.

Dhoest, A. (2015). Contextualizing diversity in TV drama: Policies, practices and discourses. *Series-International Journal of TV Serial Narratives*, 1(2), 169–180.

Hesmondhalgh, D., & Toynbee, J. (2008). Why media studies needs better social theory. In D. Hesmondhalgh & J. Toynbee (Eds.), *The media and social theory* (pp. 1–24). Routledge.

Joyrich, L. (2014). Queer television studies: Currents, flows, and (main) streams. *Cinema Journal*, 53(2), 133–139.

Kerrigan, P., & Vanlee, F. (2020). Public service broadcasting and the emergence of LGBT+ visibility: A comparative perspective on Ireland and Flanders. *European Journal of Cultural Studies*. Advance online publication. https://journals.sagepub.com/doi/abs/10.1177/1367549420935893#

Klein, B. (2011). Entertaining ideas: Social issues in entertainment television. *Media, Culture & Society*, 33(6), 905–921.

Mouffe, C. (2013). *Agonistics: Thinking the world politically*. Verso Books.

Vanlee, F. (2019). Finding domestic LGBT+ television in Western Europe: Methodological challenges for queer critics. *Continuum*, 33(4), 423–434.

Villarejo, A. (2014). *Ethereal queer: Television, historicity, desire*. Duke University Press.

REFERENCES

Abbott, A. (2018). Varieties of normative inquiry: Moral alternatives to politicization in sociology. *The American Sociologist*, 49(2), 158–180.

Amin, K. (2016). Haunted by the 1990s: Queer theory's affective histories. *Women's Studies Quarterly*, 44(3–4), 173–189.

Aslinger, B. (2009). Creating a network for queer audiences at Logo TV. *Popular Communication*, 7(2), 107–121.

Avila-Saavedra, G. (2009). Nothing queer about queer television: Televized construction of gay masculinities. *Media, Culture & Society*, 31(1), 5–21.

Bardoel, J., & d'Haenens, L. (2008). Reinventing public service broadcasting in Europe: Prospects, promises and problems. *Media, Culture & Society*, 30(3), 337–355.

Bassi, C. (2016). What's radical about reality TV? An unexpected tale from Shanghai of a Chinese Lesbian Antihero. *Gender, Place & Culture* 23(11), 1619–1630. https://doi.org/10.1080/0966369X.2015.1136809

Battles, K., & Hilton-Morrow, W. (2002). Gay characters in conventional spaces: *Will & Grace* and the situation comedy genre. *Critical Studies in Media Communication*, 19(1), 87–105.

Becker, R. (2006). *Gay TV and straight America*. Rutgers University Press.

Beirne, R. (2008). *Lesbians in television and text after the millennium*. Palgrave Macmillan.

Boelaars, B. (2008). *Benno Premsela: Voorvechter van homo-emancipatie*. Thoth.

Bond, B. J. (2015). Portrayals of sex and sexuality in gay-and-lesbian-oriented media: A quantitative content analysis. *Sexuality & Culture*, 19(1), 37–56.

Bradley, P. (2013). Romancing the soap: Representations of gay love and relationships in 'EastEnders'. In P. Demory & C. Pull (Eds.), *Queer love in film and television: Critical essays* (pp. 33–46). Palgrave Macmillan.

Caldwell, J. T. (2008). *Production culture: Industrial reflexivity and critical practice in film and television*. Duke University Press.

Cales, R. (2015). Something old & borrowed: Homonormativity and marriage in *Glee*. In B. C. Johnson & D. K. Faill (Eds.), *Glee and new directions for social change* (pp. 69–79). Sense Publishers.

Capuzza, J. C., & Spencer, L. G. (2017). Regressing, progressing, or transgressing on the small screen? Transgender characters on US scripted television series. *Communication Quarterly, 65*(2), 214–230.

Cavalcante, A. (2015). Anxious displacements: The representation of gay parenting on *Modern family* and *The new normal* and the management of cultural anxiety. *Television & New Media, 16*(5), 454–471.

Chambers, S. A. (2003). Telepistemology of the closet; or the queer politics of "Six Feet Under." *The Journal of American Culture, 26*(1), 24–41.

Chambers, S. A. (2009). *The queer politics of television*. I.B. Tauris.

Chouliaraki, L. (2011). "Improper distance": Towards a critical account of solidarity as irony. *International Journal of Cultural Studies, 14*(4), 363–381.

Cola, M., Nikunen, K., Dhoest, A., & Titley, G. (2013). "Lost in mainstreaming"? Ethnic minority audiences for public and private television broadcasting. In N. Carpentier, K. C. Schrøder, & L. Hallett (Eds.), *Audience transformations: Shifting audience positions in late modernity* (pp. 90–108). Routledge.

Cuelenaere, E. (2020). The remake industry: The practice of remaking films from the perspective of industrial actors. *Adaptation*, 1–21. https://doi.org/10.1093/adaptation/apaa016

Curtin, M., & Shattuc, J. (2017). *The American television industry*. Bloomsbury Publishing.

De Bens, E., & De Smaele, H. (2001). The inflow of American television fiction on European broadcasting channels revisited. *European Journal of Communication, 16*(1), 51–76.

Dhaenens, F. (2012). Queer cuttings on YouTube: Re-editing soap operas as a form of fan-produced queer resistance. *European Journal of Cultural Studies, 15*(4), 442–456.

Dhaenens, F. (2013). The fantastic queer: Reading gay representations in *Torchwood* and *True Blood* as articulations of queer resistance. *Critical Studies in Media Communication, 30*(2), 102–116.

Dhaenens, F. (2014). Articulations of queer resistance on the small screen. *Continuum, 28*(4), 520–531.

Dhaenens, F., & Van Bauwel, S. (2012). The good, the bad or the queer: Articulations of queer resistance in *The wire*. *Sexualities, 15*(5–6), 702–717.

Dhaenens, F., Van Bauwel, S., & Biltereyst, D. (2008). Slashing the fiction of queer theory: Slash fiction, queer reading, and transgressing the boundaries of screen studies, representations, and audiences. *Journal of Communication Inquiry, 32*(4), 335–347.

Dhoest, A. (2015). Contextualizing diversity in TV drama: Policies, practices and discourses. *Series-International Journal of TV Serial Narratives, 1*(2), 169–180.

Donders, K., Pauwels, C., & Loisen, J. (Eds.). (2016). *Private television in Western Europe: Content, markets, policies*. Springer.

Doran, S. E. (2013). Housebroken: Homodomesticity and the normalization of queerness in *Modern family*. In P. Demory & C. Pullen (Eds.), *Queer love in film and television: Critical essays* (pp. 95–104). Palgrave Macmillan.

Doty, A. (1993). Whose text is it anyway? Queer cultures, queer auteurs, and queer authorship. *Quarterly Review of Film & Video, 15*(1), 41–54.

Dow, B. (2001). *Ellen*, television, and the politics of gay and lesbian visibility. *Critical Studies in Media Communication, 18*(2), 123–140.

Dupont, W. (2019). Pas de deux, out of step: Diverging chronologies of homosexuality's (de) criminalisation in the Low Countries. *Tijdschrift voor Genderstudies, 22*(4), 321–338.

Fejes, F., & Petrich, K. (1993). Invisibility, homophobia and heterosexism: Lesbians, gays and the media. *Critical Studies in Mass Communication, 10*(4): 395–422.

Felski, R. (2015). *The limits of critique*. University of Chicago Press.

Geller, T. L., & Banker, A. M. (2017). "That magic box lies": Queer theory, seriality and *American Horror Story*. *The Velvet Light Trap, 79*(1), 36–49.

Gross, L. (2001). *Up from invisibility: Lesbians, gay men, and the media in America*. Columbia University Press.

Harrison, J., & Woods, L. M. (2001). Defining European public service broadcasting. *European Journal of Communication, 16*(4), 477–504.

Hart, K. P. R. (2000). Representing gay men on American television. *The Journal of Men's Studies, 9*(1), 59–79.

Heller, D. (2011). Visibility and its discontents: Queer television studies. *GLQ: A Journal of Lesbian and Gay Studies, 17*(4), 665–676.

Hesmondhalgh, D., & Toynbee, J. (2008). Why media studies needs better social theory. In D. Hesmondhalgh & J. Toynbee (Eds.), *The media and social theory* (pp. 1–24). Routledge.

Hess, L. M. (2017). "My whole life I've been dressing up like a man": Negotiations of queer aging and queer temporality in the TV series Transparent. [Special issue]. *European Journal of American Studies, 11*(3), 1–19. https://doi.org/10.4000/ejas.11702

Holy, M. (2012) Jenseits von Stonewall–Rückblicke auf die Schwulenbewegung in der BRD 1969–1980. In A. Pretzel & V. Weiss (Eds.), *Rosa Radikale. Die Schwulenbewegung der 1970er Jahre* (pp. 39–79). Männerschwarm Verlag.

Horsti, K., & Hultén, G. (2011). Directing diversity: Managing cultural diversity media policies in Finnish and Swedish public service broadcasting. *International Journal of Cultural Studies, 14*(2), 209–227.

Horvat, A. (2020). Queer TV. In I. Bachmann, V. Cardo, S. Moorti, & C. M. Scarcelli (Eds.), *The international encyclopedia of gender, media, and communication* (pp. 1–5). Wiley-Blackwell.

Jacobs, J. (2014). Raising gays: On Glee, queer kids, and the limits of the family. *GLQ: A Journal of Lesbian and Gay Studies, 20*(3), 319–352.

Jacobs, L., & Meeusen, C. (2020). Coming out of the closet, also on the news? A longitudinal content analysis of patterns in visibility, tone and framing of LGBTs on television news (1986–2017). *Journal of Homosexuality*, 1–25. https://pubmed.ncbi.nlm.nih.gov/32149593/

Johnson, P. M., & Holmes, K. A. (2019). Gaydar, marriage, and rip-roaring homosexuals: Discourses about homosexuality in Dear Abby and Ann Landers advice columns, 1967–1982. *Journal of Homosexuality, 66*(3), 389–406.

Joyrich, L. (2009). Epistemology of the console. In G. Davis & G. Needham (Eds.), *Queer TV: Theories, histories, politics* (pp. 15–47). Routledge.

Joyrich, L. (2014). Queer television studies: Currents, flows, and (main) streams. *Cinema Journal, 53*(2), 133–139.

Karppinen, K. (2006). Media diversity and the politics of criteria: Diversity assessment and technocratisation of European media policy. *Nordicom Review, 27*(2), 53–68.

Kerrigan, P. (2016). Respectably gay: Homodomesticity in Ireland's first public broadcast of a homosexual couple. In A. Dhoest, L. Szulc, & B. Eeckhout (Eds.), *LGBTQs, media and culture in Europe* (pp. 27–41). Routledge.

Kerrigan, P. (2019). Projecting a queer republic: Mainstreaming queer identities on Irish documentary film. *Studies in Documentary Film, 13*(1), 1–17.

Kerrigan, P., & Vanlee, F. (2020). Public service broadcasting and the emergence of LGBT+ visibility: A comparative perspective on Ireland and Flanders. *European Journal of Cultural Studies*. https://journals.sagepub.com/doi/abs/10.1177/1367549420935893#

Kies, B. (2016). First comes love, then comes marriage: (Homo)normalizing romance on American television. *Journal of Popular Romance Studies, 5*(2), 1–13.

Klein, B. (2011). Entertaining ideas: Social issues in entertainment television. *Media, Culture & Society, 33*(6), 905–921.

Kooijman, J. (2005). They're here, they're queer, and straight America loves it. *GLQ: A Journal of Lesbian and Gay Studies, 11*(1), 106–109.

Latour, B. (2004). Why has critique run out of steam? From matters of fact to matters of concern. *Critical Inquiry, 30*(2), 225–248.

Lovelock, M. (2017). Call me Caitlyn: Making and making over the "authentic" transgender body in Anglo-American popular culture. *Journal of Gender Studies, 26*(6), 675–687.

Malici, L. (2011). Queer in Italy: Italian televisibility and the "queerable" audience. In L. Downing & R. Gillett (Eds.), *Queer in Europe: Contemporary case studies* (pp. 113–128). Routledge.

Malici, L. (2014). Queer TV moments and family viewing in Italy. *Journal of GLBT Family Studies, 10*(1–2), 188–210.

Martin Jr., A. L. (2015). Scripting black gayness: Television authorship in black-cast sitcoms. *Television & New Media, 16*(7), 648–663.

Martin Jr., A. L. (2018). Introduction: What is queer production studies/why is queer production studies? *Journal of Film and Video, 70*(3–4), 3–7.

Marshall, D. (2016). Reading queer television: Some notes on method. *Review of Education, Pedagogy, and Cultural Studies, 38*(1), 85–101.

McCarthy, A. (2001). *Ellen*: Making queer television history. *GLQ: A Journal of Lesbian and Gay Studies, 7*(4), 593–620.

Meyer, M. D., & Wood, M. M. (2013). Sexuality and teen television: Emerging adults respond to representations of queer identity on *Glee*. *Sexuality & Culture, 17*(3), 434–448.

Miller, S. D. (2000). The (temporary?) queering of Japanese TV. *Journal of Homosexuality, 39*(3–4), 83–109.

Mitchell, D. (2005). Producing containment: The rhetorical construction of difference in *Will & Grace*. *Journal of Popular Culture, 38*(6), 1050.

Mouffe, C. (2013). *Agonistics: Thinking the world politically*. Verso Books.

Munt, S. R. (2006). A queer undertaking: Anxiety and reparation in the HBO television drama series *Six feet under*. *Feminist Media Studies, 6*(3), 263–279.

Nelson, R. (2007). HBO premium: Channelling distinction through TVIII. *New Review of Film and Television Studies, 5*(1), 25–40.

Netzley, S. B. (2010). Visibility that demystifies: Gays, gender, and sex on television. *Journal of Homosexuality, 57*(8), 968–986.

Ng, E. (2013). A "post-gay" era? Media gaystreaming, homonormativity, and the politics of LGBT integration. *Communication, Culture & Critique, 6*(2), 258–283.

O'Brien, A., & Kerrigan, P. (2020). Gay the right way? Roles and routines of Irish media production among gay and lesbian workers. *European Journal of Communication, 35*(4), 355–369.

Panis, K., Paulussen, S., & Dhoest, A. (2019). Managing super-diversity on television: The representation of ethnic minorities in Flemish non-fiction programmes. *Media and Communication, 7*(1), 13–21.

Peters, W. (2011). Pink dollars, white collars: *Queer as folk*, valuable viewers, and the price of gay TV. *Critical Studies in Media Communication, 28*(3), 193–212.

Pickard, V. (2017). A social democratic vision of media: Toward a radical pre-history of public broadcasting. *Journal of Radio & Audio Media, 24*(2), 200–212.

Raats, T., & Pauwels, C. (2013). Best frienemies forever? Public and private broadcasting partnerships in Flanders. In K. Donders, C. Pauwels, & J. Loisen (Eds.), *Private television in Western Europe* (pp. 199–213). Palgrave Macmillan.

Raley, A. B., & Lucas, J. L. (2006). Stereotype or success? Prime-time television's portrayals of gay male, lesbian, and bisexual characters. *Journal of Homosexuality, 51*(2), 19–38.

Ramírez, R. (2020). Simplified identities: Four 'types' of gays and lesbians on Chilean telenovelas. *Sexualities, 23*(8), 1480–1498.

Rohn, U., & Evens, T. (2020). Media management as an engaged scholarship. In U. Rohn & T. Evens (Eds.), *Media management matters: Challenges and opportunities for bridging theory and practice*. Routledge.

Sarkissian, R. (2014). Queering TV conventions: LGBT teen narratives on *Glee*. In C. Pullen (Ed.), *Queer youth and media cultures* (pp. 145–157). Palgrave Macmillan.

Sedgwick, E. K. (1997). Paranoid reading and reparative reading, or, you're so paranoid, you probably think this introduction is about you. In M. A. Barale, J. Goldberg, & M. Moon (Eds.), *Novel gazing: Queer readings in fiction* (pp. 1–40). Duke University Press.

Seidman, S. (1995). Deconstructing queer theory or the under-theorization of the social and the ethical. In L. Nicholson & S. Seidman (Eds.), *Social postmodernism: Beyond identity politics* (pp. 116–141). Cambridge University Press.

Serano, J. (2013). *Excluded: Making feminist and queer movements more inclusive*. Seal Press.

Shaw, A. (2017). What's next? The LGBTQ video game archive. *Critical Studies in Media Communication*, 34(1), 88–94.

Strangelove, M. (2015). *Post-TV: Piracy, cord-cutting, and the future of television*. University of Toronto Press.

Straubhaar, J. D. (2007). *World television: From global to local*. SAGE.

Sundet, V. S. (2020). From "secret" online teen drama to international cult phenomenon: The global expansion of *Skam* and its public service mission. *Critical Studies in Television*, 15(1), 69–90.

Thorfinnsdottir, D., & Jensen, H. S. (2017). Laugh away, he is gay! Heteronormativity and children's television in Denmark. *Journal of Children and Media*, 11(4), 399–416.

Vanlee, F. (2019a). Finding domestic LGBT+ television in Western Europe: Methodological challenges for queer critics. *Continuum*, 33(4), 423–434.

Vanlee, F. (2019b). Acknowledging/denying LGBT+ difference: Understanding homonormativity and LGBT+ homogeneity in Flemish TV fiction through production research. *European Journal of Communication*, 34(5), 520–534.

Vanlee, F., Dhaenens, F., & Van Bauwel, S. (2018). Understanding queer normality: LGBT+ representations in millennial Flemish television fiction. *Television & New Media*, 19(7), 610–625.

Vanlee, F., Dhaenens, F., & Van Bauwel, S. (2020a). Indifference and queer television studies: Distinguishing norms of existence and coexistence. *Critical Studies in Media Communication*, 7(2), 1–15.

Vanlee, F., Dhaenens, F., & Van Bauwel, S. (2020b). LGBT+ televisibility in Flanders: The presence of sexual and gender diversity in Flemish television fiction (2001–2016). *DiGeSt: Journal of Diversity and Gender Studies*, 7(1). https://doi.org/10.21825/digest.v7i1.16507

Villarejo, A. (2008). Ethereal queer: Notes on method. In G. Needham & G. Davis (Eds.), *Queer TV: Theories, histories, politics* (pp. 48–62). Routledge.

Villarejo, A. (2014). *Ethereal queer: Television, historicity, desire*. Duke University Press.

Vipond, E. (2015). Resisting transnormativity: Challenging the medicalization and regulation of trans bodies. *Theory in Action*, 8(2), 21–44.

Walsh, F. (2016). *Queer performance and contemporary Ireland: Dissent and disorientation*. Springer.

Walters, S. D. (2003). *All the rage: The story of gay visibility in America*. University of Chicago Press.

Warner, M. (2000). *The trouble with normal: Sex, politics, and the ethics of queer life*. Harvard University Press.

Wiegman, R., & Wilson, E. A. (2015). Introduction: Antinormativity's queer conventions. *differences*, 26(1), 1–25.

NOTES

1. Flanders is the northern Dutch-speaking region of Belgium. Because Belgium is a federal state and cultural mandates have been transferred to the regions, it is more accurate to speak of Flemish rather than Belgian television.
2. British Broadcasting Corporation; Nederlands Publiek Omroepbestel; Danmarks Radio; Raidió Teilifís Éireann.

3. Vlaamse Radio- en Televisieomroeporganisatie.
4. Arbeitsgemeinschaft der öffentlich-rechtlichen Rundfunkanstalten der Bundesrepublik Deutschland; Westdeutscher Rundfunk.

Florian Vanlee

BLACK GAY MEN IN TELEVISION COMEDY

INTRODUCTION

Without question, there are more representations of gay men and lesbians on narrative television (although the same is not always true of bisexual and trans characters). The increased representation has become a fertile ground of study for scholars working across a variety of fields, including English, mass communication, communication studies, sociology, psychology, and media studies, among others. Within these fields of inquiry, media texts from *Queer Eye for the Straight Guy* (Bravo, 2003–2007; Netflix, 2018–), *Queer as Folk* (Showtime, 2000–2005), *The L Word* (Showtime, 2004–2009), and *The L Word: Generation Q* (Showtime, 2019–) to *Will & Grace* (NBC, 1998–2006, 2017–2020), *Glee* (Fox, 2009–2015), and *Modern Family* (ABC, 2009–2020) have been studied extensively. In other words, the object of inquiry has largely focused on White televisual gays and lesbians. Perhaps there are at least two reasons for this focus. First, it involves numbers—there have simply been more White LGBTQ characters on television. Looking at the televisual landscape, there are more White heterosexual characters on television than Black heterosexual characters, which realistically should translate into more White gay characters than Black, particularly in an industry in which televisual Blackness equals "Black show," whereas televisual Whiteness equals "mainstream show." In addition, within this notion of mainstream Whiteness is also an assumption that gayness and Whiteness are inextricably linked. As Allan Bérubé (2001) notes, "In the United States today, the dominant image of the typical gay man is a white man who is financially better off than most everyone else" (p. 234). Second, the corpus of shows that have received the most scholarly attention are those that have achieved ratings and/or critical success, regardless of the myriad ways networks, channels, and platforms define notions of "success." For example, according to the website Reality TV World (2003a, 2003b), *Queer Eye for the Straight Guy* premiered on Bravo, where it garnered 1.6 million viewers—a record number of viewers for the niche cable network—before moving over to its sister network NBC, where it garnered 6.3 million viewers its first airing, incidentally following an episode of *Will & Grace*. In addition, series like *Modern Family* and *Will & Grace* have routinely won Emmy Awards, which, however problematically, stand in for notions of quality and excellence.

This article centers the importance of race within discussions of LGBTQ identities but also works to highlight the different trajectories of Black gay characters within comedic television and the ways imaginations of audiences shape the production practices of Black gay characters across White-/multicultural-cast and Black-cast television comedy. The article explores the historical rise of explicit gayness (and gay stereotypes) in television comedy and its relationship with Whiteness before interrogating those stereotypes as they are related—or perhaps more accurately, how they do not relate—to Black gayness in television comedy. For the purposes of this article, the use of "gay" or "gayness" speaks specifically to a homosexual, masculine positionality (with the understanding that this term can and has been used as shorthand or personal identifiers for a myriad of non-straight identities). An engagement with the existing literature on Black gayness, specifically in White/multicultural television comedies, illuminates not only television's, and thus scholars', limited engagement with Black gayness but also the need for more varied methodological interrogations that center and prioritize cultural studies, audience studies, and production studies, among others.

BLACK GAYNESS/WHITE GAYNESS: A TALE OF TWO TELEVISUAL SEXUALITIES IN TELEVISION COMEDY

This section provides a brief history of gayness in television comedies. Specifically, the distinct engagements—both televisual and scholarly—with the history and trajectory of Black gayness alongside that of White gayness are discussed. In doing so, this article's historical analysis of gayness in television comedy is connected to the Stonewall Riots and tracks the chronological (re)iterations of gayness in television comedy through character tropes predicated on the "pedagogical gay," the "sissy regular," and homonormative gayness. Throughout this section, the articulation of Whiteness and gayness is highlighted.

Comedic representations of explicit gayness on television began on mostly the same ground in the 1970s, racially speaking. Although there had been White gay male representation on television as early as 1954's television adaptation of the musical *Lady in the Dark*, television comedies did not engage with explicit White gay male characters until after the 1969 Stonewall Riots, which are often cited as the beginning of the modern gay rights movement. Prior to the 1970s, male gayness had been largely mass-mediated using techniques associated with gender inversion. In this context, gender inversion speaks to widely accepted societal understandings of homosexuality—as opposed to queerness more broadly—being understood within the reversal of the gender binary. In other words, gay men in media were largely depicted as feminine and employed in "women's professions" such as cosmetology and interior design, or what Matthew Murray (2001) called the "lavender gentleman."

Stonewall marked the beginning of broader inclusion of gay men and lesbians on television. In the wake of Stonewall, Rodger Streitmatter (2009) argues that news media "continued to portray gay men as objects of ridicule by describing the events at the Stonewall Inn as a place where the homosexual element could congregate, drink and do whatever little girls do when they get together" (p. 19), prompting some gay rights organizations to complain about the ways gay men were being represented in media.

At the same time, Stonewall coincided with television's attempt to rehabilitate its image as a "vast wasteland" by taking what is widely known as a turn to relevance, whereby television shows began to reflect the issues of the day. As Todd Gitlin (2000) details, Robert D. Wood engineered this turn to relevance because he thought television should "shift from cornball comedy to expressions—however ambiguous—of liberal ideas" (p. 206). This turn to gay and lesbian relevance could be seen in episodes of shows such as *All in the Family* (CBS, 1971–1979), *Room 222* (ABC, 1969–1974), and some Black-cast series such as *Sanford Arms* (NBC, 1977) that began to be constructed as "positive" representations. These representations included gay men who did not demonstrate markers of homosexuality that had long been associated with gayness. These men were not feminine, nor did they have careers in hegemonically "feminine careers." Martin (2021) has called this set of characters "pedagogical gay characters" because these White gay characters were primarily tasked with educating "mainstream" culture about gayness and attempting to break the semiotic chain between gay men and effeminacy and flamboyance. As would also become the norm for televisual representations of gay men and lesbians, once this issue was "tackled," the gay character was never heard from again. In this way, the main heterosexual characters could be constructed as "liberal" on gay issues without having to deal with the baggage of gayness on a weekly basis. In 1970s television, it seemed, as Chuck Hoy asserts, "as if television program creators were attempting to instruct the American public in Homosexuality 101" (as quoted in Johnson & Keith, 2001, p. 145). The pedagogical gay character largely remains the dominant model for episodic Black gay characters across Black-cast and "multicultural"-cast television.

Soon thereafter, White gay men transition into what Stephen Tropiano (2002) calls the "sissy regular." These White gay characters embodied more stereotypically feminine behaviors (and were almost always portrayed by heterosexual men) and, most important, were series regulars. ABC was the first network to feature a gay "sissy regular" on its sitcom *The Corner Bar* (1972–1973). Although the series was undoubtedly groundbreaking (particularly for the era in which it occurred), the series was not without its problems. Because its gay character, Peter Panama, was not going to simply "drop in" on the show, the network and writers needed to figure out how to make such a characterization palatable for its presumed heterosexual viewership. Much to the ire of many gay rights organizations, the solution was to make Peter a slightly updated version of the "lavender gentleman," a radio creation known for his coded homosexuality via mannerisms and modes of speech. Also significant about *The Corner Bar* is its distinction as the first television show wherein producers agreed to negotiate White gay televisual representations with gay rights groups, namely the Gay Activists Alliance's president Rich Wandel, who called Peter, the series' gay character "the worst stereotype of a gay man I've ever seen" (as quoted in Capsuto, 2000, p. 72). Show producer Alan King agreed to make changes to the character if ABC continued to air the show. The show returned in the summer of 1973 with Peter and most of the other characters having been written out of it.

Two years after the cancellation of *The Corner Bar*, Norman Lear's T.A.T. Communications entered the gay programming fray with two "sissy regulars" on *Hot l Baltimore* (ABC, 1975). The series featured a White gay couple who were residents of the Hot l Baltimore (the "e" had burned out on the residential hotel's sign and had never been replaced). However, the series that would put the sitcom's "sissy regular" on the map premiered in 1977. ABC's *Soap* (1977–1981) featured Billy Crystal's portrayal of Jodie, as a gay man who wants to undergo a sex change in order to be with his partner, a closeted professional football player. Even before the first episode aired, the network received 32,000 letters demanding the show's cancellation, mostly from people who had yet to see an episode of the show. Although the show went on to run for four seasons, the initial protests about its content prompted Baltimore's WJZ-TV to refuse to air the show's first two episodes (Shale, 1977). For groups concerned about the representation of gay men on television, one of *Soap*'s worrisome developments was writer Susan Harris' "apparent confusion" about the differences between "homosexuality, transvestism, and transexualism" (Capsuto, 2000, p. 139). On September 8, 1977, the National Gay Task

Force issued a call to have the Federal Communications Commission survey representations of gays on television, and the International Union of Gay Athletes also demanded to meet with ABC to protest the gay representations on *Soap* (Brown, 1977). In addition, *Soap* continues to be derided for its dialogue that liberally used derogatory terms for gay men, including "Fruit Loop," "homo," "pansy," and "Tinkerbell."

From the 1980s until the mid-1990s, White-cast sitcoms would vacillate between pedagogical gay characters and "sissy regulars." When the "gay 90s" hit television (led in many ways by the [short-lived] success of New Queer Cinema), a hybrid White gay character emerged. This hybrid character embodied many of the characteristics of the pedagogical gay character, namely his "masculinity," but was a series regular or, in some cases, star. Within this discourse of "respectable gays" are five general characteristics of gay men on television, which build upon Streitmatter's (2009) work with slight modifications for television. According to Streitmatter (2009), in order for White gay representations to be understood as "respectable gays," they must fit into at least two of the following categories: (1) Gay men are charming, (2) gay men are physically attractive, (3) gay men have taste, (4) gay men are successful, and (5) gay men are chaste. White-cast sitcoms such as *Will & Grace* (NBC, 1998–2006), *Normal, Ohio* (Fox, 2000), and *Some of My Best Friends* (CBS, 2001) attempted to capitalize on the new "gay chic" for what Ron Becker (2006) calls socially liberal, urban-minded professionals (or the SLUMPY) demographic. These series regulars/co-stars/stars were masculine, single, and well-adjusted within mainstream (read: White) heteronormative culture. These characterizations mirrored the pedagogical gay character who was still in circulation as a one-off representation of gayness within White-cast sitcoms.

The next wave of White gay characterizations for series stars and co-stars emerged toward the end of *Will & Grace*'s successful run. After much criticism related to Will's lack of romantic entanglements, Will began to date. These characters are the "homonormative gay characters." Lisa Duggan (2003) defines homonormativity as

> a politics that does not contest dominant heteronormative assumptions and institutions, but upholds and sustains them, while promising the possibility of a demobilized gay constituency and a privatized, depoloticized gay culture anchored in domesticity and consumptions. (p. 50)

Los Angeles Times writer Don Kilhefner (2007) adds,

> Homonormative gays are defined by a model of gay assimilation that includes a married [gay] couple with a home, a child or two and a schedule of PTA meetings and ballet lessons (for the child), a dog, a parrot, a few goldfish and tickets to a fundraising dinner at the Beverly Hilton.

In both Duggan's (2003) and Kilhefner's (2007) definitions of homonormativity, the construction of the queer couple is no different from the socially constructed image of a heterosexual married couple. The poster representation for this kind of televisual White gayness can be seen in *Modern Family* (ABC, 2009–2020), and *The New Normal* (NBC, 2012–2013). Suzanna Danuta Walters (2014) suggests, "In this era of liberal gay visibility, contemporary culture has other motifs to choose from, and the coming-out story no longer represents both the beginning and the end of how gay identity is imagined in popular media" (p. 36). Walters's assertion appears to be true for White-cast sitcoms when they feature Black gay characters. White-cast sitcoms tend to subscribe to post-racial and post-gay ideologies so that when Black gay men (rarely) appear within their ranks, there is little, if any, discussion of their Blackness or gayness. However, they broadly fit these models. *Spin City* (ABC, 1996–2002), *Brooklyn Nine-Nine* (Fox, 2013–2018; NBC, 2018–2021), and *Sirens* (USA, 2013–2015) fit within the "respectable gay" model, and *Don't Trust the B**** in Apartment 23* (ABC, 2012–2013) employed the "sissy regular" model. But how, if at all, do these models and Walters's assertions work for Black gay men within Black-cast sitcoms?

In this instance, Walters's (2014) assertion is patently false. Her imagining of televisual Blackness seems completely out of step with her efforts to critique the gay rights movement for its lack of inclusivity. She rightly observes that the modern gay rights movement has created a charmed circle of acceptance that tends to exclude "those gays and other gender and sexual minorities, such as transgendered [sic] folks and gays of color, who don't fit the posterboy image of nonstraight people and who can't be—or don't want to be—assimilated" (p. 3). Whereas White gay men in White-cast sitcoms have become post-gay (which implicitly gestures toward a post-coming-out state of being), that move has not been extended to Black gay men in Black-cast sitcoms.

Part of the different trajectories for Black gay characters in White-/multicultural-cast comedy and those in Black-cast comedy is rooted in the television industry's imagination of White audiences as more liberal viewers, or what Becker (2006) calls a SLUMPY demographic. As Martin (2018a) has argued, television comedies have "made no space for the imagining of a BLAMPY viewer—ones who are Black, liberal, affluent, metropolitan professionals and who understand that gayness can be a part of the fabric of Black television families" (p. 233). Thus, this imagining of audiences becomes key in discussing how Black gayness appears across White-/multicultural-cast comedy versus Black-cast comedy.

BLACK GAY CHARACTERS IN WHITE-/MULTICULTURAL-CAST SITCOMS

Following the discussion of the differences between Black gayness and White gayness in television comedies, this section focuses on scholarship on Black gay characters in White- or multicultural-cast sitcoms. First, this section examines how scholarship focused on *Spin City*'s Carter Heywood often ignores how his gayness was divorced from his Blackness. Similarly, it is argued that scholarship on *The Unbreakable Kimmy Schmidt*'s Titus Andromedon remains fixated on his position within a positive/negative representational binary and, specifically, detached from his Blackness and the Black gay characters that came before him. In the analysis of these characters, it is also argued that scholarship on Carter and Titus remain tethered to the image, prioritizing the text with little consideration of audiences, industries, or sociohistorical contexts.

In 1996, *Entertainment Weekly* writer Jess Cagle dubbed the 1990s the "gay 90s" because of the plethora of gay and lesbian representation across the television landscape. As Ron Becker (2006) detailed in his work, the networks—ABC, CBS, Fox, and NBC—used gay and lesbian content to court coveted 18- to 49-year-old viewers. These SLUMPY viewers consumed "edgy" LGBTQ content as a means of differentiating their taste cultures from those of more plebian viewers who consumed broad-based sitcom content. In addition to this hunt for more "edgy" content, many series moved from domestic settings to workplace settings in order to "make way for the inclusion of a differently-raced character. In other words, series regular Black gay characters on television comedies coincided with the television industry's pursuit of slumpies via the workplace sitcom" (Martin, 2018a, p. 235). One early example of this shift can be seen in the short-lived multicultural-cast series *Cutters* (CBS, 1993) that featured a Black gay character named Troy King. However, regardless of the industrial changes that occurred to make space for LGBT characters, such characters forcefully emerged from what George Gerbner (1972, p. 44) calls "symbolic annihilation" or the absence of representation and into mainstream television. As scholars attempted to make sense of these representations, they turned to the textual features of such representations. The rest of this section is devoted to a discussion of the scholarship on *Spin City* and *Unbreakable Kimmy Schmidt*, two programs that have been the focus of much of the research around Black queers in White- and multicultural-cast television comedy.

Stephen Tropiano (2002) calls *Spin City*'s Carter Heywood, who was the Black gay head of minority affairs for the New York mayor's office,

> The most intelligent and respectable gay professional on television... Carter is a rarity on television because he's gay, African American, and political. He's never afraid of speaking his mind and in the first season alone challenges the mayor on such issues as needle exchange programs ("Pride and Prejudice"), gay marriage ("Grand Illusion"), and police discrimination ("In the Heat of the Day"). (p. 244)

Although Carter seemingly possessed agency as a character and represented the White-cast sitcom's attempt at engaging race, Ron Becker (2006) argues that Carter's

> racial identity was far less salient to his narrative function than his gayness. While the show's writers and Carter's coworkers seemed blind to his Blackness, his homosexuality was a constant source of narrative development and jokes. Conversely, on the few occasions the series did explicitly deal with Carter's race, it didn't deal with his sexual identity. In other words, the series never addressed what the specific experiences of being a Black gay man or a gay Black man might have been. Carter was usually gay, sometimes Black, but never really both at the same time. (p. 180)

Thus, although *Spin City* attempted to represent a Black gay character that broke from the all-encompassing Whiteness of "gay 90s" representation, it could not reconcile how those identities could coexist rather than oscillating between them.

Breaking from Becker's (2006) assertions about the ways Carter's gayness is privileged over his racialization, Steven Capsuto (2000, p. 375) argues that *Spin City* offered a "full-fledged gay male regular who played a key role in almost every episode" and was never reduced to just being "the gay guy" in his brief textual analysis. The assertion of the fullness of the representation is attributed to the notion that Carter Heywood was politically active, was not segregated from gay populations, and was allowed to have romantic entanglements.

Similarly, Walters (2001) calls Carter "one of the most truly integrated gay characters on television" and asserts that *Spin City* stands apart from other sitcoms' engagement with gayness because it is treated as "a *subject*, certainly, but not a *topic* that is framed by coming-out stories" (p. 105). Walters's praise for Carter is rooted in a post-gay logic that suggests that the character not having to "dwell" in his own identity development should be understood within a progress narrative of gay representations. However, Walters's reading of Carter is also rooted in post-racial ideologies that attempt to erase or ignore his Blackness. In so doing, Walters positions Carter as what Catherine Squires (2009, p. 219) calls a "race neutral" character—Black characters who present a "constrained vision of Blacks in White society that promotes assimilation, not integration" because he is one of the few token characters of color on the show.

In her praise of Carter, Walters (2001) also notes that unlike many characters before him, Carter is allowed some semblance of a romantic life for the sake of the relationships, rather than as a comedic opportunity for the heterosexual characters on the show. Thus, Walters seemingly draws on Cedric Clark's (1969) stages of representation, in which a minority group's representation is understood as having ascended to the "respect" stage when its members are depicted as having interactions with children (sometimes as parents) and within committed and monogamous relationships. At the same time, Walters (2001) identifies that within *Spin City* and the character Carter, gayness continues to "be seen through the eyes of confused heterosexuals, struggling with their own reactions and feelings" (p. 104). In this way, as scholars including Becker (2006), Martin (2021), and Tropiano (2002) have argued, homosexuality becomes a conduit to center heterosexual and heterocentrist concerns, not queer ones.

The research on *Spin City* employs textual analysis of the series to make sense of Carter. Generally, the authors locate Carter on the "positive" end of the problematic positive/negative representational binary. The guiding research question for many of the authors was: How is Carter constructed with respect to long-held stereotypes of gayness? While paying attention to stereotypes, the authors broadly excluded race within their analyses. In other words, many of the authors treat Carter as a gay man versus a *Black* gay man, ignoring that although he may have been integrated into a gay community, he was segregated from a Black gay community, which is particularly troubling given that he lives in New York City.

Only Becker's (2006) research gestures toward some of the industrial and demographic shifts that made gay characters possible in the 1990s. In his theorization of the liberal viewers who became the darlings of the advertising industry in the 1990s, he suggests that gay characters, broadly construed, were a tool to attract "hip" and "cool" consumers to television content. In other words, while textual analyses asked "how" questions about Carter, Becker seemingly also asked "why" Carter (and other White gay characters) was on television in the 1990s.

In 2015, another Black gay character emerged that sparked scholarly attention: Titus Andromedon on Netflix's *Unbreakable Kimmy Schmidt*. Carmen Dexl and Katrin Horn (2017) argue that Titus is "a Black queen whose use of camp distances him from stereotypes, but connects him with audiences, whereby he not only adds to a more diverse representation of Black experience on TV but also interrogates prevailing TV tropes" (p. 442). In engaging camp to understand Titus, the authors deploy a textual analysis that reads the character as transcoding stereotypes associated with Blackness and gayness. Thus, stereotype remains the heuristic through which the authors attempt to understand the character. Embedded within their interest in Titus and an attempt to treat him as a character who is both Black and gay, the authors engage Black television histories as well as queer television histories, but not Black queer television histories. Although, admittedly, the list of representations is short, the authors, for instance, do not suggest there are any antecedents of Titus in Eddie Murphy's "Dion" from *Saturday Night Live* (NBC, 1975–) or David Alan Grier and Damon Wayans' Blaine Edwards and Antoine Merriwether from *In Living Color* (Fox, 1990–1994). In particular, *In Living Color* made liberal use of Black queer camp through comedic modes. Thus, the authors remain so tightly engaged with the text at hand (*Unbreakable Kimmy Schmidt*) that they lose sight of the broader history on which Titus builds.

Dexl and Horn (2017) briefly attempt to move outside of textual analysis by suggesting that Titus's use of camp helps audiences connect with him. However, although the authors importantly highlight that audience reception is important, particularly when engaging with a character that might embody "negative" stereotypes, they provide no evidence of having conducting audience research, or a corpus of tweets or online posts to support the claim. Thus, it reads almost as their call for future research to engage this line of inquiry.

In passing, Dexl and Horn (2017) suggest that part of what makes Titus an important character is that he is also played by an out, Black gay actor. On the one hand, this gesture toward the importance of a Black gay actor playing a Black gay role centers an "interrelated set of ideological and industrial factors that contribute to an understanding of televisual representation and its material effects on employment, activism and performance" (Martin, 2018b, p. 285). On the other hand, the authors only give casting a passing consideration in their examination of Titus but do not necessarily include this as an integral point in their analysis. Ultimately, the authors' interest in camp engages a reading of Titus that is particularly situated in their own subject positions and dissociated from industrial and reception contexts. And it is the fact that out, Black gay actor Tituss Burgess was cast as Titus which partly allows for not only their reading of the stereotypes he embodies as camp but also likely the audience's reading of him.

In a larger work on what television can teach viewers, Ava Laure Parsemain (2019) suggests that "the representation of queerness in popular culture is important because it contributes to the formation of identities and influences views and attitudes" (p. 2). Thus, with an eye toward television's pedagogical properties, and perhaps an imagination of television audiences as passive rather than active viewers, Parsemain finds that Titus reifies "the stereotype of gay men as comically flamboyant and desexualized" (p. 246). Parsemain gestures toward the industrial and economic structures of the media industries and recognizes the importance of parsing network, cable, and streaming representations; however, that is not necessarily the focus of her work. Rather, she is ultimately focused on the representational, concluding that television—across network, cable, and streaming platforms—"has a long way to go to respectfully and inclusively represent queerness" (p. 249). At the same time, she does not recognize/center Titus's Blackness. That is not to suggest that Parsemain does not know Titus is Black. Rather, she seemingly constructs him as a gay Black character rather than a Black gay character. The distinction suggests that gay Black men's (and characters') allegiance is to gay communities first, whereas Black gay men (and characters) define themselves through Blackness (Scott, 1994, p. 300). Thus, for Parsemain, studying Titus presumably teaches something about gayness, but not necessarily Black gayness.

David Oh (2020) focuses his work on a Titus-centered storyline within *Unbreakable Kimmy Schmidt*. In the narrative, Titus performs a one-person show in which he plays a geisha that is subject to backlash from Asian American communities for its insensitivities toward those of Asian descent. Oh suggests that the storyline is autobiographical for series creator Tina Fey in that both Fey and *Unbreakable Kimmy Schmidt* had been accused of being racially insensitive. Instead of having a White woman at the epicenter of the controversies within the series, Oh (2020) argues that Fey positions "Asian American protesters as intolerant and ignorant of a Black queer man's performance of Japanese femininity, shifting the target of White racial marginalization onto Asian Americans and shifting the target of White appropriation onto Black performers" (p. 60). In such a move, Oh suggests that the series, and Fey as an extension of the series, eschews a nuanced discussion of race. At the same time, Oh's focus on the substitution of Titus for Fey, and the ultimate rescuing of White feminism, decenters Titus' gayness from his analysis. To be sure, Oh is concerned with how 21st-century White feminism functions, but in so doing, he continues to make Black gayness a secondary concern. Although Oh does not necessarily pay attention to industrial or reception contexts, his essay gestures toward broader cultural events to situate his reading of *The Unbreakable Kimmy Schmidt*, thus situating Titus and the series within its cultural context.

The research on Black gay characters within White-/multicultural-cast sitcoms has broadly remained mired in discussions of the image without much attention to the cultural, production, industrial, and reception contexts in which these Black gay characters were created. Certainly, there are gestures toward the importance of these contexts in considering Black gay characters, and much of the early work on Black gay characters such as Carter Heywood is laying the groundwork for this area of inquiry. However, stereotypic analyses do not necessarily provide any real insight into these characterizations aside from the particular reading each of the authors has offered.

BLACK GAYNESS IN SKETCH COMEDY

Although perhaps there is not a distinction in methodology or approaches to comedy between sketch comedy and sitcoms (discussed in the section on "Black Gayness in Black-Cast Sitcoms"), the discussion is separated to provide intentional analysis of the scholarship based on genre. To further focus this analysis, this section discusses *In Living Color*'s "Men on..." skits. Unlike the research previously examined, the scholarship on Black gayness in sketch comedy moves beyond the text itself to prioritize the cultural context within which they are produced.

Jasmine Nichole Cobb and Robin Means Coleman (2007) perhaps take the broadest view of television in the late 20th and early 21st century in their examination of network and cable representations of Black gayness. They assert that television "is now willing to conceptualize a Black sexuality that does not threaten White women, [but] depictions of Black queer identities frequently involve interpersonal problems, violence, and (someone's) destruction" (p. 2). They frame representations of Black gayness within Patricia Hill Collins' theory of the "controlling image" and argue that, particularly within the comedy genre (which is where most Black gay televisual representations are situated), these images are "properly contained and controlled" (p. 4). As evidence of this controlling imagery, Cobb and Means Coleman point to *In Living Color*'s Blaine Edwards and Antoine Merriweather, who they posit are represented as "insufficiently masculine," which helps to televisually and thus, culturally, determine how we think about Black gay men.

Representing a critical cultural studies approach, E. Patrick Johnson examines *In Living Color* and Eddie Murphy's performances of what Marlon Riggs calls "negro faggotry" on *Saturday Night Live* (NBC, 1975–) and in his stand-up comedy film *Delirious* (HBO, 1983). Johnson (2003a) concludes that mass-mediated images of heterosexual Black masculinity are part of the "complex process through which Black male heterosexuality conceals it reliance on the Black effeminate homosexual for its status" (p. 232). In other words, Johnson argues that notions of Black gayness work in binary opposition to normative Black masculinity. Importantly, drawing from a cultural studies approach to media, Johnson culturally places Murphy's representations of Black gay men within its cultural landscape, including the Black Nationalist and Black Arts movements as well as the conservative response (or lack thereof) to the HIV/AIDS epidemic. Thus, while Johnson is focused on images of Black gayness, he places them within larger cultural discourses.

Johnson furthers his work in a chapter in *Appropriating Blackness*, wherein he conducts a close textual analysis of the "Men on..." skits from *In Living Color*. He argues the skits displace misogyny onto Black gay men and further homophobia. Johnson (2003b) posits that the characters, Blaine Edwards and Antoine Merriweather, "demonstrate random misogyny when they review works by or for women" by replying "in unison, 'Hated it'" (p. 66). In addition, he argues the skits forward, reify, and encourage homophobic ideas and rely on "the epistemology of homophobia" by presenting images of Black "gay men [who are] lascivious dick suckers who enjoy the taste of and swallowing semen" (p. 69), as evidenced by the line in one of the "Men On..." skits: "Don't tempt my tummy with the taste of nuts and honey." Johnson also finds that the skits reify homosexual codes through wardrobe. For Blaine and Antoine, their clothing and mannerisms become code for gay, despite the idea that their homosexuality is never explicitly named. Thus, Johnson employs a semiotic analysis of the ease with which gayness is/can be read onto Blaine and Antoine's bodies. Picking up on this thread, Cobb and Means Coleman (2007) assert that Blaine and Antoine offer "a new popular stereotype in their treatment of gay Black men, [whereby] the combination of hypersexuality and misogyny works to control Black gayness as something to be ridiculed" (p. 5).

Herman Gray (1995) also takes a cultural studies approach to *In Living Color*. Within that examination, he discusses "Men on..." and their reification of heterosexual masculine power. He posits that the men's attire works to code gayness and conflate homosexuality with dressing in "delicate fabrics with bright colors" (p. 141). Just as these costume choices code gayness, through binary opposition, they also contain heterosexual masculinity. Therefore, an "appropriately" masculine man cannot wear "delicate fabrics and bright colors." Particularly interesting in Gray's work is that he acknowledges that these characters are never explicitly identified as gay: rather, to borrow from Stuart Hall (2005), these "signifying practices" code them as gay.

Essex Hemphill (1995) conducts a brief reception study of *In Living Color*'s "Men on..." sketches. Interviewing Black gay men and lesbian patrons in Washington, DC, and Philadelphia, Hemphill is necessarily disinterested in how he reads Antoine and Blaine. Rather, he lets the Black gay men and lesbians tell him what they think the representations mean. The previous scholars discussed in this section read the "Men on..." sketches in a particular way because they are armed with a particularly scholarly toolkit. Hemphill attempts to engage the "Men on..." sketches as a text that "real" people engage and understand. In so doing, Hemphill found that whereas scholars find Antoine and Blaine troubling for the ways they recycled stereotypes associated with gayness, the people who they are supposed to represent engage a more negotiated response. One of Hemphill's respondents, Anthony Owens, understands the show as "a parody... [and it] should be taken as such" (p. 293). Thus, Owens put little to no importance on this representation of Black gay men. However, Alan Bell told Hemphill that he found the sketches "frightfully funny, and I enjoy looking at it, but at the same time I recognize that these portrayals are going out to people who don't have another context to put them in" (p. 394). In other words, Bell could find humor in Antoine and Blaine but has reservations about them being mediated for the Fox audience, which in the late 1980s and early 1990s was composed of primarily young, White adult male and Black heterosexual viewers.

The authors who engage in discussions of sketch comedy and Black gayness adopt an approach that centers the cultural contexts in which they appear. At the same time, although they certainly make meanings as Black spectators of the programming, they largely eschew discussions of production practices. Partly, that elision is rooted in sketch comedy generally, and *In Living Color* specifically, comprising a small portion of the work they are conducting. With the exception of Hemphill, the authors imagine an audience receiving the ideological messages the "Men on..." sketches mediate, but do not engage "real" viewers.

BLACK GAYNESS IN BLACK-CAST SITCOMS

Little research specifically addresses gay Black televisual representation in the Black-cast sitcom. Much of the literature available focuses on a single representation of Black gay maleness within a single media text rather than putting the representations in conversation with one another. In addition, the vast majority of the studies conducted have been textual analyses of representations within televisual spaces. The Black-cast sitcoms that form the basis for this section are *Moesha* and *Noah's Arc*. This section examines scholarship on *Moesha* and *Noah's Arc* to interrogate the intersections of Black gayness through the coming out process (*Moesha*) and the confluence of Blackness, gayness, and masculinities (*Noah's Arc*). In doing so, it also highlights differing methodological approaches to media studies, in general, and Black gayness, specifically.

Black gay men have appeared in 27 episodes of Black-cast sitcoms since 1977. Although they have appeared across a plethora of series and broadcast eras, they have remained narratively and industrially "trapped" in the "pedagogical gay" model. From the first Black gay character on the short-lived *Sanford & Son* spinoff *Sanford Arms* (NBC, 1977) to the multi-episode arc on *Let's Stay Together* (BET, 2012–2017), these Black gay men are narratively charged with educating the characters within the series as well as the audience about gayness. Once that "lesson" has been delivered, there is no narrative utility for the character, and he can be discarded.

This pedagogical model can take on several forms. From the first Black gay character in a Black-cast sitcom in a 1977 episode of the short-lived NBC series *Sanford Arms* titled "Phil's Assertion School" to the six-episode arc featuring a Black gay man on BET's *Let's Stay Together*, these Black characters' function within their respective series is to educate its (presumably

Black) audience about homosexuality while concomitantly reifying hegemonic Black masculinity. Because of this overarching narrative function, coupled with the imagination of Black audiences as less liberal/more anti-gay than White audiences, Black-cast sitcoms are deemed "not ready" for a recurring Black gay character. This "industry lore" about Black viewers shapes "what gets produced as well as how, where, and when productions get watched" (Havens, 2013, p. 4). This section examines not only what gets produced but also Black gay men's reception practices.

Moesha was one of the first Black-cast series to feature a Black gay character in the "gay 90s." *Moesha* broke new ground in its inclusion of Omar, a Black, gay teenager. Previously, homosexuality within television had mostly dealt with gay adults, not teenagers. Although the 1990s would see an explosion of gay characters as well as an increased production of Black-cast sitcoms, few Black-cast sitcoms included Black gay characters, and when they did include such characters, these characters were presented episodically and never as part of the ongoing casts of Black-cast sitcoms. In 1996, a year before *Spin City* debuted, *Moesha* engaged with Black gayness in its "Labels" episode. The episode concerns the suspicion that series regular Hakeem's cousin (Omar) might be gay. Although Becker (2006) only mentions *Moesha*'s "Labels" episode in the appendix of his book, simply stating that "Moesha goes on a date with Hakeem's cousin, who turns out to be gay" (p. 230), his interest is in *why* gay characters appear on television with such frequency in the 1990s. For *Moesha* and other sitcoms of the 1990s, Becker argues that gayness (and gay characters by extension) became a marketing tool to reach trendier, hipper, and cooler audiences. In this way, then, Becker was interested in the industrial utility of gayness to television marketing.

Turning more to *Moesha*'s textual features, Tropiano (2002) read the "Labels" episode as ambiguous because Omar never declares his homosexuality and instead whispers something to his cousin. Situated within a section of his book on "the coming out episode," Tropiano focuses on the textual features of episodes that feature gay characters. For Tropiano,

> the ending [of the "Labels" episode] skirts the gay issue by making it more about Hakeem and Moesha's friendship. Omar's "coming out" and Hakeem's reaction are never fully played out, which makes the ending all the more confusing. Hakeem and Moesha's silence in the end…can also be read…as if they're mourning [Omar's] gayness. (pp. 205–206)

Tropiano ultimately criticizes the episode because it did not include a declarative speech act that would settle Omar's gayness definitively for *Moesha*'s audience. Thus, for Tropiano, the ambiguity of the coming out offers an opportunity for ambiguous decodings of the episode.

However, in a study on the production practices associated with Black gay characters within Black-cast sitcoms, of which the *Moesha* "Labels" episode is one, Martin (2015) interviewed episode writer Demetrius Bady about how his script troubled the notion of the coming out episode and its insistence on the speech act of gay declaration. Bady recalled,

> The idea that Omar whispers [something] in Hakeem's ear and the audience never hears him say [he's gay] is a mirror reflection of how I was living my life…. The idea that I was saying it shouldn't matter meant [Omar did] not acknowledge himself in a very verbal and definitive way. (quoted in Martin, 2015, p. 656)

On the one hand, Bady suggests that Omar is somewhat autobiographical as a character and thus has made decisions similar to those Bady himself has made. On the other hand, and perhaps more important, Bady decenters the importance of the speech act, recognizing that it is mostly rooted in Foucauldian-style knowledge production that has more to do with the hearer of the speech act than with the speaker.

There is admittedly little work on *Moesha*, likely due to it having had only one episode that discussed Black gayness. However, unlike much of the research focused on Black gayness in White-/multicultural-cast sitcoms, Martin pay attention to industrial aspects such as the writers' room and audience imaginations for the series alongside the textual features of the episode.

Noah's Arc was a series that aired on Logo (the Viacom-owned network narrowcasted to reach lesbian, gay, bisexual, and transgender viewers) from 2005 to 2006. It was groundbreaking for its distinction as the first series to feature four Black gay men as central protagonists. Mark Cunningham (2013) argues that the series—with the main characters comprising Noah and his friends Alex, Ricky, and Chance—is "a symbolic suggestion of the familial nature of queer kinship networks that uses the 'arc' in the title not only represents the continuing storylines...but also [to reflect] the first letter in each of his friend's names" (p. 175). Via a contextual analysis that considers the series preproduction and production, Cunningham argues that *Noah's Arc* ultimately existed beyond the boundaries of a stereotypic analysis and instead engages with the multifaceted nature of Blackness, Black masculinity, and Black gayness that depicted "Black gay male relationships in an uncensored and honest manner" (p. 173). Although Cunningham's analysis is mostly textual, he begins his work by engaging historical representations of Black gayness within television as well as a brief engagement with Logo's initial value proposition rooted in providing a diversity of LGBTQ voices on the new network.

Michael Johnson (2010) explores notions of Black authenticity within *Noah's Arc* via textual analysis. Johnson asserts that the first season of *Noah's Arc* refuses to deal with the lived experience of Blackness or graphic depictions of same-sex sex, particularly in comparison to Showtime's *Queer as Folk*. One of Johnson's conclusions is his assertion that *Noah's Arc* "is important because it undermines the potential deconstruction of hegemonic masculinity associated with African American identity and the framework that...supports...the femininity equals gay arithmetic" (p. 43).

Gust Yep and John Elia (2007) examine notions of "authentic Blackness" on *Noah's Arc* and how the series both queered and quared those notions along class, gender, and sexuality lines. They take E. Patrick Johnson's notion of "quaring" as "a vernacular rearticulation and deployment of queer theory to accommodate racialized sexual knowledges" (p. 30). The authors forward that authentic Blackness is linked to social class in its association with working classedness and its segregation from White hegemony. Concomitantly, they find that *Noah's Arc* complicates these notions by allowing for a certain degree of code switching. However, the authors believe that in terms of gender, the show upholds notions of "proper" gender performativity rooted in notions of acceptable male and female behaviors and therefore does not quare gender. In the final analysis, the authors find that homosexuality and Black authenticity are incompatible on *Noah's Arc*. However, both Johnson and Yep and Elia never contend with the notion that "authenticity" is partly an affective audience response rather than something that can be observed universally because the very definition—like positive/negative—is slippery.

In a later study, Yep and Elia (2012) use homonormativity as a framework for their close reading of *Noah's Arc*. They conclude that "the characters emulate their White middleclass counterparts and their material possessions (e.g., homes, cars, clothes, products, etc.) [and] are highly characteristic of the much cherished and sought after American middle-class life with all of its benefits including social capital" (p. 907). Thus, they argue, the series seeks to flatten gayness, as evidenced by an episode in which Noah is called "faggot" before being beaten by a group of White men. For them, the series frames the violence as a gay bashing, thus ignoring that Noah is gay *and* Black, thereby acknowledging his intersectional identity.

Ben Aslinger (2009) uses *Noah's Arc*, alongside network-mate *Round Trip Ticket* (Logo, 2005), to help "move queer media studies toward an increased interrogation of mainstream media industries and the cultural labor performed by out gay and lesbian producers, writers, and executives" (p. 108). Aslinger suggests that although Logo positions itself as progressive for a "diverse queer audience" through programming such as *Noah's Arc*, those efforts "are undermined by textual choices...that reinscribe class, race, and national hierarchies in queer cultures" (p. 107). His work is mostly interested in the industrial circulation of *Noah's Arc* as the only Black gay-cast sitcom on an LGBT-focused network. However, he places *Noah's Arc* within discourses related to the blinding Whiteness of mediated gay culture by examining the industrial, reception (via reviews of the series), and textual contexts.

CONCLUSION

There remains relatively little work on Black gayness within television comedy. On the one hand, there is some work that addresses Black gayness in "prestige" drama, including *The Wire* and *Six Feet Under*, as well as reality television, including *Love and Hip Hop*. On the other hand, this work is largely textual. Thus, scholars continue to treat Black gay representation as if it is unencumbered by social, cultural, industrial, and reception contexts. Ignoring these contexts results in participation in what Tony Bennett (1982, p. 9) calls a "methodological fiction." At the same time, the research examined in this article has demonstrated that Black gayness within television comedy is not only visible but also a fascinating area of scholarly inquiry. Hopefully this body of research will come to be known as the first phase in the study of Black gayness within television comedy. Within the second phase, researchers should amplify their insistence on examining not just Black gay representation but also the systems that have produced those images. The second phase should include more methodological attention paid to the relationships between Black gayness and television industrial practices, audiences, and sociohistorical contextual analysis. Simply stated, instead of asking how Black gayness is represented, it should be asked why Black gayness is represented.

FURTHER READING

Aslinger, B. (2009). Creating a network for queer audiences at Logo TV. *Popular Communication*, 7(2), 107–121.

D'Acci, J. (2004). Cultural studies, television studies, and the crisis in the humanities. In L. Spigel & J. Olsson (Eds.), *Television after TV: Essays on a medium in transition* (pp. 418–446). Duke University Press.

Hall, S. (2005). Encoding/decoding in the television discourse. In D. M. Hunt (Ed.), *Channeling Blackness: Studies on television and race in America* (pp. 46–59). Oxford University Press.

Hemphill, E. (1995). *In Living Color*: Toms, coons, mammies, faggots and bucks. In C. K. Creekmur & A. Doty (Eds.), *Out in culture: Gay, lesbian, and queer essays on popular culture* (pp. 389–402). Duke University Press.

Johnson, E. P. (2003). The specter of the Black fag: Parody, blackness, and hetero/homosexual b(r)others. *Journal of Homosexuality, 45*(2–4), 217–234.

Martin, A. L., Jr. (2015). Scripting Black gayness: Television authorship in Black-cast sitcoms. *Television and New Media, 16*(7), 648–663.

Martin, A. L., Jr. (2020). For scholars…when studying the queer of color image alone is not enough. *Communication and Critical/Cultural Studies, 17*(2), 69–74.

Martin, A. L., Jr. (2021). *The generic closet: Black gayness and the Black-cast sitcom*. Indiana University Press.

Riggs, M. (1995). Black macho revisited: Reflections of a Snap Queen! In C. K. Creekmur & A. Doty (Eds.), *Out in culture: Gay, lesbian, and queer essays on popular culture* (pp. 470–475). Duke University Press.

Warner, K. J. (2017). In the time of plastic representation. *Film Quarterly, 71*(2), 32–37.

Yep, G. A., & Elia, E. P. (2007). Queering/quaring Blackness in *Noah's Arc*. In T. Peele (Ed.), *Queering popular culture* (pp. 27–40). Palgrave Macmillan.

REFERENCES

Aslinger, B. (2009). Creating a network for queer audiences at Logo TV. *Popular Communication, 7*(2), 107–121.

Becker, R. (2006). *Gay TV and straight America*. Rutgers University Press.

Bennett, T. (1982). Text and social process: The case of James Bond. *Screen Education, 41*(Winter/Spring), 3–14.

Bérubé, A. (2001). How gay stays White and what kind of White it stays. In B. Brander Rasmussen, E. Kineberg, I. J. Nexica, & M. Wray (Eds.), *The making and unmaking of whiteness* (pp. 234–265). Duke University Press.

Brown, L. (1977, August 8). Homosexuals move to protect civil rights on TV. *The New York Times*, p. 35.

Capsuto, S. (2000). *Alternative channels: The uncensored story of gay and lesbian images on radio and television*. Ballantine.

Clark, C. (1969). Television and social controls: Some observation of the portrayal of ethnic minorities. *Television Quarterly, 9*(2), 18–22.

Cobb, J., & Means Coleman, R. (2007). *Two snaps and a twist: Controlling images of Black male homosexuality on television* [Paper presentation]. International Communication Association.

Cunningham, M. (2013). Nigger, coon, boy, punk, homo, faggot, Black man: Reconsidering established interpretations of masculinity, race, and sexuality through *Noah's Arc*. In B. Smith Shomade (Ed.), *Watching while Black: Centering the television of Black audiences* (pp. 172–186). Rutgers University Press.

Dexl, C., & Horn, K. (2017). "Beef jerky in a ball gown": The camp excesses of Titus Andromedon in *Unbreakable Kimmy Schmidt*. *Open Cultural Studies, 1*(1), 442–453.

Duggan, L. (2003). *The twilight of equality? Neoliberalism, cultural politics, and the attack on democracy*. Beacon.

Gerbner, G. (1972). Violence in television drama: Trends and symbolic functions. In G. A. Comstock & E. Rubinstein (Eds.), *Television and social behavior. Vol. 1: Content and control*. US Government Printing Office.

Gitlin, T. (2000). *Inside prime time*. University of California Press.

Gray, H. (1995). *Watching race: Television and the struggle for Blackness*. University of Minneapolis Press.

Hall, S. (2005). Encoding/decoding in the television discourse. In D. M. Hunt (Ed.), *Channeling Blackness: Studies on television and race in America* (pp. 46–59). Oxford University Press.

Havens, T. (2013). *Black television travels: African American media around the globe.* New York University Press.

Hemphill, E. (1995). In living color: Toms, coons, mammies, faggots and bucks. In C. K. Creekmur & A. Doty (Eds.), *Out in culture: Gay, lesbian, and queer essays on popular culture* (pp. 389–402). Duke University Press.

Johnson, E. P. (2003a). The specter of the Black fag: Parody, blackness, and hetero/homosexual b(r)others. *Journal of Homosexuality, 45*(2–4), 217–234.

Johnson, E. P. (2003b). *Appropriating blackness: Performance and the politics of authenticity.* Duke University Press.

Johnson, M., Jr. (2010). After *Noah's Arc*: Where do we go from here? In J. Elledge (Ed.), *Queers in American popular culture* (pp. 35–46). ABC-CLIO.

Johnson, P. A., & Keith, M. C. (2001). *Queer airwaves: The story of gay and lesbian broadcasting.* Sharpe.

Kilhefner, D. (2007, December 5). Gay—the new straight—I don't think so!. *Los Angeles Times.* http://www.latimes.com/news/opinion/la-oew-kilhefner5dec05,0,2467579.story

Martin, A. L., Jr. (2015). Scripting Black gayness: Television authorship in Black-cast sitcoms. *Television and New Media, 16*(7), 648–663.

Martin, A. L., Jr. (2018a). Generic closets: Sitcoms, audiences, and Black male gayness. In N. Marx & M. Sienkiewicz (Eds.), *The comedy studies reader* (pp. 222–233). University of Texas Press.

Martin, A. L., Jr. (2018b). The queer business of casting gay characters on U.S. television. *Communication, Culture & Critique, 11*(2), 282–297.

Martin, A. L., Jr. (2021). *The generic closet: Black gayness and the Black-cast sitcom.* Indiana University Press.

Murray, M. (2001). "The tendency to deprave and corrupt morals": Regulation and irregular sexuality in Golden Age radio comedy. In M. Hilmes & J. Loviglio (Eds.), *Radio reader: Essays in the cultural history of radio* (pp. 135–156). Routledge.

Oh, D. C. (2020). "Opting out of that": White feminism's policing and disavowal of anti-racist critiques in *The Unbreakable Kimmy Schmidt. Critical Studies in Media Communication, 37*(2), 58–70.

Parsemain, A. L. (2019). *The pedagogy of queer TV.* Palgrave Macmillan.

Reality TV World. (2003a, July 16). *Queer Eye for the Straight Guy* premiere smashes Bravo ratings records. http://www.realitytvworld.com/news/queer-eye-for-straight-guy-premiere-smashs-bravo-ratings-records-1414.php

Reality TV World. (2003b, July 23). Ratings: Special NBC airing of *Queer Eye for the Straight Guy* draws 6.7 million viewers. http://www.realitytvworld.com/news/ratings-special-nbc-airing-of-queer-eye-for-straight-guy-draws-67-million-viewers-1465.php

Scott, D. (1994). Jungle fever: Black identity politics, White dick and the utopian bedroom. *GLQ: A Journal of Lesbian and Gay Studies, 1*(3), 299–321.

Shale, T. (1977, July 16). Fred Silverman on the cleanliness of *Soap. Washington Post.*

Squires, C. (2009). *African Americans and the media.* Polity.

Streitmatter, R. (2009). *From "perverts" to "Fab Five": The media's changing depiction of gay men and lesbians.* Routledge.

Tropiano, S. (2002). *The prime time closet: A history of gays and lesbians on TV.* Applause Books.

Walters, S. D. (2001). *All the rage: The story of gay visibility in America.* University of Chicago Press.

Walters, S. D. (2014). *The tolerance trap: How God, genes, and good intentions are sabotaging gay equality.* New York University Press.

Yep, G. A., & Elia, E. P. (2007). Queering/quaring Blackness in *Noah's Arc*. In T. Peele (Ed.), *Queering popular culture* (pp. 27–40). Palgrave Macmillan.

Yep, G. A., & Elia, E. P. (2012). Racialized masculinities and the new homonormativity in Logo's *Noah's Arc*. *Journal of Homosexuality*, 59(7), 890–911.

Cameron Lynn Brown and Alfred L. Martin

GAY PORNOGRAPHY

INTRODUCTION

Linda Williams (2014a), in the augural edition of *Porn Studies* (PS)—the field's first (and still only) dedicated journal, its conception itself an exercise in the organization of an emerging discipline—described the *field* of pornography studies as "weedy," those who attend to it as tending to "dabble," and attentions in the gay regard as an "(over)abundance." This final observation that in 2014 there was an "(over)abundance of work on gay pornography versus the surprising paucity on heterosexual pornographies" (Williams, 2014a, p. 24) was, frankly, absurd. That the statement came from a figure whose 1989 monograph was "groundbreaking" (as characterized by *PS* founding editors Feona Attwood and Clarrisa Smith [2014, p. 1]; Mercer, 2017b, p. 15, calls it "agenda-setting," even though it omits gay porn from its discussion) in porn studies' emergence was problematic. Especially so given it came as part of a field-wide survey for the inaugural issue of porn studies' first dedicated journal—in the abstract, no less. At best, it was a misunderstanding of the history of the gay porn studies subfield; at worst, it was an erasure of *the fact of erasure* in the literature and, therefore, in this author's view, a necessary first point of redress.

Commercial, moving-image (initially, American) hardcore all-male pornography (simply "gay porn" hereafter) emerged in the 1970s when, for the first time, many of the cultural inhibitions and legal restrictions on explicit gay sexual content were "swept away" with the current of a sexual revolution—prompted in large part by the 1969 Stonewall riots (Escoffier, 2009, p. ii). Straight varieties of hardcore pornography ("heteroporn" hereafter; a deconstructive reaction to the "exnomination" of heterosexual positions in "porn"—studies and texts [see Fiske & Hartley, 1978, p. 176, for a discussion of exnomination, the evacuation of privileged positions]) also entered mainstream American culture around this time (Escoffier, 2009, p. ii). Yet the gay variety came as part of a wider, gay sexual subcultural "explosion" of explicit homosexual representation (Escoffier, 2009, p. 383) and with a social history and narrative activism (i.e., Burger, 1995) that labored against a violent past and historical-present precedence for hidden-ness, prejudice, and criminalization. In fact, Wakefield Poole's "Hollywoodian" 1971 *Boys in the Sand* preceded the heteroporn hit *Deep Throat*.

Gay porn soon forged unique relations with the community whose sex it put on screen. One example of its place in gay culture has been the "highly social and communicative" adoption of it in gay spaces—especially important during times of discriminatory hostility, where it was played in bathhouses, sex clubs, bars, and discos. Such traditions are ongoing and evolving today, via the "hook-up culture" home, for instance (Adams-Thies, 2015). Within the scholarship that followed the 1970s emergence of hardcore gay and heteroporn also came a *tendency*—that ran into the early 1990s (and beyond, in some instances)—to "ignore" and "erase" or "exclude" (Gubar, 1987) the gay tradition. In some cases, to aid explicit efforts—in the view of Gubar (1987)—to focus the scholarly agenda on women being dehumanized as sexual objects or degraded as the victims in heteroporn (see Garry, 1978, for a reading of this type). In rare instances where gay porn was addressed by scholars, it was often "defined" (see Mosher, 1988) as similar in psychology and sexual acts to the degradation of a feminine object, as was argued to be taking place in heteroporn. Such reified positions persisted into the present century where, following Andrea Dworkin, Christopher N. Kendall (2004b) surmised, "Gay male pornography merges with an identity… [politic where] gay men are not only penetrated like women but are expected to lust after pain and degradation like women are thought to under male dominance" (p. 67).

In summary, gay porn was *under*represented in scholarship, and it would seem a distraction, especially in the social sciences, from the main theater. Such a position is supported by Todd G. Morrison et al.'s (2016) own survey of the subject (written at a critical moment of transformation in the literature). My survey acknowledges foundational essays (Dyer, 1985; Waugh, 1985) that helped *shape, inspire,* and *move* the gay porn studies subfield away from pathological perspectives and toward the critical mass of scholarship it enjoys today. I accept that in the 2020s, "gay porn studies comprises one of the largest and more active subfields within porn studies itself" (Ruszczycky, 2021, p. 13) while asserting from the outset that the attention and contribution of this subfield (to "porn studies" and beyond, including the wider humanities and social sciences) is a more recent and hard-fought status than Williams's statement (and her 2014 survey overall; see Mercer, 2017b, pp. 9–10, for additional critiques) implied.

SCOPE; OR PATHWAYS *TOWARD* ABUNDANCE

Let us start, as Richard Dyer (1985) famously did, by "coming to terms." While this survey is named "gay pornography," adopting "gay porn" throughout not only embraces simplicity over "grandiloquence" (see Mercer, 2017b, pp. 9–10) but exnominates as well. "Gay *male* pornography" recurs in the literature but I find it antiquated—like "gay male *video* pornography" (i.e., Burger, 1995), and "cinema," too, which belong with "pre-web, pre-digital" phases (Mercer, 2017b, pp. 11–14)—and at odds with the more contemporary, inclusive "gay porn studies." Comparing cross-decade monographs by Kendall (2004b; *Gay Male Pornography*) and Mercer (2017b; *Gay Pornography*) reveals the connections of "gay male" with a certain social-scientific (read: Morrison et al.'s [2016] *GMP*) and legal framework (read: Kendall's [2004a] *SJD*), where it is joined in the literature by terms like "MSM (Men Who Have Sex With Men)," "SEM (Sexually Explicit Media)," or even "all-male." Extraction of "male" here, in other words, comes with a cognizance for its implications.

"Lesbian porn" and "queer porn," among other areas (i.e., "trans porn") as lesser-explored and more recent subfields, respectively, are excluded, and deserving of their own surveys. Also excluded are non-moving-image media forms, such as gay porn fiction (see Ruszczycky, 2021). "Gay" is a loaded term that, some might argue, excludes non-gay-identifying performers and representations like gay-for-pay as well as producers and audiences of this pornography, which are diverse (i.e., women; McCutcheon & Bishop, 2015). That is to say, I am aware of the arguments of some scholars (i.e., Cante & Restivo, 2004) around the "multi-layered problems" (p. 111) of "gay" porn, especially outside of the Anglo-sphere and in gay-for-pay contexts; all productive points, for this diversity rubs up against some of the themes charted, such as connections (and challenges of these) with the gay community, real or imagined.

Williams's (2014a) *PS* essay advocated "critical distance" between scholars and the porn industry, to ensure the field is not automatically "pro-porn" in its stance (p. 24). It's a fair point, yet in a version of the same essay, she also makes the following observation about the "male side of the queer continuum" (2014b, p. 31): "There seems to me no doubt that this particular subfield of pornography studies will continue to flourish, for the people who write about it have found these pornographic texts crucial to who they are" (pp. 31–32). Nguyen Tan Hoang (2004) provides a powerful example of this in a Williams-collection essay via the "poignancy in 'saying good-bye'" gay men may feel in viewing a 1995 Robert Blanchon "recathexis of early 1980s gay pornography" (p. 261).

Of course, not all scholars or gay men see gay porn as crucial to who they are. See, for example, John Champagne's (1995, pp. 28–56) construction of gay porn as "nonproductive expenditure," together with Kendall's oeuvre of harms-based arguments—including rejection of the idea that gay porn is identity-forming and liberating (Kendall, 2004c, p. 877)—perspectives that have also been picked up more recently for contemplation by scholars such as Shannon Gilreath (2011, pp. 169–203). Yet gay cultures are especially "pornified" (an "axiomatic" consensus reached by Maddison, 2017, following immersion with 30 years of gay porn scholarship) and I don't shy away from a personal stake in the subject.

Williams's 2014 essay also called on porn studies scholars to invest less in one-off pieces—journal articles and book chapters—and adopt a more disciplined investment in larger, encompassing works—monographs. Reflected here is both the disciplinary core of *PS*, as envisioned by Williams, and the evolution of the discipline itself—namely, as seeded in the "film tradition" and the humanities more broadly, where fellow humanities researchers will be painfully aware of single-author books as the benchmark of success and serious contribution. Single-author monographs have a place, certainly, and there are important books, both confined to gay porn (i.e., Goss, 2021; Mercer, 2017b) and with a broader scope, yet which have nevertheless made a considerable impact (i.e., Dean, 2009, who explores bareback). Not all scholars who write on gay porn in journals alone can be seen to dabble at the surface, however. Dyer's profound contribution is often charted "through a succession of articles" (Mercer, 2017b, p. 13), and the closest we have to a gay porn scholarly canon are the so-called dabbles of daring film scholars. Dyer and Thomas Waugh may not have been the first to publish on gay porn—(Blachford, 1978) Gregg Blachford's Marxist critique appeared in *Gay Left* in 1978, for instance—but these men were the most influential.

THE CLASSIC "DABBLES"

Dyer (1985) asserted gay porn's importance as an object of textual study through an analysis of sexual narrative constructions built on the premise that narrative exists in even the simplest of pornographic loops. Writing in a context where porn discussions had tended "to start off by being either for or against all porn and to be caught up in equally dubious libertarian or puritanical ideas" (p. 27), by his own assessment, Dyer's main suggestions in the essay are "quite brief and simple" (p. 27), and necessarily so; they set out a working definition for gay porn. Dyer's contribution (together with his early writings in general) was influential because it did not discount the critiques of feminists, putting forward the view that scholars should resist "pure sex" notions and defending porn based on a position that it released a sexuality "repressed" by bourgeois society (Dyer, 1985, p. 123). In fact, in a subsequent essay, Dyer (1989) calls to dismiss views of a "small chorus of gay individualists [who] resent intrusions from feminism upon their pleasures" (p. 199), which can be read in line with cultural studies principles.

In the same edition of *Jump Cut* (*JC*), "Tom" Waugh (1985) takes a post-sixties, "relatively loose comparison of gay male pornography to straight male pornography, referring wherever relevant to its major product divisions" with the comparison organized by relations of production (making), exhibition (showing), consumption (looking), and representation (depicting). As with Dyer, a filmic disciplinary intention is clear—a characteristic of the publishing venue—with the study ending via consideration of a specific pornographer (Curt McDowell) and a call on pornographic cinema to "attain an eroticism worthy of our political ideals." Lofty ambitions are not much reflected in subsequent scholarship or the films to be released—and can, as with Dyer's analytic frame, be read in line with the influence of cultural studies on reading gay porn: such as a conscious move to "decenter" texts and a greater interest in broader issues of power and identity formation over a search for intrinsic value of certain texts, including over others (Johnson, 1986–1987).

Waugh (2017) undertook "a personal revisit" of his classic essay more than 30 years later, where he considered its relevance to the "sex wars" and pondered "the water and other fluids" to flow through the field since (p. 131). The political dimension of his original essay returns, as Waugh outlines the hectoring backdrop experienced with *JC*'s editors, Chuck Kleinhans and Julia Lesage: to defy censorship by "boldly reproducing the images under analysis" and, ultimately, to show pictures of hard cock (p. 133). Published in *PS*, Waugh takes aim at the journal as evidence of a "partial victory"—with Gail "Dines, our twenty-first-century Dworkin" (p. 132). Most valuable for our present purposes, however, is Waugh's reflection that his original essay's comparative analysis, "with gay and straight being on a continuum rather than in separately lived worlds…might be the piece's standout contribution, especially in today's 'gay-for-pay' world" (p. 132)—the latter of which has constituted a key area of gay porn scholarship. If Dyer and Waugh constitute the "first wave" of gay porn scholarship, I count three journal special issues (and their editors) as forming and agenda setting the second.

THE SPECIAL ISSUES

John Hartley (2009) describes journal special issues as "indispensably," "devoted to field-shaping initiatives." There is perhaps no greater truism of this than for gay porn scholars, who found themselves reliant on aligned or wider disciplines like cultural studies to publish—such as *International Journal of Cultural Studies* that, under Hartley's founding direction, proved itself a furtive forum for such scholarship (i.e., McKee, 1999). Hartley also conceives of the special as "an extreme version of running order," which highlights the important curatorial role of special editors in advancing underexamined areas. As of 2022, there have been three gay porn specials (Mercer, 2017a; Morrison, 2004a; Morrison et al., 2015), and they deserve separate and in-sequence attention.

2004, Journal of Homosexuality (Editor: Todd G. Morrison). By the start of the current century, gay porn had still received only limited academic attention. As redress, in 2001, Todd G. Morrison started compiling submissions for a *Journal of Homosexuality* (*JH*) special (Morrison, 2004a). Opting for an interdisciplinary approach, it drew on perspectives from fields such as history, film studies, law, psychology, and sociology. It's difficult to overstate the contribution of Morrison's project, which provided a blueprint for how gay porn studies could proceed as a subfield and is the clearest demonstration of what Mercer (2017b) describes as the "second wave of gay porn research" that emerged in the early 2000s (p. 15).

In the spirit of "eclectic" curation, Morrison included as well as departed from harms-based positions (read: antipornography feminist framework), notably with a polemic essay by Kendall (2004a) on the 2000 Canadian Supreme Court *Little Sisters Book and Art Emporium* case that had the impacts on gay youth self-respect in its sights. Working in the tradition of Dworkin and Catharine MacKinnon, 2004 was a pivotal year in Kendall's contribution to the field with his book (2004b) published, using this case among others as a springboard for harms-based positions.

Robert Jensen (2004) also adopts radical feminist ideas in the special and Karen Busby (2004) challenges Kendall's arguments around the *Little Sisters* case, bringing a balanced perspective on the complexities of gay porn. Scott J. Duggan and Donald R. McCreary's (2004) survey research lends some empirical support for criticisms in Kendall's essay around gay porn's valorization of muscle as increasing social physique anxiety for gay men, while Morrison's (2004b) own research showed, via a focus group, the active reading strategies of gay audiences, who adopt a "utilitarian perspective," seeing potentially negative influences of the gay porn texts as transitory and impacts on attitudes and behaviors of gay men as minimal.

Qualitative text-based and ethnographic contributions are also represented, via the analysis of cross-generational producer and/or actor memoirs (Cohler, 2004); behind-the-scenes (Scuglia, 2004), autobiographic-viewing (Hallam, 2004), and contributor perspectives (Ellis & Whitehead, 2004); and analyses of place, via exotic transnational locations in the works of Kristen Bjorn (Westcott, 2004) and the popularity of the prison setting (Mercer, 2004).

2015, Psychology & Sexuality (Editors: Todd G. Morrison, C. J. Bishop, & Mark Kiss). Morrison, joined this time by C. J. Bishop and Mark Kiss, contributed a second special a decade later titled "*More* Eclectic Views on Gay Male Pornography" (emphasis added) and appearing in *Psychology & Sexuality* (*P&S*). As the title suggests, it is in conversation with the earlier special, with the editors using the introduction (Morrison et al., 2015, pp. 2–3) to draw out three key differences: technological advances (notably, [continued] pervasiveness of the Internet and social media), changes to evaluative lens (notably, [continued] state of condomlessness in gay porn and shift in attitudes on the absence of condoms within the industry and gay community), and burgeoning interest in gay porn as a field of scholarship (notably, via the diversity of topics covered in the special—diversity that has also continued).

The first three essays are evidence of a maturing field, devoted to taxonomical work: Bishop (2015) undertakes a literature review, modifying Paul J. Wright's (hetero)porn frameworks; Darin J. Erickson et al. (2015) use latent class analysis to categorize users; and Richard Silvera et al. (2015) consider how "outness" might influence porn use among MSM via an online survey. The edition's remaining essayists continue the 2004 *JH* conversation and capture the *more* eclectic, "burgeoning interest" that characterized the mid-2010s (Morrison et al., 2015, p. 3). This includes two phenomenological perspectives accounting for women's (McCutcheon & Bishop, 2015) and self-conceived (Hald et al., 2015) perceptions; industry-insider-cum-scholar Scuglia (2015) returns with another reflective piece, a doomsday reading of gay porn's "point and purpose" in the internet age; contributor perspectives are again canvassed, this time as "a virtual discussion" (Nielsen & Kiss, 2015); and auteur contributions are considered in aligned-though-fresh directions, including of "new flavor" indie porn (Nielsen, 2015) and exotic visions of Arab place and national identity (Tziallas, 2015b).

Conspicuous in their absence are pathologizing perspectives in the spirit of Dworkin, which can be read as a gesture to keep the "porn wars" in the past, departing from the perspectives of Kendall while not foreclosing considerations of gay porn problematics. Keeping Kendall in the past is possible courtesy of robust challenges—within his own legal-regulatory framework—in the early 1990s, such as from Carl F. Stychin (1991–1992), who develops several lines of argument around the "failure of the feminist anti-pornography approach to differentiate" between gay and heteroporn (p. 857), namely, that gay porn ceases to be oppressive—in fact becomes liberating rather than objectifying—and destabilizes the coherence of the male subject through a subversion of phallocracy. Notably, contributors across Morrison's two specials, such as Mercer and Tziallas, went on to do much more than "dabble" in the field—Mercer most significantly.

2017, Porn Studies (Editor: John Mercer). Morrison (with Daragh T. McDermott) "assumed the reins" of *P&S* in 2017 and *PS*—then in its fourth year—published its first gay porn special (Mercer, 2017a), "Gay Porn Now!" This "hyperbolic title" sought to "capture the sense of excitement and vibrancy" of the time: "50 years after homosexuality was no longer criminal and over 30 years since Waugh provided a critical framework to discuss gay porn" (Mercer, 2017a, p. 128). Mercer's introduction and, on balance, this special, was clearly curated with an eye to history. It stands as an unusual omission, therefore, that Morrison's contributions receive no mention by Mercer here.

Waugh's (2017) "personal revisit" leads the special, aiding Mercer's account for the past while the "now!" is written in "new modes of production and emerging aesthetic and discursive patterns" (Mercer, 2017a, p. 129) that, following and expanding upon Morrison et al., are markers of the dominance of the internet and social media and evidence of changes in evaluative lenses revealing the richness of burgeoning interest.

The special includes exploratory taxonomical work (Mowlabocus & Medhurst, 2017, with sonics); interrogation of assumptions, namely a continued (following McCutcheon & Bishop, 2015) account for female heterosexual audiences for gay porn (Ramsay, 2017) and the role of porn in gay culture, as read through the lens of social media platforms (Maddison, 2017); evaluative lens changes, from auteur analyses to textual qualities of internet-based "extreme" texts (Young, 2017 reading *Gag the Fag*) and performer trajectories that account for social media celebrities trying a hand at gay porn (Arroyo, 2017, reading Chris Crocker), endemic in the 2020s; and, perhaps most significantly, account for the "new" conditions of circulation (Tsika, 2017, on streaming platforms) and production (Mercer, 2017c, on amateur porn-making practices). As of 2022, Mercer is coeditor of *PS*, a position he accepted a year after his special published.

METHOD: TEXT, INDUSTRY, AUDIENCE—THRUSTS & BULGES

As Nathaniel B. Burke (2016a) observes, "Scholarship on pornography generally falls into one of three broad categories: studies that explore films' content (e.g., *text*ual or content analysis of meaning), those that investigate *audience* reception, and studies of the *industry* itself, its means of production, and the patterns of labor and power" (p. 587, emphasis added). Jane Stokes (2003) states something similar in the context of media and cultural studies research, naming *text*, *audience*, and *industry* as the broad categories that *organize* (p. 17) and make up the *complete picture* (p. 60) of media research. I adopt these categories to organize the state of gay porn scholarship as it stands in 2022.

My aim is not exhaustiveness but instead utility, to be purposeful, embracing the digital affordances of an updateable survey of an interdisciplinary subfield's scholarly coverage of moving-image examples, underscored by a method of my own. Textual analysis in the cultural studies tradition is uniquely suited to a project such as this. Unlike quantitative content analysis, it does not strive to cleanly categorize within a confined sample; in fact, I allow for slippage across the categories in developing the key themes identified. Notably, and advantageously, I, as textual analyst, seek to identify broader trends via strategic selection of key scholarship.

There is a "reflective practice" that underscores this review. Following the ideas of Donald A. Schön's (1983) reflective practitioner, I recognize the problematics that come with the study of gay porn and the challenges of a single author undertaking a thematic reading, which is why this review is concerned more with *problem setting*: "a process in which, interactively, we *name* the things to which we will attend and *frame* the context in which we will attend to them" (p. 40). My naming and framing process is as follows: to set out many (not all) of the key gay porn *bulges* (the critically amassed interest that has comprised the core concerns of scholars across each of the three broad categories), followed by some noteworthy *thrusts* (the emergent or developing areas of the literature), with scope for future attention and adjustment, as "the 'things' of the situation" that have set the boundaries of scholarly attention up to 2022 change (Schön, 1983 p. 40). Herein lies the unique opportunity of the present project and its structure, namely: *It is written and set up to be updated.*

DOMINANT CONDITIONS

A need for taxonomical work was a key theme across the specials, given the blossoming scholarly interest in the area from the mid-2010s (Morrison et al., 2015, p. 3) and the historical prevalence of antiporn positions prior to the current century. In framing their own taxonomical project—during this critical mid-2010s period of scholarly swell—Simon Corneau and Emily van der Meulen (2014) defined, distinguished, and conceptualized gay porn types via interviews and thematic analysis with 20 Canadian consumers. The resultant five categories—mellow, commercial, raunch, amateur, and bareback—were broad conceptualizations, yet ones that demonstrate the profound impact of "bareback" (the onscreen abandonment of the condom) as a category within itself, worthy of separate consideration.

Bareback. Bareback has been (and arguably remains) the key battleground of gay porn scholarship, providing both the most compelling rationale for the *need* for research and the clearest pathway to broader concerns of gay culture and lived experience. From its origins, it's been seen as a *sub*text of gay porn and gay life, an especially radical/fringe/also-raunchy (and potentially dangerous) gay porn variant and sexual practice that rose to the level of moral panic for its potential to undermine safer-sex messaging (Jonas et al., 2014) and—in, as well as beyond, the representational sense—the workplace safety of performers (Silvera et al., 2009). Fears that bareback porn might undo progress made in the fight against AIDS led to instances of industry regulation, such as California's 2012 "Measure B," which prohibited bareback production. Such measures gave rise to legal debate on bareback porn as sufficiently "expressive" to warrant First Amendment protections (Ramos, 2013), underscored by perspectives on the practice as a form of homosociality among men (Nielsen & Morrison, 2019).

There's connective tissue—and polarizing promises of intimacy and diminishing controversy—tied with bareback porn that, returning to Hoang (2004, p. 261), point in complex ways to the wild sexual abandon of the 1970s; the grim tempering of AIDS in the 1980s and 1990s, bringing the death drive back to gay sexual representation via a revival of ideas by the likes of Leo Bersani (McKittrick, 2010); and, more recently, the return of condomless porn off the back of treatment and preventative technologies of the current age (the "bareback momentum," Brennan, 2020), ushering us into the present "post-crisis" period (Florêncio, 2020a).

Bareback porn, in order words, is a "dream screen" of radical gay lived experience (McKittrick, 2010, p. 76), an experience of profound trauma and shifting sexual fortunes. In 2007, Corita R. Grudzen and Peter R. Kerndt proffered that male viewers would likely "not tolerate" condomless gay porn depictions, for (quoting from the *Los Angeles Times Magazine*) watching condomless gay porn would be akin to "watching death on the screen" (p. e126). In a "heterotopic" (a concept Morris & Paasonen [2014, p. 27] apply to bareback porn), previously unimaginable manner, gay porn's ubiquity has turned to the condom's absence, in porn and sexual practice, leaving historical conceptions of the genre—even within the past decade (i.e., Morris & Paasonen, 2014, as "risky sex")—in need of a rethink. In ubiquity, bareback now oscillates across the other categories of gay porn (commercial, raunch, amateur, mellow).

Tim Dean's (2009) *Unlimited Intimacy* deserves to be recognized as the key text here. Dean delves into the barebacking subculture more broadly, but with discussion of bareback porn specifically (pp. 97–144), inclusive of aesthetics and the politics of this representation. Separating bareback out here is a deliberate recognition of its status as a *defiant* concept, supported by alignment among many scholars between bareback porn with queer theory (Davis, 2015). Bareback defies even received wisdoms on it as a category of gay porn, including its inception. Nostalgic constructions of the period *before* the term entered common parlance—of the "precondom" era (often referred to as the "Golden Age" of gay porn)—cannot exclude bareback; as Storms (2015) points out, the performers of those 1970s and 1980s features that are now marketed as precondom classics "were at risk of contracting HIV, regardless of whether it was a known risk at the time" (p. 388)—as indeed were/are the health threats *other than* HIV that are heightened when the condom is abandoned.

Such understanding anchors texts that might, on the surface or via their marketing, have otherwise been separated from bareback ("precondom" video porn, for example) and "contextualizes" these texts with bareback, both in a familiar—as by-products of safer-sex campaigns (Mowlabocus, 2007, p. 218)—and in a more porous way, such as with what Storms

(2015) describes as the "longer history of HIV" (p. 392). The condom's presence and absence, in other words, puts all gay porn performers, texts, and audiences in ahistorical situ with bareback. Bareback porn, its production, reception, and analysis-as-text, is, in a pinch, unstable.

This instability is especially pronounced in the industry tradition. The 2006 anti-bareback stance of pornographer Michael Lucas of Lucas Entertainment, for example, published in the *Yale Journal of Law and Feminism*, now rubs alongside scholarship reading his studios' 2013 bareback transition (Brennan, 2020, pp. 17–19) and event marketing of the condom's absence (Tziallas, 2015a, pp. 386–393) in Lucas films since. While from an audience standpoint, comparatively early studies of reactions to bareback porn that deemed such texts dangerous for "making unsafe sex sound exciting and glamorous and cool, and it's none of those" (quoted in Carballo-Diéguez & Bauermeister, 2004, p. 9) now need to be understood in line with that critical moment in which this discourse was created and current conditions.

Textually, and at the point of reception (as Mowlabocus et al., 2014, found through textual analysis and focus group methods), subcultural understandings of bareback porn are dependent on a variety of factors that include "the age, body type, and racial identities of the performers; the setting, context, and mise-en-scène of the pornographic scene; and the deployment of power relations between the insertive and receptive partners" (p. 1462). The "'cool' deviancy" (Mowlabocus, 2007, p. 218) and resolutely taboo dimensions connoted by bareback and "HIV-risks contexts" (Carballo-Diéguez & Bauermeister, 2004) in the 1990s and early 2000s now need to be tempered with changing attitudes to the practice-as-risk, such as from the mid-2010s when the iconography of bareback as connected with "the North American cowboy and his quintessential masculinity" (Gilreath, 2011, p. 169) seemed to linger while some of its harder-edged health connotations started to fall away.

Bareback's "cool" connotations lingered even as *perceptions* of risk faded as a "succession to a state of increasing 'condomlessness'" (Brennan, 2020, p. 128) swept through gay porn to make the condom's absence the "center" (Mowlabocus et al., 2013, p. 525) once more. Bareback became a key gay porn selling point, in order words. A marker of intimacy that carried a degree of expectation. As Kiss (in Nielsen & Kiss, 2015, p. 132) observed, acts of visualized internal ejaculation (known as "anal creampies"), which would have been deemed extreme—and the exclusive purview of "back-alley" studios like Treasure Island Media (TIM)—a decade earlier, were in 2015 generally considered "vanilla" in mainstream sources like *Sean Cody* (see Tollini, 2017, for readings across these sources).

Across the literature, performances and subversions of masculinity (i.e., Florêncio, 2020b; Tollini, 2017) and queer theoretical positions, especially around time/temporality (i.e., Brennan, 2022b; Florêncio, 2020a), are some of the more dominant textual concerns, while key audience arguments have addressed risky/safer-sex behavioral effects (Eaton et al., 2011) and accounted for national contexts (Vörös, 2014) in the reception and sensemaking of this porn. Recently, scholars (i.e., Longstaff, 2019) have also expanded understanding of the above themes through account for bareback in context with other gay porn representations of "risky" sex, such as chemsex porn, while ideas like "becoming-pig" (Florêncio, 2020b) and consent quandaries like "stealthing" (Brennan, 2017b) capture an inherent impulse of bareback (porn and practice) to keep a presence at the fringe—holding space alongside antiretroviral therapies, online porn, and sexual drug use, even as condomlessness has spread into the commercial mainstream. Bareback's symbolism, accounting for its "important function among gay men" and inclusive of its "deviant" dimensions that carry a "more multifaceted view" today, in sexual practice and gay porn, is as "a form of communal bonding and a challenge to gay assimilation and homonormativity" (Nielsen & Morrison, 2019, p. 215).

Gay-for-Pay. "Gay-for-pay" receives separate consideration because it has been a dominant and recurrent condition of gay porn, it has attracted concentrated and ongoing scholarly interest, and it is unique to the gay tradition—all factors that apply to bareback as well. As is suggested by Kiss and Morrison's (2021) recent definition, gay-for-pay is a "strictly for remuneration" gay porn fantasy with distinctive text ("inauthentic narratives") and industry ("male performers are heterosexual") contours that defy clean categorization in either (p. 1509). Compared with bareback, which has a messier relationship between its representation and lived identities/sexual practices, and without ignoring entirely meaning at the point of reception, gay-for-pay is, by definition, *representational* (even at the level of performance)—making it a bridge to larger debates, such as the relations between porn and fantasy (see Barker, 2014).

Drawing on Jane Caputi's definition of porn as a "worldview" that genders domination and submission, Gilreath (2011) points out the paradox for gay men, namely, that "in gay pornography we see what heterosexuality is" (pp. 169–170). Though part of "the problem with gay pornography" agenda (see Gilreath, 2011, pp. 169–203), situating gay porn within a straight supremacist system does explain the staying power of a sizable number of its stars—from Jeff Stryker and Ryan Idol (Bozelka, 2013) to Johnny Rapid (Brennan, 2022b), whose across-decades successes are connected with gay-for-pay identities and, especially in early cases, being "'made' by directors (Matt Sterling and John Travis for Stryker) or agents (David Forest with Idol[ ])" (Escoffier, 2007, p. 179); the past decade's most popular (in terms of visitor traffic) sources of gay porn, too, that take "ostensive straightness" as a narrative aim—that is, *Sean Cody*, *Gay Hoopla*, *Corbin Fisher*, and *Chaos Men*, to draw from a 2018 list of the top 10 Internet sources (Brennan, 2018b, p. 914).

Longer, "softcore" histories can be traced via "beefcake to hardcore" (Escoffier, 2009) social and production conditions. These gesture to (among other sources) the need-for-the-hetero-guise of McCarthy-era physique magazines—and are conditions, especially today, not confined to the "stars." In the Internet porn age, one way this prevalence presents itself is in the corn-fed, all-American, first-name-only,-please college "dudes" of the likes of *Sean Cody* and *Corbin Fisher*—read: nonstars, on the down low, only available to gay men through gay porn. Jane Ward's (2015) *Not Gay* is a key text in the Internet context, Chapter 5 especially (pp. 153–190), which reads *Haze Him* in connection with gay fetishization of hypermasculinity and "straight-acting" performances. On the men of *Haze Him*, Ward remarks, these "most likely gay or 'gay for pay' actors, know enough about the exceptionalizing logics that facilitate sex between straight men to be able to engage in believable not-gay sex on screen" (p. 181)—a point illustrative of the longer history of sex between men and the constructedness of these performances, serving as a useful parallel with extant understandings of gay-for-pay porn: namely as "inauthentic narratives" (Kiss & Morrison, 2021), "believably" (Ward, 2015, p. 181) and "credibly" (Escoffier, 2003) gay-sexually performed—the actual sexuality (gay or "gay for pay") of these men, notwithstanding.

Reticence and coercion through financial incentive have been key narrative drivers in gay-for-pay porn, both in American (Bozelka, 2013; Mercer, 2012b; Stadler, 2013) and non-Western contexts (Brennan, 2019a). On its industry contours, and the "making" of gay-for-pay performers in particular, implications include the promotion of a hegemonic ideal of masculinity, as Burke's (2016a) 11-month 2012/2013 participant-observation study at From Behind Films revealed. Such studies support a view of gay-for-pay performers as polished professionals, stars of whom are consciously developed and marketed—starting with Stryker in the mid-1980s, who emerged as "a new type of gay porn superstar" (Escoffier, 2007, p. 178). Escoffier's (2003) essay is a key text in this regard, using scripting theory to support the place of gay-for-pay personas within the industry, and more recent textual studies support the continued professionalization of gay-for-pay as a profitable marketing strategy (i.e., Burke, 2016b, with a content analysis of "str8" performers).

Kiss et al. (2019) explored the "believability and erotic value" of the gay-for-pay male in gay porn from a gay audience perspective, showing that narrative and performer strategies such as reluctance to engage in certain acts (i.e., bottoming) were read by viewers as markers of believability. Interestingly, the authors also observed few statistically significant associations for internalized homonegativity. Though scholars have read certain sources of gay-for-pay porn in line with a homophobic framework (i.e., Henze, 2013, with *Broke Straight Boys*) and stars such as Stryker have sometimes spoken publicly in favor of a more fluid understanding of sexuality, the issue of reception and potential *effects* of this pornography on gay men is an area in need of further research, and generally, scholars beyond the antiporn framework have favored a view of gay porn, including scenes that might appear to carry homophobic undertones, as having a "complex range of discourses at play" (Mercer, 2004, p. 166, regarding prison narratives).

Complexity has generally been served by the textual tradition, traced especially to Dyer, and carried through in the gay-for-pay context via two essays in a 2013 *JC* issue. Kevin John Bozelka (2013) examined the "gaze" in classic Stryker and Idol films, while John Paul Stadler (2013) adopted a more contemporary, pressing perspective, considering how digital production and dissemination of gay-for-pay reorients spectatorship toward amateurism and metanarratives. Mercer's (2012b) perspective on gay-for-pay in the Internet era is also valuable, his reading of *Bait Bus* and the "predatory gay male" (pp. 545–549) that connects with more recent evaluations of the genre, such as Kiss and Morrison (2021): both *readings* in the textual tradition.

TEXT

In a somewhat alarmist 1997 essay in *Cinema Journal*, Champagne (1997) set out "polemically the absurdity and perhaps even perniciousness of submitting gay porno films in particular to close textual analysis," believing the method to carry "dangers" to the film studies discipline should its scholars treat these texts as "just another film genre to be covered" (p. 76). Writing 20 years later, Mercer (2017b) argued that a proliferation of close textual readings of gay porn did not come to pass, something that in fact constituted "a blind spot for the field" (p. 18, noting exceptions including Hoang, 2004; Pronger, 1990) that he sought to redress through the "sustained fashion" (2017b, p. 18) of his monograph.

Michael C. Bolton (2004) critiques Champagne, including his preference for a "culturally-minded analysis of gay porn," with sites like gay porn theaters or arcades seen as more meaningful points for interpretation than the confines of texts themselves, something

Bolton connects with extant conceptions of porn more broadly as a "body genre" (Williams, 1991, p. 3). Certainly, queer theory would come to offer much to close reading—Eve Kosofsky Sedgwick's paranoid and reparative reading lenses, for example (published in the same year as Champagne's essay), are now widely adopted in gay porn readings (i.e., essays in Waugh & Arroyo, 2019).

In my view, Champagne's critique blinded itself to the active nature of reading texts (especially media texts beyond film, i.e., television; Fiske & Hartley, 1978) and the ability—of scholars and audiences alike—to engage in sensitive, context- and culturally minded reading. Also, to be able to engage with ideological problematics without necessarily being harmed by these; in fact, to draw them out for contemplation and understanding, positions and competencies at odds with an assessment of close reading as tending toward "value neutral and free from ideological underpinning" analyses and that are also suggestive of Champagne's wider project of anti–gay porn scholarship (p. 76).

By the second decade of the 21st century, the qualitative textual tradition in gay porn became more significant across the literature, helped in large part by Mercer's monograph. But the tradition had a wider-reaching and earlier impact than Mercer suggested. Notably, via his own investigations of gay porn iconography that came prior to 2017, but also through textual readings of decidedly problematic aspects of gay porn pointed to in the "Dominant Conditions" section (in the abandon of the condom and eroticization of ostensive straightness across bareback and gay-for-pay conditions), and further through founding voices such as Dyer—through which the film tradition origins of gay porn studies is often traced.

Bulge: Iconography (& Prototypes). Following Dyer's 1993 views around the "stereotype," Mercer (2003) offered the field "homosexual prototypes" to understand repetition and the construction of the generic, and to identify and define "the characteristics of the iconography and types deployed in contemporary American gay video pornography" (p. 280). Importantly, Mercer made clear that his use of the term placed emphasis on "textual qualities rather than the responses to them" (p. 280) and that performers are not prototypes; rather, prototypes are "a conjunction of specific presentational characteristics, iconography and physical attributes that emerges within the location of a specific text" (p. 283). While audience (responses) and industry (performers) dimensions exist, Mercer's primarily textual concerns of presentational characteristics and locations in gay porn is an important distinction, one that connects with broader definitions of porn (as fantasy, as *text*) and with it continues the departure from harms-based readings (while not foreclosing considerations of "harmful" or problematic texts regarding race or online discourse, for instance).

Prototypes are inclusive of positionalities, which, in gay porn, have been to the general exclusion of versatility—an aspect Young (2017) demonstrates via a reading of *Gag the Fag*, which, in Mercer's (2017a) assessment, "reminds readers of the staged and performed nature of the sexual acts represented in gay porn" (p. 129). A preference for top/bottom textual representations demonstrates the fantasy contours of the form—not always aligned with the lived reality of gay men. I (Brennan, 2018b) supported this via a reading of 6,900 gay porn performer profiles in line with disclosed penis size and sexual position, where, by combining qualitative and quantitative textual approaches, a sample-wide correlation in the most popular online gay porn sites between smaller penis sizes (5–6.5 inches) and receptive sexual acts (bottoming), and larger (8.5–13 inches) with penetrative acts (topping), showed representations of versatility to be at odds with survey research of gay men's sexual practices and identifications, which has favored versatility.

A top or bottom gay porn preference helps explain the popularity of the "power bottom" prototype, "an autonomous sexual adventurer" who "orchestrates sexual situations that will result in him getting what he wants, which is usually a well-endowed, prototypical top who will satisfy his need for anal sex" (Mercer, 2012c, p. 220). Other popular gay porn prototypes include the eroticized older man or "daddy" (Mercer, 2012a) and the seemingly submissive and usually slender (and White) youth or "twink" (Tortorici, 2008, p. 205), with combinations also common, especially in line with performative masculinity, as well as transitions over the course of a career, as I (Brennan, 2016a) show via a study of lollipop/muscle/power bottom twink Jake Lyons and the performer's transition to cum dumpster/piss pig. The "jock" persona is also frequently conjured through use of costumes connoting competitive (often violent, i.e., American football) sport and locker room eroticism (Pronger, 1990, pp. 125–176).

Mercer (2003) posits two questions in relation to gay porn prototypes: first, what *forms* these take and, second, *why* they exist and their *function* (p. 287). His schema and these two questions encompass both fixtures of gay porn culture and more ideological (including possibly exploitative) implications, respectively. Exemplars of "strident masculinity" such as soldiers, sailors, and construction workers are pointed to as populating gay porn texts (p. 287), as gay porn embraces what Jamie Gough (1989) describes as "masculinity as a sexual fetish" (p. 121; examples of alternative and nonnormative body types in the literature is a generally underexamined area, though exceptions do exist, i.e., Highberg, 2011, on fat and Thorneycroft, 2021, on crip representation). Such fetishization was made famous by the illustrations of Tom and Finland, among others, who rose to prominence in the pages of publications like *Physique Pictorial*. Shaun Cole (2014)—using the example Colt Studio founder Jim French's films, 1967–1981—connects the way "characters" are dressed in gay porn with such icons of masculinity and gay culture (such as the leatherman, motorcycle cop, and "gay clone," i.e., Al Parker).

Settings/spaces are another key dimension of gay porn iconography, with scene set pieces as rich in symbolism as character costume. It is in this arena that Mercer (2004) continued his textual analysis with a consideration of "the myth" of the prison in American gay porn via 110 commercially available videos produced between 1987 and 2002, confirming these as "idealized spaces" for acts of "voyeurism, narcissistic display and active/passive role-play" (p. 152). Dyer (1994) had read the prison setting a decade earlier in relation to a performance by Stryker in John Travis's 1986 *Powertool*, where he describes the pleasure of this feature "for many" as "the willing suspension of disbelief, the happy entering into the fantasy that *Powertool* is all happening in a prison cell" (p. 50).

Prison settings have been popular in gay porn and scholarship because—like barracks, boarding schools, and naval vessels—they are all-male spaces that create a degree of same-sex eroticism all their own, as captured by Escoffier's (2003) concept of "situational homosexuality" (p. 531). More *queer* spatial considerations have also been explored, such as the clubs, porn stores, and hotel rooms of TIM videos that have been conceived as "analogies to the men in the porn" (Morris & Paasonen, 2014, p. 227), together with the on-the-road urban spaces of gonzo-reality sites like *Bait Bus* and frat-house aesthetics of *Fraternity X/Frat X* (Brennan,

2016b). Mercer's (2004) use of myth was in a more literal, *forms* sense—gay mythologies drawn from diverse textual references—though he does cite Roland Barthes, and Mercer's work on prototypes helps inform work on place and constructions of national identity in gay porn texts.

Thrust: Race (& Place).
Mercer (2017b) wrote,

> I want to argue that whiteness is not just presented as a fact, as Dyer [1997, p. 2] describes it as 'non-raced' and as an ideal, but is demonstrably positioned as the default or 'exnominated' reading position from which masculinity is to be understood in gay porn. (p. 150)

Mercer's take, including the presentation of an "American version of whiteness," can be usefully applied to a range of studies, especially those grappling with national myths (i.e., McKee, 1999, on Australian; Brennan, 2019a, on Czech). Clare N. Westcott's (2004) reading of Australian, Canadian, and South American national identity in gay porn as part of Morrison's first special embodied a certain transnational spirit that has increased in the current century through readings of men and locales *outside* the Anglo-European sphere. This has included constructions of Arab (Cervulle & Rees-Roberts, 2009, via French gay porn), Indian (Baas, 2021, admittedly, using ethnographic methods and a focus on the popularity of the bodybuilder prototype), and Latino men (Subero, 2010). At an individual level, star studies have also proved increasingly popular, most notably the analyses of "transnational, ethno-flexible" (Tziallas, 2015b) François Sagat, who, in the current decade, Gabriel Ojeda-Sagué (2021) read in line with the "both racial and professional crossover potential" of his "whiteness" (p. 107).

The classic text here, however, is Richard Fung's (1991) essay on the eroticized Asian in gay porn, while historically, the aspect in greatest need of dedicated scholarship has been consideration of the Black man, which Mercer (2017b) described as "perhaps one of the most potent of the sexual prototypes of gay porn" (p. 150). Although inroads had been made toward consideration of the Black prototype in gay porn prior to the 2020s, generally this was part of broader (i.e., McBride, 2005, pp. 88–132) and aligned (i.e., Dean, 2009, pp. 159–160) gay projects. This gap in scholarship was redressed in 2021 through Desmond Francis Goss's monograph, which unpacked the stereotypes of Black men on which gay porn relies, including as "missing links" through excessive focus on their dark phalluses and essentialist representations of sexual aspects of racial identity—aspects, Goss noted, that are more prevalent in commercial gay porn compared with user-submitted content. Also recently, the representation of racial abuse by White "police officers" on Black male bodies has been explored (i.e., Brennan, 2019c; Smith et al., 2022).

INDUSTRY

It is unsurprising that celebrity and stardom have attracted attention in the literature—stars being an object of analysis Dyer is particularly well known for. The status of the gay porn "star" formed a key part of understanding the economics and constructions of gay porn's *performers*. I use "performer" rather than "actor" as a deliberate separation of these men from the *work* of men in other entertainment media, something that captures the multimodal nature of gay porn appearances and the implications of such appearances, which have been a divisive avenue of debate in the literature. Mercer (2017b) describes Escoffier's (2009) *Bigger Than Life* as "belonging to the lineage of Waugh's historical work" and as "ostensibly written for a popular readership" (Mercer, 2017b, p. 13); Escoffier's critical approaches to gay porn outside of the academy that captures something of his significance to *industry* understandings, work conditions particularly.

Bulge: Work Conditions (& Stakeholder Insights). Kendall and Funk (2004) argue that gay porn, like heteroporn, "*is* degradation, violence, and harm," chiefly because it "uses real people, many vulnerable and easily exploited" (p. 93). Powerfully, the authors follow this statement with words by 1980s gay porn star Joey Stefano, who died of a drug overdose in 1994, aged 26:

No job.
No money.
No self-esteem.
No confidence.
All I have is my looks and body.
And that's not working anymore.
I feel washed up.
Drug problem.
Hate life.
HIV-positive! (Kendall & Funk, 2004, p. 93)

Stefano serves as poster boy in Kendall and Funk for the dangers of gay porn to its "many vulnerable and easily exploited" performers, inclusive of the star's rejection by the industry after testing positive for HIV—a disease whose career and health impacts on additional performers such as Casey Donovan and Parker were charted in late-2000s biographies by Roger Edmonson. Gilda Padva (2019) applies the Frankfurt School's 1940s notion of a "culture industry" as mass deception to porn and links in the criticisms of Kendall and Funk (among others) to place the gay variant within a harms rubric—that is, via its "phallic cult" status (p. 1309) and (supposedly) top or bottom "without consent" power nonchoice contouring (p. 1310).

Though Padva was careful to include counterpositions, the "real people" point—buoyed by a steady output of scholarly collections delving into the changing complexities of male sex work—has, arguably, kept considerations of potential harms at the fore of industry-based gay porn studies. Certainly, when compared with other fields of a similar age and lineage (i.e., fan studies and "aca–fans"), the importance of "critical distance" between scholars and industry seems more pronounced for social, historical, and political reasons. This is not to discount the contributions of industry stakeholders to the literature, however, which have been significant.

Pornographers have found a voice through scholarship, particularly on high-stakes subjects like bareback (Lucas, 2006). In this regard, TIM's Paul Morris, arguably gay porn's most controversial figure, has also been the most influentially vocal of "academic–pornographers": as a single author in an academic journal's "forum" (Morris, 2016) and in "dialogue" (see Morris &

Paasonen, 2014) and collaboration (Morris & Paasonen, 2019) with Susanna Paasonen, a key voice in porn studies more broadly. Such a presence, however, should not foreclose scrutiny, as criticism of Lucas has shown (Brennan, 2020).

Industry "insider" perspectives (Scuglia, 2004, 2015) have also appeared in a limited way in the literature, while the recollections of canonical filmmakers like Poole and writings of performers like Aaron Lawrence—especially the more radical voices from the AIDS era, of which Scott O'Hara is the most notable—have been mined for scholarly insight (i.e., Race, 2010, reading O'Hara in the context of bareback, the term's genesis that has been attributed to this performer). Such contributions have made self-life-writing a valuable resource for understanding social change and life circumstances of gay porn's producers and performers (see Cohler, 2004, who reads the works of Poole, O'Hara, and Lawrence).

Self-life-writings, those of Lawrence particularly, have helped demonstrate "the retrogressive dynamic," a 1930s concept from Paul Cressey that Escoffier (2007) applied to gay porn and has been a major influence on the literature. Escoffier charts the ways in which performers attempt to confront the retrogressive dynamic by limiting the number of filmic performances, diversifying sexual repertoire or shifting to "economically complementary forms of sex work," either within or outside gay porn (2007, p. 173). The concept offers insight into the economic realities performers face—gay economic, historic, and politic foci of which have been dominant threads throughout Escoffier's scholarship—along with changing conditions, captured by gay porn turns of men from reality television and social media (Arroyo, 2017). Escoffier's concept is suggestive of the pressures on performers, particularly as these relate to the lived experience of sex work, something that has resulted (in the past decade especially) in some growth of ethnographic studies—inclusive of gay porn individuals (Johnson, 2013) and studios, with both performers (Burke, 2016b) and producers/managers (Law, 2021) being considered. Each of these studies can be seen to seek to understand, through various lenses (from love to stigma, in the case of Johnson and Law), the consequences of intimate labor.

Gay-for-pay positions have also been explored. Building on ideas from his 2017 monograph, Nicolas de Villiers (2019) explores how the behind-the-scenes motel interviews with gay porn workers in two documentaries create "a hybrid mode of *confession porn* or *gay-for-pay confessional*" and advocate a shift in scrutiny, from those who have gay-for-pay sex to the "ethics and motives of the filmmakers and the 'knowingness' and fascination of their mostly gay male audience," highlighting the persistent ethical quandaries surrounding the "real men" who contribute to the creation of gay porn and its fantasies (p. 178). Complexities borne of real-people pressures have invited reflection across text and audience as well. Returning to Stefano, Jeffreys (2002) reads pain in one of his performances, recognition of pain that, she suggests, would be rejected by gay men as it is incongruent with gay culture's commitment to gay-porn-as-liberation readings.

Thrusts: Medium, Spaces, Archives. Whitney Strub (2019) argues in a similar vein to Jeffreys, tracing the transgressive sex acts that were "sanitized" from the 1970s porn oeuvre (gay porn films included) during the U.S. sex wars. He argues that porn edited its own history, especially when access and academic attention increased following VHS. Mercer (2017b) is among those to recognize medium's significance to the literature, dividing gay porn scholarship into two "phases": "pre-web, pre-digital" and "post-web" (pp. 11–18). The first phase is inclusive of film and its spaces—gay porn theaters, for instance, have been a vibrant avenue to account for gay-culture connections, especially via ethnographic approaches (i.e., Capino, 2005)—and VHS and its store/home spaces.

The "VHS revolution" was also a porn revolution, marking a radical shift in both studio and amateur porn. Concerning the latter, the concept of the "home movie" took on a whole new meaning and represented a decisive shift in what has been described as the "democratizing of porn" (Tziallas in Nielsen & Kiss, 2015, p. 125) and the *experience* of porn (i.e., in domestic spaces; Bolton, 2004). But this also came with certain anxieties that new media often face—as captured by the "video nasty" moral panic, whereby porn entering households was seen to gnaw at the fabric of the once-wholesome home.

It was a revolution that persists, converging in the digital or "post-web" age, and disrupting certain industry conditions. Such disruption has been observed both through modes of gay porn production and distribution (i.e., with the rise of piracy and tube sites; Tsika, 2017) and through the experience and pressures on performers, whose agency, arguably, has increased via self-presentation opportunities—via social media and with the rise of new platforms for self-production, such as OnlyFans (Ryan, 2019, pp. 119–136). Such shifts have allowed gay porn performers to speak directly with their audiences in a new world of "networked intimacy" (Wang, 2021), all conditions of gay porn's *medium*.

Arrival at the commercial "DIY gay porn" that circulates on tube sites and via social platforms has been an emerging post-web phenomenon that, most recently, has included crossovers with social media influencers and microcelebrities, and contexts outside of the Anglo-sphere (i.e., in China; Song, 2021). These industry conditions have come with due acknowledgment of intersections with text and audience positions in the literature. Textual positions that are inclusive of "aesthetics" of amateur and "gonzo" forms of commercial gay porn and narrative inclusion of technology, such as "hook-up apps" on *Sketchy Sex* (Brennan, 2016b) or earlier-period throwbacks through a mobilization of VHS aesthetics (Brennan, 2022a).

In the audience stakes, while the affordances of online gay porn consumption—and "flow to float" of tube sites (Arroyo, 2016)—have led some scholars (i.e., Poole & Milligan, 2018) to the conclusion that there is greater diversity and new opportunities for personal connection with expressions and identities presented in gay porn, others have observed anxieties and a "paranoid pleasure" that may arise in a viewer as he peeps through "the keyholes of technology" as part of his ever-converging, and often participatory, gay porn consumptive practices (Vanderwees, 2019, p. 23); the commercial/amateur aspects of the content—especially as circulated "decontextualized" across tubes sites—have meant that the commercial/amateur provenance of the gay sex recordings may not always be clear (Brennan, 2018a).

I count among attention-to-medium groundswell development of and account for the "archival value" (Barriault, 2009) of gay porn, inclusive of personal collections, both amateur and studio. Such archives that are inclusive of, returning to Strub (2019), revisiting received wisdoms via the critical reading and reevaluation of these archives and some of the "historical fantasies" (Hilderbrand, 2016) that characterized 1970s-era gay porn. To this end, memory studies has offered up productive inroads for the subfield to aid in the understanding and rethinking of the past: to, especially, demystify the so-called "Golden Age" of gay porn (Herron, 2021).

AUDIENCE

In the past decade, accounting for user perspectives on gay porn has been a powerful means of demonstrating complexity at the point of reception and dissuading a sole conception of the genre using a gay affirmative or harms-based dichotomy. Corneau et al. (2017) found this in their survey research, concluding that such dichotomies "may not do justice to users' experiences, since various levels of agreement are present in users' perspectives when confronted with contrasting and often contradictory arguments" about gay porn (p. 223). Arguably, the contribution of social scientists—Morrison chief among these—who, empirically, have explored potential "effects" of gay porn for its (gay male) viewers has been most influential in moving the subfield along, both away from its dichotomist "media effects" roots and the textual, film studies tradition.

Bulge: Effects. The success of scholars in shaking gay porn's harms-based connotations can be seen as anchored in a key received wisdom about these texts. Namely, that gay porn "participates in the cultural construction of desire" (Dyer, 1994, p. 49) and "has always had a more exalted (and accepted) position in gay culture than in straight" (Thomas, 2000, pp. 61–62). Contrary perspectives, such as John Stoltenberg's (1990) argument that gay porn communicates to its spectators a sexual disconnecting that divorcees the sexual spectacle from concepts such as "communion" (p. 253), were generally positions of diminishing returns across the literature, and in fact, as with Stoltenberg, could be argued to also anchor gay porn to gay lived identity (even if it is a discounted one). Jacques Rothmann (2013) uses the U.S. and South African contexts to engage in "theoretical contemplation" with the conventional wisdom on gay porn's importance to gay men, especially the ways in which "gay men may possibly 'do' and 'use' their sexual orientation" (p. 22).

Studies seeking empirical *proof* for such wisdom among consumers were, however, late to emerge. As Morrison et al. observed in 2007: "Although perceived to be a ubiquitous and profitable element of gay culture, to date, only one published study [Duggan & McCreary, 2004] has investigated the correlates of gay men's exposure to pornography" (p. 33). Jochen Peter and Patti M. Valkenburg's (2016) 20-year survey of empirical studies exploring the prevalence, predictors, and implications of young people's use of porn offers further support for this view, finding that in the mid-2010s, research "suffered" from a heteronormativity bias, the authors only citing one exception within their youth-focused survey—Renata Arrington-Sanders et al. (2015), who examined the role of gay porn in the sexual development of Black same-sex-attracted male youth. The result of a scholarly corpus that was, until fairly recently, almost wholly focused on heteroporn was that "knowledge about the functions, meanings, and implications of pornography use" among gay men was "restricted" (Peter & Valkenburg, 2016, p. 527, speaking in this instance about gay and other nonheteronormative youth specifically).

Morrison's (2004b) focus group exploratory study in his special was an important first step in addressing neglect of the gay perspective among social scientists, a neglect that had created a situation whereby "little is known about how gay men perceive this medium" (p. 167). Morrison found that discussants tended to view gay porn from a "utilitarian perspective," namely as a masturbatory aid with little significance "vis-à-vis gay men's attitudes and behaviours" (p. 167). Morrison has continued to be a key voice in the empirical search for correlates between gay men's exposure to gay porn and, I believe, has been foundational to the diversification of the subfield. A Morrison et al. (2007) Internet-based survey, for example, found little support for anecdotal harms-based perspectives on gay porn (i.e., Kendall & Funk, 2004).

Starting in the mid-2010s (around the time of Morrison's second special), there was a notable increase in scholars (especially social scientists using an online survey method) exploring, via testable methods, the *effects* of gay porn. In particular, scholars explored effects pertaining to body image/ideals (i.e., Gleason & Sprankle, 2019), bareback/sexual risk behavior (i.e., Galos et al., 2015), and, an emerging area of concern, internalized homonegativity (Kiss et al., 2019). Such studies are vital to many of the extant arguments against harms-based perspectives (Gleason & Sprankle, 2019, for example, who were left to conclude that sexual minority men in their study did not report greater social physique anxiety, greater drive for muscularity, or reduced genital body image through their exposure to gay porn).

Recent review articles (i.e., Paslakis et al., 2022) continue to note a "scarcity of studies" (p. 743) exploring porn effects among nonheterosexual samples, however, confirming that there remains work to be done in this space, especially outside of the Anglo-European sphere. Though race has been a popular "problematic" object of analysis in textual research, the audience aspect has been lacking. As Corneau et al. (2021) note, very few studies have focused on the role porn plays in influencing and modeling sexual desire based on race and ethnicity, with these authors' study pointing to some concrete grounds for the "race problem" in gay porn and coming up with user profiles (from a sample of 974) for racialized desire among audiences.

Qualitative studies also have much to offer here, and Joseph N. Goh's (2017) interviews with 30 Malaysian men is an example of welcome expansion of understandings on gay porn audiences. Goh (2017) found support for the view that gay porn can function as "a means to perform and make sense of sexuality [and] a self-validated avenue of pleasure," as well as attending to the struggles born of a national context where sexuality remains taboo and porn is restricted by law (p. 447).

Thrust: Discourse. William L. Leap (2011), via online audience discourse on the 2009 Lucas film *Men of Israel*, argued for complexity at the point of reception, pointing to his study's analyzed discourse as evidence that the film's audience was engaging in "a broader framework" than Lucas had necessarily intended, with viewers "using transnational rather than film-specific criteria to guide their 'reading' of the Israeli-centered narrative" (p. 932). Since then, language and specifically Internet-based discourse analyses have been a key thrust in understanding the sense-making practices of audiences.

I have been a key figure in promoting online discourse as a key site of knowledge generation that provides insight into the diverse perspectives of gay porn viewers, attending especially to ideological implications of certain "extreme" pornographies. My first analysis came around the mid-2010s spike in scholarly interest and combined star study of Lyons with textual analysis of online discourse to make sense of a culture of "disposal and disgust" that surrounded Lyons's career-ending transition to bareback porn (Brennan, 2016a, p. 20). A strength of my contribution has been the advancement of understandings across time. Recently, for example, I reevaluated my 2016 analysis through concepts of time and aging and a more recent performer's (Rapid) bareback transition that was read quite differently by audiences (Brennan, 2022b).

Sustained attention to audience discourse—notably in journal articles spanning a number of years rather than via a single monograph—has aided in understanding the complex and shifting sense-making positions of audiences and helped me demonstrate a growth in "extreme" gay porn, notably, incremental advancement that avoids reification at the same time as I grapple—often through combined text- and audience-based methods—with the ethical quandaries in fantasy areas that include "abuse" in institutional settings (Brennan, 2017a), sex addiction (Brennan, 2016b), nonconsensual condom removal (Brennan, 2017b, pp. 327–329), sex tourism in Eastern Europe (Brennan, 2019a), and intergenerational familial relationships in the gay youthful-adult category (Brennan, 2022a).

GAY PORN NOW (& BEYOND!)

Thrusts and *bulges* organize gay porn's scholarship into eminent and emerging concerns in this qualitative project, with scope to be updated. What is a thrust now may bulge in successive updates, and colleagues—serial and one-off "dabblers" and career scholars akin—it is hoped, will be served by the thematic organizations within: to stake their own position on and contribution to the advancement of gay porn scholarship. Across each of the three categories are numerous topics not addressed here in detail but that may come to feature more prominently in the literature in future. These include political dimensions of parodies (Brennan, 2019b) in *text*, impending impacts and shakeups of "platform death" (Floegel, 2022) in *industry*, and how other fields and disciplines (i.e., fandom studies; McKee, 2018) may continue to challenge media effects dichotomies in *audience*, to name just a few potential growth areas. Following Mercer (2017a), this survey sought to capture something of gay porn *now!*, with due acknowledgment to history. The study of gay porn overcame erasure and underrepresentation to thrive today. To appropriate Laura Kipnis (1996, p. 167), through the present survey's structure profoundly and paradoxically social and acutely historical dimensions of gay porn's *future!* seem not only assured, but may be accounted for as well.

FURTHER READING

Escoffier, J. (2007). Scripting the sex: Fantasy, narrative, and sexual scripts in pornographic films. In M. S. Kimmel (Ed.), *The sexual self: The construction of sexual scripts* (pp. 61–79). Vanderbilt University Press.

Mercer, J. (2006). Seeing is believing: Constructions of stardom and the gay porn star in U.S. gay video pornography. In S. Holmes & S. Redmond (Eds.), *Framing celebrity* (pp. 145–160). Routledge.

Rzepczynski, B. (2015). Pornography, gay male. In A. Bolin & P. Whelehan (Eds.), *The international encyclopedia of human sexuality*. Wiley-Blackwell. https://onlinelibrary.wiley.com/doi/10.1002/9781118896877.wbiehs365

REFERENCES

Adams-Thies, B. (2015). Choosing the right partner means choosing the right porn: How gay porn communicates in the home. *Porn Studies*, 2(2–3), 123–136. https://doi.org/10.1080/23268743.2015.1060007

Arrington-Sanders, R., Harper, G. W., Morgan, A., Ogunbajo, A., Trent, M., & Fortenberry, J. D. (2015). The role of sexually explicit material in the sexual development of same-sex-attracted Black adolescent males. *Archives of Sexual Behavior*, 44(3), 597–608. https://doi.org/10.1007/s10508-014-0416-x

Arroyo, B. (2016). From flow to float: Moving through porn tube sites. *Porn Studies*, 3(3), 308–310. https://doi.org/10.1080/23268743.2016.1148328

Arroyo, B. (2017). An amplification of being: Chris Crocker and the becoming of a transindividual porn star. *Porn Studies*, 4(2), 193–209. https://doi.org/10.1080/23268743.2017.1317970

Attwood, F., & Smith, C. (2014). *Porn Studies*: An introduction. *Porn Studies*, 1(1–2), 1–6. https://doi.org/10.1080/23268743.2014.887308

Baas, M. (2021). Capitalizing on desire: (Re)producing and consuming class in Indian "gay" pornography. *Porn Studies*. https://doi.org/10.1080/23268743.2021.1977174

Barker, M. (2014). The "problem" of sexual fantasies. *Porn Studies*, 1(1–2), 143–160. https://doi.org/10.1080/23268743.2013.863656

Barriault, M. (2009). Hard to dismiss: The archival value of gay male erotica and pornography. *Archivaria*, 68, 219–246.

Bishop, C. (2015). "Cocked, locked and ready to fuck?" A synthesis and review of the gay male pornography literature. *Psychology & Sexuality*, 6(1), 5–27. https://doi.org/10.1080/19419899.2014.983739

Blachford, G. (1978). Looking at pornography: Erotica and the socialist morality. *Gay Left*, 6, 16–20.

Bolton, M. (2004). Cumming to an end: The male orgasm and domestic consumption of gay pornography. *M/C Journal*, 7(4). https://doi.org/10.5204/mcj.2398

Bozelka, K.J. (2013). The gay-for-pay gaze in gay male pornography. *Jump Cut*, 55. http://www.ejumpcut.org/archive/jc55.2013/BozelkaGayForPay/1.html

Brennan, J. (2016a). "Bare-backing spoils everything. He's spoiled goods": Disposal and disgust, a study of retired power bottom twink Jake Lyons. *Porn Studies*, 3(1), 20–33. https://doi.org/10.1080/23268743.2015.1074867

Brennan, J. (2016b). The "gonzo aesthetic" in gay porn: Fraternity X and Sketchy Sex. *Porn Studies*, 3(4), 386–397. https://doi.org/10.1080/23268743.2016.1241156

Brennan, J. (2017a). Abuse porn: Reading reactions to Boys Halfway House. *Sexuality & Culture*, 21(2), 423–440. https://doi.org/10.1007/s12119-016-9397-3

Brennan, J. (2017b). Stealth breeding: Bareback without consent. *Psychology & Sexuality*, 8(4), 318–333. https://doi.org/10.1080/19419899.2017.1393451

Brennan, J. (2018a). Microporn in the digital media age: Fantasy out of context. *Porn Studies*, 5(2), 152–155. https://doi.org/10.1080/23268743.2017.1306453

Brennan, J. (2018b). Size matters: Penis size and sexual position in gay porn profiles. *Journal of Homosexuality*, 65(7), 912–933. https://doi.org/10.1080/00918369.2017.1364568

Brennan, J. (2019a). Exploitation in all-male pornography set in the Czech Republic. *European Journal of Cultural Studies*, 22(1), 18–36. https://doi.org/10.1177/1367549417719012

Brennan, J. (2019b). Gay porn (horror) parodies. In S. Holland, R. Shail, & S. Gerrard (Eds.), *Gender and contemporary horror in film* (pp. 101–115). Emerald.

Brennan, J. (2019c). Gay pornography, in-custody abuse and the CCTV POV. *Jump Cut*, 59. http://ejumpcut.org/archive/jc59.2019/BrennanParoleHim/index.html

Brennan, J. (2020). Gay porn's bareback momentum. *Journal of Homosexuality*, 67(1), 127–157. https://doi.org/10.1080/00918369.2018.1525947

Brennan, J. (2022a). "Almost looks illegal": Family Dick's *Daddy's Little Boy* gay pornography series and its too-young look. *Journal of Homosexuality*, 69(9), 1576–1601. https://doi.org/10.1080/00918369.2021.1919477

Brennan, J. (2022b). Going bareback: Time and aging in a gay-for-pay porn career. *Sexuality & Culture*, 26(1), 373–396. https://doi.org/10.1007/s12119-021-09897-8

Burger, J. R. (1995). *One-handed histories: The eroto-politics of gay male video pornography*. Routledge.

Burke, N. B. (2016a). Hegemonic masculinity at work in the gay adult film industry. *Sexualities*, 19(5–6), 587–607. https://doi.org/10.1177/1363460716629333

Burke, N. B. (2016b). Intimate commodities: Intimate labor and the production and circulation of inequality. *Sexualities, 19*(7), 780–801. https://doi.org/10.1177/1363460715616948

Busby, K. (2004). The queer sensitive interveners in the *Little Sisters* case: A response to Dr. Kendall. *Journal of Homosexuality, 47*(3–4), 129–150. https://doi.org/10.1300/J082v47n03_07

Cante, R., & Restivo, A. (2004). The "world" of all-male pornography: On the public place of moving-image sex in the era of pornographic transnationalism. In P. C. Gibson (Ed.), *More dirty looks: Gender, pornography and power* (pp. 110–126). BFI Publishing.

Capino, J. B. (2005). Homologies of space: Text and spectatorship in all-male adult theaters. *Cinema Journal, 45*(1), 50–65. https://doi.org/10.1353/cj.2006.0003

Carballo-Diéguez, A., & Bauermeister, J. (2004). "Barebacking": Intentional condomless anal sex in HIV-risk contexts. Reasons for and against it. *Journal of Homosexuality, 47*(1), 1–16. https://doi.org/10.1300/J082v47n01_01

Cervulle, M., & Rees-Roberts, N. (2009). Queering the Orientalist porn package: Arab men in French gay pornography. *New Cinemas, 6*(3), 197–208. https://doi.org/10.1386/ncin.6.3.197_1

Champagne, J. (1995). *Ethics of marginality: A new approach to gay studies.* University of Minnesota Press.

Champagne, J. (1997). "Stop reading films!": Film studies, close analysis, and gay pornography. *Cinema Journal, 36*(4), 76–97. https://doi.org/10.2307/1225614

Cohler, B. J. (2004). Memoir and performance: Social change and self life-writing among men who are gay pornography producers and actors. *Journal of Homosexuality, 47*(3–4), 7–43. https://doi.org/10.1300/J082v47n03_02

Cole, S. (2014). Costume or dress? The use of clothing in the gay pornography of Jim French's Colt Studio. *Fashion Theory, 18*(2), 123–147. https://doi.org/10.2752/175174114X13890223974461

Corneau, S., Beaulieu-Prévost, D., Bernatchez, K., & Beauchemin, M. (2017). Gay male pornography: A study of users' perspectives. *Psychology & Sexuality, 8*(3), 223–245. https://doi.org/10.1080/19419899.2017.1360931

Corneau, S., Beaulieu-Prévost, D., Murray, S. J., Bernatchez, K., & Lecompte, M. (2021). Gay male pornography and the racialisation of desire. *Culture, Health & Sexuality, 23*(5), 579–592. https://doi.org/10.1080/13691058.2020.1717630

Corneau, S., & van der Meulen, E. (2014). Some like it mellow: On gay men complicating pornography discourses. *Journal of Homosexuality, 61*(4), 491–510. https://doi.org/10.1080/00918369.2014.865452

Davis, O. (Ed.). (2015). Bareback sex and queer theory across three national contexts (France, UK, US) [Special section]. *Sexualities, 18*(1–2), 120–249.

de Villiers, N. (2019). The videomaker and the rent boy: Gay-for-pay confessional in *101 Rent Boys* and *Broke Straight Boys TV*. In T. Waugh & B. Arroyo (Eds.), *I confess! Constructing the sexual self in the Internet age* (pp. 177–192). McGill-Queen's University Press.

Dean, T. (2009). *Unlimited intimacy: Reflections on the subculture of barebacking.* University of Chicago Press.

Duggan, S. J., & McCreary, D. R. (2004). Body image, eating disorders, and the drive for muscularity in gay and heterosexual men: The influence of media images. *Journal of Homosexuality, 47*(3–4), 45–58. https://doi.org/10.1300/J082v47n03_03

Dyer, R. (1985). Male gay porn: Coming to terms. *Jump Cut, 30*, 27–29.

Dyer, R. (1989). A conversation about pornography. In S. Shepherd & M. Wallis (Eds.), *Coming on strong: Gay politics and culture* (pp. 198–212). Unwin.

Dyer, R. (1994). Idol thoughts: Orgasm and self-reflexivity in gay pornography. *Critical Quarterly, 36*(1), 49–62. https://doi.org/10.1111/j.1467-8705.1994.tb01012.x

Dyer, R. (1997). *White.* Routledge.

Eaton, L. A., Cain, D. N., Pope, H., Garcia, J., & Chauncey, C. (2011). The relationship between pornography use and sexual behaviours among at-risk HIV-negative men who have sex with men. *Sexual Health, 9*(2), 166–170. https://doi.org/10.1071/SH10092

Ellis, S. R., & Whitehead, B. W. (2004). Porn again: Some final considerations. *Journal of Homosexuality*, 47(3–4), 197–220. https://doi.org/10.1300/J082v47n03_12

Erickson, D. J., Galos, D. L., Smolenski, D. J., Iantaffi, A., & Rosser, B. S. (2015). Typologies of sexually explicit media use among MSM: An application of latent class analysis. *Psychology & Sexuality*, 6(1), 28–43. https://doi.org/10.1080/19419899.2014.984515

Escoffier, J. (2003). Gay-for-pay: Straight men and the making of gay pornography. *Qualitative Sociology*, 26(4), 531–555. https://doi.org/10.1023/B:QUAS.0000005056.46990.c0

Escoffier, J. (2007). Porn star/stripper/escort: Economic and sexual dynamics in a sex work career. *Journal of Homosexuality*, 53(1–2), 173–200. https://doi.org/10.1300/J082v53n01_08

Escoffier, J. (2009). *Bigger than life: The history of gay porn cinema from beefcake to hardcore*. Running Press.

Fiske, J., & Hartley, J. (1978). *Reading television*. Methuen & Co.

Floegel, D. (2022). Porn bans, purges, and rebirths: The biopolitics of platform death in queer fandoms. *Internet Histories*, 6(1–2), 90–112. https://doi.org/10.1080/24701475.2021.1985833

Florêncio, J. (2020a). Antiretroviral time: Gay sex, pornography and temporality "post-crisis." *Somatechnics*, 10(2), 195–214. https://doi.org/10.3366/soma.2020.0313

Florêncio, J. (2020b). *Bareback porn, porous masculinities, queer futures: The ethics of becoming-pig*. Routledge.

Fung, R. (1991). Looking for my penis: The eroticized Asian in gay video porn. In B. Object-Choices (Eds.), *How do I look? Queer film and video* (pp. 145–168). Bay Press.

Galos, D. L., Smolenski, D. J., Grey, J. A., Iantaffi, A., & Rosser, B. S. (2015). Preferred aspects of sexually explicit media among men who have sex with men: Where do condoms fit in? *Psychology & Sexuality*, 6(2), 147–165. https://doi.org/10.1080/19419899.2013.851108

Garry, A. (1978). Pornography and respect for women. *Social Theory and Practice*, 4(4), 395–421. https://doi.org/10.5840/soctheorpract1978446

Gilreath, S. (2011). *The end of straight supremacy: Realizing gay liberation*. Cambridge University Press.

Gleason, N., & Sprankle, E. (2019). The effects of pornography on sexual minority men's body image: An experimental study. *Psychology & Sexuality*, 10(4), 301–315. https://doi.org/10.1080/19419899.2019.1637924

Goh, J. N. (2017). Navigating sexual honesty: A qualitative study of the meaning-making of pornography consumption among gay-identifying Malaysian men. *Porn Studies*, 4(4), 447–462. https://doi.org/10.1080/23268743.2017.1371066

Goss, D. F. (2021). *Race and masculinity in gay men's pornography: Deconstructing the big Black beast*. Routledge.

Gough, J. (1989). Images of sexual identity and the masculinization of the gay man. In S. Shepherd & M. Wallis (Eds.), *Coming on strong: Gay politics and culture* (pp. 119–136). Unwin Hyman.

Grudzen, C. R., & Kerndt, P. R. (2007). The adult film industry: Time to regulate? *PLoS Medicine*, 4(6), e126. https://doi.org/10.1371/journal.pmed.0040126

Gubar, S. (1987). Representing pornography: Feminism, criticism, and depictions of female violation. *Critical Inquiry*, 13(4), 712–741. https://doi.org/10.1086/448418

Hald, G. M., Træen, B., Noor, S. W., Iantaffi, A., Galos, D., & Rosser, B. S. (2015). Does Sexually Explicit Media (SEM) affect me? Assessing first-person effects of SEM consumption among Norwegian men who have sex with men. *Psychology & Sexuality*, 6(1), 59–74. https://doi.org/10.1080/19419899.2014.984516

Hallam, P. (2004). If you look at it long enough.... *Journal of Homosexuality*, 47(3–4), 59–74. https://doi.org/10.1300/J082v47n03_04

Hartley, J. (2009). Lament for a lost running order? Obsolescence and academic journals. *M/C Journal*, 12(3). https://doi.org/10.5204/mcj.162

Henze, P. (2013). Porn 2.0 utopias—Authenticity and gay masculinities on Cam4. *Media, Communication and Cultural Studies Association*, 6(1), 48–62. https://doi.org/10.31165/nk.2013.61.295

Herron, A. (2021). *Times Square Strip*: Queer memories of New York and Jack Deveau's Hand In Hand Films. *Porn Studies, 8*(3), 270–279. https://doi.org/10.1080/23268743.2020.1856002

Highberg, N. P. (2011). More than a comic sidekick: Fat men in gay porn. *Performing Ethos, 2*(2), 109–120. https://doi.org/10.1386/peet.2.2.109_1

Hilderbrand, L. (2016). Historical fantasies: 1970s gay male pornography in the archives. In C. Bronstein & W. Strub (Eds.), *Porno chic and the sex wars: American sexual representation in the 1970s* (pp. 327–348). University of Massachusetts Press.

Hoang, N. T. (2004). The resurrection of Brandon Lee: The making of a gay Asian American porn star. In L. Williams (Ed.), *Porn studies* (pp. 223–270). Duke University Press.

Jeffreys, S. (2002). *Unpacking queer politics: A lesbian feminist perspective*. Polity.

Jensen, R. (2004). Homecoming: The relevance of radical feminism for gay men. *Journal of Homosexuality, 47*(3–4), 75–81. https://doi.org/10.1300/J082v47n03_05

Johnson, M. (2013). Negotiating love and work: A critical ethnography of a gay porn star. In P. Demory & C. Pullen (Eds.), *Queer love in film and television: Critical positions* (pp. 181–192). Palgave Macmillan.

Johnson, R. (1986–1987). What is cultural studies anyway? *Social Text, 16,* 38–80. https://doi.org/10.2307/466285

Jonas, K. J., Hawk, S. T., Vastenburg, D., & de Groot, P. (2014). "Bareback" pornography consumption and safe-sex intentions of men having sex with men. *Archives of Sexual Behavior, 43*(4), 745–753. https://doi.org/10.1007/s10508-014-0294-2

Kendall, C. N. (2004a). Educating gay male youth: Since when is pornography a path towards self-respect? *Journal of Homosexuality, 47*(3–4), 83–128. https://doi.org/10.1300/J082v47n03_06

Kendall, C. N. (2004b). *Gay male pornography: An issue of sex discrimination*. UBC Press.

Kendall, C. N. (2004c). Gay male pornography and sexual violence: A sex equality perspective on gay male rape and partner abuse. *McGill Law Journal, 49*(4), 877–923.

Kendall, C. N., & Funk, R. E. (2004). Gay male pornography's "actors": When "fantasy" isn't. *Journal of Trauma Practice, 2*(3–4), 93–114. https://doi.org/10.1300/J189v02n03_05

Kipnis, L. (1996). *Bound and gagged: Pornography and the politics of fantasy in America*. Grove Press.

Kiss, M. J., & Morrison, T.G. (2021). Eroticizing desperation: Poverty gay-for-pay porn. *Sexuality & Culture, 25*(4), 1509–1528. https://doi.org/10.1007/s12119-021-09828-7

Kiss, M., Morrison, T. G., & Parker, K. (2019). Understanding the believability and erotic value of "heterosexual" men in gay pornography. *Porn Studies, 6*(2), 169–192. https://doi.org/10.1080/23268743.2018.1559091

Law, T. (2021). A different kind of risky business: Men who manage men in the sex industry. *Sexualities, 24*(7), 941–956. https://doi.org/10.1177/13634607211026312

Leap, W. L. (2011). Language, gay pornography, and audience reception. *Journal of Homosexuality, 58*(6–7), 932–952. https://doi.org/10.1080/00918369.2011.581944

Longstaff, G. (2019). "Bodies that splutter"—Theorizing jouissance in bareback and chemsex porn. *Porn Studies, 6*(1), 74–86. https://doi.org/10.1080/23268743.2018.1559090

Lucas, M. (2006). On gay porn. *Yale Journal of Law and Feminism, 18*(1), 299–302.

Maddison, S. (2017). Comradeship of cock? Gay porn and the entrepreneurial voyeur. *Porn Studies, 4*(2), 139–156. https://doi.org/10.1080/23268743.2017.1304235

McBride, D. (2005). *Why I hate Abercrombie & Fitch: Essays on race and sexuality*. NYU Press.

McCutcheon, J. M., & Bishop, C. (2015). An erotic alternative? Women's perception of gay pornography. *Psychology & Sexuality, 6*(1), 75–92. https://doi.org/10.1080/19419899.2014.983740

McKee, A. (1999). Australian gay porn videos: The national identity of despised cultural objects. *International Journal of Cultural Studies, 2*(2), 178–198. https://doi.org/10.1177/136787799900200202

McKee, A. (2018). Porn consumers as fans. In P. Booth (Ed.), *A companion to media fandom and fan studies* (pp. 509–520). Wiley.

McKittrick, C. (2010). Brothers' milk: The erotic and the lethal in bareback pornography. In D. Monroe (Ed.), *Porn—Philosophy for everyone: How to think with kink* (pp. 66–77). Blackwell.

Mercer, J. (2003). Homosexual prototypes: Repetition and the construction of the generic in the iconography of gay pornography. *Paragraph, 26*(1–2), 280–290. https://doi.org/10.3366/para.2003.26.1-2.280

Mercer, J. (2004). In the slammer: The myth of the prison in American gay pornographic video. *Journal of Homosexuality, 47*(3–4), 151–166. https://doi.org/10.1300/J082v47n03_08

Mercer, J. (2012a). Coming of age: Problematizing gay porn and the eroticized older man. *Journal of Gender Studies, 21*(3), 313–326. https://doi.org/10.1080/09589236.2012.681187

Mercer, J. (2012b). Gay for pay: The Internet and the economics of homosexual desire. In K. Ross (Ed.), *The handbook of gender, sex, and media* (pp. 535–551). Blackwell-Wiley.

Mercer, J. (2012c). Power bottom: Performativity in commercial gay pornographic video. In C. Hines & D. Kerr (Eds.), *Hard to swallow: Hard-core pornography on screen* (pp. 215–228). Columbia University Press.

Mercer, J. (Ed.). (2017a). Gay porn now! [Special section]. *Porn Studies, 4*(2), 127–256.

Mercer, J. (2017b). *Gay pornography: Representations of sexuality and masculinity*. I. B. Tauris.

Mercer, J. (2017c). Popperbate: Video collage, vernacular creativity and the scripting of the gay pornographic body. *Porn Studies, 4*(2), 242–256. https://doi.org/10.1080/23268743.2017.1304237

Morris, P. (2016). Oznog the great and powerful. *Porn Studies, 3*(4), 411–419. https://doi.org/10.1080/23268743.2016.1259579

Morris, P., & Paasonen, S. (2014). Risk and utopia: A dialogue on pornography. *GLQ, 20*(3), 215–239. https://doi.org/10.1215/10642684-2422656

Morris, P., & Paasonen, S. (2019). Strange optimism: Queer rage as visceral ethics. In R. Varghese (Ed.), *Raw: PrEP, pedagogy, and the politics of barebacking* (pp. 143–162). University of Regina Press.

Morrison, T. G. (Ed.). (2004a). Eclectic views on gay male pornography: Pornucopia [Special section]. *Journal of Homosexuality, 47*(3–4), 1–220.

Morrison, T. G. (2004b). "He was treating me like trash, and I was loving it...": Perspectives on gay male pornography. *Journal of Homosexuality, 47*(3–4), 167–183. https://doi.org/10.1300/J082v47n03_09

Morrison, T. G., Bishop, C., & Kiss, M. (Eds.). (2015). More eclectic views on gay male pornography [Special section]. *Psychology & Sexuality, 6*(1), 1–146.

Morrison, T. G., Bishop, C. J., Kiss, M., & Nielsen, E. J. (2016). Gay male pornography. In A. Wong, M. Wickramasinghe, R. Hoogland, & N. A. Naples (Eds.), *The Wiley Blackwell encyclopedia of gender and sexuality studies*. Wiley-Blackwell. https://onlinelibrary.wiley.com/doi/full/10.1002/9781118663219.wbegss618

Morrison, T. G., Morrison, M. A., & Bradley, B. A. (2007). Correlates of gay men's self-reported exposure to pornography. *International Journal of Sexual Health, 19*(2), 33–43. https://doi.org/10.1300/J514v19n02_03

Mosher, D. L. (1988). Pornography defined: Sexual involvement theory, narrative context, and goodness-of-fit. *Journal of Psychology & Human Sexuality, 1*(1), 67–85. https://doi.org/10.1300/J056v01n01_06

Mowlabocus, S. (2007). Life outside the latex: HIV, sex, and the online barebacking community. In K. O'Riordan & D. J. Phillips (Eds.), *Queer online: Media technology and sexuality* (pp. 217–234). Peter Lang.

Mowlabocus, S., Harbottle, J., & Witzel, C. (2013). Porn laid bare: Gay men, pornography and bareback sex. *Sexualities, 16*(5–6), 523–547. https://doi.org/10.1177/1363460713487370

Mowlabocus, S., Harbottle, J., & Witzel, C. (2014). What we can't see? Understanding the representations and meanings of UAI, barebacking, and semen exchange in gay male pornography. *Journal of Homosexuality, 61*(10), 1462–1480. https://doi.org/10.1080/00918369.2014.928581

Mowlabocus, S., & Medhurst, A. (2017). Six propositions on the sonics of pornography. *Porn Studies, 4*(2), 210–224. https://doi.org/10.1080/23268743.2017.1304236

Nielsen, E. (2015). Fucking with distinction: A contextualised film review of *I Want Your Love*. *Psychology & Sexuality*, 6(1), 140–146. https://doi.org/10.1080/19419899.2014.984519

Nielsen, E., & Kiss, M. (2015). Sexercising our opinion on porn: A virtual discussion. *Psychology & Sexuality*, 6(1), 118–139. https://doi.org/10.1080/19419899.2014.984518

Nielsen, E., & Morrison, T.G. (2019). Barebacking as a form of homosociality? Notes on *Bottom*. In S. Petrella (Ed.), *Erotic subjects and outlaws: Sketching the borders of sexual citizenship* (pp. 215–237). Brill.

Ojeda-Sagué, G. (2021). The whiteness of François Sagat. *Porn Studies*, 8(1), 107–120. https://doi.org/10.1080/23268743.2020.1744476

Padva, G. (2019). Pornography as culture industry: "Adult entertainment" in the age of obscene reproduction. In U. H. Bittlingmayer, A. Demirović, & T. Freytag (Eds.), *Handbuch kritische theorie* (pp. 1301–1315). Springer.

Paslakis, G., Actis, C. C., & Mestre-Bach, G. (2022). Associations between pornography exposure, body image and sexual body image: A systematic review. *Journal of Health Psychology*, 27(3), 743–760. https://doi.org/10.1177/1359105320967085

Peter, J., & Valkenburg, P. M. (2016). Adolescents and pornography: A review of 20 years of research. *Journal of Sex Research*, 53(4–5), 509–531. https://doi.org/10.1080/00224499.2016.1143441

Poole, J., & Milligan, R. (2018). Nettersexuality: The impact of Internet pornography on gay male sexual expression and identity. *Sexuality & Culture*, 22(4), 1189–1204. https://doi.org/10.1007/s12119-018-9521-7

Pronger, B. (1990). *The arena of masculinity: Sports, homosexuality, and the meaning of sex*. St. Martin's Press.

Race, K. (2010). Engaging in a culture of barebacking: Gay men and the risk of HIV prevention. In M. Davis & C. Squire (Eds.), *HIV treatment and prevention technologies in international perspective* (pp. 144–166). Palgrave Macmillan.

Ramos, C. A. (2013). Wrapped in ambiguity: Assessing the expressiveness of bareback pornography. *New York University Law Review*, 88(5), 1839–1872.

Ramsay, G. (2017). Straight women seeing gay porn: "He's too good looking!" *Porn Studies*, 4(2), 157–175. https://doi.org/10.1080/23268743.2017.1299037

Rothmann, J. (2013). "Doing" and "using" sexual orientation: The role of gay male pornographic film in the identity construction of gay men. *South African Review of Sociology*, 44(3), 22–41. https://doi.org/10.1080/21528586.2013.817048

Ruszczycky, S. (2021). *Vulgar genres: Gay pornographic writing and contemporary fiction*. University of Chicago Press.

Ryan, P. (2019). *Male sex work in the digital age: Curated lives*. Palgrave Macmillan.

Schön, D. A. (1983). *The reflective practitioner: How professionals think in action*. Basic Books.

Scuglia, B. (2004). Sex pigs: Why porn is like sausage, or the truth is that—behind the scenes—porn is not very sexy. *Journal of Homosexuality*, 47(3–4), 185–188. https://doi.org/10.1300/J082v47n03_10

Scuglia, B. (2015). The last days of gay porn. *Psychology & Sexuality*, 6(1), 111–117. https://doi.org/10.1080/19419899.2014.984517

Silvera, R., Stein, D. J., Hagerty, R., & Marmor, M. (2009). Condom use and male homosexual pornography. *American Journal of Public Health*, 99(10), 1732–1733. https://doi.org/10.2105/AJPH.2009.169912

Silvera, R. J., Grov, C., Stein, D. J., Hagerty, R., & Marmor, M. (2015). Level of "outness" and pornography use among men who have sex with men: Results from an online survey. *Psychology & Sexuality*, 6(1), 44–58. https://doi.org/10.1080/19419899.2014.984907

Smith, J. G., Liz, E., & Addy, P. (2022). F*ck the police: Resistance, agency, and power in Black male racial-sexual pleasure. *Porn Studies*, 9(2), 241–261. https://doi.org/10.1080/23268743.2021.1969991

Song, L. (2021). Desire for sale: Live-streaming and commercial DIY porn among Chinese gay microcelebrities. *Convergence*, 27(6), 1753–1769. https://doi.org/10.1177/13548565211047341

Stadler, J. P. (2013). Dire straights: The indeterminacy of sexual identity in gay-for-pay pornography. *Jump Cut, 55.* https://www.ejumpcut.org/archive/jc55.2013/StadlerGayForPay/1.html

Stokes, J. (2003). *How to do media and cultural studies.* SAGE.

Stoltenberg, J. (1990). Gays and the pro-pornography movement: Having the hots for sex discrimination. In M. S. Kimmel (Ed.), *Men confront pornography* (pp. 248–262). Meridian.

Storms, G. (2015). Bare-ing witness: Bareback porn and the ethics of watching. In L. Comella & S. Tarrant (Eds.), *New views on pornography: Sexuality, politics, and the law* (pp. 381–394). Praeger.

Strub, W. (2019). Sanitizing the seventies: Pornography, home video, and the editing of sexual memory. *Feminist Media Histories, 5*(2), 19–48. https://doi.org/10.1525/fmh.2019.5.2.19

Stychin, C. F. (1991–1992). Exploring the limits: Feminism and the legal regulation of gay male pornography. *Vermont Law Review, 16,* 857–900.

Subero, G. (2010). Gay Mexican pornography at the intersection of ethnic and national identity in Jorge Diestra's *La Putiza. Sexuality & Culture, 14*(3), 217–233. https://doi.org/10.1007/s12119-010-9071-0

Thomas, J. A. (2000). Gay male video pornography: Past, present, and future. In R. Weitzer (Ed.), *Sex for sale: Prostitution, pornography, and the sex industry* (pp. 49–66). Routledge.

Thorneycroft, R. (2021). "Facefuck me": Exploring crip porn. *Porn Studies.* https://doi.org/10.1080/23268743.2021.1961603

Tollini, C. (2017). Different portrayals of masculinity in gay bareback pornographic videos: Comparing Sean Cody with Treasure Island Media. *Porn Studies, 4*(4), 419–432. https://doi.org/10.1080/23268743.2017.1358654

Tortorici, Z. J. (2008). Queering pornography: Desiring youth, race, and fantasy in gay porn. In S. Driver (Ed.), *Queer youth cultures* (pp. 199–216). SUNY Press.

Tsika, N. (2017). Blue transfusions: Internet porn and the pirating of queer cinema's sex scenes. *Porn Studies, 4*(2), 225–241. https://doi.org/10.1080/23268743.2016.1174074

Tziallas, E. (2015a). *Between the gothic and surveillance: Gay (male) identity, fiction film, and pornography (1970–2015)* [Unpublished PhD thesis, Concordia University, Montréal, Canada].

Tziallas, E. (2015b). The new "Porn Wars": Representing gay male sexuality in the Middle East. *Psychology & Sexuality, 6*(1), 93–110. https://doi.org/10.1080/19419899.2014.983741

Vanderwees, C. (2019). Paranoid pleasure: Surveillance, online pornography, and scopophilia. *Porn Studies, 6*(1), 23–37. https://doi.org/10.1080/23268743.2018.1559084

Vörös, F. (2014). Raw fantasies. An interpretative sociology of what bareback porn does and means to French gay male audiences. In S. E. Lewis, R. Borba, B. F. Fabrício, & D. de Souza Pinto (Eds.), *Queering paradigms IV: South-north dialogues on queer epistemologies, embodiments and activisms* (pp. 321–343). Peter Lang.

Wang, Y. (2021). The twink next door, who also does porn: Networked intimacy in gay porn performers' self-presentation on social media. *Porn Studies, 8*(2), 224–238. https://doi.org/10.1080/23268743.2020.1841019

Ward, J. (2015). *Not gay: Sex between straight white men.* NYU Press.

Waugh, T. (1985). Men's pornography: Gay vs. straight. *Jump Cut, 30,* 30–35.

Waugh, T. (2017). "Men's pornography, gay vs. straight": A personal revisit. *Porn Studies, 4*(2), 131–138. https://doi.org/10.1080/23268743.2017.1298898

Waugh, T., & Arroyo, B. (2019). *I confess! Constructing the sexual self in the Internet age.* McGill-Queen's University Press.

Westcott, C. N. (2004). Alterity and construction of national identity in three Kristen Bjorn films. *Journal of Homosexuality, 47*(3–4), 189–196. https://doi.org/10.1300/J082v47n03_11

Williams, L. (1991). Film bodies: Gender, genre, and excess. *Film Quarterly, 44*(4), 2–13. https://doi.org/10.2307/1212758

Williams, L. (2014a). Pornography, porno, porn: Thoughts on a weedy field. *Porn Studies*, 1(1–2), 24–40. https://doi.org/10.1080/23268743.2013.863662

Williams, L. (2014b). Pornography, porno, porn: Thoughts on a weedy field. In T. Dean, S. Ruszczycky, & D. Squires (Eds.), *Porn archives* (pp. 29–43). Duke University Press.

Young, D. R. (2017). *Gag the fag*, or tops and bottoms, persons and things. *Porn Studies*, 4(2), 176–192. https://doi.org/10.1080/23268743.2017.1307138

Joseph Brennan

HOMONATIONALISM AND MEDIA

INTRODUCTION

Homonationalism is a 21st-century concept, addressing a historically and culturally specific constellation of views on the nation and on homosexuality. Although it may seem simple at face value, suggesting forms of nationalism that embrace homosexuality, it is theoretically complex. Moreover, it is applied to a variety of countries and situations, proving to be adaptable and productive as an analytical and heuristic tool, but losing some of its specificity and critical edge in the process. This article provides an overview of some of the literature and research on homonationalism, which is recent but quickly expanding. Although the theoretical ramifications of the concept are disentangled, this article does not aim to open a theoretical discussion, but rather to explore the lay of the field. In particular, it aims to show how the concept has been applied in a variety of settings involving a range of nations and fields of research.

To start, some preliminary remarks are in place. First, it is important to point out that the concept of homonationalism is most used in queer studies as well as cultural and political analysis, also appearing in other fields like sociology and geography, but only rarely in media studies. Although media are often used as a source of research, the research itself is rarely situated in media studies, and the specific role of media in originating and circulating homonationalist discourse is hardly reflected on, let alone studied systematically. Hence, one of the aims of this article is to chart the role of media in (the study of) homonationalism, focusing in particular on the (limited) amount of research explicitly studying media, and to suggest further avenues of research in this respect. Second, it is important to point out that this article does not offer a comprehensive overview of all literature on the topic, as it only discusses English-language literature on the topic. Although the article aims to include a wide range of international literature, the emphasis is still on U.S. and Europe-based authors. Third, a note on terminology: as a general rule, the original terms used by the authors referenced in this article are adopted, which leads to a variety of terms referring to sexual and gender minorities. When no particular author is referenced and no specific group is referenced, the umbrella term "LGBT" is used, as this is the most commonly used term in the literature discussed here.

DEFINING HOMONATIONALISM

Jasbir Puar's (2007) *Terrorist Assemblages: Homonationalism in Queer Times* is the seminal text on homonationalism. In this ambitious book, she tackles a number of issues in a rich theoretical and cultural analysis. Rather than giving a full overview of the book, a number of key elements are presented here as a foundation and background for the discussion of subsequent literature drawing on Puar's work. Puar's work is extensively quoted here, to evoke her style and vocabulary; in later sections, some of the threads introduced in this first section are further disentangled.

Before beginning, it is worth noting the central but implicit role of media in her account. When listing her sources, among other things she names governmental texts, films, documentaries and television shows, print media (especially LBGTIQ regional, national, and international newspapers and magazines), organizational press releases, manifestos, and ethnographic data (Puar, 2007, p. xv). Media figure prominently in this list, but Puar does not focus on media as such, rather reading them discursively as part of a broader cultural field, which is typical of most of the research discussed in this article: different media constitute a key source of data, but they are seldomly reflected on or analyzed in a systematic way, considering their specificity as media.

It is also important to situate Puar's writing in cultural and historical terms, for this context is crucial for her argument and it also cautions against too easy transpositions to other settings. Writing in the United States in the early 21st century, the post-9/11 American "war on terror" is an explicit reference point in Puar's book, including its title. At this particular time and place, Puar observes a rise of what she calls "homonationalism," briefly defined as "the dual movement in which certain homosexual constituencies have embraced U.S., nationalist agendas and have also been embraced by nationalist agendas" (Puar, 2007, p. xxiv). There are two sides to this equation: on the one hand, Puar states that "homosexual constituencies" are complicit with nationalist politics, and on the other hand, she states that they have been embraced by nationalist agendas.

Starting with the latter, Puar observes a growing American "benevolence to sexual others" which, however, "is contingent upon ever-narrowing parameters of white racial privilege, consumption capabilities, gender and kinship normativity, and bodily integrity" (xii). Although the inclusion of queer subjects in self-images of the nation could be seen as a positive evolution, Puar is critical of the normative and exclusionary nature of this inclusion. In relation to its normativity, Puar is indebted to the notion of (new) "homonormativity" as defined by Lisa Duggan (2002), who uses the term to describe a neoliberal sexual politics "that does not contest dominant heteronormative assumptions and institutions but upholds and sustains them while promising the possibility of a demobilized gay constituency and a privatized, depoliticized gay culture anchored in domesticity and consumption" (p. 179). This notion is revisited in the discussion of the first part of Puar's equation, queer complicity with nationalism, but for now it can be observed, with Puar, that not any kind of queer sexuality is embraced by the U.S. nation. Moreover, the inclusion of (some) queer people is inseparably connected to the exclusion of others: "National recognition, here signaled as the annexation of homosexual jargon, is contingent upon the segregation and disqualification of racial and sexual others from the national imaginary" (Puar, 2007, p. 2). These racial others, in the United States after 9/11, are mostly defined as Muslims.

All of this leads to the self-presentation of the U.S. nation as exceptionally accepting of homosexuality, which Puar describes as a form of sexual exceptionalism:

As the U.S. nation-state produces narratives of exception through the war on terror, it must temporarily suspend its heteronormative imaged community to consolidate national sentiment and consensus through the recognition and incorporation of some, though not all or most, homosexual subjects. (Puar, 2007, p. 3)

This self-presentation is accompanied by a process of sexual othering, targeted mostly at Muslims, who are presented as homophobic, in a new form of Orientalism: "Religion, in particular Islam, has now supplanted race as one side of the irreconcilable binary between queer and something else" (Puar, 2007, p. 13).

Returning to the first part of the equation, Puar is particularly critical of the complicity of the "gay left," stating that gay, homosexual, and queer national subjects aligned themselves with U.S. imperial interests in the context of the war on terror, which she connects to homonormativity: "America is narrated by multiple progressive sectors as embodying exceptional multicultural heteronormativity, one that is also bolstered by homonormativity" (Puar, 2007. p. xxv). She argues that "some homosexual subjects are complicit with heterosexual nationalism formations rather than inherently or automatically excluded from or opposed to them" (Puar, 2007, p. 4). Broadening the scope to the Global North, Puar observes the rise of homonormative Islamophobia, "whereby homonormative and queer gay men can enact forms of national, racial, or other belongings by contributing to a collective vilification of Muslims" (Puar, 2007, p. 21).

After this initial broad exploration of the concept, Puar offers a more succinct reflection on the topic in her 2013 article "Rethinking Homonationalism." Here, she presents homonationalism as a conceptual frame "for understanding the complexities of how 'acceptance' and 'tolerance' for gay and lesbian subjects have become the barometer by which the right to and capacity for national sovereignty is evaluated" (Puar, 2013, p. 336). To Puar, acceptance of homosexuality has not only become an important part of the American national self-image but is also used to (mostly negatively) assess other nations. This, as such, is historically interesting as it implies that being seen as "gay-friendly" has become desirable in the first place, which for a long time was not, and in many countries still is not, the case. As most clearly illustrated by the war on terror, homonationalism has implications for international politics, "as it undergirds U.S. imperial structures through an embrace of a sexually progressive multiculturalism justifying foreign intervention" (Puar, 2013, p. 336).

While Puar's critique on queer complicity was pronounced in "Terrorist Assemblages," in the 2013 article she clarifies that it is not simply an accusation of "gay racism." Rather, she develops the idea that it is a facet of modernity, "the historical shift marked by the entrance of (some) homosexual bodies as worthy of protection by nation-states" (Puar, 2013, p. 337). Moreover, she draws attention to the racial dimension inherent in the inclusion of some and the exclusion of others: "The narrative of progress for gay rights is thus built on the back of racialized others, for whom such progress was once achieved, but is now backsliding or has yet to arrive." She also discusses pinkwashing, which is often connected to homonationalism, stating that pinkwashing is a manifestation of, and made possible by, homonationalism. The term is most applied to Israel, criticizing its promotion of a LGBT-friendly image "to reframe the occupation of Palestine in terms of civilizational narratives measured by (sexual) modernity" (Puar, 2013, p. 337), which leads to "the cynical promotion of LGBT bodies as representative of Israeli democracy" (Puar, 2013, p. 338). Finally, Puar also situates homonationalism in the broader discussion of the globalization of Western identity constructs:

> The gay and lesbian human rights industry continues to proliferate Euro-American constructs of identity (not to mention the notion of sexual identity itself) that privilege identity politics, "coming out," public visibility, and legislative measures as the dominant barometers of social progress. (Puar, 2013, p. 338)

All these threads are further explored in the discussion of later research. For now, it is worth reflecting on the temporal specificity of Puar's analysis, which is very much connected to the Bush and Obama presidencies, the latter in particular embracing LGBT rights in the national self-image. Since Trump, the climate has radically changed, so one wonders to what degree LBGTQ rights and individuals are still included in the national self-image, by whom, and under which conditions. What clearly remains, however, is the nationalist logic of identifying external others threatening "our" norms and values, the key dynamic in homonationalist policies and discourses.

UNPACKING HOMONATIONALISM

Although the term "homonationalism" is strongly associated with Puar's work, as the account above illustrates, she builds on a wide legacy of scholarship and brings together a number of ideas that were developed across a wide range of fields, in particular, (intersectional) feminist theory and postcolonial queer theory. Therefore, first, while acknowledging the originality of her work, it is also important to recognize how she is indebted to a broad range of authors who developed similar analyses using different theoretical concepts. Second, as a consequence of these diverse roots and components, homonationalism has a lot of ramifications, which makes it a rich and inspiring concept but also leads to diverse uses as well as debate over the applicability and limitations of the concept.

Thus, it is worth taking a closer look at the "nationalism" in homonationalism, which is rather under-theorized in writing on homonationalism. On the one hand, Puar's initial definition suggests LGBT individuals and associations that are complicit with nationalist politics, but this ramification has remained relatively underexplored. Only some research has specifically focused on homonationalist attitudes and voting behavior among LGBTs, which will be discussed below. On the other hand, one could consider homonationalism as a specific form of nationalist politics, but it is certainly not limited to explicitly nationalist parties or politicians. Rather, "nationalism" is to be understood in a broader sense here, related to representations of and discourses about the nation, not limited to nationalist or rightwing politics nor even politics. In this sense, Puar's work builds on and contributes to a broader literature exploring the connection between (homo-)sexuality and (mostly Western) nations. As discussed by Pryke (1998), one important thread in research on the connection between nationalism and sexuality concerns the role of sexuality in nation-building, whereby the nation aims to delimit what is acceptable sexual behavior on behalf of national citizens. Historically, this mostly led to the marginalization of and violence toward sexual minorities, as these were seen as a threat to the national community "by undermining the family, failing to adhere to national gender stereotypes, challenging its internal homogeneity and deviating from shared social norms, especially those derived from religious teaching" (Mole, 2017, p. 660).

In more recent times, certain sexual minorities have acquired "sexual citizenship" in (mostly Western) nations, through the cultural normalization and social inclusion of lesbians and gay men (Richardson, 2017). Like Puar, Richardson (2005, 2017) connects this to neoliberalism and (homo-)normativity, also noting the use of sexual citizenship as a symbolic marker of tolerant and intolerant countries, opposing "modernity" to "backwardness." Haritaworn (2008) agrees, reiterating the notion of exceptionalism: "Sexual freedom has moved from the realm of the immoral or perverse to the realm of the morally superior, a central ingredient of U.S. and Western exceptionalism." Sabsay (2012) elaborates on the notion of Orientalism, which implies a process of cultural othering, distinguishing Western democracies from "undeveloped others." In their edited collection, Haritaworn, Kuntsman, and Posocco (2014) further discuss the exclusionary nature of Western gay rights discourses, which exclude non-White and non-Western groups and thus perpetuate inequality.

Although the notion of homonationalism was quickly adopted by many authors across a number of fields, it was also criticized, partly because of its original formulations but also and particularly because of the way it was broadened and applied by other authors. Schotten (2016) tracks the evolution of the notion of homonationalism throughout Puar's writing, and she is critical of the broadening of the concept beyond its original theoretical frame and the U.S. political context. She observes two main evolutions in Puar's use of the concept: an expansion beyond the U.S. context, considering homonationalism as a more general feature of Western sexual exceptionalism; and the abandonment of the critique on LGBT people's complicity with the (U.S., nationalist) state. As a consequence, Schotten (2016) argues, the concept loses its specificity and critical force.

Zanghellini (2012) does not criticize Puar's work as such, but she does question the way homonationalism is used as a critical tool. To her, the term is applied too easily to a variety of situations, leading to a "near-ubiquity" of homonationalism. As a consequence, gay rights discourses and activism are too easily discredited as complicit with homonationalism and Islamophobic, in line with Massad's (2002) influential but controversial critique of the "Gay International," Western LGBT nongovernmental organizations (NGOs) defending queer people in the Middle East but at the same time imperialistically imposing Western concepts and politics on them. Zanghellini is critical of the way this discredits "local" queers who may find the language of gay rights promising, while also excluding racialized and Muslim queers. Dhawan (2015) is also critical of some forms of "anti-homonationalism," which to her too easily dismiss each form of critique on homophobia in postcolonial contexts as Orientalism. Moreover, she criticizes the "state-phobia" of anti-homonationalism, which considers any collaboration with the state as suspect, not considering different historical and cultural contexts, even if negotiations with the state are indispensable for emancipatory politics in many states.

A recurrent thread in these critiques on the way the notion of homonationalism has been applied is related to its broad use, not considering the specificity of national, historical, and cultural contexts. In this vein, Ritchie (2014) states that homonationalism is elevated to a kind of "master narrative that explains all things in all places" (Ritchie, 2014, p. 620). In such a broad use, homonationalism becomes an oversimplified, homogenous, global external entity, which does not help in understanding the everyday experiences of LGBT people in specific contexts and does not pay sufficient attention to particular local micro contexts. For this reason, in what follows, studies from different national contexts are discussed, drawing attention to their local specificities. Where possible, the focus is on empirical research operationalizing and applying the concept, and particular attention is paid to the role of media in these analyses. In the "Conclusion," these scattered insights on the role of media are brought together as a first step toward developing a research agenda on media and homonationalism.

MUSLIM OTHERS

A first cluster of research focuses on discourses about and representations of the own nation as LGBT-friendly as opposed to Muslims as a threat to "our" sexual values, very much in line with Puar's initial analysis. Starting in the United States, Meyer (2019) explores homonationalism in online reporting on the Pulse nightclub shooting, qualitatively analyzing reporting on five LGBT websites, using a grounded theory approach. His analysis discloses that the shooter, Omar Mateen, is represented as a Muslim outsider rather than as a U.S. citizen. Even when these mostly left-leaning websites condemn Islamophobia, they do simultaneously link Islam with terrorism and homophobia while overlooking Mateen's Americanness, thus setting up the us versus them divide that is typical of homonationalist discourses.

Homonationalism and pinkwashing in Israel are also a rich source of writing and debate, for instance, in Hartal and Sasson-Levy's (2017) analysis of the way the Gay-Center, a LGBT community in Tel Aviv, is presented as a symbol of Israel as a modern Western liberal country, in contrast to Palestine and other Arab countries. Using ethnographic analysis, they show how dynamics of inclusion and exclusion are at work in presenting the Gay-Center as a clean, normative space. In the process, certain LGBT individuals are included in the nation but also normalized, while (perverse) others remain excluded, illustrating the homonormativity discussed by Puar. Writing from the perspective of queer people themselves, and focusing on online media, Kuntsman (2009) did ethnographic research on an online portal for Russian-speaking queer immigrants in Israel, disentangling the complexities of sexual, ethnic, and national belonging in online discussions.

Besides Israel, Western Europe is a particularly fertile ground for research on homonationalism. At the EU level, Ammaturo (2015) studied how the "queer liberal subject," which is presented as integral part of the nation, is constituted through the practices of the Council of Europe. She argues that the promotion of LGBT rights by the Council of Europe is part of a broader "Pink Agenda," which works by "creating and promoting lines of fracture between presumably queer-friendly and homo-transphobic countries within and outside the European borders" (Ammaturo, 2015, p. 1152). In line with Puar's argumentation, she states that the Pink Agenda is used as a yardstick to measure the progress of other states, instrumentalizing LGBT identities while also creating norms of sexual citizenship. She applies this analysis to two contexts: the way asylum for LGBTs is instrumentalized (persecuted queers becoming "trophies" of the West), and discussions over Pride marches in Eastern Europe (a region that is further discussed below). Overall, Ammaturo argues that the Council of Europe, particularly through the European Court of Human Rights, "plays a crucial role in portraying Europe as a tolerant, open and respectful continent for LGBT persons while, simultaneously, identifying intolerant and homo-transphobic 'others' both within and outside its borders" (Ammaturo, 2015, p. 1161).

Indeed, the "others" in homonationalist discourse can be situated within and outside of "the nation"—while the latter, as became clear in the writing of Ammaturo, can encompass larger regions such as the EU. Europe's "others" are mostly situated in the East, both within its borders (Eastern Europe) and outside its borders. Turkey occupies a liminal position, as it is situated on the border between Europe and Asia, and Szulc and Smets (2015) explore how this is reflected in Western reviews of *Zenne Dancer* (2012), a Turkish film dealing with gay honor killing. Based on a broad sample of Western film reviews, they identify a Western progressive narrative, focusing on conservatism, tradition, and Islam as key elements explaining the honor killing in the film, homogenizing and othering Turkey, thus setting up a simplifying opposition between the West and the East.

Within Europe, Islam also occupies a central position in discourses about sexuality, as argued by Mepschen and Duyvendak (2012). They state that gay issues moved to the center of the European cultural imagination: "Cases of homophobia among Muslim citizens are highlighted, epitomized as archetypal, and cast within Orientalist narratives that underwrite the superiority of European secular modernity" (Mepschen & Duyvendak, 2012, p. 71). Meanwhile, gay culture was strongly normalized, changing "from a deviant other to the mirror image of the ideal heterosexual" (Mepschen & Duyvendak, 2012, p. 73). The national cultures of Europe are framed as in need of protection against globalization and immigration, while Muslims are framed as "backward, intolerant and incongruous with 'European' secular modernity" (Mepschen & Duyvendak, 2012, p. 74).

The Netherlands is one of the countries where homonationalism is most pervasive, a situation which is further investigated by Mepschen, Duyvendak, and Tonkens (2010). They observe a number of broader European tendencies: the culturalization of citizenship in Western European societies, that is, the growing importance of culture and morality in citizenship and integration policy, and Islamophobia. They also note a number of specific Dutch contexts: strong secularization, a focus on sexual freedom, and the normalization of gay sexuality. Within these contexts, the Netherlands is one of the countries whose acceptance of homosexuality is strongly opposed to Muslim citizens, who are depicted as backward and homophobic, in particular by populist politicians like Geert Wilders. Kešić and Duyvendak (2019) frame this form of nationalism in a broader pattern of nativism, a number of right-wing parties strengthening the opposition between natives and immigrants, focusing in particular on Islam in relation to norms around gender and sexuality.

Bracke (2012) also discusses the Dutch situation, drawing a parallel between women's rights and sexual rights. Referencing Spivak's rescue script "white men saving brown women from brown men," she broadens the argument to "rescue gays" and in particular "rescue brown gays," identifying the gay Muslim as a victim figure in Western civilizational discourses. This leads to a situation where queer Muslim asylum seekers are welcomed in the Netherlands because of their sexuality, whereas Dutch-Islamic people who have lived in the Netherlands for several generations are still considered as outsiders. Other authors have also addressed the precarious position of queer Muslims in the Netherlands (and beyond). For instance, Jivrai and de Jong (2011) state that the discourse on Muslim homophobia silences queer Muslims, imposing Western standards of sexual identity on them while creating a false dichotomy between religious or cultural and sexual rights. Similarly, El-Tayeb (2012) criticizes the opposition between the implicitly gay White community and the straight Muslim community, whereby queer Muslims are represented as undeveloped others, racialized queers who need to be liberated. Also including media in the analysis, Yildiz (2017) analyzes a documentary about a Turkish boat participating in the Amsterdam Canal Pride, criticizing the strong media association of the Dutch Muslim community with gay bashing, presenting gay and ethnic identity as mutually exclusive.

All of this research focuses on the second part of Puar's equation, the incorporation of LGBT rights in national discourses, but some researchers also focus on the first part, LGBT "complicity" with such politics and discourses. Thus, Mepschen (2016) did ethnographic research on everyday expressions of Dutch sexual nationalism, reporting on discussions with gay men who replicate the culturalist framework discussed above, which rest "on collective representations of reified 'groups' whose members are thought to be defined by social stereotypes that are seen as inherent to their groups' collective life and culture" (Mepschen, 2016, p. 161) Spierings, Lubbers, and Zaslov (2017) researched voting behavior among nativist voters, exploring whether "sexually modern nativists," who support LGBT rights but hold anti-immigration attitudes, tend to vote for populist radical right parties, which in some European countries such as the Netherlands strongly support LGBT rights. While anti-immigration attitudes are more prevalent and decisive in voting behavior, they indeed do find that sexually modern nativists are more likely to vote for populist radical right parties then more sexually traditional nativists. Spierings (2020) continues this line of research, further reinforcing the idea that homonationalist citizens are ardent populist radical right voters.

While the Netherlands is the most prominent country in literature on homonationalism in Europe, other countries are also discussed. For instance, Kehl (2018) analyzes how a Swedish right-wing publicist and politician, Jan Sjunnesson, talked about Pride Järva, a "gay pride" march he organized. She situates his speech in broader homonationalist discourses presenting Sweden as particularly progressive in relation to gay rights, as opposed to threatening Islamic and racialized others, discourses which are also shared by certain LGBT associations and activists who aim to "protect" LGBTs against immigrant homophobia. To Kehl, this is a clear instance of Swedish (and more broadly European) exceptionalism, constructing Swedishness along lines of progress, secularism, enlightenment, and rationality.

Although homonationalism is mostly connected to nation-states like the United States or the Netherlands, and also occasionally connected to broader regions such as the EU or Western Europe, the concept has also been applied to smaller, subnational regions. For instance, Bilge (2012) discusses sexual nationalism in Québec, defining sexual nationalism as "the incorporation of gender-and-sexual normativities into the governmentality of migrant/Muslim integration and the politics of the nation" (Bilge, 2012, p. 304). She observes how women's and gay-and-lesbian rights have become core values in Western nations, constituting a new form of Orientalism, not associating Muslims culture with sexual excess, as before, but with gender and sexual oppression. Drawing on theories on homonationalism and homonormativity, she connects the opposition to Islam in Québec to the importance of secularism, as well as nationalist and separatist discourses presenting Québec as a vulnerable minority nation to be protected from religious others. In the Catalan context, Sadurní, Montengro, and Pujol (2019) similarly connect homonationalism to Catalan nationalism that presents Catalonia as a progressive minority seeking emancipation from the more traditionalist Spanish nation-state. Drawing on the analysis of newspapers and public documents from actors of the Catalan independence movement, they observe a form of Catalan exceptionalism which connects Catalonia to the European protection of LGBTI rights.

Flanders, the northern Dutch-speaking community in Belgium, offers another instance of a subnational region where homonationalism has been analyzed. Eeckhout (2014) cautions against the straightforward application of homonationalist critiques to Flanders. LGBT rights are widely supported across the political spectrum, with the exception of the extreme right, both in Belgium (as a nation-state) and in Flanders (as a subnational region), so it is not possible to connect support of LGBT rights to nationalism, and it is necessary to consider the varied ways in which different parties support LGBT rights. Research by the author of this article (Dhoest, 2020b) explored how Flemish newspapers report on homosexuality and Islam, identifying some explicit homonationalist discourses explicitly connecting Muslims with homophobia and opposing them to "our" LGBT-friendliness. However, the national in-group often remains unspecified, and when it is named it can be Flanders, Belgium, or even Europe. Even when Flemish nationalist politicians talk about homophobia and Islam, they often do not refer to Flanders explicitly, partly because Flanders is self-evident as a reference point in their political discourse, but also because most legal realizations in relation to LGBT rights were effectuated at the Belgian level. Besides explicitly homonationalist discourses, also identified were partial discourses, where Islam is connected to homophobia but not contrasted to an in-group; and counter-discourses, which question the binary opposition inherent in homonationalism. Overall, however, the connection between Islam and homophobia is pervasive, corresponding to most research discussed in this section where a clear opposition was found between a LGBT-friendly "us" and a homophobic, Muslim "them."

OTHER OTHERS

Although Muslims and Islam figure most prominently in homonationalist discourses and research on the topic, it is clear that not only can the (subnational, national, or regional) in-group vary but also the out-group. Radically shifting contexts, Yue (2012) discusses how Indian students and Malaysian transgender refugees are discussed in Australian media, analyzing newspapers and websites as well as policy and parliamentary reports. She argues that Australia's homonational modernity normalizes homosexuality, which regulates the Indian student migrant and the transgender Asian refugee:

> on the one hand, mainstream media such as newspapers have queered the straight student migrant through associations with racial and sexual prejudice, and, on the other hand, alternative media such as gay websites and social media have valorized the transgendered refugee through racial assimilation and fetishization. (Yue, 2012, p. 283)

Several authors have also written about homonationalism in discourses about Africa. Returning to Sweden, Jungar and Peltonen (2017) discuss the "spectacle" that was made in Western media about African homophobia, in particular in writing about Uganda. Analyzing reporting in Swedish daily newspapers, they argue that Sweden is presented as the epitome of progress, democracy and the civilized West, whereas Africa is represented as a homogeneous homophobic other. Rao (2014) is equally critical about neo-Orientalist narrative strategies in media reporting on homophobia in Africa, and particularly Uganda. For instance, he discusses two documentaries presenting a White, Western journalist visiting Uganda and comparing it to Britain, which is presented as a space of gay freedom.

Wahab (2016a) also analyzes discourses around Uganda's so-called "Anti-Homosexuality Act," which presents homosexuality as "un-African." He signals the strong influence of U.S. evangelism in stimulating homophobia, while also criticizing the role of transnational LGBT activists, in line with Massad's (2002) critique as well as Puar's criticism on the complicity of LGBT activists. Wahab states that the whole discussion is strongly influenced by Western discourses about sexual rights, universalizing Western views while culturalizing African differences. He sees this as an instance of "homotransnationalism," where the Euro-American discourse on gay rights as human rights is used on a global scale to oppose the progressive West to the homophobic Rest (i.e., the Global South). Wahab (2016b) also applies this line of thought to Jamaica, which is similarly presented as uniformly homophobic in Canadian homonationalist discourse. As elsewhere, homophobia "at home" (i.e., in Canada) is made invisible while homophobia abroad (in Jamaica) is naturalized and discussed without any consideration for local contexts.

On this global map of homonationalist discourses, generally opposing the West to the East and South, in Europe there is a particular dynamic of Western Europe talking about Eastern Europe and Russia. Central and Eastern Europe (CEE) figures prominently in these discourses and is generally presented as a "poor cousin," which is trying to "catch up" with the West after coming out of the closet in 1989 (Mizielinska & Kulpa, 2012). These discourses frame CEE as "permanently post-communist," in transition, and homophobic (Kulpa, 2014). Analyzing three resolutions of the European Parliament, Kulpa (2014) argues that CEE is othered by presenting homophobia as a problem extending uniformly across all of CEE, presenting the EU as non-homophobic and tolerant. Kahlina (2015) focuses on Croatia and Serbia, arguing that sexual citizenship has been instrumentalized both by sexual rights activists and by pro- and anti-EU proponents, the latter protesting against Pride marches in order to defend national values. She concludes that homonationalist discourses externalize homophobia and may be responsible for increased resistance to the struggles for sexual equality.

Russia is another prominent focal point in European homonationalist discourses opposing the West and the East. Wiedlack (2017) investigates discourses on Russian LGBTIQ+ issues in Anglophone media, focusing on the visual politics, which tend to present victimized bodies of Russian dissidents. As in Uganda, legislation (in this case the so-called "anti-homosexual propaganda law" of 2013) prompted this discourse, which presents Russia as brutal, backward, and anti-modern as opposed to the European North and West, which is presented as tolerant. Persson (2015) studied Russian media, highlighting the importance of media in creating the spectacle around the 2013 law. He found three tropes in Russian reporting on the homosexual propaganda bill: presenting homosexuals as a threat to the survival of the nation; representing homosexuals as an influential minority enforcing its values and lifestyle on the majority; and the refusal of Western modernity and values, proposing an alternative form of modernity. Overall, Russian media present homosexuality as alien to the nation, thus offering a counter-narrative to the homonationalist discourses in Western media.

Edenborg (2017) confirms this analysis, also discussing the 2014 Sochi Winter Olympics as an instance of Russian national self-presentation in the face of LGBT protests. Indeed, Sochi—and the Olympics more broadly—feature prominently in the literature on homonationalism. Le Blanc (2013) discusses the calls for a boycott of the Sochi games, acknowledging the problems in relation to gay rights in Russia but questioning the limited attention to other human rights issues in Russia as well as Western states' idealized self-image as progressive and liberal. Travers and Shearman (2017) studied reporting on the Sochi Olympics in American and Canadian LGBT publications, concluding that these celebrated the Olympics and presented Western countries as human rights leaders and safe havens for LGBT people, without any consideration of inequality and racialized violence, while they "othered" Russia as antigay but stayed silent about racism and ethnic violence in Russia. Duholke (2016) agrees, also drawing a line between the Sochi Olympics and the 2012 London Summer Olympics, which celebrated the inclusion of LGBT people, an equally homonationalist discourse presenting the West as uniformly LGBT-friendly. Hubbard and Wilkinson (2015) similarly argue that the London Olympics promoted an image of gay-friendliness, but that inclusion was conditional and normative, framing this not only as homonationalist but also as homonormative, an undercurrent in much writing on homonationalism: LGBT rights are promoted as a key value in the West, but are normative and conditional, excluding some forms of (racialized and/or "perverse") sexual diversity.

Another recurrent topic in the literature on homonationalism in relation to the East–West divide in Europe is the European Song Contest. Baker (2017) calls it the "gay Olympics" and considers it as a node in the geopolitics about LGBT rights symbolically opposing "Western Europe" and "Eastern Europe" as well as "Europe" and "Russia." Since the 1990s, she argues, national and European history have been reconfigured around supposedly exceptional levels of sexual and gender diversity, presenting an "essentialistic binary between an inherently tolerant West and an inherently homophobic Russia, reducing complex politics of gender and sexuality in any of these countries to a simple national us–them" (Baker, 2017, p. 107). While not explicitly using the framework of homonationalism, Cassiday (2014) does discuss the strong gay appeal of the Eurovision Song Contest and the changes in the way Russia positioned itself in this context, observing the initial strategic use of Eurovision's gay identity politics but also a subsequent backlash and distancing, in line with Russia's broader counter-discourse previously discussed in relation to the Sochi games.

In this author's own research (Dhoest, 2020a), Russia and Eastern Europe were found to figure in a similar way in Flemish newspapers. In an analysis of three months of reporting, a small number of articles were found explicitly connecting Russia and Eastern Europe to homophobia in contrast to an LGBT-friendly in-group. However, hardly any counter-discourses (questioning this binary opposition by questioning the in-group's gay-friendliness) were found either, and all articles discussing Russia and Eastern Europe in relation to LGBT issues framed those regions as a homogeneous homophobic "Eastern Bloc." Again, as with reporting on Islam, the in-group varied and often remained unnamed, which may suggest a weaker form of homonationalism but at the same time underlines that it is self-evident that "we" (however defined) are LGBT-friendly. Even partial discourses only talking about homophobia abroad implicitly create a self-image of tolerance, reinforcing a taken-for-granted binary opposition.

CONCLUSION

Despite its relatively recent introduction, the concept of "homonationalism" has inspired a rich literature. In the process, it was extended from the United States to other national contexts, and the "outgroups" identified in research also extended from Muslims to other (mostly Eastern) "others." This has led to discussions about the applicability of the term to different contexts and to critiques on the overuse of the term. At the same time, homonationalism has shown its strong heuristic value as a tool for empirical research. Although the term may lose some of its conceptual complexity and distinctiveness through its operationalization in much of the research discussed in this article, it has allowed the identification of strong and recurrent patterns of opposition between the in-group and out-group, which are inherent in nationalism but get a new and problematic slant here, as the inclusion of some is actively used to justify the exclusion of others. LGBTs, which are typically considered as an "out-group," suddenly become part of the "in-group," but at a heavy price.

Despite frequent references to media in writing on homonationalism, the account above illustrates the lack of substantive argumentation about the specific role of media in relation to homonationalism. Although a lot of work on homonationalism does heavily draw on media as a source of data (including Puar's own writing), there is only limited interest in the workings of media, which tend to be considered as mere "vessels" for homonationalist discourse. Media are mostly treated as a way to access and analyze discourse, leading to a rather vague notion of "media" as a unified realm. Some literature, however, does explicitly focus on particular media, often singling out a specific medium such as newspapers, magazines, or TV. While more explicitly acknowledging the role of media in spreading homonationalist discourse, the workings of these media are hardly reflected on, leaving a number of questions unanswered.

Thus, first, it remains unclear which media in particular play a role in spreading homonationalism discourse. Most research to date focuses on mainstream "legacy" media such as newspapers and television, but other media and platforms, also online, may be equally important. In particular, despite their central position in the contemporary landscape, social media are remarkably absent from discussions about homonationalism, although they may be instrumental in spreading homonationalist discourse beyond the journalistic and political realms that are mostly studied. Second, by either talking about the media in generic terms or only focusing on a single medium, the broader circulation of homonationalist discourse across media remains undetected. In the current era of mediatization, where a multiplicity of interconnected media occupies a central position in all areas of life, it is important to better understand the interplay of different media, particularly in a field such as politics which is so heavily mediatized. Thirdly, most research is qualitative and explores the form and content of homonationalist discourse, but this leaves the question of the prevalence of homonationalist discourse unanswered. Particularly in a comparative perspective, it remains unclear to what degree homonationalist discourses circulate in different national contexts. This relates to a fourth issue, that of sampling: most research to date has analyzed a small, purposive sample of media texts, deliberately selected to discuss homonationalism, but this makes it hard to assess how homonationalist discourses circulate beyond these specific instances. Fifth, there is the matter of genre: most research to date has focused on informative, factual media genres such as (political) news reporting or print journalism. As a consequence, research may have underestimated the importance of media in spreading homonationalist discourse in other genres, prioritizing explicit (homo-)nationalism over "banal," everyday reconfirmations of the LGBT-friendly nation. Sixth, all of these unanswered questions relate to a more fundamental question concerning the role of media: Do media only circulate pre-existing homonationalist discourse, for instance, by giving a platform to certain politicians? Or do they actively initiate homonationalist discourse? Based on the existing research, it seems like media do both, but a lot of further research is needed to disentangle which actors develop homonationalist discourse on which platforms and how these discourses further circulate across different media.

FURTHER READING

Baker, C. (2017). The "gay Olympics"? The Eurovision Song Contest and the politics of LGBT/European belonging. *European Journal of International Relations, 23*(1), 97–121.
Dhawan, N. (2015). Homonationalism and state-phobia: The postcolonial predicament of queer modernities. In M. A. Viteri & M. Lavinas Picq (Eds.), *Queering narratives of modernity* (pp. 51–68). Peter Lang.
Dhoest, A. (2020a, April 23). Eastern others: Homonationalism in the Flemish press. *International Communication Gazette*, 1748048520918495. https://doi.org/10.1177/1748048520918495
Dhoest, A. (2020b). LGBTs in, Muslims out: Homonationalist discourses and counterdiscourses in the Flemish press. *International Journal of Communication, 14*, 155–175.
Kahlina, K. (2015). Local histories, European LGBT designs: Sexual citizenship, nationalism, and "Europeanisation" in post-Yugoslav Croatia and Serbia. *Women's Studies International Forum, 49*, 73–83.
Mepschen, P., Duyvendak, J. W., & Tonkens, E. H. (2010). Sexual politics, orientalism and multicultural citizenship in the Netherlands. *Sociology, 44*(5), 962–979.
Puar, J. (2007). *Terrorist assemblages: Homonationalism in queer times*. Duke University Press.
Puar, J. (2013). Rethinking homonationalism. *International Journal of Middle East Studies, 45*(2), 336–339.
Zanghellini, A. (2012). Are gay rights Islamophobic? A critique of some uses of the concept of homonationalism in activism and academia. *Social & Legal Studies, 21*(3), 357–374.

REFERENCES

Ammaturo, F. R. (2015). The "Pink Agenda": Questioning and challenging European homonationalist sexual citizenship. *Sociology, 49*(6), 1151–1166.
Baker, C. (2017). The "gay Olympics"? The Eurovision Song Contest and the politics of LGBT/European belonging. *European Journal of International Relations, 23*(1), 97–121.
Bilge, S. (2012). Mapping Québécois sexual nationalism in times of "crisis of reasonable accommodations." *Journal of Intercultural Studies, 33*(3), 303–318. https://doi.org/10.1080/07256868.2012.673473
Bracke, S. (2012). From "saving women" to "saving gays": Rescue narratives and their dis/continuities. *European Journal of Women's Studies, 19*(2), 237–252.
Cassiday, J. A. (2014). Post-Soviet pop goes gay: Russia's trajectory to Eurovision victory. *The Russian Review, 73*(1), 1–23.
Dhawan, N. (2015). Homonationalism and state-phobia: The postcolonial predicament of queer modernities. In M. A. Viteri & M. Lavinas Picq (Eds.), *Queering narratives of modernity* (pp. 51–68). Peter Lang.
Duggan, L. (2002). The new homonormativity: The sexual politics of neoliberalism. In R. Castronovo & D. D. Nelson (Eds.), *Materializing democracy: Toward a revitalized cultural politics* (pp. 175–194). Duke University Press.

Duholke, J. (2016). The gay-friendly games: Homonationalism and the Olympics. *Sprinkle: An Undergraduate Journal of Feminist and Queer Studies, 9*, 21–32.

Edenborg, E. (2017). *Politics of visibility and belonging. From Russia's "homosexual propaganda" laws to the Ukraine Wars.* Routledge.

Eeckhout, B. (2014, April 22). What might a queer critique of homonormalization and homonationalism in Flanders look like? *CritCom: A Forum for Research and Commentary on Europe.* https://critcom.councilforeuropeanstudies.org/what-might-a-queer-critique-of-homonormalization-and-homonationalism-in-flanders-look-like/

El-Tayeb, F. (2012). "Gays who cannot properly be gay": Queer Muslims in the neoliberal European city. *European Journal of Women's Studies, 19*(1), 79–95.

Haritaworn, J. (2008, May 2). Local repetitions of the nation: Gay assimilation and the "war on terror." *Darkmatter.* http://www.darkmatter101.org/site/2008/05/02/loyal-repetitions-of-the-nation-gay-assimilation-and-the-war-on-terror/

Haritaworn, J., Kuntsman, A., & Posocco, S. (2014). *Queer necropolitics.* Routledge.

Hartal, G., & Sasson-Levy, O. (2017). Being [in] the center: Sexual citizenship and homonationalism at Tel Aviv's Gay-Center. *Sexualities, 20*(5–6), 738–761.

Hubbard, P., & Wilkinson, E. (2015). Welcoming the world? Hospitality, homonationalism, and the London 2012 Olympics. *Antipode, 47*(3), 598–615.

Jivrai, S., & de Jong, A. (2011). The Dutch homo-emancipation policy and its silencing effects on queer Muslims. *Feminist Legal Studies, 19*, 143–158. https://doi.org/10.1007/s10691-011-9182-5

Jungar, K., & Peltonen, S. (2017) Acts of homonationalism: Mapping Africa in the Swedish media. *Sexualities, 20*(5–6), 715–737.

Kahlina, K. (2015). Local histories, European LGBT designs: Sexual citizenship, nationalism, and "Europeanisation" in post-Yugoslav Croatia and Serbia. *Women's Studies International Forum, 49*, 73–83.

Kehl, K. (2018). "In Sweden, girls are allowed to kiss girls, and boys are allowed to kiss boys": Pride Järva and the inclusion of the "LGBT other" in Swedish nationalist discourses. *Sexualities, 21*(4), 674–691.

Kešić, J., & Duyvendak, J. W. (2019). The nation under threat: Secularist, racial and populist nativism in the Netherlands. *Patterns of Prejudice, 53*(5), 441–463. https://doi.org/10.1080/0031322X.2019.1656886

Kulpa, R. (2014). Western *leveraged pedagogy* of Central and Eastern Europe: Discourses of homophobia, tolerance, and nationhood. *Gender, Place & Culture, 21*(4), 431–448. https://doi.org/10.1080/0966369X.2013.793656

Kuntsman, A. (2009). *Figurations of violence and belonging: Queerness, migranthood and nationalism in cyberspace and beyond.* Peter Lang.

Le Blanc, F. J. (2013). Sporting homonationalism: Russian homophobia, imaginative geographies and the 2014 Olympic Games. Paper presented at the Sociology Association of Aotearoa New Zealand Annual Conference. https://www.academia.edu/5318682/Sporting_Homonationalism:Russian_Homophobia_Imaginative_Geographies_and_the_2014_Sochi_Olympic_Games

Massad, J. (2002). Re-orienting desire: The gay international and the Arab world. *Public Culture, 14*(2), 361–385.

Mepschen, P. (2016). Sexual democracy, cultural alterity and the politics of everyday life in Amsterdam. *Patterns of Prejudice, 50*(2), 150–167. https://doi.org/10.1080/0031322X.2016.1164426

Mepschen, P., & Duyvendak, J. W. (2012). European sexual nationalisms: The culturalization of citizenship and the sexual politics of belonging and exclusion. *Perspectives on Europe, 42*(1), 70–76.

Mepschen, P., Duyvendak, J. W., & Tonkens, E. H. (2010). Sexual politics, orientalism and multicultural citizenship in the Netherlands. *Sociology, 44*(5), 962–979.

Meyer, D. (2019). Omar Mateen as US citizen, not foreign threat: Homonationalism and LGBTQ online representations of the Pulse nightclub shooting. *Sexualities, 23*(3), 249–268. https://doi.org/10.1177/1363460719826361

Mizielinska, J., & Kulpa, R. (2012). Guest editors' introduction: Central and Eastern European sexualities "in transition": Reflections on queer studies, academic hegemonies, and critical epistemologies. *Lambda Nordica*, *17*(4), 19–29.

Mole, R. C. M. (2017). Homonationalism: Resisting nationalist co-optation of sexual diversity. *Sexualities*, *20*(5–6), 660–662.

Persson, E. (2015). Banning "homosexual propaganda": Belonging and visibility in contemporary Russian media. *Sexuality & Culture*, *19*, 256–274. https://doi.org/10.1007/s12119-014-9254-1

Pryke, S. (1998). Nationalism and sexuality, what are the issues? *Nations and Nationalism*, *4*(4), 529–546.

Puar, J. (2007). *Terrorist assemblages: Homonationalism in queer times*. Duke University Press.

Rao, R. (2014). The locations of homophobia. *London Review of International Law*, *2*(2), 169–199.

Richardson, D. (2005). Desiring sameness? The rise of a neoliberal politics of normalisation. *Antipode*, *37*(3), 515–535. https://doi.org/10.1111/j.0066-4812.2005.00509.x

Richardson, D. (2017). Rethinking sexual citizenship. *Sociology*, *51*(2), 208–224.

Ritchie, J. (2014). Pinkwashing, homonationalism, and Israel–Palestine: The conceits of queer theory and the politics of the ordinary. *Antipode*, *47*(3), 616–634. https://doi.org/10.1111/anti.12100

Sabsay, L. (2012). The emergence of the other sexual citizen: Orientalism and the modernisation of sexuality. *Citizenship Studies*, *16*(5–6), 605–623. https://doi.org/10.1080/13621025.2012.698484

Sadurní, N., Montenegro, M., & Pujol, J. (2019). National construction and LGBTI rights: Exploring Catalan homonationalism. *Sexualities*, *22*(4), 605–621.

Schotten, C. H. (2016). Homonationalism. *International Feminist Journal of Politics*, *18*(3), 351–370. https://doi.org/10.1080/14616742.2015.1103061

Spierings, N. (2020, March 24). Homonationalism and voting for the populist radical right: Addressing unanswered questions by zooming in on the Dutch case. *International Journal of Public Opinion Research*. https://doi.org/10.1093/ijpor/edaa005

Spierings, N., Lubbers, M., & Zaslov, A. (2017). Sexually modern nativist voters': Do they exist and do they vote for the populist radical right? *Gender and Education*, *29*(2), 216–237. https://doi.org/10.1080/09540253.2016.1274383

Szulc, L., & Smets, K. (2015). Homonationalism and Western progressive narrative: Locating "conservative heartlands" with Zenne Dancer (2012) and its Western reviews. *Asian Journal of Communication*, *25*(6), 551–566. https://doi.org/10.1080/01292986.2015.1007334

Travers, A., & Shearman, M. (2017). The Sochi Olympics, celebration capitalism, and homonationalist pride. *Journal of Sport and Social Issues*, *41*(1), 42–69. https://doi.org/10.1177/0193723516685273

Wahab, A. (2016a). Calling "homophobia" into place (Jamaica). *Interventions*, *18*(6), 908–928. https://doi.org/10.1080/1369801X.2015.1130641

Wahab, A. (2016b). "Homosexuality/homophobia is un-African"? Un-mapping transnational discourses in the context of Uganda's Anti-Homosexuality Bill/Act. *Journal of Homosexuality*, *63*(5), 685–718.

Wiedlack, M. K. (2017). Gays vs. Russia: Media representations, vulnerable bodies and the construction of a (post)modern West. *European Journal of English Studies*, *21*(3), 241–257. https://doi.org/10.1080/13825577.2017.1369271

Yildiz, A. (2017). "Turkish, Dutch, gay and proud": Mapping out the contours of agency in homonationalist times. *Sexualities*, *20*(5–6), 699–714.

Yue, A. (2012). Queer Asian mobility and homonational modernity: Marriage equality, Indian students in Australia and Malaysian transgender refugees in the media. *Global Media and Communication*, *8*(3), 269–287.

Alexander Dhoest

HOMONATIONALISM'S VIRAL TRAVELS

INTRODUCTION

Homonationalism is a viral concept. Since Puar (2007) coined the term in the now-seminal text *Terrorist Assemblages: Homonationalism in Queer Times*, homonationalism has traversed transnational academic and activist conversations alike (Winer & Bolzendahl, 2021), perhaps because the concept captures conditions that resonate across geopolitical contexts. In its simplest iteration, homonationalism refers to the way that national recognition and inclusion of certain LGBTQ subjects and rights reinforces racism, nationalism, and imperialism.[1] This original definition of homonationalism emphasizes how LGBTQ complicity with nationalism relies on Orientalist constructions of Muslim and Arab "others" as rightful targets for imperialist violence due to their alleged homophobia or deviant sexuality (Puar, 2007). The concept thus refers to "the convivial, rather than antagonistic, relations between presumed nonnormative sexualities and the nation" (Puar, 2007, p. 49). As Puar (2007) wrote, "some homosexual subjects are complicit with heterosexual nationalist formations rather than inherently or automatically excluded from them" (p. 4). Through its conceptual evolution, homonationalism has also come to refer to "a facet of modernity and a historical shift marked by the entrance of (some) homosexual bodies as worthy of protection by nation-states" (Puar, 2013, p. 337).

By elaborating on the desirability—and deployability—of certain nonnormative sexualities to the nation in order to both produce and make disposable a host of racial and sexual others, the concept and history of homonationalism provide an answer to questions about how and why certain gay, lesbian, and (in more recent iterations) trans subjectivities are mobilized in service of modernity's capitalist, imperial, and colonial projects, such as the U.S. "War on Terror." Homonationalism also points to the way LGBTQ rights have become a barometer to measure certain populations' ascendance into modernity and subsequent right (or lack thereof) to sovereign governance (Puar, 2017).

At the same time, homonationalism's viral uptake has led to a proliferation of perspectives that complicate, challenge, and expand the concept's usage; though the conditions it names emerge across contexts, its instantiations inevitably vary based on historical and geopolitical context. These differences in application have informed critiques of the concept, which tend to focus on the overextension and universalization of the concept at the expense of its clarity, context specificity, and utility for movements seeking to contest homonationalist policies and practices (Currah, 2013; Leksikov & Rachok, 2020; Moss, 2014; Ritchie, 2015; Schotten, 2016; Zanghellini, 2012).

This article thus proceeds through the following sections: a discussion of homonationalism's original formulation, an elaboration of the foundational theoretical concepts of bio- and necropolitical assemblage upon which it draws, a summary of the contexts to which the concept has been applied and the criticisms it has engendered, an account of the related concept of pinkwashing with a particular emphasis on the Palestinian context, a discussion of homonationalism's relationship to settler colonialism, and finally, an elaboration of homonationalism's possible conceptual and political futures. Woven throughout these sections are references to the literatures that homonationalism has produced and the debates it has inspired. As homonationalism's viral scholarly and activist travels evidence, and as new homonationalist formations of power continue to emerge, the project of understanding how the nation's normalization and sanctioning of certain sexualities and genders directly contributes to the creation of disposable populations—in short, the project of understanding homonationalism—remains critical.

CONCEPTUAL, POLITICAL, HISTORICAL ORIGINS

Narratives of the scholarly lineage of homonationalism often identify two distinct definitions of the term (Schotten, 2016; Winer & Bolzendahl, 2021). The first is Puar's (2007) initial elaboration of the concept, which defined homonationalism as complicity between LGBTQ subjects or rights discourses and nationalism, specifically in a U.S. context. The second emerges out of Puar's revisitations of the topic, which emphasized that homonationalism is not a specific set of practices, nor an accusation of bad politics to be leveraged at individuals, but a condition of modernity that accords "some populations access to cultural and legal forms of citizenship at the expense of the partial and full expulsion from those rights of other populations" (Puar, 2015, p. 320). While Puar herself acknowledges such a conceptual shift (see Puar 2013, 2015), a deep read of her work does not indicate a clear binary division between the definitions of homonationalism, as is sometimes implied. For that reason, this section traces the origins of homonationalism without placing Puar's earlier and later writings in opposition to one another, instead addressing different—but interrelated—facets of the concept that emerge across them. However, it is important for readers to be aware that homonationalism has never been static or singularly defined; rather, it continues to evolve, including in ways that have sparked the debates and critiques.

Both the term and the concept of homonationalism build on Duggan's (2004) theorization of homonormativity, which refers to a form of neoliberal sexual politics that supports certain LGBTQ communities so long as they uphold and align with economies of privatization, consumption, free markets, and domesticity. Puar (2007) posited that, just as nonnormative sexualities can be conditionally accepted when advantageous for neoliberal economies, they can also be sanctioned for national recognition and inclusion if and when they serve projects of nationalism and imperial expansion. As she wrote, "homonormativity... ties the recognition of homosexual subjects, both legally and representationally, to the national and transnational political agendas of U.S. imperialism" (p. 9). She calls this "national form of homonormativity" homonationalism (p. 2). In defining homonationalism this way, Puar (2013) issued a corrective to transnational feminist and queer discourses that claim the nation is inherently heteronormative and queers are outlaws to the nation-state. Homonationalism, especially in its later iterations, also explains and historicizes how acceptance of LGBTQ subjects has become a measure of populations' capacity for national sovereignty, or "how and why a nation's status as 'gay-friendly' has become desirable in the first place" (Puar, 2013, p. 336).

Importantly, homonationalism is not just about inclusion; while "some homosexual subjects are complicit with heterosexual nationalist formations rather than inherently excluded from or opposed to them" (Puar, 2007, p. 4), homonationalism's employment of liberal LGBTQ rights discourses also produces populations that are undesirable to the nation, which in turn facilitates the management of and violence against those populations. As Puar (2015) wrote, "homonationalism is the concomitant rise in legal, consumer, and representative recognition of LGBTQ subjects *and* [emphasis added] the curtailing of welfare provisions, immigrant rights, and the expansion of state power to engage in surveillance, detention, and deportation" (p. 320). Thus, "the narrative of progress for gay rights is built on the backs of racialized and sexualized others" specifically "Muslim others, upon whom Orientalist and neo-Orientalist projections are cast" (Puar, 2015, pp. 320–321). In this way, Puar's analysis resonates with what Massad (2002) calls the "Gay International," comprised of global LGBT rights organizations and discourses that, in seeking to "liberate" Arab and Muslim LGBTQ people, reinforce imperialist designs and formations of power. However, whereas Massad foreclosed the possibility of Arab or Muslim LGBTQ subjectivities altogether, arguing that the categories of homo and hetero universalize European and U.S. settler colonial specific terms and thus inherently uphold imperialism, Puar's analysis holds space for queer opponents of homonationalism (Boggio Éwanjé-Épée & Magliani-Belkacem, 2013).

Homonationalism thus refers both to the nation's embrace of LGBTQ subjectivities, as well as rights discourses, that serve nationalist projects, and also to the way those subjectivities and discourses are deployed to create disposable populations—often constructed as sexually perverse—within larger, transnational formations of power and nation-state sovereignty. Here Puar (2007) posited a contrast between the national homosexual subject, produced as citizen, and the nation's disavowal of racial-sexual others, imagined as terrorists.

This production of citizen and terrorist bodies, in Puar's (2007) original formulation, involves three interrelated manifestations. First, homonationalism entails a sexual exceptionalism that ties certain LGBTQ subjectivities to the imperialist political agendas of the nation (in this case the United States) in ways that sustain gender, racial, and class norms of acceptability (pp. 2–3, 9). Sexual exceptionalism allows "progressive sexuality" to be "championed as a hallmark of U.S. modernity" (p. 41). Second, she elaborated queer as regulatory, which focuses on the way that queerness enacts forms of discipline and control, folding some subjects into national life in ways that target other populations for death (p. 24), a point tied to the discussion of bio- and necropolitics in the section Homonationalism as Bio-Necropolitical Assemblage. Third, and finally, homonationalism entails the ascendancy of whiteness. Here, Puar (2007) built on Chow's (2002) extension of Michel Foucault to suggest that homonationalism serves modernity's epistemological project of micromanaging and objectifying information and bodies to the benefit of White European subjectivities. She noted that just as homosexual subjects can serve heteronormative projects, the production and management of racial difference can also serve the ascendancy of whiteness in contexts of homonationalism. Liberal projects of multiculturalism, diversity, and inclusion, she therefore wrote, are mediated by "huge realms of exclusion" for populations that do not conform, for example, to norms of class and gender (Puar, 2007, pp. 25–26). As she summarized, "the project of whiteness is assisted and benefited by homosexual populations that participate in the same identitarian and economic hegemonies as those hetero subjects complicit with this ascendancy" in ways that undercut alliances "in favor of adherence to the reproduction of class, gender, and racial norms" (Puar, 2007, p. 32).

By laying out these three intertwined facets of how homonationalism produces a complicity between certain nonnormative sexualities and the state and capitalism, Puar (2007) was quick to caution that homonationalism is not a "mechanistic explanatory device that may cover all the bases" (p. 2), in part because it emerges out of and shifts in accordance with particular historical, geographical, and political circumstances.

Indeed, the original elaboration of homonationalism is deeply tied to the political context out of which the term emerged, and it is helpful to ground its conceptual framework in some examples. Puar (2015) emphasized that homonationalism's history precedes the September 11, 2001 (9/11) attacks on the Twin Towers and the United States' subsequent "War on Terror" because the concept "names a historical shift in the production of nation-states from the insistence on heteronormativity to the increasingly inclusion of homonormativity" that emerged prior to 9/11. Nevertheless, homonationalism punctuated the years following 9/11, as part of a larger rhetorical environment in which U.S. nationalism ballooned, also employing feminist discourses toward justifications for U.S intervention and imperial projects in Iraq, Afghanistan, and beyond (see Anker, 2012; Bhattacharyya, 2008; Grewal, 2005; Mohanty, 2008). This made possible liberal political discourses that tethered populations' right to self-determination and freedom from imperialism and colonization to their embrace of LGBTQ rights, while at the same time positioning the United States and Europe as exceptional for the way they fold queer subjects into life while disregarding the violence endemic to liberal inclusion.

Such liberal discourses continue to be commonplace today, and they produce a binary in which "the homosexual other is white, and the racial other is straight" (Puar, 2007, p. 32). They often take the form of exceptionalism; to use Puar's (2015) examples,

> Of course we oppose the war on terror, but what about the homophobia of Muslims? Of course we oppose the occupation of the Middle East, but the Iranians keep hanging innocent gay men... Of course we support the Palestinians in their quest for self-determination, but what about how sexist and homophobic they are? (p. 322)

In addition to utilizing LGBTQ rights as a measure by which to determine who deserves imperialist violence, these discourses make queer and Muslim or Arab mutually exclusive categories. This binary split is "a primary facet of homonationalism," which presumes "the whiteness of gay, homosexual, and queer bodies, and the... heterosexuality of colored bodies" (Puar, 2007, p. 44).

Homonationalism's binary and deployment as a metric for acceptability to the nation still proliferate in contemporary discourses. The binary was prominent, for example, in the Trump administration's so-called "Muslim Ban," which blocked immigrants from seven majority-Muslim countries from entering the country. Trump rhetorically justified the ban in part based on Muslims' allegedly homophobic views, in spite of his own policies and rhetoric against LGBTQ people (Aftab, 2017). Such instances evidence the persistence of homonationalism as an analytic that makes sense of the shifting, complicit relationship between nonnormative sexualities and genders and the nation-state.

Because of its continued applicability to various political contexts, the conceptual framework of homonationalism has circulated widely—including substantial activist uptake outside of scholarly conversation and beyond the original context of the United States in which it was theorized—to refer to LGBTQ complicity with otherwise conservative nationalisms and imperial and colonial projects. Puar, however, stressed that homonationalism does not just refer to "gay racism." In her writing after *Terrorist Assemblages*, she clarified that "instead of thinking of homonationalism as an accusation, an identity, a bad politics" it must be understood "as an analytic to apprehend state formation and a structure of modernity" (Puar, 2013,

p. 337). To understand Puar's insistence that homonationalism is not an accusation of bad politics but in fact a "condition of possibility for national and transnational politics" requires deeper insight into the theoretical frameworks she draws and expands upon, particularly her discussion of bio- and necropolitical assemblages.

HOMONATIONALISM AS BIO-NECROPOLITICAL ASSEMBLAGE

Puar's (2013) repeated insistence that homonationalism be understood as "a constitutive and fundamental reorientation of the relationship between the state, capitalism, and sexuality" (p. 337) relies on a set of theoretical references related to the management of life and death under contemporary formations of sovereign power. Homonationalism centers sexuality in understanding contemporary manifestations of biopower, which Michel Foucault first theorized as an 18th-century shift in sovereign power in Europe such that the state was no longer primarily concerned with killing but with cultivating life (Foucault, 2003; Puar, 2007). Biopolitical concern with perpetuating life, in turn, displaces death as sovereign power's central concern; as Foucault (2003) formulated it, biopower is "the right to make live and to let die" (p. 241). Death, in this formulation, is simply a side effect of the management of life. This management of life, moreover, takes two opposite forms. While biopolitical intervention happens at the level of individual bodies that are surveilled and disciplined, it is also concerned with the production and governance of populations (Foucault, 2003, pp. 242–243).

Puar (2007) defined homonationalism as a regulatory facet of biopower that situates sexuality precisely within this division between subject and population; in homonationalist configurations of power, some LGBTQ individuals are made "celebratory queer liberal subjects folded into life" while others are made "sexually pathological and deviant populations targeted for death" (p. 24). Here we see, again, the binary between citizen and terrorist that characterizes homonationalism. However, the explanatory power of Foucauldian biopolitics is insufficient to fully understand homonationalism's production of citizen-subjects and terrorist-populations.

A secondary concern with death that comes from biopolitics' emphasis on the management of life does not adequately address the way that homonationalist formations of power explicitly mark certain populations for death by using progressive discourses around sexuality to justify imperialist projects such as U.S. military intervention in the Middle East (Puar, 2013, p. 336). For this, Puar turned to Achille Mbembe's theory of necropolitics. Mbembe posited that the exercise of sovereign power, particularly in colonial and neo-colonial contexts, is better characterized as necropolitical in character. While Foucault (2003) argued that "power ignores death" (pp. 247–248), Mbembe (2003) countered that power also instrumentalizes and materially destroys certain populations, offering nothing *but* death to those deemed disposable (p. 14). On the colonial flipside of modernity's biopolitics, necropolitics thus aims for total destruction, constantly exposing its targeted populations (the racialized, colonized, and enslaved) to the potential for death, as well as conditions of life that Mbembe called deathworlds (p. 40). Necropower inverts the Foucauldian formula, *making* some populations die (or relegating them to a deathly existence) in order to let subjects live. Queer necropolitics in particular, as homonationalism demonstrates, ties the ascendance of some subjects to "continued or renewing forms of disposability, death, and abandonment for others" (Haritaworn et al., 2015, p. 20).

Because it involves both bio- and necropolitics, the theoretical framework of homonationalism sutures the two together, with Puar writing of bio–necro collaboration. She stated that, "it is precisely within the interstices of life and death that we find the differences between queer subjects who are being folded…into life and the racialized queernesses that emerge through the naming of populations" (Puar, 2007, p. 35). By addressing the relationship between race, sexuality, and gender that shapes different possibilities for different populations, homonationalism asks "how the production of identity categories such as gay, lesbian, and even queer work in service of the management, reproduction, and regeneration of life rather than being predominantly understood as implicitly or explicitly targeted for death" (Puar, 2007, p. 35), and answers that the securitization of life for some LGBTQ subjects entails death for racialized others. In this way, homonationalism holds bio and necro in tension, describing the production of desirable subjects and disposable populations, which does not preclude nonnormative genders and sexualities from being complicit with the nation. Understanding homonationalism as a particular formation of power that harnesses sexuality and gender to produce proper citizens and disposable populations at the conjunction between bio- and necropolitics means that "homonationalism can be resisted and re-signified, but not opted out of: we are all conditioned by and through it" (Puar, 2013, p. 336).

Homonationalism is not only a theory of how sexuality is deployed toward nationalist projects; it is also part of queer studies' larger radical reorientation of how we understand sexuality and the larger politics around identification (Eng & Puar, 2020). Relying on Gilles Deleuze and Félix Guattari's (1987) theory of assemblage, Puar resisted any reliance on a static notion of identity throughout her writing on homonationalism. Against the notion of fixed, unchanging categories of identity (such as race, class, gender, sexuality) that intersect and can be disaggregated from one another, Puar (2007) suggested that "assemblage is more attuned to the interwoven forces that merge and dissipate time, space, and body against linearity, coherency, and permanency" (p. 212). For this reason, she suggested that homonationalism is "an assemblage of de- and re-territorializing forces, affects, energies and movements…a field of power rather than an activity or property of any one nation-state, organization, or individual" (Puar, 2015, p. 321). Put otherwise, as an assemblage, homonationalism tracks ever-shifting interactions of geopolitical practices, relations, shifts, conditions, and possibilities but it is neither singularly definable nor the responsibility of any one individual actor.

On the one hand, this fluidity makes it a challenge to delimit what is and is not homonationalism and, as Schotten (2016) pointed out, Puar occasionally seemed to contradict herself on that account. On the other, conceptual flexibility is part of why the term has found enduring resonance across contexts. As Puar (2015) wrote, homonationalism's conceptual virality is "a virality of mutation and replication rather than the banal reproduction of its analytic frame across different national contexts" (p. 334). The assemblage of the concept of homonationalism, along with the relations and practices it names, shifts in contingency with historical, geopolitical, and contextual circumstance, but nevertheless endures as an academic and activist analytic. The section Homonationalism's Circulation and Contestation therefore addresses the continued uptake and circulation of homonationalism as a framework, while also addressing some of the critiques and debates the concept has engendered.

HOMONATIONALISM'S CIRCULATION AND CONTESTATION

The theoretical framework of homonationalism was developed primarily in application to the Unites States and, as described in the section Palestine, Pinkwashing, and Homonationalism's Limits, Israel. However, scholars from an array of fields apply it to contexts all over the world. For just a few examples, these contexts and topics range from settler colonial institutions, the legal system, and refugee resettlement in Canada (Dryden & Lenon, 2015; Greensmith & Giwa, 2013; Murray, 2014; Smith, 2020; Sykes, 2016) to global sporting events in England (Hubbard & Wilkinson, 2015), South Africa, and Brazil (Mitchell, 2016) to the education system (Reimers, 2017) and journalistic rhetoric about Africa in Sweden (Jungar & Peltonen, 2017) to the rise of the populist right (Spierings, 2020) and the criminalization of Moroccans in the Netherlands (Aydemir, 2012) to Flemish press representation (Dhoest, 2020) to Italian imaginaries of Europe (Colpani & Habed, 2014) to gentrification in Germany (Haritaworn, 2015) to LGBTQ migrants in Serbia (Badali, 2019) to narratives of becoming European in Kosovo (Rexhepi, 2016) to South Africa's assertion of its democracy via a gay-friendly image (Lewis, 2021; Tucker, 2020) to Singapore's relaxation of restrictions on homosexual activity in the early 2000s (Treat, 2015) to queer Asian diasporas in Australia (Bao, 2013; Yue, 2012).

This brief survey does not approximate a comprehensive view of the thousands of ways the concept has been cited across disciplines and in application to hundreds of distinct geopolitical contexts. It does, however, begin to surface some of the tensions and debates endemic to homonationalism's applications; despite the widespread use of the term, questions emerge about its applicability in contexts not as neatly imperialist as those Puar analyzed. For instance, Leksikov and Rachok (2020) challenged the explanatory potential of homonationalism when it comes to Eastern Europe, suggesting that the postsocialist space is too distinct for the concept to map on neatly. Similarly, Moss (2014) highlighted the variety of configurations of politics in relation to sexuality and gender in Europe, pointing out that treating Europe as a singular, homonationalist category can obfuscate the Central and Eastern European queer experience. Dhawan (2016) meanwhile argued that a narrow focus on homonationalism in the Global North makes it a challenge to address homophobia and heteronormativity in the postcolonial world. By focusing on postapartheid South Africa, Tucker (2020) made a similar point, emphasizing the need to consider how homonationalism both translates and is reconfigured in locations outside of global centers of power.

Such questions around applicability across contexts arise in broader critiques of homonationalism. Ritchie (2015) posited that homonationalism has become a "totalizing theory" that relies on a "dangerously simplistic construction of reality" (p. 621), echoing Currah's (2013) assertion that a lack of attention to local particularities results in homonationalist analyses that fetishize a generalized idea of the state. Zanghellini (2012) argued that, while valuable, the framework of homonationalism is overused to such an extent that it results in inaccurate claims and undermines gay rights discourses and activism. In a similar vein, Schotten (2016) sustained that the concept itself, especially as Puar formulated it in later writings, has become so expansive that it undercuts its utility for activist agendas seeking to problematize LGBTQ complicity with the state. Many of these critiques take special issue with Puar's arguments related to "pinkwashing," a corollary of homonationalism that refers to nation-states promoting a "gay-friendly" record in order to obscure other types of political violence including colonialism, apartheid, and ethnic cleansing (Mikdashi, 2011; Schulman, 2011). The debates around pinkwashing offer a grounded example from which to understand some of the most prominent applications and criticisms of homonationalism.

PALESTINE, PINKWASHING, AND HOMONATIONALISM'S LIMITS

Critiques of pinkwashing have been leveraged at myriad nation-states, but perhaps none so much as Israel. This has to do with its history and geopolitical context: Puar wrote that "Israel is a pioneer of homonationalism as its particular position at the crosshairs of settler colonialism, occupation, and neoliberalist accommodationism creates the perfect storm for the normalization of homosexuality through national belonging" (2017, p. 97). She further noted that LGBTQ rights rose to prominence in Israel at the same time as the first intifada, meaning that increased mobility for LGBTQ Israelis occurred concomitantly with the increased segregation and containment of Palestinians (Puar, 2017, p. 97). This history demonstrates how homonationalism pins the national acceptance of some LGBTQ subjects to death and destruction for racialized and colonized populations, framed as "terrorists" incapable of self-governance and thus deserving of violence. Pinkwashing can therefore be understood as a part of the larger assemblage of homonationalism, illustrating the point that homonationalism is a condition of modernity that makes possible practices like the use of LGBT rights as a metric for denying a population's right to self-determination (Puar, 2013, p. 337). As Puar put it, "homonationalism-as-assemblage creates a global field within which pinkwashing takes hold" (2017, p. 118).

Given its exemplary nature, Palestine–Israel is one of the sites where the related concepts of homonationalism and pinkwashing have taken hold amongst activists seeking to problematize the use of liberal LGBT rights discourses to obscure Israel's colonial violence. For instance, Al Qaws for Sexual and Gender Diversity in Palestinian Society (Al Qaws, 2020) argued that pinkwashing in the Palestinian–Israeli context goes beyond propaganda that brands Israel as gay-friendly and instead speaks to the structural roots of settler colonial oppression. As they wrote, "recognizing pinkwashing as colonial violence can help us understand how Israel divides, oppresses, and erases Palestinians on the basis of gender and sexuality."

Crucially, Al Qaws (2020) pointed out pinkwashing's contradictions, because it puts LGBTQ Palestinians in an impossible bind by pushing "the racist idea that sexual and gender diversity are unnatural and foreign to Palestinian society" and compelling "queer Palestinians to interpret their experiences and pain through the lens of victimhood and powerlessness, which contributes to the broader disempowerment and suppression of all Palestinians under colonial domination." Al Qaws refused, as LGBTQ Palestinians, to disavow their larger communities, instead situating pinkwashing within a broader settler colonial context that does harm to all Palestinians, regardless of gender and sexual identity. In effect, Al Qaws refused the binary split endemic to homonationalist projects, in which racial others—especially Arabs and Muslims—are deemed straight (Puar, 2007). They also moved beyond identitarian politics, suggesting that "Palestinian queerness is not simply an identity, but a radical approach to political mobilization and decolonization" (Al Qaws, 2020). In this way, Al Qaws's analysis emphasizes the point that pinkwashing is not an exclusively queer issue, in the sense that it is "a powerful manifestation of the regulation of identity in an increasingly homonationalist world—a world that evaluates nationhood on the basis of the treatment of its homosexuals" (Puar, 2017, p. 124).

Because pinkwashing in the Palestinian–Israeli context plays the function of folding some subjects into life while disposing of whole populations along racial and colonial lines, it evidences the larger intervention into theories of power that Puar made with the concept of homonationalism. However, it would be incorrect to suggest that analyses of pinkwashing are the domain of homonationalism alone for two reasons. First, Al Qaws drew on their own rich history of resistance which does not rely on the analyses of U.S. academics. Second, contention around pinkwashing highlights some of the tensions between homonationalism as a theoretical framework and the politics of organizing to confront pinkwashing in practice.

Al Qaws and other antipinkwashing efforts have at times been at odds with Puar's analysis in ways that echo and inform debates around the larger concept of homonationalism. For example, Puar and Mikdashi (2012a) argued that counternarratives to pinkwashing (known as pinkwatching) end up unwittingly reinforcing discourses of homonationalism by making claims that take for granted that "the right to…sovereignty is now evaluated by how a nation treats its homosexuals." In response, Schotten and Maikey (2012) asserted that Puar and Mikdashi rely too heavily on the conceptual framework of homonationalism in ways that undercut the material struggles of antipinkwashing activists, especially queer Palestinians like Maikey, who cofounded Al Qaws and Palestinian Queers for BDS. Analyzing this same debate, Ritchie (2015) argued that homonationalism "now means so many things that it no longer means much of anything." In a rejoinder to the debate, Puar and Mikdashi (2012b) reasserted that pinkwashing is a facet of homonationalism and that their caution around pinkwatching was not directed at regional Palestinian organizers. Nonetheless, critiques about the way the concept can undercut efforts to organize against pinkwashing still warrant consideration from anyone looking to engage the framework of homonationalism.

Finally, though Puar (2017) referred to Israel and the United States as the "greatest beneficiaries of homonationalism in the current global order" (p. 97), she also cautioned against any impulse to exceptionalize Israel as uniquely homonationalist. Rather, she emphasized the centrality of history and the global international context in shaping which nation-states utilize pinkwashing as an effective strategy. Pinkwashing, as she wrote, "is only one more justification for imperial/racial/national violence that has a long history preceding it" (Puar, 2015, p. 328). The conversations around pinkwashing thus demonstrate some of the central tenets of the concept of homonationalism, emphasizing the critique of static identity and the utility of assemblage theory, the importance of geopolitical context, and the function of homonationalism as an aspect of bio-necropolitical power that conditions all of us, not just LGBT subjects. They also bring up some of homonationalism's most pointed critiques, particularly with regard to the framework's utility for activist politics on the ground; Puar's insistence that homonationalism is not a state practice, as this section has noted, does not always easily align with efforts to hold perpetrators of pinkwashing accountable. This tension contributes to another prominent critique and extension of homonationalism, which focuses on the function of settler colonialism not just externally to the United States but within it.

SETTLER COLONIAL COMPLICATIONS

In response to Schotten and Maikey's (2012) criticism that their analysis of pinkwashing undermines Palestinian organizing against Israel's settler colonial violence, Puar and Mikdashi

(2012b) asserted that their critique of pinkwatching was directed at U.S.-based activists. They argued that "one should question, for example, U.S.-based activists who fight settler colonialism in Israel without acknowledging the ongoing settling of the United States." In conversation with this claim, Morgensen (2013) stressed that there are generative dialogues, coalitions, and synergies to be built between queer and trans Palestinian resistance to Israeli settler colonialism and Indigenous queer, trans, and Two-Spirit resistance to settler colonialism in the United States and Canada. Indeed, a focused attention on settlement is one area of study that has productively complicated and expanded the framework of homonationalism.

While a focus on colonialism inheres in the original definition(s) of homonationalism, much writing on homonationalism imagines colonial and imperial dynamics to occur outside of the United States geographically and only after 9/11 historically. In contrast, Morgensen (2010) turned to the necropolitical management of Native peoples throughout the history of U.S. settler colonialism in order to extend Puar's elaboration of homonationalism toward an understanding of the way that settlement conditions the formation of modern sexuality. His theorization of a specific settler homonationalism in turn invites queer studies to denaturalize settlement by centering settler colonialism "as a condition of the formation of modern queer subjects, cultures, and politics in the United States" (Morgensen, 2010, p. 106). In demonstrating the complicity between LGBTQ sexualities and U.S. settler colonialism, Morgensen offered a longer history of homonationalism. Such an intervention has important implications for the study of homonationalism, histories of settler colonialism, and Indigenous and LGBTQ studies alike.

Morgensen (2010) argued that homonationalism refers not just to the contemporary complicity between nonnormative sexualities and nationalist or imperialist projects, but that homonationalism in fact undergirds the biopolitics of modern sexuality in the United States, which was only made possible through the ongoing regulation and subjugation of Native genders and sexualities. Adding to the formulation of citizen-subjects folded into life and their counterpart terrorists targeted for death, he asked: "What might 'terrorists' figured as foreign, have to do with 'savages,' figured as domestic, when the state identifies objects of colonial or imperial control?" (Morgensen, 2010, p. 107). In conversation with queer and feminist Native studies and histories, Morgensen emphasized that gender and sexuality informed colonial expansion in the Americas, with sexual regulation and discipline as a cornerstone of settler colonial terror. As he wrote, "under colonial rule, Native people faced constant condemnation of gender and sexual transgression, which at times took shape as a violent education in a new life" (Morgensen, 2010, p. 115). It is important to recognize that the bio- and necropolitical management of Indigenous sexualities and genders did not go uncontested; as Morgensen has emphasized, settler colonial regulation and disciplining of sexual and gender diversity was met with not just individual but collective resistance. Much like the example of Al Qaws's insistence that Palestinian queer liberation necessarily entails decolonization for all Palestinians, Native gender and sexual diversity in the United States has "persistently troubled the boundaries of sexual colonization" (Morgensen, 2010, pp. 116–117). This collective resistance to settler systems and institutions that harm all colonized people, furthermore, speaks to the way that settler homonationalism not only disciplines gender and sexuality but actively produces them, marking some populations for life and targeting (racial, sexual) others for death.

Morgensen's (2010) elaboration of settler homonationalism reiterated that homonationalism does not just describe the regulation and deployment of static, given identities in service of nationalist and settler colonial projects. Gender and sexuality, as well as settler colonialism itself, are formed through that regulation. He wrote that "scholars must recognize that modern sexuality is not a *product* of settler colonialism... modern sexuality arose in the United States as a method to *produce* settler colonialism, and settler subjects by facilitating ongoing conquest and naturalizing its effects" (Morgensen, 2010, p. 117). This means that not only the management but the very creation of modern sexuality is mutually constitutive with colonial processes of settlement. Processes of settlement, in turn, presume Native disappearance and absence to such an extent that even when LGBTQ people across the racial spectrum have been assigned a degenerate status in the United States as they were in the early 20th century, such a framing assumes that they are non-Native, presuming that "Native people had already disappeared from the modern and settled spaces where queer degenerates would be found" (Morgensen, 2010, p. 119). When non-Native queers become citizens, folded into life, they "do so by joining a colonial biopolitics of modern sexuality that functions to produce modern queers as settler subjects in relation to Native peoples" (Morgensen, 2010, p. 121). By articulating the relationship that modern, even nonnormative, sexualities and genders have to the erasure of Native people and the perpetuation of settlement, Morgensen thus profoundly reoriented the history of homonationalism, taking a long view of the way that it has undergirded formations of gender, sexuality, and biopower since the inception of the United States. This also means that homonationalism cannot be meaningfully challenged without denaturalizing settler colonialism; "theorizing settler homonationalism indicates how U.S. queer claims on national belonging stabilize settlement and participate in reinventing its lessons within new imperial projects" (Morgensen, 2010, p. 125). The only way to disrupt settler homonationalism, therefore, is to challenge settlement itself.

Because it ties a thread between the United States' production of "terrorists" through external imperial projects and the disciplining of gender and sexuality through internal settler colonial projects, the concept of settler homonationalism has embarked on a series of viral travels itself. While Morgensen focused on the United States, with some references to Indigenous communities in the broader Americas, the theory of settler homonationalism has clear explanatory power for settler colonial contexts across the world. One prominent example is the context of Canada, where the concept of settler homonationalism has been applied to illuminate the way that Canadian queer politics and pinkwashing policies simultaneously uplift White queer settlers while disavowing Indigenous queer, trans, and Two-Spirit subjectivities and obscuring the ongoing violence of settlement (Dryden & Lenon, 2015; Greensmith & Giwa, 2013; Sykes, 2016). In Puar's (2017) revisiting of the concept of homonationalism, she cited Morgensen to write that settler colonialism must be differentiated within theorizations of the biopolitics of colonialism, lest we end up treating colonialism as a foregone conclusion (p. 138). At the same time, settler homonationalism has not been without its own criticisms. For example, Oswin (2012) asked if Native Two-Spirit and queer communities necessarily resist homonationalism or if they are also complicit with it. This question resonates with the critique that if homonationalism is a condition of modernity that shapes all of us, then the concept is too broad to meaningfully leverage in critiques of specific politics. Such concerns merit attention in future scholarship on settler homonationalism.

Efforts to theorize homonationalism must grapple with settlement and its implications for the complicity between discourses of LGBTQ rights and the necropolitical violence unique to settler colonialism. Morgensen (2010) recommended that queer projects and scholarship, especially, denaturalize settlement in favor of studying "the past and present activity of settler colonialism as a contradictory and contested process, which even now produces and fractures homonationalism" (p. 107). In addition to Morgensen's fundamental expansion of homonationalism, there are several emergent reorientations and extensions of homonationalism that will likely shape study around the concept into the future.

FUTURES

Homonationalism is fixed neither in its definition nor in its expression through formations of power, as Puar has repeated and as is clear in tracing the uptake of the term. While this flexibility has resulted in the critiques of the concept's imprecision and lack of practical political utility referenced here, it has also propelled homonationalism's viral travels, provoking a wide array of theorizations related not only to homosexual subjectivities and rights discourses but also to how identitarian politics of all stripes—whether around transness, disability, or other lines of identification—can become complicit with nationalist and imperialist projects. This section therefore discusses some of the most prominent extensions of the concept of homonationalism beyond gender and sexuality, then concludes with a discussion of its (always shifting) future possibilities and limitations, both for the field of communication studies and more broadly.

Much of the literature on homonationalism remains ambiguous around the degree to which the concept applies to trans and gender nonconforming subjectivities and rights discourses. The literature summarized here reflects this dynamic; Puar's (2007) initial elaboration of homonationalism insisted on the term "homosexual" in reference to those folded into life to differentiate from the forms of queerness that mark "terrorists" and others as improperly sexual and therefore appropriate targets for death (p. 14). However, much of the literature on homonationalism uses LGBT or queer as an umbrella under which any of those subject markers or communities' rights can be mobilized toward homonationalist ends (see, for example: Winer & Bolzendahl, 2021). Myriad analyses of homonationalism, moreover, rely on examples in which some trans subjects (typically those who conform to norms of race, class, and linear transition) are folded into life in service of the nation's necropolitics. For instance, Puar (2017) referenced then-U.S. Vice President Joe Biden's statement that "transgender rights are the civil rights of our time" and the array of antidiscrimination laws passed during Obama's presidency, which coincided with the ongoing murder of Black trans women and the continuation of U.S. imperialist projects (pp. 33–34). This example indicates that homonationalism is not limited to homosexuality, which coincides with Puar's (2015) analysis of homonationalism as assemblage.

Despite the implicit suggestion in much writing on homonationalism that the term refers to LGBTQ complicity in general, however, there are meaningful distinctions to be made between gender and sexuality when it comes to understanding how nonnormative practices or identities are mobilized toward homonationalist ends. For this reason, scholars and activists increasingly ask if and how transness, specifically, can be channeled toward nationalist and imperialist projects. Puar's (2017) elaboration of homonationalism does not answer this question, but asked if Biden's remarks on trans rights "signal the uptake of a new variant of homonationalism—a 'trans(homo)nationalism'? Or is transgender identity a variation of processes of citizenship and nationalism through disciplinary normativization rather than a variation of homonationalism?" (p. 34). Either way, she argued, trans rights discourses will inevitably produce new targets for bio–necropolitical management.

The claim that trans rights discourses can create conditions of disposability for racialized and colonized populations resonates with other theorizations of transnormativity and transnormative subjects, particularly Snorton and Haritaworn's (2013) assertion that the universalizing discourse of transition and trans visibility "largely remains uninterrogated in its complicities and convergences with biomedical, neoliberal, racist, and imperialist projects" (p. 67). They emphasized the way that trans of color subjectivities are so barely conceivable that transnormativity has yet to be critiqued in a meaningful way, and that when trans of color positions *are* made visible it is often through capitalization on the death of trans people of color in service of carceral and other exploitative systems (Snorton & Haritaworn, 2013, pp. 67–68). This intervention—along with similar efforts to articulate the role of trans subjectivities and rights discourses in nationalist, necropolitical projects (Bacchetta & Haritaworn, 2016; Haritaworn, 2015; Haritaworn et al., 2015)—contributes to a small but powerful literature elaborating trans-specific applications and complications of homonationalism.

Another pressing area of consideration attends to the convergences between disability rights rhetoric and nationalist designs. In conversation with Puar, Snyder and Mitchell (2010) coined the term "ablenationalism" to refer to "the degree to which treating people with disabilities as an exception valorizes able-bodied norms of inclusion as the naturalized qualification of citizenship" (p. 113). In a similar vein, but with particular attention to how disability can be differentially included in projects of nationalism rather than wholesale excluded, McRuer (2010) wrote of "disability nationalism in crip times." He argued that disability studies must better attend to the geopolitics of disability, specifically the way that global phenomena problematize identity-based and nationalist frameworks—such as the able-bodied versus disabled binary—that shape the field (pp. 163–164). Further elaborating on this point, Markotić and McRuer (2012) theorized "crip nationalism," a term that marks "an emergent, neoliberal form of nationalism that works in and through contemporary forms of disability identity, community, and solidarity" (p. 167). These analyses in turn inform Puar's (2017) work which theorized debility as a way to complicate disability studies' general inattention to the ways that racism, colonial, and capitalism actively disable populations while capacitating others, including by folding certain disabled subjects into life. Puar (2017) also wedded this theory of debility to an understanding of trans(homo)nationalism, writing that the racialized and gender nonconforming bodies abjected by legal and nation-state recognition of normative transness are also debilitated (p. 35). Thus, theories of the way that discourses around trans and disabled identities can be mobilized toward the necropolitical disposal of populations continue the larger project of homonationalism: accounting for the way that everyone is positioned in webs of bio- and necropolitical control through neoliberal rights frameworks and identity discourses that uplift some (even historically oppressed or nonnormative) subjects in service of violence at the expense of others along racial, colonial, and capitalist lines.

In spite of the concept's popularity as a way to name the shifting complicities of LGBTQ and other rights discourses with nationalist and imperialist political aims, homonationalism has found limited uptake within the field of communication studies in the United States. This has to do, perhaps, with what some have noted as the field's larger lack of attention to LGBTQ studies (Manning et al., 2020; Yep, 2003), combined with its overrepresentation of White perspectives that do little to challenge racial and colonial constructs (Chakravartty et al., 2018). There are a few notable exceptions. For example, Yue (2012) wrote on the homonational regulation of queer diasporic Asian subjects under modernity, Chávez (2015) analyzed post-9/11 rhetoric for the way that they construct queerness as inherently terrorist, and Calafell (2017) responded to the 2016 massacre during Latin Night at the LGBT nightclub Pulse by stressing the need to consider how homonationalism, imperialism, and colonialism shape reality for queers of color. However, the communication of homonationalism—how it is expressed through discourses of power that co-opt nonnormative genders and sexualities toward the bio–necropolitical management of populations and through resistance to that management—remains relatively undertheorized, especially in terms of engaging the critiques, debates, and extensions of the concept. Within the field of communication studies, there is thus opportunity—and a need—to analyze how homonationalism is discursively expressed, justified, and challenged with a particular attention to settlement and colonialism, as well as the debates the concept has provoked.

Finally, though this account has focused primarily on the scholarly lineage of the term homonationalism, some of its most prominent circulations are not published through academic channels or written down at all. Many queer of color communities, as well as people whose self-determination is undercut by forms of colonialism and imperialism that weaponize LGBTQ rights discourses toward imperialist ends, recognize and resist homonationalism in everyday practice. For example, on Transgender Day of Visibility on March 31, 2021, President Biden (2021) tweeted that, "Transgender rights are human rights." In response, Familia: Trans Queer Liberation Movement (2021), an organization fighting for trans, queer, and gender nonconforming Latinxs, responded "Believing transgender rights are human rights means taking action to protect transgender people from gender based violences they face inside detention centers while in ICE custody. We demand you #EndTransDetention now!" Familia effectively rejected Biden's embrace of a liberal trans rights discourse of national acceptance, instead highlighting the way that the racialized violence of detention is also a form of violence against trans people. In doing so, Familia's argument rejected homo(trans)nationalism's embrace of normative trans communities at the expense of the racialized, noncitizen migrants, whom discourses of trans visibility might otherwise make disposable.

Instances like these indicate that whether or not the specific term "homonationalism" continues to have purchase, the shifting dynamics it names persist. The mobilization of LGBTQ rights discourses in service of bio–necropower and the struggles of those who confront such dynamics as part of their organizing against settler colonialism, imperialism, incarceration, and debility merit further scholarly attention in general (Winer & Bolzendahl, 2021), as well as in the specific field of communication studies.

REFERENCES

Aftab, A. (2017, February 6). Queering Islamophobia: The homonationalism of the Muslim ban. *Bitch Media*. https://www.bitchmedia.org/article/one-nation-under-hate/homonationalism-donald-trump

Al Qaws. (2020, October 10). Beyond propaganda: Pinkwashing as colonial violence. http://www.alqaws.org/articles/Beyond-Propaganda-Pinkwashing-as-Colonial-Violence?category_id=0

Anker, E. (2012). Feminist theory and the failures of post-9/11 freedom. *Politics & Gender, 8*(2), 207–215. https://doi.org/10.1017/S1743923X12000177

Aydemir, M. (2012). Dutch homonationalism and intersectionality. In E. Boehmer & S. de Mul (Eds.), *The postcolonial Low Countries: Literature, colonialism, and multiculturalism* (pp. 187–202). Lexington Books.

Bacchetta, P., & Haritaworn, J. (2016). There are many transatlantics: Homonationalism, homotransnationalism and feminist-queer-trans of colour theories and practices. In M. Evans & K. Davis (Eds.), *Transatlantic conversations: Feminism as travelling theory* (pp. 127–143). Routledge.

Badali, J. (2019). Migrants in the closet: LGBT migrants, homonationalism, and the right to refuge in Serbia. *Journal of Gay & Lesbian Social Services, 31*(1), 89–119. https://doi.org/10.1080/10538720.2019.1548330

Bao, H. (2013). A queer "comrade" in Sydney. *Interventions, 15*(1), 127–140. https://doi.org/10.1080/1369801X.2013.771012

Bhattacharyya, G. (2008). *Dangerous brown men: Exploiting sex, violence, and feminism in the war on terror.* Zed Books.

Biden, J. R. [@POTUS]. (2021, March 31). *Transgender rights are human rights—and I'm calling on every America to join me in uplifting the worth… #TransDayofVisibility* [Tweet]. Twitter. https://twitter.com/POTUS/status/1377255646651908102

Boggio Éwanjé-Épée, F., & Magliani-Belkacem, S. (2013, March 5). *The empire of sexuality: An interview with Joseph Massad*. Jadaliyya. https://www.jadaliyya.com/Details/28167

Calafell, B. (2017). Brownness, kissing, and US imperialism: Contextualizing the Orlando Massacre. *Communication & Critical/Cultural Studies, 14*(2), 198–202. https://doi.org/10.1080/14791420.2017.1293957

Chakravartty, P., Kuo, R., Grubbs, V., & McIlwain, C. (2018). #CommunicationSoWhite. *Journal of Communication, 68*(2), 254–266. https://doi.org/10.1093/joc/jqy003

Chávez, K. R. (2015). The precariousness of homonationalism: The queer agency of terrorism in post-9/11 rhetoric. *QED, 2*(3), 32–58. https://doi.org/10.14321/qed.2.3.0032

Chow, R. (2002). *The protestant ethnic and the spirit of capitalism*. Columbia University Press.

Colpani, G., & Habed, A. J. (2014). "In Europe it's different": Homonationalism and peripheral desires for Europe. In P. M. Ayoub & D. Paternotte (Eds.), *LGBT activism and the making of Europe: A rainbow Europe?* (pp. 73–93). Palgrave Macmillan. https://doi.org/10.1057/9781137391766_4

Currah, P. (2013). Homonationalism, state rationalities, and sex contradictions. *Theory & Event, 16*(1).

Deleuze, G., & Guattari, F. (1987). *A thousand plateaus: Capitalism and schizophrenia* (B. Massumi, Trans.). Columbia University Press.

Dhawan, N. (2016). Homonationalism and state-phobia: The postcolonial predicament of queering modernities. In M. A. Viteri & M. L. Picq (Eds.), *Queering paradigms V: Queering narratives of modernity* (pp. 51–68). Bern.

Dhoest, A. (2020). Eastern others: Homonationalism in the Flemish press. *International Communication Gazette, 83*(6), 1–20. https://doi.org/10.1177/1748048520918495

Dryden, O. H., & Lenon, S. (2015). *Disrupting queer inclusion: Canadian homonationalisms and the politics of belonging*. University of British Columbia Press.

Duggan, L. (2004). *The twilight of equality? Neoliberalism, cultural politics, and the attack on democracy.* Beacon Press.

Eng, D. L., & Puar, J. K. (2020). Introduction: Left of queer. *Social Text, 38*(4), 1–23.

Familia: Trans Queer Liberation Movement [@familiatqlm]. (2021, March 31). *@potus Actions speak louder than words. Believing transgender rights are human rights means taking action to protect transgender… #TransDayofVisibility* [Tweet]. Twitter. https://twitter.com/familiatqlm/status/1377286457556090882

Foucault, M. (2003). *Society must be defended: Lectures at the College de France, 1975–1976* (D. Macey, Trans.). Picador.

Greensmith, C., & Giwa, S. (2013). Challenging settler colonialism in contemporary queer politics: Settler homonationalism, Pride Toronto, and Two-Spirit subjectivities. *American Indian Culture and Research Journal, 37*(2), 129–148. https://doi.org/10.17953/aicr.37.2.p4q2r84l12735117

Grewal, I. (2005). *Transnational America: Feminisms, diasporas, neoliberalisms*. Duke University Press.

Haritaworn, J. (2015). *Queer lovers and hateful others: Regenerating violent times and places*. Pluto Press.

Haritaworn, J., Kuntsman, A., & Posocco, S. (2015). *Queer necropolitics*. Routledge.

Hubbard, P., & Wilkinson, E. (2015). Welcoming the world? Hospitality, homonationalism, and the London 2012 Olympics. *Antipode, 47*(3), 598–615. https://doi.org/10.1111/anti.12082

Jungar, K., & Peltonen, S. (2017). Acts of homonationalism: Mapping Africa in the Swedish media. *Sexualities, 20*(5–6), 715–737. https://doi.org/10.1177/1363460716645806

Leksikov, R., & Rachok, D. (2020). Beyond Western theories: On the use and abuse of "homonationalism" in Eastern Europe. In R. Buyantueva & M. Shevtsova (Eds.), *LGBTQ+ activism in Central and Eastern Europe: Resistance, representation and identity* (pp. 25–49). Springer International.

Lewis, D. (2021). Governmentality and South Africa's edifice of gender and sexual rights. *Journal of Asian and African Studies, 56*(1), 109–119. https://doi.org/10.1177/0021909620946854

Manning, J., Asante, G., Huerta Moreno, L., Johnson, R. LeMaster, B., Yachao, L., Rudnick, J., Stern, D., & Young, S. (2020). Queering communication studies: A *Journal of Applied Communication Research* forum. *Journal of Applied Communication Research, 48*(4), 413–437. https://doi.org/10.1080/00909882.2020.1789197

Markotić, N., & McRuer, R. (2012). Leading with your head: On the borders of disability, sexuality, and the nation. In R. McRuer & A. Mollow (Eds.), *Sex and disability* (pp. 165–182). Duke University Press. https://doi.org/10.1215/9780822394877-009

Massad, J. (2002). Re-Orienting desire: The gay international and the Arab world. *Public Culture, 14*(2), 361–385.

Mbembe, A. (2003). Necropolitics (A. Meintjes, Trans.). *Public Culture, 15*(1), 11–40.

McRuer, R. (2010). Disability nationalism in crip times. *Journal of Literary and Cultural Disability, 4*(2), 163–178. https://doi.org/10.3828/jlcds.2010.13

Mikdashi, M. (2011, December 16). *Gay rights as human rights: Pinkwashing homonationalism*. Jadaliyya. https://www.jadaliyya.com/Details/24855/Gay-Rights-as-Human-Rights-Pinkwashing-Homonationalism

Mitchell, G. (2016). Evangelical ecstasy meets feminist fury: Sex trafficking, moral panics, and homonationalism during global sporting events. *GLQ, 22*(3), 325–357. https://doi.org/10.1215/10642684-3479306

Mohanty, C. (2008). *Feminism and war*. Zed Books.

Morgensen, S. L. (2010). Settler homonationalism: Theorizing settler colonialism within queer modernities. *GLQ, 16*(1–2), 105–131. https://doi.org/10.1215/10642684-2009-015

Morgensen, S. L. (2013, April 3). *Settler colonialism and alliance: Comparative challenges to pinkwashing and homonationalism*. Jadaliyya. https://www.jadaliyya.com/Details/28372/Settler-Colonialism-and-Alliance-Comparative-Challenges-to-Pinkwashing-and-Homonationalism

Moss, K. (2014). Split Europe: Homonationalism and homophobia in Croatia. In P. M. Ayoub & D. Paternotte (Eds.), *LGBT activism and the making of Europe: A rainbow Europe?* (pp. 212–232). Palgrave Macmillan. https://doi.org/10.1057/9781137391766_10

Murray, D. A. B. (2014). Real queer: "Authentic" LGBT refugee claimants and homonationalism in the Canadian refugee system. *Anthropologica, 56*(1), 21–32.

Oswin, N. (2012). Book review: Scott Lauria Morgensen's *Spaces between us: Settler colonialism and indigenous decolonization. Gender, Place and Culture, 19*, 691–693.

Puar, J. K. (2007). *Terrorist assemblages: Homonationalism in queer times*. Duke University Press.

Puar, J. K. (2013). Rethinking homonationalism. *International Journal of Middle East Studies, 45*(2), 336–339. https://doi.org/10.1017/S002074381300007X

Puar, J. K. (2015). Homonationalism as assemblage: Viral travels, affective sexualities. *Revista Lusófona de Estudos Culturais*, 3(1), 319–337.

Puar, J. K. (2017). *The right to maim: Debility, capacity, disability*. Duke University Press.

Puar, J., & Mikdashi, M. (2012a, August 9). *Pinkwatching and pinkwashing: Interpenetration and its discontents*. Jadaliyya. https://www.jadaliyya.com/Details/26818/Pinkwatching-And-Pinkwashing-Interpenetration-and-its-Discontents

Puar, J., & Mikdashi, M. (2012b, October 10). *On positionality and not naming names: A rejoinder to the response by Maikey and Schotten*. Jadaliyya. https://www.jadaliyya.com/Details/27195/On-Positionality-and-Not-Naming-Names-A-Rejoinder-to-the-Response-by-Maikey-and-Schotten

Reimers, E. (2017). Homonationalism in teacher education—Productions of schools as heteronormative national places. *Irish Educational Studies*, 36(1), 91–105. https://doi.org/10.1080/03323315.2017.1289703

Rexhepi, P. (2016). From Orientalism to homonationalism: Queer politics, Islamophobia and Europeanization in Kosovo. *Southeastern Europe*, 40(1), 32–53. https://doi.org/10.1163/18763332-03903014

Ritchie, J. (2015). Pinkwashing, homonationalism, and Israel-Palestine: The conceits of queer theory and the politics of the ordinary. *Antipode*, 47(3), 616–634. http://doi.org//10.1111/anti.12100

Schotten, C. H. (2016). Homonationalism. *International Feminist Journal of Politics*, 18(3), 351–370. https://doi.org/10.1080/14616742.2015.1103061

Schotten, H., & Maikey, H. (2012, October 10). *Queers resisting Zionism: On authority and accountability beyond homonationalism*. Jadaliyya. https://www.jadaliyya.com/Details/27175/Queers-Resisting-Zionism-On-Authority-and-Accountability-Beyond-Homonationalism

Schulman, S. (2011, November 22). Israel and "pinkwashing." *New York Times*. https://www.nytimes.com/2011/11/23/opinion/pinkwashing-and-israels-use-of-gays-as-a-messaging-tool.html

Smith, M. (2020). Homophobia and homonationalism: LGBTQ law reform in Canada. *Social & Legal Studies*, 29(1), 65–84. https://doi.org/10.1177/0964663918822150

Snorton, C. R., & Haritaworn, J. (2013). Trans necropolitics. In S. Stryker & A. Aizura (Eds.), *The transgender studies reader 2*. Routledge.

Snyder, S., & Mitchell, D. (2010). Ablenationalism and the geo-politics of disability. *Journal of Literary & Cultural Disability Studies*, 4(2), 113–125. https://doi.org/10.3828/jlcds.2010.10

Spierings, N. (2020). Homonationalism and voting for the populist radical right: Addressing unanswered questions by zooming in on the Dutch case. *International Journal of Public Opinion Research*, 33(1), 1–12. https://doi.org/10.1093/ijpor/edaa005

Sykes, H. (2016). Gay pride on stolen land: Homonationalism and settler colonialism at the Vancouver Winter Olympics. *Sociology of Sport Journal*, 33(1), 54–65. https://doi.org/10.1123/ssj.2015-0040

Treat, J. W. (2015). The rise and fall of homonationalism in Singapore. *Positions: Asia Critique*, 23(2), 349–365. https://doi.org/10.1215/10679847-2861026

Tucker, A. (2020). What can homonationalism tell us about sexuality in South Africa? Exploring the relationships between biopolitics, necropolitics, sexual exceptionalism, and homonormativity. *Journal of Gender Studies*, 29(1), 88–101. https://doi.org/10.1080/09589236.2019.1692192

Winer, C., & Bolzendahl, C. (2021). Conceptualizing homonationalism: (Re-)Formulation, application, and debates of expansion. *Sociology Compass*, e12853, 1–11. https://doi.org/10.1111/soc4.12853

Yep, G. A. (2003). The violence of heteronormativity in communication studies: Notes on injury, healing, and queer world-making. *Journal of Homosexuality*, 45(2–4), 11–59. https://doi.org/10.1300/J082v45n02_02

Yue, A. (2012). Queer Asian mobility and homonational modernity: Marriage equality, Indian students in Australia and Malaysian transgender refugees in the media. *Global Media and Communication*, 8(3), 269–287. https://doi.org/10.1177/1742766512459122

Zanghellini, A. (2012). Are gay rights Islamophobic? A critique of some uses of the concept of homonationalism in activism and academia. *Social & Legal Studies, 21*(3), 357–374. https://doi.org/10.1177/0964663911435282

NOTE

1. There is an inherent tension in the use of LGBTQ here. This is due both to larger debates within the field around LGBT versus queer studies and also to Puar's (2007) analysis of the way that homonationalism embraces homosexual subjectivities at the direct expense of others, themselves often figured as (undesirably) queer. However, as the term homonationalism circulates it is most often used to refer to LGBTQ genders and sexualities in general, rather than the exclusive focus on homosexuality that Puar (2007) initially emphasizes, hence the use of the acronym here.

Hana Masri

LGBTQ YOUTH CULTURES AND SOCIAL MEDIA

INTRODUCTION

Social media use is almost ubiquitous among young people (Pew Research Center, 2021), and the current younger generation is often referred to as "digital natives" (Prensky, 2001) or the "net generation," which designates that they have grown up in a predominantly digital world. This is not to say that all young people are immersed in digital and social media. Young people continue to make up the highest proportion of social media users, but how they use social media and what platforms they prefer is far from static. The use of Facebook, for example, continues to drop among teenagers. Furthermore, ownership of smartphones among adolescents and emerging adults has increased, and this has brought changes in their social media use; for example, app-based social media, such as Instagram, TikTok, and Snapchat, have become more popular. Research has established that access to the internet and social media is vital for many lesbian, gay, bi, trans, queer + (LGBTQ+) young people (Hillier & Harrison, 2007; Selkie et al., 2020). This has manifested in even more acute ways during the COVID-19 pandemic (Paceley et al., 2021), when many LGBTQ+ young people were impacted by social isolation and in some cases confined to hostile housing environments (Melvin et al., 2021). Social media offer opportunities for self-expression and for connecting with other LGBTQ+ young people, as well as support services for LGBTQ+ youth (Jenzen & Karl, 2014). Social media platforms also function as repositories of information and provide entertainment. LGBTQ+ social media youth cultures form around and through all these functions. Oftentimes, these are enmeshed, meaning that the separate "social modalities of individualism and community" (Macintosh & Bryson, 2008) concur. Fu and Cook (2021) note that research about young people's social media use predominantly focuses on two categories: the use of social media in relation to political engagement and the use of social media for "social interaction, self-expression, and identity formation" (p. 1236). These are relatively broad categories, and in the case of LGBTQ+ youth, the focus of this essay, these domains are not separable. For LGBTQ+ youth, self-expression, identity formation, and social interaction often mesh with activism and other forms of political discourse. This essay seeks to explore LGBTQ+ youth social media cultures to nuance our understanding of how young people make use of social media in different ways. It thus makes an important contribution to the literature on adolescents' social media use and social media youth cultures, which is predominantly produced through hetero-cisgender perspectives. Theorizing the digital and social media cultures of LGBTQ+ youth, this essay draws on three main bodies of literature: scholarship on young people's social media use, LGBTQ+ digital cultures, and the less researched field of LGBTQ+ youth media cultures, which have been exemplified by projects such as Scrolling Beyond Binaries, led by Robards and Churchill, or Mary L. Gray's (2009a) work on media and rural LGBTQ youth (see also Berliner, 2018; Pullen, 2014; Pullen & Cooper, 2010). Through a digital cultural studies approach—which centers on how digital media technologies form part of our everyday life (Hjorth, 2018), recognizes the materiality of digital practices (van Doorn, 2011), and seeks to understand how our digital and social media imaginaries and practices produce new forms of socialites—the essay explores the key themes of identities, affinities, communities, and youth voices. The following sections introduce key debates around young people's social media use as framed by discourses of risk and moral panics, followed by a discussion about how young LGBTQ+ people use social media for self-expression and community formation. The essay then looks at some of the differences between social media platforms to illustrate how LGBTQ+ youth use different platforms for different purposes. Further, some of the important contextual aspects relating to LGBTQ+ youth cultures and social media are dealt with, such as the hidden pressures brought by the pervasive image that our society is open and tolerant to diversity in terms of sexual identity and that being lesbian, gay, or bisexual in this "post-homophobic" world should be completely unproblematic. This is reinforced across social media discourse and interaction, where the imperative is not to be "normal" as in straight but to be "normal" as in happy. Against this background, further sections look at identity work and self-representation on social media, including a discussion of YouTube and TikTok subgenres such as the coming-out video and gender-transitioning vlogs. The essay also looks at digital trans youth cultures specifically, noting the particular importance of online communities and resources for trans and gender-diverse young people to mitigate the lack of support and recognition in education, health care, leisure, and so on and to build community resilience in the face of rampant transphobia, frequently targeting youth specifically. Relatedly, the essay ends with a discussion of how young LGBTQ+ people operationalize "affinity spaces" (Wargo, 2017b) across social media that form the basis for social change, such as transforming genders and sexualities as well as the basis for digital and social media activism around global LGBTQ+ rights.

LGBTQ+ YOUTH AND RETHINKING RISK

The fact that young people carve out their online worlds and form their own social media cultures has, for as long as social media have existed, caused concern in adult society. This takes several different expressions: Increased screen time among youth is widely debated as a health concern (Festl, 2021); social media have been charged with causing mental health problems in young people (Keles et al., 2020; Rideout et al., 2018); concerns for adolescents' exposure to explicit material are frequently voiced (Cameron et al., 2005; Livingstone et al.,

2012); youth and children's use of the internet is associated with "stranger danger," often with homophobic overtones (Robinson & Davies, 2018); and various online platforms have been associated with negative influences. These anxieties about youth social media use and cultures variably intersect with public feelings about children and young people's sexuality, and LGBTQ+ youth social media cultures present us with public manifestations of sexuality. "Youthful sexuality," Talburt (2018) notes, "confounds and upsets the comfortable binary of youth and adult" (p. xiii), and these feelings are intimately linked with "fantasies and fears of the future, the nation, class mobility and security and, always, race" (p. xiv). As scholars like Kathryn Bond Stockton (2009) have demonstrated, societal anxieties around LGBTQ+ youth sexualities and the "queer child" are pervasive and heightened. Such fears reverberate in contemporary neoconservative discourse (Robinson & Davies, 2018) in ways that put LGBTQ+ youth at the sharp end of debates about gender and gender and sexuality minority rights and affect their life situation, for example, through the impact on policies in education environments. Alleged risks of young people's use of social media are frequently evoked in media panics. A case in point is the media attention given to the concept of "rapid-onset gender dysphoria," a (discredited) theory that claims "social contagion" causes children to become transgender (Serano, 2019). In media debates, social media youth cultures are often implicated in such "social contagion," as exemplified in tabloid newspapers running stories with claims such as "Teenage YouTube stars who enthuse about changing sex are making being transgender 'cool'" (*The Mail Online*, October 29, 2017).[1]

While concerns about both youth sexualities and youth social media cultures continue to cause debate in popular media, scholars have demonstrated that youth navigate online spaces and content in complex ways that undermine any simplistic models for risk and so on (Livingstone, 2008). Further breaking away from the overwhelming focus on online risk, youth studies scholars have also given attention to positives, such as how social media use provides opportunities for social connection and interaction with other young people (Pascoe, 2011). Further recent research has also demonstrated that making generalizing assumptions about the effects of social media on adolescents is problematic, because any link between social media use and "affective well-being" differs significantly between individuals (Beyens et al., 2020; Valkenburg et al., 2022).

Nevertheless, mass media continue to portray young people's relationship with social media in negative terms, emphasizing risks over benefits. Online bullying is a risk factor for LGBTQ+ youth, but the internet also offers opportunities for help-seeking, not always present in their lives otherwise. Hillier et al. (2012) suggest that LGBTQ+ youth may take greater risks online than non-LGBTQ+ youth but also recognize that many LGBTQ+ young people live in hostile or unsafe environments offline. In other words, to LGBTQ+ young people, the online context is not experienced as a higher risk than their offline world. What we also need to consider here is that any categorical distinction between online and offline is of course increasingly meaningless as in lived reality, these worlds mesh, and for LGBTQ+ youth, risk is a factor to negotiate across these environments. In the case of LGBTQ+ youth, discourses of risk thus need to be understood in the context of their overall lived experience. By focusing on mainstream and adult-centric debates about online risk, often limited to discussing sexual content or bullying, we may overlook less apparent, yet commanding aspects of risk for this group. For example, we also need to consider the risk of lack of access to online content. Due to issues of sexual politics and LGBTQ+ rights "increasingly materialising within technical functions of internet governance and architecture rather than at the surface level of content" (DeNardis & Hackl, 2016, p. 753), relevant content may be difficult to find. As Rodriguez (2022) has highlighted, LGBTQ+ content on YouTube is often subject to age restriction, which means viewers must be signed in and 18 years of age or older to view, in effect excluding many young people from accessing community-based educational content. The impact of such technological policies and tools on young people, in particular, is illustrated across examples of "net safety software" used by parents or schools (e.g., the much-criticized Kiddle) or platform policies that routinely categorize LGBTQ+ topics as "unsafe," TikTok's "shadowbanning" (i.e., hiding) of LGBTQ+ hashtags in some regions (Fox, 2020) and similar moderation techniques used by Instagram affecting queer and feminist activists (Are, 2021; Duguay et al., 2020), and search engines and social media platforms' opaque algorithms that work to reproduce biases about gender, race, and sexuality (Bridges, 2021; Fosch Villaronga et al., 2021; Nakamura, 2013).[2]

SELF-EXPRESSION AND COMMUNITY FORMATION

Despite cultural and technological constraints, there are many examples of how young LGBTQ+ people "resist prescribed user protocols of mainstream social networking sites (SNS) as well as employ pragmatic strategies for navigating a binary gendered online world, staking out their own methods and aesthetics for self expression and community formation" (Jenzen, 2017, p. 1627). Herein lies one of the key potentials of social media for LGBTQ+ youth: the expansion of a possibility for self-representation, both at an individual and a collective level. Online participation can be enabling of self-expression and community building in significant ways (see Duguay, 2022). These opportunities are prised open to produce corrective narratives that seek to offer alternatives to mainstream media representations of queer life or indeed make up for a lack of relevant media content about LGBTQ+ young people's lives. The impetus to this creative impulse can be traced back to LGBTQ+ subcultures that predate social and digital media, but the combined platform features of ease of uploading user-generated content and connectivity are stimulating and supporting LGBTQ+ youth cultures. The self-publishing mechanisms of social media platforms like YouTube, Tumblr, or TikTok enable stories of diverse queer lives to be told, and the platforms' searchability and algorithms along with the use of hashtags (Duguay, 2022) facilitate audiences to find content that resonates with them. Such self-publishing bypasses the gatekeepers of mainstream media and in some cases works to amplify LGBTQ+ youth voices. Examples include YouTube web series produced around the world, representing local LGBTQ+ lives and experiences; queer documentary films distributed via social media to circumvent censorship in China (Shaw & Zhang, 2018); several queer-inclusive sex education channels on YouTube, produced by influencers like Stevie Boebi or medical doctors like @thatgaydoctor and @doctorcarlton on TikTok along with many young people who seek to mitigate the lack of LGBTQ+ perspectives in school curricula (Sill, 2022); and a vast amount of fan fiction and fan art queering mainstream popular culture, across online "participatory, networked communities of interpretation" (J. Duggan, 2022, p. 148).

On the other hand, it is important not to overstate the emancipatory potential of digital and social media for marginalized youth. As Berliner (2018) warns, assumptions about young people and the "self-actualizing, self-empowered youth that is precipitated through empowerment discourse" (p. 4) are far from the full reality for most marginalized LGBTQ+ young people. Similarly, Wei (2021) challenges the notion of LGBTQ+ youth globally being served by the internet and social media has created a "borderless world where gay culture flows freely without restrictions, resistance, and transnational power hierarchies and asymmetries" (p. 6). In their study of Spanish gay male subjectivity on Instagram, Gras-Velázquez and Maestre-Brotons (2021) found that the production of gay subjectivities was dominated by neoliberal understandings of identity with a heavy emphasis on individual and commodifiable attributes and "self-engineering" with limited scope for the formation of collective identity and civic mobilization. They argue that "as a technology of subjectivity, Instagram may threaten the activists' efforts to seek equality by strongly individualising gay men" (p. 5). As this illustrates and as this essay goes on to discuss, mechanisms of visibility and information management online are ideologically constituted. It is not only the case that digital and social media are not inherently empowering, but empowerment also means different things for different young people in different contexts (Berliner, 2018).

LGBTQ+ youth use the internet and social media differently from non-LGBTQ youth (Hillier et al., 2012), and there are differences across different LGBT sexual and gender identities too (Pew Research Center, 2013). In their study with trans youth (15–18 years), Selkie et al. (2020) found that YouTube was the most used site for seeking out trans-specific content (80%) but also that the relatively small platform Tumblr is really important to this group, with 44% accessing it for trans-specific content. LGBTQ+ youth's extensive use of online resources and social media platforms shows how these meet LGBTQ+ young people's needs in ways that schools and health services fail to do (including but not limited to sex education, mental health support, etc.). This situation is indicative of how far we still have to go in terms of equity for LGBTQ+ youth who are clearly not having their needs met by education providers or health services and at the same time demonstrates the central place of social media in their everyday lives. More broadly, we see that LGBTQ+ youth's social media activities are often orientated toward social interactions they are less likely to access in their offline lives, due to stigma and marginalization, including self-expression and affirmation, building community, finding information and support (Adkins et al., 2018; Lucassen et al., 2018), and relationships and romance (Hillier et al., 2012).

Research also suggests that common everyday social media practices, such as taking and posting selfies, take on different and often political meanings for LGBTQ+ youth. Again, this needs to be understood in the context of lacking mainstream media representation (Vivienne, 2017), which makes social media opportunities for self-representation critical, both as a tool of community building and as a corrective to often sensationalizing or dramatized mainstream media representation, particularly of gender-nonconforming youth. But the division is not as clear-cut, as Susan Driver (2008) argues in her book *Queer Youth Cultures*: LGBTQ+ youth's "cultural practices are not classifiable as either mainstream or marginal, they are neither inside nor outside dominant cultural institutions; rather, they criss-cross commercial mass media, grassroots subcultural, and activist realms" (p. 1).

THE PLURALITY OF SOCIAL MEDIA

The social media sphere is growing and diversifying, and there is an increasing flow of content and interaction between traditional broadcast, lifestyle, and news media and social media.

Lindgren's (2022) definition of social media as "large-scale, internet-based, environments for making connections and sharing content, either by linking or self-creation, as well as responding to that content" highlights how social media are frameworks for participation and community building. Social media platform characteristics vary to a great degree. Different platforms have different functionalities, affordances, purposes, modalities of self-expression, user uptake, and levels of privacy. Social networking sites (SNS) like Facebook emphasize connectivity by foregrounding features like friends; encouraging frequent mundane social interactions via "likes," emoji expressions, and/or written messages; and offering the option of joining different groups. SNS are thus distinct from other forms of social media where the relationship between users is more indirect, perhaps clustered around a thematic hashtag (#) or formed around exchanges in the comments box relating to a YouTube video, for example. "The Plurality of Social Media" offers different modes of engagement, and LGBTQ+ youth use different platforms for different purposes and with different expectations. This can perhaps be illustrated by looking at the different styles of images and register of language typically used on Instagram in contrast to Snapchat. Instagram is often associated with a highly curated and idealized or aspirational mediation of the self, where conformity to dominant notions of taste, beauty, attractiveness, and so on is prevalent. But neoliberal ideological imperatives like "individualism" and self-entrepreneurialism also shape the style and content of what users post. Snapchat, on the other hand, is associated with the ugly, silly, insignificant, and sometimes profane. Such differences are partly due to the distinct affordances of the platforms. The aesthetic filters of Instagram and associated apps allow users to edit and improve the look of their images and thus encourage attractive stylizations. On the other hand, the Snapchat function that allows users' content to be automatically deleted after a set amount of time encourages spontaneity and, some would argue, realism in expression. The ephemeral nature of Snapchat content and interaction in turn produces its own norms and culture—protocols that are not just effects of platform affordances. Similarly, we see different platform vernacular and cultures emerging, for example, around different styles of selfies on Instagram or around playful skits on TikTok. Many examples from TikTok illustrate how LGBTQ+ youth make full use of the creative potentials of the platform's affordances and vernacular to index and communicate identities. A working example of such "circumscribed creativities" (Zeng & Abidin, 2021, p. 4) would be TikToks where the creator illustrates how they have experienced moving between "straight," "confused," "bi," and "gay" by jumping across the floor while making it appear they move back and forth between these "identities" over time.[3] The performativity of sexuality is captured in this playful meme while also authentically expressing how the unstable and layered nature of identity is experienced from the young person's perspective.

LGBTQ+ youth cultures on social media have a precursor in early internet culture (O'Riordan & Phillips, 2007; Robards et al., 2019), including the LGBTQ+ blogosphere, numerous listservs, and LGBTQ+ online forums, some specifically for LGBTQ+ youth (Cserni & Talmud, 2015; Gray, 2009a). These sites served community needs, often as hubs of information and knowledge exchange. However, they lacked the fluency and more lively interaction of social media. LGBTQ+ communities are among the early adopters of online networked digital media, including earlier versions of social media such as MySpace (launched 2003), to mention one (Macintosh & Bryson, 2008). A trans YouTube community emerged around 2006 (Raun, 2016), and at around the same time (2007), LGB coming-out videos, where individuals disclose their sexual identity, also appeared on the platform (Wuest, 2014).

Having reviewed platform affordances that shape youth engagement and use of social media as well as looking at the trajectory of the development of LGBTQ+ social media cultures, we can note four particular elements of social media affordances have been instrumental to the formation of LGBTQ+ social media youth cultures: first, peer networking and community building as facilitated by platform-specific opportunities for social connections; second, how social media offer the space for visual self-expression and storying of the self; third, how semi-anonymous user profiles enable youth to explore gender and sexual identities; and fourth, the possibility to participate in counterpublics and civic discourse (Jenzen, 2017). We may think of these as key categories in a broader "typology of uses" (Hanckel et al., 2019) informed by platform affordances as well as the needs of LGBTQ+ youth. The next section contextualizes LGBTQ+ youth cultures and experiences in contemporary society, after which we return to the key concepts outlined here and explore them more in detail by situating them in relation to different social media.

GROWING UP QUEER IN A POST-HOMOPHOBIC WORLD

Today's LGBTQ+ young people are growing up in a world that is presupposed as post-homophobic (see Boulila, 2019). Recent advancements in legal rights, particularly centered around same-sex marriage, have accumulated a wide-ranging symbolic meaning of "equality" in Western liberal public discourse. Combined with greater visibility of some LGBTQ+ identities and/or experiences in mass media and popular culture, a discourse of a post-homophobic society is emerging, purporting that coming out as lesbian, gay, or bisexual is unproblematic and no longer associated with the risk of harassment, discrimination, or shaming. This assimilation does not pose a challenge to heteronormativity. Rather, degrees of homotolerance are incorporated into the ideological status quo where heterosexuality is a taken-for-granted good and "natural," but explicit acceptance of LGB identities is also seen as a majority position (Svendsen et al., 2018). The notion of a modern society being characterized by an open and tolerant attitude to diversity in terms of sexual identity is increasingly mobilized across both commercial and political spheres. This is also integrated into the commercial profile of some of the major social media platforms, such as YouTube, a company that "selectively incorporates...LGBTQ stories and producers useful for its business purposes" (Rodriguez, 2022, p. 11). For young people, homotolerance brings the expectation that being LGBTQ+ is no longer an issue. Young people are interpellated, in the Althusserian sense, to think of themselves as equal and unproblematically socially accepted. A stunning example is how this message is implied even in Stonewall's (the United Kingdom's leading LGBTQ+ rights organization) statement slogan: "Some people are gay. Get over it!" The campaign—we are meant to understand—addresses homophobia by calling out those who have "issues" with gay people.[4] However, at the same time, the slogan interpellates LGBTQ+ people to get over themselves, to act up to the assimilation on offer. There are several issues at stake here. First, young LGBTQ+ people who do experience stigmatization because of their gender or sexual identity are implicitly discouraged to address this as an external, institutional, or societal issue and therefore more likely to think the problem lies with them as individuals. Second, young

LGBTQ+ people are increasingly faced with "performative progressiveness" (Brodyn & Ghaziani, 2018), a concept that identifies the gap between generally accepting attitudes of LGBTQ+ progressiveness that "lack behavioural backing" and LGBTQ+ youth's individual struggle or negative experiences in everyday life. This landscape where overt and "old-fashioned" condemnations of homosexuality have been replaced by subtle and often covert forms of prejudice and microaggression (Clarke, 2019) is complex and can be difficult for youth to navigate. Contradictions abound, and it can be difficult to raise concerns about homophobia and transphobia in an environment that disavows the existence of such intolerance (O'Riordan et al., 2022). As Svendsen et al. (2018) conclude, "Becoming queer after homotolerance involves negotiating old stigmas that have been severed from common-sense understandings of homophobia" (p. 276). Both Berliner (2018) and Gras-Velázquez and Maestre-Brotons (2021) direct our attention to how across social media produced by LGBTQ+ youth, the desire to be included in the narrative of the happy and affirmed queer youth is vocalized. Drawing on Ahmed (2010), Gras-Velázquez and Maestre-Brotons (2021) suggest that for LGBTQ+ youth today, the normativizing imperative is not to be normal as in straight but to be normal as in happy. Thus, it is the specter of unhappiness rather than nonheterosexuality that causes shame.

A similar message of how to achieve a "successful" LGBTQ+ identity is repeated in the prolific online video campaign It Gets Better, started in 2010 by Dan Savage and Terry Miller in response to reports about queer youth suicides, related to bullying.[5] The original YouTube video by Savage and Miller describes their struggles as gay youth and how they overcame hardships such as harassment in college and pressure from their religiously conservative families. The video campaign has had a phenomenal global response and its narrative format replicated thousands of times by individuals recording and uploading their own personal videos in the same testimonial style, repeating the core message of the original video. Today, a dedicated web portal hosts over 60,000 videos, including many by celebrities. Undeniably such a vast repository of life testimonials and messages to LGBTQ+ youth reflects a wide range of diverse voices. However, as many critics have pointed out (see Goltz, 2013, for a summary), the rhetoric of not only Savage and Miller's video message but a sizable proportion of the campaign as a whole is one steeped in neoliberal ideologies (Meyer, 2017), its essential message prescribing assimilation (Gal et al., 2016) and homonormativity (Grzanka & Mann, 2014) through upward mobility. Simplified, the dominant narrative equates a successful future life with White middle-class aspirations and respectable coupledom. This is also reflected in the visual language of the videos. Brandon-Friedman and Kinney (2021) found that minorities were excluded in imagery, as were those who do not "fit social standards of physical attractiveness, and those who challenge heteronormativity and adherence to gender norms" (p. 421).

More problematic, however, is perhaps the implied message of the campaign that it is the responsibility of the individual to overcome homophobia and that it is the (brave and positive) attitude of the young person that is going to bring success. As Gal et al. (2016) note, the key themes of the videos, such as experiencing bullying and loneliness, are "vastly attributed to the personal realm," and "most participants mention these phenomena without any direct criticism or demands for social change" (p. 1705). This illustrates how in an overwhelming amount of rhetoric addressing young people, by young people themselves or others, there is a very strong tendency to individualize or privatize negative experiences.

Relatedly, the It Gets Better narratives also illustrate the prevailing expectation to live up to the post-homophobic subject position; you should embrace your right to express who you are—your individualism. Freedom in the post-homophobic world is defined predominantly by an increase in individualism. The campaign is not unique in mobilizing both the individualizing frame and the universalizing notion of progress, the "getting better"; these frames are found also in policy language (Lawrence & Taylor, 2020). The pervasiveness of the progressive narrative is problematic in contemporary society because collective mobilization in response to "developing and galvanizing" resistance to LGBTQ+ rights and citizen equalities (Browne & Nash, 2014, p. 327) is still necessary. This is particularly crucial for trans youth who experience constant threats to legal and state-level recognition and protection. The risk of such systemic failures reaches far beyond celebrating and expressing one's individualism.

IDENTITY WORK ON SOCIAL MEDIA

Identity development is a central process for all youth. For LGBTQ+ youth, it typically involves a more active construction of identity than their straight and/or cisgender peers, which requires them to seek out points of reference beyond their immediate environment. The formal institutions in a young person's life, such as the family or school, do not offer LGBTQ+ enculturation (Goodwin, 1989; Wuest, 2014). Despite the increased social acceptance of LGBTQ+ people in many parts of the world, exploring gender and sexual identities outside the heterosexual cisgender norms is still an uncertain and sometimes lonely journey for many young people, and opportunities for LGBTQ+ youth to openly express or live their gender and sexual identity remain restricted (Hillier & Harrison, 2007). To overcome these limiting factors, LGBTQ+ youth construct their own social media cultures. Social media offer spaces to explore and express aspects of LGBTQ+ identities and lives, and young people use social media for informal learning and teaching as part of their identity development (Fox & Ralston, 2016). Engaging in everyday creative practices associated with social media, such as taking and posting selfies or other images and using mobile phones, is connected to processes of forming individual subjectivities that are laminated or sedimented rather than fixed and singular (Wargo, 2017b). These activities, understood as performative elements of identity, are social in nature and the self is in part constructed through mediatized interactions with other people on social media and therefore also conditioned by the commercial logic of the social media platform (Simpson & Semaan, 2021).

Ok and Kang's (2021) research shows how gender-diverse children and young people use social media to explore and learn about their gender identity. This includes sharing experiences around not just gender dysphoria but also social acceptance (or lack of), as well as discussing a wide range of aspects of gender as embodied and culturally produced. This may revolve around questions such as "Am I trans?" or a more diffuse sense of feeling out of place. Many use social media to seek out a vocabulary to be able to describe what they feel or experience, as well as a sense of belonging to a community.

Particular social media contexts may offer the opportunity for young people to be known in ways that feel more authentic to them. In Wargo's (2017b) case study, exploring identity work across three queer or trans identifying young persons' social media posts, this sense of authenticity or realness came from how in the online production of their selves, their "sexuality and gender, alongside their youth status, were not peripheral to their everyday lives, but central" (p. 576). Others have highlighted how the tagging function on Tumblr offers trans users "the unique possibility to both unobtrusively make their transness relevant in personal, quotidian moments while also rendering their self-narratives more complex" (Dame, 2016, p. 30) and constitutes, as Oakley (2016) suggests, an "excellent example of affordances shaping usage" (p. 6). However, a contrasting scenario is suggested by Simpson and Semaan (2021), who highlight how TikTok's algorithm, which regulates what content users see, is privileging homonormative (L. Duggan, 2002) intersections of LGBTQ+ identities (e.g., body size, ability, race) as well as stereotypes and thus, via a mechanism of "algorithmic exclusion" (Simpson & Semaan, 2021; also see Duguay, 2022, and for a study about YouTube, see Rodriguez, 2022), contributing to further normalization of some identities while excluding others. Such exclusion, Cover (2019) argues, is "implicated in the production of certain kinds of unliveabilities" (p. 603) affecting youth and, as Erlick (2018) shows, disproportionally impacts the lives of trans youth of color.

These practices also offer opportunities for identity validation. Marston (2019) highlights how comments on images posted by LGBTQ+ youth can "foster feelings of affirmation" (p. 283) while the polysemic nature of images offers ways to avoid "labels," thus retaining the possibility of fluidity in terms of sexual or gender identities. We also see how social media play a part in collective or shared identities being articulated. An example of this is how on Instagram, specific cultures of femininity have become visible, including queer femme cultures, characterized by aesthetics of hyperfemininity, softness, and vulnerability (Schwartz, 2020). Rob Cover's (2018, 2019) work on emerging sexualities offers an exploration into how social media spaces are used by youth to expand and challenge rather than seek affirmation and validation of established LGBT identities and representations. Social media spaces have been used by youth to produce new diverse gender and sexuality categories (Cover, 2019). This emerging new taxonomy of gender and sexuality is acknowledged in Facebook expanding its range of profile gender options (thus further finetuning their collection of demographic data; Burgess et al., 2016) and increasingly incorporated in related commercial digital spheres such as dating apps (Burgess et al., 2016), and this is framed as a departure from binary understandings of gender and sexuality, as in, for example, #OkBoomer TikTok, where young people confront the efforts of the parental generation to dictate and police restricting gender norms (Zeng & Abidin, 2021). Thus, as Cover (2019) points out, this identity work "contests both homophobic and liberal LGBT-affirmative discourses" (p. 603) while retaining an attachment to identity language (e.g., pansexual, asexual, nonbinary, agender), and despite being mobilized through a "less deliberate cultural shift" (Cover, 2018, p. 285) than queer politics of sexual liberation, they are deeply felt by the youth producing and embodying such new identities.

Fox and Ralston (2016, p. 636) note several further aspects of how social media intersect with identity work, including constructing, expressing, and managing one's identity. Different platforms provide different opportunities and challenges in this respect, due to their different affordances and structures. Platforms that require very little personal information for creating a user profile, like Tumblr, offer opportunities to be visible as a self that may be difficult to embody in other spheres of a young LGBTQ+ person's life and enable them to express individual subjectivity (Wargo, 2017b) to others and themselves predominantly via an open-ended style of text, images, and quotes/reposts. Such "lifestreaming" brings the self into being as an "ontological act of being and composing the self" (Wargo, 2017b, p. 572) that is fragmented, fluid and multilayered, and also in dialogue with others. As Wargo (2017b) describes, "through selfies, artefactual literacies, and video, LGBTQ+ youth are creating new spaces not only to express their thought and identities but also to be known differently" (p. 575). These opportunities to produce selves where one's sexual identity and gender identity can be expressed iteratively and in queer ways appeal to LGBTQ+ youth. School and college environments, like some home environments, often work to enforce heteronormative norms and can be oppressive and curtailing for LGBTQ+ youth, and their online sociality may offer alternatives and buffer the impact of enforced normativity. In contrast to Tumblr, platforms that tend to have close links to offline worlds, like Facebook, may not offer the same freedom to explore and articulate gendered and sexual selves but can in different ways be useful for LGBTQ+ youth to communicate about their identity to established social circles, such as friends and family, in a relatively controllable way. This may include performative acts like changing one's profile's pronouns or gender (Jenzen, 2017), altering a relationship status, adding an LGBTQ-themed filter to one's profile picture or a rainbow emoji next to one's name, or posting a more considered announcement, such as a "coming out" statement or video (Alexander & Losh, 2010; De Ridder & Dhaenens, 2019; Wuest, 2014). Duguay (2022) summarizes these processes under the concept of "identity modulation" and emphasizes how "people, *together with* platforms negotiate the gray area between being private and public with personal information" (p. 13, emphasis added), like sexual identity. Youth also use social networking sites for everyday learning through social interaction with LGBTQ+ interest groups they may have joined or pages they are following. A key aspect here is the extent to which young people feel they can define and express their identity on their terms (Fox & Ralston, 2016). Negotiating visibility on SNS is a part of managing one's identity that can be both useful and challenging for LGBTQ+ youth. As described above, to some young people, SNS provide a relatively safe and nonconfrontational space to "come out" to friends and family. However, self-disclosure can still generate negative reactions, and this can be difficult to handle in a semi-public environment like SNS. There is also the challenge of context collapse (boyd, 2011), which signifies the lack of control we may have over how information about ourselves travels across social media networks. As suggested above, young people typically use different social media platforms and SNS for different purposes, engaging with different social circles, on different terms. The following analogy, expressed by some young LGBTQ+ people discussing social media, illustrates this:

> Facebook is a pub where Tumblr is more like a chi chi bar...
> What does that make Reddit?
> Reddit is a club. Everyone is there, nobody knows each other, they all just sort of exist.
> (cited in Jenzen, 2017)

Here the young people express how they see Facebook as more of an everyday "familiar" type of public space that is also cross-generational and, to an extent, "local" to them. The quotation also indicates how they associate different platforms with different types of social relationships and different social protocols, expressed as the cultural difference between, respectively, a pub, a more "select" and stylized bar, and a nightclub with a big anonymous crowd. For some young people, sharing is one of the primary modes of participating (Marwick & boyd, 2014), and merging contexts may be relatively unproblematic, while for others, it may be very important to keep different online social environments separate. Context collapse is also linked to how, across different social media, there are different affordances for managing privacy settings and information control. Marwick and boyd (2014) argue that "engagement with social media has shifted conceptions of privacy from an individualistic frame to one that is networked" (p. 1052) but challenge the idea that teenagers do not care about privacy online. Consequently, negotiating online privacy is a central part of identity management for LGBTQ+ youth, and when privacy is violated online, it may force situations of self-disclosure at a point in time when they were not quite ready. Privacy violation in other cases has resulted in youth being outed by others, which may have severe consequences, such as harassment or bullying. It is also an issue that is exasperated by intersectionality. Multiple marginalizations mean that some groups and individuals are less in control of their privacy than others and ultimately put at higher risk than others. In sum, the anonymity offered by some social media sites, by using a pseudonym or avatar, may be advantageous for LGBTQ+ youth exploring different aspects of their identity or accessing community resources and seeking friendship. However, in some circumstances, it may be more important to feel validated and "known" as a whole person by others, in which case anonymity is not prioritized (Jenzen & Karl, 2014). Similarly, the reactions young people receive when they "come out" on social media or observe others receiving impact their identity development.

Coming Out. As mentioned in the above section, social media technologies may be helpful for youth across their coming-out processes. "Coming Out" is a multiple, ongoing, and variable process for young people who may identify as lesbian, gay, bi, trans, or queer or seeking to express a nonbelonging or discomfort with genderism and compulsory heterosexuality. There is a host of literature on the conditions and implications of coming out for LGBTQ+ youth (e.g., D'amico et al., 2015; Klein et al., 2015; Kosciw et al., 2015; Mayeza, 2021; Orne, 2011), including critiques of associated linear identity development models (i.e., Cass, 1979) as well as of pressures to come out that the normative dichotomy of being out or being "in the closet," to use the popular phrase, may create alongside the notion of individuals coming out to a "coherent final subject" (Klein et al., 2015, p. 300). These critiques are relevant for youth experiences and understandings of coming out. Social media platforms are one of the social worlds where youth perform coming-out processes. This includes the process of coming out to oneself, which may involve a range of activities, including observing online reactions to other young people's openness, gravitating toward LGBTQ+ representations and online affiliations (Gray, 2009a; Marston, 2019), and finding likeness with other LGBTQ+ people's mediated presences and experiences (Craig & McInroy, 2014). Giano (2021) argues that for gay men, such online experiences "catalysed" and "expedited" their coming out and that "early milestones about the realization of homosexuality came largely from online experiences" (p. 872). Gray (2009b) finds in her work on rural LGBTQ+ youth identities in the United States that increasingly, young people "weave media-generated source materials into their identity work, particularly as they master the politics of visibility's master narrative event: 'coming out.'" Similarly, participants in Craig and McInroy's (2014) study reported that they became more comfortable with their own identities, through watching or reading the stories of other

LGBTQ+ youth online, which also supports the argument that online resources are particularly important to LGBTQ+ people around the coming-out process. Social media are thus a resource for young people in various aspects of identity work and may also offer reassurance in terms of the livability of LGBTQ+ lives. However, as De Ridder and Dhaenens (2019) argue, we should be careful not "to take the emancipatory potentials of an online coming out for granted" (p. 43). Furthermore, there are differences between LGB experience and trans experience in terms of coming out on YouTube. Intersectional systems of oppression and privilege in society produce different opportunities and risks online. Trans women are targeted with online sexist, gender-based harassment to a higher degree than cisgender women and to a higher degree than others in the LGBTQ+ community (Powell et al., 2020, also see Hines, 2019). Trans-misogyny is prevalent in discourse across social media platforms and may impact negatively on young people, even when the focus is on a public figure like an artist, an athlete, or a celebrity coming out as trans, rather than targeting the young person themselves because it normalizes dehumanizing and derogatory language when talking about trans women. Trans vloggers on YouTube have also been subjected to targeted actions by anti-trans campaigners, seeking to have their videos removed by flagging them as violating community guidelines (Rodriguez, 2022). I will return to the topic of anti-trans discourse on social media in the section on "Trans Youth Social Media Cultures."

To some young people, coming out on social media simply offers a practical mechanism for informing most of their social relations in one moment, about their sexual identity or chosen gender. Some may find that coming out via a written or recorded message on social media is less emotionally charged than in a face-to-face situation and can alleviate stress. The time delay implicit in such asynchronous communication also offers opportunities to reflect before one responds, which may somewhat neutralize affective reactions. Beyond these pragmatic aspects of managing the affective dimensions of coming out, the act of visualizing oneself as queer or trans may more fundamentally contribute to the sense of being "real" (Wuest, 2014). Young people also look to social media for examples of the actual coming-out speech act (Craig & McInroy, 2014) and parental reactions (Wei, 2021). The YouTube subgenre of coming-out videos responds to this need (Alexander & Losh, 2010). As Wei (2021) argues,

> The process of 'coming out on video' has been acknowledged and celebrated as empowerment and emancipation for queer people, and as highly public and political spectacles that often draw a large crowd for democratic participation where the 'YouTubers' are seen as role models who encourage and support other queer youths to come out (p. 1).

This form of "participatory storytelling" (Wei, 2021, p. 2) accumulatively affords a collective archive of LGBTQ+ youth's experience that holds a tension of representing diverse and personal experiences while also contributing to a rhetorical trope of a formulaic coming out, combining a revelation of a true (assumed inner) self with normative predictive notions of a successful outcome. Wei (2021, p. 5) notes two constitutional parts of the mediated coming-out narrative: first, the confession of difference, which has caused hurt and made the young person hide parts of themselves, and second, the "imagining" of a "better future." This mediated "effort of queer youths to transform a shameful identity into one of pride in order to gain value from a coming out story," De Ridder and Dhaenens (2019, p. 56), underline is a form of emotional labor, and we need to consider this to better understand the complexities of how young LGBTQ+ youth make productive use of social media within a wider framework of affective capitalism.

Some YouTube coming-out videos have reached wide circulation and received over a million views, and this is one way in which LGBTQ+ youth have become more visible (Wuest, 2014). However, due to cultural and algorithmic factors, particular coming-out narratives are more visible or readily available than others, leading Wei (2021) to conclude that the YouTube genre is "stunningly and overwhelmingly white and male dominated" (p. 6). It is therefore important that researchers in this area do not conflate high rates of views or popularity with what is meaningful to different youth in different contexts (Jenzen, 2017). The searchable tagging system used on social media platforms such as YouTube nevertheless helps direct audiences to the coming-out videos by YouTubers tagging their videos with widely recognizable terms such as "coming out," "coming out gay," and so on (Wuest, 2014), while also being used to narrow down the content of specific relevance or interest, which also functions to "locate the video's story in a particular situation" (Wuest, 2014, p. 24) by adding tags that are more descriptive or localized. Tagging is here used by producers and audiences as a tool to overcome the algorithmic biases, as well as a mechanism for producing identity (Wargo, 2017b) and publics (Dame, 2016).

At a more detailed level of the structural organization of YouTube coming-out videos, there are further constituting factors that shape the narrative, including incentives to present as a likeable personality (Wei, 2021, p. 7), projecting entrepreneurial positivity, and creating possibilities for viewer positions that are agreeable to non-LGBTQ+ viewers. These aspects are linked to how coming-out videos have become media spectacles but also speak to how the specific media context of YouTube structures the style and meanings of young people's coming-out stories (De Ridder & Dhaenens, 2019; Lovelock 2017). However, adopting a personal address and encouraging viewers to interact with the video, both significant features of the coming-out video, are at once connected to the marketplace model of YouTube as a platform and signal a profound desire to connect with other LGBTQ+ youth. Many vloggers use the coming-out video to both connect with others for support and to offer support (Wuest, 2014). Their videos thus not only function to achieve visibility but also tell other young people "I see you" and encourage community building through connection and dialogue. Such connections also happen at an aesthetic level; for example, on TikTok, we see young people performing their coming out using memetic remixes (Zeng & Abidin, 2021) of lyrics of a particular song to put the message across, and the layering of the song and their performance become a meme format that other youths replicate in their videos. On the one hand, the much shorter coming-out TikToks are a further stylization of the dramatized coming-out moment, but on the other hand, because of how they are shot casually on a mobile phone, while bopping about with a friend, or in an everyday setting like sitting down for tea, they come closer to the messiness of everyday life.

With the emergence of social media influencers and the semi-professionalism of some LGBTQ+ vloggers, we also see the more practiced take on the coming-out video. These, as Wuest (2014) notes, tend to be more didactic in style, offering advice and role modeling rather than asking for help from others while retaining a personal address and narrating the "authentic" self. De Ridder and Dhaenens (2019) point to a range of stylistic strategies in YouTuber influencers or celebrities' coming-out videos that aim to draw audiences in and increase data traffic on their channel. Influencers are an increasingly important part of LGBTQ+ social media culture (Chen & Kanai, 2021; Duguay, 2019), amplifying queer culture and fostering community (Abidin & Cover, 2019) while operating at the intersection of political visibility and publicity (Berliner, 2018). Two instructive case studies are presented by John Wei (2021) in their comparison of two sets of popular YouTubers, the Rhodes brothers from the United States and the Huang brothers in Taiwan. Both have incorporated their coming out into their already established channels, and the analysis shows how the centering of the emotional register and the narrative structure featuring the suspense of the "reveal" and the reaction from their parents effectively dramatize social relations in the everyday in line with other forms of social media and reality TV entertainment. This may be perceived as a spectacle, but an enduring appeal of such coming-out archetypes to many LGBTQ+ audiences may be because of how they manifest a collective ritual.

Wei's case study also offers an interesting illustration of how central the parental reaction is. For youth coming out during their teens, the quest for autonomy overlaps with the process of coming out, and due to having both emotional and financial ties to their parents or caregivers, their partial dependence is a major factor in how they feel able to express their sexual or gender identities. There is therefore also a major interest in this group to gain insight into how other people's parents have reacted, which these YouTube and TikTok videos, rehearsing the thick texture of the emotional process, including body language, tone of voice, emotive expressions, and so on, provide. Again, mirroring key themes of many coming-out videos, the parental reaction videos exclaim some of the same desires of the youth—as they revolve around being supportive of their children realize themselves, articulating acceptance and "unconditional love" and seeking to reassure by playing down the child's difference (Wei, 2021, pp. 12–13). Ultimately, Wei (2021) argues, both types of videos "are still trapped in the normative rhetoric for social integration and assimilation rather than the more fundamental change of underlying social structures" (p. 14). The coming-out videos and the parental reaction videos arguably perform important work—for the individuals who record and share them and for audiences who feel seen, feel less lonely, and experience community belonging. But despite their public nature, in their narrative, they persistently orientate the process of coming out toward the private sphere. Personal relations are foregrounded over systemic marginalization. The (heroic) individual's overcoming of internalized fears is foregrounded over more messy negotiations with parents and family over the disclosure of nonnormative sexualities and genders that many teenagers live.

For a marginalized group, self-representation is a powerful political act, and the YouTube genre of LGBTQ+ youth coming-out stories forms part of this. Despite its "simplifying, essentializing discursive strategy, identity is important in practice," argues Wuest (2014, p. 22), and to LGBTQ+ youth, these videos not only offer necessary and important alternatives to mainstream media's representation of them from which they are shut out but also represent the political act of taking charge of the means of media production to challenge the prevailing narrative by telling their own story firsthand. This has become important to trans and gender-diverse youth, who are experiencing more intense forms of epistemic injustice (Fricker, 2007, p. 1), in which they are wronged "specifically in their capacity as a knower." On an individual level, trans and gender-diverse youth are routinely questioned about their ability to "know" their gender (Jenzen, 2017). On a wider systemic level, trans people's existence is often put into question as "debatable," mainstream media representations of trans youth (McInroy & Craig, 2015; Trans Media Watch, 2010) are rife with stereotypes and sensationalizing and are dominated by cisgender perspectives, and knowledge about trans and gender-diverse lives from within the community is completely underrepresented in the mainstream domain. The way trans youth are underserved by mainstream media, but also by school curricula, makes it especially important for them to produce and share their own media. The next section furthers the discussion on trans youth social media as information activism, responding to epistemic injustice by centering trans knowledge.

Trans Youth Social Media Cultures. Both YouTube and Tumblr have been identified as particularly important social media spaces for trans youth's cultural production (Fink & Miller, 2014; Miller, 2017; Raun, 2016).

However, without subcultural knowledge about how to navigate online information about transgender people, gender dysphoria, gender transitioning, and so on, young people are first and foremost directed to ciscentric content because of how search engines and "digital gatekeepers" (Baker & Potts, 2013, p. 188) work. A participant in Jenzen's (2017) research with trans youth noted about other young trans or gender-questioning people that

> [the] people who really need positive support are those not yet part of the community and they are not helped by mainstream media. They just see all the crap, the negative stuff that the [mainstream] media show.

From this, it is clear to see the motivation of trans youth to make full use of social media platforms to ensure that when other trans and gender-questioning youth go online to seek information and explore gender, they can find helpful and relevant information (Erlick, 2018). Telling their own stories, and representing their realities visually, also helps to counter misinformation and misrepresentation. For example, in contrast to mainstream media representations of trans lives, which overwhelmingly emphasize passing as the main ambition, user-generated trans vlogs instead typically center on feeling comfortable in oneself as an aim.

Scholarship considering user-generated content on YouTube, such as trans vlogs (Horak, 2014; Jenzen, 2017; Raun, 2016), emphasizes how "these videos are enormously productive for the trans youth who make and watch them" (Raun, 2016). Trans youth vloggers address a wide range of topics, in a variety of styles. Recurring topics include relationships, using public toilets, school, family, mental health, gender dysphoria, clothes, makeup, exercise, and other forms of self-care. Kosenko et al. (2018) note how visual representations are particularly important, and Jenzen's (2017) study noted how trans youth garnered a lot of practical life knowledge from other trans vloggers, like how to get hold of a binder if you are too young to make online purchases. Taken together, these YouTube videos can be seen as a collective effort to problem solve situations that trans and gender-diverse youth face in their everyday lives and harbor a valuable educational capacity (Miller, 2017).

Raun's (2016) comprehensive research on trans vlogs made some important inroads into this underresearched area but is mainly concerned with autobiographical vlogging focusing on individuals' encounters with transitioning processes. This is an established YouTube genre, with many vlogs adopting the format of personal video diaries documenting gender transitioning over time. As such, these videos can function in different ways for different audiences. To some audiences, YouTube videos by trans vloggers provide them with vital "how-to" information (Raun, 2015) about hormone treatments, navigating gender-affirming health care, using a binder, "masculinizing" workout exercises, "femininizing" makeup techniques, and so on, but as Raun (2015) points out, others come to these videos because of what they offer as a living archive of trans experiences and broader trans knowledge. By now, there is a multitude and diversity in experiences and perspectives represented across a sizable volume of videos, and it is important to note that there are both competing positions as well as normative pressures emerging (Miller, 2019; Tortajada et al., 2021). There are also differences between trans masculine and trans feminine vlogging, in terms of how the audiovisual affordances of the video format are used to mediate bodies and the interaction with audiences. For example, Raun (2015) notes how many "trans male vloggers use the camera to construct what testosterone does" (p. 705) by visually privileging the upper body, muscle, and facial hair. Studying the #GirlsLike Us network, Jackson et al. (2018) highlights how the "technological affordances of Twitter simultaneously served as a conduit through which trans women connected and supported one another and a channel for broadcasting their messages to broad audiences" (p. 1870), pointing to how trans women use social media to support each other in a community facing "internal" communication mode as well as to speak to wider audiences. Discussing watching YouTube vlogs, some of the trans youth participants in Jenzen's (2017) ethnographic research commented that they found that the subgenre of transitioning vlogging tended to emphasize a particular transnormative narrative of a "successful" gender transitioning they did not necessarily subscribe to themselves, but they still highly valued the visual "evidence" of other trans young people these videos provided and the community conveyed through and forming around these videos. This is also evident from the numerous comments on trans youth's videos by other young people, often commenting that they can relate as a trans person and that they find the video inspiring and a source of hope. More artful and playful approaches to the transitioning vlog also exist, such as vlogger Jamie Rainer's video "FTM Transgender: Photo a day transition timelapse" where he has created a fast montage of thousands of selfies to document his transition in a hypercompressed temporality, but also "evidencing" or marking his existence every day, day by day.[6] This daily evidencing takes on a particular meaning for trans youth who are routinely challenged at an ontological level. So, where many may primarily see a focus on body transition in these videos, how trans youth audiences engage is more complex, and we currently do not have a very good understanding of what these audiences actually take away from them.

There are differences in how vloggers address audiences. Some vloggers mainly address peer audiences, for example, Alex Bertie's "Transman problems!" video, where he revisits, through anecdotes, cringeworthy social situations assuming an "in the know" audience who may recognize themselves while using humor to deconstruct stereotypes and gain a critical distance to issues such as misgendering or deadnaming. Other videos primarily serve to educate non-trans audiences (Jenzen, 2017; Miller, 2017), for example, Chase Ross's "Trans 101" playlist or other "explainer" videos using a Q&A format. Both types of videos engage in awareness raising, pedagogy, and the articulation of critical consciousness while the peer-to-peer videos also work to produce a sense of community belonging. These videos exist on a continuum of user-generated media by trans youth, which also includes comics (Jenzen, 2017), infographics (Erlick, 2018), memes, and fan art circulated across social media platforms.

An additional aspect of trans youth's digital lives is to be confronted with anti-trans campaigning on social media platforms. Attacks on trans rights come from politically differently positioned quarters, including socially conservative voices, right-wing populist movements, and trans-exclusionary feminists, and are sometimes referred to as the "gender wars." As Finn Mackay (2021) notes about the so-called gender wars: "If you have been anywhere near social media recently, you are likely to have encountered them; high-profile celebrities and public figures have joined in and also furthered mainstream awareness of debate and disagreement around gender identities and trans rights" (p. 1). The conflict between trans-inclusive and trans-exclusionary feminism is fueled by a circular flow of content between traditional media and social media. Discourse across these spheres divides those who advocate for trans rights and those who claim these rights will limit their own (see Halberstam, 2018; Hines, 2019, 2020; Mackay, 2021; Pearce et al., 2020). These dynamics are further amplified by social media echo chambers (Hines, 2019), and online content from blogs and social media is recirculated and reframed in a range of other online political discourse, often to make an ideological stance against liberalization. Anti-trans sentiment on social media (and beyond) is associated with the broader contemporary political developments as described above but is also typically clustered around particular flashpoints, such as the debates around the proposed reform of the Gender Recognition Act 2004 (GRA) in the United Kingdom, which has been met with significant backlash (Pearce et al., 2020), or the Trump administration's reversal of policy that allowed transgender students in public schools to use toilets that correspond with their gender in the United States. As the latter example illustrates, these debates frequently center on trans youth and have a direct impact on trans youth's livability. Trans youth are portrayed as both victims without agency (see earlier section on "social contagion") and a threat to other young people, such as in debates about schools and toilets or trans inclusion in sports. The media are perpetuating the idea that trans inclusion means the presence of (dangerous) boys in the girls' toilets or the eradication of girls' safe spaces. The rhetoric is deeply gendered in that it is overwhelmingly concerned with the figure of the "deceptive" trans girl as a potential perpetrator and the figure of the cis girl as the innocent victim, and such emotive and dramatized narratives resonate with the attention economy of social media. The voices of trans youth are conspicuously absent from mainstream media debates on trans rights (Jenzen et al., 2022). For young trans people, as I discuss below, social media are the main sphere for countering campaigns to curtail trans rights, voice their demands that trans rights are human rights, and build community resilience in the face of anti-trans sentiment.

YOUTH COMMUNITIES AND YOUTH VOICES

LGBTQ+ youth rely extensively on social media for connecting with the community, both locally and globally. Wikke Jansen notes in a blog:

> If it weren't for social media, I probably wouldn't have had half the queer network I do now. I might never have met any of my Indonesian friends from the LGBTQ community there, who started out as WhatsApp friends of Facebook friends of people I knew

personally... Without Bumble BFF, a dating app function for meeting new friends, I wouldn't have had any place to advertise my little rainbow flag emoji, signalling that I was ready to meet other queers in my new hometown of Berlin back in 2018. (Jansen, 2022)

This quote illustrates not just how different networks across platforms are sometimes interconnected but how LGBTQ+ community making is intertwined with social media. LGBTQ+ youth are "operationalizing affinity spaces" on social media (Wargo, 2017b, p. 574) in ways that they have fewer opportunities to do in school or other everyday spaces. But, as Jansen (2022) goes on to note, there are multiple differences too, in terms of how individuals find themselves "at home" in different LGBTQ+ online spaces and in terms of "the limitations imposed by our material environment and our embodied selves" that manifest also in virtual, social media environments.

The use of social media for social support is very important to LGBTQ+ youth. This includes aspects such as gaining validation of their experiences, emotional support from peers, and access to information produced from within the community (Selkie et al., 2020). However, what constitutes emotional support on social media platforms, in the form of comments, emoticons, and likes, is also bound up with what generates value in the platform economy. Expressions of support build the status of the online persona, on YouTube or Instagram, or may generate more followers on Twitter, for example. Relatedly, the more users emote and express their support, the higher the value to the platform as both users' reputation and emotional bonds are valorized and ultimately monetized through the affective economy of social media (Murphy, 2018).

Informational support may range from providing information on young people's citizens and human rights around gender and sexual identity to lifestyle topics (dress, makeup, consumer ethics), health (sexual health, mental health, exercise, and well-being), and culture (TV, movies, books, comics, games, music, etc.). Information on such topics as they pertain to LGBTQ+ youth and youth cultures may not be readily available in the mainstream, may not be part of school curricula, and may be pathologizing or ostensibly hetero- and cisnormative in nature. This is partly why informational support from peers and community sources is very important to LGBTQ+ youth. Mitchell et al.'s (2014) study noted that 78% of gay, lesbian, and queer youth compared to 19% of heterosexual youth reported relying on online sources for sexual health information, which indicates a clear need and preference for LGBTQ+ youth.

The term *online community* is somewhat diffuse and perhaps utopian in that it does not recognize the geographical, cultural, and linguistic delimitations of people's social media experiences. Nevertheless, researchers have demonstrated via different *situated* studies the emancipatory power and social value of LGBTQ+ community formations across different platforms. Andrews (2021) notes that for LGBTQ+ people, YouTube offers a "space to share, reflect on and demonstrate support for the experiences of others" (p. 84), which he argues functions as a heterotopia, where heterocentric mainstream ideals and oppressive power structures can be challenged. Relatedly, platforms such as Tumblr, while remaining one of the "smaller" social media sites with mainstream audiences, have played a significant role for LGBTQ+ youth and their creation of counterpublics (Jenzen, 2017). Online counterpublics are discursive spaces that enable marginalized groups' articulations and "interpretations of its members' identities, interests, and needs" (Warner, 2002, p. 119) in opposition to a dominant public. Cavalcante (2016) and others have emphasized the importance of such spaces for "organized care and concern, that facilitate transgender identity work and everyday survival" (p. 109).

Young LGBTQ+ people's commitment to social change can be found across all social media platforms, including participating in Facebook campaigns, posting about LGBTQ+ human rights issues on Twitter, and having creative outputs on Tumblr, Instagram, and YouTube. The degree of political awareness and activist intention varies significantly across the multitude of LGBTQ+ YouTubers (Tortajada et al., 2021) and other social media, but the extent to which LGBTQ+ youth participate in civic discourse across social media and beyond arguably challenges the "hegemony of the pessimistic disaffected citizen perspective" (Caron et al., 2019, p. 697), a view that contends that there is a decline in civic participation among today's younger generations because of lower levels of voting and engagement with formal politics. Robinson and Schmitz (2021) point to how

> understanding how LGBTQ youth resist and challenge dominant relations in society—such as heteronormativity, the gender binary, white supremacy, and capitalism—promotes a more dynamic and complicated look at how marginalized groups navigate their social worlds and exert power in shaping these worlds. (p. 1)

Today, the use of social media for civic engagement is an important political sphere, and as suggested earlier, for LGBTQ+ youth, to make oneself visible is often not just a personal but a political act. Across the world, LGBTQ+ youth activates the audio/visual affordances of social media to document, depict, and bear witness to their existence, against their invisibility or misrepresentation in mainstream media (Lewin & Jenzen, in press) and more broadly against a society that dehumanizes or pathologizes them. Wargo (2017a) relatedly foregrounds the activities of collecting and curating visual and textual content on Tumblr as a primary form of LGBTQ+ youth activism, which creates community and is engaged with "public discourse surrounding equity and injustice" (p. 28). However, as Lewin and Jenzen point out, "increased visibility of a marginalised group is not...the same as increased rights or end of discrimination, is often compromised, and can even bring increased victimization."

A particular vein of online LGBTQ+ youth activism is tackling hate, by responding to hateful comments on social media. The category of "haters" is a part of social media nomenclature, a general term for those posting hypercritical or hurtful comments on Facebook and Instagram posts or spreading hate speech across comment fields on YouTube. It is often the case that the term encompasses homo- and transphobic, racist, or sexist attacks or bullying. As Elsa, a trans vlogger in Tortajada et al.'s (2021, p. 1003) study, comments about the online attacks she routinely is the target of: "I would rather call my haters 'hater,' in singular. There are different people attacking me, but in the end, they reproduce the same old rusty stereotypes about trans people." What is interesting about the term *hater* is how it offers a rhetorical purchase on a fluctuating neoconservative ideological position that can otherwise be elusive. The hater, once given a label, in the context of social media platforms, can be signified using a hashtag (#haters), meaning it can be understood and addressed as a specific phenomenon, rather than operating as a diffuse intolerance masking as the commonsense position of hegemonic whiteness/masculinity and so on. Having this new category also opens new forms of alliances among those targeted by hate speech and encourages new strategies for dealing with racism, sexism, and homo- and transphobia. One creative strategy is in the emerging practice of vloggers addressing haters, which is evolving as a social media subgenre. Examples would include Fox Fisher and Lewis Hancox's "Response to Haters" video, where they read out and respond to a small portion of the transphobic comments they receive on social media, or the Gay Beards' "How to Respond to Haters" video where they similarly "model" responses to effemiphobic and homophobic remarks about their appearance by drawing on LGBTQ+ subcultural tropes of ironic and self-deprecating humor while confidently reasserting the value of their queer masculinities.[7]

CONCLUDING REMARKS

Fu and Cook (2021, p. 1248) argue that research needs to push beyond the limited "utility view" of social media use, by which they mean that social media cannot simply be understood as a tool that young people use for various purposes and that we need to consider how young people's whole "social ontology" changes with changes in media technologies. Mapping social, cultural, and political aspects of LGBTQ+ youth social media cultures, this essay has sought to nuance the "utility view" by illustrating how identity work and media technologies enmesh and how youth form both pragmatic and affective relationships to social media when moving between individual concerns and collective affinities, as well as across subcultural and mainstream platform economics.

Several aspects of LGBTQ+ youth social media cultures are yet to be fully interrogated. The most obvious limitation of this essay is despite a critical articulation of whiteness, its focus is on English-language Western contexts. Further studies of LGBTQ+ youth social media cultures located beyond this limited context are needed alongside theoretical work situated at the nexus of decolonial, queer, and digital studies. While Black digital feminist scholarship is emerging as a key field (Sobande, 2020; Steele, 2021), the project of decolonizing our understanding of digital and social media cultures should be further prioritized. We also see emerging work at the intersection of disability and sexuality studies that will further our understanding of the digital cultures and media production of LGBTQ+ disabled and neurodiverse youth (Allsopp, 2022). Furthermore, the discussion here has given priority to platforms for social and affective and activist connections. LGBTQ+ youth online cultures also encompass dating apps and participation in online gaming communities, for example, which are further areas of sociality and digital intimacy for consideration.

FURTHER READING

Berliner, L. S. (2018). *Producing queer youth: The paradox of digital media empowerment*. Routledge.

Cover, R. (2019). Competing contestations of the norm: Emerging sexualities and digital identities. *Continuum, 33*(5), 602–613. https://doi.org/10.1080/10304312.2019.1641583

De Ridder, S., & Dhaenens, F. (2019). Coming out as popular media practice: The politics of queer youth coming out on YouTube. *DiGeSt. Journal of Diversity and Gender Studies, 6*(2), 43–60. https://doi.org/10.11116/digest.6.2.3

Fink, M., & Miller, Q. (2014). Trans media moments: Tumblr, 2011–2013. *Television & New Media, 15*(7), 611–626. https://doi.org/10.1177/1527476413505002

Fu, J., & Cook, J. (2021). Everyday social media use of young Australian adults. *Journal of Youth Studies*, 24(9), 1234–1250. https://doi.org/10.1080/13676261.2020.1828843

Gras-Velázquez, A., & Maestre-Brotons, A. (2021). Spanish gay male subjectivity, body, intimacy, and affect on Instagram. *Sexualities*, 136346072110314. https://doi.org/10.1177/13634607211031418

Gray, M. L. (2009). *Out in the country: Youth, media, and queer visibility in rural America*. New York University Press.

Jenzen, O. (2017). Trans youth and social media: Moving between counterpublics and the wider web. *Gender, Place & Culture*, 24(11), 1626–1641. https://doi.org/10.1080/0966369X.2017.1396204

McCracken, A., Cho, A., Stein, L. E., & Hoch, I. N. (Eds.). (2020). *A Tumblr book: Platform and cultures*. University of Michigan Press.

Pullen, C., & Cooper, M. (2010). *LGBT identity and online new media*. Routledge. http://prism.librarymanagementcloud.co.uk/brighton-ac/items/1387175

Raun, T. (2016). *Out online: Trans self-representation and community building on YouTube*. Routledge.

Simpson, E., & Semaan, B. (2021). For you, or for "you"? Everyday LGBTQ+ encounters with TikTok. *Proceedings of the ACM on Human-Computer Interaction*, 4(CSCW3), 1–34. https://doi.org/10.1145/3432951

Wargo, J. M. (2017). "Every selfie tells a story…": LGBTQ youth lifestreams and new media narratives as connective identity texts. *New Media & Society*, 19(4), 560–578. https://doi.org/10.1177/1461444815612447

Wei, J. (2021). Out on YouTube: Queer youths and coming out videos in Asia and America. *Feminist Media Studies*, 1–16. https://doi.org/10.1080/14680777.2021.1950797

REFERENCES

Abidin, C., & Cover, R. (2019). Gay, famous and working hard on YouTube. In P. Aggleton, R. Cover, & D. Leahy (Eds.), *Youth, sexuality and sexual citizenship* (pp. 217–231). Routledge, Taylor & Francis Group.

Adkins, V., Masters, E., Shumer, D., & Selkie, E. (2018). Exploring transgender adolescents' use of social media for support and health information seeking. *Journal of Adolescent Health*, 62(2), S44. https://doi.org/10.1016/j.jadohealth.2017.11.087

Ahmed, S. (2010). *The promise of happiness*. Duke University Press.

Alexander, J., & Losh, E. (2010). A YouTube of one's own? "Coming out" videos and rhetorical action. In C. Pullen & M. Cooper (Eds.), *LGBT identity and online new media* (pp. 37–51). Routledge.

Allsopp, J. (2022). *Amateur Filmmaking and the Practice of Neuroqueer Refusal at the Intersection of Queer Learning Disability* [Unpublished PhD thesis]. University of Brighton, UK.

Andrews, G. (2021). YouTube queer communities as heterotopias: Space, identity and "realness" in queer South African vlogs. *Journal of African Cultural Studies*, 33(1), 84–100. https://doi.org/10.1080/13696815.2020.1792275

Are, C. (2021). The Shadowban Cycle: An autoethnography of pole dancing, nudity and censorship on Instagram. *Feminist Media Studies*, 1–18. https://doi.org/10.1080/14680777.2021.1928259

Baker, P., & Potts, A. (2013). "Why do white people have thin lips?" Google and the perpetuation of stereotypes via auto-complete search forms. *Critical Discourse Studies*, 10(2), 187–204. https://doi.org/10.1080/17405904.2012.744320

Barker, M. J. (2017, December 27). A trans review of 2017: The year of transgender moral panic. *The Conversation*. http://theconversation.com/a-trans-review-of-2017-the-year-of-transgender-moral-panic-89272

Berliner, L. S. (2018). *Producing queer youth: The paradox of digital media empowerment*. Routledge.

Beyens, I., Pouwels, J. L., van Driel, I. I., Keijsers, L., & Valkenburg, P. M. (2020). The effect of social media on well-being differs from adolescent to adolescent. *Scientific Reports*, 10(1), 10763. https://doi.org/10.1038/s41598-020-67727-7

Boulila, S. C. (2019). *Race in post-racial Europe: An intersectional analysis*. Rowman & Littlefield International.

boyd, d. (2011). Social network sites as networked publics: Affordances, dynamics, and implications. In Z. Papacharissi (Ed.), *A networked self: Identity, community and culture on social network sites* (pp. 39–58). Routledge.

Brandon-Friedman, R. A., & Kinney, M. M. K. (2021). Does it get better? Exploring "It Gets Better" videos using visual sociology. *Journal of LGBT Youth, 18*(4), 421–437. https://doi.org/10.1080/19361653.2019.1691107

Bridges, L. E. (2021). Digital failure: Unbecoming the "good" data subject through entropic, fugitive, and queer data. *Big Data & Society, 8*(1), 205395172097788. https://doi.org/10.1177/2053951720977882

Brodyn, A., & Ghaziani, A. (2018). Performative progressiveness: Accounting for new forms of inequality in the gayborhood. *City & Community, 17*(2), 307–329. https://doi.org/10.1111/cico.12298

Browne, K., & Nash, C. J. (2014). Resisting LGBT rights where "we have won": Canada and Great Britain. *Journal of Human Rights, 13*(3), 322–336. https://doi.org/10.1080/14754835.2014.923754

Burgess, J., Cassidy, E., Duguay, S., & Light, B. (2016). Making digital cultures of gender and sexuality with social media. *Social Media + Society, 2*(4), https://doi.org/10.1177/2056305116672487

Cameron, K. A., Salazar, L. F., Bernhardt, J. M., Burgess-Whitman, N., Wingood, G. M., & DiClemente, R. J. (2005). Adolescents' experience with sex on the web: Results from online focus groups. *Journal of Adolescence, 28*(4), 535–540. https://doi.org/10.1016/j.adolescence.2004.10.006

Caron, C., Raby, R., Mitchell, C., Théwissen-LeBlanc, S., & Prioletta, J. (2019). How are civic cultures achieved through youth social-change-oriented vlogging? A multimodal case study. *Convergence: The International Journal of Research Into New Media Technologies, 25*(4), 694–713. https://doi.org/10.1177/1354856518795094

Cass, V. (1979). Homosexual identity formation: A theoretical model. *Journal of Homosexuality, 4*(3), 219–235.

Cavalcante, A. (2016). "I did it all online": Transgender identity and the management of everyday life. *Critical Studies in Media Communication, 33*(1), 109–122. https://doi.org/10.1080/15295036.2015.1129065

Chen, S. X., & Kanai, A. (2021). Authenticity, uniqueness and talent: Gay male beauty influencers in post-queer, postfeminist Instagram beauty culture. *European Journal of Cultural Studies*. https://doi.org/10.1177/1367549421988966

Clarke, V. (2019). "Some university lecturers wear gay pride T-shirts. Get over it!": Denials of homophobia and the reproduction of heteronormativity in responses to a gay-themed T-shirt. *Journal of Homosexuality, 66*(5), 690–714. https://doi.org/10.1080/00918369.2017.1423217

Cover, R. (2018). Micro-minorities: The emergence of new sexual subjectivities, categories and labels among sexually-diverse youth online. In S. Talburt (Ed.), *Youth sexualities: Public feelings and contemporary cultural politics* (Vol. 1, pp. 279–301). Praeger.

Cover, R. (2019). Competing contestations of the norm: Emerging sexualities and digital identities. *Continuum, 33*(5), 602–613. https://doi.org/10.1080/10304312.2019.1641583

Craig, S. L., & McInroy, L. (2014). You can form a part of yourself online: The influence of new media on identity development and coming out for LGBTQ youth. *Journal of Gay & Lesbian Mental Health, 18*(1), 95–109. https://doi.org/10.1080/19359705.2013.777007

Cserni, R. T., & Talmud, I. (2015). To know that you are not alone: The effect of Internet usage on LGBT youth's social capital. In L. Robinson, S. R. Cotten, & J. Schulz (Eds.), *Studies in media and communications* (Vol. 9, pp. 161–182). Emerald Group Publishing Limited. https://doi.org/10.1108/S2050-206020150000009007

Dame, A. (2016). Making a name for yourself: Tagging as transgender ontological practice on Tumblr. *Critical Studies in Media Communication, 33*(1), 23–37. https://doi.org/10.1080/15295036.2015.1130846

D'amico, E., Julien, D., Tremblay, N., & Chartrand, E. (2015). Gay, lesbian, and bisexual youths coming out to their parents: Parental reactions and youths' outcomes. *Journal of GLBT Family Studies, 11*(5), 411–437. https://doi.org/10.1080/1550428X.2014.981627

DeNardis, L., & Hackl, A. M. (2016). Internet control points as LGBT rights mediation. *Information, Communication & Society, 19*(6), 753–770. https://doi.org/10.1080/1369118X.2016.1153123

De Ridder, S., & Dhaenens, F. (2019). Coming out as popular media practice: The politics of queer youth coming out on YouTube. *DiGeSt. Journal of Diversity and Gender Studies, 6*(2), 43–60. https://doi.org/10.11116/digest.6.2.3

Driver, S. (Ed.). (2008). *Queer youth cultures*. State University of New York Press.

Duggan, J. (2022). Transformative readings: Harry Potter fan fiction, trans/queer reader response, and J. K. Rowling. *Children's Literature in Education, 53*(2), 147–168. https://doi.org/10.1007/s10583-021-09446-9

Duggan, L. (2002). The new homonormativity: The sexual politics of neoliberalism. In R. Castronovo & D. D. Nelson (Eds.), *Materializing democracy* (pp. 175–194). Duke University Press. https://doi.org/10.1215/9780822383901-007

Duguay, S. (2019). "Running the numbers": Modes of Microcelebrity labor in queer women's self-representation on Instagram and Vine. *Social Media + Society, 5*(4), https://doi.org/10.1177/2056305119894002

Duguay, S. (2022). *Personal but not private: Queer women, sexuality, and identity modulation on digital platforms*. Oxford University Press.

Duguay, S., Burgess, J., & Suzor, N. (2020). Queer women's experiences of patchwork platform governance on Tinder, Instagram, and Vine. *Convergence, 26*(2), 237–252. https://doi.org/10.1177/1354856518781530

Erlick, E. (2018). Trans youth activism on the Internet. *Frontiers, 39*(1), 73–92. https://doi.org/10.5250/fronjwomestud.39.1.0073

Festl, R. (2021). Social media literacy & adolescent social online behavior in Germany. *Journal of Children and Media, 15*(2), 249–271. https://doi.org/10.1080/17482798.2020.1770110

Fink, M., & Miller, Q. (2014). Trans media moments: Tumblr, 2011–2013. *Television & New Media, 15*(7), 611–626. https://doi.org/10.1177/1527476413505002

Fosch Villaronga, E., Poulsen, A., Søraa, R., & Custers, B. (2021). Gendering algorithms in social media. *ACM SIGKDD Explorations Newsletter, 23*, 24–31. https://doi.org/10.1145/3468507.3468512

Fox, C. (2020, September 10). TikTok admits restricting some LGBT hashtags. *BBC News*. https://www.bbc.com/news/technology-54102575

Fox, J., & Ralston, R. (2016). Queer identity online: Informal learning and teaching experiences of LGBTQ individuals on social media. *Computers in Human Behavior, 65*, 635–642. https://doi.org/10.1016/j.chb.2016.06.009

Fricker, M. (2007). *Epistemic injustice: Power and the ethics of knowing*. Oxford University Press.

Fu, J., & Cook, J. (2021). Everyday social media use of young Australian adults. *Journal of Youth Studies, 24*(9), 1234–1250. https://doi.org/10.1080/13676261.2020.1828843

Gal, N., Shifman, L., & Kampf, Z. (2016). "It Gets Better": Internet memes and the construction of collective identity. *New Media & Society, 18*(8), 1698–1714. https://doi.org/10.1177/1461444814568784

Giano, Z. (2021). The influence of online experiences: The shaping of gay male identities. *Journal of Homosexuality, 68*(5), 872–886. https://doi.org/10.1080/00918369.2019.1667159

Goodwin, J. P. (1989). *More man than you'll ever be: Gay folklore and acculturation in middle America*. Indiana University Press.

Goltz, D. B. (2013). It Gets Better: Queer futures, critical frustrations, and radical potentials. *Critical Studies in Media Communication, 30*(2), 135–151. https://doi.org/10.1080/15295036.2012.701012

Gras-Velázquez, A., & Maestre-Brotons, A. (2021). Spanish gay male subjectivity, body, intimacy, and affect on Instagram. *Sexualities*, https://doi.org/10.1177/13634607211031418

Gray, M. L. (2009a). *Out in the country: Youth, media, and queer visibility in rural America*. New York University Press.

Gray, M. L. (2009b). Negotiating identities/queering desires: Coming out online and the remediation of the coming-out story. *Journal of Computer-Mediated Communication*, 14(4), 1162–1189. https://doi.org/10.1111/j.1083-6101.2009.01485.x

Grzanka, P. R., & Mann, E. S. (2014). Queer youth suicide and the psychopolitics of "It Gets Better". *Sexualities*, 17(4), 369–393. https://doi.org/10.1177/1363460713516785

Halberstam, J. (2018). *Trans*: A quick and quirky account of gender variability*. University of California Press.

Hanckel, B., Vivienne, S., Byron, P., Robards, B., & Churchill, B. (2019). "That's not necessarily for them": LGBTIQ+ young people, social media platform affordances and identity curation. *Media, Culture & Society*, 41(8), 1261–1278. https://doi.org/10.1177/0163443719846612

Haynes, C. (2021, October 8). Opinion: The real problem with Instagram. *ARTnews.Com*. https://www.artnews.com/art-news/artists/opinion-instagram-outage-1234606496/

Hillier, L., & Harrison, L. (2007). Building realities less limited than their own: Young people practising same-sex attraction on the Internet. *Sexualities*, 10(1), 82–100. https://doi.org/10.1177/1363460707072956

Hillier, L., Mitchell, K. J., & Ybarra, M. L. (2012). The Internet as a safety net: Findings from a series of online focus groups with LGB and non-LGB young people in the United States. *Journal of LGBT Youth*, 9(3), 225–246. https://doi.org/10.1080/19361653.2012.684642

Hines, S. (2019). The feminist frontier: On trans and feminism. *Journal of Gender Studies*, 28(2), 145–157. https://doi.org/10.1080/09589236.2017.1411791

Hines, S. (2020). Sex wars and (trans) gender panics: Identity and body politics in contemporary UK feminism. *The Sociological Review*, 68(4), 699–717. https://doi.org/10.1177/0038026120934684

Hjorth, L. (2018). Digital cultures and critical studies. *Oxford Research Encyclopedia of Communication*. Oxford University Press. https://doi.org/10.1093/acrefore/9780190228613.013.648

Horak, L. (2014). Trans on YouTube: Intimacy, visibility, temporality. *TSQ*, 1(4), 572–585. https://doi.org/10.1215/23289252-2815255

Jackson, S. J., Bailey, M., & Foucault Welles, B. (2018). #GirlsLikeUs: Trans advocacy and community building online. *New Media & Society*, 20(5), 1868–1888. https://doi.org/10.1177/1461444817709276

Jansen, W. (2022). *Queer freedoms online? On the embodiment of our virtual presence—queer/disrupt*. https://www.queerdisrupt.com/index.php/2022/01/20/queer-freedoms-online/

Jenzen, O. (2017). Trans youth and social media: Moving between counterpublics and the wider web. *Gender, Place & Culture*, 24(11), 1626–1641. https://doi.org/10.1080/0966369X.2017.1396204

Jenzen, O., Collier, M., & Trenner, M. (2022, April). *UK media representation of transgender and gender diverse youth* [Paper presented]. Living Gender in Diverse Times Conference: Feminist Gender Equality Network, London, UK.

Jenzen, O., & Karl, I. (2014). Make, share, care: Social media and LGBTQ youth engagement. *Ada New Media*, 5. https://adanewmedia.org/2014/07/issue5-jenzenkarl/

Keles, B., McCrae, N., & Grealish, A. (2020). A systematic review: The influence of social media on depression, anxiety and psychological distress in adolescents. *International Journal of Adolescence and Youth*, 25(1), 79–93. https://doi.org/10.1080/02673843.2019.1590851

Klein, K., Holtby, A., Cook, K., & Travers, R. (2015). Complicating the coming out narrative: Becoming oneself in a heterosexist and cissexist world. *Journal of Homosexuality*, 62(3), 297–326. https://doi.org/10.1080/00918369.2014.970829

Kosciw, J. G., Palmer, N. A., & Kull, R. M. (2015). Reflecting resiliency: Openness about sexual orientation and/or gender identity and its relationship to well-being and educational outcomes for LGBT students. *American Journal of Community Psychology*, 55(1–2), 167–178. https://doi.org/10.1007/s10464-014-9642-6

Kosenko, K. A., Bond, B. J., & Hurley, R. J. (2018). An exploration into the uses and gratifications of media for transgender individuals. *Psychology of Popular Media Culture*, 7(3), 274–288. https://doi.org/10.1037/ppm0000135

Lawrence, M., & Taylor, Y. (2020). The UK government LGBT action plan: Discourses of progress, enduring stasis, and LGBTQI+ lives "getting better". *Critical Social Policy*, 40(4), 586–607. https://doi.org/10.1177/0261018319877284

Lewin, T., & Jenzen, O. (2023). LGBTQ+ visual activism. In D. Lilleker & A. Veneti (Eds.), *Research handbook on visual politics*. Edward Elgar, 283–296.

Lindgren, S. (2022). *Digital media and society* (2nd ed.). SAGE.

Livingstone, S. (2008). Taking risky opportunities in youthful content creation: Teenagers' use of social networking sites for intimacy, privacy and self-expression. *New Media & Society*, 10(3), 393–411. https://doi.org/10.1177/1461444808089415

Livingstone, S. M., Haddon, L., & Gorzig, A. (2012). *Children, risk and safety on the Internet: Research and policy challenges in comparative perspective*. Policy Press. https://go.exlibris.link/shSTM8Jc

Lovelock, M. (2017). "Is every YouTuber going to make a coming out video eventually?": YouTube celebrity video bloggers and lesbian and gay identity. *Celebrity Studies*, 8(1), 87–103. https://doi.org/10.1080/19392397.2016.1214608

Lucassen, M., Samra, R., Iacovides, I., Fleming, T., Shepherd, M., Stasiak, K., & Wallace, L. (2018). How LGBT+ young people use the Internet in relation to their mental health and envisage the use of e-therapy: Exploratory study. *JMIR Serious Games*, 6(4), e11249. https://doi.org/10.2196/11249

Macintosh, L., & Bryson, M. (2008). Youth, MySpace, and the interstitial spaces of becoming and belonging. *Journal of LGBT Youth*, 5(1), 133–142. https://doi.org/10.1300/J524v05n01_11

Mackay, F. (2021). *Female masculinities and the gender wars: The politics of sex*. Bloomsbury Publishing.

Marston, K. (2019). Researching LGBT+ youth intimacies and social media: The strengths and limitations of participant-led visual methods. *Qualitative Inquiry*, 25(3), 278–288. https://doi.org/10.1177/1077800418806598

Marwick, A. E., & boyd, danah. (2014). Networked privacy: How teenagers negotiate context in social media. *New Media & Society*, 16(7), 1051–1067. https://doi.org/10.1177/1461444814543995

Mayeza, E. (2021). South African LGBTPQ youth: The perceptions and realities of coming out and parental reactions. *Journal of GLBT Family Studies*, 17(3), 292–303. https://doi.org/10.1080/1550428X.2021.1897051

McInroy, L. B., & Craig, S. L. (2015). Transgender representation in offline and online media: LGBTQ youth perspectives. *Journal of Human Behavior in the Social Environment*, 25(6), 606–617. https://doi.org/10.1080/10911359.2014.995392

Melvin, J., Jenzen, O., Bonner-Thompson, C., & Harvey, L. (2021, June 16). *How the increased use of digital technology during the COVID19 pandemic is transforming the way that LGBTQ+ youth work is practised in the UK*. Youth Work in Flux, University of Rijeka.

Meyer, D. (2017). "One day I'm going to be really successful": The social class politics of videos made for the "It Gets Better" anti-gay bullying project. *Critical Sociology*, 43(1), 113–127. https://doi.org/10.1177/0896920515571761

Miller, B. (2017). YouTube as educator: A content analysis of issues, themes, and the educational value of transgender-created online videos. *Social Media + Society*, 3(2), https://doi.org/10.1177/2056305117716271

Miller, J. F. (2019). YouTube as a site of counternarratives to transnormativity. *Journal of Homosexuality*, 66(6), 815–837. https://doi.org/10.1080/00918369.2018.1484629

Mitchell, K. J., Ybarra, M. L., Korchmaros, J. D., & Kosciw, J. G. (2014). Accessing sexual health information online: Use, motivations and consequences for youth with different sexual orientations. *Health Education Research*, 29(1), 147–157. https://doi.org/10.1093/her/cyt071

Murphy, C. (2018). *Like, post, share, buy: The commercial value of effective networking on social media*. Dublin Institute of Technology.. https://doi.org/10.21427/D76Q8B

Nakamura, L. (2013). *Glitch racism: Networks as actors within vernacular Internet theory*. https://culturedigitally.org/2013/12/glitch-racism-networks-as-actors-within-vernacular-internet-theory/

Oakley, A. (2016). Disturbing hegemonic discourse: Nonbinary gender and sexual orientation labeling on Tumblr. *Social Media + Society*, 2(3), 205630511666421. https://doi.org/10.1177/2056305116664217

Ok, C., & Kang, H. J. (2021). To be defined or not to be? Addressing internal questions in the online community for gender diverse youth. *Interaction Design and Children*, 552–557. https://doi.org/10.1145/3459990.3465200

O'Riordan, K., Jenzen, O., & Nelson, S. L. (2022). Liveability, environment and policy: Reflections on trans student experience of entering UK higher education. *Sexualities*, 136346072210881. https://doi.org/10.1177/13634607221088148

O'Riordan, K., & Phillips, D. J. (Eds.). (2007). *Queer online: Media technology & sexuality*. Peter Lang.

Orne, J. (2011). "You will always have to 'out' yourself": Reconsidering coming out through strategic outness. *Sexualities*, 14(6), 681–703. https://doi.org/10.1177/1363460711420462

Paceley, M. S., Okrey-Anderson, S., Fish, J. N., McInroy, L., & Lin, M. (2021). Beyond a shared experience: Queer and trans youth navigating COVID-19. *Qualitative Social Work*, 20(1–2), 97–104. https://doi.org/10.1177/1473325020973329

Pascoe, C. J. (2011). Resource and risk: Youth sexuality and new media use. *Sexuality Research and Social Policy*, 8(1), 5–17. https://doi.org/10.1007/s13178-011-0042-5

Pearce, R., Erikainen, S., & Vincent, B. (2020). TERF wars: An introduction. *The Sociological Review*, 68(4), 677–698. https://doi.org/10.1177/0038026120934713

Pew Research Center. (2013). *A survey of LGBT Americans: Attitudes, experiences and values in changing times*. https://www.pewresearch.org/social-trends/2013/06/13/a-survey-of-lgbt-americans/

Pew Research Center. (2021). *Social media use in 2021*. https://www.pewresearch.org/internet/2021/04/07/social-media-use-in-2021/

Powell, A., Scott, A. J., & Henry, N. (2020). Digital harassment and abuse: Experiences of sexuality and gender minority adults. *European Journal of Criminology*, 17(2), 199–223. https://doi.org/10.1177/1477370818788006

Prensky, M. (2001). Digital natives, digital immigrants Part 1. *On the Horizon*, 9(5), 1–6. https://doi.org/10.1108/10748120110424816

Pullen, C. (2014). *Queer youth and media cultures*. Palgrave Macmillan.

Pullen, C., & Cooper, M. (2010). *LGBT identity and online new media*. Routledge.

Raun, T. (2015). Archiving the wonders of testosterone via YouTube. *TSQ*, 2(4), 701–709. https://doi.org/10.1215/23289252-3151646

Raun, T. (2016). *Out online: Trans self-representation and community building on YouTube*. Routledge.

Rideout, V., Fox, S., & Wellbeing Trust. (2018). *Digital health practices, social media use, and mental well-being among teens and young adults in the U.S.* (No. 1093; Articles, Abstracts, and Reports). Providence St. Joseph Health Digital Commons. https://digitalcommons.psjhealth.org/cgi/viewcontent.cgi?article=2092&context=publications

Robards, B., Churchill, B., Vivienne, S., Hanckel, B., & Byron, P. (2019). Twenty years of "cyberqueer": The enduring significance of the Internet for young LGBTIQ+ people. In P. Aggleton, R. Cover, D. Leahy, D. Marshall, & M. L. Rasmussen (Eds.), *Youth, sexuality and sexual citizenship* (pp. 151–167). Routledge.

Robinson, B. A., & Schmitz, R. M. (2021). Beyond resilience: Resistance in the lives of LGBTQ youth. *Sociology Compass, 15*(12), 1–15. https://doi.org/10.1111/soc4.12947

Robinson, K. H., & Davies, C. (2018). A history of child and youth sexualities: Innocence, vulnerability, and the construction of the normative citizen subject. In S. Talburt (Ed.), *Youth sexualities: Public feelings and contemporary cultural politics* (Vol. 1, pp. 3–30). Praeger.

Rodriguez, J. A. (2022). LGBTQ Incorporated: YouTube and the management of diversity. *Journal of Homosexuality*, 1–22. https://doi.org/10.1080/00918369.2022.2042664

Schwartz, A. (2020). Soft femme theory: Femme Internet aesthetics and the politics of "softness". *Social Media + Society, 6*(4), 1–10. https://doi.org/10.1177/2056305120978366

Selkie, E., Adkins, V., Masters, E., Bajpai, A., & Shumer, D. (2020). Transgender adolescents' uses of social media for social support. *Journal of Adolescent Health, 66*(3), 275–280. https://doi.org/10.1016/j.jadohealth.2019.08.011

Serano, J. (2019, February 20). *Origins of "social contagion" and "rapid onset gender dysphoria"*. https://juliaserano.blogspot.com/2019/02/origins-of-social-contagion-and-rapid.html

Shaw, G., & Zhang, X. (2018). Cyberspace and gay rights in a digital China: Queer documentary filmmaking under state censorship. *China Information, 32*(2), 270–292. https://doi.org/10.1177/0920203X17734134

Sill, J. M. (2022). "I wouldn't have ever known, if it wasn't for porn"—LGBT+ university students' experiences of sex and relationships education, a retrospective exploration. *Sex Education*, 1–14. https://doi.org/10.1080/14681811.2022.2036604

Simpson, E., & Semaan, B. (2021). For you, or for "you"? Everyday LGBTQ+ encounters with TikTok. *Proceedings of the ACM on Human-Computer Interaction, 4*(CSCW3), 1–34. https://doi.org/10.1145/3432951

Sobande, F. (2020). *The digital lives of black women in Britain*. Palgrave Macmillan.

Steele, C. K. (2021). *Digital Black feminism*. New York University Press.

Stockton, K. B. (2009). *The queer child, or growing sideways in the twentieth century*. Duke University Press.

Svendsen, S. H. B., Stubberud, E., & Farstad Djupedal, E. (2018). Becoming queer after homotolerance: Youth affective worlds. In S. Talburt (Ed.), *Youth sexualities: Public feelings and contemporary cultural politics* (Vol. 1, pp. 255–278). Praeger.

Talburt, S. (Ed.). (2018). *Youth sexualities: Public feelings and contemporary cultural politics* (Vol. 1). Praeger.

Tortajada, I., Willem, C., Platero Méndez, R. L., & Araüna, N. (2021). Lost in transition? Digital trans activism on Youtube. *Information, Communication & Society, 24*(8), 1091–1107. https://doi.org/10.1080/1369118X.2020.1797850

Trans Media Watch. (2010). *How transgender people experience the media*. https://transmediawatch.org/wp-content/uploads/2020/09/How-Transgender-People-Experience-the-Media.pdf

Valkenburg, P. M., Beyens, I., Pouwels, J. L., van Driel, I. I., & Keijsers, L. (2022). Social media browsing and adolescent well-being: Challenging the "passive social media use hypothesis". *Journal of Computer-Mediated Communication, 27*(1), zmab015. https://doi.org/10.1093/jcmc/zmab015

van Doorn, N. (2011). Digital spaces, material traces: How matter comes to matter in online performances of gender, sexuality and embodiment. *Media, Culture & Society, 33*(4), 531–547. https://doi.org/10.1177/0163443711398692

Vivienne, S. (2017). "*I will not hate myself because you cannot accept me*": Problematizing empowerment and gender-diverse selfies. *Popular Communication, 15*(2), 126–140. https://doi.org/10.1080/15405702.2016.1269906

Wargo, J. M. (2017a). #donttagyourhate: Reading collecting and curating as genres of participation in LGBT youth activism on Tumblr. *Digital Culture & Education, 9*(1), 14–30.

Wargo, J. M. (2017b). "Every selfie tells a story…": LGBTQ youth lifestreams and new media narratives as connective identity texts. *New Media & Society, 19*(4), 560–578. https://doi.org/10.1177/1461444815612447

Warner, M. (2002). *Publics and counterpublics*. Zone Books.
Wei, J. (2021). Out on YouTube: Queer youths and coming out videos in Asia and America. *Feminist Media Studies*, 1–16. https://doi.org/10.1080/14680777.2021.1950797
Wuest, B. (2014). Stories like mine: Coming out videos and queer identities on YouTube. In C. Pullen (Ed.), *Queer youth and media cultures* (pp. 19–33). Palgrave Macmillan UK. https://doi.org/10.1057/9781137383556_2
Zeng, J., & Abidin, C. (2021). "#OkBoomer, time to meet the Zoomers": Studying the memefication of intergenerational politics on TikTok. *Information, Communication & Society*, 24(16), 2459–2481. https://doi.org/10.1080/1369118X.2021.1961007

NOTES

1. See for example *Mail Online* "NHS pressured out kids to change sex (https://www.dailymail.co.uk/news/article-5027927/NHS-pressured-kids-change-sex.html)" 29 October 2017.
2. See, for example, "The issue of queer art and Instagram censorship" (Haynes, 2021).
3. See Tiktok by @juanagustin (https://www.tiktok.com/@juanagustin__/video/6777825486501399813) or Tiktok by /@cristiandennis (https://www.tiktok.com/@cristiandennis/video/6777893272661658886).
4. See Stonewall (https://www.stonewall.org.uk/our-work/campaigns/2007-some-people-are-gay-get-over-it-campaign-breaks-new-ground).
5. See the It Gets Better project (https://itgetsbetter.org).
6. See "FTM Transgender: Photo a day transition timelapse" by Jamie Rainer (https://www.youtube.com/watch?v=o9ZXvmwQxGE) or similar from Chase Ross, e.g., "Picture Every Day for 11 Years (https://www.youtube.com/watch?v=vPz4R68V-KY&list=PL7SgbxvTR7N6gpGXdTdSL9HKNzUZMtcnw)".
7. See "Response to Haters" by Fox Fisher and Lewis Hancox (https://youtu.be/27am280AFKI) and "How to Respond to Haters" by the Gay Beards (https://youtu.be/27am280AFKI).

Olu Jenzen

LGBTQ+ EPISTOLARY RHETORIC/LETTER WRITING

INTRODUCTION

In the early 21st-century terrain of Grindr—of Bumble, Chappy, Growlr, Her, Hornet, Jack'd, Lex, LGBTQutie, OkCupid, Scissr, Scruff, and Tinder—letters may seem like an obsolete form of communication, a romantic relic of the past. Romantic letters were indeed central forms of communication within relationships of the past, including and perhaps especially for people who participated in same-sex and other forms of queer, as in nonnormative, relations. Considering "the love that dare not speak its name" in the 19th-century West, for instance, the erotic letters that served as communication between Oscar Wilde and Lord Alfred Douglas became objects of blackmail and then evidence in court (Holland, 2003). As another example, letters exchanged between Addie Brown and Rebecca Primus, both freeborn African American women, constituted their romantic and erotic relationship over the course of nine years while carving out space for discussions of labor and racial politics (Hansen, 1996). Continued interest in epistolary communication from the past is apparent in not only the work of historians but also the present-day media landscape. The 2018 film *The Favourite*, which was nominated for the most Academy Awards in the history of films that center queer stories between women, dramatized the intimate as well as political consequences of communication through same-sex letters (VanHaitsma, 2019b).

Approaching letter writing through the lens of rhetoric is not an obvious priority for queer studies in communication. Rhetorical scholars have centered instead on more clearly public forms of queer communication. Scholarly attention tends to focus on the representation of LGBTQ+ communities in the media, as well as the social movement rhetoric of gay liberation, lesbian feminists, HIV/AIDS activists, and so on. Yet, particularly through examination of the latter, the importance of letters has come to the fore in two important ways. A first approach in rhetorical studies mirrors that of interdisciplinary histories of LGBTQ+ life more broadly. In this approach, letters are recognized as vital primary sources of information *in* histories of LGBTQ+ rhetoric.

A second rhetorical approach involves understanding LGBTQ+ letter writing as a rhetorical practice. Scholars taking this approach have begun to analyze LGBTQ+ letters *as* rhetoric. These two approaches are in productive tension with each other. Realizing how LGBTQ+ letters are themselves rhetorical may be taken to undermine established scholarly practices of consulting letters as evidence of past romantic relationships and sexual identities. However, even among those scholars who argue that LGBTQ+ letters should be understood as a vein of epistolary rhetoric, they rely necessarily on letters as sources of information about the past in order to develop their approach. Rather than expecting that it will or should replace the first approach, the second approach is better understood as nuancing and refining how letters are read as evidence of the past and, at the same time, as opening up new analytical approaches and sources for the study of LGBTQ+ communication.

LETTERS IN STUDIES OF LGBTQ+ RHETORIC

The importance of letters as primary sources has been recognized since the earliest days of gay and lesbian history as an academic subfield. The need to examine letters is particularly pressing within histories of same-sex and other nonnormative relations because they are less likely to be acknowledged in public records that document life events like birth, marriage, and death. Moreover, same-sex and queer relations often have been deliberately "hidden" from public view, whether by the participants themselves, their families and kinship networks, or later historians (Duberman et al., 1989). As such, and because letters are associated with "secrets and sexuality," scholars who are motivated to examine the LGBTQ+ past "investigate authentic letter correspondence for evidence of homoerotic and homosexual relationships" (Garlinger, 2005, p. ix). The investigation of such correspondence is by no means a straightforward question, and scholars often debate how to interpret letters (Smith-Rosenberg, 2000). Still, letters are crucial sources that document romantic, erotic, and sexual life. So too within histories of LGBTQ+ rhetoric. In this sense, rhetorical scholars approach letters as primary sources *in* studies of LGBTQ+ rhetoric. Within such scholarship, letters are understood as evidence of gendered romantic, erotic, and sexual relations from the past. Letters also serve as evidence of other aspects of the rhetorical situations under study.

Evidence of Gendered Relations. In rhetorical scholarship on LGBTQ+ history, the turn to letters as primary sources requires what Charles E. Morris has characterized as a methodological "queering" of the discipline of rhetoric (2007a).[1] Within early histories of rhetoric, the predominant focus on public address, at least as it was narrowly conceived, obscured the relevance of sexuality during periods prior to LGBTQ+ social movements and their public-facing activism. With this historiographic focus on great orators speaking from public platforms about issues deemed of grand historical significance, Morris explained, "it is easy to fathom the long absence of queer texts, especially the presumed void of discourse prior to the homophile movements of the 1950s and 1960s, prior to the 'out' culture and politics that emerged from the Stonewall 'revolution'" (Morris, 2007a, p. 3). Not surprisingly, communication scholarship prior to Morris's groundbreaking historical interventions tended to focus on "contemporary queer culture, media, and politics" (p. 5). To even study sexuality, historians of rhetoric needed to "queer…the objects, methods, and theories within this field of inquiry" (p. 5). Study of relations previously conceived of as private or intimate, especially as those relations are evidenced in letters, has played an important part in this methodological queering of rhetorical studies.

Approaching letters as both historians and rhetorical critics, scholars have recognized these primary sources as evidence of romantic, erotic, and/or sexual relations from the past and, at the same time, considered critically how letters are used to construct the public memory of historical figures in the present. This strand of scholarship tends to focus on well-known and relatively privileged public figures. For these figures, their significance is already presumed, yet there are contests of memory over whether they can be understood as having participated physically and sexually in same-sex relations. Scholars turn analytic attention to the ways that the correspondence of these historical figures is interpreted to justify (or not) the recovery of their roles in LGBTQ+ history. Abraham Lincoln and Eleanor Roosevelt are two such figures.

Conflicting interpretations of letters are at the heart of debates about how to remember Lincoln's intimate friendship with Joshua Speed. Morris pointed to this centrality of correspondence in his analysis of the "homosexual panic" that followed when activist and author Larry Kramer "claimed to have new documentary evidence" of Lincoln and Speed's relationship, including "letters and diary entries allegedly found buried beneath the floorboards of Speed's old store and housed currently in a private, unnamed collection" (2007b, pp. 96, 102). "Kramer without qualification concluded that Lincoln and Speed were gay," according to Morris, and "substantiated his interpretation in part by reference to extent correspondence" between the two men (p. 102). Even with respect to the extant letters, Lincoln scholars have interpreted the same texts differently, defending against any queer possibilities through what Morris theorized as "queer mnemonicide" (p. 103). One Lincoln scholar concluded, for example, that "Lincoln's letters to Speed 'are totally lacking in expressions of warm affection'" (p. 109). In critical analysis of the contest over Lincoln's public memory, Morris too relied necessarily on his own interpretations of Lincoln's "flurry of passionate correspondence to Speed in January and February of 1842" (p. 98). Whether a rhetorical critic examines letters for evidence of romantic, erotic, and sexual relations—or to analyze how *others* have leveraged letters as such evidence—it is clear that the epistolary genre serves an important evidentiary function when claiming historical figures for rhetoric's LGBTQ+ public memory.

The epistolary genre plays a similar role within contests over the public memory of Eleanor Roosevelt and her intimate friend, Lorena Hickok. Dana Cloud (2007) has considered how the two women's letters are interpreted within biographical debates about the nature of their relationship. "When, in 1978, the Franklin D. Roosevelt Library opened eighteen cartons containing Eleanor's correspondence with Hick," Cloud explained, "the public was shocked to discover numerous erotic passages exchanged between them" (p. 26). Similar to the case of Lincoln, some have interpreted the letters as evidence of "a long-term, intimate, homosexual relationship," whereas others insisted the relationship was "passionate" but "nonsexual" (pp. 26–27). Moreover, Cloud's analysis emphasized the role of critics in bringing supposedly "private" texts like letters into considerations of rhetoric and public life, noting the critical possibilities of "outing" texts rather than individual historical figures.

> Rather than claiming Roosevelt, we can *queer* her by pointing out how her private life, if brought by rhetorical criticism into public memory—which has sublimated, if not erased, this relationship—can trouble the assumptions of heteronormativity. We may out the *texts* of Eleanor Roosevelt, but we may not out *Eleanor*. (p. 39)

Here Cloud offered a crucial framing of epistolary texts that anticipated later scholarship on romantic letters as rhetoric.

Qwo-Li Driskill (2016) has demonstrated further the importance of letters to the construction of LGBTQ+ public memory. Whereas most work along these lines has focused on the public memory of privileged figures, examining letters written *by* them, Driskill's scholarship on Cherokee story, history, and memory considered the role of letters written *about* Southeastern Indigenous and Two-Spirit people. Driskill's research involved consulting, for example, the records of Spanish colonialists during the 16th century, which included expedition letters written by Fray Domingo and Fray Pedro about the bodies and genders of Indigenous people in Coosa.[2] In one letter from Domingo,

> we can see the process of a colonial gaze examining and classifying the bodies and genders of Indigenous people not only as a kind of exoticization of Indigenous bodies, but also in order to describe to Spanish powers Indigenous people as their obstacles, resources, or allies in colonization. (Driskill, 2016, p. 71)

Examining another letter from Pedro, Driskill observed, "his letter reveals more about sexual and gender violence than other accounts of Spanish invasions, as he argues for colonization" (p. 71). What Driskill's analysis of these and other letters makes clear is how, as primary sources, the letters evidence the gendered and sexualized violence of settler colonialism. At the same time, s/he showed how the letters have been used to remember—and, in Driskill's own work, to counter settler colonial memories of—Two-Spirit people. In recognizing how the letters constructed not only documentation but also arguments, hir work—like Cloud's—gestured toward the second scholarly approach to letters as rhetoric. Before turning to that scholarship, it is necessary to consider other ways that letters function as evidence in studies of LGBTQ+ rhetoric.

Evidence of Rhetorical Situations. Studies of LGBTQ+ rhetoric approach letters as evidence of not only sexuality and gender but also other aspects of rhetorical situations. Studies in the latter category usually focus on late-20th-century rhetors around whom there is less contest over their public memory with respect to belonging in LGBTQ+ history. These studies draw on letters as sources of background and behind-the-scenes information about the situations navigated by LGBTQ+ rhetors.

Along these lines, Isaac West's (2014) study of transgender rhetors and their negotiations of citizenship and the law offered an instructive theorization of letters as "hidden transcripts" (p. 39).[3] These hidden transcripts are in contrast with "public texts such as judicial decisions or legislative debates about statutes" (p. 38). West discussed hidden transcripts in his case study of "Debbie Mayne, a male-to-female transsexual" who was arrested in 1955 "for 'masquerading as a woman' and 'outraging public decency'" (p. 37). The public transcripts in this case include "press reports and court documents," while the hidden transcripts consist of her "correspondence with and between her friends and acquaintances" (p. 39). What makes this distinction so important is that, within the public transcripts, the legal case seems relatively straightforward, whereas the hidden transcripts "paint a different picture" through letter writing that "reveals a resistant rather than a passive subject, and one who actively sought a confrontation with the law" (p. 39). "Mayne's correspondence," West explained, "provides concrete evidence of the operation of agency in a world of constraints" (p. 39). Consider, for example, letters Mayne exchanged in 1953 with "Harry Benjamin, who was at that time one of the world's only medical experts on transsexuality" (p. 46). As explicated by West, "in her letters to Benjamin, Mayne oftentimes presented a public transcript of deference while pursuing a hidden transcript of defiance and resistance" (p. 46). Part of what letters may reveal within studies of LGBTQ+ rhetoric, as in West's analysis of Mayne's correspondence, is the rhetorical agency of LGBTQ+ rhetors who navigate constraints in ways that may not be visible through attention to more public transcripts alone.

Unpublished letters from LGBTQ+ readers to editors also function as hidden transcripts, offering critics and historians information about the rhetorical situations of publications and the broader social movements with which they are aligned. Consider, for example, Jean Bessette's (2018) research on the lesbian homophile organization Daughters of Bilitis (DOB), and their curation of "an *archive* of lesbian experience" through anecdotes published in founders Del Martin and Phyllis Lyon's 1972 book *Lesbian/Woman*. Letters are significant to the book in that its published anecdotes of experience were drawn "from hundreds of women the couple had corresponded with through their work with the DOB during the 1950s and 1960s" (Bessette, 2018, p. 25). Yet Bessette's examination of the women's letters in unpublished form is revealing of the rhetorical situation of *Lesbian/Woman* in other ways. Specifically, Bessette uncovered the effects of the book in relation to its audience. Letters written in response to the book's publication show "how readers responded to and made use of its collections of anecdotes" (p. 26). These letters "evince the heuristic potential" of the book "to prompt a process of *archival consciousness raising*" (p. 27). At the same time, with the DOB primarily serving the interests of middle-class White women who subscribed to norms of femininity, study of unpublished letters allows for consideration of "more diverse lesbian readers" (p. 27). Bessette was able to show the "limits" of the book's consciousness-raising potential for these readers through analysis of the letters they wrote to Lyon and Martin (p. 52). Such study of unpublished letters as "hidden transcripts" allows scholars to develop a fuller view of rhetorical situations, analyzing the interactions between published texts and their intended audiences and, at the same time, considering the perspectives of LGBTQ+ rhetors whose interests were not represented by movement organizations like the DOB.

Through consideration of those LGBTQ+ rhetors who were more likely to read and respond to, rather than create, movement publications, the "hidden transcripts" of letters offer an expanded view of social movement rhetoric itself. Elizabeth Groeneveld's (2018) analysis of letters written to *On Our Backs* (*OOB*) points to this ability of letters to record information not available through study of "public transcripts" alone. "Letters provide documentation of social and political movements written not from the perspective of reporters, theorists, or social movement rock stars," Groeneveld wrote, "but from people who felt compelled enough to respond to a story or an image" in a movement publication (p. 153). Within this enlarged view of participation, letters also document its emotional and affective dimensions. As Groeneveld characterized "the epistolary form of the letter to the editor," it is "often motivated by strong feelings, like love, fury, or confusion" (2018, p. 157). These feelings, far from being a "private" concern beyond the domain of rhetorical studies, played an important role within lesbian counterpublics: "The letters to the editor section of *OOB* became...a forum for readers to express their feelings about the sex wars and to build a different kind of lesbian public culture, which they did in every issue of the magazine" (p. 157). The "hidden transcripts" of letters are rhetorically significant in offering a multidimensional view of specific rhetorical situations as well as LGBTQ+ social movements more broadly.

Letters serve as sources of background information in countless other ways as wide-ranging as LGBTQ+ rhetoric itself. A few additional examples suggest this range. One is John M. Sloop's (2007) study of the historical discourse surrounding "the transformation of Lucy Lobdell into the Reverend Joseph Israel Lobdell," as well as debate about whether Lobdell should be understood as "lesbian" and/or "transgender" (p. 149). Sloop's analysis cites letters from the woman with whom Lobdell lived "as a married couple," Marie Louise Perry (p. 151). Sloop recounted, "When Lobdell was arrested in 1876 and committed to jail...Perry is said to have written a letter beseeching authorities to release him" (p. 156). Her "ability to write such a beautiful note," including her chirography and grammar, was interpreted by others as evidence of her "normal" femininity (p. 156). Another example is Erin J. Rand's (2014) research on the late-20th-century rhetoric of Larry Kramer. Rand cited a 1990 letter from Kramer, an open letter in which he "reasserts his significance to ACT UP," as evidence of his generally "contentious" role "as a provocateur" in the gay community (p. 69). Whether consulted for background information on interpretations of gender, or on conflicts within LGBTQ+ social movement groups, letters serve as crucial evidence.

These available sources of evidence take on additional significance in part because they are too often intentionally destroyed or simply absent (Freedman, 1998; Gladney, 1998). In Eric Darnell Pritchard's (2017) research on Black queer literacy and rhetorical practices, they discussed a research participant who initially wrote notes to his high school boyfriend "'because it was a way for us to express the feelings that we have for each other without the whole world having to know'" (p. 77). The writer quickly stopped, however, after the notes were discovered by his parents who confronted him about being gay. In this case, the epistolary record was foreclosed in anticipation of further unwanted discovery. In another example, in his study of queer public memory, Thomas R. Dunn (2016) described the experience of conducting archival research in the papers of Alexander Wood, a Toronto man who "excelled in his position [as a magistrate] until a scandalous incident in 1810 that would forever link the name Wood with *molly*" (p. 37). Dunn experienced "exhilaration" when first discovering that there were "several good-sized boxes" of Wood's "letters and notes," with the "letters...almost all dated," only to learn that a folder for 1810, the year marked by scandal, was absent (p. 187). Dunn was left to speculate about who may have destroyed the letters from that single year and why, yet ultimately, "where an 1810 folder should have been, there was literally a gap in the records" (p. 188). While similar absences exist in all intimate archives, they are particularly common in documentation of LGBTQ+ lives—and most especially the lives of those multiply marginalized at the intersections of gender, sexuality, race, class, and so on.

Working with these absences in the historical record of LGBTQ+ rhetors and rhetorical practices, scholars have invented creative, imaginative methods for reconstructing that which is not documented in extant letters. In Saidiya Hartman's (2019) history of the "wayward lives" of early-20th-century Black women, including those who pursued "intimacy outside the institution of marriage, and queer and outlaw passions," she posed crucial questions that also animate rhetorical scholarship that imaginatively navigates epistolary absences (p. xiv). Writing about Mattie Jackson née Nelson, who, though the "letters are missing from the case file," was "punished" while incarcerated "for passing notes to a girl in another cottage," Hartman asked: "What stories were shared in all the letters lost and disappeared, the things whispered, and never disclosed? Is it possible to conjure the sentences and paragraphs and poems contained in the lost archive?" (p. 75). Hartman's scholarship has done just that, "conjur[ing]" a "lost archive" of queer Black women and their letters, "reconstructing the experience of the unknown and retrieving minor figures from oblivion" (Hartman, 2019, p. 31), including through a method she previously termed "critical fabulation" (Hartman, 2008, p. 11).

In rhetorical studies, scholars also have developed critical and creative methods for navigating the archival absences that mark LGBTQ+ letters as sources of information. For example, Pamela VanHaitsma (2016) theorized gossip as a method for speculating when the available evidence is replete with epistolary absences. Drawing on Jacqueline Jones Royster's (2000) theorization of "critical imagination," along with queer studies of gossip like Kwame Holmes's (2015), VanHaitsma proposed "gossip as another rhetorical methodology that may desire to embrace rather than seek to revolve the uncertainties that define both history and sexuality," particularly where letters are coded or simply absent (2016, p. 136). Ames Hawkins (2019) has offered another approach in a "genre-bending visual memoir and work of literary nonfiction" that creatively collects and speculates about the courtship letters written by their father to their mother before he later came out and was diagnosed with HIV.

In examining and speculating about letters as a source of information, rhetorical scholars have approached these texts as documentation of LGBTQ+ life. Consider, as a final example on this point, Julia M. Allen's (2013) history of the loving partnership and shared political and rhetorical work of Anna Rochester and Grace Hutchins during the early 20th century. Allen considered the "expressions of devotion" in the women's letters and notes to each other in order to understand the nature of their same-sex love and 45-year relationship (p. 1). In the same history, Allen also consulted as evidence a range of letters to and from other correspondents. These letters are revealing of the rhetorical situations and strategies engaged by Rochester and Hutchins as they "work[ed] to create a more egalitarian world" through involvement and leadership in Christian, feminist, and socialist groups (p. 1). Across LGBTQ+

rhetorical scholarship, as in Allen's study, letters serve as evidence of both LGBTQ+ relations and the broader situations that LGBTQ+ rhetors navigate. Yet letters are not only evidence in studies of LGBTQ+ rhetoric, they also have been approached *as* LGBTQ+ rhetoric.

LETTERS AS LGBTQ+ RHETORIC

From the start, LGBTQ+ rhetorical studies has approached letters as sources of information. More recent work continues to do so, relying on letters as primary evidence for investigating LGBTQ+ rhetoric. But these scholars nuance interpretations of such evidence by emphasizing how letters themselves serve *as* LGBTQ+ rhetoric. Rhetorical genre studies offers helpful frameworks for theorizing how LGBTQ+ letters amount to rhetoric. Rhetorical theorists have conceived of genres as rhetorical and social action that emerges through repeated responses to rhetorical situations that recur within broader cultural and historical contexts (Bawarshi & Reiff, 2010; Miller, 1984). Conceiving of the letter as a rhetorical genre—as a conventionalized or normative form of textual and social life—holds important implications for studies of LGBTQ+ letters that might otherwise be dismissed as merely private or individualized writing. Not surprisingly, obviously public and political letters have been most studied as LGBTQ+ rhetoric. Yet, especially in the case of LGBTQ+ life, such letters often blur the lines between genres that are public and intimate, political and romantic. As such, even intimate and romantic letters have been examined as a form of epistolary rhetoric.

Public and Political Letters. Examining clearly public and political LGBTQ+ letters as rhetoric follows in the Western rhetorical tradition of *ars dictaminis*, or the art of epistolary writing (Bizzell & Herzberg, 2001, pp. 492–495; Poster & Mitchell, 2007). In this tradition, well-known rhetorical theorists and rhetoricians have used the epistle form to address political rhetoric to public audiences. Feminist studies of rhetoric show how women especially have capitalized on the blurring of boundaries between public and private through the epistolary genre in order to advance arguments even in historical periods and cultural contexts where public participation was largely discouraged (Bizzell & Herzberg, 2001, pp. 9, 494). In studies of LGBTQ+ rhetoric, scholars consider individual rhetors who develop open letters that are made public through social movement publications and political campaigns, as well as organizations that advance their political agendas through letter-writing campaigns.

Whereas letters to the editor that are available mainly through archival holdings may serve as "hidden transcripts," published letters to the editor function more like "public transcripts," circulating as they do within movement publications (West, 2014). Along these lines, Lisbeth Lipari (2007) examined the epistolary rhetoric of Lorraine Hansberry in her 1957 letters to the *Ladder*, the first national lesbian periodical that was published in the United States by the already discussed homophile organization DOB. Lipari made clear the status of the letters as rhetoric. "A letter is a relational act of address," she wrote,

> to write a letter is to place oneself in a dialogue with an explicitly acknowledged addressee. To write a public letter is to situate oneself in relation to a public, a real or imagined community of auditors who share, at the very least, the experience of the address. (Lipari, 2007, p. 229)

Lipari's approach reflects the move within rhetorical criticism to treat letters not simply as evidence of LGBTQ+ identities or relations, but as epistolary rhetoric. "Rather than undergo a search for evidence of Hansberry's personal identity," Lipari explained, she "instead explore[d] Hansberry's publicly constructed rhetorical voice for its articulations of counter-hegemonic perspectives on sexuality, race gender, and class" (p. 221). Specifically, Lipari's analysis showed how Hansberry's public letters developed and deployed a "rhetoric of intersectionality" decades before the Combahee River Collective's statement and subsequent Black feminist theories of intersectionality (p. 221).[4] Here Lipari's analysis of Hansberry's intersectional rhetoric parallels Bessette's analysis of unpublished letters responding to Martin and Lyon's *Lesbian/Woman*. Whether functioning as hidden or public transcripts, letters to the authors and editors of early LGBTQ+ movement publications were well positioned to offer the perspectives of more diverse readerships—and especially those perspectives that were critical of the lack of intersectional approaches in predominantly middle-class and White-edited and -authored publications.

In addition to public letters addressed to social movement publications, scholars consider the epistolary rhetoric of political campaigns and elected public officials. An example is the epistolary rhetoric of Harvey Milk, who was elected in 1977 as the first openly gay city supervisor in San Francisco. Jason Edward Black and Charles E. Morris's (2013) edited collection of materials drawn from Milk's archive of speeches and other writing includes more than 10 letters, the majority of which are open and/or public letters. Early in Milk's political career, when he needed "to argue for a platform itself, to use rhetorical artistry in order to attract audiences," Milk deployed public letters to such ends (Black & Morris, 2013, p. 75). One open letter (1973) put San Francisco's "Mayor Joseph Alioto on the spot, for instance, rather melodramatically, regarding fundamental democratic principles of electioneering" (Black & Morris, 2013, p. 75). Another public letter (1974) decried "police harassment of gays" and "police brutality...against the homosexuals who are undesirables" through comparison to "Nazi Germany in the '30s" (p. 93). Along with these early public letters, Black and Morris's collection includes a campaign letter (1975) from Milk's second bid for election (p. 117). Milk began, "Dear Friends, It probably comes as no surprise to most of you, but I am going to run for Supervisor again this year" (p. 118). After appealing to "the Gay vote" and "the straight community," as well as insisting that he would not "be a 'one issue' candidate," Milk commented on the limitations of the letter: "I regret that this is a form letter and not the individual one I would like it to be" (pp. 119–120).

Several of the letters collected by Black and Morris are from 1978, after Milk was elected on his third attempt. In a public letter, Milk countered the homophobic campaign by Senator John Briggs for California Proposition 6, which sought to "constitutionalize bigotry" by prohibiting gays and lesbians from serving as public school teachers (p. 234). In another from a couple months later, Milk, along with his friend and speechwriter Frank Robinson, "rearticulated the anti-Briggs arguments one last time on the morning of the referendum," serving as "Milk's last public, discursive push for [its] defeat" (p. 240). Like many public officials, Milk deployed epistolary rhetoric, and especially the open letter form, to build audiences, advance campaigns for his own election, and use his public platform to argue for legislative actions.

Scholars also have considered how LGBTQ+ advocacy groups utilize epistolary rhetoric through targeted letter-writing campaigns. Karma R. Chávez (2013) discussed two such campaigns within her study of coalitional rhetorics by the LGBTQ+ movement and migrant youth movement. The first letter-writing campaign was initiated in 2010 by "*Citizen Orange*, a global justice blog committed to supporting the pro-migrant movement in the United States" (Chávez, 2013, p. 79). The DREAM Now campaign "featured letters written to [President] Barack Obama by migrant youth who requested his support for the DREAM Act," with *Citizen Orange* posting these public letters to its blog along with movement updates (pp. 79–80). As Chávez explained, DREAM Now was "modeled" after another letter-writing campaign: the 2010 OutServe-Service Members Legal Defense Network's (SLDN) campaign. This second campaign "consisted of letters written to Obama each day by current and former gay, lesbian, and bisexual members of the US armed forces and their straight allies who requested the repeal" of the military's "Don't Ask, Don't Tell" policy (p. 79). Chávez characterized the "strategic decision" to model DREAM Now after the SLDN campaign (p. 80). As the founder of *Citizen Orange* observed, " any migrant youth leader will tell you, just as racism is inextricable from nativism, so is the LGBT movement inextricable from the migrant youth movement. A disproportionate number of migrant youth leaders identify as queer " (qtd. in Chávez, 2013, p. 80). Whereas DREAM Now was modeled after the SLDN's campaign, SLDN in turn "announced and backed DREAM Now," as did other LGBTQ+ blogs (p. 80). These coalitional rhetorics of LGBTQ+ and migrant youth movements demonstrate the persistent role of activist letter-writing campaigns, even into the 21st century and conjoined with strategies of digital rhetoric.

The LGBTQ+ letters most familiar within the present-day media landscape are those circulated digitally. In one of the only studies of epistolary rhetoric to focus entirely on transgender letters, Joe Edward Hatfield (2019) considered digital suicide letters. Hatfield examined letters that were written by Leelah Alcorn in 2014 and Zander Mahaffey in 2015. The letters were auto-posted to Tumblr and then recirculated across digital networks in order to address the exigencies of transphobia and memorialize Alcorn and Mahaffey. Hatfield's analysis of these "letters as an emergent rhetorical form I name the *digital transgender suicide letter*" demonstrates the potential for transgender epistolary studies to queer rhetorical theories of form, agency, *kairos*, circulation, and digitality (Hatfield, 2019, p. 27). A less common yet important kind of digital open letter is that written by scholars and published on various open access sites.[5] Critical cultural communication scholar Shadee Abdi (2014) embedded such a letter, handwritten and addressed to her mom, within a narrative essay that included discussion of her identities and experiences as an Iranian-American lesbian (pp. 18–19). As Abdi (2020) explained in a later publication, "that letter ... offered the reasons why I was unable to share my queer identity with my mother" (p. 51). Publication of the letter was accompanied by risks, especially because of Abdi's "decision to publish in an open access journal" that is available to anyone who finds the essay or searches with Abdi's name online (p. 51). Abdi's mother has since read the letter (p. 52). Indeed, the nature of audiences primary and secondary, intended and not, varies in different forms of the open letter, whether published in print alone or circulated digitally. Across LGBTQ+ open letters, however, individuals and organizations use epistolary rhetoric to address publics and counterpublics about exigencies facing LGBTQ+ people.

Whereas open letters by definition call attention to their simultaneous address—as letters made available to the public even if addressed to an individual—most letters actually blur lines, in at least some ways, between communication that is public or interpersonal, political or intimate. Lipari (2007) pointed out how even Hansberry's already discussed open letters crossed the boundaries between public and private epistolary rhetoric, in part because they were initially published anonymously (p. 220). Hansberry's epistolary authorship was identified publicly by former *Ladder* editor Barbara Grier only after Hansberry had passed away—and then her place within LGBTQ+ history and literature became a subject of scholarly investigation (p. 220). Hansberry's anonymous letters to the *Ladder* are "at once both public and private," Lipari explained, and "thus occupy a liminal space—not quite public and not quite private, yet at the same time, both public and private" (p. 229). Although Lipari's analysis hinges on the initial anonymity of Hansberry's letters, a liminal status marks most epistolary rhetoric. As previously mentioned, feminist rhetorical scholars in particular have investigated this potential for the epistolary genre to be appropriated in variously public and private ways (Bordelon, 2018a; Bordelon, 2018c; Donawerth, 2002; Johnson, 2002; Gring-Pemble, 1998). Following this nuanced feminist understanding of epistolary rhetoric—as occupying a complex space that may traverse public and private domains—scholars have begun to consider how not only overtly public and political letters but also intimate and even romantic letters may be theorized as LGBTQ+ rhetoric.

Intimate and Romantic Letters. Current scholarship in LGBTQ+ rhetorical studies underscores how those letters understood as private—letters between friends, acquaintances, and lovers—are rhetorical in nature.[6] These letters are rhetorically crafted by writers. In other words, letter writers address audiences within specific situations, deploying rhetorical strategies to accomplish their purposes. Of course, this rhetorical perspective often is not brought to bear with respect to specifically intimate letters. As Poster (2007) noted, these letters generally are perceived as developing "conviction…based primarily on relationships rather than argument" (p. 2). In the words of Hawkins (2019), who recognized "the love letter as a rhetorical genre," the purpose of personal letters operates according to a different "logic": "The goal is to reinforce or restructure a relationship; to offer an apology, condolences, thanks; to declare to a particular person, 'I love you'" (pp. 56–57).

Yet a range of rhetorical strategies, including and beyond argumentative ones, may be utilized *in tandem* with intimate and romantic relationships in order to develop convictions, or for any purpose along the persuasive continuum. This understanding of intimate letters as epistolary rhetoric both presumes an expansive definition of rhetoric itself and pushes back on the presumption that argument may develop outside of the context of relationships between rhetors and audiences. E. Patrick Johnson's (2019) oral history of Black Southern women who love women discussed, for instance, letters written by a research participant to her family and especially her mother in which the writer "did mention being lesbian" (p. 47). In doing so, she inserted into the epistolary conversations of those relationships a reality that her family members found difficult to acknowledge in person. In another example, the already mentioned analysis of Mayne's correspondence with Benjamin, West (2014) discussed rhetorical strategies used within letters in the context of a relationship. West pointed out how Mayne "learned how to frame her actions in such a way that they conformed to Benjamin's politics, such as portraying herself as a victim of police harassment" (p. 47). Her rhetorical crafting of letters to him also involved "performing an act of deference to Benjamin's expertise." West's analysis makes clear that Mayne's agency includes the rhetorical agency of crafting her letters in order to achieve her goals within the context of her relationships.

While letters are crafted by their writers, it is important to understand the agency of LGBTQ+ rhetors as a negotiation of heteronormative conventions for the epistolary genre. Informed by rhetorical genre theory, VanHaitsma's (2014, 2019a) research on queer romantic epistolary rhetoric in the 19th-century United States has emphasized this simultaneous force of genre conventions and ingenuity of rhetors in navigating those conventions. Whereas romantic letters usually "are presumed to be natural and unstudied expressions of heartfelt love," VanHaitsma argued the letters are "a rhetorically taught, learned, and crafted practice" (2019a, p. 14). With this attention to rhetorical teaching and learning, VanHaitsma examined popular letter-writing manuals, showing how they "taught not only the genre or form of the romantic letter but also heteronormative ends and even ways of being" (p. 10).[7] More specifically, manual "instruction in genre conventions for epistolary address taught normatively gendered romantic coupling, instruction in conventions for the pacing of exchange taught normative restraint, and instruction in conventions for rhetorical practice taught a normative marriage *telos*" (p. 28). At the same time, letter-writing manuals taught invention strategies that rendered heteronormative genre conventions "prone to challenge through gender-crossing address, unrestrained outbreaks, and queer repurposing," especially by letter writers participating in same-sex and other nonnormative romantic relationships (p. 37).

In crafting LGBTQ+ romantic letters that subvert the genre conventions taught by heteronormative forms of rhetorical education and cultural pedagogy, rhetors enact queer rhetorical practices. VanHaitsma defined as "queer" those "relational and rhetorical practices that were nonnormative within the context of 19th-century manual instruction in cultural norms and genre conventions" for the romantic letter, including epistolary "practices that were unconventional in their transgressions of generic boundaries while pursuing nonnormative romantic relations" (pp. 12–13). Thus situating queer epistolary practices in relation to heteronormative genre conventions, VanHaitsma analyzed the practices of rhetors who developed correspondence constitutive of same-sex and nonnormative romantic relations. She considered, for instance, the same-sex, cross-class romantic correspondence of the previously introduced Addie Brown and Rebecca Primus. These freeborn African American women exchanged well over a hundred extent romantic letters between 1859 and 1868. The letters suggest that the women "challenged the heteronormative gendering, pacing, and *telos* embedded within the genre instruction" of letter-writing manuals (p. 50). Rather than writing letters in pursuit of normative opposite-sex marriage, Brown and Primus developed a same-sex romantic and erotic relationship in which they used their epistolary exchange to discuss not only their relationship but also labor and racial politics.

Though archival collections of same-sex letters between 19th-century Black women are rare, Brown and Primus were by no means alone in developing epistolary rhetoric that queered cultural norms and genre conventions. Hawkins (2019) has observed how other women composed love letters in defiance of norms, considering "letters from Janet Flanner to Natalia Danesi Murray, from Vita Sackville-West to Virginia Woolf, from Emily Dickenson to Susan Huntington Dickinson, from Radclyffe Hall to Evguenia Souline, from Gertrude Stein to Alice B. Toklas" (p. 86). Hawkins interpreted these "letters as a practice of unmaking historical assumptions regarding sexuality and gender" (p. 87). Reading these historical letters alongside those by their father and even themself, Hawkins has envisioned "the love letter itself" as a genre "or form that always provides an aperture to the queer" (p. 144).

In recognizing LGBTQ+ romantic letters as a rhetorical genre, recent scholarship has made clear how love letters are not only evidence of LGBTQ+ rhetors, relations, and rhetorical situations, but also instances of LGBTQ+ rhetorical practice. Hawkins (2019) observed, for example, that they "learned the art of syntactical love making" through writing letters that were not "explicitly sexual" (p. 104). The rhetorical practice of writing was itself an act of love making, in other words, rather than mere documentation of whether or not sexual acts occurred outside the letters. In VanHaitsma's (2019a) case, instead of offering an interpretation of Brown and Primus's letters "that characterizes the nature of their romantic relations by trying to determine their erotic practices and what they did *outside* the letters," she focused "on their rhetorical practices and what they did *within* the letters themselves" (p. 54). In these ways, scholars have shown how the most personal LGBTQ+ letters—intimate, romantic, and erotic letters—should be approached as rhetoric.[8] Even at their most heartfelt or heated, LGBTQ+ letters must rhetorically navigate the generic conventions that recur within a culture and evolve over time, along with the social norms for gender and sexuality that are embedded in those conventions.

This rhetorical approach to LGBTQ+ letters has begun to inform studies of gender and sexuality with respect to opposite-sex romantic correspondence as well. Suzanne Bordelon (2018b) examined, for instance, the 19th-century "courtship-by-correspondence" of Louise Amelia Knapp Smith Clappe and Alexander Hill Everett (p. 296). Bordelon approached Clappe and Everett's opposite-sex epistolary practices as rhetorically learned and crafted, as subject to genre conventions for the romantic letter (p. 304). In doing so, her analysis was able to show how both writers deployed generic conventions, and how Clappe in particular developed "the ability to directly and indirectly resist gendered expectations and the capacity to negotiate power and even benefit from it" (p. 318). Along similar lines, J. P. Hanly (2019) examined the courtship letters of another opposite-sex couple, Lucy Stone and Henry B. Blackwell. Hanly asked,

> Did nineteenth-century romantic letters exchanged between women and men, like women's letters to family and to female friends and lovers, serve as an important site for the sort of rhetorical work aimed at contesting the genre and gender conventions that VanHaitsma describes? (p. 286)

Hanly's analysis of the Stone-Blackwell correspondence found that they "use[d] their letters to: explore their views on rhetoric; contest the genre and gender conventions being taught by manuals; and engender the possibility of forming a rhetorical alliance" (p. 285). Significantly, this alliance exceeded the heteronormative conception of marriage that was embedded in conventional courtship letters. Theirs was "a lifelong rhetorical and romantic alliance animated by shared aims and characterized by a commitment to thinking about and speaking on behalf of those aims together" (p. 293). As Hanly and Bordelon's analyses of opposite-sex romantic letters have made clear, approaches developed for the study of LGBTQ+ letters as rhetoric have implications for understanding the rhetorical (re)gendering of romantic relations writ large.

CONCLUSIONS AND FUTURE DIRECTIONS FOR RESEARCH

Informed by rhetorical genre theory, recent communication scholarship focused on queer intimate and romantic letters not only emphasizes the rhetorical dimensions of the genre but also informs studies of opposite-sex romantic epistolary rhetoric. Other scholarship typically is not focused on letters as a subject, yet considers correspondence as a hidden transcript relevant to understanding the rhetorical agency of LGBTQ+ people. Rhetorical scholarship more predictably concerned with overtly public and political communication considers the significance of letters to the editor, open letters, and letter-writing campaigns by LGBTQ+ communities and social movements. While all of these approaches treat LGBTQ+ letters as rhetoric, scholars have long examined letters as primary sources of information in histories of LGBTQ+ life and rhetoric. For this historical research, letters preserve and make available information about gendered relations from the past, while serving as key sites of contest over the queer public memory of historical figures. Letters also document a wide range of other kinds of background information about the rhetorical situations navigated by LGBTQ+ rhetors. In these ways, to repurpose the language of Angela G. Ray (2016) for queer rhetorical studies, a letter may be read "as a fragment of evidence, to support claims about historical context," or "as a focal text" for "rhetorical analysis" (p. 55). Whether a LGBTQ+ letter functions as "context" or "text" depends "not on its physical or formal features but on the analytic purposes and processes of the scholar" (p. 43). Whether scholars underscore how LGBTQ+ letters are rhetoric, or simply draw on letters as records of information, letters are indispensable sources for the development of LGBTQ+ histories of rhetoric, studies of public memory, and research on communication.

Future studies of LGBTQ+ letters as rhetoric may address at last three underdeveloped areas of the extant scholarship. First, as in much LGBTQ+ scholarship, attention has gone mainly to lesbian, gay, and queer letter-writing practices. There have been few analyses of transgender epistolary rhetoric, though it is important to acknowledge the exception of work by Hatfield (2019), Sloop (2007), and West (2014), and virtually no analysis of bisexual, intersex, and Two-Spirit letter writing as such (VanHaitsma, 2021). Trans* coming out letters are an overlooked subgenre of LGBTQ+ epistolary rhetoric, to offer just one example, and other potential primary sources for analysis are included in the "Links to Digital Materials" and "Further Reading" sections. A second area for additional research involves LGBTQ+ epistolary rhetoric that is Indigenous, international, and/or written in languages other than English. Again, exceptional work by Abdi (2014, 2020), Chávez (2013), and Driskill (2016) needs to be recognized, but studies of LGBTQ+ epistolary rhetoric, like much of rhetorical studies writ large, remain stubbornly North American and Eurocentric. The "Further Reading" section offers some resources for developing scholarship on Indigenous and international LGBTQ+ epistolary rhetoric in multiple languages. Doing so, however, will require challenging the colonialist and settler colonial conceptions of gender, sexuality, and rhetoric that undergird Western epistolary traditions (Driskill, 2016; VanHaitsma, 2019a, p. 106). Finally, building on Hatfield's (2019) work, there is considerable room to expand the study of LGBTQ+ epistolary rhetoric through analyses of open letters that are circulated digitally. From social movement organizations and coalitions, to individuals coming out as various LGBTQ+ identities, people continue to harness the rhetorical power of the open letter form while capitalizing on the technical affordances of social media. These letters are published on organizational websites as well as circulated by social media accounts using hashtags that draw attention to the pressing exigencies that continue to face LGBTQ+ communities.

DIGITAL MATERIALS

Arizona Queer Archives (https://azqueerarchives.org/).
Digital Collections, Lesbian Herstory Archives (https://lesbianherstoryarchives.org/digital-resources/).
Digital Transgender Archive (https://www.digitaltransgenderarchive.net/).
Gay and Lesbian History, The New York Public Library Digital Collections (https://digitalcollections.nypl.org/collections/lane/gay-lesbian-history).
interACT's open letter re: "gender" in the draft Crimes Against Humanity Convention (https://interactadvocates.org/interacts-open-letter-re-gender-in-the-draft-crimes-against-humanity-convention/).
Lesbian, Gay, Bisexual, Transgender and Queer Studies, University of Michigan Library Research Guides (https://guides.lib.umich.edu/c.php?g=282858&p=1884817).
LGBTQ Issues in Records (https://www.archives.gov/research/lgbt), U.S. National Archives.
Mazer Lesbian Archives (https://www.mazerlesbianarchives.org/).
ONE National Gay and Lesbian Archives (http://digitallibrary.usc.edu/cdm/landingpage/collection/p15799coll4), USC Digital Library.
Online Collections, GLBT Historical Society Museum and Archives (https://www.glbthistory.org/online-collections).
Robinson, R. (2019). *Dear my black, bisexual, freshman self: You are enough* (https://www.glsen.org/blog/dear-my-black-bisexual-freshman-self-you-are-enough).
Sexuality and Gender Identity History (https://www.nationalarchives.gov.uk/help-with-your-research/research-guides/gay-lesbian-history/), U.K. National Archives.
Szabo, S. (2013, March 8). "And I do mean all my life": A trans* coming out letter (https://www.autostraddle.com/and-i-do-mean-all-my-life-a-trans-coming-out-letter-160349/). *Autostraddle*.

FURTHER READING

Ahearn, L. M. (2001). *Invitations to love: Literacy, love letters, and social change in Nepal*. University of Michigan Press.
Bazerman, C. (2000). Letters and the social ground of differentiated genres. In D. Barton & N. Hall (Eds.), *Letter writing as social practice* (pp. 15–29). John Benjamins Publishing.
Garlinger, P. P. (2003). Pleasurable insurrections: Sexual revolution and the anarchy of writing in lluís fernàndez's L'anarquista nu. *Bulletin of Hispanic Studies, 80*(1), 83–104.
Griffin, F. J. (Ed.). (1999). *Beloved sisters and loving friends: Letters from Rebecca Primus of Royal Oak, Maryland, and Addie Brown of Hartford, Connecticut, 1854–1868*. Ballantine.
Jones, C. (Ed.). (1997). *The love of friends: An anthology of gay and lesbian letters to friends and lovers*. Simon & Schuster.
Loftin, C. M. (Ed.). (2012). *Letters to ONE: Gay and lesbian voices from the 1950s and 1960s*. State University of New York Press.
Marchal, J. A. (2020). *Appalling bodies: Queer figures before and after Paul's letters*. Oxford University Press.

McDonald, C., & Tinsley, O. N. (2017). "Go beyond our natural selves": The prison letters of CeCe McDonald. *TSQ, 4*(2), 243–265.

Norton, R. (1998). *My dear boy: Gay love letters through the centuries*. Leyland Publications.

Syrett, N. L. (2012). A busman's holiday in the not-so-lonely crowd: Business culture, epistolary networks, and itinerant homosexuality in mid-twentieth-century America. *Journal of the History of Sexuality, 21*(1), 121–140.

VanHaitsma, P. (2018). African American rhetorical education and epistolary relations at the Holley School, 1868–1917. *Advances in the History of Rhetoric, 21*(3), 293–313.

VanHaitsma, P. (2017). Romantic correspondence as queer extracurriculum: The self-education for racial uplift of Addie Brown and Rebecca Primus. *College Composition and Communication, 69*(2), 182–207.

REFERENCES

Abdi, S. (2014). Staying I(ra)n: Narrating queer identity from within the Persian closet. *Liminalities, 10*(2), 1–20. http://liminalities.net/10-2/

Abdi, S. (2020). Revisiting a letter for someday: Writing toward a queer Iranian diasporic potentiality. In S. Eguchi & B. M. Calafell (Eds.), *Queer intercultural communication: The intersectional politics of belonging in and across differences* (pp. 47–61). Rowman & Littlefield.

Allen, J. M. (2013). *Passionate commitments: The lives of Anna Rochester and Grace Hutchins*. State University of New York Press.

Allen, J. S., & Tinsley, O. N. (2019). After the love: Remembering black/queer/diaspora. *GLQ, 25*(1), 107–112.

Bannet, E. T. (2005). *Empire of letters: Letter manuals and transatlantic correspondence, 1688–1820*. Cambridge University Press.

Bawarshi, A. S., & Reiff, M. J. (2010). *Genre: An introduction to history, theory, research, and pedagogy*. Parlor Press.

Bennett, J. A. (2009). *Banning queer blood: Rhetorics of citizenship, contagion, and resistance*. University of Alabama Press.

Bessette, J. (2018). *Retroactivism in the lesbian archives: Composing pasts and futures*. Southern Illinois University Press.

Bessette, J. (2019, November 14). Queering the "begging letter": Maimie Pinzer's resistant appeals for charity in epistolary autobiography [Conference session]. National Communication Association, Baltimore, MD.

Bizzell, P., & Herzberg, B. (Eds.). (2001). *The rhetorical tradition: Readings from classical times to the present* (2nd ed.). Bedford.

Black, J. E., & Morris, C. E., III (Eds.). (2013). *Harvey Milk: An archive of hope*. University of California Press.

Bordelon, S. (2018a). "Courtship-by-correspondence": Seduction through mentoring. *Rhetorica, 36*(3), 295–319.

Bordelon, S. (2018b). Louise Clappe and *The Shirley Letters*: Indirect feminist rhetoric and the contradictions of domestic space. *College English, 80*(5), 449–470.

Bordelon, S. (2018c). "Private letters" for public audiences: The complexities of *ethos* in Louise Clappe's *The Shirley Letters* from the California mines, 1851–1852. *Rhetoric Review, 37*(1), 77–89.

Chávez, K. R. (2013). *Queer migration politics: Activist rhetoric and coalitional possibilities*. University of Illinois Press.

Chávez, K. R. (2015). Beyond inclusion: Rethinking rhetoric's historical narrative. *Quarterly Journal of Speech, 101*(1), 162–172.

Cloud, D. (2007). The first lady's privates: Queering Eleanor Roosevelt for public address studies. In C. E. Morris (Ed.), *Queering public address: Sexualities in American historical discourse* (pp. 23–44). University of South Carolina Press.

Cooper, B. (2015). Intersectionality. In L. Disch & M. Hawkesworth (Eds.), *The Oxford handbook of feminist theory* (pp. 1–12). Oxford University Press. http://doi.org/10.1093/oxfordhb/9780199328581.001.0001

Donawerth, J. (2002). Nineteenth-century United States conduct book rhetoric by women. *Rhetoric Review, 21*(1), 5–21.

Driskill, Q. (2016). *Asegi stories: Cherokee queer and Two-Spirit memory*. University of Arizona Press.

Duberman, M., Vicinus, M., & Chauncey, G. (Eds.). (1989). *Hidden from history: Reclaiming the gay and lesbian past*. Meridian.

Dunn, T. (2016). *Queerly remembered: Rhetorics for representing the GLBTQ past*. University of South Carolina Press.

Freedman, E. B. (1998). "The burning of letters continues": Elusive identities and the historical construction of sexuality. *Journal of Women's History, 9*(4), 181–200.

Garlinger, P. P. (2005). *Confessions of the letter closet: Epistolary fiction and queer desire in modern Spain*. University of Minnesota Press.

Gladney, M. R. (1998). Biographical research on lesbigay subjects: Editing the letters of Lillian Smith. In J. V. Carmichael Jr. (Ed.), *Daring to find our names: The search for lesbigay library history* (pp. 47–54). Greenwood Press.

Gring-Pemble, L. M. (1998). Writing themselves into consciousness: Creating a rhetorical bridge between the public and private spheres. *Quarterly Journal of Speech, 84*(1), 41–61.

Groeneveld, E. (2018). Letters to the editor as "archives of feeling": *On Our Backs* magazine and the sex wars. *American Periodicals, 28*(2), 153–167.

Hanly, J. P. (2019). "Then alone could the morning stars sing together for joy": Engendering alliance in the Stone-Blackwell courtship correspondence. *Rhetoric Review, 38*(3), 285–296.

Hansen, K. (1996). "No *kisses* is like yours": An erotic friendship between two African-American women during the mid-nineteenth century. In M. Vicinus (Ed.), *Lesbian subjects* (pp. 178–207). Indiana University Press.

Hartman, S. (2008). Venus in two acts. *Small Axe, 16*(2), 1–14.

Hartman, S. (2019). *Wayward lives, beautiful experiments: Intimate histories of social upheaval*. W. W. Norton.

Hatfield, J. E. (2019). The queer kairotic: Digital transgender suicide memories and ecological rhetorical agency. *Rhetoric Society Quarterly, 49*(1), 25–48.

Hawkins, A. (2019). *These are love(d) letters*. Wayne State University Press.

Holmes, K. (2015). What's the tea: Gossip and the production of black gay social history. *Radical History Review, 122*, 55–69.

Holland, M. (Ed.). (2003). *Oscar Wilde: A life in letters*. Fourth Estate.

Johnson, E. P. (2019). *Honeypot: Black Southern women who love women*. Duke University Press.

Johnson, N. (2002). *Gender and rhetorical space in American life, 1866–1910*. Southern Illinois University Press.

Keeanga-Yamahtta, T. (Ed.). (2017). *How we get free: Black feminism and the Combahee River Collective*. Haymarket Books.

Kennerly, M. (2019, November 14). *The queer temporalities of classical reception: The love letters of Fronto and Aurelius in the 19th century* [Conference session]. National Communication Association, Baltimore, MD.

Lipari, L. (2007). The rhetoric of intersectionality: Lorraine Hansberry's 1957 Letters to the *Ladder*. In C. E. Morris (Ed.), *Queering public address: Sexualities in American historical discourse* (pp. 220–248). University of South Carolina Press.

Miller, C. (1984). Genre as social action. *Quarterly Journal of Speech, 70*, 151–167.

Miller, S. (1998). *Assuming the positions: Cultural pedagogy and the politics of commonplace writing*. University of Pittsburgh Press.

Morris, C. E., III. (2007a). Introduction: Portrait of a queer rhetorical/historical critic. In C. E. Morris III (Ed.), *Queering public address: Sexualities in American historical discourse* (pp. 1–19). University of South Carolina Press.

Morris, C. E., III. (2007b). My old Kentucky homo: Abraham Lincoln, Larry Kramer, and the politics of queer memory. In C. E. Morris (Ed.), *Queering public address: Sexualities in American historical discourse* (pp. 93–120). University of South Carolina Press.

Olson, L. (2012). Intersecting audiences: Public commentary concerning Audre Lorde's speech, "Uses of the erotic: The erotic as power." In K. R. Chávez & C. L. Griffin (Eds.), *Standing in the intersection: Feminist voices, feminist practices in communication studies* (pp. 125–146). State University of New York Press.

Poster, C. (2007). Introduction. In C. Poster & L. C. Mitchell (Eds.), *Letter-writing manuals and instruction from antiquity to the present: Historical and bibliographic studies* (pp. 1–6). University of South Carolina Press.

Poster, C., & Mitchell, L. C. (Eds.). (2007). *Letter-writing manuals and instruction from antiquity to the present: Historical and bibliographic studies*. University of South Carolina Press.

Pritchard, E. D. (2017). *Fashioning lives: Black queers and the politics of literacy*. Southern Illinois University Press.

Rand, E. J. (2014). *Reclaiming queer: Activist and academic rhetorics of resistance*. University of Alabama Press.

Ray, A. G. (2016). Rhetoric and the archive. *Review of Communication, 16*(1), 43–59.

Royster, J. J. (2000). *Traces of a stream: Literacy and social change among African American women*. University of Pittsburgh Press.

Sloop, J. M. (2007). Lucy Lobdell's queer circumstances. In C. E. Morris (Ed.), *Queering public address: Sexualities in American historical discourse* (pp. 149–173). University of South Carolina Press.

Smith-Rosenberg, C. (2000). Diaries and letters. In B. Zimmerman (Ed.), *Lesbian histories and cultures: An encyclopedia* (pp. 234–236). Garland Publishing.

Trasciatti, M. A. (2009). Letter writing in an Italian immigrant community: A transatlantic tradition. *Rhetoric Society Quarterly, 39*(1), 73–94.

VanHaitsma, P. (2014). Queering "the language of the heart": Romantic letters, genre instruction, and rhetorical practice. *Rhetoric Society Quarterly, 44*(1), 6–24.

VanHaitsma, P. (2016). Gossip as rhetorical methodology for queer and feminist historiography. *Rhetoric Review, 35*(2), 135–147.

VanHaitsma, P. (2019a). *Queering romantic engagement in the postal age: A rhetorical education*. University of South Carolina Press.

VanHaitsma, P. (2019b, February 22). What can "The Favourite" tell us about the rhetoric of queer letters? *Citizen Critics*. https://citizencritics.org/2019/02/what-can-the-favourite-tell-us-about-the-rhetoric-of-queer-letters/

VanHaitsma, P. (2021) An archival framework for affirming Black women's bisexual rhetorics in the Primus Collections. *Rhetoric Society Quarterly, 51*(1), 27–41.

West, I. (2014). *Transforming citizenships: Transgender articulations of the law*. New York University Press.

Woods, C. S. (2019, November 14). *In praise of "abnormal women": Reclaiming the letters of "girls who answer personals" for queer and feminist rhetorical history* [Conference session]. National Communication Association, Baltimore, MD.

NOTES

1. For another important intervention in normative conceptions of the history of rhetoric, see Chávez (2015).

2. As explained by Driskill (2016), Coosa was "a Muskogeean 'chiefdom' that would later become the Cherokee town of Coosawattee in the eighteenth century" (p. 68).
3. On the relationship between hidden and public transcripts within studies of queer rhetoric, also see Bennett (2009, p. 4).
4. The statement is reprinted and contextualized in Keeanga-Yamahtta (2017). Sources that consider the complexity of Black feminist theories of intersectionality and interlocking oppressions, while also accounting for questions of sexuality, include Olson (2012) and Cooper (2015).
5. For another form of published scholarly letter involving queer, Black, and diasporic "epistolary reflection," see Allen and Tinsley (2019).
6. Other scholars of rhetoric, communication, and composition who consider romantic letters, at least in brief, include Miller (1998, pp. 201–206) and Trasciatti (2009, pp. 85–88).
7. While countless scholars have examined letter-writing manuals, studies that consider instruction in specifically romantic letters include Bannet (2005) and Trasciatti (2009).
8. New and yet unpublished scholarship on queer epistolary rhetorics includes Bessette (2019), Kennerly (2019), and Woods (2019).

Pamela VanHaitsma

MEDIA DEPICTIONS OF SEXUAL ATTITUDES

INTRODUCTION

Sexual content in the media has garnered much scholarly attention in the last four decades due to its high prevalence. Content analyses have shown that sexual content is common on television, appearing in at least 70% and even 80% of prime-time shows in different countries (e.g., Eyal et al., 2014; Farrar et al., 2003; Kunkel et al., 2005). Much of the content in television programming appears in the form of conversations about sex and sexuality, and a smaller proportion depicts sexual behaviors, mostly passionate kissing and light intimate touching or flirting (Rousseau et al., 2018; Timmermans & Van den Bulck, 2018). Much less frequent in television content is the portrayal of sexual intercourse and more explicit sexual behaviors (Dillman Carpentier et al., 2017). Similar findings have been identified in content analyses of television shows popular among adolescents, with some studies identifying as much as 70% of television shows portraying some sexual content (Eyal et al., 2007) and more recent research classifying 50% of all main characters on such shows as being sexually active (Signorielli & Bievenour, 2015). Still, most of the sexual content in teen-preferred television programming is in the form of sexual talk, innuendo, kissing, and flirting. In approximately the last one-and-a-half decades, with the rise in viewing of televised content through streaming services (e.g., Rideout & Robb, 2019), sexual content has been found to be prevalent in streamed content as well (e.g., Dudek et al., 2022; Letort, 2019) and has been receiving increased scholarly attention, also with regard to live streaming of video game play (Ruberg, 2021).

Popular films also include much sexual content, with sexual behaviors appearing in 82% of U.S. films (Willis et al., 2020). In contemporary Mexican films, too, the most prevalent sexual behavior was found to be kissing, with sexual intercourse portrayed far less commonly (Kollath-Cattano et al., 2018). As media technologies and content become more digital and interactive in nature, scholars have also been examining technologies such as video games. According to the Entertainment Software Rating Board data, among the top-selling video games between 1994 and 2013, 13% included sexual content, with increases in its prevalence over the years in the M (Mature) and T (Teen) rating categories (Vidana-Perez et al., 2018). Music videos, too, often include sexual content, with variations across musical genres (Wright, 2009). Most references to sexuality in music videos are implicit, similar to other television programming content.

The current article reviews the peer-reviewed published literature relevant to the depiction of sexual attitudes in mainstream entertainment media content. It begins by defining sexual attitudes. The definition is followed by a consideration of relevant theoretical perspectives that help explain the central effects likely to take place among audience members as a result of exposure to such portrayals. Then, the different ways through which sexual attitudes have been found to be conveyed in the content are reviewed. The media in focus throughout this article include television, film, music, and—as entertainment media has evolved—also streaming services and video games. The article does not address print media, news content, pornography, and social media because it focuses on constructed entertainment narratives that are likely to convey and impact attitudes. The article centers largely on the literature published since the new millennium (since 2000), with a stronger emphasis on the period from 2015 to the present.

DEFINING SEXUAL ATTITUDES

An attitude is an evaluation of an object, a pro- (like) or anti- (dislike) tendency associating attributes with a certain referent (Maio et al., 2019). Although not always consistent with behaviors, attitudes are considered important influencers in behavioral decision-making. Attitudes originate in diverse ways, including through direct experiences and behaviors for which one receives reinforcements and appraisals, but also through observation of how others perform certain behaviors, experience emotions, or convey attitudes in the real-world environment or through the media (Olufemi, 2012). Narratives—stories that "contain information about setting, characters, and their motivations" (Braddock & Dillard, 2016, p. 446)—which are prevalent in entertainment media, are especially likely to play a role in attitude formation and change because they are potent conveyors of messages, both informative and evaluative, about the topic they address (Moyer-Gusé, 2008).

In the context of media and sexual content, attitudes have often been studied as important outcomes likely to result from one-time or repeated exposure to sexual portrayals. Among the common attitudes examined are permissive sexual attitudes (e.g., attitudes endorsing casual sexual relations, extrarelational sex, sexual activity with multiple partners), attitudes accepting of sexualization, attitudes supportive of abuse or harassment, especially against women, attitudes supportive of rape myths, and attitudes toward safer sex practices (e.g., attitudes toward abstinence and toward contraception use; Baams et al., 2015; Dillman Carpentier & Stevens, 2018; Eyal & Kunkel, 2008; Seabrook et al., 2019).

THE EFFECTS OF MEDIA PORTRAYALS OF SEXUAL ATTITUDES ON AUDIENCES: MAIN THEORETICAL PERSPECTIVES

The Creation of Sexual Scripts. One of the main ways in which media depictions of attitudes can impact the audience is by constructing scripts (Rousseau et al., 2018). Scripts are sense-making structures (Rubinsky & Cooke-Jackson, 2017) that provide a road-map of sorts for navigating through social situations (Dillman Carpentier et al., 2017). Alongside information about the situations, scripts also convey norms and cultural messages about them. Examples of sexual scripts studied in the context of media portrayals are the heterosexual script, which conveys information about the culturally accepted gender-role sexual inclinations of men and women (Kim et al., 2007) and scripts about casual sex (Timmermans & Van den Bulck, 2018), which will be reviewed when addressing attitudes conveyed through mere presence, below. A central model used in recent research to theorize about the effects of sexual scripts presented in media content on audiences is Wright's (2011) 3AM model. Building on theories of cognitive scripts (Huesmann, 1986) and on theories of sexual scripting (Gagnon & Simon, 1973), the model details three main roles that the media play in the development of sexual scripts: the acquisition (i.e., learning of a new script), activation (i.e., priming or retrieval of an existing script, which often happens in future encounters with sexual media content), and application (i.e., acting upon the script) of sexual scripts.

The Cultivation of a Worldview Consistent With the Sexual Reality Portrayed in the Media. Cultivation theory (Gerbner et al., 1994) suggests that cumulative exposure to repetitive and consistent themes in media content can lead, through a long-term process, to the development of a worldview that is consistent with that presented in the content. The themes prevalent in media content present not only information about the world (e.g., what percentage of the population is made up of certain groups or which behaviors are more commonplace) but also convey attitudes about the acceptability and normativity of such groups or actions. Thus, Gerbner et al. (1994) considered television the main cultural storyteller, the conveyor of society's priorities and values.

Though initially focused on television, cultivation theory has since been expanded to encompass other platforms and content in the mediated environment. Indeed, studies have shown that patterns of portrayals across different genres and technologies can lead to cultivation effects, namely, impacting the real-world beliefs and perceptions of audiences (e.g., Morgan & Shanahan, 2010). Whereas cognitive effects are termed first-order cultivation effects, second-order cultivation effects address attitudinal and emotional effects that result from such repeated media exposure (e.g., the mean world syndrome; Morgan et al., 2014). Indeed, studies applying cultivation theory to the context of sexual media content have found that exposure to nonexplicit sexual media content is associated with small-yet-significant first-order effects in the form of perceptions of peer sexual experience (Coyne et al., 2019; Martino et al., 2005). Moreover, in a study of Flemish adult women, Custers and Van den Bulck (2013) found that exposure to televised crime drama series predicted second-order perceived risk and fear of sexual violence.

The Teaching of Sexual Behaviors and the Attitudes and Emotions That Underlie Them. Social cognitive theory (Bandura, 2009) has often been applied to the study of sexual media effects. According to this theory, the long-term exposure to sexual role modeling in the media can lead to the learning of the rules and norms that underlie social behaviors, among them those associated with sex. As part of the learning process, behaviors are cognitively stored in memory, rehearsed, and coupled with internal and external reinforcements that are often learned from cues about rewards or punishments that the behaviors accrue. Along with information stored in memory about past experiences and personal inclinations, a decision-making process can lead to a decision to enact (or avoid) these behaviors by the person. In a meta-analysis on the effects of exposure to nonexplicit portrayals of sexual content in the media, Coyne et al. (2019) confirmed that there have been identified small but significant effects of media use on the age of sexual initiation, overall sexual experience, and engagement in risky sexual behaviors, with stronger effects manifested among adolescents, boys, and White participants. Similar findings have emerged from studies of exposure to music videos with sexually objectifying content (Herd, 2015) and of exposure of college students to music lyrics (Wright & Rubin, 2020). Self-efficacy is a central mechanism driving behaviors according to the social cognitive perspective. Behm-Morawitz and Mastro (2009) found that playing a sexualized female character in a video game led to lowered efficacy perceptions among female undergraduate students compared to playing a nonsexualized video game character.

Though behaviors were the initial outcome of concern in social cognitive theory, later theoretical developments have placed an emphasis also on the underlying attitudes and emotions involved in and guiding the social learning process. Coyne et al.'s (2019) meta-analysis found small but significant effects of exposure to nonexplicit sexual media content and permissive sexual attitudes and acceptance of rape myths. Consistent findings have emerged from studies of adolescents' and emerging adults' exposure to teen sex romps (Alexopoulos & Taylor, 2020) and video games (Collins et al., 2017), including positive links with tolerance for harassment against women. Attitudes toward condom use have also been found to be negatively linked to media exposure (Alexopoulos & Taylor, 2020). Emotions such as shame or fear, which are sometimes conveyed through media content may transfer to the audience member and impact their learning and execution of (or decision to not execute) social behaviors and even identity development and self-concept (Collins et al., 2017; McInroy & Craig, 2015; Rubinsky & Cooke-Jackson, 2017). Among sexual minority youth, especially gay, lesbian, bisexual, transsexual, and queer youth, the lack of interpersonal communication about sex may lead them even more than heterosexual youth to turn to the media for information and messages about sexuality that contribute to their identity development (Bond, 2014, 2015).

Importantly, it should be noted that, although the main focus in the literature on sexual media content effects has been on negative outcomes, largely reviewed in the section of the article below about the effects of media portrayals of sexual attitudes on audiences, positive outcomes of exposure are also possible, including adults' increased awareness of and understanding of some sexual health issues (e.g., Sisson et al., 2021) and minimizing college student's felt sexual stigma (Johnson, 2017). Such positive outcomes are especially likely to result from positive representations of sexuality in the media, including those that address sexual health and responsibility (Maes & Vandenbosch, 2022) and those that represent sexual diversity and provide information about nonheterosexual sexuality (e.g., Bond et al., 2009).

THE DEPICTION OF SEXUAL ATTITUDES IN MAINSTREAM ENTERTAINMENT MEDIA

Sexual Attitudes Conveyed Through Mere Presence (or Lack Thereof).

Although attitudes are abstract constructs difficult to concretely portray on the screen, sexual attitudes are conveyed through both scenes with sexual behaviors as well as in scenes with conversations about sex (Kunkel et al., 2005). First, the mere presence of certain depictions on screen conveys attitudes toward sexuality. The fact that about 70% of television shows (Eyal et al., 2014) and over 80% of films (Willis et al., 2020) include sexual talk and behavior confirms the importance and interest in this topic.

One focus within content analyses of sexual depictions in entertainment media has been the relational context within which sexual behaviors occur. Some studies have found that popular television shows depict sexuality nearly equally in committed relationships as in casual relationships. In teen sex romps, Alexopoulos and Taylor (2020) found that most sexual behaviors occur outside of committed relationships. Even in teen-oriented drama series, there is a common depiction of commitment-free, casual sexual relations among teen characters (Van Damme, 2010). Scholars suggest that this prevalence of casual sex supports an attitude permissive and encouraging of sex in noncommitted relationship, a behavior that often inevitably involves less familiarity with the sexual partner's sexual history and background.

In contrast, the absence of certain sexual topics from the media tends to convey the opposite: that the topic is unimportant or insignificant. Such an argument was advanced by Gross's (1994) discussion of the absence of nonheterosexual characters from media portrayals, a situation he termed symbolic annihilation. According to Gross, the choice to exclude sexual minorities from the media reflects a biased preference, an attitude of decision-makers in the industry who choose through such invisibility to impact audience perceptions and evaluations. Since their emergence in approximately the last 15 years, and more so in the last five years, streaming content has been analyzed for the increased prevalence of queer representations (e.g., Symes, 2017). Still, recent content analyses have confirmed that despite increases in media portrayals of sexual minorities over the years, the majority of sexual or intimate portrayals in mainstream entertainment media are still heterosexual. The range of nonheterosexual sexual identities is also still limited in mainstream entertainment media (Bond, 2015). For example, Thorfinnsdottir and Jensen (2017) found that only six incidents of sexuality in Danish public television shows targeting 7–12-year-olds were nonheterosexual and none of these incidents involved a romantic or relational interest. The authors concluded that such minimal representation does not validate nonheterosexual relations.

Sexual Attitudes Conveyed Through the Focus of Mediated Depictions.

The focus within sexual depictions in the media can also convey attitudes toward sex and sexuality. Much like framing, placing an emphasis on certain elements in portrayals by elaborating upon them, giving them more screen time, or developing their related storylines in greater depth can communicate messages about the importance or relevance of the topics for audience members' lives. This article will address two important foci within entertainment media sexual depictions and discuss the attitudes communicated through such portrayals: sexual health and sexual abuse versus consent.

Media's Depiction of Attitudes Toward Sexual Health. A topic that has received much attention in the sexual media literature in the last two decades is the inclusion of messages about sexual health in mainstream entertainment media content. Sexual health, sometimes also termed sexual risks and responsibilities (Kunkel et al., 2005), acknowledges that sexuality is a topic of importance both personally and from a public health perspective, and that along with the pleasure which it can provide participants, it can also lead to less desired and even negative consequences in different dimensions, emotionally, physically, relationally, and socially. Despite the real-world understanding that engaging in sexual behaviors should involve a consideration of the risks they pose as well as a serious consideration of the precautions that can be taken to minimize or avoid such risks, mainstream entertainment media has not been realistically representing such issues in its content.

The lack of serious consideration of sexual risks and responsibilities and the minimal promotion of low-risk sexual activity have been found in content analyses of popular television programming, popular films, and teen sex films (Alexopoulos & Taylor, 2020; Kinsler et al., 2019; Kollath-Cattano et al., 2018). In a study of Israeli prime-time television shows, Eyal et al. (2014) found that only 19% of shows with sexual content also included scenes with sexual risk and responsibility portrayals. Only 2% of shows with sexual content placed a central emphasis on the topic of sexual health as a major theme. In other studies, the number of scenes of sexual content that involve information about sexual health can be counted on less than two hands (Dillman Carpentier et al., 2017). In a content analysis of media content popular among young teens, Hust et al. (2008) found that less than 1% of the content addressed sexually healthy behaviors. Even the show *16 and Pregnant*—an MTV production focusing on the story of teen mothers, their (largely unintended) pregnancies, and their lives and relationships upon pregnancy—has been found to include little information about safer sex practices or precaution (Lance et al., 2012).

Interestingly, the content that seems to have the greatest prevalence of sexual health, risks, and responsibilities messages embedded within it is television shows that address sex as a central theme within the show, such as the premium channel HBO's *Sex and the City* and *Girls* (Jensen & Jensen, 2007; Stevens & Garrett, 2016). In an analysis of the Netflix series *Elite*, Maes and Vandenbosch (2022) reported that positive sexual messages—that is, messages that convey a responsible and accepting stance toward sexuality, mutuality in sexual relationships, resilience to negative sexual effects, and the promotion of open communication about sex and sexuality—were common within this series, appearing on average four times per episode and conveyed by 64% of the characters. Maes and Vandenbosch did note that such positive sexual messages often co-occurred in scenes with antisocial sexual messages (e.g., messages about sexual violence or messages that ignored the serious consequences of sexual behavior). Some scholars have argued that the attitude conveyed about sex and sexuality in most of the limited portrayals is that sex is merely recreational, that sexual health and sexual topics are not topics worthy of consideration, and that they are not serious or relevant for viewers (Dillman Carpentier et al., 2017). Indeed, audience effects investigations have documented a positive effect of exposure to condom depictions in televised drama shows on emerging adult females' attitudes toward condom use (Farrar, 2006). In contrast, studies have found a negative relationship between exposure to mediated sexual content that lacks a serious consideration of risks and responsibilities and adolescents' lowered perceived personal sexual risks (Aubrey et al., 2014).

Media's Depiction of Attitudes Toward Sexual Abuse Versus Sexual Consent. A few years into the new millennium, scholars have documented an increase in the representation of sexual crimes and abuse in entertainment content, especially in the burgeoning genre of law-and-order television drama shows (Cuklanz & Moorti, 2006). Such shows placed a greater emphasis on unwanted, coercive, and illegal behaviors in the realm of sex than before and often also depict the treatment of these crimes by the law enforcement forces and the just punishment for the perpetrators of these crimes. Exposure to scenes with certain depictions of sexual violence against women that were taken from such crime drama television shows was found to be associated with undergraduate students' lower acceptance of rape myths (Lee et al., 2011).

However, the law-and-order crime drama genre has greatly expanded in the following years and has developed into multiple franchises; with this expansion came great variations in portrayals. Some of the shows have been critiqued for the inclusion of gendered stereotypes (Cuklanz & Moorti, 2006) and others, such as *CSI: Crime Scene Investigation*, have been accused of promoting the rape myth by presenting women victims as responsible, in some way, for the sexual crime (e.g., by acting in a sexually suggestive manner or spending time in "dangerous" locations; Foss, 2010). Kinsler et al. (2019) similarly found that storylines that addressed sexual violence, abuse, or harassment in prime-time television shows viewed by teens or young adults were not coupled by a message about the negative consequences of such behaviors, although in real life such incidents carry meaningful implications for the victims. Letort (2019) analyzed sexual content in the Netflix series *13 Reasons Why* and found that the show endorsed and perpetuated the rape myth. Such sanitized portrayals of sexual abuse may convey the impression that harassment or violence are inconsequential or are not significant enough to be addressed. Indeed, later effects investigations have pointed to more complex and nuanced outcomes with regard to college student viewers' attitudes toward sexual violence and rape myth acceptance (Hust et al., 2015).

Related to the topics of sexual violence and abuse is the topic of sexual consent, which has been receiving greater attention in the academic scholarship in recent years. According to Jozkowski et al. (2019), young people report that in real life, the process of sexual consent—or the agreement of two people to engage in sexual activity with one another—may take time to develop, often starting in one public location and advancing to a private one in which the behavior actually takes place. However, popular mainstream films tend to depict the sexual consent process as a much more simplified and quick process. Most often, sexual consent is conveyed implicitly and nonverbally, and often, it takes place immediately before the sexual act itself. Willis et al. (2020) also found that sexual consent in films, especially those rated R (Restricted), was largely unmodeled. When consent cues were present, more often in PG-13 (Parents strongly cautioned—Some material may be inappropriate for children under 13)- rated movies, the cues tended to be implicit or nonverbal and were often followed by consensual sexual activity. Jozkoski et al. and Willis et al. argue that such portrayals can normalize an attitude that sexual consent is unimportant or obvious, that one should not pay close attention to obtaining consent prior to sexual behaviors, and that nonverbal or implicit consent is normative and sufficient.

Sexual Attitudes Conveyed Through the Consequences of Sex Depicted in Media Content. The depiction of consequences to sexual behaviors has been suggested to carry important implications for audience members' sexual perceptions, attitudes, and behavioral decision-making (Eyal & Finnerty, 2007). Such importance is ascribed to the depiction of consequences because it tends, through the focus and valence associated with such portrayals, to convey attitudes toward the sexual behaviors, such as whether they are normative, acceptable, positive, and so forth. Kinsler et al. (2019) found that television shows viewed by youth do not involve many narratives about the consequences of sex and sexual behaviors. Bond et al. (2018) similarly found that only less than 30% of sexual references were depicted as resulting in clear consequences and that consequences—especially negative ones—were significantly more likely to take place within heterosexual contexts that in those involving gay, lesbian, or bisexual characters. Ortiz and Brooks (2014) found that in teen television shows, sexual talk was associated largely with negative consequences, whereas sexual behaviors were solely linked with positive outcomes. Although early studies tended to examine and emphasize the physical consequences of sexual activity (e.g., pregnancy, contraction of sexually transmitted diseases), later studies have consistently found that emotional and social/relational consequences are far more common in televised narratives than physical ones (Aubrey, 2004; Eyal & Finnerty, 2009).

Sexual Attitudes Conveyed Through the Emotions Associated With Sexuality and Sexual Behaviors in Media Content. The attachment of emotional expressions to social behaviors portrayed in the media can convey important information about the attitudes associated with those behaviors. Emotions may communicate to the audience that a certain behavior is undesirable, dangerous, or rather positive. The few content analyses examining emotions associated with sexual depictions in the media have focused on the emotional outcomes of sexual behaviors, primarily sexual intercourse. Aubrey (2004) analyzed the consequences depicted for sexual references or behaviors in teen television programming. She found that the large majority of consequences depicted in these television shows were negative and emotional or social in nature, far outnumbering positive or physical outcomes. The portrayals of sexual consequences were led by the emotions of guilt/anxiety, humiliation, and disappointment. In examining sexual intercourse behaviors depicted on television programs, more specifically, Eyal and Finnerty (2009) found that the majority of consequences portrayed to these behaviors were emotional. Of the emotional consequences identified in the study, 73% were positive (happiness or excitement) and 27% were negative (guilt or regret). Interestingly, Dillman Carpentier et al. (2017) found that in television shows popular among emerging adults in the United States, only 7% of scenes depicted both sex and love together in the scene.

One sexual context that is intrinsically linked with emotions is the initiation of sexual activity, also known as virginity loss. First-time intercourse is "one of the major turning points in sexual life" (Carpenter, 2009, p. 804) and is also a common storyline in films and television shows, especially those that focus on or target adolescents. Carpenter identified three main scripts associated with virginity loss in narrative media content: (1) virginity as a gift—one's virginity is seen as a valuable possession given to someone else who is expected to reciprocate with love or commitment; (2) virginity as stigma—virginity is seen as something of which one needs to dispose and quickly as it negatively impacts one's reputation; and (3) virginity as a step in the process of growing up, of identity development, personal insight gaining, and individual transformation.

Another typology of sexual initiation scripts in narrative media content was constructed by Kelly (2010) in her analysis of teen drama television shows. Kelly identified three main representations of virginity loss: (1) abstinence (delaying virginity loss) as an important value, (2) virginity as a social stigma that needs to be tossed in order to maintain personal and social benefits, and (3) a management script that focuses on the handling of risks associated with the inevitable virginity loss. In both Carpenter's (2009) and Kelly's (2010) typologies it is clear that emotions are involved in virginity management, maintenance, and loss. Emotions are involved in the decision-making process, the actual experience of virginity loss, and the consequences that ensue from that experience, especially the emotional risks it involves. Indeed, studies have found that mediated narratives—both in film and in television shows—play a role in adolescents' interpretation of sexual initiation scripts and even their real-life virginity loss experiences (Carpenter, 2009; Eyal & Ben-Ami, 2017). The mediated stories about virginity loss serve as comparison points and as sources for information.

Sexual Attitudes Conveyed Through Humor. Humor is an interesting context in mediated presentations. Humor can come in many forms: through puns, understatements, comical jokes, or one-liners that lighten up the atmosphere, through satire or irony, or through demeaning and manipulating comments that make fun of people or situations (e.g., Stevens & Garrett, 2016). Humor is common in the media's portrayal of sex and sexuality. Dillman Carpentier et al. (2017) found that 25% of scenes with sexual content in television shows popular among emerging adults used comedic one-liners about sexual organs; such jokes or puns were, in fact, the most common type of talk about sex identified in their study. Even in the entertainment media content consumed by young teens, humor is prevalent when addressing even serious topics such as sexual health, as reported by Hust et al. (2008). Among the main themes they identified in the presentation of sexual health topics, they found that puberty was depicted as funny, accompanied by jokes and satirical images, and contraception was portrayed as embarrassing or humiliating. Hust et al. suggested that humor served to ease the discomfort sometimes associated with the discussion of sexuality but could have also led the young audience members to feel less comfortable with their own bodies and sexuality and could have undermined the importance of safer sex practices.

Indeed, scholars' interpretations of the role of humor in conveying sexual attitudes in media content have been as diverse as the forms of humor in content. On the one hand, Stevens and Garrett (2016) analyzed the HBO series *Girls* about which they write that "critics and academics alike have argued that *Girls* is a pivotal point for how sexuality is depicted on television" (p. 931). They found that 17% of scenes with sexual behavior and 63% of scenes with talk about sex in the series involved humor. A slightly higher percentage (66%) of scenes with sexual risk and responsibility messages involved humor. And among scenes that addressed sexual crimes, 53% were coded as humorous. Stevens and Garrett, although not providing information about what type of humor was used in these contexts, seemed to perceive humor in this context as nonjudgmental. They concluded that humor is an effective strategy for learning about sex as it draws attention to the messages and presents often taboo topics in nonthreatening ways.

Other scholars, however, have raised questions about the effectiveness of using humor in media content to convey sexual attitudes. Thorfinnsdottir and Jensen (2017) reported that Danish public television shows targeting children ages 7–12 included scenes with nonheterosexual content only in the context of humor, as a comic relief or a funny misunderstanding, thus reinforcing, in their view, a heteronormative attitudinal preference. Moyer-Gusé et al. (2011) found that embedding humor within a sexual narrative about an unintended pregnancy on a television sitcom led to greater intentions among undergraduates to engage in unprotected sex in comparison to the same storyline without the humorous context. They argued that humor associated with sexual mediated narratives may lead to decreased counterarguing and to the trivialization of the seriousness of sexual risks.

Similarly, Collins et al. (2003) analyzed an episode of the popular television sitcom *Friends* in which condoms were present and centrally focused upon in multiple scenes, a rare occurrence on television. About half of adolescent viewers who had seen the episode had changed their attitude toward condom effectiveness relative to the pre-viewing measure; however, the attitudes were changed in both directions—about half of viewers had more positive perceptions of condom effectiveness after viewing the episode and about half had more negative perceptions. The authors wrote that "although the Friends episode was entirely correct in the facts it presented, the implications of these facts were ambiguous" (p. 1120). Perhaps the humorous context within which the topic of condoms was presented in the episode blurred the clarity regarding their effectiveness or importance in sexual risk prevention, thus not communicating a clear attitude toward their use.

Sexual Attitudes Conveyed Through Stereotypes in Media Depictions. Stereotypes are sets of beliefs and expectations one holds about certain groups in society; they are prevalent in media representations and can impact the development of beliefs, attitudes, and behaviors of media audiences (Mastro, 2009). Stereotypes in the media convey cultural norms and reflect societal attitudes toward certain groups or phenomena and may nurture perceptions and attitudes in viewers (Wahl, 2003). Studies of stereotypical representation in the context of sexuality have focused on several topics, which will be reviewed in the following sections below: stereotypes of sexual minorities, stereotypes of sexual gender roles, and the stereotyping of women through sexualization.

Attitudes Conveyed Through Stereotyping of Sexual Minorities. Content analyses have found that minority sexuality has been underrepresented in mainstream media, both with regard to its prevalence as well as with regard to the diversity it involves (Bond, 2015). Content analyses conducted in the mid teen years of the new millennium have documented an increase in sexual minority representation in mainstream media, especially television, relative to the 1970s (McInroy & Craig, 2015). Still, minority sexuality tends to be biased and stereotypical in its presentation and also sanitized, meaning that often, a minority sexual identity is stripped of the sexuality altogether (Bond, 2015). Bond's content analysis of mainstream media popular among gay and lesbian youth (gay-and lesbian-oriented media [GLO] media), focusing on television shows, films, and music, have shown that this content includes many more sexual minority representations than portrayals of heterosexuality, especially among gay men. GLO media were shown to include a greater variety of minority sexuality representations with diverse outcomes and more realistic portrayals of gay culture than in traditional media. GLO media were found to portray a more validating picture of minority sexuality with few demeaning portrayals.

Attitudes Conveyed Through Sexual Gender-Role Stereotyping. Sexual attitudes are often linked to gender and gender-role portrayals (Sink & Mastro, 2017), for example, by linking sexuality to hypermasculinity (e.g., stringent sexual norms for heterosexual romantic partners and sexual dominance by males) and hyperfemininity (e.g., women serving as sexual titillation to men and female sexual submission to men). Sink and Mastro found that, alongside a new trend to objectify men in prime-time television programming, it was still the female characters who were more likely to behave in sexually provocative ways and serve as the object of men's heterosexual desires, thus supporting hegemonic masculinity.

A common form of a stereotypical presentation of sexual attitudes as linked to gender has been the heterosexual script (Kim et al., 2007). In this script, which has been found in diverse television narratives, including television shows involving young characters (Aubrey et al., 2020) and even children's television programs (Kirsch & Murnen, 2015), gender-appropriate sexual and relational norms are commonly promoted in mediated narratives. The script is manifested through the following common themes: (1) sex as masculinity versus the good girls: men are presented as sexual initiators who are obsessed with sex whereas women are sexually passive and serve as the sexual gate-keepers; (2) masculine versus feminine courting strategies: men's active and powerful courting maneuvers are pitted against women's, yet again, passive and self-sexualizing strategies for securing the men's attention; (3) masculine versus feminine commitment: men are portrayed as avoiding relational commitment and prioritizing sex whereas women prioritize their romantic relationships; and (4) male-oriented homophobia versus appropriation of female homosexuality: homosexuality is something to be avoided and ridiculed whereas women's sexual relationships are perceived as arousing. Overall, the heterosexual script ascribes men and women fixed sexual roles that involve female passivity and a diminished sexual agency (Seabrook et al., 2017).

Attitudes Conveyed Through Female Sexual Objectification. Another aspect of stereotypically gendered portrayals of sexuality in the media is the objectification and sexualization of female characters. Sexual objectification refers to the forcing of a sexual role on a character, eliminating their agency in the context of sexuality, forcing unwanted sexual actions upon them, or making disparaging remarks about their sexual appeal (Rousseau et al., 2018). It further refers to the treatment of one's body as a collection of body parts to be evaluated by others and geared toward satisfying others' desires rather than one's own (Hirschman et al., 2006).

The American Psychological Association (2007) pointed out that even young girls are sexualized in diverse forms of media. Rousseau et al. (2018) found that in shows popular among Dutch young teens, 10% of sexual acts involved objectification of both men and women. In an analysis of two television teen drama shows (*One Tree Hill* and *Gossip Girl*), Van Damme (2010) found that female characters were often sexualized and even engaged in self-sexual objectification. In video games, too, Downs and Smith (2010) reported that in top-selling video games, female characters, although underrepresented relative to men, tended to be sexualized and their bodies objectified. Similarly, Lynch et al. (2016) found that despite a decrease in the sexualization of female characters since the 1990s, sexualization is still common especially in male-oriented genres and in M (Mature)-rated video games. Surprisingly, in T (Teen)-rated video games, sexualization was just as prevalent as in M-rated ones.

Similarly, Smiler et al. (2017) analyzed top songs between 1960 and 2008 and found that male performers were more likely then female performers to sing about sex and objectify both men and women, with an increase in objectifying bodies over the years. And in Belgian music television, too, in both videos and programs, 40% of scenes included sexualization, most of them of women (Vandenbosch et al., 2013). McDade-Montez et al. (2017) found that in television shows popular among 6–11-year-old Dutch girls, sexualization was present in every single episode analyzed in their study. In fact, each episode in their sample included at least three instances of sexualization with an average of four instances per episode. Most of the sexualization (72%) was addressed toward girl characters and most of it occurs in the form of sexualized clothing but also through sexualizing comments and body exposure. Galdi and Guizzo (2021) summarized literature on exposure to sexually objectifying media content and identified exposure to such content as a factor implicating both engagement in sexual harassment as well as increasing attitudes accepting of sexual harassment and discouraging bystander interventions to prevent such behaviors.

CONCLUSION

Mainstream entertainment media content commonly involves sexual portrayals, both in the form of conversation and in the form of behaviors. Such depictions convey sexual attitudes in myriad ways. From the mere presence of sexual content and the focus it receives in the narrative to the portrayal of sexual health, sexual consequences, and sexual emotions, messages are communicated to the audience about the importance of the topic of sex and about the seriousness with which it should be considered (or not). Whether presented in a humorous context, as is often the case, or through the reliance on sexual stereotypes, sexual attitudes are conveyed to audiences. From these depictions, audiences can learn about societal norms and expectations, develop sexual scripts, learn about the emotions involved in sex and sexuality, and, in turn, adopt and cultivate attitudes, behaviors, and a worldview that is similar to that presented in the media.

FURTHER READING

Aubrey, J. S., Dajchaes, L., & Teran, L. (2021). Media as sources of sexual socialization for emerging adults. In E. M. Morgan & M. H. M. van Dulmen (Eds.), *Sexuality in emerging adulthood* (pp. 312–332). Oxford University Press.

Aubrey, J. S., Harrison, K., Kramer, L., & Yellin, J. (2003). Variety versus timing: Gender differences in college students' sexual expectations as predicted by exposure to sexually oriented television. *Communication Research*, 30(4), 432–460. https://doi.org/10.1177/0093650203253365

Brown, J. D., Halpern, C. T., & L'Engle, K. L. (2005). Mass media as a sexual super peer for early maturing girls. *Journal of Adolescent Health*, 36(5), 420–427. https://doi.org/10.1016/j.jadohealth.2004.06.003

Common Sense Media. (2020). *How much sexual content in media is appropriate for kids?*, https://www.commonsensemedia.org/articles/how-much-sexual-content-in-media-is-appropriate-for-kids

Daniels, E. A., Zurbriggen, E. L., & Ward, L. M. (2020). Becoming an object: A review of self-objectification in girls. *Body Image*, 33, 278–299. https://doi.org/10.1016/j.bodyim.2020.02.016

Kunkel, D., Farrar, K. M., Eyal, K., Biely, E., Donnerstein, E., & Rideout, V. (2007). Sexual socialization messages on entertainment television: Comparing content trends 1997–2002. *Media Psychology*, 9(3), 595–622. https://doi.org/10.1080/15213260701283210

Manganello, J. A., Henderson, V. R., Jordan, A., Trentacoste, N., Martin, S., & Hennessy, M. (2009). Adolescent judgment of sexual content on television: Implications for future content analysis research. *Journal of Sex Research*, 47(4), 364–373. https://doi.org/10.1080/00224490903015868

Pinkleton, B. E., Weintraub Austin, E., Chen, Y.-C. Y., & Cohen, M. (2012). The role of media literacy in shaping adolescents' understanding of and responses to sexual portrayals in mass media. *Journal of Health Communication*, 17(4), 460–476. https://doi.org/10.1080/10810730.2011.635770

Ward, L. M. (2015). Media and sexualization: State of empirical research, 1995–2015. *Journal of Sex Research*, 53(4–5), 560–577. https://doi.org/10.1080/00224499.2016.1142496

REFERENCES

Alexopoulos, C., & Taylor, L. D. (2020). Risky business: Sexual risk and responsibility messages in teen sex romps. *Sexuality & Culture*, 24(6), 2161–2182. https://doi.org/10.1007/s12119-020-09742-4

American Psychological Association. (2007). *Report of the APA task force on the sexualization of girls*.

Aubrey, J. S. (2004). Sex and punishment: An examination of sexual consequences and the sexual double standard in teen programming. *Sex Roles*, 50(7–8), 505–514. https://doi.org/10.1023/B:SERS.0000023070.87195.07

Aubrey, J. S., Behm-Morawitz, E., & Kim, K. (2014). Understanding the effects of MTV's *16 and Pregnant* on adolescent girls' beliefs, attitudes, and behavioral intentions toward teen pregnancy. *Journal of Health Communication*, 19(10), 1145–1160. https://doi.org/10.1080/10810730.2013.872721

Aubrey, J. S., Teran, K. Y. L., & Roberts, L. (2020). The heterosexual script on tween, teen, and young-adult television programs: A content analytic update and extension. *Journal of Sex Research*, 57(9), 1134–1145. https://doi.org/10.1080/00224499.2019.1699895

Baams, L., Overbeek, G., Semon Dubas, J., Doornwaard, S. M., Rommes, E., & van Aken, M. A. G. (2015). Perceived realism moderates the relation between sexualized media consumption and permissive sexual attitudes in Dutch adolescents. *Archives of Sexual Behavior*, 44(3), 743–754. https://doi.org/10.1007/s10508-014-0443-7

Bandura, A. (2009). Social cognitive theory of mass communication. In J. Bryant & M. B. Oliver (Eds.), *Media effects: Advances in theory and research* (3rd ed., pp. 94–124). Routledge.

Behm-Morawitz, E., & Mastro, D. (2009). The effects of the sexualization of female video game characters on gender stereotyping and female self-concept. *Sex Roles*, 61(11), 808–823. https://doi.org/10.1007/s11199-009-9683-8

Bond, B. J. (2014). Sex and sexuality in entertainment media popular with lesbian, gay, and bisexual adolescents. *Mass Communication & Society, 17*(1), 98–120. https://doi.org/10.1080/15205436.2013.816739

Bond, B. J. (2015). Portrayals of sex and sexuality in gay and lesbian oriented media: A quantitative content analysis. *Sexuality & Culture, 19*(1), 37–56. https://doi.org/10.1007/s12119-014-9241-6

Bond, B. J., Hefner, V., & Drogos, K. L. (2009). Information-seeking practices during the sexual development of lesbian, gay, and bisexual individuals: The influence and effects of coming out in a mediated environment. *Sexuality & Culture, 13*(1), 32–50. https://doi.org/10.1007/s12119-008-9041-y

Bond, B. J., Miller, B., & Aubrey, J. S. (2018). Sexual references and consequences for heterosexual, lesbian, gay and bisexual characters on television: A comparison content analysis. *Mass Communication & Society, 22*(1), 72–95. https://doi.org/10.1080/15205436.2018.1489058

Braddock, K., & Dillard, J. P. (2016). Meta-analytic evidence for the persuasive effect of narratives on beliefs, attitudes, intentions, and behaviors. *Communication Monographs, 83*(4), 446–467. http://dx.doi.org/10.1080/03637751.2015.1128555

Carpenter, L. M. (2009). Virginity loss in reel/real life: Using popular movies to navigate sexual initiation. *Sociological Forum, 24*(4), 804–827. https://www.jstor.org/stable/40542597

Collins, R. L., Elliott, M. N., Berry, S. H., Kanouse, D. E., & Hunter, S. B. (2003). Entertainment television as a healthy sex educator: The impact of condom-efficacy information in an episode of *Friends*. *Pediatrics, 112*(5), 1115–1121. https://doi.org/10.1542/peds.112.5.1115

Collins, R. L., Strasburger, V. C., Brown, J. D., Donnerstein, E., Lenhart, A., & Ward, M. (2017). Sexual media and childhood well-being and health. *Pediatrics, 140*(S2), S162–S166. https://doi.org/10.1542/peds.2016-1758X

Coyne, S. M., Ward, M., Kroff, S. L., Davis, E. J., Holmgren, H. G., Jensen, A. C., Erickson, S. E., & Essig, L. W. (2019). Contributions of mainstream sexual media exposure to sexual attitudes, perceived peer norms, and sexual behavior: A meta-analysis. *Journal of Adolescent Health, 64*(4), 430–436. https://doi.org/10.1016/j.jadohealth.2018.11.016

Cuklanz, L. M., & Moorti, S. (2006). Television's "new" feminism: Prime-time representations of women and victimization. *Critical Studies in Media Communication, 23*(4), 302–321. https://doi.org/10.1080/07393180600933121

Custers, K., & Van den Bulck, J. (2013). The cultivation of fear of sexual violence in women: Processes and moderators of the relationship between television and fear. *Communication Research, 40*(1), 96–124. https://doi.org/10.1177/0093650212440444

Dillman Carpentier, F. R., & Stevens, E. M. (2018). Sex in the media, sex on the mind: Linking television use, sexual permissiveness, and sexual concept accessibility in memory. *Sexuality & Culture, 22*(1), 22–38. https://doi.org/10.1007/s12119-017-9450-x

Dillman Carpentier, F. R., Stevens, E. M., Wu, L., & Seely, N. (2017). Sex, love, and risk-n-responsibility: A content analysis of entertainment television. *Mass Communication & Society, 20*(5), 686–709. https://doi.org/10.1080/15205436.2017.1298807

Downs, E., & Smith, S. L. (2010). Keeping abreast of hypersexuality: A video game character content analysis. *Sex Roles, 62*(11–12), 721–733. https://doi.org/10.1007/s11199-009-9637-1

Dudek, D., Woodley, G., & Green, L. (2022). "Own your narrative": Teenagers as producers and consumers of porn in Netflix's *Sex Education*. *Information, Communication & Society, 25*(4), 502–515. https://doi.org/10.1080/1369118X.2021.1988130

Eyal, K., & Ben-Ami, Y. (2017). It only happens once: Adolescents' interpretations of mediated messages about sexual initiation. *Mass Communication & Society, 20*(1), 68–91. https://doi.org/10.1080/15205436.2016.1187754

Eyal, K., & Finnerty, K. (2007). The portrayal of consequences of sexual intercourse on prime-time programming. *Communication Research Reports, 24*(3), 225–233. https://doi.org/10.1080/08824090701439125

Eyal, K., & Finnerty, K. (2009). The portrayal of consequences of sexual intercourse on television: How, who, and with what consequences? *Mass Communication & Society, 12*(2), 143–169. https://doi.org/10.1080/15205430802136713

Eyal, K., & Kunkel, D. (2008). The effects of television drama shows on emerging adults' sexual attitudes and moral judgments. *Journal of Broadcasting & Electronic Media, 52*(2), 161–181. https://doi.org/10.1080/08838150801991757

Eyal, K., Kunkel, D., Biely, E., & Finnerty, K. (2007). Sexual socialization messages on television programs most popular among teens. *Journal of Broadcasting & Electronic Media, 51*(2), 316–336. https://doi.org/10.1080/08838150701304969

Eyal, K., Raz, Y., & Levi, M. (2014). Messages about sex on Israeli television: Comparing local and foreign programming. *Journal of Broadcasting & Electronic Media, 58*(1), 42–58. https://doi.org/10.1080/08838151.2013.875021

Farrar, K., Kunkel, D., Biely, E., Eyal, K., & Donnerstein, E. (2003). Sexual messages during prime-time programming. *Sexuality & Culture, 7*(1), 7–37. https://doi.org/10.1007/s12119-003-1001-y

Farrar, K. M. (2006). Sexual intercourse on television: Do safe sex messages matter? *Journal of Broadcasting & Electronic Media, 50*(4), 635–650. https://doi.org/10.1207/s15506878jobem5004_4

Foss, K. (2010). Gender, victimization, and responsibility in *CSI: Crime Scene Investigation*. *Journal of Research on Women & Gender, 1*(1), 98–115. https://digital.library.txstate.edu/handle/10877/12806

Gagnon, J. H., & Simon, W. (1973). *Sexual conduct: The social sources of human sexuality*. Aldine.

Galdi, S., & Guizzo, F. (2021). Media-induced sexual harassment: The routes form sexually objectifying media to sexual harassment. *Sex Roles, 84*(11–12), 645–669. http://doi.org/10.1007/s11199-020-01196-0

Gerbner, G., Gross, L., Morgan, M., & Signorielli, N. (1994). Growing up with television: The cultivation perspective. In J. Bryant & D. Zillmann (Eds.), *Media effects: Advances in theory and research* (pp. 17–41). Erlbaum.

Gross, L. (1994). What is wrong with this picture? Lesbian women and gay men on television. In R. J. Ringer (Ed.), *Queer words, queer images: Communication and the construction of homosexuality* (pp. 143–156). New York University Press.

Herd, D. (2015). Conflicting paradigms on gender and sexuality in rap music: A systematic review. *Sexuality & Culture, 19*(3), 577–589. https://doi.org/10.1007/s12119-014-9259-9

Hirschman, C., Impett, E. A., & Schooler, D. (2006). Dis/embodied voices: What late-adolescent girls can teach us about objectification and sexuality. *Sexuality Research & Social Policy, 3*(4), 8–20. https://doi.org/10.1525/srsp.2006.3.4.8

Huesmann, L. R. (1986). Psychological processes promoting the relation between exposure to media violence and aggressive behavior by the viewer. *Journal of Social Issues, 42*, 125–139.

Hust, S. J. T., Brown, J. D., & L'Engle, K. L. (2008). Boys will be boys and girls better be prepared: An analysis of the rare sexual health messages in young adolescents' media. *Mass Communication & Society, 11*(1), 3–23. https://doi.org/10.1080/15205430701668139

Hust, S. J. T., Garrigues Marett, E., Lei, M., Ren, C., & Ran, W. (2015). *Law & Order*, *CSI*, and *NCIS*: The association between exposure to crime drama franchises, rape myth acceptance, and sexual consent negotiation among college students. *Journal of Health Communication, 20*(12), 1369–1381. https://doi.org/10.1080/10810730.2015.1018615

Jensen, R. E., & Jensen, J. D. (2007). Entertainment media and sexual health: A content analysis of sexual talk, behavior, and risks in a popular television series. *Sex Roles, 56*(5–6), 275–284. https://doi.org/10.1007/s11199-006-9167-z

Johnson, E. K. (2017). Erasing the scarlet letter: How positive media messages about sex can lead to better sexual health among college men and women. *American Journal of Sexuality Education, 12*(1), 55–71.

Jozkowski, K. N., Marcantonio, T. L., Rhoads, K. E., Canan, S., Hunt, M. E., & Willis, M. (2019). A content analysis of sexual consent and refusal communication in mainstream films. *Journal of Sex Research*, 56(6), 754–765. https://doi.org/10.1080/00224499.2019.1595503

Kelly, M. (2010). Virginity loss narratives in "teen drama" television programs. *Journal of Sex Research*, 47, 479–489. https://doi.org/10.1080/00224490903132044

Kim, J. L., Sorsoli, C. L., Collins, K., Zylbergold, B. A., Schooler, D., & Tolman, D. L. (2007). From sex to sexuality: Exposing the heterosexual script on primetime network television. *Journal of Sex Research*, 44(2), 145–157. https://www.jstor.org/stable/25701753

Kinsler, J. J., Glik, D., de Castro, S., Malan, H., Nadjat-Haieme, C., Wainwright, N., & Papp-Green, M. (2019). A content analysis of how sexual behavior and reproductive health are being portrayed on prime-time television shows being watched by teens and young adults. *Health Communication*, 34(6), 644–651. https://doi.org/10.1080/10410236.2018.1431020

Kirsch, A. C., & Murnen, S. K. (2015). "Hot" girls and "cool dudes": Examining the prevalence of the heterosexual script in American children's television media. *Psychology of Popular Media Culture*, 4(1), 18–30. https://doi.org/10.1037/ppm0000017

Kollath-Cattano, C. L., Mann, E. S., Moreno Zegbe, E., & Thrasher, J. F. (2018). Sexual scripts in contemporary Mexican cinema: A quantitative content analysis. *Sexuality & Culture*, 22(1), 90–105. https://doi.org/10.1007/s12119-017-9454-6

Kunkel, D., Eyal, K., Biely, E., Finnerty, K., & Donnerstein, E. (2005). *Sex on TV 4: A biennial report to the Kaiser Family Foundation*. Henry J. Kaiser Family Foundation.

Lance, A., Wallett, S., Lorber, B., & Harris, L. (2012). *16 and Pregnant*: A content analysis of a reality television program about unplanned teen pregnancy. *Contraception*, 86(3), 292. https://doi.org/10.1016/j.contraception.2012.05.028

Lee, M. J., Hust, S. J. T., & Zhang, L. (2011). Effects of violence against women in popular crime dramas on viewers' attitudes related to sexual violence. *Mass Communication & Society*, 14(1), 25–44. https://doi.org/10.1080/15205430903531440

Letort, D. (2019). *13 Reasons Why*: The rape myth survives. *Girlhood Studies*, 12(2), 17–31. https://doi.org/10.3167/ghs.2019.120203

Lynch, T., Tompkins, J. E., van Driel, I. I., & Fritz, N. (2016). Sexy, strong, and secondary: A content analysis of female characters in video games across 31 years. *Journal of Communication*, 66(4), 564–584. https://doi.org/10.1111/jcom.12237

Maes, C., & Vandenbosch, L. (2022). "Consent is sexy": Exploring the portrayal of prosocial sexuality messages in youth-oriented series. *Journal of Children & Media*, 16(3), 332–351. https://doi.org/10.1080/17482798.2021.1982741

Maio, G. R., Haddock, G., & Verplanken, B. (2019). *The psychology of attitudes and attitude change* (3rd ed.). SAGE.

Martino, S. C., Collins, R. L., Kanouse, D. E., Elliott, M., & Berry, S. H. (2005). Social cognitive processes mediating the relationship between exposure to television's sexual content and adolescent's sexual behavior. *Journal of Personality & Social Psychology*, 89(6), 914–924. https://doi.org/10.1037/0022-3514.89.6.914

Mastro, D. E. (2009). Racial/ethnic stereotyping and the media. In R. L. Nabi & M. B. Oliver (Eds.), *The SAGE handbook of media processes and effects* (pp. 377–391). SAGE.

McDade-Montez, E., Wallander, J., & Cameron, L. (2017). Sexualization in U.S. Latina and White girls' preferred children's television programming. *Sex Roles*, 77(1), 1–15. https://doi.org/10.1007/s11199-016-0692-0

McInroy, L. B., & Craig, S. L. (2015). Transgender representation in offline and online media: LGBTQ youth perspectives. *Journal of Human Behavior in the Social Environment*, 25(6), 606–617. https://doi.org/10.1080/10911359.2014.995392

Morgan, M., & Shanahan, J. (2010). The state of cultivation. *Journal of Broadcasting & Electronic Media, 54*(2), 337–355. http://dx.doi.org/10.1080/08838151003735018

Morgan, M., Shanahan, J., & Signorielli, N. (2014). Cultivation theory in the twenty-first century. In R. S. Fortner & P. M. Fackler (Eds.), *Handbook of media and mass communication theory* (pp. 480–497). Wiley.

Moyer-Gusé, E. (2008). Toward a theory of entertainment persuasion: Explaining the persuasive effects of entertainment-education messages. *Communication Theory, 18*, 407–425. https://doi.org/10.1111/j.1468-2885.2008.00328.x

Moyer-Guse, E., Mahood, C., & Brookes, S. (2011). Entertainment-education in the context of humor: Effects on safer sex intentions and risk perceptions. *Health Communication, 26*(8), 765–774. https://doi.org/10.1080/10410236.2011.566832

Olufemi, T. D. (2012). Theories of attitudes. In M. I. Hodges & C. D. Logan (Eds.), *Psychology of attitudes* (pp. 61–78). Nova.

Ortiz, R. R., & Brooks, M. E. (2014). Getting what they deserve? Consequences of sexual expression by central characters in five popular television teen dramas in the United States. *Journal of Children & Media, 8*(1), 40–52. https://doi.org/10.1080/17482798.2014.863477

Rideout, V. J., & Robb, M. B. (2019). *The Common Sense Census: Media use by tweens and teens.* Common Sense Media. https://www.commonsensemedia.org/research/the-common-sense-census-media-use-by-tweens-and-teens-2019

Rousseau, A., Eggermont, S., Bels, A., & Van den Bulck, H. (2018). Separating the sex from the object: Conceptualizing sexualization and (sexual) objectification in Flemish preteens' popular television programs. *Journal of Children & Media, 12*(3), 346–365. https://doi.org/10.1080/17482798.2018.1425888

Ruberg, B. (2021). "Obscene, pornographic, or otherwise objectionable": Biased definitions of sexual content in video game live streaming. *New Media & Society, 23*(6), 1681–1699. https://doi.org/10.1177/1461444820920759

Rubinsky, V., & Cooke-Jackson, A. (2017). "Where is the love?" Expanding and theorizing with LGBTQ memorable messages of sex and sexuality. *Health Communication, 32*(12), 1472–1480. https://doi.org/10.1080/10410236.2016.1230809

Seabrook, R. C., Ward, L. M., Cortina, L. M., Giaccardi, S., & Lippman, J. R. (2017). Girl power or powerless girl? Television, sexual scripts, and sexual agency in sexually active young women. *Psychology of Women Quarterly, 41*(2), 240–253. https://doi.org/10.1177/0361684316677028

Seabrook, R. C., Ward, L. M., & Giaccardi, S. (2019). Less than human? Media use, objectification of women, and men's acceptance of sexual aggression. *Psychology of Violence, 9*(5), 536–545. https://doi.org/10.1037/vio0000198

Signorielli, N., & Bievenour, A. (2015). Sex in adolescent programming: A content analysis. *Communication Research Reports, 32*(4), 304–313. https://doi.org/10.1080/08824096.2015.1089856

Sink, A., & Mastro, D. (2017). Depictions of gender on primetime television: A quantitative content analysis. *Mass Communication & Society, 20*(1), 3–22. https://doi.org/10.1080/15205436.2016.1212243

Sisson, G., Walter, N., Herold, S., & Brooks, J. J. (2021). Prime-time abortion on *Grey's Anatomy*: What do US viewers learn from fictional portrayals of abortion on television. *Perspectives on Sexual Reproductive Health, 53*(1–2), 13–22. https://doi.org/10.1363/psrh.12183

Smiler, A. P., Shewmaker, J. W., & Hearon, B. (2017). From "I Want to Hold Your Hand" to "Promiscuous": Sexual stereotypes in popular music lyrics, 1960–2008. *Sexuality & Culture, 21*(4), 1083–1105. https://doi.org/10.1007/s12119-017-9437-7

Stevens, E. M., & Garrett, K. P. (2016). Girls and sex: A content analysis of sexual health depictions in HBO's Girls. *Sexuality & Culture, 20*(4), 923–935. https://doi.org/10.1007/s12119-016-9365-y

Symes, K. (2017). *Orange is the New Black:* The popularization of lesbian sexuality and heterosexual modes of viewing. *Feminist Media Studies, 17*(1), 29–41. https://doi.org/10.1080/14680777.2017.1261836

Thorfinnsdottir, D., & Strandgaard Jensen, H. (2017). Laugh away, he is gay! Heteronormativity and children's television in Denmark. *Journal of Children & Media*, *11*(4), 399–416. https://doi.org/10.1080/17482798.2017.1312470

Timmermans, E., & Van den Bulck, J. (2018). Casual sexual scripts on the screen: A quantitative content analysis. *Archives of Sexual Behavior*, *47*(5), 1481–1496. https://doi.org/10.1007/s10508-018-1147-1

Van Damme, E. (2010). Gender and sexual scripts in popular US teen series: A study of the gendered discourse in *One Tree Hill* and *Gossip Girl*. *Catalan Journal of Communication & Cultural Studies*, *2*(1), 77–92. https://doi.org/10.1386/cjcs.2.1.77_1

Vandenbosch, L., Vervloessem, D., & Eggermont, S. (2013). "I might get your heart racing in my skin-tight jeans": Sexualization on music entertainment television. *Communication Studies*, *64*(2), 178–194. https://doi.org/10.1080/10510974.2012.755640

Vidana-Perez, D., Braverman-Bronstein, A., Basto-Abreu, A., Barrientos-Gutierrez, I., Hilscher, R., & Barrientos-Gutierrez, T. (2018). Sexual content in video games: An analysis of entertainment software rating board classification from 1994–2013. *Sexual Health*, *15*(3), 209–213. https://doi.org/10.1071/SH17017

Wahl, O. F. (2003). Depictions of mental illness in children's media. *Journal of Mental Health*, *12*(3), 249–258. https://doi.org/10.1080/0963823031000118230

Willis, M., Jozkowski, K. N., Canan, S. N., Rhoads, K. E., & Hunt, M. E. (2020). Models of sexual consent communication by film rating: A content analysis. *Sexuality & Culture*, *24*(6), 1971–1986. https://doi.org/10.1007/s12119-020-09731-7

Wright, C. L., & Rubin, M. (2020). Sexualized popular music and risky sexual behaviors among emerging adults from the United States and Australia. *Howard Journal of Communications*, *31*(1), 1–19. https://doi.org/10.1080/10646175.2019.1567407

Wright, P. J. (2009). Sexual socialization messages in mainstream entertainment mass media: A review and synthesis. *Sexuality & Culture*, *13*(4), 181–200. https://doi.org/10.1007/s12119-009-9050-5

Wright, P. J. (2011). Mass media effects on youth sexual behavior: Assessing the claim for causality. *Annals of the International Communication Association*, *35*(1), 343–385. https://doi.org/10.1080/23808985.2011.11679121

Keren Eyal

QUEER CHINESE MEDIA AND POP CULTURE

(RE)DEFINING QUEER CHINESE MEDIA AND POP CULTURE

In the past two decades, transcultural and global information flows into and within the Chinese and Sinophone worlds, Chinese-speaking netizens' enhanced accessibility to various kinds of social media, and China's active participation in the global neoliberal economy have contributed to a flourishing of representations of nonnormative genders and sexualities and related pop cultural practices. Consequently, the 21st century has witnessed not only a wealth of queer Chinese media and pop cultural productions but also an increase in and greater diversity of scholarship on queer Chinese media and pop cultural studies (Bao, 2021; Zhao, 2019, 2020b; Zhao & Wong, 2020). A growing number of English-language scholarly publications in the area of global LGBTQ studies have focused on Chinese literature and print magazines (Bao, 2018, 2020; Feng, 2013; Han, 2021; Yang & Xu, 2015), cinema (Bao, 2018;

Berry, 2000, 2004; Chao, 2010, 2020; Leung, 2008, 2012; Lim, 2006; Schoonover & Galt, 2016; Spencer, 2012; Zhou, 2014), TV (Ng & Li, 2020; Wang, 2015; Wong, 2020; Zhao, 2016, 2020a), theatrical spaces and performances (Bao, 2020a; He, 2013, 2014), fandoms (Lavin et al., 2017; Xu & Yang, 2013; Yang & Bao, 2012; Zhao, 2017a, 2017b, 2018c), and digital media (Chan, 2021; Liao, 2019; Wang, 2020a, 2020b).

However, far from being a contemporary cultural phenomenon triggered by the boom in consumerist, global entertainment cultures and widespread internet access, queer Chinese media and pop cultures have their own local traditions, some of which can be traced back to rituals of the elitist, artistic groups and aesthetic and religious philosophies of ancient China (e.g., see Goldman, 2012; Kam, 2016; Wu, 2004). Both implicit and explicit portrayals of same-sex desire and intimacies are found in imperial and modern Chinese visual and literary productions, such as local operas, paintings, poetry, novels, and (Republican) films (Bullough & Bullough, 1978; Girchner, 2011; Hinsch, 1990; Ruan & Bullough, 1992; Sang, 2003; van Guilik, 1961; Volpp, 2011; Wong, 2012; Wu, 2003). Moreover, same-sex relations had generally been "tolerated" if they had not directly disrupted heterosexual marital systems and class-based patrilineal–familial structures (Guo, 2016; Kong, 2016; Zhang, 2014, 2015). Even in the Maoist era (1949–1976), when the People's Republic of China (PRC) experienced decades-long social–political turmoil and upheavals, unconventionally gendered images and nonnormative practices were still widespread, if not unexpectedly encouraged (Honig, 2002; Jiao, 2021; Sang, 2003, p. 163; Ye, 2018).

It is difficult to comprehensively and exhaustively capture in a brief encyclopedia entry the scholarly debates surrounding LGBTQ identities, media, and spaces in premodern and modern Chinese-speaking societies. One of the main reasons for this is that the concepts of homosexuality (as well as other forms and performances of nonheterosexuality), queerness, and Chineseness have been constructed and understood in vastly different ways in diverse temporal–historical and geolinguistic contexts. Therefore, rather than mapping out the entire history and development of LGBTQ media in China, this entry mainly strives to (re)define queer Chinese media and pop culture and map out the main streams of scholarship on the topic that have emerged and proliferated since the late 1990s. In doing so, it highlights the transcultural traveling, mutations, and (mis)interpretations of the meanings of "queerness" and "Chineseness" in contemporary Chinese-language media and pop cultural studies.

Although many scholarly works in the fields of queer Asian, queer Chinese, and queer Sinophone studies (Chiang, 2012, 2014; Chiang & Heinrich, 2014; Chiang & Wong, 2016, 2017; Huang, 2011; Kong, 2011; Leung, 2008; Lim, 2006; Liu, 2010, 2015; Liu & Rofel, 2010; Martin, 2009, 2010, 2014; Pecic, 2016; Rofel, 1999, 2007; Tan, 2013; Wong, 2012, 2020; Yue, 2012, 2014; Zhao & Wong, 2020) have highlighted the significance and richness of queer media and pop cultures in contemporary Hong Kong, Taiwan, and other Sinitic-language communities throughout the world, due to space limitations, this entry largely focuses on queer media and pop culture in mainland China (PRC). However, it briefly touches on the broader topic of queer Sinophone media and pop culture to emphasize the transcultural linkages and mutual shaping of queer information and politics in the Sinophone sphere, Asia, and the West. In so doing, it strives to "right an imbalance in the scholarly literature on queer East Asia" and highlights the intricacies and paradoxes of queer Chinese media and pop culture, which have been "less often written about than more visible, queer-influenced, public [and pop] cultural aspects in" other Sinitic-language spaces and communities (Zhao et al., 2017, p. xiii).

HOMOSEXUALITY AND *TONGZHI* (COMRADE)

To understand queer Chinese media and pop culture, it is necessary to first trace the genealogy of the closely related term "homosexuality" in the Chinese-speaking world. Even though mainstream Chinese society has remained heteropatriarchal and heavily indoctrinated by traditional Confucian values, same-sex erotic relations and desires, such as the famous case of "passions of the cut sleeve" (*duanxiu zhi pi*), were widespread in premodern classical literature, theatrical performances, and historical records (Chao, 2020; Chiang, 2012; Chou, 2001; Guo, 2016; Hinsch, 1990; Kang, 2009; Rocha, 2010; Sang, 2003; C. Wu, 2004; J. Wu, 2003). In premodern Chinese contexts, male same-sex eroticism was often described as "*pi*" (obsession), whereas the female equivalent was referred to as "*mojing*" (mirror-rubbing) (Kang, 2009; Rocha, 2010, p. 610; Shi, 2014). The Chinese neologisms *tongxing'ai* ("homosexuality") and *nü tongxing'ai* ("lesbianism") have only existed since the 1920s (the Republican period). These terms came into circulation through the subjective negotiations of local May Fourth New Culture intellectuals with European sexological knowledge and discourses, such as those on modern conceptualizations of "sex" and "love" (Rocha, 2010, p. 610; Sang, 1999, p. 277, 2003). It was during this period that modern understandings of the "pathology" and "abnormality of homosexuality," which aimed "to establish love between man and woman at the center of human affection," were introduced to the general public in China (Sang, 1999, pp. 277, 281). Thus, "a new sexual taxonomy centered on the dichotomy of heterosexuality and homosexuality" was constructed during the Republican era (1919–1949) (Shi, 2020, p. 264).

As mentioned in the section on "Re(Defining) Queer Chinese Media and Pop Culture," a large body of English-language historiography has acknowledged the existence of same-sex eroticism in premodern China (e.g., Chou, 2000, 2001; Furth, 1994; Hinsch, 1990; Sommers, 2000; van Gulik, 1961; Vitiello, 2011; Volpp, 2011). However, this does not mean that premodern Chinese society was entirely friendly to same-sex eroticism, as suggested (and even romanticized) in earlier English-language academic literature on Chinese indigenous traditions of same-sex desire, such as the book *Passions of the Cut Sleeve* by Bret Hinsch (1990).[1] On the contrary, research has shown that female same-sex intimacy in premodern China was often only tolerated as a stimulant of heteromarital harmony and heterosexual male sexual fantasy (Sang, 2003, pp. 48–50). Moreover, some scholars have demonstrated that both Republican and Socialist China manipulated imported ideas of modern (homo)sexuality to reject an essentialized Western bourgeoisie and distinguish China from what was perceived as Western cultural decadence and moral decline (Zhang, 2014, 2015). For instance, Sang (1999) mapped a complex linkage between modern Chinese understandings of homosexuality and Republican and Socialist Chinese discourses of self-modernization and political progress. As she elaborates,

> The medical stigma on homosexuality in Republican China was moderate, however, and one cannot foretell from its mildness that the Chinese Communist Party, after 1949, would harshly denounce homosexuality either as Western capitalist corruption or a heinous feudalist crime. (p. 281)

Republican Chinese discussion on same-sex love, with its preponderant attention to the intersubjective and the circumstantial, can be viewed as providing an alternative modern discourse on homosexuality rather than as a deformed version of Western sexology, deficient and falling far behind Western knowledge. (p. 299)

Similarly, Qingfei Zhang (2015) noted that "from a socialist Oriental gaze," homosexuality was imaged as Western capitalist darkness and spiritual pollution in Maoist official media (p. 98).

In the postsocialist years up to the 1990s, *tongxing'ai* (sometimes also *tongxinglian*, "*lian*" meaning "love/in love") was a common term for homosexuality (Bao, 2018, p. 29; Lim, 2006, p. 11). Since the mid-1990s, another term, *tongzhi* (meaning "comrade") has become more common for referring to nonheterosexual desire and subjectivity in both Chinese LGBTQ communities and official media (Lim, 2006, p. 12).

The term *tongzhi* was "effectively mobilized to refer to people sharing the same political ideals" (Bao, 2018, p. 69). It was closely "associated with rebelliousness during its use in anti-Qing uprisings at the end of the imperial period and continued to be used by both Nationalists and Communists" (Engebretsen & Schroeder, 2015, pp. 4–5). However, as Engebretsen and Schroeder (2015) noted,

> After 1949, the term took on the socialist character of "comrade" that the English term also carries because of its implementation as a preferred non-hierarchical form of address. It was used throughout the Maoist period in mainland China as an everyday appellation and is still used as a formal way of introducing people, especially in public ceremonies. (p. 5)

Chinese-language film scholar Song Hwee Lim (2006) describes the term's politically charged link to homosexuality within Chinese-speaking contexts in a more elaborate and transculturally mediated way:

> Up until the 1990s, *tongxinglian* and *tongxing'ai* remained the most commonly used Chinese discursive terms for homosexuality. This began to change with the appropriation of the term *tongzhi* (literally "same will"), the Chinese translation of the Soviet communist term "comrade," as a discursive term for same-sex sexuality.... The term *tongzhi* was first publicly appropriated for same-sex sexuality by the organizers of Hong Kong's inaugural lesbian and gay film festival in 1989 and introduced to Taiwan in 1992 when the Taipei Golden Horse International Film Festival featured a section on lesbian and gay films. It has since gained popular currency in Taiwan, Hong Kong, overseas Chinese communities, and on the World Wide Web, where it is widely used to refer to lesbian- and gay-related activities and publications.... Even in China, where there is potential ambiguity and confusion in its use resulting from the conflation of its appropriated meaning with its political reference, the term is increasingly used to refer to same-sex sexuality. (p. 11)

Lim's (2006) theorization of *tongzhi* emphasizes not only transcultural appropriation across Chinese-speaking communities and spaces but also the simultaneous emergence, convergence, and cross-geopolitical circulation of visual and linguistic languages devoted to "marginal elements and identities" (p. 12). He noted that the popularity of the use of *tongzhi* in the Chinese-speaking world helps "acknowledge the temporal coevality (the 1990s) of its circulation with the emergence of representations of male homosexuality in cinemas from China, Taiwan, and Hong Kong" (p. 12).

Similarly, the work of Chinese media scholar Hongwei Bao (2018) demonstrates a surge in transcultural *tongzhi* media and activism in the Sinophone sphere. Bao suggested that the creative use of the mainstream, socialist term "reflects both a conscious departure from the socialist past and the desire to become fully a member of global neoliberal capitalism on the part of many members of the varied LGBT communities in Chinese-speaking contexts" (Bao, 2011, p. 133; see also Rofel, 2007). He highlights the fact that *tongzhi* conferences were held in Hong Kong, Taiwan, and then Beijing in the late 1990s (Bao, 2018, p. 78). Following China's decriminalization and depathologization of homosexuality in 1997 and 2001, respectively, *tongzhi* conferences, *tongzhi* literature, *tongzhi* films, and *tongzhi* online and offline public spaces have flourished in mainland China, a trend that has accelerated with widespread internet access (Bao, 2018, p. 78). Focusing largely on mainland Chinese LGBTQ politics and media, Bao (2018) describes *tongzhi* "as an identity category and as a form of activism" (p. 4). He explains that whereas LGBTQ identities and communities (and those associated with the term *tongxinglian*) were still widely stigmatized and pathologized in mainstream Chinese society and media during the 1990s and 2000s, the dialogue program *Youhua Haoshuo* produced by Hunan TV presented an episode titled "Approaching Homosexuality" in 2000 in which the guest speakers first popularized the term *tongzhi* as a "positive self-identification [of LGBTQ people] in mainland China's official media" (p. 78).

In the post-2010 years, a growing number of studies devoted to Chinese LGBTQ groups have used "*tongzhi*" in their title to refer to nonnormatively gendered and sexualized identities and life experiences. Examples include the monographs *Chinese Male Homosexualities: Memba, Tongzhi and Golden Boy*, by Travis Kong (2011); *Shanghai Lalas: Female Tongzhi Communities and Politics in Urban China*, by Lucetta Yip Lo Kam (2012); *Queer Comrades: Gay Identity and Tongzhi Activism in Postsocialist China*, by Hongwei Bao (2018); *Tongzhi Living: Men Attracted to Men in Postsocialist China*, by Tiantian Zheng (2015); and the anthology *Queer/Tongzhi China: New Perspectives on Research, Activism, and Media Cultures*, edited by Elisabeth Engebretsen and Williams Shroeder (with Hongwei Bao) (2015).

However, the use of the term *tongzhi* as an umbrella term to describe different kinds of Chinese LGBTQ cultures, communities, and media remains problematic. For instance, *tongzhi* is often considered a gendered term that refers exclusively to gay men. In mainland China, the terms *lala* (a translinguistic mutated term from the English term lesbian) and *nü tongzhi* (female comrade) are often used to refer to lesbian-related identities and cultures (Engebretsen, 2013; Kam, 2012). Moreover, *tongzhi* (comrade) is explicitly associated with identity politics and carries strong politically provocative and subversive meanings, thereby implicating a pejorative use of Socialist Chinese vocabularies (Bao, 2018; Engebretsen & Schroeder, 2015). These meanings and connotations of the term are not compatible with the anti-identitarian and "depoliticized" media and cultural productions about and for nonnormative genders and sexualities that have burgeoned in post-2010 China (Zhao, 2016, 2018b). For instance, Zhao (2016, 2018b) has identified this depoliticization of nonnormative images and performances in mainland Chinese reality TV competition shows that are mostly adapted from South Korean and Euro-American formats, such as the long-lasting, most influential female participant-only singing competition program, *Super Voice Girl* (2004–2006, 2009, 2011, 2016; Hunan TV). These norm-defying representations (tomboyish images and celebrity personas in the case of *Super Voice Girl*) often heavily draw on inter-Asian and Western beauty standards and fashion cultures (e.g., East Asian androgyny and soft masculinity widely circulated through the global popularity of "flower beautiful boys" [*hua mei nan*] or the high-fashion, cosmopolitan elements closely associated with non-Chinese identities and cultures) to legitimize these gender norm-defying images and disassociate them from signs and connotations of nonheterosexuality in a Chinese context. This tendency to "de-lesbianize" and "de-gay" gender nonnormativity proliferating in entertainment media and pop cultural industries led to a "queer pop" scene in today's mainland China (Zhao, 2020b). Similarly, as Cai (2017) finds in the media performances of the famous female impersonator in contemporary China, Li Yugang, his cross-gender impersonation often invokes both pop music and traditional Chinese operatic elements. This kind of gender-norm-transgressive performance in Chinese media and pop cultural industries is often framed as "transient and artistic" and thus "produce[s] 'fantasy' and 'disidentification,'" which cannot be considered as nor fully understood through real-world LGBTQ identity and body politics largely defined by Western scholarship and knowledge (Cai, 2017, para. 6). Considering this complexity of queer Chinese media and pop culture, the following section of "Queer Theory and Queer/*ku'er* in Chinese Media and Pop Culture" discusses the transcultural circulation, use, and reconfigurations of another term, "queer" (*ku'er*), which is commonly used in the Chinese-speaking world in connection with nonnormative gender and sexual representations and productions in contemporary Chinese entertainment media and pop culture.

QUEER THEORY AND QUEER/*KU'ER* IN CHINESE MEDIA AND POP CULTURE

One of the most influential scholarly definitions of "queer" in Anglophone queer theory comes from Eve Kosofsky Sedgwick. In her monograph *Tendencies*, Sedgwick (1993) defines "queer" as "the open mesh of possibilities, gaps, overlaps, dissonances and resonances, lapses and excesses of meaning when the constituent element of anyone's gender, of anyone's sexuality aren't made (or can't be made) to signify monolithically" (p. 8). Similarly, Annamarie Jagose (1996) defines "queer" as "gestures or analytical tools which dramatize incoherences in the allegedly stable relations between chromosomal sex, gender, and sexual desire" (p. 3). Many Western media and pop cultural studies scholars have adopted this understanding of "queer" as both a norm-disruptive logic and an analytical angle in their film, TV, music, and audience studies. For instance, in *Making Things Perfectly Queer*, queer media scholar Alexander Doty (1993) extended the uses of queer and queer theory to a study of the nontraditional "positions, pleasures, and readings" of the media audience (p. xviii). Later, discussing Hollywood cinema, Jack (Judith) Halberstam (2005) theorized queer as "non-normative logics and organizations of community, sexual identity, embodiment, and activity in space and time" (p. 6).

Indeed, a large body of existing Anglophone cinema, TV, and media spectator and fan scholarship has employed queer theory (Aaron, 2004; Benshoff & Griffin, 2004; Brennan, 2019; Davis & Needham, 2009; Doty, 1993; Driver, 2006; Kohnen, 2016; Lovelock, 2019; Mennel, 2012; Schoonover & Galt, 2016; Sender, 2004; Villarejo, 2014) to explore not only the possibilities of nonnormative genders and sexualities but also postmodern "temporality" and active "place-making practices," which disrupt and reconfigure mainstream hegemonic orders (Halberstam, 2005, p. 6). Similarly, some global queer and feminist studies scholars (e.g., Berry et al., 2003; Boellstorff, 2005; Jackson, 2011; Martin et al., 2008;

McLelland, 2018; Yue, 2014) employ *queer* or *queerness* to refer to "extensive diversities of homoerotic, bi, trans, and other nonnormative sexualities and genders, identities [and] cultures" (Engebretsen, 2013, p. xvi).

The application of queer theory in Chinese-language cultures has been the subject of academic debate. For instance, as Andrea Bachner (2014) noted, a direct, uncritical use of Western-derived queer theory in Chinese cultural studies is believed to "risk becoming a weapon in reiteration of the West's global hegemony" (p. 201). However, although a straightforward refusal of Western-originated queer-related terminology and theories can emphasize "a discrete set of historical and sometimes transcultural explanations for difference," it can also dismiss productive conversations that lead to a "more global synthesis" (Chiang, 2014, pp. 354–355).

Other studies have highlighted the cultural translation and transformation of the English word "queer" in Chinese-speaking LGBTQ and media cultures. In particular, Lim (2006) finds that unlike the word *tongzhi*, which was appropriated from Republican and Socialist China, since the mid-1990s the Western-originated word "'queer' has also become popular in Taiwan, where it is translated as *ku'er* (literally 'cool kid') or *guaitai* (meaning weirdo, or literally 'strange fetus')" (p. 12). In a later commentary, Bao (2018, pp. 29–30) recorded that after its emergence in Taiwan and Hong Kong, the word *ku'er* was imported into mainland China by Chinese gender studies scholar Li Yinhe through her scholarly translation of Western feminist and queer theories in 2003. Although Li's translation of "queer" carries a certain celebratory tone and connotations of rebelliousness, freedom, fashion, and coolness, the term was quickly appropriated by filmmakers, artists, and activists in mainland China, who interpreted it quite differently (Bao, 2018, pp. 30, 80; Engebretsen & Schroeder, 2015, p. 6). In the late 1990s and early 2000s, most of the *ku'er*-labeled Chinese films (some of which were produced by heterosexual filmmakers), art, and scholarship were "abstruse, if not depressing, for community consumption because of their theoretical density and aesthetic avant-gardism" (Bao, 2018, p. 30; Bao, 2020b, p. 363). The double meanings of *ku'er* as either fashionable, subversive, cosmopolitan, and avant-guarde or a self-identification point for nonnormative gender and sexual minorities (or both) have led to at least two main streams of queer Chinese media and pop culture scholarship in the post-2000 years.

More often than not, the term *ku'er*/queer does not have the same heavily political tone of *tongzhi*/comrade. Indeed, the former is sometimes used to describe the kind of gender and sexual minority culture (e.g., LGBTQ cinema, literature, art, and social activism) in China that "embodies identitarian and anti-identitarian aspects at the same time"—aspects that are "mutually constitutive and transformative" (Bao, 2020, p. 6). This line of research also emphasizes that "*tongzhi* and *ku'er* are not always rigidly separate in meaning and are sometimes used interchangeably" (Engebretsen & Schroeder, 2015, p. 8). It considers "queer" as both a reference point for gender and sexual identification (the Q in LGBTQ) and a non-reproductive practice or moment (fleeting nonheterosexual desire that is widespread in a predominantly heterosexual world).[2] In other words, "queer" in this body of scholarship can be used to denote media culture and activism based on identity politics (produced by, about, and/or for self-identified LGBTQ minority groups), as well as nonnormatively gendered, eroticized media and cultural productions that might not be explicitly presented or identified as homosexual in character.

For instance, in juxtaposing "queer" and "*tongzhi*," Engebretsen and Schroeder (2015) appropriate "an English and a Chinese term, each with a complex history and contested interpretations regarding sexual politics" to create the new conceptual term, "queer/*tongzhi*," thereby highlighting "the necessarily symbiotic relationship between languages, identifications and positionalities, politics, locations and theories" in queer Chinese media and cultural studies (p. 8). Their 2015 co-edited anthology, *Queer/Tongzhi China* comprises studies dedicated to both grassroots activism of gender and sexual minority groups and mainstream pop music and celebrities analyzed through a queer lens. Similarly, Bao (2020) explores what he calls "'queer comrade' activism," which holds "the promise of developing a radical, progressive, Left and socialist politics by building on socialist ideals of egalitarianism and justice as well as revolutionary experiences of mass mobilisation" (p. 16). As Bao (2020) explains, the creation of "'queer comrade' assemblage" aims to highlight both "socialist modes of 'comrade' subjectivity and politics" and "postsocialist queer identity formation and LGBTQ social movements" in Chinese media and cultural activism (p. 13), which ultimately challenge "neoliberal gay identity born out of global capitalism" (p. 16).

In the post-2010 years, another line of queer Chinese media and pop culture scholarship has gained momentum, most of which focuses on mainstream Chinese TV, music, and celebrity industries, cyber fan cultures, and online fiction writing and reading (Lavin & et al., 2017; Wang, 2015, 2018; Wei, 2014; Xu & Yang, 2013; Yang, 2010; Yang & Bao, 2012; Yang & Xu, 2015, 2016; Zhao, 2016, 2017a, 2017b, 2018b, 2018c, 2019, 2020a, 2020b; Zhao & Wong, 2020). This body of research employs "queer" mainly as "a productive analytical lens" to interrogate "any perspectival norms and ideals in both contemporary public cultural and scholarly discourses surrounding nation-states, linguistics, geopolitics, ethnicities, genders, and sexualities" and thus uses it to "loosely refer to all kinds of nonnormative representations, viewing positions, identifications, structure of feelings, and ways of thinking" (Zhao et al., 2017, p. xii). Highlighting the disruptive, negotiative, and pejorative potential of queer culture, this research does not necessarily emphasize the linkage of queer media and culture to gay identity and LGBTQ politics and activism. Instead, it looks exclusively at the media and cultural representations, productions, and celebrity and fan cultures situated within and contradictorily "enabled, commodified, celebrated, and carefully regulated" by the largely heteronormative environment of contemporary China's mainstream globalist media industries and neoliberal public spaces (Zhao, 2020b, p. 464). In doing so, it strives to demystify the essentialist imaginaries of post-2000 China as either a Euro-American–defined heteropatriarchal, homophobic world or one that is "becoming more liberal and less heteronormative" (Zhao, 2020b, pp. 464–465).

In particular, in her studies of the rise and transformation of gender-norm-defying images on Chinese TV in the past decade (between 2006 and 2016), Zhao has identified a complex queer Chinese TV phenomenon in which gender-nonnormative celebrities intentionally disidentify with restrictive LGBTQ identities and politics in real life to escape censorship while deliberately playing out and playing with same-sex desire and intimacies for commercial interests onstage (Zhao, 2018b, 2020a). As Zhao and Wong (2020) argue, to better understand this kind of Chinese-specific media and pop culture, "queer" itself should be viewed "as both a creative visual–cultural–industrial technology and a fertile analytical tool" (p. 476). This requires "moving beyond seeing 'queer' as merely an identitarian, restrictive category" and excavating the multivalent potential of Chinese-language media and pop cultures in "forming disruption to and negotiation with normative... imaginations of desiring, being, and belonging" surrounding not only gender and sexuality but also geocultural, ethnic, and linguistic identities (Zhao & Wong, 2020, pp. 476–477). These scholars find the concept of queer especially fruitful for overturning Western-centrism in queer studies and revealing how China and its related sociocultural identities and spaces "have never operated in a Western-imagined normative way" (Zhao, 2020b, p. 465). As the following section on "Chineseness in Queer Media and Pop Culture" reveals, this is because queerness and Chineseness are two mutually implicative and constitutive concepts (Chiang, 2014; Leung, 2008; Liu, 2010, 2015; Liu & Rofel, 2010; Martin, 2009, 2014).

CHINESENESS IN QUEER MEDIA AND POP CULTURE

Exploring the co-implicative relationship between queerness and Chineseness has always been a central focus of queer China and queer Sinophone studies. This escalating scholarly interest indicates "a continuing effort of global queering theory in debunking the hegemonic, imperialist, universalist tendency in Eurocentric queer scholarship" (Zhao & Wong, 2020, p. 475). Therefore, it is necessary to contextualize the burgeoning development of queer China and queer Sinophone studies in the post-2010 years within the debates surrounding global queering theory since the late 1990s.

As the Australia-based queer Asian studies scholar Mark McLelland (2018) recalled in his article published as a contribution to the 20th anniversary of the journal *Sexualities*, a growing number of Anglophone scholarly publications "about sexual minority issues in Asia" have emerged "in the late 1990s and early 2000s" (p. 1272). Many of these publications strove to respond to, if not explicitly criticize, the earlier generation of "global queering theory" that was marked by Dennis Altman's (1996) deeply problematic Euro-American-centric position originally elaborated in his article "On Global Queering" in *Australian Humanities Review*.

In his original theory, Altman (1996) proposed "a newly universal sense of homosexuality as the basis for identity and lifestyle"—especially in the non-Western world—which resulted from media, cultural, and economic–political globalizations of Western modernity. In response to Altman's controversial proposal, queer Chinese film scholar Chris Berry (1996) criticized that both the universalization (or homogenization) of gender and sexual identities throughout the world and the indigenization of various cultures of gender and sexuality as sheer reflections of local traditions should be particularly alarming to queer scholars. As Berry (1996) noted, these two scholarly responses

> continu[e] to reinforce the post-Stonewall model of White, middle-class, respectable lesbian and gay cultures as the original, the true identity against which all others are measured, rather than recognising that, however powerful it has been and continues to be thanks to its alliance with consumer capitalism, it is as historically and locally specific as any other way of "conceptualising sexuality and gender."

Berry, along with Fran Martin and Audrey Yue, published a more elaborate anthology, *Mobile Cultures: New Media in Queer Asia* (Berry et al., 2003), which paved the way for the development of queer Asian studies. Calling attention to a glocal process, rather than a one-way globalizing or localizing one, the editors proposed a productive way of researching the gendered, sexualized bodies, desire, technologies, and media information flows within Asia (Berry et al., 2003, p. 7). This approach rejects the reductive binarism of local traditions and Western origins of earlier global queering theory.

Developing the anti-Western-centric lens in global queering research further, another anthology, *AsiaPacifiQueer: Rethinking Genders and Sexualities* (Martin et al., 2008), outlined the analytical position of the most recent evolution of global queering theory, "the queer hybridization model" (p. 6). Martin et al. (2008) proposed that this research model

> moves beyond the reductiveness of earlier approaches that located the sexual cultures and practices of other societies along a continuum of sameness versus difference from those of the West. Instead, it underscores the way in which both Western and non-Western cultures of gender and sexuality have been, and continue to be, mutually transformed through their encounters with transnationally mobile forms of sexual knowledge. In seeking to challenge the simplistic opposition of local essentialist and global homogenization views of global queering, the queer hybridization model offers a productive framework for understanding transformations of sexual cultures and knowledges today. (p. 6)

This theorization of the queer hybridization model, along with a number of influential publications in the late 2000s,[3] led to an escalation of scholarly debate over the relationship between queerness and Chineseness in the second decade of the 21st century.

As Yue (2014) explained in her reflective piece published in *Cinema Journal*, although there has been a "mainstreaming" of queer Asian studies after its rise in the 2000s, two entangled strands of research have emerged: "queer hybridity" and "critical regionality" (p. 146). Among the most fruitful endeavors in the latter direction are the academic writings of a growing number of queer Sinophone studies scholars. Their efforts are built upon the fertile ground of Sinophone studies, which examine "Sinitic-language cultures on the margins of geopolitical nation-states and their hegemonic productions" (Shih, 2011, p. 710) by "foregrounding the values of difficulty, difference, and heterogeneity" (Shih, 2007, p. 5).

For instance, following Shih's theorization, queer Sinophone scholar Howard Chiang (2014) highlighted the importance of reconceptualizing and amalgamating the notions of queerness and Chineseness:

> Taking a cue from the intellectual endeavor of denaturalizing categories of gender and sexuality, a non-hegemonic subversive definition of "Chineseness" is essential to the concept of queer Sinophonicity. It encompasses the perspectives of queer people living outside China and in locales not traditionally associated with Chinese studies (Singapore, Malaysia, etc.) and pays closer attention to the cultural differences between Sinitic-language communities on the margins of China (Taiwan, Hong Kong, etc.) and those within the People's Republic of China (PRC), rather than flattening out these unique cultural identifications with the bias of China-centrism. (p. 31)

Adopting this analytical lens, in his later work, Chiang (2019) examines one of the most famous Chinese-language gay films, *Lan Yu* (2001), directed by Hong Kong director Stanley

Kwan and set in postsocialist Beijing, the capital of the PRC, as a queer Sinophone story. The film's narration of a Chinese gay romance during local political upheaval and economic transformation (particularly the film's presentations of the government's crackdown on the student-led demonstrations in the Tiananmen Square on June 4, 1989, and the country's later rapid economic development and urban construction) ridicules both traditional heteronormative Chinese (Confucian) familial–marital values and the authoritarian party-state that have underpinned the essentialized imaginary of a heterosexual China. Similarly, from a queer Sinophone perspective, Alvin Wong (2012) examines the synthesized representations of gender, sexual, political, and national–cultural–linguistic others in the Chinese-language lesbian films *Butterfly* (directed by Yan Yan Mak, 2004, Hong Kong) and *Saving Face* (directed by Alice Wu, 2005, United States). A. Wong (2012) argues that the transregional and transnational constructions of a "lesbian" imaginary and history in the Sinophone world, as narrated in the two films, fundamentally trouble the dictatorial, heteropatriarchal manifestation of "Chinese nationalism" and reconfigure a queer Sinophone identity based on "critical gender and sexual heterogeneity and difference" (pp. 314, 319). Considering the films through a queer Sinophone approach reveals that the meanings of lesbianism and Chineseness, rather than being coherent and stable across time and space, have been "mutually constituted" and changing in the Chinese and Sinophone worlds (Wong, 2012, p. 320).

Whereas earlier queer Sinophone works focused largely on media and public cultures and social activism in Hong Kong, Taiwan, and other Sinitic communities in Southeast Asia (Chiang & Heinrich, 2014), more recent queer Sinophone studies have broadened their scope and diversified their methodologies to underline the possibilities and necessity of including in their discussions queer media about geocultural–ethnic–linguistic minority groups living within mainland China or in a "transpacific" context (Chen, 2020; Shernuk, 2020; Wong, 2020a, 2020b).

Some scholars also emphasize the "anti-essentialist, post-national" nature of both queerness and Chineseness (Martin, 2014, p. 36; see also Kong, 2011; Leung, 2008, p. 129). In particular, drawing on the understanding of Chineseness presented by Rey Chow (1998), the transnational queer research of Martin (2014) understands Chineseness as a concept that is "multiple, contradictory and fragmented: not the expression of a timeless national essence but instead the product of disjunctive regimes of cultural regulation across the multiple transnational contexts where claims to various forms of Chineseness are made" (p. 35; see also Lim, 2006, p. 2; Yau, 2010). The conceptual approach of Martin (2014) highlights the "tensions between what might be called centripetal versus centrifugal understandings [of Chineseness]" (which might be understood as the roots and routes of Chinese culture in imagining queer lives) in studies of transnational Chinese queer living experiences and politics of the 21st century (p. 36).

Another line of research engaged in unraveling the tensions and entanglement between queerness and Chineseness—queer China/Chinese studies—underscores the significance and intricacy of Western-originated queer theory and politics in shaping how people understand Chinese and nonnormative gender and sexual identities in Chinese-language queer media and public cultures (Liu, 2010; Rofel, 2007). For instance, in his widely cited journal article, "Why Does Queer Theory Need China?" Petrus Liu (2010) claims,

The possibility of practicing queer theory in Chinese contexts demonstrates that critical attention to local knowledges and concerns does not immediately constitute a categorical rejection of "the queer"; rather it shows that what is "queer" is constantly expanded, supplemented, and revised by what is "Chinese." (p. 297)

Drawing on, yet also diverging from, queer Sinophone approaches in his most recent book, *Queer China*, Bao (2020) focuses mainly on mainland Chinese queer media, creating a "'queer China' assemblage that undoes identity politics, unsettles conventional ways of thinking and creates spaces for critical reflection and autonomous living" (p. 18). Bao proposes that this "disidentification" characteristic of queer China studies "epitomizes a post-identitarian trajectory of thinking" and "recognize[s] that identification for minority cultures and marginalized communities is never complete, uncompromising and without failure throughout the world" (p. 18). Other queer China scholars have also used this non-identitarian understanding of queer to identify norm-defying cultures and groups as deeply rooted in, or even as indispensable contours of, official, mainstream imaginaries about China as a global, modern nation-state (Zhao, 2020a, 2020b; Zhao & Wong, 2020). Interestingly, this queer culture that paradoxically disidentifies with LGBTQ minorities has often successfully avoided censorship and has been largely encouraged and exploited by contemporary mainland Chinese media and celebrity industries.

CHINESE MEDIA CENSORSHIP OF HOMOSEXUAL AND QUEER CONTENT

The Chinese government's media and cultural policies on same-sex intimacy have greatly contributed to the rise of queer media images and pop cultures, albeit indirectly. China's media and online censorship systems have been characterized by ambiguity, inconsistency, and "generative"-ness within a "panoptic" social structure (Ng, 2015; Tsui, 2003). The often contradictory attitudes of official censors at various levels of media production and broadcasting, as well as the self-censorship of media practitioners who "tend to produce materials [that are] commercially successful" and less politically offensive to "the conservative morals of mainstream Chinese consumers" (Gorfinkel, 2018, p. 75), often lead to the censoring of information that is incompatible with the political–ideological projects of the state and to unreasonable (self-) crackdowns on "politically innocuous" content in public spaces (Balding, 2017).

In the post-2000 years, China's media censorship system has undergone a series of structural changes, and official policies regarding homosexuality in mass media have been regularly revised. To date, however, explicit portrayals of homosexual topics are generally either censored or carefully regulated in official, legal, educational, and media discourses (Bai, 2021; Bao, 2021; Bram, 2017; Pulver, 2019; Yang & Xu, 2016; Zhao, 2018a). The government has shown an ambiguous attitude, claiming that it does not encourage, discourage, or promote LGBTQ culture (Jia & Zhou, 2015). As Jia and Zhou (2015) noted, official media policies since 2008 have deemed homosexual content "abnormal" and "perverted." They also observed that some official guidelines directly associate homosexuality with "pornography, sex, and vulgarisms" and claim that it should be excluded from Chinese mass media and public spaces. Meanwhile, the state's anti-pornography campaigns since early 2000s have "continue[d] to follow outdated, homophobic regulations" and categorized homosexuality as "obscene" and "abnormal sexual behavior" (Yang & Xu, 2016, p. 169; see also Yan, 2015, p. 389). As Bao (2021, p. 31) opined, this problematic linkage of homosexuality to vulgar and pornographic content in China's regulatory regimes and public domains can also be partly explained through a tracing of the legal discourse and social recognition of gender and sexual minorities in contemporary China. Bao (2021) found that male homosexuality was "often punished under the category of 'hooliganism (*liumang zui*)" in pre-1997 China (p. 32). Even in the post-2000 years,

> due to its long history of stigmatization and the general public's lack of knowledge about it, homosexuality is still seen in some parts of Chinese society as a form of abnormality (*bu zhengchang*), deviance (*biantai*), disease (*youbing*), or even criminality (*liumang*), despite the increasing acceptance of homosexuality among the younger generation. (p. 33)

For example, alongside the significant change in public attitudes toward homosexuality in China since 2000 (David & Friedman, 2014, pp. 17–18), LGBTQ film festivals and communicative platforms, as well as fan sites dedicated to same-sex fantasies, have been subject to periodic crackdowns (Zhao et al., 2017, pp. xi–xxxiii).

Similarly, Gareth Shaw and Xiaoling Zhang (2017) pointed out that in 2016, SAPPRFT (the State Administration of Press, Publication, Radio, Film, and Television) issued a set of new stipulations expressing unequivocal disapproval of media materials that "express or display abnormal sexual relations or sexual behavior, such as incest, homosexuality, perversion, sexual assault, sexual abuse, and sexual violence" or "promote unhealthy views of marriage and relationships, including extramarital affairs, one-night stands, and sexual freedom" (p. 273). One notable censorship case was that of the 2016 popular online gay-themed TV drama, *Addicted* (*Shangyin*; iQiyi, China). The show, also known as *Heroin*, was about a gay high school romance. It premiered on January 29, 2016, and was removed from all video-streaming sites in China before the online distribution of its final three episodes in late February 2016. It was taken off the air for its portrayals of homosexuality and was accused of promoting "vulgar, immoral, and unhealthy content" and "the dark side of society" (Ellis-Petersen, 2016). The two main actors who played a gay couple in the series were also banned from Chinese TV screens (Ennis, 2016).

Some research also noted that this state-enforced censorship and waves of crackdown on homosexual content might be necessary, especially considering that some popular forms of queer Chinese media and cultural productions (e.g., boys' love [BL], also known as *danmei* in China; a media and literary genre featuring male homoerotic relationships) contain heavy portrayals of pedophilia and incest (Bai, 2021; Xu & Yang, 2013; Yang & Xu, 2016). As Ling Yang and Yanrui Xu (2016) observed, some people believe that the campaigns might "help curb the deluge of thoughtless and distasteful works... and minimize the potential harm of the [BL] genre to younger" generations (p. 171). Nevertheless, this body of scholarship also acknowledged that the censorship of homosexual and pornographic content often discursively serves the interests of "the government to tighten its grip on public opinion and stamp out anti-government voices" (Yan, 2015, p. 395) or helps the state oppose a self-imagined foreign cultural imperialism (e.g., Japanese cultural values and beliefs circulated through BL to China), which would erode local traditions and normative values on gender and sexuality (Yang & Xu, 2016, pp. 166–167).[4] Sometimes, both official and self-practiced censorial systems unexpectedly encourage an internal reporting (*jiefa*) mechanism in different groups of media producers and consumers/fans who are in "personal conflicts" with each other, which are ultimately underpinned by misogynistic and patriarchal ideals in mainstream Chinese society (Bai, 2021, p. 9; Zheng, 2019). For example, as Xiqing Zheng (2019) recorded, many reports to the police that made the BL writers the target of government censorship were done by "informants inside the community, especially anti-fans of a certain genre of writing, or even anti-fans of certain slash pairings [meaning 'same-sex coupling']." The destructive competition and official and internal bans on certain sexual and political topics in online Chinese BL production and consumption circles "have reinforced the public image of the outlaw nature" of this form of queer media and encouraged rampant plagiarism and "a weary sameness and insipidity of many" BL productions (Yang & Xu, 2016, pp. 170, 174).

The ambiguous attitudes, inconsistent structures, and "generative" (rather than repressive) regulatory practices of Chinese official censorship systems often lead to self-censorship not only by celebrities, netizens, the grassroots public, and LGBTQ-identified media practitioners but also by mainstream media producers and communicative platforms (Amar, 2018; Ho, 2010; Ng, 2015, pp. 87–103). However, research has also found that in response to the state's practices of "morality" regulation, media producers and directors often "embrac[e] resilience" and pragmatically tailor modes of media production and distribution to circumvent censorship (Guo, 2017, p. 488). For instance, Shaw and Zhang (2017, p. 285) found that Chinese independent filmmakers often use social networks and video-streaming sites to circulate LGBTQ-themed documentaries. Moreover, some Chinese netizens and social media users use homosexual-related hashtags to form "an alternative discourse about LGBTQ rights and free speech," which also challenges "the government's hegemonic censorship" (Liao, 2019, p. 2314). In addition, in 2014, in response to the government's sudden interest in and crackdowns on some online BL fan communities, one of the most large-scale literature websites based in mainland China also quickly renamed its BL subsite as "*chun'ai*" (literally meaning "pure love") to evade the government surveillance (Yang & Xu, 2016, p. 173). This renaming interestingly drew on the complex discourses of love (*ai*) and sex (*xing*) in the May Fourth period to legitimize BL as a form of spiritual love fantasy instead of a genre of erotica.[5]

As discussed in the section on "Queer Theory and Queer/*ku'er* in Chinese Media and Pop Culture," numerous cultural productions from mainland China show that LGBTQ cultures cannot simply be regarded as taboo in the local entertainment industry, despite the fact that homosexual content is banned from mainstream media. On the contrary, queer performances, meanings, and desires have not only been visible but also constantly fashionized, commercialized, normalized, and "straightened" in Chinese mass media (Zhao, 2016, 2020a, 2020b). Such a case in point is the local media framing of a large number of Chinese model female workers, female stars, and female Olympic athletes with visible masculine personas. Their queer performances of female gender (in the form of female masculinity) and sexuality (in the form of female singledom or female homosociality/sisterhood) are sometimes engineered as Chinese-specific feminist expressions or cosmopolitan Chinese women's fashion styles, which have been shaped by traditional gender values and modern Chinese social–political projects on female gender and sexuality (Zhao, 2018b, 2021). Also, some films (including both Chinese and imported ones), which feature heavy queer connotations yet without explicit depictions of homosexual relationships and characters, were successfully released in mainland China's commercial cinemas in late 2010s. A notable example is the 2018 musical film *Bohemian Rhapsody* (directed by Byran Singer), with its gay content removed from its Chinese version (Bao, 2021, p. 34). Sometimes, "politically innocuous" queer pop (including commercialized signs of gender and sexual nonnormativities, such as images of rainbow flags and clothes and representations of homosociality), which have disidentified with more politically sensitive homosexual content, are widely seen in film and on TV and contribute to the government's political–ideological imaginaries of a global, cosmopolitan China (Zhao, 2016, 2020b). Although this queer pop scene can be viewed as manifestations of intricate "social relations and creative agency the censorship mechanism enables and mobilizes" (Bao, 2021, p. 34), it also largely contributes to the queerbaiting and "queer sensationalism"—both are media industries' strategies to commercialize queer cultures as fantasies or aesthetics for LGBTQ audiences' attention and consuming power without fully acknowledging the existence, political importance, and equal rights of gender and sexual minorities—prevalent in contemporary China's commercial media and cultural industries (Zhao, 2018b, 2021).

CONCLUSION

This article challenges Western-centric scholarship on Chinese-language LGBTQ cultures, which often claims that nonheterosexual desires, identities, and intimacies in the Chinese-speaking context have been rigidly banned and thus not promoted and encouraged in mainstream mediascapes and pop cultural spaces. Using multiple cases and rich scholarly discussions on relevant examples and concepts, it was shown that in the contemporary Chinese worlds, queer practices, images, and narratives that have been actively voiced, either explicitly or implicitly, by media producers, performers, consumers, and fans who do not necessarily self-identify as LGBTQ people are commonly seen in both online and offline public and popular spaces. The discussion of glocalized concepts, such as *tongzhi* (comrade) and *ku'er* (queer), as well as ambivalent geocultural-identity-based notions, such as "Chineseness," presented here also maps out the transcultural traveling and mutations of the meanings of these English terms in Chinese-language media studies and cultures. In addition, the discussions of Chinese media censorial practices, policies, and ambiguities concerning homosexual and queer content also help challenge the dyad of Western-centrism and local essentialism. Thus, this article (re)defines queer Chinese media and pop culture as a continuous, negotiative cultural discourse that is affected by many global and local forces and factors and that is fluid, performative, and hybrid in nature.

FURTHER READING

Bao, H. (2020). "A cool kid": Queer theory travels to China. *Translation and Interpreting Studies, 16*(2), 219–239.
Berry, C. (1998). East palace, west palace: Staging gay life in China. *Jump Cut, 42,* 84–89.
Berry, C. (2001). Asian values, family values: Film, video, and lesbian and gay identities. In G. Sullivan & P. A. Jackson (Eds.), *Gay and lesbian Asia: Culture, identity, community* (pp. 211–231). Harrington Park Press.
Chi, D. T. (1997). *Queer archipelago: A reader of the queer discourses in Taiwan* (酷儿启示录:台湾当代 Queer 论述读本). Yuanzuen Wenhua.

Chi, D. T. (2017). *A history of tongzhi literature: A queer invention in Taiwan* (同志文学史:台湾的发明). Lianjing.

Chiang, H., & Wang, Y. (Eds.). (2018). *Perverse Taiwan*. Routledge.

Chiang, H., & Wong, A. K. (Eds.). (2020). *Keywords in queer Sinophone studies*. Routledge.

Eng, D. (2009). The queer space of China: Expressive desire in Stanley Kwan's *Lan Yu*. In O. Khoo & S. Metzger (Eds.), *Futures of Chinese cinema: Technologies and temporalities in Chinese screen cultures* (pp. 193–222). Intellect.

Jeffreys, E. (Ed.). (2006). *Sex and sexuality in China*. Routledge.

Jeffreys, E., & Yu, H. (Eds.). (2015). *Sex in China*. Polity Press.

Lavin, M., Yang, L., & Zhao, J. J. (Eds.). (2017). *Boys' love, cosplay and androgynous idols: Queer fan cultures in Mainland China, Hong Kong, and Taiwan*. Hong Kong University Press.

Leung, H. H. (2001). Queerspaces in contemporary Hong Kong cinema. *positions*, 9(2), 423–448.

Li, S. (2003). *Cross-dressing in Chinese opera*. Hong Kong University Press.

Li, Y. (1998). *The homosexual subculture* (同性恋亚文化). Jinri zhongguo.

Li, Y., & Wang, X. (1993). *Their world* (他们的世界). Tiandi tushu.

Liou, L. (2003). At the intersection of the global and the local: Representation of male homosexuality in fiction by Pai Hsien-yung, Li A. Chu T. and Chi T. *Postcolonial Studies*, 6(2), 191–206.

Marchetti, G. (2011). Between comrade and queer: Stanley Kwna's *Hold You Tight*. In E. Cheung, G. Marchetti, & S. K. Tan (Eds.), *Hong Kong screenscapes* (pp. 197–212). Hong Kong University Press.

Martin, F. (2003). *Situating sexualities: Queer representation in Taiwanese fiction, film and public culture*. Hong Kong University Press.

Pang, L., & Wong, D. (Eds.). (2005). *Masculinities and Hong Kong cinema*. Hong Kong University Press.

Rojas, C. (2003). "Nezha was here": Structures of dis/placement in Tsai Ming-liang's *Rebels of the Neon God*. *Modern Chinese Literature and Culture*, 15(1), 63–89.

Shiau, H. (2008). Marketing boys' love: Taiwan's independent film, *Eternal Summer*, and its audiences. *Journal of Asian Cinema*, 19(1), 157–171.

Sun, W., & Yang, L. (2019). Introduction. In W. Sun & L. Yang (Eds.), *Love stories in China: The politics of intimacy in the twenty-first century* (pp. 1–21). Routledge.

Wu, J. (2003). From "*Long Yang*" and "*Dui Shi*" to tongzhi: Homosexuality in China. *Journal of Gay & Lesbian Psychotherapy*, 7(1–2), 117–143.

Xu, Y., & Yang, L. (2014). Rotten girls "rotten" boys: *Danmei*, rotten culture, and the remaking of male masculinity in transnational cultural flows (腐女"腐"男:跨国文化流动中的耽美、腐文化与男性气质的再造). *Cultural Studies* (文化研究), 3, 3–25.

Yang, L. (2009). All for love: The corn fandom, prosumers, and the Chinese way of creating a super star. *International Journal of Cultural Studies*, 12(5), 527–543.

Yau, C. (2005). *Sexing shadows: Genders and sexualities in Hong Kong cinema* (性/别光影:香港电影中的性与性别文化研究). Hong Kong Film Critics Society.

Yue, A. (2012). Mobile intimacies in the queer Sinophone films of Cui Zi'en. *Journal of Chinese Cinemas*, 6(2), 95–108.

Zhang, C. Y. (2017). When feminist falls in love with queer: Dan Mei culture as a transnational apparatus of love. *Feminist Formations*, 29(2), 121–146.

Zhao, J. J. (Ed.). (2020). Queer pop in post-2000 China [Special issue]. *Feminist Media Studies*, 20(4), 463–581.

Zhao, J. J., & Wong, A. K. (Eds.). (2020). Making a queer turn in Chinese-language media studies [Special issue]. *Continuum*, 20(4), 475–555.

REFERENCES

Aaron, M. (Ed.). (2004). *New queer cinema: A critical reader*. Rutgers University Press.
Altman, D. (1996, July 1). On global queering. *Australian Humanities Review, 2*. http://australianhumanitiesreview.org/1996/07/01/on-global-queering/
Amar, M. (2018). "Ni you freestyle me?" (Do you freestyle?): The roots of censorship in Chinese hip-hop. *China Perspectives, 1–2*, 107–114.
Bachner, A. (2014). Queer affiliations: Mak Yan Yan's *Butterfly* as Sinophone romance. In H. Chiang & A. L. Heinrich (Eds.), *Queer Sinophone culture* (pp. 201–221). Routledge.
Bai, M. (2021, May 3). Regulation of pornography and criminalization of BL readers and authors in contemporary China (2010–2019). *Cultural Studies*. https://www.tandfonline.com/doi/full/10.1080/09502386.2021.1912805
Balding, C. (2017, November 6). The soft power of Chinese censorship. *IAPS Dialogue*. https://theasiadialogue.com/2017/11/06/the-soft-power-of-chinese-censorship/
Bao, H. (2011). "Queer Comrades": Transnational popular culture, queer sociality, and socialist legacy. *English Language Notes, 49*(1), 131–137.
Bao, H. (2018). *Queer comrades: Gay identity and tongzhi activism in postsocialist China*. NIAS Press.
Bao, H. (2020a). *Queer China: Lesbian and gay literature and visual culture under postsocialism*. Routledge.
Bao, H. (2020b). Screening sexualities, identities and politics: Queer cinema in contemporary China. In K. Latham (Ed.), *Routledge handbook of Chinese culture and society* (pp. 361–375). Routledge.
Bao, H. (2021). *Queer media in China*. Routledge.
Benshoff, H., & Griffin, S. (Eds.). (2004). *Queer cinema: The film reader*. Routledge.
Berry, C. (1996). Chris Berry responds to Dennis Altman. *Australian Humanities Review, 2*. http://australianhumanitiesreview.org/2008/05/01/chris-berry-responds-to-dennis-altman/
Berry, C. (2000). Happy alone? Sad young men in East Asian gay cinema. *Journal of Homosexuality, 39*(3–4), 187–200.
Berry, C. (2004). The sacred, the profane, and the domestic in Cui Zi'en's cinema. *positions, 12*(1), 195–201.
Berry, C., Martin, F., & Yue, A. (Eds.). (2003). *Mobile cultures: New media in queer Asia*. Duke University Press.
Boellstorff, T. (2005). *The gay archipelago: Sexuality and nation in Indonesia*. Princeton University Press.
Bram, B. (2017, April 7). How China keeps gay people off TV. *Dazed*. https://www.dazeddigital.com/artsandculture/article/35487/1/how-china-censors-gay-lgbt-film
Brennan, J. (2019). *Queerbaiting and fandom: Teasing fans through homoerotic possibilities*. University of Iowa Press.
Bullough, V. L., & Bullough, B. L. (1978). *Prostitution: An illustrated social history*. Crown.
Cai, S. (2017, December). Li Yugang and his transgender performance: Body politics, entertainment and aesthetic ambiguity. *Intersections, 41*. http://intersections.anu.edu.au/issue41/shenshen.pdf
Chan, L. S. (2021). *The politics of dating apps: Gender, sexuality, and emergent publics in urban China*. MIT Press.
Chao, S. (2010). Coming out of the box, marching as dykes. In C. Berry, X. Lv, & L. Rofel (Eds.), *The new Chinese documentary movement: For the public record* (pp. 77–96). Hong Kong University Press.
Chao, S. (2020). *Queer representations in Chinese-language film and the cultural landscape*. Amsterdam University Press.
Chen, M. (2020). Recognition, reproach, repression: The Ren Likui case in 1947 Tianjin and the cultural politics of homosexual murder in the Sinophone world. In H. Chiang & A. K. Wong (Eds.), *Keywords in queer Sinophone studies* (pp. 153–174). Routledge.
Chiang, H. (Ed.). (2012). *Transgender China*. Palgrave Macmillan.

Chiang, H. (2014). Queering China: A new synthesis. *GLQ: A Journal of Lesbian and Gay Studies, 20*(3), 353–378.

Chiang, H. (2019). Sinophone modernity: History, culture, geopolitics. In C. Zhang (Ed.), *Composing modernist connections in China and Europe* (pp. 142–167). Routledge.

Chiang, H., & Heinrich, A. L. (Eds.). (2014). *Queer Sinophone cultures*. Routledge.

Chiang, H., & Wong, A. K. (2016). Queering the transnational turn: Regionalism and queer Asias. *Gender, Place & Culture, 23*(11), 1643–1656.

Chiang, H., & Wong, A. K. (2017). Asia is burning: Queer Asia as critique. *Culture, Theory and Critique, 58*(2), 121–126.

Chou, W. (2000). *Tongzhi: Politics of same-sex eroticism in Chinese societies*. Haworth.

Chou, W. (2001). Homosexuality and the cultural politics of *tongzhi* in Chinese societies. *Journal of Homosexuality, 40*(3–4), 27–46.

Chow, R. (1998). On Chineseness as a theoretical problem. *Boundary, 25*(3), 1–24.

David, D. S., & Friedman, S. L. (2014). Deinstitutionalizing marriage and sexuality. In D. S. Davis & S. L. Friedman (Eds.), *Wives, husbands, and lovers: Marriage and sexuality in Hong Kong, Taiwan, and urban China* (pp. 1–38). Stanford University Press.

Davis, G., & Needham, G. (Eds.). (2009). *Queer TV: Theories, histories, politics*. Routledge.

Dikotter, F. (1992). Book review of *Passions of the Cut Sleeve*. *Journal of Asian Studies, 55*(1), 170.

Doty, A. (1993). *Making things perfectly queer*. University of Minnesota Press.

Driver, S. (2006). *Queer girls and popular culture: Reading, resisting, and creating media*. Lang.

Ellis-Petersen, H. (2016, March 4). China bans depictions of gay people on television. *The Guardian*. https://www.theguardian.com/tv-and-radio/2016/mar/04/china-bans-gay-people-television-clampdown-xi-jinping-censorship

Engebretsen, E. L. (2013). *Queer women in urban China: An ethnography*. Routledge.

Engebretsen, E. L., & Shroeder, W. F. (2015). Queer/tongzhi China: Introduction. In E. L. Engebretsen & W. F. Shroeder (with H. Bao) (Eds.), *Queer/tongzhi China: New perspectives on research, activism, and media cultures* (pp. 1–17). NIAS.

Engebretsen, E. L., & Shroeder, W. F. (with Bao, H.) (Eds.). (2015). *Queer/tongzhi China: New perspectives on research, activism, and media cultures*. NIAS.

Ennis, D. (2016, March 4). WATCH: The show that has China banning all gay couples from TV. *Advocate*. https://www.advocate.com/world/2016/3/04/watch-china-bans-gay-couples-tv

Feng, J. (2013). *Romancing the Internet: Producing and consuming Chinese web romance*. Brill.

Furth, C. (1994). Rethinking van Guilk: Sexuality and reproduction in traditional Chinese medicine. In C. Gilmartin, G. Hershatter, L. Rofel, & T. White (Eds.), *Engendering China* (pp. 125–146). Harvard University Press.

Girchner, L. E. (2011). *Erotic aspects of Chinese culture*. Literary Licensing.

Goldman, A. S. (2012). *Opera and the city: The politics of culture in Beijing, 1770–1900*. Stanford University Press.

Gorfinkel, L. (2018). *Chinese television and national identity construction: The cultural politics of music entertainment programmes*. Routledge.

Guo, S. (2017). When dating shows encounter state censors: A case study of *If You Are the One*. *Media, Culture & Society, 39*(4), 487–503.

Guo, T. (2016). Translating homosexuality into Chinese: A case study of Pan Guangdan's translation of Havelock Ellis's *Psychology of Sex: A Manual for Students* (1933). *Asia Pacific Translation and Intercultural Studies, 3*(1), 47–61.

Halberstam, J. (2005). *In a queer time and place: Transgender studies, subcultural lives*. New York University Press.

Han, L. (2021, July 19). Alternative media and the queer feminist community: The lesbian print magazine in China. *Journal of Homosexuality*. https://doi.org/10.1080/00918369.2021.1940013

He, C. (2013). Trespassing, crisis and renewal: Li Yugang and cross-dressing performance. *Differences*, 24(2), 150–171.

He, C. (2014). Performance and the politics of gender: Transgender performance in contemporary Chinese films. *Gender, Place & Culture*, 21(5), 622–636.

Hinsch, B. (1990). *Passion of the cut sleeve: The male homosexual tradition in China*. University of California Press.

Ho, L. W. W. (2010). *Gay and lesbian subculture in urban China*. Routledge.

Honig, E. (2002). Maoist mappings of gender: Reassessing the red guards. In S. Brownell & J. N. Wasserstrom (Eds.), *Chinese femininities, Chinese masculinities: A reader* (pp. 255–268). University of California Press.

Huang, H. T. (2011). *Queer politics and sexual modernity in Taiwan*. HKUP.

Jackson, P. A. (Ed.). (2011). *Queer Bangkok*. Hong Kong University Press.

Jagose, A. (1996). *Queer theory: An introduction*. New York University Press.

Jia, L., & Zhou, T. (2015, July 28). Regulation of homosexuality in the Chinese media scene. *IAPS*. https://theasiadialogue.com/2015/07/28/regulation-of-homosexuality-in-the-chinese-media-scene/

Jiao, L. (2021, February). Reconciling femininities and female masculinities: Women's premarital experiences of breast-binding in the Maoist era. *Modern China*. https://doi.org/10.1177/0097700421992314

Kam, L. (Ed.). (2016). *Changing Chinese masculinities: From imperial pillars of state to global real men*. Hong Kong University Press.

Kam, L. Y. L. (2012). *Shanghai lalas: Female tongzhi communities and politics in urban China*. Hong Kong University Press.

Kang, W. (2009). *Obsession: Male same-sex relations in China, 1900–1950*. Hong Kong University Press.

Kohnen, M. E. S. (2016). *Queer representation, visibility, and race in American film and television: Screening the closet*. Routledge.

Kong, T. S. K. (2011). *Chinese male homosexualities: Memba, tongzhi and golden boy*. Routledge.

Kong, T. S. K. (2016). The sexual in Chinese sociology: Homosexuality studies in contemporary China. *Sociological Review*, 64(3), 495–514.

Leung, H. H. (2008). *Undercurrents*. UBC Press.

Leung, H. H. (2012). Homosexuality and queer aesthetics. In Y. Zhang (Ed.), *A companion to Chinese cinema* (pp. 518–534). Wiley-Blackwell.

Liao, S. (2019). "#IAmGay# What About You?": Storytelling, discursive politics, and the affective dimension of social media activism against censorship in China. *International Journal of Communication*, 13, 2314–2333.

Lim, S. H. (2006). *Celluloid comrades*. University of Hawai'i Press.

Liu, P. (2010). Why does queer theory need China? *positions*, 18(2), 291–320.

Liu, P. (2015). *Queer Marxism in two Chinas*. Duke University Press.

Liu, P., & Rofel, L. (2010). Beyond the strai(gh)ts: Transnationalism and queer Chinese politics. *positions*, 18(2), 281–289.

Lovelock, M. (2019). *Reality TV and queer identities: Sexuality, authenticity, celebrity*. Palgrave Macmillan.

Martin, F. (2009). That global feeling: Sexual subjectivities and imagined geographies in Chinese-language lesbian cyberspaces. In G. Goggin & M. McLelland (Eds.), *Internationalizing internet studies* (pp. 285–301). Routledge.

Martin, F. (2010). *Backward glances: Contemporary Chinese cultures and the female homoerotic imaginary*. Duke University Press.

Martin, F. (2014). Transnational queer Sinophone culture. In M. McLelland & V. Mackie (Eds.), *Routledge handbook of sexuality studies in East Asia* (pp. 35–58). Routledge.

Martin, F., Jackson, P. A., McLelland, M., & Yue, A. (Eds.). (2008). *AsiaPacifiQueer: Rethinking genders and sexualities*. University of Illinois Press.

McLelland, M. (2018). From queer studies on Asia to Asian queer studies. *Sexualities, 21*(8), 1271–1275.

Mennel, B. (2012). *Queer cinema: School girls, vampires and gay cowboys.* Wallflower.

Ng, E., & Li, X. (2020). A queer "socialist brotherhood": The *Guardian* web series, boys' love fandom, and the Chinese state. *Feminist Media Studies, 20*(4), 479–495.

Ng, H. W. (2015). Rethinking censorship in China: The case of *Snail House*. In R. Bai & G. Song (Eds.), *Chinese television in the twenty-first century: Entertaining the nation* (pp. 87–103). Routledge.

Pecic, Z. L. (2016). *New queer Sinophone cinema: Local histories, transnational connections.* Palgrave Macmillan.

Pulver, A. (2019, February 28). China to remove LGBT scenes from *Bohemian Rhapsody*. *The Guardian*. https://www.theguardian.com/film/2019/feb/28/china-to-remove-lgbt-scenes-from-bohemian-rhapsody

Rocha, L. A. (2010). Xing: The discourse of sex and human nature in modern China. *Gender & History, 22*(3), 603–628.

Rofel, L. (1999). Qualities of desire: Imagining gay identities in China. *GLQ, 5*(4), 451–474.

Rofel, L. (2007). *Desiring China: Experiments in neoliberalism, sexuality, and public culture.* Duke University Press.

Ruan, F. F., & Bullough, V. L. (1992). Lesbianism in China. *Achieves of Sexual Behavior, 21*(3), 217–226.

Sang, T. D. (1999). Translating homosexuality: The discourse of *Tongxing'ai* in Republican China (1912–1949). In L. Liu (Ed.), *Tokens of exchange* (pp. 276–304). Duke University Press.

Sang, T. D. (2003). *The emerging lesbian: Female same-sex desire in modern China.* University of Chicago Press.

Schoonover, K., & Galt, R. (2016). *Queer cinema in the world.* Duke University Press.

Sedgwick, E. K. (1993). *Tendencies.* Duke University Press.

Sender, K. (2004). *Business, not politics: The making of the gay market.* Columbia University Press.

Shaw, G., & Zhang, X. (2017). Cyberspace and gay rights in a digital China: Queer documentary filmmaking under state censorship. *China Information, 32*(2), 270–292.

Shernuk, K. (2020). A queerness of relation: The plight of the "ethnic minority" in Chan Koon-Chung's *Bare Life*. In H. Chiang & A. K. Wong (Eds.), *Keywords in queer Sinophone studies* (pp. 80–102). Routledge.

Shi, L. (2014). *Chinese lesbian cinema: Mirror rubbing, lala, and les.* Lexington.

Shi, L. (2020). Constructing a new sexual paradigm: Emergence of a modern subject. *Prism, 17*(2), 264–276.

Shih, S. (2007). *Visuality and identity: Sinophone articulations across the pacific.* University of California Press.

Shih, S. (2011). The concept of the Sinophone. *Publications of the Modern Language Association of America, 126*(3), 709–718.

Sigley, G. (2006). Sex, politics and the policing of virtue in the People's Republic of China. In E. Jeffreys (Ed.), *Sex and sexuality in China* (pp. 43–61). Routledge.

Sommers, M. H. (2000). *Sex, law, and society in late imperial China.* Stanford University Press.

Spencer, N. A. (2012). Ten years of queer cinema in China. *positions, 20*(1), 373–383.

Tan, E. K. (2013). *Rethinking Chineseness: Translational Sinophone identities in the Nanyang literary world.* Cambria Press.

Tsui, L. (2003). The panopticon as the antithesis of a space of freedom: Control and regulation of the internet in China. *China Information, 17*(2), 65–82.

van Gulik, R. H. (1961). *Sexual life in Ancient China: A preliminary survey of Chinese sex and society from ca. 1500 B.C. till 1644 A.D.* Brill.

Villarejo, A. (2014). *Ethereal queer: Television, historicity, desire*. Duke University Press.
Vitiello, G. (2011). *The libertine's friend: Homosexuality and masculinity in late imperial China*. University of Chicago Press.
Volpp, S. (2011). *Worldly stage: Theatricality in seventeenth-century China*. Harvard University Asian Center.
Wang, Q. (2015). Queerness, entertainment, and politics: Queer performance and performativity in Chinese pop. In E. L. Engebretsen & W. F. Shroeder (with H. Bao) (Eds.), *Queer/tongzhi China: New perspectives on research, activism, and media cultures* (pp. 153–178). NIAS.
Wang, Q. (2018). Flower in the mirror and moon in the water: The ambiguity of gender, genre, and politics of Li Yugang. In G. Lee (Ed.), *Rethinking difference in gender, sexuality, and popular music: Theory and politics of ambiguity* (pp. 71–88). Routledge.
Wang, S. (2020a). Chinese gay men pursuing online fame: Erotic reputation and internet celebrity economies. *Feminist Media Studies*, 20(4), 548–564.
Wang, S. (2020b). Live streaming, intimate situations, and the circulation of same-sex affect: Monetizing affective encounters on Blued. *Sexualities*, 23(5–6), 934–950.
Wei, J. (2014). Queer encounters between Iron Man and Chinese boys' love fandom. *Transformative Works and Cultures*, 17. http://journal.transformativeworks.org/index.php/twc/article/view/561/458
Wong, A. K. (2012). From the transnational to the Sinophone: Lesbian representations in Chinese-language films. *Journal of Lesbian Studies*, 16(3), 307–322.
Wong, A. K. (2020). Towards a queer affective economy of boys' love in contemporary Chinese media. *Continuum*, 34(4), 500–513.
Wong, L. (2020a). *Transpacific attachments: Sex work, media networks, and affective histories of Chineseness*. Columbia University Press.
Wong, L. (2020b). Transfiguring Asian North American and the Sinophonic in Jia Qing Wilson-Yang's *Small Beauty*. In H. Chiang & A. K. Wong (Eds.), *Keywords in queer Sinophone studies* (pp. 16–37). Routledge.
Wu, C. (2004). *Homoerotic sensibilities in late Imperial China*. Routledge.
Wu, J. (2003). From "*long yang*" and "*dui shi*" to tongzhi: Homosexuality in China. *Journal of Gay & Lesbian Psychotherapy*, 7(1–2), 117–143.
Xu, Y., & Yang, L. (2013). Forbidden love: Incest, generational conflict and the erotics of power in Chinese BL fiction. *Journal of Graphic Novels and Comics*, 4(1), 30–43.
Yan, M. N. (2015). Regulating online pornography in mainland China and Hong Kong. In M. McLelland & V. Mackie (Eds.), *Routledge handbook of sexuality studies in East Asia* (pp. 387–401). Routledge.
Yang, L. (2010). "Bent" romance: Super Girl's GL literature, female desire, and feminism (弄弯的"罗曼史:超女同人文、女性欲望与女性主义). *Cultural Studies* (文化研究), 9. https://www.cnki.com.cn/Article/CJFDTotal-SWWH200900011.htm
Yang, L., & Bao, H. (2012). Queerly intimate: Friends, fans and affective communication in a *Super Girl* fan fiction community. *Cultural Studies*, 26(6), 842–871.
Yang, L., & Xu, Y. (2015). Queer texts, gendered imagination, and popular feminism in Chinese web literature. In E. L. Engebretsen & W. F. Shroeder (with H. Bao) (Eds.), *Queer/tongzhi China: New perspectives on research, activism, and media cultures* (pp. 131–152). NIAS.
Yang, L., & Xu, Y. (2016). Danmei, Xianqing, and the making of a queer online public sphere in China. *Communication and the Public*, 1(2), 251–256.
Yang, L., & Xu, Y. (2016). "The love that dare not speak its name": The fate of Chinese *danmei* communities in the 2014 anti-porn campaign. In M. McLelland (Ed.), *The end of cool Japan: Ethical, legal, and cultural challenges to Japanese popular culture* (pp. 163–183). Routledge.
Yau, C. (Ed.). (2010). *As normal as possible: Negotiating sexuality and gender in mainland China and Hong Kong*. Hong Kong University Press.

Ye, S. (2018). A reparative return to "Queer Socialism": Male same-sex desire in the cultural revolution. In H. Chiang (Ed.), *Sexuality in China: Histories of power & pleasure* (pp. 142–162). University of Washington Press.

Yue, A. (2012). Mobile intimacies in the queer Sinophone films of Cui Zi'en. *Journal of Chinese Cinemas*, 6(1), 95–108.

Yue, A. (2014). Queer Asian cinema and media studies: From hybridity to critical regionality. *Cinema Journal*, 53(2), 145–151.

Zhang, Q. (2014). Representation of homoerotism by the *People's Daily* since 1949. *Sexuality & Culture*, 18(4), 1010–1024.

Zhang, Q. (2015). Sexuality and the official construction of Occidentalism in Maoist and early post-Mao China. *European Journal of Cultural Studies*, 18(1), 86–107.

Zhao, J. J. (2016). A splendid Chinese queer TV? "Crafting" non-normative masculinities in formatted Chinese reality TV shows. *Feminist Media Studies*, 16(1), 164–168.

Zhao, J. J. (2017a). A queerly normalized Western lesbian imaginary: Online Chinese fans' gossip about the Danish fashion model Freja Beha Erichsen. *Feminist Media Studies*, 17(1), 42–58.

Zhao, J. J. (2017b). Queerly imagining *Super Girl* in an alternative world: The fannish worlding in FSCN femslash romance. *Transformative Works and Cultures*, 24. http://dx.doi.org/10.3983/twc.2017.870

Zhao, J. J. (2018a). Censoring "rainbow" in China. *IAPS*. http://theasiadialogue.com/2018/06/01/censoring-rainbow-in-china/

Zhao, J. J. (2018b). Queer, yet never lesbian: A ten-year look back at the reality TV singing competition show *Super Voice Girl*. *Celebrity Studies*, 9(4), 470–486.

Zhao, J. J. (2018c). The ebb and flow of female homoeroticism in the online Chinese queer fandom of the 2006 *Super Voice Girl*. *Journal of Fandom Studies*, 6(1), 33–45.

Zhao, J. J. (2019). Queer TV China as an area of critical scholarly inquiry in the 2010s. *Critical Asian Studies*, 26.

Zhao, J. J. (2020a). Queerness within Chineseness: Nationalism and sexual morality on and off the rap competition *The Rap of China*. *Continuum*, 34(4), 484–499.

Zhao, J. J. (2020b). It has never been "normal": Queer pop in post-2000 China. *Feminist Media Studies*, 20(4), 463–478.

Zhao, J. J. (2021). Blackpink queers your area: The global queerbaiting and queer fandom of K-pop female idols. *Feminist Media Studies*, 21(6), 1033–1038. https://doi.org/10.1080/14680777.2021.1959373

Zhao, J. J. (2021). Doing it like a tomboy on post-2010 Chinese TV. *Communication, Culture & Critique*, 15(3). https://doi.org/10.1093/ccc/tcab053

Zhao, J. J., & Wong, A. K. (2020). Introduction: Making a queer turn in contemporary Chinese-language media studies. *Continuum*, 34(4), 475–483.

Zhao, J. J., Yang, L., & Lavin, M. (2017). Introduction. In M. Lavin, L. Yang, & J. J. Zhao (Eds.), *Boys' love, cosplay, and androgynous idols: Queer fan cultures in mainland China, Hong Kong, and Taiwan* (pp. xi–xxxiii). Hong Kong University Press.

Zheng, T. (2015). *Tongzhi living: Men attracted to men in postsocialist China*. University of Minnesota Press.

Zheng, X. (2019). Survival and migration patterns of Chinese online media fandoms. *Transformative Works and Cultures*, 30. https://doi.org/10.3983/twc.2019.1805

Zhou, Y. (2014). Chinese queer images on screen: A case study of Cui Zi'en's films. *Asian Studies Review*, 38(1), 124–140.

NOTES

1. Criticism of this book can be found in a number of reviews, such as that by Frank Dikotter (1992) in the *Journal of Asian Studies*.

2. For a detailed discussion of the differences between the two, see Martin's (2010) discussion on the differences between female homoeroticism and lesbianism in her monograph *Backward Glances: Contemporary Chinese Culture and the Female Homoerotic Imaginary*.
3. These include the widely cited monograph *Desiring China: Experiments in Neoliberalism, Sexuality, and Public Culture* by Lisa Rofel (2007), which includes a chapter titled "Imagining Gay Identities in China" that was published as early as 1999 in a special issue of *GLQ*. In the original journal article, Rofel (1999) explored the "contingent processes and performative evocations that do not presume equivalence but ask after confrontations charged with claims of power" (p. 457).
4. This imagined "cultural erosion," as discussed by Yang and Xu (2016, p. 170), is believed by the party-state to misguide young Chinese generations to a sexual liberalism, which eventually will lead to a political liberalism among the general public and thus risk the social stability of the country. For a detailed discussion about the convergence of sexual and political liberalization in China's public culture and regulatory practices, see Sigley (2006, pp. 44–48).
5. For a discussion of modern Chinese discourses on love and sex, see Rocha (2010).

Jamie J. Zhao

QUEER COMICS

INTRODUCTION

Queer theory is inseparable from queer culture. This article focuses on one aspect of queer culture: comics. The meanings and uses of the term "queer" emerge from both inside and outside the academy. And as the article "Queer Perspectives in Communication Studies (https://doi.org/10.1093/acrefore/9780190228613.013.81)" has documented, "more often than not, political and cultural developments outside academia informed" queer scholars and intellectuals. Queer scholars are themselves members of queer communities, influenced by the creative expression, joys, and struggles of those communities. This influence is clear when the focus of scholarship is on queer cultural production, but it is present and operating in the background even when scholarship is more conceptual or theoretical. As Fawaz (2019) claimed, "Queerness as a form of deviation from prescribed gender and sexual norms is a literal part of the sequential logic of comics" (p. 593).

It is beyond the scope of this article to provide a comprehensive history of queer comics, as this is an important task which has been taken up by other cartoonists and scholars (Chute, 2017; Hall, 2013). This article analyzes the particular affordances of comics as a medium of communication that make it especially potent for telling queer stories and challenging the status quo. I use the term affordance to describe that which the form of comics, specifically, makes possible. This study speaks to studies of community archives, zines and DIY media cultures, visual rhetoric, queer autoethnography, and queer feminist pedagogy. The focus of this article is comics made by queer cartoonists for queer audiences, and the examples used in the analysis just scratch the surface of the depth and breadth of queer comics. In addition to those that are widely circulated and belonging to an evolving canon of queer comics, there are scores of comics in notebooks, stashed in drawers, scratched on bathroom stall doors, and circulated among friends. There are underground comics in volunteer-run queer and zine archives, including the Queer Zine Archive Project (https://archive.qzap.org/)

in the United States and the Queer Zine Library (https://www.queerzinelibrary.com/) in the United Kingdom, some digitized, some not. This article does not reflect non-English-language scholarship, an important direction for future study, as queer comics are created internationally and transnationally in a wide variety of contexts.

The medium of comics, particularly in the form of self-published zines, offers what Licona (2012) called "a technology of potentially transformative recording, which can produce, promote, and/or reveal diverse community and grassroots literacies" (p. 19). However, this radical potentiality does not diminish the fact that comics have had a largely White creator and reader base, which is also reflected in scholarship about comics. Recently, this has been shifting, with scholar-artists like John Jennings, whose graphic novel adaptations of Octavia Butler's *Kindred* and *Parable of the Sower* have been widely popular, and whose book *The Blacker the Ink: Constructions of the Black Identity in Comics and Sequential Art* (2015), coedited with Frances Gateward, offers a collection of essays on Blackness in comics. Writer Ta-Nehesi Coates has authored the Marvel comic *Black Panther* since 2016, and Gabby Rivera wrote the Marvel comic book *America* that ran from 2017 to 2018, featuring queer Latina superhero America Chavez. Still, as Howard and Jackson (2013) noted, "oftentimes comics tell a story about white heroes and minority villains, white victors and minority losers, white protagonists and perhaps a minority sidekick" (p. 2). The underlying messages within comics, like many other forms of media, have been based in "white patriarchal universalism" (Howard & Jackson, 2013, p. 2), which is also heteronormative. Comics in the United States have been nearly synonymous with the superhero genre, which, as Gateward and Jennings (2015) argued, does not utilize the potency and power of the form. The radical, queer, anti-racist potential of the comics form, which this article seeks to uplift, cannot be considered outside comics' historical reinforcement of White patriarchal norms.

THE COMIC FORM

Comics have no set definition, but most often, the singular term "comics" describes pictures and words that together create a narrative—though there are exceptions to this, like Shaun Tan's wordless graphic novel *The Arrival*, from 2006. Comics have been defined as sequential art, where the passage of time is marked through visual space on the page. Eisner (1985), in his landmark work *Comics and Sequential Art*, called comics "a means of creative expression, a distinct discipline, an art and literary form that deals with the arrangement of pictures or images and words to narrate a story or dramatize an idea" (p. 5). From Sunday newspaper comics sections to comic books, the medium has historically been considered a "low" art form, one that is cheaply made and easily reproducible. Comics do not require expensive equipment to produce—at their most simple, pen and paper.

With comics, readers can control the pace and direction of their consumption of images, which is unique among sequential, visual forms, and important for readers from marginalized communities. Does one read the words or pictures first? They may choose. Kuttner et al. (2017) wrote that "Different readers approach them in different ways, and may alter their approach depending on how a particular page is structures. Viewing a comic is a cyclical process—a back and forth between seeing and reading, with image informing text and text informing image" (p. 398). In film, for example, viewers are at the mercy of the filmmaker's editing and pacing, while "time in the static form of comics unfolds in space, allowing the reader to experience it at a much more individual pace" (Kuttner et al., 2017, p. 400).

Comics are typically made up of frames, known as panels, on the page, and the space, called the gutter, between them. Chute (2010) wrote, "the effect of the gutter, the rich empty space between the selected moments that direct our interpretation, is for the reader to project causality in these gaps that exist between the punctual moments of the frames" (p. 8). Comics artists use the gutter as innuendo, allowing the reader to imagine what is happening between and beyond what is pictured in the panels. This absence, McCloud (1994) noted, is unique to the medium: "what's between the panels is the only element of comics that is not duplicated in any other medium" (p. 13). Gardner (2006) wrote that "comics do open up (inevitably and necessarily) a space for the reader to pause, between the panels, and make meaning out of what she sees and reads" (p. 791), serving as "collaborative texts between the imagination of the author/artist and the imagination of the reader who must complete the narrative" (Gardner, 2006, p. 800). Chute (2010) argued that the form of comics enables a feminist ethic, in which the reader controls their experiences with the images on the page, something that is particularly important with stories of trauma. They may look, close the book, and then look again—read quickly, read slowly, read again and again.

While comics are popularly associated with humor, there are many creators of comics who deal with more serious and complex issues. Comics are not just for kids, and they are not just funny. Art Spiegelman (1996) won a Pulitzer Prize in 1992 for his graphic novel *Maus*, in which he narrated his family's experience of the Holocaust and his relationship with his father. Many, if not most, comics outside the superhero realm today do deal with serious subjects, and not necessarily without humor. The *Drawing Power: Women's Stories of Sexual Violence, Harassment, and Survival, A Comics Anthology* by Noomin (2019) is a collection of works by 64 noted comics artists that won the 2020 Eisner Award for Best Anthology. Rendering serious stories as comics allows authors to utilize a rich multimodal vocabulary, and the form also broaden the story's readership.

While "serious comics" have gone mainstream, there is also a long history of independent, underground, and self-published comics, which continues today. Comics are a cultural medium that emerges from earlier forms of media, offering powerful modes to tell stories and address significant issues. "Zines are cheaply made printed forms of expression on any subject.... Zines are not a new idea. They have been around under different names (chapbooks, pamphlets, flyers). People with independent ideas have been getting their word out since there were printing presses" (Todd & Watson, 2006, p. 12). The advent of the widely available photocopier in the 1970s, and now, of course, the internet, made it possible for people to create their own comics and reproduce and circulate them inexpensively, which enabled the creation of radical and queer zine cultures. The ability to self-publish content without the approval of mainstream cultural institutions was critical in maintaining and creating community without conforming to social norms of respectability—something impossible for queer-identified people anyway. Zines are countercultural (Licona, 2012) and counterpublic (Brouwer, 2005), resisting dominant modes of communication and commerce. Often, zines are given away, traded, or sold for a small fee, with the foremost goal of creating community, not profit. Not all zines are comics, and, of course, not all zines are queer, though, as Sender (2020) argued, "they can embody metaphors for queer productivity: the importance of self-representation while making do with what we have" (p. 136). While some queer comics have gone mainstream, their most significant potential is in the world of self-publishing, independent, and small presses, where the aim is not so much widespread acclaim as it is queer affirmation, community- and world-building.

COMICS IN AND AS SCHOLARSHIP

In the field of communication, comics have been taken up by some scholars, particularly in the areas of visual rhetoric and health communication (Cox, 2016; King, 2017; Palczewski, 2005). Eisner (1985), examining the medium of comics, wrote that it was "an 'art of communication' more than simply an application of art" and that "comics communicate in a 'language' that relies on a visual experience common to both creator and audience" (pp. 6 and 7). Comics have long been considered artifacts worthy of analysis by historians, literature and cultural studies scholars (Chute, 2010, 2014, 2017; Eisner, 1985; Fawaz, 2016). Entire journals are dedicated to their study, including the *Journal of Graphic Novels and Comics*, *Studies in Comics*, *The Comics Journal*, *The Comics Grid: Journal of Comics Scholarship*, and *ImageTexT: Interdisciplinary Comics Studies*. Graphic medicine, which encompasses comics about experiences of illness, health care, and caregiving, has become its own field; many of its practitioners are also scholars, health care, and public health professionals (see Czerwiec et al., 2015; Green, 2010; Williams, 2014). The *Annals of Internal Medicine*, one of the most widely cited journals in the world, began publishing comics monthly in 2015. Within the field of communication, a special issue dedicated to graphic medicine in *Health Communication* 32(5) was published in 2017. Comics studies scholars in communication often publish their work in journals from other disciplines, including pop culture, media studies, literature, and visual arts journals.

In contrast to scholarship about comics, scholarship done in comic form is less prevalent, though gaining some traction. Ebony Flowers (2017a) and Nick Sousanis (2015) both published their dissertations in comics form, and Sousanis's *Unflattening* was then published by Harvard University Press in 2015. Popular history texts have been published as comics, notably *A People's History of American Empire: A Graphic Adaptation* by Howard Zinn et al. (2008) and the *March* trilogy by John Lewis (2013, 2015, 2016) about the civil rights movement. Journalist and cartoonist Joe Sacco has reported on some of the world's great conflicts—including Palestine, Bosnia, indigenous North America, and Iraq—in the form of comics. Scholarly comics, what Kuttner et al. (2017) called "comics-based research," has been published in journals including the *Annals of Internal Medicine*, *Qualitative Inquiry*, the *Harvard Educational Review*, *Women's Studies in Communication*, *Teachers College Record*, and *QED*, not to mention in online spaces.

A growing number of scholars have begun to do scholarship in comic form, which is a challenge to text-primary academia (Councilor, 2018, 2019; Flowers, 2017a, 2017b; Sousanis, 2015). Anthropologist Katz creates comic field notes, which she has published in their original comic form. Describing the reasoning behind doing so, Katz (2013) wrote, "Rather than a single monographic narrative that airbrushes—when it does not obscure entirely—what it means to be 'in the field' in an embodied way, written in the sanctioned language of social science, which can make it all seem straightforward, clean and deliberate, these other records exposed the anxiety, discomfort, muddied thinking, bafflements, exquisite joys, and stunning beauty of doing research" (p. 768). They are untranslated into typeset text, maintaining their embodied and complex form, from the content itself to the shaky pen lines that compose it. In their study of bisexuality and bi erasure, Berbary and Guzman (2018) represented their data in comics "because they have a long history in queer culture for being politically educative, creative, social justice-oriented contributions that bring previously silenced lived experiences of LGBTQ individuals to the forefront of popular social culture through an accessible, relatable, contextualized, and easily distributed genre" (p. 481). They model a queer form of scholarship, telling the stories of bisexual women, and doing so in a hybrid scholarly–comics format, as well as through the creation of a zine for popular distribution. Their academic research article and community zine project are a dual-authored partnership between a bisexual-identified scholar and a queer cartoonist. This kind of project prompts the question: How might scholarship produced in comic form queer academic writing in ways that keep the material body present? The sections to follow will elaborate on the presence and potentiality of the body in queer comics.

QUEER COMICS

Often in colloquial speech, queer is used to describe LGBTQIA+ identities, or non-normative sexualities and gender identities. Queer is also defined outside of identity, as a verb rather than a noun. Barker and Scheele (2016) wrote that "queering is something we do rather than something we are (or are not)" (p. 14). Gumbs (2016) has defined queer as "that which fundamentally transforms our state of being and the possibilities for life. That which is queer is that which does not reproduce the status quo" (p. 115). In this article, "queer" is used in both of these ways—as a verb, to queer, as in to challenge the status quo, and as a descriptor of LGBTQIA+ content and creators.

Cartoonist and comics scholar Hall (2013) has defined queer comics as "comic books, strips, graphic novels, and webcomics that deal with LGBTQIA+ themes from an insider's perspective... queer comics have been primarily created for their own communities, and they have been neither interested in, nor able to gain, a wider market" (Editor's note). This definition of comics differs from those about queer subjects by straight artists for straight audiences, which have historically been fetishistic and reductive (Scott & Kirkpatrick, 2015). While it is important for LGBTQIA+ characters to be represented within mainstream comics and other forms of media, "it falls to queer comics to dissect queer identities and examine in more profound ways the queer experience" (Hall, 2013, Editor's note). Queer self-representation through comics is an important corrective to stereotyping and erasure in dominant media. Queer cartoonists create characters and stories that represent themselves and their communities as valid, believable, and real. Fawaz (2019) wrote that "Comics is a medium in which anything that can be drawn can be believed" (p. 589), making it an essential medium for queer worldmaking.

There are some key dialectics within the study of queer comics that will be elaborated on throughout this article. The first is the function of queer comics anthologies which offers important visibility for diverse creators and stories while also decontextualizing the origins of that work. There are many more graphic artists than there are single-authored graphic works, especially when it comes to queer comics; therefore, anthologies play a key role in introducing readers to more artists telling more kinds of stories. At the same time, especially for comics that were syndicated in local or independent publications, an active reading community was part of what kept that strip in print; sometimes the actual content of a strip was created in response to or in relation to that reading community. Like listening to a song plucked from an album and included on a "Best of" collection, it is possible to enjoy a piece and discover a new artist, even if that first encounter is devoid of original context. The second tension centers around the derivation of meaning in comics. On the one hand, the creator's agency and individuality are paramount to comics—especially in hand-drawn, hand-lettered work. The author's presence is felt through the style of drawing, writing, shading, color, narration, even the shape of a nose. On the other hand, as some scholars have argued, the author ought to be decentered in favor of the queer reading community that takes up the comic(s). Certainly, one of the most important features of comics is the active role readers must take in the meaning-making process, and queer communities often take up cultural artifacts in ways for which they were not originally intended, which raised an important question: How has this comic been taken up by and circulated within a community in a particular time and place? This article does not resolve these tensions, but it expands on them as important areas of inquiry. The following section takes up the role of the reader in meaning making.

QUEER READERS

More than with other visual art forms, the reader of comics plays an active role in constructing meaning and in the pace and direction of their reading. Comics scholar Køhlert (2019) noted that "the multimodal hybridity of the comics form—consisting, as it does, of multiple overlapping, independent, and often competing verbal and visual codes—creates a distinctively unstable and decentered reading experience that enables the drawn performance of the autobiographical self as a site of ideological struggle" (p. 4). He argued that, in autobiographical comics, the author renders themselves over and over throughout, the sequential form meaning that the self is not singular and not stable. In each panel, the character is drawn anew, and the reader is invited to identify with the multiply drawn self. This decentered reading experience means that comics are a particularly powerful form of media for marginalized communities, allowing audiences to read themselves into the pages in complex and diverse ways. Johnson (2018) argued that comics are powerful because they are enthymematic, but this quality also makes the form unstable: "It is the radical contingency of closure, not its universality, that makes the medium of comics so generative" (p. 6). The reader fills in the gaps—the literal gaps of what is called the "gutter," the space between panels. Comics, in other words, force readers to be highly active in the meaning-making process, and it is this—not universally relatable characters or storylines—that makes the form powerful.

Comics are well-suited for queer stories because the medium allows for an intimacy between author and reader. The thought bubble allows the reader to experience a character's inner world, and comics make it possible to read oneself into the story. The way comics are read, Chaney (2011) wrote, "as a pleasurable alternative to high seriousness, also affords occasions for reader identification with characters and situations that solicit our autobiographical intimacy" (p. 125). This intimacy is particularly significant for queer readers, those who do not see their lived experience reflected in mainstream culture. As Chaney (2011) said,

"Representation of the artist's face in particular...may serve as an icon that elicits identifications with our own image, thereby changing the reader-viewer experience" (p. 125). The reader thus co-creates the story, reading their own on top of or alongside the printed comic. As Chute (2010) explained, "what feels so intimate about comics is that it looks like what it is; handwriting is an irreducible part of its instantiation" (p. 11). Although comics are reproduced through print, they are not translated into type, but remain in their original form. The lines and shapes the creator made on the page are visible. "There is an intimacy to reading handwritten marks on the printed page, an intimacy that works in tandem with the sometimes visceral effects of presenting 'private' images" (Chute, 2010, p. 10). Lewkowich and Jacobs (2019) wrote about the reparative psychic work the reader of comics does, particularly through the unique affordance of the gutter:

> Rather than simply a blank canvas, upon which the reader projects unconscious thoughts, the gutter functions as a liminal space between the concerted influence of multiple aesthetic forces. It is therefore a powerfully persuasive textual gap that, due to its structural indeterminacy—an emptiness that will be, must be filled, but not with anything that can ever be fully or safely predicted—may lead readers to question where the text ends and where they themselves begin. (pp. 25–26)

The gutter is a narrative tool for the creator, and it calls forth the reader's participation like a call and response.

While much of comics studies has, like literary studies, embraced and lifted up a canon by focusing on a set of individual authors, queer comics are both products and reflections of their reading communities. Galvan (2018) theorized queer comics in ways that "shift our focus from canons to the collective practices that shape the production and circulation of queer comics art" (p. 409). She argued that Alison Bechdel's early publishing in New York feminist newspaper *WomaNews* and her fans' engagement with the strip shaped her work, examining "the visual theorizing that her comics perform in dialogue with grassroots networks" (p. 408). Anthologies including *Gay Comix* (1980–1998), *Strip AIDS USA* (1988), *Dyke Strippers* (1995), *Juicy Mother* (2005), *Juicy Mother 2* (2007), *No Straight Lines* (2013), *QU33R* (2014), and *Alphabet* (2016) have collected queer strips and made them available to readers, but in doing so, removed them from their original grassroots publication contexts. Galvan's methodological intervention here is crucial, urging scholars to decenter the individual and foreground the collectivity—the rich context and grassroots network in which any queer single-authored work comes to be. Rhetorical field methods—like participant observation, ethnography, and interviewing—which are embodied and focused on lived experience, offer important approaches to these rich, emergent communities. Anyone who seeks to fully understand a particular artist or strip must attend to the context out of which that artist emerged, how the work circulated, and how reading communities have taken it up.

Comics offer the ability to capture subtle moments, which is very important for queer-identified people because that kind of representation is healing to create and validating to read. Squier (2018) wrote that "Comics have a remarkable ability to embrace and reveal experiential ambivalence and complexity because of their multilayered, visual and verbal, linear and looping narrative capacity" (p. 208). Hatfield (2009) has called comics "the art of tensions." The kinds of tensions queer people encounter in daily life, the complexities and ambivalences that take place in an instant, are powerfully represented through comics. Two of the most basic comics-making tools that enable this simultaneity are the thought bubble and the speech bubble, which enable the cartoonist to depict what a character is thinking and saying (or not saying) at once within a single frame. In comics, time unfolds across space on the page, which means the form allows for microaggressions to be slowed down, shown from multiple angles, and yet still "gotten" by a reader in a moment. As Johnson (2018) explained, "If one of the unique affordances of comics is the capacity to depict embodiment over time, closely related is the power of comics to depict the complexity of emotions at a single moment" (p. 11).

QUEER AND TRANS SELF-REPRESENTATION

The act of self-representation is an important one for queer cartoonists. El Refaie (2012) wrote that the "requirement to produce multiple drawn versions of one's self necessarily involves an intense engagement with embodied aspects of identity" (p. 51). In a comics essay, Councilor (2018) demonstrated this intense engagement with his own embodied identity—importantly without processing through verbal language—that led to his gender transition (figure 1). Comics can be aspirational in this way as well—cartoonists can render their gendered selves without being mediated through medical or social institutions—drawing a squarer jaw, wider hips, clothing that they may not feel comfortable wearing in public. There is the freedom, too, to depict futures that have not yet been realized, to build new, queer worlds. This can be accomplished through other art forms, of course, but it is difficult to match the potency, accessibility, and immediacy of comics. Fawaz (2016) explained, "As a low-tech visual form requiring only pencil and paper, comics allow for the visual depiction of extraordinary scales of existence and embodiment without the need for costly technical special effects" (p. 17). Comics offer the tools for queer and trans people to author and shape their own identities.

The affective component of drawing oneself and others in scenes that unfold through time requires the artist to inhabit, and thus come to understand, each of these elements. Flowers (2017b) argued that "Comic making calls attention to movement and affect in an imaginative

Figure 1. Panel from comic by Councilor (2018).
Source: Councilor (2018). Used with permission of the author.

form of dwelling. By making comics I put myself in a unique and precarious position to experience a liveliness... that carries over into the finished comic. Comics making uniquely requires (re)imagining lived experience through inhabitation" (p. 31). Alison Bechdel famously dressed up as all of the characters in creating her memoirs, taking photographs and then drawing from them. While she quite literally inhabited her characters through dress, posture, and facial expression, this inhabitation happens through the cartoonist's act of drawing on the page. Comics journalist Joe Sacco has said that "drawing is a weird thing because you just inhabit everything you draw. And that means you sort of have to appreciate holding up a bat to hit someone over the head. You have to appreciate holding up your arm to stop the bat. And you kind of have to go through the motions of it so you can get the shoulders right as it turns up.... When you're drawing, you can't put yourself out of it. To get it better you have to be in it. Drawing is harder than hearing it. Drawing is a lot harder than being there" (as quoted in Wilson, 2013, pp. 151–152).

The embodied engagement inherent to the form makes it important for healing and representing the complexities and evolutions of identity, from aging and exploring sexuality to transitioning one's gender. Køhlert (2019) wrote,

> the comics form's sequential nature makes it exceptionally well equipped for the task of representing marginalized selves, because no single image is ever made to stand in for the totality of identity. By visually performing changing and often confrontational selves throughout the pages of their comics, artists can take control of representation and insist on establishing new ways of experiencing and seeing subjectivities and/or bodies marked by the various cultural discourses of gender, trauma, homosexuality, and disability. (pp. 158–159)

Trauma and struggle are common structural and interpersonal experiences for queer and trans people and are often powerfully rendered in comics. Queer self-representation leads to far more nuanced portrayals of queer lives. Cartoonists like Gillman (2020) use comics to express both the pain and confusion of growing up in a world where there were not available representations for who they were and to create those representations. In their comic "Witch Camp," Gillman (2020) wrote, "I'm a queer, nonbinary person, and always have been. I didn't always know it, though. Growing up in a community where words like 'queer' and 'nonbinary' are never talked about, can make it seem like queer, nonbinary people simply don't exist. Except for that persistent, nagging feeling that something's 'wrong' with you" (p. 212). In the images alongside this narration, the narrator as a young person is getting out of the car with a dinosaur on their shirt and nervous look on their face, the Christian camp building looming large in the background; at the same time, a group of girls with Christian fish on their shirts whispers about the narrator, "I don't think that is a girl!" While the text of the comic does not identify the camp as Christian, the repeated drawings of Christian symbols makes this immediately clear. This representation captures the way people experience the world—context rendered through signs, symbols, feelings, and observations that are often not expressed through written or spoken language.

As a growing number of queer cartoonists shares their stories, they provide roadmaps for young queers—names for their strong and perhaps amorphous feelings, role models, and identities to try on. Like Gillman, Brager (2020) also expressed confusion about growing up with minimal queer and trans representation. Their comic "LiveJournal Made Me Gay" begins with the text, "Was your adolescent experience as *confusing* as mine was? I didn't recognize myself in anything I encountered. Most of the ideas I had about queer and trans people came from surreptitiously watching TV in my parents' basement. I kept my finger on the power button just in case" (p. 169). In the first panel, Brager depicts *Queer as Folk* on the TV surrounded by a dark background. A person in a ponytail and glasses has their face up to the screen, finger on the power button, open journal in front of them. It can be quite confusing to understand your developing gendered and sexual self when you cannot recognize yourself in any representations, leaving you to piece together a sense of self using minimal clues (figure 2).

In "When You're Invisible in Pop Culture," Bianca Xunise and Sage Coffey (2020) rendered their conversation about queer visibility in popular culture as a comic, allowing them to nonverbally cite other media texts, like *Mulan* and *Goofy*. The cartoonists' characters begin the strip in the roles of talk show host and guest, then during the conversation, move seamlessly through wildly different settings. They discuss having to piece together their identities, often identifying with the outcast or even evil characters. Sage asks whether Bianca sees herself more in older movies or more recent ones, and Bianca responds, "Honestly I'm on the fence. I see myself here and there but I've yet to see a full version of myself. That's why I write comics" (Xunise & Coffey, 2020, p. 111). A few panels later, Bianca explains, "Often I feel like I have to piece myself together through film and TV" (Xunise & Coffey, 2020, p. 112). She sees herself

Figure 2. Panel from Brager (2020).
Source: Brager (2020). Used with permission from the publisher.

represented in *Moonlight*, but mostly through race—a partial reflection of who she is (figures 3 and 4).

Bianca and Sage speak to futurity, asking, "What are your hopes for our media?" Sage, now lying on the talk show desk, says, "A big thing for me is just having a sincere nonbinary character on screen. I cannot think of a single nonbinary character from a film other than Benedict Cumberbatch's joke character in *Zoolander 2*." Bianca responds, "Yikes." Sage continues, "Also, trans stories that aren't about transitioning and whose identities aren't used as some twist or act of betrayal. Just give me someone who's trans and living their life. They can have conflict, sure but going back to what you said, there just needs to be more than one narrative for these characters!" As the comic concludes, the two characters talk about continuing to hope for representation before the final panel, which is a parody image of themselves within the Warner

Figure 3. Panel from Xunise and Coffey (2020).
Source: Xunise and Coffey (2020). Used with permission from the publisher.

Figure 4. Panels from Xunise and Coffey (2020).
Source: Xunise and Coffey (2020). Used with permission from the publisher.

Figure 5. Panel from Xunise and Coffey (2020).
Source: Xunise and Coffey (2020). Used with permission from the publisher.

Brothers' *Looney Tunes* "That's all folks" circle. The comic is not an expression of hope, however, as much as it is a creation of what they are calling for in the piece. They are calling out their exclusion in the same breath (or brushstroke) as they are writing themselves in. This strip demonstrates the power of comics as a way to write yourself in, to create futures, to imagine, to see oneself and be seen. As their characters shapeshift through the comic, they take of the visual cues—of *Goofy*, for example—to literally show how they see themselves in media portrayals. In this way, they use the 2D form of comics to cite the visual language of popular culture texts, to queer their representations, and to make a case for the importance of widely available queer stories by queer artists (figure 5).

QUEER SPATIALITY AND TEMPORALITY

Comics have been compared to music, the panels representing beats. Eisner (1985) explained, "In music or the other forms of auditory communication where rhythm or 'beat' is achieved, this is done with actual lengths of time. In graphics, the experience is conveyed by the use of illusions and symbols and their arrangement" (p. 26). Brown (2013) pointed out that "while this is true for comics, it is also true of music when represented graphically, as notation must also represent timing and rhythm via space" (n.p.). Lynda Barry is one of many cartoonists who makes this comparison: "Comics are more like music to me than like plain old reading, and music changes the more you hear it because there are so many elements—from lyrics to melody to rhythm to duration in time" (as quoted in Spurgeon, 2008). What the many queer comics anthologies do is effectively create mixtapes, bringing together strips like songs from different decades, genres, and contexts—slow songs and fast, sexy songs and sad ones, bringing together A-sides and B-sides to new readers. Queer comic anthologies can help contemporary queer readers better understand the mindset of those living through the early days of the AIDS crisis, or gay life, dating, and hookup culture before the advent of the internet.

The spatial nature of comics allows for the expression of queerness, which, as Ahmed (2006) rightly noted, is itself "a spatial term, which then gets translated into a sexual term, a term for a twisted sexuality that does not follow a 'straight line,' a sexuality that is bent and crooked" (p. 67). Fawaz (2019) argued that comics is "an art form that constantly asks how sequential visual panels unfolding in space might formally be like the embodied experience of transitioning between genders, like the psychic disorientation of racial double consciousness, like the temporal reality of aging or moving between states of physical ability and disability" (p. 592). The form, then, lends itself to an embodied experience both for author and audience. Cartoonists use visual cues like panel size and shape to speed up or slow down the passage of time across the space of the page. They can merge two temporalities into a single frame, sweep back and forth between past, present, and future. And, importantly, they can set the terms of those timelines and re-orient the story.

Comics are well suited to the nonlinear, nonchronological nature of images, something cartoonist Barry has spoken and written much about:

> In our heads we have it that we're rolling into the future. There's this feeling that there's a chronological order to things because there's an order to the years, and there is an order to our cell division from the time we're a little embryo until we're dust again. But I think the past has no order whatsoever. We think of time, or the past, as moving from one point to another. If you think of these images, they can move every which way, so you don't know they're coming to you. (as quoted in Chute, 2014, p. 77)

The study of trauma has shown that for the body, the recollection of traumatic memory is not remembering the past, but experiencing the present. Freeman (2010) has described queer time as "nonsequential," which might seem to put queer time at odds with the common definition of comics as sequential art. Panels unfold in sequence, which can also function as resistance to sequence. Comics rely on the reader's understanding of the passage of time. Even if the panels on a page are placed in chronological order, a reader may move through the comic in a nonlinear fashion, circling their eye around the page, looping forward and backward throughout the book. They may read it queerly.

Halberstam (2005) wrote that one component of queer time is that it is "about the potentiality of a life unscripted by the conventions of family, inheritance, and child rearing" (p. 2). It is precisely the temporal affordances of comics that makes the form so well-suited for queer stories: exploring and representing the potentialities of queer lives lived on queer time. In comics and in life, queers push back on what Freeman (2010) called chrononormativity, "the use of time to organize individual human bodies toward maximum productivity" (p. 3), synchronizing the behaviors of whole populations around the clock in service of wage work, and state and economic functions. McCullough (2018) argued that Bechdel's *Fun Home* is a particularly potent example of the reparative queer worldmaking possible in the comics form: "the queer temporal openings inherent in the comics form provide a generative medium for queer world making and a potentially reparative one at that; comics' unique combination of the visual and textual allows for the articulation of aspects of a queered temporality that cannot be achieved by other solely visual or textual forms" (p. 378).

QUEER CONVERSATIONS

Comics allow for cartoonists to speak to one another through recreating others' visual languages, and, in this way, images can travel through time and space, from one cartoonist to another. There are many ways that cartoonists cite and speak to one another in their comics, among them crossover character references, book reviews, and copying an artist's style. Jeff Keane, the cartoonist who took over his father, Bil Keane's long-running weekly strip *Family Circus*, drew cartoonist and avowed fan Lynda Barry into the circle in 2017; he created a character of Lynda in the iconic style of the strip but with enough markers of Barry's own iconic look that her fans would recognize the crossover. Trans cartoonist Dylan Edwards has drawn a comic about Alison Bechdel's *Fun Home* in which he draws himself reading the book in addition to recreating one of her panels as he considers how books with bigger publishers are subject to more scrutiny and censure.

In a 2019 piece, cartoonist Nicole J. Georges depicts her interview with Bechdel as a comic. The two cartoonists' characters begin outside of the house where Bechdel grew up, a funeral home and the setting for her 2006 memoir *Fun Home*. Georges uses teal, echoing the color of *Fun Home*'s cover and the interior ink wash, and cites Bechdel's text by redrawing one of her panels in Bechdel's style (figure 6). Bechdel's character explains that she hoped writing the book would help heal her family, that they would finally talk about her father's homosexuality and his suicide. In the second panel, as the two characters begin to walk, Bechdel explains that it didn't. Instead, it was met with critique by her mother about small details, which Georges depicts in the copied panel where Bechdel's mother says, "you got the wallpaper wrong." In the following panels, Bechdel explains that what did bring healing was the experience of watching *Fun Home* as a musical with her brothers and crying together, when it debuted on Broadway in 2015. This queer story, told first in comics, changed form, was told on stage and in song, and now reflected on by another queer cartoonist in an interview. As Georges' comic continues, she explains that Bechdel supported her in the writing process of her own graphic memoir, *Calling Dr. Laura*, particularly about "betraying an instilled family creed of burying all shame." At this point, the two authors are sharing a blanket on the beach. Georges says, "That's why I draw, I think. I didn't feel seen, so I had to reflect my own experience back," to which Bechdel replies, "That's it!" (figure 7).

Georges begins the strip outside of Bechdel's childhood home in rural central Pennsylvania, then as the characters walk, they end up at the beach. While there's no explicit signification for what beach this is, it is quite possible that it represents the California coast, one of the places where Georges lives and works. They discuss not being seen as children, and the power in authoring their own experiences to validate them. Georges merges her memoir and Bechdel's in a single panel, showing each of them as a child (figure 8). Depicting each child in the visual language of the cartoonist, Georges merges two different moments in time and space into the space of a single panel; this narrative choice is highly complex, yet a seamless move in comic form, a fleeting moment in which these queer children, lonely and unheard in their real lives, get to share a space on this page as their adult selves get to do. The piece exemplifies queer community in comics, as Bechdel's work and support enabled Georges to create and share her graphic memoir. They represent two generations of queer cartoonists. In the final panel of the strip, Georges says, "I've come to think of my creative family as my extended family,"

Figure 6. Nicole J. Georges.
Source: Georges (2019). Used with permission from the publisher.

Figure 7. Nicole J. Georges.
Source: Geroges (2019). Used with permission from the publisher.

Figure 8. Nicole J. Georges.
Source: Georges (2019). Used with permission from the publisher.

representing the common queer kinship practice of chosen family. Bechdel echoes her, saying "for many years, the *Dykes to Watch Out For* characters were sort of my family." The interview and Georges's creative visual interpretation of it demonstrate the importance of queer self-representation, and the potential for healing familial trauma through comics.

Georges's comic interview is a reparative text, according to Sedgwick (1997), demonstrating the affordance of comics to visit and own painful pasts and create new potential futures.

COMICS IN THE CLASSROOM AS QUEER FEMINIST PEDAGOGY

Many comics are being adopted as texts for study in high school and college classrooms, particularly graphic memoirs and graphic histories. Expanding encounters with comics has the potential to increase student engagement in learning through both reading and creating comics. As the readership of comics continues to grow in print and online, so will the reach of queer comics, thus expanding their impact. In addition to having students read comics, however, having them draw by hand offers radical potential as a queer feminist pedagogy. Queer media scholar Sender (2020) has adopted creative practices in her classroom, having students create weekly handmade zine pages instead of written reflections. She wrote,

> I want the class to consider what it takes to make a queer world through the kinds of disorientation that creative work requires (being outside our comfort zone, being wrong-footed), to continue to engage theoretically while shifting our locus of perspective.... Queer experience shows us that once we wrench ourselves, or are wrenched sometimes unwillingly, from the well-trodden path, the normative groove, everything becomes reimaginable. (Sender, 2020, p. 134)

Sender's account shows that queer worldmaking is a hands-on, messy, and often disorienting practice. It does not happen through traditional analytical modes of reading texts and writing papers. In classrooms, teachers can create the space for inquiry that is multimodal and complex, giving students the embodied experience of creative engagement toward building new futures.

Hand-producing comics interrupts the typical modes through which students produce academic work (Morrison & Chilcoat, 2002). Sealey-Morris (2015) wrote, "Comics-making, however, is a labor-intensive production, physically and mentally. Encouraging students to produce comics as essays is another means of encouraging students to slow down, to consider the power of their rhetorical productions, and to own their authorship in a more palpable way than typing glowing dots onto a screen" (p. 48). Drawing by hand offers no delete button, no copy and paste, and fundamentally changes the pace at which they are processing and representing ideas. Much of 21st-century academic work—and life—takes place in front of a computer, a tablet, or a phone. Asking students to create material objects rather than digital files requires a multidimensional understanding of the material.

A return to material embodiment can expand the audiences and impact of comics that reflect and share stories of queer lived experiences. The expansion of queer stories by queer cartoonists in mainstream media is important, but might also come with increased scrutiny and pressure to adhere to heteronormative social norms. The queerest and most important comics may be those that are seen only by their creators, or only shared within communities. No matter the scope of their circulation, comics is a powerful means of representing oneself and one's community, of telling queer stories, and building new worlds. Muñoz (2009) wrote that queerness is "a structuring and educated mode of desiring that allows us to see and feel beyond the quagmire of the present" (p. 1), and artists are the visionaries at the vanguard of queer worldmaking. Comics are spaces for building and expanding queer utopias (Fawaz et al., 2017). As Cardell (2014) wrote, "Comics *literally* enable new ways of seeing, new ways of being seen, and new ways of representing the self" (p. 121). In a world that is increasingly in crisis, new ways of seeing and new ways of being in relation to one another are precisely what we need.

FUTURE DIRECTIONS

In addition to the notable pedagogical opportunities for using comics in the classroom and scholarship in comics form, there are a number of directions for research on queer comics. While the interdisciplinary field of comics studies is vibrant and longstanding, there are two significant areas that are underdeveloped, particularly within the field of communication. Certainly, comics provide rich archives for case studies of particular political, cultural, and rhetorical events—political cartoons, public health comics, and newspaper strips provide valuable artifacts for study. Comics are important historical archives for queer communities and increasingly widespread in popular culture globally. More centrally, however, communication scholars have important perspectives and theories with which to analyze comics as a unique form of communication in which image and text are inextricably linked. What might visual communication scholars, who have focused predominantly on the function of images in public discourse, bring to the table in analyses of comics? How might we build on communication studies of other "low" or underground art forms like graffiti, zines, and tattoos, particularly in relation to queer and other marginalized communities? How do comics as an iterative form relate to gender performativity and embodiment? As comics continue to grow in popularity and cultural status, their functions will diversify, and their influence will grow. As is already happening, there will become an increasingly dominant canon of graphic narratives, which will make it important for scholars to pay attention to comics in queer networks and local contexts. There will be increasingly diverse queer representations, making comics an important site for liberatory self and community representation and the continued expansion of gender identities and sexual orientations. In short, queer comics as a multimodal form offer many opportunities for communication scholars in advancing research in the field, engaging students in the classroom, and extending scholarship to new audiences.

FURTHER READING

Barker, M. J., & Scheele, J. (2020). *Gender: A graphic guide.* Icon Books.
Brunetti, I. (2007). *Cartooning: Philosophy & practice.* Yale University Press.
Camper, J. (Ed.). (2004). *Juicy mother: Celebration.* Soft Skull Press.
Cruse, H. (1995). *Stuck rubber baby.* Paradox Press.
Duffy, D., & Jennings, J. (2010). *Black comix: African American independent comics, art and culture.* Mark Batty.
Duffy, D., & Jennings, J. (2020). *Black comix returns.* Magnetic Press.
Mady, G., & Zuckerberg, J. (2019). *A quick & easy guide to queer & trans identities.* Limerence Press.
Sacco, J. (1993). *Palestine.* Fantagraphics Books.
Sousanis, N. (2018). Frames of thought. *PMLA, 133*(1), 154–159. https://doi.org/10.1632/pmla.2018.133.1.154
Szép, E. (2020). *Comics and the body: Drawing, reading, and vulnerability.* Ohio State University Press.
Syma, C. K., & Weiner, R. G. (Eds.). (2013). *Graphic novels and comics in the classroom: Essays on the educational power of sequential art.* McFarland.
Wilson, J., & Jacot, J. (2013). Fieldwork and graphic narratives. *Geographical Review, 103*(2), 143–152. https://doi.org/10.1111/gere.12003

REFERENCES

Ahmed, S. (2006). *Queer phenomenology: Orientations, objects, others.* Duke University Press.
Barker, M.-J., & Scheele, J. (2016). *Queer: A graphic history.* Icon Books.
Barry, L. (2014). *Syllabus: Notes from an accidental professor.* Drawn and Quarterly.

Barry, L. (2019). *Making comics*. Drawn and Quarterly.
Bechdel, A. (2007). *Fun home: A family tragicomic*. Mariner Books.
Bechdel, A. (2008). *The essential dykes to watch out for*. Houghton Mifflin Harcourt.
Berbary, L. A., & Guzman, C. (2018). We exist: Combating erasure through creative analytic comix about bisexuality. *Qualitative Inquiry, 24*(7), 478–498. https://doi.org/10.1177/1077800417735628
Brager, J. (2020). LiveJournal made me gay. In M. Bors (Ed.), *Be gay, do comics: Queer history, memoir, and satire* (pp. 169–172). The Nib.
Bronson, A. A., & Aarons, P. (Eds.). (2013). *Queer zines, Vol. 1* (2nd ed.). Printed Matter.
Bronson, A. A., & Aarons, P. (Eds.). (2014). *Queer zines, Vol. 2*. Printed Matter.
Brouwer, D. (2005). Counterpublicity and corporeality in HIV/AIDS zines. *Critical Studies in Media Communication, 22*(5), 351–371. https://doi.org/10.1080/07393180500342860
Brown, K. M. (2013). Musical sequences in comics. *The Comics Grid, 3*(1). https://doi.org/10.5334/cg.aj
Cardell, K. (2014). *Dear world: Contemporary uses of the diary*. University of Wisconsin Press.
Carrington, A. (2018). Desiring blackness: A queer orientation to Marvel's Black Panther, 1998–2016. *American Literature, 90*(2), 221–250. https://doi.org/10.1215/00029831-4564286
Chaney, M. (2011). *Graphic subjects: Critical essays on autobiography and graphic novels*. University of Wisconsin Press.
Chute, H. (2010). *Graphic women: Life narrative and contemporary comics*. Columbia University Press.
Chute, H. (2014). *Outside the box: Interviews with contemporary cartoonists*. University of Chicago Press.
Chute, H. (2017). *Why comics: From underground to everywhere*. HarperCollins.
Councilor, K. (2018). Drawing the body in: A comic essay on trans mobility and materiality. *Women's Studies in Communication, 41*(4), 441–453. https://doi.org/10.1080/07491409.2018.1556979
Councilor, K. (2019). Standing on the shoulders of Stonewall. *QED: A Journal in GLBTQ Worldmaking, 6*(2), 40–43.
Cox, T. L. (2016). The postwar medicalization of <family> planning: Planned Parenthood's conservative comic, *Escape from Fear*. *Women's Studies in Communication, 39*(3), 268–288. https://doi.org/10.1080/07491409.2016.1194936
Czerwiec, M. K., Williams, I., Squier, S. M., Green, M. J., Myers, K. R., & Smith, S. T. (2015). *Graphic medicine manifesto*. Penn State University Press.
D'agostino, A. M. (2018). "Flesh-to-flesh contact": Marvel comics' rogue and the queer feminist imagination. *American Literature, 90*(2), 251–281. https://doi.org/10.1215/00029831-4564298
Duncombe, S. (1997). *Notes from underground: Zines and the politics of alternative culture*. Verso.
Eisner, W. (1985). *Comics & sequential art*. Poorhouse Press.
El Refaie, E. (2012). *Autobiographical comics: Life writing in pictures*. University of Mississippi Press.
Friedman, R. S. (Ed.). (1997). *The factsheet five zine reader: The best writing from the underground world of zines*. Three Rivers Press.
Fawaz, R. (2016). *Superheroes and the radical imagination of American comics*. New York University Press.
Fawaz, R. (2019). A queer sequence: Comics as a disruptive medium. *PMLA, 134*(3), 588–594.
Fawaz, R., Hall, J., & Kinsella, H. M. (2017). Discovering paradise islands: The politics and pleasures of feminist utopias, a conversation. *Feminist Review, 116*(1), 1–21. https://doi.org/10.1057/s41305-017-0065-8
Flowers, E. (2017a). *DrawBridge* [Ph. D. Dissertation]. University of Wisconsin.
Flowers, E. (2017b). Experimenting with comics making as inquiry. *Visual Arts Research, 43*(2), 21–57.
Freeman, E. (2010). *Time binds: Queer temporalities, queer histories*. Duke University Press.
Galvan, M. (2018). "The lesbian Norman Rockwell": Alison Bechdel and queer grassroots networks. *American Literature, 90*(2): 407–438. https://doi.org/10.1215/00029831-4564358

Gardner, J. (2006). Archives, collectors, and the new media work of comics. *Modern Fiction Studies*, *52*(4), 787–806. https://doi.org/10.1353/mfs.2007.0007

Gateward, F., & Jennings, J. (Eds.). (2015). *The blacker the ink: Constructions of Black identity in comics and sequential art*. Rutgers University Press.

Georges, N. (2019). The Nib interview with Alison Bechdel. *Nib*, *1*(2), 30–31

Gillman, M. (2020). Witch camp. In M. Bors (Ed.), *Be gay, do comics: Queer history, memoir, and satire* (pp. 212–218). The Nib.

Gumbs, A. P., Martens, C., & Williams, M. (Eds.). (2016). *Revolutionary mothering: Love on the front lines*. PM Press.

Green, M. J., & Myers, K. R. (2010). Graphic medicine: Use of comics in medical education and patient care. *BMJ (Online)*, *340*(7746), 574–577.

Halberstam, J. (2005). *In a queer time and place: Transgender bodies, subcultural lives*. New York University Press.

Hall, J. (Ed.). (2013). *No straight lines: Four decades of queer comics*. Fantagraphics.

Hatfield, C. (2009). The art of tensions. In J. Heer & K. Worcester (Eds.), *A comics studies Reader* (pp. 132–148). University of Mississippi Press.

Howard, S. C., & Jackson, R. (Eds.). (2013). *Black comics: Politics of race and representation*. Bloomsbury Academic.

Johnson, J. (Ed.). (2018). *Graphic reproduction: A comics anthology*. Penn State University Press.

Katz, C. (2013). Playing with fieldwork. *Social & Cultural Geography*, *14*(7), 762–772.

King, A. (2017). Using comics to communicate about health: An introduction to the symposium on visual narratives and graphic medicine. *Health Communication*, *32*(5), 523–524. https://doi.org/10.1080/10410236.2016.1211063

Køhlert, F. (2019). *Serial selves: Identity and representation in autobiographical comics*. Rutgers University Press.

Kumbier, A. (2014). *Ephemeral material: Queering the archive*. Litwin Books.

Kuttner, P., Sousanis, N., & Weaver-Hightower, M. (2017). How to draw comics the scholarly way: Creating comics-based research in the academy. In P. Levy (Ed.), *Handbook of arts-based research* (pp. 396–423). Guilford Press.

Lewis, J., Aydin, A., & Powell, N. (2013). *March: Book 1*. Top Shelf Productions.

Lewis, J., Aydin, A., & Powell, N. (2015). *March: Book 2*. Top Shelf Productions.

Lewis, J., Aydin, A., & Powell, N. (2016). *March: Book 3*. Top Shelf Productions.

Lewkowich, D., & Jacobs, N. (2019). A silent production, both of text and self: Conceptualizing the psychic work of comics reading. *Language and Literacy*, *21*(3), 18–37.

Licona, A. C. (2012). *Zines in third space: Radical cooperation and borderlands rhetoric*. State University of New York Press.

McCloud, S. (1994). *Understanding comics: The invisible art*. HarperPerennial.

McCullough, K. (2018). "The complexity of loss itself": The comics form and *Fun Home*'s queer reparative temporality. *American Literature*, *90*(2), 377–405.

Morrison, T., Bryan, G., & Chilcoat, G. (2002). Using student-generated comic books in the classroom. *Journal of Adolescent & Adult Literacy*, *45*(8), 758–767. https://www.jstor.org/stable/40012828

Muñoz, J. (2009). *Cruising utopia: The then and there of queer futurity*. New York University Press.

Noomin, D. (Ed.). (2019). *Drawing power: Women's stories of sexual violence, harassment, and survival, a comics anthology*. Abrams ComicArts.

Palczewski, C. (2005). The male Madonna and the feminine Uncle Sam: Visual argument, icons, and ideographs in 1909 anti-woman suffrage postcards. *Quarterly Journal of Speech*, *91*(4), 365–394.

Schlund-Vials, C. J., & Cutter, M. J. (2017). *Redrawing the historical past: History, memory, and multiethnic graphic novels*. University of Georgia Press.

Scott, S., & Kirkpatrick, E. (2015). Trans representations and superhero comics: A conversation with Mey Rude, J. Skyler, and Rachel Stevens. *Cinema Journal, 55*(1), 160–168. https://doi.org/10.1353/cj.2015.0060

Sealey-Morris, G. (2015). The rhetoric of the paneled page: Comics and composition pedagogy. *Composition Studies, 43*(1), 31–50. http://search.proquest.com/docview/1753216901/

Sedgwick, E. K. (1997). Paranoid reading and reparative reading; or, you're so paranoid, you probably think this introduction is about you. In E. K. Sedgwick (Ed.), *Novel gazing: Queer readings in fiction* (pp. 1–37). Duke University Press.

Sender, K. (2020). Creative practice as queer media pedagogy. In A. Atay & S. L. Pensoneau-Conway (Eds.), *Queer communication pedagogy* (pp. 130–151). Routledge.

Sousanis, N. (2015). *Unflattening*. Harvard University Press.

Spiegelman, A. (1996). *The complete maus: A survivor's tale*. Pantheon.

Spurgeon, T. (2008, June 29). Interview with Lynda Barry. *Comics Reporter*. https://www.comicsreporter.com/index.php/index/cr_sunday_interview_lynda_barry/

Squier, S. (2018). Afterward. In J. Johnson (Ed.), *Graphic reproduction: A comics anthology* (pp. 205–208). Penn State University Press.

Stanley, M. (2010). Drawn out: Identity politics and the queer comics of Leanne Franson and Ariel Schrag. *Canadian Literature, 205*, 53–68.

Tan, S. (2006). *The Arrival*. Hodder & Stoughton.

Todd, E., & Watson, M. (2006). *Whatcha mean, what's a zine? The art of making zines and mini comics*. Houghton Mifflin Harcourt.

Williams, I. (2014). *The bad doctor*. Myriad.

Wilson, J., & Jacot, J. (2013). Fieldwork and graphic narratives. *Geographical Review, 103*(2), 143–152.

Xunise, B., & Coffey, S. (2020). When you're invisible in pop culture. In M. Bors (Ed.), *Be gay, do comics: Queer history, memoir, and satire* (pp. 109–113). IDW Publishing.

Zinn, H., Konopacki, M., & Buhle, P. (2008). *A people's history of American empire: A graphic adaptation*. Metropolitan Books.

KC Councilor

QUEER MELODRAMA

INTRODUCTION

Throughout history, melodrama has centered narratives about women and queer people and has long been popular among marginalized audiences. Melodrama's storytelling, disruption, critique, and potential impacts on audiences render the genre a particularly useful communication tool for marginalized groups such as queer people. Creators across the world have incorporated and reconfigured elements of melodrama for queer stories and audiences. These adaptations of melodrama constitute a subtype of melodrama: queer melodrama, which can be broadly defined as melodrama by, for, and/or about queer people.

Scholarship about melodrama and queer melodrama is deeply interdisciplinary and international, as scholars engage with media from around the world (e.g., Chairetis, 2017; Champagne, 2015; Stewart, 2014; Williams, 2004). Queer genre scholarship remains somewhat limited in communication and rhetoric.[1] Despite substantial contributions from communication and rhetoric scholars in media, television, and film studies, communication and rhetoric scholarship about queer melodrama is exceedingly rare in comparison to scholarly engagement in other fields (e.g., Elliott-Smith, 2014; Kiliçbay, 2008; Pidduck, 2013; Sánchez Vilela, 2020).[2] In addition to scholarship from communication and rhetoric, scholarship on queer melodrama includes works from within the disciplines of film, literature, media studies, cultural studies, and women's, gender, and sexuality studies as well as disciplines associated with specific languages, cultures, geographies, and identities. Queer melodrama appears in various forms and mediums, but most scholarly analyses focus on film and television due to the emergence of cinema (and, later, television) as the primary medium(s) through which the "blood and thunder" stories of melodrama circulate (Singer, 2001, p. 217).

Queer melodrama scholarship is deeply indebted to literary theory, which has been foundational to the study of genre and melodrama. In addition to literary theory, this entry depends on foundational rhetorical genre studies scholarship from Carolyn Miller (1984), Karlyn Kohrs Campbell and Kathleen Hall Jamieson (1978, 1990), and Anis Bawarshi and Mary Jo Reiff (2010). Rhetorical genre studies focuses on how genres "enable their users to carry out situated symbolic actions rhetorically and linguistically, and in so doing, to perform social actions and relations, enact social roles, and frame social realities" (Bawarshi & Reiff, 2010, p. 59).

Scholarship on queer melodrama stands out as a significant resource for understanding queer media, storytelling, and critique. Queer melodrama scholarship consists of two primary areas of inquiry and research. First, most queer melodrama scholarship works to define the genre and identify artifacts within the genre. Second, scholars of queer melodrama scholarship analyze the purposes, benefits, and problems of queer melodrama. These areas of inquiry demonstrate the value of existing queer melodrama scholarship while indicating areas for further research in communication studies.

MELODRAMATIC CHARACTERISTICS, STRUCTURES, AND STYLES

Scholars studying melodrama repeat variations of a common refrain: Melodrama is not simply uniform or easily reduced to a singular definition (LeBlanc, 2006).[3] As with many genres, melodrama itself is difficult to define and prone to a range of interpretations, each centering and decentering different aspects of the genre. Due to the unwieldiness of the genre of melodrama, scholars have often heavily invested in identifying melodrama and queer melodrama. Because "queer" often denotes a marginal or nonnormative positioning that resists categorization, queer melodrama can be even more difficult to define. Indeed, the unruliness of queerness, queer theory, and queer scholarship contributes to such taxonomical and definitional difficulties. Compared to other areas of scholarship, queer scholarship has been more reluctant to prioritize definitional and categorical work. This difference is likely due in part to queer scholars' enhanced awareness of how definitions and categories can be normative, harmful, and limiting. In the face of this, queer melodrama scholarship maintains two primary foci: the queerness of queer melodrama and queer melodrama's relationship to the broader genre of melodrama. This section outlines the three main ways scholars identify and conceptualize melodrama and queer melodrama: generically in terms of characteristics, formulaically in terms of plot, and stylistically in terms of affect and aesthetic. Following the unruliness of the genre, scholars regularly deploy various combinations of these three frames. However, for the sake of clarity, this chapter approaches the three frames separately.

First, melodrama and queer melodrama are generic forms and thus come with expectations of a genre's relative consistency. In other words, works in a certain genre tend to exhibit most of the genre's characteristics most of the time. Defining melodrama generically allows scholars to focus on a loose set of recognizable characteristics while avoiding the potential exclusions that might be caused by other, narrower definitions. Generic definitions of melodrama list common themes, tropes, plot devices, and characteristics associated with the genre. One of the most widely cited scholars of melodrama, Peter Brooks (1976), locates the following themes and plot devices as central to the melodramatic repertoire: "hyperbolic figures, lurid and grandiose events, masked relationships and disguised identities, abductions, slow acting poisons, secret societies, [and] mysterious parentage" (p. 4). Traditional melodramas commonly feature depictions of women, family, home, and passion (Mulvey, 1989). Moreover, melodramas examine relationships and moral questions. Moral themes in melodramas include victims, villains, moral triumphs, and self-righteous endings (Frye, 1957), as well as moral polarization between good and evil (Singer, 2001). This diverse repertoire of characteristics exemplifies the difficult genre-defining work of examining melodrama.

Queer melodramas incorporate queer experiences—like coming out—into the familiar genre of melodrama. Communication scholar Gilad Padva (2004) lists "situational homosexual," "assimilated gay," and "confused teen" as tropes of queer melodrama (p. 357). Netflix's first Spanish drama, *Las chicas del cable* (2017–2020), exemplifies many generic trends in queer melodrama: coming-out narratives, "transgender love triangles, criminal enterprise, and an attempt to kidnap the Spanish King, Alfonso XIII, and force him to abdicate the throne" (Divine, 2022, p. 63). With queer melodrama's emphasis on relationality, plots frequently draw upon romance, community, kinship, and friendship. For example, *Queer as Folk* (2000–2005) deeply values friendships based on respect, affection, support, and loyalty (Cramer, 2007). Queer melodramas engage with morality in terms of interpersonal relationships and societal injustice. Protagonists in queer melodramas are almost always victims of an "evil or morally corrupt society" that denies rights to minority groups (Richardson & Smith, 2022, p. 91).

Second, melodrama and queer melodrama rely upon formulaic narrative features. The most distinctly melodramatic plots are those characterized by a dramatized and tragic climax paired with an eerily pleasant, abrupt, and/or contrived ending resembling a deus ex machina. Such elements may appear in "narratives of coincidence, reverses and sudden happy endings organized around rigid opposition between good and evil" (Mulvey, 1989, p. 73). One primary formulaic plot of queer melodrama involves the anguish of being closeted or outed followed by the simplified resolution of coming out. In queer melodramas, coming-out narratives represent a "pivotal moment in the challenging, but ultimately empowering process known as coming of age" (Monaghan, 2010, p. 56). In queer melodramas, coming out becomes a simplified, one-time event and destination rather than a repetitive process or highly contextual collection of experiences. Such simplified resolutions appear elsewhere in melodrama where there is typically an easy, obvious, or even illogical solution that may require increased or renewed suspension of disbelief from audience members. For example, one subplot in *Queer as Folk* (2000–2005) initially portrays a character's experience of overdose in an anxiety-inducing, jarring, and cacophonous way that seemingly overshadows the event itself. In the next moment, this character's recovery is portrayed as a short-term process with the whole ordeal having little long-term impact on the character or his relationships with others (Johnson, 2013). While the entire show exemplifies queer melodrama, this example homes in on melodrama's dramatization of real, deeply serious issues paired with nonsensically and unbelievably easy resolutions. By directing attention to melodrama's specific combination of types of climax and resolution, formulaic frames for understanding melodrama can help identify the way melodrama differs from other types of narratives like tragedy.

Third, melodrama and queer melodrama can be understood stylistically via the affective and aesthetic excess typically found in melodramatic storytelling. Echoing colloquial uses of the term "melodramatic," melodrama is characterized by intense emotional displays such as "extravagant and rampageous spectacles of tears, cries, and emotional collapse" (Padva, 2004, p. 359). Feminist film scholar Christine Gledhill (1991) describes melodrama as a genre with notoriously excessive expressiveness in the form of "hyperbolic emotions, extravagant gesture, high-flown sentiments, declamatory speech, and spectacular settings" (p. 212). Through these melodramatic affective displays, audiences come to know the characters' essential selves and see the truth within melodrama's fictional portrayals (Brooks, 1976). In this way, melodrama can be thought of as exaggerated and embellished depictions of true and relatable life experiences (Brooks, 1976). For example, *Una mujer fantástica* (*A Fantastic Woman*, 2017) tells of grief, rage, and catharsis following the death of the trans woman protagonist's lover (Popescu, 2022).

The extreme emotionality of queer melodrama primarily manifests in bodily expressions of emotion, aggression, crisis, and desire. Desire plays a particularly crucial role in the affective repertoire of queer melodrama. The extreme, polarized emotions of melodrama "mark and are marked by the vicissitudes of desire" as desire arises and is fulfilled, blocked, or abandoned (Neale, 1986, p. 12). In *Call Me by Your Name* (2017), Timothée Chalamet writhes in lusty, lovelorn agony that exemplifies the bodily expressions of desire and suffering that are often central to queer melodrama. Queer desire persists as a source of commonality or relatable experience among many queer people, and portrayals of such desire can facilitate queer audience identification with media and a sense that they too are represented in media. With a preference for bodily performances of emotion over verbal descriptions or interpretations, queer melodrama invites curiosity and empathy over analytical thinking. Queer melodrama's embodied performances of emotion and desire can be more sexual and erotic than those portrayed in other types of melodrama. By symbolically demonstrating desire and critique through multiple dances, *Una mujer fantástica* exemplifies the style of melodrama in this way as well (Popescu, 2022).

Alongside emotional excess, scholars including Michael LeBlanc (2006) and Margaret Johnson (2013) highlight the role of aesthetic excess in melodrama. The aesthetics of melodrama relates to the meaning of term "melodrama," which combines two Greek derivations, "melo" and "drama," that together indicate a multimedia form that combines music with play and/or action (Rooney, 2013). Aesthetic excess surfaces in the sonic and visual dimensions of media including music and other sound effects as well as rapid cuts, distorted imagery, and camera movements. LeBlanc (2006) builds on David Mayer's (1980) and Caryl Flinn's (1992) work on music in melodramatic film to argue that melodrama centrally exhibits aesthetic excess through music. The Chinese films *Farewell My Concubine* (1993) and *Happy Together* (1997) demonstrate melodramatic aesthetics in their uses of musical and auditory elements from Beijing opera and Argentine tango, respectively (Tan, 2021).

The generic, formulaic, and stylistic understandings of melodrama and queer melodrama offer a foundation for more than identification, categorization, and definition. Engaging with the established characteristics, narrative structures, and affective and aesthetic excesses of queer melodrama also enables scholars to better interpret examples of queer melodrama and grapple with what melodrama and queer melodrama can signify, offer, and do.

DISMISSIVE CRITIQUES OF (QUEER) MELODRAMA

Queer melodrama scholarship is deeply invested in demonstrating the value and potential of the genre. The valuation of queer melodrama counters sexist and logocentric critiques of melodrama that continue to haunt queer melodrama scholarship. Before turning to the purposes, impacts, and problems of queer melodrama, this section provides a brief overview of those dismissive, unnuanced, and prejudiced critiques.

Melodrama is oftentimes considered the "most maligned genre" in Hollywood (Cagle, 2008, p. 85). Popular understandings of melodrama regard it as a genre of "women's film" and as associated with marginalized characters and audiences (e.g., Cagle, 2008; Elsaesser, 1987; Williams, 2003). Negative attitudes toward melodrama derive, in part, from melodrama's associations with marginalized groups as well as judgments about the intellectual capacity and aesthetic preferences of those groups. For example, Ruth Harris (1988) analyzes how critics link the emotionality and perceived femininity of melodrama to fears of hysteria and feminine crimes of passion.[4] Some people use "melodrama" as a pejorative term for any media they do not believe should be taken seriously or as a term that implies "unrealistic, pathos-filled, campy tale[s] of romance or domestic situations with stereotypical characters" (Dirks, n.d., para. 1).[5] Some melodramas include "heavy doses of sex, violence, and emotion" that some critics consider sensationalist or meaningless (Williams, 2003, p. 142). Shallow and dismissive critiques of melodrama frequently depend on logocentrism. Logocentric readings of melodrama consider drama, sensationalism, and emotionality less masculine, deep, meaningful, and/or serious than other affective registers. This type of criticism incorrectly assumes that emotions are frivolous, unimportant, and lacking in purpose or usefulness.

Queer melodramas are similarly critiqued for lack of substance, political engagement, and deeper meaning—issues associated with the sensationalism and emotionality of melodrama. Williams (2003) identifies descriptions of gratuitous sex, violence, terror, and emotion as a common basis for misinformed critiques of melodrama's sensationalism. Queer melodrama is susceptible to similar critiques. For example, some critique *Queer as Folk* (2000–2005) for uncritically portraying sexual promiscuity, drug culture, party/bar culture, and so forth (Cramer, 2007). Like most logocentric criticism of sensationalism and excess, these critiques generally fail to acknowledge more explicitly political content and the potential for the seemingly hedonistic content to critique and comment on such behaviors and cultural concerns within the queer community.

PURPOSES, IMPACTS, AND PROBLEMS

The continual scholarly defense of melodrama as a valuable genre and object of study demonstrates the pervasiveness of logocentric and sexist critiques in popular criticism and academia. A substantial amount of scholarship has articulated significant political defenses and critiques of melodrama and queer melodrama. Queer melodrama scholarship works against critiques of melodrama that render the genre as unserious, apolitical, frivolous, excessively emotional, meaningless, useless, and/or unworthy of rigorous study. Instead, queer melodrama scholarship deeply values the genre's purposes and impacts while also underscoring the problems associated with the genre.

Purposes: Storytelling, Disruption, and Critique. As a genre, queer melodrama is a rhetorical tool. Genre is political and has long been important for communication and rhetoric scholars. As rhetoric scholar Carolyn Miller (1984) famously argued, genre is a form of social action. According to rhetorical genre studies scholarship, genres "dynamically maintain, reveal tensions within, and help reproduce social practices and realities" (Bawarshi & Reiff, 2010, p. 59). The genre of queer melodrama is a rhetorical tool with three main purposes: storytelling, disruption, and critique.

Queer melodrama's contemporary ubiquity and popularity is due in part to its focus on queer storytelling, which contrasts with the many historical silences and erasures in mainstream media (Johnson, 2013). Through queer storytelling, queer melodrama makes queer subjects, desires, emotions, experiences, and meanings legible. Queer melodramas tend to include stories about coming out, being out, being closeted, and/or having various kinds of queer relationships. These narratives provide queer audiences, especially queer youth, representations of themselves, their lives, and their potential life choices (Padva, 2004). For example, communication and media scholar Murat Akser (2016) analyzes the Turkish film *Zenne Dancer* (*Zenne, The Male Dancer*, 2012) which depicts a friendship shared by three gay men who live very different lives. Inspired by true events, the film revolves around three characters: a German photojournalist who lives in Istanbul and lacks familiarity with Turkish values, a "flamboyant, openly gay and proud male belly dancer who enjoys the love and support from his family," and a university student who comes from a conservative Eastern family and "seeks dignity, honesty and personal liberty" but is tragically murdered by his homophobic father (Akser, 2016, p. 7). This example shows that much of the significant disruptive and critical potential of melodramatic queer storytelling stems from the fact that queer stories are frequently shaped by experiences with power and violence.

Melodrama has long been established as a disruptive and critical genre. Melodrama scholarship has persistently stressed the genre's "ability to perform ideological work for mainstream audiences" (LeBlanc, 2006, p. 109). Since the 1970s, feminist film theorists have built upon psychoanalytic theory and Marxist theory to show how melodrama disrupts and critiques the status quo. Melodrama refuses repression and seeks to create disruptive moments through persistent, vulnerable expressions including thoughts and emotions that are often reserved or concealed (Brooks, 1976, 1994).

Queer melodrama disrupts many types of normativity and political projects associated with hegemonic values and institutional power. Queer melodramas primarily push back against (cis)heteronormativity, the process by which (cisgender) heterosexuality becomes the hegemonic standard "for legitimate, authentic, prescriptive, and ruling social, cultural, and sexual arrangements" (Yep, 2003). For instance, *Queer as Folk* (2000–2005) resists respectability politics through its disruptive refusal to "sanitize" or simplify queer cultures or provide respectable role models (Rasmussen & Kenway, 2004, p. 55). By rejecting heteronormative conceptualizations of respectability, the show refuses homonormative assimilation to heteronormative values. Other queer melodramas disrupt cisheteronormativity specifically by carefully attending to the gendered aspects of heteronormativity. One such example is the Senegalese film *Karmen Geï* (2001), which proffers bisexuality as a "complex, queer site that destabilizes stereotyped gender roles and monosexuality" by depicting a bisexual protagonist who disruptively wreaks havoc on other characters as well as audience members (Stobie, 2016, p. 100). Similarly, the Greek film *Angelos* (*Angel*, 1982) is a family melodrama that queers the concept of family with attention to gender and allows the characters to take on a variety of desires, sexualities, and public and private roles. Together *Queer as Folk* (2000–2005), *Karmen Geï* (2001), and *Angelos* (*Angel*, 1982) demonstrate how queer melodrama uses disruption to reveal aspects of hegemonic (cis)heteronormativity that would otherwise remain "opaque, reinforced, and unquestioned" (Yep, 2003).

In addition to disruptiveness that implies critique, melodrama also engages in more explicit criticism. Scholars such as Landy (1991) have argued that critique of society is melodrama's central purpose. Melodrama's social critique is particularly attuned to temporal politics in relation to social change (Cawelti, 1991; Deleyto, 2012). Melodrama commonly performs moral criticism and critiques of violence and injustice, often by using narratives that assign blame, guilt, and innocence. The importance of melodrama is largely due to its capacity to represent culturally significant moral questions (Deleyto, 2012; Williams, 2001). Melodrama's potential for critique makes the genre a particularly useful tool for queer media.

Queer melodrama adopts mainstream melodrama's proclivity for critique and applies it to queer political concerns and moral questions. Queer melodrama critically engages with topics such as gay parenting, drug addiction, party culture, HIV/AIDS, gay marriage, sexual harassment, economic instability, gay clergy, pornography, sexual consent, domestic violence, and trans issues such as transantagonism and needs for affirmative care (Divine, 2022; Johnson, 2013). For example, Heather McPherson, the first out lesbian in New Zealand to publish a collection of poetry, uses queer melodrama to engage with lesbian feminism and critique informed by Adrienne Rich's (1980) critical concepts of compulsory heterosexuality and the lesbian continuum (Lyons, 2019). Many queer melodramas engage in both disruptiveness and critique such as *Karmen Geï* (2001). Here, the bisexual criminal Karmen uses melodrama and dance to critique inequity, the institution of marriage, consumerism, and state corruption (Stobie, 2016). Like *Karmen Geï* (2001), queer melodrama's critique regularly encompasses a variety of intersectional political and moral concerns. For example, Murat Akser (2016) demonstrates how Turkish films featuring LGBT narratives critique bigotry, hatred, and violence. In *Güneşi Gördüm* (*I Saw the Sun*, 2009), director Mahsun Kirmizigül grapples with the "futility of hatred" by telling the story of a Kurdish family's forced migration as a result of decades of ethnic and political conflicts. In the melodramatic film, Kirmizigül positions the death of a transgender drag queen who was murdered for dishonoring their family name in relation to the ongoing conflict (Akser, 2016). These examples of more explicit critique in queer melodrama exemplify the genre's usefulness as a versatile tool for social critique, ideological commentary, and social engagement with moral questions. The purposes of queer melodrama ultimately lie in the genre's ability to use queer storytelling to disrupt and critique (cis)heteronormativity as well as various other institutions, norms, values, attitudes, and behaviors.

Impacts: Awareness, Empathy, Hope, and Imagination. Scholarship about melodrama and queer melodrama frequently presumes creators' intentions and audience members' responses. These claims are especially helpful considering melodramas rarely invoke direct calls-to-action for behavioral or ideological changes. Instead, the emotionality and storytelling within melodrama allow for a wide range of responses including emotional responses, awareness, empathy, hope, and imagination. In rhetorical genre studies, these potential responses may be understood in terms of the actions that genres help people produce (Miller, 1984).

Queer melodrama can elicit emotional responses, which makes the genre especially useful for addressing an audience's potential apathy, ambivalence, or prior ignorance toward a social issue or identity group. Melodrama scholars regularly defend dramatism and emotionality as useful and productive, especially for these characteristics' potential impacts on and meanings for audiences. Melodramas are capable of arousing intense emotional responses (Kaplan, 1983; Landy, 1991). Based on analysis of coming-out narratives in queer melodramas, Padva (2004) argues that the climax of melodramatic plots is a "spectacle of emotional crisis" used to generate a sense of tragedy (p. 360). Melodrama's affective impact relies on bodily expressions of emotion such as tears, which can cause strong, even painful emotional responses from audience members (Duncan, 2011). The disruptive nature of melodrama causes "discomfort with the familiar" and allows audience members to feel "new feelings" (Goldberg, 2016, pp. 26–27).

One of melodrama's greatest strengths is its ability to make the ineffable legible to audiences, thereby generating new awareness or understanding. Melodrama primarily generates awareness and comprehension by relentlessly revealing, amplifying, and exaggerating thoughts and feelings that would otherwise be withheld (Johnson, 2013). For example, *Una mujer fantástica* (2017) "visualise[s] trans liminality on the screen" in a way that may be more comprehensible to cisgender audience members who might be unfamiliar with the concept (Richardson & Smith, 2022, p. 106). The emotional dimensions of melodrama guide audience interpretations and help them focus on the text's main ideas (Johnson, 2013). The drama and emotionality of melodrama can provide audience members with clear, direct, and consistent understandings that other genres may not be able to provide as easily.

In large part due to the emotional dimensions of the genre, melodrama encourages audience empathy for, identification with, acceptance of, and internalization of melodramatic texts, characters, and ideas (Padva, 2004). Queer melodramas frequently invite audience identification with queer and trans characters regardless of audience members' sexual identities or gender identities. For example, *Una mujer fantástica* tells the story of a trans woman named Marina as she reclaims her right to grieve the death of her lover despite the heteronormative and cisnormative rejections of their relationship (Ortiz-València, 2022). By dramatizing emotions and tying those emotions to more general experiences such as grief, queer and trans melodrama makes its characters and their emotions feel familiar, real, raw, and relatable. By foregrounding Marina's emotions, *Una mujer fantástica* makes "the experiences and struggles transgender individuals encounter on a daily basis" not only legible but also relatable to audiences (Ortiz-València, 2022, pp. 33–34). In the process, the film makes trans identification both "understandable and sympathetic" to cisgender spectators (Richardson & Smith, 2022, p. 106).

Queer melodrama also has the potential to generate hope. The hopefulness of melodrama can be attributed to the genre's many formulaically happy endings that contrast with other more emotionally devastating and/or abusive representations. Until the mid-1990s, mainstream portrayals of queer characters in film and television were frequently quite paternalistic and punishing (Padva, 2004). They portrayed "gay and lesbian teens as freaks or unfortunates, perverts or victims" thereby "maintain[ing] and reaffirm[ing] the oppressing gender and sexual dichotomies reproduced by the straight dominance" (Padva, 2004, pp. 356–357). *Love, Simon* (2018) exemplifies the cheeriest of queer melodramatic endings. The film depicts Simon's suffering in the closet, unsatisfied desire for romantic love and platonic acceptance, and experiences with homophobic blackmail and being outed to his entire high school. After Simon comes out to his loved ones and openly pursues his crush, nearly everyone responds with understanding and acceptance, all conflicts are resolved, and Simon and his crush share a kiss at the top of a Ferris wheel while throngs of fellow high school students applaud the new couple from the ground below. Unbelievably happy endings such as this can "demonstrate maturity, acceptance, pride, and happiness" and "express empathy, comfort, and compassion" while "encouraging the young viewers not to feel devastated but to celebrate their gay identity" (Padva, 2004, p. 369).

Queer melodramas can also inspire imaginative audience responses focused on how society could change for the better. For example, Richard Oswald's Weimar German film *Anders als die Andern (Different from the Others*, 1919) is a hygiene film intended to guide viewers to recognize and seek social reform to end the suffering of homosexual men due to prejudice and criminalization (Malakaj, 2017). Media scholar Ervin Malakaj (2017) argues the film is better understood as a "hygiene-melodrama film" or "hygienic melodrama" (p. 218) because the film also uses the stylistic Goldberg (2016) calls "melodramatic impossibility" to inspire viewers to imagine alternative ways of being.[6] In other words, this queer hygienic melodrama goes beyond encouraging empathy to help viewers experience the "possibilities in the impossible" and grapple with the potential for change (Goldberg, 2016, p. 156). In an analysis of the AIDS melodrama *Philadelphia* (1993), Cherniavsky (1998) argues that, despite the devastating ending of the film, the gay HIV-positive protagonist "broaches a new and more hopeful spectrum of melodramatic affect" through his demand for community and recognition (p. 397). Similarly, queer melodramas such as *Las chicas del cable* (2017–2020) focus on community relationships based on care and solidarity (Divine, 2022). This show demonstrates how such communities benefit the female and gender-nonconforming characters and allow them to transcend the nuclear family (Divine, 2022). Together, *Anders als die Andern (Different From the Others*, 1919), *Philadelphia* (1993), and *Las chicas del cable* (2017–2020) illuminate several ways queer melodrama advocates for change by encouraging audience members to imagine something better. Despite queer melodrama's potential to generate emotional responses, awareness, empathy, hope, and imagination, the genre is marked by several weaknesses which are outlined in the following section.

Problems: Exclusion, Normativity, and Assimilationism. Audiences continually rally around queer melodrama as a fresh, hopeful alternative to otherwise harsh, punishing depictions of queer people. Queer melodrama also stands out as a corrective to the outright erasure of queerness and transness as well as portrayals that reduce queer and trans people to subtext, queer coding, innuendo, and normativity. Unfortunately, historically damaging representations provide a low standard for evaluating queer media. While earlier portions of this encyclopedia entry outlined how scholarship regularly refutes critiques of melodrama, many scholars have significant concerns about the weaknesses, limits, failures, and potential harms of queer melodrama. Many of these critiques center around the genre's patterns of exclusion, normativity, and assimilationism.

Although queer melodrama can apply to a plethora of intersectional identities and experiences, mainstream queer melodramas from the United States and the United Kingdom tend to be quite exclusionary. Such mainstream queer melodramas frequently center white, wealthy, cisgender, able-bodied gay men. Depictions of queerness as solely, primarily, and/or centrally intersecting with identities of privilege and power pervade queer melodrama. Thus, the queerness of queer melodrama is somewhat aspirational as varied or fluid queer identities do not appear prominently in the genre. Citing fellow communication scholar Rob Cover's (2000) analysis of mainstream queer films, Padva (2004) argues queer melodrama often presents a "rigid dichotomy between heterosexuality and homosexuality that is contrasted to any notion of real or latent bisexuality or, alternatively, of a sexual fluidity or a sexuality that might be understood along lines other than gender-object-choice" (p. 368). Fewer queer melodramas engage with multiply marginalized intersectional identities, and corresponding scholarship is similarly lacking. For example, queer melodramas and disability melodramas divide sharply and are rarely discussed as potentially overlapping genres.[7] Scholars often address lacking diversity of representation as an aside, such as Johnson's (2013) remark about the "limitations in representation" in *Queer as Folk* (2000–2005) (p. 422). Scholarship about queer melodrama often fails to adequately engage with questions of why or how this exclusion occurs or to what potential impacts. The pervasiveness of these so-called representational limitations reveals that exclusion is not the result of separate privileged creators doing semi-autobiographical work but rather the result of serious, powerful, and alarming systemic and cultural forces. Because representations are limited in most queer melodramas, the genre's positive potential audience impacts are also somewhat limited to certain kinds of queer people. Furthermore, the problems of normativity and assimilationism pair with exclusionary portrayals of queerness to have additional harmful effects.

Queer melodrama can construct a harmful, unobtainable representation of queer normalcy. In an analysis of recent trans representation in Latin American telenovelas, communication scholar Rosario Sánchez Vilela (2020) argues that, in the process of facilitating change, "melodrama organizes, embraces, controls and standardizes" in ways that are "prescriptive and moralizing" and that fail to adequately address hegemony (para. 3). Padva (2004) argues many tropes of queer melodrama such as the "confused homosexual" developed to express "a burning desire" "to be a part of the mainstream, reflecting a more desperate than affirmational attitude" (p. 357). *Love, Simon* (2018) exemplifies the assimilationist thread in mainstream queer melodrama. The film opens with Simon stating in voiceover to the audience, "I'm just like you. For the most part, my life is totally normal" (Berlanti, 2018). While scenes of upper-middle-class suburban life play across the screen, Simon describes his nuclear family including his "annoyingly handsome quarterback" father and "hot valedictorian" mother who were high school sweethearts. In addition to the opening scenes, most of the film focuses on aligning Simon with mainstream, straight, white, suburban normalcy. Queer melodramas often receive public praise for their normalization of queer characters, as was the case with the portrayal of two proud, unnamed lesbian partners within the Turkish thriller *NAR* (*Pomegranate*, 2011) (Akser, 2016). Normalizing portrayals of certain types of queerness and queer people can further ostracize others as unsympathetic or "abnormal."

Much of the normativity of queer melodrama can be linked to attempts to be perceived as relatable and respectable to certain types of audience members. (Berlanti, 2018). In summarizing his opening narration, Simon states, "So, like I said. I'm just like you. I have a totally, perfectly normal life. Except I have one huge-ass secret..." (Berlanti, 2018). *Love, Simon* (2018) normalizes the queer teen protagonist as innocent, shy, sexless, normal, and "just like you...but gay" (Berlanti, 2018). Simon's homosexuality is portrayed as anomalous to his otherwise privileged and normative life. Furthermore, these normalizing attempts to relate to certain straight audiences can erase the complexities of queerness such as when Simon describes his fear of coming out as not "just a gay thing" because "[n]o matter what, announcing who you are to the world is pretty terrifying because what if the world doesn't like you?" (Berlanti, 2018). By reducing the fears associated with coming out to the general fear of not being liked, Simon suggests even straight people are closeted about something and that coming out is a normal, everyday, and even straight experience. This film is a prime example of how queer melodramas remain products of the culture and society in which they are produced and can replicate the very politics they seek to critique (King, 2002).

The normativity of queer melodrama involves expanding existing norms and structures to fit more people and differences while maintaining hegemonic power and requiring at least partial assimilation. In addition to being homonormative, queer melodrama can also be transnormative. In an analysis of the American film *Transamerica* (2005) and the Canadian television series *Degrassi: The Next Generation* (2001–2015), Cael Keegan (2013) theorizes that these mainstream, melodramatic texts have made "transgender difference accessible and consumable" in transnormative ways (para. 28). Keegan argues that transnormativity is "an expression of hegemonic cultural expansion, a sign of the enduring assimilative power of liberal democratic ideology and its gendered logics" (para. 28). Transnormative queer melodramas suggest that "trans difference" can be resolved through inclusion within heteronormative structures (Keegan, 2013, para. 3). Furthermore, transnormativity is offered as an oversimplified solution to the "bad feelings of being transgender" including gender dysphoria (para. 17).[8] Together, exclusion, normativity, and assimilationist politics limit the political power of queer melodrama and increase the genre's potential to cause harm.

CONCLUSION AND OPPORTUNITIES FOR FUTURE SCHOLARSHIP

Queer melodrama centers queer characters, stories, and politics that, in turn, queer the broader genre's characteristics, structures, and affects. Extant scholarship has spent substantial time, energy, and space refuting sexist, otherwise bigoted, and critically unengaged assumptions about the value, meaningfulness, and impact of melodrama and queer melodrama. This is not to say that queer melodrama scholarship is totally uncritical of the genre. Instead, scholars see opportunities for queer melodrama to demonstrate greater critical awareness and have deeper impacts on audiences. Yet, these conversations in and of themselves reflect the already rich potential of queer melodrama. The genre has been heralded as a tool for oppositional queer politics in the form of storytelling, disruption, and critique that encourages audiences to engage emotionally and become more aware, empathetic, hopeful, and imaginative.

While scholars of communication and rhetoric continue to engage with queer genres, communication scholarship has not yet fully attended to the pervasiveness of melodrama in queer rhetoric and media. The political and social dimensions of queer melodrama offer numerous rich opportunities for scholars of queer communication. To further our understanding of how queer melodrama functions and what its capabilities are, more queer communication scholarship is needed in several areas. Scholars of queer communication are uniquely equipped to analyze more thoroughly the limits and weaknesses of queer melodrama especially in terms of the genre's ethics, political potential, and relationships to power. Moreover, the breadth of queer melodramas and scholarship on queer melodramas from various disciplines and from around the world offer scholars of queer communication endless opportunities to engage in transdisciplinary and transnational scholarship.

With an eye toward the future, there are several underdeveloped areas of queer melodrama scholarship that would benefit from future research in communication and rhetoric. Extant queer melodrama scholarship has primarily attended to melodramas about gay, lesbian, and queer people while largely ignoring other sexual and gender identities in melodrama. In response to the dearth of bisexual melodrama scholarship, scholars might build productively upon Stobie's (2016) work. Scholars should continue to explore transness in queer and/or trans melodrama with special attention to foundational work by Richardson and Smith (2022). Disability melodrama and queer melodrama are often explored almost entirely separately, or with only surface-level analyses linking the two. Additional queer melodrama scholarship should draw upon scholarship on disability melodrama in order to explore how melodrama engages with both queerness and disability together. While some scholars such as LeBlanc (2006) and Tan (2021) have attended to visual and musical aesthetics of excess in queer melodrama, rhetoric scholars may be uniquely able to expand this area of research by analyzing the visual and sonic rhetoric of queer melodrama. Communication and rhetoric scholars' continued engagement with affect theory offers additional opportunities to explore the affective dimensions of queer melodrama. In particular, scholars might build upon Keegan's (2013) and Popescu's (2022) work on trans feelings in melodrama as well as Needham's (2010) work on negative affect in queer melodrama in order to critically examine trans and queer melodramas in relation to trans affect scholarship.[9] By exploring these opportunities, communication scholars of queer communication will unfurl the nuances and complexities of this genre and contribute greatly to the future of queer melodrama scholarship.

PRIMARY SOURCES

Berlanti, G. (Director). (2018). *Love, Simon* [Film]. 20th Century Fox.
Guadagnino, L. (Director). (2017). *Call me by your name* [Film]. Buena Vista International.

FURTHER READING

Brooks, P. (1976). *The melodramatic imagination: Balzac, Henry James, melodrama, and the mode of excess.* Yale University Press.
Brooks, P. (1994). Melodrama, body, revolution. In J. Bratton, J. Cook, & C. Gledhill (Eds.), *Melodrama: Stage, picture, screen* (pp. 11–24). British Film Institute.

Byars, J. (2003). *All that Hollywood allows: Re-reading gender in 1950s melodrama*. Routledge.
Gledhill, C. (Ed.). (1987). *Home is where the heart is: Studies in melodrama and the woman's film*. British Film Institute.
Hayward, S. (2012). *Cinema studies: The key concepts* (5th ed.). Routledge.
Kapurch, K. (2015). Rapunzel loves Merida: Melodramatic expressions of lesbian girlhood and teen romance in *Tangled, Brave,* and *Femslash. Journal of Lesbian Studies, 19*(4), 436–453.
Padva, G. (2004). *Edge of Seventeen*: Melodramatic coming-out in new queer adolescence films. *Communication and Critical/Cultural Studies, 1*(4), 355–372.
Popescu, I. (2022). Structures of empathy: Transgender rights, personhood, and melodrama in *Una mujer fantástica. Canadian Journal of Latin American and Caribbean Studies, 48*(1), 1–19.
Richardson, N., & Smith, F. (2022). *Trans representations in contemporary, popular cinema: The transgender tipping point*. Taylor & Francis.
Singer, B. (2001). *Melodrama and modernity: Early sensational cinema and its contexts*. Columbia University Press.
Smith, J. L. (2017). *Melodrama*. Routledge.
Stewart, M. (Ed.). (2014). *Melodrama in contemporary film and television*. Springer.
Stobie, C. (2016). "She who creates havoc is here": A queer bisexual reading of sexuality, dance, and social critique in *Karmen Geï. Research in African Literatures, 47*(2), 84–103.
Tan, Y. Y. (2021). Echo and resonance in *Farewell my concubine* and *Happy together. Ex-Position, 45*, 167–192.
Williams, L. (1998). Melodrama revised. In N. Browne (Ed.), *Refiguring American film genres: Theory and history* (pp. 42–88). University of California Press.

REFERENCES

Akser, M. (2016). Changing LGBT narratives in Turkish cinema. *Reconstruction: Studies in Contemporary Culture, 16*(2), 1–9.
Ang, I. (2013). *Watching* Dallas: *Soap opera and the melodramatic imagination*. Routledge.
Arnold, S. (2016). *Maternal horror film: Melodrama and motherhood*. Springer.
Bawarshi, A. S., & Reiff, M. J. (2010). *Genre: An introduction to history, theory, research, and pedagogy*. Parlor Press.
Brooks, P. (1976). *The melodramatic imagination: Balzac, Henry James, melodrama, and the mode of excess*. Yale University Press.
Brooks, P. (1994). Melodrama, body, revolution. In J. Bratton, J. Cook, & C. Gledhill (Eds.), *Melodrama: Stage, picture, screen* (pp. 11–24). British Film Institute.
Cagle, R. L. (2008). The mechanical reproduction of melodrama: Matthias Müller's "home" movies. In R. Griffiths (Ed.), *Queer cinema in Europe* (pp. 93–104). Intellect Books.
Campbell, K. K., & Jamieson, K. H. (1978). *Form and genre: Shaping rhetorical action*. Speech Communication Association.
Campbell, K. K., & Jamieson, K. H. (1990). *Deeds done in words: Presidential rhetoric and the genres of governance*. University of Chicago Press.
Cawelti, J. G. (1991). The evolution of social melodrama. In M. Landy (Ed.), *Imitations of life: A reader on film & television melodrama* (pp. 33–49). Wayne State University Press.
Chairetis, S. (2017). Negotiating heteronormativity in the family melodrama: A case study of Giorgos Katakouzinos's *Angelos/Angel* (1982). *Filmicon: Journal of Greek Film Studies*, (4), 7–28.
Champagne, J. (2015). *Italian masculinity as queer melodrama: Caravaggio, Puccini, contemporary cinema*. Springer.

Cherniavsky, E. (1998). Real again: Melodrama and the subject of HIV/AIDS. *GLQ, 4*(3), 375–401.
Cornelio-Marí, E. M. (2020). Mexican melodrama in the age of Netflix: Algorithms for cultural proximity. *Comunicación y Sociedad, 17*, 1–26.
Cover, R. (2000). First contact: Queer theory, sexual identity, and "mainstream" film. *International Journal of Sexuality and Gender Studies, 5*(1), 71–89.
Cramer, J. M. (2007). Discourses of sexual morality in *Sex and the City* and *Queer as Folk Journal of Popular Culture, 40*(3), 409–432.
Deleyto, C. (2012). Film genres at the crossroads: What genres and films do to each other. In B. K. Grant (Ed.), *Film genre reader IV* (pp. 218–237). University of Texas Press.
Desilet, G., & Appel, E. C. (2011). Choosing a rhetoric of the enemy: Kenneth Burke's comic frame, warrantable outrage, and the problem of scapegoating. *Rhetoric Society Quarterly, 41*(4), 340–362.
Dhaenens, F. (2013). The fantastic queer: Reading gay representations in *Torchwood* and *True Blood* as articulations of queer resistance. *Critical Studies in Media Communication, 30*(2), 102–116.
Dirks, T. (n.d.). *Melodramas/weepers: Melodrama films*. Filmsite. https://www.filmsite.org/melodramafilms.html
Divine, S. (2022). Melodrama and visual archives of Madrid in *Las chicas del cable*. *Hispanic Issues on Line, 29*, 63–79.
Duncan, P. (2011). Tears, melodrama and "heterosensibility" in *Letter From an Unknown Woman*. *Screen, 52*(2), 173–192.
Elliott-Smith, D. (2014). "Blood, sugar, sex, magik": Unearthing gay male anxieties in queer gothic soaps *Dante's Cove* (2005–2007) and *The Lair* (2007–2009). In M. Stewart (Ed.), *Melodrama in contemporary film and television*. Palgrave Macmillan.
Elsaesser, T. (1987). Tales of sound and fury: Observations on the family melodrama. In C. Gledhill (Ed.), *Home is where the heart is: Studies in melodrama and the woman's film* (pp. 43–69). British Film Institute.
Fisher, M., & Jacobs, A. (2011). Debating *Black Swan* Gender and horror. *Film Quarterly, 65*(1), 58–62.
Flinn, C. (1992). *Strains of utopia: Gender, nostalgia, and Hollywood film music*. Princeton University Press.
Frye, N. (1957). *Anatomy of criticism: Four essays*. Princeton University Press.
Gledhill, C. (1991). Signs of melodrama. In C. Gledhill (Ed.), *Stardom: Industry of desire* (pp. 229–252). Routledge.
Gledhill, C. (1992). Speculations on the relationship between soap opera and melodrama. *Quarterly Review of Film and Video, 14*(1–2), 103–124.
Gledhill, C. (2016). Interview with Christine Gledhill. In J. Metelmann & S. Loren (Eds.), *Melodrama after the tears: New perspectives on the politics of victimhood* (pp. 297–310). Amsterdam University Press.
Gledhill, C., & Williams, L. (Eds.). (2018). *Melodrama unbound: Across history, media, and national cultures*. Columbia University Press.
Goldberg, J. (2016). *Melodrama: An aesthetics of impossibility*. Duke University Press.
Harris, R. (1988). Melodrama, hysteria and feminine crimes of passion in the fin-de-siècle. *History Workshop Journal, 25*(1), 31–63.
Holmes, M. S. (2010). *Fictions of affliction: Physical disability in Victorian culture*. University of Michigan Press.
Johnson, M. E. (2013). "Never the same one twice": Melodrama and repetition in *Queer as Folk Genre: Forms of Discourse and Culture, 46*(3), 419–442.
Kaplan, E. A. (1983). Theories of melodrama: A feminist perspective. *Women & Performance: A Journal of Feminist Theory, 1*(1), 40–48.
Karlyn, K. R. (1995). Comedy, melodrama, and gender: Theorizing the genres of laughter. In K. B. Karnick & H. Jenkins (Eds.), *Classical Hollywood comedy* (pp. 39–62). Routledge.

Keegan, C. M. (2013). Moving bodies: Sympathetic migrations in transgender narrativity. *Genders, 57*, 1–12.
Kiliçbay, B. (2008). Queer as Turk: A journey to three queer melodramas. In R. Griffiths (Ed.), *Queer cinema in Europe* (pp. 117–128). Intellect Books.
King, G. (2002). *New Hollywood cinema: An introduction*. Columbia University Press.
Klinger, B. (1994). *Melodrama and meaning: History, culture, and the films of Douglas Sirk*. Indiana University Press.
Kuhn, A. (2008). Women's genres: Melodrama, soap opera and theory. In L. Spigel & C. Brunsdon (Eds.), *Feminist television criticism: A reader* (pp. 220–234). Open University Press.
Kuzniar, A. A. (1999). Zarah Leander and transgender specularity. *Film Criticism, 23*(2/3), 74–93.
Kuzniar, A. A. (2019). Hesitancy and hovering: Irony, camp, and fetishism in *Mädchen in uniform*. *Seminar: A Journal of Germanic Studies, 55*(2), 94–109.
Landy, M. (Ed.). (1991). *Imitations of life: A reader on film & television melodrama*. Wayne State University Press.
LeBlanc, M. (2006). Melancholic arrangements: Music, queer melodrama, and the seeds of transformation in *The hours*. *Camera Obscura, 21*(1), 105–145.
Lewis, V. (2010). *Crossing sex and gender in Latin America*. Springer.
Lyons, E. (2019). The melodrama of Heather McPherson's "for her thirtysixth year, a breakout." *Journal of New Zealand Literature, 37*(1), 144–158.
Malakaj, E. (2017). Richard Oswald, Magnus Hirschfeld, and the possible impossibility of hygienic melodrama. *Studies in European Cinema, 14*(3), 216–230.
Malatino, H. (2022). *Side affects: On being trans and feeling bad*. University of Minnesota Press.
Manning, J. (2015). Communicating sexual identities: A typology of coming out. *Sexuality & Culture, 19*(1), 122–138.
Mayer, D. (1980). The music of melodrama. In D. Bradby, L. James, & B. Sharratt (Eds.), *Performance and politics in popular drama: Aspects of popular entertainment in theatre, film and television, 1800–1976*. Cambridge University Press.
Mercer, J., & Shingler, M. (2013). *Melodrama: Genre, style and sensibility*. Columbia University Press.
Merritt, R. (1983). Melodrama, postmortem for a phantom genre. *Wide Angle: A Quarterly Journal of Film History Theory Criticism and Practice, 5*(3), 24–31.
Miller, C. R. (1984). Genre as social action. *Quarterly Journal of Speech, 70*(2), 151–167.
Moeschen, S. C. (2006). Suffering silences, woeful afflictions: Physical disability, melodrama, and the American charity movement. *Comparative Drama, 40*(4), 433–454.
Monaghan, W. (2010). "It's all in a day's work for a 15-year-old gay virgin": Coming out and coming of age in teen television. *Colloquy*, (19), 56–69.
Mulvey, L. (1989). *Visual and other pleasures*. Springer.
Murphy, J. M. (2022). Melodrama, William Barr, and the imperial presidency. *Quarterly Journal of Speech, 108*(1), 75–101.
Nancy, R. K. (2022). Genre fluidity as a queer rhetorical practice of activists: A play/chapter in multiple acts. In J. Rhodes & J. Alexander (Eds.), *The Routledge handbook of queer rhetoric* (pp. 346–355). Routledge.
Neale, S. (1986). Melodrama and tears. *Screen, 27*(6), 6–23.
Needham, G. (2010). *Brokeback Mountain* Edinburgh University Press.
Ortiz-València, S. (2022). A fantastic woman (2017) by Sebastián Lelio: A transnational portrait of transgender experience. *Hispanófila, 195*(1), 33–45.
Padva, G. (2004). *Edge of Seventeen*: Melodramatic coming-out in new queer adolescence films. *Communication and Critical/Cultural Studies, 1*(4), 355–372.
Pidduck, J. (2013). The times of *The Hours*: Queer melodrama and the dilemma of marriage. *Camera Obscura: Feminism, Culture, and Media Studies, 28*(1), 37–67.

Popescu, I. (2022). Structures of empathy: Transgender rights, personhood, and melodrama in *Una mujer fantástica*. *Canadian Journal of Latin American and Caribbean Studies*, 1–19.
Rasmussen, M. L., & Kenway, J. (2004). Queering the youthful cyberflâneur. *Journal of Gay & Lesbian Issues in Education*, 2(1), 47–63.
Rich, A. (1980). Compulsory heterosexuality and lesbian existence. *Signs: Journal of Women in Culture and Society*, 5(4), 631–660.
Richardson, N., & Smith, F. (2022). *Trans representations in contemporary, popular cinema: The transgender tipping point*. Taylor & Francis.
Rooney, M. 2013. Voir venir: The future of melodrama? *Australian Humanities Review*, (54), 81–102.
Sánchez Vilela, R. (2020). New wine in old wineskins: The melodramatic matrix of the telenovela and contemporary cultural changes in gender identities. *Comunicación y Sociedad*, 17.
Schatz, T. (1981). *Hollywood genres: Formulas, filmmaking, and the studio system*. Temple University Press.
Schwarze, S. (2006). Environmental melodrama. *Quarterly Journal of Speech*, 92(3), 239–261.
Singer, B. (2001). *Melodrama and modernity: Early sensational cinema and its contexts*. Columbia University Press.
Stewart, M. (Ed.). (2014). *Melodrama in contemporary film and television*. Springer.
Stobie, C. (2016). "She who creates havoc is here": A queer bisexual reading of sexuality, dance, and social critique in *Karmen Geï*. *Research in African Literatures*, 47(2), 84–103.
Strengell, H. (2005). The ghost: The gothic melodrama in Stephen King's fiction. *European Journal of American Culture*, 24(3), 221–238.
Tan, Y. Y. (2021). Echo and resonance in *Farewell My Concubine* and *Happy Together Ex-Position*, (45), 167–192.
VanHaitsma, P. (2019). *Queering romantic engagement in the postal age: A rhetorical education*. University of South Carolina Press.
Velie, A. R. (1991). Gerald Vizenor's Indian Gothic. *Melus*, 17(1), 75–85.
Williams, L. (1998). Melodrama revised. In N. Browne (Ed.), *Refiguring American film genres: Theory and history* (pp. 42–88). University of California Press.
Williams, L. (2001). *Playing the race card: Melodramas of black and white from Uncle Tom to O. J. Simpson*. Princeton University Press.
Williams, L. (2003). Film bodies: Gender, genre, and excess. In B. K. Grant (Ed.), *Film genre reader III* (pp. 141–159). University of Texas Press.
Williams, L. (2004). Melancholy melodrama: Almodóvarian grief and lost homosexual attachments. *Journal of Spanish Cultural Studies*, 5(3), 273–286.
Yep, G. A. (2003). The violence of heteronormativity in communication studies: Notes on injury, healing, and queer world-making. *Journal of Homosexuality*, 45(2–4), 11–59.

NOTES

1. For examples of queer communication scholarship about other queer genre(s), see Dhaenens (2013), Nancy (2022), and VanHaitsma (2019).
2. Most communication and rhetoric scholarship that engages with the concept of melodrama relies substantially on Kenneth Burke's category of melodrama in order to analyze political discourse and public address (e.g., Desilet & Appel, 2011; Schwarze, 2006). For an analysis that engages a wide range of melodramatic scholarship in order to analyze the melodramatic mode in traditional, nonfictional rhetoric, see Murphy (2022).
3. Melodrama is sometimes erroneously conflated with the subgenre of "family melodrama" (Williams, 1998). Elsaesser (1987), Schatz (1981), and Williams (1998) offer foundational works on family

melodrama specifically. Broad and loose conceptualizations of melodrama have resulted in the use of "melodrama" as a sort of umbrella term (LeBlanc, 2006; Mercer & Shingler, 2013; Merritt, 1983). For a critique of perfunctory uses of the term "melodrama," see Neale (1986).
4. For melodrama scholarship centering masculinity, see Champagne (2015).
5. For more on melodrama and camp, see Kuzniar (1999, 2019) and Klinger (1994).
6. Melodrama scholarship frequently links melodrama to various genres such as the gothic genre (Elliott-Smith, 2014; Strengell, 2005; Velie, 1991), thrillers (Cornelio-Marí, 2020; Lewis, 2010), horror (Arnold, 2016; Fisher & Jacobs, 2011), romance (Gledhill, 1992; Padva, 2004), comedy (Cornelio-Marí, 2020; Karlyn, 1995), Western (Needham, 2010), and soap opera (Ang, 2013; Gledhill, 1992; Kuhn, 2008). For more information on melodrama as a "transgeneric mode," see Gledhill and Williams (2018). For more on the queerness of genre fluidity, see Nancy (2022).
7. For more information on disability melodrama, see Holmes (2010) and Moeschen (2006).
8. Oversimplification is somewhat common in queer melodrama and can be linked to victim-blaming of queer and trans protagonists. See Padva's (2004) work on coming out and closetedness portrayed as moral failure and Richardson and Smith's (2022) work on a trans protagonist's transition being portrayed as selfish and harmful to a cisgender secondary character.
9. See Hil Malatino (2022) for more on negative affect and trans experience.

Cora Butcher-Spellman

QUEER MEMORY AND FILM

MEMORY AND THE MEDIA: A GENERAL INTRODUCTION

When contemplating the matter of queer memory and how it is shaped by the screen, it is first necessary to take into account how the very notion of memory has been transformed by memory studies scholars from an individual to a collective matter. For scholars such as Maurice Halbwachs (1952/1992), most commonly considered the field's founding father, the concept of memory could be thought of not only with reference to the individual and their personal recollections, but rather as a way of describing how social groups and nations conceive of their own past—which stories they tell about their own history, and which present needs these stories serve. Far from being an objective document of the past, what Halbwachs terms "collective memory" can thus be considered an issue of both emotional and political relevance to the social group to which it pertains. He therefore argues that "the past is not preserved but is reconstructed on the basis of the present" (Halbwachs, 1952/1992, p. 40), therein pointing toward the ways in which a group's collective memory is continually remade anew. Moreover, such continually created collective memories play a key role in inspiring a sense of belonging and collectivity among social groups, and in crafting the very "imagined communities" which Benedict Anderson (1986/2006) points to as the basis of nation-states.

In turn, memory can be passed on among different generations via different methods, ranging from interpersonal contact (the generational dynamics of which have been perceptively encapsulated in Marianne Hirsch's (1999) concept of "postmemory," which she uses to describe the ways in which younger generations internalize the traumatic memories of their forebears), to what Pierre Nora (1989) has termed *lieux de mémoire* or "sites of memory," which range from physical monuments and archives, to less palpable but affectively powerful methods such as a minute of silence. Of particular relevance to this article is the potential of media such as film to serve as memory sites, and therein to influence how viewers think of the past. As numerous memory studies scholars have noted (Edgerton, 2001; Grainge, 2003; Landsberg, 2004; Sturken, 1997), it is the widespread nature of technologies like cinema and television among millions of people, as well as the immersive and affectively powerful nature of the mediums, that enables them to have a particular influence on audiences. For Marita Sturken (1997, p. 9), film and television are thus "technologies of memory, not vessels of memory on which memory passively resides so much as objects through which memories are shared, produced, and given meaning." While the affective potency of the medium has prompted writers such as Michel Foucault (1975) to warn of the negative influence of cinema, others have emphasized its potential to move beyond group lines, and to create memories in the viewer which they could not have accessed through interpersonal contact. In this regard, the work of Alison Landsberg (2004) is of particular importance, with Landsberg's concept of "prosthetic memory" describing the particular qualities of memory formed through one's engagement with such media. She writes that:

> Prosthetic memory, then, rejects the notion that all memories—and, by extension, the identities that those memories sustain—are necessarily and substantively shaped by lived social context. Prosthetic memories are not "socially constructed" in that they do not emerge as the result of living and being raised in particular social frameworks. At the same time, prosthetic memories are transportable and hence not susceptible to biological or ethnic claims of ownership.... These memories, like an artificial limb, are actually worn on the body; these are sensuous memories produced by an *experience* of mass-mediated representations.... Calling them "prosthetic" signals their interchangeability and exchangeability and underscores their commodified form. (Landsberg, 2004, pp. 19–20)

Through commenting both on the commodification of filmic and televisual memory, as well as the potential of such commodified memory to cross group borders, Landsberg's work describes the complex dynamics inherent in mediated memory representation. On the one hand, these representations have the potential to uphold heterosexist, nationalist visions of the past. On the other, they also have the potential to present visions of the past which do not stem from the viewer's own social group, and therein to inspire identification and empathy toward these groups. While not specifically focused on queer memory, Landsberg's concept of prosthetic memory nonetheless illustrates the potential relevance of filmic and televisual memory representation for minority communities.

QUEER MEMORY AND THE SCREEN

As has been noted, lesbian, gay, bisexual, transgender, and queer (LGBTQ) histories have often been and continue to be systematically and deliberately excluded from the "official" memory narratives of nation-states, whether it be within the context of education or other commemorative projects (Dunn, 2016; Horvat, 2021). Moreover, as a group whose very survival has often depended on going unnoticed (Dunn, 2016; Muñoz, 1996), LGBTQ people have not often been allowed the luxury of preserving the memories of their communities. In spite of this, the desire to preserve LGBTQ histories has led many activists and academics to queer historiographic work, creating community archives, as well as unprecedented commemorative projects such as the NAMES Project AIDS Quilt, composed of 48,000 individual panels, each sewn in memory of a person who has died of AIDS. It is therefore relevant here to note the difference between work on historiography and that on memory, as these often-overlapping concepts can nonetheless be distinguished by historiography's focus on the realities of the past, the historical permutations of sexuality, and how they are now documented by historians, while memory has more to do with how the past is represented and (mis)remembered outside the discipline of history, as well as the present function these memories serve (Assmann, 2006; Lowenthal, 1985).

While this article will focus in detail on the relationship between queer memory and the screen, it is relevant to note that memory has been an underutilized concept within the different branches of queer studies, with authors often privileging concepts such as the archive (Cvetkovich, 2013), nostalgia (Kies & West, 2017; Padva, 2014), temporality, and futurity (Dinshaw, 1999; Edelman, 2004; Freccero, 2006; Freeman, 2010; Halberstam, 2005; Muñoz, 2009). Work which does privilege the concept of memory has nonetheless focused on a diverse array of issues, looking at how queer histories are forgotten, remembered, and commemorated in archives (Cram, 2015, 2016a, 2016b), in public space and education (Dunn, 2016), as well as how activist action is being remembered (Morris, 2011). Authors looking specifically at queer memory in relationship with the cinema have predominantly done so in single case studies and book chapters (Bao, 2020; Brunow, 2019; Cheng, 2016; Jelača, 2016; Kagan, 2013; Shahani, 2012), with particular auteurs such as Pedro Almodóvar (Gutiérrez-Albilla, 2013; Ibáñez, 2013; Melgosa, 2013), Isaac Julien (Bravmann, 1993; Freeman, 2010; Summers, 2016), and Cheryl Dunye (Horvat, 2021; Reid-Pharr, 2006; Richardson, 2011; Sullivan, 2000; Wills Foote, 2007) receiving a notable amount of scholarly attention with respect to how they engage with the past. Monographs on the subject of queer memory which also deal with cinema have been rare, with the exception of Castiglia and Reed's (2012) work on gay male memory in *If Memory Serves: Men, AIDS, and the Promise of the Queer Past*, which focuses on numerous types of memory sites including film and television; Scott McKinnon's (2016) *Gay Men at the Movies: Cinema, Memory and the History of a Gay Male Community*, which analyses the memories of a group of gay cinemagoers in Sydney, Australia; and the monograph *Screening Queer Memory: LGBTQ Pasts in Contemporary Film and Television* (Horvat, 2021), which presents the first book to undertake a sustained analysis of how film and television have themselves represented and commented on queer memory. This section will thus map how these authors have addressed the subject, as well as looking at how specific case studies have looked at particular examples of queer onscreen memory.

In their work on gay male memory in *If Memory Serves*, Castiglia and Reed (2012) argue that queer culture is subject to what they term "degenerational unremembering"; a term they use to denote conservative and homonormative approaches which seek to demonize the sexual freedom which marked gay communities prior to the advent of AIDS. In their analysis of the U.S. context, Castiglia and Reed (2012, p. 40) argue that

> the years following the onset of the AIDS epidemic witnessed a discursive operation that instigated a cultural forgetting of the 1960s and 1970s, installing instead a cleaned-up

memory that reconstitutes sanctioned identity out of historical violence...turning gays and lesbians into a "respectable" (fit for assimilation) constituency.

Within such a context, Castiglia and Reed (2012, p. 2) locate cinema and television as a way to fight back against this "assault on gay memory" through creating resources of gay counter-memory, noting how films such as *Longtime companion* (1989), *The dead boys' club* (1992), and *Milk* (2008) engage with the past in ways which do not seek to erase or deprecate the sexual liberation of the pre-AIDS era.

While Castiglia and Reed's work emphasizes the deliberate forgetting of pre-AIDS cultures, Scott McKinnon's (2016) *Gay Men at the Movies* examines the history of gay male cinema-going in Sydney, tracing both how the landscape of the city's cinemas has changed throughout the decades, as well as how he himself and the men he interviews remember formative examples of gay cinema and acts of cinema-going. McKinnon's book thus points toward the importance of studying queer audience recollections, with its examination of the role film played in the lives of gay men presenting an important step toward a broader interrogation of LGBTQ audience memories. As the book argues, films can not only form the focus of deeply personal memories of perceiving one's own sexuality, but the social experience of seeing them also creates deeply relevant memories of either social belonging or exclusion. Both he and his interviewees therefore look back at their own memories of cinema, their own relationship to the broader homophobic context in which these memories are enclosed, as well as the changing technologies which have affected how and where films are consumed. The book therefore approaches memory primarily through the lens of historiography, audience studies and auto-ethnography, with its final chapters also pointing toward the relevance of queer historical cinema such as *Alexander* (2004) and *Milk* (2008) due to how it reimagines queer histories.

While Castiglia, Reed, and McKinnon all focus on gay male memory, *Screening Queer Memory* (Horvat, 2021) looks more broadly at how cinema and television have represented LGBTQ histories, therein both commenting on and creating queer memory.[1] It argues that the particular relevance of media such as film and television as technologies of queer memory stems not only from the ways in which histories have often been systematically excluded from more officially sanctioned narratives of history (such as national curricula or commemorative projects (Dunn, 2016)), but from the lack of intergenerational contact (Russell & Bohan, 2005) which marks the LGBTQ community more broadly. On the one hand, the family is often not a safe space for queer individuals (Schulman, 2009), with LGBTQ histories often being deliberately omitted from familial memory (Gelfand, 2018) instead of being passed on from generation to generation. On the other hand, the "chosen families" formed within LGBTQ communities are often formed among individuals from the same generation, leading to a diminished contact between community "elders" and younger queer individuals. As Russell and Bohan (2005) have argued, in LGBTQ communities, "contacts between youths and elders are not an intrinsic element of social systems [as these] tend to be age-segregated (youths cannot go to bars; adults cannot participate in youth coming-out groups)" (p. 2). Such generational segregation is thus deemed by researchers like Russell and Bohan as precisely what differentiates LGBTQ communities from other minority communities such as those formed along ethnic, racial, national, or religious lines, though the LGBTQ community will, of course, find itself formed along multiple intersections of these communities. This generational segregation carries particular implications with respect to the passage of memory from one generation of queers to another, with LGBTQ people therefore being forced to look elsewhere in order to be able to find what can be termed queer memory.

The particular importance of media such as film and television for the construction of queer memory therefore stems not only from the ways in which LGBTQ memory has been excluded from national memory narratives, but also from the generational segregation which impedes the passage of memory from one generation of queers to another. As *Screening Queer Memory* argues, "this does not mean that cinema and television are the sole channels through which queer memory is passed on, with LGBTQ groups working diligently to preserve and excavate their histories, and creating numerous community archives" (Horvat, 2021, p. 6). In spite of this, community archives and LGBTQ history books usually require a person to deliberately seek them out, "while cinema and television function as technologies of memory a person can even stumble upon accidentally" (Horvat, 2021, p. 6), therein making certain cinematic works a far more accessible sources of memory than, for example, community archives usually located in large urban centers, many of which have yet to be digitized. The fact that queer cinema so often engages with and reimagines LGBTQ pasts thus points toward the relevance of understanding how it comments on the construction of queer memory, as well as what sort of visions of the past it promotes, particularly in relation to the history of queer activism.

It is worth noting here the importance attributed to queer memorial cinema and television by activists and viewers, as is, for example, evident from the boycott of the film *Stonewall* (2015) due to its marginalizing approach to trans and lesbian BAME (Black, Asian, and minority ethnic) activists who had been crucial to the Stonewall Riot (Horvat, 2021). Moreover, the showrunners behind these projects often speak explicitly of their work as an intervention into LGBTQ memory, noting a "lack" of memory within the community as an impetus for their work. For example, director David Weissman (2010) has positioned his own documentary on the U.S. AIDS crisis *We were here* as a response to the lack of history which permeates LGBTQ communities, arguing that "in families and in ethnic groups, history is passed on from generation to generation ... we don't have that as queers, we don't have any direct lineage from older queers to younger queers" (Kagan, 2013, p. 151). Similarly, when commenting on the relevance of his series *Pose*, which depicts trans ballroom communities during the AIDS crisis, Ryan Murphy has argued that "we," as LGBTQ people, "have very little history. All of the men who would probably be our mentors were taken away at the prime of their life.... What I'm trying to do with a lot of my work is leave a living history and educate people" (Bentley, 2018). While Murphy's gendered notion of queer memory stands in conflict with the mainly female protagonists of *Pose*, what binds both of these statements together is the conscious use of film and television as technologies of queer memory; as interventions into what both directors perceive as a lack of memory within the community.

While projects which reimagine LGBTQ pasts have for long been a part of queer cinema and television, with films like *Strawberry and Chocolate* (*Fresa y Chocolate*, 1993), *Aimée & Jaguar* (1999), the oeuvre of Derek Jarman (Parsons, 2014; Tweedie, 2003), and the New Queer Cinema movement (Aaron, 2006) all displaying a marked preoccupation with the past, there has nonetheless been a particular preponderance of such projects in the 21st century (Horvat, 2021; Ryberg, 2020). Examples of this include films such as *Carol* (2015),

Battle of the Sexes (2017), *Call Me by Your Name* (2017), *The Happy Prince* (2018), *Colette* (2018), *The Miseducation of Cameron Post* (2018), *Lizzie* (2018), *Rocketman* (2019), and *Ammonite* (2020), all of which reimagine different time periods from queer vantage points. Moreover, as exemplified by the Swedish *The Circle* (*Der Kreis*, 2014), the South Korean *Handmaiden* (*Ah-ga-ssi*, 2016), the Finnish *Tom of Finland* (2017), the French *120 Beats per Minute* (*120 battements par minute*, 2017) and *Portrait of a Lady on Fire* (*Portrait de la jeune fille en feu*, 2019), this tendency of cinematic looking back is anything but limited to one cinematic region, but is rather a distinctly transnational trend.

Work looking at specific national cinemas and how these depict queer memory can sometimes be found within larger studies of particular regions, as is, for example, the case with Dijana Jelača's (2016) work on memories of trauma in the cinema of former Yugoslavian countries, which also explores the connection between national memory and queerness. For Jelača, films such as Želimir Žilnik's *Marble Ass* (Serbia, 1995), Dalibor Matanić's *Fine Dead Girls* (Croatia, 2002), and Ahmed Imamović's *Go West* (Bosnia, 2005) are particularly significant as they engage "in the establishment of affective regimes by which to deny the primacy of heteronormative understandings of and responses to trauma" (Jelača, 2016, p. 104). Differently put, they subvert the expectation that national memory can be conceived of only through a heteronormative lens, therein addressing the question of trauma and memories of war through focusing on LGBTQ protagonists. Drawing from this, it is clear that work looking at specific national cinemas and how they address queer memory is indispensable in order to gain a broader understanding of how LGBTQ memory is constructed through and in film.

MEMORY AND NOSTALGIA

In looking at how cinema has represented the queer past, some authors (Kies & West, 2017; Padva, 2014, 2017; Windle, 2016) have preferred to utilize the theoretical lens of nostalgia instead of memory. Gilad Padva's (2014) *Queer Nostalgia in Cinema and Popular Culture* is here particularly relevant, with Padva's monograph looking at films such as *Velvet Goldmine* (1998), *Looking for Langston* (1989), and *Brother to Brother* (2004) in order to examine the nostalgic pleasure these films find in the past. In a 2017 special issue of *Queer Studies in Media and Popular Culture*, editors Bridget Keis and Thomas J. West also ask "why popular media [is] so eager to turn to the past to tell stories about queer people and for whom these stories were being told" (Kies & West, 2017, p. 161), therein arguing for nostalgia as the best theoretical lens through which this cinematic focus can be explored. While nostalgia has been criticized for presenting an idealized version of the past and for lacking objectivity, Padva (2014) argues for its reparative potential, both with respect to how we experience the present and the future. For Padva, cinematic "nostalgia is useful precisely because it glorifies yesterday's successes, victories, struggles, braveness, and devotedness and can stimulate reconsideration of the past *and* the future. In this respect," he argues, "nostalgia, especially for discriminated and persecuted minorities, is like a beacon, a ray of light in the darkness... [and] encourages optimism because it revives the pursuit of happiness and inspires resistance to the horrors of the present" (Padva, 2014, p. 228). Thus, while some authors have dismissed nostalgia as regressive and politically reactionary, Padva finds virtue in precisely nostalgia's idealized approach to the past, arguing on behalf of its creative and political potential. He argues that:

Nostalgia does not necessarily hide or underestimate painful history, however, but rather plays its own part in mediating and modifying the past in order to make it more bearable. In this respect, nostalgia is not about denial of reality and its sordid experiences, but rather about new horizons and recollection of valuable heroes and positive occurrences that encourage pride and faith in the community's own legacy and power. (Padva, 2014, pp. 228–229)

As this approach to nostalgia shows, the concept of nostalgia differs from memory with respect to its approach to the past and how it is represented. While nostalgia describes a romanticized version of the past that can, for authors like Padva, serve as a source of resilience for the future, memory is a broader term, therein encompassing both nostalgic and traumatic recollections (Horvat, 2021; Padva, 2014). As such, while both concepts share an emphasis on affect, as well as a consequent lack of objectivity, they cannot be used interchangeably due to their differing approach to the past. Nonetheless, both authors working on queer nostalgia (Padva, 2014) and those whose work has focused more on memory (Muñoz, 2009) have stressed the positive potential of imaginative engagement with the past with respect to both the present, and for queer futurity. As Jose Esteban Muñoz writes in his own work on queer utopia, "our remembrances and their ritualized tellings—through film, video, performance, writing, and visual culture [have] world-making potentialities [and can therefore be useful resources to] help us carve out a space for actual, living sexual citizenship" (Muñoz, 2009, p. 35). This is particularly relevant with respect to cinematic commemorations of LGBTQ activism and their potential to influence collective political action (Horvat, 2021), as shall be seen in more detail in the next section "Queer Activist Memory and the Screen."

QUEER ACTIVIST MEMORY AND THE SCREEN

The documentary genre has for long retained a particular importance with respect to how the past of queer activism has been memorialized. Whether it be formative queer documentaries such as the Oscar-winning *The Times of Harvey Milk* (1984) and *Before Stonewall* (1984), or later works such as *We Were Here* (2010), *How to Survive a Plague* (2012), and *United in Anger: A History of ACT UP* (2012), all of which depict the history of the AIDS crisis in the United States and the queer activism which responded to it, the documentary genre has consistently offered viewers a chance to engage with the history of LGBTQ political action. While American documentaries tend to receive the most media attention, transnational cinema and television has also continued to document queer history, with works such as the British *Prejudice and Pride: The People's History of LGBTQ Britain* (BBC, 2017), the Chilean *Lemebel* (2019), the Argentinian *Carlos Jauregui: The Unforgettable Fag* (*El Puto Inolvidable*, 2019), and Spanish documentary series *We Are* (*Nosotrx Somos*, 2018) tracing the development of LGBTQ rights movements and the lives of specific activists in their respective contexts. In contrast to the considerable number of documentary works presenting the LGBTQ past, historical dramas based on queer activism have been few and far between, with a greater number of such works only being made since the success of Gus Van Sant's *Milk* (2008). Prominent dramatizations of queer political action can thus be found in films such as Robin Campillo's *120 Beats Per Minute* (*120 battements par minute*, 2017), Matthew Warchus' *Pride* (2014),

Roland Emmerich's much-critiqued *Stonewall* (2015), and Stefan Haupt's docudrama *The Circle* (*Der Kreis*, 2014).

In both documentaries and historical dramas, the question of how the past is represented, whose activism takes center-stage, and how this depicts the LGBTQ rights movement is paramount (Horvat, 2021). Critical work examining these films and television series has thus often focused on specific cinematic works and has examined how faithfully they present the past, as well as which activist histories get left out (Als, 2009; Bao, 2020; Bronski, 2009; Cheng, 2016; Dillard, 2017; Lenon, 2013; Valdivia, 2010). Such academic work raises questions about what types of narratives about the queer past are being promoted by these films, often paying particular attention to what types of present needs these narratives serve. For example, a number of authors have looked at Van Sant's *Milk* in order to assess its portrayal of the activist, with Michael Bronski (2009) arguing that the film misrepresents Milk as a *sui generis* activist, therein minimizing the role of other activists who composed the movement in the same period. For Bronski,

> *Milk* fails politically because it sacrifices and substitutes the communal work of political organizing with the false image of a gay political savior and martyr, [therein negating or obscuring] the work of multitudes of gay activists who did make change happen. (Bronski, 2009, p. 73)

While other writers analyzing *Milk* did not have quite the same assessment of the film, a number of authors did note the ways in which it minimizes the role of women (Als, 2009) and activists of color (Dillard, 2017; Lenon, 2013; Valdivia, 2010), therein raising the question of the relative (un)importance attributed to activists who were not white gay men within the scope not only of Van Sant's film, but queer commemorative cinema more broadly (Horvat, 2021).

Work on representations of activist memory has focused on the narrative trends marking U.S. and U.K. dramatizations of queer activism (Horvat, 2021), and has looked at which types of narratives are likely to be granted attention, and whose activism is more likely to be forgotten. Since the making of *Milk*, it is possible to observe in historical drama a distinct shift from privileging only the story of one activist, to a more collectivist approach in films like *Pride* and *120 BPM*, both of which center on the activism of multiple individuals, therein depicting the collectivity of the queer rights movement. At the same time, the question of *whose* activism is depicted remains vital, as some representations nonetheless continue privileging the activism of white gay men, while marginalizing the political work of other members of the LGBTQ community. In doing so,

> representations of queer activist history as a white, male, monosexual and cisgendered endeavour risk obfuscating the ways in which women, transgender men, and people of other races and ethnicities have shaped LGBTQ history, therein relegating them to a secondary role in the movement's present as well as its past. (Horvat, 2021, p. 105)

The tendency of privileging the activism of white men is notable not only in historical drama, but can also be found in documentary film, as is, for example, made evident in Jih-Fei Cheng's (2016) analysis of the documentary *How to survive a plague*, which shows how the documentary draws on a large archive of AIDS-related activist action, and yet depicts almost solely the activism of white gay men.

In a similar vein, the question of which paradigms pervade queer commemorative cinema also pertain to issues of cultural colonialism and local LGBTQ histories. Within a Chinese context, Hongwei Bao has written on Zhao Jing and Shi Tou's documentary *We are here* (China, 2015), looking in particular at how the documentary depicts the history of lesbian feminist activism in China through tracing it back to the Fourth United Nations World Conference on Women. In analyzing this depiction, Bao points toward the ways in which it ignores the local history of Chinese feminism, instead misremembering the movement as a Western import. Taken together, the works mentioned here exemplify the stakes involved in representing the past of queer activism and in commemorating particular narratives about the past at the expense of others. Consequently, "the emphasis placed on certain parts of activist history, as well as on certain activists themselves can influence not only how a movement is conceived of, but also *to whom* it is thought to belong" (Horvat, 2021, p. 105).

While all the films mentioned here thus far look back at the past of queer activism, it is important also to note the ways in which activist cinema *from* the past also acts as a technology of memory (Hallas, 2009). As Robert Hallas's work on activist cinema during the AIDS crisis shows, films produced during the crisis have now been "reframed by time … [and have] therefore come to serve as a repository of collective memory" (Hallas, 2009, p. 76). In this sense, the very act of creating archives and of curating them needs to be understood as activist labor, and has itself also been the subject of documentary work (Cvetkovich, 2002). In Megan Rossman's *The Archivettes* (2019), for example, the history of the volunteers leading the New York Lesbian Herstory Archives is thematized, with the film presenting archiving as not only linked to, but itself a form of activism. Rossman's film thus echoes Jack Halberstam's (2005, p. 169) arguments that "the archive is not simply a repository, [but is rather] a theory of cultural relevance, a construction of collective memory," underscoring the political relevance of both archiving and, implicitly, of representing this process through documentary. Similarly, Ann Cvetkovich's (2002) work on documentary depictions of queer archives engages with how these films expand the archives themselves through depicting them, therein underscoring the ways in which LGBTQ archives themselves function not only as collections of material traces of queer life, but also serve an emotional purpose, tracing the affective legacies which compose queer history. As will be seen in the next section, "Film Preservation, Exhibition, and Home Video," questions of digitalization, curation, and preservation are thus particularly relevant for filmic repositories of queer memory, and for preserving the films made by activist themselves.

FILM PRESERVATION, EXHIBITION, AND HOME VIDEO

As authors working on queer video and film archives have shown, the preservation and archiving of LGBT film poses unique challenges, as these works are often produced without the necessary support that makes restoration and archiving possible (Pepe, 2011), and are liable not to be curated accurately (Brunow, 2019). In Kristin Pepe's (2011) work on the preservation of American lesbian film, she shows the effects of a lack of funding and institutional support, with even influential works such as the activist documentary *Tom of Finland* (1978) suffering from missing scenes and scratched film prior to the organization of larger projects of preservation. In order to combat such losses of queer film history, the Legacy Project for LGBT Moving Image Preservation was founded, bringing together Outfest and the UCLA Film & Television Archive in order to remaster and digitize both documentary works such as *The Word is Out* and *Choosing Children* (1985), as well as works from The ONE National Gay & Lesbian Archives Collection. In their aim of preserving queer film history, projects such as Legacy and the Lesbian Home Movie Project have also worked on digitizing LGBTQ home videos, and on creating virtual sites of queer memory through which the quotidian aspects of the LGBTQ past can also be claimed as part of queer heritage (Brunow, 2019; Pepe, 2011).

Such newly digitized material brings forth its own challenges of curation, as Dagmar Brunow's work on memory and LGBT+ archives makes clear. As Brunow (2019, p. 100) argues, lesbian "home movies and amateur film-making can offer fresh perspectives of LGBT+ pasts beyond dominant representations framed by criminalizing discourses, such as images of raids and police surveillance." In acting as a record of queer everyday life and love, such media serve as valuable resources for queer memory, therein underscoring the relevance of how they are curated, especially as their queer meaning may not be readily apparent to the viewer without the context of curation. Brunow (2019, p. 109) therefore highlights how the "contextualization provided by archivists can frame the meaning of films, [while] an act of unqueering the film images results in an erasure of LGBT+ lives," therein halting the formation of queer memory.

LGBTQ home videos have also been remediated in queer documentary films like Stu Maddux's *Reel in the Closet* (2015), transforming private archives of queer memory into more public filmic formats. In reference to *Reel*, Brunow (2019, p. 105) notes it is "by making the footage available to global audiences, [that the film] has become a travelling archive for queer memories," thus highlighting the role which film festivals play in the creation of such memory. The relevance of filmic distribution and curation for queer memory has also been noted in work dealing with queer film festivals, with Antoine Damiens's (2020) monograph highlighting the ways in which these "festivals [function] *as* archives—as a visual historiographical device that uniquely refracts queer cultural memory and affects" (p. 158).

Like Maddux's *Reel in the closet*, another example of documentary remediation can be seen in Chris Bolan's *A Secret Love* (2020), which transforms the private archive of one aging lesbian couple (mostly composed of photographs, letters, and a small amount of home videos) into a new commemorative work. *A Secret Love* is particularly significant here because it exemplifies the ways in which new distribution technologies can influence the potential reach of a queer commemorative work, with the film being purchased by Netflix and thus being granted further media attention in newspapers such as *The Guardian* (Clarke, 2020), *Time* (Gajanan, 2020), and *The New York Times* (Winkelman, 2020). While the significance of documentary film in shaping how one thinks of activist histories has already been emphasized in this article, the place granted to Bolan's film on a streaming platform as popular as Netflix shows both the influence of distribution and the significance of granting space to cinematic memory projects which also commemorate the more private, sometimes closeted, everyday realities of queer life.

When viewed in conjunction, the challenges presented to queer film in terms of preservation, distribution, and curation demonstrate the active and constantly shifting role which these processes play in the creation of LGBTQ filmic memory. While even projects exclusively dedicated to the preservation of LGBTQ film and video archives are unable to preserve many of the materials with which they come into contact (Pepe, 2011), work on the remediation and curation of these materials has demonstrated how their meaning can be remade and resignified depending on the manner in which they are presented. Moreover, the means of distributing these works also shape how visible and, by extension, influential they may be. Taken together, the emphasis which the authors mentioned here place on curation, remediation, representation, and audience reaction highlights how queer filmic memory remains anything but fixed. Rather, it is a constantly evolving process, continually remade by directors, writers, archivists, and viewers themselves.

CONCLUSION

In many ways, the study of how queer memory has been and continues to be shaped by cinema is only at its inception, with monographs on the subject only beginning to appear. As such, more work remains to be done on specific national and transnational manifestations of queer commemorative cinema, as well as on processes of curation and cinema preservation, and on LGBTQ audience memories. The hegemonic position of Anglophone and particularly American film needs also to be taken into account here, as the transnational reach of cinema stemming from this area also influences the prominence of certain memory narratives. Differently put, while numerous national cinemas have engaged with and reimagined LGBTQ pasts, there exists a danger of these works and histories nonetheless remaining marginalized in favor of narratives of the LGBTQ past which focus almost exclusively on American history. As *Screening Queer Memory* argues, "it is precisely [due to] the cultural colonialism inherent in the over-representation of media stemming from the United States and Britain... [that] it is relevant to understand precisely what type of narratives is being promoted" (Horvat, 2021, pp. 11–12) by these films, as well as for further academic attention to be granted to often-marginalized media contexts. Considering the prominent focus on LGBTQ pasts in contemporary queer cinema, as well as the specific challenges surrounding the preservation of queer film and home video, such academic work is of vital relevance if the role which cinema continues to play in the formation of queer memory is to be fully comprehended.

FURTHER READING

Brunow, D. (2019). Amateur films and LGBT+ memory. In Ingrid Stigsdotter (Ed.), *Making the invisible visible: Reclaiming women's agency in Swedish film history and beyond* (pp. 97–117). Nordic Academic Press.

Castiglia, C., & Reed, C. (2012). *If memory serves: Gay men, AIDS, and the promise of the queer past*. University of Minnesota Press.

Dunn, T. R. (2016). *Queerly remembered: Rhetorics for representing the GLBTQ past*. University of South Carolina Press.

Hallas, R. (2009). *Reframing bodies: AIDS, bearing witness, and the queer moving image*. Duke University Press.

Horvat, A. (2021). *Screening queer memory: LGBTQ pasts in contemporary film and television*. Bloomsbury Academic.

Kagan, D. (2013). How to have memories in an epidemic: Recent documentaries about HIV/AIDS. *Kill Your Darlings*, 13, 141–152.

McKinnon, S. J. (2016). *Gay men at the movies: Cinema, memory and the history of a gay male community.* University of Chicago Press.

Padva, G. (2014). *Queer nostalgia in cinema and pop culture.* Palgrave Macmillan.

REFERENCES

Aaron, M. (2006). New queer cinema. In L. R. Williams & M. Hammond (Eds.), *Contemporary American cinema* (pp. 398–409). Open University Press.

Akhavan, D. (Director). (2018). *The miseducation of Cameron Post* [Film]. Beachside Films.

Als, H. (2009). Revolutionary road. *New York Review of Books*, March 12. https://www.nybooks.com/articles/2009/03/12/revolutionary-road/

Amos, K. S., & Calman, S. (Creators). (2017). *Prejudice and pride: The people's history of LGBTQ Britain* [Documentary Mini Series]. BBC.

Anderson, B. (2006). *Imagined communities: Reflections on the origin and spread of nationalism.* Verso Books. (Original work published 1986)

Assmann, A. (2006). Memory, individual and collective. In R. E. Goodin & C. Tilly (Eds.), *The Oxford handbook of contextual political analysis* (pp. 210–226). Oxford University Press.

Bao, H. (2020). "We are here": The politics of memory in narrating China's queer feminist history. *Continuum, 34*(4), 514–529. https://doi.org/10.1080/10304312.2020.1785079

Bentley, J. (2018). *Pose*: 10 surprising facts about Ryan Murphy's trans-inclusive series. *The Hollywood Reporter*, July 11. https://www.hollywoodreporter.com/live-feed/pose-10-surprising-facts-ryan-murphys-trans-inclusive-series-1126281

Bolan, C. (Director). (2020). *A secret love* [Film]. Beech Hill Films.

Bravmann, S. (1993). Isaac Julien's *Looking for Langston*: Hughes, biography and queer(ed) history. *Cultural Studies, 7*(2), 311–323.

Bronski, M. (2009). Milk. *Cineaste, 34*(2), 71–73.

Brunow, D. (2019). Amateur films and LGBT+ memory. In Ingrid Stigsdotter (Ed.), *Making the invisible visible: Reclaiming women's agency in Swedish film history and beyond* (pp. 97–117). Nordic Academic Press.

Campillo, R. (Director). (2017). *120 BPM (120 battements par minute)* [Film]. Les Films de Pierre.

Canals, S., Falchuk, B., & Murphy, R. (Creators). (2018–2021). *Pose* [Television Series]. FX.

Castiglia, C., & Reed, C. (2012). *If memory serves: Gay men, AIDS, and the promise of the queer past.* University of Minnesota Press.

Chan-wook, P. (Director). (2016). *The handmaiden* (아가씨) [Film]. Moho Film.

Chasnoff, D., Klausner, K., & Lazarus, M. (Directors). (1985). *Choosing children* [Film]. Groundspark.

Cheng, J.-F. (2016). How to survive: AIDS and its afterlives in popular media. *Women's Studies Quarterly, 44*(1–2), 73–92.

Christopher, M. (Director). (1992). *The dead boys' club* [Flim]. Frameline Distribution.

Clarke, C. (2020). *A Secret Love* review: Moving portrait of two women's 60-year romance. *The Guardian*, April 29. https://www.theguardian.com/film/2020/apr/29/a-secret-love-review-netflix-documentary-terry-donahue-pat-henschel

Cram, E. (2015). *Violent inheritance: Landscape memory, materiality, and queer feelings in the Rocky Mountain West.* Indiana University Press.

Cram, E. (2016a). Archival ambience and sensory memory: Generating queer intimacies in the settler colonial archive. *Communication and Critical/Cultural Studies, 13*(2), 109–129. https://doi.org/10.1080/14791420.2015.1119290

Cram, E. (2016b). Imaging rurality in Matthew Shepard's memory. In M. L. Gray, C. R. Johnson, & B. J. Gilley (Eds.), *Queering the countryside: New frontiers in rural queer studies* (pp. 267–289). New York University Press.

Cvetkovich, A. (2002). In the archives of lesbian feelings: Documentary and popular culture. *Camera Obscura, 17*, 107–147. https://doi.org/10.1215/02705346-17-1_49-107

Cvetkovich, A. (2013). *An archive of feelings: Trauma, sexuality, and lesbian public cultures*. Duke University Press.

Damiens, A. (2020). *LGBTQ film festivals: Curating queerness*. Amsterdam University Press.

Dayton, J., & Faris, V. (Directors). (2017). *Battle of the sexes* [Film]. Cloud Eight Films.

Dillard, C. (2017). Un-quaring San Francisco in Milk and Test. *European Journal of American Studies, 11*(3), 1–16. http://ejas.revues.org/11714

Dinshaw, C. (1999). *Getting medieval: Sexualities and communities, pre- and postmodern*. Duke University Press.

Dunn, T. R. (2016). *Queerly remembered: Rhetorics for representing the GLBTQ past*. University of South Carolina Press.

Edelman, L. (2004). *No future: Queer theory and the death drive*. Duke University Press.

Edgerton, G. R. (2001). Television as historian: A different kind of history altogether. In G. R. Edgerton & P. C. Rollins (Eds.), *Television histories: Shaping collective memory in the media age* (pp. 1–18). University Press of Kentucky.

Emmerich, R. (Director). (2015). *Stonewall* [Film]. ACE Entertainment.

Epstein, R. (Director). (1984). *The times of harvey milk* [Film]. Black Sand Productions.

Evans, R. (Director). (2004). *Brother to brother* [Film]. Miasma Films.

Everett, R. (Director). (2018). *The happy prince* [Film]. Maze Pictures.

Färberböck, M. (Director). (1999). *Aimée & Jaguar* [Film]. Senator Film Produktion.

Fletcher, D. (Director). (2019). *Rocketman* [Film]. Paramount Pictures.

Foucault, M. (1975). Film and popular memory: An interview with Michel Foucault. *Radical Philosophy, 11*, 24–29.

France, D. (Director). (2012). *How to survive a plague* [Film]. Public Square Films.

Freccero, C. (2006). *Queer/early/modern*. Duke University Press.

Freeman, E. (2010). *Time binds: Queer temporalities, queer histories*. Duke University Press.

Gajanan, M. (2020). The story behind Netflix's coming-out doc A Secret Love. *Time*, April 24. https://time.com/5824910/a-secret-love-netflix/

Gelfand, R. (2018). *Nobody's baby: Queer intergenerational thinking across oral history, archives, and visual culture* (PhD thesis). University of North Carolina.

Grainge, P. (2003). *Memory and popular film*. Manchester University Press.

Guadagnino, L. (Director). (2017). *Call me by your name* [Film]. Frenesy Film Company.

Gutiérrez-Albilla, J. D. (2013). Scratching the past on the surface of the skin: Embodied intersubjectivity, prosthetic memory, and witnessing in Almodóvar's *La mala educación*. In M. D'Lugo & K. M. Vernon (Eds.), *A companion to Pedro Almodóvar* (pp. 322–344). Wiley-Blackwell.

Gutiérrez Alea, T., & Tabío, J. C. (Directors). (1993). *Strawberry and chocolate (Fresa y Chocolate)* [Film]. Instituto Cubano del Arte e Industrias Cinematográficos (ICAIC).

Halberstam, J. (2005). *In a queer time and place: Transgender bodies, subcultural lives*. New York University Press.

Halbwachs, M. (1992). *On collective memory*. University of Chicago Press. (Original work published 1952)

Hallas, R. (2009). *Reframing bodies: AIDS, bearing witness, and the queer moving image*. Duke University Press.

Haupt, S. (Director). (2014). *The circle (Der Kreis)* [Film]. Contrast Film.

Haynes, T. (Director). (1998). *Velvet goldmine* [Film]. Goldwyn Films.

Haynes, T. (Director). (2015). *Carol* [Film]. The Weinstein Company.

Hirsch, M. (1999). Projected memory: Holocaust photographs in personal and public fantasy. In J. C. Mieke Bal & L. Spitzer (Eds.), *Acts of memory: Cultural recall in the present* (pp. 3–23). University Press of New England.

Horvat, A. (2021). *Screening queer memory: LGBTQ pasts in contemporary film and television*. Bloomsbury Academic.

Hubbard, J. (Director). (2012). *United in anger: A history of ACT UP* [Film]. New York State Council on the Arts.

Ibáñez, J. C. (2013). Memory, politics, and the post-transition in Almodóvar's cinema. In M. D'Lugo & K. M. Vernon (Eds.), *A companion to Pedro Almodóvar* (pp. 153–175). Wiley-Blackwell.

Imamović, A. (Director). (2005). *Go West* [Film]. Comprex.

Jelača, D. (2016). *Dislocated screen memory*. Palgrave Macmillan.

Jing, Z., & Tou, S. (Directors). (2015). *We are here* (트레일러 재생) [Film]. Ford Foundation Beijing Office.

Julien, I. (Director). (1989). *Looking for Langston* [Film]. British Film Institute.

Kagan, D. (2013). How to have memories in an epidemic: Recent documentaries about HIV/AIDS. *Kill Your Darlings, 13*, 141–152.

Karukoski, D. (Director). (2017). *Tom of Finland* [Film]. Anagram.

Kies, B., & West, T. J., III. (2017). Queer nostalgia and queer histories in uncertain times. *Queer Studies in Media & Popular Culture, 2*(2), 161–165. https://doi.org/10.1386/qsmpc.2.2.161_2

Landsberg, A. (2004). *Prosthetic memory: The transformation of American remembrance in the age of mass culture*. Columbia University Press.

Lee, F. (Director). (2020). *Ammonite* [Film]. British Film Institute (BFI).

Lenon, S. (2013). White as *Milk*: Proposition 8 and the cultural politics of gay rights. *Atlantis: Critical Studies in Gender, Culture and Social Justice, 36*(1), 44–54.

Lowenthal, D. (1985). *The past is a foreign country*. Cambridge University Press.

Macneill, C. W. (Director). (2018). *Lizzie* [Film]. Powder Hound Pictures.

Maddux, S. (Director). (2015). *Reel in the closet* [Film]. Interrobang Productions.

Mariposa Film Group. (Directors). (1978). *The word is out* [Film]. Milestone Film and Video.

Matanić, D. (Director). (2002). *Fine dead girls (Fine Mrtve Djevojke)* [Film]. Alka Film Zagreb.

McKinnon, S. J. (2016). *Gay men at the movies: Cinema, memory and the history of a gay male community*. University of Chicago Press.

Melgosa, A. P. (2013). The ethics of oblivion: Personal, national, and cultural memories in the films of Pedro Almodóvar. In M. D'Lugo & K. M. Vernon (Eds.), *A companion to Pedro Almodóvar* (pp. 176–199). Wiley-Blackwell.

Morris, C. E., III. (Ed.) (2011). *Remembering the AIDS Quilt*. Michigan State University Press.

Muñoz, J. E. (1996). Ephemera as evidence: Introductory notes to queer acts. *Women and Performance, 8*(2), 5–16. https://doi.org/10.1080/07407709608571228

Muñoz, J. E. (2009). *Cruising utopia: The then and there of queer futurity*. New York University Press.

Nora, P. (1989). Between memory and history: Les Lieux de Mémoire. *Representations, 26*, 7–24. https://doi.org/10.2307/2928520

Padva, G. (2014). *Queer nostalgia in cinema and pop culture*. Palgrave Macmillan.

Padva, G. (2017). A fantastic fabrication of Weimar Berlin: Queer nostalgia, timeless memories and surreal spatiality in the film *Bent*. *Queer Studies in Media & Popular Culture, 2*(2), 167–182. https://doi.org/10.1386/qsmpc.2.2.167_1

Parsons, A. (2014). History, activism, and the queer child in Derek Jarman's *Queer Edward II* (1991). *Shakespeare Bulletin, 32*(3), 413–428. https://doi.org/10.1353/shb.2014.0040

Pepe, K. K. (2011). Outside the Hollywood canon: Preserving lesbian moving images. *GLQ: A Journal of Lesbian and Gay Studies, 17*(4), 632–638. https://doi.org/10.1215/10642684-1302433

Reid-Pharr, R. F. (2006). Makes me feel mighty real: *The Watermelon Woman* and the critique of Black visuality. In A. Juhasz & J. Lerner (Eds.), *F is for phony: Fake documentary and truth's undoing* (pp. 130–142). University of Minnesota Press.

René, N. (Director). (1989). *Longtime companion* [Film]. American Playhouse.
Reposi Garibaldi, J. (Director). (2019). *Lemebel* [Film]. Solita Producciones.
Richardson, M. (2011). Our stories have never been told: Preliminary thoughts on Black lesbian cultural production as historiography in *The Watermelon Woman*. *Black Camera*, 2(2), 100–113. https://doi.org/10.2979/blackcamera.2.2.100
Rossman, M. (Director). (2019). *The archivettes* [Film]. Lucky Duck Pictures.
Russell, G. M., & Bohan, J. S. (2005). The gay generation gap: Communicating across the LGBT generational divide. *Angles*, 8(1), 1–8.
Ryberg, I. (2020). Queer cultural memory. *Lambda Nordica*, 25(1), 122–126.
Santa Ana, L. (Director). (2019). *Carlos Jauregui: The Unforgettable Fag (El Puto Inolvidable)* [Film]. Sombracin.
Schiller, G., & Robert Rosenberg, R. (Directors). (1984). *Before Stonewall* [Film]. Before Stonewall Inc.
Schulman, S. (2009). *Ties that bind: Familial homophobia and its consequences*. New Press.
Sciamma, C. (Director). (2019). *Portrait of a lady on fire (Portrait de la jeune fille en feu)* [Film]. Lilies Films.
Shahani, N. (2012). Getting off (on) the *Shortbus* (John Cameron Mitchell, 2006): The politics of hypothetical queer history. *New Cinemas: Journal of Contemporary Film*, 10(2–3), 101–114. https://doi.org/10.1386/ncin.10.2-3.101_1
Stone, O. (Director). (2004). *Alexander* [Film]. Warner Bros.
Sturken, M. (1997). *Tangled memories: The Vietnam War, the AIDS epidemic, and the politics of remembering*. University of California Press.
Sullivan, L. L. (2000). Chasing Fae: *The Watermelon Woman* and Black lesbian possibility. *Callaloo Literature and Culture*, 23(1), 448–460.
Summers, I. (2016). Montage of a queering deferred: Memory, ownership, and archival silencing in the rhetorical biography of Langston Hughes. *Journal of Homosexuality*, 63(5), 667–684. https://doi.org/10.1080/00918369.2015.1111106
Tomás, P., & Vallejo, C. (Creators). (2018). *We are* [Film]. *Nosotrx Somos*, Playz.
Tweedie, J. (2003). The suspended spectacle of history: The tableau vivant in Derek Jarman's *Caravaggio*. *Screen*, 44(4), 379–403. https://doi.org/10.1093/screen/44.4.379
Valdivia, A. N. (2010). *Latino/as in the media*. Polity Press.
Van Sant, G. (Director). (2008). *Milk* [Film]. Focus Features.
Warchus, M. (Director). (2014). *Pride* [Film]. Pathe.
Weissman, D., & Weber, B. (Directors). (2010). *We were here* [Film]. Weissman Projects.
Westmoreland, W. (Director). (2018). *Colette* [Film]. Number 9 Films.
Wills Foote, T. (2007). Hoax of the lost ancestor: Cheryl Dunye's *The Watermelon Woman*. *Jump Cut*, 49. https://www.ejumpcut.org/archive/jc49.2007/WatermelonWoman
Windle, E. (2016). "It never really was the same": *Brother to Brother*'s Black and White and queer nostalgia. *Melus*, 41(4), 6–31. https://doi.org/10.1093/melus/mlw042
Winkelman, N. (2020). "A Secret Love" review: A lesbian couple's enduring affection. *New York Times*, April 29. https://www.nytimes.com/2020/04/29/movies/a-secret-love-review.html
Žilnik, Ž. (Director). (1995). *Marble ass (Dupe od Mramora)* [Film]. Radio B92.

NOTE

1. By using the term queer memory, this article aims at once to encapsulate the diverse memories of groups which fall under the LGBTQ umbrella, as well as to point toward the specifically queer nature of such memories—i.e., how they evade, subvert, and differ from the heteronormative perceptions of the past which are actively promoted by heteropatriarchal national, educational, and familial memory regimes.

Anamarija Horvat

QUEER MUSIC PRACTICES IN THE DIGITAL REALM

INTRODUCTION

In a time when music culture is produced, distributed, and consumed increasingly in digital spaces, relations between music and LGBTQ+ identities are meaningfully informed by these spaces and are deserving of scholarly attention. A considerable number of theoretical and empirical studies can serve as background and inspiration for researchers broadly interested in, and occupied with, queer music-reception practices in the digital realm. These music practices can be related to fandom, listening, curation, music taste, etc.—in short, "anything music-related" from an audience perspective.[1]

Amid digital practices and cultures, a broad range of digital music practices can be discerned, including watching music videos, streaming music, engaging in fan cultures on social media, and connecting with artists. At the same time, many offline music practices (e.g., live performances, singing, nightlife) remain important and meaningful, and the digital and the offline continuously inform each other.

As for the terminology used, in general, the adjective "LGBTQ+" is used to include all identities that do not meet, or that somehow challenge, heteronormative and binary societal norms. When practices or cultures, rather than people or identities, are referred to, the adjective "queer" is generally used. In discussion of certain literature, the terms are used in correspondence with the particular work of literature.

Since the very intersection of topics (identity, LGBTQ+ identity, music, and digital media) has not been widely explored in the existing literature, the literature presented in this article usually does not include all three perspectives. The article cannot be a straightforward history of a coherent field of research; instead, it presents theories, ideas, and literature from different relevant fields and angles. All presented literature, however, explicitly or implicitly touches topics and employs perspectives relevant and inspiring to researchers interested in the relations between LGBTQ+ identities and music in times when music consumption (and production) mainly happens through digital media. It presents broader literature on music and identity, the rich body of literature on LGBTQ+ identities and music, and theoretical and empirical research in new media studies. Covering a variety of fields that are not always naturally related, the overview aims to situate the respective literature historically within the academic landscape and critically link it to the topics at hand.

Depending on the research question at hand, some sections might be of more interest to certain readers than to others, so readers can look for sections specifically relevant to them, as well as read the piece in its entirety. Also, the literature presented here is of course not exhaustive and integrally representative for the respective fields. Readers who think a certain theory or approach might be helpful to them are invited to let the literature presented here, and the references, further guide them.

POPULAR MUSIC STUDIES: MUSIC AND IDENTITIES

Before focusing on digital and/or queer music practices, it is relevant to present broader popular music studies literature that explores the relations between music, identities, and society and that remains profoundly instrumental and inspiring for music researchers today. While not focusing on LGBTQ+ identities per se, the presented popular music studies have paved the way for identity-focused and socially sensitive research and have provided helpful perspectives and lenses.

While musicology has been a respected and established branch of academic study for centuries, for a long time it has been focusing almost solely on the strictly musical aspects of music, with a strong disdain for popular music and extramusical and societal contexts. The object of studies has been the "transcendent" work of "geniuses" like Mozart and Beethoven, supposedly worthy of strictly aesthetic scrutiny and devoid of societal interference.

One of the first to draw attention to, and seriously examine, music's social role and ties to identities was the Frankfurter Schüle scholar Theodor Adorno. In several essays on music (translated and bundled in 2002), Adorno laid out a bleak analysis of popular music (and other art) as standardized, formulaic, commercial products without much artistic merit (Adorno, 2002). Adorno's elitist and all-too-pessimistic views have been widely criticized but they have provided an opening for music studies to take seriously music's social implications.

A significant development for the serious treatment of popular music was the foundation of the Centre for Contemporary Cultural Studies in Birmingham in 1964. Scholars there were devoted to the social analysis of contemporary (sub)cultures, and many (such as Angela McRobbie) increasingly saw popular music as a substantial aspect of the (sub)cultures. A key example of such subculture analysis with a focus on the role of popular music was Willis's *Profane Culture* (2014), a sociological study of a biker gang. Such studies, applying a broader sociological lens to popular music, have become central to, and characteristic of, popular music studies.

Equally significant was the development of what was dubbed "new musicology" (Bennett & Waksman, 2014), in which musicology scholars were trying to reconcile their music-theoretical perspectives with more social concerns and urged their colleagues to do the same. A key work here was Leppert and McClary's aptly titled *Music and Society: The Politics of Composition, Performance and Reception* (1989). A third important development was that of popular music itself: from the 1960s onward, artists like the Beatles and Bob Dylan were sparking major popular attention as well as (consequently) serious academic rigor (Cloonan, 2005).

The combination of these developments led to the emergence of the loosely demarcated field of popular music studies, which crystalized in the International Association for the Study of Popular Music (IASPM) in 1981. Following a conference on popular music research in Amsterdam (Lacasse, 2014), a group of European (Swedish, Italian, British) and American scholars founded the association and at the same time (the predecessor of) the journal *Popular Music* was founded (for the U.K. branch). American counterparts were *Popular Music and Society* (founded in 1971) and the *Journal of Popular Music Studies* (1988), and all three journals have remained prominent outlets for the study of popular music (Cloonan, 2005).

Characteristic of popular music studies is its multidisciplinarity. In 1982, Philip Tagg foregrounded this in the first newsletter of the IASPM, and the IASPM still emphasizes its interprofessional and interdisciplinary character on its website. Throughout its many approaches and angles, popular music studies developed some key themes and concepts during the 1980s and 1990s: musical meaning, studies of audiences, studies in the music industries, and questions of place, as well as an increasing interest in questions of identity (Cloonan, 2005; Hesmondhalgh & Negus, 2002).

It wasn't until the 1990s that broad theoretical accounts of music and identity were published. Leading musicology scholar Middleton's *Studying Popular Music* (1990) aimed to carve out a theoretical basis for the study of popular music at a time where musicology still too often rejected popular music and cultural studies had trouble dealing with "the forbiddingly special character of music" (1990, p. v). Middleton theoretically explored the role of popular music and popular music studies, historically and socially, touching upon often disregarded themes like politics and pleasure, and suggested what the future of popular music studies might look like.

Frith's *Performing Rites* (1996), with the telling subtitle *On the Value of Popular Music*, both defended and examined the value of popular music. In twelve chapters, Frith examined the different sides of popular music, ranging from its meaning and its performance to the role of the voice. Frith ambitiously asked the most profound questions (Where do sounds come from? [Chapter 5]; How can one understand "songs as texts"? [Chapter 8]), always paying attention to the socially informed meanings and mechanisms attached to the various musical aspects.

In *After Adorno* (2003), DeNora explicitly took on and criticized Adorno's analyses to ask the question where popular music studies should go, while further aiming to dissolve the paradox between the strictly musical and the socially informed aspects of popular music. Next to that, DeNora acknowledged and examined the role of *Music in Everyday Life* (2000) and its important relations to mood, emotion, and intimacy. In a way, the latter book took the study of the extramusical dimensions of music one step further, from wide social and political contexts into the very personal realm of intimacy and identity. The book is a landmark of music and identity, and DeNora's ideas of mood cultivation and the use of music as a technology of self are especially relevant for researchers wanting to explore gender and sexual identity music practices.

Searching for a lens to profoundly explore the relations between music and identities, Hargreaves et al. introduced a useful concept in *Musical Identities* (2002), which encompassed both the role of identities in music and the role of music in identities. Musical identities usefully bring together aesthetic preferences, music taste, and broader social identities. With a specific interest in the development of musical identities, the chapters focus on how young people's identities can develop through music and how different social identities relate to music.

Much of the contemporary work in popular music studies is somehow indebted to the theoretical literature. Establishing that music has informative and meaningful ties to people's social lives, and vice versa, the theoretical works have opened up an almost infinite range of possibilities for researchers to explore and to examine these ties. The specific paragraphs on music and gender, and music and LGBTQ+ identities, should help guide and inspire future research.

Popular Music and Gender.   When an awareness of, and interest in, the role of music in people's social lives and identities started to gain ground, several scholars turned their attention toward the relations between music and gender. In their 1978/1990 groundbreaking, influential essay, titled "Rock and Sexuality," Frith and McRobbie explored the gendered nature of certain music genres. Examining music (performance) as a means of sexual expression and control, they set the masculinized cock rock in opposition to the feminized teenybop music. While their account has since been criticized by some for being too rigid in its binary oppositions, the essay remains a seminal (first) account of music's powerful gender dimensions, and importantly it installed the idea that music and music taste always carry with them gendered meanings and connotations, even when these are implicit or hidden.

In 1997, Whiteley edited the book *Sexing the Groove*, a powerful collection of gender in music studies featuring several chapters that tackle music's gendered dimensions. Focusing on several gender performances, both hegemonic and resistant, and a wide range of genres and scenes, the book takes into account fan practices, instruments, live performance, "subcultures," music videos, and the like. *Sexing the Groove* does not try to paint a coherent, exhaustive image of gender in music; instead, it aims to thoroughly examine several sides of the matter and encourages others to do the same. Several chapters pay considerable attention to the roles of sexual identities and meaningful intersections of identities. The collection is a culmination of the study of gender in popular music at that time and remains an inspiration for scholars.

Other notable works in this regard, carrying somewhat more implicit links to gender or music but emphasizing the relations between them, arose at the turn of the century. Think of Thornton's *Club Cultures: Music, Media and Subcultural Capital* (1996), McRobbie's *Postmodernism and Popular Culture* (1994), and McRobbie's "Post-feminism and Popular Culture" (2004), among many others. As was increasingly acknowledged, music and music culture can be important mediators of gender discourses, in both reactionary and counterhegemonic ways. Halberstam, for example, took the case of the artist Lady Gaga as a lens to analyze the state of gender politics, dubbing it "gaga feminism" (2012), "a form of political expression that masquerades as naïve nonsense but that actually participates in big and meaningful forms of critique" (p. xxv).

A particular field of study focuses on the more explicitly political Riot Grrrl scene, sparking interests from both feminist and queer perspectives: the abovementioned *Sexing the Groove* featured chapters on Riot Grrrl from Leonard (1997) and Kearney (1997), and Halberstam's influential work on queer subcultural lives (2005) included some insightful analyses of Riot Grrrl scenes. Schilt also offered a sharp exploration of what the exact meaning of the Riot Grrrl movement (2004) has been and an analysis of "the appropriation of Riot Grrrl politics by mainstream female musicians" (2003). Schilt focused on conflicts and political dynamics within the scene, as well as on the role of popular media in creating an image of Riot Grrrl that led to its devaluation and recuperation.

In line with the latter study, another interesting angle on music and gender is to focus more on the production side, examining the gendered dynamics and experiences of musicians. For example, for *Gender in the Music Industry* (2017), Leonard interviewed several professional "musicians in female-centered bands" (p. 16), not to treat their narratives "as testimony of 'the way it really is' but as individual and revealing responses by musicians in female-centered bands" (p. 16). Applying a production-focused approach, Leonard explored and questioned the widespread masculinization of rock music and offered a powerful counternarrative.

POPULAR MUSIC AND LGBTQ+ IDENTITIES

Somewhat parallel to the developments in music and gender literature, music and LGBTQ+ literature emerged in the 1970s with some inspiring essays and studies, featured a first notable edited volume in the 1990s, and has since been producing numerous studies from very diverse angles. This literature has provided both works celebrating the queer potential and undervalued significance of certain music and artists, and studies criticizing and dismantling the reproduction of power and hierarchy.

A key early work was the essay "In Defense of Disco" (1979/2005), in which Dyer urged fellow scholars to take seriously the then widely popular genre of disco. While acknowledging disco's capitalist origins and production backgrounds, Dyer pointed out the political potential that lay in its reception. Disco remains one of queer culture's prominent phenomena, and decades later, Kooijman (2005) revisited Dyer's defense of the genre and proposed that its revolutionary ideas have been, and should further be, used in queer (popular music) studies, while Hughes (2014) examined the political potential for African American and queer culture that lies in disco's ties to desire. Dyer's essay paved the way for many other (queer) authors to take seriously the social and political value in the pleasure, physicality, and eroticism of music, which was, and is, often rejected.

In *The Queen's Throat* (1993), Koestenbaum explored the worshipping of opera divas by gay men. While focusing on nonpopular music, Koestenbaum made some inspiring and influential statements on the gay political potential of music, the importance of the voice, and the significance of *jouissance* in enjoying music. Koestenbaum's exploration of diva worshipping has inspired many other queer fan studies (e.g., Jennex, on Lady Gaga, 2013), and, much like Dyer, has foregrounded the political value of these seemingly private fan practices. The meaningfulness of the voice in music, and queer music in particular, also inspired other scholars. Bonenfant (2010) sharply explored the elusive but meaningful act of "queer listening to queer vocal timbres" and provided some insightful handles to tackle the recurrent importance of the voice in queer music experiences and studies.

In 1994, *Queering the Pitch: The New Gay and Lesbian Musicology* appeared. Compiled by Brett et al., the book marked an ambitious attempt to capture and fully launch the then-new field of gay musicology and featured chapters by now-prominent writers in the field of queer music studies, such as Philip Brett, Susan McClary, and Jennifer Rycenga. While innovative in its themes and approaches, the volume was still heavily indebted to traditional musicology in its focus on "highbrow" music and its heavy theoretical wonderings. Also, as the subtitle suggests, the book focused primarily on gay and lesbian musicology, leaving little room for more queer approaches and theorizations. To a certain extent, there was more attention for such queer perspectives in new editions, and *Queering the Pitch* remains a landmark in queer music studies and an excellent starting point for later academic research.

Peraino's *Listening to the Sirens* (2005), tried to sidestep the classic versus popular and ancient versus modern dichotomies, examining, as its subtitle suggests, "musical technologies of queer identity from Homer to Hedwig." Peraino explored various articulations and practices of queerness in the broadly defined field of music. The objects of study ambitiously span three millennia, covering ancient and medieval music, as well as 1970s disco and Madonna.

In an attempt to tackle the absence of popular music and profoundly queer perspectives in *Queering the Pitch*, Whiteley and Rycenga edited *Queering the Popular Pitch* (2006). Acknowledging the inherent diversity within gender and sexuality and taking as research objects a wide variety of popular music, the editors compiled a highly diverse collection of work. *Queering the Popular Pitch* featured several chapters on non-Western music cultures, such as Hebrew music and Latin house, and it took a much more intersectional approach throughout, exploring gender and sexual identity's interplay with religion, diaspora, race, and other identities. In its broad collection of essays, the writers see popular music as "a catalyst for different truths, for different interpretations that have worked to free the queer imaginary" (p. xiv). Queer popular music studies from the 1990s onward have been shot through with a similar queer, dynamic perspective that often draws upon feminist theory, postcolonial theory, critical race theory, and the like.

Dyer's *The Culture of Queers* "deal[t] with aspects of the culture produced by and/or about men in the category queer" (2002, p. 1). In the book's essays, Dyer investigated the representations of LGBTQ+ people in literature, television, and film, spotting and deconstructing trends, stereotypes, and powerful narratives. While the book did not focus on music per se, many of the representations and discourses it touched upon are relevant across media representations.

Readers looking for a more theoretical and focused introduction into queer theory and queer music studies are invited to take up the following literature. In *Playing It Queer* (2012b), Taylor presented extensive and thorough research into three Australian queer music groups and scenes. Apart from the incisive case studies, Taylor's work offered a very broad theoretical exploration of queer music studies literature and a critical and dynamic reflection on this very literature. The literature review and case studies, as well as Taylor's sharp and sometimes (semi) personal analysis, together painted an inspiring image of what queer music studies are and what they can be. With regard to queer music scenes, Taylor's article on middle-age queers (2010) and her theoretical "queerly reframing of the music scenes perspective" (2012a) are interesting, too.

For a more concise introduction to the field of LGBTQ+ identities and popular music, the following introductory articles in anthologies or special issues can be helpful. Maus's contribution to Routledge's *The Cultural Study of Music: A Critical Introduction* (2011) laid out relevant terminology and theory concerning gender and sexuality, both in general and in popular music. A number of special issues on LGBTQ+ identities have been published in popular music journals. The introductory essays in these issues often provide a concise and lucid account of the state of the art of LGBTQ+ studies and some suggestions for further directions. Bradby and Laing's (2001) introduction to the "gender and sexuality" issue of *Popular Music* explored popular music studies' "difficult and intermittent relationship" with gender and sexuality and asked for the deconstruction of several persistent ideas that complicate this relationship. Lecklider's introduction in the *Journal of Popular Music Studies* (2006) described popular music as "an arena where marginalized voices can be heard and sexual identities shaped, challenged, and renegotiated" (p. 117) and emphasized the importance of a thorough examination of the definitions of "queerness."

THE DIGITAL REALM

Studying popular music in the 21st century must take into account the role of new digital media. An overwhelming share of people's music practices can now be situated in the digital realm. Music streaming and music video platforms are obvious sites, but social media and other "nonmusical" new media are profoundly meaningful, too, because so much of social, musical, and sexual life is mediated by new media. The sheer magnitude and multiplicity of new media, as well as the various ways through which they relate to identities and to music, open up many possibilities and angles for researchers to examine queer music practices in the digital realm. This section presents a number of angles and hopes to inspire new ones.

With new technologies claiming more and more place in society, scholars increasingly theorized about their social and sociological implications. While social scientists long directed their attention to technology's "effects on society," MacKenzie and Wajcman's (1999, p. 1) influential edited volume *The Social Shaping of Technology* saw the relationship between technology and society as one of mutual shaping. After a first edition appeared in 1985, the 1999 second edition was emblematic for a more social constructionist approach toward technology, and it remains an inspiration for social technology scholars. Its central claim—that technology and society should be seen in junction, shaping each other in constant interaction—remains instructive for much literature on new media.

Key Concepts: Affordances and Mediation. In this vein of thought, a concept used by many new media scholars is that of affordances. The term *affordances* originated in perceptual psychology, in the critical work of James Gibson, who aimed to step away from the tradition of "cognitivist thinking that privileged perception as the foundation for the value of objects" (Prior, 2018, p. 17). The affordances concept nuanced this perspective, in privileging which uses and practices objects afford (Norman, 1988). A stone, a bridge, a computer, and a Spotify profile all offer a wide range of possible uses and practices, stretching out beyond their most obvious qualities and leaving considerable room for the agency and creativity of users. A stone affords to be used to build houses or to be bounced on water for leisure purposes, even though these uses are not necessarily inscribed into its very core.

The affordances concept was transferred to human–computer interaction by Norman (1988), becoming a key concept of both theory and methodology in technology and new media studies. Today, an affordances lens is used to explore technologies' many complex sociomaterial and contextual interpretations, leaving room for users' agency (Bucher & Helmond, 2017). It is a useful lens for exploring the ways in which agency, society, and identities relate to technologies.

Another concept often used to grasp the tensions between technologies, cultures, and society is mediation. In popular music studies, Hennion (2003) wrote, the concept of mediation was mainly introduced to overcome difficulties in the sociological study of art. A focus on music itself was deemed by some as insufficient for studying its social implications, while a sociological study of popular music would neglect and ignore its inherent, meaningful musical qualities. The mediation approach brought to popular music studies a more practical theory that focused on very concrete phenomena to make broader sociological claims. Hennion defined mediation as "reciprocal, local, heterogeneous relations between art and public through precise devices, places, institutions, objects, and human abilities, constructing identities, bodies, and subjectivities" (p. 250). Mediation is a fruitful concept in offline contexts, but it is especially helpful in digital contexts because it, like affordances, takes into account an environment's specific qualities, while avoiding technological determinism and acknowledging contextual factors and users' agency. It allows social and identity-related analyses that value technology and society's nuanced and complex characters.

Social Media. Within the immense world of digital and new media, social media, of course, take up a major role. Whether one considers predecessors like blogs and forums, early social media like MySpace, or established giants like Facebook and Twitter, these platforms are important and meaningful mediators of social and cultural phenomena. Furthermore, they are ever-changing, both in their composition and their position in the social world. Social media, whether they are somehow music-oriented (MySpace, TikTok) or not, have strong ties to popular music, through their affordances of engaging in self-presentation, taking part in cultural discussions, performing fan practices (see below), and the like. Moreover, music streaming platforms share many characteristics and affordances with social media, such as datafication, connectivity, interaction, and self-presentation.

Concerns about social media's growing role in political processes and media giants' handling of users' privacy and data gave way to some razor-sharp critical analyses of social media. Pariser famously coined the concept of the "filter bubble" (2011), painting a somber image of the internet as a highly segregated space in which timelines and interfaces are monitored heavily by the respective services, which are primarily informed by commercial interests. Barberá et al. (2015) introduced the related concept of the "echo chamber" to describe segregated virtual spaces where opinions are simply echoed, with little room for contestation or negotiation. While their ideas primarily concern the distribution of news and information, their analyses might provide useful tools for thinking about music streaming platforms and the ways in which they mediate which music and musical identities are foregrounded, and which aren't.

A number of scholars take a less pessimistic and negative approach to social media platforms, leaving more space for users' agency. Van Dijck and Poell (2013), aiming to understand social media logic, acknowledged and critically analyzed the power of social media, for example in affecting journalistic and political processes, despite—or precisely because of—their "tendency [...] to present themselves as neutral platforms that fairly represent different public voices and opinions" (p. 4). At the same time, they emphasized the agency of users and the mutuality of the relationship. They discerned four main elements in social media logic (programmability, popularity, connectivity, and datafication) that are to some extent applicable to most social media platforms, and, in fact, to music streaming platforms.

Van Dijck et al. broadened their perspective and sharpened their analysis in *The Platform Society* (2018). Again, they argued that the "mutual shaping of platforms and society is not predetermined or irreversible" (p. 32), and "ultimately, the fate of a platform is determined by the collective behavior of users" (p. 47). Building upon their earlier work, this time they boiled it down to three "platform mechanisms": datafication, commodification, and selection. These concepts serve as tools for social scientists to get a grip on the misty ways in which platforms (including Spotify, Apple, and YouTube) guide, monitor, and steer online actions, discoveries, and representations while retaining a pseudo neutral front.

Considering the central role of music and music taste in people's identities, Hogan's (2010) sharp and influential analysis of online self-presentation is relevant here. Hogan's theory built upon Goffman's dramaturgical approach to social interaction (1959), which states that social practices can be seen as performances taking place on a stage. Applying this to a social media context, Hogan saw chatting and video calling as staged performances, and importantly added the idea of an exhibition with artifacts, where a virtual audience can come by at any time.

Facebook, Instagram, and Spotify profiles are such exhibitions, and considerable work may take place backstage to monitor impression management, in which gender and sexual identity are important factors.

Algorithms. Enabling and monitoring social media and music media practices and doing much of the datafication and selection work are algorithms. Throughout the 2010s, algorithms landed front and center in the social media debate, not the least in popular media. This debate, however, often remains limited to its two extremes. On the one hand, there is the techno-optimist stance, admiring the powers of algorithms and praising them for making our lives more convenient. On the other hand, the apocalyptic stance describes algorithms as evil forces, continuously and profoundly tracking and influencing our lives, determining who we are becoming and how we socially interact. The field of algorithm studies aims to bring some much-needed nuance to these debates and to explore the wide expanse between the two extremes.

Cheney-Lippold argued that algorithms (and the new media they inform) engage in a "cybernetic relationship to identification" (2011, p. 168). People are no longer (solely) identified through rigid, fixed demographic qualities (e.g., age, location, gender) as these essentialist notions of identity are replaced by "pliable behavioral models" (p. 168). One's virtual identity depends on the things one does online and the choices and decisions one makes, small as they may be. This approach to identification brings about issues of intrusion, inaccuracy, and privacy, while also not erasing the discriminatory problems of previous identification approaches. Prey (2018) applied these ideas to music streaming platforms, arguing that they employ "algorithmic individuation." On music streaming platforms, one's "taste profile" is algorithmically shaped (based on plays, likes, skips, playlists, etc.), so every decision users make implicitly and invisibly affects their future recommendations.

It is important, as Gillespie argued, to "unpack the warm human and institutional choices that lie behind these cold mechanisms" (2014, p. 3), to be aware of the humanity in algorithms and the fact that algorithms are always to some extent written and monitored by people. This also entails going beyond "the promise of algorithmic objectivity," to not take algorithmic interferences and recommendations for granted, but to try to understand where they come from and what assumptions and categorizations they are based on.

Seaver elaborated on the humanity of algorithms by suggesting an anthropology of algorithms (2017). According to Seaver, since algorithms should no longer be seen in culture, but as culture, researchers should also treat them anthropologically, as instances of human culture, and as inherently human phenomena. Responding to this call, Bonini and Gandini interviewed and observed people working as curators in music streaming platforms. They argued that human and algorithmic curation go hand in hand, creating "algotorial playlists," "combining human activity 'augmented' by algorithms and non-human activity designed, monitored, and edited by humans" (Bonini & Gandini, 2019, p. 6). There are complex curation mechanisms behind playlists, which are curated not only on aesthetic grounds, but also often on social grounds (e.g., Pride playlists, Black History Month playlists).

Striphas had a more somber, critical outlook on algorithms and "algorithmic culture" (2015). Where the aforementioned scholars looked at what was underneath algorithms, Striphas pointed out the secrecy and the power of algorithmic processing, which is "increasingly becoming a private, exclusive and indeed profitable affair" (p. 407), making profound critical analyses almost impossible. Pelly, a prominent voice in popular media debates on Spotify, published some sharp, hypercritical accounts of Spotify's recommender systems (2017, 2018), arguing that an algorithmic approach to music discovery favors Muzak and unadventurous, mainstream (and thus hegemonic) music, which Pelly deemed undesirable from both an artistic and a social perspective.

Trying to get a grip on the ways in which algorithms mediate users' experiences and identities, without reducing users to defenseless entities, Seaver suggested the metaphor of the "trap" (2019). Sidestepping the dichotomy between the "voluntary and the coerced" (p. 423), the trap metaphor implies that algorithms try profoundly to persuade users into certain uses, but whether users allow themselves to be persuaded remains dependent on their agency.

Similarly, Bucher's *If... Then: Algorithmic Power and Politics* (2018) explored this middle ground between coercive force and voluntary agency. Bucher argued that "life is not merely infused with media but increasingly takes place in and through an algorithmic media landscape" (p. 1), but he puts emphasis on the transience and the ever-changing nature of algorithms. Algorithms, by definition, rely on the actions of users, and, consequently, users and algorithms evolve alongside each other. "Just as algorithms and platforms are perpetually changing, so are the worlds created in and around them. In other words, as the 'if' changes, so does the 'then'" (p. 159). Scholars studying identities in algorithmic environments should thus pay attention to both the "if" and the "then" and how they relate to social power hierarchies.

Queer Digital Practices. Digital and social media have considerably affected people's social practices and social lives. As social scientists, quite early on, began to acknowledge the informative and meaningful role of digital media in people's identities and social interactions, a share of scholars have explored digital media's specific relations to queer identities. Their work aims to understand what affordances of new media might pose opportunities or constraints for queer world-making.

Just like the new media landscape itself, critical new media studies are constantly changing and evolving. The first works were either departing from, or reacting against, the idea of the internet as a progressive, democratic force, a "cyberspace" where offline identities could be shaken off and inequalities would be largely excluded. The objects of study in early works were early internet phenomena, such as blogs, forums, and file-sharing platforms, which seemed to carry a more bottom-up, democratic potential. As the internet, social media, and more specifically music-related new media evolved, these expectations soon lost their relevance; new media have become so strongly intertwined with the offline social world that thinking of new media as an exotic, secluded space seems nonsensical. New media studies, and queer new media studies in particular, therefore, mostly treat digital media as mediators, with both positive and negative implications for individual and social identities.

While some of this work might not have direct or explicit links to music practices and cultures, note that music permeates the digital realm significantly beyond the confines of music streaming platforms. Social media platforms like Facebook and Instagram, as well as video platforms like YouTube and TikTok, are important sites for fan practices and music-related creation. Just like in the offline world, music's social (and political) powers transcend the strictly musical.

Early works focused on how LGBTQ+ people explored "cyberspace" in the search for opportunities to articulate and to live out their sexual identities in ways that weren't always available offline. One of the prominent early contributions in the field of queer internet studies was Campbell's *Getting It on Online: Cyberspace, Gay Male Sexuality, and Embodied Identity* (2004). The title clearly suggests the then-prevalent view of the internet as a cyberspace and the rather delineated perspective on gay male sexualities. In a very similar approach, Fox published *Gays in (Cyber-) Space: Online Performances of Gay Identity* (2007), using a rather optimist discourse on the internet's "opportunities for gay men to affirm their identities in digital contexts."

More open and more dynamic in approach and opting for the more inclusive concept of "queer" rather than "gay" identities, *Queer Online: Media Technology and Sexuality* (2007), edited by O'Riordan and Philips, provided another early account of queerness in the online context. The collection included several empirical case studies, but also, in dedicated chapters and throughout, examined more theoretical debates surrounding queer theory and new media studies. As the authors explicitly stated, the collection did "not seek to provide a homogenous view of either queer theory or communication technologies but [aimed] to bring together a range of diverse positions" (p. 1), resulting in a thought-provoking analysis of the relations between queerness and media technologies, at a time when new media were only just gradually becoming what they are today. Gray's *Out in the Country: Youth, Media and Queer Visibility* (2009) also aimed to transcend the segregation of cyberspace by placing it in a very concrete geographical context.

A similar perspective was adopted by Pullen and Cooper (2010) in their edited volume *LGBT Identity and Online New Media*. Interdisciplinary in approach, the extensive collection aimed to examine both the positive and the negative implications of online new media for LGBT identities. The chapters focused on a very wide range of media, including YouTube, health websites, and MySpace, and the five chapters in Part III focused specifically on LGBT fan cultures.

As Szulc pointed out in a triple book review (2014), the geographical scope of the chapters featured in these monographs and collections remained largely limited to the United States and United Kingdom. Overall, this literature often ignores or takes for granted its Anglo- and Western-centric focal points, implicitly confirming the idea that "U.S.-based studies are presumed to be primary and general while non-U.S. studies are framed as particular and secondary" (p. 2928). While case studies set in North America obviously remain important and valuable (see Wargo, 2017, among many others), a series of studies have provided a counterweight to this trend and have foregrounded queer online practices all over the world. Much like in popular music studies, scholars have gradually stepped away from their rigid scope and perspectives in favor of more open, diverse, and queer perspectives.

As early as 2003, Berry et al. carved the path for a less Western-centric examination of queer digital cultures with *Mobile Cultures: New Media in Queer Asia*, studying a number of early queer new media phenomena in Singapore, Korea, and Japan. In examining the online experiences of post-Soviet queers in Israel/Palestine, Kuntsman's *Figurations of Violence and Belonging* (2009) addressed issues of queerness, migranthood, and nationalism in "cyberspace and beyond" (subtitle). Kuntsman and Al-Qasimi also edited a special issue of the *Journal of Middle East Women's Studies* on "Queering Middle-Eastern Cyberscapes" (2012), countering "imperialist Western narratives about oppressed Middle Eastern queers" (p. 1) and the role of the Internet in this.

Enteen's *Virtual English: Queer Internets and Digital Creolization* explicitly refused to treat new media and the internet as "static documents in predominantly English-language environments that possess unchanging and atemporal geo-political coordinates" (2010, p. 10), and it is illustrative of multiple studies employing a more queer approach toward new media. Pullen's (2014) edited volume *Queer Youth and Media Cultures* focused on a variety of queer youth practices and representations across different media. In 19 chapters, the book explored notions of performance and representation of queer youth, both in traditional media such as film and TV, and in new media and social media contexts. The volume adopted a transnational perspective and featured studies of Indian, Turkish, and Ugandan cases, presenting a broad and diverse account of queer youth's roles in media cultures.

Other researchers have examined the more conscious, explicit discourses and narratives of queer people on new media. In a series of articles, De Ridder (2017) and De Ridder and Van Bauwel (2013, 2015) researched the ways in which queer people themselves, and youth in particular, negotiate and make sense of the relations between sexual identities and new media.

Less focused on queer identities per se, the work of Marwick and Boyd addressed notions of privacy and intimacy on social media. In "I tweet honestly, I tweet passionately" (Marwick & Boyd, 2011), they explored how users navigate "imagined audiences" to avoid the "context collapse" of different social contexts in social media environments where the intimate and the social are always connected. In "Networked Privacy: How Teenagers Negotiate Context in Social Media," Marwick and Boyd (2014) applied these ideas to social media in general, stating that privacy online, just like the environments in which it is embedded, has become networked. Because sexual identities, especially those that are nonnormative, are almost by definition intimate matters over which people desire a certain degree of control, scholars have taken these concepts and applied them to queer practices and lives. Duguay, for example, researched how LGBTQ+ people negotiate sexual identity disclosure and context collapse on Facebook (2016). Since music also attains a rather intimate position in many people's lives and is often linked to social identities, and music practices exist in a range of new media environments, the work of Marwick and Boyd has considerable relevance to sexual identities and music in the digital realm.

(LGBTQ+) Audiences and Digital Media. With the advent of the internet and its many affordances for social interaction and self-presentation (e.g., blogs, forums, social media), opportunities arose for audiences and fans, who quickly found their way to the new media, often even before artists did (Baym, 2018, p. 95). Sandvoss (2005) stated that "(under the influence of new media) fandom became an ordinary aspect of life from the early 2000s" (in Wasserbauer & Dhoest, 2016). These "new" fan practices have received significant scholarly attention, because of their increasing prominence in the lives of audiences and because "practices hidden in private spaces for decades became visible and accessible, amplifying their impact" (Baym, 2018, p. 79) and, consequently, providing interesting, accessible study material for social scientists. The field of audiences and digital media soon became rather large, so the focus here is on studies examining the topic with an emphasis on notions of identity, community, resistance, and/or music.

In *Tune in, Log on* (2000), early instances of online fandom of soap series were examined by Baym, who has been studying audiences' and fan practices in the online world for decades. While Baym did not focus explicitly on gender and sexual identity, crucial notions in these studies are intimacy, community, and connection. Baym is interested in the ways online environments mediate personal and intimate engagements between people (or between fans and their favorite arts) and the communities emerging in these new media environments.

Focusing on television fandom, texts by Andrejevic (2008) and Booth (2010) urged fandom scholars to take online fandom seriously. Andrejevic (2008) pointed out the relevance of social media responses to television series, responses that provide a form of instant feedback that is often taken into consideration in the production of new episodes, granting the art–fan relationship an increasingly mutual character. Booth's *Digital Fandom* (2010) aimed to "integrat[e] digital scholarship into fan studies, ... to provide a text that offers a unique view of contemporary audiences" (p. 5) and suggested stepping away from treating the fan as individual in favor of an analysis of fandoms as communities (p. 22). Like Andrejevic, Booth advanced to see fans not merely as consumers, but also as producers.

Driver's (2007) *Queer Girls and Popular Culture* examined the various ways in which young queer women try to "make sense of their lives and communicate their differences" (p. 1) by using popular culture and media that are, after all, embedded in heteronormativity and aimed at straight, gender-normative girls. As the subtitle *Reading, Resisting, and Creating Media* suggests, Driver gave considerable weight to the agency and practices of the girls, who are "making do with what is available within mass culture while also seeking out possibilities beyond its normalizing and commercial scope" (p. 16). The book's chapters focus on films, TV series, magazines, and the like, but especially relevant here is Chapter 6, which explores how communities are performed online in "creative spaces of self-representation."

In *Personal Connections in the Digital Age* (2015), Baym explored the "new forms of personal connection" mediated by digital media. In chapters focusing on community creation, identities, and relationships, Baym dealt with and nuanced both utopian and dystopian rhetorics of digital media. Applying ideas about intimate digital connections to musicians and fans is *Playing to the Crowd: Musicians, Audiences, and the Intimate Work of Connection* (2018), a book that aimed to find out "how artists and audiences can relate to one another in ways that help them flourish within the decidedly modern context that calls on them to exploit their feelings and selves for commercial gain" (p. 33) and that offered an examination of how age-old artist–fan relations are reworked in digital spaces.

To research fan cultures and fan practices in a 21st-century context, is to at least partly take into account new media practices, whether as a specific focus or as a helpful way to gain access to fan practices. Scholars researching a wide range of LGBTQ+ fandom (e.g., Lavin et al., 2017 for China, Hong Kong, and Taiwan; Waggoner, 2018 for a North-American context; Wasserbauer & Dhoest, 2016, for Belgium), have paid attention to new media fan practices. Likewise, scholars examining the fandom of one specific artist have taken social media as their focal point (e.g., Bennett, 2014; Click et al., 2013, on Lady Gaga fandom).

Music Streaming and Identities. In 2023, music streaming has been established as the primary tool for music consumption. After the tumultuous reign of the MP3 file and the associated (illegal) file-sharing technologies that disrupted the music industries, access-based streaming platforms have re-installed a relative peace in the music industries. Scholars have researched both streaming and its predecessors from several angles: the implications for the music industries, the legal relevance in terms of copyright and ownership, the philosophical meanings in transforming the ways music is defined or understood, and the mediation of social, sociological, and identity-related cultures and practices. Here, the latter perspective is most relevant, but some works focusing more on the industry and the corporate side can provide interesting backgrounds and contexts. After all, economic, legal, philosophical, and sociological dimensions should not, and cannot, be seen as operating separately from each other.

Eriksson et al.'s *Spotify Teardown* (2019) is a broad analysis of Spotify, the world-leading music streaming platform in terms of paying subscribers. The writers aimed to situate and analyze Spotify within the history of music distribution and within the contemporary music industry landscape. Central in their analysis is the "curatorial turn" Spotify made when it started to focus more on recommendation and personalization, to distinguish Spotify from its competitors. Eriksson and colleagues also dived into Spotify's more identity-related and sociological implications, in examining its corporate self-presentation and its editorial playlists, arguing that Spotify "implicitly position[s] the ideal user as a millennial with progressive values" (p. 127) and frames music streaming as a "personal and intimate—even happiness-inducing—practice" (p. 136).

An industries lens was applied more strictly in Wikström's *The Music Industry: Music in the Cloud* (2019). The 2019 book was an update of the first edition, published in 2009, when single-song downloads threatened the music industries' revenue model. Wikström argued that music in the 21st century underwent a shift "from the Disc to the Cloud" (p. 5) and that the three shifts already observed in the 2009 music industries have intensified: from control to connectivity, from product to service, and from professional to amateur. Extensive in range, *The Music Industry* provided a thorough but highly accessible account of the complex developments leading to the current state of the music industry and a firm background for researchers interested in the contemporary music landscape.

Other scholars have taken a much more sociological approach to digital music phenomena, aiming to understand how new music media mediate how audiences construct, negotiate, and/or present their identities. This body of scholarly work, in essence, explores how important "predigital" music-related practices and phenomena work through digital environments, albeit in a (somewhat) different way. Again, in line with theories on technologies and algorithms, music streaming platforms and video platforms are analyzed as new mediators with certain (new) distinct qualities, rather than disruptive forces bringing about a drastic shift in music consumption.

Some scholars have published book-length broad examinations of a variety of issues related to digital music practices. Prior's *Popular Music, Digital Technology and Society* (2018) aimed to understand the changing, and less changing, ways in which popular music and societies relate in the age of digital technology. Drawing on insights from the new media and algorithm literature and paying attention to historical evolutions in both technology and popular music, Prior's ambitious work of theory provided a very helpful, thorough guide for music studies in the digital age.

Nowak's *Consuming Music in the Digital Age* (2016) explored the different roles of music in the digital age. The book is broad and ambitious in scope and came rather early in the era of streaming. Nowak examined the role of music in everyday life (drawing upon DeNora, 2000), the affective possibilities of music, and music taste as assemblage. Johansson et al. (2017) specifically focused on streaming music, taking into account its implications for practices, media, and cultures, and covering a broad range of theoretical debates on everyday life, connectivity, and so on. Leijonhufvud's *Liquid Streaming* (2018) focused solely on Spotify and described "the Spotify way to music" as a liquid phenomenon that converges smoothly with music's increasing role in everyday life.

Some scholars have specifically turned their attention to the role of music in everyday life in the digital age. Bull's *Sound Moves: iPod Culture and Urban Experience* was an early analysis of "the aural experience of the social, mediated through mobile technologies of communication" (2007/2015, p. i). Bull's account remains influential and thought-provoking in pointing out and making sense of the role of technologies in everyday contexts and in examining the very loose boundaries between the online and the offline, the musical and the nonmusical, which may have only increased since the rise of the smartphone.

In *Ubiquitous Listening* (2013), Kassabian observed how music is everywhere (at home, through headphones, in stores and public transport environments) and argued that the consequent ubiquitous listening has important implications for our music-related affect and attention, resulting in distributed subjectivity. In many ways precisely because of its ubiquity and the inattentive listening it often inspires, music affords a way to negotiate everyday life, and to "know ourselves in and through musical engagement" (p. 18).

Some scholars have directed their attention toward music streaming platforms and their architecture, interface, and algorithmic infrastructure, to analyze their implications for users' music practices. Morris (2015) explored what it means when aesthetic–human phenomena like curation and taste become datafied and coded. Morris and Powers (2015) examined what this implies for the notion of control: who or what exactly controls taste and music discovery in the streaming age and how may this affect musical experiences? Prey (2020) went a step further and took on the question of power in times of "platformization," situating Spotify not only in the music market, but also in the advertising and finance market.

A limited but strong body of scholarly literature has researched streaming practices (mostly on Spotify) and their implications for identities, trying to determine how people navigate and negotiate music streaming platforms. In a multiyear project, Anja Nylund Hagen and colleagues explored these issues, drawing on interviews and focus groups with Spotify users. The studies (Hagen, 2015, 2016; Hagen & Lüders, 2017) provide meaningful and sharp analyses of audiences' engagements with streaming platforms and the meanings they assign to them. The audience studies reveal that Spotify (and similar streaming platforms) occupy an important intimate and social position for many people, although articulations and discourses may diverge considerably among users. For example, people may hold quite divergent views on what they want to share, how they curate their playlists, and how they use streaming platforms in everyday life.

Another Scandinavian multiyear project has done similar research, but with a specific focus on the gendered dimensions of online music practices. Werner and Johansson (2016) researched the ways that music streaming technology is embedded in gendered discourses. In focus groups they found that the knowledgeable, active music fan is still often framed as a man (e.g., the boyfriend, the father). Departing from research on new media and taking a feminist approach toward new technologies, Werner and Johansson contended that the consumption of music (and) technologies has indeed partly led to more individual, "neutral" engagements with music, but at the same time "continue[s] to be firmly situated in discourse and social contexts" (2016, p. 189). Eriksson and Johansson (2017) and Werner (2020) used a similar feminist approach to examine Spotify's algorithmic architecture, laying bare the ways in which the supposedly neutral data processors in fact "organize gender" (Werner, 2020). Music streaming's gendered meanings are relevant and meaningful for queer music practices, because they demarcate intended or "acceptable" music and practices for respective genders.

Focusing more on the increasing importance of context and mood in music streaming (see Eriksson et al., 2019; Hagen, 2016), Siles et al. drew upon interviews with Spotify users to contend that genres are containers of social affect (2019). Building on DeNora's pre-streaming work on mood cultivation (2000), they argued that playlists often serve to negotiate everyday life and intimate emotions, as enabled through the increasing prominence of mood in Spotify's recommendations and interface.

One of the very few studies that focused specifically on queer music practices on digital media was Dhaenens and Burgess's (2019) exploration of the diverse cultural logics behind LGBTQ-themed playlists on Spotify. Examining a sample of 37 playlists, they found that "the curation of LGBTQ-themed playlists engages with LGBTQ culture and identity politics in three distinctive ways" (p. 1206). First, the curation of such playlists contributes to a library of libraries, through which "a canon is created and consolidated" (p. 1207). Second, the platform is involved in community-building, offering "role models, allies, LGBTQ music to dance to, politically themed songs or personal stories with which to identify" (p. 1207). Third, the playlists suggest varying identity politics—"playlists that are politically queer, homonormative, or ideologically ambiguous" (p. 1194). Dhaenens and Burgess's research suggested that music cultures remain "an important resource for LGBTQ people to find and express comfort, pleasure, belonging, and recognition" (p. 1206).

CONCLUSION

The literature overview presented in this article aims to be a starting point, a helpful guide, and a source of inspiration for readers interested in the relations between LGBTQ+ identities and popular music in the digital age. It illustrates that these themes have inspired a rich body of scholarly work, in which exciting debates and theories are continuously revisited and continue to evolve alongside the societal contexts in which they are embedded.

Both popular music studies and new media studies have evolved from rather rigid perspectives to more open, dynamic, and social-critical ones, often inspired by ideas from gender and queer studies. Scholars have provided profound and exciting accounts of how people, and LGBTQ+ people in particular, use music and new media to make sense of, negotiate, and express identities and what the potentials and constraints are. While the roles of music and the potential of the Internet and new media in queer lives have thus been frequently researched, the intersection of the two remains largely unexplored.

Some authors (such as Dhaenens and Burgess) have already delved into queer digital music practices, and hopefully, the work presented here can serve as an invitation to study the wide array of issues, practices, and cultures that remain to be explored. Building upon the existing body of valuable literature and adding new perspectives and approaches, researchers of diverging backgrounds can continue to sharpen our understanding of how identities and sexualities relate to popular music and digital media, and vice versa.

REFERENCES

Adorno, T. (2002). *Essays on music* (R. Leppert, Trans). University of California Press.
Andrejevic, M. (2008). Watching television without pity: The productivity of online fans. *Television & New Media, 9*(1), 24–46.
Barberá, P., Jost, J. T., Nagler, J., Tucker, J. A., & Bonneau, R. (2015). Tweeting from left to right: Is online political communication more than an echo chamber? *Psychological Science, 26*(10), 1531–1542.
Baym, N. K. (2000). *Tune in, log on: Soaps, fandom, and online community.* SAGE.
Baym, N. K. (2015). *Personal connections in the digital age.* John Wiley & Sons.
Baym, N. K. (2018). *Playing to the crowd: Musicians, audiences, and the intimate work of connection* (Vol. 14). New York University Press.
Bennett, A., & Waksman, S. (Eds.). (2014). *The SAGE handbook of popular music.* SAGE.
Bennett, L. (2014). Fan/celebrity interactions and social media: Connectivity and engagement in Lady Gaga fandom. In L. Duits, K. Zwaan, & S. Reijnders (Eds.), *The Ashgate research companion to fan cultures* (pp. 109–120). Ashgate.
Berry, C., Martin, F., Yue, A., & Spigel, L. (Eds.). (2003). *Mobile cultures: New media in queer Asia.* Duke University Press.
Bonenfant, Y. (2010). Queer listening to queer vocal timbres. *Performance Research, 15*(3), 74–80.
Bonini, T., & Gandini, A. (2019). "First week is editorial, second week is algorithmic": Platform gatekeepers and the platformization of music curation. *Social Media + Society, 5*(4), 1–11.
Booth, P. (2010). *Digital fandom: New media studies.* Peter Lang.
Bradby, B., & Laing, D. (2001). Introduction to "gender and sexuality" [Special issue]. *Popular Music, 20*(3), 295–300.
Brett, P., Wood, E., & Thomas, G. C. (Eds.). (1994). *Queering the pitch: The new gay and lesbian musicology.* Taylor & Francis.
Bucher, T. (2018). *If... then: Algorithmic power and politics.* Oxford University Press.
Bucher, T., & Helmond, A. (2017). The affordances of social media platforms. In J. Burgess, T. Poell, & A. Marwick (Eds.), *The SAGE handbook of social media* (pp. 231–253). SAGE.
Bull, M. (2015). *Sound moves: iPod culture and urban experience.* Routledge. (Original work published 2007)
Campbell, J. E. (2004). *Getting it on online: Cyberspace, gay male sexuality, and embodied identity.* Harrington Park Press.
Cheney-Lippold, J. (2011). A new algorithmic identity: Soft biopolitics and the modulation of control. *Theory, Culture & Society, 28*(6), 164–181.
Click, M. A., Lee, H., & Holladay, H. W. (2013). Making monsters: Lady Gaga, fan identification, and social media. *Popular Music and Society, 36*(3), 360–379.
Cloonan, M. (2005). What is popular music studies? Some observations. *British Journal of Music Education, 22*(1), 77–93.
DeNora, T. (2000). *Music in everyday life.* Cambridge University Press.
DeNora, T. (2003). *After Adorno: Rethinking music sociology.* Cambridge University Press.
De Ridder, S. (2017). Social media and young people's sexualities: Values, norms, and battlegrounds. *Social Media + Society, 3*, 1–11.
De Ridder, S., & Van Bauwel, S. (2013). Commenting on pictures: Teens negotiating gender and sexualities on social networking sites. *Sexualities, 16*(5–6), 565–586.

De Ridder, S., & Van Bauwel, S. (2015). The discursive construction of gay teenagers in times of mediatization: Youth's reflections on intimate storytelling, queer shame and realness in popular social media places. *Journal of Youth Studies, 18*(6), 777–793.

Dhaenens, F., & Burgess, J. (2019). "Press play for pride": The cultural logics of LGBTQ-themed playlists on Spotify. *New Media & Society, 21*(6), 1192–1211.

Driver, S. (2007). *Queer girls and popular culture: Reading, resisting, and creating media* (Vol. 1). Peter Lang.

Duguay, S. (2016). "He has a way gayer Facebook than I do": Investigating sexual identity disclosure and context collapse on a social networking site. *New Media & Society, 18*(6), 891–907.

Dyer, R. (2002). *The culture of queers*. Routledge.

Dyer, R. (2005). In defense of disco. In R. Dyer (Ed.), *Only entertainment* (pp. 151–160). Routledge. (Original work published 1979)

Enteen, J. B. (2010). *Virtual English: Queer Internets and digital creolization*. Routledge.

Eriksson, M., Fleischer, R., Johansson, A., Snickars, P., & Vonderau, P. (2019). *Spotify teardown: Inside the black box of streaming music*. MIT Press.

Eriksson, M., & Johansson, A. (2017). Tracking gendered streams. *Culture Unbound: Journal of Current Cultural Research, 9*(2), 163–183.

Fox, R. (2007). *Gays in (cyber-) space: Online performances of gay identity*. AV Akademikerverlag.

Frith, S. (1996). *Performing rites: On the value of popular music*. Oxford University Press.

Frith, S., & McRobbie, A. (1990). Rock and sexuality. In S. Frith & A. Goodwin (Eds.), *On record: Rock, pop and the written word* (pp. 371–389). Routledge. (Original work published 1978)

Gillespie, T. (2014). The relevance of algorithms. In T. Gillespie, P. J. Boczkowski, & K. A. Foot (Eds.), *Media technologies: Essays on communication, materiality, and society*. MIT Press.

Goffman, E. (1959). *The presentation of self in everyday life*. Doubleday.

Gray, M. L. (2009). *Out in the country: Youth, media, and queer visibility in rural America*. New York University Press.

Hagen, A. N. (2015). The playlist experience: Personal playlists in music streaming services. *Popular Music and Society, 38*(5), 625–645.

Hagen, A. N. (2016). The metaphors we stream by: Making sense of music streaming. *Journal on the Internet, 21*(2), 1–13.

Hagen, A. N., & Lüders, M. (2017). Social streaming? Navigating music as personal and social. *Convergence, 23*(6), 643–659.

Halberstam, J. J. (2005). *In a queer time and place: Transgender bodies, subcultural lives* (Vol. 3). New York University Press.

Halberstam, J. J. (2012). *Gaga feminism: Sex, gender, and the end of normal* (Vol. 7). Beacon Press.

Hargreaves, D. J., Miell, D., & MacDonald, R. A. (2002). What are musical identities, and why are they important? In R. A. MacDonald, D. J. Hargreaves, & D. Miell (Eds.), *Musical identities* (pp. 1–20). Oxford University Press.

Hennion, A. (2003). Music and mediation: Toward a new sociology of music. In M. Clayton, T. Herbert, & R. Middleton (Eds.), *The cultural study of music: A critical introduction* (2nd ed., pp. 249–260). Routledge.

Hesmondhalgh, D., & Negus, K. (Eds.). (2002). *Popular music studies*. Oxford University Press.

Hogan, B. (2010). The presentation of self in the age of social media: Distinguishing performances and exhibitions online. *Bulletin of Science, Technology & Society, 30*(6), 377–386.

Hughes, W. (2014). In the empire of the beat: Discipline and disco. In T. Rose & A. Ross, (Eds.), *Microphone fiends* (pp. 147–157). Routledge.

Jennex, C. (2013). Diva worship and the sonic search for queer utopia. *Popular Music and Society, 36*(3), 343–359.

Johansson, S., Werner, A., Åker, P., & Goldenzwaig, G. (2017). *Streaming music: Practices, media, cultures*. Routledge.

Kassabian, A. (2013). *Ubiquitous listening: Affect, attention, and distributed subjectivity*. University of California Press.

Kearney, M. C. (1997). Riot Grrrl—Feminism—Lesbian Culture. In S. Whiteley (Ed.), *Sexing the groove: Popular music and gender* (pp. 207–229). Routledge.

Koestenbaum, W. (1993). *The queen's throat: Opera, homosexuality and the mystery of desire*. Da Capo Press.

Kooijman, J. (2005). Turn the beat around: Richard Dyer's "in defence of disco" revisited. *European Journal of Cultural Studies, 8*(2), 257–266.

Kuntsman, A. (2009). *Figurations of violence and belonging: Queerness, migranthood and nationalism in cyberspace and beyond*. Peter Lang.

Kuntsman, A., & Al-Qasimi, N. (Eds.). (2012). Queering Middle-Eastern cyberspace. *Journal of Middle East Women's Studies, 8*(3), 1–157.

Lacasse, S. (2014). (Re)generations of popular musicology. In A. Bennett, & S. Waksman (Eds.), *The SAGE handbook of popular music* (pp. 62–76). SAGE.

Lavin, M., Yang, L., & Zhao, J. J. (Eds.). (2017). *Boys' love, cosplay, and androgynous idols: Queer fan cultures in Mainland China, Hong Kong, and Taiwan*. Hong Kong University Press.

Lecklider, A. (2006). Introduction. *Journal of Popular Music Studies, 18*(2), 117–123.

Leijonhufvud, S. (2018). *Liquid streaming: The Spotify way to music* [Dissertation, Luleå University of Technology].

Leonard, M. (1997). Feminism, 'subculture', and grrrl power. In S. Whiteley (Ed.), *Sexing the groove: Popular music and gender* (pp. 230–255). Routledge.

Leonard, M. (2017). *Gender in the music industry: Rock, discourse and girl power*. Routledge.

Leppert, R., & McClary, S. (Eds.). (1989). *Music and society: The politics of composition, performance and reception*. Cambridge University Press.

MacKenzie, D., & Wajcman, J. (Eds.). (1999). *The social shaping of technology* (2nd ed.). Open University Press.

Marwick, A. E., & boyd, d.. (2011). I tweet honestly, I tweet passionately: Twitter users, context collapse, and the imagined audience. *New Media & Society, 13*(1), 114–133.

Marwick, A. E., & boyd, d.. (2014). Networked privacy: How teenagers negotiate context in social media. *New Media & Society, 16*(7), 1051–1067.

Maus, F. E. (2011). Music, gender, and sexuality. In M. Clayton, T. Herbert, & R. Middleton (Eds.), *The cultural study of music: A critical introduction* (pp. 317–329). Routledge.

McRobbie, A. (1994). *Postmodernism and popular culture*. Psychology Press.

McRobbie, A. (2004). Post-feminism and popular culture. *Feminist Media Studies, 4*(3), 255–264.

Middleton, R. (1990). *Studying popular music*. Open University Press.

Morris, J. W. (2015). Curation by code: Infomediaries and the data mining of taste. *European Journal of Cultural Studies, 18*(4–5), 446–463.

Morris, J. W., & Powers, D. (2015). Control, curation and musical experience in streaming music services. *Creative Industries Journal, 8*(2), 106–122.

Norman, D. (1988). *The design of everyday things*. Basic Books.

Nowak, R. (2016). *Consuming music in the digital age: Technologies, roles and everyday life*. Springer.

O'Riordan, K., & Philips, D. J. (2007). *Queer online: Media technology and sexuality*. Peter Lang.

Pariser, E. (2011). *The filter bubble: What the Internet is hiding from you*. Penguin Press.

Pelly, L. (2017, December). The problem with muzak. *The Baffler*. https://thebaffler.com/salvos/the-problem-with-muzak-pelly

Pelly, L. (2018, June 4). Discover weakly. *The Baffler*. https://thebaffler.com/latest/discover-weakly-pelly

Peraino, J. A. (2005). *Listening to the sirens: Musical technologies of queer identity from Homer to Hedwig*. University of California Press.

Prey, R. (2018). Nothing personal: Algorithmic individuation on music streaming platforms. *Media, Culture and Society, 40*(7), 1086–1100.

Prey, R. (2020). Locating power in platformization: Music streaming playlists and curatorial power. *Social Media and Society, 6*(2), 1–11.

Prior, N. (2018). *Popular music, digital technology and society*. SAGE.
Pullen, C. (Ed.). (2014). *Queer youth and media cultures*. Springer.
Pullen, C., & Cooper, M. (Eds.). (2010). *LGBT identity and online new media*. Routledge.
Sandvoss, C. (2005). *Fans: The mirror of consumption*. Polity Press.
Schilt, K. (2003). "A little too ironic": The appropriation and packaging of Riot Grrrl politics by mainstream female musicians. *Popular Music and Society, 26*(1), 5–16.
Schilt, K. (2004). Riot Grrrl is: Contestation over meaning in a music scene. In A. Bennett & R. Peterson (Eds.), *Music scenes: Local, translocal, and virtual* (pp. 115–130). Vanderbilt University Press.
Seaver, N. (2017). Algorithms as culture: Some tactics for the ethnography of algorithmic systems. *Big Data & Society, 4*(2), 1–12.
Seaver, N. (2019). Captivating algorithms: Recommender systems as traps. *Journal of Material Culture, 24*(4), 421–436.
Siles, I., Segura-Castillo, A., Sancho, M., & Solís-Quesada, R. (2019). Genres as social affect: Cultivating moods and emotions through playlists on Spotify. *Social Media and Society, 5*(2), 1–11.
Striphas, T. (2015). Algorithmic culture. *European Journal of Cultural Studies, 18*(4–5), 395–412.
Szulc, L. (2014). The geography of LGBTQ internet studies. *International Journal of Communication, 8*, 2927–2931.
Taylor, J. (2010). Queer temporalities and the significance of "music scene" participation in the social identities of middle-aged queers. *Sociology, 44*(5), 893–907.
Taylor, J. (2012a). Scenes and sexualities: Queerly reframing the music scenes perspective. *Continuum, 26*(1), 143–156.
Taylor, J. (2012b). *Playing it queer: Popular music, identity and queer world-making*. Peter Lang.
Thornton, S. (1996). *Club cultures: Music, media, and subcultural capital*. Wesleyan University Press.
Van Dijck, J., & Poell, T. (2013). Understanding social media logic. *Media and Communication, 1*(1), 2–14.
Van Dijck, J., Poell, T., & De Waal, M. (2018). *The platform society: Public values in a connective world*. Oxford University Press.
Waggoner, E. B. (2018). Bury your gays and social media fan response: Television, LGBTQ representation, and communitarian ethics. *Journal of Homosexuality, 65*(13), 1877–1891.
Wargo, J. M. (2017). "Every selfie tells a story...": LGBTQ youth lifestreams and new media narratives as connective identity texts. *New Media & Society, 19*(4), 560–578.
Wasserbauer, M., & Dhoest, A. (2016). Not only little monsters: Diversity in music fandom in LGBTQ lives. *Iaspm Journal, 6*(1), 25–43.
Werner, A. (2020). Organizing music, organizing gender: Algorithmic culture and Spotify recommendations. *Popular Communication, 18*(1), 78–90.
Werner, A., & Johansson, S. (2016). Experts, dads and technology: Gendered talk about online music. *International Journal of Cultural Studies, 19*(2), 177–192.
Whiteley, S. (1997). *Sexing the groove: Popular music and gender*. Routledge.
Whiteley, S., & Rycenga, J. (Eds.). (2006). *Queering the popular pitch*. Routledge.
Wikström, P. (2019). *The music industry: Music in the cloud* (3rd ed.). Polity Press.
Willis, P. E. (2014). *Profane culture*. Princeton University Press.

NOTE

1. Researchers more interested in the production side of music will certainly find interesting starting points in Whiteley's *Sexing the Groove*, Frith's *Performing Rites*, Whiteley and Rycenga's *Queering the Popular Pitch*, Leonard's *Gender in the Music Industry*, and Wikström's *The Music Industry* (see references).

Ben De Smet

QUEER PRODUCTION STUDIES

INTRODUCTION

This article describes queer production studies as a relatively new subfield within media studies, while also contextualizing its emergence in a longer history of studies of media production. Reflecting existing scholarship, the bulk of the discussion focuses on televisual production in legacy and digital platforms, with some mention of other media forms, such as radio. It also focuses on entertainment programming, while acknowledging the significance of content produced more explicitly for didactic or political purposes. In addition, it is worth noting that the "queer" in queer production studies refers to media content as well as to producers and users when they are something other than cisgendered or heterosexual. As Martin (2018a, p. 7) summarized, queer production studies examines "the production of LGBTQ imagery, the ways queers produce their own media both within and outside the 'mainstream' culture industries, and the ways queers work as oppositional readers of texts and paratexts."

SITUATING QUEER PRODUCTION STUDIES WITHIN MEDIA STUDIES

In situating queer production studies within media studies as a whole, it is useful to understand it both in relation to production studies more generally and as its own developing subfield. Partly in response to a focus on textual analysis by many media studies scholars, production studies has directed attention to the identities and practices of workers in the media industries, including not just actors, directors, and producers, but also those in "below-the-line" occupations, all of whom are often referred to as "producers" or "cultural producers" in a broader sense than the occupational role usually denoted by "producer." One goal has been to provide deeper context for how and why media producers create particular kinds of media texts. Another is to better understand how producers both help create and become shaped by the production cultures that they are part of, or as Mayer et al. (2009, p. 2) put it, "how media producers make culture, and, in the process, make themselves into particular kinds of workers in modern, mediated societies."

Queer production studies emerged as an explicitly named subfield in a 2018 special issue of the *Journal of Film and Video*, edited by Alfred Martin Jr. Martin's (2018a) introductory article argued for the utility of distinguishing it from production studies more generally, for several reasons. First, much production studies scholarship examining the identities of media producers has paid little attention to the significance of nonnormative gender and sexual expression. Second, there has been no coherent approach to queer media production that examines the economic scale from major commercial to independent domains or that includes fan production. A third reason, which this article should make clear, is the significance of examining queer cultural production in relation to the politics of marginality in both media and society more broadly.

Another pertinent differentiation is between production studies and media industry studies. There is some overlap, as studies of the media industries also include some attention to production while production studies necessarily refers to conditions of the media industry. However, much media industries studies research focuses more on broad economic, regulatory, and technological developments while production studies research frequently makes use of interviews and ethnographic research with producers, often combined with analysis of relevant industry documents and media texts, to center the practices of cultural producers and the outcomes of these practices. In these ways, production studies draws from methods of both the humanities and social sciences, and such mixed-method and interdisciplinary approaches are also reflected in queer production studies.

Before moving on to discuss queer production studies research, it is therefore useful to note a separate body of work in media industry studies about LGBTQ media that examines changes such as commercialization and conglomeration or the significance of how media consumers are imagined and sought by media producers, but is not focused on production practices and producers themselves. For example, Becker (2006) discussed how U.S. television networks began producing gay-themed programming in the 1990s to appeal to a segment of educated, liberal heterosexual viewers who would be attracted to content seen as edgier. Aslinger (2009) discussed the emergence of LGBTQ television networks in the United States also from a media industry studies perspective, highlighting trends in the television industry to carve out niche audiences in a "post-network" era (Lotz, 2007) and the role of emergent digital technologies. Comparable approaches have been taken by Aslinger (2010), Campbell (2005), and Gamson (2003) about the trajectories of LGBTQ websites in the United States during the 1990s. For radio, Martin's (2018b) account of OutQ, the now defunct LGBTQ-focused satellite station, discussed how it was imagined by its producers as a "queer listening public" that was not an overtly resistant "counterpublic" (Fraser, 1990) the way that some queer spaces have been theorized to be (Warner, 2005), but which still functioned importantly as a live space of what Tongson (2011, p. 130) had termed the "remote intimacies" of community formation via radio listening.

The outcomes of media deregulation and globalization have meant that a media text (such as a film or television program) is often distributed in multiple countries. However, this does not mean that different national contexts all have the same production environments. In particular, there remain important differences with respect to how acceptable LGBTQ identity and expression are within a country, and the prominence of government-funded ("public") broadcasters, which may produce media that includes LGBTQ content. The next section provides an overview of transnational perspectives on queer production studies, followed by sections on queer production in the domains of major commercial media, public media, independent production, and fan production. Taken together, these show that queer production studies addresses a number of issues in media and cultural theory to do with how the identities of media producers influence their work, inclusion and marginality in different production domains, and the relationship of media production and media texts to society more generally.

TRANSNATIONAL PERSPECTIVES

The conditions for the production of LGBTQ content vary across different national contexts for at least two major kinds of reasons. One is the degree to which gender and sexual nonnormativity are accepted at a legal and societal level, as this affects both the regulatory conditions for queer content and the ability of queer media to be distributed even if it can be legally produced. A crude measure for societal acceptance is whether homosexuality is legal, although in terms of its outcomes for queer media production, the relationship is not entirely predictable. For example, homosexuality is legal in China, but there is substantial censorship of media for queer (and other sexual) content (Lavin et al., 2017; Zhou, 2017). Thus, several Chinese series revolving around a male–male relationship, even when not explicitly romantic, have been the target of government censorship (Ng & Li, 2020). In contrast, homosexuality is illegal in Singapore, but there is more leeway for LGBTQ media (Chua, 2014; Ng, 2018).

Unsurprisingly, the majority of queer production studies scholarship has been conducted in countries where homosexuality is legal and there are substantial amounts of LGBTQ media being produced, particularly the United States. Queer production studies research remains relatively new even for the European context, and so far, it has centered on Ireland and Belgium based on research by Páraic Kerrigan, Anne O'Brien, and Florian Vanlee (see also the section "Queer Production in Public Media"). For example, drawing on interviews, Kerrigan and O'Brien (2020) and O'Brien and Kerrigan (2020) investigated how LGBTQ-identified workers in Irish film and television production have negotiated the heteronormative conditions of the industry, finding that some of them adopted a more assimilationist, "homonormative" (Duggan, 2002) approach, while others asserted their queer identities during production practices, such as editing. Also, while there were experiences of bias and discrimination sidelining the workers or blocking career advancement, many were also able to form useful professional networks with each other and sometimes successfully challenged the heteronormativity of their work environments.

National contexts are also important with regard to prominence that state-supported media has in content production, particularly television. Even as public service broadcasting has become increasingly driven by commercial considerations (Dornfeld, 1998; Johnson, 2013), official mandates for public service broadcasters have retained language about producing a slate of programming that reflects the country's diversity. Thus, while in the United States, which has no equivalently significant public service broadcaster, it is commercial media that has led the way in the production of LGBTQ-themed television; in the United Kingdom, both the primarily state-funded British Broadcasting Corporation (BBC) as well as the commercially supported Independent Television (ITV) and the independent Channel 4 channels have contributed significantly to LGBTQ content.

Unfortunately, there is little scholarship centered on queer media production outside of the Global North or Asia, especially in places where homosexuality is illegal, although there are occasional references to production conditions in primarily text-focused analyses of LGBTQ media, such as Harvey's (2012) discussion about AIDS documentaries in sub-Saharan Africa. Given the availability of digital technologies and the internet, there may well be queer media production occurring under the radar of current scholarly attention.

QUEER PRODUCTION IN THE COMMERCIAL DOMAIN

A large amount of queer production occurs in the commercial domain, and it is the topic of most queer production studies scholarship. Central issues addressed include how LGBTQ workers have shaped the content and marketing of queer media and the relationship of commercial LGBTQ media to independent queer media and to LGBTQ activism. A key work is

Sender's (2004) account of how gay and lesbian print media in the United States, which had mostly begun as independent publications, developed into national, commercialized magazines. Sender interviewed a number of mostly gay-identified workers associated with producing and marketing these new publications and discussed how their activities had become increasingly professionalized in comparison to the more grass-roots activist, community-based newspapers that had preceded them. The tastes and dispositions of these workers regarding how queer sexual identity should or should not be presented resulted in major publications such as the *Advocate* and *OUT* magazines shifting away from overtly sexual content (such as ads for commercialized sexual services), while constructing more sexually "tasteful" representations of gay men and lesbians intended to make the publications attractive for major corporate advertisers.

Several subsequent projects have examined the significance of having LGBTQ-identified cultural workers involved in creating or marketing LGBTQ content for television. Farrell (2008) interviewed gay professionals at three LGBTQ-centric U.S. television networks—Logo, Here TV, and the now defunct Q Television Network—as well as workers at GLAAD (formerly the Gay and Lesbian Alliance Against Defamation) and queer producers of LGBTQ media. Overall, she noted that although many of them discussed their work in both political and economic terms, there was a tendency to evaluate their contributions to LGBTQ equality optimistically without sufficient recognition of the constraints from operating within contexts of commercial production. In another study of U.S. television, Ng (2013, 2013b) described how a new cohort of LGBTQ workers became part of the Logo network during a period of website acquisitions, resulting in a more complex mix of cultural producers that included those who had previously been active only in fan and nonprofessional domains. Initially, Logo's strategies for acquiring content also contributed to a burgeoning of independently produced LGBTQ media, although eventually the network shifted toward a mix of lifestyle-oriented reality programming intended to draw a broader viewership. However, these developments, Ng argued, still constituted significant changes to queer production culture.

Himberg (2018) interviewed a different set of U.S.-based LGBTQ workers across a range of media occupations, including network executives, producers of television programming, and marketing and public relations professionals, discussing how these industry insiders helped generate "common-sense" concepts about LGBTQ identity and politics seen on television. Arguing against assumptions that workers within mainstream media would fail to advance LGBTQ issues, Himberg presented a more complex picture of how they navigated commercial production, both in terms of more visible practices, such as GLAAD advocacy work, and "under-the-radar" activism by network executives invested in effecting significant social change.

In a different line of inquiry looking behind the scenes of television production, Martin (2018c) interviewed Hollywood casting directors to investigate the casting of gay male characters, finding a persistent discourse that the "best actor" would be chosen regardless of an actor's sexuality. However, commercial considerations, such as how well-known an actor was, also shaped the decisions made. Furthermore, gay roles were sometimes described with language such as "masculine" that seemed designed to exclude gay actors by virtue of the stereotypical association of male gayness with effeminacy. Thus, Martin argued that the industry must address the structural conditions that mean that heterosexual actors play gay far more than gay actors play heterosexual roles.

Well before LGBTQ media content had become prevalent, there have been activists criticizing mainstream LGBTQ representations and seeking to shape commercial production cultures in this regard. In an early account of such activism in the United States, Montgomery (1981) examined how gay activists, particularly those working for the New York-based National Gay Task Force (now the Washington, D.C.-based National LGBTQ Task Force), established "routine, informal relations with network personnel" (p. 55) at the three major U.S. television networks at the time—ABC, CBS, and NBC—to provide feedback about LGBTQ content and exert pressure for improvements. Johnson and Keith's (2001) history of queer radio also highlights the contribution of activists to LGBTQ media production, concentrating on U.S.-based independent radio but also noting efforts to reach international audiences. Juhasz (1995) focused more specifically on media arising out of U.S. AIDS activism, some of which was in response to problematic mainstream representations. For example, dissatisfied with the first television movie about AIDS, *An Early Frost* (NBC, 1985), AIDS activists produced several documentaries "which attempted to provide accurate information and expose the distortions of the mainstream press" (p. 47). Doyle's (2015) research on the U.S. organization GLAAD traced a shift from the more militant queer activism of some AIDS activists in the 1980s to a "politics of respectability" in the next two decades as LGBTQ media advocacy became professionalized and institutionalized. While this enabled a certain level of influence on mainstream media as GLAAD leveraged carefully calibrated public criticism and successfully fundraised from wealthy donors, it also entailed a skew toward the participation of White middle-class gay men and pushed GLAAD away from a more strongly inclusive agenda around gender, race, and class, although the organization now takes a more comprehensive approach to diversity in its critiques of media representation (e.g., see GLAAD, 2020).

QUEER PRODUCTION IN PUBLIC MEDIA

Within television, production of LGBTQ content by state-supported broadcasters is similar in certain respects to LGBTQ media that is solely commercially funded in that there is typically a substantial enough budget for higher-quality production values and longer programming. However, public service broadcasters are mandated to serve their viewers in particular ways, including reflecting a nation's diversity. For example, in the United Kingdom, the Communication Act of 2003, which applies to the BBC (British Broadcasting Corporation), ITV (Independent Television), and Channel 4, states that these media services must ensure that the "cultural activity in the United Kingdom, and its diversity, are reflected, supported and stimulated by the representation in those services" (Communication Act, 2003, p. 235). In Ireland, the 2004 Public Service Broadcasting Charter for RTÉ (Raidió Teilifís Éireann) states that it should "reflect fairly and equally the regional, cultural and political diversity of Ireland and its peoples" and that "no editorial or programming bias shall be shown in terms of gender, age, disability, race, sexual orientation, religion or membership of a minority community" (Kerrigan & Vanlee, 2020, p. 4). In the Flanders region of Belgium, the 1997 management agreement for the Flemish public service broadcaster VRT (Vlaamse Radio-en Televisieomroeporganisatie [Flemish Radio-and Television Broadcasting Organisation]) stated that "the diversity of the Flemish population should be fairly represented," although so far neither sexuality nor gender expression have been explicitly listed the way that ethnic and cultural minorities and people with disabilities were later added (Kerrigan & Vanlee, 2020, p. 5).

These public service broadcasting remits came to be interpreted to include content with diverse gender and sexual identities around the time when activism around LGBTQ rights began having an impact on mainstream acceptance of LGBTQ people (Edwards, 2010; Kerrigan, 2021; Kerrigan & Vanlee, 2020) and, in the case of Ireland's RTÉ, also in setting a preliminary goal of having 4% of its employees be LGBTQI-identified (see Kerrigan & O'Brien, 2020; the "I" in "LGBTQI" stands for "intersex"). Drawing in part from interviews with producers at RTÉ and Flanders' VRT, Kerrigan and Vanlee (2020) outlined how the emergence of LGBTQ content at these broadcasters was influenced by LGBTQ activists and outside expertise such as academics with progressive views on gender and sexuality. Early programming around LGBTQ issues on RTÉ and VRT was thus often explicitly pedagogical or didactic, taking the form of talk shows and documentaries, which was also true of British television (see Buckle, 2018; Edwards, 2010). Scripted programming with LGBTQ content on British and European public service broadcasters increased partly in response to competition from commercial content, as media deregulation and globalization made programming from the United States and elsewhere readily available.

Scholarship, including interviews with producers at public service broadcasters, reveals issues around the scripting of LGBTQ characters despite intentions to create diverse representations. Examining television in Flanders, Vanlee (2019) discussed how producers at VRT were conscious about the need to integrate diversity of sexuality into its programming, but generally wrote characters who had fully assimilated and displayed no conventional markers of queerness. This homonormative presentation of LGBTQ characters arose from the writers' desire to avoid negative stereotyping, but also resulted in a paradoxical lack of diversity. In Ireland, Kerrigan (2021) described how LGBTQ representations on RTÉ's sitcoms and soap operas soon after the decriminalization of homosexuality in 1993 continued to be queer-coded through stereotypes, ambivalently depicted, or problematically conservative in terms of what sexual behaviors were shown, due at least in part to the writers' uncertainties on how to represent queer characters. In the following decade, RTÉ did better with more complex depictions of LGBTQ characters, although these representations were entwined with discourses associating the characters with a cosmopolitanism consonant with the turn of Ireland as a nation toward neoliberal globalization.

QUEER PRODUCTION IN THE INDEPENDENT DOMAIN

Despite the increase in LGBTQ production in mainstream media in recent decades, much queer media production has continued to occur within an independent realm of modestly budgeted production. Scholars have examined how producers negotiate the issue of resources and the relationships between the independent and mainstream domains of production, including producer trajectories across the divide, and how independent queer producers can distinguish their content to appeal to sufficient viewers. In an early example of such research, Henderson (2008) discussed the making of the short film *Desert Motel*, centered on a lesbian couple and a transgender support group. In terms of the creators' professional trajectories and the funding of the film, the producers discussed the possibility of a distribution deal with the Viacom-owned Logo television network, and several crew members had worked in commercial media before making *Desert Motel* or took on positions in commercial media after the completion of the film. Thus, Henderson argued that even for an ostensibly independent film, producers of such content actually tend to "move in a cultural middle range" (p. 572) rather than simply at one pole of an industry-independent opposition.

In another study, Coon (2018) interviewed the founders of Mythgarden, an independent production company established by several gay Hollywood producers and actors to produce queer content specifically for queer audiences. Mythgarden had one moderately successful film, *Save Me*, a critical look at the ex-gay movement, which played on the festival circuit and helped the company garner additional pitches, However, facing a challenging financial environment, the company disbanded without producing more content. Still, Coon argued that *Save Me* illustrated the potential for queer-made LGBTQ-themed media to contribute to positive social change. However, Martin (2018a, p. 6) noted that Mythgarden's trajectory "exposes the inherent marketplace contradictions between producing queer content for queers and producing queer content that might have more 'mainstream' appeal," thus also illustrating the struggles faced by independent queer filmmakers working in legacy media. In a different study on how the independent film distributors sought to define the category of "LGBT film," Wuest (2018) discussed how the "packaging, promoting, framing, and naming" of various films with LGBTQ content reflected the still fraught status of queer media. Still, independent producers prioritizing grass-roots queer aesthetics and community over market appeal, as Nault (2018) discussed for Three Dollar Cinema's "DIY" (do-it-yourself) approach in the Austin, TX indie film scene, remain able to produce content distinctive in form and purpose from mainstream LGBTQ media. There has also been some work on the production of queer independent video games, which provide alternatives to mainstream games in terms of not just queer representation, but also the function of the games, which frequently have an explicitly political and/or pedagogical purpose (see Wonica, 2017). Additionally, here it is worth mentioning again Juhasz's (1995) account of independent media production by AIDS activists, much of which was also educational and political in orientation.

Digital platforms have offered important alternatives to producers of queer media, as they have for many communities that have often found mainstream production inaccessible due to economic and other barriers. Christian (2018) discussed various independent web series in the late 2000s and 2010s centered on queer characters, which contributed to the emergence of websites dedicated to LGBTQ content. For example, GLO, The Arthouse, and SLAY TV hosted multiple series about queer people of color, while Between Women TV streamed web series centered on queer women, and the Open TV platform, which helps fund and host diverse web series, includes several centered on queer characters of color. However, many such websites do not survive beyond a few years, with producers facing the challenges of securing funding and attracting viewers amidst an increasingly competitive streaming landscape, not just from the major streaming services, but also general video sites such as YouTube, which has a large amount of LGBTQ content available for free. The sites that have persisted the longest have depended either on user subscriptions or have significant funding from nonprofit organizations.

Radio has been important for independent queer media (see Johnson & Keith, 2001), even in the era of digital technologies, and there has been some research incorporating a production studies perspective. For example, Bosch (2007) conducted participant observation and interviews in examining the South African program *In the Pink*, which aired on the Cape Town community radio station Bush Radio. While there was a range of content on *In the Pink* intended to create an alternative space for LGBTQ listeners, Bosch noted that the majority of the program's producers were middle class, and there were also gender and racial asymmetries: White gay men and Black lesbians constituted the bulk of the production team, but many of the Black lesbians were hesitant to go on air. In another study, examining the LGBTQ-oriented Irish radio station Open FM, Kerrigan and O'Brien (2018) found a programming approach intended to appeal to both LGBTQ and heterosexual listeners, a strategy that Sender (2007) had termed "dualcasting" in relation to U.S. cable network Bravo's goal of attracting straight women and LGBTQ viewers. Thus, Open FM's producers recruited volunteers from radio and media students without requiring them to be queer-identified and generally prioritized presenting content in a "professional" manner over a more overtly queer political vision.

QUEER PRODUCTION WITHIN FAN CULTURES

A sizable amount of queer production occurs within the domain of media fandoms. General production studies scholarship, with a focus on industrial practice, does not typically address fan cultural production. However, attention to fan production that has significant points of intersection with industrial producers and texts is consonant with the goal of queer production studies to address areas traditionally neglected within general production studies. One set of issues revolves around fan–official producer boundaries, including how queer fan producers interact with official producers as well as how fan texts relate to canonical (i.e., official) texts and industrial production. Another line of discussion concerns the extent to which queer fan texts challenge dominant norms of gender and sexuality that are prevalent in mainstream media.

In this vein, a number of older studies on queer fan videos can be considered through a queer production studies lens. Research on fan-produced "slash" music videos featuring the Kirk and Spock characters of the *Star Trek* series by Bacon-Smith (1992), Jenkins (1992), and others discussed the practices of remixing segments of the show's episodes with a music soundtrack, creating new homoerotic narratives that suggested a romantic relationship between the two men. Fans have also produced music videos for pairings that are canonically queer, sometimes because the representation on the official media text is found to be inadequate (Ng, 2008). While fans producing videos about pairings between two women are typically queer women themselves (Ng, 2008; Russo, 2017), videos about pairings between men are mostly made by heterosexual women, reflecting a broader trend in fan cultures (Bacon-Smith, 1992; Jenkins, 1992). Thus, although the narratives of queer-themed fan videos may contest the heteronormativity of the canonical texts to some extent, the interest of straight-identified women in eroticizing male–male relationships has also been argued to arise less from progressive conceptualizations of gender and sexuality than from a depoliticized interest in male homoeroticism that may even veer toward misogyny (Jenkins, 1992; Scodari, 2003). Fan videos about lesbian pairings made by queer women, which are more clearly examples of content creation by members of a marginalized community, also offer alternatives to heteronormative narratives, but they also frequently fail to challenge various mainstream norms around gender roles, sex, and romance (Ng, 2008; Russo, 2013).

Fans also produce paratextual commentary (i.e., verbal or graphic content and other creative works that engage with a canonical text and its official paratexts), such as marketing materials, cast interviews, and producer commentary on DVD releases (Gray, 2010). Similar to fan videos, queer-themed paratexts can be examined for the extent to which their production "seeks to neutralize social, cultural, and industrial anxieties around mediated homosexuality" and how they "contest 'preferred' readings of LGBTQ texts" (Martin, 2018a, p. 5). A variety of digital platforms are now important, although not all have garnered equal scholarly attention; as Tsika (2016) argued in an account of fan paratexts around cinematic depictions of queer men, while corporate media is invested in "affirm[ing] male homosexuality as a fixed identity category" to maintain a commercially appealing, recognizable gay male consumer (p. 18), this is challenged by "a proliferation of short, extractive media such as GIFs, Vines, photomontages, tweets, Facebook uploads, Instagram renderings, Tumblr productions, and various other forms of digital encoding" (pp. 25–26).

Drawing on such sources, Ng (2018) examined fan-produced paratexts about the lesbian-themed films *Carol* (2015) and *Freeheld* (2015), finding that while official promotional materials and mainstream media reviews stressed themes of "universality" that downplayed the nonnormative content of the films, fans reworked segments of the original texts and offered commentary that explicitly asserted the queer specificities of both films, including the "Harold, they're lesbians" meme about *Carol* that briefly went viral. Tsika (2016) argued that the paratexts he examined constituted understudied "'perverse archives'" that are "unauthorized, openly fetishistic, libelous, and downright pornographic" (p. 20). For example, screenshots of Jude Law's feet from the film *The Talented Mr. Ripley* (1999) were circulated on "a foot-fetish Tumblr" blog (p. 63), and clips of James Franco's character in his 2011 master's thesis film *The Broken Tower* performing oral sex on another man were featured in a sex blog video post entitled "Here's That Video of James Franco Sucking a Dick."

Another genre of paratextual commentary is the videographic essay involving the combining of remixed material, mainly from television and film, with analysis to produce critical readings of these texts in audiovisual format. Such essays about LGBTQ media are commonly made by fans and shared on video platforms (e.g., see NINTH SHOW, PrideBrary, and Rowan Ellis's YouTube channels), as well as being authored by scholars and published in videographic journals (e.g., Daigle, 2018; Francis, 2018). The production of such commentary has not to date received significant attention in production studies scholarship, although remix is an important topic in fan studies. On this note, Navar-Gill and Stanfill (2018) explicitly pushed back against the traditional separation of fan studies from production studies, arguing that fan activist hashtags criticizing certain television representations of LGBTQ characters should be theorized as "production interventions" (p. 98) rather than simply insular fan practices that are only tangentially related to media production.

The emergence of digital technologies has to some extent increased the permeability of the boundary between industry and fan production (Jenkins, 2006). While scholars such as Ng (2017) and Navar-Gill and Stanfill (2018) described instances of fans criticizing industry producers via social media, in other cases, there have been more collaborative relationships. In a study about the mainland Chinese series *Guardian* (*Youku.com*, 2018), adapted from a novel in the "boys' love" genre popular in several East Asian countries (Suter, 2013; Zhao et al., 2017), Ng and Li (2020) examined how fan interactions with the series producers as well as fan paratexts about the series demonstrated a careful negotiation of the conditions for expressing enthusiasm for the central relationship between the two male characters; fan discourses in the more public online platforms generally hewed to the official producers' line that the relationship was brotherly rather than romantic, while only in less well-known fan spaces did fans more openly circulate explicitly homoerotic content. Online fan works have also crossed over to industrial production. Examples of non-LGBTQ fan fiction being adapted into mainstream media forms in the West, such as *Fifty Shades of Grey*, are well-known, but the phenomenon has emerged elsewhere too. For example, in China, several works of popular online fiction have come to the attention of television producers and been made into series (Gong & Yang, 2017). Some of these belong to the "boys' love" category (see Chen & Hu, 2018), including *The Untamed* (*Tencent Video*, 2019), which was distributed globally by Netflix.

AREAS FOR FURTHER RESEARCH

To date, research on LGBTQ media, as in much analysis of the media in general, remains primarily focused on textual content as opposed to production, no doubt due in part to the fact that meaningful access to media producers and the processes of their work, particularly those in the commercial domain, is often challenging to obtain. Furthermore, queer production studies is a relatively new subfield within media studies. As such, there are many research settings that require further examination in terms of the type of production domain (e.g., mainstream commercial or independent), the form of media text (e.g., film vs. television), and the geographical location of the production, all of which significantly shape the particular conditions of production. With a larger body of work, scholars would be better able to theorize the significance of nonnormative sexual and gender identity within different production contexts, including the key issues of the relationship between producer identities and the media texts they produce. It is also important to investigate how queerness intersects with other axes of marginality, such as class, race and ethnicity, and language, especially given existing scholarship suggesting that particular forms of LGBTQ identity are positively associated with consumerism and neoliberal cosmopolitanism (Ng, 2013; Sender, 2004).

At another level, Martin (2018a) proposed queer production studies as a framework encompassing areas of research that have not been consistently theorized together, particularly the inclusion of fan paratexts alongside industrial production (although texts such as fan videos have been discussed within scholarship about the media industries; e.g., see Jenkins, 2006). The existing research in queer production studies suggests this is a promising theoretical endeavor that can reconfigure traditional subdisciplinary boundaries, but more work is needed to see how theoretically generative such an approach will be.

PRIMARY SOURCES

The key reference for demarcating queer production studies as a subfield is the 2018 special issue of the *Journal of Film and Video*, 70 (pp. 3–4). Martin's introductory essay outlines the rationale and goals and situates it against general production studies. Also in this special issue are articles about official and fan paratexts around queer media (Navar-Gill & Stanfill; Ng; Wuest) and queer independent film production (Coon; Nault) focused on the U.S context. Since then, the work of Páraic Kerrigan, Anne O'Brien, and Florian Vanlee has extended the queer production studies framework to European contexts (Kerrigan & O'Brien, 2020; Kerrigan & Vanlee, 2020; O'Brien & Kerrigan, 2020; Vanlee, 2019).

As the article mentions earlier, there are a number of studies about queer production prior to this special issue that did not explicitly name themselves as queer production studies. Important examples include Sender (2004), Henderson (2008), Ng (2013), Himberg (2018), and Christian (2018), which are producer- and production-focused studies of mainstream and independent queer media in the United States. There are also a number of studies on fan production of queer media, both of narrative forms such as music videos (Ng, 2008; Russo, 2017) and various forms of paratextual content, as noted. See also Lavin et al. (2017) for a discussion of fan cultural production in China, Hong Kong, and Taiwan.

Additionally, it may be helpful to refer to a couple of key texts for general production studies, such as Banks et al. (2015), Caldwell (2008), Mayer et al. (2009), and Mayer (2018). Although these do not address queer production, they lay out the theory and methods of industry-focused production studies.

FURTHER READING

Christian, A. (2018). *Open TV: Innovation beyond Hollywood and the rise of web television*. New York University Press.
Henderson, L. (2008). Queer relay. *GLQ, 14*(4), 569–597. https://doi.org/10.1215/10642684-2008-005
Kerrigan, P., & O'Brien, A. (2020). Camping it up and toning it down: Gay and lesbian sexual identity in media work. *Media, Culture & Society, 42*(7–8), 1061–1077. https://doi.org/10.1177/0163443720908149
Kerrigan, P., & Vanlee, F. (2020). Public service broadcasting and the emergence of LGBT+ visibility: A comparative perspective on Ireland and Flanders. *European Journal of Cultural Studies* 25(1), 183–200. https://doi.org/10.1177/1367549420935893
Lavin, M., Yang, L., & Zhao, J. J. (2017). *Boys' love, cosplay, and androgynous idols: Queer fan cultures in Mainland China, Hong Kong, and Taiwan*. Hong Kong University Press.
Ng, E. (2013). A "post-gay" era? Media gaystreaming, homonormativity, and the politics of LGBT integration. *Communication, Culture, & Critique, 6*(2), 258–283. https://doi.org/10.1111/cccr.12013
Ng, E. (2018). Contesting the queer subfield of cultural production: Paratextual framings of *Carol* and *Freeheld*. *Journal of Film and Video, 70*(3–4), 8–23. https://doi.org/10.5406/jfilmvideo.70.3-4.0008
O'Brien, A., & Kerrigan, P. (2020). Gay the right way: Roles and routines of Irish media production among gay and lesbian workers. *European Journal of Communication, 35*(4), 355–369. https://doi.org/10.1177/0267323120903684
Sender, K. (2004). *Business, not politics: The making of the gay market*. Columbia University Press.
Vanlee, F. (2019). Acknowledging/denying LGBT+ difference: Understanding homonormativity and LGBT+ homogeneity in Flemish TV fiction through production research. *European Journal of Communication, 34*(5), 520–534. https://doi.org/10.1177/0267323119874250

REFERENCES

Aslinger, B. (2009). Creating a network for queer audiences at Logo TV. *Popular Communication, 7*(2), 107–121. https://doi.org/10.1080/15405700902776495
Aslinger, B. (2010). PlanetOut and the dichotomies of queer media conglomeration. In C. Pullen & M. Cooper (Eds.), *LGBT identity and online new media* (pp. 113–124). Routledge.
Bacon-Smith, C. (1992). *Enterprising women: Television fandom and the creation of popular myth*. University of Pennsylvania Press.
Banks, M., Conor, B., & Mayer, V. (2015). *Production studies, the sequel! Cultural studies of global media industries*. Routledge.
Becker, R. (2006). *Gay TV and straight America*. Rutgers University Press.
Bosch, T. (2007). *In the Pink*: Gay radio in South Africa. *Feminist Media Studies, 7*(3), 225–238. https://doi.org/10.1080/14680770701477859

Buckle, S. (2018). *Homosexuality on the small screen: Television and gay identity in Britain.* I.B. Tauris.

Caldwell, J. (2008). *Production culture: Industrial reflexivity and critical practice in film and television.* Duke University Press.

Campbell, J. (2005). Outing PlanetOut Surveillance, gay marketing and internet affinity portals. *New Media & Society, 7*(5), 663–683. https://doi.org/10.1177/1461444805056011

Chen, W., & Hu, Q. (2018). Research on the types of *danmei* internet dramas in China in the new century [新世纪中国耽美网络剧类型化研究]. *Media Observer* (传媒观察), *417*(9), 71–77. https://www.cnki.net/kcms/doi/10.19480/j.cnki.cmgc.2018.09.011.html

Chua, L. (2014). *Mobilizing gay Singapore: Rights and resistance in an authoritarian state.* Temple University Press.

Communication Act 2003, Chapter 21. (2003). *Legislation.gov.uk.* https://www.legislation.gov.uk/ukpga/2003/21/pdfs/ukpga_20030021_en.pdf

Coon, D. R. (2018). Mythgarden: Collaborative authorship and counter-storytelling in queer independent film. *Journal of Film and Video, 70*(3–4), 44–62. https://doi.org/10.5406/jfilmvideo.70.3-4.0044

Daigle, A. (2018). Of love and longing. *Journal of Videographic Film & Moving Image Studies, 5*(2). http://mediacommons.org/intransition/2018/05/02/love-and-longing

Dornfeld, B. (1998). *Producing public television, producing public culture.* Princeton University Press.

Doyle, V. (2015). *Making out in the mainstream: GLAAD and the politics of respectability.* McGill-Queen's University Press.

Duggan, L. (2002). The new homonormativity: The sexual politics of neoliberalism. In R. Castronovo & D. Nelson (Eds.), *Materializing democracy: Toward a revitalized cultural politics* (pp. 175–194). Duke University Press.

Edwards, N. (2010). *Queer British television: Policy and practice, 1997–2007* [Unpublished doctoral dissertation]. University of Nottingham. http://eprints.nottingham.ac.uk/11113/

Ellis, R. (n.d.). Home [Video]. YouTube. https://www.youtube.com/user/muppetmadness

Farrell, K. (2008). *Backstage politics: Social change and the "gay TV" industry* [Unpublished doctoral dissertation]. Syracuse University. https://surface.syr.edu/soc_etd/5/

Francis, M. (2018). Cruising différance in 3 scenes. *Journal of Videographic Film & Moving Image Studies, 5*(3). http://mediacommons.org/intransition/cruising-diff%C3%A9rance-3-scenes

Fraser, N. (1990). Rethinking the public sphere: A contribution to the critique of actually existing democracy. *Social Text, 25/26,* 56–80. https://doi-org.proxy.library.ohio.edu/10.2307/466240

Gamson, J. (2003). Gay Media Inc.: Media structures, the new gay conglomerates, and collective sexual identities. In M. McCaughey, & M. Ayers (Eds.), *Cyberactivism: Online activism in theory and practice* (pp. 255–278). Routledge.

GLAAD. (2020). Where we are on TV report: 2020–2021. *GLAAD.* https://www.glaad.org/whereweareontv20

Gong, H., & Yang, X. (2017). Constructing gendered desire in online fiction and web dramas. In *Reconfiguring class, gender, ethnicity and ethics in Chinese internet culture* (pp. 72–88). Routledge.

Gray, J. (2010). *Show sold separately: Promos, spoilers, and other media paratexts.* New York University Press.

Guardian [镇魂]. (2018). *Youku.com.* https://v.youku.com/v_show/id_XMzY2MDI5NDM0MA==.html

Harvey, D. (2012). Sub-Saharan African sexualities, transnational HIV/AIDS educational film and the question of queerness. In C. Pullen (Ed.), *LGBT transnational identity and the media* (pp. 67–83). Palgrave Macmillan.

Himberg, J. (2018). *The new gay for pay: The sexual politics of American television production.* University of Texas Press.

Jenkins, H. (1992). *Textual poachers: Television fans and participatory culture.* Routledge.

Jenkins, H. (2006). *Convergence culture: Where old and new media collide.* New York University Press.

Johnson, C. (2013). From brand congruence to the "virtuous circle": Branding and the commercialization of public service broadcasting. *Media, Culture & Society, 35*(3), 314–331. https://doi.org/10.1177/0163443712472088

Johnson, P. A., & Keith, M. C. (2001). *Queer airwaves: The story of gay and lesbian broadcasting*. M.E. Sharpe.

Juhasz, A. (1995). *AIDS TV: Identity, community and alternative video*. Duke University Press.

Kerrigan, P. (2021). *LGBTQ visibility, media and sexuality in Ireland*. Routledge.

Kerrigan, P., & O'Brien, A. (2018). "Openness through sound": Dualcasting on Irish LGBT radio. *Journal of Radio & Audio Media, 25*(2), 224–239. https://doi.org/10.1080/19376529.2018.1477779

Lafferty, P. (Producer), & Erman, J. (Director). (1985). *An early frost* [Motion picture]. NBC.

Lotz, A. (2007). *The television will be revolutionized*. New York University Press.

Martin, A. L., Jr. (2018a). Introduction: What is queer production studies/why is queer production studies? *Journal of Film and Video, 70*(3–4), 3–7. https://doi.org/10.5406/jfilmvideo.70.3-4.0003

Martin, A. L., Jr. (2018b). Queer (in)frequencies: SiriusXM's OutQ and the limits of queer listening publics. *Feminist Media Studies, 18*(2), 648–663. https://doi.org/10.1080/14680777.2017.1315735

Martin, A. L., Jr. (2018c). The queer business of casting gay characters on U.S. television. *Communication, Culture and Critique, 11*(2), 282–297. https://doi.org/10.1093/ccc/tcy005

Martin, A. L., Jr. (2021). *The generic closet: Black gayness and the Black-cast sitcom*. Indiana University Press.

Mayer, V. (2018). Cultural and creative industries. In J. Nussbaum (Ed.), *Oxford research encyclopedia of communication*. Oxford University Press. https://doi.org/10.1093/acrefore/9780190228613.013.552

Mayer, V., Banks, M., & Caldwell, J. (2009). *Production studies: Cultural studies of media industries*. Routledge.

Montgomery, K. (1981). Gay activists and the networks. *Journal of Communication, 31*(3), 49–57. https://doi.org/10.1111/j.1460-2466.1981.tb00427.x

Nault, C. (2018). Three dollar cinema: The down and dirty DIY of queer production. *Journal of Film and Video, 70*(3–4), 63–84. https://doi.org/10.5406/jfilmvideo.70.3-4.0063

Navar-Gill, A., & Stanfill, M. (2018). "We shouldn't have to trend to make you listen": Queer fan hashtag campaigns as production interventions. *Journal of Film and Video, 70*(3–4), 85–100. https://doi.org/10.5406/jfilmvideo.70.3-4.0085

Ng, E. (2008). Reading the romance of fan cultural production: Music videos of a television lesbian couple. *Popular Communication, 6*(2), 103–121. https://doi.org/10.1080/15405700701746525

Ng, E. (2013b). *Rebranding gay: New configurations of digital media and commercial culture* [Unpublished doctoral dissertation]. University of Massachusetts, Amherst.

Ng, E. (2017). Between text, paratext, and context: Queerbaiting and the contemporary media landscape. *Transformative Works and Cultures, 24*. https://doi.org/10.3983/twc.2017.917

Ng, E. (2018). LGBT advocacy and transnational funding in Singapore and Malaysia. *Development and Change, 49*(4), 1093–1114. https://doi.org/10.1111/dech.12406

Ng, E., & Li, X. (2020). A queer "socialist brotherhood": The *Guardian* web series, boys' love fandom, and the mainland Chinese state. *Feminist Media Studies, 20*(4), 479–495. https://doi.org/10.1080/14680777.2020.1754627

NINTH SHOW. (n.d.). *Home* [Video]. YouTube. https://www.youtube.com/channel/UCxWCv-lsRqkNvH44VUyLg2A

PrideBrary. (n.d.). *Home* [Video]. YouTube. https://www.youtube.com/c/PrideBrary

Russo, J. L. (2013). Textual orientation: Queer female fandom online. In C. Carter, L. Steiner, & L. McLaughlin (Eds.), *The Routledge companion to media and gender* (pp. 450–460). Routledge.

Russo, J. L. (2017). Femslash goggles: Fan vids with commentary by creators. *Transformative Works and Cultures, 24*. http://dx.doi.org/10.3983/twc.2017.1026

Scodari, C. (2003). Resistance reexamined: Gender, fan practices, and science fiction television. *Popular Communication, 1*(2), 111–130. https://doi.org/10.1207/S15405710PC0102_3

Sender, K. (2007). Dualcasting: Bravo's gay programming and the quest for women audiences. In S. Banet-Weiser, C. Chris, & A. Freitas (Eds.), *Cable visions: Television beyond broadcasting* (pp. 302–318). New York University Press.

Suter, R. (2013). Gender bending and exoticism in Japanese girls' comics. *Asian Studies Review*, 37(4), 546–558. https://doi.org/10.1080/10357823.2013.832111

The Untamed [陈情令]. (2019). *Tencent Video*. https://v.qq.com/x/cover/vbb35hm6m6da1wc.html

Tongson, K. (2011). *Relocations: Queer suburban imaginaries*. New York University Press.

Tsika, N. (2016). *Pink 2.0: Encoding queer cinema on the internet*. Indiana University Press.

Warner, M. (2005). *Publics and counterpublics*. Zone Books.

Wonica, P. (2017). Ending the cycle: Developing a board game to engage people in social justice issues. In B. Ruberg & A. Shaw (Eds.), *Queer game studies* (pp. 45–53). University of Minnesota Press.

Wuest, B. (2018). A shelf of one's own: A queer production studies approach to LGBT film distribution and categorization. *Journal of Film and Video*, 70(3–4), 24–43. https://doi.org/10.5406/jfilmvideo.70.3-4.0024

Zhao, J. J., Yang, L., & Lavin, M. (2017). Introduction. In M. Lavin, L. Yang, & J. J. Zhao (Eds.), *Boys' love, cosplay, and androgynous idols: Queer fan cultures in Mainland China, Hong Kong, and Taiwan* (pp. xi–xxxiii). Hong Kong University Press.

Zhou, S. (2017). From online BL fandom to the CCTV spring festival gala: The transforming power of online carnival. In M. Lavin, L. Yang, & J. J. Zhao (Eds.), *Boys' love, cosplay, and androgynous idols: Queer fan cultures in Mainland China, Hong Kong, and Taiwan* (pp. 91–110). Hong Kong University Press.

Eve Ng

QUEER(ING) POPULAR MUSIC CULTURE

INTRODUCTION

In this contribution, crucial explanations of queer theory are given, and developments in musicology presented, for example, how (sub)cultural studies helped to queer musicology. Furthermore, it provides insights from non-U.S. and U.K. queer scholarship and points to the Whiteness of this scholarship. After this, various selected periods in popular music culture are analyzed to find queer characteristics and ways of queering music, for example: blues and jazz in the early 20th century, glam rock during the late 1960s and 1970s, Riot Grrrls during the 1990s, and their ladyfests, which lasted until 2010s; Black hip-hop feminism; and the most recent development is that many trans and nonbinary musicians are coming out publicly and sing about their trans experiences. The selection of these periods and genres was made according to the relevance for contemporary queer music culture. The first queer period in the blues, jazz, and vaudeville culture proves that many working-class African American musicians were actively queering music. This Black queering of music is happening now again in hip-hop culture. Glam rock had a big impact on LGBTIQ-life and politics and is still here today, as seen in the recent winners of the Eurovision song contest 2021, Måneskin—an Italian rock band imitating glam rock performances and playing with gender nonconformity and queer sexual orientation, whose same-sex kiss on the stage at the end of their concert in Poland is a critique of the current anti-LGBTIQ politics happening there. Due to the limited space in this contribution, it was not possible to include further examples of queer music, but a look in the archives, which are mentioned later, will show many more contributions to queer music culture. Another impossible task was to narrow down some simple central questions which could be used methodologically for finding out what is queer music, as the complexity of gender and sexuality performances and performativity in different cultural and temporal context gets in the way.

Queer Theory. Queer theory originated through the AIDS movement in the United States, but critically distanced itself from gay and lesbian studies through its strong antiessentialism (Teresa de Lauretis, 1991), antiassimilation, and aims to subvert fixed identities, normativity (even homonormativity), and classifications (see "Queer Perspectives in Communication Studies," Isaac N. West, 2018, in this encyclopedia). Already in 1981, Gloria Anzaldúa, a feminist of color, used the term "queer" to describe the overlapping of complex forms of oppression, which builds the basis for alliances that are not based on a certain identity. Thus, queer feminists of color anticipated the main political impact of queer activism and theory as a reconceptualization of gender, sexuality, and other intersectionalities in order to overcome identity politics. Despite the involvement of people of color in queer activism and theory, queer theory was seen at the beginning as mainly White dominated. The White antisocial strand in queer theory was most influential during the late 1990s and early 2000s with Lee Edelman's punk ideology in *No Future* (2004) and J. Halberstam's works *Female Masculinity* (1998) and *In a Queer Time and Place* (2005). Queer academics of color gave a powerful rebuttal to the dominant White voices with a more positive utopian attitude, such as in the works of Sara Ahmed, for example, *Queer Phenomenology* (2006), José Esteban Muñoz, *Cruising Utopia* (2009), and Juana María Rodríguez, *Sexual Futures* (2014). A positive queer future is crucial for queer and trans people of color, for whom the struggle to be able to survive is still important.

Two examples of how these antisocial and pro-utopian queer strands have been integrated in musicology and cultural studies will be given in this paragraph. Robin James discusses the "No Future" attitude connected with music in her book *Resilience and Melancholy* (2015) and uses Atari Teenage Riot's (ATR), a German digital hardcore cyberpunk band, *Delete Yourself (You Have No Chance to Win)* as an example of how, for White people, death is the effect of a deliberate divestment (which is queer because it does not invest in the neoliberal demand of a "normal" life) and not of exclusion (pp. 49–77). However, Marlon M. Bailey shows how Black and Latina LGBTIQ people created in the ballroom culture of Detroit, a place for survival for queers of color to affirm and support each other, also through HIV prevention activities (Bailey, 2014, 2013). They did this through building a positive space with its own kind of kinship structure (called houses, which are led by mothers and fathers) to secure a future for their community.

QUEER(ING) MUSICOLOGY

Similar developments happened when queer theory gained a foothold in musicology. In the early 1990s, queer music was still seen as a gay and lesbian enterprise and the music world seemed to be dominated mainly by successful White gay, lesbian, and bisexual musicians, and female and male impersonators (Brett & Wood, 2001). The anthology *Queering the Pitch: The*

New Gay and Lesbian Musicology (Brett et al., 1994) is an example of this. The achievement of this book was to open up the field of popular music studies beyond the study of White male performers and to widen the research perspective in musicology, which was before mainly concerned with White male composers and the study of notations. After the editors had been criticized for their lack of attention paid to race and class and to trans individuals (Baitz, 2009), they published the second edition with an additional "Coda" addressing these critiques. In the 2006 *Queering the Popular Pitch* anthology by different editors (Whiteley & Rycenga) similar issues are covered, but genuine trans experiences still do not form part of the chapters. No edited or authored book focusing on these intersectionalities (e.g., race, class, or trans) in queer music culture exists so far, only some examples of articles and chapters, for example in the section "Challenging hegemonic practices: New masculinities, queerness, and transgenderism" in Stan Hawkins's edited book *The Routledge Research Companion to Popular Music and Gender* (2017), some contributions of *The Oxford Handbook of Music and Queerness* (2018/2022) edited by Fred Everett Maus and Sheila Whiteley, or parts of the authored book *Queer Tracks* (Leibetseder, 2012). Other music scholars, whom I did not mention so far, publishing multidisciplinary work at the crossroads of queer theory and musicology are Lori Burns and Mélisse Lafrance, *Disruptive Divas* (2002); Judith Peraino, *Listening to the Sirens* (2006); Freya Jarman-Ivens, *Queer Voices* (2011); and Stan Hawkins, *Queerness in Pop Music* (2016).

Queering Musicology With (Sub)Cultural Studies. The queering of musicology happened mainly with the help of queer (sub)cultural studies. Their study of queer subjectivities and their (sub)culture consists of recognizing when "queer sexualities, identities, sensibilities, and diversities" occur (Hawkins, 2017, p. 5; Taylor, 2013, p. 195). Jodie Taylor confirms that queering became an accepted hermeneutic method in many fields (Taylor, 2013) and the same holds true for musicology through incorporating (sub)cultural studies' analysis of queer people and their cultural sensibilities. This interdisciplinary character of more contemporary popular music studies, which bridges musicologist and cultural studies approaches, is seen in Taylor's book *Playing It Queer* (2012). In her empirical research she analyzes local musicians and the queer (sub)cultural style in everyday lives in Australia, Berlin and London. Her work gives an account of how "music-making, performance and consumption" form "identities and political imagination" (see cover text of the book). Another research project on the influence of music on LGBTIQ people in their daily life was based in Belgium and the outcome, including playlists from the interviewed people, is presented at QueerVoices.be.

The development of queer subcultural studies started with the studies of youth subcultures by the Centre for Contemporary Cultural Studies (CCCS) at the University of Birmingham in the 1970s. Those studies suggested that subcultural music scenes were in opposition to the dominant culture and to parent cultures. Although, J. Halberstam, a queer theorist, sees a different relationship of queer subcultures to parent cultures (Frith, 1983; Halberstam, 2005; Hall & Jefferson, 1976; Hebdige, 1979; Reitsamer, 2008, p. 213) and notes that in queer subcultures "they oppose not only the hegemony of dominant culture but also mainstreaming of gay and lesbian culture" (Halberstam, 2005, p. 161). An example of one such queer subculture is queercore, a queer punk movement in the 1980s in Toronto. Their artists were against the homophobia of mainstream punk and the exclusionary strategies of the dominant gay and lesbian scene (Curran, 2018). This queer punk subculture is analyzed in the book *Queer Feminist Punk* by Katharina Wiedlack who "seeks to bring queer-feminist punks of color, Riot Grrrls, and Queercore, Homocore or Dykecore to the fore" (2015, p. 11) and focuses on the queer-feminist and antiracist punk movements in the United States and Canada.

In many countries outside the United States and the United Kingdom, the visibility and mainstreaming of gay and lesbian culture did not even happen before queer subculture emerged. Thus, the opposition of queer subcultures depends on where the queer subculture is placed geographically and culturally. As for example, Rosa Reitsamer explains with the queer-feminist music events happening in the 1990s and 2000s in Vienna, where the intergenerational dialogue was part of the opposition to the dominant (male-dominated) culture, and the (lesbian) "first" generations visited the "new" queer festivals (Reitsamer, 2008, p. 227). This corroborates another insight of Halberstam, who says that the recent women's music festivals are "clear inheritors of lesbian feminist music festivals and they revive an earlier model of feminism for a new generation of grrrls" (Halberstam, 2005, p. 180; Reitsamer, 2008, p. 225; see also the Riot Grrrls and Ladyfest section in this article).

HISTORY OF QUEER(ING) POPULAR MUSIC CULTURE

Dominant approaches to reconstructing popular music's past tend to neglect queer, female, or African American performers and queer music subculture. The primarily White male music critics and rock historians have praised only certain musicians (Regev, 1994) and erased many female and African American artists from written and audio history (Reitsamer, 2018, p. 28; Zuberi, 2018). As counterarchives to the dominant popular music history, several individual and collective digital archives were built in a DIY way to document and disseminate "women's, feminist and queer music-making in the past and present" (Reitsamer, 2018, p. 31).

In popular music culture, the historical roots are found in the African American blues and jazz tradition. The queering happened early on as the performance character of those concerts stem from vaudeville variety shows including crossdressers playing the role of the other genders on stage (Howells, 1869). The representation of women done by men was in a respectful and appropriate way (Callen, 2006, p. 187). During the 1920s and 1930s many of the working-class African American blues singers such as Ma Rainey were lesbian or gay. Their sexual orientation was presented publicly as in the advertisement for Rainey's song *Prove it on Me Blues*, showing a drawing of the singer who tries to seduce two women in man's clothing on the street (Callen, 2006, p. 190). The blues music of the Black vaudeville women from that time reflects the lived experiences and the sexual politics of Black working-class women (Davis, 1999; Hayes, 2010, p. 27).

Later on as rock and pop music developed further, Janis Joplin's bisexuality and ambiguous gender presentation were mentioned in the 1960s (O'Brien, 2002, pp. 104–105). Signs of gender parody could be already seen in Elvis Presley's legendary hip swing (Whiteley, 2006, p. 249), his makeup, and golden suits (Hoskyns, 1998, p. 32). The Beatles' hairstyles were another contribution to the "feminization" of men during the conservative late 1950s and early 1960s. Little Richard, who started his career with vaudeville shows and blues, was a very glittering, African American, and homosexual representative of rock music. He was the forerunner of the glam rock period, and even David Bowie mentioned that Little Richard was his boyhood idol.

Glam Rock. Glam rock was the sexual and gender revolution in popular music culture and an outburst of queer(ing) rock and pop music in the late 1960s and early 1970s. Norms for both gender performance and sexual orientation were subverted by musicians such as Marc Bolan from T. Rex, David Bowie, Lou Reed, and Iggy Pop. Wearing glitter, makeup, and feminine clothes, those artists performed a different sexual desire on stage, for example when Bowie "went down on" Mick Ronson's guitar (Haynes, 1998, pp. X–XI). Bowie said in an interview in 1972 that he was gay, which was only five years before the laws on homosexuality had been reformed in the United Kingdom (Watts, 2006). The androgynous look and the bisexuality of the glam rockers corresponded to a camp aesthetic. Susan Sontag explained in her *Notes on Camp* (1964, reprinted 2018) more on the characteristics of this kind of sensibility, as Sontag describes it. In a nutshell, for her it is an exaggerated and extravagant style occurring in objects and in people's behavior, a kind of homosexual taste. To camp is a mode of seduction, seeing androgyny as sexually attractive and not being moralistic. Camp is a form of enjoyment and appreciation; it does not differentiate between a mass-produced or unique object, which according to Oscar Wilde (whom she dedicated the 58 notes to) shows the democratic esprit of camp (Leibetseder, 2012, p. 61). Freya Jarman-Ivens explains how musical gestures can be camp. Jarman-Ivens analyzes, among others, two performances of the same piece of music, of Tchaikovsky's *Piano concerto No. 1 in B flat minor* (op. 23, 1975), one played by Vladimir Horowitz in 1943 and the other by Liberace in 1969. In Liberace's musical performance, she found an exaggerated production of anticipation through particular attacks and decays on relevant notes. Liberace holds an accented note longer than Horowitz, just a bit too long—as Sontag describes the extravagance or theatricality of camp. In the opening, Liberace's hands seem to bounce off the keyboard from one chord to the next attack, thereby increasing the dramatic sound of the music (Jarman-Ivens, 2009).

Eve Kosofsky Sedgwick, a literary scholar, included the audience in her analysis of camp and sees it as a strategy of self-empowerment if the audience recognizes the camp quality of the author's work. She therefore uses the term "camp recognition" (1990, p. 156). Not only the camp performance is important, but also the performativity—the repetition of camp gestures—which are recognized by the right, queer, audience, and led to self-empowerment of queer people. For example, a song could help a young queer person growing up in the countryside to find his/her/their queer community (even if the internet does not yet exist there). To recognize that one likes the song *Somewhere Over the Rainbow* by Judy Garland, is a moment of feeling different from others, but also finding recognition of the community of people who also like this song. Thus, a feeling of empowerment comes with this collective appreciation (Michasiw, 1994, pp. 151–154). The influence of the gender and sexual fluidity of glam rockers on the queer community was important and helped many to express themselves in their daily lives or as a musician. This could be seen after David Bowie's death, when many queer and trans people, and also LGBTIQ organizations, mentioned how much influence his music and performances had on their lives (Oppenheim, 2016; Rogers, 2016). The glam rock movement was mainly dominated by men (although being in drag) and had its origin in the U.K. Despite this, a few female glam rock bands such as Suzi Quatro and The Runaways with Joan Jett came to global fame. In contrast, the U.S. music scene in the late 1970s and early 1980s was more into glam metal (a sort of glam version of hard rock or heavy metal), but it was not queer or trans friendly or inclusive.

Riot Grrrls and Ladyfest. In the early 1990s, the feminist queer revolution started in the punk scene in Olympia, Washington, and in Washington, D.C. Young female musicians expressed their discontent with the male-oriented punk scene. Female creativity in popular music in general was and still is limited and pressed into a heteronormative scheme. Different sexual and gendered lifestyles add to the experience of feeling excluded from certain music cultures as musicians, whereas one is only being included as a consumer (Bayton, 1998; Frith & McRobbie, 1978; Gottlieb & Wald, 1994; Reitsamer, 2008, p. 213). Riot Grrrls felt alienated and marginalized and started their own empowerment through the formation of bands and producing fanzines, according to the old DIY punk ethos, but with a queer-feminist twist (Piepmeier, 2009). In the Riot Grrrl scene there was a strong lesbian element and links to the gay punk homocore or queercore movement, which had a focus on LGBTIQ issues during the 1980s and 1990s. Examples of some of the lesbian bands were Tribe 8 and Team Dresch (Wiedlack, 2015). They wanted to create a space for young women to be free to express themselves. It was unsatisfactory to be just one of the guys; they did not want to assimilate into the male music culture (Gottlieb & Wald, 1994; Leibetseder, 2012, pp. 27–30). In their songs, they reclaimed insults such as dyke, bitch, and slut, similar to what happened to the term "queer" in the queer movement. Kathleen Hanna, one of the most influential Riot Grrrls, sang in her band Bikini Kill the song "Rebel Girl" with the lines "The queen of my world... in her kiss I taste the revolution" (Reynolds, 1995, p. 330). The documentary *The Punk Singer* (2013) shows her life and how she started the Riot Grrrl movement. Riot Grrrls started to run their own indie labels (e.g., Mr. Lady Records) to avoid the mainstream male- and heterosexual- dominated music industry. The second option was to use smaller indie labels, which were supportive of their cause, and the third to bring back the 1980s cassette culture in punk's DIY mode.

Essential for the Riot Grrrls was and is to organize and participate in ladyfests in many countries, where queer-feminist workshops (against sexism, sexual abuse, rape, homo- and transphobia, etc.) took and are still taking place. The first Ladyfest happened in Olympia, Washington, in 2000, and within 10 years it spread to 34 countries (most of them in Europe, though some in North and South America, Australia and New Zealand, Africa and Asia) with over 264 ladyfests (Zobl, 2011, p. 212). Each Ladyfest is noncommercial, nonhierarchical, and locally self-organized (DIY), but is conducive to transnational networking for musicians, activists, and artists with the main focus on music, workshops, discussions, exhibitions, film-shows, presentations, artistic and online-projects, social media events, and so forth (e.g., Ladyfest (http://www.ladyfest.org/), Ladyfest Europe, Ladyfest Myspace, the Facebook group "I am/was a Ladyfest organizer," and "Ladyfest Archive Project"; Zobl, 2011, p. 221). These local, transnational, and virtual networks helped to diversify the subcultural music scene (Downes, 2007, 2012). The politics is/was to be genderqueer and trans inclusive. This is the difference to the previous lesbian and women's music scene, as the younger queer-feminist musicians have a more inclusionary gender politics (Reitsamer, 2008, p. 216). Ladyfest organizers attempted to go beyond the battle for cultural visibility for (lesbian) women (Reitsamer, 2008, p. 222) and focus instead on fluid femininity and masculinity and "(un)doing gender" (Reitsamer, 2008, p. 227). However, it shares one feature of the male punk movement; it was/is still predominantly White and middle-class (Nguyen, 2012; Wiedlack, 2015; Zobl, 2011, p. 214).

Some of the most prominent bands were Bikini Kill with Kathleen Hanna, Bratmobile, Sleater-Kinney, Gossip, Heavens to Betsy, Huggy Bear, Mambo Taxi, and so forth. Later on (mostly in the 2000s) the queer-feminist ideology continued in more electroclash-based bands such as Le Tigre (with Kathleen Hanna, Johanna Fateman, and genderqueer JD Samson, who both formed MEN in 2007) Scream Club, Peaches, Chicks on Speed, and so forth. JD Samson in Le Tigre and MEN brought LGBTIQ topics to the front, such as visibility for LGBTIQ people in the song "Viz" (2004) or different kinds of queer reproduction in "Credit Card Babie$" (2010). Queer-feminist electroclash bands expanded globally as well and can be found in Austria (e.g., *pop:sch*) or Poland (e.g., *Zrada Palki*), and even *Pussy Riot* claims to have their roots in the Riot Grrrl movement.

The same locally organized DIY strategy, though globally connected (Bennett, 2009, p. 483; Cantillon et al., 2017) led to the creation of queer-feminist digital archives that aim to resist normative historical formations (Reitsamer, 2018, p. 31). Their collections include a variety of even ephemeral materials that reflect everyday life in a certain time (Eichhorn, 2013, p. 98; Reitsamer, 2018). These archives documented the queer performativity of music culture by showing how musical performances had an impact on daily life and vice versa. Another queer strategy is seen here, as the artist/audience and production/consumption scheme is not so clear-cut in a dichotomous way anymore. Thus, the local community helped through participatory and collaborative activities, first in that queer-feminist musicians are able to perform in those ladyfests, and second in that these solidary achievements are archived in a corresponding and inspiring way for many others to come (Flinn, 2011; Reitsamer, 2015). Such archives include *Women's Liberation Music Archive* (WMLA) for the 1970s and 1980s in the U.K. and Ireland, *Queer Music Heritage Archive, Her Noise Archive, Jenny Woolworth Women in Punk Archive*, and the *Grassroots Feminism Archive* with interviews of the organizers of ladyfests in Europe and South America and other materials used at these events.

Queer(ing) Black Hip-Hop Feminism.

Although women's festivals provided some space for women of color—for example the Women of Color Tent at the Michigan Womyn's festival—the experience of Black women was still one of "White overload" (Hayes, 2010, p. 22 f.). However, these festivals "give participants the chance to see and hear outstanding black musicians" (Hayes, 2010, p. 7). Hayes writes that the types of songs Black musicians perform at this festival are songs "with a lesbian content" and some of them are love songs or songs reflecting intersectional "axes of oppression," and songs about the heritage of Black women (Hayes, 2010, p. 80). They often performed songs with apparent lesbian connotations, but which were never recorded (Hayes, 2010). In 1991, a Black lesbian festival called Sistahfest took place (Hayes, 2010, p. 89) in Malibu, California, and was organized by United Lesbians of African Heritage (Hayes, 2010, p. 103). In 2005 Serafemme, a (queer) Women of Color Music Festival, was held during the Black Pride in LA on the parking lot of the National Gay and Lesbian Archives (Hayes, 2010, p. 90). Marquita Thomas, the organizer of Serafemme, said she wanted "particularly black lesbians to feel empowered, to know what the issues are for us, to bridge the gap between older and younger women, to have a safe network, to have everything that they deserve" (Hayes, 2010, p. 93).

Miss Money, "the gay Missy Elliott," performed at Serafemme and revealed that she was drawn to hip-hop because they accepted more diversity of women's physical appearances

(Hayes, 2010, p. 95 f.). Later on during the interview she admitted that once she got into the music industry she experienced humiliation, as she confused their gender expectations, because of her butch haircut and clothes (Hayes, 2010, p. 97). She experienced sexism in hip-hop working in the background as a writer, producer, and singing hooks as she was not convinced at the beginning that she could have a career as a singer (Hayes, 2010, p. 97 f.). As soon as she was invited as a singer to festivals, men did not accept her success first and did not understand why her work for them had to wait (Hayes, 2010, p. 98). Talking about her intersectionalities, Miss Money self-defines as being a "gay black female" and explains that being gay for her is inconsequential, because "you don't see it in our faces" (Hayes, 2010, p. 100). However, being Black is very consequential, which she is reminded of everyday, as it is a more visible marker in society than sexual identity (Hayes, 2010, p. 101).

Malika, a Black female musician, played at ladyfests and other women's music festivals in the United States (Hayes, 2010, p. 117) in the early 2000s and owned her own record label. She said at that time that in African American culture the "queer thing" was a taboo (Hayes, 2010, p. 121) and there was a generational divide in the use of this word (Hayes, 2010). Malika preferred "queer" to "lesbian," because it is an umbrella term and "lesbian" is too confining (Hayes, 2010, p. 122). However, even in the grassroots community, such as at the ladyfests, she still found racism and backstabbing, but she learned that many hip-hop and R&B artists sound better performing there than on their albums (Hayes, 2010, p. 127 f.).

Since 1990 hip-hop feminism, seen from artists such as Meshell Ndegeocello, Lauryn Hill, Lil' Kim, Erykah Badu, and Queen Latifah, articulates Black feminist consciousness (Clay, 2008; Durham et al., 2013; Morgan, 1999) and has successfully combined knowledge from inside and outside the academy (social justice grassroots movements) to challenge and transform power structures and social and cultural practices (Durham, 2010, p. 134; Durham et al., 2013, p. 721). Their focus is on "living with contradictions," to "refuse easy and essentialist political stances" (Durham et al., 2013, p. 723) and on a "pro-sex framework" (e.g., the songs, videos, and performances of Yo! Majesty; Hernandez, 2014), within a politics of "respectability" (Durham et al., 2013, p. 724). However, challenging the silencing of queer and trans people of color has been harder for queer cis and trans women than for cis queer men (e.g., Frank Ocean, Lil Nas X). Nicki Minaj had to renounce her comment on her own bisexuality (Durham et al., 2013, p. 725). Ndegeocello's coming out as bisexual and having minimal acceptance in the mainstream culture—she even ended up on MTV—has barely been mentioned in popular or academic publications (Clay, 2008, pp. 55, 58). For example, in her song *Leviticus: Faggot* (1996), she speaks up against the homophobia in the Black community, especially in the Black church (Clay, 2008, p. 64 f.). Ndegeocello is featured in the song *Girlfriend* (1997) by Queen Pen, for which both have received homophobic comments (Jamison, 1998).

The ongoing necessary queering and transing of hip-hop feminism (Glover & Glover, 2019; Love, 2017) transforms this popular culture genre into public pedagogy. Queer and trans hip-hop feminism influences the everyday life of young Black girls and queer Black youth, as they use the hip-hop language and performances (e.g., Big Freedia's twerking "free your ass and your mind will follow" Ross, 2015) to confront heteronormative structures (Berggren, 2014; Carney et al., 2015; Durham et al., 2013, p. 728; Lindsey, 2015; Love, 2017). The queer afrofuturist (Murchison, 2018) investment in digital media (e.g., digital mixing and sampling; De Kosnik, 2019) and social media helped to queer and trans hip-hop and connect it with social justice movements (Durham et al., 2013, p. 731 ff.), for example, the Crunk Feminist Collective blog (Dutheley, 2017) and Janelle Monáe's #BlackLivesMatter anthem "Hell You Talmbout" (2015).

TRANS(ING) MUSIC CULTURE

Trans studies emphasize that their methods are different from queer methods, because trans methods see the body as a primary source of knowledge, which differs from queer methods that transcend the body, whereas trans methods invest in the body (Baitz, 2018). In order to show how music culture is influenced and changed by trans musicians nowadays, both queer and trans methods are used. Queer insights explain how instable identity labels concerning gender or sexuality are, and trans strategies focus on the materiality of the body (Wasserbauer, 2019).

Since the 2000s, more and more transgender, and more recently nonbinary, musicians have come out showing the diversity of genders (Välimäki, 2017). It is easier for transgender people working in cultural industries to come out as the work environment is mostly progressive and allows for more gender flexibility (Hines, 2010, pp. 602–604). The rockumentary *Riot Acts: Flaunting Gender Deviance in Music Performance* (2009) gives a good insight in the "trans fabulous" life of gender-variant musicians. During the interviews, several issues are raised, which are specific to their trans identity and being a musician. For most of them transitioning is a very rich experience inspiring their musical work. Here, the materiality of their body and their voice comes into play. For most singers, especially, their trans voice is a concern, while others do not care if their voice matches their gendered appearance at all. For transwomen it is easier, as they can opt for a voice training to match their image, but for transmen if they take testosterone, it gets more adventurous. Their voice will break at one point and will sound different afterwards. Hence, this creates insecurity for a singing career because transmen do not know when their voice will crack, they have to change the key of most of their songs, and might end up singing in an octave lower (compare: Joe Steves in *Riot Acts*). However, there are also still ambiguous trans voices (compare: singer of *The Shondes* in *Riot Acts*; Leibetseder, 2017, p. 305f). For trans men it is recommended to exercise their voice regularly during a more gradual increase of testosterone doses and more compositions for trans voices should exist (Constansis, 2013, pp. 4–11). Thus, the auditory component of trans people should be more recognized and focused on, and not only on the visual one.

The history of trans people's contribution to music culture is presented in the chapter on "Trans" in the book *Queer Tracks* (Leibetseder, 2012). Three examples of trans and nonbinary musicians coming out recently include Laura Jane Grace of the White punk rock band *Against Me!* who came out as a woman in 2012. Her trans experience was the inspiration for their sixth album *Transgender Dysphoria Blues* (2014) of which the song *True Trans Soul Rebel* functions as a trans anthem. Her voice does not sound more feminine, nor does the music, but the lyrics narrate the story of her transition and emotions. The second is Ezra Fuhrman, who self-defines as trans, came out in 2018 and uses the pronouns she/her and they/their.[1] In the same year she released her seventh album *Transangelic Exodus* with songs about gender, love, acceptance, sexuality, and religion. In this album, she reflects on her being trans, queer, and Jewish in songs such as "Driving Down to L. A.," "Love You So Bad," and "I Lost My Innocence." The video of the first song expresses her fear of living in the United States during Trump's presidency, as she has to escape a group of White neo-Nazis on her road tour, while an angel is accompanying her. The video is dedicated to Heather Heyer, who was killed while protesting White supremacists just one day before this video was shot (Dresden, 2017). The third musician is the Austrian hip-hopper Mavi Phoenix who came out as a trans man with his album *Boys Toys* in 2020. He uses a distorted voice and tells different masculine narratives in each song. In "Bullet in My Heart" he sings about his experience of gender dysphoria.

This music by trans people has an influence on the queer and trans community in their daily life. The Belgium LGBTIQ-identity and music research project by Wasserbauer includes a focus on trans people and their life stories on how "music works as a cultural means of identity creation and reflection" for them (Wasserbauer, 2019). The music used by trans people in the interviews is found in the playlists of this website: Queer Voices (https://queervoices.be/).

CONCLUSION

This contribution has shown what queer(ing) popular music culture entails. It started with explanations from queer theory, clarifying crucial terminology such as the performance and performativity of gender and sexuality, and how queer theory influenced musicology. This was done mainly through (sub)cultural studies and analyzing queer identities and their culture and everyday life. Thus, not only queer musicians make queer music culture, but also the audience and queer people's everyday lives contribute to queer music. Challenges in researching queer popular music culture lie in the predominantly White and male scholarship on this topic. Queer popular music culture archives are therefore crucial in order to preserve the diversity of existing materials, which might in future be analyzed by a more diverse scholarship.

Queer popular music culture is still thriving (as, e.g., Christine and the Queens or Perfume Genius show) and undergoing changes toward being more inclusive again for queer and trans people of color (e.g., Janelle Monáe, Frank Ocean) after a period of mainly well-known White cis musicians. Research is still lagging behind and more musicological studies on queer and trans people of color and other non-Western queer music culture would be particularly welcome (e.g., Moshe Morad's *Fiesta de diez pesos: Music and Gay Identity in Special Period Cuba* (2016) or Gregory Barz and William Cheng's *Queering the Field: Sounding Out Ethnomusicology*).

PRIMARY AND ADDITIONAL RESOURCES

Queer Music Heritage. https://www.queermusicheritage.com/
Queere Musik (German website). https://www.queermdb.de/musik.html
Queer Noise: The History of LGBT+ Music and Club Culture in Manchester. https://www.mdmarchive.co.uk/exhibition/id/77/QUEER_NOISE.html
Queer Voices: LGBTQ Identity and Music (Belgium). https://queervoices.be/

WOMEN'S ARCHIVES

Women's Liberation Music Archive. https://womensliberationmusicarchive.co.uk/
Her Noise Archive; and the other Crisap noise Archive: Online Archive is closed for maintenance, but there is a physical archive in London.

Jenny Woolworth: Women in Punk Archive. https://jennywoolworth.com/women-in-punk
Grassroots Feminism Archive (Ladyfest). https://www.grassrootsfeminism.net/cms/sortable_node_list_digital_fest/125
Riot Grrrl Collection: Mimi Thi Nguyen Zine Collection, in Collaboration with the People of Color Zine Project 1992–1998; MSS365; Series I: Zines; Fales Library and Special Collections, New York Libraries. http://dlib.nyu.edu/findingaids/html/fales/nguyen/admininfo.html

TRANS ARCHIVE

Digital Transgender Archive (The keyword search for "music" has over 140 entries). https://www.digitaltransgenderarchive.net/inst/0611cd89-5b24-4237-b11b-e63939a9bb76

BLACK LGBT CULTURAL ARCHIVE

Rukus! (UK): Life website does not work anymore, but there is an physical archive in London: https://egcrichton.sites.ucsc.edu/migrating-archives-delegates/rukus/
Black Gay and Lesbian Archive (New York, physical Archive). http://archives.nypl.org/scm/21212

FURTHER READING

Bailey, M. M. (2013). *Butch queens up in pumps: Gender, performance, and ballroom culture in Detroit*. University of Michigan Press.
Barz, G., & Cheng, W. (2020). *Queering the field: Sounding out ethnomusicology*. Oxford University Press.
Brett, P., Wood, E., & Thomas, G. C. (Eds.). (1994). *Queering the pitch: The new gay and lesbian musicology*. Routledge.
Geffen, S. (2020). *Glitter up the dark: How pop music broke the binary*. University of Texas Press.
Halberstam, J. (2006). *In a queer time and place: Transgender bodies, subcultural lives*. New York University Press.
Hawkins, S. (2002). *Settling the pop score: Pop texts and identity politics*. Ashgate.
Hawkins, S. (2009). *The British pop dandy: Masculinity, popular music and culture*. Ashgate.
Hawkins, S. (2016). *Queerness in pop music: Aesthetics, gender norms and temporality*. Routledge.
Hawkins, S. (Ed.). (2017). *The Routledge research companion to popular music and gender*. Routledge.
Hayes, E. M. (2010). *Songs in black and lavender: Race, sexual politics, and women's music*. University of Illinois Press.
Hoskyns, B. (1998). *Glam! Bowie, Bolan and the glitter rock revolution*. Pocket books.
James, R. (2015). *Resilience and melancholy: Pop music, feminism, neoliberalism*. Zero Books.
Jarman-Ivens, F. (Ed.). (2007). *Oh boy! Masculinities and popular music*. Routledge.
Jarman-Ivens, F. (2011). *Queer voices: Technologies, vocalities, and the musical flaw*. Palgrave Macmillan.
Leibetseder, D. (2012). *Queer tracks: Subversive strategies in rock and pop music*. Ashgate.
Maus, F. E., & Whiteley, S. (Eds.). (2018/2022). *The Oxford handbook of music and queerness*. Oxford University Press. https://www.oxfordhandbooks.com/view/10.1093/oxfordhb/9780199793525.001.0001/oxfordhb-9780199793525
Morad, M. (2015). *"Fiesta de diez pesos": Music and gay identity in special period Cuba*. Ashgate.
Peraino, J. A. (2006). *Listening to the sirens: Musical technologies of queer identity from Homer to "Hedwig."* University of California Press.
Reynolds, S., & Press, J. (1995). *The sex revolts: Gender, rebellion and rock'n'roll*. Serpent's Tail.

Rodríguez, J. M. (2014). *Sexual future, queer gestures, and other Latina longings*. NYU-Press.
Taylor, J. (2012). *Playing it queer: Popular music, identity and queer world-making*. Peter Lang.
Whiteley, S. (Ed.). (1997). *Sexing the groove: Popular music and gender*. Routledge.
Whiteley, S., & Rycenga, J. (Eds.). (2006). *Queering the popular pitch*. Routledge.
Wiedlack, K. M. (2015). Queer-feminist punk: An anti-social history. Zaglossus. https://library.oapen.org/handle/20.500.12657/33098

REFERENCES

Ahmed, S. (2006). *Queer phenomenology: Object, orientation, others*. Duke University Press.
Anzaldúa, G. (1981). La Prieta. In C. Moraga, & G. Anzaldúa (Eds.), *This bridge called my back: Writings by radical women of color* (pp. 189–209). Women of Color Press.
Bailey, M. M. (2013). *Butch queens up in pumps: Gender, performance, and ballroom culture in Detroit*. University of Michigan Press.
Bailey, M. M. (2014). Engendering space: Ballroom culture and the spatial practice of possibility in Detroit. *Gender, Place & Culture, 21*(4), 489–507.
Baitz, D. (2009). Queering the pitch: Review. *Women and Music: A Journal of Gender and Culture, 13*(1), 109–112.
Baitz, D. (2018). Toward a Trans* Method in Musicology. In F. E. Maus & S. Whitely (Eds.), *The Oxford handbook of music and queerness* (pp. 365–381). Oxford University Press. https://www.oxfordhandbooks.com/view/10.1093/oxfordhb/9780199793525.001.0001/oxfordhb-9780199793525-e-44
Bayton, M. (1998). *Frock rock: Women performing popular music*. Oxford University Press.
Bennett, A. (2009). "Heritage rock": Rock music, representation and heritage discourse. *Poetics, 37*, 474–489.
Berggren, K. (2014). Hip hop feminism in Sweden: Intersectionality, feminist critique and female masculinity. *European Journal of Women's Studies, 21*(3), 233–250.
Brett, P., & Wood, E. (2001). Gay and lesbian music. *Grove Music Online, Oxford Music Online*. Oxford University Press. https://doi.org/10.1093/gmo/9781561592630.article.42824
Brett, P., Wood, E., & Thomas, G. C. (Eds.). (1994). *Queering the pitch: The new gay and lesbian musicology*. Routledge.
Burns, L., & Lafrance, M. (2002). *Disruptive divas: Feminism, identity & popular music*. Routledge.
Callen, J. (2006). Gender crossings: A neglected history in African American music. In S. Whiteley & J. Rycenga (Eds.), *Queering the popular pitch* (pp. 185–198). Routledge.
Cantillon, Z., Baker, S., & Buttigieg, B. (2017). Queering the community music archive. *Australian Feminist Studies, 32*(91–92), 41–57.
Carney, C., Hernandez, J., & Wallace, A. M. (2015). Sexual knowledge and practiced feminisms: On moral panic, black girlhoods, and hip hop. *Journal of Popular Music Studies, 28*(4), 412–426.
Clay, A. (2008). Like an old soul record. *Meridians, 8*(1), 53–73.
Constansis, A. N. (2013, March). The female-to-male (ftm) singing voice and its interaction with queer theory: Roles and interdependency. *Transposition. Musique et Sciences Sociales, 3*, 1–27. https://journals.openedition.org/transposition/353?lang=en
Curran, N. (Ed.). (2018). *Queer core: Queer punk media subculture*. Routledge.
Davis, A. Y. (1999). *Blues legacies and black feminism*. Vintage Books.
De Kosnik, A. (2019). Why it matters that black men and queer women invented digital remix culture. *JCMS: Journal of Cinema and Media Studies, 59*(1), 156–163.
de Lauretis, T. (1991). Queer theory: Lesbian and gay studies. An introduction. *Differences—a Journal of Feminist Cultural Studies, 3*(2), iii–xviii.

Downes, J. (2007). Riot grrrl: The legacy and contemporary landscape of DIY feminist cultural activism. In N. Monem (Ed.), *rot grrrl; revolution grrrl style now!* (pp. 12–51). Black Dog Publishing.

Downes, J. (2012). The expansion of punk rock: Riot grrrl challenges to gender power relations in British indie music subcultures. *Women's Studies, 41*(2), 204–237.

Dresden, H. (2017, September 27). Ezra Furman Escapes Neo-Nazis in 'Driving Down to L.A.'. *Out Magazine*. https://www.out.com/music/2017/9/27/ezra-furman-escapes-neo-nazis-driving-down-la

Durham, A. (2010). Hip hop feminist media studies. *International Journal of Africana Studies, 16*(1), 117–140.

Durham, A., Cooper, B. C., & Morris, S. M. (2013). The stage hip-hop feminism built: A new directions essay. *Signs: Journal of Women in Culture and Society, 38*(3), 721–737.

Dutheley, R. (2017). Black feminist hip-hop rhetorics and the digital public sphere. *Changing English, 24*(2), 202–212.

Edelman, L. (2004). *No future: Queer theory and the death drive*. Duke University Press.

Eichhorn, K. (2013). *The archival turn in feminism: Outrage in order*. Temple University Press.

Flinn, A. (2011). Archival activism: Independent and community-led archives, radical public history and the heritage professions. *InterActions, 7*(2), 1–20.

Frith, S. (1983). *Sound effects: Youth, leisure and the politics of rock*. Constable.

Frith, S. & McRobbie, A. (1978). Rock and sexuality. In S. Frith & A. Goodwin (Eds.), *On record: Rock, pop and the written word* (pp. 371–389). Routledge.

Glover, S. T., & Glover, J. K. (2019). "She ate my ass and my pussy all night": Deploying illicit eroticism, funk, and sex work among black queer women femmes. *American Quarterly 71*(1), 171–177.

Gottlieb, J., & Wald, G. (1994). Smells like teen spirit: Riot grrrls, revolution and women in independent rock. In A. Ross & T. Rose (Eds.), *Microphone friends: Youth music and youth culture* (pp. 250–270). Routledge.

Halberstam, J. (1998). *Female masculinity*. Duke University Press.

Halberstam, J. (2005). *In a queer time and place: Transgender bodies, subcultural lives*. New York University Press.

Hall, S., & Jefferson, T. (Eds.). (1976). *Resistance through rituals: Youth subcultures in post-war Britain*. Hutschinson.

Hawkins, S. (2016). *Queerness in pop music: Aesthetics, gender norms and temporality*. Routledge.

Hawkins, S. (Ed.). (2017). *The Routledge research companion to popular music and gender*. Routledge.

Hayes, E. M. (2010). *Songs in black and lavender: Race, sexual politics, and women's music*. University of Illinois Press.

Haynes, T. (1998). Foreword. In B. Hoskyns (Ed.), *Glam! Bowie, Bolan and the glitter rock revolution* (pp. X–XI). Pocket books.

Hebdige, C. (1979). *Subculture: The meaning of style*. Routledge.

Hernandez, J. (2014). Carnal teachings: Raunch aesthetics as queer feminist pedagogies in Yo! Majesty's Hip Hop practice. *Women & Performance: A Journal of Feminist Theory, 24*(1), 88–106.

Hines, S. (2010). Queerly situated? Exploring negotiations of trans queer subjectivities at work and within community spaces in the UK. *Gender, Place and Culture, 17*(5), 597–613.

Hoskyns, B. (1998). *Glam! Bowie, Bolan and the glitter rock revolution*. Pocket Books.

Howells, D. W. (1869). The new taste in theatricals. *Atlantic Monthly, 16*, 640–644.

James, R. (2015). *Resilience and melancholy: Pop music, feminism, neoliberalism*. Zero Books.

Jamison, L. (1998, January 18). A feisty female rapper breaks a hip-hop taboo. *New York Times*. https://www.nytimes.com/1998/01/18/arts/pop-jazz-a-feisty-female-rapper-breaks-a-hip-hop-taboo.html

Jarman-Ivens, F. (2009). Notes on musical camp. In D. B. Scott (Ed.), *The Ashgate research companion to popular musicology* (pp. 189–204). Ashgate.

Jarman-Ivens, F. (2011). *Queer voices: Technologies, vocalities, and the musical flaw*. Palgrave Macmillan.
Leibetseder, D. (2012). *Queer tracks: Subversive strategies in rock and pop music*. Ashgate.
Leibetseder, D. (2017). Express yourself! Gender euphoria and intersections. In S. Hawkins (Ed.), *The Routledge research companion to popular music and gender* (pp. 300–312). Routledge.
Lindsay, T. B. (2015). Let me blow your mind: Hip hop feminist futures in theory and praxis. *Urban Education*, 50(1), 52–77.
Love, B. L. (2017). A ratchet lens: Black queer youth, agency, hip hop, and the black ratchet imagination. *Educational Researcher*, 46(9), 539–547.
Maus, F. E., & Whitely, S. (2022). *The Oxford Handbook of Music and Queerness*. Oxford University Press. https://www.oxfordhandbooks.com/view/10.1093/oxfordhb/9780199793525.001.0001/oxfordhb-9780199793525
Michasiw, K. (1994). Camp, masculinity, masquerade. *differences*, 6(2+3), 146–173.
Morad, M. (2016). *Fiesta de diez pesos: Music and gay identity in special period Cuba*. Routledge.
Morgan, J. (1999). *When chickenheads come home to roost: A hip-hop feminist breaks it down*. Simon & Schuster Paperbacks.
Muñoz, J. E. (2009). *Cruising utopia: The then and there of queer futurity*. NYU Press.
Murchison, G. (2018). Let's flip it! Quare emancipations: Black Queer traditions, afrofuturisms, Janelle Monáe to Labelle. *Women and Music: A Journal of Gender and Culture*, 22(1), 79–90.
Nguyen, M. T. (2012). Riot grrrl, race and revival. *Women and Performance: A Journal of Feminist Theory*, 22(2–3), 173–196.
O'Brien, L. (2002). *She bop II. The definitive history of women in rock, pop and soul*. Continuum.
Oppenheim, M. (2016, January 11). How David Bowie became an LGBT icon. The pioneering star revolutionised attitudes to sexuality in his six-decade career. *The Independent*. https://www.independent.co.uk/news/people/how-david-bowie-became-gay-icon-a6806041.html
Peraino, J. A. (2006). *Listening to the sirens: Musical technologies of queer identity from Homer to "Hedwig."* University of California Press.
Piepmeier, A. (2009). *Girl zines: Making media, doing feminism*. New York University Press.
Regev, M. (1994). Producing artistic value: The case of rock music. *The Sociological Quarterly*, 35(1), 85–102.
Reitsamer, R. (2008). These islands where we came from: Notes on gender and generation in the Viennese lesbian-queer subculture. In M. Gržinić & R. Reitsamer (Eds.), *New feminism. Worlds of feminism, queer and networking conditions*. Löcker.
Reitsamer, R. (2015). Alternative histories and counter-memories: Feminist music archives in Europe. In S. Baker (Ed.), *Preserving popular music heritage*. Routledge.
Reitsamer, R. (2018). Gendered narratives of popular music history and heritage. In S. Baker, C. Strong, L. Istvandity, & Z. Cantillon (Eds.), *The Routledge companion to popular music history and heritage*. Routledge.
Reynolds, S., & Press, J. (1995). *The sex revolts: Gender, rebellion and rock'n'roll*. Serpent's Tail.
Rodríguez, J. M. (2014). *Sexual future, queer gestures, and other Latina longings*. NYU Press.
Rogers, K. (2016, January 13). Was he gay, bisexual or Bowie? Yes. David Bowie's gender-bending performances and cultural fluidity inspired a generation of gay, lesbian and transgender people. *The New York Times*. https://www.nytimes.com/2016/01/14/style/was-he-gay-bisexual-or-bowie-yes.html
Ross, F. (2015). *Big Freedia: God save the Queen Diva*. Gallery Books.
Sedgwick, E. K. (1990). *Epistemology of the closet*. University of California Press.
Sontag, S. (2018). *Notes on camp*. Penguin Random House.
Taylor, J. (2012). *Playing it queer: Popular music, identity and queer world-making*. Peter Lang.

Taylor, J. (2013). Claiming queer territory in the study of subcultures and popular music. *Sociology Compass*, 7(3), 194–207.

Välimäki, S. (2017). Confronting the gender trouble for real: Mina Caputo, metal truth and transgender power. In S. Hawkins (Ed.), *The Routledge research companion to popular music and gender* (pp. 326–346). Routledge.

Wasserbauer, M. (2019). "Bivouacking in the borderlands": Gender nonconforming trans persons on music and identity. *Tijdschrift voor Genderstudies*, 22(1), 67–84.

Watts, M. (2006, January 22). Flashback: 22 January 1972. On the cusp of fame, Bowie tells Melody Maker he's gay—and changes pop for ever. *The Guardian*. https://www.theguardian.com/music/2006/jan/22/popandrock.davidbowie

Whiteley, S. (2006). Popular music and the dynamics of desire. In S. Whiteley & J. Rycenga (Eds.), *Queering the popular pitch* (pp. 249–262). Routledge.

Whiteley, S., & Rycenga, J. (Eds.). (2006). *Queering the popular pitch*. Routledge.

Wiedlack, K. M. (2015). Queer-feminist punk. An anti-social history. Zaglossus. https://library.oapen.org/handle/20.500.12657/33098

Zobl, E. (2011). Zehn Jahre Ladyfest. Rhizomatische Netzwerke einer lokalen, transnationalen und virtuellen queer-feministischen Szene. In R. Reitsamer & W. Fichna (Eds.), *"They Say I'm Different…" Popularmusik, Szenen und ihre Akteur_innen*. Löcker.

Zuberi, N. (2018). Sounding out popular music history: A musicological approach. In S. Baker, C. Strong, L. Istvandity, & Z. Cantillon (Eds.), *The Routledge companion to popular music history and heritage*. Routledge.

NOTE

1. Furman, E. [@ezrafurman]. (2018, October 21). It's been slowly dawning on me (and this dawning took a jump forward right after I sent that first tweet) that it's for-sure accurate to refer to myself as trans (https://twitter.com/ezrafurman/status/1054067597233184768) [Tweet]. Twitter.

Doris Leibetseder

REPRESENTATIONS OF DRAG CULTURE

DRAG, GENDER PERFORMATIVITY, AND CAMP

According to Butler (1990), performativity underpins constructs of gender. Gender, rather than being an inherent feature of our beings, is a self-conception that we develop and re-create through acts and performances which work as "hallucinatory effect[s] of naturalized gestures" (Butler, 1990, pp. xv–xvi). Drag further complicates performing gender as it brings into play biological sex, gender identities, and *gender-performed* identities enacted in drag performance. Drag therefore simulates and intensifies constructs of gender by parodying displaced meanings ascribed to "original" notions of gender, thereby imitating myths of gender itself (Butler, 1990, p. 188). Drag, conceived from Butler's perspective, thus becomes a deliberate, conscious performance of gender, predicated on the ways in which we perform gender unconsciously every day. In a study of American female impersonators, Newton (1972, p. 108) relates Greta Garbo playing women to gay men "passing" by playing straight men. Both Greta Garbo role-playing female characters and gay men passing as straight men are in drag, and from which "drag" assumes broader signification to encompass many expressions not only of gender performativity but also of parodying performing gender to underscore the performance itself as taken for granted.

In her influential essay, Sontag (1967, p. 275) depicts camp as a "sensibility" rather than an idea and as something which is exhibited rather than analyzed. Moreover, as sensibilities are difficult to articulate and work as "private code," to attempt to articulate camp therefore betrays it (Sontag, 1967, p. 275). Medhurst (1991) also sees camp as experiential and not as analytical, as "a set of attitudes, a gallery of snapshots, an inventory of postures" which, despite camp's illusive nature, "most of us know...when see, hear, feel or do it" (Medhurst, 1997, p. 276). However inexact the definition, scholars take different positions on describing what camp is. For some, camp is not about taste or sensibilities but rather about the politics of the gay liberation movement of the 1960s and 1970s (Dyer, 1999, p. 5). Thus, camp responds to heterosexual censure through strategies of "defensive offensiveness" on the part of queers who not only "dare to exist but... actively flaunt and luxuriate in their queerness" (Medhurst, 1997, p. 276). For others (Britton, 1999; Simpson, 1999), camp has been diluted by heteronormative culture, thereby abnegating the political weight that camp once held. Davis (2004, p. 56) notes that while the mainstream appeal of camp is prevalent, thus weakening its political foundations, it is far from defunct. Rather, the recognition of camp's inception in 1960s gay political culture should account for a distinction between gay camp and its dilution into the widespread dissemination of straight camp (Davis, 2004). Moreover, although gay camp arose from transgressive gay politics, it has since been appropriated for arbitrary use and imitation, particularly by "mercenary profit-oriented straight people" (Davis, 2004, p. 56). A more useful distinction between *gay* and *straight* uses of camp may therefore be *queer* and *gay* deployments of camp, where the former retains the political foundations of camp, and the latter references camp through the mechanisms of mainstream appropriation, appeal, and profitability. Illustrative of queer and gay deployment of camp are, respectively, John Waters's (1988) film *Hairspray* and Adam Shankman's (2007) remake; although the latter "clearly touts itself as a remake," it nonetheless discards "the queer politics of the original, producing instead a sanitized exemplar of normative nostalgia" (Woodward, 2012, p. 116). Still, camp's grounding in revolutionary queer politics, as epitomized by Divine, Waters's underground drag queen, muse, and star of the original *Hairspray* and transformed by Hollywood celebrity John Travolta into "family-friendly" drag in Shankman's remake, underscores the continued need for the political work that queer camp does, if only by virtue of its erasure (Woodward, 2012).

While it is useful to discern queer, political versions of camp from ones that take from subculture re-conceived notions of the transgressive (Robertson & Wojcik, 1996, p. 129), we are left with the idea that "legitimate" camp is used only by queers to speak to other queers; thus, camp cannot be used by anyone from "outside" queerness (Davis, 2004, p. 57). Newton's (1972) groundbreaking study of American female impersonators in the late 1960s reveals a less dichotomized definition of camp. Rather than designating a "thing," camp designates a *relationship* between actors, activities, and qualities of things (Newton, 1972, p. 105). Moreover, from these various actors, activities, and qualities emerge camp's *incongruity, theatricality*, and *humor*, where "Incongruity is the subject matter of camp, theatricality its style, and humor its strategy" (Newton, 1972, p. 106). Newton's definition of camp is likely the most adaptable and lasting.

CROSS-DRESSING, TRANSVESTISM, GENDER, RACE, AND ETHNICITY

In American popular culture, as early as 1903, Edward S. Porter featured a cross-dressing character in one of his films, and as successors to vaudevillian histories, male actors cross-dressed as women in films such as *Miss Fanny's Seaside Lovers* (1915), *Spit-Ball Sadie* (1915), and *Bumping into Broadway* (1919) for comedic effect (Russo, 1987). A large part of this effect rested on characters who were seen as "less than men or more than women" and on "the zany farce of mistaken identity and transvestite humor" adopted from older American theatrical traditions (Russo, 1987, p. 6). Cross-dressing assumed more nuanced tones in early American films, such as *A Woman* (1915), featuring Charlie Chaplin, and the drag persona of Stan Laurel, who related to Oliver Hardy as the more "feminine" of the pair, yet both Chaplin and Laurel "hinted at the deeper levels of a visual language that could at times capture the possibility of pure androgyny" (Russo, 1987, p. 10). "Amatory confusion" (Ginibre, 2005, p. 12) provided the basis of cross-dressing in early American film, in which naïve heterosexual men fall for duplicitous heterosexual men dressed as women. Remade over 20 times in 10 different countries, *Charley's Aunt* (1925) set the precedent for ushering in the humorous precepts of false identity, gullibility, and duplicity of cross-dressing for global audiences (Ginibre, 2005).

Other "classic drag films" include *Some Like It Hot* (1959), *Victor and Victoria* (1933, 1935, 1957, 1982), the United Kingdom's *Carry On* series (1958–1972, 1992), *The Rocky Horror Picture Show* (1975, 2016), *Tootsie* (1982), and the French/Italian *La Cage aux Folles* (1978) and its American remake, *The Birdcage* (1996) (Ginibre, 2005). These films deploy drag in several overlapping and consistent ways: as the basis of an entire story line or a narrative twist; as a means for characters to hide from pursuers; as a way to facilitate a hoax; as a technique for going undercover; and as a platform for gay visibility, viewpoints, and "lifestyles" catalyzed by the gay rights movement (Ginibre, 2005, p. 9). However, the largely buoyant deployment of cross-dressing in film contrasts, and becomes conflated with, more complex representations of transvestism. Alfred Hitchcock's *Murder* (1930) features a transvestite trapeze artist who murders a woman to prevent her from disclosing his "half-caste" status, where half-caste signifies both "mixed-race" and sexual preference; in *Caprice* (1967), another murderous transvestite gets her comeuppance when she is pushed from a balcony by Doris Day (Russo, 1987); and *The Silence of the Lambs* (1991) features the transsexual serial killer Buffalo Bill, who skins her female victims to fashion a new epidermis. Tharp (1991, p. 110) identifies the transvestites of *Psycho* (1960) and *The Silence of the Lambs* in Freudian terms as mother-obsessed, desirous of, and repelled by femininity; transvestites whose "gender dilemmas" become "aberrations of nature" or pathologies. While trickster cross-dressers may be distinct from transvestites, who in cross-dressing nevertheless wish to carefully protect their original gender identity, or antiquated transsexuals, who wish to publicly assume the role of the sex opposite to which they were born (Bullough et al., 1983), these distinctions gloss over how cross-dressing and transvestism are largely coterminous in film representations. Discerning between cross-dressing and transvestism is further complicated by "temporary transvestite films," in which the humorous "failure of the disguise" that serves as a curative response to real-life gender transgressions becomes the more convincing transvestism, "less funny and yet more demonstrative of the cultural power of gender and the superficiality of costume" (Straayer, 1992, pp. 423–424). The transvestite requires grappling with the inability to identify that figure as male or female; therefore, lacking "*one* gender, he/she effectively has *no* subjectivity" (Straayer, 1992, p. 424; original emphasis) and becomes more prone to depictions of aberration.

Cross-dressing also involves women performing as men. From *The Female Highwayman* (1906) and *Glen or Glenda* (1953) to *Yentl* (1983), *The Ballad of Little Jo* (1983), and *Osama* (2003), film has addressed the cultural power attached to male dress and women assuming roles as men. Characteristic of cross-dressing, whether men are performing as women or women as men, is that it provides sources of amusement and erotic attraction (de Lauretis, 1990). However, in either case, erotic attraction seems to favor men, which suggests that in addition to reflecting the parodic (Butler, 1990), cross-dressing reflects more male than female desires and aesthetics (de Lauretis, 1990; Modleski, 1997). Thus, the "seriousness" (Straayer, 1992) by which transvestism suggests greater subjective investment in performing another gender than the anodyne role-playing of cross-dressing (men) equally suggests greater seriousness involved in depictions of women performing as men. In *The Ballad of Little Jo*, the transvestism of Jo, the male-identified female protagonist, is situated in the Western genre, signaling a radical departure from the all-male milieu of the Old West, with its occasional, parodic appearance of the male cross-dresser. In contrast, *Ballad* is a non-parodic narrative about "the pleasures of transsex identification," yet Jo resists being "'wholly absorbed' in and by the role" (Irigaray, 1985; Modleski, 1997, p. 541). Moreover, Jo is a woman who, in acquiring the more "admirable traits" of a man, proves herself "more manly than the men" while revealing darker aspects of masculinity, such as homophobia and misogyny (Modleski, 1997, p. 541). Different discourse informs the transvestism of women performing as men. Women's "non-parodic" performance means drawing on a gamut of prevailing masculine modes rather than reducing masculinity to its most farcical or aberrant modes, as often happens with men performing as women. Halberstam's (1997, 1998) studies of drag kings find that the presence (or absence) of theatricality in performing rests on attempts to reproduce majority or minority masculinities; thus, whether drag kings rely on "impersonation or whether [their] own masculinity flavors the act" (1997, p. 115). Arguments supporting the idea that women's cross-dressing performances are more serious and complex than those of men do not suggest that men are unable to invoke their own femininities to complicate cross-dressing. Rather, there is greater latitude in women drawing on representational modes of masculinity in order to perform its already privileged effects.

Television takes fewer risks than film (Garber, 1997) to suggest lessened efforts by television creators to portray complexity in cross-dressing characterizations and themes. Nonetheless, portrayals of cross-dressing in early television anticipate how the visibility of and interest in drag have peaked in contemporary television. In a study of transvestism and the cultural anxieties it has produced within numerous texts and contexts, Garber (1997) reveals three themes that have dependably resurfaced in television. One is that of the transsexual killer (see also Mogul et al., 2011), also depicted in film, who in television appears in a broader array of forms and genres, from anodyne (*Murder, She Wrote*, 1984–1986), auteurist (*Twin Peaks*, 1990–1991), and grisly (*Criminal Minds*, 2005–2020) fiction to true-crime and made-for-television reenactments (*48 Hours*, 1988– and *The Jinx: The Life and Deaths of Robert Durst*, 2015). Garber (1997, p. 187) finds that the process of "detecting" the transvestite as behind criminal acts relies on (false) assumptions made about attire, hairstyle, and other modes of presentation, which create a "necessary stage in the unravelling of the plot." More persistent, however, is the proclivity to "look *through* rather than *at* the cross-dresser" as a fundamental element of the detective narrative, which serves to obscure understanding of how transvestism can operate as a cultural intervention rather than as a heteronormative foil (Garber, 1997, p. 187, original emphasis).

Another theme is cross-dressing as comedic, which again does not diverge from film but which does evidence the steady trope of cross-dressing within the variety of television forms. American sitcoms from *McHale's Navy* (1962–1966), *All in the Family* (1971–1979), *M*A*S*H* (1972–1983), *Bosom Buddies* (1980–1982), *Three's Company* (1977–1984), *On Our Own* (1994–1995), and *Friends* (1994–2004) to *Arrested Development* (2003–2006), *The Big Bang Theory* (2007–2019), and *Work It* (2012) have consistently used cross-dressing for plot and character twists. Comedy-dramas, which humorize cross-dressing within weightier themes, include *Glee* (2009–2015), *Baskets* (2016–2019), and *Master of None* (2015–); and cross-dressing appears in the animated television series *The Simpsons* (1989–), *Dexter's Laboratory* (1996–2003), *The Powerpuff Girls* (1998–2005), and *SpongeBob SquarePants* (1999–).

Cross-dressing has left its largest impression on the sketch/satire comedy genre with implications for representing not only gender but also ethnicity and race in relation to power. Milton Berle regularly appeared in drag as host of NBC's *Texaco Star Theatre* (1948–1955), and in 1959, also dressed as Auntie Mildred, he appeared in *The Lucy-Desi Comedy Hour* (1957–1960), where he flirts with Ricky and Fred to Lucy and Ethel's chagrin. Far from subversive, Berle's *schtick* mocked the supposed characteristics of gay men to entertain steadfastly heterosexual American audiences (Pasternack, 2017). Contrastingly, Berle's drag *was* transgressive in bringing transvestism and its implications of homosexuality to American television in the first instance. In the face of being "too Jewish" for audiences, and with program makers' disdain for and racial difference in television content and actors' appearance (Antler, 1988), Berle, a Jewish American cross-dresser, exceeded the parameters of 1950s American television.

Berle made cross-dressing a standard of ensemble sketch routines, to manifest in the recurring cross-dressing characters of *The Carol Burnett Show* (1967–1978), *Saturday Night Live* (1975–), *The Drew Carey Show* (1995–2004), and *Kids in the Hall* (1989–1995). With the exception of Tracy Morgan's and Kenan Thompson's characters in *Saturday Night Live*, both the comics and their personas in these ensemble sketch series are White, which underscores Garber's third theme of cross-dressing: the transvestite Black man. The transvestite Black man inevitably summons the American, antebellum minstrel tradition, in which White male actors "double-crossed" into role-playing not only as women but also as Black women. Moreover, the Black male transvestite contradicts the largely comedic tradition of viewers "knowing" the true gender identity of the (white) cross-dressing actor by carrying the mantle of having to "pass" both as a Black woman and, more acutely, as a neutered and therefore "broken" Black man (Garber, 1997). In this light, the number of television and film productions starring transvestite Black men is unsurprising. These productions include Flip Wilson as Geraldine Jones on *The Flip Wilson Show* (1970–1974); Jamie Foxx as Wanda Wayne on *In Living Color* (1991–1994); Martin Lawrence as Sheneneh Jenkins and Mama Payne on *Martin* (1992–1997) and as Big Momma Pierce in the *Big Momma's House* franchise (2000, 2004, 2011); Eddie Murphy as Mama and Grandma Klump in *The Nutty Professor* franchise (1996, 2000) and as Rasputia Latimore in *Norbit* (2007); Ving Rhames as Holiday Heart in *Holiday Heart* (2000); Tracy Morgan as Maya Angelou on *Saturday*

Night Live (2002); Shawn and Marlon Wayans as White sisters Brittany and Tiffany Wilson in *White Chicks* (2004); Kenan Thompson as Barbara Birmingham, Virginica Hastings, Whoopi Goldberg, Maya Angelou, and Mo'nique on *Saturday Night Live* (2007, 2008, 2009, 2010); Tyler Perry as Mabel Madea Simmons in the *Madea* franchise (2005, 2006, 2008, 2009); and Brandon T. Jackson as Charmaine Daisy Pierce in *Big Mommas: Like Father, Like Son* (2011) (Sanfiorenzo, 2011). That Black male transvestism ensures profitability for the American television and film industries is clear, if evidenced only by film franchises. Along the same lines, Little Richard, Luther Vandross, Michael Jackson, and Prince guaranteed success for the American music industry through their gender androgyny and sexual ambiguity as Black men (Garber, 1997, pp. 273–274). Moreover, while Black male transvestism benefits culture industries at the cost of neutering Black masculinities, Boyd (2006) argues that the *agency* of Black male actors is also implicated in mainstream comedic cross-dressing:

> Perhaps by feminizing the image of Black masculinity, some people are made to feel less threatened and more comfortable. Perhaps the cross-dressing Black man is a way to neutralize the image of empowered Black men that hip-hop culture provides on a regular basis. Perhaps some entertainers will do anything for a laugh and a dollar. I'm sorry. I don't want to see any more Black men in dresses. Though the entertainment industry is far from being a racial utopia…performers do have a choice. What is so frustrating about all of these contemporary figures…is that they all seemed to willingly don the dress themselves.

Of equal significance are the implications of Black male transvestism for representations of Black women. Thompson Moore (2020, p. 87) finds that in caricaturing the Black macho woman (BMW), Black male comedians depict Black women as "creatures of sexualization, victimization, ridicule, and aggression." Furthermore, the BMW trope compounds Black men's marginalization in White society by shifting blame to the stereotype of the "angry Black woman," thereby fueling existing tensions between Black women and Black men while contributing to Black male comics' fame in "allowing for the expression of anger, bitterness, and strife towards Black women" (Thompson Moore, 2020, p. 98). Garber (1997, p. 303) counterargues narratives of Black suppression vis-à-vis transvestism by identifying their use of ambiguous elements "as a strategy of economic, political, and cultural achievement" to translate "oppression and stigmatization into a supple medium for social commentary and aesthetic power." Black transvestism thus becomes a means of liberation from historically oppressive gendered, sexual, and racialized conditions, but given the contexts in (and profits from) which its performances occur, Black transvestism and any liberties it affords remain paradoxically limited.

REPRESENTATIONS OF DRAG IN *RUPAUL'S DRAG RACE*

RuPaul's Drag Race first aired in 2009 in the United States on the VH1-owned, LGBTQ-oriented cable channel Logo TV, migrated to VH1 itself in 2017, and has generated multiple American and international spin-offs (Brennan & Gudelunas, 2017). RuPaul Charles, originator and host of *Drag Race* and self-proclaimed "supermodel of the world," invites onto the reality/competition series semi-professional drag queens who contend for the title of "America's next drag superstar" (Brennan, 2017). RuPaul also serves as a "GuRu" for the

LGBTQ+ community through self-help books and physical DragCon gatherings, and RuPaul's familiar catchphrases include "If you can't love yourself, how in the hell you gonna love somebody else?" and "We're all born naked and the rest is drag." The diverse, inclusive environment that *Drag Race* fosters is reflected in close to three-quarters of its contestants representing Black, Latinx, and Asian Pacific Islander communities (Marcel, 2014), and nonwhite queens have won the title nine times in the series's first 13 seasons. However, RuPaul has circumscribed *Drag Race*'s inclusivity by barring transfeminine contestants from competing in the series. Although Gottmik, a transmasculine drag queen, competed through to the season 13 finale, the series has paradoxically confined gender performativity, alongside determining what constitutes prevailing (that is, winning) drag modalities.

Authenticity, Consumption, and Competition. At the core of *Drag Race*, like virtually all formats and genres of reality television, is the notion of authenticity, or reality television's claim to present social realities and frame the ways in which we access realities that matter most to us as social beings (Couldry, 2004, p. 83). Reality television, like fictional forms of television, is often scripted; thus, the authentic quality of the genre particularly emerges when contestants' artifice breaks down and their "true" selves are revealed (Hill, 2002, 2005). Moreover, authenticity would contradict the parodic nature of drag, yet *Drag Race* relies on authentic performances of femaleness (Edgar, 2011) as well as on consistently authentic performances of femaleness in consistently different ways. Put differently, authenticity in *Drag Race* particularly reveals itself when fissures appear in contestants' performance of femaleness, resulting in queens' elimination from the competition, or their "sashaying away." Authenticity in *Drag Race* also operates through the strength and legitimacy of relationships established between queens and their fans, similar to the ways in which the popular arts discerned meaningful popular culture from valueless mass culture through artist and performer relations (Hall & Whannel, 1964). Additionally, since *Drag Race* claims a place in the small space of dedicatedly queer reality television, its authenticity is further substantiated by the "exclusivity" of queer viewership, which "legitimates and authenticates" the series vis-à-vis its proximity to queer sensibilities (Edgar, 2011, p. 135). The notion of "realness" also applies to *Drag Race*'s authenticity, in that realness is a criterion by which the African American and Latinx drag queens of Jennie Livingston's (1990) documentary *Paris Is Burning* are judged for their abilities to emulate the world of the straight, White elite and from which *Drag Race* takes its inspiration.

In *Drag Race*, authenticity is facilitated by drag queens' performance, but consumption serves as another premise of the series. Silverstone (1999, p. 78) asserts that play and performance are "mobilized in the service of our participation in economic life" and that consumption as a form of "work" aids us in navigating our ways as "global consumer-citizens" to both create "personal meanings" and "participate in local cultures." Thus, consumption entails "an acting out," a "play of fantasy," and a "display of identity" (Silverstone, 1999, p. 80) in which, by extension, the ephemeral and illusionary nature of drag is both expressed and contained by the series's contestants. Economic and social factors also govern who participates in consumption practices and in what ways (Stearns et al., 2011), which has distinct implications for the race, ethnicity, class, and gender identity of the series's contestants as well as for the kinds of consumption promoted by *Drag Race* as queer reality television.

Scholars (Andrejevic, 2004; Deery, 2015; Hill, 2015; Marwick, 2015) have identified consumption as a framework for self-promotion specific to reality television, in which contestants commodify themselves *and* the program's commercial value. Self-promotion, however, characterized drag culture well before the indispensable role it plays in reality television. Newton (1972) observes how drag queens' professional environment is formed by different types of (self-)promotion: through audience response to acts, drag queens' response to patrons, alcohol and drug use, and management and payment schemes. Berkowitz and Belgrave (2010, p. 173) observe of Miami Beach drag queens that while drugs pervade the scene, they may serve as "a coping mechanism to counter the marginalization and harassment" that couple with systemic "homophobia and gender nonconformity," or they may be "something that simply comes with the territory." The intersections of consumption, self-promotion, and drag culture therefore manifest in both anodyne and potentially destructive ways.

More than being characterized by participants competing with each other (and against themselves), reality television is characterized by cost-effective techniques and high-ratings elements that seek to compete with traditional, prime-time programming (Kavka, 2012). Furthermore, reality television came to compete with *itself* by displacing human-experiment (*Big Brother*, *Survivor*) with theme-based (*American Idol*, *The Bachelor*) productions and "by openly combining actuality and artifice in ways that broke rating records and caused widescale debate" within a new generational, cultural imaginary (Kavka, 2012, p. 76). Competition in reality television, *Drag Race* included, also rests on neoliberal precepts, in which "individual responsibility" supplants community support, and "the benefits of choice—especially consumer choice"—are equated with "individual fulfillment" (Sender, 2006, p. 135). What becomes clearer, then, are the ways in which competition overlaps with authenticity and consumption not only in reality television generally but also in *Drag Race* specifically.

Specifically, competition informs the historical context of drag culture in ways that anticipate the premises of *Drag Race*. Of late-1960s American drag circuits, Newton (1972, p. 46) observes that "homosexual subculture values visual beauty, and beating women at the glamour game is a feat valued by all female impersonators and by many homosexuals in general." Moreover, given the clandestine work of drag queens in highly policed environments in tandem with the marginalized experience of gay men and lesbians in general, the "greatest source of tension was inherent in the life-situation of most female impersonators. Cut-throat motives of gain and competition were allowed free play and even encouraged in a…loosely structured situation whose only certainties were uncertainties" (Newton, 1972, p. 115). Fifty years later, reality television has transformed the premises of competition from modes of subsistence to those of entertainment, but within the realm of *Drag Race* in particular, Newton's observations are still relevant.

Global Audiences, Fandom, and Participation.

Drag Race has significantly reconfigured the intersections of race, gender, and sexuality within the landscape of reality television, and these intersections have been received by global viewers and fans of *Drag Race* in varying ways. In the growing, convergent "Runiverse" of *Drag Race* television franchises, live events, and social media channels, *Drag Race* has been exported to Thailand, the United Kingdom, Chile, Canada, The Netherlands, Spain, Australia, and New Zealand. Three themes tie together *Drag Race*'s local and global incarnations. First, it has transformed drag culture from transgressive, anti-establishment cultural critique, such as that embodied by The Cockettes troupe in 1960s San Francisco, to projects of self-branding and entrepreneurism (Feldman & Hakim, 2020). Second, *Drag Race* has mobilized geopolitical identity and gender performativity in ways that both facilitate and constrain expressions of race, ethnicity, sexuality, and physicality while underscoring feminist concerns with misogyny (Brennan & Gudelunas, 2017). Third, the series has solidified official and unofficial global performances of and participation in drag culture, especially in the space of social media, to exceed situating drag in the physical, gay bar/club scene (Brennan & Gudelunas, 2017; Gudelunas, 2017).

Drag Race markedly reverberates outside of the United States. In Brazil, this is due in large part to the country's historically visible, and demonized, *travesti* community (Green, 2020). Millions of Brazilians constitute a dedicated *Drag Race* fan base, which has grown substantially since the series appeared on Netflix in Brazil in 2014. Many former *Drag Race* contestants include Brazilian cities in their tour circuits, and the success of the series has prompted the creation of two Brazilian imitations: *Glitter: Em Busca de um Sonho* and *Academia de Drags* (Castellano & Leal Machado, 2017). Apart from reflecting the success of *Drag Race* in Brazil, the Brazilian derivatives signal increased visibility and radicalization of LGBTQ+ discourse as the country's political landscape turns increasingly conservative, with profound implications for Brazil's LGBTQ+ communities (Castellano & Leal Machado, 2017). In Mexico, *Drag Race* has not been as eagerly received, at least by traditional Mexican society characterized by sexism, misogyny, homophobia, and male chauvinism (de la Garza Villareal et al., 2017). More telling of *Drag Race*'s reception in Mexico, however, is not the expected repudiation by straight, middle-class society but rather critique by young, gay, middle-class Mexican men for whom the series represents a superficial reinforcement of gay stereotypes and caters to viewers who like "'faggy' things" (de la Garza Villareal et al., 2017, p. 193). What young, gay Mexican men's appraisal of *Drag Race* reveals is less an indictment of the series and the host themselves and more an implicit acknowledgment of Mexican society's circumscription of (straight) men performing queerness.

In the European context, Greek viewers' responses to *Drag Race* better align with those of Latin Americans than northern Europeans in that the queer themes of the series contradict well-established heterosexual narratives in a predominantly conservative society. The influence of the European Union, however, has shifted Greek attitudes concerning homosexuality from secrecy to acceptance of long-term relationships, if only as a reflection of homonormativity (Duggan, 2003), and still within a discourse of marginalized visibility (Chronaki, 2017). *Drag Race*'s depictions of drag as a profession requiring hard work and talent, rather than simply a lifestyle choice, resound with Greek viewers, as does RuPaul's agility in switching between male and female guises and her witty neologisms, all of which suggest the discursive resonance of self-governmentality in Greek society (Chronaki, 2017). In Italy, *Drag Race* has been programmed as subcultural fare, relegated to the late-night, schedule-fillers of reality television, and undeserving of critical appraisal (Barra et al., 2020). What Italian network television (and not Italian viewers) has underestimated, however, is the cultural-linguistic complexity of drag as conveyed through *Drag Race*, as well as a history of Italian drag culture legitimized by RuPaul herself. The paradox of importing *Drag Race* to Italian television as fulfilling a subcultural space is that the mainstream success of the series has warranted re-examining the significance of drag culture in Italy (Barra et al., 2020).

Drag Race has put Australian drag on the global map, due to season six contestant Courtney Act and her particularly "managed" appeal by virtue of the mainstream, normative framework of Australian media (McIntyre, 2017, p. 89). Perth, Australia, is also noteworthy as the most isolated, provincial capital in the world and as a locus for witnessing explosive interest in drag because of the success of *Drag Race* (Alexander, 2017). With *Drag Race*'s mainstream appeal in Australia has come the idea that any (provincial) drag queen can enjoy the celebrity of a former *Drag Race* contestant. Moreover, by circumventing the complex structure of the drag family as a locus for defying and reaffirming the dominant norm of the heterosexual family (Butler, 1999), the internet and social media provide space for aspiring Australian queens to pursue instantaneous visibility and fame (Alexander, 2017). Social media and other digital platforms—arguably more so than the highly regulated, largely nationalized medium of television itself—have indeed facilitated *Drag Race*'s global success (Gudelunas, 2017). Furthermore, contestants, including former ones, leverage their fan bases through social media platforms to simultaneously promote themselves and the *Drag Race* universe (Gudelunas, 2017), reaffirming the ways in which both drag culture and social media have followed a similarly corporatized trajectory (Feldman & Hakim, 2020).

Subjectivity, (Self-)Transformation, and Queer Pedagogy. *Drag Race* is recognized as having changed heteronormative assumptions about the proscriptive, exclusively "gay" place of drag culture and therefore as having raised awareness of the diversity of LGBTQ+ historical and contemporary experience (Brennan & Gudelunas, 2017). However, *Drag Race*'s now mainstream, corporatized framework contradicts the platform it espouses for vocalizing the complexity of LGBTQ+ identities. Both the merits and shortcomings of *Drag Race* assume the interpretive potential of queer representation, thereby evading the ways in which representation itself operates as a productive agent (Yudelman, 2017). Butler (1990) argues that power (re)produces what it claims to represent, prompting questions of how representing drag in reality television reifies the power of the latter over the "reality" of drag performance as subject matter. Similarly, Bratich (2006) sees reality television as a performative mechanism that seizes on and recirculates (self-)transformation as discourse. In *Drag Race*, self-betterment and self-regulation underscore neoliberal, entrepreneurial discourse contingent on the transformative process, and self-transformation supplants the ethos of community and interdependence characteristic of the drag family network (Yudelman, 2017). Moreover, as *Drag Race* continues to grow in popularity through reality television's mechanisms, subjectification to self-transformation will continue to inform the ways in which drag is understood as contemporary practice.

In the social media universe of Facebook, YouTube, Twitter, and Instagram, performativity also rests on the transformative capacity of the self, a process facilitated by the ability to continually (re)invent one's self through social media's tools and technologies. In semiotic terms, this means that infinite readings of the self can defy reduction to a single corporeality (Colapietro, 1989), aided by social media's (self-)transformational logic. When the self-transformational capacities of social media are located in the digital spaces of *Drag Race*, the key idea is spreadability (Jenkins et al., 2013), in which drag queens' performativity generates limitless, (re)interpretable, and highly circulated meanings (Henn et al., 2017). Moreover, as Henn and colleagues (2017, p. 301) argue, when a semiosphere (Lotman, 1999), characterized by (self-)transformational signs processed and metabolized into structures that organize culture, is located in the digital spaces of *Drag Race*, a social network of signification opens up, enabling "a rich set of performances that give more meaning to semiodiversity" (p. 301). Given the performative and self-transformative nature of drag, compounded by the reinventing capabilities of social media, however, semiodiverse meanings can remain unstable and highly disputed amongst both drag queens and their fans, and transformative discourse can remain in the realm of visibility for only a handful of prevailing drag queens.

For some, *Drag Race* provides a pedagogical space. Pensoneau-Conway (2006) finds that drag is replete with the educational potential to explore constructs of gender and sexuality, while performativity is mediated in ways that decide which modes of performing gender and sexuality are seen as socially acceptable (Baumann & Briggs, 1990; Case, 2009). The idea that, as a media text, *Drag Race* carries queer educational potential resonates with hooks's (1996) assertion that film facilitates as much as it inhibits understanding race, gender, and class as social constructs. Whitworth (2017) suggests a few questions in seeking to identify the educational potential of *Drag Race* for its viewers' exploration of queerness. In what ways has *Drag Race*'s espoused platform of queer pedagogy changed because of the series's increased visibility? How does the growing, mainstream popularity of the series implicate its ability to continue serving diverse, queer educational interests? How can the contradictions of a highly produced reality television series educating viewers about the complexities of queer identity, history, and community be resolved? Answers to questions such as these lie in the way *Drag Race* contestants may embrace or rebuff RuPaul's exemplar of drag practice; some choose to "stay in the style and form of femininity and drag superstardom modeled by RuPaul," while others "take the opportunity to sashay away, to depart from the roots that have nourished them" (Fine & Shreve, 2014, p. 185). The potential of drag to serve as a platform for queer pedagogy vis-à-vis reality television remains limited, however, as within the reality/competition television format the multiple articulations of queer performativity are reduced to winning and losing possibilities (Brennan, 2017, p. 42).

Daggett (2017) also argues that *Drag Race* has enabled queer education, including through its increasingly mainstream online and live spaces. As drag culture becomes more commercial and profitable, however, discourses of queer self-love and community-building clash with the neoliberalism tenets of individualism and self-transformation. Put differently, while *Drag Race* affectively engages viewers in embracing self and community, as a reality television form it simultaneously advances self-interest and rivalry. Additionally, *Drag Race*'s dialogue between communitarianism and competition occurs in both virtual and live settings. These dual settings are where the idea of mimicry (Bhabha, 1994), mobilized to subvert dominant paradigms from within their own orders, and rooted in the drag families of *Paris Is Burning*, capture *Drag Race*'s dual humanizing and profiting strategies. *Drag Race*'s live moments (DragCon, Battle of the Seasons tour) reveal how physical immersion in drag culture differs from the screened experience yet how community and individualism nonetheless coexist in both spaces. As space between the virtual and the physical becomes increasingly indistinct in the *Drag Race* universe, so too does the division between community support and self-promotion, as the series continues to pursue the effects of both strategies (Daggett, 2017).

Hetero- and Homonormativity. The connections between performativity, (self-)transformation, and individualism suggest *Drag Race*'s invocations of American exceptionalism, particularly through the neoliberal tenets of private competition and personal responsibility (Goldmark, 2015). Duggan (2003, p. 45) traces how American political culture has unfolded with implications for "gay and lesbian civil rights, lobbying and litigation organizations" which have "moved away from constituency mobilization and community-based consultation." Furthermore, "pressed by the exigencies of fundraising for survival, gay civil rights groups have adopted neoliberal rhetoric and corporate decision-making models" (Duggan, 2003, p. 45). To look at the incorporation of racial, national, and linguistic others into *Drag Race*'s self-transforming discourse indeed suggests its adherence to a neoliberal model (Goldmark, 2015). Moreover, contestants have been challenged with transforming butch women, masculine men, and armed forces veterans as "outsiders" into *Drag Race*-sanctioned "versions" of themselves. With the veterans, Ferrante (2017, p. 161) reads an amalgam of American patriotism, homonormativity, and drag community at work:

> In one short step, the drag mother is turned into the motherland. The denaturalization of femininity, and the reconfiguration of bonds of solidarity and support as alternatives to the traditional family, can be represented and celebrated on [*Drag Race*] as long as they are...attributable to a matrix of national pride.

Brusselaers (2017, p. 57) argues that in its increasingly mainstream visibility, *Drag Race* attempts to represent and cater to gay camp sensibilities at odds with the respectability and legitimacy of "accepted" artistry. This contradiction connects with Newton's (1972) observations of female impersonators' disapproval of straight incursions into gay male culture, from which it could be argued that transforming drag into a "legitimate" form of art inevitably "straightens" it by extricating drag from the transgressive, subaltern contexts from which it originated (Brusselaers, 2017). As discussed above, camp (see also Meyer, 1994), as a sensibility purportedly "exclusive" to gay male culture, creates environments averse to the unironic and "serious," *Drag Race* included. The series's decontextualized references to LGBTQ+ history and obscurely premised challenges decenter the legitimacy of drag as a contemporary, cosmopolitan set of practices. As Halperin (2012, p. 63) describes the borderline essentialism of homonormative gay male culture, it is "the stubborn but ultimately untenable belief that social identities are grounded in some inherent property or nature or quality common to all the members of an identity-based group." In looking at *Drag Race* vis-à-vis subcultural/mainstream dialectics, we can begin to see not only how its homonormative codes start to approximate heteronormative cultural standards but also the hazy area that exists between (gay male) subculture and (straight) mainstream media.

The "drag family" is based not on biological bonds but on an equivalent sense of community and reciprocity. Drag families refer to the houses of drag with which drag queens are often affiliated, as closely depicted in *Paris Is Burning* (Livingston, 1990), and create a sense of kinship that runs against the hetero-patriarchal familial institution (Weston, 1997). In *Drag Race*, constant citations to families and familial roles ("Mama Ru," "sister"), while clearly referencing traditional familial structures, nevertheless upend the notion of family and subvert its meaning in the symbolic order of society (Butler, 2000). At the same time, *Drag Race* creates a "domesticated" discourse that configures the tradition of the drag family to post-9/11, American sociopolitical ideology to aid in constructing a homonormative regime of queer visibility (Ferrante, 2017). This regime, as a set of norms governing representations of subjectivity, becomes homonormative by putting queer bodies to work within structured, segregated processes of meaning-creation to deftly reconfigure hegemonic power (Duggan, 1994, 2003; Ferrante, 2017; Puar, 2007). The "eccentric subject" (Slaner, 1996) that once disrupted heteronormative society has been supplanted with *Drag Race* queens who become assimilated into a national body if they prove productive, and indeed winning, in that body's re-conception of family.

Race, Nationality, Language, and Body. Discourses of race, nationality, language, and body significantly inform *Drag Race*'s portrayals of drag culture. These discourses intersect in the acceptability by which Asian queens adopt Native American–inspired "global" looks or mimic the image of wealthy Filipinas; Latinx queens adhere to the guise of high-glamour pageantry; White queens play with goth or kooky aesthetics; yet Black queens must discard the dualities of performing femininity on the runway and masculinity at home and in the community (Marcel, 2014), which *Paris Is Burning* again captures and from which *Drag Race* supposedly takes inspiration.

Across its 14 seasons to date, *Drag Race* has featured a diverse range of contestants, many of whom, in various seasons, have been referred to as "Puerto Rican drag queens." Most notable of queens who fit into this category is an emphasis on their English-language capabilities and, relatedly, their knowledge of queer popular culture of the United States. If the skills or knowledge of Puerto Rican queens is lacking in these areas, they are often the butt of other contestants' jokes. The consistency of these inter-contestant relations raises questions about "border control" and homonationalistic tactics on the part of White and nonwhite queens from the continental United States when referring to their Global South counterparts (McIntyre & Riggs, 2017, p. 61). Scholars (Anthony, 2014; Mayora, 2014) have noted how native Spanish-speaking *Drag Race* contestants are treated with a degree of otherness, which more specifically suggests "the colonial contours of Puerto Rican citizenship" and more broadly establishes the series's "implicit English proficiency requirement" in determining "success on the set" (Goldmark, 2015, p. 502). Policing of language and nationality in *Drag Race* has implications beyond the underscored limited cultural capital of queens from outside the continental United States. It also has implications for the ways in which some queer lives are made to matter more than others (McIntyre & Riggs, 2017).

Although season one *Drag Race* contestant BeBe Zahara Benet won the crown of America's Next Drag Superstar, RuPaul nonetheless prefaced her every runway entrance with "Cameroon!" in reference to BeBe's birth country (despite coming to the competition from Minneapolis, MN) and reminded BeBe that she was carrying "all of Africa on her shoulders" in reference to the continent with which Bebe was associated during the entire season (Tucker Jenkins, 2017). Unsurprising, then, may be Black drag's equation with a modern-day blackface minstrelsy (Magubane, 2002).

The fat body and fat stigma have also discursively figured into *Drag Race*'s representations of drag performativity (Darnell & Tabatabai, 2017; Pomerantz, 2017). Imperative is that the producers of the series include at least one fat queen each season, as they do with representatives of other underrepresented faces of drag. *Drag Race* presents viewers with a mix of contradictory attitudes and references toward the fat body. Some contestants (and judges) appear supportive of fat empowerment, while others clearly identify with idealized body types. Apparent, too, is that although fat queens and fat-supportive views seem to be embraced within *Drag Race*'s ecumenical ethos, such views are belied by statements that reveal contestants' and judges' real views. As constantly in transition, popular culture is also gradually relinquishing hegemonic standards to allow for diversity in body shapes and positions on the body, which may account for more fat queens and more *successful* fat queens over *Drag Race*'s seasons (Pomerantz, 2017). Gay men have developed strategies to deal with fat stigma, such as emphasizing the large, masculine body common in Bear communities. For fat queens in *Drag Race*, however, strategies that combine masculinity and corpulence are at odds with the series's paradigmatic, idealized vision of drag performativity.

Transgender Subjectivity. In the first six seasons of *Drag Race*, RuPaul used the recorded line "You've Got She-Mail," a reference to the 1998 film *You've Got Mail* and a nod to "Tyra Mail" of *America's Next Top Model* (Oleksiak, 2021), to gather contestants around RuPaul on a monitor in which she gives instructions for the episodes' mini-challenges. Additionally, a season six mini-challenge entitled "Female or She-male?" had contestants guess whether photo pairings depicted a drag queen or a cisgender female. In a *Guardian* interview, RuPaul was asked whether he would accept transgender contestants to the series, to which he responded:

> Probably not. You can identify as a woman and say you're transitioning, but it changes once you start changing your body. It takes on a different thing; it changes the whole concept of what we're doing. We've had some girls who've had some injections in the face and maybe a little bit in the butt here and there, but they haven't transitioned. (Aitkenhead, 2018)

In a since-deleted tweet, RuPaul reiterated his position on transgender women being accepted to the series, posting, "You can take performance enhancing drugs and still be an athlete, just not in the Olympics" (quoted in Framke, 2018).

The *Drag Race* segments, and RuPaul's comments, met with objections from nonbinary, former contestants and from the LGBTQ+ community. As a result of the controversy, then-broadcaster Logo removed all "she-mail" references from episodes, and RuPaul replaced the line with "She done already done had herses." In their podcast *What's the Tee?*, however, RuPaul and cohost Michelle Visage joke, "Did you call me a granny, girl? That is your new thing, because we can't say it with a 'T' anymore…We're just going to say it for everything that's T-related" (quoted in Duffy, 2015). RuPaul apologized for barring transgender contestants from appearing on the series, tweeting: "I understand and regret the hurt I have caused. The trans community are heroes of our shared LGBTQ movement. You are my teachers" (quoted in Nolfi, 2018). Although *Drag Race* cast transmasculine contestant Gottmik in season 13, the decision does not resolve RuPaul's ambivalence about accepting transfeminine contestants to the series (Sonoma, 2021). The liminality of *Drag Race*'s transgender contestants, as they seem to be selected as (fully) transmasculine and not (partially) transfeminine, warrants highlighting several contestants who self-identify as transfeminine, both on the series and since their departures from it.

Kylie Sonique Love was *Drag Race*'s first transgender contestant. Sonique was asked by episode judges to remove her mask after a runway show, as she appeared to be "hiding something." During a reunion episode and a talk with RuPaul, Sonique reflected, "I don't really feel that people got a chance to know who Sonique is," to which RuPaul responded, "I've heard there's something you want to share with us concerning that." Sonique continued:

> I haven't been happy for a really long time in my life, and I've never understood why. I just had to be honest with myself…I'm…a woman. I'm not a boy who dresses up…I feel like the only thing I've ever done right was go to a doctor and start transitioning. I've never been more happier in my entire life.

When RuPaul responded, "I know a lot of people get confused [about] what a transsexual is…" Sonique interjected:

> There's a line between drag and transgender. Most transgender girls do not do drag…They want to live their life solely as a woman. Where drag queens want to get out of drag and be a man, when I go home…I dread taking off my makeup.

Carmen Carrera competed on *Drag Race* season three and was warned by cohost Visage not to over-rely on her burlesque performance in order to win the competition. Unlike Sonique, whose status as a nonbinary and unpopular contestant approaches other within otherness (Ahmed, 2002), Carmen became part of the "Heathers" clique, in reference to the 1988 film featuring four domineering, self-obsessed young women. Carmen came out as transgender in 2012, one year after competing on *Drag Race*. Similar to Sonique, the arbiters of her deemed that performance as obscuring a "true" sense of who Carmen really is. Subsequently, Carmen condemned the "Female or She-male?" challenge as well as *Drag Race*'s transphobic discourse:

> "Shemale" is an incredibly offensive term, and this whole business about if you can tell whether a woman is biological or not is getting kind of old…We live in a new world where understanding and acceptance are on the rise. *Drag Race* should be a little smarter about the terms they use and comprehend the fight for respect trans people are facing every minute of today. They should use their platform to educate their viewers truthfully on all facets of drag performance art. (Molloy, 2014)

Jiggly Caliente of season four was portrayed and often ridiculed on the series for her stature and weight. Jiggly found herself at the receiving end of fat jokes during her run, compounded by her passion for food and her Filipina heritage. Jiggly came out as a transgender woman in 2016 and has since integrated her Filipina identity with her drag persona to inform her music.

> That's one thing I wanted to make sure that people see the culture. I want people to know there is a voice behind this woman…I am proud to be Filipina and I wanted my album to represent that too. (Youtt, 2018)

Monica Beverly Hillz self-identified as a transgender woman during *Drag Race*'s fifth season. As with her predecessors, the series's judges saw Monica as "disconnected" in her appearances. At one point, RuPaul asked Monica, "What's going on?," to which Monica tearfully replied, "I've just been holding a secret in, I've been trying so hard…" RuPaul pursued with, "What secret?" Monica, erupting in tears, responded, "I'm not just a drag queen. I'm a transgender woman."

Gia Gunn competed on *Drag Race* season six, was eliminated early, and returned in 2018 after coming out as transgender to compete in *RuPaul's Drag Race All Stars*. As the first transgender contestant invited to compete on *All Stars*, Gia may have been asked to appear in response to the transphobic comments of earlier that year. Gia provided her own response to RuPaul's position:

> Does this mean as a trans woman I will no longer be considered for future seasons of *All Stars*?…I respect that this is RuPaul's decision, but at the end of the day I don't feel that my transness has anything to do with me as an artist. If you're a fierce queen and you bring it to the runway you should be accepted as one and nothing more and nothing less. (Blackmon, 2018)

On *Race Chaser*, a podcast hosted by former contestants Willam and Alaska, Gia reflected on her *All Stars* experience:

> I felt completely disregarded…I didn't feel acknowledged. I didn't feel wanted, to be there in the competition. And truthfully it…hurt my feelings and I had a really big breakdown in between sets and I was just like, 'If I'm getting this feeling from her and I don't feel very welcome then what the fuck am I doing here.'

Gia continued:

> If we were going to bring somebody on the show to, basically, you know, clean up somebody's mess, obviously that fell on me, right? Because months before [RuPaul] had made a statement that was completely opposite of what they did. And I knew by being casted that I was going on there to basically show the world that this show does, quote-unquote, support trans and that [RuPaul] does see trans people as drag queens. So for me to get there and…never have eye contact with [RuPaul], never have any sort of acknowledgement of, "Oh, you've come so far", or "Your journey has been so beautiful to watch", or anything of that sort, I just felt really hurt. (Katz, 2019)

During *Drag Race* season nine, Peppermint entered the competition and later self-identified as a transgender woman, placing runner-up in the finale. Less the result of runner-up status and more a reflection on her transfeminine identity, Peppermint writes:

> in the words of Monica Beverley Hillz, who so bravely came out in season five of *Drag Race*, that "Drag is what I do and trans is who I am." And I think that's the simplest way to put it. I know that there's a lot of nuances, just as there are in the human experience – there's no one way to describe everyone…It's really easy, especially when we're talking

about minorities, to kind of paint the entire community with one broad stroke and just say 'all gay people are this' or 'all trans people are that.' And this is primarily because we have very limited examples of who these people are in our media. So I think once we start to expand the different shades and shapes and sizes of the people in our queer community in media, then people will see that there are different types of trans people – some of whom are drag queens and some of whom are not. Drag is a job or career – it's a way to make money, but it's not necessarily the be all end all of a trans person's existence. (Nichols, 2017)

From the liminal positions in which Sonique, Carmen Carerra, Jiggly Caliente, Monica Beverly Hillz, Gia Gunn, and Peppermint were placed in *Drag Race* as transfeminine contestants, many of these women have advocated for greater visibility and awareness of transgender experience since their time on the show, especially in social media.

Reality television generally and *Drag Race* specifically are vehicles that do not simply stage but rather construe the ways in which gender performativity is articulated through contestants' lived experience. Specifically, *Drag Race*'s construal of gender performativity rests on the existing liminality of gay men, which more recently has become the liminality of gay men transgressing cisgender, homonormative boundaries to become women. In essence, drag is premised on the act of performing a gendered other. Yet, when performing a gendered other is transgressed by *becoming* and indeed *being* a gendered other, construing performativity becomes limited, if not foreclosed, by *Drag Race*. The performativity of transfeminine drag queens in intersecting with Latinx, Asian, African American, and other underrepresented identities assumes greater potency in social media space than within the construed premises of *Drag Race* and reality television. More than what drag represents within the circumscribed boundaries of reality television, transfeminine queens have mobilized their post-*Drag Race* fame and the discomfort of their presence within the series to achieve visibility and political mobility for transgender identities in social media. Finally, even if transgender drag queens' ephemeral political alignments in social media space may at times approximate *Drag Race*'s neat reduction of complex LGBTQ+ histories and identities (Brennan, 2021), social media offers fertile space for enabling the articulation of intersecting subjectivities that more realistically constitutes drag performativity, at least more so than in representing drag in reality television's now mainstream space.

CONCLUSION

As a representational act, drag has continually mobilized gender performativity to draw out, parody, and complicate how gender is already enacted in "natural" and taken-for-granted ways. Drag also has the potential to become *political* representational acts in not only complicating naturalized constructs of gender but also in subverting heteronormative positions and exchange and even in drag's most anodyne and "knowingly" straight ways. The political potency of drag lies in its roots in camp as more a strategy of gay liberation than mere "sensibility." Moreover, even at the frequent points at which drag is coopted by heteronormative culture industries at the expense of queer agency, the appropriation and dilution of drag continue to implicate its political space by virtue of its queer potency. The same could be argued for the ways in which drag is deployed to further compound essentializing constructs of race, ethnicity, gender, and sexuality by the mainstream American cultural industries. To invoke drag in constructing female, Black, Jewish, transgender, and other "others" in American popular characterizations—whether for humorous or "serious" ends—is to reaffirm systemic mechanisms of oppression *and* to suggest subverting those mechanisms from within their same performative assertions.

While drag has consistently straddled subversive cultural expression and popular appeal, both the transgressive and the mainstream meet in *RuPaul's Drag Race*, the American reality/competition television series that has achieved global, commercial success as a queer text. *Drag Race* imparts the ecumenical inclusivity of different racial, ethnic, geo-linguistic, and physical identities uniting around contemporary drag practice. However, the neoliberal premises of individualism and self-transformation vis-à-vis entrepreneurialism and consumer agency, even as persistent qualities of reality television, nevertheless belie the communitarian, "drag family" ethos of *Paris Is Burning*, from which *Drag Race* purportedly draws inspiration. *Drag Race* has come to paradigmatically represent contemporary drag practice by occupying not only mainstream televisual but also physical and online space. For some viewers, congregants, and users, *Drag Race*'s occupation of traditionally heteronormative space reveals the series's unparalleled value as a queer pedagogical text, and even in some nationally and culturally mediated contexts, *Drag Race* defies encapsulation as merely fulfilling subcultural programming quotas to represent drag as modalities of dexterity and artistry over "gay lifestyle" or "choice." *Drag Race*'s precipitous ascent to occupy the role of paradigmatically representing drag in diverse media spaces has generated commensurate, local-to-global discourse, from the notion that any provincial queen can become the next face of drag superstardom to the idea that the "semiodiversity" of drag should be arbitrated by global, online fan communities.

However, if we are to adequately consider drag as straddling queer agency and heteronormative structure, then we must consider how the 2023 face of drag negotiates transgender subjectivity. Left to the representational paradigm of *Drag Race*, transgender drag queens must adhere to the cisgender, homonormative ideas of what the series and RuPaul Charles proscribe as within the limits of gender performativity. Transgender drag queens themselves, and in spaces outside of *Drag Race* and reality television, reveal that drag is political, intersectional, and communal. The challenge, in 2023, lies in seeking out the ways in which drag has moved beyond the humorous, anodyne, and cisgender/homonormatively "knowing," and the contradiction lies in the ways drag has come to paradigmatically represent the limits over the possibilities of gender performativity.

FURTHER READING

Andrews, H. (2020). Drag celebrity impersonation as queer caricature in "The Snatch Game." *Celebrity Studies*, *11*(4), 417–430. http://doi.org/10.1080/19392397.2020.1765082

Brennan, N., & Gudelunas, D. (Eds.). (2023). *Drag in the global digital public sphere: Queer visibility, online discourse and political change*. Routledge.

Collie, H., & Commane, G. (2020). "Assume the position: Two queens stand before me": RuPaul as ultimate queen. *Celebrity Studies*, *11*(4), 402–416. http://doi.org/10.1080/19392397.2020.1765081

Disemelo, K. (2015). *Black men as pink consumers? A critical reading of race, sexuality and the construction of the pink economy in South African queer consumer media* [Doctoral dissertation, University of the Witwatersrand].

Escudero-Alías, M. (2011). Ethics, authorship, and the representation of drag kings in contemporary US popular culture. *Journal of Popular Culture, 44*(2), 256–273.

Ferreday, D. (2020). "No one is trash, no one is garbage, no one is cancelled": The cultural politics of trauma, recovery and rage in RuPaul's Drag Race. *Celebrity Studies, 11*(4), 464–478. http://doi.org/10.1080/19392397.2020.1765101

Heller, M. (2020). *Queering drag: Redefining the discourse of gender-bending*. Indiana University Press.

LeMaster, L., & Tristano, M., Jr. (2021). Performing (Asian American trans) femme on *RuPaul's Drag Race*: Dis/orienting racialized gender, or, performing trans femme of color, regardless. *Journal of International and Intercultural Communication, 16*(1), 1–18. http://doi.org/10.1080/17513057.2021.1955143

Litwiller, F. (2020). Normative drag culture and the making of precarity. *Leisure Studies, 39*(4): 600–612.

Mercer, J., & Sarson, C. (2020). Fifteen seconds of fame: *RuPaul's Drag Race*, camp and "memeability." *Celebrity Studies, 11*(4), 479–492. http://doi.org/10.1080/19392397.2020.1765102

Middlemost, R. (2020). Rewriting "herstory": Sasha Velour's drag as art and activism. *Celebrity Studies, 11*(4), 431–446. http://doi.org/10.1080/19392397.2020.1765083

Moreman, S. T., & McIntosh, D. M. (2010). Brown scriptings and rescriptings: A critical performance ethnography of Latina drag queens. *Communication and Critical/Cultural Studies, 7*(2), 115–135.

O'Connell, R. (2020). "Labouring in the image": Celebrity, femininity, and the fully commodified self in the drag of Willam Belli. *Celebrity Studies, 11*(4), 447–463. http://doi.org/10.1080/19392397.2020.1765085

Strings, S., & Bui, L. T. (2014). "She Is Not Acting, She Is": The conflict between gender and racial realness on *RuPaul's Drag Race*. *Feminist Media Studies, 14*(5), 822–836.

Zervigon, A. M. (2009). Drag shows: Drag queens and female impersonators. *GLBTQ Arts, 1*, 89–103.

REFERENCES

Ahmed, S. (2002). This other and other others. *Economy and Society, 31*(4): 558–572.

Aitkenhead, D. (2018, March 3). RuPaul: "Drag is a big f-you to male-dominated culture." *The Guardian*. https://www.theguardian.com/tv-and-radio/2018/mar/03/rupaul-drag-race-big-f-you-to-male-dominated-culture

Alexander, C. (2017). What can drag do for me? The multifaceted influences of *RuPaul's Drag Race* on the Perth drag scene. In N. Brennan & D. Gudelunas (Eds.), *RuPaul's Drag Race and the shifting visibility of drag culture: The boundaries of reality TV* (pp. 245–269). Palgrave Macmillan.

Andrejevic, M. (2004). *Reality TV: The work of being watched*. Rowman & Littlefield.

Anthony, L. (2014). Dragging with an accent: Linguistic stereotypes, language barriers and translingualism. In J. Daems (Ed.), *The makeup of RuPaul's Drag Race: Essays on the queen of reality shows* (pp. 49–66). McFarland.

Antler, J. (1988). Jewish women on television: Too Jewish or not enough? In J. Antler (Ed.), *Talking back: Images of Jewish women in popular American culture* (pp. 242–252). Brandeis University Press.

Barra, L., Brembilla, P., Rossato, L., & Spaziante, L. (2020). Lip-sync for your life (abroad): The distribution, adaptation and circulation of *RuPaul's Drag Race* in Italy. *VIEW Journal of European Television, History & Culture, 9*(17): 119–133.

Bauman, R., & Briggs, C. (1990). Poetics and performance as critical perspectives on language and social life. *Annual Review of Anthropology, 19*, 59–88.

Berkowitz, D., & Belgrave, L. L. (2010). She works hard for the money: Drag queens and the management of their contradictory status of celebrity and marginality. *Journal of Contemporary Ethnography, 39*(2): 159–186.

Bhabha, H. (1994). *The location of culture*. Routledge.
Blackmon, M. (2018, November 9). RuPaul reversed himself and is now allowing a trans "Drag Race" contestant to compete. *BuzzFeedNews*. https://www.buzzfeednews.com/article/michaelblackmon/rupaul-drag-race-all-stars-gia-gunn-trans
Boyd, T. (2006, August 8). A Black man in a dress: No laughing matter [Radio broadcast]. *National Public Radio*. https://www.npr.org/templates/story/story.php?storyId=5626512
Bratich, J. Z. (2006). "Nothing is left alone for too long": Reality programming and control society subjects. *Journal of Communication Inquiry*, 30(1), 65–83.
Brennan, N. (2017). Contradictions between the subversive and the mainstream: Drag cultures and *RuPaul's Drag Race*. In N. Brennan & D. Gudelunas (Eds.), *RuPaul's Drag Race and the shifting visibility of drag culture: The boundaries of reality TV* (pp. 29–43). Palgrave Macmillan.
Brennan, N. (2021). Performing drag in a pandemic: Affect in theory, practice and (potential) political mobilization. *Consumption Markets & Culture*, 25(4), 369–381. http://doi.org/10.1080/10253866.2021.1974010
Brennan, N., & Gudelunas, D. (2017). Drag culture, global participation and *RuPaul's Drag Race*. In N. Brennan & D. Gudelunas (Eds.), *RuPaul's Drag Race and the shifting visibility of drag culture: The Boundaries of reality TV* (pp. 1–11). Palgrave Macmillan.
Britton, A. (1999). For interpretation: Notes against camp. In F. Cleto (Ed.), *Camp: Queer aesthetics and the performing subject* (pp. 136–142). University of Michigan Press.
Brusselaers, D. (2017). "Pick up a book and go read": Art and legitimacy in *RuPaul's Drag Race*. In N. Brennan & D. Gudelunas (Eds.), *RuPaul's Drag Race and the shifting visibility of drag culture: The boundaries of reality TV* (pp. 45–59). Palgrave Macmillan.
Bullough, V., Bullough, B., & Smith, R. (1983). A comparative study of male transvestites, male to female transsexuals, and male homosexuals. *The Journal of Sex Research*, 19(3): 238–257.
Butler, J. (1990). *Gender trouble: Feminism and the subversion of identity*. Routledge.
Butler, J. (1999). Gender is burning: Questions of appropriation and subversion. In S. Thornham (Ed.), *Feminist film theory: A reader* (pp. 336–349). New York University Press.
Butler, J. (2000). *Antigone's claim: Kinship between life & death* (Vol. 8). Columbia University Press.
Case, S. E. (2009). *Feminist and queer performance: Critical strategies*. Palgrave Macmillan.
Castellano, M., & Leal Machado, H. (2017). "Please come to Brazil!" The practices of *RuPaul's Drag Race*'s Brazilian fandom. In N. Brennan & D. Gudelunas (Eds.), *RuPaul's Drag Race and the shifting visibility of drag culture: The boundaries of reality TV* (pp. 167–177). Palgrave Macmillan.
Chronaki, D. (2017). Mainstreaming the transgressive: Greek audiences' readings of drag culture through the consumption of *RuPaul's Drag Race*. In N. Brennan & D. Gudelunas (Eds.), *RuPaul's Drag Race and the shifting visibility of drag culture: The boundaries of reality TV* (pp. 197–212). Palgrave Macmillan.
Colapietro, V. (1989). *Peirce's approach to the self: A semiotic perspective on human subjectivity*. State University of New York Press.
Couldry, N. (2004). Teaching us to fake it: The ritualized norms of television's "reality" games. In S. Murray & L. Ouellette (Eds.), *Reality TV: Remaking television culture* (pp. 82–99). New York University Press.
Daggett, C. (2017). "If you can't love yourself, how in the hell you gonna love somebody else?" Drag TV and self-love discourse. In N. Brennan & D. Gudelunas (Eds.), *RuPaul's Drag Race and the shifting visibility of drag culture: The boundaries of reality TV* (pp. 271–285). Palgrave Macmillan.
Darnell, A. L., & Tabatabai, A. (2017). The werk that remains: Drag and the mining of the idealized female form. In N. Brennan & D. Gudelunas (Eds.), *RuPaul's Drag Race and the shifting visibility of drag culture: The boundaries of reality TV* (pp. 91–101). Palgrave Macmillan.
Davis, G. (2004). Camp and queer and the new queer director: Case study—Gregg Araki. In M. Aaron (Ed.), *New Queer Cinema: A critical reader* (pp. 53–67). Edinburgh University Press.
Deery, J. (2015). *Reality TV*. Polity Press.

de la Garza Villareal, N. A., Valdez García, C. & Rodríguez Fernández, G. K. (2017). Reception of queer content and stereotypes among young people in Monterrey, Mexico: *RuPaul's Drag Race*. In N. Brennan & D. Gudelunas (Eds.), *RuPaul's Drag Race and the shifting visibility of drag culture: The boundaries of reality TV* (pp. 179–195). Palgrave Macmillan.

de Lauretis, T. (1990). Eccentric subjects: Feminist theory and historical consciousness. *Feminist Studies*, 16(1): 115–150.

Duffy, N. (2015, March 2). *RuPaul's Drag Race* axes "You've Got She-Mail" catchphrase. *PinkNews*. https://www.pinknews.co.uk/2015/03/02/rupauls-drag-race-axes-youve-got-she-mail-catchphrase/

Duggan, L. (1994). Queering the state. *Social Text*, 39(39), 1–14.

Duggan, L. (2003). *The twilight of equality? Neoliberalism, cultural politics, and the attack on democracy*. Beacon Press.

Dyer, R. (1999). It's being so camp as to keep us going. In F. Cleto (Ed.), *Came queer aesthetics and the performing subject: A reader* (pp. 110–116). University of Michigan Press.

Edgar, E. (2011). Xtravaganza! Drag representation and articulation in *RuPaul's Drag Race*. *Studies in Popular Culture*, 34(1), 133–146.

Feldman, Z., & Hakim, J. (2020). From *Paris is Burning* to #dragrace: Social media and the celebrification of drag culture. *Celebrity Studies*, 11(4), 386–401.

Ferrante, A. A. (2017). Super troopers: The homonormative regime of visibility in *RuPaul's Drag Race*. In N. Brennan & D. Gudelunas (Eds.), *RuPaul's Drag Race and the shifting visibility of drag culture: The boundaries of reality TV* (pp. 153–165). Palgrave Macmillan.

Fine, D. J., & Shreve, E. (2014). The prime of miss RuPaul Charles: Allusion, betrayal and charismatic pedagogy. In J. Daems (Ed.), *The makeup of RuPaul's Drag Race: Essays on the queen of reality shows* (pp. 168–187). McFarland.

Framke, C. (2018, March 7). How RuPaul's comments on trans women led to a Drag Race revolt—And a rare apology. *Vox*. https://www.vox.com/culture/2018/3/6/17085244/rupaul-trans-women-drag-queens-interview-controversy

Garber, M. B. (1997). *Vested interests: Cross-dressing and cultural anxiety*. Psychology Press.

Ginibre, J.-L. (2005). *Ladies or gentlemen: A pictorial history of male cross-dressing in the movies*. Filipacchi.

Goldmark, M. (2015). National drag: The language of inclusion in *RuPaul's Drag Race*. *GLQ*, 21(4), 501–520.

Green, J. (2020). LGBTQ history and movements in Brazil. *Oxford Research Encyclopedia of Latin American History*. https://doi.org/10.1093/acrefore/9780199366439.013.840

Gudelunas, D. (2017). Digital extensions, experiential extensions and hair extensions: *RuPaul's Drag Race* and the new media environment. In N. Brennan & D. Gudelunas (Eds.), *RuPaul's Drag Race and the shifting visibility of drag culture: The boundaries of reality TV* (pp. 231–243). Palgrave Macmillan.

Halberstam, J. (1997). Mackdaddy, superfly, rapper: Gender, race, and masculinity in the drag king scene. *Social Text*, 52/53, 105–131.

Halberstam, J. (1998). *Female masculinity*. Duke University Press.

Hall, S., & Whannell, P. (1964). *The popular arts*. Hutchinson Educational.

Halperin, D. M. (2012). *How to be gay*. Belknap Press of Harvard University Press.

Henn, R., Viero Kolinski Machado, F., & Gonzatti, C. (2017). "We're all born naked and the rest is drag": The performativity of bodies constructed in digital networks. In N. Brennan & D. Gudelunas (Eds.), *RuPaul's Drag Race and the shifting visibility of drag culture: The boundaries of reality TV* (pp. 287–303). Palgrave Macmillan.

Hill, A. (2002). *Big Brother*: The real audience. *Television & New Media*, 3(3), 323–340.

Hill, A. (2005). *Reality TV: Audiences and popular factual television*. Routledge.

Hill, A. (2015). *Reality TV*. Routledge.

hooks, b. (1996). *Reel to real: Race, sex, and class at the movies*. Routledge.

Irigaray, L. (1985). *Speculum of the other woman* (G. C. Gill, Trans.). Cornell University Press.

Jenkins, H., Ford, S., & Green, J. (2013). *Spreadable media, creation, value and meaning in a networked culture.* New York University Press.

Katz, E. R. (2019, January 1). Gia Gunn allegedly had an unaired confrontation with RuPaul on "All Stars 4." *Out.* https://www.out.com/entertainment/2019/1/01/gia-gunn-allegedly-had-unaired-confrontation-rupaul

Kavka, M. (2012). *Reality TV.* Edinburgh University Press.

Livingston, J. (1990). *Paris Is Burning.* Off White Productions.

Lotman, Y. (1999). *Culture and explosion, predictable processes of social change.* Gedisa Editorial.

Magubane, Z. (2002). Black skins, Black masks or "the return of the white Negro": Race, masculinity, and the public personas of Dennis Rodman and RuPaul. *Men and Masculinities, 4*(3), 233–257.

Marcel, M. (2014). Representing gender, race and realness: The television world of America's next drag superstars. In J. Daems (Ed.), *The makeup of RuPaul's Drag Race: Essays on the queen of reality shows* (pp. 13–30). McFarland.

Marwick, A. E. (2015). You may know me from YouTube: (Micro-)celebrity in social media. In P. D. Marshall & S. Redmond (Eds.), *A companion to celebrity* (pp. 333–350). John Wiley & Sons.

Mayora, R. G. (2014). Cover, girl: Branding Puerto Rican drag in 21st-century U.S. popular culture. In J. Daems (Ed.), *The makeup of RuPaul's Drag Race: Essays on the queen of reality shows* (pp. 106–123). McFarland.

McIntyre, J. (2017). Transgender idol: Queer subjectivities and Australian reality TV. *European Journal of Cultural Studies, 20*(1), 87–103.

McIntyre, J., & Riggs, D. (2017). North American universalism in *RuPaul's Drag Race*: Stereotypes, linguicism, and the construction of "Puerto Rican queens." In N. Brennan & D. Gudelunas (Eds.), *RuPaul's Drag Race and the shifting visibility of drag culture: The boundaries of reality TV* (pp. 61–75). Palgrave Macmillan.

Medhurst, A. (1991). Batman, deviance and camp. In R. E. Pearson & W. Uricchio (Eds.), *The many lives of the Batman: Critical approaches to a superman and his media* (pp. 149–163). Routledge and British Film Institute.

Medhurst, A. (1997). Camp. In A. Medhurst & S. R. Munt (Eds.), *Lesbian and gay studies: A critical introduction.* Cassell.

Meyer, M. (1994). Introduction: Reclaiming the discourse of camp. In M. Meyer (Ed.), *The politics and the poetics of camp* (pp. 1–22). Routledge.

Modleski, T. (1997). A woman's gotta do...what a man's gotta do? Cross-dressing in the Western. *Signs, 22*(3), 519–544.

Mogul, J. L., Ritchie, A. J., & Whitlock, K. (2011). *Queer (in)justice: The criminalization of LGBT people in the United States.* Beacon.

Molloy, P. M. (2014, April 1). Carmen Carrera slams *Drag Race* over transphobic slur. *Advocate.* https://www.advocate.com/politics/transgender/2014/04/01/carmen-carrera-slams-idrag-racei-over-transphobic-slur

Newton, E. (1972). *Mother camp: Female impersonators in America.* University of Chicago Press.

Nichols, J. M. (2017, April 29). Peppermint opens up about coming out as trans on "RuPaul's Drag Race." *HuffPost.* http://tinyurl.com/1c71urg7

Nolfi, J. (2018, March 5). RuPaul tweets "regret" over controversial transgender comments: "The trans community are heroes." *Entertainment Weekly.* https://ew.com/news/2018/03/05/rupaul-apology-transgender-comments/

Oleksiak, T. (2021). It's too late to Rupaulogize: The lackluster defense of an occasional unlistener. In C. Crookston (Ed.), *The cultural impact of RuPaul's Drag Race: Why are we all gagging?* (pp. 194–211). Intellect.

Pasternack, D. (2017, December 7). Cross-dressing at the crossroads: A brief history of drag in comedy. *Paste.* https://www.pastemagazine.com/comedy/drag/cross-dressing-at-the-crossroads-a-brief-history-o/

Pensoneau-Conway, S. (2006). *Gender and sexual identity: A reflexive ethnographic account of learning through drag* [Doctoral dissertation]. Southern Illinois University.

Pomerantz, A. (2017). Big-girls don't cry: Portrayals of the fat body in *RuPaul's Drag Race*. In N. Brennan & D. Gudelunas (Eds.), *RuPaul's Drag Race and the shifting visibility of drag culture: The boundaries of reality TV* (pp. 103–120). Palgrave Macmillan.

Puar, J. K. (2007). *Terrorist assemblages: Homonationalism in queer times*. Duke University Press.

Robertson, P., & Wojcik, P. R. (1996). *Guilty pleasures: Feminist camp from Mae West to Madonna*. Duke University Press.

Russo, V. (1987). *The celluloid closet*. Harper & Row.

Sanfiorenzo, D. (2011, February 18). Crossing over: A history of Black comedians dressing in drag. *Complex*. https://www.complex.com/pop-culture/2011/02/crossing-over-a-history-of-black-comedians-dressing-in-drag/

Sender, K. (2006). Queens for a day: *Queer Eye for the Straight Guy* and the neoliberal project. *Critical Studies in Media Communication, 23*(2), 131–151.

Shankman, A. (2007). *Hairspray*. New Line Cinema.

Silverstone, R. (1999). *Why study the media?* SAGE.

Simpson, M. (1999). *It's a queer world: Deviant adventures in pop culture*. Haworth Press.

Slaner, S. E. (1996). "Eccentric Subjects": de Lauretis and Rossellini. *The Review of Education, Pedagogy, and Cultural Studies, 18*(1), 61–72.

Sonoma, S. (2021, January 8). RuPaul says the first transmasculine contestant on *Drag Race* changed his mind about drag. *Them.* https://www.them.us/story/rupaul-first-transmasculine-contestant-drag-race-changed-mind-about-drag-gottmik

Sontag, S. (1967). *Notes on Camp*. Penguin UK.

Stearns, J., Sandlin, J. A., & Burdick, J. (2011). Resistance on aisle three? Exploring the big curriculum of consumption and the (im)possibility of resistance in John Updike's "A&P." *Curriculum Inquiry, 41*(3), 394–415.

Straayer, C. (1992). Redressing the "natural": The temporary transvestite film. *Wide Angle, 14*(1), 402–427.

Tharp, J. (1991). The transvestite as monster: Gender horror in *The Silence of the Lambs* and *Psycho*. *Journal of Popular Film and Television, 19*(3), 106–113.

Thompson Moore, K. (2020). Fallacy of the nut pussy: Cross dressing, Black comedy, and women. *Popular Culture Studies Journal, 8*(2), 85–103.

Tucker Jenkins, S. (2017). Spicy. Exotic. Creature. Representations of racial and ethnic minorities on *RuPaul's Drag Race*. In N. Brennan & D. Gudelunas (Eds.), *RuPaul's Drag Race and the shifting visibility of drag culture: The boundaries of reality TV* (pp. 77–90). Palgrave Macmillan.

Waters, J. (1988). *Hairspray*. New Line Cinema.

Weston, K. (1997). *Families we choose: Lesbians, gays, kinship*. Columbia University Press.

Whitworth, C. (2017). Sissy that performance script! The queer pedagogy of *RuPaul's Drag Race*. In N. Brennan & D. Gudelunas (Eds.), *RuPaul's Drag Race and the shifting visibility of drag culture: The boundaries of reality TV* (pp. 137–151). Palgrave Macmillan.

Woodward, S. (2012). Taming transgression: Gender-bending in *Hairspray* (John Waters, 1988) and its remake. *New Cinemas, 10*(2+3), 115–126.

Youtt, H. (2018, July 13). Jiggly Caliente talks *Pose* cameo and new music: "I am going for it all." *Billboard*. https://www.billboard.com/culture/pride/jiggly-caliente-interview-pose-new-music-drag-race-8465386/

Yudelman, J. (2017). The "RuPaulitics" of subjectification in *RuPaul's Drag Race*. In N. Brennan & D. Gudelunas (Eds.), *RuPaul's Drag Race and the shifting visibility of drag culture: The boundaries of reality TV* (pp. 15–28). Palgrave Macmillan.

Niall Brennan

SPECULATIVE FICTION AND QUEER THEORY

> The question of whether the queer, for queer theory, has ever been human must, then, be answered, not equivocally but deliberately, Yes and No. Yes, because this sustained interrogation of the unjust dehumanization of queers insistently, if implicitly, posits the human as standard form, and also because many queer theorists have undeniably privileged the human body and human sexuality as the locus of their analysis. But No because queer theory has long been suspicious of the politics of rehabilitation and inclusion to which liberal-humanist values lead, and because "full humanity" has never been the only horizon for queer becoming. We might see the "Yes/No" humanity of the queer less as an ambivalence about the human as status than as a queer *transversal* of the category. The queer, we could say, runs across or athwart the human. As Eve Kosofsky Sedgwick reminds us, "The word 'queer' itself means across—it comes from the Indo-European root-*twerkw*, which also yields the German *quer* (transverse), Latin *torquere* (to twist), English *athwart*." To say that queer transverses the human is to understand their relation as contingent rather than stable: it needs to be read up from particular situations, not proclaimed from above.
>
> —Luciano and Chen (2015), "Has the Queer Ever Been Human?" (pp. 186–187)

INTRODUCTION

This article examines the ways in which queer theory can help to illuminate depictions of sexuality, gender, and their intersectionalities as they are represented in speculative fictions of all kinds. As the epigram implies, if applied to speculative fiction, what is at the heart of queer speculative writing (and other art forms) is the question of queer inclusion in the category of human; however, the near boundless imaginative possibilities of speculative fiction, in all its forms, allow us both to recognize the limitations of this question (Is "human" the be all and end all?) and to ask if there are other horizons for queer becoming. Like queer itself, speculative fiction can transverse multiple epistemological and ontological categories, of which "human," although it may be the prime category, is still only one possibility. The often queer categories of being encountered in speculative fiction, from the aliens that permeate science fiction to the elves and fairies in fantasy and folk tales, remind us that "human" may not be the sole way of defining good, livable, intelligible modes of being.

In opening up some very large questions, queer speculative fiction, taken as a body of work, speaks to several specifically queer theoretical interventions, including: questions of queer representation; histories in which queer representation has been suppressed; queer dismantling of all types of normativity; queer theorizing about intimacy, kinship, reproduction, and family; questions of posthumanism and the queering of embodiment and/through technology; and issues of queer time and the ability to critique chrononormativity (the normative sense of time across the lifespan) to subvert assumptions about linear time and "normal" life. Speculative fiction is a powerful medium for both queer readers and queer writers because it uses its ability to go beyond the limitations of mimetic, realist approaches to fiction to empower narratives, characters, and/or settings that disrupt the many ways in which dominant assumptions about "human nature," notably in terms of sexuality, gender, and race, are produced by, and in turn reinforce, capitalist and colonialist aspirations and expectations. Some speculative fiction may be dystopian, but it may also read the past—or the future—reparatively, in order to imagine possibly more hopeful and certainly queerer futures for both the human and the un/inhuman.

SPECULATING ABOUT SPECULATIVE FICTION: DEFINITIONS AND CONUNDRUMS

Given the nature of this encyclopedia, there is no need here to begin by defining what queer theory is, does, or means. However, it may still be useful to explain what is meant by the term *speculative fiction*. *Speculative fiction* (like *queer*) can be something of an omnibus term. It gathers the similarities between specific genres, including science fiction (sf), fantasy (in all its iterations), horror, and the Gothic.[1] However, it is capacious enough to include more liminal works—works that, for example, flirt with the tropes of sf while remaining on its margins. Within the context of sf genre scholarship, to some extent these liminal texts are collected under the term *slipstream*. However, almost all magic realist texts can be considered forms of speculative fiction, as can many texts that play with fairy tales, traditional oral narratives, etc. The common tropes of all speculative fiction involve some form of imagination beyond the contemporary world or its dominant history (histories). In fact, the term *speculative fiction* was created in 1947 by science fiction writer Robert A. Heinlein (1947) to encompass works that did not fit neatly into the fairly "hard science" ethos espoused by many of the predominant voices in the sf genre at the time.

As is often the case, the question of definition is not wholly objective, but takes on a distinct political valence in the context of a literary history in which genre fiction has been variously dismissed as childish, trite, "girly" (particularly if focused on romance), obsessed with "boys' toys," and generally written significantly less well than Capital-L Literature. While one might hope that this trite distinction between genre fiction and literature is grossly outdated, it still raises its head repeatedly. Indeed, the best-known case in point is Margaret Atwood's determination that her science-fictional works—including *The Handmaid's Tale* (1985), its recent sequel, *The Testaments* (2019), and the entire MaddAdam trilogy (2003–2013)—are not sf. However, if we look back at critical attempts to define speculative fiction, the late sf writer and editor Judith Merril used the term to distinguish "the essence of science fiction." Merril (2017) classified sf into a threefold typology: "teaching stories" (often with the explicit goal of getting American boys—not girls—involved with science for the sake of the space race), "preaching stories," which either allegorize or satirize (or both) contemporary society, and "speculative fiction," which aims "to explore, to discover, to *learn*, by means of projection, extrapolations, analogue, hypothesis-and-paper experimentation, something about the nature of the universe, of man [*sic*], of 'reality'" (p. 27).

This discussion reiterates Marek Oziewicz's definition but adds a greater emphasis on the ways in which genre fiction is constructed in some sort of opposition to literature. Oziewicz wrote:

The term "speculative fiction" has three historically located meanings: a subgenre of science fiction that deals with human rather than technological problems, a genre distinct from and opposite to science fiction in its exclusive focus on possible futures, and a super category for all genres that deliberately depart from imitating "consensus reality" of everyday experience.... Rather than seeking a rigorous definition, a better approach is to theorize "speculative fiction" as a term whose semantic register has continued to expand. (Oziewicz, 2017)

This expansion of the semantic register includes the ways in which Merril's discussion turns on its head what has become a normative assumption among many readers that speculative fiction is the broader field ("supercategory") to which sf belongs. Some earlier scholarship, particularly in the 1970s, also cast fantasy (usually as Fantasy) in the role of supercategory. Farah Mendlesohn (2014) began *Rhetorics of Fantasy* by noting that the lengthy debates over definition have largely resolved through the acceptance of "a viable 'fuzzy' set."[2] Rather than focusing on defining fantasy, Mendlesohn centered her work on the question of how the genre is constructed.

John Rieder referred to traditional (European) categories of writing in *Science Fiction and the Mass Cultural Genre System* (2017) as the "academic-classical genre system" and contrasted them to what he referred to as the "mass cultural genre system," which includes works whose definitional categories both produce and contribute to their commercial value. Rieder described sf, specifically, as arising organically from mass culture and argued that

literary and cultural studies scholars in general, and science fiction studies scholars in particular, ought to be making [effects of stratification] part of the object of their inquiries into the workings of contemporary culture and the powers exercised by various forms of narrative within it. (pp. 9–10)

In other words, Rieder argued that there is a tendency to create hierarchies based on genre and that these stratifications should be part of scholarship on speculative fiction. Queer theory is similarly conscious of, and critical about, forms of cultural hierarchy, particularly those that take as their bases assumptions about sexual, gender, and racial hierarchies (better to be heterosexual, better to be cisgender, better to be White).

Queer Theory, Paraliterature, and Literary Hierarchies.

In one response to the hierarchical tendencies of literary and cultural scholarship to value "literature" above genre fiction, the gay African American writer and critic Samuel R. Delany argued that genre fiction can be understood as "paraliterature." Delany's own work spanned several genres, including sf, fantasy, pornography, and literary criticism. As Carl Freedman (2001) pointed out, Delany normally regarded definitions with skepticism but nonetheless proposed paraliterature as a term to gather "written genres traditionally excluded by the limited, value-bound meaning of 'literature' and 'literary' " (Delany, 1999, p. 236). While Freedman argued that Delany established an unnecessary binarism that divided literature from paraliterature, Delany's distinction is not one that allows literary fiction to seize the high ground. Delany argued that, "In literature, the odder or more fantastical or surreal it is, the more it's assumed to be about mind or psychology" (Delany, "Semiology," p. 143). Earl Jackson (1995) has pointed out that

> Literature's preoccupation with the inner states of the characters, its representation of the subject as the perceptual focus, the phenomenological frame, of the object, underwrites an ideological investment in the centrality of the subject as a self-evident unity; It is through this ideological investment that 'literature' serves as what Louis Althusser has termed an 'Ideological State Apparatus', ('ISA'), a mode of representation that interpellates the individual as a specifically fixed subject." (pp. 101–102)

In other words, one might argue that paraliterary genres are those that are able to spring writing free of its interpellation in the process of subjectification by removing the focus on the psychology of the "hero" and placing it, instead, on the systemic and the structural, the contexts within which the hero's journey is made possible.[3]

However, if we link this argument back to this article's epigram by Luciano and Chen, we might also note that, by removing a certain focus on individual psychology and its attendant assumptions about the nature of the human, we allow in multiple forms of queerness, both those that focus on the inclusion of the queer within the human and those that long for more capacious options for both becoming and belonging. The notion of paraliterature becomes in its own right a queering both of generic categories and of the use of those categories to constrain and limit our conceptions of humanity. To finish this section with a concrete example, one could consider the relationship between humanity and animality in Charlie Jane Anders's *All the Birds in the Sky* (2016), in which the distinction between human and animal is constantly slipping, particularly among the animals who talk to Patricia Delfine, but so also is the distinction between organic and inorganic and specifically between the artificial intelligence CH@NG3M3 and the World Tree, a slippage commemorated in CH@NG3M3's choice to name itself Peregrine. The novel raises the question of whether the bird Dirp or the AI Peregrine is less "human" than Patricia and Lawrence Armstead, the novel's other protagonist, and what it means to ask that question.

Queer Orientations: From Paraliterature to Fuzzy Sets. To borrow from Sarah Ahmed's *Queer Phenomenology* (2006), one might then suggest looking to see both the directions in which genres are oriented and the ways in which questions of humanity are posed. While the notion of the paraliterary has been taken up rather spottily in literary criticism, it seems possible to argue that all speculative fiction is, in one way or another, oriented toward understanding systemic and social contexts, contexts able to tackle big questions—like "What does it mean to be human?"—rather than individual psychology. In sf, those contexts likely have some relationship to technology and the future; in fantasy, despite its rather frequent reference to an often vague notion of the medieval, these contexts are rarely historical, but rather may use roughly historical tropes to imagine alternatives to the present. In queer speculative fiction, these alternatives are themselves usually queer, although not necessarily in obvious ways—to take one example, Naomi Novik's dragon series (2006–2016) is a queerish speculative fiction work in which the focus is very much on the romantic, but asexual, relationship between the human, Will Laurence, and the dragon, Temeraire. In depicting the deep love between human and dragon, Novik also reinvented the Napoleonic era in ways that call into question its colonialism and its assumptions of European supremacy (the Chinese are much more knowledgeable about dragons and willing to assign them leadership roles). Laurence, already predisposed to detest slavery due to his politician father's involvement in the abolitionist movement, is further influenced to understand its moral depravity by Temeraire's appalled reaction to learning about the legal enslavement of humans and the de facto enslavement of dragons. The depiction of the consequences of Laurence's and Temeraire's love for each other creates a situation in which Novik effectively demonstrates the connections between colonialism, racism, misogyny, and homophobia that Siobhan Somerville (1994) explicated in "Scientific Racism and the Emergence of the Homosexual Body"—to sum it up, colonialist expansion requires the subjection of non-White bodies and the policing of White bodies as (re)productive, both of which necessitate the control of women's bodies and the eradication or conversion of queer ones. Novik's series brings into question any distinction between Laurence and Temeraire that rules one human and the other not. "Human" is rather randomly used in speculative fiction, sometimes to indicate *Homo sapiens* and, at other times, to indicate membership in an intelligent, sentient species, which is a broader and more generous definition of human-ness than is often the case in reality; in the latter sense, however, Temeraire is every bit as "human" as Laurence. Despite its characters' heterosexual practices, the series thus demonstrates the ways in which queerness transverses the category of the human, with its implicit assumption of the superiority of the human animal over all other animals.

Queer theory, as an inherently contestatory field, is a place where arguments about the nature of genre and assumptions of what constitutes "quality" can be understood as discursive assertions precisely intended to construct and empower hierarchy. Indeed, speculative fiction in its most common usage is currently branching out to embrace such alternative forms to the traditional literary text as the graphic novel—a medium that has been increasingly taken seriously by readers and researchers alike since the publication of works like Art Spiegelman's *Maus* (1980), Alan Moore's *V for Vendetta* (1990), and Neil Gaiman's *Sandman* (1991). *V* is post-apocalyptic and primarily science fictional; *Sandman* is probably best described as dark fantasy. *Maus*, however, is based on the experiences of Spiegelman's family in and after the Holocaust and probably has more in common with Alison Bechdel's graphic memoirs, *Fun Home* (2007) and *Are You My Mother?* (2012) than with either genre or nongenre forms of graphic fiction; indeed, its nonfictional qualities may have helped legitimate graphic narratives. These early graphic novels paved the way for works like Tillie Walden's *On a Sunbeam* (2018), which is partially set in space and involves nonbinary and queer characters.

We can now define speculative fiction as any writing in which "reality" is not mimetically represented; in other words, a fuzzy set. That includes sf, fantasy, horror, and most or all magic realist writing. It includes *slipstream*, a term apparently invented by writer Bruce Sterling and bibliophile Richard Dorsett to categorize a certain surreal, postmodern sensibility in works that are neither quite mainstream (literature) nor clearly sf or fantasy (Sterling, 1989). Rob Latham (2014) summarized their argument by describing slipstream as nonrealistic fiction with a postmodern sensibility (p. 119), even though Sterling went on to argue that slipstream hasn't, and in his opinion may never, come to fruition (Sterling, 2011). What all these variants have in common is a degree of nonrealism—while Atwood tried to distinguish her writing from sf on the grounds that it could happen, in practice, much sf could happen (Mancuso, 2016).

There is a whole movement among sf writers, jump-started by Geoff Ryman with the "Mundane Manifesto" in 2004, that focuses on what could happen; the essence of the Mundane science fiction movement is the belief that humanity and the planet are both in such a state of crisis that there is an ethical imperative to write fiction that tackles contemporary issues with a focus on Earth and our solar system—in other words, with readily imaginable and possible futures (Ryman, 2004).

The distinction between genres that can be coalesced under the label of speculative fiction is less one of events and worlds than of rationales: in speculative fiction, if a hammer floats, there will be a scientific explanation (zero gravity, for example); in fantasy, if a hammer floats, it is most likely a spell or other form of magic; in horror, if a hammer floats, there will be a supernatural force behind it. Both slipstream and magic realism may take up any or all of these rationales—or indeed none at all, as in the notorious start of Salman Rushdie's *The Satanic Verses* (1988), which gives no explanation for the protagonists' miraculous survival of a terrorist attack that destroys their plane in mid-air.

Understanding speculative fiction as a fuzzy set also makes it possible to understand that individual readers may identify the works they are comfortable reading or excited or challenged by without feeling compelled to accept any given author's or critic's determination of its genre identity. Indeed, for at least some LGBTQ2SI readers, the attraction may be less the specifics of genre than the types of characters and stories that address the issues and lived experiences of queer and trans people or that allow queer and/or trans characters to explore new worlds and new timelines while, in most cases, offering critiques of the present.[4] In fact, one of the things queer theory may help us to understand is the possibility of queering genres categories, whether by reading without reference to them or by reading/writing in ways that transcend boundaries and rigid categories; generic identity need be seen as no more fixed than gender identity or sexuality within the overall rubric of queer theory. Reading outside of genre conventions may also open possibilities for what Eve Kosofsky Sedgwick called "reparative reading," since the generic definitions may or may not allow space/time for queerness (Sedgwick, 1997).[5]

A BRIEF AND INCOMPLETE QUEER GENEALOGY OF SPECULATIVE FICTION

The question that underlies this article is what queer theory can tell us about ways of reading (and potentially writing) speculative fiction. This question can be broken down in several ways, including asking what is queer about speculative fiction, whether there is such a thing as specifically queer speculative fiction (with the corollary that some, if not most, speculative fiction is more normative, particularly in terms of gender and sexuality), if there are queer ways of reading speculative fiction that illuminate whether the work and/or its author(s) is or does anything that can be labeled queer, whether reparative reading, as a queer strategy, empowers readers differently from the critical habit of what Sedgwick labeled "paranoid" (or deconstructive) reading, what a queer history of speculative fiction might look like, and so on. This article looks briefly at these questions before moving on to consider some specific areas in which queer theory can shine a light on aspects of speculative fiction, including the question of queer representation and/or queering representation, the question of queer concepts of intimacy and kinship, the question of posthumanism, embodiment, and technology, and the question of queer temporality, which is particularly central in sf as a genre, where concepts of futurity (and its alternatives) play a large role. Queer theory's critique of heteronormativity threads through the entirety of the article.

Is there a specifically queer speculative fiction? And, if so, can we construct a genealogy of when, where, and how queer speculative fiction appeared? One answer might even be the commonest origin story of sf, which is usually to locate the genre's beginnings with Mary Shelley's *Frankenstein* (1818). It would be hard to deny that much about *Frankenstein* looks very queer from a contemporary perspective. Not only do we have a man using technology to bypass heterosexual reproduction and produce his own "child," but the crux of the novel is Frankenstein's inability to recognize that he has any responsibility for his progeny's "birth," education, or ability to live in the world. Steven Bruhm noted that for Shelley's society, children were not only symbols of innocence, but also of sin (in the story of the expulsion from Eden). Furthermore, while the contemporary world sees children as a symbol of futurity, in a period before adequate contraception and safe abortion, reasonable pre- and postnatal care for mothers, and vaccinations against common, but lethal, childhood ailments, "Children = Death" (Bruhm, 2018). Not only is *Frankenstein* amenable to a variety of queer readings, but the figure of monstrosity the creature supposedly represents has resounded for trans theorists and activists as well, beginning with Susan Stryker's important 1994 article "My Words to Victor Frankenstein Above the Village of Chamonix: Performing Transgender Rage." Stryker originally gave an early version of the article as a performance piece, saying that she "sought to reclaim Frankenstein's monster as an empowering figure, thereby directly challenging popular transphobic readings of the infamous character, particularly by TERFS" (Sanders, 2019).

Queer theory tends to be skeptical of origin stories, following Michel Foucault in preferring a more genealogical approach (Foucault, 2021). Given the breadth covered by speculative fiction, one could also look at other origin stories told about various genres; again, to use sf as an example, origin stories usually encompass primarily European and/or American texts, generally anglophone, so that one approach sees sf as originating from such works as Lucian of Samosata's 2nd-century *True History*, or from Francis Godwin's *The Man in the Moone* (1638/2009), or from Margaret Cavendish's *The Blazing World* (1666/1994). *True History* involves a narrator who finds himself unexpectedly on the moon, among many other adventures; Moonites have no women and exist as an all-male society. Earlier in his adventures, Lucian discovers an island where rivers flow with wine and women grow on trees—but sex with them is lethal. Whether one locates the origins of sf in Lucian of Samosata or *Frankenstein*, it remains striking just how queer those origins are. An almost entirely different approach focuses more on the "science" in sf and locates sf's origins on the one hand in the works of H. G. Wells and Jules Verne, primarily, or on the other hand in the pulp fiction of the early 20th century, notably the short stories published in Hugo Gernsback's *Amazing Stories*, which began monthly publication in 1926 (and is still publishing today). What both these approaches and others (for example, those that trace the utopian strand in sf from Plato's *Republic* through Thomas More to Shakespeare [*The Tempest*] and beyond) have in common is that they tend to focus on, first, anglophone work and, second, Euro-American work. Another genealogy might locate both sf and the larger genre of speculative fiction in a timeline that begins with the

Sumerian *Epic of Gilgamesh* and includes such fantastical works as the *Tales of the Arabian Nights*—both have elements that are susceptible to queer readings, even though *Gilgamesh* tends to depict heterosexual sex as a civilizing force, all the while Enkidu and Gilgamesh wrestle with each other.

Global Genealogies and Indigenous Interventions. Increasingly, the globalized and transnational nature of sf means that scholars are beginning to pay more attention to a genealogy that recognizes non-Western or non-anglophone ancestors of contemporary sf as a worldwide phenomenon. Wu et al. (2018) for example, trace the origins of Chinese sf in folklore and mythology, but they focus primarily on early 20th-century writers influenced by "the influx of Western scientific culture that brought about the flourishing of science fiction literature in China" (p. 45). That is one account and, as with the various genealogies and histories existing simultaneously in Western culture, there are others that place more emphasis on earlier Chinese texts. Certainly, Lu Xun's 1903 translation of Jules Verne's *From the Earth to the Moon* was influential in spurring an interest in sf as a genre. As Mimi Mondal pointed out, understanding how genres interact with each other and knowing something about their history is important because,

> without it, it's impossible to recognize which works from a primarily non-Western but also postcolonial culture were written *clearly* to be genre, or even fiction. South Asia had a significant culture of letters in several languages for centuries before British colonization. (Mondal, 2018)

According to Mondal, Indian culture did not make clear distinctions between religious and secular works or between realist and nonrealist works. Only in the mid-19th century did novels and short stories become recognized and sought-after cultural forms, and it is only since the 1980s that speculative fiction has taken off in India, primarily published in English, but also in Hindi, Bengali, etc. In Japan, as in China, one sees a long tradition of myth, religious writing (notably the *mirai-ki*, which presumes a reader in the future), oral narrative, fairy tale, and so on. Some scholars trace the arrival of speculative fiction, and particularly sf, in Japan to the 1860s and the Meiji dynasty's commitment to modernization and technologization, coinciding with decreasing tolerance for homosexual practices in Japan (see McLelland & Dasgupta [2005]; Pflugfelder [2007]); others trace Japanese interest in mass cultural genres primarily to the post-WWII period and the influence of pulp magazines imported by American soldiers. Outside of a purely written tradition, however, one should also note the importance and prevalence of graphic and visual media in the forms of anime and manga, whose popularity has spread these Japanese narrative modes globally. Furthermore, both anime and manga include powerful queer and trans elements, from the gender transformations of Ranma in *Ranma ½* to the depiction of men having sex with men in *yaoi*, a genre usually written by women for girls (McLelland, 2005, 2006).

Before moving on from the question of the history and dissemination of speculative fiction and the genres that fall under its umbrella, it is important to note that in the last decade or so, Indigenous speculative fiction has also exploded as a field. Not only are Indigenous writers publishing widely in sf, fantasy, horror, and the like, but also Indigenous authors already recognized as literary figures are turning to speculative fiction, as, for example, with award-winning novelist Louise Erdrich's *Future Home of the Living God* (2017), which riffs on Atwood's *Handmaid's Tale*. In Canada, many First Nations and Inuit writers, including Cherie Dimaline, Eden Robinson, Thomas King, Daniel Heath Justice, Drew Haydn Taylor, and Waubgeshig Rice, have taken up speculative fiction, whether fantasy, horror, sf, Gothic, cyberpunk, or magic realism, as a way to comment on the present and to imagine (generally dystopian) futures within the context of resistance and decolonization.

Justice's Kynship trilogy (2005–2007) mixes the traditions of high fantasy with science fiction tropes and the history of the Cherokee and the Trail of Tears both to represent the horrors of colonization and to imagine how a different relationship to nature and the planet might be a powerful tool for decolonization. As a Two-Spirit writer, Justice tackles issues of gender and sexuality throughout the trilogy, distinguishing between Indigenous practices and the constrained normativities of the colonizer. In 2020, Joshua Whitehead's *Love after the End: An Anthology of Two-Spirit & Indigiqueer Speculative Fiction* (2020), the first major collection of its kind, won the Lambda Literary Award. Queer Indigenous speculative fiction takes up the non-normative focus of queer theory and uses it in the service of an anticolonial and decolonizing praxis.

CRITICAL INVESTIGATIONS OF QUEER SPECULATIVE FICTION

In the critical literature of queerness and speculative fiction, it makes sense to begin where the research largely began: with working out what is actually there. As a result, some of the earliest critical work was about locating depictions of alternative sexualities, usually under the rubric of homosexuality, in specific genres. Eric Garber and Lyn Paleo's comprehensive bibliography, *Uranian Worlds: A Reader's Guide to Alternate Sexuality in Science Fiction and Fantasy* (1983, second edition in 1990), lists every work the authors could identify as having primarily characters who are homosexual, bisexual, or have some other form of alternative sexuality, as having an LGBTQ2SI author, or as taking on issues of gender and sexuality in non-normative ways.[6] They also interpreted genre broadly. As the editors pointed out, in earlier works, particularly in the late 19th and early 20th centuries, authors often found alibis for their characters' sexuality: lesbians became vampires, gay men became monsters, and so on. Nicholas Mirzoeff (1999) pointed out that the figure of the alien is a tremendously useful floating signifier "that takes on complex resonances of race, gender, and politics" (p. 191) and often stands in for a culture's particular obsession, whether it be women, queers, or communists.

During the middle of the 20th century, publishers would allow openly LGBT characters so long as they came to sticky ends; the Hays Code in Hollywood censored any overt representation of alternative sexualities, yet it was never able to stop writers, directors, and actors from sneaking it in by using cultural codes and references recognizable to queer people, but not generally to the straight community. In 1957, the Wolfenden Report recommended the decriminalization of male homosexuality in the United Kingdom, yet even the revised Hays Code, as Larry Gross (2001) indicated, permitted depictions of homosexuals "only as long as they were unhappy" (p. 60).[7]

Garber and Paleo agreed with other critics of the period in identifying the sf writer Theodore Sturgeon as more or less single-handedly opening "the science-fiction field to explicitly gay images with the publication of 'The World Well Lost'" (1983, p. x). Garber and Paleo concentrated on this short story (Sturgeon, 1965), which features an alien couple known on Earth as the "loverbirds", being extradited in the hope of favorable trade relations with their home planet, Dirbanu; one of the two-person crew of the ship returning them is a closeted gay man (named Grunty) secretly in love with his captain. Upon realizing that the loverbirds are a gay couple, Grunty sets them free in an escape pod. His homophobic captain assumes he did this to prevent the captain from getting into trouble for killing them, as would any truly manly man. However, the true twist in the story is the revelation that the Dirbanu are homophobes who assume all humans are gay because our sexes look far more similar than theirs do. Sturgeon's work also focuses significantly on alternative genders and specifically on the deliberately self-manufactured transgender humans at the heart of the novel *Venus Plus X*.[8] Samuel Delany has also called Sturgeon's *The Dreaming Jewels* "the most effective/satisfying story of transgender revenge I've ever read".

Following the work of Garber and Paleo came Donald Palumbo's two collections, *Erotic Universe: Sexuality and Fantastic Literature* (1986b) and *Eros in the Mind's Eye: Sexuality and the Fantastic in Art and Film* (1986a). Both collections took a largely essentialist view of sexuality and identity and neither has since been taken up much by scholars applying queer theory to speculative fiction. The 1990s was, of course, the efflorescence of queer theory, yet it was a relatively quiet period for considerations of sexuality in speculative fiction. Most of the critical emphasis at the time was on feminist approaches to speculative fiction in both literature and cinema, while work on the recent emergence of fictional explorations of alternate genders and sexualities tended to focus on gender more than on sexuality. This was the era in which serious critical focus was applied to writers like Joanna Russ, whose novel *The Female Man* (1975) brought both lesbian characters and a de facto lesbian world (because Whileaway has no men) to fascinated readers; Ursula K. Le Guin, whose *The Left Hand of Darkness* (1969) explored what life would be like for a cisgender human male alone on a planet of hermaphrodites; Samuel R. Delany, whose *Triton* (1976) presupposed future recognition of nine sexual orientations and 40–50 genders; Thomas Disch, whose *334* (1972) is set in a future housing project full of lesbian and gay residents; Suzie McKee Charnas, whose *Motherlines* has another all-female society; Anne Rice, whose *Interview with the Vampire* (1976) abounds with homoeroticism and has an alternative vampire family; Elizabeth Lynn, whose *A Different Light* (1978) depicts a male spacefarer in search of his same-sex lover; Vonda McIntyre, whose *Dreamsnake* (1978) shows the reader a gender egalitarian bisexual future world; and Marion Zimmer Bradley, whose Darkover series contains a coming-out story set among gay male aristocrats in *Heritage of Hastur* (1975).[9]

Toward the end of the millennium, feminist criticism that had focused primarily on the status of women in sf also started to include queer approaches to speculative writing and, to a lesser extent, film and television. Wendy Gay Pearson's "Alien Cryptographies: The View from Queer" and Veronica Hollinger's "(Re)reading Queerly: Science Fiction, Feminism, and the Defamiliarization of Gender" were both published by *Science Fiction Studies* in 1999 in a special section on sf and queer theory. *Foundation* published a special issue on LGBT sf in 2002, edited by Andrew M. Butler, with articles on a spectrum of lesbian, gay, and queer issues both in sf literature and in film and television. In 2008, Pearson et al. published *Queer Universes: Sexualities in Science Fiction*. One of the critical moves in that book was signaled in its title, which no longer designates queerness as "alternative." *Queer Universes* takes up Sedgwick's contention that the homo–hetero binary has so dominated Western culture that it is impossible to escape its influence, even as queer theory calls into question the ways in which the very idea of binary sexual orientation has been naturalized.

Lewis Call's *BDSM in American Science Fiction and Fantasy* was published in 2012 and offers a long-overdue investigation of kinky sexualities in speculative fiction. *The Sex Is Out of This World: Essays on the Carnal Side of Science Fiction*, edited by Sherry Ginn, Michael Cornelis, and Donald Palumbo, also published in 2012, offered a mixed bag of essays (there are two on Octavia Butler, but nothing on Delany or Russ, among others) split between literature and other media (mostly television). Stephen Kenneally's doctoral dissertation, "Queer Be Dragons: Mapping LGBT Fantasy Novels 1987–2000" (2016), provides a comprehensive overview of queer and trans fantasy in the late 20th century. Also in 2018, Alexis Lothian published *Old Futures: Speculative Fiction and Queer Possibility*, which is the book most informed by queer theory in the last decade. In terms of fantasy and other areas of speculative fiction, there are few dedicated book-length studies. Notable among them are Paulina Palmer's *The Queer Uncanny: New Perspectives on the Gothic* (2012) and *The Lesbian Fantastic: A Critical Study of Science Fiction, Fantasy, Paranormal and Gothic Writings* (2014) by Phyllis Betz. However, much of the work on queer fantasy focuses on it as either a young adult (YA) or children's genre (see, for example, Abate & Kidd, 2011; Roberts & MacCallum-Stewart, 2016). Most work on queer horror focuses on film; the classic work in this area is probably Harry Benshoff's *Monsters in the Closet* (1997). However, a recent special issue of *Research on Diversity in Children's Literature* included three articles dealing with different aspects of YA speculative fiction, including one on YA horror. This reflects the fact that the bulk of the critical work in every aspect of queer speculative fiction lies in articles on specific authors/directors/artists, works, or themes.

REPRESENTING QUEER(LY)

In terms of queer theory's applicability to reading and understanding speculative fiction, it makes sense to start with one of the most basic issues: the question of representation. Since queer theory, despite the name, is not about LGBTQ2SI people, but rather about the discursive and social structures that shape our understanding of sexuality (including the fact that we understand the randomness and diversity of sex acts by humans as "sexuality"), the question of representation, while basic, is not simple. When we talk about queer representation, what are we talking about? Certainly, it's the place scholarship on sexuality in speculative fiction began, with locating and to some extent categorizing works that do represent forms of homosexuality, bisexuality, or, relatedly, the lives of transgender people. However, we could also talk about queer theory's applicability to representation of sexuality and gender in speculative fiction not in terms of how fictional works illustrate contemporary life for those who fit into these identity categories but rather in terms of how fiction takes up queer theory's broader pertinency to systems of thought and their enactment in social structures and cultural practices. Thus, for example, some of the first works to apply queer theory to science fiction, such as Pearson's "Alien Cryptographies," were focused less on the representation of LGBTQ2SI people and more on the epistemological and ontological practices that make categories such as "gay" and "lesbian" meaningful, whether those cultural meanings are inclusive or whether they work to exclude LGBTQ2SI people from the category of the intelligibly human. One of the ways in which speculative fiction can interrogate and/or subvert sexual and gender epistemologies and their potentially exclusionary effects is by relocating them to different worlds, different futures, and even different species.

Let's begin, however, with the representation of practices and identities that today fall under the LGBTQ2SI rubric. How does speculative fiction represent queer people and their interactions with their own and others' cultures? Representation matters in part because of the way it moderates both widespread cultural responses and political decision-making. The current "debate" between transgender-positive people and those who oppose trans people (usually referred to by the acronym TERF, although the term's use is not without its own opposition) is an excellent example.[10] Trans people have traditionally been represented, particularly by Hollywood, as either deeply confused or evil. But trans people have often simply been excluded, even from misrepresentation; in many cultural forms, trans people either do not exist or are significantly underrepresented. As a result, it is relatively easy for anti-trans activists to spread misinformation, so long as it conforms to existing stereotypes, and to enact legislation that is intended to make trans life difficult, if not impossible.[11]

Judith Butler (2016) noted that life becomes unlivable when one's existence is not culturally intelligible. "The epistemological capacity to apprehend a life is partially dependent on that life being produced according to norms that qualify it as a life or, indeed, as part of life" (p. 4). If one's life or belonging as human is not recognized, that has material consequences that increase one's experience of precarity and vulnerability to insult and harm. Indeed, Butler wrote that unrecognized lives are inherently ungrievable, as they are apprehensible neither epistemologically nor ontologically; this is readily understood in relation to the epidemic of murders of trans women of color in places like the United States and Brazil. In so far as trans people or queer people are unintelligible culturally, the material consequences on their possibilities for life are immense. Representation is one of the ways cultural intelligibility is created or denied. Nonrepresentation and misrepresentation both do harm.

Speculative fiction has a long history of representing queer people that is quite different from its history of tackling issues that are at the heart of queer theory (the cultural existence and nature, if any, of sexuality; the function of discourse in shaping our understanding of sex; the implications of Foucault's ideas about biopower and power/knowledge; the need to resist multiple forms of normativity; the importance of an intersectional approach to gender and sexuality, especially in relation to race and indigeneity). Queer representation often rests on a series of assumptions about what matters (including the way in which both senses of "matter" inform theoretical work on bodies). Speculative fiction allows us to imagine times/spaces where queer and/or trans bodies matter, both in having their material existence recognized and made possible and in terms of their identities, philosophies, relationships, and desires being credited as meaningful. This is the space in which we locate the aporia between same-sex marriage as a mode of homonormative assimilationist politics ("We're just like you") and marriage equality as a symbolic dismantling of the cultural hierarchy that overvalues heterosexuality.[12] Equality, despite its limitations, is a powerful force for recognition, particularly for those too often deemed not to be fully human.

Athwart the Human: Queering Discourses of Health and Disease. In the 1980s, with the advent of the AIDS crisis, questions of representation became very clearly linked to the questions of who counts as human, whose lives matter, and how queer people are represented, especially in popular media. Queer speculative fiction engaged with many aspects of the situation, from a resurgence of public homophobia resulting in calls for quarantine and even concentration camps, to subversive political action that resulted in the creation of organizations like ACT-Up and AIDS Action Now, to reflections on the ways in which community came together to care for the ill and dying. Geoff Ryman's *Was* (1992) featured in one of its three narratives a gay B-movie actor dying of AIDS who becomes obsessed with finding Dorothy from the *Wizard of Oz*; Jonathan travels to Manhattan, Kansas (home of nuclear silos) where Dorothy lived (the novel depicts her as an abused child in a settler colonial world where the Indigenous peoples are being caused to vanish). Arriving in Manhattan, Jonathan mistakes DZ for OZ, believes he has found OZ Magic, and vanishes himself. The third narrative features a young Judy Garland. All three protagonists have to negotiate childhoods that are difficult in different ways, including Dorothy's sexual abuse by her uncle and Judy's family's constant relocations as her closeted father's relations with young men are repeatedly exposed. The novel focuses more on the difficulties of family life than on AIDS per se, but it does so in a cultural context in which HIV+ gay men were frequently abandoned by their birth families and were supported only by their chosen families. Ryman finished the novel with an afterword in which he said that it is necessary to distinguish between history and fantasy and to "use them against each other." Susan Knabe noted that,

> As neither overtly political nor obviously elegiac, the two most common responses of mimetic fiction to the epidemic, the fantastic works to undo the certainties both of these mimetic responses entail (particularly with respect to appeals to identity), while at the same time recognising the historical, social and psychic truths that underwrite these responses.... [F]antastic writing about AIDS offers an important, even necessary, alternative to mimetic responses. (Knabe, 2008, p. 216)

Knabe's point resonates with much speculative fiction dealing with AIDS. Where mimetic responses have tended to offer a steady diet of tragedy (sometime tinged with implicit homophobia, as in the film *Philadelphia*, in which the gay lovers are so muted as to seem unbelievable), fantasy and speculative fiction generally offer alternative perspectives and even possibilities for reparative reading. Early speculative works dealing with AIDS include not only *Was*, but also Tony Kushner's two-part play *Angels in America: A Gay Fantasia on National Themes* (1994), Gary Indiana's *Gone Tomorrow* (1993), John Greyson's AIDS musical *Zero Patience* (1993), in which the ghost of Patient Zero meets up with the historical figure of Sir Richard Burton, who has found the Fountain of Youth, Samuel Delany's *The Mad Man* (1994) and "The Tale of Plagues and Carnivals" in his Nevèrÿon fantasy series (1985), Elizabeth Hand's *Glimmering* (1997/2021), Peg Kerr's *The Wild Swans* (1999), and Ryman's *The Child Garden* (1989), which contemplates the nature of both disease and cure and the difficulties, in some cases, of distinguishing between them (Pearson, 2002). Speculative fiction can address, and has addressed, the issues of HIV/AIDS in very different ways, many of them involving the use of allegory, but also other, sometimes quite subtle, ways of imagining the relationships between AIDS as a disease, sexuality (and, obviously, homosexuality understood historically—mostly—as a disease in both medicine and psychiatry), and the contemporary world.

Changing Contexts: Queer Intersectionalities and Representation. One of the most powerful ways in which speculative fiction opens up space and time for queer representation lies in its ability to change the context. The producers of *Star Trek* were at one time notorious not only for their refusal to include an openly gay character (at a time when mimetic cinema and television were increasingly representing LGBTQI people in shows like *Six Feet Under* and *Will & Grace*), but also for their torqued rationale: homosexuality will not be an issue in the future, so we cannot represent it, because doing so would make it an issue.[13] By contrast, much of the most powerful speculative fiction simply ignores the homosexuality-as-problem trope and instead constructs worlds in which people's same-sex desires and other alternative sexualities are completely unremarkable. An interesting iteration of this occurs in Ursula Le Guin's Tiptree Award-winning story "Mountain Ways" (1996/2002). Le Guin starts the story with an explanatory note:

> Ki'O society is divided into two halves or moieties, called (for ancient religious reasons) the Morning and the Evening. You belong to your mother's moiety, and you can't have sex with anybody of your moiety.
> Marriage on O is a foursome, the sedoretu—a man and a woman from the Morning moiety and a man and a woman from the Evening moiety. You're expected to have sex with both your spouses of the other moiety, and not to have sex with your spouse of your own moiety. So each sedoretu has two expected heterosexual relationships, two expected homosexual relationships, and two forbidden heterosexual relationships. (Le Guin, 1996/2002)

This is a radically different form of social organization that disrupts every heteronormative impulse of contemporary Western society. The power of taking supposedly alternative sexualities and forms of desire for granted is significant, in part because it allows readers minoritized in their everyday lives the momentary experience of being in a space where they would not be noticeably different nor have to worry about the negative reactions to supposedly "alternative" sexualities inherent in heteronormative approaches to the world.

Other speculative fiction works explore what would happen if anti-queer attitudes continued as a norm or, indeed, became worse. An example of this, written from a queer perspective, is River Solomon's *An Unkindness of Ghosts* (2017), in which the intergenerational starship setting involves slavery, segregation, racism, homophobia, and transphobia. Contemporary speculative fiction is far more aware of intersectional issues and less likely to depict future worlds, or fantastical ones, as primarily or entirely White. In fact, this has long been the case with some writers. Le Guin, whose protagonists are almost always people of color, notoriously disagreed with the producers of the televisual adaptation of her Earthsea novels (*Earthsea*, 2004) when they turned the protagonist, Ged, who is described in the novels as a slight youngster with brown skin, into a muscular blue-eyed blond hero.[14] While this was an unusually overt case of whitewashing, it reflected a certain trend in viewer expectation, notable also in the number of complaints inspired by the casting of Rue, described in *The Hunger Games* as Black, with a Black actor (Holmes, 2012).

Fantasy and sf are not discrete classifications, which is why speculative fiction can be a useful term for work that moves across and between borders. Queer sf and fantasy has always been written and read by people of color and Indigenous peoples, just as it has—if discursively denied in parts of the sf world—by women.[15] Such newer generic classifications as Afrofuturism, a term coined by Mark Dery in 1994, bring the perspectives of people racialized in the Western world to the forefront. Afrofuturism is defined as "a way of imagining possible futures through a Black cultural lens" (Ingrid LaFleur, quoted in Womack, 2013, p. 9). Afrofuturism is a form peculiar to the African diaspora and refers to a specific aesthetic, rather than a specific medium. Thus, work like Beyoncé's short film *Lemonade* (2016) is both feminist and Afrofuturist, as are Janelle Monáe's "emotion pictures," such as the film that accompanied her *Dirty Computer* album (2018). The ways in which speculative fiction can foreground alienation, as an individual experience, a cultural manifestation, and a literary/dramatic technique, enables consideration of the past's effects on the present and speculation about the future, important when one's past may have been entirely shaped by one's ancestors' experience of the Middle Passage and subsequent enslavement and dehumanization. Although the term didn't come into being until 1993, a fair number of extant works have since been collected under its aegis, notably work by African American sf writers like Octavia Butler—particularly in terms of *Kindred* (1979/2003), her time-travelling and remarkably queer exploration of the complicated relationships created by race-based slavery—Samuel R. Delany, Nancy Farmer, and Steven Barnes.[16] Both the comic book and film versions of *Black Panther* are now considered Afrofuturist, while Ralph Ellison's *Invisible Man* can be understood as a precursor to Afrofuturism (Yaszek, 2005).

It is impossible to discuss issues of queer representation in speculative fiction, and the concomitant recognition of LGBTQ2SI-identified authors, particularly in the context of race, without mentioning the series of events happening in the sf and fantasy world about the question of representation. RaceFail was a conversation that happened, largely on Twitter, beginning in 2009, about the issue of "writing the Other." The arguments spilled over onto such questions as cultural appropriation, which is a particular issue in fantasy, where some writers have taken the myths, legends, folk tales, and even religious texts of other races and cultures as the groundwork for their own fiction. Multiple Hugo Award-winning author N. K. Jemisin pointed out in a 2010 blogpost that the "fail" in RaceFail was not, as some White people seemed to think, that it happened at all. Indeed, Jemisin describes RaceFail as a good and necessary thing for the speculative fiction community since it forced people to look around them and see who was, and who was not, present in any given conversation. However, RaceFail was followed by the eruption of two largely White, largely patriarchal, and largely homophobic groups who insisted (and continue to insist) that women, queers, and people of color have ruined "their" genre. Both groups, the original Sad Puppies and the derivative, but more extreme, Rabid Puppies, attempted to game the Hugo Awards (based on fan votes) in order to promote the work of cisgender straight White men—the real speculative fiction writers according to them. Anna Oleszczuk has a good account of these events in "Sad and Rabid Puppies: Politicization of the Hugo Award Nomination Procedure" (2017). Nobody watching the conservative backlash against human rights gains and social acceptance of queer, trans, and racialized people in Western cultures (and elsewhere) can be surprised that these White supremacist and heterosexist ideologues should be violently opposed to the presence, and worse yet the success, of queer, trans, and racialized speculative fiction writers and their works. Representation is political, and the politics of representation also shape the potential for the future to be imagined in more or less inclusive ways, to broaden or to narrow the definition of "human" itself.

WON'T ANYONE THINK OF THE CHILDREN?

How does speculative fiction writing provide (or not) space and time for queerness in a world that still reads queerness as antireproductive by necessity and as lacking a future? In part because of these questions, queer theory has a particular interest in children, both real and symbolic. Informed by two decades of fighting HIV/AIDS and the social and political structures that permitted it to ravage gay male communities, Lee Edelman argued in *No Future: Queer Theory and the Death Drive* (2004) that reproductive futurism (the investment of a culture's ideas and hopes for the future in the children, particularly the White cisgender male children, it produces) both valorizes and reinforces heteropatriarchy.[17] The child (or "Child" in Edelman's usage) remains entirely available for the discursive hegemony of reproductive heterosexuality. The Child, in this formulation, has become wholly symbolic of life in the West and has lost (largely due to medical and social improvements) the association with danger and potential death, for both mother and child. For Edelman, this future holds no space for queers and should be resisted, which Edelman argued involves rethinking our queer relationship both to futurity and to the death drive. Edelman's interest in the Child as a symbol of the cultural and political status quo certainly resonates with the ways in which the figure of the child has been mobilized politically in the United States: obvious examples include Anita Bryant's notorious homophobic "Save Our Children" campaign in the 1970s, which rolled back hard-fought human rights gains in places like Dade County, Florida, and the rhetorical use of the "innocent" child, largely figured as a big-eyed blonde White girl, whose life will be hopelessly, if inexplicably, damaged by marriage equality.[18] At the same time, however, queer speculative fiction proposes many alternative ideas about reproduction, children, and the future. An obvious alternative is the recourse to technology, either by choice or necessity. Thus, Victor Frankenstein uses science and technology to create a new being who, in Victor's fervid imagining, will experience deep gratitude for his creation. Victor's vision of his creation's future neatly replicates in many ways Mary Shelley's labeling of the novel itself as her "hideous progeny" (Shelley, 1818, p. 284).

Fast forward to the late 20th century and we see reproduction addressed variously, but often queerly, in much speculative fiction. In P. D. James's novel, *The Children of Men* (1992/2010), the mainstream cultural fear of losing the future that Edelman addressed comes to life in a world where women are simply unable to conceive, for reasons both unknown and untreatable. The most queer thing about the novel is the situation itself: a species that cannot reproduce is effectively queered. But James takes for granted the desirability of restarting human reproduction and her novel is largely an exploration of the psychological effects of despair that the human race is ending and hope that a sudden and singular pregnancy might augur its survival. The film adaptation directed by Alfonso Cuarón (2006) further queered the narrative by locating the future hope of the human race in the racialized, classed, and largely abjected body of a Black teenaged refugee.

By contrast, in *Woman on the Edge of Time* (2016), Marge Piercy took up feminist writer Shulamith Firestone's argument in *The Dialectic of Sex* (1970) that gender equality is impossible while women bear the burden of reproduction. In Piercy's utopian future Mattapoissett, gender equality has been achieved, binary heterosexuality has broken down, and fetuses are grown in artificial wombs so that no one person has to become pregnant and give birth. Instead, families of three adults (gender both unspecified and unimportant) take on the job of creating and then raising the new child. Piercy contrasted this future, with its high-tech reproductive process and environmentally sustainable lifestyle, with a glimpse of a dystopian world in which women are property used solely for sex, breeding, and male display. Piercy's bottle-raised fetuses are not dissimilar to those in Aldous Huxley's *Brave New World* (1932), except that their reason for being is much queerer; in Huxley's world, it is only about controlling fetal development to fit the future adults uncomplainingly into their social hierarchy, from ruler to elevator operator.

Queer forms of reproduction also mean queer forms of maternity and, as we see with Piercy, of family and kinship. In "Is Kinship Always Already Heterosexual?" Judith Butler (2002) took up the somewhat awkward relationship between marriage and kinship.[19] In 2002, marriage equality had been achieved in only a very few countries, not including Canada and the United States. Butler specifically looked at both French and American arguments around marriage and kinship and noted that these battles produce a "contemporary predicament in which the state is sought for the recognition it might confer on same-sex couples and countered for the regulatory control on normative kinship that it continues to exercise" (p. 17). The idea of families of choice, as alternatives to unwelcoming biological families, continues to exercise considerable valence for many members of the LGBTQ2SI community. Speculative fiction provides space to imagine alternative forms of kinship and family. Not only does *Frankenstein* depict a potentially very queer family (a single father and his non-heterosexually-reproduced progeny), as does Novik with her closely bonded dragon/human pairing, but many other speculative fiction works imagine alternative forms of reproduction and kinship, almost always tied either to a vision of at least quasi-utopian alternatives or to a thoroughly dystopian vision of contemporary trends projected into fictional, often futuristic, spaces/times.

Brave New Worlds of Queer Kinship. Larissa Lai's *Salt Fish Girl* (1999) plays with cyberpunk and particularly *Blade Runner* (Scott, 1982) to create a dystopian corporate-controlled world in which female clones are used for slave labor; some of these slaves, called Sonias, escape their corporate owner and learn to reproduce parthenogenetically. The futuristic story is mirrored by a second narrative grounded in Chinese mythology in which the goddess Nu Wa, who creates humans, also opts to become human herself and falls in love with a seller of salt fish. The novel juggles two queer relationships, the one with Nu Wa in human form and the salt fish girl, and the near-future one with Miranda and her lover, Evie Xin, and ends with Miranda giving birth to a non-heterosexually-produced baby, who may or may not be the start of a "brave new world." *Salt Fish Girl* (1999) is distinctly a generic blend, bringing together the literary qualities of magic realism with the use of myth and folk tale and with riffs on both literary and cinematic sf. The novel uses the freedoms of speculative fiction to consider queer reproduction and queer family in the context of decolonization, something that Lai's more recent novel, *The Tiger Flu* (2018) continues. In contesting normative reproductive and kinship structures, speculative fiction not only provides space for queer potentialities, but also allows writers and readers alike to consider the relationship between heteronormativity, misogyny, racism, and colonialism.

Similarly, Hiromi Goto's *The Kappa Child* (2001) described the most liminal of pregnancies: the kappa fetus talks directly to the reader, yet the pregnancy is both invisible and undetectable by modern medicine. The kappa is a genderless reptilian trickster figure from Japanese mythology and the nameless narrator conceives during a very equivocal encounter with a nippleless, belly-buttonless but otherwise apparently human stranger on the runway of Calgary airport during a lunar eclipse. Kappa like to wrestle humans, and the narrator and the stranger wrestle/have sex on the runway—the narrator is quite confused about what has happened. Unsurprisingly, a pregnancy resulting from an ambivalently sexual encounter with a mythical figure does not follow normal developmental models nor is the kappa ever actually born in any recognizable sense. Goto's novel comments on both traditional and nontraditional family structures; the narrator's family home and relationship with her mother and three sisters are dominated by her father's abuse while the narrator finds family among her friends and lesbian lover. All of this consideration of reproduction and family is framed by the story's generic references to sf and by the narrator's childhood reading of *Little House on the Prairie* (1935) in her quest to understand how to negotiate life in the gender normative, heteronormative, and racially hostile world of the prairies. The crux of the story is the narrator's realization that *Little House on the Prairie* is a lie—it not only erases the Indigenous presence, but also whitewashes the hardship and poverty faced by many White settlers; it absolutely cannot function as a guidebook to Canadian prairie life for a differently gendered child of Japanese descent trying to claim intelligibility in an uncomprehending world (Pearson, 2019).

A more recent exploration of queer possibilities to rethink reproduction and family occurred in Annalee Newitz's (2017) novel, *The Future of Another Timeline*. Newitz described a world in which five ancient Machines allow time travel to the past. Time travelers can go back and "edit" the timeline to produce specific effects. The conflict in the novel circulates around attitudes toward gender and reproduction: one group, led by a fictional version of the real historical figure of Anthony Comstock (Postal Inspector and Secretary of the New York Society for the Suppression of Vice, which campaigned against sex education, birth control, and abortion), is trying to produce a future in which men have total control over women and reproduction; the other group, who call themselves the Daughters of Harriet, are trying to edit the past so as to create a present in which all women have the vote, Harriet Tubman was able to become a U.S. senator, and abortion is legal. The novel presents the reader with a group of protagonists that includes at least one nonbinary person, a lesbian couple (one of whom is murdered by the Comstockers, until an edit reverses that particular version of history), and a strong emphasis on the value of friendship and close bonds between women/nonbinary people that may or may not be sexual.

Even before marriage equality triumphed in some nations, including the United States, many speculative fiction authors incorporated same-sex marriages into their fictions. In fantasy, this may take the form of royalty negotiating marriages between their eligible sons, to take one example, or it can take the form of Cinderella triumphing but abandoning the prince for something better than a royal marriage, as in Malinda Lo's *Ash* (2009), in which Ash chooses the fairy huntress, Kaisa, over the prince. Diane Duane, in her trilogy *The Tale of the Five* (1979–1992), ended the third novel, *Door into Sunset* (1992), with the triumphant marriage of Prince Freelorn to both his long-standing male love, Herewiss, and their pregnant partner, Segnbora.[20] Duane is clear that her Middle Kingdoms' universe accepts marriages with multiple partners and that marriage may or may not include sexual relationships between the various individuals involved. In another of the earlier LGBT-focused fantasy trilogies, *The Chronicles of Tornor* (1975, 1979, 1980), Elizabeth Lynn explored same-sex relationships both in the context of the brutal patriarchal world of the Keeps and a gender egalitarian society that opposes it. The three novels have multiple same-sex relationships, both male and female (and, in one case, incestuous), none of which are remarked on as in any way out of the ordinary. Fantasy often naturalizes same-sex attraction, treating it as an ordinary part of a fantastical world, but it can also play with such tropes as the evil queer or transgender character.

In sf, same-sex attraction (and potentially marriage) is more commonly part of the background. Becky Chambers's Wayfarer series (2015–2021), which is not only sf, but also space opera, depicts a future in which sexual relationships between people of the same or similar genders is completely normative, but so are sexual and romantic relationships with or between alien species, where physically possible.[21] Chambers also reimagined sex work as a free and respected profession that some people choose; this is possible because her one mostly human society, formed by people who have chosen to remain on multigeneration ships that fled Earth centuries ago, is also a completely noncapitalist world in which everyone has the basic right to air, food, water, clothing, living quarters, medical care, etc. The scenario in the Wayfarer novels reverses the TANSTAAFL ideology of Robert A. Heinlein's *The Moon Is a Harsh Mistress* (1966/1997), in which the triumph of free-market capitalism means that not even air is a human right.[22] Furthermore, Heinlein's very unqueer attempts to imagine new forms of kinship and relationship (such as "line marriages" in which husbands and wives alternate and heterosexuality reigns supreme) are genuinely queered by the multiple forms of kinship and sexual relationship in Chambers' novels. In *Record of a Spaceborn Few* (2018), the sex worker is a man and the client a woman, setting contemporary discourses about sex work on their heads, albeit it is hard to know if one should label this prostitution, since, in a noncapitalist society, the transaction involves neither buying nor selling.

From a queer theoretical perspective, then, speculative fiction provides space/time to explore the very things queer theorists focus on, including critiques of reproductive heteronormativity, of the relationship between heterosexuality and the state sanction or control of kinship in all its forms, of the relationship between capitalism and sexuality (not only in sex work, but also in the financial coercion that has historically underwritten much heterosexual marriage), of the relationship between gender and sexuality that is perhaps summed up by the question of whether one can have homosexuality without a binary gender system, and, finally, of the possibilities for sexuality and the idea of sexual orientations in times/spaces that might have quite different sociocultural and political contexts—spaces that, in some cases, are not so much literally situated in, as made possible by, the very unknowability of the future.

Strange Matings: No Future or Cruising Utopia? The very idea of the future has been a hotly contested debate within queer studies for some time. Lee Edelman's *No Future* is widely cited, even by those who ignore its psychoanalytic framing, as setting out the case that queers should ignore or dismiss futurity since, according to Edelman, there is no way to separate political and sociocultural futurity from reproductive futurity. So long as children are posed as necessary to a future, any future, Edelman argued that heteropatriarchy remains inescapable. One might argue that this is an inevitable consequence of Edelman's Lacanian leanings, since, for Lacan, the possession of the phallus is what guarantees symbolic meaning and thus the very existence of culture. Heteropatriarchy seems largely inescapable. Conversely, José Esteban Muñoz (2009) argued that queer theory is inherently utopian and thus inherently invested in futurity. Muñoz quoted Oscar Wilde's maxim that "A map of the world that does not include Utopia is not worth even glancing at" (p. 1) to argue that queers do need a sense of futurity and, following Wilde, that humanity is constantly in search of a more utopian world. Muñoz summed up his project in *Cruising Utopia* by writing,

> We may never touch queerness, but we can feel it as the warm illumination of a horizon imbued with potentiality. We have never been queer, yet queerness exists for us as an ideality that can be distilled from the past and used to imagine a future. (p. 1)

The concept of utopia as something one cruises (with all its connotative ramifications) is particularly useful for considering the potential of queer speculative fiction to imagine other times and places.[23] Not all these necessarily engage with identity politics, an idea about which queer theory is deeply skeptical. Many do not assume an essential gender identity or an essential sexual orientation. But all imagine futures that, while necessarily informed by past and present, give queer writers and readers (and other seekers of queerer worlds) a more capacious room of their own than society normally allows or legitimates.

Queer theory has since the early 2000s developed a strong critique of what has come to be called "chrononormativity," a term that summarizes the normative life path expected of humans, at least in contemporary capitalist cultures (Knabe & Pearson, 2013; Lothian, 2018). Chrononormativity tracks the life path from birth to school to (heterosexual) dating to graduation, job, marriage, children, a house with a white picket fence, and eventually grandchildren, old age, and death, a very stereotypical narrative. While the queering of familial and kinship relations that has taken place since the 1990s means that more LGBTQ2SI people may be living a homonormative version of this life path, it is not, by and large, one that is amenable to queerness. Queers have a strange—or perhaps estranged—relation to time. And as Katherine Bond Stockton (2009), among others, has pointed out, queer childhoods enact a very different relationship to time than do heterosexual ones. Stockton referred to this as "growing sideways" (p. 1), because of the nonlinear relationship to chrononormative time experienced by queer children and adolescents. Indeed, notions of queer time also take up, often satirically, the Freudian notion of arrested development. Consequently, ideas about time and about queer futurity thread through speculative fiction in manifold and often exciting ways. Even writers identified as straight find queerness all over the future.

For example, the editors of a collection on African American sf writer Octavia Butler chose her phrase "strange matings" for the title of their book (Holden & Shawl, 2013). Butler's work is full of strange matings—between contemporary humans and ancient ones, between slave owners and slaves, between humans and aliens, many of them nonconsensual. Two examples of human/alien matings should suffice: in the much-fêted story "Bloodchild" (1984a), a human boy expects to be impregnated by a female Tlic, a giant insectoid alien species. Butler has said that she wished specifically to experiment with the notion of male pregnancy. She wrote the story at a time when pregnant trans men had not yet become news; instead, she looked at impregnating a biologically male body.[24] While the concept of a human male implanted with the eggs of a female alien has been addressed primarily in terms of gender, it is also very queer—particularly in the way T'Gatoi trades on the boy, Gan's, affection for her. On the one hand, this could be read as an attempt to ease the process for him; on the other hand, the contemporary context suggests a kind of grooming of a child by an exploitative adult (although the impregnation does not involve sex).

In the Xenogenesis trilogy (Butler, 2012b), the queerness of the human protagonists' situation is indeed sexual, although again not directly identified as queer. Humans from a dying Earth are scooped up by the Oankali, aliens for whom genetic information is wealth, collected by blending species. In the process of pursuing their trade, the Oankali, who have three sexes, male, female, and Ooloi, offer humans help saving the planet—but the price is creating a new species of hybrid referred to as "constructs." Lilith Ayapo, the protagonist of the first novel, *Dawn* (1987), is initially repulsed by both the tentacled bodies of the Oankali and the prospect of a "sexual" relationship with an Ooloi that is not immediately comprehensible in terms of binary human genders. While neither the short story nor the trilogy, like the time-travel novel *Kindred*, deals overtly with the idea of queerness, queerness permeates every aspect of these works and shapes the potential for futurity in the last Xenogenesis book, *Imago* (1989). Only through accepting the queer creation of a new hybrid species are humans enabled to save the Earth and have an actual future. Butler's map of the world includes a potential utopia made possible by the creation of Oankali constructs. Alexis Lothian (2018) pointed out that "within most genealogies of queer studies, [queer] belongs to the histories and cultures of gay men's sexual activity" (p. 130), yet much of the queerest work in speculative fiction comes from women and people of color, not all of them queer-identified. The work of writers like Octavia Butler opens up more generous spaces of queerness, even though many readers might not recognize how queer her works are.

SPECULATING (ABOUT) FUTURES: QUEERING THE CHRONONORMATIVE

Several subgenres of speculative and science fiction lend themselves to pondering questions of chrononormativity and forms of queer futurity that may not be dependent on reproduction. Time travel and alternative histories both question how humans apprehend and experience time and the ways in which forms of governmental and societal power exploit chrononormativity to keep people "on the straight and narrow." Neither author not characters need to be queer for the queering of the chrononormative to be central to the narrative, as for example in Kate Atkinson's *Life after Life* (2013) and Jo Walton's *My Real Children* (2014). *Life after Life* tells the story of Ursula Todd, who is born and dies immediately, is born and lives to childhood, is born and lives to adulthood, each time experiencing a different life and, for the baby, a different future. The cover blurb for the novel asks, "What if you could live your life again and again until you got it right?" Of course, this begs the question of what is "right." For Ursula Todd, it seems to be reinventing herself until she finds herself in 1930, in a cafe in Munich, pointing a gun at Hitler and pulling the trigger. Yet this apparent denouement is not exactly the end, as the novel returns twice more to the moment of Ursula's birth in 1910. Yet Hitler's apparent death is precisely where the novel starts—before moving on (or back) to Ursula's birth during a snowstorm and immediate death from asphyxiation, as the umbilical cord is wrapped around her neck. In the final 1910 sequences, the doctor and midwife remain stuck in the snowstorm, yet Ursula lives because her mother has secreted surgical scissors in her night table and is able to cut the cord herself. "Practice makes perfect" (p. 568).

The recursive structure of the narrative effectively queers any notion of time as linear and of the life course as chrononormative; little could be less chrononormative than the constant repetition of birth and death that Ursula experiences throughout the novel—and of which she has very vague, fuzzy memories. Since she cannot be sure that she is changing history, Ursula finishes the last section in 1945 both rejoicing that this time her brother Ted has made it through the war, and uncomfortably, if not entirely consciously, aware of the precarity of any timeline. The novel is both deadly serious and remarkably funny, combining a meta-commentary on the author's power to create, manipulate, and destroy with serious reflections on the state of English middle-class life through two world wars, particularly in relation to gender-based violence, the limitations placed on women, and her society's normative expectations of how a woman's life should unspool.

Atkinson is largely regarded as a literary writer, although her five Jackson Brodie novels are mysteries, which means that *Life after Life* received more critical attention than Jo Walton's *My Real Children* (2014). In her review of Walton's novel, science fiction writer Gwyneth Jones (2014) noted its similarities to both *Life after Life* and Audrey Niffenegger's *The Time Traveler's Wife* (2003), referring to all three as "high-concept modern fairytales." Generically, Walton's novel contains more science fictional references—in one of Patricia Cowan's two pasts (the novel is framed by Patty's attempt to handle her dementia while coping with remembering two distinct pasts—and two discrete families), humanity has a base on the Moon, suggesting a degree of futurity not present in *Life after Life*. *My Real Children* is also more obviously queer, because in one life, Tricia marries a bully named Mark and endures a horrible, impoverished heterosexual relationship, while in the other Pat meets the love of her life, Bee, and lives with her in Italy, as well as England, while pursuing a fulfilling career and raising their three children.

Normative time is queered both by the movement between the two life stories and sets of memories and by the fact that the less chrononormative life is the happy one. In some senses, both novels offer us not alternative histories, but alternative genealogies in which the bending of time creates multiple pasts. Linear history can make sense of neither novel; instead, what they produce are affective histories that embrace, rather than obscure, "the continuities, contacts, contradictions among past, present, and future" (Freeman, 2010, p. xx). Jack Halberstam (2005) made the point that "Queer time and space are useful frameworks in assessing political and cultural change in the late 20th and early 21st centuries (both what has changed and what must change)" (p. 4). This is apt in terms of both novels, each of which uses repeated changes to dominant history as a way of understanding gender, sexuality, family, kinship, and the complications of human relationships under different sociocultural regimes; even small changes may make visible the costs and damages of life with bullying men, for example. Patty's life with Bee seems, by contrast, positively utopian—so much so that Jones was reminded of Luciente's life in Mattapoissett in Marge Piercy's *Woman on the Edge of Time* (1976), another anti-chrononormative novel in which the racialized protagonist travels to two very different futures and ends by making choices in the present intended to bring Mattapoisett into being and prevent a dystopian misogynist patriarchal world (something of a precursor to the world of the Comstockers in Newitz's *The Future of Another Timeline*).

REPAIRING THE PAST: READING TO TRANSVERSE THE HUMAN

Nisi Shawl's (2016) novel *Everfair* narrates a complex, richly populated, alternative past set largely in the Congo while King Leopold II of Belgium is attempting to gain control of the land, its resources, and its peoples.[25] Its history begins to diverge from ours at the moment when, instead of putting its money into founding the London School of Economics, the Fabian Society in the United Kingdom instead opts to use its wealth to purchase land from Leopold in order to house Congolese refugees. Amin El-Mohtar (2016) usefully noted that,

> The cast of characters is beautifully diverse in terms of faith, ability, ethnicities, sexual orientation and nationalities, making the web of relationships intricate and fraught; Shawl is brilliant at showing where the various ideals, motivations and desires for Everfair as a utopian experiment bump up against each other. From wealthy White families whose free attitudes towards sexuality and plural marriage compromise their return to England, to light-skinned characters deciding not to pass, to queer characters struggling to understand each other across racial lines, to Indigenous characters coming to terms with their new prosthetics, the depth and breadth of experience represented in a richly imagined setting is a huge achievement.

Because *Everfair* is so crammed with both character and incident, it is difficult to summarize succinctly. Important from the perspective of queer theory are the multiple ways in which *Everfair* queers its characters, its situation, its relationship to history, and even its genre. An offshoot of cyberpunk, *Everfair* falls squarely within the conventions of steampunk, a genre that, as El-Mohtar pointed out, is often "sepia-toned, gear-ridden, and frustratingly nostalgic toward empire and colonialism." *Everfair* might be gear-ridden, but it is anything but sepia-toned, and it has neither nostalgia nor tolerance for empire and colonialism. Like much other Afrofuturist work, *Everfair* reimagines the past in order to make space for racialized, and particularly for Black, people in a future from which they have often been excluded. That it does so in the queerest of contexts and while debunking both colonial history and chrononormativity only makes it a more powerful critique of the ways in which colonialism has mobilized racism, misogyny, and homophobia together on behalf of its White supremacist goals. In this case, however, Shawl also directly took on the need to represent racialized queer people in the past (and, by projection, in the future). Her characters are often pansexual, polyamorous, and disinclined, in some cases, to obey the conventions of normative gender any more than they obey those of normative sexuality. *Everfair* is a useful work with which to end this article because it pulls together so many of the topics queer theory itself addresses and does so in ways that allow queer and racialized readers the option of reading (or perhaps re-reading) the past reparatively. As Sedgwick herself pointed out, there is both power and relief in realizing that the past could have happened differently. Understanding that one does not have to paranoidly refuse the potential pain of hope (because it is so easily disappointed) allows the reader to rethink the relationship between past and present and to consider the ways in which queerness has the potential to torque humanity into more inclusive and more generous modes of life.

CONCLUSION

This article examines the ways in which queer theory provides insights into speculative fiction, both as a category of genres that can be queer/ed and as a reading practice that can look at queer, nonqueer, and even antiqueer work with an eye to understanding how these works question, subvert, or simply reproduce normative epistemologies of sexuality and gender. That these normativities cannot themselves be separated from further questions of race, Indigeneity, and anticolonialism is amply demonstrated in the many ways in which queer racialized people have taken up speculative fiction genres to think about the inclusions and exclusions that variably define them as fully human, partially human, or not human at all. Queer theory allows insight into questions of how sexuality (and the people it categorizes as outside the sexual norm) can be represented in speculative fiction. It allows us to interrogate normative ideas of intimacy and kinship and to contemplate alternative understandings and potential practices of reproduction. It demonstrates the ways in which "human" itself is a limited definition that may ignore or deny the sentience and affective capacities of nonhumans, including terrestrial animals and the aliens we may someday meet. And, finally, it questions the ways in which chrononormative approaches to time limit our ability to imagine alternative life courses that may be infinitely queerer than cultural stereotypes suggest. In the end, however, just as the definition of speculative fiction is itself largely up to the reader, the queerness of speculative fiction will inevitably be understood differently by different readers. For those who read reparatively, or wish to do so, queer speculative fiction opens up possibilities of hope; it may even bring the horizon of queerness closer, leading to the potentiality of at least imagining a queer utopia athwart the very unqueer dailyness of contemporary culture and politics. The possibilities are endlessly queer.

FURTHER READING

Balay, A. (2012). "Incloseto Putbacko": Queerness in adolescent fantasy fiction. *The Journal of Popular Culture*, 45(5), 923–942.
Benshoff, H. M., & Griffin, S. (Eds.). (2004). *Queer cinema: The film reader*. Psychology Press.
Bradley, M. Z. (1975). *The heritage of Hastur*. DAW Books.
Butler, A. M. (2002). Proto-sf/proto-queer: The strange cases of Dr Frankenstein and Mr Hyde. *Foundation*, 86, 7–16.
Butler, A. M. (Ed.). (2002). Special issue: Gay and Lesbian science fiction. *Foundation: The International Review of Science Fiction*, 86, 1–118.

Butler, A. M. (2016). Strange boys, queer boys: Gay representations in young adult fantastic fiction. In J. Roberts & E. MacCallum-Stewart (Eds.), *Gender and sexuality in contemporary popular fantasy* (pp. 53–67). Routledge.

Clay, D., & Brusuelas, J. H. (2021). *Lucian, true history: Introduction, text, translation, and commentary.* Oxford University Press.

Collins, S. (2011). *The hunger games trilogy.* Scholastic Australia.

Delany, S. R. (1985). *Flight from Nevèrÿon.* Bantam.

Delany, S. R., Gregory, S., & McCaffery, L. (1987). The semiology of silence. *Science Fiction Studies, 14*(2), 134–164.

Elliott-Smith, D. (2016). *Queer horror film and television: Sexuality and masculinity at the margins.* Bloomsbury.

Evans, R. (2017). Fantastic futures? Cli-fi, climate justice, and queer futurity. *Resilience: A Journal of the Environmental Humanities, 4*(2–3), 94–110.

Faucheux, A. H. (2017). Race and sexuality in Nalo Hopkinson's oeuvre; Or, queer Afrofuturism. *Science Fiction Studies, 44*(3), 563–580.

Foster, B. R. (Ed.). (2001). *The epic of Gilgamesh* (B. R. Foster, Trans.). W. W. Norton.

Grantham, M. (2015). *The transhuman antihero: Paradoxical protagonists of speculative fiction from Mary Shelley to Richard Morgan.* McFarland.

Haggerty, G. E. (2006). *Queer Gothic.* University of Illinois Press.

Justice, D. H. (2011). *The way of thorn and thunder: The kynship chronicles.* UNM Press.

Keeling, K. (2019). *Queer times, black futures.* NYU Press.

Keneally, S. (2016). *Queer be dragons: Mapping LGBT fantasy novels* [Doctoral dissertation, University of Dublin, Trinity College].

Kim, M. (2017). *Afrofuturism, science fiction, and the reinvention of African American culture.* Arizona State University.

Le Guin, U. K. (2010). *The birthday of the world and other stories.* Hachette UK.

Le Guin, U. K. (2012). *A wizard of Earthsea.* Houghton Mifflin Harcourt.

Murchison, G. (2018). Let's flip it! Quare emancipations: Black queer traditions, Afrofuturisms, Janelle Monáe to Labelle. *Women and Music: A Journal of Gender and Culture, 22,* 79–90.

Novik, N. (2006). *His majesty's dragon: A novel of Temeraire* (Vol. 1). Del Rey.

Pascual, M. C. (2021). *The Tiger Flu*: A critical posthumanist response to the illusion of transhumanism. *Hélice, 7*(1), 99–110.

Pearson, W. G. (2003). Queer theory. In E. James & F. Mendlesohn (Eds.), *The Cambridge companion to science fiction* (pp. 55–68). Cambridge University Press.

Pearson, W. G. (2008). Towards a queer genealogy of sf. *Queer Universes: Sexualities in Science Fiction, 37,* 72.

Reid, R. A. (2009). Thrusts in the dark: Slashers' queer practices. *Extrapolation, 50*(3), 463–483.

Sturgeon, T. (1953). *E pluribus unicorn: A collection of short stories of Theodore Sturgeon.* Abelard Press.

Tyler, J. (2017). *The trail of blood: Queer history through vampire literature.* The University of Alabama in Huntsville.

Wells, H. G. (2005). *The time machine.* Berkley. (Original work published 1895)

Wisker, G. (2017). Devouring desires: Lesbian Gothic horror. In W. Hughes & A. Smith (Eds.), *Queering the Gothic* (pp. 123–141). Manchester University Press.

REFERENCES

Abate, M. A., & Kidd, K. B. (Eds.). (2011). *Over the rainbow: Queer children's and young adult literature.* University of Michigan Press.

Ahmed, S. (2006). *Queer phenomenology: Orientations, objects, others.* Duke University Press.

Anders, C. J. (2016). *All the birds in the sky*. Tor Books.
Arnason, E. (1993). *Ring of swords*. Tor Books.
Atkinson, K. (2013). *Life after life*. Doubleday.
Atwood, M. (1985). *The handmaid's tale*. McClelland & Stewart.
Bechdel, A. (2012). *Are You My Mother?* Random House.
Bechdel, A. (2007). *Fun home: A family tragicomic*. Houghton Mifflin Harcourt.
Benshoff, H. M. (1997). *Monsters in the closet: Homosexuality and the horror film*. Manchester University Press.
Berlant, L. (1997). *The queen of America goes to Washington City*. Duke University Press.
Betz, P. M. (2014). *The lesbian fantastic: A critical study of science fiction, fantasy, paranormal and Gothic writings*. McFarland.
Beyoncé. (Director). (2016). *Lemonade*. Parkwood Entertainment, Columbia Records.
Bruhm, S. (2018). *Frankenstein's creature: Or, Yes Sir, That's My Baby!* Words.
Butler, J. (2002). Is kinship always already heterosexual? *differences*, 13(1), 14–44.
Butler, J. (2016). *Frames of war: When is life grievable?* Verso Books.
Butler, O. E. (2003). *Kindred*. Beacon Press. (Original work published 1979)
Butler, O. E. (2012a). *Bloodchild: And other stories*. Open Road Media.
Butler, O. E. (2012b). *Lilith's brood: The complete Xenogenesis trilogy*. Open Road Media.
Call, L. (2012). *BDSM in American science fiction and fantasy*. Springer.
Cavendish, M. (1994). *The blazing world and other writings*. Penguin UK. (Original work published 1666)
Chambers, B. (2018). *Record of a spaceborn few: Wayfarers 3*. Hodder & Stoughton.
Charnas, S. M. (1978). *Motherlines*. Berkley/Putnam.
Cuarón, A. (Director). (2006). *Children of men*. Strike Entertainment.
Delany, S. R. (1976). *Triton*. Bantam.
Delany, S. R. (1994). *The mad man*. Richard Kasak/Masquerade Books.
Delany, S. R. (1999). *Shorter views: Queer thoughts & the politics of the paraliterary*. Wesleyan University Press.
Dery, M. (1994). Black to the future: Interviews with Samuel R. Delany, Greg Tate, and Tricia Rose. In S. Bukatman, M. Laidlaw, P. Schwenger, & V. Sobchack (Eds.), *Flame wars* (pp. 179–222). Duke University Press.
Derry, C. (2018). Lesbianism and feminist legislation in 1921: The age of consent and 'gross indecency between women'. *History Workshop Journal*, 86, 245–267.
Disch, T. M. (1972). *334*. MacGibbon & Kee.
Duane, D. (1992). *Door into sunset*. Corgi.
Edelman, L. (2004). *No future: Queer theory and the death drive*. Duke University Press.
El-Mohtar, A. (2016, September 7). "Everfair" looks into steampunk's dark heart. Tor.com.
Eng, D. L. (2010). *The feeling of kinship: Queer liberalism and the racialization of intimacy*. Duke University Press.
Erdrich, L. (2017). *Future home of the living god*. Hachette UK.
Firestone, S. (1970). *The dialectic of sex: The case for feminist revolution*. Morrow.
Foucault, M. (1980). *The history of sexuality: 1: The will to knowledge*. Vintage.
Foucault, M. (2021). Nietzsche, genealogy, history. In Bouchard, D. F. & Simon, S. (Eds.), *Language, counter-memory, practice* (pp. 139–164). Cornell University Press.
Freedman, C. (2001). Adventures of the dialectic: Or, on Delany as critic. *Science Fiction Studies*, 28(1), 107–118.
Freeman, E. (2010). *Time binds: Queer temporalities, queer histories*. Duke University Press.
Gaiman, N. (1991). *The Sandman* (Vol. 1). *Preludes & nocturnes*. DC Comics.

Garber, E., & Paleo, L. (1983). *Uranian worlds: A reader's guide to alternative sexuality in science fiction and fantasy*. Hall Reference Books.

Ginn, S., Cornelius, M. G., & Palumbo, D. E. (Eds.). (2012). *The sex is out of this world: Essays on the carnal side of science fiction* (Vol. 36). McFarland.

Godwin, F. (2009). *The man in the Moone*. Broadview Press. (Original work published 1638)

Goto, H. (2001). *The kappa child*. Red Deer Press.

Gross, L. (2001). *Up from invisibility: Lesbians, gay men, and the media in America*. Columbia University Press.

Halberstam, J. (2005). *In a queer time and place: Transgender bodies, subcultural lives*. NYU Press.

Hand, E. (2021). *Glimmering*. Open Road Media. (Original work published 1997)

Heinlein, R. A. (writing as L. Monroe). (1947). On the writing of speculative fiction. In L. A. Eshbach (Ed.), *Of worlds beyond: The science of science-fiction writing* (pp. 9–17). Fantasy Press.

Heinlein, R. A. (1997). *The moon is a harsh mistress*. Macmillan. (Original work published 1966)

Hollinger, V. (1999). (Re) reading queerly: Science fiction, feminism, and the defamiliarization of gender. *Science Fiction Studies*, 26(1), 23–40.

Holmes, A. (2012, March 30). White until proven Black: Imagining race in *Hunger Games*. *The New Yorker*.

Huxley, A. (1932). *Brave new world*. Vintage.

Jackson, E., Jr. (1995). *Strategies of deviance: Studies in gay male representation*. Indiana University Press.

James, P. D. (2010). *The children of men*. Vintage. (Original work published 1992)

Jemisin, N. K. (2010, January 18). Why I think RaceFail was the bestest thing evar for SFF. In N. K. Jemisin's blog.

Jones, G. (2014, September, 27). My *Real Children* review—A high-concept modern fairytale. *The Guardian*.

Kenneally, S. C. (2016). *Queer be dragons: Mapping LGBT fantasy novels 1987–2000* [Doctoral dissertation, Trinity College Dublin].

Kerr, P. (1999). *The wild swans*. Aspect.

Kim, M. (2017). *Afrofuturism, science fiction, and the reinvention of African American culture*. Arizona State University.

Knabe, S. (2008). History and AIDS in *Was* and *Angels in America*. *Extrapolation*, 49(2), 214–239.

Knabe, S., & Pearson, W. G. (2013). "Gambling against history": Queer kinship and cruel optimism in Octavia Butler's *Kindred*. In Holden R. & Shawl N. (Eds.), *Strange matings: Science fiction, feminism, African American voices, and Octavia E. Butler* (pp. 51–78). Aqueduct Press.

Kushner, T. (1992). *Angels in America: A gay fantasia on national themes, Part One: Millennium approaches*. Theatre Communications Group.

Kushner, T. (1994). *Angels in America: A gay fantasia on national themes, Part Two: Perestroika*. Theatre Communications Group.

Lai, L. (1999). *The salt fish girl*. Tessera.

Lai, L. (2018). *The tiger flu*. Arsenal Pulp Press.

Larbalestier, J. (2002). *The battle of the sexes in science fiction*. Wesleyan University Press.

Latham, R. (Ed.). (2014). *The Oxford handbook of science fiction*. Oxford University Press.

Lavietes, M., & Ramos, S. (2022, March 20). Nearly 240 anti-LGBTQ bills filed in 2022 so far, most of them targeting trans people. *NBC News*.

Le Guin, U. K. (1969). *The left hand of darkness*. Ace.

Le Guin, U. K. (2002). *Mountain ways. The birthday of the world and other stories*. Harper Collins. (Original work published 1996)

Le Guin, U. K. (2004). A whitewashed Earthsea: How the Sci Fi Channel wrecked my books. *Slate.com*.

Le Guin, U. K. (2009, August 29). *The Year of the Flood* by Margaret Atwood. *The Guardian*.

Lo, M. (2009). *Ash*. Little, Brown Books for Young Readers.

Lothian, A. (2018). *Old futures: Speculative fiction and queer possibility* (Vol. 10). NYU Press.
Luciano, D., & Chen, M. Y. (2015). Introduction: Has the queer ever been human? *GLQ, 21*(2), iv–207.
Lynn, E. A. (1978). *A different light*. Berkley.
Lynn, E. A. (2017). *The chronicles of Tornor trilogy: Watchtower, The Dancers of Arun, and The Northern Girl*. Open Road Media. (Original work published 1979, 1979, 1980)
Mancuso, C. (2016, August 10). Speculative or science fiction? As Margaret Atwood shows, there isn't much distinction. *The Guardian*.
McIntyre, V. N. (1978). *Dreamsnake*. Houghton Mifflin.
McLelland, M. (2005). The world of Yaoi: The Internet, censorship and the global "boys' love" fandom. *Australian Feminist Law Journal, 23*(1), 61–77.
McLelland, M. (2006). Why are Japanese girls' comics full of boys bonking? *Refractory, 10*(4), 1–14.
McLelland, M., & Dasgupta, R. (Eds.). (2005). *Genders, transgenders and sexualities in Japan*. Routledge.
Mendlesohn, F. (2014). *Rhetorics of fantasy*. Wesleyan University Press.
Merril, J. (2017). What do you mean? Science? Fiction? In Latham, R. (Ed.), *Science fiction criticism: An anthology of essential writings* (pp. 22–36). Bloomsbury.
Mirzoeff, N. (1999). *An introduction to visual culture*. Psychology Press.
Monáe, J. (Director). (2018). *Dirty computer*. Wondaland.
Mondal, M. (2018, January 30). *A short history of South Asian speculative fiction: Part I*. Tor.com.
Moore, A., & Lloyd, D. (1990). V for vendetta. DC Comics.
Muñoz, J. E. (2009). *Cruising utopia: The then and there of queer futurity*. NYU Press.
Newitz, A. (2017). *The future of another timeline*. Tor Books.
Oleszczuk, A. (2017). Sad and rabid puppies: Politicization of the Hugo Award nomination procedure. *New Horizons in English Studies, 2*(1), 127–135.
Oziewicz, M. (2017). Speculative fiction. In Rabinowitz, P. (Ed.), *Oxford research encyclopedia of literature*. Oxford University Press.
Palmer, P. (2012). *The Queer uncanny: New perspectives on the Gothic*. University of Wales Press.
Palumbo, D. (Ed.). (1986a). *Eros in the mind's eye: Sexuality and the fantastic in art and film* (Vol. 21). Praeger.
Palumbo, D. (Ed.). (1986b). *Erotic universe: Sexuality and fantastic literature* (Vol. 18). Praeger.
Pearson, W. G. (1999). Alien cryptographies: The view from queer. *Science Fiction Studies, 26*(1), 1–22.
Pearson, W. G. (2002). Science fiction as pharmacy: Plato, Derrida, Ryman. *Foundation: The International Review of Science Fiction, 86*, 66–75.
Pearson, W. G. (2002). Sexuality and the hermaphrodite in science fiction, or, the revenge of Herculine Barbin. In Hollinger, V. & Gordon, J. (Eds.), *Edging into the future: Science fiction and contemporary cultural transformation* (pp. 108–123). University of Pennsylvania Press.
Pearson, W. G. (2019). Cruising Canadian sf's queer futurity: Hiromi Goto's *The Kappa Child* and Larissa Lai's *Salt Fish Girl*. In Ransom, A. J. & Grace, D. (Eds.), *Canadian science fiction, fantasy, and horror* (pp. 185–201). Palgrave Macmillan.
Pearson, W. G., Hollinger, V., & Gordon, J. (Eds.). (2008). *Queer universes: Sexualities in science fiction* (Vol. 37). Liverpool University Press.
Pflugfelder, G. M. (2007). *Cartographies of desire: Male-Male sexuality in Japanese discourse, 1600–1950*. University of California Press.
Piercy, M. (2016). *Woman on the edge of time*. Random House.
Rice, A. (1976). *Interview with the vampire*. Alfred A. Knopf.
Rieder, J. (2017). *Science fiction and the mass cultural genre system*. Wesleyan University Press.
Roberts, J., & MacCallum-Stewart, E. (2016). *Gender and sexuality in contemporary popular fantasy: Beyond boy wizards and kick-ass chicks*. Routledge.

Rushdie, S. (1988). *The satanic verses*. Viking Penguin.
Russ, J. (1975). *The female man*. Bantam.
Ryman, G. (1989). *The child garden*. Unwin Hyman.
Ryman, G. (1992). *Was: A novel*. Harper Collins.
Ryman, G. (2004). The mundane manifesto. *The New York Review of Science Fiction, 19*, 4–5.
Sanders, W. (2019, November 14). Theorist Susan Stryker on one of her most groundbreaking essays, 25 years later. *Them*.
Scott, R. (Director). (1982). *Blade runner*. The Ladd Company, Shaw Brothers, Blade Runner Partnership.
Sedgwick, E. K. (1997). Paranoid reading and reparative reading, or, You're so paranoid, you probably think this introduction is about you. In M. A. Barale, J. Goldberg, & M. Moon (Eds.), *Novel gazing: Queer readings in fiction* (pp. 1–37). Duke University Press.
Shawl, N. (2016). *Everfair: A novel*. Macmillan.
Shelley, M. (1818). *Frankenstein, or the modern Prometheus*. Simon & Schuster.
Solomon, R. (2017). *An unkindness of ghosts*. Akashic.
Somerville, S. (1994). Scientific racism and the emergence of the homosexual body. *Journal of the History of Sexuality, 5*(2), 243–266.
Sterling, B. (1989). Slipstream. *SF Eye, 5*(July), 77–80.
Sterling, B. (2011). Slipstream 2. *Science Fiction Studies, 38*(1), 6–10.
Stockton, K. B. (2009). *The queer child, or growing sideways in the twentieth century*. Duke University Press.
Stryker, S. (1994). My words to Victor Frankenstein above the village of Chamonix: Performing transgender rage. *GLQ, 1*(3), 237–254.
Sturgeon, T. (1950). *The dreaming jewels*. Greenberg.
Sturgeon, T. (1960). *Venus plus X*. Pyramid Books.
Sturgeon, T. (1965). The world well lost. In *E pluribus unicorn* (pp. 52–70). Ballantine Books. (Original work published 1953)
Sun, S. (2019). Stop using phony science to justify transphobia. *Scientific American*.
Takahashi, R. (1987–1996). *Ranma 1/2*. Weekly Shōnen.
Walden, T. (2018). *On a sunbeam*. First Second.
Walton, J. (2014). *My real children*. Tor Books.
Weaver, H. (2015). Pit bull promises: Inhuman intimacies and queer kinships in an animal shelter. *GLQ, 21*(2–3), 343–363.
Whitehead, J. (Ed.). (2020). *Love after the end: An anthology of two-spirit & Indigiqueer speculative fiction*. Arsenal Pulp Press.
Womack, Y. (2013). *Afrofuturism: The world of black sci-fi and fantasy culture*. Chicago Review Press.
Wu, Y., Yao, J., & Lingenfelter, A. (2018). A very brief history of Chinese science fiction. *Chinese Literature Today, 7*(1), 44–53.
Yaszek, L. (2005). An Afrofuturist reading of Ralph Ellison's *Invisible Man*. *Rethinking History, 9*(2–3), 297–313.

NOTES

1. General practice in the world of science fiction criticism is to use the acronym "sf" (lowercase). Oziewicz provided a quite extensive list: "In this latter sense, speculative fiction includes fantasy, science fiction, and horror, but also their derivatives, hybrids, and cognate genres like the Gothic, dystopia, weird fiction, post-apocalyptic fiction, ghost stories, superhero tales, alternate history, steampunk, slipstream, magic realism, fractured fairy tales, and more" ("Speculative Fiction"; online, March 29, 2017).

2. Oziewicz also took up the idea of the "fuzzy set": "First applied to genre studies by Brian Attebery, a fuzzy set is a category defined not by clear boundaries but by resemblance to prototypical examples and degrees of membership: from being *exactly like* to being *somewhat* or *marginally like*. Likewise, speculative fiction in its most recent understanding is a fuzzy set supercategory that houses all non-mimetic genres—genres that in one way or another depart from imitating consensus reality" ("Speculative Fiction"; online, March 29, 2017).
3. Although the kind of literary criticism that understands literature as about the hero's journey tends to use *hero* very much in a masculinely gendered way, it is used here as a gender-neutral term with a little more weight than *protagonist*.
4. There are many acronyms working as umbrella terms for people with non-normative genders and sexualities; this one was chosen for its inclusion of Two-Spirit and intersex people. LGBT and LGBTQ are more common variants.
5. Sedgwick (1997) contrasted "reparative reading"—reading for the dangers and possibilities of hope—to the more common academic practice of "paranoid reading"—reading to reveal what concepts and ideologies underlie specific texts. The latter practice is deconstructive and often revealing, although Sedgwick noted that what is revealed may not be much of a revelation.
6. *Uranian Worlds* is the only print bibliography of queer speculative fiction. There have since been several online bibliographies of alternative sexualities in sf; currently the main one is Wikipedia's less than comprehensive list of "LGBT-themed speculative fiction," while Feministspeculativefiction.org also maintains lists of both fiction and nonfiction (criticism).
7. Lesbianism was never criminalized in the United Kingdom; when a motion to include it was bruited in 1921, Members of Parliament concluded that it was safer not to criminalize it, since doing so would publicize its existence (and presumably women would flock to it by the thousands). See, for example, Derry 2018.
8. For more on the depiction of transgender people in *Venus Plus X*, see Pearson 2002.
9. Bradley's work has never attracted much critical attraction and critics have been ambivalent about how to address her work since her children, Mark and Moira Bradley, spoke out in 2014 about sexual abuse by both their parents and about their mother's facilitation of their father's pedophilia.
10. "TERF" stands for "trans exclusionary radical feminist." While this is, on the face of it, merely descriptive, many of the people it describes have labeled it a slur and are attempting to rebrand themselves as "gender critical feminists." The name does not alter their focus on denying the existence and rights of trans people.
11. For example, one could question whether it is accidental that the timing of J. K. Rowling's now notorious pronouncements about trans women coincided with the passage of a bill in the United Kingdom in 2020 (and overturned by court ruling in 2021) restricting access to puberty blockers to people 16 and over, thus rendering these agents pointless. To make clear how pervasive legal assaults on LGBTQ2SI people are, one need only note that between January 1 and March 20, 2022, some 240 anti-LGBT laws were tabled across the USA, bringing to 670 the total of proposed anti-LGBT laws proposed since 2018 (Lavietes & Ramos, 2022).
12. Notably, the Canadian LGBT rights organization EGALE waited for the symbolic recognition premised by marriage equality before starting a campaign to help queer youth and to end bullying.
13. The issue of queering *Star Trek* is addressed in Pearson's *Alien Cryptographies*; much has changed since 1999, but it took until the 2017 season of *Star Trek: Discovery* for openly gay characters to appear on the show.
14. See Le Guin's "A Whitewashed Earthsea" in *Slate*.
15. For a good account of attempts to erase women's presence in sf as authors, illustrators, readers, and fans, see particularly Justine Larbalestier's *The Battle of the Sexes in Science Fiction* (2002).

16. For a discussion of the queerness of *Kindred*, see Susan Knabe and Wendy Gay Pearson's "Queer Kinship and Cruel Optimism in Octavia Butler's *Kindred*."
17. The initial identification of AIDS with the "Four Hs" produced stigmatization of three groups (homosexuals, heroin drug users, and Haitians—standing in for racialized people generally); only hemophiliacs were discursively constructed as "innocent" victims of the virus. The very idea of "risk groups" was debunked early in the AIDS crisis.
18. The term *marriage equality* is preferable to the terms *same-sex marriage* and *gay marriage* because both of the latter sound like they're alternate and possibly unequal forms of marriage. Nobody talks about "heterosexual marriage" outside of the political debate over marriage equality. The same symbolic use of the figure of the child occurs in other places, notably the fight in Ontario against a revised sex education curriculum that would have taught children that LGBT people exist and that gender is a complex thing experienced differently by different people, as well as by different cultures. Lauren Berlant also discussed the political uses of the symbolic, but definitely not real, child in *Queen of America Goes to Washington City* (p. 20), although Berlant sees this occurring primarily through the depiction of a slightly multiracial girl, as opposed to a White boy. Either way, the "innocence" of the child, which must be preserved at all costs, serves to torque politics in ways that do not serve minoritized peoples.
19. Butler's (2015) argument in this article has been taken up by many other queer scholars in a variety of fields. Eng 2010 for example, considers queer kinship in the context of liberalism and racialization, while Weaver 2015 extends the kinship question beyond the human species.
20. A fourth novel, *Door into Starlight*, remains unpublished.
21. In Eleanor Arnason's *Ring of Swords* (1993), the male protagonist, Nick, makes the point that his relationship with a male alien should not be called "homosexuality" but "hom*e*osexuality" since they are like ("homeo") not the same ("homo").
22. Heinlein's acronym stands for "There ain't no such thing as a free lunch."
23. To be clear, in gay parlance "cruising" refers to the practice of looking for sex in public areas, such as parks and public washrooms.
24. From a trans perspective, the phrase "biological sex" is always fraught; indeed, science is increasingly less certain that there are clear-cut distinctions between "biological" sexes. See, for example, Sun 2019.
25. Shawl is an African American writer who identifies as genderfluid.

Wendy Gay Pearson

Queer Methods

ARTS-BASED QUEER COMMUNICATION STUDIES

INTRODUCTION

In Manning et al. (2020), the authors begin by stating that the "communication discipline needs more scholarship that explores genders and sexualities in meaningful ways" (p. 1). The blending of queer communication studies and arts-based research (ABR) offers a unique way to engage in this exploration and critique dominant structures and institutions that influence social lives. Queer ABR relies on aesthetic qualities to reveal the unseen and unspoken aspects of situations and experiences that remain invisible to traditional approaches (Eisner, 2008). Queer ABR also privileges the personal, emotional, experiential, and embodied knowledge and values alternative and nonnormative ways of knowing (Browne & Nash, 2016; Faulkner & Trotter, 2017). By emphasizing these diverse ways of knowing, researchers can deconstruct the strict boundaries imposed by traditional research processes. Queer ABR puts critical theory into action with an emphasis on the use of the aesthetic power of art. In addition, queer ABR allows individuals to question the taken-for-granted conventions that shape social understanding of gender, sex, and sexuality in a subjective and participatory way. This article provides an overview of arts-based approaches to queer communication studies, including queer methodology, autoethnography, poetic inquiry, performance, and documentary and film.

QUEER METHODOLOGY

Methodologies consist of the rules and procedures that shape how researchers investigate a particular phenomenon (Browne & Nash, 2016). Methodological processes are also informed by a project's epistemological and ontological groundings. This process also influences the chosen research methods and means of data collection. With these ideas in mind, queer methodologies give attention to "how social categories of being, and lived experience, are constituted within certain historical, cultural and spatialized contexts, including normative ideas about what are deemed to be embodied gendered and sexual practices and behaviours" (Nash, 2016, p. 133). For these reasons, communication studies research must critically examine and, if need be, alter existing methodologies so that the study of queer bodies acknowledges the interanimation of oppressive and liberatory practices embedded within contemporary culture (Manning et al., 2020; Murphy et al., 2016).

Given that some traditional methodologies exclude queer populations (LeMaster et al., 2019; Manning et al., 2020), Halberstam (1998) proposed the idea of scavenger methodology, which

> uses different methods to collect and produce information on subjects who have been deliberately or accidentally excluded from traditional studies of human behavior. The queer methodology attempts to combine methods that are often cast as being at odds with each other, and it refuses the academic compulsion toward disciplinary coherence. (p. 13)

In other words, in a queer methodology, queerness stems from the research subject, data, and multiplicity of methods that fall outside the parameters of traditional research (Dahl, 2016). From the perspective of Halberstam (1998), a queer methodology entails that the researcher scavenges among methods and approaches and takes what is most useful for the project at hand. This approach makes sense given that "lived practices rarely, if ever, fit into our theoretical binaries" (West, 2013, p. 539).

Queer methodologies seek to challenge and critique the taken-for-granted normative structures and practices that constitute our social world (Browne & Nash, 2016; Chevrette, 2013). As Holman Jones and Harris (2019) explain, "Queer not only points to an activist stance toward the theorizing of (gay, lesbian, bi and in some instances intersex and trans*) identities and the workings of power, but also the relationally lived experience of queer as fluid and unfinished, playful and political" (p. 3). A queer methodology does not attempt to impose boundaries on the research process; instead, it welcomes fluidity and accepts the diverse perspectives and approaches to research situations (Berry, 2014). By deviating from conventional research processes, queer methodologies provide researchers with the means to explore and interrogate the "the messiness of social lives, experiences, power relations, and hierarchies" (Holman Jones & Harris, 2019, p. 15). Given the pervasiveness of cisnormativity and heteronormativity, other forms are often delegitimized or erased (Elia, 2003). Rather than trying to fit queer research into a cisnormative and heteronormative framework, a queer methodological approach questions traditional perspectives and allows for a more nuanced exploration of identity (Chevrette, 2013; Yep, 2003). Based on existing scholarship, the primary queer methodologies include queer criticism; activist research; historical research; social scientific research; and the focus of this article, arts-based research (Browne & Nash, 2016; Manning, 2017).

ARTS-BASED RESEARCH

The idea of arts-based research (ABR) as a methodology started in the 1970s, 1980s, and 1990s as art therapists and researchers conceptualized how artistic inquiry could be used as a research method (Bresler, 2011). ABR initially centered on the literary arts such as fiction and poetry before expanding to nonlinguistic arts forms such as dance, film, and drama. According to Faulkner and Trotter (2017), "arts-based research (ABR) represents diverse qualitative methodologies that rely on an aesthetic process of imagination and artistic expression through various art mediums as a way to understand and examine a research problem, subject, or text" (p. 1). ABR practices are a set of methodological tools that scholars use in all phases of a research project from conceptualization to presentation and draw on literary and visual art forms such as dance, drama, writing, painting, poetry, and drawing (Leavy, 2015). Simply put, ABR practices use a systematic process to incorporate art in the research process, or as McNiff (2008) notes, "the actual making of artistic expressions in all of the different forms of the arts, as a primary way of understanding and examining experience by both researchers and the people that they involve in their studies" (p. 29). The most distinguishing feature of ABR is the use of aesthetic qualities to illuminate often unseen/unspoken situations and experiences, things that we cannot talk about in other forms (Eisner, 2008). ABR offers scholars a means to understand in more imaginative ways by creating space for personal, emotional, experiential, and embodied expressions of knowledge that value alternative, participatory, and indigenous ways of knowing. ABR can also expand our pedagogical practices by providing new and innovative ways to talk about research, connect to an individual's experience, and evoke empathic responses (Faulkner & Trotter, 2017).

Tracing the history of ABR in media and communication is difficult, as much work is not explicitly labeled as ABR. Scholars have taken ABR approaches in areas such as critical rhetoric (e.g., Johnson & LeMaster, 2020), interpersonal communication (e.g., Berry, 2014), and intercultural communication (e.g., Atay, 2018). What the work has in common is the use of ABR as a methodological practice to focus on the power of aesthetic presentation, which allows for multiple viewpoints and multiple meanings. Furthermore, ABR as a methodological tool does not require researchers to treat their artistic self and research self as separate entities. ABR and queer methodologies offer an opening up of research and new ways of thinking about traditional research methods and approaches, making ABR an appropriate methodology for queer research. "ABR utilizes the aesthetic qualities of emotion and sensation to illuminate undiscovered, ineffable, invisible, and unspoken experiences that are not easily talked about in other forms. It is useful for the study of identity, subjugated perspectives, and difficult experiences" (Faulkner & Trotter, 2017, p. 3). Often, media and communication scholars use arts-based approaches to "make visible and critique unjust operations of power, and work toward more equitable realities" (Moore, 2017, p. 13). Scholars also use ABR as activist work to create a space where alternative knowledge can be developed and shared and serve as a form of public scholarship (Faulkner & Squillante, 2020). For instance, as Faulkner and Trotter (2017) explain:

Arts-based research persuades the audience to move beyond their existing assumptions regarding phenomena and challenges them to examine the world from different perspectives and alternate points of view. The arts address the qualitative nuances of situations by addressing what is subtle but significant, by developing dispositions and habits of mind that reveal to the individual a world [they] may not have noticed. (p. 5)

Given the tenets of ABR and its openness to alternative knowledges, it aligns well with the work of scholars in queer studies.

According to Ahmed (2006), "to make things queer is to disturb the order of things" (p. 161). Queer studies examine relationships of power relative to gender, sex, and sexuality (Berry, 2014; Manning, 2017). Queer studies also attempt to deconstruct the dominant cultural labels that stigmatize and shame nonnormative individuals and/or groups and provide an alternative to the heterosexual norm (Berry, 2014; Elia, 2003; West, 2018; Yep, 2003). Manning (2017) notes that "queer art-based research can challenge stereotypes, stimulate and expand awareness, build empathy, and promote dialogue. Art-based research also can allow for unique forms of expression of sexual pleasure, something endorsed by queer theory" (p. 7; see also Yep, Lovaas, & Elia, 2014). Specific methods of ABR include visual and literary arts such as creative nonfiction and autoethnography, poetic inquiry, performance, and documentary and film. We now turn to a discussion of these methods, staring with queer autoethnography.

QUEER AUTOETHNOGRAPHY

Autoethnography is a type of academic writing in which a researcher uses insights about their personal experience to connect to larger culture. Autoethnographers use personal experience to make sense of and critique lived experience, and the method offers "researchers and readers alike an opportunity to witness the effect/affect of cultural performance on the individual" (Santoro, 2016, p. 109). It is a method focused on writing as research practice and using the power of personal story and theory to show how our stories can be the change we need in the world (Holman Jones, 2016). The researcher's experience is central in autoethnography: "Autoethnography, simply put, is an observational, participatory, and reflexive research method that uses writing about the self in contact with others to illuminate the many layers of human social, emotional, theoretical, political, and cultural praxis" (Poulus, 2021, pp. 4–5). Furthermore, Poulus (2021) describes autoethnography as:

An autobiographical genre of academic writing that draws on and analyzes or interprets the lived experience of the author and connects researcher insights to self-identity, cultural rules and resources, communication practices, traditions, premises, symbols, rules, shared meanings, emotions, values, and larger social, cultural, and political issues. (p. 4)

Johnson and LeMaster (2020) consider autoethnography as a means for "inserting the bodily flesh and its many positions as ways of (not)knowing via autopoetic narrative, autocritography, performance, and rhetorical autoethnography" (p. 5). While most autoethnography, especially that in media and communication is not framed as ABR, we argue that it can be an inherently queer method because of the aesthetic focus on personal lived experience that often differs from expected cultural scripts. Adams and Holman Jones (2011) suggest that autoethnography is a queer method in and of itself because of its commitment "to uncertain, fluid, and becoming subjectivities, multiple forms of knowledge and representations" (p. 108). In their conceptualization of queer autoethnography, Adams and Bolen (2017) note the potential of this approach:

> Queer autoethnographies offer representations of personal/cultural experience that identify and celebrate queer values; complicate taken-for-granted cultural norms and expectations tied to relationships and desires; offer strategies for reappropriating bad sentiments; and provide ways of using personal experience at the service of social justice. (p. 107)

When engaging with the possibilities indicated above, autoethnographers use various means of data gathering and qualitative research such as participant observation, interviews, focus groups, narrative analysis, archival research, journaling, and storytelling (Poulus, 2021), as well as varied literary and visual forms in their autoethnography ranging from creative nonfiction, fiction, video and film, comics, poetry, opera, hybrid work, to memoir and personal narrative. This work may include more informal writing and presentation such as social media posts, which Atay (2018) considers to be a type of life writing. Atay (2018) presents digital life writing as a space for queer scholars of color to make sense of and represent their identities and "since digital life writing is narrative based, it enables queer scholars to articulate the notion of affect and how queer relationships, stories and emotions are presented in online domains" (p. 184).

Autoethnography also offers researchers access to a method for studying difficult to observe phenomena and intersectionality as Adams and Bolen (2017) point out:

> ...given the vulnerable, intimate, and taboo topics associated with queer theory, it can be difficult to do fieldwork, participant observation, and deep hanging out in natural settings related to these topics. For example, where do we go to participate in same-sex attraction, gender nonconformity, or heteronormativity? Where can we hang out to observe monogamy, barebacking, melancholy, or failure? Working with personal experience in autoethnography offers important access to these topics, as everyday life becomes an important site for data. (p. 105)

Holman Jones and Harris (2019) argue "From its beginnings, autoethnography sought to challenge temporal and geographical and biographical claims and objectivities, in favor of a queer power of subjectivity in which the self was the only (if shifting) lens through which one could see" (p. 5). Queer autoethnographies give researchers the opportunity to blend the "ideas, intentions, practices, and affects of queer theory with the purposes and practices of autoethnography" (Adams & Bolen, 2017, p. 105). Johnson and LeMaster (2020) discuss the power of intersectional autoethnography to allow "authors to unpack the complex layers of power systems that chaperone experience" (p. 8); power systems include patriarchy, racism, sexism, binary gender, and colonialism. Thus, queer autoethnography is a literary form of ABR that focuses on theory, story, narrative, aesthetics, knowledge building, and how the personal connects to larger culture in an attempt "to evoke empathic and affective responses at a time of political numbness"; it expands the political and scholarly potential of autoethnography by queering research practices (Holman Jones & Harris, 2019, p. 4). It is not an apolitical endeavor. According to Holman Jones and Harris (2019),

> Queering autoethnography draws on the practices and politics of queer and queering to offer narrative and theoretical disruptions of taken-for-granted knowledges that continue to marginalize, oppress and/or take advantage of those of us who do not participate or find ourselves reflected in mainstream cultures and social structures—which includes research methodologies. (p. 4)

Furthermore, Browne and Nash (2016) note that "queer autoethnography allows for journeys of self-understanding that are relational and not restricted by the limits of categories while proposing challenges to normative ideologies and discourses" (p. 21). Autoethnography has been critiqued for being too personal and queer theory has been critiqued for being too abstract (Adams & Bolen, 2017). Queer autoethnography addresses these critiques by focusing on the autoethnographic, the reflexive, and the queer:

> The autoethnographic means telling a story about how much we—children and parents, researchers and subjects, authors and readers—worry about fitting in, about normal, about being accepted, loved, and valued. The queer means telling a story about being half in and half out of identities, subject positions, and discourses and having the courage to be fluid in a world relentlessly searching for stability and certainty. The reflexive means understanding the way stories change and can change, recognizing how we hide behind and become inside the words we speak and writing the possibilities created by our means and modes of address. (Adams & Homan Jones, 2011, p. 114)

For some, queer autoethnography is a space of transformation and liberation that can create space for alternate ways of being and knowing. While not framed as ABR, Johnson and LeMaster (2020) take a critical rhetorical approach in their volume of queer intersectional autoethnography to imagine a queer futurity in which "the gender future is rooted in pleasure" and readers can think "about their own gender free futures, what potential exist within and beyond their own constraints, and how gender moves through the world" (pp. 10–11). Their focus on intersectional praxis makes the text an activist project. Autoethnographers can give attention to intersectionality by "focusing on experience in relationships of power" (Holman Jones & Harris, 2019, p. 2).

Queer autoethnography is necessarily critical autoethnography because of its focus on social justice, praxis, and change, and the critique of unjust cultural practices, use of critical theory as action, and focus on building new knowledge to transform social practices. "Arts-based research (ABR), ethnographic, and narrative research methods can realize the potential of critical work to critique, expand, and alter dominant discourse that circumscribes family communication research and praxis" (Faulkner, 2016, p. 9). In a collaborative autoethnography, Eguchi and Long (2019) use intersectional reflexivity to imagine a queer relationality "that work on and against hegemonic, heteronormative, and homonormative paradigms of relating and push toward an embrace of queer family" (pp. 1591–1592). They write about their experiences as a Queer Fat Femme and a Queer Asian Femme:

> We together call for queer family as a temporal and present mode of relational and political resistance to interrupt existing power relations that structurally constrain the multiple fluidity of queerness across space, time, and history. This allows possibilities of coalitions within and among different kinds of queers to be further promoted. (p. 1603)

In another example of queer autoethnography, Abdi and Cuomo (2020) write about the possibilities and constraints queer bodies of color experience in the communication classroom and detail their experiences as queer instructors of color "to showcase the ways in which coalition can be built between our intersectional selves, in an effort to sustain queer relationality" (p. 40). These examples show how scholars have used queer autoethnography to challenge the status quo and give visibility to marginalized discourses.

In addition, queering autoethnography is also a queering of method. Faulkner (2018c) uses poetic collage as queer methodology, manipulating headlines of current events around women's reproductive health and justice, curriculum from liberal sexuality education, and conversations with her daughter about sex and sexuality to critique sexuality education and policies about women's health in the United States. The use of autoethnography in the form of dialogue poems between mother and daughter demonstrates reflexivity. Social science "research questions" frame and push the poetic analysis to show critical engagement with sexuality literature, and the collaging of news headlines about sexuality connects personal experience about sexuality education to larger cultural issues. Santoro (2016) uses queer auto/ethnography to show how the actual geography of a fieldwork site can be a space of heteronormativity and how sexualities matter in a variety of contexts. They reflexively write about having to try and "pass" when doing fieldwork in a rural setting: "When I perceive my body—my sexuality—as a threat to others, I adjust my presence to take on the characteristics of a less queer performance" (p. 119). In an ethnography in a dance studio, Olzman (2020) highlights how a fat queer body is seen as out of place in dance spaces: "The way are bodies are read and move always affect the space we are in, and the communication we participate in" (p. 57). "I love to dance. But my body is not a body expected to do dance. As a fat feminine person, it seems that most would prefer I follow the whispers of my fatness and die" (p. 57). They use autoethnography to show how fatness is connected to gender and heterosexual normativities. These autoethnographers use personal experience in service of cultural and methodological critique, which is also present in poetic inquiry.

POETIC INQUIRY AND QUEER COMMUNICATION STUDIES

Poetic inquiry is a feminist methodology focused on doing, showing, and teaching embodiment and reflexivity, refusing the mind-body dialectic, and urging social agitation and change and can be framed using feminist, queer, narrative, and identity theories (Faulkner, 2018a). Poetic inquiry as a form of ethnography and qualitative research is "the use of poetry crafted from research endeavors, either before project analysis, as a project analysis, and/or poetry that is part of or that constitutes an entire research project" (Faulkner, 2020, pp. 3–4). Researchers can use poetry as a research method, to represent research and the research process, and as praxis (Faulkner, 2020). Poetry used as research is a method of turning research interviews, transcripts, observations, personal experience, and reflections into poems or poetic forms. Scholars in communication studies have been using poetic inquiry to study identities and identity negotiation processes (Faulkner, 2006; LeMaster, 2020), critique dominant understandings of motherhood (Faulkner, 2017), show reflective research practices (Faulkner, 2005), and as a form of public memory (Harris & Holman Jones, 2017; Johnson, 2020).

There are numerous examples of scholars using poetic inquiry in identity projects as a way to critique, alter, render visible, and demonstrate the fluid nature of identity negotiation processes. For example, Johnson and LeMaster (2020) include nine poems in their volume on gender futurity and intersectional autoethnography that present intersectional identities. In one poem, McNeill (2020) writes about the constraints of having to fit their nonbinary gender into binary expectations, and Green (2020) presents the struggle of traveling as a Black trans man. Faulkner (2020) explains how poetry is a useful tool for exploring one's identity because of the possibilities of form:

> Poetry defies singular definitions and explanations, it mirrors the slipperiness of identity, the difficulty of capturing the shifting nature of who we are and want to be, and resonates more fully with the way identity is created, maintained, and altered through our interacted narratives. (p. 27)

Faulkner (2006) crafted poems from narrative interviews with LGBTQ+ Jewish Americans on their experiences of being gay and Jewish, and then analyzed the poems for themes and connections to identity theories using poetic analysis. Faulkner used poetry as embodied research practice to show being LGBTQ+ and Jewish in ways that pay attention to the senses and offer some narrative and poetic truths about the experience of multiple stigmatized identities. The poem, "Reconstructionist", is a sonnet that depicts enactments of new and different Jewish rituals that affirm queer and Jewish identities by rewriting them into compatible identities. The poem shows the story of isolation, stigmatized identities, and the promise of love that illustrates persistence and the search for acceptance of identities despite a tumultuous struggle in the absence of wide social support.

Reconstructionist
She thinks it's different now, and asks me how
I find the rallies, picnics, police, gay
lovers with youth who walk in the open now.
She found no path, no help with the labels,
the parties of conservative newspapers
that print *Jewish activist lesbian*
as if boxes can contain her labors
to make Seders and new year with new kin.
Now she tells mom, keeps a job, says enough

and buys a house with oaks and shaded jade,
makes a *minyan* and trims a holly bough
with a Christian woman. The years they've made,
are like the book club books read together
for 12 years when they had nothing better. (Faulkner, 2006, p. 104–105)

In a forum in the *Journal of Autoethnography* titled, " 'We Don't See LGBTQ Differences': Cisheteronormativity and the Concealing of Phobias and Irrational Fears behind Rhetorics of Acceptance," LeMaster (2020) uses three haiku poems about engaging "preferred" gender pronouns, ally theatre, and the politics of citationality to unmask the violence of racialized cisheterosexism in the academy and to render the invisible workings of white supremacy and trans* phobia visible. LeMaster writes that critical love for folks of color is about recognizing and affirming how the "(not so) subtle man-ifestations of cisheterosexist violence organize mundane life" (p. 76). For example, LeMaster writes in "A note on 'preferred'": To be fucking clear/My pronouns are not preferred/They are what they are" (p. 77). They tell us that their "intent for using haiku regards my desire to implicate the point while punctuating my (not so) subtle dissatisfaction in a focused and playful manner" (pp. 76–77). The use of the haiku form works as a pointed critique given the brevity of the form. Using poetry to make cisheterosexism visible works as an act of critical love.

In the poetry chapbook, *Bringing Up Baby*, Faulkner (2023) uses erasure poetry as feminist poetic inquiry to critique white middle-class notions of being a mother and motherhood as an institution by queering the idea of the baby book and pages in *What to Expect When You're Expecting*, a popular pregnancy advice manual. The project includes 12 erasure and collage poems about pregnancy and mothering created from felted wool, applique pins, crayon, markers, stickers, photos, book pages, crib placards, pediatrician instructions, language, and family artifacts. The collection contains two types of collage and erasure poetry: *What to Expect*, which are erasure poems from a pregnancy advice manual and *Baby Book*, which includes erasure and collage of feminist texts, Faulkner's baby book, and material scraps of Faulkner's daughter's early years. Faulkner (2017) suggests that "taking an expected activity—scrapbook making—and queering it by naming the personal detritus of crafting as scholarship, as queer feminist praxis, and as cultural critique, blurs the lines separating art, scholarship, and mothering" (p. 167). The erasure of advice from parenting authorities and pediatricians uncovers what is elided in popular discourse about pregnancy and mothering, critiques the dominant discourse of expected positive feelings about pregnancy and being a mother, and resists the dominant understanding of White middle-class motherhood by queering MotherWork, by situating MotherWork as raced and gendered, and by querying what mother identities mean.

> The baby book as queer enterprise refuses the binary of *mother* versus every other role. This project embraces the nonbinary dialectic surrounding MotherWork, the dominant discourses of self-abnegation, breeding as feminine fulfillment, child as star in a mother's play, women as never good enough, and the marginalized discourses of mothering as painful, unfulfilling, and boring. The use of "scavenger methodology" shows the promise of nonbinary queer autoethnography for expanding disciplinary boundaries. (Faulkner, 2017, p. 176)

Poetic inquiry is also used as a reflective research practice to acknowledge a researcher's contributions to the meaning making process. Faulkner (2005) presents the method section of a study on LGBTQ+ Jewish American identity as a series of poems in order to make the research process transparent, to demonstrate reflexivity, to show more than the formal neatly presented research project, and how identities shift in field work. We see the internal dialogue not expressed to research participants in the following confessional poem:

> *I'm not what Lesa Expected*
> no blonde bunned hair
> like the researcher in her mind,
> like my second grade teacher, glasses,
> but blue and stylish and young.
> I'm 31 and old enough to teach,
> ask others about their identity,
> though I have scant lines on face and vita,
> wear shirts without collars.
> I talk like a friend- except those questions
> about being gay and Jewish-
> as I shift, catch words with my tape recorder,
> khaki cargo pants belie my worry with uniform.
> Another participant says I walked lesbian-
> like, confident stride and spiky cut hair,
> down 7th Avenue into the diner where we ate
> rice pudding and talked about family. She knew
> who I was without my description–
> short red hair, 5 feet 5 inches, sapphire spectacles–
> How do I tell them that I live and flirt
> and fight with a man now, that my
> ex-girlfriend called me semi-straight
> or semi-gay and interested in labels? (Faulkner, 2005, pp. 943–944)

Poetry has been used as a form of public memory and memorialization and a way to address questions about the public sphere. Harris and Holman Jones (2017) use poetry as a vehicle to present queer terror, "an affective condition not limited to LGBT or other minoritarian subjects, and its relationship to fear, hate and factionalism (or isolationism)," in the massacre at the Pulse nightclub in Orlando, Florida on June 12, 2016. They ask "whether, through the act and its viral media representations, queer terror creates minoritarian public sphere that can be shared by queer people of color (QPOC) and allies alike" (p. 562). Harris and Holman Jones use found poems constructed from media accounts of the massacre and queer theory to demonstrate what queer allyship can look like against a backdrop of queer terror.

> Feeling and doing the work of allyship means insisting on an end to the conditions that made Orlando possible. This allyship must look beyond narrowing and homogenizing media representations, calls for gun control or apocalyptic notions of a United States (and world) riddled by crime, extremism, and isolationist politics. (p. 566)

In a similar vein, Johnson (2020) wrote a poem about the Pulse massacre from a people-of-color point of view that shows the connectedness of brown, black, and queer bodies: "After the pulse of a rhythm enters your body,/Your body is never the same." In the poem "Pulse," Johnson uses bolded text to emphasize the pain of stigma and being unwelcome that QPOC experience in everyday spaces and the horror of violence perpetrated in a seemingly sanctified safe space like a queer nightclub: **STAY OUT, WE ARE DYING**, and **They are mine to grieve this time**. Johnson also uses cascading lines to mirror the rhythms of a racing pulse and the growing violence against QPOC. These poems about the Pulse massacre perform grief, hope, and memorialization showing that poetic inquiry is closely tied to the performative given that much poetry is meant to be performed orally to bear witness to our experiences. We now turn to an explicit discussion of queer performance.

QUEER PERFORMANCE

Performances are "highly reflexive, highly personal approaches to research that allow for an intriguing blurring between modernist forms of understanding and traditionally art-oriented forms" (Manning & Kunkel, 2014, p. 7). Performance studies represent explicit examples of ABR in media and communication. Performances can include, but are not limited to, dance, plays, film, songs, collage, and expressions. Performance functions as an art event in that the performer and audience cocreate the artwork (Fischer-Lichte, 2018). For instance, "one's relation to works of art...involves something other than passive reception. We are never simply consumers of popular cultural texts, but in and through our very 'reading' of them we actively (re)create them" (Sullivan, 2003, p. 189). In this sense, the completion of the performance depends on the active engagement of the audience. Through this engagement, both performers and audiences can learn more about the self and the other (Johnson, 2011). According to Sullivan (2003), to queer means "to make strange, to frustrate, to counteract, to delegitimize, to camp up-heteronormative knowledges and institutions, and the subjectivities and socialites that are (in)formed by them and that (in)form them" (p. vi). Therefore, this section will show how performance and performative writing can function as queer methodologies in that they provide space for queer worldmaking; a space for expression that is not constrained by cisgender and heteronormative standards.

Muñoz (2006) writes that the culture of (cis)heteronormativity "makes queers think both the past and future do not belong to them. All we are allowed to imagine is barely surviving the present" (p. 19). To cope with this cisheteronormative culture, LeMaster et al. (2019) blends the art of collage with autoethnography (e.g., collaged relational autoethnography) "to explore the performative constitution of nonbinary gender subjectivity in relational contexts" (p. 342). The authors explain how the practice of collaged relational autoethnography creates a relational context committed to unlearning cisheteronormative practices and resulted in the "performance of queer worldmaking" (p. 347). In addition, performative writing can challenge cisheteronormative traditions. For instance, Pollack (1998) suggests that "as the effect of social relations and as a mode of cultural, historical action, performative writing throws off the norms of conventional scholarship for an explicit, alternative normativity" (p. 96).

Pérez (2019) notes that to understand performance, one must understand that it occurs "on stages and in stages" (p. 371). As Pérez further explains, the notion of stage and staging merges texts and contexts "in ways that allow for attention to the dynamic intersections of the discursive, embodied, and relational dimensions of performance" (p. 371). We can witness these intersections in queer autobiographical performances of family, which promote the exposure, negotiation, and reconsideration of conceptualizations of families and the practices enacted in families (Pérez, 2019). Queer performance aligns with the guiding tenets of Critical Interpersonal and Family Communication, or CIFC, primarily the need to accept alternative family forms beyond the nuclear family model and the call to collapse the binary between public and private (Suter et al., 2015). By bringing issues of family to the forefront of the stage, queer performers can not only challenge the dominant family narrative but also shift these discourses from the "private and familiar to the public and unfamiliar" (Pérez, 2019, p. 373). This space of the unfamiliar, then, provides room for exploration and growth. In addition, Brouwer (1998) describes the different manifestations of the stage beyond that of a theatrical performance. In research about HIV/AIDS tattoos and self-stigmatization, Brouwer (1998) notes that "tattoo wearers textualize the surface of the body" (p. 115) and the body thus becomes a stage of different productions that move beyond the theater into the spaces of work and home.

The queer genre depicts the "positive and generative aspects of queer lives" (Giannini, 2011, p. 302). Within the theatre industry, the antigay genre "focuses on issues relating to homophobia and the coming out or unwanted outing of a troubled gay character" (p. 302). However, some queer plays directed toward younger audiences counter the myth that all LGBTQ+ youth will have troubled lives. As Giannini (2011) explains:

> A queer play for young audiences breaks away from the restrictions of the anti-gay bashing genre by including: 1) the articulation and representation of same-sex desire; 2) manifestations of homosexuality both inside and outside of sexual identity categories; 3) fun in homosexuality; 4) communities that embrace homosexuality; 5) the extension of queerness beyond able-bodied, white, middle-class males. (p. 303)

In this way, performances have the potential to intervene in problematic and/or limited representations of queerness and offer alternative portrayals that give visibility to the multifaceted nature of queer lives (Johnson, 2014).

Among the scholars who expanded queer studies into the performance domain, E. Patrick Johnson (2001) calls out the Whiteness of queer theory and its failure to recognize White privilege and the contributions of QPOC. That said, performance can also function as a "site of agency" that enables QPOC to disidentify from the dominant cultural structures and institutions (Johnson, 2001, p. 12; see also Johnson, 2014). According to Muñoz (1999), disidentification means to work for "permanent structural change while at the same time valuing the importance of local and everyday struggles of resistance" (p. 12). Beyond performance in the traditional sense, such as artistic expressions in the theater or concert venue, locations such as streets and picket lines can also serve as spaces for disidentificatory performances (Johnson, 2001, 2011). Furthermore, QPOC can use "practices such as vogueing, snapping, 'throwing shade,' and 'reading'" to demonstrate resistance and counter to the status quo (Johnson, 2001, p. 13). That said, Johnson (2016) explains that despite the advantages of performance, it is unable to break free from the politics of representation. Even so, performance can still expose the oppression ingrained within aspects of everyday life that "the gaze of objectivity" cannot always identify (Johnson, 2016, p. 64).

For researchers who want to expand the purview of traditional approaches, Muñoz (2006) explains that "aesthetic practices and performances offer a particular theoretical lens to understand the ways in which different circuits of belonging connect" (p. 6). Performance can shed light on how relational and cultural experiences shape one's identity and vice versa (Manning et al., 2020). In addition to performance, these connections can also be witnessed in documentary and film.

DOCUMENTARY AND FILM

Queer documentary and film go against conventional modes of storytelling and reevaluate the societal expectations relative to representations of queer lives (Brook, 2018; Geiger, 2020). These artistic forms enable individuals to "*work through and within* the process of identification and community formation" (Tan, 2016, p. 39). Toward the end of the 20th century, queer documentary and film were instrumental in deconstructing heteronormativity, drawing attention to broader issues of inequality and invisibility, and challenging "monocultural thinking while delving further into the complexities of intersectional lives" (Geiger, 2020, p. 180). It is important to note that like queer theory, queer documentary and film do not only apply to individuals who identify as queer (Manning et al., 2020).

While Nichols (2017) conceptualizes six types of documentary modes, the following section focuses on the performative mode, poetic mode, and reflexive mode. First, performative documentaries encourage the audience to "feel or experience the world in a particular way as vividly as possible" (p. 151). The performative mode centers on the subjective embodied experiences that are not always visible in everyday interactions. Unlike other modes, performative documentaries can show the "emotional reality of a particular subject's experiences while simultaneously making connections to the social, cultural, and political world in which that subject is historically situated" (Goldstein, 1997, p. 176). For instance, the documentary *My Prairie Home* draws on performances, interviews, and music to show how Rae Spoon—a trans person—navigates their coming-of-age journey (McMullan, 2014). This approach enables the filmmaker to capture the experiences that conventional documentaries would fail to notice. The audience, then, can reach an "affective and critical understanding of both a particular subject and themselves in the moment of viewing" (Goldstein, 1997, p. 176).

Second, the poetic mode emphasizes mood, affect, and tone as opposed to knowledge displays (Nichols, 1994, 2001). This mode centers on how the voice of the filmmaker gives different aspects of the "historical world a formal, aesthetic integrity peculiar to the film itself" (Nichols, 2017, p. 119). The poetic mode allows the audience to learn by helping individuals understand how it feels to "see and experience the world in a particular, poetic way" (Nichols, 2017, p. 117).

Finally, the reflexive mode seeks to bring the viewers to a heightened awareness about their relation to the film and what it means. What separates the reflexive modes from previous modes is its "intensified reflection on what representing the world involves" (Nichols, 2017, p. 125).

Reflexive documentaries can draw attention to the pervasive discrimination toward LGBTQ+ individuals/groups as well as counter predominant stereotypical and/or oppressive representations of nonnormative genders, sexualities, and identities. For instance, *Call Me Kuchu* (2012) follows David Kato, the first man to be openly gay in Uganda, and Christopher

Senyonjo, an Anglican Bishop, as they work to combat Ugandan legislation that would make homosexuality a crime punishable by death. Reflexive documentaries "challenge assumptions about gender identity and sexual orientation that are often presented as natural and obvious within the dominant, heteronormative culture and are shown to be open to question" (Nichols, 2017, p. 130). Reflexive documentaries emphasize the agency of the audience, not the film itself, in enacting social transformation.

Overall, queer documentaries and films provide an alternative view into queer lives and experiences. This section does not present an exhaustive overview of approaches to queer documentary and film. Documentaries and film can also take on a testimonial lens, for instance, the documentary *Disclosure* examines depictions of transgender people in the television and film industry (Feder, 2020). The film includes commentaries from trans actors and actresses who share their thoughts and experiences about Hollywood's representation of trans people and trans issues.

As a queer ABR methodology, documentaries and film can visually represent the personal narratives and/or the collective experiences of marginalized groups. These representations not only give visibility and voice to these marginalized groups but also counter heteronormativity on a visceral level.

CONCLUSION

In sum, ABR approaches to queer communication studies allow individuals to combine queer concepts, content, and methodologies with subjective lived and embodied experiences. ABR offers several avenues to disrupt and transform the taken-for-granted cisheteronormative foundations of research as well as the "rules and rituals imposed by heteronormative attitudes, structures, and expectations" (Manning et al., 2020, p. 21). ABR alongside queer communication studies encourages individuals to challenge their perceptions of gender and sexuality as well as the conventions that shape these perceptions. ABR, unlike other research methodologies, creates a space where individuals can explore and confront difficult topics in a more digestible and non-traditional manner. Through creative practices such as autoethnography, poetic inquiry, performance, and film, individuals can resist and critique the status quo while simultaneously providing an alternative perspective that recognizes the highly personal and fluid nature of one's identities and relationships.

FURTHER READING

Adams, T. (2011). *Narrating the closet: An autoethnography of same sex attraction*. Routledge.
Faulkner, S. L. (2014). Bad mom(my) litany: Spanking cultural myths of middle-class motherhood. *Cultural Studies ↔ Critical Methodologies*, 14(2), 138–146. https://doi.org/10.1177%2F1532708613512270
Johnson, E. P. (2019). *Honeypot: Black southern women who love women*. Duke.
Johnson, E. P. & Rivera-Servera, R. H. (Eds.). (2016). *Blacktino queer performance*. Duke.
Leavy, P. (2020). *Method meets art: Arts-based research practice* (3rd ed.). Guilford.
Mingé, J. M., & Zimmerman, A. M. (2013). *Concrete and dust: Mapping the sexual terrains of Los Angeles*. Routledge.
Perez, K. (2015). Performing queer latinidad: Dance, sexuality, politics. *Text and Performance Quarterly*, 35(4), 419–421. https://doi.org/10.1080/10462937.2015.1073785

Yep, G. A. (2013). Queering/quaring/kauering/crippin'/transing "other bodies" in intercultural communication. *Journal of International and Intercultural Communication, 6*(2), 118–126. https://doi.org/10.1080/17513057.2013.777087

REFERENCES

Abdi, S., & Cuomo, A. P. (2020). On possibility: Queer relationality. In A. L. Johnson & B. LeMaster (Eds.), *Gender futurity, intersectional autoethnography: Embodied theorizing from the margins* (pp. 37–54). Routledge.

Adams, T. E., & Bolen, D. M. (2017). Tragic queer at the urinal stall, who, now, is the queerest one of all? Queer theory|Autoethnography|Doing queer autoethnography. *QED: A Journal in GLBTQ Worldmaking 4*(1), 100–113. https://doi.org/10.14321/qed.4.1.0100

Adams, T. E., & Holman Jones, S. (2011). Telling stories: Reflexivity, Queer theory, and autoethnography. *Cultural Studies ↔ Critical Methodologies, 11*(2), 108–116. https://doi.org/10.1177/1532708611401329

Ahmed, S. (2006). *Queer phenomenology: Orientations, objects, others*. Duke University Press.

Atay, A. (2018). Digital life writing: The failure of a diasporic, queer, blue Tinker Bell. *Interactions: Studies in Communication & Culture, 9*(2), 183–193. https://doi.org/10.1386/iscc.9.2.183_1

Berry, K. (2014). Introduction: Queering family, home, love, loss/relational troubling. *Cultural Studies ↔ Critical Methodologies, 14*(2), 91–94. https://doi.org/10.1177/1532708613512258

Bresler, L. (2011). Arts-based research and drama education. In S. Schonmann (Ed.), *Key concepts in theatre/drama education* (pp. 321–326). Sense Publishers.

Brook, E. D. (2018). Un/queering family in the media. In A. Harris, S. H. Jones, S. L. Faulkner, & E. Brook (Eds.), *Queering families, schooling publics: Keywords* (pp. 49–67). Routledge.

Brouwer, D. (1998). The precarious visibility politics of self-stigmatization: The case of HIV/AIDS tattoos. *Text and Performance Quarterly, 18*(2), 114–136. https://doi.org/10.1080/10462939809366216

Browne, K. & Nash, C. J. (2016). Queer methods: An introduction. In K. Browne & C. J. Nash (Eds.), *Queer methodologies: Intersecting queer theories and social science research* (pp. 1–23). Routledge.

Chevrette, R. (2013). Outing heteronormativity in interpersonal and family communication: Feminist applications of queer theory "beyond the sexy streets." *Communication Theory 23*, 170–190. https://doi.org/10.1111/comt.12009

Dahl, U. (2016). Femme on femme: Reflections of collaborative methods and queer femme-inist ethnography. In K. Browne & C. J. Nash (Eds.), *Queer methodologies: Intersecting queer theories and social science research* (pp. 143–166). Routledge.

Eisner, E. (2008). Art and knowledge. In J. G. Knowles & A. L. Cole (Eds.), *Handbook of the arts in qualitative research: Perspectives, methodologies, examples, and issues* (pp. 3–12). SAGE.

Eguchi, S., & Long, H. R. (2019). Queer relationality as family: Yas fats! Yas femmes! Yas Asians!. *Journal of Homosexuality, 66*(11), 1589–1608. https://doi.org/10.1080/00918369.2018.1505756

Elia, J. P. (2003). Queering relationships: Toward a paradigmatic shift. In G. A. Yep, K. E. Lovaas, & J. P. Elia (Eds.), *Queer theory and communication: From disciplining queers to queering the discipline* (pp. 61–86). Harrington Park Press.

Faulkner, S. L. (2005). Method: Six poems. *Qualitative Inquiry, 11*(6), 941–949. https://doi.org/10.1177%2F1077800405276813

Faulkner, S. L. (2006). Reconstruction: LGBTQ and Jewish. *International and Intercultural Communication Annual, 29*, 95–120.

Faulkner, S. L. (2016). Postkarten aus Deutschland: A chapbook of ethnographic poetry. *Liminalities, 12*(1). http://liminalities.net/12-1/postkarten.html

Faulkner, S. L. (2017). MotherWork collage (A queer scrapbook). *QED: A Journal in GLBTQ Worldmaking, 4*(1), 166–179. https://doi.org/10.14321/qed.4.1.0166

Faulkner, S. L. (2018a). Crank up the feminism: Poetic inquiry as feminist methodology. *Humanities*, 7(3), 85. https://doi.org/10.3390/h7030085

Faulkner, S. L. (2018b). Mother-poems: Using the confessional as critique in autoethnographic poetry. In S. Holman Jones & M. Pruyn (Eds.), *Creative selves/creative cultures: Critical autoethnography, performance, and pedagogy* (pp. 103–111). Palgrave Macmillan.

Faulkner, S. L. (2018c). Queering sexuality education and family and schools. In A. Harris, S. Holman Jones, S. L. Faulkner, & E. Brook (Eds.), *Queering families, schooling publics: Keywords* (pp. 25–41). Routledge.

Faulkner, S. L. (2020). *Poetic inquiry: Craft, method, and practice, 2nd ed.* Routledge.

Faulkner, S. L. (2023). Setting the agenda: Poetic inquiry as critical family and interpersonal methodology. *Journal of Family Communication*, 23(1), 75–87.

Faulkner, S. L., & Squillante, S. (2020). Creative approaches to writing qualitative research. In P. Leavy (Ed.), *The Oxford handbook of qualitative methods* (2nd Ed., pp. 1023–1044). Oxford University Press.

Faulkner, S. L., & Trotter, S. P. (2017). Arts-based methods in qualitative research. In C. S. Davis & R. F. Potter (Eds.), *International encyclopedia of communication research methods* (pp. 1–8). Wiley-Blackwell. http://doi.org/10.1002/9781118901731.iecrm0250

Feder, S. (Director). (2020). *Disclosure* [Film]. Disclosure Film, Bow & Arrow Entertainment, and Field of Vision.

Fischer-Lichte, E. (2018). Introduction: Transformative aesthetics—Reflections on the metamorphic power of art. In E. Fischer-Lichte & B. Wihstutz (Eds.), *Transformative aesthetics* (pp. 1–25). Routledge

Geiger, J. (2020). Intimate media: New queer documentary and film. *Studies in Documentary and Film* 14(3), 177–201). https://doi.org/10.1080/17503280.2019.1632161

Giannini, A. (2011). Queer representations in TYA. In S. Schonmann (Ed.), *Key concepts in theatre/drama education* (pp. 301–306). Sense Publishers.

Goldstein, L. (1997). Getting into lesbian shorts: White spectators and performative documentaries by makers of color. In C. Holmlund & C. Fuchs (Eds.), *Between the sheets, in the streets: Queer, lesbian, gay documentary* (pp. 175–189). University of Minnesota Press.

Green, K. M. (2020). Poem: Black. Queer. Fly. In A. L. Johnson & B. LeMaster (Eds.), *Gender futurity, intersectional autoethnography: Embodied theorizing from the margins* (pp. 85–86). Routledge.

Halberstam, J. (1998). *Female masculinity*. Duke University Press.

Harris, A., & Holman Jones, S. (2017). Feeling fear, feeling queer: The peril and potential of queer terror. *Qualitative Inquiry*, 23(7), 561–568. https://doi.org/10.1177%2F1077800417718304

Holman Jones, S. (2016). Living bodies of thought: The "critical" in critical autoethnography. *Qualitative Inquiry*, 22(4), 228–237. https://doi.org/10.1177/1077800415622509

Holman Jones, S., & Harris, A. M. (2019). *Queering autoethnography*. Routledge.

Holmlund, C. & Fuchs, C. (1997). Introduction. In C. Holmlund & C. Fuchs (Eds.), *Between the sheets, in the streets: Queer, lesbian, gay documentary* (pp. 1–12). University of Minnesota Press.

Johnson, A. L. (2020). Pulse. In A. L. Johnson & B. LeMaster (Eds.), *Gender futurity, intersectional autoethnography: Embodied theorizing from the margins*. Routledge.

Johnson, E. P. (2001). "Quare" studies, or (almost) everything I know about queer studies I learned from my grandmother. *Text and Performance Quarterly*, 21(1), 1–25. https://doi.org/10.1080/10462930128119

Johnson, E. P. (2011). Queer epistemologies: Theorizing the self from a writerly place called home. *Biography*, 34(3), 429–446. https://doi.org/10.1353/bio.2011.0040

Johnson, E. P. (2014). To be young, gifted, and queer: Race and sex in the new black studies. *The Black Scholar* 44(2), 50–56. https://doi.org/10.1080/00064246.2014.11413687

Johnson, E. P. (2016). Put a little honey in my sweet tea: Oral history as quare performance. *Women's Studies Quarterly*, 44(3–4), 51–67. https://www.jstor.org/stable/44474062

Johnson, A. L., & LeMaster, B. (2020) *Gender futurity, intersectional autoethnography: Embodied theorizing from the margins*. Routledge.

Leavy, P. (2015). *Method meets art: Arts-based research practice* (2nd ed.). Guilford.
LeMaster, B. (2020). Notes on some especially (not so) subtle dissatisfactions. *QED: A Journal in GLBTQ Worldmaking* 7(1), 75–82. https://doi.org/10.14321/qed.7.1.0075
LeMaster, B., Schultz, D., McNeill. J., Bowers, G., Rust, R. (2019). Unlearning cisheteronormativity at the intersections of difference: Performing queer worldmaking through collaged relational autoethnography. *Text and Performance Quarterly*, 39(4), 341–370. https://doi.org/10.1080/10462937.2019.1672885
Manning, J. (2017). Queer methods. In M. Allen (Ed.), *The SAGE encyclopedia of communication research methods*. SAGE. http://dx.doi.org/10.4135/9781483381411
Manning, J., Asante, G., Huerta Moreno, L., Johnson, R., LeMaster, B., Li, Y., Rudnick, J., Stern, D.M., & Young, S. (2020). Queering communication studies: A *Journal of Applied Communication Research* forum. *Journal of Applied Communication Research* 48(4), 413–437. https://doi.org/10.1080/00909882.2020.1789197
Manning, J., & Kunkel, A. (2014). *Researching interpersonal relationships: Qualitative methods, studies, and analysis*. SAGE.
McMullan, C. (Director). (2014). *My prairie home* [Film]. National Film Board of Canada.
McNeill, J. N. (2020). Poem: Are you boy or girl? In A. L. Johnson & B. LeMaster (Eds.), *Gender futurity, intersectional autoethnography: Embodied theorizing from the margins* (p. 23). Routledge.
McNiff, S. (2008). Art-based research. In J. G. Knowles & A. L. Cole (Eds.), *Handbook of the arts in qualitative research: Perspectives, methodologies, examples, and issues* (pp. 29–40). SAGE.
Moore, J. (2017). Where is the critical empirical interpersonal communication research? A roadmap for future inquiry into discourse and power. *Communication Theory*, 27, 1–20. http://doi.org/10.1111/comt.12107
Muñoz, J. E. (1999). *Disidentifications: Queers of color and the performance of politics*. University of Minnesota Press.
Muñoz, J. E. (2006). Feeling brown, feeling down: Latina affect, the performativity of race, and the depressive position. *Signs* 31(3), 675–688. https://doi.org/10.1086/499080
Murphy, K. P., Pierce, J. L., & Ruiz, J. (2016). What makes queer oral history different. *The Oral History Review*, 43(1), 1–24. https://doi.org/10.1093/ohr/ohw022
Nash, C.J. (2016). Queer conversations: Old-time lesbians, transmen and the politics of queer research. In K. Browne & C. J. Nash (Eds.), *Queer methodologies: Intersecting queer theories and social science research* (pp.129–142). Routledge.
Nichols, B. (1994). *Blurred boundaries: Questions of meaning in contemporary culture*. Indiana University Press.
Nichols, B. (2001). *Introduction to documentary*. Indiana University Press.
Nichols, B. (2017). *Introduction to documentary* (3rd ed.). Indiana University Press.
Olzman, M. D. (2020). Dancing at the intersections. In A. L. Johnson & B. LeMaster (Eds.), *Gender futurity, intersectional autoethnography: Embodied theorizing from the margins* (pp. 55–68). Routledge.
Perez, K. (2019). Staging the family unfamiliar: The queer intimacies in ramble-ations: A one D'lo show. *Text and Performance Quarterly*, 39(4), 371–387. https://doi.org/10.1080/10462937.2018.1457174
Pollack, D. (1998). *Writing as performance: Poeticizing the researcher's body*. Southern Illinois University Press.
Polous, C. N. (2021). *Essentials of autoethnography*. American Psychological Association.
Santoro, P. (2016). Queerscape: Embodying landscape and rupture in auto/ethnography. *International Review of Qualitative Research*, 9(1), 107–136. https://doi.org/10.1525%2Firqr.2016.9.1.107
Sullivan, N. (2003). *A critical introduction to queer theory*. Edinburgh University Press.
Suter, E. A., Seurer, L. M., Webb, S., Grewe, B., Jr., & Koenig Kellas, J. (2015). Motherhood as contested ideological terrain: Essentialist and queer discourses of motherhood at play in female-female co-mothers' talk. *Communication Monographs*, 82(4), 458–483. https://doi.org/10.1080/03637751.2015.1024702

Tan, J. (2016). Aesthetics of queer becoming: *Comrade Yue* and Chinese community-based documentaries online. *Critical Studies in Media Communication, 33*(1), 38–52. http://dx.doi.org/10.1080/15295036.2015.1129064

West, I. (2013). Queer generosities. *Western Journal of Communication, 77*(5), 538–541. https://doi.org/10.1080/10570314.2013.784351

West, I. (2018). Queer perspectives in communication studies. In J. Nussbaum (Ed.), *Oxford Research Encyclopedia of Communication.* Oxford University Press. https://doi.org/10.1093/acrefore/9780190228613.013.81

Yep, G. A. (2003). The violence of heteronormativity in communication studies. *Journal of Homosexuality, 45*(2–4), 11–59. https://doi.org/10.1300/J082v45n02_02

Yep, G. A., Lovaas, K. E., & Elia, J. P. (2014). Introduction: Queering communication: Starting the conversation. In G. A. Yep, K. E. Lovaas, & J. P. Elia (Eds.), *Queer theory and communication: From disciplining queers to queering the discipline(s)* (pp. 1–10). Routledge.

Sandra L. Faulkner and Madison A. Pollino

METHODOLOGICAL AND STATISTICAL CONSIDERATIONS IN STUDYING SEXUAL MINORITY AND GENDER DIVERSE RELATIONSHIPS

INTRODUCTION

Sexual minority and gender diverse (SMGD) individuals have been historically underrepresented in social science research and related disciplines for reasons both external and internal to the science (Andersen & Zou, 2015; Reczek, 2020).[1] Antagonism and heterosexist bias against SMGD individuals were present in early versions of the clinical diagnostic manual of the American Psychiatric Association (1952, 1968) wherein such identification was grounds for a psychiatric diagnosis. Consequently, nonclinical community samples of SMGD couples and families have been underrepresented and often excluded by most researchers, all while relationships composed of heterosexual-identified and/or cisgender-identified partners became the archetypal frame for our view of human connection (Drescher, 2015; Williamson et al., 2022).

Only in the early 21st century has there been a rise in SMGD relationship research; Hartwell et al. (2012) found there were 239% more studies on lesbian, gay, and bisexual (LGB) populations published in the couple and family literature from 1997 to 2012 relative to an earlier review of work published from 1975 to 1995 (Clark & Serovich, 1997). A review of SMGD studies found that of a sample of 632 studies published between 2000 and 2015, the primary topic of study was "social well-being" (36.3%; e.g., stigma, discrimination, marriage, family, parenting, etc.), surpassing topics related to mental and psychological health (21.8%; e.g., mood, anxiety, mood image) and sexual behavior (19.2%; e.g., HIV prevention, condom use, etc.). Furthermore, the proportion of SMGD studies focused on social well-being relative to other topics has grown from 2000 to 2020, suggesting that interest in SMGD relationships continues to rise (Walch et al., 2020).

Despite the increase in empirical science conducted with SMGD samples and interest from clinicians and policymakers aiming to rectify social inequities, traces of heterosexist biases, at one time inculcated by societal forces, continue to impact how researchers approach studying topics and analyzing data with this population. Namely, the predominant methodological and statistical paradigms used within relationship science continue to drive the implicit exclusion of SMGD individuals from relationship research. A review of 591 studies on couples and well-being published between 2002 and 2012 found that 88.7% excluded sexual minority couples, a trend consistent throughout the decade (Anderson & Zou, 2015). The authors speculate that SMGD couples may be excluded because sampling biological and psychological data from couples (or dyads) requires greater funding and labor (e.g., neuroimaging of couples; Zeki & Romaya, 2010). Because dyadic data acquisition can be costly, researchers often elect to only sample non-SMGD couples because they presuppose their analyses will be underpowered to detect between group differences at the level of the couple (Blair, 2014; Walch et al., 2020).

To study romantic relationships, processes, and outcomes, researchers will often collect individual data from one partner or dyadic data from both partners (for a discussion related to this, see Barton et al., 2020). Dyadic data has long been considered the "gold standard" in relationship research, which allows for the examination of how partners' experiences are linked (i.e., interdependence) (Machia et al., 2020). However, to collect and analyze these data, binary categories for gender (i.e., female and male) are often used and assigned to distinguish partners' reports. The use of only two gender categories, and possibly three (i.e., "Other"), lends itself to cross-partner analyses and the testing of interaction effects. However, accommodating the plurality of SMGD identities beyond "female" and "male" in these analytical frameworks can cause analyses to be underpowered and generate models that are difficult to interpret, with multiple interactions between diverse SMGD identities and other identity factors such as age, race, socioeconomic status, ability status, and more.

Accounting for the heterogeneity in SMGD samples while maintaining adequate statistical power has been a pernicious problem for researchers, and simply increasing sample size, especially for traditionally underrepresented samples, is rarely a feasible option. Unfortunately, most studies of SMGD populations do not employ methods that compensate for small sample size while capturing the diversity among SMGD individuals. Systematic reviews of research with SMGD populations indicate that most studies rely on relatively basic analytical procedures such as descriptive analysis, t-tests, linear regression, and analysis of variance (ANOVA) which provide limited insight into the unique experience of any given individual or relationship (Goodrich et al., 2015; van Eeden-Moorefield et al., 2018). Simple analytic procedures are the norm in research with SMGD populations in part because data collection is mostly cross-sectional and nonexperimental, lending itself to research questions focused on simple group differences. For example, of a sample of SMGD studies published between 2000 and 2015, a large majority of quantitative studies were nonexperimental (96.5%; $N = 627$), used retrospective or cross-sectional data (88.8%; $N = 577$), and employed convenience sampling or self-selected sampling (Meyer & Wilson, 2009; Walch et al., 2020). Only 7.8% ($N = 51$) of 650 unique samples employed a longitudinal nonexperimental design, and even fewer employed an experimental design (2.6%; $N = 17$). In contrast, another review of publications in relationship science from 2014 to 2018 found a wider array of research methods and designs. Compared to SMGD studies, a larger majority were longitudinal (24%; $n = 188$), experimental (19%; $n = 143$), observational (11%; $n = 86$), and intensively sampled (9%; $n = 71$; Williamson et al., 2022). Taken together, the types of methods and designs used in SMGD studies (apart from the samples that inform the generalizability of results) do not lend themselves to understanding the relationship initiation and maintenance behaviors that unfold in real time, yielding a dearth of information in the understanding of SMGD couples and families, broadly defined.

The goal of this article is to outline methodological and statistical considerations salient for those interested in conducting relationship research with SMGD populations, and to present analytical tools that may circumvent issues specific to research questions with SMGD samples. This article first begins by presenting issues related to sampling procedures in SMGD research, followed by a brief discussion of how multilevel modeling can be utilized as an accessible solution to account for between-person heterogeneity (i.e., differences in partner's reports). Next, dyadic relationship sampling and data analyses are presented, with a specific focus on partner interdependence, distinguishability, and statistical applications using multilevel modeling and structural equation modeling. This is followed by a discussion of longitudinal analysis in dyadic research and emerging paradigms for studying relationships as dynamic systems, which can capture the idiosyncratic features of SMGD relationships otherwise overlooked by cross-sectional research. Finally, several novel techniques for analyzing relationship dynamics are presented with references for further reading. Given that the content presented draws on empirical literature, references to technical definitions and guides are included throughout to direct the reader to more thorough analytical descriptions.

BETWEEN-PERSON HETEROGENEITY IN SMGD INDIVIDUALS

For those interested in conducting relationship research with SMGD individuals, a major challenge can be defining the inclusion criteria for sexual minority and gender diverse individuals, respectively (Matsuno & Budge, 2017; Moradi et al., 2009).[2] Many researchers choose to aggregate sexual minority and gender diverse individuals together as a singular group to maximize group-level sample size; however, doing so further marginalizes these individuals as a singular, and often "other," identity group. Indeed, pooling SMGD individuals together limits the generalizability of findings to other populations that differ in sexual orientation (Galupo et al., 2015), sexual identity (Galupo et al., 2017), perceived experiences of prejudice (Mitchell et al., 2015), minority stress (Randall et al., 2017), and relational ties across the life-course (Reczek, 2020). Variations among individuals' experiences may be further confounded by other intersectional identities, which include, but are not limited to, age (Samrock et al., 2021), race (Hayes et al., 2011), and socioeconomic status (Shangani et al., 2020). While broadening the inclusion criteria may allow for increased sample sizes, doing so presents challenges for methodologists to parse between-person and between-group differences.

Qualitative research aims to circumvent issues of small sample size by employing intersectionality-informed and grounded theory paradigms that offer insights from "the ground up," allowing participants to be more accurately represented during final analysis (Rouhani, 2014). For example, focus groups (Suen et al., 2020), thematic analysis (Rossman et al., 2019), check-lists and open-ended questions (Matsuno et al., 2021), and semistructured interviews (Araya et al., 2021; Brown, 2010) have been used across populations of SMGD individuals in close relationships (e.g., romantic, family, etc.). Qualitative research methods are well suited to account for nuances in the relationships of SMGD individuals, however, the dissemination of inclusive quantitative designs has been more stagnant (Fehrenbacher & Patel, 2020; van Eeden-Moorefield et al., 2018). As such, the current article aims to explicate emerging techniques in quantitative research that avail themselves to the study of SMGD individuals in relationships.

MULTILEVEL MODELING (MLM) AND SMGD HETEROGENEITY

Multilevel modeling (MLM), also called mixed-effects modeling or hierarchical linear modeling, offers a solution to disentangle between-group differences (e.g., differences between same-gender male dyads and same-gender female dyads) and between-dyad differences (e.g., differences between individual same-gender male dyads) in SMGD samples. MLM regression works by separating linear effects into fixed and random components (Hox et al., 2017). The fixed effects are assumed to be constant across all groups, whereas the random component varies across groups, and represents the degree to which an effect differs from the group average. For example, the stress that marginalized groups may experience due to their identity (i.e., minority stress; Meyer, 2003) predicts lower personal displays of affect in same-gender relationships (i.e., the fixed effect), but this effect may be slightly stronger or weaker across individual couples in the sample (i.e., the random effect; Hocker et al., 2021). MLM can accommodate data nested within subpopulations, or time-points nested within individuals across time (Snijders & Bosker, 2011).

An example of a basic MLM regression would take the form:

$$y_{ij} = \beta_{0j} + \beta_{1j}(x_{1ij}) + e_{ij}$$
$$e_{ij} = N(0, \sigma^2)$$

where the outcome for person i in group j is predicted by some intercept $(\beta-_{0j})$ and an effect of $x_{1ij} (\beta_{1j})$ for person j. Errors are assumed to be person-specific and independently distributed with a mean of zero and a variance of σ^2. The between-group part of the model would take the form:

$$\beta_{0j} = \gamma_{00} + \mu_{0j}$$
$$\beta-_{1j} = \gamma_{10} + \mu_{1j}$$

where the intercept and slope terms are further separated into fixed effects (γ_{00} and γ_{10}), which are the same across all subgroups, and random (μ_{0j} and μ_{1j}) effects, which are unique to each group. The effect of x_{1ij} can be further separated into between-group and within-group components by including a group-level variable and a person-level variable, separating deviation of one's group from the grand mean (i.e., group-level variable) and deviation of an individual from their group-mean (i.e., person-level variable). The new model would take the form:
Within

$$y_{ij} = \beta_{0j} + \beta_{1j}(\bar{x}_{1j}) + \beta_{2j}(\bar{x}_{1j} - \bar{x}_{1ij})e_{ij}$$
$$e_{ij} = N(0, \sigma^2)$$

Between

$$\beta_{0j} = \gamma_{00} + \mu_{0j}$$
$$\beta_{1j} = \gamma_{10} + \mu_{1j}$$
$$\beta_{2j} = \gamma_{20} + \mu_{2j}$$

where $\bar{x}_{1j}$ is the average value of x in group j, and $(\bar{x}_{1j} - \bar{x}_{1ij})$ the deviation of person i in group j from the average value of x in group j. Therefore, in this model, β_{1j} represents a *between*-group effect (e.g., $+\beta_{1j}$ = groups with higher x are expected to have higher y) and β_{2j} represents a *within*-group effect (e.g., $+\beta_{2j}$ = individuals with higher x, *relative to others in their group*, are expected to have higher y). In this way, MLM can directly model differences between SMGD groups, and differences between individuals within a specific group. For example, SMGD individuals experience depressive symptoms at a disproportionately higher rate compared to heterosexual and cisgender individuals (see Plöderl & Tremblay, 2015 for a review). Therefore, those who identify as SMGD may suffer a greater negative effect of depressive symptoms on relationship satisfaction, relative to other groups (i.e., between-group effect; Gilmour et al., 2021). Furthermore, SMGD individuals reporting higher depressive symptoms *relative to other SMGD individuals* may be at an even greater risk of experiencing lower relationship satisfaction (i.e., within-group). Thus, MLM allows for variance in the outcome (e.g., relationship satisfaction) to be decomposed into between- and within-group effects. Curran and Hancock (2021, pp. 67–68) introduce the handy "*for a ...*" concept to explain between- and within-group effects: For example, gender congruence (i.e., similarity between physical presentation and one's gender identity) may have a negligible effect on sexual satisfaction in a community sample, but *for a* sample of transgender men, this effect may be quite appreciable, especially in those reporting high internalized transphobia (i.e., internalization of negative messages that devalue one's gender identity; Kline & Randall, 2021).

Random effect estimates from MLM models (e.g., $\mu_{0j}, \mu_{1j} \ldots \mu_{nj}$) can be used to extract group-specific effects known as Empirical Bayes (EB) estimates (Liu et al., 2021). This procedure essentially takes a weighted average between the fixed effect (i.e., average effect across all groups) and the effect from an ordinary least squares (OLS) regression used with only a single group (i.e., only same-gender male couples). If effects vary considerably across groups (i.e., large random effect), then the OLS is more heavily weighted; conversely, if effects are consistent across groups (i.e., small random effect), then the fixed effect from the MLM model is more heavily weighted. EB estimates can be graphed with confidence intervals to visually depict differences in between-group effects (see Randall et al., 2021). Researchers interested in studying SMGD populations using an intersectional lens (Cole, 2009; Crenshaw, 1989) could employ EB to compare differences in relational functioning across groups of SMGD individuals with multiple, overlapping social identities. For example, a sample may be separated into subgroups based on race (e.g., Asian, Black, Latinx, White, etc.), gender (e.g., cis-female, trans-female, etc.), and sexual orientation (e.g., bisexual, gay, heterosexual, lesbian, etc.) and EB estimates can be derived for each intersectional identity (e.g., Black, trans-female, lesbian) even if there are a very small number of individuals in this group (Bell et al., 2010). A more thorough discussion of EB estimation, including limitations of the approach, can be found in Liu et al. (2021).

Another advantage of MLM is that it allows researchers to circumvent the need for very large sample sizes, depending on the type of effect researchers are aiming to test. Number of groups is more important for maximizing power at the between-group level, and number of individuals determines power at the within-group level (Snijders & Bosker, 2011). In longitudinal research, number of individuals determines the power for between-person comparisons, and number of time-points determines the power to detect within-person differences across time. While MLM tends to require moderate to large numbers of groups as model complexity increases (Hox et al., 2017), estimations using restricted maximum likelihood and EB estimation have proven to limit relative bias with samples that have less than 10 groups (McNeish, 2016, 2017; Van de Schoot & Miocevic, 2020).

DYADIC ANALYSIS IN SMGD RELATIONSHIPS

Romantic partners' experiences are inextricably linked to one another (for a review, see research on interdependence theory; Machia et al., 2020). Given this, many researchers opt for the collection and analysis of dyadic data (i.e., data collected from both partners; Kenny et al., 2006). In short, dyadic data analysis suggests that data collected from both partners in a romantic relationship may covary systematically across different variables and across time (Kenny et al., 2006). Members of a dyad are expected to be interrelated and mutually influential of each other's thoughts, emotions, and behavior (Randall & Schoebi, 2018). ANOVA and OLS regression assume that scores across subjects are independent, and therefore these techniques are a poor fit for data nested within a dyadic structure. Dyadic data analysis is a series of techniques used to model relational processes in dyads cross-sectionally and longitudinally (see Kenny et al., 2006).

INDISTINGUISHABLE DYADIC ANALYSIS FOR SMGD RELATIONSHIPS

A distinction is made in dyadic analysis between dyads are that *distinguishable* or *indistinguishable* (Kenny & Ledermann, 2010). Dyads that are distinguishable can be separated by some discrete, stable, trait-like factor, wherein the default has traditionally been a binary gender term (i.e., female or male). However, any dichotomous variable could theoretically be used, depending on the research question (e.g., partner diagnosed with cancer and the undiagnosed partner). As previously alluded to, the dichotomization of gender inadequately translates to SMGD dyadic research where binary categorizations of sexual orientation and gender identity are less applicable (West et al., 2008). A solution is dyadic analysis that treats dyads as *indistinguishable*.

Actor-Partner Interdependence Model (APIM) for Indistinguishable Dyads in MLM.
The actor-partner interdependence model (APIM) is a method used to model dyadic data, and such methods have also been applied to the study of indistinguishable (Kashy et al., 2008) and same-sex dyads (Randall et al., 2017). The APIM explicitly models *actor* and *partner* effects (Kenny & Lederman, 2010). Actor effects refer to effects of predictor x from Partner A on outcome y from Partner A, and vice versa for Partner B. Conversely, partner effects are cross-partner effects, referring to the effect of predictor x from Partner B on outcome y from

Partner A, and vice versa. These effects can be modeled in an MLM framework to account for the nested structure of partners within dyads. Let's consider an example where researchers want to understand if romantic partners' life satisfaction can be predicted by each partners' minority stress (actor effect) and the minority stress of their partner (partner effect). A partner-level model (Level 1) from an APIM with one predictor would take the form:

$$Life\ Satisfaction_{ij} + \beta_{0j} + \beta_1(Actor\ Stress)_{ij} + \beta_2(Partner\ Stress)_{ij} + \epsilon_{ij}$$

where the outcome *Life Satisfaction* for person i nested within dyad j is predicted by the sum of a random intercept (β_{0j}) which varies across dyads, an actor effect of one's own minority stress (β_2), a partner effect of partner's minority stress (β_2), and a random error term (ϵ_{ij}). At the dyad-level (Level 2), the model takes the form:

$$\beta_{0j} = \gamma_{00} + \mu_{0j}$$
$$\beta_1 = \gamma_{10}$$
$$\beta_2 = \gamma_{20},$$

where the intercept term from Level 1 consists of a fixed component that is consistent across all dyads and a random component (μ_{0j}) that accounts for differences between each dyad and the average intercept. Notice, there are no random components for either β_1 and β_2 (i.e., slope coefficients). MLM requires there to be more members of each group than random variables. Therefore, in the case of dyadic analysis, there are only two members in each group so only one random variable can be included, and it is often the case that a random intercept is the best choice for modeling dyadic data (Kenny et al., 2006). However, other fixed effects can be added to the model to account for covariates at either Level 1 or Level 2. For example, a person-specific factor such as stress communication may be added as a Level 1 covariate:

$$Life\ Satisfaction_{ij} + \beta_{0j} + \beta_1(Actor\ Stress)_{ij} + \beta_2(Partner\ Stress)_{ij}$$
$$+ \beta_3(Stress\ Communication_{ij}) + \epsilon_{ij}$$

Furthermore, researchers may be interested to assess if the effect of an individual's stress on their life satisfaction varies as a function of their stress communication with their partner. To explore such a hypothesis, interaction terms between fixed effects may also be added to the model:

$$Life\ Satisfaction_{ij} + \beta_{0j} + \beta_1(Actor\ Stress)_{ij} + \beta_2(Partner\ Stress)_{ij}$$
$$+ \beta_3(Stress\ Communication_{ij}) + \beta_4(Stress\ Communication_{ij}) * (Actor\ Stress_{ij}) + \epsilon_{ij}$$

similarly, covariates that are the same for each member of the dyad, such as household income, can be included at Level 2:

$$\beta_{0j} = \gamma_{00} + \gamma_{01}(Household\ Income_{ij}) + \mu_{0j}$$
$$\beta_1 = \gamma_{10}$$
$$\beta_2 = \gamma_{20}$$

The drawback of using MLM to conduct an APIM is that the model is unable to accommodate factor analysis and the inclusion of latent variables, which are used to measure various dimensions of a particular construct (Kline, 2015). For example, while one may include minority stress in the model, types of minority stress can include acts of discrimination, perceptions of lack of family support, and negative internalized feelings about one's identity; all types that are not explicitly included in the model (see Lewis et al., 2003). To address such concerns, APIM can be fit using structural equation modeling (SEM), a framework that offers latent variable modeling and path analysis to model covariates among factors (Kashy et al., 2008).

Actor-Partner Interdependence Model in SEM. SEM allows latent variables to be included in the APIM as either outcomes or predictors (Gistelinck & Loeys, 2019). Factor analysis is used to model the association each item has with the underlying latent factor. Using latent variables in path analysis is optimal because it accounts for differences in how strongly each item relates to the latent variable, rather than assuming all items are related to the latent variable equally. For example, negative internalized feelings about one's sexual identity may be a stronger indicator of minority stress compared to perceived lack of social support from family. Accounting for such differences in factor structure (i.e., weighting each item appropriately) minimizes estimation biases and increases the trustworthiness of the estimates (Kline, 2015). Moreover, factor analysis directly accounts for measurement error (i.e., the difference between a measured score and the true score), further improving model estimates.

Despite the benefits, a drawback of SEM is that it is less readily adapted to the analysis of indistinguishable compared to distinguishable dyads. As an example, consider a study applying the APIM to model the association between different-cisgender romantic partners' perceived stress and their relationship satisfaction. An APIM for distinguishable dyads is suitable for this task and shown in Figure 1, depicting actor (a_1, a_2) and partner effects (p_1, p_2)

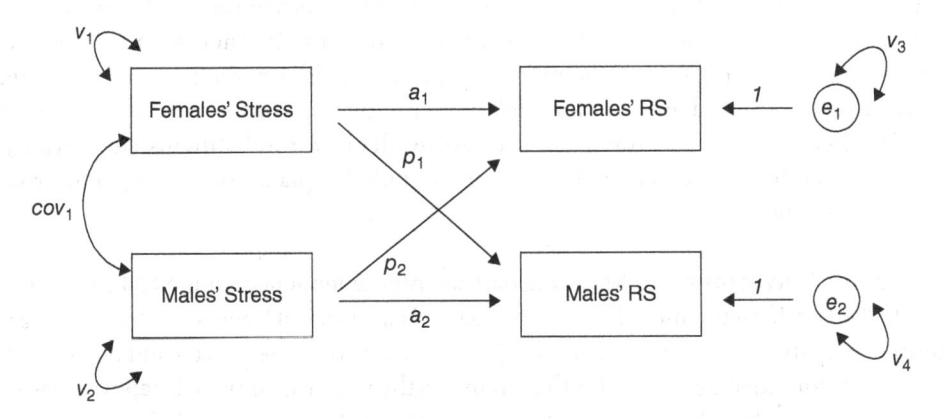

Figure 1. Actor-partner interdependence model (APIM) for distinguishable dyads.
Note: v = variances; cov = covariances; a = actor effects; p = partner effects; e = residual error term. This parameterization would be used to study interpersonal dynamics when partners' bidirectional influences are expected to differ across some distinguishing factor (e.g., gender identity, employment status, health condition, etc.).
Source: Figure adapted from Kenny et al. (2006).

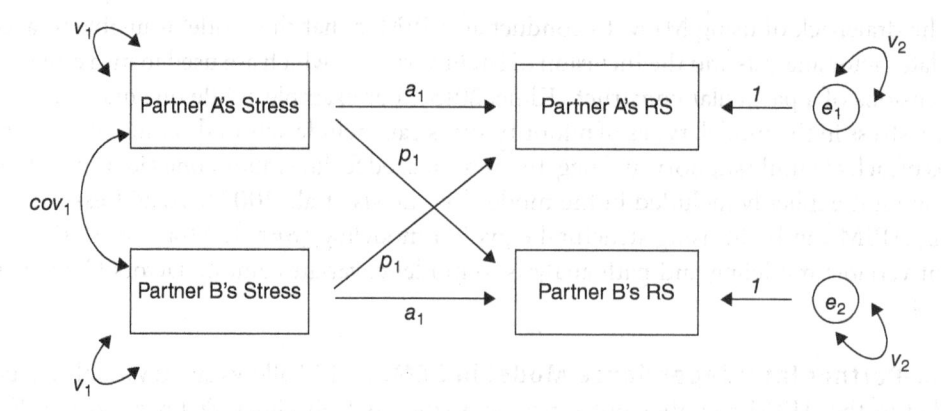

Figure 2. Actor-partner interdependence model (APIM) for indistinguishable dyads.
Note: v = variances; cov = covariances; a = actor effects; p = partner effects; e = residual error term. Notice that actor effects, partner effects, and variances are constrained to be equal across both members of the dyad. This modification allows for APIM to be applied in the SEM framework without having to categorize partners based on dichotomous gender or sexual orientation.
Source: Figure adapted from Kenny et al. (2006).

in a path model. Variances are estimated freely for females' and males' stress (v_1, v_2) and the residual errors (v_3, v_4). To apply a similar model to indistinguishable dyads, model constraints must be applied to means (not pictured), variances, and actor and partner effects. The model for indistinguishable dyads is depicted in Figure 2, renaming "female" and "male" to be inclusive to SMGD individuals (e.g., Partner A and Partner B). Notice, the variances for partners' stress and the residual error are held constant, as are the actor and partner effects. This model assumes that partners are not statistically distinguishable and therefore their designation in the model as either "female" or "male" is arbitrary. If the order of partners were to change for some of the dyads (e.g., scores for Partner A and Partner B are swapped for part of the sample), the model estimates would remain the same. Of note, the interpretation of standard indices of model fit, including the χ^2 difference test, changes significantly when applying this framework to test model fit for indistinguishable dyads, and readers should refer to Peugh et al. (2013) for a detailed explanation of proper approaches to testing model fit.

Measurement Invariance. Modeling partner interdependence using SEM affords the opportunity to test if factor models are consistent (i.e., invariant) across different subgroups (Gareau et al., 2016). Assuming researchers' samples are adequately sized and analytic procedures account for indistinguishability, there remains the issue that most self-report measures in relationship science have been validated using samples that are primarily White, heterosexual, and cisgender (Williamson et al., 2022). Therefore, it is not self-evident that these measures, while empirically validated and widely used, are valid indicators of the same construct in SMGD populations (see Totenhagen et al., 2023). Tests of measurement invariance can be used to determine if (1) latent constructs (e.g., relationship satisfaction) have the same factor structure across groups (i.e., configural invariance); (2) individual items from a measure have the same weighted relationship with the latent construct across groups (i.e., metric invariance); and (3) the scores for the latent constructs are on the same scale (i.e., scalar invariance; Vandenberg & Lance, 2000). There has been an increased awareness of the importance of measurement invariance in cross-cultural research (Han et al., 2019; Jeong & Lee, 2019), but the process of validating measures across SMGD subgroups continues to develop incrementally.

LONGITUDINAL AND DYNAMIC DYADIC ANALYSIS

While MLM and SEM arguably surpass more traditional methods such as repeated measures ANOVA, which makes more stringent statistical assumptions while providing less information about how the dynamics unfold in real time (McNeish, 2017; Snijders & Bosker, 2011), a noteworthy limitation of cross-sectional individual and dyadic analysis using MLM and SEM is that statistical power to detect effects can only be amplified by increasing the number of participants (Bolger & Laurenceau, 2013; Lane & Hennes, 2018; Wolf et al., 2013). These techniques excel at accounting for between-person and between-group differences (i.e., MLM) and latent factor structure (i.e., SEM) but demand sampling resources that may be limited given that SMGD individuals compose approximately 5.6% of the population in the United States, and large heteronormative biases exist around the world, which may make access to these samples more difficult.[3] Rather than aiming to sample more participants at one time point, an alternative solution is to sample SMGD participants repeatedly over time. By following SMGD individuals and their experiences across time, it negates the need to solicit moderate or large samples cross-sectionally to boost statistical power. Maximizing the number of time-points becomes more optimal than maximizing the number of participants, albeit dependent on resources to conduct such work.

Many variations of longitudinal dyadic data analysis can be readily implemented in both MLM (Bolger & Laureneau, 2013; Lyons & Sayer, 2005) and SEM (Gistelinck & Loey, 2019; Ram & Pederson, 2011). Dyadic latent growth modeling (D-LGM) can be used to model the interrelation between dyadic growth trajectories over time (Kashy et al., 2008), such as joint decline in partners' sexual satisfaction during the first three years of marriage (Ghodse-Elahi et al., 2021). Ghodse-Elahi et al. (2021) found that the decline in partners' sexual satisfaction tended to be synchronized, and that this decline was steeper in couples who reported lower sexual satisfaction at the outset of their marriage. As discussed previously, model constraints are required when using D-LGM in an SEM framework (see Peugh et al., 2013), but MLM offers more parsimonious applications for indistinguishable dyads (see Smith et al., 2013). Gistelinck and Loeys (2019) provide a more thorough outline of current and emerging applications of dyadic longitudinal analysis, including novel techniques designed for intensively repeated data collected from dyads from day-to-day (Vaillancourt-Morel et al., 2020) or over the course of a single conversation (Randall et al., 2021).

SMGD RELATIONSHIPS AS DYNAMIC INTERPERSONAL SYSTEMS

For decades, relationship scientists have defined close relationships as interpersonal systems that change dynamically over time (Cox & Paley, 2003; Minuchin, 1974; Vallacher et al.,

2002); however, only recently has this conceptual framework come to bear on the analysis of data collected from dyads (Gates & Liu, 2016) and groups (Ram et al., 2014). Much like any social ecosystem, relationships emerge from the dynamic interrelations between the behaviors, thoughts, and emotions that are exchanged between partners over time (Randall & Schoebi, 2018). As such, the dynamic qualities of relationships cannot be inferred by observing their constituent components in isolation, nor by studying them at a temporal resolution coarser than the process of interest (e.g., weekly self-reports failing to capture daily ebbs and flows in couples' stress). Cross-sectional self-reports may provide information of trait-like features of relationships, but the dynamic processes that undergird these global features may only be discernible by studying relationships on an hourly or daily basis.

For example, a daily diary study of romantic couples found that the positive benefits of sexual satisfaction on marital satisfaction are mediated by partners' day-to-day perceived partner responsiveness (Gadassi et al., 2016). Extending this example, consider the case where Partner A is more sexually satisfied when they perceive Partner B to be responsive (i.e., caring, validating, etc.). Suppose that Partner A perceived Partner B was responsive because, on the day prior, Partner B provided social support for Partner A after a stress-invoking incident (e.g., discrimination at work/school). Moreover, perhaps Partner B's supportive behavior was preceded by a compassionate gesture from Partner A (e.g., romantic dinner) that reinforced Partner B's belief that Partner A is committed to the longevity of the relationship (Landis et al., 2014). This illustration demonstrates that a global characteristic of the dyad (i.e., high relationship satisfaction) is an emergent byproduct of partners' daily appraisals and responses toward each other's behaviors.

Indeed, relationships arise from dynamic microprocesses, and the relationship itself can exert a regulatory influence on the same microprocesses of which it is composed (Kelledy & Lyons, 2019). This reciprocal process of *circular causality* explains why supportive relationships can serve as a protective factor against stressors endogenous to the relationship such as minority stress (Randall et al., 2017), or disintegrate in a downward spiral when partners cannot adapt to each other's negative mood (Butler, 2015; Levenson & Gottman, 1983).

In a prescient address to colleagues, psychologist Ellen Berscheid (1999) foreshadowed the burgeoning shift toward dynamics in relationship science:

> relationship scholars seek laws governing individuals' interactions with each other—or the influence each person's behavior exerts on his or her partner's behavior. Thus, the tissue of a relationship, and the object of study, is the oscillating rhythm of influence observed in the interactions of two people. This rhythm is displayed in regularities in their interaction pattern, and the goal of relationship science is to identify the causal conditions responsible for that rhythm. A relationship thus does not reside in the individual. Moreover, the rhythm of a relationship is revealed only over time; relationships are inherently temporal rather than static. Further, a relationship's rhythm is not presumed to have a direct material representation. Finally, like the other great forces of nature—such as gravity, electricity, and the four winds—a relationship itself is invisible; its existence can be discerned only by observing its effects. (p. 261)

Berscheid's words were emblematic of a push toward modeling the relationships as living, fluid connections. However, it has not been until recently that methodological developments have grown to complement this theoretical framework (for a discussion see Butler, 2018). Advances in data acquisition techniques including online data-collection, smartphone and mobile computing, sensor and wearable technology, ambulatory assessment, and multimodal intensive laboratory assessment have provided the rich data sources needed to apply a dynamic systems framework to relationship research (Bolger & Laurenceau, 2013; Lougheed & Hollenstein, 2018). As this technology has developed, methodologists in developmental science have been instrumental in adapting techniques from physics, ecology, economics, and sociology to study how human relationships grow, evolve, and respond to external stimuli.

Despite the advances in dynamic longitudinal analysis in relationship science more broadly, researchers interested in studying the relationships of SMGD individuals have only recently begun to capitalize on these designs. A few noteworthy examples are Li and colleagues (2020), who studied the dynamic linkage between same-gender male couples during health- and body image–related discussions, and Vaillancourt-Morel and colleagues (2020) who used daily diaries to determine whether the impact of pornography use on relationship satisfaction, sexual desire, and sexual activity varied in same-gender and mixed-gender relationships. Most researchers assume that intensive sampling paradigms are more resource intensive; however, advances in observational and ambulatory assessment have become feasible options for generating rich, multimodal data streams on social relationships in the laboratory and in daily life (Hilpert et al., 2020; Trull & Ebner-Priemer, 2013).

DYNAMICS IN DAILY LIFE: AMBULATORY ASSESSMENT AND ECOLOGICAL MOMENTARY ASSESSMENT

As most studies with SMGD samples have relied on cross-sectional, between-person designs, researchers are beginning to embrace intensive longitudinal designs such as ambulatory assessment (AA) to track day-to-day and moment-to-moment fluctuations in SMGD individuals' lived experience (Mereish et al., 2021; Trull & Ebner-Primer, 2013) and identify the mechanisms underlying the relationship (Mereish & Poteat, 2015). Broadly, AA refers to *active* and *passive* techniques for collecting data on individuals' daily lives outside of the laboratory (Trull & Ebner-Priemer, 2013). In *active* AA, participants are electronically prompted to provide feedback on their lived experience in the moment; these methods have been referred to, among other names, as ecological momentary assessment (EMA), experience sampling methods (ESM), and daily diaries (Trull & Ebner-Priemer, 2013). *Passive* AA refers to data collected through computers, sensors, wearables, and other devices that collect data from participants unobtrusively.

When paired together, active and passive AA have the potential to reshape the framework for studying SMGD relationships (see Carpenter et al., 2016; Timmons et al., 2017). As noted in the introduction of the current article, there is considerable between-person variability in the social identities of SMGD individuals; therefore, the dynamics of SMGD partners are likely to be idiosyncratic and not reducible to generalizations based on binary gender, which are common in relationship science, even in studies with SMGD populations (e.g., mothers provide more sensitive care than fathers to their infants; Ellis-Davies et al., 2022). Intensively sampled data provides the breadth and depth of information to study relationships *ideographically;* that is, researchers can take a bottom-up research approach (i.e., *ideographic*) by modeling the unique, nonlinear dynamics of specific relational systems (e.g., couples, families, etc.), rather than imposing a top-down approach where general inferences are used to draw conclusions about individuals (i.e., *nomothetic*).

In family research, ideographic designs can be used to study how families with SMGD individuals express their interpersonal dynamics uniquely, independent of generalizations formulated by observing family dynamics across the population (Ram et al., 2014). Similarly, couples' dynamics can be mapped by deriving dyad-specific parameters, such as coefficients that describe how partners regulate each other's emotions and behavior (Reed et al., 2015; Steele et al., 2014). While AA techniques have notable limitations and methodological considerations of their own (see Ram et al., 2017), they reduce the need for researchers to collect very large samples of SMGD subgroups, making SMGD-inclusive studies more tractable for researchers who would otherwise exclude SMGD participants (Anderson & Zou, 2015; Blair, 2014).

EMERGING TECHNIQUES IN RELATIONSHIP SCIENCE FOR ANALYZING INTENSIVE LONGITUDINAL DATA

Temporal Synchrony and Cross-correlation.

Of emerging interest to researchers is the understanding of how partners' interpersonal experiences shape relationship initiation and maintenance behaviors (see Randall & Schoebi, 2018). Members of a dyads are likely to influence each other's behavior, emotion, or physiology, and capturing these dynamics could provide information about the dyad's well-being (e.g., Saxbe & Repetti, 2010; Timmons et al., 2015). Temporal covariation among and between individual members of dyads has been classified using many terms including *linkage, synchrony, contagion, concordance, and coregulation*, each with slightly different definitions (see Butler, 2011; Timmons et al., 2015). Techniques used to model temporal synchrony differ across data type (e.g., continuous and categorical data; see Gates & Liu, 2016 for a detailed review). For continuous data, MLM is efficient for modeling temporal synchrony directionally (i.e., one partner predicts change in the other) and nondirectionally (i.e., correlation; see Gates & Liu, 2016; Helm et al., 2018). Other methods are amenable to both continuous and categorical data. For example, techniques such as cross-recurrence quantification analysis (Wallot, 2019) and state-space grids (Hollenstein, 2007) can be used to model dyad-specific behavioral sequences and represent these data graphically.

State-space grids are a noncomputational, graphical dynamic systems method for modeling behavior from n partners on an n-dimensional grid. Gradations of each partners' behavior are represented along each axis of the grid, and lines and arrows are overlayed on the grid to depict the trajectory of partners' joint behavioral state which changes dynamically as partners interact. To illustrate a use-case for state-space grids, data were simulated to depict trajectories of positive affect in romantic dyads discussing a topic of conflict in their relationship (see Figure 3; see Brinberg et al., 2017 for a tutorial). Although illuminating of qualitative differences, comparing state-space grids individually may not be scalable with large samples. Descriptive statistics can be derived from the grids (e.g., *flexibility*; see Hollenstein, 2015) as a quantitative measure of interpersonal dynamics for each dyad or group, negating the need to visually compare grids one-by-one. Among other novel research questions, this work can be applied to research with families headed by SMGD parents, for example, how systemic stigma and discrimination toward SMGD individuals influences the exchange of emotion over time between SMGD parents and their children (i.e., affective dynamics; Patterson et al., 2021).

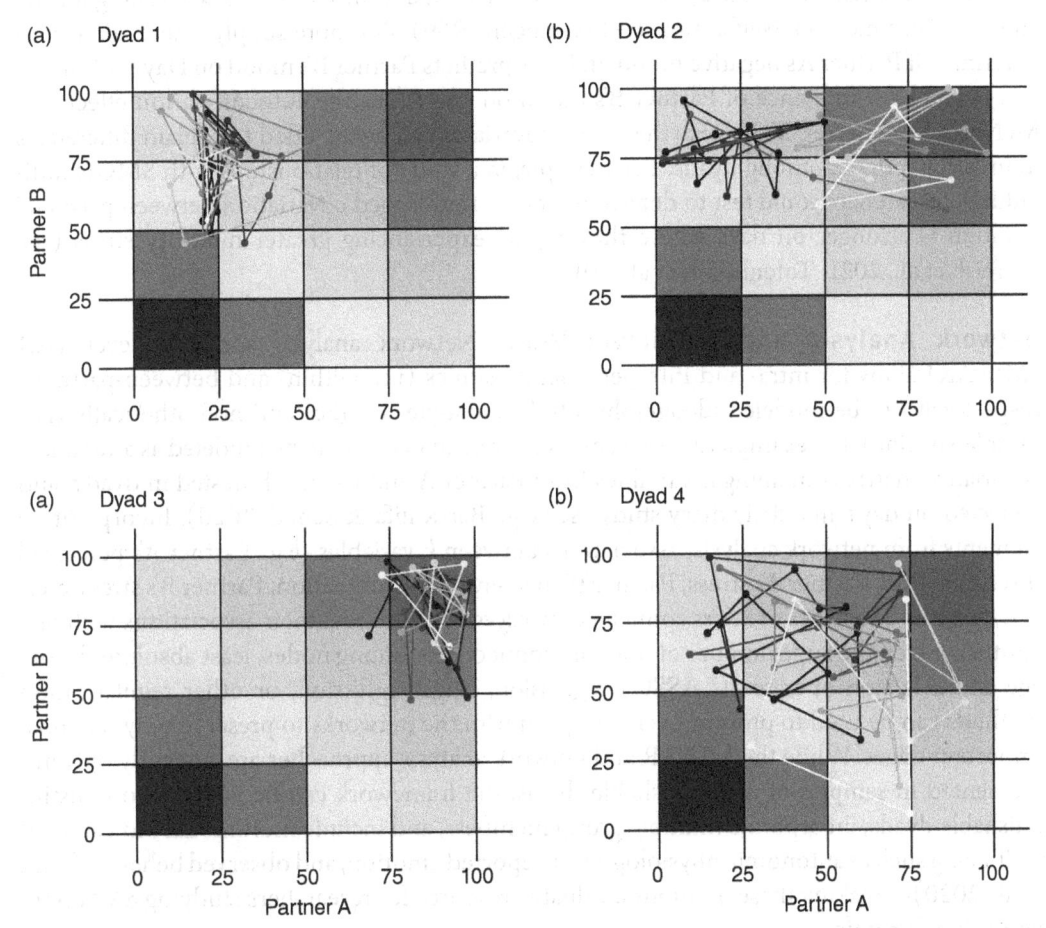

Figure 3. State-state grids of romantic partners positive affect during a conflict conversation.
Note: Panels A—D depict simulated data created to represent levels of positive affect from four separate romantic dyads as they discuss a topic of conflict in their relationship for seven minutes. Partner A and Partner B use rating dials to report their moment-to-moment levels of positive affect as the conversation unfolds (0 = lowest positive affect, 100 = highest positive affect). Dots signify levels of positive affect averaged across 10s intervals, and lines represent the trajectory of dyads' positive affect throughout the conversation. The shading of the dots and lines represent the progression of each dyad's trajectory in time (i.e., darker = earlier in the conversation, lighter = later in the conversation). Dyad 1 has one partner with consistently higher positive affect than the other. Dyad 2 resembles Dyad 1 at the outset of their conversation, but gradually Partner A's positive affect increases to match Partner B's in Dyad 2. Dyad 3 appears to remain in a joint high positive affect state for the entire interaction. Finally, Dyad 4 has a less clear temporal signature, evidencing a more chaotic pattern.
Source: Figure adapted from Brinberg et al. (2017).

Time-Lagged Interdependence. As presented earlier, the APIM is well suited for studying the cross-lagged associations between partners' experiences over time (Cook & Kenny, 2005). The cross-lagged autoregression model, also called the vector autoregressive model (VAR; Bringmann et al., 2018) or the stability and influence model (Thorson et al., 2018), allows for the testing of causal associations among variables while explicitly considering time-dependence (i.e., Granger causality). That is, predictor x is said to "Granger-cause" outcome y when a directional effect of x at time t on y is observed at time $t+1$ while controlling for the effect of x at time t on itself at time $t+1$ (Granger, 1969). Put more simply, one could test to determine if Partner A's negative mood on Day t predicts Partner B's mood on Day $t+1$, above and beyond the influence of Partner B's mood on Day t (i.e., the autocorrelation effect; see McNeish & Hamaker, 2020). Furthermore, covariates can be included to explain differences in interdependence among dyads. For example, in a study of relationships with SMGD individuals, researchers could test to determine if the cross-lagged covariation between partners' emotion is stronger on days where they report experiencing greater minority stress (see Mereish et al., 2021; Totenhagen et al., 2017),

Network Analysis and Multilevel VAR. Network analysis and multilevel VAR (MLVAR) allow for intra- and interpersonal dynamics (i.e., within- and between-partners, respectively) to be modeled ideographically (i.e., couple-specific) and nomothetically (i.e., sample-specific). For example, SMGD couples' stress dynamics can be modeled as a variance-covariance matrix containing k variables from Partner A and Partner B nested in dyad c and collected on day t in a daily diary study (see e.g., Bar-Kalifa & Sened, 2020). Incorporating elements from network analysis, associations between k variables (e.g., Partner A's perceived discrimination, Partner A's stress, Partner B's perceived discrimination, Partner B's stress, etc.) can depicted as a series of *nodes* connected by *edges* which model their associations with one another. Given the large number of possible connections among nodes, least absolute shrinkage and selection operator (LASSO) regression, ridge regression, or other regularization methods can be used to prevent overfitting and trim the networks to preserve only the most important edges. While the MLVAR and network analysis approaches are currently only implemented in samples of distinguishable dyads, the framework can be adapted to indistinguishable dyads, incorporate multiple group members, and include multimodal indicators of well-being such as autonomic physiology, self-reported emotion, and observed behavior (Park et al., 2020)—making these methods a valuable resource for researchers studying SMGD relationship dynamics.

While not specific to the study of SMGD individuals, Bar-Kalifa and Sened (2020) measured couples' daily mood ratings and used network analysis to model intrapersonal (i.e., how Partner A influence their own emotions over time) and interpersonal (i.e., how Partner A and Partner B influence each other's emotions over time) dynamics in partners' emotions. Of note, the authors were able to model time-lagged and contemporaneous effects in a single model and represent these dynamics using user-friendly network graphing in the *mlVAR* package in R (Bar-Kalifa & Sened, 2020; Epskamp et al., 2017). In relationships with SMGD individuals, this approach allows researchers to visually depict couple-specific differences, without having to collapse all participants into a single group. For example, stress regulation in couples with SMGD individuals can be compared across individuals with different adult attachment styles (i.e., patterns of emotional bonding; Hazan & Shaver, 1987) to determine if minority stress becomes more entrenched over time in couples with dismissive-avoidant partners (i.e., valuing independent and avoiding emotional attachment; Mohr et al., 2013).

Dynamic Systems Analysis. A dynamic approach commonly used to study relationship dynamics is differential equation modeling—specifically, variations of the coupled linear oscillator (CLO; Helm et al., 2018; Randall et al., 2021; Steele et al., 2014). The CLO is essentially a bivariate system of equations which predicts *change* in variables over time, rather than the value of that variable at one specific point in time. For example, suppose members of a couple rate their daily levels of positive and negative affect for one month. These ratings are expected to fluctuate over time (Chow et al., 2005), and may follow a specific oscillatory pattern such that affect is higher on some days (e.g., weekends) compared to others (e.g., weekdays). In standard regression, these affect ratings would be treated as a dependent variable and modeled as a function of some set of independent variables. However, in differential equation modeling, the first and second derivatives of these affect ratings are computed (i.e., velocity and acceleration, respectively) and used to explicitly model change in affect over time:

$$d^2 x(t)/dt^2 = \eta x(t) + \zeta (dx(t)/dt) + e(t)$$

The second derivative of affect $(d^2 x(t)/dt^2)$ at time t represents the acceleration in affect, or the change in momentary velocity, at a given time point. When plotted, this equation yields an oscillatory functional form that maps on to fluctuations in affect over time (Chow et al., 2005) and can be used to model dyadic processes using the CLO (see Randall et al., 2021). While the mathematical principles underlying this model are beyond the scope of this article, the CLO exemplifies a shift toward modeling relationships as dynamic change processes as opposed to a series of discrete, independent events. Only recently has this approach been integrated into research on SMGD couples (see Li et al., 2020) and future applications could explore the progression of continuous change processes across multiple modalities. For example, researchers interested in studying minority stress coping can model oscillations in SMGD couples' mood and autonomic physiology (e.g., HRV) to determine whether partners who help each other return to a calm physiological state after encountering an act of discrimination.

CONCLUSION

Few researchers have offered guidance on how novel methodological techniques can help to advance the study of the relationships of sexual minority and gender diverse individuals. To address this gap, the information presented on emerging statistical and methodological paradigms seeks to provide insight into how researchers can expand this body of research, with an eye toward inclusive science that will benefit these communities. To complement the continued use of qualitative methods (see Suen et al., 2020; van Eeden-Moorefield et al., 2018), the current article highlights empirical examples of research with sexual minority and gender diverse individuals that capitalized on advances in quantitative methodologies (Walch et al., 2020). Suggested readings are provided for in-depth coverage of advanced topics that offer comprehensive technical details and examples for applied research.

FURTHER READING

Bolger, N., & Laurenceau, J. P. (2013). *Intensive longitudinal methods: An introduction to diary and experience sampling research*. Guilford Press.

Gates, K. M., & Liu, S. (2016). Methods for quantifying patterns of dynamic interactions in dyads. *Assessment*, 23(4), 459–471. https://doi.org/10.1177%2F1073191116641508

Kenny, D. A., Kashy, D. A., & Cook, W. L. (2006). *Dyadic data analysis*. Guilford Publications.

Li, X., Kuelz, A., Boyd, S., August, K., Markey, C., & Butler, E. (2020). Exploring physiological linkage in same-sex male couples. *Frontiers in Psychology*, 11, 3951. https://doi.org/10.3389/fpsyg.2020.619255

Machia, L. V., Agnew, C. R., & Arriaga, X. B. (Eds.). (2020). *Interdependence, interaction, and close relationships*. Cambridge University Press.

Mereish, E. H., Miranda, R., Jr., Liu, Y., & Hawthorne, D. J. (2021). A daily diary study of minority stress and negative and positive affect among racially diverse sexual minority adolescents. *Journal of Counseling Psychology*, 68(6), 670–681. https://psycnet.apa.org/doi/10.1037/cou0000556

National Institutes of Health. (2018). *Methods and measurement in sexual & gender minority health research: Developing a research agenda and identifying research opportunities*. NIH Gender and Minority Health Office. https://dpcpsi.nih.gov/sites/default/files/MethodsMeasures_Paper_508_FV.pdf

Peugh, J. L., DiLillo, D., & Panuzio, J. (2013). Analyzing mixed-dyadic data using structural equation models. *Structural Equation Modeling: A Multidisciplinary Journal*, 20(2), 314–337. https://doi.org/10.1080/10705511.2013.769395

Randall, A. K., & Scheobi, D. (2018). *Interpersonal emotional dynamics in close relationships*. Cambridge University Press.

Thorson, K. R., West, T. V., & Mendes, W. B. (2018). Measuring physiological influence in dyads: A guide to designing, implementing, and analyzing dyadic physiological studies. *Psychological methods*, 23(4), 595–616. https://psycnet.apa.org/doi/10.1037/met0000166

Walch, S. E., Bernal, D. R., Gibson, L., Murray, L., Thien, S., & Steinnecker, K. (2020). Systematic review of the content and methods of empirical psychological research on LGBTQ and SGM populations in the new millennium. *Psychology of Sexual Orientation and Gender Diversity*, 7(4), 433–454. https://doi.org/10.1037/sgd0000364

Williamson, H., Bornstein, J. X., Cantu, V., Ciftci, O., Farnish, K. A., & Schouwiler, M. T. (2022). How diverse are the samples used to study intimate relationships? A systematic review. *Journal of Social and Personal Relationships*, 39(4), 1087–1109. https://doi.org/10.1177/02654075211053849

REFERENCES

American Psychiatric Association. (1952). *DSM-I: Diagnostic and statistical manual: Mental disorders*.

American Psychiatric Association. (1968). *DSM-II: Diagnostic and statistical manual of mental disorders*.

American Psychological Association, APA Task Force on Psychological Practice with Sexual Minority Persons. (2021). *Guidelines for psychological practice with sexual minority persons*. http://www.apa.org/about/policy/psychological-practice-sexual-minority-persons.pdf

Andersen, J. P., & Zou, C. (2015). Exclusion of sexual minority couples from research. *Health Science Journal*, 9(6), 1–9.

Araya, A. C., Warwick, R., Shumer, D., & Selkie, E. (2021). Romantic relationships in transgender adolescents: A qualitative study. *Pediatrics*, 147(2), e2020007906, https://doi.org/10.1542/peds.2020-007906

Bar-Kalifa, E., & Sened, H. (2020). Using network analysis for examining interpersonal emotion dynamics. *Multivariate Behavioral Research*, 55(2), 211–230. https://doi.org/10.1080/00273171.2019.1624147

Barton, A. W., Lavner, J. A., Stanley, S. M., Johnson, M. D., & Rhoades, G. K. (2020). "Will you complete this survey too?" Differences between individual versus dyadic samples in relationship research. *Journal of Family Psychology, 34*(2), 196–203. https://doi.org/10.1037/fam0000583

Bell, B. A., Morgan, G. B., Kromrey, J. D., & Ferron, J. M. (2010). The impact of small cluster size on multilevel models: A Monte Carlo examination of two-level models with binary and continuous predictors. *JSM Proceedings, Survey Research Methods Section, 1*(1), 4057–4067.

Berscheid, E. (1999). The greening of relationship science. *American Psychologist, 54*(4), 260–266. https://doi.org/10.1037/0003-066X.54.4.260

Blair, K. L. (2014). The state of LGBTQ-inclusive research methods in relationship science and how we can do better. *Relationship Research News, 13*(1), 7–12.

Bolger, N., & Laurenceau, J. P. (2013). *Intensive longitudinal methods: An introduction to diary and experience sampling research*. Guilford Press.

Brinberg, M., Fosco, G. M., & Ram, N. (2017). Examining inter-family differences in intra-family (parent–adolescent) dynamics using grid-sequence analysis. *Journal of Family Psychology, 31*(8), 994–1004. https://doi.org/10.1037/fam0000371

Bringmann, L. F., Ferrer, E., Hamaker, E. L., Borsboom, D., & Tuerlinckx, F. (2018). Modeling nonstationary emotion dynamics in dyads using a time-varying vector-autoregressive model. *Multivariate Behavioral Research, 53*(3), 293–314. https://doi.org/10.1080/00273171.2018.1439722

Brown, N. R. (2010). The sexual relationships of sexual-minority women partnered with trans men: A qualitative study. *Archives of Sexual Behavior, 39*, 561–572. https://doi.org/10.1007/s10508-009-9511-9

Butler, E. (2018). Next steps towards understanding interpersonal emotion dynamics. In A. K. Randall & D. Schoebi (Eds.), *Interpersonal emotion dynamics in close relationships* (pp. 179–188). Cambridge University Press.

Butler, E. A. (2011). Temporal interpersonal emotion systems: The "TIES" that form relationships. *Personality and Social Psychology Review, 15*(4), 367–393. https://doi.org/10.1177/1088868311411164

Butler, E. A. (2015). Interpersonal affect dynamics: It takes two (and time) to tango. *Emotion Review, 7*(4), 336–341. https://doi.org/10.1177%2F1754073915590622

Carpenter, R. W., Wycoff, A. M., & Trull, T. J. (2016). Ambulatory assessment: New adventures in characterizing dynamic processes. *Assessment, 23*(4), 414–424. https://doi.org/10.1177/1073191116632341

Chow, S. M., Ram, N., Boker, S. M., Fujita, F., & Clore, G. (2005). Emotion as a thermostat: Representing emotion regulation using a damped oscillator model. *Emotion, 5*(2), 208–225. https://doi.org/10.1037/1528-3542.5.2.208

Clark, W. M., & Serovich, J. M. (1997). Twenty years and still in the dark? Content analysis of articles pertaining to gay, lesbian, and bisexual issues in marriage and family therapy journals. *Journal of Marital and Family Therapy, 23*(3), 239–253. https://doi.org/10.1111/j.1752-0606.1997.tb01034.x

Cole, E. R. (2009). Intersectionality and research in psychology. *American Psychologist, 64*(3), 170–180. https://doi.org/10.1037/a0014564

Cook, W. L., & Kenny, D. A. (2005). The actor–partner interdependence model: A model of bidirectional effects in developmental studies. *International Journal of Behavioral Development, 29*(2), 101–109. https://doi.org/10.1080/01650250444000405

Cox, M. J., & Paley, B. (2003). Understanding families as systems. *Current Directions in Psychological Science, 12*(5), 193–196. https://doi.org/10.1111/1467-8721.01259

Crenshaw, K. (1989). Demarginalizing the intersection of race and sex: A Black feminist critique of antidiscrimination doctrine, feminist theory and antiracist politics. In K. T. Bartlett & R. Kennedy (Eds.), *Feminist legal theory* (pp. 139–167). Routledge.

Curran, P. J., & Hancock, G. R. (2021). The challenge of modeling co-developmental processes over time. *Child Development Perspectives, 15*(2), 67–75. https://doi.org/10.1111/cdep.12401

Drescher, J. (2015). Queer diagnoses revisited: The past and future of homosexuality and gender diagnoses in DSM and ICD. *International Review of Psychiatry, 27*(5), 386–395. https://doi.org/10.3109/09540261.2015.1053847

Ellis-Davies, K., Van Rijn-van Gelderen, L., Winstanley, A., Helmerhorst, K. O., Rubio, B., Vecho, O., Lamb, M. E., & Bos, H. M. W. (2022). Parental sensitivity and intrusiveness in gay-, lesbian-, and heterosexual-parent families with infants conceived using artificial reproductive techniques: Do parents' gender and caregiver role matter? *Early Childhood Research Quarterly, 58*, 177–187. https://doi.org/10.1016/j.ecresq.2021.09.002

Epskamp, S., Deserno, M. K., & Bringmann, L. F. (2017). *mlVAR: Multi-level vector autoregression (R package version 0.5)*. https://cran.r-project.org/web/packages/mlVAR/mlVAR.pdf

Fehrenbacher, A. E., & Patel, D. (2020). Translating the theory of intersectionality into quantitative and mixed methods for empirical gender transformative research on health. *Culture, Health & Sexuality, 22*(Supp. 1), 145–160. https://doi.org/10.1080/13691058.2019.1671494

Gadassi, R., Bar-Nahum, L. E., Newhouse, S., Anderson, R., Heiman, J. R., Rafaeli, E., & Janssen, E. (2016). Perceived partner responsiveness mediates the association between sexual and marital satisfaction: A daily diary study in newlywed couples. *Archives of Sexual Behavior, 45*(1), 109–120. https://doi.org/10.1007/s10508-014-0448-2

Galupo, M. P., Mitchell, R. C., & Davis, K. S. (2015). Sexual minority self-identification: Multiple identities and complexity. *Psychology of Sexual Orientation and Gender Diversity, 2*(4), 355–364.

Galupo, M. P., Ramirez, J. L., & Pulice-Farrow, L. (2017). "Regardless of their gender": Descriptions of sexual identity among bisexual, pansexual, and queer identified individuals. *Journal of Bisexuality, 17*(1), 108–124. https://doi.org/10.1080/15299716.2016.1228491

Gareau, A., Fitzpatrick, J., Gaudreau, P., & Lafontaine, M. F. (2016). Analyzing, interpreting, and testing the invariance of the actor-partner interdependence model. *The Quantitative Methods for Psychology, 12*(2), 101–113. https://doi.org/10.20982/tqmp.12.2.p101

Gates, K. M., & Liu, S. (2016). Methods for quantifying patterns of dynamic interactions in dyads. *Assessment, 23*(4), 459–471. https://doi.org/10.1177%2F1073191116641508

Ghodse-Elahi, Y., Neff, L. A., & Shrout, P. E. (2021). Modeling dyadic trajectories: Longitudinal changes in sexual satisfaction for newlywed couples. *Archives of Sexual Behavior*, 1–12. https://doi.org/10.1007/s10508-021-02075-9

Gilmour, A. L., Whisman, M. A., & Whitton, S. W. (2021). A dyadic analysis of relationship satisfaction and depressive symptoms among same-sex couples. *Journal of Family Psychology, 36*(3), 372–377. https://psycnet.apa.org/doi/10.1037/fam0000912

Gistelinck, F., & Loeys, T. (2019). The actor–partner interdependence model for longitudinal dyadic data: An implementation in the SEM framework. *Structural Equation Modeling: A Multidisciplinary Journal, 26*(3), 329–347. https://doi.org/10.1080/10705511.2018.1527223

Goodrich, K. M., Sands, H., & Catena, A. (2015). Journal of LGBT issues in counseling publication patterns: Author and article characteristics from 2006 to 2012. *Journal of LGBT Issues in Counseling, 9*(3), 180–198. https://doi.org/10.1080/15538605.2015.1068145

Granger, C. W. J. (1969). Investigating causal relations by econometric models and cross-spectral methods. *Econometrica, 37*(3), 424–438.

Han, K., Colarelli, S. M., & Weed, N. C. (2019). Methodological and statistical advances in the consideration of cultural diversity in assessment: A critical review of group classification and measurement invariance testing. *Psychological Assessment, 31*(12), 1481–1496. https://doi.org/10.1037/pas0000731

Hartwell, E. E., Serovich, J. M., Grafsky, E. L., & Kerr, Z. Y. (2012). Coming out of the dark: Content analysis of articles pertaining to gay, lesbian, and bisexual issues in couple and family therapy journals. *Journal of Marital and Family Therapy, 38*, 227–243. https://doi.org/10.1111/j.1752-0606.2011.00274.x

Hayes, J. A., Chun-Kennedy, C., Edens, A., & Locke, B. D. (2011). Do double minority students face double jeopardy? Testing minority stress theory. *Journal of College Counseling, 14*(2), 117–126. https://doi.org/10.1002/j.2161-1882.2011.tb00267.x

Hazan, C., & Shaver, P. (1987). Romantic love conceptualized as an attachment process. *Journal of Personality and Social Psychology, 52*(3), 511–524. https://doi.org/10.1037/0022-3514.52.3.511

Helm, J. L., Miller, J. G., Kahle, S., Troxel, N. R., & Hastings, P. D. (2018). On measuring and modeling physiological synchrony in dyads. *Multivariate Behavioral Research, 53*(4), 521–543. https://doi.org/10.1080/00273171.2018.1459292

Hilpert, P., Brick, T. R., Flückiger, C., Vowels, M. J., Ceulemans, E., Kuppens, P., & Sels, L. (2020). What can be learned from couple research: Examining emotional co-regulation processes in face-to-face interactions. *Journal of Counseling Psychology, 67*(4), 475–487. https://psycnet.apa.org/doi/10.1037/cou0000416

Hocker, L., Kline, K., Totenhagen, C. J., & Randall, A. K. (2021). Hold my hand: Associations between minority stress, commitment, and PDA for same-gender couples. *Journal of Social and Personal Relationships, 38*(9), 2742–2750. https://doi.org/10.1177%2F02654075211020501

Hollenstein, T. (2007). State space grids: Analyzing dynamics across development. *International Journal of Behavioral Development, 31*(4), 384–396. https://doi.org/10.1177/0165025407077765

Hollenstein, T. (2015). This time, it's real: Affective flexibility, time scales, feedback loops, and the regulation of emotion. *Emotion Review, 7*(4), 308–315. https://doi.org/10.1177/1754073915590621

Hox, J. J., Moerbeek, M., & Van de Schoot, R. (2017). *Multilevel analysis: Techniques and applications*. Routledge.

Jeong, S., & Lee, Y. (2019). Consequences of not conducting measurement invariance tests in cross-cultural studies: A review of current research practices and recommendations. *Advances in Developing Human Resources, 21*(4), 466–483. https://doi.org/10.1177/1523422319870726

Kashy, D. A., Donnellan, M. B., Burt, S. A., & McGue, M. (2008). Growth curve models for indistinguishable dyads using multilevel modeling and structural equation modeling: The case of adolescent twins' conflict with their mothers. *Developmental Psychology, 44*, 316–329. https://doi.org/10.1037/0012-1649.44.2.316

Kelledy, L., & Lyons, B. (2019). Circular causality in family systems theory. In J. L. Lebow & D. C. Breunlin (Eds.), *Encyclopedia of couple and family therapy* (pp. 431–434). Springer.

Kenny, D. A., Kashy, D. A., & Cook, W. L. (2006). *Dyadic data analysis*. Guilford Publications.

Kenny, D. A., & Ledermann, T. (2010). Detecting, measuring, and testing dyadic patterns in the actor–partner interdependence model. *Journal of Family Psychology, 24*(3), 359–366.

Kline, K., & Randall, A. K. (2021). The moderating effect of internalized transphobia on the association between gender congruence and sexual satisfaction for transgender men. *Journal of LGBTQ Issues in Counseling, 15*(1), 93–109. https://doi.org/10.1080/15538605.2021.1868378

Kline, R. B. (2015). *Principles and practice of structural equation modeling*. Guilford Publications.

Landis, M., Bodenmann, G., Bradbury, T. N., Brandstätter, V., Peter-Wight, M., Backes, S., Sutter-Stickel, D., & Nussbeck, F. W. (2014). Commitment and dyadic coping in long-term relationships. *GeroPsych, 24*(4), 139–149. https://doi.org/10.1024/1662-9647/a000112

Lane, S. P., & Hennes, E. P. (2018). Power struggles: Estimating sample size for multilevel relationships research. *Journal of Social and Personal Relationships, 35*(1), 7–31. https://doi.org/10.1177%2F0265407517710342

Levenson, R. W., & Gottman, J. M. (1983). Marital interaction: Physiological linkage and affective exchange. *Journal of Personality and Social Psychology, 45*(3), 587–597. https://doi.org/10.1037/0022-3514.45.3.587

Lewis, R. J., Derlega, V. J., Griffin, J. L., & Krowinski, A. C. (2003). Stressors for gay men and lesbians: Life stress, gay-related stress, stigma consciousness, and depressive symptoms. *Journal of Social and Clinical Psychology, 22*(6), 716–729. https://doi.org/10.1521/jscp.22.6.716.22932

Li, X., Kuelz, A., Boyd, S., August, K., Markey, C., & Butler, E. (2020). Exploring physiological linkage in same-sex male couples. *Frontiers in Psychology, 11*, 3951. https://doi.org/10.3389/fpsyg.2020.619255

Liu, S., Kuppens, P., & Bringmann, L. (2021). On the use of empirical bayes estimates as measures of individual traits. *Assessment, 28*(3), 845–857. https://doi.org/10.1177%2F1073191119885019

Lougheed, J. P., & Hollenstein, T. (2018). Methodological approaches to studying interpersonal emotion dynamics. In A. K. Randall & D. Schoebi (Eds.), *Interpersonal emotion dynamics in close relationships* (pp. 75–92). Cambridge University Press.

Lyons, K. S., & Sayer, A. G. (2005). Longitudinal dyad models in family research. *Journal of Marriage and Family, 67*(4), 1048–1060. https://doi.org/10.1111/j.1741-3737.2005.00193.x

Machia, L. V., Agnew, C. R., & Arriaga, X. B. (Eds.). (2020). *Interdependence, interaction, and close relationships*. Cambridge University Press.

Matsuno, E., & Budge, S. L. (2017). Non-binary/genderqueer identities: A critical review of the literature. *Current Sexual Health Reports, 9*(3), 116–120. https://doi.org/10.1007/s11930-017-0111-8

Matsuno, E., McConnell, E., Dolan, C. V., & Israel, T. (2021). "I am fortunate to have a transgender child": An investigation into the barriers and facilitators to support among parents of trans and nonbinary youth. *Journal of GLBT Family Studies*, 1–19. https://doi.org/10.1080/1550428X.2021.1991541

McNeish, D. (2016). On using Bayesian methods to address small sample problems. *Structural Equation Modeling: A Multidisciplinary Journal, 23*(5), 750–773. https://doi.org/10.1080/10705511.2016.1186549

McNeish, D. (2017). Small sample methods for multilevel modeling: A colloquial elucidation of REML and the Kenward-Roger correction. *Multivariate Behavioral Research, 52*(5), 661–670. https://doi.org/10.1080/00273171.2017.1344538

McNeish, D., & Hamaker, E. L. (2020). A primer on two-level dynamic structural equation models for intensive longitudinal data in Mplus. *Psychological Methods, 25*(5), 610–635. https://psycnet.apa.org/doi/10.1037/met0000250

Mereish, E. H., Miranda Jr, R., Liu, Y., & Hawthorne, D. J. (2021). A daily diary study of minority stress and negative and positive affect among racially diverse sexual minority adolescents. *Journal of Counseling Psychology, 68*(6), 670–681. https://psycnet.apa.org/doi/10.1037/cou0000556

Mereish, E. H., & Poteat, V. P. (2015). A relational model of sexual minority mental and physical health: The negative effects of shame on relationships, loneliness, and health. *Journal of Counseling Psychology, 62*(3), 425–437. https://psycnet.apa.org/doi/10.1037/cou0000088

Meyer, I. H. (2003). Prejudice, social stress, and mental health in lesbian, gay, and bisexual populations: Conceptual issues and research evidence. *Psychological Bulletin, 129*(5), 674. https://psycnet.apa.org/doi/10.1037/2329-0382.1.S.3

Meyer, I. H., & Wilson, P. A. (2009). Sampling lesbian, gay, and bisexual populations. *Journal of Counseling Psychology, 56*(1), 23–31. https://psycnet.apa.org/doi/10.1037/a0014587

Minuchin, S. (1974). *Families and family therapy*. Harvard University Press.

Mitchell, R. C., Davis, K. S., & Galupo, M. P. (2015). Comparing perceived experiences of prejudice among self-identified plurisexual individuals. *Psychology & Sexuality, 6*(3), 245–257. https://doi.org/10.1080/19419899.2014.940372

Mohr, J. J., Selterman, D., & Fassinger, R. E. (2013). Romantic attachment and relationship functioning in same-sex couples. *Journal of Counseling Psychology, 60*(1), 72–82. https://psycnet.apa.org/doi/10.1037/a0030994

Moradi, B., Mohr, J. J., Worthington, R. L., & Fassinger, R. E. (2009). Counseling psychology research on sexual (orientation) minority issues: Conceptual and methodological challenges and opportunities. *Journal of Counseling Psychology, 56*(1), 5–22. https://psycnet.apa.org/doi/10.1037/a0014572

Park, J. J., Chow, S. M., Fisher, Z. F., & Molenaar, P. (2020). Affect and personality: Ramifications of modeling (non-) directionality in dynamic network models. *European Journal of Psychological Assessment, 36*(6), 1009–1023. https://psycnet.apa.org/doi/10.1027/1015-5759/a000612

Patterson, C. J., Farr, R. H., & Goldberg, A. E. (2021). LGBTQ+ parents and their children. *Executive Summary*, 6(3), 1-8.

Peugh, J. L., DiLillo, D., & Panuzio, J. (2013). Analyzing mixed-dyadic data using structural equation models. *Structural Equation Modeling: A Multidisciplinary Journal*, 20(2), 314-337. https://doi.org/10.1080/10705511.2013.769395

Plöderl, M., & Tremblay, P. (2015). Mental health of sexual minorities. A systematic review. *International Review of Psychiatry*, 27(5), 367-385. https://doi.org/10.3109/09540261.2015.1083949

Ram, N., Brinberg, M., Pincus, A. L., & Conroy, D. E. (2017). The questionable ecological validity of ecological momentary assessment: Considerations for design and analysis. *Research in Human Development*, 14(3), 253-270. https://doi.org/10.1080/15427609.2017.1340052

Ram, N., & Pedersen, A. B. (2011). *Dyadic models emerging from the longitudinal structural equation modeling tradition: Parallels with ecological models of interspecific interactions* (pp. 97-116). Routledge.

Ram, N., Shiyko, M., Lunkenheimer, E. S., Doerksen, S., & Conroy, D. (2014). Families as coordinated symbiotic systems: Making use of nonlinear dynamic models. In S. McHale, P. Amato, & A. Booth (Eds.), *Emerging methods in family research* (pp. 19-37). Springer.

Randall, A. K., & Schoebi, D. (2018). Conceptual approaches to studying interpersonal emotion dynamics. In A. K. Randall & D. Schoebi (Eds.), *Interpersonal emotion dynamics in close relationships* (pp. 7-26). Cambridge University Press. https://doi.org/10.1017/9781316822944.003

Randall, A. K., Tao, C., León, G., & Duran, N. D. (2021). Couples' co-regulation dynamics as a function of perceived partner dyadic coping. *Anxiety, Stress, & Coping*, 34(6), 597-611. https://doi.org/10.1080/10615806.2021.1912740

Randall, A. K., Totenhagen, C. J., Walsh, K. J., Adams, C., & Tao, C. (2017). Coping with workplace minority stress: Associations between dyadic coping and anxiety among women in same-sex relationships. *Journal of Lesbian Studies*, 21(1), 70-87. https://doi.org/10.1080/10894160.2016.1142353

Reczek, C. (2020). Sexual-and gender-minority families: A 2010 to 2020 decade in review. *Journal of Marriage and Family*, 82(1), 300-325. https://doi.org/10.1111/jomf.12607

Reed, R. G., Barnard, K., & Butler, E. A. (2015). Distinguishing emotional coregulation from codysregulation: An investigation of emotional dynamics and body weight in romantic couples. *Emotion*, 15(1), 45-60. https://doi.org/10.1037/a0038561

Rossman, K., Sinnard, M., & Budge, S. (2019). A qualitative examination of consideration and practice of consensual nonmonogamy among sexual and gender minority couples. *Psychology of Sexual Orientation and Gender Diversity*, 6(1), 11-21. https://doi.org/10.1037/sgd0000300

Rouhani, S. (2014). Intersectionality-informed quantitative research: A primer. *American Journal of Public Health*, 103(6), 1082-1089.

Samrock, S., Kline, K., & Randall, A. K. (2021). Buffering against depression: Association between self-compassion, perceived family support, and age for transgender and non-binary individuals. *MDPI: International Journal of Environmental Research and Public Health*, 18, 7938. https://doi.org/10.3390/ijerph18157938

Saxbe, D., & Repetti, R. L. (2010). For better or worse? Coregulation of couples' cortisol levels and mood states. *Journal of personality and social psychology*, 98(1), 92-103. https://psycnet.apa.org/doi/10.1037/a0016959

Schrager, S. M., Steiner, R. J., Bouris, A. M., Macapagal, K., & Brown, C. H. (2019). Methodological considerations for advancing research on the health and wellbeing of sexual and gender minority youth. *LGBT Health*, 6(4), 156-165. https://doi.org/10.1089/lgbt.2018.0141

Shangani, S., Gamarel, K. E., Ogunbajo, A., Cai, J., & Operario, D. (2020). Intersectional minority stress disparities among sexual minority adults in the USA: The role of race/ethnicity and socioeconomic status. *Culture, Health & Sexuality*, 22(4), 398-412. https://doi.org/10.1080/13691058.2019.1604994

Smith, J. Z., Sayer, A. G., Goldberg, A. E. (2013) Multilevel modeling approaches to the study of LGBT-parent families: Methods for dyadic data analysis. In A. Goldberg, & K. Allen (Eds.), *LGBT-parent families* (pp. 307–323). Springer. https://doi.org/10.1007/978-1-4614-4556-2_20

Snijders, T. A., & Bosker, R. J. (2011). *Multilevel analysis: An introduction to basic and advanced multilevel modeling.* SAGE.

Steele, J. S., Ferrer, E., & Nesselroade, J. R. (2014). An idiographic approach to estimating models of dyadic interactions with differential equations. *Psychometrika*, 79(4), 675–700. https://doi.org/10.1007/S11336-013-9366-9

Suen, L. W., Lunn, M. R., Katuzny, K., Finn, S., Duncan, L., Sevelius, J.,... & Obedin-Maliver, J. (2020). What sexual and gender minority people want researchers to know about sexual orientation and gender identity questions: A qualitative study. *Archives of sexual behavior*, 49(7), 2301–2318. https://doi.org/10.1007/s10508-020-01810-y

Thorson, K. R., West, T. V., & Mendes, W. B. (2018). Measuring physiological influence in dyads: A guide to designing, implementing, and analyzing dyadic physiological studies. *Psychological methods*, 23(4), 595–616. https://psycnet.apa.org/doi/10.1037/met0000166

Timmons, A. C., Baucom, B. R., Han, S. C., Perrone, L., Chaspari, T., Narayanan, S. S., & Margolin, G. (2017). New frontiers in ambulatory assessment: Big data methods for capturing couples' emotions, vocalizations, and physiology in daily life. *Social Psychological and Personality Science*, 8(5), 552–563. https://doi.org/10.1177%2F1948550617709115

Timmons, A. C., Margolin, G., & Saxbe, D. E. (2015). Physiological linkage in couples and its implications for individual and interpersonal functioning: A literature review. *Journal of Family Psychology*, 29(5), 720–731. https://psycnet.apa.org/doi/10.1037/fam0000115

Totenhagen, C. J., León, G. A., & Randall, A. K. (2023). Dyadic Coping Inventory—Sexual Minority Stress: A scale validation with lesbian, gay, and bi+ men and women in same- and different-gender couples. *Psychology of Sexual Orientation and Gender Diversity*.

Totenhagen, C. J., Randall, A. K., Cooper, A. N., Tao, C., & Walsh, K. J. (2017). Stress spillover and crossover in same-sex couples: Concurrent and lagged daily effects. *Journal of GLBT Family Studies*, 13(3), 236–256. https://doi.org/10.1080/1550428X.2016.1203273

Trull, T. J., & Ebner-Priemer, U. (2013). Ambulatory assessment. *Annual Review of Clinical Psychology*, 9, 151–176. https://doi.org/10.1146/annurev-clinpsy-050212-185510

Vaillancourt-Morel, M. P., Rosen, N. O., Willoughby, B. J., Leonhardt, N. D., & Bergeron, S. (2020). Pornography use and romantic relationships: A dyadic daily diary study. *Journal of Social and Personal Relationships*, 37(10–11), 2802–2821. https://doi.org/10.1177%2F0265407520940048

Vallacher, R. R., Read, S. J., & Nowak, A. (2002). The dynamical perspective in personality and social psychology. *Personality and Social Psychology Review*, 6(4), 264–273. https://doi.org/10.1207%2FS15327957PSPR0604_01

Van de Schoot, R., & Miočević, M. (2020). *Small sample size solutions: A guide for applied researchers and practitioners.* Taylor & Francis.

van Eeden-Moorefield, B., Few-Demo, A. L., Benson, K., Bible, J., & Lummer, S. (2018). A content analysis of LGBT research in top family journals 2000–2015. *Journal of Family Issues*, 39(5), 1374–1395. https://doi.org/10.1177%2F0192513X17710284

Vandenberg, R. J., & Lance, C. E. (2000). A review and synthesis of the measurement invariance literature: Suggestions, practices, and recommendations for organizational research. *Organizational Research Methods*, 3(1), 4–70. https://doi.org/10.1177%2F109442810031002

Walch, S. E., Bernal, D. R., Gibson, L., Murray, L., Thien, S., & Steinnecker, K. (2020). Systematic review of the content and methods of empirical psychological research on LGBTQ and SGM populations in the new millennium. *Psychology of Sexual Orientation and Gender Diversity*, 7(4), 433–454. https://doi.org/10.1037/sgd0000364

Wallot, S. (2019). Multidimensional Cross-Recurrence Quantification Analysis (MdCRQA)–a method for quantifying correlation between multivariate time-series. *Multivariate Behavioral Research*, 54(2), 173–191. https://doi.org/10.1080/00273171.2018.1512846

West, T. V., Popp, D., & Kenny, D. A. (2008). A guide for the estimation of gender and sexual orientation effects in dyadic data: An actor-partner interdependence model approach. *Personality and Social Psychology Bulletin*, 34(3), 321–336. https://doi.org/10.1177%2F0146167207311199

Williamson, H., Bornstein, J. X., Cantu, V., Ciftci, O., Farnish, K. A., & Schouwiler, M. T. (2022). How diverse are the samples used to study intimate relationships? A systematic review. *Journal of Social and Personal Relationships*, 39(4), 1087–1109. https://doi.org/10.1177/02654075211053849

Wolf, E. J., Harrington, K. M., Clark, S. L., & Miller, M. W. (2013). Sample size requirements for structural equation models: An evaluation of power, bias, and solution propriety. *Educational and Psychological Measurement*, 73(6), 913–934. https://doi.org/10.1177%2F0013164413495237

Zeki, S., & Romaya, J. P. (2010). The brain reaction to viewing faces of opposite- and same-sex romantic partners. *PLOS ONE*, 5(12), e15802. https://doi.org/10.1371/journal.pone.0015802

NOTES

1. Sexual minority and gender diverse (SMGD) individuals are defined as those who endorse a non-heterosexual sexual orientation (e.g., lesbian, gay, bisexual, etc.) or a non-cisgender gender identify (e.g., transgender, nonbinary, genderqueer, etc.).
2. The American Psychological Association's *Guidelines for Psychological Practice with Sexual Minority Persons* defines sexual minority persons as individuals who identify as lesbian, gay, bi+ (e.g., pansexual, queer, etc.), asexual, or non-heterosexual (APA, 2021). Most researchers consider gender diverse individuals to be composed of individuals who identify as transgender, gender-expansive, gender-nonconforming, or non-cisgender (Matsuno & Budge, 2017; Schrager et al., 2019).
3. However, numbers of SMGD individuals are increasing, with one in six adults from Generation Z (born 1997–2012) identifying as either lesbian, gay, bisexual, or transgender (LGBT).

Gabriel A. León and Ashley K. Randall

QUEER COMMUNICATION PEDAGOGY

INTRODUCTION

Queer communication pedagogy (QCP) marks an activist-oriented educative praxis that works to dismantle racist cisheterosexism. Informed by enfleshed histories of embodied resistance to racist cisheteronormative disciplining, regulating, and policing of sex, gender, and sexual difference, QCP performs a liberatory politic committed to the abolition of the prison industrial complex (PIC), which Critical Resistance (2020) defines as "the overlapping interests of government and industry that use surveillance, policing, and imprisonment as solutions to economic, social and political problems" and that PCARE (2017) reminds us "reflects and produces racial inequality" (p. 297; see also PCARE, 2007). To be clear, QCP does not perform liberal reform politics in the form of uncritical or performative inclusionary gestures that fail to implicate the bases of racist cisheterosexist violences. Rather, QCP seeks to "interrupt settler colonialism by challenging students to study the ways in which they inherit colonial histories and to insist that they critically question the colonial institutions through which their rights are sought" (Smith, 2013, p. 469). QCP is radical pedagogical praxis that implicates the very foundation of communication studies. Still, QCP is derived largely of Western queer and trans experience and, as a result, its assumptions risk perpetuating U.S. centrism (Atay, 2020). Said quite differently, while QCP can claim the bravado of a radical, decolonial pedagogical politic, it remains a largely U.S.-centric venture that, without intersectional reflexivity, can privilege U.S. neoliberal educative modes and Western notions of "justice" (Jones & Calafell, 2010).

While rarely stated so explicitly, the drive to end the policing and disciplining of difference has long animated queer and trans existence and, in turn, is what informs QCP's abolitionist goals. Indeed, the *queer* in queer communication research is, or ought to be, activist oriented and work in service of liberatory ends (Slagle, 1995). Such ends should serve, specifically, those most lethally impacted by the PIC, including policing mechanisms that emerge through existing disciplinary knowledge, exclusionary course design, and the use of policing agents, including campus police, to remedy so-called unruly or uncivil students (LeMaster & Mapes, 2020).

Within the discipline of communication, queer approaches to pedagogy are relatively new, having emerged in the early 21st century. Prior to its emergence, queerness was largely glossed over in the communication discipline as mere outlier, deviant to those White cisheteronormative subjectivities worthy of academic interest. In his critical assessment of the communication discipline, Yep (2003) found queer and trans folks endure internalized, externalized, institutional, and discursive cisheteronormative violences at the intersections of difference. In addition to culture more generally, Yep revealed that cisheteronormative violences were performed in and through both communication scholarship and the resulting pedagogies that made their way into communication classrooms. Yep additionally argued that communication scholars are equipped to facilitate healing through criticism, performance, and pedagogy. Criticism includes demystification of cisheteronormativity while performance and pedagogy point to embodiment of difference and cultural performance as critical sites for interrogating and intervening in the performative sedimentation of cisheteronormativity (see also Pineau, 2002; Yep, 2017). In short, QCP's late emergence reflects the pervasiveness of racist cisheteronormativity organizing the foundation of the communication discipline generally and communication pedagogy more specifically.

To navigate these historically sedimented terrains, queer communication pedagogues draw on both their/our lived experiences, as folks who navigate cisheterosexist communication classrooms, in addition to a variety of interdisciplinary means used to imagine and enact queer communication pedagogies that work in service of liberatory ends. More formally, QCP reflects the convergence of critical communication pedagogy (CCP) with queer pedagogy. Informed by critical pedagogies, CCP centers the humanization, and in turn liberation, of communicative subjects. Conversely, queer pedagogies center the liberation of, specifically, queer and trans subjects most violently impacted by racist cisheterosexist carcerality. Taken together, QCP turns to communicative means to imagine and enact the liberation of intersectional sex, gender, and sexual nonnormativity in the communication classroom and beyond. This article traces the emergence of QCP as a liberatory abolitionist politic that works across the whole of communication curriculum. To accomplish this, we first story the emergence of QCP. Then, we unpack QCP's constitutive elements, including (1) locating, historicizing, and politicizing "queer"; (2) the emergence of CCP as a liberatory educative praxis that enables interdisciplinary connection with queer pedagogies; and (3) queer pedagogy as a pedagogical politic that labors to destabilize normativity with the larger goal of abolishing carcerality. Taken together, QCP marks a distinct communicative pedagogical project committed to the liberation of gender and sexual nonnormativity through the abolition of carcerality. To begin, we turn to the emergence of QCP.

THE EMERGENCE OF QUEER COMMUNICATION PEDAGOGY

Informed by enfleshed histories of resistance to racialized cisheterosexist discipline and violence at the hands of both state and local officials, including community members and educators, QCP is activist oriented and works in service of dismantling intersecting oppressions that mar the lives of marginalized identities, voices, and bodies in the communication classroom and beyond. In so doing, QCP takes as a critical point of departure the liberation of those oppressed by racist cisheterosexism at the intersections of difference. Atay and Pensoneau-Conway (2020b) formally coined QCP with the publication of their anthology *Queer Communication Pedagogy*. In it, communication scholars theorized queer paths and possibilities of and for communication pedagogy and liberation. While scant, earlier work that might be termed QCP included troubling normative renderings of gender in the classroom.

For instance, Lovaas et al. (2002) guided students to practice reflexive processing of one's own held beliefs about gender. In so doing, the authors encouraged students to interrogate their own deeply held beliefs about gender normativity and projected assumptions about gender difference and, specifically, trans bodies. Similarly, Cooks and Sun (2002) analyzed stories students tell about gender by placing in conversation the historical discourses that enable the communicative utterance with the dialogic encounter between gendered bodies. These pedagogical interventions sought to expand how students imagined and enacted gender and gender relations in communicative exchanges. While not explicitly "queer," the implications of this work are profoundly important for the liberation of sexual and gender difference in the communication classroom. Similar work during the 2000s focused on how to locate the gender and sexual nonnormative subject in the classroom highlighting the question of outness including its pedagogical and political implications (Gust & Warren, 2008; Meyer, 2005). Others reflect back on early cutting-edge courses in communication and sexuality (e.g., Charles, 2005; Lovaas & Jenkins, 2020).

Yep's (2003) important critique during this time highlighted an intense violence undergirding the communication discipline; that is cisheteronormativity (see also Yep, 2017). This critique pointed out that the discipline was not amenable to queerness or transness. The discipline did not begin to encounter queer approaches to pedagogy with increasing regularity until the 2010s. We do not want to discount the courageous and groundbreaking queer pedagogical work that occurs daily in communication classrooms but whose practices may not make it to the page due to any number of political reasons, including disinterest in publishing in academe, disinterest in formalizing queer pedagogical practices, lack of institutional resources that would allow for the space to reflect and write on pedagogical experience, and work spaces that are especially hostile to racialized sexual and gender nonnormativity.

Said differently, we cannot read the absence of a historically rich and robust explicitly named QCP body of literature as disinterest but as an indication of the racist cisheterosexism that pervasively organizes the communication discipline specifically and the academy more generally. That said, the published work that constitutes QCP provides a productive means of imagining queer and trans liberation in the communication classroom and beyond (e.g., Gingrich-Philbrook, 2002; Hobson, 2020; Lovaas, 2010; Lovaas & Jenkins, 2020; Sender, 2020; Whitworth & Wilcoxen, 2020; Young, 2020). Take for example Spieldenner and Booker (2020), who "talk sex" so as to "disrupt structures between student and teacher, between classroom and social network, and amongst sexual categories" (p. 157; see also Pensoneau-Conway, 2009). And consider the groundbreaking work of queer pedagogues who theorize the body as pedagogical intervention (Johnson & Calafell, 2020), look to queer performance art as pedagogical praxis (Pattisapu, 2020), transnationalize queer pedagogy (Atay, 2020), and read pedagogical potential in historical figures (Morris, 2013). LeMaster (2018) founded the Trans Empowerment Group, which helps to facilitate healing through critical interrogation of cisheterosexism in everyday lives of trans people, leading to queer worldmaking outside of the communication classroom (see also LeMaster et al., 2019). And consider the importance of queer mentoring, advising, and the constitution of queer families of choice in academe (Eguchi & Long, 2019; LeMaster, 2020; Pattisapu & Calafell, 2012).

Fox (2013) made an explicit link between queer pedagogy and communicative utterances in his call for queer pedagogues to attend to the "periperformative" dimensions of queer communication, or "speech *about* queer speech" (p. 73). Sedgwick (2003) coined "periperformative" and theorized it spatially: "Periperformative utterances aren't just about performative utterances in a referential sense: they cluster around them, they are near them or next to them or crowding against them; they are in the neighborhood of the performative" (p. 68). Sedgwick offered the performative example of a dare: *I dare you!* Performativity theory draws our attention to the first- and second-person persona involved in the dare, which together enable the utterance to *do*. Sedgwick, however, draws our attention to the third-person plural subject that is interpellated through a presumed alignment with the terms of engagement enabling the dare, "the 'they' of witness—whether or not literally present" (p. 69). In this regard, the subject who does not object to the dare (i.e., through silence or [presumed] absence) is assumed to align with the first-person subject enacting the scene. In the classroom, how the instructor and students talk about sexual and gender difference reveals the political scene against which "learning" is presumed to occur and in which sexual and gender nonnormative students are forced to accept the oppressive terms of their own violent exclusion. Fox set an important tone for the emergence of a communication-centered approach to queer pedagogy that attends to the communicative constitution of cisheterosexism performatively animated in and through mundane cultural performances in the classroom, a point long explored by critical communication pedagogues (see, e.g., Alexander, 1999).

More recently, and in the introduction to their co-edited special issue of *Communication Teacher* titled "Teaching Trans-Affirming, Intersectional Gender," LeMaster and Johnson (2019) called for a specifically trans-affirming queer pedagogy. To accomplish this, they modeled a critical trans-centered reading of Julia T. Wood and Natalie Fixmer-Oraiz's (2017) popular gender communication textbook *Gendered Lives*. In turn, the collection of classroom activities included in the special issue seek to radically reimagine gender in the communication classroom (see also Agid & Rand, 2011; Courvant, 2011; Enke, 2016; Muñoz & Garrison, 2008;

Nicolazzo et al., 2015; Spade, 2011). Capuzza et al. (2020) theorized trans-affirming pedagogy through a roundtable titled "Transing Communication Education: A Chorus of Voices." While queer pedagogy demands greater inclusion of queer voices and experiences, those voices and experiences often reflect *nontrans* queer experiences. This roundtable adds to LeMaster and Johnson's (2019) critical call for a specifically trans-affirming communication classroom. Reflecting on her own pedagogy in the classroom, Lucy Miller noted:

> Centering gender identity can be as simple as not relying exclusively on examples related to cisgender [non-trans] men and women and by continually reinforcing the socially constructed nature of gender, even when discussing communication patterns ascribed to a specific gender in our society. (Capuzza et al., 2020, p. 115)

Conversely, matthew heinz cautioned that "such pedagogy requires risks and a constant awareness of the inherent instability of ways of thinking about the human experience" (Capuzza et al., 2020, p. 117).

Capuzza et al. (2020) illustrated the cutting-edge work featured in Atay and Pensoneau-Conway's (2020b) edited collection just as it marked the *where* of our disciplinary conversation with regard to QCP. In the broadest sense, Atay and Pensoneau-Conway offered three paths to focus QCP efforts: (1) foster a space in which students can critically reflect on and interrogate racist cisheterosexism including the ways in which knowledge production is constrained by the terms, and their constitutive histories, themselves; (2) adopt readings and content that encourage students to question and resist racialized cisheteronormative presumptions of a "proper" text or object of study; and (3) enact curricular change that destabilizes assumptions about course content and perspective through centering queer and trans voices "as well as voices that decenter conventional curricular structures" (Atay & Pensoneau-Conway, 2020a, p. 8). To these we add a concerted focus on the interrogation of racist cisheterosexism and the resulting abolition of both policing and prison, key elements of queer and trans politics we must not forgo. The contributors to Atay and Pensoneau-Conway's volume—informed by their own intersectional political commitments to queer and trans liberation, coupled with their unique disciplinary approaches to QCP—theorized and enacted pedagogical possibilities of liberation of/for/by queer and trans subjects. QCP has rapidly developed in important ways that trouble the communication classroom and that work pedagogy in service of liberatory ends. Still, communication thinkers are only now beginning to imagine and enact QCP's liberatory possibilities. To gain a better perspective on the liberatory ends inherent in QCP, we turn our focus first to the "queer" of QCP before unpacking QCP's remaining constitutive elements: CCP and queer pedagogy.

LOCATING, HISTORICIZING, AND POLITICIZING THE "QUEER" IN QUEER COMMUNICATION PEDAGOGY

QCP is a form of critical pedagogy in that it desires liberation with a specific focus on queer and trans life, wellness, embodiment, identity, and experience at the intersections of difference. The queer of QCP marks an activist orientation that labors toward the destruction of intersectional normativities and their attending violences. Within queer communication studies, queer is articulated as both a noun and as a verb. As a noun, queer can refer to those whose embodiment or intersectional identities chafe against the dictates of racialized cisheteronormativity. These can include, for instance, sexual identities (e.g., lesbian, bisexual, pansexual, asexual, BDSM, leather, kink, gay), including erotic formations (e.g., polyamorous, aromantic, single) as well as gender identities (e.g., trans, transgender, ipsogender, nonbinary, genderqueer, agender) and including identities that center sex (e.g., transsexual, intersex) and many more intersectional identities that have yet to be imagined, felt, or relationally enacted.

Of course, these identities fail to capture the complexity of sex, gender, and sexual embodiment. Indeed, identity does not determine behavior nor presentation (nor does it determine the reverse), highlighting the reality that identities such as these reference those who are marked by others—or who identify themselves—as such (Hall, 1996). More than that, these identities represent but a small fraction of human experience (Yep, 2016). Specifically, these terms reference identity formations with colonial roots that privilege the global North and West, particularly U.S. American formations (Aizura et al., 2014; binaohan, 2014). Therefore, "queer" functions as an imperfect means of organizing and referencing large swaths of people who specifically navigate racialized cisheterosexism at the intersections of difference. In turn, "queer" is a coalitional politic that works to dismantle systemic oppression while centering an intersectional engagement with sexual politics and ideology (Cohen, 1997; Rubin, 2011). That being said, there is a particular distinction that is worth noting. And that is between that of "queer" and that of "trans," or between that of sexuality and of sex and gender (Stryker, 2004).

In the biggest sense, "queer" references that which is understood as odd, weird, and peculiar from the vantage of those who embody cultural power in the form of norms. When norms are imbued with cultural power they materialize as a compulsory cultural expectation projected onto all bodies such that those who fail—whether consciously or not—normative expectancies are dubbed sick or immoral (Rich, 1980). While queer references "oddness" in a big sense, it specifically references nonnormative sexuality. Cisheteronormativity marks the ideological ground distinguishing "good" from "bad" gendered sexualities (Yep, 2003). Rubin (2011) adds "recurrent battles [that] take place between the primary producers of sexual ideology—the churches, the family, and the media—and the groups whose experience they name, distort, and endanger"—educative spaces bearing no exception, particularly with regard to the cisheteronormative bias inherent in the communication discipline's foundation (p. 165; Yep, 2003). Queers, those whose sexualities have been dubbed "bad, abnormal, unnatural, damned," by those with the power to name (e.g., nonqueers), are embroiled in an ongoing battle of someone else's design (Rubin, 2011, p. 152).

Conversely, those subjects who otherwise mirror the "mythical norm" (White, endosex and cisgender, Christian, economically secure, able-bodied and -minded, citizen)—save for their queer sexuality—have increasingly turned to respectability politics in a bid toward assimilation into an unchanged sexual order organized by white supremacy (Lorde, 2007, p. 116). These respectable White queer subjects embody what Duggan (2003) theorizes as "homonormativity," or a neoliberal sexual politic "that does not contest dominant heteronormative assumptions and institutions, but upholds and sustains them, while promising the possibility of a demobilized gay constituency and a privatized, depoliticized gay culture anchored in domesticity and consumption" (p. 50). Homonormative subjects placate to Whiteness through a single-axis view of sexuality that refuses to engage intersectional complexity.

Homonormativity is not queer; it is a racist and unreflexive individualistic respectability politic marked by personal success in an unchanged racist cisheterosexist social order.

To be clear, the "queer" in queer pedagogy rejects untroubled bids of cultural inclusion as that encountered in homonormative politics as well as in (White) nationalist projects including homonationalism, which privileges "good" queer subjects who work in service of propping up the U.S. nation-state (Puar, 2007). Conversely, the "queer" in queer pedagogy references unruly sexual subjects dubbed "queer" as a result of their embodied difference and who, in turn, resist by way of existing against normativity. Emerging out of this context, "queer" has been historically used as an epithet and weaponized against people presumed to be lesbian, bisexual, and gay largely due to their nonnormative sexualities and gender performances (whether presumed as in the problematic use of the so-called gaydar or materialized in the form of a disclosure, i.e., *I'm not straight*). Sluts, sex workers, feminine men and masculine women, as well as "punks, bulldaggers, and welfare queens" bore/bear the brunt of these violences as subjects marked by their nonnormativity, including those marked as such in the communication classroom (Cohen, 1997, p. 463).

The 1990s ushered in a dark era of death in which a significant number of queer folks lost their lives due to an intentionally neglectful and conservative U.S. government response to HIV/AIDS. In turn, queers resisted the U.S. government-led decimation of queer subjects through activism in the form of groups like the AIDS Coalition to Unleash Power (ACT-UP) and Queer Nation (Rand, 2014). During this time, activists—targeted by racist cisheterosexism in the form of classed health disparities and death—reclaimed "queer" as a radical liberatory organizing politic. These queers used anger and rage as affective points of departure for political organizing. Queer pedagogies, so understood, are resistant, unruly, peculiar, and playful while committed to the destruction of intersectional sexual oppression. While queer subjects are policed and brutalized for the way they/we love, relate, and fuck, it is often through gender embodiment that outsiders project sexual meaning. Gender and sexuality are not the same, though they are culturally coconstitutive in a Western, U.S. context.

Like queer, "trans" functions as a broad coalitional politic that organizes large swaths of folks whose sex and gender evade cisheteronormative expectancies for bodily being and comportment (Stryker et al., 2008). The nation-state requires human reproduction for its perpetuation; it is, in this logic, a "duty" to reproduce the nation. (White) nationalist projects draw on racist cisheterosexist ideologies in order to mark humans for their capacity to reproduce. This logic forms the ground for colonial expansion historically (Stoller, 1995). The colonial project sought/seeks to control and destroy difference, both body and land (Miranda, 2013). In a colonial context, "gender" designated (White) human subjects as being either *men* or *women*, with man serving as the human exemplar and woman as his invert. Her task was to reproduce the (White) human race. Conversely, sex was used to distinguish reproductive capacity, and in turn labor promise, of nonhumans as *males* or *females*. It was into this category that colonial terrorists placed Indigenous, Black, and Brown subjects (Lugones, 2011).

While sex and gender are understood in different terms today, the colonial foundation on which contemporary gender is lived persists in the continued violence targeted at Indigenous and Black trans women and femme subjects today. Said directly, the sex and gender binaries are colonial technologies used to distinguish humans from nonhumans in racialized terms (binaohan, 2014). It is in this historical context that we locate the specificity of trans experience: As emerging in response to the colonial medical gaze that creates "sex" out of racist fantasies about genitals and the (White) nationalist shaping of human reproduction. Indeed, while trans experiences diverge in important ways (Plemons & Straayer, 2018; Prosser, 1998), it is a shared sense of resistance to normative racialized sex and gender interpellation that constructs a ground for collective organizing against the violences of racist cisheterosexism. Trans folks affirm their/our bodies in ways both similar to and different from nontrans folks; a primary difference is that trans folks are violently policed for, and restricted from, shaping their/ our bodies on their/our relative terms of engagement (Sullivan, 2006).

So, while there is overlap (especially as that experienced in trans folks whose sexualities are also queer), the distinction between queer and trans matters. When used in the broader, *universalizing* sense, yes, trans subjects might be understood as queer and the implications of queer sexual politics impact trans subjects in important ways (Sedgwick, 2008). However, trans folks can be easily erased when "queer" is understood in a narrow sense focused exclusively on sexuality sans intersectional complexity including heterosexual trans folks and trans folks who refuse to identify with/as "queer." We locate the core of this tension in White queer political resistance politics that expect nonnormative lives, bodies, and identities to work exclusively in service of dismantling normativity; this is not necessarily the goal of trans subjects who are simply trying to live life (Namaste, 2000). The expectation that a trans subject ought to challenge the gender binary, for instance, in every life choice they make not only places the onus of social change on trans bodies but it lets nontrans subjects off the hook from implicating their own complacency in maintaining the existing racist gender order. This includes nontrans subjects who have yet to interrogate their own compulsory sex assignment at birth and the resulting gender trajectory on which one finds oneself (Valentine, 2012) and queer and/ or trans subjects who refuse to interrogate the whiteness that undergirds their own relationship to binary gender (Detournay, 2019; Snorton, 2017). Whereas queer politics deconstruct culture, trans politics imagine and reconstruct possibility in a racist cisheterosexist culture (Keegan, 2020). In this regard, trans politics necessarily trouble queer assumptions of assimilation as an either/or dichotomy. In total, "queer" as a noun references a variety of subjects whose sex, gender, and/or sexuality fail to meet racist cisheterosexist standards for identity and embodiment.

As a verb, "queer" refers to the discursive dismantling, destabilization, and deconstruction of cultural normativities generally and cisheteronormativity specifically. It is the noun—the queer and trans culture makers and their mundane, even if unintentional, embodied resistance to racialized cisheteronormative carcerality—that provides the performative means enabling the verb, or the queer*ing* of culture. In this way, the impulse to critique culture from a queer vantage is informed by historical embodied resistance to the violence of intersectional normativities including racialized cisheteronormativity. Take, for instance, Joan of Arc's famed protest to being imprisoned and forced to wear clothing expected of women: "For nothing in the world will I swear not to arm myself and put on a man's dress" (quoted in Feinberg, 1992, p. 14). The Inquisition sentenced Joan of Arc to death and remarked on her unwillingness to wear clothes expected of women: "time and again you have relapsed, as a dog that returns to its vomit" (quoted in Feinberg, 1992, p. 14; see also Crane, 1996). Or take 18th-century resistance to London molly house raids wherein patrons "many of them in drag, met the raid with determined and violent resistance" (Bray, 1982, p. 91). Or the 1966 resistance to police harassment and brutality led by trans women of color at Gene Compton's Cafeteria in San Francisco or the later 1969 Stonewall Rebellion in New York, led by Black and Brown queer and trans folks of color including Stormé DeLarverie, Miss Major Griffin-Gracy, Marsha P. Johnson, and Sylvia Rivera—each are inspirational activists in their own right (see Feinberg, 1996; Stryker, 2017). Or consider that exciting moment when, in 2017, Trans Queer Pueblo, an activist group that centers trans and queer migrant voices, shut down Arizona Phoenix Pride and demanded organizers make Pride safe for queer and trans people of color by ending its ties with the police state and demanding the release of queer and trans migrants from detention (Philp, 2017). Or take the 2020 Brooklyn Liberation March of 15,000 activists asserting: *Black Trans Lives Matter!*

Those who fall outside of intersectional normativity's privileged core are forced to endure the brunt of systemic oppression (Yep, 2013). This resistance can be spectacular, as exhibited in the examples here largely led by trans culture makers, or it can look and sound and feel quite mundane in the context of violent racist cisheterosexism as illustrated in Lourde Ashley Hunter's (2015) important declaration: *Every Breath a Black Trans Woman Takes Is an Act of Revolution*. Cohen (1997) locates the "radical potential of queerness" at the "intersection of oppression and resistance," where different bodies coalesce around an intersectional politic of resistance (p. 440). Taken together, queer (as noun and verb) marks a praxiological pedagogical posture that centers the liberation of minoritized sexual subjects at the intersections of difference. Within the discipline of communication, CCP has proven amenable to queer's political edge in pedagogical terms. In the next section, we explore the ways CCP possibilizes queer's radical pedagogical potential through liberatory commitments before turning to queer pedagogy itself, which serves as a guide that directs CCP practitioners to more fully engage and resist racist cisheterosexism through abolitionist goals.

CRITICAL COMMUNICATION PEDAGOGY AS LIBERATORY

The study of communication in educational contexts has fallen into two camps: communication education and instructional communication. Staton (1989) distinguishes communication education as "the study of the teaching of speech communication" (p. 365). Studies of this sort have engaged the teaching of communication in classroom settings at all levels, from grade school through college. Communication education scholars theorize and explore effective means of teaching communication theories and skills. Conversely, instructional communication is "the study of the human communication process as it occurs in instructional contexts" or, said differently, how communication affects "instructional situation[s], classroom context[s], or school environment[s]" (p. 366). Communication education offers a narrower point of focus than that of instructional communication, which looks at communication across any number of subjects and at all levels of education.

Both communication subfields have historically relied on quantitative means to theorize effective pedagogy. Research of this sort assumes at least two things: (1) the classroom is a neutral, depoliticized site and (2) generalizable findings are dependent on essentialized notions of identity and difference such that "the student" stands in for learning experiences across learning sites (Sprague, 1992, 1993, 1994). Fassett and Rudick (2016) add that research of this sort relies on: "state/trait-based research (e.g., verbal aggressiveness), decontextualized communicative behaviors (e.g., verbal immediacy), or interpersonal-level understandings of power" (p. 576). In response, Sprague (1992) shifted the focus by asking quite simply and directly of communication scholars: "Does our current approach to scholarship have a *liberating* or a *dehumanizing* effect on students and teachers?" (p. 5, emphasis added). This question formally introduced the question of criticality to communication education and instructional communication research.

Prior to Sprague's (1993) critical call for a "renewed and reinvigorated" study of communication pedagogy, instructional communication scholars were already theorizing power in the classroom (p. 106). However, they theorized power as a tool used in service of policing student behavior so as to ensure classroom management. In the first of a series of essays titled "Power in the Classroom," McCroskey and Richmond (1983) describe the function of power and its relationship to communication in the classroom thusly:

> Power and communication are closely interrelated. Power that is not used, for all intents and purposes, is power that does not exist. The use of power requires communication. In the absence of communication, therefore, the teacher in the classroom is powerless. In the same vein, the way(s) the teacher communicates with her/his [sic] students to a major extent determine the type and extent of the power he/she [sic] *exert* over those students. Similarly, the type of power *exerted* will have a major impact on the quality of teacher-student communication. (pp. 175–176, emphasis added; see also Richmond & McCroskey, 1992)

This and resulting research offered Behavioral Alteration Messages and Behavioral Alteration Techniques as pedagogical means to control student behavior perceived to be "disruptive" or "unruly" or "uncivil" from the vantage of the authoritarian educator. Returning to Sprague's (1992) query—*Does our current approach to scholarship have a liberating or a dehumanizing effect on students and teachers?*—one will rightly note that these traditional articulations of power (as coercive and violent means to *alter* student [who are humans, after all] behavior) serve as grounds to *dehumanize* students. It is against this backdrop of oppressive compulsory pedagogical practice that Sprague asks her important question ushering in the critical interrogation of communication pedagogy.

Critical pedagogy marks less a method than it does a posture. As a posture, critical pedagogies maintain, in the words of hooks (1989), "Education is a political issue for exploited and oppressed people" (p. 98; see also Giroux 2000, 2004); it is the *practice of freedom* (hooks, 1994). To answer Sprague's (1992) query, critical pedagogies labor toward *liberating* effects for both students and teachers, regardless of the course or level of teaching/learning. Informed in part by CCP, QCP focuses its abolitionist goals toward the *liberation* of racialized gender and sexual nonnormativities specifically while CCP is amenable to a broader intersectional engagement with liberatory politics and pedagogy. A common misunderstanding is that critical pedagogies are restricted to "cultural" classrooms. Rather, critical pedagogies understand the classroom *as* a cultural site produced by, while producing, culture (Alexander, 1999, 2004a, 2004b, 2005; Alexander & Warren, 2002). As Giroux argues in McLaren (1999), "schools are more than instructional sites; they are cultural sites that are actively involved in the selective ordering and legitimization of specific forms of language, reasoning, sociality, daily experience and style" (p. xxiv). In short, schooling constructs "good" subjects based on hegemonic cultural standards including those of whiteness and cisheteronormativity.

There is no "real world" out there, but rather different cultural contexts in which the same machinations of power flow differently across our different bodies and through different course content and areas of study. As such, critical pedagogies are well suited to all communication classrooms, perhaps especially for those courses and areas of study in which antioppression is undertheorized or in which whiteness orders a hierarchy of communicative intelligibility (Chakravartty et al., 2018). Critical pedagogy reverses the assumptions undergirding traditional communication education and instructional communication research by (1) politicizing the classroom by drawing attention to cultural power, which always and already exists and animates the classroom and beyond, and (2) advancing an embodied understanding of identity as coconstitutive of culture and communication (Calafell, 2010; Hamera, 2004; Pineau, 2002; Warren, 1999). This discursive reversal of terms renders generalizable findings that attempt to make sense of "the student" in "the classroom" as suspicious at best.

While critical pedagogy has assumed many forms, it is the work of Brazilian philosopher Paolo Freire that has made the greatest critical impact on communication pedagogy. Freire (2005) famously critiqued the "banking" model of education wherein students are understood as empty vessels into which teachers deposit knowledge. This framework depends on a vertical relational power dynamic with the teacher positioned above the student wielding knowledge as a "gift bestowed by those who consider themselves knowledgeable upon those whom they consider to know nothing" (p. 72). In Freire's education philosophy, the banking model hinders what he terms *conscientização*, or critical consciousness. *Conscientização* enables students and teachers to understand themselves as historically situated in culture as opposed to as individuals navigating individual life trajectories as that advocated for in banking models of education. In the place of banking education, Freire (2005) proposed "problem-posing" education (p. 79).

A problem-posing approach to education highlights intersectional structural barriers against which we must differently toil in and out of the classroom (Kahl, 2017). Said differently, cultural criticism serves as a beginning rather than an end, pointing to the praxis undergirding critical pedagogy (Freire, 2005). For example, one such problem might include the compulsory use of an institutional language expectation (U.S. English) for public speaking courses and U.S. communication curriculum. In their important pedagogical intervention, Chawla and Rodriguez (2011) recognized that "language un/shapes and un/constitutes us" (p. 77). By interrogating the U.S. English requirement undergirding the public speaking course, which centers the *good speaker speaking well*, Chawla and Rodriguez press us to recognize the "inseparable relationship" between communication and perception as relational grounds for enacting public advocacy—as opposed to action derived of the lone persuasive orator (p. 77). Rather than assessing all students with the same rubric as they respond to the same prompt, a problem-posing approach to public speaking might include a teacher working *with* students to collaboratively "examine the historical, ontological, and epistemological forces that shape and influence how we relate and experience our bodies and that of others" (p. 86). In turn, students and teachers are equipped to coconstruct platforms that advocate against the compulsory use of U.S. English so as to open more space for more genders to emerge in the public speaking course or that advocate for greater language inclusion more generally.

It is through dialogue that students and teachers develop *conscientização*. In problem-posing education, dialogue shifts the intersectional vertical power dynamic from teacher/student to a horizontal orientation: "teacher-student" and "students-teacher" (Freire, 2005, p. 80). The student-and/as-teacher framing embodies Conquergood's (1985) notion of a "dialogical stance" that positions communicative subjects "together even while it holds them apart. It is more like a hyphen than a period" (p. 9). Said differently, students enter the classroom filled with knowledge derived from lived experience. The critical pedagogue's task is, in dialogue with/as students, to collaboratively imagine and cocreate a different world in which there is less harm and no oppression while using as a point of focus the particulars of course content; that is, how can course content be used in service of facilitating progressive social change and, ultimately, the liberation of those most oppressed and harmed by racist cisheterosexist carcerality? To be clear, critical pedagogy does not resolve power between students and teachers; this is a naïve understanding of cultural power. Rather, it draws our attention to the pervasiveness of power as students-and/as-teachers lean into one another in intersectional political coalition (Cooks, 2010). Yes, teachers have power over students. But it is also the case that intersectional identities trouble any attempt at clear identity and thus power distinctions. Indeed, a student who is also a White cisgender man has more access to cultural power relative to a Black trans femme educator even if both share the same classroom scene. Power, like culture, is complicated, and critical pedagogy labors to critique power and transform culture through the destruction of oppression and its intersectional complexities.

Fusing Freirian pedagogy to postmodern theories of identity (i.e., performativity), Fassett and Warren (2007) importantly advanced critical communication pedagogy (CCP) as "both a field of study and a pedagogical practice" that develops and refocuses communication education *and* instructional communication scholarship to embrace social justice as an overarching pedagogical goal (p. 38; see also Rudick et al., 2018). In their original articulation, Fassett and Warren (2007) advanced 10 commitments of critical pedagogy. Fassett and Rudick (2018) reconceptualized this into three thematic moves reflecting developments in CCP research, noting (1) communication as constitutive, (2) social justice as process, and (3) teaching and learning environments as meaningful sites of activism and interpersonal justice. In turn, Fassett and Rudick (2016) defined CCP as a

> critical paradigmatic approach for the study of communication and instruction—one that focuses on analysis of culture and power in the service of social justice. CCP also signals a critical paradigmatic approach to classroom practice—one that is fundamentally student-centered, dialogic, and attentive to power and privilege. (p. 579)

Finally, CCP scholarship is diverse and covers topics that include racism and race talk (Cummins & Griffin, 2012; Rudick & Golsan, 2017), neoliberalism in education (Jones & Calafell, 2012), difference (Warren & Toyosaki, 2012), mentoring (Pattisapu & Calafell, 2012), and student-teacher relationships (Rudick & Golsan, 2014). What queer pedagogy lends CCP is a concerted focus on abolition in the face of racist cisheterosexism and the concomitant liberation of queer and trans subjects at the intersections of difference. For example, CCP's focus on "social justice" presumes reliance on a given nation's justice system, which in a U.S. context has proven to be one of the primary settler forces enacting racist cisheterosexist violence against Black, Indigenous, Brown, and other queer and trans folks of color (Smith, 2013). In turn, QCP is both liberatory, as a result of its critical pedagogical influences, *and* abolitionist, in response to its queer pedagogical influences. In the final section, we turn to queer pedagogy's abolitionist impulse before closing the article with a brief meditation on QCP's horizon.

QUEER PEDAGOGY AS ABOLITIONIST

Where critical pedagogy recognizes the classroom as a political site imbued with cultural power, queer pedagogy more specifically recognizes racist cisheterosexist carceral logics as a primary political force organizing Western education (LeMaster & Mapes, 2019, 2020). The policing, disciplining, regulating, and violent repression of intersectional gender and sexual differences that divert from racialized cisheteronormative formations serve as the historically violent force that has animated, and that continues to inform, queer and trans politics. Said differently, resistance to the literal policing of nonnormative difference serves as the political ground animating queer and trans politics. In turn, the *liberatory* impulse driving queer pedagogy's critical edge is committed to, and informed by, abolitionist politics, which move us to "imagine an entirely different world—one that is not built upon the historical and contemporary legacies of the racial and gendered brutality that maintain the power" of the police state, including prison (Stanley, 2015, p. 14). As such, the queer pedagogue's task begins, at minimum, with the constant reflexive interrogation of one's own institutionally derived power as "teacher" capable of leveraging punishment whether through oppressive and exclusionary curriculum design or through agents of the state including campus police forces. Queer pedagogy is critical pedagogy is liberatory pedagogy is abolition pedagogy.

Bryson and de Castell (1993) first termed "queer pedagogy" in the early 1990s, ushering in an era of queer pedagogical interventions. Some of the earliest work in this area questioned, theorized, and troubled the politics of outness in the classroom, asking: *Should we [educators] come out?* (i.e., Khayatt, 1997; Wright, 1993; Yescavage & Alexander, 1997). The question of outness has political implications for queer educators. Russ et al. (2002) found queer educators who disclosed their sexual identity were perceived to be less credible educators and that students of queer educators perceive themselves to learn less when compared with students of nonqueer educators. These perceptions have historical precedence grounded in the pathologization of White sexual and gender formations that refused cisheteronormative expectations for human reproduction.

Foucault (1978) argued that modern cultural forces converged to construct knowledge about sexuality, which was in turn used to regulate sexuality differently across different bodies and ultimately serving political ends. Women were defined through their bodies as hypersexual creatures (pathologized as "hysteria") in need of regulation such that sex was defined through a narrow scope of reproductive intelligibility. Children became known as inherently sexual creatures in need of protection from themselves (i.e., masturbation as "evil") and from those who might take advantage of their unregulated hypersexuality. Finally, sexuality was separated from the body and understood as something to be analyzed and interrogated for its alignment with (White) nationalist expectations for human reproduction; sexual formations that did not work in service of human reproduction were pathologized as sick and in need of discipline and repair. The Western model of sexuality construct(ed/s) queer and trans subjects as sick and in need of discipline and repair. The queer and/or trans educator, then, troubles the cisheteronormative assumption informing the desexualized image of the maternal "teacher."

Specifically, the *queer* educator is understood as a *sexually perverse* educator who not only spoils the minds of youth but who also poses a sexual threat to students/children who are understood as needing protection from so-called perverts. This includes allied educators who are not queer nor trans but who center queer and trans life and liberation—these allies risk contagion through affiliation, although their access to cisheterosexual privileges can provide insulation denied the educator dubbed queer or trans. It is the trope of the sexual pervert that queer and trans educators are forced to navigate in the context of education and that serves as but one ground mediating outness; indeed, intersectional analysis reveals the Whiteness undergirding this Foucauldian observation: queer and/or trans educators of color are forced to navigate the intersectional constitution of both the trope of the sexual pervert *and* any historically sedimented racist tropes that constrain racialized sexualities (Stoller, 1995).

Some queer educators have explored the question of outness in pedagogical terms, advocating for strategic disclosures that work in service of troubling presumptions of identity and embodiment (Branfman, 2017; Kirk, 2008; Nathanson, 2009). Recent research engaging the question of outness, or manifestations of queer presence in the classroom, reveals that while White queer educators have enjoyed relative privilege to being out as educators (especially those queer educators who embody and perform homonormativity and who have the privilege to strategically disclose identity), higher education remains an unsafe space for queer and trans educators of color at the intersections of difference (Abdi & Cuomo, 2020; Calafell, 2012; Calafell & Eguchi, 2020). Embodied tensions with normative expectancies for bodily being and comportment in the classroom lie at the heart of these engagements with outness; the queer educator and student are "trouble" because they highlight the classroom as always and already inherently designed by and for White fantasies of gender and sexual regulation, being, and comportment; education is designed to fail queer and trans subjects (LeMaster, 2018).

As such, queer pedagogy is an abolitionist educative praxis committed to "the deliberate production of queer relations and to the production of subjectivities as deviant performance" and can be understood as a kind of "postmodern carnivalesque pedagogy of the underworld, as agitation <implemented deliberately to interfere with, to intervene in the production of so-called normalcy in schooled subjects>" (Bryson & de Castell, 1993, pp. 298–299; see also Shlasko, 2005). Queer pedagogy seeks to destabilize taken-for-granted (compulsory) cultural assumptions grounded in an abolitionist politic that works against carcerality. Queer pedagogies that fail to center abolitionist politics in favor of postmodern flights of fancy (e.g., "queer" as thought experiment with no grounding in the materiality of queer and trans of color life) appropriate the "odd" of "queer" and, in turn, erase the racist cisheterosexist violences, and resulting embodied resistances, that form the core of queer and trans politics. Queer pedagogies must engage both: a destabilization of knowledge production that works in service of liberating subjects that are most immediately and violently impacted by racist cisheterosexism. To accomplish this, queer pedagogy must center racialized sexual and gender differences that are marginalized by racist cisheterosexism, which requires educators to acknowledge the limits of their/our knowing (LeMaster & Fassett, 2021; LeMaster & Johnson, 2019). Loutzenheiser (2001) characterized queer pedagogy as

> a shifting tool for queer students of color and others (including teachers) to read their own marginalizations as positions from which they can act, think critically, accept and reject, no matter how contingent and partial they may be. It is in this messy, contradictory morass of not controlling the outcome that they can acknowledge the issues that make possible a queered, antiracist way of teaching. (p. 202)

Rather than working to resolve ignorance, as that advocated in the banking model of education, queer pedagogy uses racist cisheterosexist oppression as a point of critical departure for imagining and enacting a different means of relating that works in service of liberating queer and trans subjects at the intersections of difference (Britzman, 1998). These liberatory, abolitionist goals are conducive to any and all disciplinary curriculum and to communication in particular.

CONCLUSION: QUEER COMMUNICATION PEDAGOGY AS LIBERATORY AND ABOLITIONIST

As noted by Nakayama and Corey (2003), "throughout the academy, queer students idolize heteronormative theories, methods that constructed variance, deviance, discourses of abnormality, and documents of marginalization" (p. 324). This idolization reflects the racist cisheteronormative constraints that delimit how communication scholarship makes sense of sex, gender, and sexual nonnormativity. QCP provides an alternative—queer—path of possibility grounded in the liberation of queer and trans subjects through the abolition of carcerality. This path provides critically oriented students and faculty a model for imagining themselves and others as free of the constraints delimiting life chance and possibility. As a result, much of that which QCP facilitates can be located in the realm of imagination. Out of that which does not exist in the literature, queer and trans students-and/as-teachers cocreate worlds of abolitionist possibility. The racist cisheteronormative literature is not seen as a limitation, but as a critical point of departure to ask different questions that work in service of liberatory and abolitionist ends.

Indeed, QCP's concerted focus on power as a fluid, intersectional force empowers students to name not only ways in which they feel empowered by pedagogical possibility but also ways in which they feel harmed by the violence of racist cisheteronormativity as it emerges in the disciplinary literature, pedagogical practice, and communicative means by which we, as educators, seek to "control" difference through disciplinary mechanisms. QCP works in service of liberating all subjects from the compulsory constraints of sex, gender, and sexual normativities at the intersections of difference—queer, trans, nonqueer, and nontrans alike. It destabilizes the hegemony of disciplinary knowledge and neoliberal education in favor of local resistance to, and concomitant liberation from, intersectional oppressions.

Thus, QCP facilitates revolt in service of liberating those most directly impacted by racist cisheterosexism. In this regard, QCP marks a commitment to abolitionist politics, which center queer and trans of color liberation from discipline, policing, and violence. These violences often begin in the classroom from grade school to high school through the school-to-prison pipeline (GSA Network, 2014). Indeed, QCP must begin with the material recognition that those queer and trans students most impacted by the police state rarely share our classroom settings in higher education. And, thus, QCP exceeds the boundary of the classroom by centering the absence of those bodies most impacted by policing mechanisms. QCP is not a thought experiment. It is enfleshed resistance to racist cisheterosexism, particularly in regard to the violent policing and disciplining of sex, gender, and sexual nonnormativity at the intersections of difference.

PRIMARY SOURCE

Atay, A., & Pensoneau-Conway, S. L. (Eds.). (2020). *Queer communication pedagogy*. Routledge.

FURTHER READING

Atay, A., & Toyosaki, S. (Eds.). (2018). *Critical intercultural communication pedagogy*. Lexington Books.
Brim, M. (2020). *Poor queer studies: Confronting elitism in the university*. Duke University Press.
Corey, F. C., & Nakayama, T. K. (1997). Sextext. *Text and Performance Quarterly, 17*(1), 58–68. https://doi.org/10.1080/10462939709366169
Johnson, J. M., & Javier, G. (Eds.). (2017). *Queer people of color in higher education*. Information Age Publishing.
Kishimoto, K. (2018). Anti-racist pedagogy: From faculty's self-reflection to organizing within and beyond the classroom. *Race, Ethnicity, and Education, 21*(4), 540–554. https://doi.org/10.1080/13613324.2016.1248824
Kumashiro, K. (2002). *Troubling education: Queer activism and antioppressive pedagogy*. Routledge.
LeMaster, B., & Johnson, A. L. (2019). Teaching trans-affirming, intersectional gender [Special issue]. *Communication Teacher, 33*(3), 189–233. https://doi.org/10.1080/17404622.2018.1467566
Muñoz, V. (2012). Gender/sovereignty. In F. Enke (Ed.), *Transfeminist perspectives in and beyond transgender and gender studies* (pp. 23–33). Temple University Press.
Nicolazzo, Z. (2016). *Trans* in college: Transgender students' strategies for navigating campus life and the institutional politics of inclusion*. Stylus Publishing.
Nicolazzo, Z., Marine, S. B., & Galarte, F. J. (Eds.). (2015). Trans*formational pedagogies. [Special issue]. *Transgender Studies Quarterly, 2*(3), 367–518.
Stanley, E., & Smith, N. (Eds.). (2015). *Captive genders: Trans embodiment and the prison industrial complex* (2nd ed.). AK Press.
Thomas-Reid, M. (2018). Queer pedagogy. In G. Noblit (Ed.), *Oxford research encyclopedia of education*. Oxford University Press. http://doi.org/10.1093/acrefore/9780190264093.013.405
Varghese, R. (Ed.). (2019). *Raw: PrEP, pedagogy, rxand the politics of barebacking*. University of Regina Press.

REFERENCES

Abdi, S., & Cuomo, A. P. (2020). On possibility: Queer relationality and coalition-building in the university classroom. In A. L. Johnson & B. LeMaster (Eds.), *Gender futurity, intersectional autoethnography: Embodied theorizing from the margins* (pp. 37–54). Routledge.
Agid, S., & Rand, E. (2011). Beyond the special guest: Teaching "trans" now. *Radical Teacher, 92*, 5–9. https://www.jstor.org/stable/10.5406/radicalteacher.92.0005

Aizura, A. Z., Cotton, T., Balzer, C., LaGata, B., Ochoa, M., & Vidal-Ortiz, S. (2014). Decolonizing the transgender imaginary. *Transgender Studies Quarterly, 1*(3), 308–319. https://doi.org/10.1215/23289252-2685606

Alexander, B. K. (1999). Performing culture in the classroom: An instructional (auto)ethnography. *Text and Performance Quarterly, 19*(4), 307–331. https://doi.org/10.1080/10462939909366272

Alexander, B. K. (2004a). Critically analyzing pedagogical interactions as performance. In B. K. Alexander, G. L. Anderson, & B. P. Gallegos (Eds.), *Performance theories in education: Power, pedagogy, and the politics of identity* (pp. 41–62). Taylor & Francis.

Alexander, B. K. (2004b). Racializing identity: Performance, pedagogy, and regret. *Cultural Studies ⇔ Critical Methodologies, 4*(1), 12–27. https://doi.org/10.1177/1532708603251810

Alexander, B. K. (2005). Embracing the teachable moment: The black gay body in the classroom as embodied text. In E. P. Johnson & M. G. Henderson (Eds.), *Black queer studies: A critical anthology* (pp. 249–265). Duke University Press.

Alexander, B. K., & Warren, J. T. (2002). The materiality of bodies: Critical reflections on pedagogy, politics, and positionality. *Communication Quarterly, 50*(3–4), 328–343. https://doi.org/10.1080/01463370209385667

Atay, A. (2020). Transnational queer communication pedagogy. In A. Atay & S. L. Pensoneau-Conway (Eds.), *Queer communication pedagogy* (pp. 92–104). Routledge.

Atay, A., & Pensoneau-Conway, S. L. (2020a). Introduction: Queering communication pedagogy. In A. Atay & S. L. Pensoneau-Conway (Eds.), *Queer communication pedagogy* (pp. 1–13). Routledge.

Atay, A., & Pensoneau-Conway, S. L. (Eds.). (2020b). *Queer communication pedagogy*. Routledge.

binaohan, b. (2014). *Decolonizing trans/gender 101*. Biyuti Publishing.

Branfman, J. (2017). "(Un)Covering" in the classroom: Managing stigma beyond the closet. *Feminist Teacher, 26*(1), 72–82. https://www.muse.jhu.edu/article/657558

Bray, A. (1982). *Homosexuality in Renaissance England*. Columbia University Press.

Britzman, D. P. (1998). Is there a queer pedagogy? Or, stop reading straight. In W. F. Pinar (Ed.), *Curriculum: Toward new identities* (pp. 211–227). Garland Publishing.

Bryson, M., & de Castell, S. (1993). Queer pedagogy: Praxis makes im/perfect. *Canadian Journal of Education, 18*(3), 285–305. https://www.jstor.org/stable/1495388

Calafell, B. M. (2010). When will we all matter? Exploring race, pedagogy, and sustained hope for the academy. In D. L. Fassett & J. T. Warren (Eds.), *The SAGE handbook of communication and instruction* (pp. 343–360). SAGE.

Calafell, B. M. (2012). Monstrous femininity: Constructions of women of color in the academy. *Journal of Communication Inquiry, 36*(2), 111–130. https://doi.org/10.1177/0196859912443382

Calafell, B. M., & Eguchi, S. (2020). Are we queer yet? Queerness on the horizon in academia. In A. L. Johnson & B. LeMaster (Eds.), *Gender futurity, intersectional autoethnography: Embodied theorizing from the margins* (pp. 69–84). Routledge.

Capuzza, J. C., Spencer, L. G., Billard, T. J., Booth, T., heinz, m., Jones, S., & Miller, L. (2020). Transing communication education: A chorus of voices. In A. Atay & S. L. Pensoneau-Conway (Eds.), *Queer communication pedagogy* (pp. 107–129). Routledge.

Chakravartty, P., Kuo, R., Grubbs, V., & McIlwain, C. (2018). #CommunicationSoWhite. *Journal of Communication, 68*(2), 254–266. https://doi.org/10.1093/joc/jqy003

Charles, C. (2005). Queer writes. *Women's Studies in Communication, 28*(1), 32–56. https://doi.org/10.1080/07491409.2005.10162483

Chawla, D., & Rodriguez, A. (2011). Postcoloniality and the speaking body: Revisioning the English oral competency curriculum. *Cultural Studies ⇔ Critical Methodologies, 11*(1), 76–91. https://doi.org/10.1177/1532708610386923

Cohen, C. J. (1997). Punks, bulldaggers, and welfare queens: The radical potential of queer politics? *GLQ: A Journal of Lesbian and Gay Studies, 3*(4), 437–465. https://doi.org/10.1215/10642684-3-4-437

Conquergood, D. (1985). Performing as a moral act. *Literature in Performance, 85*(5), 1–13. https://doi.org/10.1080/10462938509391578

Cooks, L. (2010). The (critical) pedagogy of communication and the (critical) communication of pedagogy. In D. L. Fassett & J. T. Warren (Eds.), *The SAGE handbook of communication and instruction* (pp. 293–314). SAGE.

Cooks, L., & Sun, C. (2002). Constructing gender pedagogies: Desire and resistance in the "alternative" classroom. *Communication Education, 51*(3), 293–310. https://doi.org/10.1080/03634520216517

Courvant, D. (2011). Strip! *Radical Teacher, 92*, 26–34. https://www.jstor.org/stable/10.5406/radicalteacher.92.0026

Crane, S. (1996). Clothing and gender definition: Joan of Arc. *Journal of Medieval and Early Modern Studies, 26*(2), 297–320.

Critical Resistance. (2020). What is the PIC? What is abolition?, http://criticalresistance.org/about/not-so-common-language/

Cummins, M. W., & Griffin, R. A. (2012). Critical race theory and critical communication pedagogy: Articulating pedagogy as an act of love from Black male perspectives. *Liminalities, 8*(5), 85–106. http://liminalities.net/8-5/

Detournay, D. (2019). The racial life of "cisgender": Reflections on sex, gender, and the body. *Parallax, 25*(1), 58–74. https://doi.org/10.1080/13534645.2019.1570606

Duggan, L. (2003). *The twilight of equality: Neoliberalism, cultural politics, and the attack on democracy*. Beacon Press.

Eguchi, S., & Long, H. R. (2019). Queer relationality as family: Yas fats! Yas femmes! Yas Asians! *Journal of Homosexuality, 66*(11), 1589–1608. https://doi.org/10.1080/00918369.2018.1505756

Enke, A. F. (2016). Stick figures and little bits: Toward a nonbinary pedagogy. In Y. Martinez-San Miguel & S. Tobias (Eds.), *Trans studies: The challenge to hetero/homo normativities* (pp. 215–229). Rutgers University Press.

Fassett, D. L., & Rudick, C. K. (2016). Critical communication pedagogy. In P. Witt (Ed.), *Communication and learning* (pp. 573–598). DeGruyter Mouton.

Fassett, D. L., & Rudick, C. K. (2018). Critical communication pedagogy. In J. Nussbaum (Ed.), *Oxford research encyclopedia of communication*. Oxford University Press. http://doi.org/10.1093/acrefore/9780190228613.013.628

Fassett, D. L., & Warren, J. T. (2007). *Critical communication pedagogy*. SAGE.

Feinberg, L. (1992). *Transgender liberation: A movement whose time has come*. World View Forum.

Feinberg, L. (1996). *Transgender warriors: Making history from Joan of Arc to Dennis Rodman*. Beacon Press.

Foucault, M. (1978). *The history of sexuality: An introduction* (trans. R. Hurley). Vintage.

Fox, R. (2013). "Homo"-work: Queering academic communication and communicating queer in academia. *Text and Performance Quarterly, 33*(1), 58–76. https://doi.org/10.1080/10462937.2012.744462

Freire, P. (2005). *Pedagogy of the oppressed* (trans. Myra Bergman Ramos). Continuum.

Gingrich-Philbrook, C. (2002). The queer performance that will have been: Student-teachers in the archive. In N. Stucky & C. Wimmer (Eds.), *Teaching performance studies* (pp. 69–84). Southern Illinois University Press.

Giroux, H. A. (2000). Public pedagogy as cultural politics: Stuart Hall and the "crisis" of culture. *Cultural Studies, 14*(2), 341–360. https://doi.org/10.1080/095023800334913

Giroux, H. A. (2004). Cultural studies, public pedagogy, and the responsibility of intellectuals. *Communication and Critical/Cultural Studies, 1*(1), 59–79. https://doi.org/10.1080/1479142042000180926

GSA Network. (2014). Workshop series: Educational justice campaigns. *GSA Network.* https://gsanetwork.org/resources/workshop-series-educational-justice-campaigns/

Gust, S. W., & Warren, J. T. (2008). Naming our sexual and sexualized bodies in the classroom and the important stuff that comes after the colon. *Qualitative Inquiry, 14*(1), 114–134. https://doi.org/10.1177/1077800407308819

Hall, S. (1996). Introduction: Who needs "identity"? In S. Hall & P. du Gay (Eds.), *Questions of cultural identity* (pp. 1–17). SAGE.

Hamera, J. (2004). Exposing the pedagogical body: Protocols and tactics. In B. K. Alexander, G. L. Anderson, & B. P. Gallegos (Eds.), *Performance theories in education: Power, pedagogy, and the politics of identity* (pp. 63–81). Taylor & Francis.

Hobson, K. (2020). Hesitant to walk: Affective interventions in queer communication pedagogy. In A. Atay & S. L. Pensoneau-Conway (Eds.), *Queer communication pedagogy* (pp. 189–206). Routledge.

hooks, b. (1989). *Talking back: Thinking feminist, thinking Black*. South End Press.

hooks, b. (1994). *Teaching to transgress: Education as the practice of freedom*. Routledge.

Hunter, L. A. (2015, February 6). Every breath a Black trans woman takes is an act of revolution. *Huffington Post*. https://www.huffpost.com/entry/every-breath-a-black-tran_b_6631124

Johnson, J. A., & Calafell, B. M. (2020). Disrupting public pedagogies of bisexuality. In A. Atay & S. L. Pensoneau-Conway (Eds.), *Queer communication pedagogy* (pp. 62–72). Routledge.

Jones, R. G., Jr., & Calafell, B. M. (2012). Contesting neoliberalism through critical pedagogy, intersectional reflexivity, and personal narrative: Queer tales of academia. *Journal of Homosexuality, 59*(7), 957–981. https://doi.org/10.1080/00918369.2012.699835

Kahl, D. H., Jr. (2017). Addressing the challenges of critical communication pedagogy scholarship. *Journal of Applied Communication Research, 45*(1), 116–120. https://doi.org/10.1080/00909882.2016.1248468

Keegan, C. M. (2020). Getting disciplined: What's trans* about queer studies now? *Journal of Homosexuality, 67*(3), 384–397. https://doi.org/10.1080/00918369.2018.1530885

Khayatt, D. (1997). Sex and the teacher: Should we come out in the class? *Harvard Educational Review, 67*(1), 126–143. https://doi.org/10.17763/haer.67.1.27643568766g767m

Kirk, A. (2008). Embracing ambiguity in a critical/queer pedagogy. *Kaleidoscope, 7*, 1–22.

LeMaster, B. (2018). Pedagogies of failure: Queer communication pedagogy as anti-normative. In A. Atay & S. Toyosaki (Eds.), *Critical intercultural communication pedagogy* (pp. 81–96). Lexington.

LeMaster, B. (2020). Fostering an emerging queer consciousness. In A. Atay & S. L. Pensoneau-Conway (Eds.), *Queer communication pedagogy* (pp. 170–188). Routledge.

LeMaster, B., & Fassett, D. L. (2021). Refusing mastery, mastering refusal: Critical communication pedagogy and gender. In M. N. Goins, J. F. McAlister, & B. K. Alexander (Eds.), *The Routledge international handbook of communication and gender* (pp. 600–615). Routledge.

LeMaster, B., & Johnson, A. L. (2019). Unlearning gender: Toward a critical communication trans pedagogy. *Communication Teacher, 33*(3), 189–198. https://doi.org/10.1080/17404622.2018.1467566

LeMaster, B., & Mapes, M. (2019). Embracing the criminal: Queer and trans relational liberatory pedagogies. In S. Eguchi & B. M. Calafell (Eds.), *Queer intercultural communication: The intersectional politics of belonging in and across differences*. Rowman & Littlefield.

LeMaster, B., & Mapes, M. (2020). Refusing a compulsory want for revenge, or, teaching against retributive justice with liberatory pedagogy. *Communication and Critical/Cultural Studies, 7*(4), 401–409. https://doi.org/10.1080/14791420.2020.1829662

LeMaster, B., Shultz, D., McNeill, J., Bowers, G., & Rust, R. (2019). Unlearning cisheteronormativity at the intersections of difference: Performing queer worldmaking through collaged relational autoethnography. *Text and Performance Quarterly, 39*(4), 341–370. https://doi.org/10.1080/10462937.2019.1672885

Lorde, A. (2007). *Sister outsider: Essays and speeches by Audre Lorde*. Ten Speed Press.

Loutzenheiser, L. W. (2001). If I teach about these issues they will burn down my house: The possibilities and tensions of queered, antiracist pedagogy. In K. K. Kumashiro (Ed.), *Troubling intersections of race and sexuality: Queer students of color and anti-oppressive education* (pp. 195–214). Rowman & Littlefield.

Lovaas, K. (2010). Sexualities and critical communication pedagogy. In D. L. Fassett & J. T. Warren (Eds.), *The SAGE handbook of communication and instruction* (pp. 385–410). SAGE.

Lovaas, K. E., Baroudi, L., & Collins, S. M. (2002). Transcending heteronormativity in the classroom. *Journal of Lesbian Studies, 6*(3–4), 177–189. https://doi.org/10.1300/J155v06n03_15

Lovaas, K., & Jenkins, M. M. (2020). Queer pedagogy: Story of a course. In A. Atay & S. L. Pensoneau-Conway (Eds.), *Queer communication pedagogy* (pp. 17–43). Routledge.

Lugones, M. (2011). Methodological notes toward a decolonial feminism. In A. M. Isasi-Daz & E. Mendieta (Eds.), *Decolonizing epistemologies: Latina/o theology and philosophy* (pp. 68–86). Fordham University Press.

McCroskey, J. C., & Richmond, V. P. (1983). Power in the classroom I: Teacher and student perceptions. *Communication Education, 32*(2), 175–184. https://doi.org/10.1080/03634528309378527

McLaren, P. (1999). *Schooling as a ritual performance: Toward a political economy of educational symbols and gestures* (3rd ed.). Rowman & Littlefield.

Meyer, M. D. E. (2005). Drawing the sexuality card: Teaching, research, and living bisexuality. *Sexuality and Culture, 9*(3), 3–13. https://doi.org/10.1007/BF02908759

Miranda, D. (2013). Extermination of the Joyas: Gendercide in Spanish California. In S. Stryker & A. Z. Aizura (Eds.), *The transgender studies reader 2* (pp. 347–360). Routledge.

Morris, C. E., III. (2013). Sunder the children: Abraham Lincoln's queer rhetorical pedagogy. *Quarterly Journal of Speech, 99*(4), 395–422. https://doi.org/10.1080/00335630.2013.836281

Muñoz, V., & Garrison, E. K. (2008). Transpedagogies: A roundtable discussion. *Women's Studies Quarterly, 36*(3–4), 288–308. https://doi.org/10.1353/wsq.0.0093

Nakayama, T. K., & Corey, F. C. (2003). Nextext. *Journal of Homosexuality, 45*(2–4), 319–334. https://doi.org/10.1300/J082v45n02_15

Namaste, V. (2000). *Invisible lives: The erasure of transgendered and transsexual people*. University of Chicago Press.

Nathanson, J. (2009). Bisexual pedagogy: Bringing bisexuality into the classroom. *Journal of Bisexuality, 9*(1), 71–86. https://doi.org/10.1080/15299710802660037

Nicolazzo, Z., Marine, S. B., & Galarte, F. J. (2015). Introduction: Trans*formational pedagogies. *Transgender Studies Quarterly, 2*(3), 367–375. https://doi.org/10.1215/23289252-2926360

Pattisapu, K. (2020). Celebration, resistance, and change: Queer gender performers of color as public pedagogues. In A. Atay & S. L. Pensoneau-Conway (Eds.), *Queer communication pedagogy* (pp. 73–91). Routledge.

Pattisapu, K., & Calafell, B. M. (2012). (Academic) families of choice: Queer relationality, mentoring, and critical communication pedagogy. In N. Bardhan & M. Orbe (Eds.), *Identity and communication research: Intercultural reflections and future directions* (pp. 51–67). Lexington Books.

PCARE. (2007). Fighting the prison industrial complex: A call to communication and cultural studies scholars to change the world. *Communication and Critical/Cultural Studies, 4*(4), 402–420. https://doi.org/10.1080/14791420701632956

PCARE. (2017). PCARE @10: Reflecting on a decade of prison communication, activism, research, and education, while looking ahead to new challenges and opportunities. *Communication and Critical/Cultural Studies, 14*(3), 288–310. https://doi.org/10.1080/14791420.2017.1345577

Philp, K. (2017, June). No justice, no pride. *Echo Magazine*. https://echomag.com/tqp/

Pensoneau-Conway, S. L. (2009). Desire and passion as foundations for teaching and learning: A pedagogy of the erotic. *Basic Communication Course Annual, 21*(Article 12), 173–206. http://ecommons.udayton.edu/bcca/vol21/iss1/12

Pineau, E. (2002). Critical performative pedagogy: Fleshing out the politics of liberatory education. In N. Stucky & C. Wimmer (Eds.) *Teaching performance studies* (pp. 41–54). Southern Illinois University Press.

Plemons, E., & Straayer, C. (2018). Introduction: Reframing the surgical. *Transgender Studies Quarterly, 5*(2), 164–173. https://doi-org.ezproxy1.lib.asu.edu/10.1215/23289252-4348605

Prosser, J. (1998). *Second skins: The body narratives of transsexuality*. Columbia University Press.

Puar, J. K. (2007). *Terrorist assemblages: Homonationalism in queer times.* Duke University Press.
Rand, E. J. (2014). *Reclaiming queer: Activist and academic rhetorics of resistance.* University of Alabama Press.
Rich, A. (1980). Compulsory heterosexuality and lesbian existence. *Signs, 5*(4), 631–660. https://www.jstor.org/stable/3173834
Richmond, V. P., & McCroskey, J. C. (1992). *Power in the classroom: Communication, control, and concern.* Routledge.
Rubin, G. S. (2011). *Deviations: A Gayle Rubin reader.* Duke University Press.
Rudick, C. K., & Golsan, K. B. (2014). Revisiting the relational communication perspective: Drawing upon relational dialectics theory to map an expanded research agenda for communication and instruction scholarship. *Western Journal of Communication, 78*(3), 255–273. https://doi.org/10.1080/10570314.2014.905796
Rudick C. K., & Golsan, K. B. (2017). Civility and white institutional presence: An exploration of white students' understanding of race-talk at a traditionally white institution. *Howard Journal of Communications, 29*(4), 335–352. https://doi.org/10.1080/10646175.2017.1392910
Rudick, C. K., Golsan, K. B., & Cheesewright, K. (2018). *Teaching from the heart: Critical communication pedagogy in the communication classroom.* Cognella.
Russ, T., Simonds, C., & Hunt, S. (2002). Coming out in the classroom...an occupational hazard? The influence of sexual orientation on teacher credibility and perceived student learning. *Communication Education, 51*(3), 311–324. https://doi.org/10.1080/03634520216516
Sedgwick, E. K. (2003). *Touching feeling: Affect, pedagogy, performativity.* Duke University Press.
Sedgwick, E. K. (2008). *Epistemology of the closet.* University of California Press.
Sender, K. (2020). Creative practice as queer media pedagogy. In A. Atay & S. L. Pensoneau-Conway (Eds.), *Queer communication pedagogy* (pp. 130–154). Routledge.
Shlasko, G. D. (2005). Queer (v.) pedagogy. *Equity and Excellence in Education, 38*(2), 123–134. https://doi.org/10.1080/10665680590935098
Slagle, R. A. (1995). In defense of queer nation: From identity politics to a politics of difference. *Western Journal of Communication, 59*(2), 85–102. https://doi.org/10.1080/10570319509374510
Smith, K. (2013). Decolonizing queer pedagogy. *Affilia: Journal of Women and Social Work, 28*(4), 468–470. https://doi.org/10.1177/0886109913505814
Snorton, C. R. (2017). *Black on both sides: A racial history of trans identity.* University of Minnesota Press.
Spade, D. (2011). Some very basic tips for making higher education more accessible to trans students *and* rethinking how we talk about gendered bodies. *Radical Teacher, 92,* 57–62. https://www.muse.jhu.edu/article/463370
Spieldenner, A. R., & Booker, J. J. (2020). The queer act of talking sex: Pedagogical challenges in a communication course on pornography. In A. Atay & S. L. Pensoneau-Conway (Eds.), *Queer communication pedagogy* (pp. 155–169). Routledge.
Sprague, J. (1992). Expanding the research agenda for instructional communication: Raising some unasked questions. *Communication Education, 41*(1), 1–25. https://doi.org/10.1080/03634529209378867
Sprague, J. (1993). Retrieving the research agenda for communication education: Asking the pedagogical questions that are "embarrassments to theory." *Communication Education, 42*(2), 106–122. https://doi.org/10.1080/03634529309378919
Sprague, J. (1994). Ontology, politics, and instructional communication research: Why we can't just "agree to disagree" about power. *Communication Education, 43*(4), 254–266. https://doi.org/10.1080/03634529409378986
Stanley, E. A. (2015). Fugitive flesh: Gender self-determination, queer abolition, and trans resistance. In E. A. Stanley & N. Smith (Eds.), *Captive genders: Trans embodiment and the prison industrial complex* (pp. 7–17). AK Press.

Staton, A. Q. (1989). The interface of communication and instruction: Conceptual considerations and programmatic manifestations. *Communication Education*, 38(4), 364–371. https://doi.org/10.1080/03634528909378777

Stoller, A. L. (1995). *Race and the education of desire: Foucault's history of sexuality and the colonial order of things*. Duke University Press.

Stryker, S. (2004). Transgender studies: Queer theory's evil twin. *GLQ: A Journal in Lesbian and Gay Studies*, 10(2), 212–215. https://muse.jhu.edu/article/54599

Stryker, S. (2017). *Transgender history: The roots of today's revolution*. Seal Press.

Stryker, S., Currah, P., & Moore, L. J. (2008). Introduction: Trans-, trans, or transgender? *WSQ: Women's Studies Quarterly*, 36(3–4), 11–22. http://doi.org/10.1353/wsq.0.0112

Sullivan, N. (2006). Transmogrification: (Un)becoming other(s). In S. Stryker & S. Whittle (Eds.), *Transgender Studies Reader 1* (pp. 552–564). Routledge.

Valentine, D. (2012). Sue E. Generous: Toward a theory of non-transexuality. *Feminist Studies*, 38(1), 185–211. https://www.jstor.org/stable/23269176

Warren, J. T. (1999). The body politic: Performance, pedagogy, and the power of enfleshment. *Text and Performance Quarterly*, 19(3), 257–266. https://doi.org/10.1080/10462939909366266

Warren, J. T., & Toyosaki, S. (2012). Performative pedagogy as a pedagogy of interruption: Difference and hope. In N. Bardhan & M. P. Orbe (Eds.), *Identity research and communication: Intercultural reflections and future directions* (pp. 3–20). Lexington Books.

Whitworth, C., & Wilcoxen, A. (2020). Disclosing lives, reading bodies: A duo-autoethnography of queerness in the classroom. In A. Atay & S. L. Pensoneau-Conway (Eds.), *Queer communication pedagogy* (pp. 207–222). Routledge.

Wood, J. T., & Fixmer-Oraiz, N. (2017). *Gendered lives: Communication, gender, and culture* (12th ed.). Cengage.

Wright, J. (1993). Lesbian instructor comes out: The personal is pedagogy. *Feminist Teacher*, 7(2), 26–33. https://www.jstor.org/stable/40545647

Yep, G. A. (2003). The violence of heteronormativity in communication studies: Notes on injury, healing, and queer world-making. *Journal of Homosexuality*, 45(2–4), 11–59. https://doi.org/10.1300/J082v45n02_02

Yep, G. A. (2013). Queering/quaring/kauering/crippin'/transing "Other bodies" in intercultural communication. *Journal of International and Intercultural Communication*, 6(2), 118–126. https://doi.org/10.1080/17513057.2013.777087

Yep, G. A. (2016). Toward thick(er) intersectionalities: Theorizing, researching, and activating the complexities of communication and identities. In K. Sorrells & S. Sekimoto (Eds.), *Globalizing intercultural communication: A reader* (pp. 86–94). SAGE.

Yep, G. A. (2017). Further notes on healing from "the violence of heteronormativity in communication studies" *QED: A Journal in GLBTQ Worldmaking*, 4(2), 115–122. https://www.jstor.org/stable/10.14321/qed.4.2.0115

Yescavage, K., & Alexander, J. (1997). The pedagogy of marking: Addressing sexual orientation in the classroom. *Feminist Teacher*, 11(2), 113–122. https://www.jstor.org/stable/40545788

Young, S. L. (2020). Bi and bi: Exploring the transgressive potential of the bisexual-biracial identity in the queer classroom. In A. Atay & S. L. Pensoneau-Conway (Eds.), *Queer communication pedagogy* (pp. 44–61). Routledge.

Lore/tta LeMaster

QUEER STUDIES AND ORGANIZATIONAL COMMUNICATION

SITUATING QUEER THEORY IN ORGANIZATIONAL COMMUNICATION RESEARCH

Organizational communication, as a subfield of the larger discipline of communication studies, traces its origins to the 1960s and 1970s. Early organizational communication research adopted a functionalist and managerial lens to the relationship between communication and organization and tended to conceptualize communication as a variable that affected organizational outcomes (Nicotera, 2019). As such, organizational communication was merely the study of communication within organizations. Although some organizational communication research continues to adopt this perspective, the field is now much more theoretically diverse. Starting in the 1980s, the field underwent a paradigm shift that ushered in what is referred to as the interpretive turn (Putnam & Pacanowsky, 1983). The interpretive turn broke with the tradition of functionalist research by introducing qualitative methods to the field and making thick description, rather than establishing relationships among variables, the ultimate goal of research. Moreover, the interpretive turn set the stage for a more complex view of the relationship between communication and organization, with communication now seen as constituting organizational realities rather than merely expressing them.

The interpretive turn of the 1980s paved the way for organizational communication scholars to explore critical approaches to research that view power as a constitutive feature of organizing. Critical approaches became institutionalized in the field during what is called the critical turn of the 1990s (Mumby, 1993). It is also during this time that a tradition of feminist organizational communication research began to emerge (Buzzanell, 1994). Some of the earliest feminist organizational communication research sought to highlight the voices and experiences of women, which had until then been largely neglected in mainstream organizational research. This strain of research drew largely from cultural feminism, which views women as culturally different from men and as having unique values.

Standpoint feminism also made its way into organizational communication research in the 1990s, with studies highlighting how women have knowledge about the social world that is unknown to men due to their unique positionalities and the material conditions that affect their lives. One of the major contributions of standpoint feminism to organizational communication research has been to bring race into the purview of the field and to showcase the unique standpoint and experiences of Black women (Allen, 1996).

As early as the 1990s, postmodern feminism also found significant traction within organizational communication scholarship, and postmodern feminism remains the field's dominant approach to feminism to this day (Ashcraft, 2014). Postmodern feminism has long been seen as being highly compatible with taking a communicative perspective lens to understand social life because it views both gender and power as communicative accomplishments (Mumby, 1996). In addition, postmodern feminism critiques binary thinking, highlights the diversity of experiences among gendered subjects, and calls into question stable categories such as "women" and "men." As such, postmodern feminism shares many of its premises with queer theory. However, unlike queer theory, postmodern feminism does not center sexuality as a unit of analysis, nor does it explicitly seek to interrogate heteronormativity.

It was only in the mid-2010s that queer theory began to find a home within organizational communication. Queer theory research in organizational communication has drawn extensively from the allied field of critical management studies, which has a longer tradition of organizational scholarship that is both explicitly informed by queer theory (Gibson-Graham, 1996; Parker, 2001, 2002) and that explores sexuality as a feature of organizational life (Burrell & Hearn, 1989). Engaging with queer theory in organizational communication research entails exposing and critiquing heteronormativity in organizational life, viewing difference and intersectionality as constitutive features of organizing, adopting an anti-categorical approach to difference and intersectionality, and conceptualizing identity as fluid and performative (McDonald, 2015). Moreover, queer organizational communication research explicitly centers sexuality as a unit of analysis by interrogating how "normal" sexuality is constructed in everyday organizational life and how this functions to privilege dominant sexual identities while silencing others (Compton & Dougherty, 2017).

A key feature of organizational scholarship informed by queer theory has been to invoke queer as a verb, with the goal of this scholarship being to queer our understandings of organizational life. Used in this sense, queering is a deconstructive practice that entails espousing "an attitude of unceasing disruptiveness" (Parker, 2001, p. 58) and questioning "what is considered 'normal', 'common sense', 'healthy' and 'natural'" (Rumens et al., 2019, p. 598). As such, queering is a continual process of interrogating and destabilizing taken-for-granted norms and refusing common sense in order to always consider alternative possibilities (Parker, 2016). Organizational scholars have drawn from this conceptualization of queering to queer concepts such as gender and sexuality at work, leadership, diversity management, the closet, research methods, and even queer theory itself.

QUEERING GENDER AND SEXUALITY AT WORK

Since its inception, one of the most important contributions of queer theory has been to challenge binary and stable views of gender and sexuality in favor of a performative and fluid ontology. As organizational scholars have taken to queer theory, they have drawn from this ontology to queer the dominant identity categories through which gender and sexuality are understood in both organizational scholarship and organizational life.

Theoretically, one way through which organizational scholars have queered dominant understandings of gender and sexuality at work is by introducing the concept of cosexuality. Originally developed by Compton and Dougherty (2017), cosexuality refers to the process of how individuals communicatively organize around sexuality by developing norms for what are considered to be normative and nonnormative expressions of sexuality. Exploring cosexuality in organizational settings is consistent with queering gender and sexuality at work because it conceptualizes sexuality as a performative accomplishment, emphasizes that normative and nonnormative conceptions of sexuality are constantly evolving and negotiated through communication, and views sexuality as a constitutive feature of organizing. Indeed, cosexuality underscores that all organizational members—not just sexual minorities—participate in the process of organizing around sexuality and creating sexual norms.

Another way that organizational scholars have also sought to queer gender and sexuality at work is by critiquing conceptualizations of identity that rely on stable and binary categories in favor of a performative conceptualization of identity that is consistent with Butler's (1990) theory of gender performativity. For example, research on occupational segregation, which refers to the ways in which occupations are organized around identities such that some forms of difference are heavily overrepresented or underrepresented in certain lines of work, predominately conceptualizes identities such as gender and race through stable binary categories. McDonald (2016b) proposed queering occupational segregation research, which would entail deconstructing those fixed notions of identity and instead conceptualizing identity as performative. A queer approach to occupational segregation would examine the extent to which occupations are segregated on the lines of how individuals performatively enact various forms of identity, rather than taking those identities for granted.

Empirically, organizational scholars have contributed to queering gender and sexuality at work by exploring gender and sexual identities outside of the heterosexual matrix. In this regard, a significant amount of research has drawn from queer theory to explore the experiences of gay men in a variety of organizational settings, including white-collar professions (Rumens & Kerfoot, 2009), academia (Ozturk & Rumens, 2015), the police (Rumens & Broomfield, 2012), and the performing arts (Rumens & Broomfield, 2014). This research has highlighted the difficulties that gay men experience as they negotiate heteronormativity in organizational contexts. For instance, gay men can experience difficulties enacting "professionalism" because performances of gay identity are largely seen as incompatible with professionalism (Rumens & Kerfoot, 2009). Moreover, even in organizational contexts that are dubbed gay-friendly, such as the performing arts, the gender performances of gay men are constrained by heteronormative understandings of gender (Rumens & Broomfield, 2014).

In addition to exploring gay male identities at work, a limited amount of organizational research has drawn from queer theory to highlight the experiences of the trans community. This research effectively queers notions of gender and sexuality at work by highlighting how organizational life is experienced by those who live outside of the heterosexual matrix and binary conceptualizations of gender and sexuality. These experiences are vividly highlighted in O'Shea's (2018) autoethnographic study, which openly questions how it might be possible to organize in a way that makes trans lives more livable. Through an affective and emotive narrative, O'Shea (2018) recounts how heteronormativity constrains and marginalizes the lives of nonbinary individuals as they go about their everyday lives. In another study, Muhr et al. (2016) explore the lived experiences of Clare, a trans woman, as she negotiates heteronormativity across both work and nonwork contexts. They find that whereas Clare actively seeks to transgress gender norms outside of her professional life, she is less political and deemphasizes gendered differences in professional contexts.

Although most organizational research drawing from queer theory has highlighted the perspectives of those within the LGBTQ+ community to queer dominant notions of gender and sexuality, queer organizational theorists have also highlighted the need to also queer heterosexuality in organizational research. In particular, Rumens et al. (2019) have suggested that organizational scholars can mobilize queer theory to queer heterosexuality; that is, analyze heterosexual identities in a deconstructive manner that functions to denaturalize heterosexuality. Queering heterosexuality in this way exposes variations within the experiences of those who identify as heterosexual, shows how people who identify as heterosexual can also be constrained by heteronormativity, and illustrates how heterosexuality can be fluid and shifting just like all forms of sexuality. McDonald (2013) offers an empirical example of queering heterosexuality in organizational research by engaging in a reflexive account of his experiences conducting fieldwork at an organization where he was presumed to be gay despite identifying as heterosexual and having no same-sex experiences prior to entering the field. Through an autoethnographic tale, he shows that despite being a "straight" researcher when first entering the field, he was a particular straight researcher who shared many experiences with his gay participants. Moreover, he notes that by the end of the fieldwork, he had begun to identify as gay, thereby showing how heterosexuality can be a fleeting and unstable category.

In addition to queering heterosexuality, organizational research has sought to queer the category of bisexuality. Although there is only a limited amount of empirical research that explicitly examines bisexual identities in organizational settings, Rumens (2013) offers a research agenda for queering bisexuality that involves exploring how bisexuality manifests itself, how bisexuality identities are performed, and how bisexualities disrupt dominant understandings of gender and sexuality in organizational settings.

QUEERING LEADERSHIP

Approaches to leadership that mobilize an explicitly queer theoretical lens often draw upon poststructuralist feminist theorizing that references Butlerian and Foucauldian approaches to power, discourse, bodies, and identity. Parker (2002) muses on Butler's metaphor of drag to discuss the performative nature of "manager" as a leadership identity that must be continually accomplished through practice.

Normative inquiry largely serves as a starting point for queering the notion of leadership itself in the literature, seeking to identify how binary constructions frame what counts as normal/abject and natural/unnatural in leadership. Much of this work grounds itself in an interrogation of gender, sexuality, and the heterosexual matrix. Bowring (2004) highlights how the gender binary is inherent in constructions of leadership, noting that leadership scholarship relies on stable categories of male/female and masculine/feminine. Through an analysis of Captain Janeway from the *Star Trek: Voyager* series, she argues that leadership's reliance on the gender binary ensures that both gender and leadership are trapped in the heterosexual matrix. Queer theory provides a means of disrupting such binaries in an attempt to refigure gender, and therefore leadership, "as one of an infinite number of positions in a four-dimensional space" (Bowring, 2004, p. 383).

Other scholars shift their primary focus from gender to sexuality in applying queer theory to defining and disrupting leadership. Rottmann (2006) suggests that sexuality organizes educational leadership as a largely unacknowledged norm and that queer theory can aid in reframing effective leadership practices as distributed, emotional, and collaborative. Lee et al. (2008) find that heteronormativity and masculinity are thoroughly engrained in managerial identity. Their analysis of interviews with managers who identify as gay or men who have sex with men (MSM) reveals that participants distance themselves from their sexuality in order to construct a "gay other" against which they assert their leadership position as a manager. Heteronormativity and masculinity therefore serve as compulsory norms that all managers, including those who identify as gay men, are called to enact in order to be recognized as a manager.

Such interrogations of gender and sexuality reveal what norms are embedded in the subject position of leader. Harding et al. (2011) introduce a discussion of sexual desire as a motivating factor and unspeakable norm motivating organizational leadership. Through their analysis of interviews with male managers, they show that while the managers referenced leadership frequently, they were unable to provide a coherent definition of the concept. In exploring issues that are often unsaid and unsayable in organizational contexts, they reveal latent homoerotic desire as an animating force between leaders and followers. References to the way leaders penetrate, seduce, and incite desire among followers point to an "erotic discourse" (Harding et al., 2011, p. 937) that circulates, unacknowledged, within conceptualizations of leadership.

While much of the scholarship on queering leadership grounds itself in gender and sexuality norms, a queer approach can, and some argue should, entail normative inquiry beyond heteronormativity. For Ford et al. (2008), leadership itself figures as an organizational norm and dominant regime that institutes its own hierarchy of good and bad employees: that of the leader (the norm) and follower (the abject other). Activities characteristic of leadership development, such as 360-degree questionnaires and MBTI tests, operate as normalizing strategies that imply how leaders "ought to be" (Ford et al., 2008, p. 110). Given that leadership is a norm without a referent in the "real world," a queer lens reveals normative leadership to be a precarious positionality, one inherently entailing insecurity: "To be a leader is to constantly strive and repetitively fail to be a leader" (Ford et al., 2008, p. 113). Leaders must therefore constantly achieve their subject position through repetitive actions socially deemed to be evidence of leadership.

In addition to queering the very notion of leadership, research on queering leadership has also centered LGBTQ+ voices and experiences with leadership. Often, such work helps to reveal the difficulties that LGBTQ+ leaders face when managing their sexual identity alongside their professional identities. Tooms (2007) finds that gay and lesbian school leaders engage in extra labor attempting to be "the right kind of queer" and striving to "fit" their social contexts, and as a result they both minimize their sexual identity while also striving to be "an overachiever and workaholic" (p. 623). Lugg and Tooms (2010) inquire further into the professional norms, including dress codes, that institute self-disciplinary actions related to navigating and expressing queer identities in leadership roles.

Conducting research with participants who identify as queer brings up a host of tensions when mobilizing queer theory, an approach that in part seeks to destabilize identity categories. Courtney (2014) acknowledges and navigates these tensions when analyzing leaders who themselves identify as lesbian, gay, or bisexual, arguing that scholarship must honor participants' identities and their political importance while maintaining an expansive view of queer inquiry. To this end, Courtney (2014) frames queer:

> not as an identity which I force upon my essentially identifying participants, but rather moments of transgression, non-normative aspects of identity or practices which subvert heteronormativity in some way without denying the personal validity and usefulness of my participants' identity categories. (p. 388)

The visibility of minoritized sexual identities in positions of leadership in turn queers leadership in challenging heteronormative constructions of what it means to be a leader. As a result, leaders who identify as lesbian, gay, or bisexual can exhibit "inadvertently queer leadership" (Courtney, 2014, p. 395) as they transgress norms in their day-to-day practices.

Muhr and Sullivan (2013) draw on a case study of a transgender leader, Claire, to focus specifically on how bodies and embodied experiences navigate, transgress, and reinforce leadership norms. Through Claire's story, they explicate how the heterosexual matrix inscribes normative boundaries on all leaders that limit possibilities for embodiment. In spite of the binary gender expectations that her employees had of her leadership style, Claire's refusal to identify as solely male or female or as masculine or feminine transgresses identities rendered intelligible via the heterosexual matrix and reveals how embodiment can serve to disrupt gender binaries and open up new ways of inhabiting the role of "leader" for all people (Muhr & Sullivan, 2013).

As the above literature indicates, a queer approach to leadership has largely interrogated normative constructions of leadership and how queer-identified bodies navigate and disrupt such norms. Ashcraft and Muhr (2018) widen the lens further to examine how scholarly practices contribute to "doing gender" by utilizing gendered, and specifically masculinized, metaphors such as the military and sports to code, analyze, and theorize leadership. Using a queer approach of performativity and promiscuous coding can disrupt these familiar gender binaries entrenched in leadership studies and therefore lead toward a multiplicity of potentialities related to enacting leadership. Queer approaches to leadership must therefore engage in critical reflexivity that draws upon the embodied experiences of researchers to better interrogate normative structures and make visible new ways of enacting and recognizing leadership.

QUEERING DIVERSITY MANAGEMENT

As an established area of inquiry within organizational studies, diversity management is broadly concerned with "the practical application of how differences are and should be managed in organizations, and to what ends" (Holck & Muhr, 2017, p. 2). Queer approaches to diversity management, while limited, largely fall into the critical turn in the subfield, which seeks to challenge underlying assumptions of normative approaches to "managing diversity" in organizational contexts (Holvino & Kamp, 2009). Queer theories provide an opportunity to disrupt the profit-motivated functionalism inherent in many diversity management efforts, as a "deconstructive mode of critique that enables difference and diversity to be rearticulated and, potentially, lived in alternative ways that undermine the essentialist logic of diversity management discourse" (Rumens, 2018a, p. 59).

Before reviewing queer theoretical approaches to diversity management, it is worth noting that LGBTQ+ subjects are largely unaddressed in diversity management literature, particularly in comparison to studies of gender and race (Ozturk & Tatli, 2016). This dearth of scholarship is notable, particularly given that organizations have experienced increasing pressure in terms of public opinion and governmental influence to address diversity and inclusion of sexual and gender identities (Bowring & Brewis, 2009). Gender identity in particular remains "almost a phantom concept in the make-up of LGBT equalities literature" (Ozturk & Tatli, 2016, p. 784), necessitating a more concerted effort to bring concerns related to transgender and genderqueer subjectivities to the fore in diversity management literature. Queer theories and queer subjectivities are certainly not one and the same, yet this silence in a subfield specifically concerned with issues of organizational equity and justice nonetheless signals what lives are livable in organizational contexts. The literature cited later helps to address these gaps, while simultaneously utilizing queer theories to more broadly queer diversity management.

Existing queer scholarship has predominantly treated diversity management as a discourse, drawing upon poststructuralism to interrogate notions of identity that underpin and shape diversity management's enactments and effects in organizing. Bendl et al. (2008) provide an initial foray into queering identity in this regard, arguing that diversity management research and practices rely upon essentialist and stable identity categories that ultimately perpetuate organizational heteronormativity and binary thinking: "the dominant discourse on diversity dimensions portrays organisational members as having one sex, one sexuality and one gender, congruent with each other, fixed for life, and positioned within the heterosexual matrix" (p. 388). Echoing Parker's (2002) effort to queer management, Bendl et al. (2008) suggest a tripartite approach involving queering (1) diversity managers as a normative subjectivity; (2) diversity management as performative practices that reproduce identity binaries and social hierarchies; and (3) diversity management as a subfield engaging in knowledge production and seeking legitimacy.

Organizational documents have provided fruitful data for analyzing how diversity management discourses attempt to portray and fix identity. Bendl et al. (2009) apply a queer deconstructive approach to organizational codes of conduct, finding that such organizational documents further a host of hierarchical binaries which indicate an implicit norm and associated social hierarchy, including male/female, company/employee, nonsexual/sexual, and normative/nonnormative family structures. Accordingly, the authors conclude that the codes of conduct "do not question heteronormative categorizations nor provide equality and visibility for all subject positions and constructions of identity within organizations" (Bendl et al., 2009, p. 635). In a later and more expansive study of organizational codes of conduct, Bendl and Hofmann (2015) further argue that such documents serve as "a means of enforcing the organizational rules and of establishing the predictability of employees' behaviour in reproducing hetero- and cisnormative power relations" (p. 212). In an analysis of diversity statements from higher education institutions, Morrish and O'Mara (2011) find that such statements render queer subjectivities invisible, given the threat they pose to disrupting "the homogenization of diversity" in the institution (p. 987).

While empirical efforts to queer diversity management largely focus on document analysis, scholars are beginning to turn to other means of data collection in their research. In their call for more efforts to queer human resource development, Gedro and Mizzi (2014) suggest that organizational training spaces, often difficult to study via document analysis alone, are themselves political sites that reenact power differentials through normative practices. As one example of additional methodological approaches, Priola et al. (2018) conducted a qualitative study on heteronormative discursive practices in Italian organizations that includes participant observation, interviews, a focus group, and document analysis. Drawing from Foucault, the authors utilize genealogical analysis to understand how particular societal epistemes shape opportunities for organizational inclusion. Despite popular discourses of inclusion and the extension of government legal protections, prevailing heteronormativity in institutions helps to ensure that opportunities for inclusion remain exclusive: "LGBTQ employees who regulate themselves to fit in the normative standards are included, while those who fail in self-censuring their diversity remain under-included or even excluded" (Priola et al., 2018, p. 748).

While the aforementioned studies remain focused on interrogating heteronormativity, queer approaches to diversity management also include broader critiques of organizational normativity. Just and Christiansen (2012) conduct an analysis of organizational diversity statements utilizing Butler's notion of performativity to understand how diversity management discourses shape opportunities for agency and identity in constituting subject positions. They find that such discourses single out particular organizational members as "subjects of diversity" (Just & Christiansen, 2012, p. 322) who are positioned outside of the norm, with limited opportunities for agency and identity within diversity management discourses.

Building on Just and Christiansen's (2012) work, Holck and Muhr (2017) queer diversity management by utilizing a norm-critical approach that seeks to disrupt nondiverse/diverse binaries and the underlying assumptions about competency that they entail. Instead of fixing attention to organizational members coded as diverse, a norm-critical approach interrogates and unravels normative ways of working that establish particular social hierarchies. They argue that "by broadening the norms of competencies and allowing multiple identities to counter societal understandings of ethnic minorities, the majority norm of the ideal worker in the organization can be confronted and destabilized" (Holck & Muhr, 2017, p. 10). As such, they suggest managers pay greater attention to how normative discourses such as "us/them" and "benevolent/needy" show up in day-to-day interactions in ways that contribute to particular realities in organizing.

Developing a norm-critical approach to diversity management further, Christensen (2018) argues that queer organizing entails "continuously challenging the explicit and implicit norms that underlie organisational practices and that structure social relations, standards and expectations" (p. 106). Christensen (2018) accordingly theorizes queer as a performative mode of doing that has the ability to unseat norms from their naturalized position of "business as usual," in the hopes of altering existing organizational power relations. In the context of a training session, this can include discussing terminology that points to normative identities rather than marginalized ones, as well as reflecting on self-identity markers and how they do, or do not, align with participants' personal experiences and self-conceptualizations (Christensen, 2018). For Christensen (2018), norm critique provides a means of not taking identity categories for granted while also attending to intersectionality and the lived realities of interlocking social locations, an issue that is largely unaddressed in diversity management literature (Nkomo & Hoobler, 2014).

As this literature suggests, queering diversity management via an examination of norms and binaries extends well beyond interrogations of gender and sexual identities. Queer analytics can serve as a durable means of understanding the multitude of power relations that are dynamically at play in diversity management.

QUEERING THE CLOSET AT WORK

Organizational scholars have made contributions to queer studies by exploring how individuals negotiate closeting processes at work and the disclosure of nonnormative identities.

Because the closet and closeting processes are most often associated with the disclosure of nonnormative sexualities, this research primarily focuses on the experiences of LGBTQ+ individuals who negotiate how, when, and if to disclose their sexual identity at work (Ward & Winstanley, 2005). In this regard, negotiating whether to keep one's queer identity closeted at work is regarded as one of the most important professional and career decisions faced by LGBTQ+ workers. Many factors play into decisions about whether to come out at work, including personal factors such as the strength of one's LGBTQ+ identity and whether one has a partner, as well as organizational factors such as the overall workplace climate and culture, the perceived level of homophobia in the workplace, the presence or absence of other out LGBTQ+ individuals in that workplace, and organizational diversity policies (Bowring & Brewis, 2009, 2015; King et al., 2008; Ragins, 2004; Rumens & Broomfield, 2012; Ward, 2008).

Because sexuality is largely considered a taboo topic and antithetical to professionalism, being out as a queer person at work can be difficult—even in self-professed "gay-friendly" organizations (Rumens & Kerfoot, 2009; Williams et al., 2009). Indeed, Compton (2016) found that even LGBTQ+ workers at organizations with policies in place to support sexual minorities were selective about the individuals with whom they disclosed their queer identity, often finding that the supportive policies were not enacted by other organizational employees and managers. Yet, engaging in "passing" in an attempt to keep one's queer identity concealed at work can be challenging because it is an ongoing communicative process that must continually be (re)enacted and requires substantial effort (Mitra & Doctor, 2016; Spradlin, 1998).

Trans individuals face unique challenges in negotiating closeting processes in organizational contexts. First, for individuals who are in the process of transitioning, the physical markers of their transition may effectively out them in a way that does not enable them to conceal their trans identity (Bahadur & Kumar, 2016). Moreover, the job-seeking process can be particularly challenging because of potential background checks revealing former names and identification documents that may not represent their identity and/or pronouns (Eger, 2018).

In addition to exploring how members of the LGBTQ+ community negotiate closeting processes at work, organizational scholars have sought to queer the concept of the closet itself by reconceptualizing it in a broader, intersectional way. This work views the closet and closeting processes as omnipresent, constitutive features of organizing, not just for the LGBTQ+ community, but for all individuals who negotiate the revealing and/or concealing of stigmatized, nonnormative identities at work (McDonald et al., 2020). This expanded conceptualization of the closet and closeting processes is informed by both intersectionality and queer theory, as it recognizes that closeting can occur in relation to multiple identities, sometimes simultaneously. In addition, a queer conceptualization of the closet and closeting processes underscores that closeting processes are negotiated differently across contexts and that negotiating closeting at work is thus a fluid, unstable, interactive, and ongoing process.

A 2018 *Management Communication Quarterly* forum dedicated to queering the closet at work highlights some of the ways through which organizational communication scholars have sought to generate knowledge about how individuals with a range of stigmatized, nonnormative identities negotiate closeting processes in organizational contexts (Harris & McDonald, 2018). In this regard, workers, including but not limited to those who identify as

LGBTQ+, can negotiate closeting processes in relation to nontraditional and stigmatized family structures that are not composed of straight couples with biological children (Dixon, 2018). When applying for jobs, foreign-born workers in need of an employer-sponsored visa also negotiate closeting processes in relation to their citizenship status (McDonald, 2018). In addition, Ferguson (2018) shows how he has negotiated closeting processes as a Black man in a predominately White graduate program and how closeting has shaped his experiences of organizational socialization. Moreover, individuals can negotiate closeting processes in relation to a health and lifestyle choice such as not drinking alcohol, since not drinking is stigmatized in some workplace cultures (Romo, 2018).

Crucially, any form of difference that is subject to closeting processes can overlap and intersect with additional forms of difference that individuals may seek to closet, including but not limited to gender and sexual identities. By queering the notion of the closet, organizational communication scholars have thus been able to show how workers negotiate closeting processes in relation to multiple identities that are intersectional, overlapping, and fluid.

QUEERING ORGANIZATIONAL RESEARCH METHODS

In addition to queering concepts in organizational research, organizational scholars have contributed to interdisciplinary conversations about the methodological implications of queer theory for researchers in the social sciences (Brim & Ghaziani, 2016; Browne & Nash, 2010). Rather than suggest that any methods are inherently queer, which would go against the philosophical underpinnings of queer theory, discussions about the implications of queer theory for methodology revolve around the process of queering methodologies—that is, deconstructing taken-for-granted assumptions about research and methodology while interrogating and challenging heteronormativity. As such, queering methodologies entails destabilizing and disrupting "the methodological norms that currently govern how organisational research has been, and ought to be, carried out" (Rumens, 2018b, p. 107). Drawing from this notion of queering, organizational scholars have sought to queer methodological norms around practices such as reflexivity and coding, as well as queer methodologies such as interview research, ethnography, and autoethnography (McDonald, 2017).

Queering Reflexivity. Reflexivity, which entails reflecting on the ways in which researchers shape the research process and how the identities of researchers come to matter in fieldwork, is a common practice among qualitative organizational researchers. Queering the practice of research reflexivity breaks with the ways in which most reflexive accounts are written, which adopt a stable ontology by viewing identity as both transparent and stable throughout the research process. Instead, the practice of queer reflexivity entails reflecting on the categories that are used to identify both researchers and participants, considering how identities are performatively accomplished in the field, understanding that some researcher and participant identities may be closeted, and recognizing that identities may shift during fieldwork (McDonald, 2013). Moreover, queer reflexivity entails being reflexive about how heteronormativity shapes the research process and might be enacted and/or resisted in the field (McDonald, 2016a).

Queering Coding. Ashcraft and Muhr (2018) queer the practice of coding qualitative data through their call for promiscuous coding, which has the ability to trouble persistent binaries in research. Promiscuous coding involves embodied attunement as a means of identifying fruitful moments for embracing uncertainty in coding, involving "a kind of perpetual body scan, acknowledging and checking the researcher's conditioned defenses in order to stay open to energies arising" (Ashcraft & Muhr, 2018, p. 220). This queer coding practice also includes developing "acute 'sense-abilities', like registering flashes of discomfort, confusion, excitement or delight, shifts of mood or energy in a room, or felt but formless awareness of something 'off' or odd" (Ashcraft & Muhr, 2018, p. 220). When coding data gathered from this embodiment, Ashcraft and Muhr (2018) encourage researchers to "search for multiple, unusual partners, especially those once deemed off limits" (p. 221). Promiscuous coding invites the body into practices of ethnographic research, echoing calls for embodiment and attention to desire in other queer ethnographic works (Tweedy, 2016).

Queering Interview Research. Queering interview research entails viewing interviews as performative, constitutive, and embodied encounters rather than as a process through which researchers merely gather preexisting, objective information (Kong et al., 2003). Within organizational research, Riach et al. (2016) have developed a novel approach to queering interview research that they call anti-narrative interviewing. Anti-narrative interviewing queers the interview process by seeking to generate interview narratives that highlight the complexity and multiplicity of the participants' subjectivities rather than aspiring for a linear, coherent narrative. As such, interview narratives are not seen as reflecting reality, but rather as reflecting the ways in which participants account for and reflect on their realities and subjectivities.

Queering Ethnography. Ethnography, as a methodological practice, involves immersing oneself in a culture for an extended period of time and engaging in participant observation, with the ultimate goal of generating in-depth contextual knowledge about the culture. There is a long and rich tradition of ethnography in organizational research, dating back to the interpretive turn of the 1980s. Although there is not yet a tradition of organizational ethnography that is explicitly informed by queer theory, organizational scholars have reflected upon what queering organizational ethnography entails (McDonald, 2017).

An important implication of queering the practice of organizational ethnography is to disrupt the researcher–participant binary and view researchers as active participants in the culture that they are researching. Queering organizational ethnography also requires of ethnographers that they be reflexively aware of how they are not merely reporting disinterested knowledge about the culture, but actively constituting researcher and participant identities through the research and writing process (Rumens, 2018b). As such, researcher and participant identities are conceptualized as fluid and performative.

In line with queer theory's political impulse and critique of heteronormativity, queering organizational ethnography entails paying particular attention to how heteronormativity is enacted and/or resisted, not just in the culture being researched, but in the fieldwork process itself and in relationships between researchers and participants. An important implication of queering organizational ethnography is thus to disrupt heteronormative assumptions about fieldwork, including the assumption that sexuality and desire should be repressed in the field. Indeed, a queer approach to ethnography views researchers and participants as sexual beings and sexuality as a constitutive feature of fieldwork interactions. Critically reflecting on how sexuality and desire manifest in fieldwork is thus an important feature of the practice of queering organizational ethnography (Tweedy, 2016).

Queering Autoethnography. Out of the methods that organizational scholars use to conduct research, autoethnography is the most amenable to queering. One of the reasons for this is that autoethnography is still considered a nontraditional and emerging methodology within the realm of organizational research. Thus, autoethnographic research challenges taken-for-granted assumptions about what counts as research and queers organizational research methods. In line with the philosophical assumptions and commitments of queer theory, autoethnography also disrupts binaries such as those between researchers and participants, views the social world as performatively enacted, and deconstructs grand narratives while developing situated and contextual knowledge (McDonald & Rumens, 2020).

The practice of autoethnography itself can also be queered by rejecting assumptions about what autoethnography should be and how it should be written. In this regard, O'Shea (2019) queers autoethnography by rejecting the notion that autoethnographic narratives should be logical and coherent. Instead, O'Shea (2019) provocatively makes the case for attempting to achieve emotional resonance with the reader by "writing badly" (p. 39) rather than by attempting to create a uniform and consistent narrative. O'Shea (2018) also contributes to queering autoethnography through their vivid account of negotiating heteronormativity in both organizations and society at large as a nonbinary transsexual.

CONCLUSION AND FUTURE DIRECTIONS

Queer theory is still new to the subfield of organizational communication, with the first published articles on queer theory only emerging in the mid-2010s. Although there is a longer tradition of queer organizational scholarship in the field of critical management studies, queer organizational scholars agree that there remains a great deal of potential for queer theory to make important, substantive contributions to organizational scholarship (McDonald & Rumens, 2020; Pullen et al., 2016; Rumens, 2018a).

To date, there is a limited amount of empirical research that mobilizes queer theory to highlight LGBTQ+ subjectivities. This is largely because queer organizational scholarship has been more conceptual than empirical. Moving forward, an important contribution of queer organizational scholarship can thus be to draw attention to queer voices and ways in which heteronormativity shapes the organizational experiences of those with nonnormative sexual identities. While conducting empirical research informed by queer theory, organizational researchers can actively queer methodologies such as interview research, ethnography, and autoethnography. Whereas organizational scholars have discussed what it may look like to queer methodologies, there are only limited examples of empirical studies where organizational researchers queer methodologies.

Another future direction for queer theory in organizational research is for it to substantively address the intersections of race, sexuality, and (hetero)normativity. Just like the broader field of communication studies (Chakravartty et al., 2018), organizational communication is overwhelmingly White, as is queer organizational scholarship. Indeed, there has been little mention of race in this article because queer organizational scholarship is largely silent on race, which reifies Whiteness as a taken-for-granted norm. Outside of organizational scholarship, queer theory has also been critiqued for failing to interrogate its Whiteness and for glossing over the experiences of queer people of color. The Whiteness of mainstream queer theory has led queer of color theorists to propose an alternative—quare theory—which critiques stable notions of identity while also locating racialized and class knowledges (Eguchi & Asante, 2016; A. Johnson, 2019; E. P. Johnson, 2001). Quare theory is currently absent from organizational scholarship. Moving forward then, queer organizational scholars can work to critically interrogate Whiteness and quare queer organizational scholarship by centering queer of color subjectivities.

In conclusion, queering is an ongoing process that never reaches an end point, as queering entails refusing the common sense of the day and interrogating what seems normal and taken for granted. To prevent queer theory itself from becoming normalized, stagnant, and a cliché, Parker (2016) has suggested that queer theory itself must be continually queered and subject to critical interrogation. Queering queer is thus necessary to maintain queer theory as a dynamic, rich, and contested body of thought. Moving forward, both organizational scholarship and queer theory can continue to be queered in order to advance new understandings of social and organizational life.

FURTHER READING

Compton, C. A., & Dougherty, D. S. (2017). Organizing sexuality: Silencing and the push–pull process of co-sexuality in the workplace. *Journal of Communication, 67*(6), 874–896. https://doi.org/10.1111/jcom.12336

Dixon, J. (2017). Queer approaches. In L. K. Lewis & C. R. Scott (Eds.), *International encyclopedia of organizational communication* (pp. 1–7). Wiley. https://doi.org/10.1002/9781118955567.wbieoc174

Gilmore, S., Pullen, A., Harding, N., & Phillips, M. (Eds.). (2017). *Feminists and queer theorists debate the future of critical management studies* (Vol. 3). Emerald.

McDonald, J. (2015). Organizational communication meets queer theory: Theorizing relations of "difference" differently. *Communication Theory, 25*(3), 310–329. https://doi.org/10.1111/comt.12060

McDonald, J. (2017). Queer methodologies in qualitative organizational research: Disrupting, critiquing, and exploring. *Qualitative Research in Organizations and Management, 12*(2), 130–148. https://doi.org/10.1108/QROM-06-2016-1388

Parker, M. (2002). Queering management and organization. *Gender, Work & Organization, 9*(2), 146–166. https://doi.org/10.1111/1468-0432.00153

Pullen, A., Thanem, T., Tyler, M., & Wallenberg, L. (2016). Sexual politics, organizational practices: Interrogating queer theory, work and organization. *Gender, Work & Organization, 23*(1), 1–6. https://doi.org/10.1111/gwao.12123

Rumens, N. (2016). Towards queering the business school: A research agenda for advancing lesbian, gay, bisexual and trans perspectives and issues. *Gender, Work & Organization, 23*(1), 36–51. https://doi.org/10.1111/gwao.12077

Rumens, N. (2018). *Queer business: Queering organization sexualities*. Routledge.

Rumens, N., de Souza, E., & Brewis, J. (2019). Queering queer theory in management and organization studies: Notes toward queering heterosexuality. *Organization Studies*, 40(4), 593–612. https://doi.org/10.1177/0170840617748904

REFERENCES

Allen, B. J. (1996). Feminist standpoint theory: A Black woman's (re)view of organizational socialization. *Communication Studies*, 47(4), 257–271. https://doi.org/10.1080/10510979609368482

Ashcraft, K. L. (2014). Feminist theory. In L. L. Putnam & D. K. Mumby (Eds.), *The SAGE handbook of organizational communication: Advances in theory, research, and methods* (pp. 127–150). SAGE.

Ashcraft, K. L., & Muhr, S. L. (2018). Coding military command as a promiscuous practice? Unsettling the gender binaries of leadership metaphors. *Human Relations*, 71(2), 206–228. https://doi.org/10.1177/0018726717709080

Bahadur, A., & Kumar, K. K. (2016). I am the man for the job: The challenges of coming out as a female-to-male transgender in the Indian organizational space. In T. Köllen (Ed.), *Sexual orientation and transgender issues in organizations: Global perspectives on LGBT workforce diversity* (pp. 43–62). Springer.

Bendl, R., Fleischmann, A., & Hofmann, R. (2009). Queer theory and diversity management: Reading codes of conduct from a queer perspective. *Journal of Management & Organization*, 15(5), 625–638. https://doi.org/10.1017/S1833367200002467

Bendl, R., Fleischmann, A., & Walenta, C. (2008). Diversity management discourse meets queer theory. *Gender in Management*, 23(6), 382–394. https://doi.org/10.1108/17542410810897517

Bendl, R., & Hofmann, R. (2015). Queer perspectives fuelling diversity management discourse: Theoretical and empirical-based reflections. In R. Bendl, I. Bleijenbergh, E. Henttonen, & A. J. Mills (Eds.), *The Oxford handbook of diversity in organizations* (pp. 195–217). Oxford University Press.

Bowring, M. A. (2004). Resistance is not futile: Liberating Captain Janeway from the masculine-feminine dualism of leadership. *Gender, Work & Organization*, 11(4), 381–405. https://doi.org/10.1111/j.1468-0432.2004.00239.x

Bowring, M. A., & Brewis, J. (2009). Truth and consequences: Managing lesbian and gay identity in the Canadian workplace. *Equal Opportunities International*, 28(5), 361–377. https://doi.org/10.1108/02610150910964231

Bowring, M. A., & Brewis, J. (2015). Navigating service and sexuality in the Canadian, UK and US militaries. In F. Colgan & N. Rumens (Eds.), *Sexual orientation at work: Contemporary issues and perspectives* (pp. 28–41). Routledge.

Brim, M., & Ghaziani, A. (2016). Introduction: Queer methods. *Women's Studies Quarterly*, 44(3–4), 14–27. https://doi.org/10.1353/wsq.2016.0033

Browne, K., & Nash, C. J. (2010). Queer methods and methodologies: An introduction. In K. Browne & C. J. Nash (Eds.), *Queer methods and methodologies: Intersecting queer theories and social science research* (pp. 1–24). Ashgate.

Burrell, G., & Hearn, J. (1989). The sexuality of organization. In J. Hearn, D. L. Sheppard, P. Tancred-Sheriff, & G. Burrell (Eds.), *The sexuality of organization* (pp. 1–28). SAGE.

Butler, J. (1990). *Gender trouble: Feminism and the subversion of identity*. Routledge.

Buzzanell, P. M. (1994). Gaining a voice: Feminist organizational communication theorizing. *Management Communication Quarterly*, 7(4), 339–383. https://doi.org/10.1177/0893318994007004001

Chakravartty, P., Kuo, R., Grubbs, V., & McIlwain, C. (2018). #CommunicationSoWhite. *Journal of Communication*, 68(2), 254–266. https://doi.org/10.1093/joc/jqy003

Chang, J., & Bowring, M. A. (2017). The perceived impact of sexual orientation on the ability of queer leaders to relate to followers. *Leadership, 13*(3), 285–300. https://doi.org/10.1177/1742715015586215

Christensen, J. F. (2018). Queer organising and performativity: Towards a norm-critical conceptualisation of organisational intersectionality. *Ephemera, 18*(1), 103–130.

Compton, C. A. (2016). Managing mixed messages: Sexual identity management in a changing U.S. workplace. *Management Communication Quarterly, 30*(4), 415–440. https://doi.org/10.1177/0893318916641215

Compton, C. A., & Dougherty, D. S. (2017). Organizing sexuality: Silencing and the push–pull process of co-sexuality in the workplace. *Journal of Communication, 67*(6), 874–896. https://doi.org/10.1111/jcom.12336

Courtney, S. J. (2014). Inadvertently queer school leadership amongst lesbian, gay and bisexual (LGB) school leaders. *Organization, 21*(3), 383–399. https://doi.org/10.1177/1350508413519762

Dixon, J. (2018). Looking out from the family closet: Discourse dependence and queer family identity in workplace conversation. *Management Communication Quarterly, 32*(2), 271–275. https://doi.org/10.1177/0893318917744067

Eger, E. K. (2018). Transgender jobseekers navigating closeting communication. *Management Communication Quarterly, 32*(2), 276–281. https://doi.org/10.1177/0893318917740226

Eguchi, S., & Asante, G. (2016). Disidentifications revisited: Queer(y)ing intercultural communication theory. *Communication Theory, 26*(2), 171–189. https://doi.org/10.1111/comt.12086

Ferguson, M. W. (2018). (Re)negotiating organizational socialization: Black male scholarship and the closet. *Management Communication Quarterly, 32*(2), 282–286. https://doi.org/10.1177/0893318917741990

Ford, J., Learmonth, M., & Harding, N. (2008). *Leadership as identity: Constructions and deconstructions.* Palgrave Macmillan.

Gibson-Graham, J. K. (1996). Queer(y)ing capitalist organization. *Organization, 3*(4), 541–545. https://doi.org/10.1177/135050849634011

Gedro, J., & Mizzi, R. C. (2014). Feminist theory and queer theory: Implications for HRD research and practice. *Advances in Developing Human Resources, 16*(4), 445–456. https://doi.org/10.1177/1523422314543820

Harding, N., Lee, H., Ford, J., & Learmonth, M. (2011). Leadership and charisma: A desire that cannot speak its name? *Human Relations, 64*(7), 927–949. https://doi.org/10.1177/0018726710393367

Harris, K. L., & McDonald, J. (2018). Introduction: Queering the "closet" at work. *Management Communication Quarterly, 32*(2), 265–270. https://doi.org/10.1177/0893318917742517

Holck, L., & Muhr, S. L. (2017). Unequal solidarity? Towards a norm-critical approach to welfare logics. *Scandinavian Journal of Management, 33*(1), 1–11. https://doi.org/10.1016/j.scaman.2016.11.001

Holvino, E., & Kamp, A. (2009). Diversity management: Are we moving in the right direction? Reflections from both sides of the North Atlantic. *Scandinavian Journal of Management, 25*(4), 395–403. https://doi.org/10.1016/j.scaman.2009.09.005

Johnson, A. (2019). Quare/kuaer/queer/(e)ntersectionality. *CrossCurrents.* https://doi.org/10.1111/cros.12338

Johnson, E. P. (2001). "Quare" studies, or (almost) everything I know about queer studies I learned from my grandmother. *Text and Performance Quarterly, 21*(1), 1–25. https://doi.org/10.1080/10462930128119

Just, S. N., & Christiansen, T. J. (2012). Doing diversity: Text-audience agency and rhetorical alternatives. *Communication Theory, 22*(3), 319–337. https://doi.org/10.1111/j.1468-2885.2012.01407.x

King, E. B., Reilly, C., & Hebl, M. (2008). The best of times, the worst of times: Exploring dual perspectives of "coming out" in the workplace. *Group and Organization Management, 33*(5), 566–601. https://doi.org/10.1177/1059601108321834

Kong, T. S. K., Mahoney, D., & Plummer, K. (2003). Queering the interview. In J. A. Holstein & J. F. Gubrium (Eds.), *Inside interviewing: New lenses, new concerns* (pp. 91–110). SAGE.

Lee, H., Learmonth, M., & Harding, N. (2008). Queer(y)ing public administration. *Public Administration*, 86(1), 149–167. https://doi.org/10.1111/j.1467-9299.2007.00707.x

Lugg, C. A., & Tooms, A. K. (2010). A shadow of ourselves: Identity erasure and the politics of queer leadership. *School Leadership & Management*, 30(1), 77–91. https://doi.org/10.1080/13632430903509790

McDonald, J. (2013). Coming out in the field: A queer reflexive account of shifting researcher identity. *Management Learning*, 44(2), 127–143. https://doi.org/10.1177/1350507612473711

McDonald, J. (2015). Organizational communication meets queer theory: Theorizing relations of "difference" differently. *Communication Theory*, 25(3), 310–329. https://doi.org/10.1111/comt.12060

McDonald, J. (2016a). Expanding queer reflexivity: The closet as a guiding metaphor for reflexive practice. *Management Learning*, 47(4), 391–406. https://doi.org/10.1177/1350507615610029

McDonald, J. (2016b). Occupational segregation research: Queering the conversation. *Gender, Work & Organization*, 23(1), 19–35. https://doi.org/10.1111/gwao.12100

McDonald, J. (2017). Queer methodologies in qualitative organizational research: Disrupting, critiquing, and exploring. *Qualitative Research in Organizations and Management*, 12(2), 130–148. https://doi.org/10.1108/QROM-06-2016-1388

McDonald, J. (2018). Negotiating the "closet" in U.S. academia: Foreign scholars on the job market. *Management Communication Quarterly*, 32(2), 287–291. https://doi.org/10.1177/0893318917740428

McDonald, J., Harris, K. L., & Ramirez, J. (2020). Revealing and concealing difference: A critical approach to disclosure and an intersectional theory of "closeting." *Communication Theory*, 30(1), 84–104. https://doi.org/10.1093/ct/qtz017

McDonald, J., & Rumens, N. (2020). Queering organizational research through autoethnography. In A. F. Herrmann (Ed.), *The Routledge international handbook of organizational autoethnography* (pp. 69–83). Routledge.

Mitra, R., & Doctor, V. (2016). Passing in corporate India: Problematizing disclosure of homosexuality at the workplace. In T. Köllen (Ed.), *Sexual orientation and transgender issues in organizations: Global perspectives on LGBT workforce diversity* (pp. 307–320). Springer.

Morrish, L., & O'Mara, K. (2011). Queering the discourse of diversity. *Journal of Homosexuality*, 58(6–7), 974–991. https://doi.org/10.1080/00918369.2011.581966

Muhr, S. L., & Sullivan, K. R. (2013). "None so queer as folk": Gendered expectations and transgressive bodies in leadership. *Leadership*, 9(3), 416–435. https://doi.org/10.1177/1742715013485857

Muhr, S. L., Sullivan, K. R., & Rich, C. (2016). Situated transgressiveness: Exploring one transwoman's lived experiences across three situated contexts. *Gender, Work & Organization*, 23(1), 52–70. https://doi.org/10.1111/gwao.12093

Mumby, D. K. (1993). Critical organizational communication studies: The next 10 years. *Communication Monographs*, 60, 18–25. https://doi.org/10.1080/03637759309376290

Mumby, D. K. (1996). Feminism, postmodernism, and organizational communication studies: A critical reading. *Management Communication Quarterly*, 9(3), 259–295. https://doi.org/10.1177/0893318996009003001

Nicotera, A. M. (2019). Developments in the 20th century. In A. M. Nicotera (Ed.), *Origins and traditions of organizational communication: A comprehensive introduction to the field* (pp. 22–44). SAGE.

Nkomo, S., & Hoobler, J. M. (2014). A historical perspective on diversity ideologies in the United States: Reflections on human resource management research and practice. *Human Resource Management Review*, 24(3), 245–257. https://doi.org/10.1016/j.hrmr.2014.03.006

O'Shea, S. C. (2018). This girl's life: An autoethnography. *Organization*, 25(1), 3–20. https://doi.org/10.1177/1350508417703471

O'Shea, S. C. (2019). My dysphoria blues: Or why I cannot write an autoethnography. *Management Learning, 50*(1), 38–49. https://doi.org/10.1177/1350507618791115

Ozturk, M. B., & Rumens, N. (2015). Gay male academics in UK business and management schools: Negotiating heteronormativities in everyday work life. *British Journal of Management, 25*(3), 503–517. https://doi.org/10.1111/1467-8551.12061

Ozturk, M. B., & Tatli, A. (2016). Gender identity inclusion in the workplace: Broadening diversity management research and practice through the case of transgender employees in the UK. *The International Journal of Human Resource Management, 27*(8), 781–802. https://doi.org/10.1080/09585192.2015.1042902

Parker, M. (2001). Fucking management: Queer, theory and reflexivity. *Ephemera, 1*(1), 36–53.

Parker, M. (2002). Queering management and organization. *Gender, Work & Organization, 9*(2), 146–166. https://doi.org/10.1111/1468-0432.00153

Parker, M. (2016). Queering queer. *Gender, Work & Organization, 23*(1), 71–73. https://doi.org/10.1111/gwao.12106

Priola, V., Lasio, D., Serri, F., & De Simone, S. (2018). The organisation of sexuality and the sexuality of organisation: A genealogical analysis of sexual "inclusive exclusion" at work. *Organization, 25*(6), 732–754. https://doi.org/10.1177/1350508418790140

Pullen, A., Thanem, T., Tyler, M., & Wallenberg, L. (2016). Sexual politics, organizational practices: Interrogating queer theory, work and organization. *Gender, Work & Organization, 23*(1), 1–6. https://doi.org/10.1111/gwao.12123

Putnam, L. L., & Pacanowsky, M. E. (Eds.). (1983). *Communication and organizations: An interpretive approach*. SAGE.

Ragins, B. R. (2004). Sexual orientation in the workplace: The unique experiences of gay, lesbian and bisexual workers. *Research in Personnel and Human Resources Management, 23*, 35–120. https://doi.org/10.1016/S0742-7301(04)23002-X

Riach, K., Rumens, N., & Tyler, M. (2016). Towards a Butlerian methodology: Undoing organizational performativity through anti-narrative research. *Human Relations, 69*(11), 2069–2089. https://doi.org/10.1177/0018726716632050

Romo, L. K. (2018). Coming out as a non-drinker at work. *Management Communication Quarterly, 32*(2), 292–296. https://doi.org/10.1177/0893318917740227

Rottmann, C. (2006). Queering educational leadership from the inside out. *International Journal of Leadership in Education, 9*(1), 1–20. https://doi.org/10.1080/13603120500389507

Rumens, N. (2013). Queering men and masculinities in construction: Towards a research agenda. *Construction Management and Economics, 31*(8), 802–815. https://doi.org/10.1080/01446193.2013.765021

Rumens, N. (2018a). *Queer business: Queering organization sexualities*. Routledge.

Rumens, N. (2018b). Queered methodologies for equality, diversity and inclusion researchers. In L. A. E. Booysen, R. Bendl, & K. Pringle (Eds.), *Handbook of research methods in diversity management, equality and inclusion at work* (pp. 103–121). Edward Elgar.

Rumens, N., & Broomfield, J. (2012). Gay men in the police: Identity disclosure and management issues. *Human Resource Management Journal, 22*(3), 283–298. https://doi.org/10.1111/j.1748-8583.2011.00179.x

Rumens, N., & Broomfield, J. (2014). Gay men in the performing arts: Performing sexualities within "gay-friendly" work contexts. *Organization, 21*(3), 365–382. https://doi.org/10.1177/1350508413519766

Rumens, N., de Souza, E., & Brewis, J. (2019). Queering queer theory in management and organization studies: Notes toward queering heterosexuality. *Organization Studies, 40*(4), 593–612. https://doi.org/10.1177/0170840617748904

Rumens, N., & Kerfoot, D. (2009). Gay men at work: (Re)constructing the self as professional. *Human Relations, 62*(5), 763–786. https://doi.org/10.1177/0018726709103457

Spradlin, A. L. (1998). The price of "passing": A lesbian perspective on authenticity in organizations. *Management Communication Quarterly, 11*(4), 598–605. https://doi.org/10.1177/0893318998114006

Tooms, A. (2007). The right kind of queer: Fit and the politics of school leadership. *Journal of School Leadership, 17*(5), 601–630. https://doi.org/10.1177/105268460701700503

Tweedy, A. (2016). Openings, obstacles, and disruptions: Desire as a portable queer method. *Women's Studies Quarterly, 44*(3–4), 208–223. https://doi.org/10.1353/wsq.2016.0043

Ward, J. (2008). *Sexualities, work and organizations: Stories by gay men and women in the workplace at the beginning of the twenty-first century*. Routledge.

Ward, J., & Winstanley, D. (2005). Coming out at work: Performativity and the recognition and renegotiation of identity. *Sociological Review, 53*(3), 447–475. https://doi.org/10.1111/j.1467-954X.2005.00561.x

Williams, C., Giuffre, P., & Dellinger, K. (2009). The gay-friendly closet. *Sexuality Research & Social Policy, 6*(1), 29–45. https://doi.org/10.1525/srsp.2009.6.1.29

Jamie McDonald and Sean C. Kenney

QUEER/ING ARCHIVES

INTRODUCTION

To begin, a brief queer archive tale. Two archival queers walk into a gay bar in Phoenix called Rebar. Both being deeply constituted by queer pasts, they were delighted to see there two Sisters of Perpetual Indulgence. Beginning in 1979 in San Francisco and spreading globally over the past three and half decades, these genderfuck nuns through their cultural embodied performance, activism, and education have gifted all queer peoples with worldmaking interventions against stigma and violence, on behalf of joy and health and justice. So, naturally, the two archival queers bought the sisters a round of shots. Sister Sugar Britches chatted with them for a long time; their shared interest in queer history and memory was hilariously if also lamentably punctuated by a 20-something tipsy gay boy, who, eyeing the drag habit, approached to emphatically declare, earnestly so, that he loved the Whoopi Goldberg film *Sister Act*. As he cheerily stumbled off for another vodka, the three queer elders giggled at the misrecognition and then had a quite serious colloquy about why queer history and memory and their impoverishments matter, the archival imperative, and the complex politics at the heart of it all.

Scholars have long been interested in the relationship among archives, politics, and rhetoric, as evidenced by the multiple monographs, articles, special issues, and edited volumes devoted to issues—sometimes quite charged—concerning theory, method, and praxis. It remains the case, however, that communication studies scholars historically have been on the vanguard of the archival turn in the discipline while being, sometimes insidiously so, much slower in responding to the queer turn in the academy and the bridging initiatives of scholar-activism. For those committed to such queer interventions, the site of the archive is a productive location and means of ingress and outreach. In the introduction to their special issue, "Queering Archives: Historical Unravelings" in *Radical History Review*, Marshall et al. (2014) write, "Insofar as the archive serves as site for historical accumulation, visitation, and recognition, it has become an exemplary space for academic, activist, and community contests over the proper or desirable boundaries of sex, gender, and knowledge" (p. 2). Of course, we might add that the archive is an exemplary dynamic space of rhetorical reckoning and power, and of political promise, or, as Rawson (2015) observed in his introduction to the special issue of *Transgender Studies Quarterly* on "Archives and Archiving," echoing Howard Zinn, "leveraging the power of archives is not the 'politicization of a neural craft, but the humanizing of an inevitably political craft'" (p. 544).

Queer archives index a fraught array of investments in sexualities, holdings, and politics. They have come to include place-based understandings, text-based understandings, digitally mediated understandings, and orientations toward past and present. At their broadest, queer archives cultivate new relationships to the archive of gay and lesbian studies and the "straight" archive. Scholars engaging queer archives do so on a range of at times oppositional terms. Thus, addressing queer archives offers insights into wider archives of academic scholarship. A foundational concern of queer archival investments fittingly concerns etiology and the extent to which such a commitment is sustainable on queer terms. Public contestations over the origins and significance of Stonewall, for instance, under the queerly familiar banner of "the first pride was a riot," demonstrate the contested potential of queer archives. On one hand, activists seeking rights-based recognition from the state inaugurate Stonewall as the start of a "modern civil rights movement." On others, activists seek to retell Stonewall as a site of queer emergence, a prefiguration of a present political identity, and visions for more liberatory futures.

The partiality of any archive forms a foundational source for its queer promise and use beyond the confines of ostensibly LGBTQ identification. While *queer* modifies archive here, queer Communication scholars are adamant in asserting that queer (disciplinary) archives are of relevance to all scholarship and archival engagements. We underscore here and throughout that we focus mostly on U.S. contexts in this essay, a shortcoming that we address in the future directions section, a shortcoming widely evident in so much of the existing scholarship to date on queer/ing archives. Like the serendipitous nature of archival work and the zigzag of desire, queer scholars martial archives toward unexpected and often open ends. In communication studies, scholars have invoked queer archives to challenge and reimagine the where of archives and the standards of archival evidence, address methodologies that better attend to archived lives, shift the terms of past–present identification, retell firsthand experiences in the archive, (re)define appropriate sites of activism around sexuality, and reenvision queer possibilities for the future, through the past.

Communication studies scholars, from our perspective, also do and should understand queer archives as intentional resources for others but also, centrally, themselves as active rhetorical agents, or archival queers (Morris, 2006a), in the curation, interpretation, and mobilization of archival holdings wherever they may be found. Such "movement" requires restlessness and reflexivity, insight and ingenuity, and creativity and commitment to the ongoing intersectional prospects of queer pasts. Archival queers robustly engage and enlist, which is to say recruit, others likewise to archivally engage, requiring openness and defiance so as to traverse and trouble those borders and boundaries of exclusionary demarcation and diminishment. Archival queers seek, for instance, what David Román (2000) called "the vernacular imagination of immigrant subjects" through "mining the archives that preserve the interrelation between the social experiences of race and sexuality [which] may in fact help us perceive more critically the ways in which such norms of citizenship have been constructed and enforced historically" (p. 351). To do so, archival queers must be expansive in what they are looking for, assembling, exhibiting, for as Román observes, the "undocumented archive" "exists in oral history, cultural memory, social ritual, communal folklore, and local performance," such as his own exploration of Chay Yew's 1998 saga of Miss Visa Denied, a Malaysian immigrant drag performer (p. 352). Far from daunted by the challenges of such expansiveness and ephemerality, archival queers are venturesome, desiring to rummage through the past, buoyed by Patrick Johnson's (2008) alluring promise that "the past haunts the air" of the Black gay South, "but one does not choke on the stench of flesh as before. The scent of magnolia is not spoiled by the scent of ashen bodies, but rather broken by the savory scent of collards, cornbread, and cobbler" (p. 1). And yet even as archival queers follow the nose of their archival desire, they must remember, following Anjali Arondekar (2009), that such desire and its multifarious contexts and processes, then and now, are constitutive of the subjects that we find there; that is to say, archives of whatever sort, even under such auspicious mantles, always have consequences.

In what follows, we explore key questions, motives, domains, and practices of queer/ing archives. We derive this constellation from scholarship across decades of work inspired by the transdisciplinary archival turn that has shaped how Communication researchers have endeavored to access and imagination the meanings, doings, and potentialities of queer pasts. This is not a linear genealogy of scholarship in communication studies about queerness and archives. Like queerness itself, work in the discipline has swerved in and out of veins of research mobilized in other disciplines and in fits and starts charted its own paths inspired especially by central commitments to rhetorical and critical/cultural perspectives. This essay, then, moves through a constellation of seven issues and questions related to queer/ing archives that intersect influential work in communication studies with scholarship across disciplinary domains. In the first section, we follow the question of where the queer/ing archive can be found. Second, we address the relationship between queerness, archives, and identity/(dis)identification. Third, we survey methods and methodologies archival queers have deployed in their creative engagements. Fourth, we account for the temporal preoccupations in queer historiography and futurity implicating archival investments. Fifth, we take up the meaning and mobility of evidence shaped by archival norms. Sixth, we explore the mutually influential relationship between queer archives and activism. Finally, in the seventh section, we look to future potentialities of queer/ing archives, particularly those that decenter the United States.

THE WHERE OF QUEER ARCHIVES

For a very long time, queer people faced challenges in finding queer holdings, circumstances of erasure, injury, neglect that well warranted early narratives that claimed their yearnings, searchings, curations as projects of discovery, and rescue. No doubt archival labor felt that way to so many seeking the accumulation and visibility for queer pasts, even if queer pasts had always been there, somewhere. Critiques of that framing are also well founded and have been enabled in their transformative perspectives and visions because for two generations now, queer archives, ample and robust, have emerged in a diverse array of locations and configurations, institutional and grassroots, official and vernacular. *Where* are queer archives? Such a question, research or pilgrimage, is now easily and multiply answered: Brooklyn (Lesbian

Herstory Archives) and Manhattan (Schomburg Center for Research in Black Culture; The LGBT Community Center National History Archive; New York University's Fales Library), Boston (The History Project), Holyoke (Sexual Minorities Archives), Ann Arbor (National Transgender Archive and Museum), Chicago (Gerber/Hart Library and Archives; Leather Archives and Museum), Bloomington (Kinsey Institute at Indiana University), Minneapolis (Tretter Collection at the University of Minnesota), Portland (Gay & Lesbian Archives of the Pacific Northwest), San Francisco (GLBT Historical Society), Los Angeles (ONE National Gay and Lesbian Archives at University of Southern California), Tucson (Arizona Queer Archives), Birmingham (Invisible Histories Project at University of Alabama), and Atlanta (LGBTQ Institute at the National Center for Civil and Human Rights), to name only some of the most recognizable sites. More recently, such "brick-and-mortar" or analog repositories have been made more accessible, radically reimagined, supplemented, and complemented through generation of and by digital archives, the most prominent and pathbreaking of which in recent years has been the Digital Transgender Archive (https://www.digitaltransgenderarchive.net/), founded by K. J. Rawson.

Efforts to queer archives' objects, practices, and stories—to expand reach, accessibility, engagement, and circulation—have widened domains and proliferated sites. The where of archival queerness is now mapped onto institutional and state archives whose ideologies and structural constraints would not have historically nominated them for queer destination to domestic spaces and cultural and community venues where the stuff of the queer past is accumulated, collected, curated, and exhibited. What may be described as the ephemeral turn (Muñoz, 1996), driven by race and class critique, as well as the affective turn (Cvetkovich, 2003), emphasizing the queer archival projects that focus on the feelings, experiences, and relations elicited and constituted by encounters of the past, have deepened the promise of where queer archives and archival queering may be pursued and mobilized. The emergence of digital archives, broadly conceived, has radically transformed the where of queer archives and archiving, leading Arondekar et al., 2015 to ask, "Are we already past the tipping point when the commonsense usage of the word archive refers not to an institution housing documents but to the ubiquitously accessible location where digital copies of one's emails, MP3 files, videos, et cetera, one's so called data double, are stored? I think my students are already here" (p. 217). The generative and justice implications of this turn are worldmaking, as Rawson (2014), in speaking of the Digital Transgender Archive he founded, observes, "Taken together, these materials create a world where trans people can share their experiences, recognize their shared experiences, and contribute to the development of community knowledges" (p. 56). Queer digital archives are also classrooms, contributing to both civic participation and communal memory (VanHaitsma, 2019a).

What we describe above makes the where of queer archives relevant and significant as sites of invention (Morris, 2006b), influence, and legitimation, rhetorical scenes and funds that afford opportunities for address, engagement, and change within and beyond the location of archival experience. In the most conventional sense, where matters because these places are storehouses of materials from which (dis)identifications and rhetorical visions are formed, evidence is derived, and arguments and strategies emerge. Archival queers have also brought to the forefront the myriad ways that archives and archival spaces are themselves rhetorical. Archives are structural, both in spatial design and in their access, organization and narration of materials, procedures, norms of behavior, and staff relations with visitors (Gieseking, 2015). Indexing and description of materials, to offer for example, often constitute "invisible" but consequential rhetorical inscriptions, obfuscations, and absences, or queer routings (Bessette, 2017; Hernández, 2015; Rawson, 2015, 2018). Archives are also rhetorical places because they are embodied, people and objects, sensory experiences, and wide-ranging feelings (Cifor, 2015; Cvetkovich, 2012; Frischherz, 2020; Lee, 2019), and because "archival environments curate their memorializing context" (Cram, 2016, p. 112). "Archival ambience," as Cram (2016) experienced and conceptualizes it, "reimagines invention and circulation as the relational materiality of bodies...the generation of intimacies...affectability of bodies, sexualities, and built environments" (p. 112). The destination of the queer archival where, in short, is a matter of propinquity, sensorium, encounter, and inducement, the very grounds of rhetorical appeal.

QUEER ARCHIVAL IDENTIFICATIONS

Holdings of queer pasts are desired, pursued, mobilized, disavowed, or ignored for a variety of compelling reasons. Chief among these archival motives is identification or disidentification, historical and interpretive (mis)alignments—emotional, biographical, circumstantial, ideological, political—with people and events understood or felt as queer in some important or insufficient dimension. The implications of such connections across time and generation—the desire and efforts to "feel historical" (Nealon, 2001) and "touch history" (Dinshaw, 1999)—concern who "we" are, where we have been (both complex constructions and performances that are to say the least troublingly differential across race, class, gender, ability), and where we are going (Ramírez, 2010). This is to say that queer archival identification shapes and is shaped by individual and collective identity, community, culture, politics, and activism in the present and competing visions, initiatives, and movements influencing what queer futures might be and do.

Rohy (2010), drawing on the work of Cvetkovich (2003), claims that the queer archive is a "technology of identity" (p. 354). Identity, then, from our perspective, is an ongoing rhetorical becoming facilitated and forged by alluring and alienating archival funds. Bessette's (2017) application of Burke's (1945) rhetorical theory of identification situates what she calls the "retroactivism" of lesbian collective archival engagement and historiography, its access and ongoing adaptation, at the heart of "the complexities of sexual identity formation and narration...[through] their discursive creation and disruption—to the historical and rhetorical forces that shape contests over the definition of specific sexual identities" (p. 15). Bessette's attention to the "individual difference within identification" (p. 15) conjures Muñoz's (1999) intersectional analysis of identification founding his theory of disidentification, the "survival strategies" that queer archival resources used to craft "identities-within-difference" in projects of developing transformative queer subjects and social relations. Such is the achievement of Pritchard's (2014, 2017) communal archival wellspring, of which he writes, "Black queers use literacy to form relationships with ancestors to address historical erasure when they uncover buried histories, engender Black queer identity formation and affirmation, create genealogical links, and preserve cultural traditions. I categorize such literacy practices as 'life-fashioning,' which refers to the ways in which one achieves self-care, resistance, collective empowerment, and personal affirmation" (p. 32). In a similar vein, Johnson (2019) writes about his groundbreaking *Honeypot*, his oral history project of Black southern lesbians, observing, "I was challenged to think more creatively about false distinctions we make about myth and truth, since many of us—and especially those who are marginalized—are constantly compelled to prove the validity of our experiences or the stories we tell about them" (p. xv).

In the United States, one prominent illustration of queer archival identifications is Stonewall, the enduring and much-contested legacy of the 1969 New York City riots that "gave birth," so the mythic origin narrative goes, to modern gay liberation. "The fire at Stonewall burns still," Appiah (2019) accurately observed. "These days, the episode looms so large that it has been likened to the storming of the Bastille; we furiously debate who threw the first fist, brick, or bottle." There are many reasons for Stonewall's half-century heat and glow. Surely chief among them is Stonewall's constructed capacity to generate across generations deep identifications and disidentifications about the fact of "our" history, the defiant resistance against longstanding virulent homophobia, and the legacy of queer freedom's promise—the kindling and combustion of memory and identity, with important political implications and appropriations across the decades to date.

The rhetorical process of identification and archival sustenance of memory is perhaps most illuminating not in its inertia, the whiteness and commemorative ritual that has sustained it for so long, but in its vibrant and material challenge. Interpretive battles over the political meaning and vision, progressive or radical, have been intense in recent years. As Ryan (2015), echoing familiar rebuttals of homonormative narratives of Stonewall, has argued, "At a time when our country is once again rocked by riots demanding justice from a broken system, it's critical that we celebrate not just the sterile concept of liberation, but its messy reality. Chains don't break themselves, and they don't go quietly. By reducing the shouts of gay power to the whispers of tolerance, we prevent ourselves from understanding what it takes to actually make change in this world." Ryan, too, like many others, has decentered the White patrons drinking and dancing at the Stonewall Inn that fateful summer evening in 1969 in order to elevate and make visible those with "the least social capital (the poor, the gender queer, the people of color) who fought back," in order to reinscribe the legacy of Stonewall. Marsha Johnson and Sylvia Rivera, for instance, have been at the center of fierce archival contestations over Stonewall's narrative and who gets to claim and tell it, the identifications it creates. Piepzna-Samarasinha (2019), in advocating for disability justice in Stonewall's memory, writes of "the grassroots scholarship and cultural work of Tourmaline, who battled racist and transmisogynist security guards to access Johnson and Sylvia Rivera's archives and make their legacies accessible to a new generation of queer and trans people" (p. 58). Driskill (2019), "longing for a different memory of Stonewall" (p. 46), plumbed the New York Public Library Digital Archives to find a photographic triptych of an unidentified queer activist at a 1970 demonstration organized by Rivera and STAR: Street Transvestite Action Revolutionaries at New York University. The photographs help answer a question key to archival identifications, "Where were the Indians at Stonewall?" (p. 46) and to advance a project that recasts Stonewall's legacy with Indigenous and Two-Spirit people. Such efforts also recast the claimed vision of Stonewall and its political prescriptions in carrying the mantle. Driskill's (2016) call is to "think carefully about our own desires and assumptions, to acknowledge our own memories or lack of memories as we write and rewrite these stories in this process of this kind of memory work" (p. 51).

METHODS & METHODOLOGIES

Queer engagements with the variegated locales of queer pasts also mark a starting point for wider rewritings of archival methods and methodologies. Queer archival methods frequently focus on denying received heteronormative categories and common sense. Ghaziani and Brim (2019) argue that "*queered*" methods seek to "tweak or explode what is possible with our existing categories" (p. 15). In communication studies, self-reflexive, relational, embodied, performative, and processual methods have come to the fore in studies of queer archives.

Communication scholars' investments in interrogating questions of power have challenged the presumed neutrality of archival records, such as finding aids, by addressing the often invisible methods that make archival materials intelligible (Rawson, 2018). Like the professional discipline of archival studies, which focuses on the preservation, classification, and description of archival collections, Communication scholars have taken up these categories to highlight the queer possibilities for understanding the past on different terms. Queer archival organizing practices, those that deny linear, singular, and "official" categorizations, challenge homophobic standards by seeking accountability to queer lives (Kumbier, 2014; Sheffield, 2014). Tyburczy (2016) works between professional historical practices and academic methods, in particular as they relate to displaying archival materials. Tyburczy coins "queer curatorship" as a set of tactics used to display "unruly objects" in excess of heteronormative assumptions (p. 3). In this sense, queer archival methods foreground the participatory nature of all archival productions, highlighting how the categories of "archivist" and "researcher" must be understood as imbricated.

Alongside methods that seek to challenge neutrality through self-reflexive engagement, embodiment has emerged as a queer source of possibility. Arondekar (2009) addresses archives through their colonial logics, seeking a methodology that exceeds queers' presumed ties to historical loss. Gutierrez-Perez and Andrade (2018), for example, draw on their experiences to demonstrate that daily life exceeds the limits of legal definition through their consideration of "embodied ideographs," a method of queer of color worldmaking. Taylor (1950/2003) draws on performance studies scholarship to produce an enlivened, or at least less dead and dusty, understanding of archives. For Taylor, the archive must be understood in relation to repertoires or embodied activities, such as dance, that exist beyond textual documentation. Jaclyn Pryor (2017) takes up a queer challenge to linear (straight) historical narratives through "slips" in performances that mark those moments when past, present, and future cannot so easily be delineated. Lee (2019) takes up "(un)becomings," out of lived shifts in historical understanding alongside momentary stablizings of identity, as an aspect of a queered methodology focused on the processual nature of archival engagements. And Bessette (2017) addresses "retroactivist" impulses beyond the academy, centering how queer activists perform their own self-reflexive historiographic work by appropriating available sexual and gendered categories to their own ends (p. 8). Queer composers and critics likewise engage retroactivst methods in works such as *Fun Home, Lesbian/Woman*, and *Becoming an Image* (Bessette, 2013; Rohy, 2010).

ARCHIVES, QUEER HISTORIOGRAPHY, AND FUTURITY

Historiography, broadly understood, demands a consideration of the contextual production of historical knowledge in a past and in relation to a present. If historically oriented queer communication scholarship has largely focused on U.S. pasts, one insight of queer historiography into this archive is that queer knowledge production, as scholarship in this instance, is contextual and also worthy of study in its own right. Queer critiques of the "weight" of histories of ACT UP and Stonewall, particularly in terms of their lacking attention to class and race, also continue to thrive (Chàvez, 2012; Juhasz, 2006). And the growth in competing etiologies of queer theory also demonstrates the expansion of queer thought since the early 1990s and the attendant growth of historiographic scholarship on sexuality, focused on queer history beyond the academy, both in and outside of communication studies (Nelson, 2014; Rand, 2014; Rohy, 2014. Following Stoler (2010), queer archives must be understood both as a physical collection of materials and metaphorically as any collection of texts, in this case, scholarly narratives of queer pasts and the disciplinary norms that shape(d) them. Queer historiographies are both responsive to pasts and seek, in line with attendant sexual political commitments, opportunities to reenvision and enliven queer futures. Given queer scholars' investment in interrogating histories of sexualities generally and in self-reflexive interrogations of the "status" and history of queer scholarship in the academy, this section takes up two general themes of queer theory and thus of queer historiography. Namely, theories and methods invested in negativity and those invested futurity, to map how "the queer archive" has been differentially understood as a "resource" for queer historiographers in communication studies. These bisections of archives and historiographies, as literal or metaphorical and as scholarly or otherwise, respectively, are not to deny that reflexive academic historiographies continue on queer terms. For instance, Rand (2014) revisits the history of "queer theory" alongside attendant commitments to scholarship and activism toward a queer theory of rhetorical agency.

Queer historiography in communication studies is rooted in feminist historiographies, gay and lesbian studies histories and historiographies, and contemporary commitments to the study of queer life out of performance studies, critical theory, and as critical race scholarship— alongside contestations over these roots, or "rhizomes" (Allen, 2016), and how they have or have not been animated, enlivened, or (actively) erased. In considering scholarly texts as archives, decolonial responses to the discipline offer one site of archival and historiographic reflection, in this collection, as in uneasy tension with decolonial critiques of Western gender and sexuality (Cram, 2016; Lugones, 2007; LeMaster, 2020).

Love (2007) articulates a view of "melancholic" historiography that "does not propose a 'theory of love'" but "does take impossible love as a model for queer historiography," which demonstrates queer historiography's rootedness in queer archives in both a literal and a metaphorical sense (p. 24). Love's work on one hand responds to "queer negativity," as figured by Leo Bersani (1989) and Lee Edelman (2004), which finds some uptake in historiographic thinking as seen in Sara Edenheim's (2013 recouping of "dust," embracing the impossibilities of the past and recognizing the partial and always incomplete status of any archive. Extending these lineages toward communication studies, Bessette (2017) notes 1990s investments in queer antisociality took up centrally what it means to consider a historical subject on present terms, asking how much a historical figure is really "like us." Thus, to tell a narrative of the queer archive is to also often to tell a narrative of responses to, or denials of, trends in queer theory. Similar questions arise in communication studies particularly with regard to the terms of queer (dis)identification in the archive (Bessette, 2013). In sum, "melancholic" strands of queer historiography embrace the queer archive's always incomplete status, and its particular traumas inflicted on queer people, as a source of possibility.

In partial contrast, Muñoz's (2009) *Cruising Utopia*, alongside the work of Eng and Kazanjian (2002), and Berlant (2011), demands an account of queerness that is future oriented, without returning to a model of "anticipatory readings" wherein historical subjects, "proto-gays," are sought out to produce a teleological historical narrative of sexuality in the present (Coviello, 2013). Here, scholars have interrogated the "queer worldmaking" possibilities of the archive (Berlant & Warner, 1998). In this vein, historiography has been adopted to revisit foreclosed upon futures.

Continuing efforts to challenge the easy lines offered thus far, queer hauntologies, building on Derrida (1995) and Ballif (2013), articulate an/other more "ethical" approach to the past that demands a consideration of the archive as a site of active intersubjective engagement. In this vein, queer scholars adopt Derrida's embrace of the past despite, in fact because of, its unknowability (Bessette, 2017; Lewis, 2014). That is, Freccero (2005) shows that hauntology allows for an approach to the queer past as an often unheard "specter" in our present. Hauntology demands attention to how a past may not only "speak back" to present interpretation, but also affectively respond to and thus produce embodied experiences in the present, toward an ethics-informed understanding of the present that seeks to hear that which has been silenced. These approaches, like recent turns in queer historiographies, maintain an awareness of the likelihood of their involvement in an/other's continued dereliction by way of any archival engagement. This impulse produces and motivates wider queer historical investments. Queer scholars both assert "we are here" and assert the "here and now[ness]" of such an assertion. To read against this then can be understood to continue the same queer legacy that produced it, anew.

NORMS OF ARCHIVAL EVIDENCE

Out of the above histories, Communication scholars have marshalled the queer archive toward challenging disciplinary norms of archival evidence. Since early invocations of queer, scholars have noted and worked against norms of rigor tied frequently to documentary evidence. Muñoz's (1996) work on ephemerality draws on lived realities of queer historical erasure and marks a potent source for queer historical claims. Following Muñoz, queer scholars including Manalansan (2014) and Halberstam (2011) have come to understand queer archives and life through ephemeral traces, "messes," whose unruliness, incompleteness, and abundance challenge traditional norms of historical documentation. These queer challenges to evidence have resulted in a recouping of various claims to gossip, traces, and "ephemera" through speculation, queer absence, and "queer fictions" as sources worthy of engagement in the face of critiques of failing to meet standards of "historical rigor" (Bravmann, 1997; Reichard, 2012; VanHaitsma, 2016).

Challenges to standards of disciplinary evidence also emerged in Foucauldian and feminist Communication scholarship. As Biesecker (2006) argues, "Out of the deconstruction of the material presence of the past and, thus, in relation to what the archive cannot *authenticate* absolutely but can (be made to) *authorize* nonetheless, issues an invitation to write rhetorical histories of archives, which is to say, critical histories of the situated and strategic uses to which archives have been put" (p. 130). The feminist historiographical work of Ballif (1992), Jarratt (1992), and Sharer (1999) continues to inform queer considerations of sexuality.

Cvetkovich (2003) offers an influential extension of Munoz's work as she approaches "trauma archives." For Cvetkovich, the realities of queer historical traumas, and especially silence around AIDS, necessitate new norms from which to approach archival artifacts. Cvetkovich's focus on the public erasure of queer experiences, and thus frequent archival erasure, can also be seen as an impulse behind many "recovery" projects. These revisions of evidentiary standards also offer new readings of archives' relationships to their collections. Likewise, Wrathall (1992) attends to the stakes of silences around sexuality in archives. He argues that the structure of a given collection, alongside its provenance, can be treated as historical sources in their own right. Morris (2009) addresses the queer possibilities of what is "visible beneath the lines" of archival materials through a reading of queer consignation. In this sense, queer archival work often demands attention to (un)intentional elisions in collections that may offer more than their silences suggest.

Alongside efforts to contextualize historical materials within their archival locations, digital archives have offered queer and trans scholars an opportunity to address consignation online, in both print and practice. Rawson (2013) shows how platforms and websites, like physical archives, work on different terms to shape researchers' experiences and thus mark a unique site for rhetorical inquiry: "The lesson this offers for rhetorical historians is that by intentionally including born-digital artifacts into our histories we can also push the boundaries of where we find rhetorical histories and what they are supposed to look like" (p. 10).

More broadly, the question of queer challenges to archival evidence allows for a consideration of how queer historical materials are embedded with or challenge social norms otherwise considered "beyond" sexuality. In this vein, archivists, activists, and archival activists draw on insurgent histories to remedy contemporary public lack. Scot (2014), alongside a range of past and present archivists such as Joan Nestle, has also taught queer histories in places ranging from the archive itself, to K–12 classrooms, to public queer-centered workshops. Similarly, queer familial narratives and oral histories, while often not identified as archives, continue to function as a resource for scholars and others to revisit experiences of historical (dis)identification (Chávez, 2009; Johnson, 2001; Muñoz, 1999).

Out of a review of melancholic queer histories, those focused on loss and recovery, Arondekar (2014) poses an alternative vision of queer archival evidence with the question, "What would it mean to let go of our attachments to loss, to unmoor ourselves, as it were, from the stakes of reliable ghosts?" (p. 99). In response, she figures a queer futurity out of poetic abundance. Nelson (2014) sums up the impulse of many of the queer archival projects considered here: "We must develop tools to help others creatively intervene when faced with a seemingly vacuous or 'complete' archive... enacting queer historical futures requires us to reenvision material that does exist, expanding our present-past for future-pasts to come" (p. 134). These works on their whole also offer a larger call to communication studies' disciplinary archive, namely, to interrogate its own elisions of queer life. While not archival in its traditional sense, scholars have raised queer revisions of "professional" standards, especially as they concern silence (Corey & Nakayama, 1997; Samek & Donofrio, 2013).

ACTIVISM AND QUEER ARCHIVES

Queer activist archives have had gravitational pull for scholars, activists, creatives, and counterpublics. Arguably the conditions of marginalization, discrimination and dispossession, movement's residual verve and effervesce and intimacies, and tactical reservoirs and storied actions of protest translate, resonate, and adapt better across time and generation than other archival materials plumbed and circulated from the stores of LGBTQ history and memory. These issues of relevancy and saliency, affective relay, and accessibility are central to the question of archival potentiality, beyond the prima facie value of preservation, for worldmaking mobilization in the present and for future queer communities, culture, and political transformation. Even if these activist archives draw well academics and grassroots archivists who pursue or build them, and even if they appear to have certain temporal advantages, there remain contextual and generational challenges that constrain which materials emerge, if and how they are met, and what they might do.

The seismic trauma of the AIDS epidemic, and its generation of activist and cultural responses in the 1980s and 1990s, produced a copious and diverse archive of print and media, art, ephemera, oral history and performance, and official and vernacular collections that have with regularity garnered attention, labor, and distribution among scholars, activists, and queer communities. Juhasz and Kerr (2018) have established the ebb and flow of this archival work and its productions across the four decades of the epidemic, periods of silence and proliferation; the current moment, roughly 2008 to the present, they call a period of "AIDS Crisis Revisitation." Especially influential is ACT UP (AIDS Coalition to Unleash Power), founded in 1987 as "a diverse, nonpartisan group of individuals united in anger and committed to direct action to end the AIDS crisis" (Schulman, 2021). ACT UP's mourning and militancy, as Crimp (2002) memorably described it, can be credited with transformative political and medical interventions nationally and internationally during their prime and have captured the archival imagination and collective memory over the past two decades. As Kerr (Juhasz & Kerr, 2018) observes, "Even today, amidst a time of increased social unrest, not a month goes by where there isn't a blog post, article, or radio segment heralding ACT UP as the perfect model for what is needed now."

A wide range of writings, films, exhibitions, and public pedagogy, the ACT UP archive—its actions, verbal and visual corpus, its funerals—reveals what its creators and contributors hope might come from its ongoing generation. Sarah Schulman (2013) in her critique of AIDS gentrification, then and now, believes that "this is the most remarkable story I have ever experienced, and it should and could be a model for human behavior in all realms. The true message of AIDS is that making people with power accountable works" (p. 156). Schulman and Jim Hubbard, who founded the ACT UP Oral History Project in 2002, collecting hundreds of hours and scores of recorded interviews, have averred that its purpose is to place the movement "in the middle of mainstream U.S. history" so as not to be forgotten but perhaps more importantly to "de-mystify the process of making social change, remind us that change can be made, and help us understand how to do it." Toward that end, Hubbard continues to do public screenings of his acclaimed 2012 documentary, *United in Anger: A History of ACT UP*. On the Facebook page for the film, Hubbard posted in January 2017 that "last night, I had a wonderful screening at the City Reliquary, where we had a serious discussion not only about ACT UP strategies, but how to learn from those techniques to find ways to fight against the reactionary policies of the Trump administration." In March 2020, another post announced that "Mayday Space is doing an online screening of United in Anger followed by a discussion with me (Jim Hubbard) and Kenyon Farrow. We'll take your questions, talk about what's going on and try to figure out whether ACT UP and AIDS Activism have anything to teach us about how to deal with COVID-19." His website for the film includes an Activist Guide "designed to help groups learn from the example of ACT UP and apply the lessons of ACT UP's organizing tactics and campaign strategies to their own movements today."

ACT UP's political legacy as strategic and rhetorical repertoire is inextricably immersed in its powerful affective inheritance, an electric range of emotions, from anger to grief to lust. Cvetkovich (2003) places ACT UP's "archive of feelings," comprising especially oral histories of lesbian women in ACT UP, as crucial to understanding what keeps a movement together, its "political difficulties and challenges," and "revivifying the dead" (pp. 204, 238). Rand (2012), in remembering ACT UP's "ambivalent relationship between pride and shame," argues that there are significant political stakes in "cultivat[ing] a deep appreciation of the contradictions involved in deploying affect as an activist tactic" (p. 75). Such archival cultivation and circulation is what Hilderbrand (2006) calls "retroactivism," an "intergenerational nostalgia" that provides temporal and affective access, inspiration, and insight that can be "potentially enlivening for radical queer community" (pp. 307, 308). Emmer (2012) describes the embodiment of such work in ACT UP Philadelphia as "meta-generation," cross-generational archival engagement and relations that produce "radical mnemonic capital," and "alchemy of retro- and pro-spective imagination" that "propel us toward queer futurity" (pp. 91–93).

The promising potentialities of an activist archive such as ACT UP's provide powerful inducements, but there are troubles as well. Most of those who have curated, researched, published, and exhibited the ACT UP archive have been White, and there have been deep critiques and damaging memory presumptions that ACT UP was racist (Gould, 2012). Those such as Juhasz and Kerr (2018) and Chávez (2012, 2021), who are attempting to foreground the antiracist, feminist, and other intersectional work from the archive, are all nevertheless part of a resounding chorus of scholarly and activist critics importantly challenging the "whitewashing" of AIDS memory and history (Brier et al., 2017; Brouwer & Morris, 2021; Cheng, 2016; Hammonds, 1987; Hernández, 2019; Muñoz, 2009; Ramirez, 2010; Ryan, 2013; Shahani, 2016; Stockdill, 2018; Sturken, 1997; Woubshet, 2015). There also remain many generational challenges, affective and political, to the fulsome archival vision described above. Hallas (2003, 2009) and Juhasz (2012) have both described the differing structures of feeling and material circumstances that create obstacles to bearing witness to the epidemic or understanding its ongoing relevance. Juhasz (2012) writes of the "legacy of forgetting AIDS activism: what amnesia looks like, sounds like, and means in daily life for those of us who survived as well as for new generations of at-risk youth of color who were never reminded that others fought, lived, and died before them" (see also West, 2012).

FUTURE DIRECTIONS

At times, tense relations between queer, trans, and feminist pasts and presents mark an ongoing direction of queer archival engagement and the extent to which queer elides, aligns, or adjusts the terms of gender identification. Often against identificatory claims to sexuality and gender, scholars have turned to decolonial and Afro-realist approaches to the queer archive. In this vein, the queerness of an archive cannot be separated from its ontological investments.

Tracing the rise of sexuality as founded on a division of life into human and nonhuman, decolonial projects demand attention to the coloniality of modern sexual and gender identification itself. As this essay exhibits, communication studies needs to move beyond U.S.-specific archival projects and their Western perspectives in theoretical and political extension and disruption of what queer might mean. Cultivating and critiquing what Phillips and Reyes (2011) and Houdek (2016) call "global memoryscapes" offers a promising decentering and resituating of domains and knowledges that undoubtedly will transform our understanding of what queer/ing archives are and do (Cheng et al., 2020). For example, work in other disciplines provides important foundations for exploring AIDS memory work in Africa (Barz, 2006; Decoteau, 2013; Fassin, 2007). In communication studies, Huang (2019) has intervened and inspired such work by asking, "What does Stonewall mean to me, a Chinese diasporic lesbian residing in the United States?" (p. 69). Such efforts will further underscore the critical significance of work in/on digital archives as queer/ing archives as part of global memoryscapes expands.

We also want to imagine future expanding engagements with the disposition and provenance of queer archives. The queer archival encounter in Phoenix with which we began this essay is symptomatic of what Morris and Black (2013) described as the "where" and "please" challenges of conveying and circulating queer history and memory: the former referring to multifaceted and entrenched infrastructural constraints such as access, embodiment, ephemerality and precarity, and norms of transmission and erasure, all compounded by intersectional violences; the latter, inextricably related, concerns the rhetorical impediments to cultivating in diverse audiences a will to the past and its mobilization (p. xi). In the face of such challenges, archival queers better than many understand archives fundamentally as inventional resources, wellsprings of argument and appeal that might make the past unmistakably and palpably relevant and resonant to the felt and exigent present and future. In the interest of widening and animating these inventional funds, who bequeaths and makes good on them, then, it would be valuable to consider further archival *disposition*, echoing Martínez (2014) that "a queer approach to archives requires an exercise of the mind that endeavors hard to treat classification schemes not just as abstractions but as systems of power that have multiple effects on lives and bodies" (p. 175). As work by Rawson (2018) and Bessette (2017) demonstrate, the situatedness, ordering, and legibility of archives through their discourses, in other words, are a matter of dispositio as well as inventio.

Inspired by an essay published long ago by Wrathall (1992), we also emphasize that the notion of archival disposition is not only about institutional arrangement but also about *provenance*, that is, the *rhetorical transfer and transition "into" the archive*, the identificatory, constitutive and justificatory, epideictic and mnemonicidic discourses that attend *the giving and receiving of archival matter*, and the ongoing acquisitory memories of discovery, taking possession, ownership, bequeathing, curation, arrival, assimilation. How are archival materials narrated, framed, illuminated, and obscured, in the rhetorical performances and silences, embodiments and relations, histories and affects, of donation, gifting, purchase, salvage? *Provenance* is an underexplored conceptual and material domain in the work catalyzed by the archival turn—the telling often circuitous genealogies of collection, holding, selling, bequest, dumpster diving, eBay-ing, and so on. The paucity here, at least in terms of future archival efforts, is in *the curation of archive stories of provenance*. How individuals and collectives, if at all, have rhetorically configured materials about to archivally change hands, their meanings and memories, and, importantly, their values; what are the narratives archival agents and institutions tell about these accumulated items and collections, the complexities and implications (materially, culturally, politically) of their consignment—in short, the rhetorical histories and inventional funds of acquisitory exchange, or rhetorics of archival provenance.

One might also consider provenance curation in terms of longer tracings of affective heritage on the radically situated experience of what Cram (2016) calls ambient archival environments. Here archival disposition is also about the characteristic mood, spirit, and attitude of the agent of arrangement; the disposition of disposition, as it were—the less effable influences, including affective and ideological influences, on placement and hierarchy often rationalized as, say, objective method. Cram's phrase "generation of intimacies" is propulsive, and we would punctuate the doubling of that word "generation" to further explore the productive intersections of ambience and provenance, the deepened connections between inside and outside domains of archival rhetorics. Tracing generative genealogies of intimacy through acquisitory memory, that is, in the changing hands of archival objects and experiences, and provenance's rhetorics, is potentially one more way to meaningfully queer archives. As Cram (2016), drawing on Marshall et al. (2014) in their *Radical History Review* special issue, observes, queering the archive is a project of context, in which the critic "'recall[s] and renews the historical imperative to apply critical pressure to the type of knowledge we inherit in relation to gender and sexuality and the manner through which we inherit it'" (p. 113).

FURTHER READING

Burton, A. M. (2003). *Dwelling in the archive: Women writing house, home, and history in late colonial India.* Oxford University Press.

Carden, K. R., Vaught, S. E., Muñoz, A., Pinto, V., Vaught, C., & Zeigler, M. (2016). A critical archival pedagogy: The Lesbian Herstory Archives and a course in radical lesbian thought. *Radical Teacher, 105,* 23–32.

Castiglia, C., & Reed, C. (2011). *If memory serves: Gay men, AIDS, and the promise of the queer past.* University of Minnesota Press.

Davy, K. (2008). Cultural memory and the lesbian archive. In G. Kirsch & L. Rohan (Eds.), *Beyond the archives: Research as a lived process* (pp. 128–135). Southern Illinois University Press.

Duberman, M. B. (2002). *Left out: The politics of exclusion: Essays, 1964–2002.* South End Press.

Eichhorn, K. (2013). *The archival turn in feminism: Outrage in order.* Temple University Press.

Escoffier, J. (2018). *American homo: Community and perversity.* Verso.

Ferguson, R. A. (2018). *One-dimensional queer.* Polity.

Freeman, E. (2010). *Time binds: Queer temporalities, queer histories.* Duke University Press.

Johnson, E. P. (2019). *Honeypot: Black southern women who love women.* Duke University Press.

Kumbier, A. (2014). *Ephemeral material: Queering the archive.* Litwin Books.

Lee, J. (2020). *Producing the archival body.* Routledge.

Palladini, G., & Pustianaz, M. (Eds.). (2017). *Lexicon for an affective archive.* Intellect Press.

Rawson, K. J., & Devor, A. (Eds.). (2015). Special issue: Archives and archiving. *TSQ: Transgender Studies Quarterly, 2*(4), 539–716.

Snorton, C. R. (2017). *Black on both sides: A racial history of trans identity* (3rd ed.). University of Minnesota Press.

Steedman, C. (2002). *Dust: The archive and cultural history.* Rutgers University Press.

Stryker, S. (2008). *Transgender history.* Seal Press.

REFERENCES

Allen, J. S. (2016). Black/queer rhizomatics: Train up a child in the way ze should grow... In E. P. Johnson (Ed.), *No tea, no shade: New writings in Black queer studies* (pp. 27–47). Duke University Press.

Appiah, K. A. (2019, June 22). Stonewall and the myth of self-deliverance. *New York Times*.

Arondekar, A. R. (2009). *For the record: On sexuality and the colonial archive in India*. Duke University Press.

Arondekar, A. R. (2014). In the absence of reliable ghosts: Sexuality, historiography, South Asia. *Differences*, 25(3), 98–122.

Arondekar, A. R., Cvetkovich, A., Hanhardt, C. B., Kunzel, R., Nyong'o, T., Rodríguez, J. M., Stryker, S., Marshall, D., Murphy, K. P., & Tortorici, Z. (2015). Queering archives: A roundtable discussion. *Radical History Review*, 122, 211–231.

Ballif, M. (1992). Re/dressing histories; Or, on re/covering figures who have been laid bare by our gaze. *Rhetoric Society Quarterly*, 22(1), 91–98.

Ballif, M. (2013). Historiography as hauntology: Paranormal investigations into the history of rhetoric. In M. Ballif (Ed.), *Theorizing histories of rhetoric* (pp. 139–152). Southern Illinois University Press.

Barz, G. (2006). *Singing for life: HIV/AIDS and music in Uganda*. Routledge.

Berlant, L. (2011). *Cruel optimism*. Duke University Press.

Berlant, L., & Warner, M. (1998). Sex in public. *Critical Inquiry*, 24(2), 547–566.

Bersani, L. (1989). *Is the rectum a grave? And other essays*. University of Chicago Press.

Bessette, J. (2013). An archive of anecdotes: Raising lesbian consciousness after the Daughters of Bilitis. *Rhetoric Society Quarterly*, 43(1), 22–45.

Bessette, J. (2017). *Retroactivism in the lesbian archives: Composing pasts and futures*. Southern Illinois University Press.

Biesecker, B. A. (2006). Of historicity, rhetoric: The archive as scene of invention. *Rhetoric and Public Affairs*, 9(1), 124–131.

Bravmann, S. (1997). *Queer fictions of the past: History, culture, and difference*. Cambridge University Press.

Brier, J., Bell, J., Bost, D., Capó, J., Cheng, J. F., Fox, D. M., Hanhardt, C., Hobson, E. K., & Royles, D. (2017). Interchange: HIV/AIDS and U.S. history. *Journal of American History*, 104, 431–460.

Brouwer, D. C., & Morris III, C. E. (2021). Decentering whiteness in AIDS memory: Indigent rhetorical criticism and the dead of Hart Island. *Quarterly Journal of Speech*, 107(2), 160–184.

Burke, K. (1945). *A rhetoric of motives*. University of California Press.

Chávez, K. (2009). Remapping Latinidad: A performance cartography of Latina/o identity in rural Nebraska. *Text and Performance Quarterly*, 29(2), 165–182.

Chávez, K. (2012). ACT UP, Haitian migrants, and alternative memories of HIV/AIDS. *Quarterly Journal of Speech*, 98(1), 63–68.

Chávez, K. (2021). *The borders of AIDS: Race, quarantine, and resistance*. University of Washington Press.

Cheng, J. (2016). AIDS and its afterlives in popular media. *Women's Studies Quarterly*, 44(1 & 2), 73–92.

Cheng, J.-F., Juhasz, A., & Shahani, N. (Eds.). (2020). *AIDS and the distribution of crises*. Duke University Press.

Cifor, M. (2015). Presence, absence, and Victoria's hair: Examining affect and embodiment in trans archives. *Transgender Studies Quarterly*, 2(4), 645–649.

Corey, F. C., & Nakayama, T. K. (1997). Sextext. *Text and Performance Quarterly*, 17(1), 58–68.

Coviello, P. (2013). *Tomorrow's parties: Sex and the untimely in nineteenth-century America*. New York University Press.

Cram, E. (2016). Archival ambience and sensory memory: Generating queer intimacies in the settler colonial archive. *Communication and Critical/Cultural Studies*, 13(2), 109–129.

Crimp, D. (2002). *Melancholia and moralism: Essays on AIDS and queer politics*. MIT Press.

Cvetkovich, A. (2003). *An archive of feelings: Trauma, sexuality, and lesbian public cultures*. Duke University Press.
Cvetkovich, A. (2012). *Depression: A public feeling*. Duke University Press.
Decoteau, C. L. (2013). *Ancestors and antiretrovirals: The biopolitics of HIV/AIDS in post-apartheid South Africa*. University of Chicago Press.
Derrida, J. (1995). *Archive fever: A Freudian impression*. University of Chicago Press.
Dinshaw, C. (1999). *Getting medieval: Sexualities and communities, pre- and postmodern*. Duke University Press.
Driskill, Q. (2016). *Asegi stories: Cherokee queer and two-spirit memory*. University of Arizona Press.
Driskill, Q. (2019). All power to the people: A gay liberation triptych. *QED: A Journal of GLBTQ Worldmaking, 6*, 44–53.
Edelman, L. (2004). *No future: Queer theory and the death drive*. Duke University Press.
Edenheim, S. (2013). Lost and never found: The queer archive of feelings and its historical propriety. *Differences, 24*(3), 36–62.
Emmer, P. (2012). Talkin' 'bout meta-generation: ACT UP history and queer futurity. *Quarterly Journal of Speech, 98*(1), 89–96.
Eng, D., & Kazanjian, D. (2002). *Loss: The politics of mourning*. University of California Press.
Fassin, D. (2007). *When bodies remember: Experience and politics of AIDS in South Africa* (A. Jacobs & G. Varro, Trans.). University of California Press.
Freccero, C. (2005). *Queer/early/modern*. Duke University Press.
Frischherz, M. (2020). Queer adventures in the forum and the archive: Or, the flood made immersion possible. *Cultural Studies Critical Methodologies, 20*(2), 167–175.
Ghaziani, A., & Brim, M. (2019). *Imagining queer methods*. New York University Press.
Gieseking, J. J. (2015). Useful in/stability: The dialectical production of the social and spatial Lesbian Herstory Archives. *Radical History Review, 122*, 25–37.
Gould, D. B. (2012). ACT UP, racism, and the question of how to use history. *Quarterly Journal of Speech, 98*(1), 54–62.
Gutierrez-Perez, R., & Andrade, L. (2018). Queer of color worldmaking: In the rhetorical archive and the embodied repertoire. *Text & Performance Quarterly, 38*(1), 1–18.
Halberstam, J. (2011). *The queer art of failure*. Duke University Press.
Hallas, R. (2009). *Reframing bodies: AIDS, bearing witness, and the queer moving image*. Duke University Press.
Hallas, R. (2003). The witness in the archive. *S&F Online*.
Hammonds, E. (1987). Race, sex, AIDS: The construction of "other." *Radical America, 20*, 28–36.
Hernández, R. (2015). Drawn from the scraps. *Radical History Review, 2015*(122), 70–88.
Hernández, R. (2019). *Archiving an epidemic: Art, AIDS, and the queer Chicanx Avant-Garde*. New York University Press.
Hilderbrand, L. (2006). Retroactivism. *GLQ: A Journal of Lesbian and Gay Studies, 12*(2), 303–317.
Houdek, M. (2016). The rhetorical force of "global archival memory": (Re)situating archives along the global memoryscape. *Journal of International and Intercultural Communication, 9*, 204–221.
Huang, S. (2019). Fifty years since Stonewall: Beyond the borders of the United States. *QED: A Journal in GLBTQ Worldmaking, 6*, 69–75.
Jarratt, S. C. (1992). Performing feminisms, histories, rhetorics. *Rhetoric Society Quarterly, 22*(1), 1–5.
Johnson, E. P. (2001). "Quare" studies, or (almost) everything I know about queer studies I learned from my grandmother. *Text & Performance Quarterly, 21*(1), 1.
Johnson, E. P. (2008). *Sweet tea: Black gay men of the South*. University of North Carolina Press.
Johnson, E. P. (2019). *Honeypot: Black southern women who love women*. Duke University Press.

Juhasz, A. (2006). Video remains: Nostalgia, technology, and queer archive activism. *GLQ, 12*(2), 319–328.

Juhasz, A. (2012). Forgetting ACT UP. *Quarterly Journal of Speech, 98*(1), 69–74.

Juhasz, A., & Kerr, T. (2017). *Stacked on her office shelf: Stewardship and AIDS archives*. Center for the Humanities, City University of New York. http://www.centerforthehumanities.org/distributaries/stacked-on-her-office-shelf-stewardship-and-aids-archives

Juhasz, A., & Kerr, T. (2018). Who are the stewards of the AIDS archive? Sharing the political weight of the intimate. In A. Jones, J. N. DeFilippis, & M. W. Yarbrough (Eds.), *The unfinished queer agenda after marriage equality* (pp. 88–101). Routledge.

Kumbier, A. (2014). *Ephemeral material: Queering the archive*. Litwin Books.

Lee, J. A. (2019). A queer/ed archival methodology: Archival bodies as nomadic subjects. *Journal of Critical Library and Information Studies, 1*(2), 1–27.

LeMaster, L. (2020). "It's a … [inaudible blood-curdling screams, chaos]!": Gender reveal party fails as ideological rupture. *Peitho, 22*(4). https://cfshrc.org/article/its-a-inaudible-blood-curdling-screams-chaos-gender-reveal-party-fails-as-ideological-rupture/

Lewis, A. J. (2014). "I am 64 and Paul McCartney doesn't care": The haunting of the transgender archive and the challenges of queer history. *Radical History Review, 120*, 13–34.

Love, H. (2007). *Feeling backward: Loss and the politics of queer history*. Harvard University Press.

Lugones, M. (2007). Heterosexualism and the colonial/modern gender system. *Hypatia, 22*(1), 186–209.

Manalansan, M. F. (2014). The "stuff" of archives: Mess, migration, and queer lives. *Radical History Review, 120*, 94–107.

Marshall, D., Murphy, K. P., & Tortorici, Z. (2014). Queering archives: Historical unravelings. *Radical History Review, 120*, 1–11.

Martínez, M. E. (2014). Archives, bodies, and imagination: The case of Juana Aguilar and queer approaches to history, sexuality, and politics. *Radical History Review, 120*, 159–182.

Morris, C. E., III. (2006a). Archival queer. *Rhetoric and Public Affairs, 9*(1), 145–151.

Morris, C. E., III. (2006b). The archival turn in rhetorical studies; Or, the archive's rhetorical (re)turn. *Rhetoric and Public Affairs, 9*(1), 113–115.

Morris, C. E., III. (2009). Richard Halliburton's bearded tales. *Quarterly Journal of Speech, 95*(2), 123–147.

Morris, C. E. III, & Black, J. E. (2013). *An archive of hope: Harvey Milk's speeches and writings*. University of California Press.

Muñoz, J. E. (1996). Ephemera as evidence: Introductory notes to queer acts. *Women & Performance: A Journal of Feminist Theory, 8*(2), 5–16.

Muñoz, J. E. (1999). *Disidentifications: Queers of color and the performance of politics*. University of Minnesota Press.

Muñoz, J. E. (2009). *Cruising utopia: The then and there of queer futurity*. New York University Press.

Nealon, C. S. (2001). *Foundlings: Lesbian and gay historical emotion before Stonewall*. Duke University Press.

Nelson, L. (2014). Reanimating archiving/archival corporealities: Deploying "Big Ears" in de rigueur mortis intervention. *QED: A Journal in GLBTQ Worldmaking, 1*(2), 132–159.

Phillips, K. R., & Reyes, M.G. (2011). *Global memoryscapes: Contesting remembrance in a transnational age*. University of Alabama Press.

Piepzna-Samarasinha, L. L. (2019). Disability justice/Stonewall's legacy, or: Love mad trans Black women when they are alive and dead, let their revolutions teach your resistance all the time. *QED: A Journal of GLBTQ Worldmaking, 6*, 54–62.

Pritchard, E. (2014). "Like signposts on the road": The function of literacy in constructing Black queer ancestors. *Literacy in Composition Studies, 2*(1), 29–53.

Pritchard, E. (2017). *Fashioning lives: Black queers and the politics of literacy*. Southern Illinois University Press.

Pryor, J. (2017). *Time slips: Queer temporalities, contemporary performance, and the hole of history*. Northwestern University Press.
Ramírez, H. R. (2010). Gay Latino histories/dying to be remembered: AIDS obituaries, public memory, and the queer Latino archive. In G. Pérez, F. Guridy, & A. Burgos (Eds.), *Beyond El Barrio: Everyday life in Latina/o America* (pp. 103–128). New York University Press.
Rand, E. J. (2012). Gay pride and its queer discontents: ACT UP and the political deployment of affect. *Quarterly Journal of Speech, 98*(1), 75–80.
Rand, E. J. (2014). *Reclaiming queer: Activist & academic rhetorics of resistance*. University of Alabama Press.
Rawson, K. J. (2013). Rhetorical history 2.0: Toward a digital transgender archives. http://www.encultura tion.net/toward_digital_transgender_archive
Rawson, K. J. (2014). Transgender worldmaking in cyberspace: Historical activism on the Internet. *QED: A Journal of GLBTQ Worldmaking, 1*(2), 38–60.
Rawson, K. J. (2015). Introduction: An inevitably political craft. *Transgender Studies Quarterly, 2*(4), 544–552.
Rawson, K. J. (2018). The rhetorical power of archival description: Classifying images of gender transgression. *Rhetoric Society Quarterly, 48*(4), 327–351.
Reichard, D. A. (2012). Animating ephemera through oral history: Interpreting visual traces of California gay college student organizing from the 1970s. *The Oral History Review, 391*, 37–60.
Rohy, V. (2010). In the queer archive: Fun Home. *GLQ: A Journal of Lesbian and Gay Studies, 16*(3), iv–361.
Rohy, V. (2014). *Lost causes: Narrative, etiology, and queer theory*. Oxford University Press.
Román, D. (2000). Visa denied. In J. Boone, M. Dupis, M. Meeker, K. Quimby, C. Sarver, D. Silverman, & R. Weatherston (Eds.), *Queer frontiers: Millennial geographies, genders, and generations* (pp. 350–366). University of Wisconsin Press.
Ryan, H. (2013, August 3). How to whitewash a plague. *New York Times*.
Ryan, H. (2015, June 29). What does liberation look like? *Slate*.
Samek, A. A., & Donofrio, T. A. (2013). "Academic drag" and the performance of the critical personae: An exchange on sexuality, politics, and identity in the academy. *Women's Studies in Communication, 36*(1), 28–55.
Schulman, S. (2013). *The gentrification of the mind: Witness to a lost imagination*. University of California Press.
Schulman, S. (2021). *Let the record show: A political history of ACT UP New York, 1987–1993*. Farrar, Straus, and Giroux.
Scot, J. (2014). A Revisionist history: How archives are used to reverse the erasure of queer people in contemporary history. *QED: A Journal in GLBTQ Worldmaking, 1*(2), 205–209.
Shahani, N. (2016). How to survive the whitewashing of AIDS: Global pasts, transnational futures, *QED: A Journal in GLBTQ Worldmaking, 3*(1), 1–33.
Sharer, W. B. (1999). *Rhetorical Bodies*. University of Wisconsin Press.
Sheffield, R. T. (2014). The bedside table archives: Archive intervention and lesbian intimate domestic culture. *Radical History Review, 2014*(120), 108–120.
Stockdill, B. C. (2018). Love in the time of ACT UP: Reflections on AIDS activism, queer family, and desire. *QED: A Journal in GLBTQ Worldmaking, 5*(1), 48–83.
Stoler, A. L. (2010). Archival dis-ease: Thinking through colonial ontologies. *Communication and Critical/Cultural Studies, 7*(2), 215–219.
Sturken, M. (1997). *Tangled memories: The Vietnam war, the AIDS epidemic, and the politics of remembering*. University of California Press.
Taylor, D. (2003). *The archive and the repertoire: Performing cultural memory in the Americas*. Duke University Press. (Original work published 1950)

Tyburczy, J. (2016). *Sex museums: The politics and performance of display*. University of Chicago Press.
VanHaitsma, P. (2016). Gossip as rhetorical methodology for queer and feminist historiography. *Rhetoric Review*, 35(2), 135–147.
VanHaitsma, P. (2019a). Digital LGBTQ archives as sites of public memory and pedagogy. *Rhetoric & Public Affairs*, 22(2), 253–280.
VanHaitsma, P. (2019b). *Queering romantic engagement in the postal age: A rhetorical education*. University of South Carolina Press.
West, I. (2012). Reviving rage. *Quarterly Journal of Speech*, 98(1), 97–102.
Woubshet, D. (2015). *The calendar of loss: Race, sexuality, and mourning in the early era of AIDS*. Johns Hopkins University Press.
Wrathall, J. D. (1992). Provenance as text: Reading the silences around sexuality in manuscript collections. *Journal of American History*, 79(1), 165–178.

Morgan DiCesare and Charles E. Morris

QUEERING COLONIALISMS AND EMPIRE

INTRODUCTION

Queer theory centers marginalized sexual identities and challenges heteronormativity and its accompanying binary system of identity categorization. Its emergence in academic spaces in the late 1980s and early 1990s paralleled LGBTQ activist efforts of this era, which countered both the cisheteronormative assumptions of public space and the assimilatory impulses of earlier gay and lesbian movements.[1] Contributions of queer theory and activism included combating regulatory state structures, resisting systems of normativity and categorization that produce sexual others against a presumed heterosexual norm, and defying public–private divisions related to same-sex desire (Berlant & Warner, 1998). By directing attention to sexuality and heterosexual privilege, queer theory has had long-ranging interdisciplinary impacts, shaping critical/cultural theorizing in the humanities and social sciences.

Despite queer theory's profound impacts within and beyond the academy, its intersections with the study of colonialism and empire[2] are complex and even contradictory. Several communication scholars have called attention to queer theory's centering of White, gay, cis-male U.S. citizen subjects and its limited ability to translate into non-White and non-Western transnational contexts (e.g., Aiello et al., 2013; Asante, 2020; Eguchi & Calafell, 2020). Writing about its failure to encompass Black male subjectivities, Bryant Keith Alexander (2008) describes queer theory as "fraught with the danger of imperialism, colonialism, academic puffery, and racism" (p. 110). Illustrating imperial mobilizations of queer, scholars have demonstrated how "homonormative" and "homonationalist" rhetorics reinforce gendered and racialized hierarchies inherent to colonial projects, marking certain bodies, lives, and kinships as more valuable than others (Duggan, 2002; Eng, 2010; Morgensen, 2012; Puar, 2007; Smith, 2011).

These critiques highlight important limitations of queer theory and LGBTQ activism. However, although much of what has been called "queer theory" reflects Western-centric intellectual frameworks, Black, Indigenous, and people of color (BIPOC) and Global South scholars and activists have long contributed to understanding complex linkages between sexualities and colonial power. Queer of color scholarship and women of color feminisms have been fundamental for interrogating how heteropatriarchal systems contribute to imperialism, settler colonialism, and racialized oppressions globally and within the United States. Communication scholars' increasing participation in this interdisciplinary area of inquiry is evidenced by theoretical developments including quare theory (Johnson, 2001) and queer intercultural communication (Chávez, 2013; Eguchi & Calafell, 2020), along with contributions to areas such as queer and trans border, migration, and diaspora studies (Durham, 2004; Luibhéid & Chavez, 2020; McKinnon, 2017; Yue, 2011); Black feminist, trans, and queer of color performance pedagogies (Alexander & Warren, 2002; Gutierrez-Perez, 2018; Hall, 2021; LeMaster & Johnson, 2019); and transnational and digital LGBTQ media studies (Atay, 2021; Costanza-Chock et al., 2017; Mitra & Gajjala, 2008; Spiers, 2016; Subero, 2010). This article overviews the "queering" of the study of colonialism and empire in relation to its foundations and developments within and beyond the field of communication, identifying two broad thematics defining this scholarship. The first is *decolonizing queer theory* through research that critiques and challenges the intersections of queer theory and LGBTQ activism with Whiteness and empire. Second is *queering decolonization* through the expansion of research investigating how heteropatriarchal, binary, and normative systems of sex, sexuality, and gender have contributed to colonial processes of past and present. This article maps these thematics, identifying alignments among queer and (post)colonial inquiry,[3] reviewing historical and contemporary scholarship, and exploring directions for communication scholars interested in this expanding study.

THEORETICAL ALIGNMENTS OF QUEER AND (POST)COLONIAL INQUIRY

Queer and (post)colonial theorizing in the academy emerged alongside LGBTQ, feminist, antiracist, and decolonial social movements in the United States and throughout the world (Ferguson, 2019; Jefferess, 2008). As such, these areas of inquiry share an interest in social transformation and resistant praxis, including the critique and refusal of dominant (geo)political structures and systems of discourse and representation, and the recovery and identification of alternative knowledges and histories. These theoretical projects have methodological implications, as amplified by communication scholars' recent calls for engaging queer (post)colonial studies and transnational queer studies "as an epistemological and methodological intervention in communication" (Huang, 2021, p. 204) and "as a way to lay bare the geopolitical imbalances and colonial entanglements in which queer scholarship is done" (Asante & Hanchey, 2021, p. 213). Exploring compatibilities in the theoretical assumptions of the often separately engaged areas of queer and (post)colonial studies as well as identifying their intertwinement in queer of color scholarship and activism is useful for communication scholars wishing to engage them together.

One foundational alignment of queer and (post)colonial theorizing is their focus on critiquing binary discursive formations that fictively construct a deviant, subordinate, and objectified Other in relation to and through the gaze of a dominant, also fictive, subject or self. Early queer scholars and activists directed attention to the role of the homosexual/heterosexual binary in shaping social interaction and self-definition, and they fought against a "minoritizing view" in which lesbian and gay sexual identities and desires were imagined as deviating from "normal" sexual subjectivities (Sedgwick, 1990, p. 85). Michel Foucault's (1978) foundational scholarship, for example, identified the discourse of homosexuality in opposition to heterosexuality as a relatively new and historically Anglo-European cultural project reifying relations of power—a claim that has been further elaborated by Indigenous, (post)colonial, and transnational sexuality studies scholars who have illustrated impositions of Western sex/gender categories as central to colonial and imperial expansions (Arvin et al., 2013; Gopinath, 2005; Grewal & Kaplan, 1994; Kaplan et al., 1999; Lugonés, 2007; Morgensen, 2012; Puar, 2007; Schotten, 2018). Challenging the notion of fixed, stable sexual identities and attending to the politics of same-sex desire as articulated within national and global contexts have thus been central to queer theory's development and subsequent advancement.

Interrogations of binary identity constructions such as us/them, subject/object, center/periphery, and male/female that informed knowledge produced in "the West" regarding the "foreign" peoples and cultures of the non-Western "Third World" or Global South have also been central to (post)colonial theorizing. Foundational scholarship on colonialism and empire highlighted these categorical impositions and the construction of deviant Others as central to imperial power relations and, specifically, Anglo-European colonial rule. Early developments included, for example, Frantz Fanon's (1952/2008) argument that the material control held by White colonizers in Algeria was reinforced through the symbolically constructed Otherness of the native Black population, and Edward Said's (1978) coining of the term "Orientalism" to describe the discursive construction of Asian and especially Middle Eastern peoples and cultures in ways that embodied colonialist attitudes. Influenced by Foucault's (1971) theories of power and discourse that also significantly shaped queer theorizing, Said called attention to the binary distinction between West and East in which Western Anglo-European cultures were depicted as masculine, rational, civilized, and good, whereas Eastern cultures were depicted as feminine, irrational, uncivilized, and bad. (Post)colonial feminist scholars further identified desire as central to imperial processes, examining how exoticized fantasies proliferated by travel and anthropological accounts and extended in a variety of contemporary media forms reflect White, Western, heteromasculinist desires to possess and consume the Other (Narayan, 1997; Parameswaran, 2006; Pratt, 1992).

In addition to their critique of the discursive construction of identities, another foundational alignment of queer and (post)colonial scholarship is their emphasis on resistance. David Jefferess (2008) identified four frames of resistance in postcolonial theorizing. The first is *cultural resistance*, in which "writing back" serves as a means of resisting colonial power. This strategy, popularized in the academy by anthropological and ethnographic scholars (Ashcroft et al., 1989; Tuhiwai Smith, 1999), can be seen in the work of the Subaltern Studies Group, a group of Western-trained South Asian scholars who sought to recover histories of "subaltern" populations geographically and politically denied power and voice under colonial rule (Guha, 1982). In this manner, transforming knowledges "from below" has become an important and ongoing tool of decolonial activism. Next, is *resistance-as-subversion*. Exemplified by the writings of Homi Bhabha (1994), this frame "evokes resistance from within the 'cracks' and 'in-between spaces' of colonial power" and "enables political struggle by discursively refusing colonial identities and binary thought processes" (Shahjahan, 2011, p. 276). Similarly, Gloria Anzaldúa's (1987) conceptualization of the borderlands (*la frontera*) as an in-between space neither "here" nor "there" employs this frame of subversive refusal, with further attention to the role of sexual/gender categorization in transnational processes. A third frame envisions *resistance-as-opposition*. This frame, influenced by neo-Marxism, focuses on collective organizing against the race, class, and gender relations produced by the colonial encounter. Its strategic utility and necessity are evidenced by its successful employment in decolonial political movements; however, one limitation is its reliance on the categorical identities created by the colonial encounter. A final frame is *resistance-as-transformation*, in which colonial structures and their political effects are resisted by both dismantling discursive logics and materially transforming relationships and structures.

Queer theoretical endeavors engage similar approaches to resistance. For example, cultural resistance through writing back/against power was practiced by queer knowledge producers within and outside of academia in the late 1980s and continues today, in an effort to recover historical erasures and foreground what Robert Hill (1996) calls "fugitive knowledge" (para. 5). Confronting the authority and legitimacy of cisheteronormative knowledge production and methodological norms, queer scholars and activists have highlighted experiential, relational, and embodied knowledges—an effort that has had methodological impacts across disciplines, influencing communication scholars' use of ethnographic, autoethnographic, and performance methods in particular. Queer theory engages in resistance-as-subversion by countering the "historical notion of straight as the marker of normal against which queer sex and gender differences are to be gauged and judged" (Grace & Hill, 2001, para. 2) and affirming an array of "subversive" genders and sexualities. The use of "queering" as a verb to describe the unsettling of normalizing processes and procedures further illustrates the centrality of subversive logics to queer forms of resistance. Resistance-as-opposition can be seen in the queer activist call to "bash back" (*Queer Nation*, 2016), whereas resistance-as-transformation appears in queer scholars' rejection of a "logic of toleration or simple political interest-representation in favor of a more thorough resistance to regimes of the normal" (Warner, 1993, p. xxvi).

Alexander (2008) summarizes the "contact points" between queer and (post)colonial theorizing as follows:

> To me, each is engaged in a project of excavation and rescue of the alienated and silenced other. Each is engaged in acts of subverting regimes of the normal and systematic deconstructions of colonial legacies, to create spaces for the variable performative identities of racialized and gendered minorities to practice voice. Each is involved in a rhetoric of critique and a rhetoric of possibility that liberates alternate ways of knowing, constructing, and engaging the world through the dense particularity of being. Each moves toward illuminating and dismantling systems of oppression by engaging critical analysis of those systems and their attending manifestations in social, cultural, and political practice. (p. 105)

Despite these alignments, however, normalizing deployments of queer and (post)colonial theory as separate rather than intertwined avenues of inquiry have limited their radical potential for critiquing intersections of regulatory systems of sex and gender with White supremacist, colonial, and imperial logics and systems. Identifying queer theory and activism as "tied to and rooted in a tradition of political struggle most often identified with people of color and other marginal groups," Cathy Cohen (1997, p. 447) argued, "if there is any truly radical potential to be found in the idea of queerness and the practice of queer politics, it would seem to be located in its ability to create a space in opposition to dominant norms, a space where transformational political work can begin" (p. 438). Queer of color theorizing attends to this transformational work, offering one means of bringing together queer and (post)colonial approaches to social transformation. This approach has influenced the field of communication, contributing to scholarship in critical/cultural studies, intercultural communication, rhetoric, media studies, and performance studies.

QUEER OF COLOR CRITIQUES AND DECOLONIZING QUEERNESS IN COMMUNICATION

Queer of color scholarship contributes to the important work of decolonizing queerness by interrogating intersecting systems of oppression that continue to maintain gendered and racialized structures of colonialism and empire. One significant line of queer of color critique problematizes queer theory's reproduction of White privilege and its elisions of connections between sexualities and other modes of difference. Numerous scholars have illustrated how mainstreaming queerness through a focus on (White) gay and lesbian inclusion within a single-issue rights-based political framework has led to the incorporation of "queer" as a "one-dimensional" political subject rather than as a mode of insurgent resistance (Ferguson, 2019, p. 3; see also Duggan, 2002; Eng, 2010). Because a significant amount of the queer scholarship "taught, cited and canonized… [is] decidedly directed toward analyzing white lesbian and gay men" (Muñoz, 1999, p. 10), queerness as a theoretical and political project has been falsely separated from the intersectional struggles of "anti-racism, anti-imperialism, transgender liberation, [and] anti-poverty" from which it initially emerged (Ferguson, 2019, p. 36). For this reason, queer of color critique is itself a project of recovering elided histories and knowledges, among these the contributions of BIPOC scholars to theorizing racialized sexuality. Queer of color scholars have extended Black and women of color feminisms, including works of Anzaldúa (1987), Audre Lorde (1984), Cherríe Moraga (2001), and Alice Walker (1983), to highlight how "racist practice articulates itself generally as gender and sexual regulation, and that gender and sexual differences variegate racial formations" (Ferguson, 2004, p. 3).

For example, in Leandra Hernández and Robert Gutierrez-Perez's (2019) edited volume *This Bridge We Call Communication: Anzaldúan Approaches to Theory, Method, and Praxis*, contributors explore forms of communication that bridge cultures, identities, and practices while also creating "stories of praxis" spanning the worlds of art, activism, and academia (p. xiv). (Re)covering Anzaldúa's influence across communication subdisciplines including rhetoric, performance studies, and intercultural communication, the volume builds bridges for communication scholars to engage in decolonial critiques that cross multiple languages, locations, methods, and disciplinary conversations. Describing Anzaldúa's impact on his positioning as a critical intercultural communication scholar, Gust Yep (2019) recalls,

> The field [of communication] was—and, in many ways, still is—dominated by (post) positivism and publicly embracing the identity of a critical communication scholar was simultaneously nourishing, satisfying, risky, and hazardous. I learned to embrace and

embody liminality, or in Anzaldúa's terms, "nepantla"—"the space in-between, the locus and sign of transition." I was "caught in remonilos (vortexes), each with different, often contradictory, forms of cognition, perspectives, worldviews, belief systems," such as (post)positivistic and critical theoretical assumptions... [and] methodologies.... I had gradually become a bridge. (p. 339)

In addition to the bridgework of engaging BIPOC feminist theorizations, queer of color critique also seeks to recover the experiences of queer and trans people of color that have largely been absent within dominant theorizing. For example, in an effort to foreground the experiences of LGBTQ people of color, E. Patrick Johnson (2001) advanced the project of *quare* studies (p. 3). Calling attention to the elisions of racially situated knowledges under the false umbrella of "queer," he argued that "quare," drawing from the African American vernacular for "queer," articulates racial and sexual identities to attend to queer identities and cultural performances "both as discursively mediated and as historically situated and materially conditioned" (p. 3). This theoretical lens, which has been utilized by communication scholars for intersectional analysis of various queer texts (e.g., Eguchi & Roberts, 2015; Eguchi et al., 2014; Hatfield, 2017; Rodriguez, 2018), was also extended through Wenshu Lee's (2003) formulation of *kuaer* theory as a "transnational womanist quare studies" lens for interrogating complex linkages between culturally specific quare worlds under conditions of globalization (p. 161). Attending to the elisions of transgender experiences, Yep (2013) further argued that "queering/quaring/kauering/crippin'/transing" offer a set of distinct but interrelated analytical tools to assist intercultural communication scholars in understanding "other bodies" by attending to the geopolitical contexts in which "cultural systems of body normativity" are situated (pp. 121, 120).

The emergence of queer intercultural communication illustrates communication scholars' investments in queer of color and decolonizing queer critiques. In a special issue of *The Journal of International and Intercultural Communication*, Karma Chávez (2013) called attention to intercultural communication scholars' failures to substantively engage with queerness, noting that "in this very journal, a search of all available issues reveals no mention of queer or transgender on its pages" (p. 84). On the other hand, Shinsuke Eguchi and Bernadette Calafell (2020) note that communication scholarship bringing together queer and intercultural inquiry had long existed but failed "to receive recognition as *intercultural* because of their 'queer' elements" (p. 3). In line with queer (post)colonial efforts to counter dominant knowledges, including the ways in which disciplinary narratives are crafted, Eguchi and Calafell identified Thomas Nakayama's (1994) interrogation of Hollywood's binary media portrayals of feminized Asian male characters contrasted with performances of heteromasculinist Whiteness as an early contributor to this area of study. Heeding Chávez's call for the intersections between queer and intercultural "to be more explicitly elucidated and elaborated" (p. 84), along with Eguchi and Calafell's articulation of queer intercultural communication as a theoretical and methodological intervention attentive to intersectionality, belonging, and differences, queer intercultural communication has gained recognition as a robust area of inquiry.

Queer of color, decolonizing queer, and queer intercultural critiques together offer important ways to address imperializing tendencies resulting from the geopolitical travels of queer theory and LGBTQ activism from the United States and other Anglo-European countries and universities to non-Western cultures within and outside these nation-states. One area of concern is the globalization of U.S.-based (White) gay culture through the expansion of Western cultural and political forms that have together falsely fashioned global LGBTQ "identities, performances, and politics...as ideological products of White, Western, and U.S. American modernity" (Eguchi & Calafell, 2020, p. 6). In recent years, simultaneous global expansions of homophobia and transphobia along with Western gay and lesbian identity-based politics have reinforced colonial and imperial "White savior" relationships. This gendered structure, in which White Westerners save Brown women from Brown men (Spivak, 1985)—or save Brown queers from oppressive nation-states—is evidenced in human rights rhetorics and dialogues around LGBTQ migration, persecution, and safety. As described by Brenna Munro and Gema Pérez-Sánchez (2017),

> The increasing vulnerabilities queer people face globally have a complex relationship to the highly visible emerging legal equality and social normativity of LGBT people in North America and Europe, not to mention the global circulation of myriad cultural products from the Global North depicting queer lives. (para. 3)

Rhetorical scholars studying queer and trans migrations have therefore importantly queried how Western human rights discourses produce particular (il)legibilites relating to non-normative gendered and sexual subjectivites while reinforcing U.S. and Anglo-European exceptionalism (Luibhéid & Chavez, 2020; McKinnon, 2017).

Further tying to Western discourses of exceptionalism, endeavors to decolonize queerness have led to an interrogation of contemporary processes of homonationalism that extend colonial figurations of sexuality and masculinity to construct "modern" subjects against their "pre-modern" others. Analyzing U.S. popular media in relation to the war on terror, Jasbir Puar (2007) examined how incorporation of some U.S. White middle-class LGBTQ subjects into the heteropatriarchal and paternal U.S. nation-state reinforced arguments for protecting the nation from the feminized, hypermasculinized, or otherwise perversely sexualized and racialized terrorist other. As Schotten (2018) noted, in this manner, LGBTQ advocacy can serve as

> the sharp end of the spear of empire and colonization [as] today's wars on terror, refugees, and Islam shroud themselves in the pious guise of gay rights to justify their otherwise unjustifiable violence against the "savage," "backward," and ostensibly homophobic people and places they seek to target. (p. 21).

Morgan Bassichus and Dean Spade (2014) further (re)connect the ways "progressive queer politics participate in white supremacy's tactics of pitting 'good gays' (white, middle class, gender normative, able bodied) against 'bad queers' (black, brown, power, and disabled, which necessarily mean gender non-normative)" back to structures of anti-Blackness within the United States (p. 194). As rhetorical scholar Jenna Hanchey (2021) writes, "The dehumanization of ontological anti-Blackness and African epistemological erasure must be met with re-humanizing practices that center African being, context, thought, and materiality" (p. 13). To this end, Afrocentricity (Asante, 1988), Afrofuturist feminism (Hall, 2021), and Africanfuturism (Hanchey, 2021) offer directions for communication scholars to "decolonize queer and trans intercultural futures" (p. 1) by attending to the constitutive role of anti-Blackness as it extends beyond, and within, the United States to intersect with other colonial imperial processes.

In summary, decolonizing queerness requires recognizing that White, Western models of what queerness looks like fail to encompass the lived realities of many LGBTQ individuals and communities of color within and outside of the United States. Another broad thematic for scholarship queering colonialism and empire is bringing deeper engagement with gender and sexual identities to bear on examinations of colonial and imperial processes. As Godfried Asante (2020) notes, reorienting queer of color criticism to engage with "the bodies of those who live and enact their sexual identity from the periphery of the colonial/imperial center" presents new directions and theoretical possibilities for communication scholars (p. 165).

QUEERING DECOLONIZATION: (POST)COLONIAL APPROACHES

(Post)colonial approaches emphasize the historical impacts of Western imperial nations (or the Global North) on nations in Africa, Asia, and the Americas (or the Global South) (Young, 2001). As Raka Shome and Radha Hegde (2002) summarize, (post)colonial scholarship "studies issues of race, class, gender, sexuality, and nationality, that are of concern to contemporary critical scholarship by situating these phenomena within geopolitical arrangements, and relations of nations and their inter/national histories" (p. 252). Unlike much critical scholarship, including forms of queer, feminist, and antiracist scholarship that have tended to limit the scope of their critique within national boundaries, (post)colonial approaches propel engagement with and beyond nation-states, which entails "geopoliticizing the nation and locating it in larger (and unequal) histories and geographies of global power and culture" (Shome & Hegde, 2002, p. 252). (Post)colonial scholarship also interrogates how these histories extend into the present through "neocolonial control of the global South through cultural, economic, educational, military, and political mechanisms" (Coloma, 2009, p. 271).

Contemporary queer (post)colonial approaches are precedented by, and draw from, the work of transnational feminisms, women of color, and Indigenous theoretical critiques identifying entanglements of ethnocentric, Western, capitalist, patriarchal, White supremacist, and heterosexist structures (Anzaldúa, 1987; Grewal & Kaplan, 1994; hooks, 1994; Kaplan et al., 1999; LaDuke, 1994; Lugonés, 2007; Mohanty, 2003), while also deepening engagements with sex, gender, sexuality, and cisheteronormativity. Research in this area spans disciplines and decades, featuring an array of topics, such as the study of gender and sexual identities and expressions in (post)colonial cultures, global LGBTQ activism and social movements, BIPOC re/formulations of queerness through art and performance, state-sanctioned violences against queer and transgender individuals, LGBTQ refugees and human rights rhetoric, queer citizenship, migrations and diasporic formations, and LGBTQ tourism and queer Orientalism. Across this broad scholarship, scholars interrogate relationships among race, sexuality, gendered normativities, national imaginaries and borders, global and transnational flows, and economies of desire.

Queer (post)colonial scholarship attends to the omission of racialization within Lauren Berlant and Michael Warner's (1998) otherwise cogent observation that "national heterosexuality is the mechanism by which a core national culture can be imagined" (p. 549). Expanding on Foucault's (1978) genealogy of the discursive production of the heterosexual/homosexual binary, queer (post)colonial scholars have interrogated the production of interlocking racial and cisheteropatriarchal binaries within larger spatiotemporal formations as biopolitical technologies for governing populations (e.g., Haritaworn et al., 2014; Stoler, 1995). Likewise, queer (post)colonial approaches have mobilized feminist theorizations of the centrality of gender and sexuality in racialized geopolitics with heightened attention to the structuring roles of cisheterosexism and homophobia in the colonial encounter.

To this end, (queer)postcolonial scholars across disciplines have examined culturally specific nonnormative genders and sexualities that preexisted colonial encounters (e.g., Donham, 2002; Gopinath, 2005; Murray & Roscoe, 1998; Subero, 2010; Swarr, 2004). Extending this work into the field of communication, G. Asante (2020) examines how, prior to colonization, gender-nonconforming people in West Africa "were affectionately incorporated into the social fabric of many tribal and ethnic groups" (p. 160). Asante illustrates that same-sex sexual encounters were not criminalized historically; instead, contemporary "policing of same-sex desires, relations, and intimacies" in West Africa reveals the influence of Anglo-European cisheteropatriarchy on postcolonial nation-states (p. 161). As colonization fundamentally reshaped views of kinship and desire through the imposition of heteropatriarchal institutions, "'cultural' conflicts between Western colonizing cultures and colonized indigenous cultures" often centered on regulating gender and sexuality (Narayan, 1997, p. 17), leading to the rendering of the bodies of women, same-sex desiring, and gender-nonconforming individuals as symbolic sites of contestation as well as material sites of violent conquest. Exemplifying the need for queering decolonization is the fact that the forms of heteropatriarchy institutionalized through colonial encounters have often been further sedimented by nationalist decolonization movements using "the same militarized masculinities as a foundation for liberation, thereby maintaining the nonstatus of women and upholding heterosexuality as the basis for citizenship" (Asante, 2020, p. 160).

In addition to examining historical and ongoing regulations of gender and sexuality within nation-states as products of colonial and imperial processes, queer (post)colonial scholarship highlights global and transnational flows of people, capital, and cultural products and the impacts of these flows on symbolic and material geographies of desire and consumption. For example, Eng-Beng Lim's (2013) transnational study of Asian performance practices addresses how homoerotic practices reproduce the Orientalist gaze through stereotypes of "brown boys" and "rice queens" to construct the dyadic trope of White man/feminized native boy. Lim demonstrates continuities in this racialized fetishization across different geographic locations, time periods, and shifting colonial forms (from imperial occupation to postcolonial nation-states to neoliberal globalization). Investigating ideological entanglements of sexuality, gender, race, and nation within border-crossing performances and media representations of queer desire, communication scholars have contributed to this area by unpacking the complexities of Black video vixens (Johnson, 2014), Latina drag queen performances (Moreman & McIntosh, 2010), international queer film festivals (Mokkil, 2018), and numerous other cultural productions (e.g., Abdi & Calafell, 2017; Alexander, 2008; Chambers-Letson, 2018; Hatfield, 2017; Nakayama, 1994; Pelle, 2010; Song, 2021).

Queer (post)colonial scholars have further theorized global mobilities in relation to "queer diasporas," a term that can refer to examining multiple axes of difference within and across ethnic–diasporic formations or to transnational networks connecting queer cultures across continents (Gopinath, 2005; Puar, 1998). Communication scholars have extended this scholarship by examining codifications, negotiations, and articulations of intercultural diasporic identities as well as queer uses of social media and digital technologies to interface disparate social groups, cultural contexts, and geographic locations (Abdi & Van Gilder, 2015; Atay, 2021; Durham, 2004; Mitra & Gajjala, 2008; Prasad, 2017; Spiers, 2016; Yue, 2011). Further interrogating the travel of both bodies and representations, queer (post)colonial scholars have unpacked queer tourism as a neocolonial practice in which privileged, frequently Western, White, cisgender gay and lesbian subjects travel to "exotic" locations to experience the otherness of their cultural and sexual forms (e.g., Puar, 2002). Highlighting connections between LGBTQ tourism and inequalities produced and sustained by global capitalism, queer (post)colonial scholars thus challenge the idea of global mobility as liberatory.

The racialized hierarchies that have produced uneven queer mobilities amid enduring colonial and imperial violences have also led to the attempted universalization of rhetorical constructs of "the closet" and "coming out" to describe non-Western LGBTQ experiences. Privileging Western definitions in this manner, however, leads to views of non-Western practices "as premodern and unliberated. Practices that do not conform with Western narratives of development of individual political subjects are dismissed as unliberated or coded as homophobic" (Manalansan, 1995, p. 489). In their examination of "coming out's" ill fit for describing queer subject in mainland China, communication scholars Shuzhen Huang and Daniel Brouwer (2018) argue that the notion of "coming with" offers a more accurate representation of how Chinese queer subjects negotiate sexuality: "Coming with does not require the queer subject to preserve queer sexuality by declaring it out loud, and coming out does not share a commitment to including the family in one's queer future" (p. 108). "Coming with" thus affirms gay and lesbian sexuality while still emphasizing the importance that Asian cultures place on collectivity. Qwo-Li Driskill (Cherokee) et al. (2011) also offer an alternative metaphor to "the closet," which they argue is inaccurate for describing Indigenous experiences. They note that because queer Indigenous people have been under surveillance since contact, and due to

> the marginal spaces allotted to queer Native peoples and the theft of Native lands through the continued occupation of our lands, the space we have to hide our sexual and political desires is the space of a cupboard, not a closet. (p. 212)

QUEERING DECOLONIZATION: INDIGENOUS APPROACHES

Indigenous scholars have been integral to queering the study of colonialism and empire, offering important contributions to the queer (post)colonial analytics already discussed. Nonetheless, they have also frequently been erased by (post)colonial scholars' tendencies to focus on representational practices resulting from past colonial processes rather than on the material continuance of colonies within settler nation-states. Colonialism in settler colonial nations differs in structure and temporality from postcolonial nation-states, leading to Indigenous criticisms of postcolonial approaches as having largely failed Indigenous people for whom the colonial is anything but "post" (Byrd & Rothberg, 2011; Cook-Lynn, 1997;

Weaver, 2000). In settler colonial nation-states, which include the United States, Canada, nations in Central and South America, South Africa, Australia, New Zealand, Israel, and the Caribbean and Pacific islands, "colonizers have come to stay, which requires the ongoing epistemic and ontological disappearing of Indigenous peoples" (Chevrette, 2016, p. 77). For settlers to claim the land as their own, "Indigenous peoples must be destroyed, removed, and made into ghosts," while narratives of manifest destiny and other rhetorical erasures simultaneously "indigenize" settlers as the original inhabitants of the land (Arvin et al., 2013, p. 12; see also Tuck & Yang, 2012). In the United States and other settler nations, then, queering the study of colonialism and empire points toward the necessity of engaging with the settler nation-state formation and its impacts.

In the field of communication, scholars have examined rhetorical processes that together erase Indigenous pasts and mobilize settler colonial presents. Areas of attention have included memory places (Black, 2009; Chevrette & Hess, 2015; Dickinson et al., 2005, 2006; McCue-Enser, 2020), representations in news media and culture (LaCroix, 2011; Merskin, 2001; Roosvall & Tegelberg, 2013), political speeches and deliberation processes (Black, 2008; Na'puti & Hahn, 2013), sports mascots (Billings & Black, 2018), and other discursive phenomena that uphold material violences (Endres, 2009; Na'puti, 2019a; Siegfried, 2020). Engaging in decolonial resistance by centering Indigenous experiences, scholars have also focused attention on Indigenous voices, protests, and other self-determination strategies (Davis, 2016; Endres, 2011; Halualani, 2002; Kelly & Black, 2018; Lake, 1983, 1991; McCue-Enser, 2020), as well as utilized Indigenous epistemologies and ontologies to critique theoretical and methodological assumptions in the field (de la Garza, 2008; Lechuga, 2020; Na'puti, 2019b, 2020). Amidst this scholarship, attention to gender, sexuality, and desire as categories of analysis for understanding racialized settler colonial processes has been scarce, however, with notable exceptions found in communication scholars' interrogations of the gendered figures of Kokopelli (Rogers, 2007) and Pocahontas (Ono & Buescher, 1999), along with recent examinations of Indigenous feminist organizing against gendered violence (Mack & Na'puti, 2019; Wieskamp & Smith, 2020).

Queering communication scholarship on settler colonial processes requires extending these foundations to further engage the critical role of gendered and sexual systems in enduring violences propelled by settler colonialism's elimination and replacement logics. Queer and feminist Indigenous scholars have demonstrated the centrality of settler states' historical regulation of gender identity, kinship, intimacies, sexual relations and desires, marriage, reproduction, and genealogy to the violent conquest of Indigenous lands (e.g., Arvin et al., 2013; Driskin et al., 2011). As heteropatriarchal colonialism "sexualized Indigenous lands and peoples as violable, subjugated Indigenous kin ties as perverse, [and] attacked familial ties and traditional gender roles" (Morgensen, 2012, p. 4), forced assimilation processes "rema[de] Indigenous peoples into settler state citizens" subject to the imposed settler colonial order (pp. 14–15). Directing attention to contemporary state-sanctioned violences as enduring attempts to erase Indigenous survivance, Ashley Mack and Tiara Na'puti (2019) discuss the failures of #MeToo to encompass the particularities of racialized gender violence enacted by individuals and nation-states against Indigenous peoples. Engaging the work of two activist groups—Missing and Murdered Indigenous Women and Violence on the Land, Violence on Our Bodies—as models for decolonial feminist organizing, Mack and Na'puti urge scholars to more actively examine settler states' continued enactments of violence against Indigenous women, nonbinary, and LGBTQ/Two-Spirit individuals.

The term "Two-Spirit" demonstrates convergences between queer approaches with decolonial thought, as it was coined by Indigenous LGBTQ activists to distinguish nonnormative gender and sexual identities, practices, and desires within Indigenous cultures from universalizing White and Western-centric conceptualizations of "gay," "lesbian," and "queer" and their global travels. Two-Spirit can include but is not limited to LGBTQ, nonbinary, and intersex persons, as well as individuals who perform "alternate" genders through their social, spiritual, or relational roles. Two-Spirit and queer critiques converge around the challenges they pose to cisheteronormativity, heteropatriarchy, and heterosexual privilege while also aligning with the impetus of queer of color critiques to center BIPOC experiences. At the same time, they challenge "White-dominated queer theory and queer of color critique's near erasure of Native people and nations" (Driskill, 2010, p. 71), instead emphasizing the importance of engaging with Indigenous theories and the lived experiences of Indigenous peoples. Given that settler societies were, and continue to be, perpetuated through binary colonial constructions of difference in tandem with colonial violences committed against Indigenous women and LGBTQ/Two-Spirit peoples, Two-Spirit critiques can assist in "unsettle[ing] the terms of sexuality entangled within the mythic structures of settler societies" (Cram, 2016, p. 2). Cram (2016) has emphasized the utility of such an endeavor for guiding queer scholars of rhetoric, public memory, and archives, noting that the decolonial perspectives foregrounded by Indigenous critiques "encourage queer critics to put pressure on the modes of inheriting the imaginative metanarratives we use to guide archival practice and craft queer memories" (p. 17).

As settler colonial and Indigenous scholarship continues to gain visibility in the field of communication, there is potential for forging new synergies among communication, queer, and (post)colonial studies to craft new queer potentialities and decolonial futures. Indigenous scholars encourage this project be taken up widely, rather than only as an identity project engaged in only by queer Indigenous and settler scholars. Maile Arvin (Native Hawaiian), Eve Tuck (Unangax̂), and Angie Morrill (Klamath) write "because the United States is balanced upon notions of white supremacy and heteropatriarchy, everyone living in the country is not only racialized and gendered, but also has a relationship to settler colonialism" (Arvin et al., 2013, p. 9). Moreover, as these relationships have extended beyond national borders into the universalization of White, Western binary systems of sex and gender, the naturalization of "racial distinctions of primitive from civilized gender/sexuality" extends not only to settlers and "to the Indigenous nations they occupy, but to the whole world" (Morgensen, 2012, p. 13).

A final caution: From Indigenous perspectives, queering colonialisms and empire cannot only be about the decolonization of queer theory in any abstract sense. Tuck (Unangax̂) and K. Wayne Yang (2012) argue that "when metaphor invades decolonization, it kills the very possibility of decolonization; it recenters whiteness, it resettles theory, it extends innocence to the settler, it entertains a settler future" (p. 3). Indigenous scholars propel settler scholars to extend their work to actively question their own and their universities' roles in Indigenous dispossession and to examine and alter curriculum and research while also problematizing the notion of inclusion as an end in itself (Arvin et al., 2013). In other words, queering decolonization through Indigenous approaches requires queering, or denaturalizing, the taken-for-grantedness of the settler colonial nation-state/project and its manifestations. Because they do not rely on the nation-state for their validation, queer/Two-Spirit Indigenous critiques may further assist in complicating "one-dimensional" liberal conceptualizations of LGBTQ political identities and create new forms of queer (post)colonial communication scholarship, activism, and advocacy.

CONCLUSION

Queering colonialism and empire necessitates unsettling normalizing theories and methodologies to examine new formations. This requires undoing the epistemic violences that erase queer of color theorizing by separating queer movements and subjectivities from BIPOC decolonial struggles. Much like gender and sexuality exceed categorical definitions, there is no one way to bring queerness together with (post)colonial theorizing. Instead, alignments of these areas include challenging binary identities and communicative constructions of dominance and marginality; questioning dominant knowledges, discourse, and norms; and generating new forms of intersectional, queer, decolonial resistance. In the communication discipline, scholarship queering the study of colonialism and empire has emerged from critical–cultural studies, queer intercultural communication, rhetoric, media, and performance studies, though it need not be confined to these areas. Despite different orientations and approaches, critical communication researchers are uniquely positioned to interrogate intersecting communicative constructions of gender, sexuality, race, nation, and empire that produce rhetorical and material borders generating categorical identities. Attending to the ways symbolic and material violences produce and uphold one another, communication and critical/cultural scholars have made important contributions to investigating the discursive terrains of colonialism and empire. To continue the task of decolonizing queerness and queering colonialism not only as a metaphor but also as a process and practice requires scholars "to question, critique, and hopefully dismantle the cultural production of (hetero)sexuality as a structural body of knowledge(s) that helps sustain the *ordinary* and *normal*" (Eguchi & Calafell, 2020, p. 4). This includes resisting and delinking from the colonial logics that demarcate gender and sexuality as well as the gendered logics that maintain settler colonial, neocolonial, and imperial structures.

FURTHER READING

Ahmed, S. (2006). *Queer phenomenology: Orientations, objects, others.* Duke University Press.

Alexander, M. J. (1997). Erotic autonomy as a politics of decolonization: An anatomy of feminist and state practice in the Bahamas tourist economy. In M. J. Alexander & C. T. Mohanty (Eds.), *Feminist genealogies, colonial legacies, democratic futures* (pp. 43–100). Routledge.

Anzaldúa, G. (1992). To(o) queer the writer: Loca, escrita y chicana. In B. Warland (Ed.), *Inversions: Writing by dykes, queers, and lesbians* (pp. 251–273). Press Gang.

Asante, G. (2019). #RhetoricSoWhite and US centered: Reflections on challenges and opportunities. *Quarterly Journal of Speech, 105*(4), 484–488. https://www.tandfonline.com/doi/full/10.1080/00335630.2019.1669892

Atay, A. (2021). Charting the future of queer studies in communication and critical/cultural studies: new directions and pathways. *Communication and Critical/Cultural Studies.* https://www.tandfonline.com/doi/full/10.1080/14791420.2021.1907847

Bakshi, S., Jivraj, S., & Posocco, S. (2016). *Decolonizing sexualities: Transnational perspectives, critical interventions.* Counterpress.

Barnard, I. (2004). *Queer race: Cultural interventions in the racial politics of queer theory.* Lang.

Binnie, J. (2004). *The globalization of sexuality.* SAGE.

Carillo Rowe, A. (2017). A queer Indigenous manifesto. *QED: A Journal in GLBTQ Worldmaking, 4*(2), 93–99.

Chávez, K. R. (2010). Border (in)securities: Normative and differential belonging in LGBTQ and immigrant rights discourse. *Communication and Critical/Cultural Studies, 7*(2), 136–155. https://www.tandfonline.com/doi/abs/10.1080/14791421003763291?journalCode=rccc20

Chávez, K. R. (2013). *Queer migration politics: Activist rhetoric and coalitional possibilities.* University of Illinois Press.

Cram, E. (2019). Queer geographies and the rhetoric of orientation. *Quarterly Journal of Speech, 105*(1), 98–115. https://www.tandfonline.com/doi/abs/10.1080/00335630.2019.1553587

Cruz-Malavé, A., & Manalansan, M. F., IV. (Eds.). (2002). *Queer globalizations: Citizenship and the afterlife of colonialism.* New York University Press.

Eguchi, S., & Asante, G. (2016). Disidentifications revisited: Queer(y)ing intercultural communication theory. *Communication Theory, 26*, 171–189.

Eguchi, S., & Calafell, B. M. (2020). *Queer intercultural communication: The intersectional politics of belonging in and across differences.* Rowman & Littlefield.

Gopinath, G. (2018). *Unruly visions: The aesthetic practices of queer diaspora.* Duke University Press.

Gutierrez-Perez, R. (2018). Monstrosity in everyday life: Nepantleras, theories in the flesh, and transformational politics. *Popular Culture Studies Journal, 6*(2–3), 345–368.

Hawley, J. C. (Ed.). (2001). *Postcolonial, queer: Theoretical intersections.* State University of New York Press.

Jackson, P. A., McLelland, M., & Yue, A. (Eds.). (2008). *AsiaPacifiQueer: Rethinking genders and sexualities* (pp. 1–27). University of Illinois Press.

Johnson, A. (2019). Exploring the dark matter(s) of Wakanda: A quest for radical queer inclusion beyond capitalism. *Journal of Futures Studies, 24*(2), 5–14. https://jfsdigital.org/articles-and-essays/vol-24-no-2-december-2019/redefining-the-colonial-an-afrofuturist-analysis-of-wakanda-and-speculative-fiction/

Kuntsman, A., & Miyake, E. (Eds.). (2008). *Out of place: Interrogating silences in queerness/raciality.* Raw Nerve Books.

Lewis, E. S., Borba, R., Fabrício, B. F., & de Souza, D. (2014). *Queering paradigms: South–North dialogues on queer epistemologies, embodiments and activism.* Lang.

Moraga, C., & Anzaldúa, G. (1983). *This bridge called my back: Writings by radical women of color.* Kitchen Table.

Morgensen, S. L. (2012). Queer settler colonialism in Canada and Israel: Articulating Two-Spirit and Palestinian queer critiques. *Settler Colonial Studies, 2*(2), 167–190. https://www.tandfonline.com/doi/abs/10.1080/2201473X.2012.10648848

McClintock, A. (1995). *Imperial leather: Race, gender and sexuality in the colonial contest.* Routledge.

Pérez, H. (2015). *A taste for brown bodies: Gay modernity and cosmopolitan desire.* New York University Press.

Upadhyay, N. (2019). "Can you get more American than Native American?" Drag and settler colonialism in RuPaul's Drag Race. *Cultural Studies, 33*(3), 480–501. https://www.tandfonline.com/doi/abs/10.1080/09502386.2019.1584907

REFERENCES

Abdi, S., & Calafell, B. (2017). Queer utopias and a (feminist) Iranian vampire: A critical analysis of resistive monstrosity in *A Girl Walks Home Alone at Night*. *Critical Studies in Media Communication, 34*(4), 358–370. https://www.tandfonline.com/doi/abs/10.1080/15295036.2017.1302092

Abdi, S., & Van Gilder, B. (2015). Cultural invisibility and identity dissonance: Queer Iranian-American women and their negotiation of existence. *Journal of International and Intercultural Communication, 9*(1), 69–86. https://www.tandfonline.com/doi/abs/10.1080/17513057.2016.1120850?journalCode=rjii20

Aiello, G., Bakshi, S., Bilge, S., Kahaleole Hall, L., Johnston, L., Pérez, K., & Chávez, K. (2013). Here, and not yet here: A dialogue at the intersection of queer, trans, and culture. *Journal of International and Intercultural Communication, 6*(2), 96–117. https://www.tandfonline.com/doi/abs/10.1080/17513057.2013.778155

Alexander, B. K. (2008). Queer(y)ing the postcolonial through the West(ern). In N. K. Denzin, Y. S. Lincoln, & L. T. Smith (Eds.), *Handbook of critical and Indigenous methodologies* (pp. 101–133). SAGE.

Alexander, B. K., & Warren, J. T. (2002). The materiality of bodies: Critical reflections on pedagogy, politics, and positionality. *Communication Quarterly, 50*(3–4), 328–343.

Anzaldúa, G. (1987). *Borderlands/la frontera: The new mestiza.* Aunt Lute Books.

Arvin, M., Tuck, E., & Morrill, A. (2013). Decolonizing feminism: Challenging connections between settler colonialism and heteropatriarchy. *Feminist Formations, 25*(1): 8–34. https://muse.jhu.edu/article/504601

Asante, G. (2020). "Queerly ambivalent": Navigating global and local normativities in postcolonial Ghana. In S. Eguchi & B. M. Calafell (Eds.), *Queer intercultural communication: The intersectional politics of belonging in and across differences* (pp. 157–176). Rowman & Littlefield.

Asante, G., & Hanchey, J. N. (2021). Decolonizing queer modernities: The case for queer (post)colonial studies in critical/cultural communication. *Communication and Critical/Cultural Studies, 18*(2), 212–220. https://www.tandfonline.com/doi/abs/10.1080/14791420.2021.1907849?journalCode=rccc20

Asante, M. K. (1988). *Afrocentricity.* Africa World Press.

Ashcroft, B., Griffiths, G., & Tiffin, H. (1989). *The empire writes back: Theory and practice in post-colonial literatures.* Routledge.

Atay, A. (2021). Transnational and decolonizing queer digital/quick media and cyberculture studies. *Communication and Critical/Cultural Studies, 18*(2), 183–189. https://www.tandfonline.com/doi/abs/10.1080/14791420.2021.1913284

Bassichus, M., & Spade, D. (2014). Queer politics and anti-Blackness. In J. Haritaworn, A. Kuntsman, & S. Posocco (Eds.), *Queer necropolitics* (pp. 199–210). Routledge.

Berlant, L., & Warner, M. (1998). Sex in public. *Critical Inquiry, 24,* 547–566.

Bhabha, H. K. (1994). *The location of culture.* Routledge.

Billings, A. C., & Black, J. E. (2018). *Mascot nation: The controversy over Native American representations in sports.* University of Illinois Press.

Black, J. E. (2008). Plenary rhetoric in Indian country: The *Lone Wolf v. Hitchcock* case and the codification of a weakened Native character. *Advances in the History of Rhetoric, 11–12*(1), 59–80. https://www.tandfonline.com/doi/abs/10.1080/15362426.2009.10597380

Black, J. E. (2009). Memories of the Alabama Creek War, 1813–1814: U.S. governmental and Native identities at the Horseshoe Bend National Military Park. *American Indian Quarterly, 33*(2), 200–229. http://www.jstor.com/stable/25487928

Byrd, J. A., & Rothberg, M. (2011). Between subalternity and Indigeneity: Critical categories for postcolonial studies. *International Journal of Postcolonial Studies, 13*(1), 1–12.

Chambers-Letson, J. (2018). *After the party: A manifesto for queer of color life.* New York University Press.

Chávez, K. (2013). Pushing boundaries: Queer intercultural communication. *Journal of International and Intercultural Communication, 6*(2), 83–95. https://www.tandfonline.com/doi/abs/10.1080/17513057.2013.777506

Chevrette, R. (2016). *Assembling global (non)belongings: Settler colonial memoryscapes and the rhetorical frontiers of Whiteness in the US Southwest, Christians United for Israel, and FEMEN* [Doctoral dissertation, Arizona State University].

Chevrette, R., & Hess, A. (2015). Unearthing the Native past: Citizen archaeology and modern (non)belonging at the Pueblo Grande Museum. *Communication and Critical/Cultural Studies, 12*(2), 1–20. https://www.tandfonline.com/doi/abs/10.1080/14791420.2015.1012214

Cohen, C. (1997). Punks, bulldaggers, and welfare queens: The radical potential of queer politics? *GLQ: A Journal of Gay and Lesbian Studies, 3,* 437–465.

Coloma, R. S. (2009). Postcolonial challenges in education. *Counterpoints, 369,* 268–286.

Cook-Lynn, E. (1997). Who stole Native American studies? *Wicazo Sa Review, 12*(1), 9–28.

Costanza-Chock, S., Schweidler, C., & the Transformative Media Organizing Project. (2017). Toward transformative media organizing: LGBTQ and Two-Spirit media work in the United States. *Media, Culture, & Society, 39*(2), 159–184. https://journals.sagepub.com/doi/10.1177/0163443716674360

Cram, E. (2016). Archival ambience and sensory memory: Generating queer intimacies in the settler colonial archive. *Communication and Critical/Cultural Studies, 13*(2), 109–129.

Davis, P. (2016). Commemorative places, political spaces: Virginia Indians, the Jamestown Quadricentennial, and the quest for sovereignty. *Journal of International and Intercultural Communication, 9*(3), 222–239.

de la Garza, S. A. (2008). The four seasons of ethnography: A creation-centered ontology for ethnography. In M. K. Asante & Y. Miike (Eds.), *The global intercultural communication reader* (pp. 143–164). Routledge.

Dickinson, G., Ott, B. L., & Aoki, E. (2005). Memory and myth at the Buffalo Bill Museum. *Western Journal of Communication, 69*(2), 85–108. https://www.tandfonline.com/doi/abs/10.1080/10570310500076684

Dickinson, G., Ott, B. L., & Aoki, E. (2006). Spaces of remembering and forgetting: The reverent eye/I at the Plains Indian Museum. *Communication and Critical/Cultural Studies, 3*(1), 27–47. https://www.tandfonline.com/doi/abs/10.1080/14791420500505619

Donham, D. L. (2002). Freeing South Africa: The "modernization" of male–male sexuality in Soweto. In J. X. Inda & R. Rosaldo (Eds.), *The anthropology of globalization: A reader* (pp. 410–427). Blackwell.

Driskill, Q.-L. (2010). Doubleweaving Two-Spirit critiques: Building alliances between Native and queer studies. *GLQ: A Journal of Gay and Lesbian Studies, 16*(1–2), 69–92. https://read.dukeupress.edu/glq/article-abstract/16/1-2/69/34688/DOUBLEWEAVING-TWO-SPIRIT-CRITIQUESBuilding

Driskill, Q.-L., Finley, C., Gilley, B. J., & Morgensen, S. L. (2011). *Queer Indigenous studies: Critical interventions in theory, politics, and literature* (pp. 211–221). University of Arizona Press.

Duggan, L. (2002). The new homonormativity: The sexual politics of neoliberalism. In R. Castronovo & D. D. Nelson (Eds.), *Materializing democracy: Toward a revitalized cultural politics* (pp. 175–194). Duke University Press.

Durham, M. G. (2004). Constructing the "new ethnicities": Media, sexuality, and diasporic identity in the lives of South Asian immigrant girls. *Critical Studies in Media Communication, 21*(2), 140–161. https://www.tandfonline.com/doi/abs/10.1080/07393180410001688047

Eguchi, S., & Calafell, B. M. (2020). Introduction: Reorienting queer intercultural communication. In S. Eguchi & B. M. Calafell (Eds.), *Queer intercultural communication: The intersectional politics of belonging in and across differences* (pp. 1–16). Rowman & Littlefield.

Eguchi, S., Calafell, B. M., & Files-Thompson, N. (2014). Intersectionality and quare theory: Fantasizing African-American male same-sex relationships in *Noah's Arc: Jumping the broom. Communication, Culture, & Critique, 7,* 371–389.

Eguchi, S., & Roberts, M. (2015). Gay rapping and possibilities: A quare reading of "Throw That Boy P***y." *Text and Performance Quarterly, 35*(2–3), 142–157.

Endres, D. (2009). The rhetoric of nuclear colonialism: Rhetorical exclusion of American Indian arguments in the Yucca Mountain nuclear waste siting decision. *Communication and Critical/Cultural Studies, 6*(1), 39–60.

Endres, D. (2011). American Indian activism and audience: Rhetorical analysis of Leonard Peltier's response to denial of clemency. *Communication Reports, 24*(1), 1–11. https://www.tandfonline.com/doi/abs/10.1080/08934215.2011.554624

Eng, D. (2010). *The feeling of kinship: Queer liberalism and the racialization of intimacy*. Duke University Press.
Fanon, F. (2008). *Black skin, white masks*.(R. Philcox, Trans.). Grove Press. (Original work published 1952).
Ferguson, R. A. (2004). *Aberrations in black: Toward a queer of color critique*. University of Minnesota Press.
Ferguson, R. A. (2019). *One-dimensional queer*. Polity Press.
Foucault, M. (1971). *The order of things: An archaeology of the human sciences*. Random House.
Foucault, M. (1978). *The history of sexuality: Volume 1. An introduction* (R. Hurley, Trans.). Random House.
Gopinath, G. (2005). *Impossible desires: Queer diasporas and South Asian public cultures*. Duke University Press.
Grace, A. P., & Hill, R. J. (2001). *Using queer knowledges to build inclusionary pedagogy in adult education* [Paper presentation]. Adult Education Research Conference, East Lansing, MI. https://newprairiepress.org/aerc/2001/papers/26
Greensmith, C., & Giwa, S. (2013). Challenging settler colonialism in contemporary queer politics: Settler homonationalism, Pride Toronto, and Two-Spirit subjectivities. *American Indian Culture & Research Journal*, 37(2), 129–148. https://meridian.allenpress.com/aicrj/article-abstract/37/2/129/210862/Challenging-Settler-Colonialism-in-Contemporary?redirectedFrom=fulltext
Grewal, I., & Kaplan, C. (Eds.). (1994). *Scattered hegemonies: Postmodernity and transnational feminist practices*. University of Minnesota Press.
Guha, R. (Ed.). (1982). *Subaltern studies I: Writings on South Asian history and society*. Oxford University Press.
Gutierrez-Perez, R. (2018). Theories in the flesh and flights of the imagination: Embracing the soul and spirit of critical performative writing in communication research. *Women's Studies in Communication*, 41(4), 404–415.
Hall, A. R. (2021). Towards love as life praxis: A Black queer and feminist pedagogical orientation. *Communication Teacher*, 35(3), 262–275. https://www.tandfonline.com/doi/full/10.1080/17404622.2021.1930666
Halualani, R. T. (2002). *In the name of Hawaiians*. University of Minnesota Press.
Hanchey, J. N. (2021). "The self is embodied": Reading queer and trans Africanfuturism in *The Wormwood Trilogy*. *Journal of International and Intercultural Communication*. https://www.tandfonline.com/doi/abs/10.1080/17513057.2021.1931707
Hardt, M., & Negri, A. (2000). *Empire*. Harvard University Press.
Haritaworn, J., Kuntsman, A., & Posocco, S. (2014). *Queer necropolitics*. Routledge.
Hatfield, J. E. (2017). Dancing southern diaspora: Alvin Ailey's blood and the backwardness of quare disidentification. *Text and Performance Quarterly*, 37(1), 51–67.
Hernández, L. H., & Gutierrez-Perez, R. (Eds.). (2019). *This bridge we call communication: Anzaldúan approaches to theory, method, and praxis*. Lexington Books.
Hill, R. J. (1996). Learning to transgress: A social–historical conspectus of the American gay lifeworld as a site of struggle and resistance. *Studies in the Education of Adults*, 28(2), 253–279.
hooks, b. (1994). *Outlaw culture*. Routledge.
Huang, S. (2021). Why does communication need transnational queer studies? *Communication and Critical/Cultural Studies*, 18(2), 204–211. https://www.tandfonline.com/doi/abs/10.1080/14791420.2021.1907850
Huang, S., & Brouwer, D. C. (2018). Coming out, coming home, coming with: Models of queer sexuality in contemporary China. *Journal of International and Intercultural Communication*, 11(2), 97–116.
Jefferess, D. (2008). *Postcolonial resistance: Culture, liberation and transformation*. University of Toronto Press.
Johnson, A. (2014). Confessions of a video vixen: My autocritography of sexuality, desire, and memory. *Text and Performance Quarterly*, 34(2), 182–200. https://www.tandfonline.com/doi/abs/10.1080/10462937.2013.879991

Johnson, E. P. (2001). "Quare" studies, or (almost) everything I know about queer studies I learned from my grandmother. *Text and Performance Quarterly, 21*(1), 1–25.

Kaplan, C., Alarcón, N., & Moallem, M. (Eds.). (1999). *Between woman & nation: Nationalisms, transnational feminisms, and the state*. Duke University Press.

Kelly, C. R., & Black, J. E. (Eds.). (2018). *Decolonizing Native American rhetoric: Communicating self-determination*. Lang.

Lacroix, C. C. (2011). High stakes stereotypes: The emergence of the "casino Indian" trope in television depictions of contemporary Native Americans. *Howard Journal of Communications, 22*(1), 1–23.

LaDuke, W. (1994). An Indigenous perspective on feminism, militarism, and the environment. *Peace Now, 4*(4), 7.

Lake, R. A. (1983). Enacting red power: The consummatory function in Native American protest rhetoric. *Quarterly Journal of Speech, 69*(2), 127–142. https://www.tandfonline.com/doi/abs/10.1080/00335638309383642

Lake, R. A. (1991). Between myth and history: Enacting time in Native American protest rhetoric. *Quarterly Journal of Speech, 77*(2), 123–151. https://www.tandfonline.com/doi/abs/10.1080/00335639109383949

Lechuga, M. (2020). An anticolonial future: Reassembling the way we do rhetoric. *Communication and Critical/Cultural Studies, 17*(4), 378–385.

Lee, W. (2003). Kuaering queer theory: My autocritography and a race-conscious, womanist, transnational turn. *Journal of Homosexuality, 45*(2–4), 147–170. https://www.tandfonline.com/doi/abs/10.1300/J082v45n02_07

LeMaster, B., & Johnson, A. L. (2019). Unlearning gender—Toward a critical communication trans pedagogy. *Communication Teacher, 33*(3), 189–198. https://www.tandfonline.com/doi/full/10.1080/17404622.2018.1467566

Lim, E.-B. (2013). *Brown boys and rice queens: Spellbinding performance in the Asias*. New York University Press.

Lorde, A. (1984). *Sister outsider: Essays and speeches*. Ten Speed Press.

Lugonés, M. (2007). Heterosexualism in the colonial/modern gender system. *Hypatia, 22*(1), 186–209.

Luibhéid, E., & Chávez, K. R. (Eds.). (2020). *Queer and trans migrations: Dynamics of illegalization, detention, and deportation*. University of Illinois Press.

Mack, A. N., & Na'puti, T. R. (2019). "Our bodies are not terra nullius": Building a decolonial feminist resistance to gendered violence. *Women's Studies in Communication, 42*(3), 347–370. https://doi.org/10.1080/07491409.2019.1637803

Manalansan, M. F., IV. (1995). In the shadows of Stonewall: Examining gay transnational politics and the diasporic dilemma. *GLQ: A Journal of Lesbian and Gay Studies, 2*(4), 425–438.

McCue-Enser, M. (2020). Genocide in the sculpture garden and talking back to settler colonialism. *Quarterly Journal of Speech, 106*(2), 179–204.

McKinnon, S. (2017). *Gendered asylum: Race and violence in U.S. law and politics*. University of Illinois Press.

Merskin, D. (2001). Winnebagos, Cherokees, Apaches, and Dakotas: The persistence of stereotyping of American Indians in American advertising brands. *Howard Journal of Communication, 12*(3), 159–169. https://www.tandfonline.com/doi/abs/10.1080/106461701753210439

Mitra, R., & Gajjala, R. (2008). Queer blogging in Indian digital diasporas. *Journal of Communication Inquiry, 32*(4), 400–423. https://journals.sagepub.com/doi/10.1177/0196859908321003

Mohanty, C. T. (2003). *Feminism without borders: Decolonizing theory, practicing solidarity*. Duke University Press.

Mokkil, N. (2018). Queer encounters: Film festivals and the sensual circuits of European cinema in India. *Studies in European Cinema, 15*(1), 85–100.

Moraga, C. (2001). La güera. *Debate Feminista, 24*, 119–128.

Moreman, S., & McIntosh, D. M. (2010). Brown scriptings and rescriptings: A critical performance ethnography of Latina drag queens. *Communication and Critical/Cultural Studies*, 7(2), 115–135. https://www.tandfonline.com/doi/abs/10.1080/14791421003767912

Morgensen, S. L. (2012). Theorising gender, sexuality and settler colonialism: An introduction. *Settler Colonial Studies*, 2(2), 2–22. https://www.tandfonline.com/doi/abs/10.1080/2201473X.2012.10648839

Muñoz, J. E. (1999). *Disidentification: Queers of color and the performance of politics*. University of Minnesota Press.

Munro, B., & Pérez-Sánchez, G. (2017). Introduction: Thinking queer activism transnationally. *The Scholar & Feminist Online*, 14(2). http://sfonline.barnard.edu/thinking-queer-activism-transnationally/introduction-thinking-queer-activism-transnationally/

Murray, S. O., & Roscoe, W. (Eds.). (1998). *Boy-wives and female husbands: Studies in African homosexualities*. Palgrave Macmillan.

Nakayama, T. K. (1994). Show/down time: "Race," gender, sexuality, and popular culture. *Critical Studies in Mass Communication*, 11(2), 162–179. https://www.tandfonline.com/doi/abs/10.1080/15295039409366893

Na'puti, T. R. (2019a). Archipelagic rhetoric: Remapping the Marianas and challenging militarization from "a stirring place." *Communication and Critical/Cultural Studies*, 16(1), 4–25.

Na'puti, T. R. (2019b). Speaking of indigeneity: Navigating genealogies against erasure and #RhetoricSoWhite. *Quarterly Journal of Speech*, 105(4), 495–501. https://www.tandfonline.com/doi/full/10.1080/00335630.2019.1669895

Na'puti, T. R. (2020). Oceanic possibilities for Communication Studies. *Communication and Critical/Cultural Studies*, 17(1), 95–103. https://www.tandfonline.com/doi/abs/10.1080/14791420.2020.1723802

Na'puti, T. R., & Hahn, A. H. (2013). Plebiscite deliberations: Self-determination and deliberative democracy in Guam. *Journal of Public Deliberation*, 9(2), Article 11. https://www.publicdeliberation.net/jpd/vol9/iss2/art11

Narayan, N. (1997). *Dislocating cultures: Identities, traditions, and Third World feminism*. Routledge.

Ono, K. A., & Buescher, D. T. (1999). Deciphering Pocahontas: Unpacking the commodification of a Native American woman. *Critical Studies in Media Communication*, 18(1), 23–43. https://www.tandfonline.com/doi/abs/10.1080/15295030109367122

Parameswaran, R. (2006). Local culture in global media: Excavating colonial and material discourses in *National Geographic*. *Communication Theory*, 12(3), 287–315. https://onlinelibrary.wiley.com/doi/abs/10.1111/j.1468-2885.2002.tb00271.x

Pelle, S. (2010). The "grotesque" pussy: "Transformational shame" in Margaret Cho's stand-up performances. *Text and Performance Quarterly*, 30(1), 21–37. https://www.tandfonline.com/doi/abs/10.1080/10462930903366977

Prasad, P. (2017). Outsider orbits: Disavowal and dissent in the United States. *QED: A Journal in GLBTQ Worldmaking*, 4(2), 100–107.

Pratt, M. L. (1992). *Imperial eyes: Travel writing and transculturation*. Routledge.

Puar, J. K. (1998). Transnational sexualities: South Asian (trans)nation(alism)s and queer diasporas. In D. Eng & A. Hom (Eds.), *Q & A: Queer in Asian America* (pp. 405–422). Temple University Press.

Puar, J. K. (2002). Circuits of queer mobility: Tourism, travel, and globalization. *GLQ: A Journal of Lesbian and Gay Studies*, 8(1–2), 101–137. https://muse.jhu.edu/article/12203

Puar, J. K. (2007). *Terrorist assemblages: Homonationalism in queer times*. Duke University Press.

Queer Nation. (2016). Queer Nation NY: Our history. https://queernationny.org/history

Rodriguez, N. S. (2018). Hip-hop's authentic masculinity: A quare reading of Fox's *Empire*. *Television & New Media*, 19(3), 225–240. https://journals.sagepub.com/doi/abs/10.1177/1527476417704704

Rogers, R. A. (2007). Deciphering Kokopelli: Masculinity in commodified appropriations of Native American imagery. *Communication and Critical/Cultural Studies*, 4(3), 233–255.

Roosvall, A., & Tegelberg, M. (2013). Framing climate change and Indigenous peoples: Intermediaries of urgency, spirituality and de-nationalization. *International Communication Gazette, 75*(4), 392–409. https://journals.sagepub.com/doi/10.1177/1748048513482265

Said, E. (1978). *Orientalism*. Vintage Books.

Schotten, C. H. (2018). To exist is to resist: Palestine and the question of queer theory. *Journal of Palestine Studies, 47*(3), 13–28. https://www.tandfonline.com/doi/abs/10.1525/jps.2018.47.3.13

Sedgwick, E. (1990). *Epistemology of the closet*. University of California Press.

Shahjahan, R. (2011). Engaging the faces of "resistance" and social change from decolonizing perspectives: Toward transforming neoliberal higher education. *Journal of Curriculum Theorizing, 27*(3), 273–286.

Shome, R., & Hegde, R. S. (2002). Postcolonial approaches to communication: Charting the terrain, engaging the intersection. *Communication Theory, 12*(3), 249–270.

Siegfried, K. (2020). Making settler colonialism concrete: Agentive materialism and habitational violence in Palestine. *Communication and Critical/Cultural Studies, 17*(3), 267–284. https://www.tandfonline.com/doi/abs/10.1080/14791420.2020.1787475

Smith, A. (2011). Queer theory and Native studies: The heteronormativity of settler colonialism. In Q.-L. Driskill, C. Finley, B. J. Gilley, & S. L. Morgensen (Eds.), *Queer Indigenous studies: Critical interventions in theory, politics, and literature* (pp. 43–65). University of Arizona Press.

Song, L. (2021). Entertainingly queer: Illiberal homonormativity and transcultural queer politics in a Chinese Broadway musical. *Feminist Media Studies, 21*(1), 1834. https://www.tandfonline.com/doi/abs/10.1080/14680777.2019.1690019

Spiers, E. (2016). Performing the "quing of Berlin": Transnational digital interfaces in queer feminist protest culture. *Feminist Media Studies, 16*(1), 128–149.

Spivak, G. (1985). Can the subaltern speak? Speculations on widow sacrifice. *Wedge, 7–8*, 120–130.

Stoler, A. L. (1995). *Race and the education of desire: Foucault's history of sexuality and the colonial order of things*. Duke University Press.

Subero, G. (2010). Gay male pornography and the re/de/construction of postcolonial queer identity in Mexico. *New Cinemas, 8*(2), 119–136.

Swarr, A. L. (2004). Moffies, artists, and queens: Race and the production of South African gay male drag. *Journal of Homosexuality, 46*(3–4), 73–89.

Tuck, E., & Yang, K. W. (2012). Decolonization is not a metaphor. *Decolonization, 1*(1), 2012, 1–40.

Tuhiwai Smith, L. (1999). *Decolonizing methodologies: Research and Indigenous peoples*. Zed Books.

Walker, A. (1983). *In search of our mothers' gardens*. Harcourt.

Warner, M. (1993). *Fear of a queer planet: Queer politics and social theory*. University of Minnesota Press.

Weaver, J. (2000). Indigenousness and Indigeneity. In H. Schwarz & S. Ray (Eds.), *A companion to postcolonial studies* (pp. 221–235). Blackwell.

Wieskamp, V. N., & Smith, C. (2020). "What to do when you're raped": Indigenous women critiquing and coping through a rhetoric of survivance. *Quarterly Journal of Speech, 106*(1), 72–94. https://www.tandfonline.com/doi/abs/10.1080/00335630.2019.1706189

Yep, G. A. (2013). Queering/quaring/kuaering/crippin'/transing "other bodies" in intercultural communication. *Journal of International and Intercultural Communication, 6*(2), 118–126. https://www.tandfonline.com/doi/abs/10.1080/17513057.2013.777087

Yep, G. A. (2019). Becoming a bridge in/through critical communication scholarship: Meditations on the affective afterlife of cultural normativities. In L. H. Hernández & R. Gutierrez-Perez (Eds.), *This bridge we call communication: Anzaldúan approaches to theory, method, and praxis* (pp. 335–356). Lexington Books.

Young, R. J. C. (2001). *Postcolonialism: An historical introduction*. Blackwell.

Yue, A. (2011). Critical regionalities in inter-Asia and the queer diaspora. *Feminist Media Studies, 11*(1), 131–138.

NOTES

1. An alternative history is offered by queer of color scholar Ferguson (2019), who renarrates multidimensional queer politics as having been instrumental to U.S. gay liberation beginning with Stonewall.
2. "Colonialism" is used here to mean "the state control and conquest of peoples, lands, and resources" through territorial expansion resulting from imperial as well as settler colonial processes (Greensmith & Giwa, 2013, p. 132). "Empire" and "imperialism," often utilized by (post)colonial scholars of history to reference past political systems, are also used throughout this article in reference to transnational forms of governance and oppression theorized by Hardt and Negri (2000) as "new" processes of empire. Contemporary colonial and imperial processes include a variety of separate and interlocking forms, such as settler colonialism, neocolonialism, ecocolonialism, internal colonization, global military expansion, biopolitical and necropolitical state processes, and other forms of gendered and racialized exploitation of people, land, and labor in transnational systems of neoliberal capitalism.
3. The term "(post)colonial" is utilized throughout both as a means of encompassing the varied and enduring nature of colonial formations and in reference to the call by Asante and Hanchey (2021) for critical/cultural communication scholars to engage in "queer (post)colonial studies" (p. 213). Because "postcolonial" also often references theorizations developed by South Asian scholars almost exclusively, this usage is intended to be broad enough to incorporate decolonial theorizing originating from the Americas and other locations.

Roberta Chevrette

Directory of Contributors

Fatima Zahrae Chrifi Alaoui
San Francisco State University
    Transnational and Queer Diasporic Sexualities

Cimmiaron Alvarez
Rutgers University
    Queer People's Communication with Families of Origin

Luis M. Andrade
Santa Monica College
    Jotería Studies and/in Communication

Godfried Asante
San Diego State University
    Queer African Studies

Ahmet Atay
The College of Wooster
    Transnational Queer Translations

Jeffrey Bennett
Vanderbilt University
    Crip Theory

Joseph Brennan
Independent Scholar
    Gay Pornography

Niall Brennan
Fairfield University
    Representations of Drag Culture

Cameron Lynn Brown
University of Iowa
    Black Gay Men in Television Comedy

Randal D. Brown
Widener University
    Sexual Communication Between Queer Partners

Maria Butauski
Columbia College
  Parenting of Queer Offspring

Cora Butcher-Spellman
Pennsylvania State University
  Queer Melodrama

Bernadette Marie Calafell
Gonzaga University
  Queer Intercultural Communication: Sexuality and Intercultural Communication

Paris S. Cameron-Gardos
Independent Researcher based in the Netherlands
  Coming-Out Narratives in Audiovisual Culture

Robert Carroll
University of Texas at Austin
  Minority Stress and Relationships

Roberta Chevrette
Middle Tennessee State University
  Queering Colonialisms and Empire

Daniel Coleman
Georgia State University
  Transfeminisms

KC Councilor
Southern Connecticut State University
  Queer Comics

Yossi David
Ben-Gurion University of the Negev
  Queer Safe Spaces and Communication

Ben De Smet
Ghent University
  Queer Music Practices in the Digital Realm

Alexander Dhoest
University of Antwerp
  Homonationalism and Media

Morgan DiCesare
University of Iowa
  Queer/ing Archives

Héctor Domínguez Ruvalcaba
University of Texas at Austin
  Queer Sexualities in Latin America

Thomas R. Dunn
Colorado State University
  Queer Memory; Queer Worldmaking

Elizabeth K. Eger
Texas State University
  LGBTQ+ Workers

Shinsuke Eguchi
University of New Mexico
  Cultural Productions of Queer Asia

Brandon William Epstein
Bar-Ilan University
  Queer Safe Spaces and Communication

Victor Evans
Seattle University
  African American Queer Cinema

Keren Eyal
Reichman University
  Media Depictions of Sexual Attitudes

Carly Leilani Fabian
University of Georgia
  Sex Work, Queer Economic Justice, and Communicative Ethics

Sandra L. Faulkner
Bowling Green State University
  Arts-based Queer Communication Studies

Natalie Fixmer-Oraiz
University of Iowa
  Queer(ing) Reproductive Justice

Santiago Fouz Hernández
Durham University
  Spanish Queer Cinema

L. Brooke Friley
Texas A&M University at Corpus Christi
Sexual Orientation and Gender Identity Disclosure in the Medical Context

Michaela Frischherz
Towson University
Sexual Pleasure in Queer Communication Studies

Dustin Goltz
DePaul University
Gay Aging and Discourses of Future; Queer Temporalities

Stephen M. Haas
University of Cincinnati
Same-Sex Couple Relationship Maintenance

Jamie Hakim
King's College London
Queer Men's Bodies and Digital Media

Gilly Hartal
Bar-Ilan University
Queer Safe Spaces and Communication

Madeleine Redlick Holland
University of Texas at Austin
Divorce and Relational Termination; Sexual Satisfaction in LGB Relationships

Anamarija Horvat
Northumbria University at Newcastle
Queer Memory and Film

Shuzhen Huang
Commonwealth University of Pennsylvania
Alternatives to Coming-Out Discourses

Nicole Hudak
Maine Medical Center
Queer Healthcare Communication

Áine M. Humble
Mount Saint Vincent University
Social Support and LGBTQ+ Individuals and Communities

Olu Jenzen
University of Brighton
LGBTQ Youth Cultures and Social Media

Sierra R. Kane
University of Wisconsin–Milwaukee
LGBTQ+ Workers

Sean C. Kenney
University of Colorado Boulder
Queer Studies and Organizational Communication

Kai Kline
Arizona State University
Stress and Coping in Sexual and Gender Minority Relationships

Katrin Köppert
Academy of Fine Arts Leipzig
Molecular Images, Leaky Masculinities: Pain, Photography, and Queer Desire

Kami Kosenko
North Carolina State University
Queer Safer Sex Communication

Pamela J. Lannutti
Widener University
Divorce and Relational Termination; LGBTQ+ Marriage: Relational Communication Perspectives; Parenting of Queer Offspring

Doris Leibetseder
University of Vienna
Queer(ing) Popular Music Culture

Lore/tta LeMaster
Arizona State University
Queer Communication Pedagogy

Gabriel A. León
University of Southern California
  Methodological and Statistical Considerations in Studying Sexual Minority and Gender Diverse Relationships

Ryan M. Lescure
San Francisco State University
  Kuaer Theory

Yachao Li
The College of New Jersey
  Coming Out in Interpersonal and Relational Perspectives

Morgan L. Litrenta
Texas State University
  LGBTQ+ Workers

Alfred L. Martin
University of Iowa
  Black Gay Men in Television Comedy

Hana Masri
University of Wisconsin–Madison
  Homonationalism's Viral Travels

Jamie McDonald
University of Texas at San Antonio
  Queer Studies and Organizational Communication

Dawn Marie D. McIntosh
Independent Scholar
  Homonormativity

Taisha McMickens
Chaffey College
  Queer Intercultural Communication: Sexuality and Intercultural Communication

Shane Moreman
California State University, Fresno
  Performance of Brown Sexualities

Charles E. Morris
Syracuse University
  Queer/ing Archives

Megan Elizabeth Morrissey
University of North Texas
  Disidentification

João Nemi Neto
Columbia University
  Brazilian Queer Cinema

Eve Ng
Ohio University
  Queer Production Studies

Lucy C. Niess
Arizona State University
  Relational Communication and Consensual Non-Monogamy

Bolivar X. Nieto
Florida International University
  HIV/AIDS: The Queer Communication of HIV in the LGBTQ Community

Miranda Dottie Olzman
San Francisco State University
  Queer Intercultural Communication: Sexuality and Intercultural Communication

Hailey N. Otis
University of Maryland
  Queer Worldmaking

Brandon T. Parrillo
Widener University
  Sexual Communication Between Queer Partners

Lital Pascar
Independent Scholar
  Queer Safe Spaces and Communication

Wendy Gay Pearson
University of Western Ontario
  Speculative Fiction and Queer Theory

Madison A. Pollino
Bowling Green State University
  Arts-based Queer Communication Studies

Ashley K. Randall
Arizona State University
Methodological and Statistical Considerations in Studying Sexual Minority and Gender Diverse Relationships; Stress and Coping in Sexual and Gender Minority Relationships

Danielle C. Romo
University of Wisconsin–Milwaukee
Queering the Study of U.S. Military Family Communication

Valerie Rubinsky
University of Maine at Augusta
Relational Communication and Consensual Non-Monogamy

Erin Sahlstein Parcell
University of Wisconsin–Milwaukee
Queering the Study of U.S. Military Family Communication

Steven Samrock
Arizona State University
Stress and Coping in Sexual and Gender Minority Relationships

Kristina M. Scharp
Rutgers University
Queer People's Communication with Families of Origin

Lace D. Senegal
Texas State University
LGBTQ+ Workers

Andrew DJ Shield
Leiden University
Queer Migration and Digital Media

Andrew R. Spieldenner
California State University, San Marcos
HIV/AIDS: The Queer Communication of HIV in the LGBTQ Community

Pamela VanHaitsma
Pennsylvania State University
LGBTQ+ Epistolary Rhetoric/Letter Writing

Florian Vanlee
Ghent University
Agonistic Queer TV Studies for Western Europe

Maria K. Venetis
Rutgers University
Sexual Orientation and Gender Identity Disclosure in the Medical Context

Hilary Wermers
Widener University
LGBTQ+ Marriage: Relational Communication Perspectives

Isaac West
Vanderbilt University
Queer Perspectives in Communication Studies

Terrie Siang-Ting Wong
Pennsylvania State University, Brandywine
Chinese Pink Markets

Shui-yin Sharon Yam
University of Kentucky
Queer(ing) Reproductive Justice

Jamie J. Zhao
City University of Hong Kong, HKSAR
Queer Chinese Media and Pop Culture

Index

Notes: Page numbers printed in boldface indicate a major discussion, while those followed by "*f*" indicate figures and illustrations and those followed by "*t*" indicate tables. For the benefit of digital users, indexed terms and table entries that span two pages (e.g., 52–53) may, on occasion, appear on only one of those pages.

AA. *See* ambulatory assessment
ABC, 1066
Abdi, Shadee, 474–475, 943
A Bela Época do Cinema Brasileiro (Paula Araújo), 3–4
able-bodied identity, 231
ableism, 229–230, 235
ablenationalism, 901
ABR. *See* arts-based research
Abreu, Caio Fernando, 20
Academia de Drags (television series), 1097
academic-classical genre system, 1114
academic drag, 697
Academy Awards, 232–233
acceptance
    casual, 629
    factors in, 771
    familial, 660

    context and, 660–661
    outcomes of, 661
    of queer identities, 660–662
    global trends in, of LGBTQ+, 770–771
    Measure of Family Acceptance, 772–773
    measures of societal, of homosexuality, 1063
    parenting and journeys to, 628–630
    social support and, 771
Achter het Nieuws, 821–822
ACRJ. *See* Asian Communities for Reproductive Justice
active concealment, 304
activism, 12
    antipornography, 571–572
    disabilities and practices of, 236
    discourses of future and, 388–389
    Jotería Studies and, 422

activism (*continued*)
  by media network executives, 1065
  political, 648–650
  QAS and, 648–650
  queer archives and, 1233–1235
  queer memory and screens and, 1033–1035
  radicalization in 1970s of, 65
  social media and, 925
  trans, 502–504
actor-partner interdependence model (APIM), 1167–1169, 1176
  in SEM, 1169–1171
ACT UP. *See* AIDS Coalition to Unleash Power
ACT UP Oral History Project, 1234–1235
Adam4Adam (website), 488
ADAPT, 232
Addicted (television show), 981
additive minority stress, 617–618
adoption, 711–712
Adorno, Theodor, 1043
advice, 735
Advise and Consent (film), 366
Aerts, Saskia, 378
The Aesthetics of Hunger (Rocha), 12–13
aesthetics risks, 411
Afetos (Lopes), 86
affective turn, 1227
affective well-being, social media and, 908
affiliations, Queer Asia and, 50–53
affinity spaces, 906–907, 924
affinity ties, 716
Affirming Couples Counseling to Engage Same-Sex Partners, 330
affordances, 1048
Afifi, Tamara, 618
African American queer cinema, 791–792
  documentaries, 801–804
  future of, 804–807
  mainstream LGBTQ films, 796–797
  noteworthy independent films, 797–800
African Americans, racial minority stress and, 617–618
African feminism, 649
Africanness, 639
African sexualities
  colonialism and, 641
  essentialist approach to, 642
African studies, 643–645
Afrocentricity, 1248–1249
Afro-feminism, 501
Afrofuturism, 1126, 1248–1249
Afro-pessimism, 501–502
After Adorno (DeNora), 1044

Against Me!, 1083–1084
age
  communication and sexual satisfaction and, 761
  intersectionality and, 446–447
agentic fidelity, 558–559
The Aggressives (documentary), 215
aging
  gay, 385–388, 390–392
  heteronormativity and, 385
  intergenerational communication and, 394–396
  lesbian, 392
  research on, 392–394
  social support and, 778–779
  trans, 392
aging lesbians, 392
agonistic queer TV studies, 810–813
Ahlberg, Beth Maina, 642
Ahmed, Sara, 476–477, 1076, 1115–1116
AIDS, 243, 263, 642
  activism and archives and, 1234
  China and, 41
  discourses of future and, 388–389
  first report of, 276
  gentrification of, 1234–1235
  media disseminating information about, 65
  monogamy and, 743
  queer memory and, 169–170, 173
  speculative fiction and, 1124–1125
  television depictions of, 1066
  temporal impact of, 211
  transgender individuals and, 297
  trauma archives and, 1233
AIDS, furor do sexo (film), 15
AIDS Action Now, 1124
AIDS Coalition to Unleash Power (ACT UP), 173, 175, 188, 222–223, 244–245, 252, 388–389, 939, 1124, 1191, 1230–1231
  archives and, 1234–1235
  political legacy of, 1235
AIDS Crisis Revisitation period, 1234
AIDS epidemic, 19
  Brazilian film and, 15
AIDS Memorial Quilt, 171, 175, 177, 253–254, 1028–1029
Aiello, Giorgia, 475–476
Ai Fu Hao Zi Zai Bao (love, luck, good, self-at-ease newspaper), 418–421
Ailey, Alvin, Jr., 143–144
Aimée & Jaguar (film), 1031–1032
Aí vem os cadetes! (film), 10
Aizura, A., 214
AJAAS. *See* Association for Jotería Arts, Activism, and Scholarship

Akonga, Joseph, 646
Alarcón, Linda, 136
Alcorn, Leelah, 943
Alexander (film), 1030
Alexander, Bryant Keith, 117–118
Alexander, Jacqui, 648
Alfonso XIII (King), 1013
algorithmic culture, 1050–1051
algotorial playlists, 1050
"Alien Cryptographies" (Pearson, W. G.), 1121–1123
Alioto, Joseph, 942
Allen, Julia M., 940–941
All God's Children (documentary), 802–803
All in the Family (television series), 832–833
All the Birds in the Sky (Anders), 1115
Almodóvar, Pedro, 96–99, 1029
Althusser, Louis, 138, 193–194, 1115
Altman, Dennis, 5–7, 977
Alvarez, Rafael, 18
Amar es para siempre (film), 102–103
Amazing Stories (magazine), 1118–1119
Amazon Prime, 807
ambient intimacy, 487
Ambrossi, Javier, 101
ambulatory assessment (AA), 1173–1174
America (comic), 992
American Academy of Family Physicians, 312
American Family Association, 793
American Psychological Association, 963
American Psychosomatic Society, 768
American Society for Reproductive Medicine, 710–711
America's Next Top Model (television series), 1101–1102
Amira De La Garza, Sarah, 420
AM model, 954
Amor Maldito (film), 15
Amsterdam Canal Pride, 880–881
Anders, Charlie Jane, 1115
Anders als die Andern (film), 1019
Anderson, Benedict, 1027
Anderson, Karrin Vasby, 578
Andrade, Luis, 476, 692, 694
de Andrade, Joaquim Pedro, 4
de Andrade, Mario, 3
androgynous same-sex couples, 738
Angelos (film), 1016–1017
Angels in America (Kushner), 1124–1125
Annals of Internal Medicine (journal), 994
Anscombe, G. E., 168
antiassimilation, 1076
anticipatory readings, 1232
antiessentialism, 1076

anti-gay rhetoric, social support and, 779–780
"Anti-Homosexuality Act" (Uganda), 883
anti-LGBTQ+ marriage legislation, 523–524
anti-LGBT violence, in Africa, 645–646
"Anti-LGBT Violence and the Ambivalence (Colonial) Discourses of Ghanaian Pentecostalist Charismatic Church Leaders" (Asante), 646
antipornography activism, 571–572
antipornography feminism, 571–573
antiretroviral cocktails, 211
anti-social approaches, 693–694
anti-trans sentiment, 923
Anzaldua, Gloria, 119–120, 136, 170–171, 220, 402–404, 409, 417–418, 458–459, 475, 1076, 1246
  on borderlands, 1244–1245
Aoki, Eric, 171, 174, 420
APIM. *See* actor-partner interdependence model
Appiah, Anthony Kwame, 716
Appropriating Blackness (Johnson, E. P.), 840
Aranda, Vicente, 94–96
de Araújo, Luciana Corrêa, 8–9
archival ambience, 1227–1228
archival disposition, 1236–1237
An Archive of Hope (Black and Morris, C.), 180
archives, 698–700, 1224–1226
  activism and, 1233–1235
  gay pornography studies, 862–863
  historiography, futurity, and, 1230–1232
  letters as, 941
  methods and methodologies, 1230
  norms of evidence, 1232–1233
  queer-feminist, 1081
  trauma, 1233
The Archivettes (film), 1035
Arévalo, Carlos, 94
Are You My Mother? (Bechdel), 1116
Arondekar, Anjali, 1225–1226
Arrington-Sanders, Renata, 864
The Arrival (Tan), 992
ars dictaminis tradition, 941
ART. *See* assisted reproductive technologies
The Arthouse, 1068
arts-based queer communication studies, 1145
  documentary and film, 1157–1158
  poetic inquiry and, 1151–1155
  queer autoethnography, 1148–1151
  queer methodology, 1147–1148
  queer performance, 1155–1157
arts-based research (ABR), 1145, 1147–1148
Arvin, Maile, 1253
Asante, Godfried, 471–476, 640, 646–651, 1249–1250

asexual orientation, disclosure of, 309
As Good As It Gets (film), 233
Ash (Lo), 1129–1130
Asian Communities for Reproductive Justice (ACRJ), 707
Asian financial crisis of 1997/1998, 51
AsiaPacifiQueer (anthology), 978
Aslinger, Ben, 844
assemblage, homonationalism as, 893–894
assimilationism, melodrama and, 1019–1021
assimilationist politics, 677
assisted reproductive technologies (ART), 710, 712, 714–715
Association for Jotería Arts, Activism, and Scholarship (AJAAS), 401–402, 404, 408–409, 412, 422
assurances, 735
asylum seekers, 68, 123
    digital media platforms and, 68–69
Atari Teenage Riot (ATR), 1076
Athey, Ron, 547
Atkinson, Kate, 1132–1133
ATR. *See* Atari Teenage Riot
ATRESPlayer Premium, 102–103
attitudes
    defining, 953
    heterosexist, 262
    narratives and, 953
    sexual
        defining, 953
        media depictions of, 952–953
Attwood, Feona, 847
Atwood, Margaret, 1113, 1116–1117, 1119–1120
audiences
    digital media and, 1053–1054
    gay pornography, study of, 864–866
    RuPaul's Drag Race and, 1096–1098
Audio-Visual Law (Brazil), 15–16
Augusto Aníbal quer casar (film), 8–9
Austin, J. L., 193–194
Australia
    drag in, 1098
    same-sex marriage and, 779
authenticity
    RuPaul's Drag Race and, 1095–1096
"Authenticity, Uniqueness and Talent" (Chen and Kanai), 492
autism, 238
Autism Speaks, 236
autocritography, 418, 421
autoethnography, 420–421, 446, 695–696, 991–992, 1148–1151
    critical, 1150–1151

organizational research and, 1218
of pleasure, 589–591
queering, 1218
autohistorias, 408–410
autohistoriography, 212–213
Autran, Arthur, 14
avant-garde, in Brazilian queer cinema, 8–9
Avendaño, Lukas, 511
Avila-Saavedra, Guillermo, 818
Awkward, Michael, 418
Aydemir, Murat, 381
Aztlán (journal), 401–403

baby safe haven laws, 711–712
Bachner, Andrea, 975
Bacurau (film), 19–20
Badu, Erykah, 1082
Bady, Demetrius, 842
Bahia de todos os santos (film), 11
Bailey, Marlon M., 1076
Bailey, Steve, 171
Baldiga, Jürgen, 547
The Ballad of Little Jo (film), 1092
ballroom culture, 1076
Banana Is My Business (documentary), 18
Los bandidos de Río Frío, 66
Banning Queer Blood (Bennett), 388
Bao, Hongwei, 973, 976, 980, 1035
Barbosa, Lygia, 19
bareback porn, 853–856
Barker, Meg-John, 585–586
Barnard Conference, 572–573
Barnes, Steven, 1126
barrier-free sex, 280–281
barrier methods, 280–281
de Barros, Luiz, 8–10, 16
Barry, Lynda, 1002–1004
Bassichis, Morgan, 508
Bassichus, Morgan, 1248–1249
Bataille, Georges, 583
bathhouses, 284–285
Baudrillard, Jean, 687
Bawarshi, ANis, 1012
Baym, N., 1054
Bazán, Oswaldo, 65
BBC. *See* British Broadcasting Corporation
BDSM. *See* bondage, domination, and sadomasochism
BDSM in American Science Fiction and Fantasy (Call), 1122
bear, 484
Beasley, Vanessa, 236
Beast Mode, 141–142

Beatles, 1043, 1078
Beautiful Thing (film), 368–372, 381–382
beauty influencers, gay male, 492
Bechdel, Alison, 997–999, 1003–1006, 1116
Becker, Albrecht, 535–536
    dragz-images, 537–546
    molecularization and, 537–546
    photographic biography, 536–537
    vernacularization and, 546–548
Becker, Ron, 816–817, 834–837, 842
Behavioral Alteration Messages, 1194
Behavioral Alteration Techniques, 1194
Behavioral Risk Factor Surveillance Survey, 297–298
Belgium, 882
Benjamin, Harry, 938, 944–945
Bennett, J. A., 388
Bennett, Tony, 844
Berlant, Lauren, 211–212, 216–217, 367, 541, 585, 687–688, 1142n.18
    queer worldmaking and, 689–690, 697
    racialization and, 1249–1250
Berlanti, Greg, 806–807
Berle, Milton, 1093–1094
Bernardet, Jean-Claude, 7
Berry, Chris, 977–978, 1052–1053
Bersani, Leo, 854, 1231–1232
Berscheid, Ellen, 1172–1173
Bertie, Alex, 922–923
Bérubé, Allan, 831
Bessette, Jean, 938–939
Bessie (film), 799
Between Women TV, 1068
Bey, Marquis, 497–498, 504
Beyoncé, 1126
Bhabha, Homi, 1244–1245
Bianchi, Sergio, 15
Bichas, o documentário (documentary), 19
Biden, Joe, 725
    EEOC and, 428
    on trans rights, 900–902
Bikini Kill, 1080–1081
Bilge, Sirma, 474
biodrag, 535–537, 541
biogenetics, 711–712, 715
biological determinism, 500
biopolitics, homonationalism and, 893–894, 898
biopower, 1123
    homonationalism and, 893
BIPOC LGBTQ+ people
    marriage equality and, 523
    research on marriage and, 525
birth control, disclosure and, 310

bisexual people
    familial rejection of, 663
    queering, 1210
    workplace and, 435–436
Bishop, C. J., 851
Bixa Travesti (documentary), 18–19
Black, Jason Edward, 174–175, 180, 942
Black Arts movement, 840
Blackbird (film), 798
Black-cast sitcoms, 841–844
The Blacker the Ink (Butler, O.), 992
Black feminism, 417–418
    pleasure and, 587
    transgender studies and, 498–501
Black gay characters, 835–839
Black gay men
    in sketch comedy, 839–841
    in television comedy, 831–832
Black gayness, 832–835
Black hip-hop feminism, 1075–1076
    queering, 1081–1083
Black is, Black Ain't (film), 795
#blacklivesmatter, 489
Black Lives Matter, 412–413, 620, 622
Black macho women (BMW), 1094
Black Nationalism, 793, 840
Blackness, 831
Black Panther (comic), 992
Black Public Sphere Collective, 687
Black queer documentaries, 801–804
Black queer theory, 119–120
black sheep effect, 395
Blackwell, Henry B., 946
Black./Womyn (documentary), 802
Blade Runner (film), 1128–1129
Blair, Carole, 590
The Blair Witch Project (film), 4
Blake, Melissa, 229–230
Blanchon, Robert, 849
Blanco, José Joaquín, 83
Blaque, Kat, 806
Blaser, Mario, 507
blaxploitation films, 792–793
The Blazing World (Cavendish), 1118–1119
Blinne, Kristen, 591
blockbuster films, 800–801
Blockers (film), 584–585
"Bloodchild" (Butler, O.), 1132
Blued, 29, 40–41, 72
blues, 1075–1076, 1078
BMW. *See* Black macho women
bodily shame, 588

body
  homonormative ideas of, 251–252
  medicalization of queer, 259
  performance and, 475
  queering, 251–253
  RuPaul's Drag Race and, 1101–1102
body image, 483
body politics, networked communications and, 485
Bohemian Rhapsody (film), 800, 982–983
Bolan, Chris, 1036
Bolan, Marc, 1079
Bolton, Michael C., 857–858
bondage, domination, and sadomasochism (BDSM), 536–537, 548, 553
  CNM and, 557
Bonin-Rodriguez, Paul, 171
Bonner-Thompson, Carl, 487
Booth, P., 1054
Bordelon, Suzanne, 946
borderlands, 1244–1245
Borderlands/La Frontera (Anzaldúa), 402–404, 410
Borgeson, Kevin, 376
Bornstein, Kate, 188
Born This Way (website), 217
Boston, Nicholas, 68
boundary management, 606
Bowie, David, 1078–1079
Boyd, D., 1053
Boys Beware (video), 821–822
The Boys in the Band (film), 366, 387, 793, 796–797, 805
Boys in the Sand (film), 847
Boys Toys (album), 1083–1084
Bozelka, Kevin John, 857
Bradley, Marion Zimmer, 1121
Bradley, Peri, 819–820
Bratmobile, 1081
Brave New World (Huxley), 1128
Brazil
  cinema of, 7–8
  documentary tradition in, 18–19
  end of dictatorship in, 14
  hate crimes in, 24n.11
  military dictatorship in, 14–15
  modernization and, 3
  queer identities in, 4–7
  redemocratização, 15–17
  RuPaul's Drag Race fandom in, 1097
  same-sex civil unions in, 23n.5
  sexuality in, 4
  travesti community, 1097
Brazilian queer cinema, 3–4, 20
  AIDS epidemic and, 15

chanchada and, 9–12
contemporary genres, 16–17
first decades of, 8–9
identity and, 4–7, 12–15
in 1950s and 1960s, 10–12
in 1970s and 1980s, 14–15
retomada and after, 15–17
2019 and beyond, 19–20
Brett, Philip, 1046
This Bridge We Call Communication (Hernández, L., and Gutierrez-Perez), 1246
bridgework, 1247
Briggs, John, 942
Briggs, Laura, 711–712
Briggs Institute, 179
"Bringing Up Baby," 1153
Briones, Stephanie, 477
British Broadcasting Corporation (BBC), 821, 1063, 1066
Brokeback Mountain (film), 196, 233, 366, 382, 390, 792
A Broken Bargain for LGBT Workers of Color, 428, 430
The Broken Hearts Club (film), 807
Bronski, Michael, 368, 1034
Brooklyn Liberation March, 1192–1193
Brooks, Peter, 1013
Brotherhood (film), 368–369, 375–377, 381–382
Brothers and Sisters (television series), 218
Brother to Brother (film), 798, 1032
Brouwer, Daniel, 699–700, 1251
Brown, Addie, 175, 934–935, 945–946
brown, adrienne maree, 587
Brown, as identity grouping, 459–460, 464
Brown, Michael, 343–344
brown boys, 1250
"Brown Scriptings and Rescriptings" (Moreman and McIntosh), 407
Brown sexualities
  performance of, 457–459, 464–465
    contexts of, 458
    dance, 462–463
    everyday life and, 463–464
    teatro, 461–463
  performance studies in communication and, 460–461
Bruhm, Steven, 1118
Brum, Eliane, 19
Brunow, Dagmar, 1036
Bryant, Anita, 385–386, 1127
BTS (band), 493
Buchanan, Pat, 793
Bucher, T., 1051
Buffington, Robert, 67
built environment, disability and, 232
Bull, M., 1056

bullying, 913
Bumble, 934–935
Bumble BFF, 923–924
Bumping into Broadway (film), 1091
buo luo jia, 419
Burke, Nathaniel B., 853
Burks, Ruth Coker, 253
Burton, Richard, 641, 1124–1125
Busby, Karen, 851
Bush, George H. W., 793
Bush Radio, 1068–1069
Butch hunt competition, 56
Butler, Andrew M., 1121–1122
Butler, Judith, 138, 193–194, 212, 367, 583, 1128
  on coming out, 344
  on cultural intelligibility, 1123
  dirt and, 537, 541
  on drag, 1089–1090, 1210
  on "queer," 190
Butler, Octavia, 992, 1122, 1126, 1132
Butterflies Will Burn (Garza Carvajal), 65
Butterfly (film), 978–979

Cabaret (film/play), 218–219
Cabezas, Amalia, 574
Cadena, Marisol de la, 507
Cagle, Jess, 835–836
Calafell, Bernadette, 410–412, 420, 427, 460, 463, 471–476, 478–479, 1247
Caliente, Jiggly, 1103, 1105
California Proposition 6, 942
Call, Lewis, 1122
Calling Dr. Laura (Georges), 1004
Call Me By Your Name (film), 1014
Call Me Kuchu (documentary), 802–803, 1157–1158
Calmon, Antonio, 14–15
Calvo, Javier, 101
Cambio de sexo/Forbidden Love (film), 95–96
Cameroon, 645–646, 1101
Caminhada Lésbica por Marielle (documentary), 18
camp, 838, 1079, 1089–1090
  RuPaul's Drag Race and, 1100
  as sensibility, 1090
Campbell, John Edward, 485, 1052
Campbell, Karlyn Kohrs, 1012
Campuzano, Giuseppe, 87
Canada, 899
Cane, Clay, 803
Canto, André, 19
capitalism, 6
  disidentification and resisting and subverting logics of, 141–142

  as double-edged sword, 36
Capozzola, Christopher, 171
Caprice (film), 1091–1092
Capsuto, Steven, 836–837
Caputi, Jane, 856
Capuzza, Jamie, 818
Cárdenas, Micha, 710–711
Cardoso, David, 15
Carne (film), 19
Carol (film), 1070
Carrera, Carmen, 1103, 1105
Carrier, Joseph, 82–83
Carrillo, Héctor, 84–85
Carrillo, Juanma, 101–102
Carrillo Rowe, Aimee, 405–406
Carta para além dos muros, 19
Carter, Julian, 147
Casanova, Eduardo, 101
Castellanos, Antonio, 411–412
caste systems, in India, 47
Castiglia, Christopher, 171, 1029–1030
casting, 1065
casual acceptance, 629
CAT. *See* communication accommodation theory
Catalan nationalism, 881–882
Cather, Willa, 172–173
Catholic Church, 641, 667
Caucus on Lesbian, Gay, Bisexual, Transgender, and Queer Communication Studies Division, 407–408
Caucus on Lesbian, Gay, Bisexual, Transgender, and Queer Concerns, 407–408
cautionary narratives, 385–387, 390
Cavalcante, Andre, 490–491
Cavendish, Margaret, 1118–1119
CBS, 1066
CCET-SMS. *See* Couples Coping Enhancement Training-Sexual Minority Stress
CCP. *See* critical communication pedagogy
CDC. *See* Centers for Disease Control and Prevention
The Celluloid Closet (Russo), 7, 20
Cendrars, Blaise, 8
censorship, Chinese, of homosexual and queer content, 980–983
Center for Gay and Lesbian Studies, 250–251
Center for Reproductive Rights, 708
Centers for Disease Control and Prevention (CDC), 255, 276
Centre for Contemporary Cultural Studies, 1043, 1077–1078
CGCO. *See* Chengdu Gay Care Organization
Chalamet, Timothée, 1014

Chambers, Becky, 1130
Chambers, Ross, 373
Chambers, Samuel, 815–816
Champagne, John, 849, 857–858
Chan, Lik Sam, 493
chanchada, 9–12, 16, 18–19
Chang, Justin, 799
Channel 4, 1064, 1066
Chao, Antonia, 35
Chaplin, Charlie, 1091
Charles, James, 492
Charles, RuPaul, 1094–1095
Charley's Aunt (film), 1091
Charnas, Suzie McKee, 1121
Chávez, Karma, 118–119, 169, 173, 405–406, 446, 471–472
   on embodied translation, 477
   letters and, 942–943
   on queerness and intercultural communication, 1247
Check It (documentary), 803
chemsex porn, 855–856
Chen, Shirley Xue, 492
Chen Dongyuan, 419
Cheng, Jih-Fei, 1034–1035
Chengdu Gay Care Organization (CGCO), 39–40
Chiang, Howard, 978–979
Chicano rights movement, 402, 405–406
Las chicas del cable (television series), 1013, 1019
Chicks on Speed, 1081
The Child Garden (Ryman), 1124–1125
The Children of Men (James, P. D.), 1127–1128
The Children's Hour (film), 366
China
   HIV/AIDS economy in, 41
   lesbians in, 52
   LGBTQ population estimates, 25–26
   Open Door Policy, 28–29
   prospective migrants from, 68
   romantic love in, 52
   self-censorship in pink market in, 39–41
   speculative fiction and, 1119
China Pink Market Conference, 29
China-UK AIDS Prevention and Care Project, 35
Chinchilla, Maya, 419–420
Chineseness, in queer media and pop culture, 977–980
Chinese pink markets, 25–26
   class-based *tongzhi* visibility in, 36–37
   classed and raced *tongzhi* subjectivity in, 37–38
   common trajectories of research on, 33–39
   definitions and terminology for, 26–27
   future directions and methodological considerations for, 41–42
   genealogy of theorization on, 27–32
   political economy perspective on early research on, 27–28
   safe space needs and, 34–36
   self-censorship in PRC, 39–41
Chinese queer feminisms, 418–419
Choosing Children (documentary), 1035–1036
Chou, Wah-shan, 348–349
Chow, Rey, 979
Christenssen, Carlos Hugo, 11
The Chronicles of Tornor (Lynn), 1129–1130
chronic minority stress (CMS), 617
chrononormativity, 210–211, 1003, 1131
   queering, 1132–1134
Chueca, 92–93
CIFC. *See* critical interpersonal family communication
Cine arco-íris (Letisch), 7–8
cinema
   arts-based queer communication studies and, 1157–1158
   coming out in contemporary, 368
   exhibition of, 1035–1037
   gay and lesbian characters in, 386–387
   Latin America and, 85–86
   Queer Asia and, 56–58
   in Spain, 93–103
   as technology of memory, 1027–1028
Cinema de Invenção', 13
"Cinema Gay Brasileiro" (Lacerda Júnior), 7–8
Cinema Journal, 857, 978
Cinema Marginal, 12–14
Cinema Novo, 12–14, 18
Cinema Novo x5 (Johnson, R.), 12–13
circular causality, 1172
cisheteronormativity, 425, 431
   policies reinforcing, 443
   queer melodrama and, 1016–1017
   work relationships and, 437–438
cisheteropatriarchy, colonialism and, 1250
cisnormativity, 153–154
cissexism, 424–425, 431
   heteronormativity and, 425
cis-sexist norms, 710
citationality, 193–194
Citizen Orange (blog), 942–943
citizenship, 28
   U.S., disidentification and resisting and subverting, 142–144
civic engagement, social media and, 925
civil equality, 528
   marriage decisions and, 527

civil rights, 508
  comics about, 994
  politics and, 527
civil unions, 325
Clappe, Louise Amelia Knapp Smith, 946
Clark, Cedric, 837
Clarke, Shirley, 792
class-based visibility, *tongzhi* and, 36–37
class consciousness, 51–52
class struggle, 575
clinical recommendations, 267–268
Clinton, Bill, 724
CLO. *See* coupled linear oscillator
closet, 342
  alternatives to, 345–350
  complicating, 343–344
  critique of paradigm, 344–345
  fluid, 346–347
  glass, 343–344
  as protective, 343–344
  trans people and, work and, 1215
  work and, 433
    queering, 1214–1216
closeting communication research, 450
Cloud, Dana, 172–173, 937
Club Cultures (Thornton), 1045
CMI. *See* Community Marketing & Insights
CMS. *See* chronic minority stress
CNM. *See* consensual nonmonogamy
CNSM. *See* communicated narrative sense-making theory
coalition building, QAS and, 648–650
Coalition of Women for a Feminist Sexuality and Against Sadomasochism, 572
Coates, Ta-Nehisi, 992
Cobb, Jasmine Nicole, 839–840
Cobb, S., 768
coding, queering, 1217
Coffey, Kathryn, 422, 1001–1002
Coffey, Sage, 1000–1001
cognitive scripts, 954
Cohen, Cathy, 190, 588, 1245–1246
Cole, Shaun, 859
Colebrook, Claire, 504
Colectivo Mexicano, 248
Coleman, Robin Means, 839–840
Colichman, Paul, 805–806
collaborative autoethnography, 695–696
collaborative performance, 222
collaborative personal narrative, 222
Collins, Patricia Hill, 119–120, 839–840
Colombian Lesbian and Gay Association, 248
colonialism, 1115–1116
  African sexuality and, 641
  anti-LGBT violence in Africa and, 645–646
  cisheteropatriarchy and, 1250
  gender and, 505–506
  homonationalism and, 897–900
  queering, 1242–1243
  settler, 897–900
  theoretical alignments of, 1243–1246
"The Coloniality of Gender" (Lugones), 403–404
The Color Purple (film), 793, 797–798
Colt Studio, 859
Combahee River Collective, 942
Comella, Lynn, 587–588
comics. *See also* zines
  in classroom, 1006–1007
  defining, 992–994
  as field notes, 994–995
  layout of, 993
  multimodal hybridity of, 996
  production of, 1007
  queer, 995–996
    future research directions, 1007–1008
  queer and trans self-representation in, 998–1002
  queer conversations and, 1004–1006
  as queer feminist pedagogy, 1006–1007
  queer readers and, 996–998
  queer spatiality and temporality and, 1002–1003
  reading experience of, 992–993
  scholarship and, 994–995
Comics and Sequential Art (Eisner), 992
coming home, 348–349
coming out
  alternatives to, 345–350
  as assimilationist agent, 344–345
  audiovisual media and, scripting of, 368
  as communication behavior, 357–361
  complicating, 343–344
  in contemporary film, 368
  contents, 358–360
  conversations in 357–358, 359*f*
  CPM and, 632–633
  critique of paradigm, 344–345
  discourses of, 341–342
  disidentification and, 349–350
  empirical studies related to, 355–357
  family of origin and communicating with outside world after, 668–669
  family support and, 660–662
  future research directions, 361–362
  goals for, 360–361
  heteronormativity and, 353
  historicizing, 342–343

coming out (*continued*)
  ideological status of, 342
  initial and communicative family reactions to, 659–664
  interpersonal and relational perspectives, terminology and scope for, 353
  after migration, 70
  narratives of, 366–369
  parental reactions to, 627–628
  processes of, 341–342
  social media and, 917–921
  strategies for, 358
  theoretical models of, 354–355
  types of conversations, 309
  workplace and, 356
coming out discourse, neoliberalism and, 344–345
coming out message production (COMP), 360–361
coming with, 349–350
commercial queer spaces, 34–35, 37
commercial surrogacy, 712
commercial websites, 486
committed, unmarried couples, 528–530
communicated narrative sense-making theory (CNSM), 630–631
communicated perspective-taking (CPT), 631
communication
  CNM and, 557–560
  critiquing and decolonizing queerness in, 1246–1249
  family of origin and, with outside world, 668–669
  HIV prevention as, 245–246
  polyamory and, 560–563
  relationship maintenance and, 734–735
  sexual satisfaction and, 761
  of social support, 767–768
communication accommodation theory (CAT), 631–632
Communication Act 2003 (United Kingdom), 1066
Communication and Critical/Cultural Studies (journal), 119, 462–463
Communication Monographs (journal), 618
communication privacy management theory (CPM), 561–562, 632–633
Communications Act, Section 230, 577–578
communication studies
  cripping, 229–231
  disidentification in, 138–139
  heteronormativity in, 690, 694–695, 1186–1187
  queer
    arts-based, 1145
    poetic inquiry and, 1151–1155
  queering of memory and, 175–179
  queer worldmaking in, 690–691

sexuality scholarship in, 582–584
sex work in, 568–570
Communication Teacher (journal), 1188–1189
Communication Theory (Squires), 687
communication theory of identity, 558, 560–561
communicative ethic, 690
community archives, 991–992
community building, HIV and, 248
community climate, 774
community connectedness and support, measures of, 773–774
community-level social support, 330
Community Marketing & Insights (CMI), 29
Como era gostoso meu francês (film), 4
co-mothers, 269–270
  defining, 276n.1
COMP. *See* coming out message production
compersion, 559–560
competition, *RuPaul's Drag Race* and, 1095–1096
compulsory able-bodiedness, 237
Comstock, Anthony, 1129
concealable identity
  active concealment and, 304
  disclosure and, 301–304
concealment, 324
  active, 304
  CPM and, 632–633
  as information management, 304–306
  LGBTQ+ marriage and, 523
  motivations for, 305
  relationship quality and, 615
Conde, Maite, 7
condom use, 279, 751, 753
  negotiation strategies and, 279
  pornography and, 853–854
conflict management, 735
Confucianism, 55–56, 347–348
connective affects, 459
Conquergood, Dwight, 407, 1196
conscientização, 1195–1196
consensually nonmonogamous relationships, 552–553
consensual nonmonogamy (CNM), 552–553, 601–602, 743
  BDSM and, 557
  communication and relational maintenance and, 557–560
  family disclosure and, 561–563
  future research directions, 563–564
  interpersonal skills and, 557–559
  jealousy communication and, 559–560
  LGBTQ communities and, 556–557
  open relationships, 554

polyamory, 555–556
   swinging relationships, 553–554
   terms and definitions for, 553–557
Consensual Non-Monogamy Attitude Scale, 552–553
consensual sex work, 570
consent, media depictions and, 958–959
Constitutive Model of Coming Out, 355
consumer culture, 159
consumerism, 575
Consuming Music in the Digital Age (Nowak), 1055–1056
consumption, *RuPaul's Drag Race* and, 1095–1096
contact advertisements, 65–66
content analysis, 952
controlling image, 839–840
Cooper, Dennis, 209–210
coparenting, 606
coping skills, relationship quality and, 616
Corbin Fisher (film), 856
Corey, Frederick, 171, 220, 589, 696
Corneau, Simon, 853, 865
Cornejo, Giancarlo, 11
Cornelis, Michael, 1122
The Corner Bar (television series), 833
corporeal refusals, 508–510
Cosenza Krell, Elías, 502, 511
cosexuality, 1208
Cosmopolitan (magazine), 584–585
Council of Europe, 879–880
counterculture, zines and, 993–994
counter-discourse, 209n.7
counterpublics, 137–139, 689, 924–925
   zines and, 993–994
coupled linear oscillator (CLO), 1177
Couples Coping Enhancement Training-Sexual Minority Stress (CCET-SMS), 330–331
Coutinho, Laerte, 19
Cover, Rob, 915, 1020
COVID-19 pandemic, 127, 277, 287, 412–413, 1234–1235
   digital spaces and, 680
   film production delays due to, 19–20
   safe spaces and, 681
Cox, Laverne, 803
CPM. *See* communication privacy management theory
CPT. *See* communicated perspective-taking
Cram, E., 180, 1237, 1253
CrashPad, 509
C-Real, 645–646
Creating Change Conference, 446
Crenshaw, Kimberlé Williams, 119–120, 410, 473, 499, 707–708

Cressey, Paul, 862
criminalization, 251–252
cripistemologies, 230
crip theory, 229–231, 239–240
   definitions and, 231–239
   performance, narrative, and embodiment and, 237–239
   politics, public culture, and critiques of productive body, 235–237
Crip Theory (McRuer), 233
#CripTheVote, 236
critical autoethnography, 1150–1151
critical communication pedagogy (CCP), 1186–1187, 1196
   as liberatory, 1193–1197
critical consciousness, 922–923
critical interpersonal family communication (CIFC), 725–728, 1155–1156
critical pedagogy, 1195
critical race scholarship, 66
critical race theory, 499
critical regionality, 978
Critical Resistance, 1185–1186
critical theory, minority stress and, 621–622
critical turn, 1207
Crónica de las destrucciones (Debroise), 82
Cronin, Patricia, 175
cross-correlation, 1174–1176
cross-dressing, 1091–1094
cross-generational experiences and, 395
Crowley, Mart, 796–797
Cruising Utopia (Muñoz), 86–87, 460, 1076, 1232
Cruz, Joelle, 649
Cruz, Victoria, 803
The Crying Game (film), 800–801
crypto-normativity, queer TV studies and, 817–819
Crystal, Billy, 833–834
CSI (television series), 956
Cuarón, Alfonso, 1127–1128
Cuelenaere, Eduard, 820
cultivation theory, 954
cultural assimilation, 33
cultural constructs, about sexuality, 106
cultural erotophobia, 583
cultural feminism, 1207
cultural globalization, 28
cultural identity
   diaspora and, 109
   formations in, 120–122
cultural intelligibility, 1123
cultural production, of Queer Asia, 44–46
cultural resistance, 1245

cultural scripts
　"harder path," 386, 393–394
　intergenerational communication and, 394
　internalized, 393–394
cultural studies, 420, 547
　digital, 906–907
The Cultural Study of Music, 1047
culture. *See also* visual culture
　globalization of, 493
　vernacular, 547
Culture Clash (Montoya), 461–462
culture industry, 861
The Culture of Queers (Dyer), 1047
Cunningham, Mark, 843
curatorship, 1230
The Curious Incident of the Dog in the Nighttime (Haddon), 238
curry queen, 484
Cutters (television series), 835–836
Cvetkovich, Ann, 171, 1035, 1233, 1235
CW (network), 806–807
cybercarnality, 486
cyberspace, 1052
cyberutopia myth, 66
cyberutopian tendencies, 485

daddy, 484
DADT. *See* Don't Ask, Don't Tell
Dalits, 47
Dambuza, Lasizwe, 806
Damiens, Antoine, 1036
dance, Brown sexuality and, 462–463
dandyism, 67
Dan Lan/Blued, 29, 40
danmei, 981–982
dating websites, race and racism and, 487–489
Daughters of Bilitis (DOB), 938–939, 941
Davis, Angela, 119–120, 402, 795
Davis, Glyn, 343
Davis, Sid, 821–822
Davis, Vaginal, 419–420
Dawn (Butler, O.), 1132
Dawson's Creek (television show), 389–390
Day, Doris, 1091–1092
Day, Fred Holland, 546–547
Day, Iyko, 499, 501
DDM. *See* Disclosure Decision Model
DD-MM. *See* Disclosure Decision-Making Model
The dead boys' club (film), 1030
Deaf Queers, 162–163
deaf queer world-making, 477
Dean, Tim, 588, 854

The Death and Life of Marsha P. Johnson (film), 791, 803, 805
Debroise, Olivier, 82
D.E.B.S. (film), 796, 804
Decena, Carlos, 84
decolonial feminisms, 504–507
decoloniality, 478
decolonization
　disidentification and, 146
　queering
　　colonial and postcolonial approaches, 1249–1251
　　indigenous approaches, 1251–1254
　of queerness in communication, 1246–1249
　of queer theory, 1242–1243
Decolonizing the Sodomite (Horswell), 64–65
deconstructive reading, 1117–1118
decriminalization, of sex work, 577–580
Deep Throat (film), 847
defamation, HIV-related stigma as, 246–247
Defense of Homosexuals in Cameroon, 645–646
Defense of Marriage Act (DOMA), 724–725
defensive offensiveness, 1090
definitions for, definitions for, 295–300
degenerational unremembering, 1029
DeGeneres, Ellen, 196
Degrassi: The Next Generation (television series), 1021
Dehesa, Rafael de la, 81–82
DEKKOO, 805–806
Delany, Samuel, 484, 1114–1115, 1120–1121, 1124–1126
DeLarverie, Stormé, 1192–1193
Delete Yourself (song), 1076
Deleuze, Gilles, 535–536, 545–546, 548, 894
Delgado, Fernando P., 420
Delgado, Luis María, 94
Delgado Huitrón, Cynthia Citlallin, 510
Delirious (film), 840
De los otros (Carrier), 82–83
Del Otro lado del espejo (Sierra Madero), 67
Del Priore, Mary, 4
D'Emilio, John, 6, 342–343
Deng Xiaoping, 28–29
DeNora, T., 1044
Department of Homeland Security, impact of policies, 443–444
"Depoliticized Pleasures and the Construction of (White) Queer Utopia in Netflix's *Sense8*" (Asante et al.), 650
derealization, 551n.9
deregulation, media impacts of, 1063
Derrida, Jacques, 193–194, 1232
Dery, Mark, 1126
Desert Motel (film), 1067–1068
designated spaces, as sites of resistance, 677

De Sodoma a Chueca (Mira), 92–93
Devassos no paraíso (Trevisan), 12
DeWaele, Alexis, 378
Dewey, John, 686–687
Dexl, Carmen, 837–838
Dhaenens, Frederik, 815–816
Dhoest, Alexander, 820
diabetes, 237
Diagnose van het Anders-Zijn (documentary), 821–822
Diagnostic and Statistical Manual of Mental Disorders, 251, 259, 551n.8
The Dialectic of Sex (Firestone), 1128
diaspora
    cultural identity and, 109
    global mobility and, 1250–1251
diasporic communities
    online, 71
    queer, 71
diasporic identities, 121
diasporic migration, 106
diasporic sexualities, themes in, 109–113
Diawara, Manthia, 794
Dickenson, Emily, 945–946
The Dickson Experimental Sound Film, 5
Díez, Jordi, 81–82
Diferente/Different (film), 94–95
difference, 136
differences (journal), 417
A Different Light (Lynn), 1121
digital cultural studies, 906–907
digital cultures, racism in, 70–71
Digital Fandom (Booth), 1054
digital gatekeepers, 921
digital intimate publics, 483
digital media, 64, 483–484, 493, 1068
    algorithms and, 1050–1051
    audiences and, 1053–1054
    emancipatory potential of, 909–910
    migration and, 68–69
    popular music and, 1047–1057
    queer music practices and, 1042
    settling in after migration and, 69–71
digital natives, 906–907
digital platforms, queer affect monetization in, 38–39
digital pornography, 568
digital sex work, 568–569
digital spaces, 485
    constructing queer safe spaces and, 679–680
    COVID-19 pandemic and, 680
Digital Transgender Archive (DTA), 180–181, 1226–1227
digital transgender suicide letter, 943

Dimarco, Nyle, 477
Ding Naifei, 343
DiPIetro, P. J., 511
direct disclosure, 308, 310
dirt, 536–537, 541–542, 544–545
Dirty Computer (album), 1126
disability, 231–232
    activist practices and, 236
    built environment and, 232
    media representations of, 232–235
    social model of, 232
disability melodrama, 1022
disability nationalism, 901
disabled subjectivities, 237
Disch, Thomas, 1121
disciplinary paternalism, 577
disclosure
    considerations for, 657
    CPM and, 632–633
    direct, 308, 310
    double, 303
    factors in in decisions, 657
    family, 561–563
    family of origin and communicating with outside world after, 668–669
    future opportunities, 313–314
    in healthcare, 265–266
    to heterosexual families of origin, 656–659
    initial and communicative reactions, 659–664
    HIV, 308, 751–752
    information management and, 304–306
    LGBTQ+ marriage and, 523
    motivations for, 306–307
    patient-provider, 300–310
    practices, 658–659
    recipients of, 657–658
    recommendations, guidelines, and programs, 310–313
    relevance and, 307
    of sexual orientation and gender identity, 265, 303–304
    stigma and, 301–303
    strategies for, 307–310
    typology for, 658
    at work, 432–437, 450
        navigating complexities of, 435–437
Disclosure (documentary), 804–805, 1158
Disclosure Decision-Making Model (DD-MM), 306
Disclosure Decision Model (DDM), 306
disclosure target-oriented goals, 360
discourse, Foucault and, 191–193
discovery, 176–177
discreditable, 301–302

discrimination, 767
  healthcare and, 263–265, 296–297
  minority stress and, 323–325
  non-verbal behavior and, 263–264
discriminatory pricing, 35–36
discursive negotiations, of identity, 646–648
discursive representation, 534–536
disidentification, 86–87, 149–150, 162, 1156
  broadening theory with, 148–149
  coming out and, 349–350
  in communication studies, 138–139
  cultural understandings of space and, 147–148
  decolonization and, 146
  defining, 135–136
  intellectual traditions informing, 136–138
  negotiating hybridity and, 145–147
  normative ideology and, 147
  quare, 143–144
  queer futures and utopias and, 693
  as queer of color worldmaking process, 144–145
  as subversion/subsistence mode, 140–144
    capitalism and, 141–142
    heteronormativity and, 140–141
    whiteness and U.S. citizenship, 142–144
  as survival mode, 139–140
  worldmaking and, 692–693
Disidentification (Muñoz), 460, 687–688
disjunctive modernities, Queer Asia as, 49–58
  identifications and affiliations, 50–53
  media and popular culture, 56–58
  relationalities and spatialities, 53–56
distal-proximal nature of stress, 614
diverse queer visibility, lack of, 118–120
diversity management
  document analysis and, 1213–1214
  norm-critical approaches, 1214
  queering, 1212–1214
divestment, 142
Divinas Divas (documentary), 19
divorce, 599–600
  experiences of, 604–605
  future research directions, 606–608
  gender composition and, 600–601
  minority stress and, 603–604
  relational arrangements and, 601–602
  relationships after, 605–606
  resources and, 602–603
  risk factors for, 600
  terminology and scope, 600
DIY gay porn, 863
DIY media cultures, 991–992, 1068, 1080–1081
D-LGM. *See* dyadic latent growth modeling

D'Lo, 693
DOB. *See* Daughters of Bilitis
document analysis, diversity management and, 1213–1214
documentaries
  arts-based queer communication studies and, 1157–1158
  Brazil traditions of, 18–19
Dolan, Jill, 221–222
DOMA. *See* Defense of Marriage Act
Dompierre, Jean-Marc, 394
Doña Herlinda y su hijo (film), 85–86
Donato, Nicolo, 375
Donofrio, Theresa, 697
Donovan, Casey, 861
Don't Ask, Don't Tell (DADT), 443–444, 448, 724, 728–729, 942–943
Door into Sunset (Duane), 1129–1130
Doran, Steven, 823–824
Dornelles, Juliano, 19–20
Dorsett, Richard, 1116–1117
Doty, Alexander, 4, 215–216, 974
double disclosure, 303
double jeopardy, 617–618
Douglas, Alfred, 934–935
Douglas, Mary, 537, 541
Douleur d'amour (film), 15
Dowling, Aydian, 492
down low, 345–346
DR, 821
drag, 541–546, 1089–1090
  leadership and, 1210
  representations of, in *RuPaul's Drag Race*, 1094–1105
DragCon, 1094–1095
drag family, 1100–1101
dragz-images, 537–546
The Drawing Power (Noomin), 993
DREAMers, 147, 161, 419–420
The Dreaming Jewels (Sturgeon), 1120–1121
DREAM Now campaign, 942–943
Dreamsnake (McIntyre), 1121
dress codes, 431
"dress for success" discourses, 431
Driskill, Qwo-Li, 937, 1251
Driver, Susan, 910, 1054
DTA. *See* Digital Transgender Archive
dualcasting, 1068–1069
Duane, Diane, 1129–1130
Duggan, Lisa, 7, 576, 714–715, 834, 875, 890
Duggan, Scott J., 851
Dunn, Thomas R., 170, 175, 177, 698–699, 939–940
Dunye, Cheryl, 793, 795–798, 1029

Duplechan, Larry, 798
DuVernay, Ava, 798–799
Dworkin, Andrea, 573, 847–848, 851
dyadic analysis, 1167
　dynamic, 1170–1171
　indistinguishable, 1167–1171
　longitudinal, 1170–1171
dyadic coping, 329
dyadic latent growth modeling (D-LGM), 1171
Dyer, Richard, 368, 848–850, 857–861, 1046–1047
dying, queering of, 253–254
Dylan, Bob, 1043
dynamic dyadic analysis, 1170–1171
dynamic systems analysis, 1177
dysfertility, 712
Dzi Croquetes (documentary), 18

Eakins, Thomas, 546–547
An Early Frost (film), 1066
Earthsea (television show), 1125–1126
Earthsea novels (Le Guin), 1125–1126
EastEnders (television series), 819–820
"Eating the Other" (hooks), 650
ecological momentary assessment (EMA), 1173–1174
economic justice, 446
　queer, 569
　sex work and, 569
economies of visibility, 40–41
Ecuadorian LGBT Movement, 248
Edelman, Lee, 211–214, 216–219, 1076, 1127, 1131
Edenheim, Sara, 1231–1232
Edge of Seventeen (film), 368
Edmonson, Roger, 861
Edwards, Dylan, 1004
EEOC. *See* Equal Employment Opportunity Commission
effeminacy, 67
Efya, Wanlov Kubolo, 645–646
Eguchi, Shinsuke, 471–474, 478, 693, 1247
Eisner, W., 992, 994, 1002
Ele, Ela Quem (film), 8–9
electroclash, 1081
Elia, John, 843–844
Eliana, 9
Elite (television series), 957–958
Ellen (television show), 389–390, 816–817
Ellison, Ralph, 1126
Ellison, Treva, 501
EMA. *See* ecological momentary assessment
embodied homonormativity, 157–158
embodied ideograph, 692, 1230
embodied translation, 477–478

embodiment
　crip theory and, 237–239
　queer intercultural communication and, 475–478
Embrafilme, 14
EMERJ. *See* Expanding the Movement for Empowerment and Reproductive Justice
Emilinha, 9
emotional support, 768
emotions
　in melodrama, 1014
　sexuality in media content and, 959–960
empire, queering, 1242–1243
enclaves, 676
Eng, David, 715
Enguix, Begonya, 487, 490
enslaved women, reproduction by, 498–499
Ensler, Eve, 585
Enteen, J., 1053
Entertainment Software Rating Board, 952–953
Entertainment Weekly (magazine), 835–836
entitlement racism, 70–71
A Entrevista (documentary), 12–13, 18–19
environmental stressors, 614
Enzensberger, Christian, 542–544
"Ephemera as Evidence" (Muñoz), 688
ephemerality, 177–178, 1232
ephemeral turn, 1227
Epic of Gilgamesh, 1118–1119
Epistemology of the Closet (film), 367
epistolary rhetoric, 934–935
　evidence of gendered relations and, 936–937
　future research directions, 947–948
epistolary writing, 941
Epprecht, Marc, 642
Equal Employment Opportunity Commission (EEOC), 427–428
eQuality curriculum, 313
equal marriage laws, 6, 23n.5, 91–92
Erdrich, Louise, 1119–1120
Eribon, Didier, 209n.7
Erickson, Darin J., 851–852
Eriksson, M., 1055
Eros in the Mind's Eye (Palumbo), 1121
erotic comedies, 14
Erotic Universe (Palumbo), 1121
erotophobia, 583
Escobar, Arturo, 507
Estavillo, Manolo, 84
Estou com AIDS (documentary), 15
ETA. *See* Euskadi Ta Askatasuna
ethnicity, cross-dressing, transvestism, and, 1091–1094
ethnography, 1217–1218

Eubanks, Virginia, 713
Eunuka Posporno, 509
European Court of Human Rights, 709–710, 879–880
European Song Contest, 884
European Union, 880
Europride, 93
Eurovision Song Contest, 884
Euskadi Ta Askatasuna (ETA), 100–101
Evans, Rodney, 798
Everett, Alexander Hill, 946
Everfair (Shawl), 1134–1135
everyday racism, 70–71
Ewalt, Joshua, 698
exceptionalism, 878, 892, 1099–1100
exclusion, queer melodrama and, 1019–1021
exclusionary workplace cultures, 438
exclusive policies, 442–444
exoticization, 427
Expanding the Movement for Empowerment and Reproductive Justice (EMERJ), 716–717
extradyadic relationships, 552–554
El extraño viaje/The Strange Journey (film), 95

Facebook, 64, 66–67, 650–651, 679–680, 916–917, 925, 1049, 1051, 1053
  connectivity emphasized in, 910–911
  performativity and, 1098–1099
  real names policy, 443–444
Falconí Trávez, Diego, 83
Familia, 902
familial acceptance, 660
  context of, 660–661
  outcomes, 661
familialism, ideology of, 715–716
familial rejection, 662–664
  context and, 662–663
  forms of, 663–664
  outcomes, 664
familial transitions, 659–660
La Familia: Trans Queer Liberation Movement, 419–420
familism, 777
Family Circus (comic), 1004
family communication, 195
family disclosure, CNM and, 561–563
family dynamics, polyamory and, 561–562
family formation, RJ and, 709–714
family identity, marriage and, 527–528
family justice, 714
family-of-origin relationships
  adjustment in, 664–668
    parents, 665–667
    siblings, 667–668
  communicating with outside world and, 668–669
  disclosure, 656–659
    considerations for, 657
    practices, 658–659
    recipients of, 657–658
  initial and communicative reactions, 659–664
  LGBTQ+ marriage and, 530
  polyamory and, 562–563
family readiness, 728–729
family research, 1174
family support, 660–662
  measures of, 773
Family Watch International, 641–642
The Famous 41, 403–404
The Famous 41 (Irwin, McCaughan, and Rocío Nasser), 67
fan cultures, 1069–1071
fandom, *RuPaul's Drag Race* and, 1096–1098
Fanon, Frantz, 1244
fantasy, 1113–1114, 1126
fan texts, 1069
Farewell My Concubine (film), 1014
Far From Heaven (Hayne), 215
Farmer, Nancy, 1126
Farrow, Kenyon, 1234–1235
fat, stigma, 1101–1102
FatClub.com, 140–141
Fateman, Johanna, 1081
The Favourite (film), 934–935
FDA. *See* Food and Drug Administration
Federal Communications Commission, 833–834
The Female Man (Russ), 1121
Female Masculinity (Halberstam), 1076
female sexual objectification, media and, 962–963
Fembook, 31
feminism, 570–571
  African, 649
  Afrofuturist, 1248–1249
  antipornography, 571–573
  Black hip-hop, 1075–1076, 1081–1083
  cultural, 1207
  decolonial, 504–507
  indigenous, 504–507
  Marxist, 575
  material, 574
  postmodern, 1207–1208
  sex-positive, 573
  standpoint, 1207
  trans-exclusionary, 923
feminist historiographies, 1231
The Feminist Porn Book, 586
Fenelon, Moacyr, 10

Ferguson, Roderick, 148–149
Fernández, Bibiana, 95–96
Fernández de Lizardi, Joaquín, 65–66
Fernán Gómez, Fernando, 95
Ferris, Jim, 238–239
fertility, 710–712
Festival Mix Brasil de Cultura da Diversidade, 16
Fey, Tina, 839
fidelity, agentic, 558–559
field notes, comic, 994–995
Fiestas, baños y exilios (Rapisardi and MOdarelli), 83
Fifty Shades of Grey, 584–585, 1070–1071
Files-Thompson, Nicole, 473–474, 478
Filho, Daniel, 16
film. *See* cinema
Filme para poeta cego (documentary), 19
film preservation, 1035–1037
filter bubbles, 1049
financial domination, 574–575
Finlay, Michael, 571
Fiol-Matta, Licia, 87
Firestone, Shulamith, 1128
first/third world binary, blurring, 112–113
first-time intercourse, 960
Fisher, André, 16
Fisher, Diana, 343–344, 346
Fisher, Fox, 925–926
Fitz, C., 803
Fixmer-Oraiz, Natalie, 1188–1189
Flaming Classics (Doty), 4
Flanagan, Bob, 547
Flanner, Janet, 945–946
Flemish TV, 820
FLH. *See* Frente de Liberación Homosexual
Flinn, Caryl, 1014
Flor, Dana, 803
Florentine Codex, 64
Flores, Lisa A., 420
Flores, R. R., 459
Flowers, Ebony, 994, 998–999
Floyd, George, 620
fluid bonding, 280–281
fluid closet, 346–347
de Fluvià, Armand, 92
Fly Young Red, 693
da Fontoura, Antonio Carlos, 14
Food and Drug Administration (FDA), 255
  PrEP and, 285–286
Ford, Yance, 807
formal social support, 780
FOSTA/SESTA, 577–578
Foster, David William, 12–13, 85

foster care, 711–712
Foucault, Michel, 83, 170–171, 191–195, 209–210, 583, 891, 893, 1123, 1243–1244
  on cinema, 1027–1028
  on closet, 344
  genealogical approach and, 1118–1119
  public realm theory and, 687
  on state paternalism, 577
Fountain (performance), 143
Fourth World Conference on Women, 708, 1035
Fox, Ragan, 697
France, David, 803
Franco, Jess, 94–95
Franco dictatorship, 92
  cinema during, 94–95
Frankenstein (Shelley), 1118–1119, 1128
Freebie and the Bean (film), 387
Free CeCe (documentary), 803
Freedman, Carl, 1114–1115
Freeheld (film), 1070
Freeman, Elizabeth, 210–212
Freire, Paolo, 1195
French, Jim, 859
Frente de Liberación Homosexual (FLH), 67
Fresa y chocolate (film), 85–86
Freud, Sigmund, 137, 667
Friday Night Lights (television series), 234
Friends (television series), 961
Frith, S., 1044–1045
From Behind Films, 856–857
From the Earth to the Moon (Verne), 1119
Front Cover (film), 56–57
fugitive knowledge, 1245
Fuhrman, Ezra, 1083–1084
Fun Home (Bechdel), 1003–1004, 1116
Fury, Gran, 252–254
Fuss, Diana, 137, 343
future
  AIDS and queer activism in discourses of, 388–389
  archives and, 1230–1232
  children and, 1118
  constructing, 385–386
  discursive construction of queer doom, 386–387
  intergenerational communication and, 394–396
  internalized scripts, 393–394
  queer, 396
  queer media criticism and, 389–392
  research on LGBTQ aging and, 392–394
Future Home of the Living God (Erdrich), 1119–1120
The Future of Another Timeline (Newitz), 1129
fuzzy sets, 830n.2
  speculative fiction and, 1115–1117

gaige kaifang, 28–30
gaisen bars, 54
Gaius Media, 806
Gamson, Joshua, 714, 716
Ganga Bruta (film), 8
gangsta rap, 794–795
Garber, Eric, 1120–1121
Garbo, Greta, 1089–1090
García, Lia, 510
Garland, Judy, 792, 1079, 1124
Gary, Indiana, 1124–1125
Garza Carvajal, Federico, 65
Gateward, Frances, 992
Gay, Lesbian, and Straight Education Network (GLSEN), 678
Gay Activists Alliance, 833
gay aging, 385–388, 390–392, 395–396
    research on, 392–394
Gay and Lesbian Acceptance and Support Index (GLASSI), 773
Gay and Lesbian Alliance Against Defamation (GLAAD), 388–389, 800, 807
    media advocacy by, 1065–1066
Gay and Lesbian Dominican Empowerment, 248
Gay and Lesbian Studies, 1076
gay bars, 679–680
Gay Beards, 925–926
gay beauty ideal, 483–484
    hookup apps and, 487
    online cultures and, 491
    predigital media cultures and, 484–485
gayborhoods, 676, 679–680
gaycapitalism, 6
Gay-Center, 879
#gaychub, 485
Gaydar (website), 486–487, 489
Gaydar Culture (Mowlabocus), 486
gay erotica, 484
gay-for-pay, 856–857, 862
Gay International, 878, 890–891
Gay Latino Studies (collection), 402–403
gay left, 876
gay liberation movement, 341–343
gay male beauty influencers, 492
gay marriage, 82, 1142n.18
Gay Men at the Movies (McKinnon), 1029–1030
#gaymuscle, 485–486
#gaymusclebears, 485
Gay Museum in Berlin, 536
gaypitalism, 93
gay pornography, 847–848
    bareback, 853–856
    DIY, 863
    gay-for-pay, 856–857, 862
    prison settings in, 859–860
    study of
        audience, 864–866
        discourse, 865–866
        dominant conditions in, 853–857
        early studies, 849–850
        effects, 864–865
        iconography and prototypes, 858–860
        industry, 860–863
        medium, spaces, archives, 862–863
        methods of, 853
        race and place, 860
        scope of, 848–849
        special issues on, 850–852
        text, 857–860
        work conditions, 861–862
Gay Pride Parade, 768–769
gay refugees, 68
gay-related immune disease (GRID), 243–245
#gayspain, 490
Gay Star News, 40
gay-straight alliances (GSA), 616
gaystreaming, 156–157
gay-supportive policies, 441, 443
gay-themed television programming, 1063
gender
    as biotechnological artifact, 535
    caste and, 47
    colonialism and, 505–506
    cross-dressing, transvestism, and, 1091–1094
    popular music and, 1044–1045
    production of, 535
    sexual scripts and, 759
    work and, 1208–1210
gender affirmation, 629–630
gender bending, 9
gender composition, relational termination and, 600–601
gender dysphoria, rapid-onset, 907–908
Gendered Lives (Wood, J. T. and Fixmer-Oraiz), 1188–1189
gendered relations, evidence in letters of, 936–937
gender identity, 296
    disclosure in medical context, 265, 295
    disclosure of, 303–304
    inclusive policies and, 442
    patient-provider disclosure and, 300–310
    stigma on, 246–247
gendering, 499
Gender in the Music Industry (Leonard), 1045
gender-neutral terms, 261

gender nonconformity, 47
    homonormativity and, 155
gender performativity, 1089–1090
gender-performed identity, 1089–1090
Gender Recognition Act 2004 (United Kingdom), 923
gender roles, 738
    media and stereotyping of, 962
gender wars, 923
Gene Compton's Cafeteria, 1192–1193
generational segregation, 1030–1031
generativity, 223
Geng Le, 36, 40
geography
    of sexualities, 677
geolocative apps, 67
George, Lynell, 802, 1006
Georges, Nicole J., 1004
Gerbner, George, 387, 835–836
Gernsback, Hugo, 1118–1119
Getting It on Online (Campbell), 485, 1052
G.G. v. Gloucester County School Board, 143
Ghana, 645–646, 651
Ghanaian Pentecostalist Charismatic Church (GPCC), 646
Gibbon, Edward, 641
Gibson, James, 1048
Gill-Peterson, Julian, 504–505
Gilreath, Shannon, 849, 856
GinGin, 31
Ginn, Sherry, 1122
Giorgi, Gabriel, 81
Girlfriend (song), 1082
Girls (television series), 957–958, 961
A Girl Walks Home at Night (film), 217
Gitlin, Todd, 832–833
GLAAD. *See* Gay and Lesbian Alliance Against Defamation
glam rock, 1075–1076, 1079
glass closet, 343–344
GLASSI. *See* Gay and Lesbian Acceptance and Support Index
Gledhill, Christine, 1014
Glee (television series), 815–816, 831
Glimmering (Hand), 1124–1125
Glitter (television series), 1097
G&L Magazine, 27, 31, 34, 38–39
GLO, 1068
global audiences, *RuPaul's Drag Race* and, 1096–1098
globalization, 44–46
    cultural, 28
    of culture, 493
    media and popular culture and, 56

media impacts of, 1063
online media and, 66
queer, 46–49
science fiction and, 1119
transnationalism and, 109
Global Measure of Sexual Satisfaction, 757–758
global memoryscapes, 1235–1236
global mobilities, 1250–1251
global queering thesis, 27–28, 33–34, 977
Globo Films, 16
GLSEN. *See* Gay, Lesbian, and Straight Education Network
Goal-Driven Model of Interpersonal Influence, 281
Gods and Monsters (film), 394
Godwin, Francis, 1118–1119
Goh, Joseph N., 865
going public, 36
Goldberg, Whoopi, 797, 1224
Goltz, Dustin Bradley, 693–694
Gomez-Narvaez, Erick, 487, 490
Gómez Peña, Guillermo, 419–420, 461–462
Gone Tomorrow (Indiana), 1124–1125
Gosling, Ryan, 234–235
The Gospel according to Andre (documentary), 803
Gossip, 1081
Gothic fiction, 1113
Goto, Hiromi, 1129
Gottlieb, Michael, 276
Gough, Brendan, 374
Gough, Jamie, 859
GPCC. *See* Ghanaian Pentecostalist Charismatic Church
Grace, Laura Jane, 1083–1084
Granger causality, 1176
graphic medicine, 994
Grassroots Feminism Archive, 1081
Gras-Velázquez, Adrián, 490
Gray, F. Gary, 797
Gray, Herman, 840
The Great Woman Singer (Fiol-Matta), 87
Greece, *RuPaul's Drag Race* fandom in, 1097
Green, Kai M., 497–498, 501
Greyson, John, 1124–1125
GRID. *See* gay-related immune disease
grief, queering of, 253–254
Grier, Barbara, 943–944
Grier, David Alan, 837–838
Griffin-Gracy, Major, 1192–1193
Grindr, 64, 67, 229, 487–489, 934–935
Groeneveld, Elizabeth, 939
Gross, Larry, 342–343, 387, 1120
grounded theory, 775
group sex events (GSE), 284–285

Grudzen, Corita R., 854
GSA. *See* gay-straight alliances
GSE. *See* group sex events
guaitai, 975
Guardian (television series), 1070–1071
Guattari, Félix, 535–536, 545–546, 548, 894
"La Guerra declarada contra el niño afeminado" (Cornejo), 11
Guerrero, Ed, 792
Guevara, Ernesto, 67
Gumbs, Alexis Pauline, 714
Güneşi Gördüm (film), 1017
Gunn, Gia, 1104–1105
Gustavo, Paulo, 16
Gutiérrez, Jennicet, 419–420
Gutiérrez, Laura G., 86
Gutierrez-Perez, Robert, 476, 692, 694, 1246
Guzmán, Manolo, 84

Habermas, Jürgen, 686–688
Haddon, Mark, 238
Hagen, Anja Nylund, 1056
Hairspray (film), 16, 1090
Halberstam, J. Jack, 171, 213–214, 223, 235, 974, 1003, 1035, 1045, 1076–1078, 1133–1134
    on drag, 1092
    on scavenger methodology, 1146
Halbwachs, Maurice, 170, 1027
The Half of It (film), 805
Hall, Radclyffe, 945–946
Hall, Stuart, 420, 547, 840–841
Hall, Todrick, 806
Hallas, Robert, 1035
Halliburton, Richard, 174–175
Hammers, Michele, 585
Hanchey, Jenna, 649, 1248–1249
Hancox, Lewis, 925–926
Hand, Elizabeth, 1124–1125
Handbook on Queer African Studies (Nyeck), 640
The Handmaid's Tale (Atwood), 1113, 1119–1120
Hanly, J. P., 946
Hanna, Kathleen, 1080–1081
Hansberry, Lorraine, 174–175, 941–944
Happy Together (film), 1014
Harbord, Janet, 382
"harder path" cultural script, 386
hardscape monuments and memorials, 177
Hardy, Oliver, 1091
Hargreaves, D., 1044
Haritaworn, Jin, 502–503
¡Harka! (film), 94–95
Harlem Renaissance, 794, 798

harm reduction, 249
Harris, Ruth, 1015
Harris, Susan, 833–834
Harris Interactive, 299
Hartford, Jason, 379
Hartley, John, 850
Hartman, Saidiya, 940
Hartmann-Tews, Ilse, 373
hate, social media and, 925–926
hate crimes, 376
    in Brazil, 24n.11
Hatfield, Joe Edward, 943
hauntologies, 1232
Hawkins, Deion, 472–473
Hawkins, Stan, 1076–1077
Hayne, Todd, 215
Hays Code, 386–387, 1120
Haze Him (film), 856
Head On (film), 368
HEAL Project, 502
health behavior theories, 281
health-card systems, 579
healthcare
    discrimination in, 263–265, 296–297
    heterosexism in, 262
    lack of insurance and, 297–298
    provider education and, 298–299
    provider knowledge and, 262–263
    provider recommendations, 267–268
        queer pregnancy and, 271–272
    queer identity disclosure in, 265–266
    queer invisibility and, 264–265
    seeking queer-friendly, 266–267
    sex work and, 579
    transgender, 268
healthcare communication
    disclosing queer identity and, 265–266
    medical forms and, 266
    provider knowledge and, 262–263
    queer pregnancy and, 269–272
    special topics in, 268–272
Health Communication (journal), 994
health education
    heterosexism in, 259
    queer-focused, 261
health expertise, queering, 254–255
Heavens to Betsy, 1081
Hebard, Grace, 170
Hegde, Radha, 1249
hegemonic masculinity, 435, 550n.3
hegemonic representations, 585–586
    pornography and, 586

hegemony, 110–112
Heinlein, Robert A., 1113, 1130
Hemphill, Essex, 188, 793, 840–841
Henderson, Mae G., 119–120
Hepple, Josh, 229
HereTV, 805–806, 1065
Heritage of Hastur (Bradley), 1121
Hernández, Leandra, 1246
Hernández, Roxsana, 236–237
Her Noise Archive, 1081
"Hetero Barbie" (Roger), 215–216
heteronormativity, 11, 105–106, 110–112, 153–154, 195, 220, 223–224, 367
   aging and, 385
   camp and, 1090
   cissexism and, 425
   coming out and, 353
   in communication studies, 690, 694–695, 1186–1187
   defining, 208n.3
   disidentification and resisting and subverting, 140–141
   diversity management and, 1213
   marriage and, 527
   motherhood and, 712
   in organizational contexts, 1209
   parents and, 666
   patient disclosure and, 300–301
   queer melodrama and, 1016–1017
   queer studies and, 639
   RuPaul's Drag Race and, 1099–1101
   sexual scripts and, 759
   social support and, 778
   time and, 210–211
   work and, 424
   youthism and, 390–391
heteropatriarchal recolonization, 648–649
heterophobia, 447
heteroporn, 847
heterosexism, 426
   defining, 276n.1
   in healthcare, 262
   in health education, 259–262
   language and, 261
   terminology of, 431
heterosexual identity, 231
heterosexual partner studies, 752–753
heterosexual script, 962
Heyer, Heather, 1083–1084
Hick, Jochen, 15
Hickok, Lorena, 937
hijras, 47, 56–57
Hill, Lauryn, 1082
Hill, Robert, 1245

Hilliard, Shelly, "Treasure," 803
Hillz, Monica Beverly, 1104–1105
HIM. *See* Homosexual Identity Model
Hindu nationalism, 47
Hinsch, Bret, 971
HIPAA, 426
hip-hop culture, 1075–1076
   sexism in, 1081–1082
Hirsch, Marianne, 1027–1028
Hirschfeld, Magnus, 23n.3, 65
Historia de la homosexualidad en Argentina (Bazán), 65
historiography, archives and, 1230–1232
History of Sexuality Vol. 1 (Foucault), 209–210
Hitchcock, Alfred, 1091–1092
HIV, 83–84, 236–237, 243, 255–256, 262, 472–473
   China and, 41
   community building and, 248
   disclosure, 308
   as epidemic of signification, 246
   federal government responses and, 248–249
   gay pornography and, 854
   healthcare communication and research on, 268–269
   identity creation and, 252
   impact on organizations and technologies, 247–250, 252
   international programs for, 642
   IPV and, 283
   LGBTQ relationship impact of, 243–247
   maintenance behaviors and, 740
   marginalization and, 243
   media disseminating information about, 65
   medical education and, 260–261
   monogamy and, 743
   pharmaceutical industry impacts of, 249–250
   prevention of, 278, 280–281
      as communication, 245–246
      secondary, 280
   queering body and, 251–253
   queering dying and grief and, 253–254
   queering health expertise and, 254–255
   queer memory and, 169–170
   status disclosures, 280, 751–752
   thinking about body and, 250–255
   transgender individuals and, 297
HIV-related stigma, as queer defamation, 246–247
Hoad, Neville, 643–644
Hoang, Nguyen Tan, 849
Hoekstra, Pieter, 795
Hoggart, Richard, 547
Holler if You Hear Me (documentary), 803
Holliday, Tess, 698

Holling, Michelle, 420
Hollinger, Veronica, 1121–1122
Hollywood Diversity Report, 807
Holmes, Kwame, 940
Holocaust, 993
  memory boom and, 170
Hombres sin mujer (Montenegro), 66
home video, 1035–1037
homo-colonialism, 160–162
homonationalism, 107, 160–161, 446, 680–681, 874, 885–886, 1242
  as bio-necropolitical assemblage, 893–894
  circulation and contestation of, 895–896
  conceptual, political, and historical origins, 890–893
  critiques of, 895–896
  defining, 874–877
  futures for, 900–902
  limits of, 896–897
  Muslim others and, 879–882
  other others, 882–884
  settle colonial complications, 897–900
  as totalizing theory, 895–896
  unpacking, 877–879
  as viral concept, 889–890
homonegativity, 615
homonormative gay characters, 834
homonormative whiteness, 158–160
homonormativity, 7, 152–153, 163–164, 507–508, 714–715, 834–835, 875–876, 1190–1191, 1242
  archival identifications and, 1229
  in coming out narratives, 371
  deconstructing, 162–163
  defining, 153–157
  embodied, 157–158
  homonationalism and, 890
  ideas of body and, 251–252
  intersectional, 157–158
  masculinity and, 550n.3
  RuPaul's Drag Race and, 1099–1101
  transnational, 160–162
homophile movement, 546–547
homophile publications, 65
homophobia, 65–66, 637, 913, 1115–1116
  defining, 276n.1
  evangelism and, 883
  healthcare and, 262
  heteronormativity and, 153
  queer pregnancy experiences and, 270
  sports and, 374
  xenophobia and, 67
homophobic insults, political uses of, 65–66
homophobic language, 426

homosexual identity, 5, 23n.3
Homosexual Identity Model (HIM), 354
homosexuality
  in Chinese-speaking world, 971
  Diagnostic and Statistical Manual of Mental Disorders and, 259
  in film, 386–387
  measures of societal acceptance of, 1063
  pathologization of, 551n.8
  universal, 158–159
Homosexual Lifespan Development Model, 354–355
homosexual masculinity, 539, 548, 550n.3
homosexual rights, 6
homosociality, 375–376
homotransnationalism, 883
Honeypot (Johnson, E. P.), 591, 1228–1229
Hong Kong, 55–56
  class consciousness in, 51–52
  economic status in, 51
  media and popular culture and, 56–57
  political economy of, 51
Hong Kong pink market, 30–31
hooks, bell, 119–120, 417, 650, 795
hookup apps, 487, 863
  race and racism and, 487–489
Hoover, J. Edgar, 172–173, 699
hormones, 505, 535
Horn, Katrin, 837–838
"Horny Lil Devil" (song), 794–795
Horowitz, Vladimir, 1079
horror, 1113
Horswell, Michael, 64–65
Horvat, Anamarija, 66
hostile workplace communication, 438–439
Hot l Baltimore (television series), 833–834
Howard, Sheena, 474
How to Have Sex in an Epidemic (guidebook), 245
"How to Respond to Haters" (video), 925–926
How to survive a plague (film), 1034–1035
Hoy, Chuck, 832–833
HPV. *See* human papillomavirus
HRC. *See* Human Rights Campaign
Huang, Shuzhen, 1251
Hubbard, Jim, 1234–1235
Huerta, Dolores, 402
Huggy Bear, 1081
Hughes, Holly, 222, 794
Hughes, Langston, 794
Hugo Awards, 1126–1127
Hulu, 807
human-computer interaction, 1048
human papillomavirus (HPV), 278

human rights
  having children as, 709–713
  queer globalization and, 46–49
Human Rights Campaign (HRC), 620
Hunan TV, 973
Hungochani, 637–638
Hunt, Darnell, 807
Hunt, Helen, 233
Hunter, Lourde Ashley, 1193
Hunting Season (documentary), 18
Huntington Dickenson, Susan, 945–946
Hutchins, Grace, 940–941
Huxley, Aldous, 1128
hybridity, 137
  disidentification and negotiating, 145–147
  of identity, 138–139

IASPM. *See* International Association for the Study of Popular Music
ICD. *See* International Classification of Diseases
ICE. *See* Immigration and Customs Enforcement
Ice Cube, 794–795
iconography, gay pornography and, 858–860
IDAHO. *See* International Day Against Homophobia, Transphobia, and Biphobia
identifications, 136–137, . *See also* disidentification
  Queer Asia and, 50–53
identity, 194–195, . *See also* social identity
  able-bodied, 231
  archives and, 1228–1229
  Brown as grouping for, 459–460, 464
  communicating, in interpersonal work relationships, 438–440
  communication theory of, 558, 560–561
  cultural formations, 120–122
  diasporic, 121
  discursive negotiations of, 646–648
  family of origin adjustment and, 664–668
  gender-performed, 1089–1090
  heterosexual, 231
  HIV creation of, 252
  hybridity of, 138–139
  Jotería, 407
  LGBTQ+ marriage and, 524–525
  music and, 1042–1045
    LGBTQ+, 1045–1047
  music streaming and, 1054–1057
  performative, 1209
  polyamory and, 560–563
  QCP and, 1189–1190
  rejection forms and, 663
  resistance and, 192

  social, 619–620, 665
  social media and work in, 914–923
  sovereign, 665
  transnational queer as category of, 124–126
identity-building, 69
identity concealment, 324
identity conflicts, 667
identity development, 914
identity formation, 136
identity gaps, 558, 560
identity management theory, 560–561
identity validation, 915
ideographic designs, 1174
Ideological State Apparatus (ISA), 1115
ideology
  of familialism, 715–716
  power and, 191
Idol, Ryan, 856
IEMSS. *See* Interpersonal Exchange Model of Sexual Satisfaction
If Memory Serves (Castiglia and Reed), 1029
If… Then (Bucher), 1051
Iggy Pop, 1079
Iglesia, Eloy de la, 96–99
IGRA. *See* International Gay Rodeo Association
Imago (Butler, O.), 1132
IMF crisis, 51
"Imitation and Gender Insubordination" (Butler, J.), 367
immigrant justice, 446
Immigration and Customs Enforcement (ICE), 236–237, 412–413, 446, 902
imperialism, 6
In and Out (film), 7
In a Queer Time and Place (Halberstam), 1076
inclusionary workplace cultures, 438
inclusive language, 442
inclusive policies, 441–442
The Incredibly True Adventures of 2 Girls in Love (film), 796
"In Defense of Disco" (Dyer), 1046
Independent Television (ITV), 1064, 1066
Index of Sexual Satisfaction, 757–758
India
  caste system in, 47
  media and popular culture and, 56–58
  speculative fiction and, 1119
Indiana, Gary, 1124–1125
indigenous decolonization approaches, 1251–1254
indigenous feminisms, 504–507
Indigenous speculative fiction, 1119–1120
indignados, 142–143
infertility, 712

informal social support, 769
informational assistance, 768, 924
information management, concealment as, 304–306
In Living Color (television program), 837–840
#instagays, 489–490
Instagram, 489–490, 906–907, 909–910, 924–925, 1051
  identity validation and, 915
  mediation of self and, 910–911
  performativity and, 1098–1099
Instinct Magazine, 391
institutionalized heterosexuality, 110–111
instrumental support, 768
insult, 64
intercultural communication, 195–196
  Jotería Studies and, 407–408
  queerness and, 1247
  queer worldmaking and, 697–698
  sexuality and, 471–473
intercultural slippage, 477–478
intergenerational communication, 394–396
intergroup communication, 631–632
internalized homonegativity, 615
  sexual satisfaction and, 760
internalized scripts, 393–394
internal migration, 64
International Association for the Study of Popular Music (IASPM), 1043
International Classification of Diseases (ICD), 551n.8
International Conference of Population and Development, 706–708
International Day Against Homophobia, Transphobia, and Biphobia (IDAHO), 770
international dissidence, 508–510
International Gay Rodeo Association (IGRA), 162–163
International Journal of Cultural Studies, 850
international students, 123–124
international tourism, 65
International Union of Gay Athletes, 833–834
International Women's Day, 91–92
internet, 485–486
  FOSTA/SESTA impacts on, 577–578
  hookup apps, 487
Internet Relay Chats (IRCs), 483, 485–486, 493
Interpersonal Exchange Model of Sexual Satisfaction (IEMSS), 758–759
interpersonal factors, in marriage decisions, 528
interpersonal relationships, work and navigating, 437–440, 450–451
  communicating LGBTQ+ identities in, 438–440
interpersonal skills, in CNM communities, 557–559
interpretive turn, 1207
intersectional homonormativity, 157–158

intersectionality, 119–120, 157, 322
  age and, 446–447
  disidentification and, 137
  international students and, 123–124
  LGBTQ+ workers and, 444–447
  minority stress and, 621
  queer intercultural communication and, 473–475
  RJ and, 707–708
  social support studies and, 775–777
  transfeminisms and, 499–501
intersectional LGBTQ+ organizing, 447–449
intersectional reflexivity, 695–696
intersectional work experiences, 444–449
intersex, 505, 535
interview research, queering, 1217
Interview with the Vampire (Rice), 1121
In the Pink (television program), 1068–1069
intimate and romantic letters, 944–946
intimate justice, 584–585
intimate partner violence (IPV), 283–284
intimate relationships, social support and, 778
invisibility
  healthcare and, 264–265
invisibilization, 64
Invisible Man (Ellison), 1126
Ipas, 708–709
IPV. *See* intimate partner violence
IRCs. *See* Internet Relay Chats
Irwin, Robert M., 67
ISA. *See* Ideological State Apparatus
"Is Kinship Always Already Heterosexual?" (Butler, J.), 1128
Islamophobia, 876, 880
Israel, 879, 897–898
Issa, Tatiana, 18
It Gets Better (video campaign), 216–217, 698, 913–914
I Thought People Like That Killed Themselves (Rofes), 391–392
It's All Relative (television series), 818
ITV. *See* Independent Television
"I tweet honestly, I tweet passionately" (Marwick and Boyd), 1053

Jackson, Mattie, 940
Jagose, Annamarie, 189, 366–367, 582–583
James, P. D., 1127–1128
James, Robin, 1076
Jamieson, Kathleen Hall, 1012
Jansen, Wikke, 923–924
Japan, 54–56
  ethnocentrism in, 54–55
  lesbians in, 52–53

media and popular culture and, 57
queer formations in, 48–49
speculative fiction and, 1119
Jarchow, Stephen, 805–806
Jarman, Derek, 1031–1032
Jarman-Ivens, Freya, 1079
Jaws (film), 800
jazz, 1075–1076, 1078
JC. See *Jump Cut*
jealousy, 559–560
jealousy communication, 559–560
Jefferess, David, 1244–1245
Jelača, Dijana, 1032
Jemisin, N. K., 1126–1127
Jennings, John, 992
Jenny Woolworth Women in Punk Archive, 1081
Jensen, Helle, 820
Jensen, Robert, 851
Jett, Joan, 1079
Jewel's Catch One (documentary), 803
jin lan hui (golden orchid association), 418–419
jock persona, 859
Johnson, Amber, 421
Johnson, E. Patrick, 108, 117–120, 171, 194–195, 417–418, 420–421, 591, 840, 843–844, 1225–1226, 1228–1229
  on letters, 944–945
  racially situated knowledges and, 1247
  on representation in *Queer as Folk*, 1020
  on whiteness of queer theory, 1156
Johnson, Margaret, 1014
Johnson, Marsha P., 502, 1192–1193, 1229
Johnson, Michael, 843
Johnson, Randal, 7, 12–13
Johnston, Jill, 586
Joint United Nations Program on AIDS (UNAIDS), 249, 254–255, 642
Jolly, Jallicia, 708
Jones, Gwyneth, 1133
Joplin, Janis, 1078
Jotería, 476, 694
  aesthetics, 411–412
  defining, 400–401
  identity, 407
Jotería Communication Studies, 407
Jotería-historia, 409
joteríastoria, 409
Jotería Studies, 412–413
  aesthetics and, 411–412
  authors and writings in, 402–403
  documenting and fighting oppression and, 403–404

entry into and influence on communication, 405–408
history of, 401–405
intercultural communication and, 407–408
methodologies, 408–412
  personal, 408–410
  theories in the flesh, 410–411
origins of, 402
praxis and transformation and, 422
safe spaces and, 404
Joto Caucus, 404
Journal of Autoethnography, 1153
Journal of Film and Video, 1062, 1071
Journal of GLBT Family Studies, 777, 780
Journal of Homosexuality, 851
Journal of International and Intercultural Communication, 118–119, 471–472, 1247
Journal of Popular Music Studies, 1043–1044, 1047
Juhasz, Alexandra, 173
Julien, Isaac, 793–794, 796, 801–802, 1029
Jump Cut (*JC*) (journal), 850, 857
Jumping the Broom (film), 798
Just Between Us (Núñez Noriega), 83–84
Justice, Daniel Heath, 1120

Kafka, Franz, 548
kaifang, 28–29
Kälin, Matthias, 15
Kanai, Akane, 492
The Kappa Child (Goto), 1129
Karimi, Aryan, 68
Karmen Geï (film), 1016–1017
Kassabian, A., 1056
Kato, David, 802–803, 1157–1158
Katter, Camila, 19
Keane, Bil, 1004
Keane, Jeff, 1004
Keegan, Cael, 214, 492, 1021
Keis, Bridget, 1032
Kendall, Christopher N., 847–848, 851–852
Kenya, 648
Kerndt, Peter R., 854
Kerr, Peg, 1124–1125
Kerrigan, Páraic, 819–820, 822–823, 1063, 1071
Khuntha, 637–638
Kiki (documentary), 803
Kilhefner, Don, 834
Kimmel, Michael, 376
Kindr campaign, 488
Kindred (Butler, O.), 992, 1126, 1132
Kinear, Greg, 233
King, Alan, 833
King, Sisco, 698

kinship
  queering, 713–717
  ritualized relations of, 459
Kipnis, Laura, 866
Kirchhoff, Herbert, 547–548
Kirmizigül, Mahsun, 1017
Kiss, Mark, 851, 856–857
Kleinhans, Chuck, 850
Kline, Kevin, 7
Kluge, Alexander, 687
Knabe, Susan, 1124–1125
knowledge
  Foucault and, 191–193
  fugitive, 1245
  racially situated, 1247
Koestenbaum, W., 1046
Kotsur, Troy, 232–233
K-Pop, 493
Kramer, Larry, 171–172, 936, 939
Krasteva, Anna, 375–376
Kuaer, 108, 421
kuaer theory, 418
  influence of, 421–422
  three awakenings and, 418–421
ku'er, 26–27
  in Chinese media and pop culture, 974–977
Kunzel, Regina, 155–156
Kushner, Tony, 1124–1125
Kuusisto, Stephen, 238–239
Kwan, Stanley, 978–979

L (app), 29
Labaki, Amir, 18
labor
  defining, 574
  reproductive, 574
  sex work and, 573–576
de Lacerda Júnior, Luiz Francisco Buarque, 7–8, 10, 14–15
Ladder (periodical), 941, 943–944
Ladyfests, 1075–1076, 1080–1082
Lady Gaga, 1045
Lady in the Dark (television program), 832
Laerte-se (documentary), 19
La Fountain-Stokes, Lawrence, 84–85, 87
Lai, Larissa, 1128–1129
lala, 52
Lambda Legal, 296–297
Lampião da Esquina (publication), 14–15
Landa, Alfredo, 95
Landsberg, Alison, 1027–1028
Lane, Nikki, 475–476

language
  changes for, 431
  heterosexism and, 261
  homophobic, 426
  inclusive, 442
  RuPaul's Drag Race and, 1101–1102
Lan Kwai Fong (LKF), 34–35, 38
Lan Yu (film), 978–979
Larrañaga, Carlos, 95
Lars and the Real Girl (film), 234–235, 693–695
LASSO. *See* least absolute shrinkage and selection operator
Latham, Rob, 1116–1117
Latin America, 64
  future research directions, 87–88
  gay marriage in, 82
  LGBT organizations in, 67
  modern adversities of queer, 64–67
  political uses of homophobic insult, 65–66
  queer as performance and, 86–87
  queer cinema of, 85–86
  queer ethnographies and, 82–84
  sexile or queer migration, 84–85
Latin American Studies Association, 404
Latina/o Communication Studies Division, 407–408
Latinidad, 459, 462–463
Latinx, emergence of term, 464
Latinx sexuality, political identification of, 112
Latitud 0, 248
Latour, Bruno, 824–825
Lauer, Samantha, 799
Laurel, Stan, 1091
de Lauretis, Teresa, 137, 188, 212, 217–218, 417
Law, John, 507
Law, Jude, 1070
Lawrence, Aaron, 862
Lawrence, Denasia, 144
Laws of Desire (Smith, P. J.), 93
lazi, 27
Le, Peter, 58, 159
leadership
  drag and, 1210
  performativity and, 1212
  queering, 1210–1212
  sexual desire and, 1211
Leal, Antonio, 3–4
Leal, Leandra, 19
Leap, William L., 865
Lear, Norman, 833–834
least absolute shrinkage and selection operator (LASSO), 1176
LeBlanc, Michael, 1014

Lee, Ang, 422
Lee, Carl, 792
Lee, Wenshu, 418, 421, 1247
   three awakenings of, 418–421
The Left Hand of Darkness (Le Guin), 1121
Legacy Project for LGBT Moving Image Preservation, 1035–1036
legalization, of sex work, 577–580
Le Guin, Ursula K., 1121, 1125–1126
Leidolf, Esther Morris, 505
Leijonhufvud, S., 1055–1056
LeMaster, Benny, 474, 695
LeMaster, Lore/tta, 590
Lemebel, Pedro, 83
Lemonade (film), 1126
Leonard, M., 1045
Leopold II (King), 1134
Lesage, Julia, 850
Lesbian, BiMujeres, and Trans Caucus, 404
Lesbian, Gay, Bisexual, and Transgender Climate Inventory (LGBTCI), 774
Lesbian Home Movie Project, 1035–1036
Lesbianismo-Feminismo (documentary), 18
lesbian liberation movement, 342
lesbian motherhood, 195
Lesbian Mothers (documentary), 18
lesbian porn, 848–849
lesbian pregnancy, 269–272
Lesbian/Woman (Martin, D., and Lyon), 938–939, 942
Letisch, Stevan, 7–8
Let's Stay Together (television series), 841–842
letters, 934–935
   evidence of gendered relations in, 936–937
   intimate and romantic, 944–946
   as LGBTQ+ rhetoric, 941–946
   LGBTQ+ rhetoric studies and, 935–941
   public and political, 941–944
letter-writing campaigns, 942–943
Levine, Adam, 492
Lewis, Desiree, 641
Lewis, John, 994
Lewis, Ryan, 698
"Ley de Vagos y Maleantes" (Vagrancy Law), 92
"Ley sobre peligrosidad y rehabilitación social" (Law of dangerousness and social rehabilitation), 92
"Ley Trans" (Trans Law), 91–92
"Ley Zerolo," 91–92
LGBTCI. *See* Lesbian, Gay, Bisexual, and Transgender Climate Inventory
LGBT Health Certificate program, 313
LGBT Identity and Online New Media, 1052
LGBT Outreach Center (LOC), 447

LGBTQ+
   background information for, 295–300
   barriers to healthcare for, 299–300
   disclosure motivations, 306–307
   disclosure strategies, 307–310
   discrimination, 296–297, 323–325
   emotional experience in romantic relationships, 321–323
   global trends in acceptance of, 770–771
   health behaviors, 297
   healthcare and provider education, 298–299
   health issues, 297–298
   televisability of, 820
   terminology and scope, 521–522
   uninsured, 297–298
LGBTQ aging
   queer future and, 396
   research on, 392–394
LGBTQ centers, 244–245
LGBTQ+ cinema, in Spain, 93–103
LGBTQ+ communities
   CNM and, 556–557
   inclusiveness in, 525
   minority stress and, 615
LGBTQ films, 792–796
   blockbusters, 800–801
   mainstream African American, 796–797
LGBTQ+ letters
   future research directions, 947–948
   intimate and romantic, 944–946
   public and political, 941–944
LGBTQ+ marriage, 522–525, 601–602
   background for, 522
   deciding to marry, 526–529
   family identity and, 527–528
   future research directions, 531
   identity and, 524–525
   individuals and, 522–525
   psychological impacts on individuals of, 523–524
   relationship-related perceptions and, 526
   relationships and, 525–530
      experiences within, 526–529
      with friends and families, 529–530
      impact of, 529
   terminology and scope, 521–522
LGBTQ+ POC, minority stress and, 617–618
LGBTQ politics, 107–108
LGBTQ+ relationships
   emotional experiences of, 321–323
   minority stress and, 603–604
   models for stress in, 326–327
   partners coping with stress, 328–330

LGBTQ+ marriage (*continued*)
  population-based survey studies, 323
  psychosocial impacts of legal recognition of, 325–326
  relationship science scholarship on, 322–323
  research in, 734
  stress in, 326
LGBTQ+ rhetoric
  letters as, 941–946
  letters in studies of, 935–941
LGBTQ television networks, 1063
LGBTQ+ workers, 424–425
  disclosure and, 432–437
    closeting, 433
    navigating complexities of, 435–437
    outing, 434–435
    passing, 433–434
  future research directions, 449–451
  inclusive and exclusive policies, 440–444
  interpersonal relationship navigation and, 437–440
    communicating identities and, 438–440
  intersectionality and, 444–447
  intersectional work experiences and organizing, 444–449
  workplace discrimination and, 425–432
    actions for change and, 431–432
    material consequences of, 429–430
    microaggressions, 425–427
    worker protection laws, 427–429
LGBTQ+ youth cultures
  growing up in post-homophobic world, 912–914
  rethinking risk and, 907–909
  self-expression and community formation, 909–910
  social media and, 906–907
    coming out and, 917–921
    early Internet precursors to, 911–912
    trans cultures, 921–923
    youth voices and, 923–926
Liberace, 1079
lieux de mémoire (sites of memory), 1027–1028
Life after Life (Atkinson), 1132–1133
lifestreaming, 915–916
Lil' Kim, 1082
Lily, Shangay, 6, 93
Lim, Eng-Beng, 1250
Lim, Song Hwee, 972, 975
Limite (film), 8–9
Lincoln, Abraham, 936
Lindenstraße (television series), 819–820
Lipari, Lisbeth, 174–175, 941–944
Liquid Streaming (Leijonhufvud), 1055–1056
Listening to the Sirens (Peraino), 1046
literary hierarchies, 1114–1115

Little House on the Prairie, 1129
Little Richard, 1078
Little Sisters Book and Art Emporium case, 851
Liu, Petrus, 347
Liu Jen-peng, 343
livability, 678
Livermon, Xavier, 643–644
Livingston, Jennie, 802, 1095
Li Yinhe, 975
Li Yugang, 973–974
LKF. *See* Lan Kwai Fong
Lo, Malinda, 1129–1130
Lobdell, Lucy/Joseph Israel, 939
LOC. *See* LGBT Outreach Center
LOGO, 804, 1065
loneliness, 913
long-distance information, 67–68
longitudinal dyadic analysis, 1170–1171
Longtime companion (film), 1030
Looking for Langston (film), 794, 796, 801–802, 1032
Lopes, Denilson, 8–9, 86
López, Nando, 102–103
López Vázquez, José Luis, 95
Lorde, Audre, 119–120, 170–171, 174–175, 402, 417, 587, 590, 1246
Los Javis, 101
Lothian, Alexis, 1132
Louro, Guacira Lopes, 5
Love, Kylie Sonique, 1103, 1105
Love, Simon (film), 800, 807, 1018–1020
Love after the End (Whitehead), 1120
Love and Hip Hop (television show), 139–141, 844
Lozano-Reich, Nina Maria, 584–585
Lucas, Michael, 855
Lucas Entertainment, 855, 865
Lucian of Samosata, 1118–1119
El lugar sin límites (film), 85–86
Lugones, Maria, 403–404, 505–507, 512
Luiz, Samuel, 93
Lu Xun, 1119
The L Word (television series), 831
Lynch, David, 821–822
Lynch, John, 174
Lynch, Marshawn, 141–142
Lynes, George Platt, 546–547
Lynn, Elizabeth, 1121, 1129–1130
Lyon, Phyllis, 938–939, 942
Lyons, Jake, 859, 865
Lyotard, Jean-François, public realm theory and, 687

Macdonald, Hettie, 369
Macías-González, Victor, 67

Mack, Ashley, 1252–1253
Mackay, Finn, 923
MacKenzie, D., 1048
Mackie, Anthony, 798
MacKinnon, Catherine, 573, 851
Macklemore, 698
MacLennan Incident, 30–31
Macunaíma (film), 4
Maddux, Stu, 1036
Madison, D. Soyini, 221–222
The Mad Man (Delany), 1124–1125
Mad Max: Fury Road (film), 234–235
Madrid, Spain, 93
Maestre-Brotons, Antoni, 490
Magai, 637–638
Maggenti, Maria, 796
magic realism, 1117
Mahaffey, Zander, 943
major life events, social support and, 769
Making Things Perfectly Queer, 974
Malakaj, Ervin, 1019
Malici, Luca, 819–820
Malika, 1082
Maluco, Capadócio, 4
Mama, Amina, 649
"Mama's baby, Papa's maybe" (Spillers), 498–499
Mambo Taxi, 1081
Management Communication Quarterly (journal), 1215–1216
Manalansan, Martin, 343
Måneskin, 1075–1076
Manifesto Entendido (Trevisan), 13
The Man in the Moone (Godwin), 1118–1119
Mann, Abby, 387
Manning, Chelsea, 174–175
Manning, Jimmy, 583–584, 587
Mansur, Fauzi, 15
Mao Zedong, 28–29
Mapes, Meggie, 474
March for Women's Lives, 707
marching, 236
March trilogy (Lewis, J.), 994
marginalization
    HIV and, 243
    parenting and, 713
mariposa, 411–412
marriage, 601–602
marriage equality, 523, 527, 1142n.18
marriage resistance, 418–419
Martin, Alfred, 814–815, 837, 1062, 1065
Martin, Del, 938–939, 942
Martin, Fran, 342, 977–979

Martin, Trayvon, 141–144, 620
Martinez, Jacqueline M., 407–408
Martinez Correa, Luiz Antonio, 18
Martínez-San Miguel, Yolanda, 84
martyrdom, 546–547
Marwick, A. E., 1053
Marxist feminism, 575
masculinity
    gay pornography and, 855–856
    hegemonic, 550n.3
    homosexual, 539, 548, 550n.3
masking, 347, 776–777
mass cultural genre system, 1114
"The Mass Public and Mass Subject" (Warner, Mark), 687–688
Mateen, Omar, 879
mate-guarding behaviors, 559–560
material feminism, 574
maternity care, 710
Matlin, Marlee, 232–233
Matlovich, Leonard, 174–175
Matoso, Glauco, 19
Mauro, Humberto, 8
Maus (Spiegelman), 993, 1116
Maus, Fred Everett, 1076–1077
Mayday Space, 1234–1235
Mayer, David, 1014
Mayer-Rokitansky-Küster-Hauser syndrome (MRKH), 505
Mayne, Debbie, 938, 944–945
Mayo, Alfredo, 94
Mbembe, Achille, 503, 893
McCarthy, Kevin, 213, 217–218
McCaughan, Edward J., 67
McClary, Susan, 1046
McClodden, Tiona, 802
McConatha, Melina, 473–474, 478
McCreary, Donald R., 851
McDermott, Daragh T., 852
McDonald, Chrishaun Reed, "CeCe," 803
McGlotten, Shaka, 71, 488, 586
McIntosh, Dawn, 407, 471, 475
McIntyre, Vonda, 1121
McKinnon, Scott, 1029–1030
McLelland, Mark, 977
McPherson, Heather, 1017
McRobbie, Angela, 1043–1045
McRuer, Robert, 231, 233, 237, 901
Measure B, 853–854
measurement invariance, 1170–1171
Measure of Family Acceptance, 772–773
Meccia, Ernesto, 82

media. *See also* digital media
   Chinese censorship of, 980–983
   Chineseness in queer, 977–980
   cultivation theory and, 954
   deregulation and globalization impacts on, 1063
   disability representations in, 232–235
   female sexual objectification and, 962–963
   geolocative turn in, 67
   homonationalism and, 874
   memory and, 1027–1028
   online transition, 66–67
   predigital, transnational flows and, 65–66
   QAS and, 650–651
   Queer Asia and, 56–58
   queer/*ku'er* in Chinese, 974–977
   safe spaces and, 679
   sexual attitude depictions in, 952–953
      abuse *versus* consent, 958–959
      consequences and, 959
      emotions and, 959–960
      focus in, 956–959
      humor in, 960–961
      mainstream, 956
      sexual health depictions, 957–958
      stereotypes in, 961–963
      theoretical perspectives on effects of, 954
      worldview cultivation and, 954
   sexual content in, 952
   Stonewall and representation in, 832
   transnational queer networks and, history of, 64–67
media culture
   DIY, 991–992, 1068
   predigital, gay beauty ideal in, 484–485
media studies, queer production studies and, 1062–1063
mediated sex advice, 585–586
media text, distribution of, 1063
mediation, music and, 1048
medical education
   discussions of sex in, 261
   heterosexism in, 259
   HIV and, 260–261
   transgender people and, 261
medical forms, 266
medicalization
   of queer bodies, 259
   of sexual communication research, 753
Meier, Pierre-Alain, 15
Melero, Alejandro, 94–95
de Mello, Fernando Collor, 14
melodrama, 1011–1012
   characteristics, structures, and styles, 1012–1015
   critiques of, 1015
   defining, 1013
   narrative features, 1013–1014
   purposes, impacts, and problems, 1015–1021
Melrose Place (television show), 389–390
Mema's House, Mexico City (Prieur), 83
memba, 27
memorable messages, 767
Memorial to Marriage (installation), 175
memory
   archival identifications and, 1229
   ephemerality of, 177–178
   media and, 1027–1028
   methods of passing on, 1027–1028
   nostalgia and, 1032–1033
   prosthetic, 1027–1028
   queer, screens and, 1028–1032
   queering of, 175–179
   technologies of, 1027–1028
memory booms, 170
memoryscapes, 1235–1236
Memory's Caretaker (Bonin-Rodriguez and Bailey), 171
memory studies, 170, 1027
MEN, 1081
Men, Women and Muxe' in the Isthmus of Tehuantepec (Miano Borruso), 65
Mendelsohn, Farah, 1114
Mendonça, Kléber, 19–20
Men of Israel (film), 865
Menon, Alok V., 493–494
mental health, 238, 251
Mercer, John, 852, 857, 859–860, 862–863, 866
Merril, Judith, 1113–1114
Meruane, Lina, 5–6
mestizaje subjectivity, 458–459
mestiza queer, 417
metageneration, 222–223
methodology
   defining, 1146
   queer, 1146–1147
   scavenger, 1147–1148
#MeToo, 1252–1253
Meu corpo é político (documentary), 19
Meulen, Emily van der, 853
The Mexican (film), 390
Mexico, political cartoons in, 67
Mexico marimacho (Quevedo y Zubieta), 66
de Meyer, Adolphe, 546–547
Miano Borruso, Marinella, 65
Miao, Vera, 420
microaggressions, 425–427
   exoticization, 427
   forms of, 425

homophobic language and, 426
invalidation tactics, 663
organizational structure and, 426
policies for counteracting, 441
workplace policies and, 426
Middle Passage, 1126
Middleton, R., 1044
Midnight Cowboy (film), 387
migration, 64, 446
   coming out after, 70
   decisions and paths to, 67–69
   diasporic, 106
   digital media and, 68–69
   identity-building and belonging and, 69
   practicalities of, 68–69
   queer identities and, 70
   reasons for, 123
   settling in after, 69–71
military children, 729
military family communication, 723
   study of, 723–724
      future of queer, 727–729
      queer, 725–727
Milk (film), 1030, 1034
Milk, Harvey, 174–175, 180, 942
Miller, Carolyn, 1012, 1016
Miller, Lucy, 1188–1189
Miller, Terry, 216–217, 913
Miller, Tim, 222
Millet, Ignasi, 100–101
Minaj, Nicki, 1082
Minha mãe é uma peça (film trilogy), 16
minority, 545–546
   media and stereotyping of, 962
minority stress, 327–329, 767
   additive, 617–618
   defining, 614–618
   discrimination and, 323–325
   experiencing and coping with, 321–323
   intersectionality and, 621
   LGBTQ+ communities and, 615
   LGBTQ+ related processes, 767
   limitations of research, 619
   queer theory and, 621–622
   relational termination and, 603–604
   relationships and, 613–614
      calls for change and, 618–619
      future research directions, 621–622
      quality of, 615–617
   romantic partner and coping with, 324–325
   same-sex couples and, 736–737
   sexual satisfaction and, 758–759

   social identity and, 619–620
   social support and, 741
   stigma and, 736–737
minor literature, 535–536, 545–546, 548
minor photography, 535–536, 546–548
Mi querida señorita/My Dearest Lady (film), 95
Mira, Alberto, 92–93, 95
Miranda, Carmen, 9, 18
Mirzoeff, Nicholas, 1120
Miskolci, Richard, 5
misogyny, 1115–1116
   marriage and, 527
Miss Fanny's Seaside Lovers (film), 1091
Missing and Murdered Indigenous Women, 1252–1253
Miss Money, 1081–1082
Miss Visa Denied, 1225–1226
Mitchell Brothers Theater, 571
MLM. *See* multilevel modeling
MLVAR. *See* multilevel VAR
mnemonicide, 176
Mobile Cultures (Berry, Martin, F., and Yue), 977–978, 1052–1053
Mobile Homecoming Experimental Archive, 222–223
mobility
   global, 1250–1251
Modarelli, Alejandro, 83
model minority, 604
Modern Family (television series), 815–816, 823–824, 831, 834–835
modernism, in Brazilian queer cinema, 8–9
modernization, Brazil and, 3
Modern Language Association, 404
Moesha (television series), 841–843
Mogrovejo, Norma, 84
El-Mohtar, Amin, 1134–1135
molecularization, 537–546
   of photography, 535–536
Molly House raids, 1192–1193
Monáe, Janelle, 1126
Mondal, Mimi, 1119
monogamish relationships, 743
Monsiváis, Carlos, 83
Montenegro, Carlos, 66
Montoya, Richard, 461–462
"Monumental" (exhibition), 143
monuments, 698–700
The Moon Is a Harsh Mistress (Heinlein), 1130
Moonlight (film), 791, 799–800, 805
"Moonlight: A Tale of Heartbreak, Brilliance, and Interhuman Artistry" (Lauer), 799
Moore, Alan, 1116
Moraga, Cherríe, 136, 170–171, 402, 417, 475, 1246

moral insubordination, 64
moralizing timelines, 223
Morbidity and Mortality Weekly Report (CDC), 276
More, Thomas, 1118–1119
Moreira, Rita, 18
Moreman, Shane T., 407, 471, 477
Moreno, Antonio, 7, 10–11, 14–15
Morgan, Joan, 587
Morgan, Tracy, 1093–1094
Morrill, Angie, 1253
Morris, Charles E., III, 169, 171–175, 177, 179–180, 584, 694, 696–699, 936, 942
Morris, Paul, 861–862
Morris, Wesley, 794
Morrison, Todd G., 848, 851–852, 856, 864–865
Morrisroe, Mark, 547
Mosbacher, Dee, 802
motherhood, heteronormativity and, 712
Motherlines (Charnas), 1121
MotherWork, 1153
"Mountain Ways" (Le Guin), 1125
Movement Advancement Project, 428
moviment gai, 92
Mowlabocus, Sharif, 486, 488–489, 493
MRKH. *See* Mayer-Rokitansky-Küster-Hauser syndrome
Mudimbe, V. Y., 641
Mugabe, Robert, 640–641
Una mujer fantástica (film), 1014, 1018
multilevel modeling (MLM), 1165–1167
multilevel VAR (MLVAR), 1176–1177
Mumbai Pride March, 58
"Mundane Manifesto" (Ryman), 1117
mundane science fiction, 1117
"El Mundo Zurdo," 220
Muñoz, José Esteban, 85–87, 170–171, 190, 212–213, 217–218, 457–458, 460, 475, 1076, 1156, 1232
  on memory, 1033
  on queer theory as utopian, 1131
  queer worldmaking and, 687–690, 692
Munro, Brenna, 1247–1248
Murder (film), 1091–1092
Murderball (film), 233–234
Murphy, Eddie, 837–838, 840
Murphy, Ryan, 807, 815, 1031
Murray, Matthew, 832
Murray, Natalia Danesi, 945–946
Museveni, Yoweri, 645–646
music
  affordances and, 1048
  digital realm and, 1047–1057
    algorithms, 1050–1051
    social media, 1049–1050
  DIY culture and, 1080–1081
  gender and, 1044–1045
  identity and, 1042–1045
    LGBTQ+, 1045–1047
  mediation and, 1048
  popular
    queering, 1075–1076
    transing, 1083–1084
  social media and, 1049–1050
Musical Identities (Hargreaves et al.), 1044
music culture, 1042
  transing, 1083–1084
The Music Industry (Wikström), 1055
Music in Everyday Life (DeNora), 1044
musicology, 1042–1045
  queering, 1076–1078
    subcultural studies and, 1077–1078
music streaming platforms, 1050, 1054–1057
Muslim others, 879–882
Mutua-Mambo, Consolata, 649
muxeidad, 511
Muxe identity, 511
muxerista consciousness, 410
My Beautiful Laundrette (film), 366
"My Old Kentucky Homo" (Morris, C.), 171–172
My Prairie Home (documentary), 1157
My Real Children (Walton), 1132–1133
MySpace, 911–912, 1049, 1052
Mythgarden, 1068
mythical norm, 1190–1191
myth-making, 695
"My Words to Victor Frankenstein Above the Village of Chamonix" (Stryker, S.), 1118

NACCS. *See* National Association for Chicana and Chicano Studies
Nagib, Lucia, 7, 15–16
Nakayama, Thomas, 171, 220, 471, 479, 589, 694, 696, 1247
name changes, structural barriers of, 426
NAMES Project, 175, 253–254, 1028–1029
nanshoku, 48–49
Na'puti, Tiara, 1252–1253
NAR (film), 1020
narcocorridos, 141
narrative
  attitudes and, 953
  cautionary, 385–387, 390
  crip theory and, 237–239
  internalized scripts, 393–394
  melodrama and, 1013–1014
  personal, 220, 420
    collaborative, 222

of queer developmental failure and punishment, 387
of self-destructive behavior, 391–392
narrative film, 366
Nash, Jennifer C., 500, 588
National Association for Chicana and Chicano Studies (NACCS), 404
National Center for Transgender Equity, 429
National Coming Out Day program, 341–342
National Communication Association (NCA), 404, 407–408
National Endowment for the Arts (NEA), 793–795
National Gay and Lesbian Archives, 1081
National Gay Task Force, 833–834, 1066
National HIV/AIDS Strategy, 249
nationalism, 875, 877–878
    Catalan, 881–882
    disability, 901
    sexual, 881
nationality, *RuPaul's Drag Race* and, 1101–1102
National Latina Institute for Reproductive Health, 708
National Lesbian Health Organization, 299
National LGBTQ+ Task Force, 446, 708–709
    "Queering Reproductive Justice" tool kit, 705
nation-statehood, refusing neoliberal capitalist logics of, 507–510
Nazis, 65, 375–376, 536–537, 541, 551n.4, 551n.8
NBC, 1066
NCA. *See* National Communication Association
Ndegeocello, Me'shell, 1082
NEA. *See* National Endowment for the Arts
necropolitics, 502–504
    homonationalism and, 893–894
Needham, Gary, 343
Negt, Oskar, 687
Nelson, Lydia, 700
neoliberalism, 236–237, 493–494
    anti-LGBT violence in Africa and, 645–646
    coming out discourse and, 344–345
    consequences of, 576
    refusing logics of, 507–510
    sexual politics and, 875
    sex work and, 576–577
neoliberal market economy, 27–28
Neon (documentary), 804
neo-Nazis, 375–376, 381–382
Nestle, Joan, 1233
Netflix, 19, 805–806
    RuPaul's Drag Race and, 1097
the Netherlands, 880–881
Neto, Trigueira, 11
net safety software, 908–909
network analysis, 1176–1177

"Networked Privacy" (Marwick and Boyd), 1053
The New Black (documentary), 802–803
Newitz, Annalee, 1129
New Maricón Cinema (Venkatesh), 86
The New Normal (television series), 834–835
New Queer, 1031–1032
New Queer Cinema, 368, 792, 794, 796, 802, 805, 834
New Sexual Satisfaction Scale, 757–758
Newton, Esther, 188
New York Dance and Performance Awards, 253–254
New York Lesbian Herstory Archives, 1035
New York Public Library Digital Archives, 1229
NGOs. *See* nongovernmental organizations
Nicholson, Jack, 233
Nicht der Homosexuelle ist pervers, sondern die Situation, in der er lebt (film), 821–822
Nietzsche, Friedrich, 193
Niffenegger, Audrey, 1133
Nkom, Alice, 645–646
Noah's Arc (television series), 797–798, 841, 843–844
No desearás al vecino del quinto/Though Shalt not Covet Thy Fifth Floor Neighbor (film), 95
No Future (Edelman), 211–212, 1076, 1127, 1131
"No Future" attitude, 1076
nonbinary people
    disclosure at work and, 436
    reproduction and, 710
nondiscrimination policies, 356
nongovernmental organizations (NGOs), 29–30, 878
nonrealism, 1116–1117
nonromantic relational goals, 360
non-verbal behavior
    discrimination and, 263–264
Noomin, D., 993
Nora, Pierre, 170, 1027–1028
Normal, Ohio (television series), 834
normalization, 534
normalizing ethic, 690
normative heterosexuality, 110–111
normative ideology, disidentification and, 147
normative inquiry, 1210
normative orgasmic imperative, 587–588
normative public discourses, pleasure and resisting, 586–589
normativities, 231
    designated spaces and, 677
    policies reinforcing, 443–444
    queer melodrama and, 1019–1021
    queer TV studies and, 817–819
norm-critical approaches, 1214
Norris, David, 821–822
North Sea Texas (film), 368–369, 377–382

nostalgia, memory and, 1032–1033
Notes on Camp (Sontag), 1079
Novack, Kate, 803
Novik, Naomi, 1115–1116, 1128
Nowak, R., 1055–1056
Nowlan, Bob, 370–371
NPO, 821–822
Nujoma, Sam, 640–641
Núñez Noriega, Guillermo, 83–84
nü tongzhi, 973–974
Nyanzi, Stella, 637–639, 645–646, 649
Nyeck, S. N., 640

Oaks, Laury, 711–712
Obama, Barack, 724–725, 942–943
O Bandido da Luz Vermelha (film), 13–14
O Beijo (film), 11
Obergefell v. Hodges, 325, 522, 599, 724–725, 737, 742
"Obito travesti" (film), 509
objectification, 962–963
O'Brien, Anna, 1063, 1071
occupational segregation, 1209
Ochoa, Marcia, 87
Office of National Policy, 249
Oh, David, 839
O'Hara, Scott, 862
Ojeda-Sagué, Gabriel, 860
Okech, Awino, 649
Oleszczuk, Anna, 1126–1127
O menino do Gouveia (Maluco), 4
O menino e o vento, 11
On a Sunbeam (Walden), 1116
O negócio do michê (Perlongher), 82–83
120 BPM (film), 1034
The ONE National Gay & Lesbian Archives Collection, 1035–1036
"On Global Queering" (Altman), 977
online bullying, 908–909
online community, 924–925
online cultures, gay beauty ideal and, 491
online diasporic communities, 71
online disembodiment thesis, 485
online self-presentation, 1049–1050
online visual culture, 486
OnlyFans, 568, 863
On Our Backs (*OOB*) (publication), 939
ontology, 501–502
OOB. See *On Our Backs*
Open Door Policy, 28–29
Open FM, 1068–1069
openness, 735
open relationships, 554, 743

Open TV platform, 1068
O Personagem Homossexual do Cinema (Moreno), 7
Oppenheimer, Toby, 803
opposition, resistance as, 1244–1245
oral history, 403
organizational communication, 439, 450
 critical turn, 1207
 documents, diversity management and, 1213–1214
 future research directions, 1218–1219
 interpretive turn in, 1207
 queering closet and, 1214–1216
 queer studies and, 1207–1208
 trans community and, 1209
organizational ethnography, 1217–1218
organizational research methods
 autoethnography and, 1218
 coding, 1217
 ethnography, 1217–1218
 interviews, 1217
 queering, 1216–1218
 reflexivity, 1216
organizational structure, microaggressions and, 426
Orgia ou o homem que deu cria (film), 4, 12–14
Orientalism, 1244, 1250
Ortiz, José Mario, 14
Oscarito, 9
Os Trapalhões, 24n.18
Oswald, Richard, 1019
Otelo, Grande, 9
othering, 121
othermothering, 714
otherness, 1244
Otis, Hailey Nicole, 698
O torturador, 14–15
Ott, Brian, 171, 174, 589
Out (magazine), 708–709
Outfest, 1035–1036
outing, 252
 work and, 434–435
Out Online (Raun), 491
OutQ, 1063
OutServe-Service Members Legal Defense Network (SLDN), 942–943
Owens, Anthony, 840–841
Oyěwùmí, Oyèrónkẹ́, 500, 506–507

packing, 127–128
Padva, Gilad, 370–372, 861, 1013, 1020, 1032
pain, 548, 551n.8
 in visual culture, 546–547
Paleo, Lyn, 1120–1121
Palestine, 896–898

Palestinian Queers for BDS, 897
Palumbo, Donald, 1121–1122
Parable of the Sower (Butler, O.), 992
paraliterature, 1114–1115
paranoid reading, 1117–1118, 1141n.5
paratextual commentary, 1069–1070
parental suspicion, 666–667
Parente, Marlon, 19
parenting
   centering communication, 630–634
   family of origin adjustment and, 665–667
      parental pride, 667
      parental suspicions, 666–667
      perceived blame, 667
   journeys to acceptance, 628–630
   marriage decisions and, 527
   of queer offspring, 627
   reactions to children coming out, 627–628
   right to safe and healthy environments for, 713–714
   social support and, 778–779
Parents and Allies for Gay Empowerment, 666–667
Parents and Friends of Lesbians and Gays (PFLAG), 629
Pariah (film), 474, 791, 798–799
Paris is Burning (documentary), 802–803, 805, 1095, 1099–1101
Parsemain, Ava Laure, 838
participation, *RuPaul's Drag Race* and, 1096–1098
participatory storytelling, 918–919
Partido Popular (PP), 91
Partido Socialista Obrero Español (PSOE), 91
Partner Sexual Communication Scale, 279
partus sequitur ventrem, 498–499
passing
   archival labor and, 700
   strategies of, 433–434
   work and, 433–434
Passion of Christ, 546–547
Passions of the Cut Sleeve (Hinsch), 971
passive-aggressive invalidation tactics, 663
Passos, Pereira, 3
paternalism, 576–577
Pathways of Desire (Carrillo), 84–85
patient-provider disclosure, 300–310
   future opportunities, 313–314
   recommendations, guidelines, and programs, 310–313
Patton, Cindy, 188
Patton-Imani, Sandra, 715
de Paula Araújo, Vicente, 3–4
Payno, Manuel, 66
PBS, 793–794
PCARE, 1185–1186
Peaches, 1081

Pearson, Kyra, 584–585, 1122–1123
Pearson, Wendy Gay, 1121–1122
Pêcheux, Michel, 138
pedagogical space, 678
Peixoto, Mario, 8–9
Pelliccione, Damian, 806
penny press, 67
Pentecostalist Charismatic Churches, 641, 646
A People's History of American Empire (Zinn), 994
Pepe, Kristin, 1035–1036
PEPFAR. *See* President's Emergency Plan for AIDS Relief
Peppermint, 1104–1105
Peraino, J., 1046
perceived blame, 667
Pereira dos Santos, Nelson, 4
Pérez, Kimberlee, 693, 695
Pérez, Miriam Zoila, 705–706, 708–709
Pérez-Sánchez, Gema, 1247–1248
performance
   body and, 475
   of Brown sexualities, 457–459, 464–465
      contexts of, 458
      dance, 462–463
      everyday life and, 463–464
      teatro, 461–463
   collaborative, 222
   crip theory and, 237–239
   of possibilities, 221–222
   queer, 86–87
      arts-based queer communication studies and, 1155–1157
   relational, 695–696
performance studies, 238
   Brown in, 460–461
   queer temporalities in, 219–222
Performance Studies in Communication (PSC), 460–461
performative identity, 1209
performative progressiveness, 912–913
performative writing, 220
   of pleasure, 589–591
performativity, 193–194, 1188
   gender, 1089–1090
   leadership and, 1212
   social media and, 1098–1099
Performing Mexicanidad (Gutiérrez), 86
Performing Queer Latinidad (Rivera-Servera), 87
Performing Rites (Frith), 1044
periperformative statements, 380
periperformative utterances, 1188
El Periquillo Sarniento (Fernández de Lizardi), 65–66
Perlongher, Néstor, 6, 67, 82–83

Perry, Marie Louise, 939
Personal Connections in the Digital Age (Baym), 1054
personal narrative, 220, 420
    collaborative, 222
Peter, Jochen, 864
Petit, Jordi, 92
PFLAG. *See* Parents and Friends of Lesbians and Gays
phantom public, 686–687
pharmaceutical industry, 249–250
pharmacopornographic turn, 535
phenomenology, 775
Philadelphia (film), 196, 1019, 1124–1125
Philosophical Investigations (Wittgenstein), 168
Phoenix, Mavi, 1083–1084
Phoenix Pride, 1192–1193
photographic representation, 534–536
photography
    dirt and, 544
    dragz-images, 537–546
    minor, 535–536, 546–548
    molecularization of, 535–536
    studio, 552n.14
PIC. *See* prison industrial complex
pictivism, 775
pictorialism, 546–547
Piercy, Marge, 1128, 1133–1134
Pindi, Gloria, 649
Pink Agenda, 879–880
pink economy, 26
    Hong Kong *tongzhi* subject formation and, 30–31
    Taiwan *tongzhi* subject formation and, 31–32
pink herring, 172–173
pink market, 26
    class-based *tongzhi* visibility in, 36–37
    classed and raced *tongzhi* subjectivity in, 37–38
    self-censorship in PRC, 39–41
pinkwashing, 879, 895–898
PISSAR, 235–236
PISSED (installation), 143
place
    gay pornography and, 860
    queer safer sex communication and, 284–285
Placeres Ocultos (film), 94–95
PlanetRomeo, 66
planned behavior theory, 281
The Platform Society (Van Dijck et al.), 1049
Plato, 1118–1119
Playing it Queer (Taylor, J.), 1047, 1077
pleasure
    performative writing and authoethnographies of, 589–591
    representations of, 584–586

Pleasure Activism (brown, a. m.), 587
Pleasure Ninjas collective, 587
Plummer, Kenneth, 341–342
La Pocha Nostra, 419–420
Poeira de Estrelas (film), 10
poetic autoethnography, 446
poetic inquiry, 1151–1155
Poland, cross-border exchanges and local publications in, 65–66
Police Academy (film series), 394
policy dissemination, 442–443
political activism, QAS and, 648–650
political cartoons, 67
political economy
    early Chinese pink market research and, 27–28
    of sexuality, 28
political memory, 170–171
political polarization, 631
politics
    camp and, 1090
    crip theory and, 235–237
    marriage decisions and, 527
    progressive, 1248–1249
    QAS context and, 640–643
    of time, 209–211
The Politics of Dating Apps (Chan), 493
The Politics of Gay Marriage in Latin America (Díez), 82
politics of visibility, 40–41
Polk, Patrik-Ian, 797–798
polyamory, 554–556, 743
    communicating jealousy and, 560
    communication, identity, and, 560–563
    compersion and, 559–560
    family disclosure and, 561–563
    family dynamics and, 561–562
polycules, 555
polyfidelitious relationships, 555
Pons, Ventura, 96–101
Pontes, Norma Bahia, 18
Poole, Wakefield, 847
popular culture
    Chineseness in queer, 977–980
    music
        history of queering, 1078–1083
        queering, 1075–1076
        transing, 1083–1084
    Queer Asia and, 56–58
    queer Chinese media and, 969–970
    queer/ku'er in Chinese, 974–977
popular media, queer temporality and, 216–217
Popular Music (journal), 1043, 1047
Popular Music, Digital Technology and Society (Prior), 1055

Popular Music and Society (journal), 1043–1044
popular music culture, queering, 1075–1076
popular music studies, 1042–1045
popular press, 67
Porfiriato, 67
PornHub, 568
pornochanchada, 14, 16
pornography, 571
    hegemonic representations and, 586
    as worldview, 856
Porn Studies (*PS*) (journal), 847, 849, 852
porn wars, 852
Porter, Edward S., 1091
Portrait of Jason (film), 792, 801–802
Pose (television series), 807, 1031
positive relationship functioning, relationship maintenance and, 735–736
positivity, 735
postcolonialism
    anti-LGBT violence in Africa and, 645–646
    queering decolonization and, 1249–1251
    theoretical alignments of, 1243–1246
"Post-feminism and Popular Culture" (McRobbie), 1045
posthumanism, 1112–1113
postmemory, 1027–1028
postmodern feminism, 1207–1208
Postmodernism and Popular Culture (McRobbie), 1045
Post-Op, 508–509
postporn, 508–509
poststructuralism, 1213
POV (television series), 793
power
    Foucault and, 191–193
    homonationalism and, 893
    organizing and, 1207
    queer intercultural communication and, 478–479
    sovereign, 893
power bottom prototype, 859
power dynamics, 738–739
Powertool (film), 859
PP. *See* Partido Popular
praxis
    Jotería Studies and, 422
PRC *tongzhi*
    subject formation, 28–30
    subjectivity, 28
preaching stories, 1113
precariousness, 52
Preciado, Paul, 10–11, 535–536, 541
predigital media, transnational flows and, 65–66
predigital media cultures, gay beauty ideal in, 484–485

pre-exposure prophylaxis (PrEP), 248, 250, 268–269, 281, 298, 303, 472–473
    queer safer sex communication and, 285–286
pregnancy
    provider recommendations and, 271–272
    queer-friendly healthcare and, 267
    queer healthcare communication and, 269–272
Pregnancy (art installation), 710–711
Premsela, Benno, 821–822
PrEP. *See* pre-exposure prophylaxis
President's Emergency Plan for AIDS Relief (PEPFAR), 249, 642
Presley, Elvis, 1078
Price, Kimala, 708
Pride (film), 1034
Pride Järva, 881
La Prieta (Anzaldúa), 170–171
Prieur, Annick, 83
Primer Movimiento Peruano, 248
The Primetimers, 395
Primus, Rebecca, 175, 934–935, 945–946
Prior, N., 1055
prison culture, 155
prison industrial complex (PIC), 1185–1186
prison settings, 859–860
prison sexual politics, 155–156
Pritchard, Eric Darnell, 939–940
privacy rule decisions, 562–563
private information, 632–633
private sex parties, 284–285
procreative liberty, 712
Profane Culture (Willis), 1043
professionalism, 431, 1209, 1215
Professor Marston and the Wonder Women (film), 804
Program for LGBTQ Health, 313
progressive politics, 1248–1249
progressive sexuality, 891
promiscuity
    assumptions of, 262
prosperity gospel, 641–642
prosthetic memory, 1027–1028
prostitution, 578
prototypes, gay pornography and, 858–860
Prove it on Me Blues (song), 1078
Proyecto 10Bis, 510
Pryor, Jaclyn, 1230
PS. See Porn Studies
PSBs. *See* public service broadcasters
PSC. *See* Performance Studies in Communication
PSOE. *See* Partido Socialista Obrero Español
Psycho (film), 1091–1092
psychoanalytic theory, 137

Psychology & Sexuality (journal), 851–852
Puar, Jasbir, 367, 378–379, 874–878, 881, 883, 889–893, 895–897, 900–901
　assemblage and, 893–894
　on bio-necropolitics, 894
The Public and Its Problems (Dewey), 686–687
public and political LGBTQ+ letters, 941–944
Public Broadcasting Charter (Ireland), 1066
Public Culture (journal), 687–688
public culture, crip theory and, 235–237
public discourse, television rules and, 822
public emergence, 137–138
public memory, queering, 699
public rituals, 459
Publics and Counterpublics (Warner, Mark), 687–688
public service broadcasters (PSBs), 811–813, 821, 1063, 1066–1067
　LGBT+ expertise and, 821–823
public sphere, 686–687
Pulse Nightclub shooting, 584, 678, 695–696, 879, 901–902, 1154–1155
Punks (film), 797–798
The Punk Singer (documentary), 1080
"Purity and Endangerment" (Douglas), 541
"Pushing Boundaries" (Chávez), 118–119
Pussy Riot, 1081

QAM. *See* Queer Azaadi Mumbai
QAS. *See* Queer African studies
Al Qaws for Sexual and Gender Diversity in Palestinian Society, 896–898
QCP. *See* queer communication pedagogy
QED (journal), 694, 696, 699–700
QEJ. *See* Queers for Economic Justice
Q Television Network, 1065
QTPOC. *See* queer and trans people of color
Qualitative Inquiry (journal), 462–463
quare disidentification, 143–144
quare studies, 171, 194–195, 417–418, 421, 693, 1247
quare theory, 108
quaring, 843–844
　intersectionality and, 478
Quarterly Journal of Speech (journal), 175, 687–688
Québec, 881–882
da Quebrada, Linn, 18–19
Quechua, 64–65
Queen for a Day (Ochoa), 87
Queen Latifah, 797, 799, 1082
The Queen of America Goes to Washington City (Berlant), 211–212
Queen Pen, 1082

The Queen's Throat (Koestenbaum), 1046
queer
　in Chinese media and pop culture, 974–977
　definitions and, 231–239, 276n.1, 637–640, 974
　in QCP, 1189–1193
　ranges of meanings in, 583–584
　as regulatory, 891
queer affect, monetization of, in digital platforms, 38–39
queer Africa, 161
"Queer African and African Feminist Coalitional Possibilities" (special forum), 649
Queer African Reader (anthology), 639
Queer African studies (QAS), 637
　coalition building and political activism, 648–650
　colonial, postcolonial, and neoliberal entanglements of anti-LGBT violence, 645–646
　definitions for, 637–640
　　queerness, 639–640
　discursive negotiations of identity and, 646–648
　future research directions, 651–652
　history and political contexts, 640–643
　incorporating in queer communication studies, 645–651
　media representation and social media connections, 650–651
queer and trans people of color (QTPOC), 449, 794
queer archives, 698–700, 1224–1226
　activism and, 1233–1235
　future research directions, 1235–1237
　historiography, futurity, and, 1230–1232
　identifications, 1228–1229
　methods & methodologies, 1230
　norms of evidence, 1232–1233
　where of, 1226–1228
Queer as Folk (television series), 390–392, 831, 843, 999–1000, 1013–1017
　representation and, 1020
Queer Asia, 44–46, 59
　cinema and, 56–58
　class and economic status in, 51
　as disjunctive modernities, 49–58
　　identifications and affiliations, 50–53
　　media and popular culture, 56–58
　　relationalities and spatialities, 53–56
　interdisciplinary venues discussing, 45
queer as performance, 86–87
queer asylum cases, 68
queer autoethnography, 1148–1151
Queer Azaadi Mumbai (QAM), 58
queer bodies
　medicalization of, 259

Queer China (Bao), 980
queer Chinese media and pop culture, 969–970
queer cinema
    African American, 791–792
        documentaries, 801–804
        future of, 804–807
        mainstream LGBT films, 796–797
        noteworthy independent films, 797–800
    blockbuster films, 800–801
    in Brazil, 3–7
    defining, 792
    history, 792–796
    as identity, birth of, 12–15
    Latin American, 85–86
    in Spain, 93–103
queer coloniality, 64
queer comics, 991–992, 995–996
    self-representation and, 998–1002
queer commemorations, 178
queer communication pedagogy (QCP), 1185–1187
    emergence of, 1187–1189
    as liberatory and abolitionist, 1199–1200
    locating, historicizing, and politicizing "queer" in, 1189–1193
queer communication studies
    arts-based, 1145
    incorporating QAS in, 645–651
    poetic inquiry and, 1151–1155
    queer studies and African studies implications for, 643–645
queercore, 1077–1078
queer curatorship, 1230
queer diaspora, 109, 1250–1251
queer diasporic communities, 71
queer digital cultures, racism in, 70–71
queer digital practices, 1051–1053
queer doom, discursive construction of, 386–387
queer economic justice, 569
queer ephemeral archives, 179–180
queer ethnographies, Latin America and, 82–84
Queer Eye for the Straight Guy (television show), 196, 584–585, 814, 818, 831
queer families
    RJ and formation of, 709–714
    transnational and diasporic, 112
queer-feminist digital archives, 1081
queer feminist pedagogy, 1006–1007
Queer Feminist Punk (Wiedlack), 1077–1078
queer film, 792–796
    defining, 792
queer-focused health programs, 261

queer-friendly healthcare
    provider recommendations and, 267–268
    seeking, 266–267
queer futurity, 221, 396
    worldmaking and, 693–694
Queer Girls and Popular Culture (Driver), 1054
queer globalization, 46–49
queer hauntologies, 1232
queer hybridity, 978
queer identities
    in Brazil and national cinema, 4–7
    disclosure
        considerations for, 657
        to family of origin, 656–659
        in healthcare, 265–266
        initial and communicative reactions to, 659–664
        practices, 658–659
        recipients of, 657–658
    family acceptance of, 660–662
    family of origin adjustment and, 664–668
    family rejection of, 662–664
    migration and, 70
    parental acceptance of, 628–630
    sibling reactions to, 667–668
    terminology and, 5–6
queering, 476
    archives, 1224–1226
    autoethnography, 1218
    bisexuality, 1210
    Black hip-hop feminism, 1081–1083
    body, 251–253
    chrononormativity, 1132–1134
    coding, 1217
    colonialism, 1242–1243
    decolonization
        colonial and postcolonial approaches, 1249–1251
        indigenous approaches, 1251–1254
    diversity management, 1212–1214
    dying and grief, 253–254
    empire, 1242–1243
    ethnography, 1217–1218
    health expertise, 254–255
    intersectionality and, 478
    kinship and family, 713–717
    leadership, 1210–1212
    minority stress and relationships and, 622
    musicology, 1076–1078
        subcultural studies and, 1077–1078
    occupational segregation, 1209
    organizational research methods, 1216–1218

queering (*continued*)
   popular music culture, 1075–1076
      history of, 1078–1083
   public memory, 699
   reflexivity, 1216
   reproductive justice, 705–706
   work and, 1208–1210
      closet, 1214–1216
queering Africa, 638–639
Queering Public Address (Morris, C.), 171–172, 177
"Queering/Quaring/Kuaring/Crippin'/Transing 'Other Bodies' in Intercultural Communication" (Yep), 646–647
"Queering Reproductive Justice" (Pérez, M. Z.), 705–706
"Queering Reproductive Justice" tool kit, 705
Queering the Pitch (Brett), 1046–1047, 1076–1077
Queering the Popular Pitch (Whiteley and Rycenga), 1046–1047, 1076–1077
Queering the Public Sphere in Mexico and Brazil (de la Dehesa), 81–82
queer intercultural communication, 471–473, 479–480
   embodiment and, 475–478
   intersectionality and, 473–475
   power and, 478–479
"Queer Intercultural Communication" (Yep et al.), 472
queer invisibility, 264–265
queer kinship, 1128–1130
queer Lincoln, 171–173, 177, 179, 699, 936
"Queerly Ambivalent" (Asante), 647–648
Queerly Remembered (Dunn), 172
queer material culture, 170
queer media criticism, 389–392
queer melodrama, 1011–1012
   characteristics, structures, and styles, 1012–1015
   critiques of, 1015
   defining, 1013
   future scholarship opportunities, 1021–1022
   narrative features, 1013–1014
   purposes, impacts, and problems, 1015–1021
   storytelling in, 1016
queer memory, 168–170, 698–700
   activist, 1033–1035
   archives of, 179–181
   diversity and, 178
   emergence of, 170–172
   framing, in communication, 172–181
   pedagogical potential, 179
   screens and, 1028–1032
   temporality and, 179
queer men's bodies, 483–484, 493–494
   gay male beauty influencers, 492
queer methodology, 1146–1147

queer migration, 64
   decisions and paths to, 67–69
   Latin America and, 84–85
Queer Migration Politics (Chávez), 405–406
queer military family communication research, 725–727
   future of, 727–729
queer monuments and memorials, 698
Queer Music Heritage Archive, 1081
queer music practices, digital realm and, 1042
Queer Nation, 188, 197, 1191
queerness
   cultural context and critical potential of, 345
   defining, 639–640
   in film, 386–387
   intercultural communication and, 1247
   mediated representations of, 196
   politics of time and, 209–211
   representations of violence in, 387
   self-destructive behavior and, 391–392
   socially performed character of, 347–348
   as umbrella term, 190
   Western Europe television and, 823–825
Queer Nostalgia in Cinema and Popular Culture (Padva), 1032
queer of color
   coming out discourse critique and, 344
   critiquing and decolonizing queerness in communication, 1246–1249
   digital media critique and, 488
   disidentification as worldmaking process, 144–145
   worlds and theories, 692–696
queer offspring
   parental journeys to acceptance, 628–630
   parental reactions to coming out, 627–628
   parenting of, 627
      centering communication, 630–634
Queer Online, 1052
queer origin stories, 187–189
queer partner studies, 751–752
queer pedagogy
   as abolitionist, 1197–1199
   RuPaul's Drag Race and, 1098–1099
queer people, 194–196
queer performance, 1155–1157
Queer Phenomenology (Ahmed), 1076, 1115–1116
queer porn, 848–849
Queer Praxis, 218–219
queer production studies, 1062
   commercial domain and, 1064–1066
   fan cultures and, 1069–1071
   further research areas, 1071
   independent domain and, 1067–1069

primary sources for, 1071
public media and, 1066–1067
situating in media studies, 1062–1063
transnational perspectives in, 1063–1064
queer readers, comics and, 996–998
queer relationality, 694–696
queer representation, 9–12, 196–197
queer reproductions, 706
queer rhetorical pedagogy, 179
queer safer sex communication, 276–277
    conceptual and definitional issues in, 277–281
    future research considerations, 286–287
    main findings from literature, 281–286
        age, 281–282
        contextual issues, 283–286
        demographics, 281–283
        intimate partner violence, 283–284
        place, 284–285
        PrEP, 285–286
        race, 282–283
queer safe spaces, 674, 676–682
    constructing within online contexts, 679–680
    offline contexts, 677
    spatial perspective, 676–677
queer scholarship
    television production and, 813–815
    U.S.-centric nature of, 814–815
Queers for Economic Justice (QEJ), 446, 569
Queer Sites in Global Contexts (Ramos and Mowlabocus), 493
queer slippages, 126
queer social movements, 197
queer spaces, commercial, 34–35, 37
queer speculative fiction, critical investigations of, 1120–1122
queer studies, 582–583, 643–645
    defining, 107–108
    heteronormativity and, 639
    organizational communication and, 1207–1208
    politics and, 197
Queer Studies in Media and Popular Culture (journal), 1032
queer temporal camp, 215–216
queer temporalities, 209–211
    AIDS crisis and, 211
    Edelman and, 211–214
    expansive scope of, 214–215
    in performance studies, 219–222
    rhetorical studies of, 215–219
queer temporality, popular media and, 216–217
queer theory, 137, 170–171, 187–188, 209–210, 479–480, 1076

    Black, 119–120
    Chinese pop culture and, 974–977
    communications studies and, 117–118
    decolonizing, 1242–1243
    defining queer in, 189–191
    first-generation, 417–418
    Foucault and, 191–193
    LGBTQ politics and, 107–108
    minority stress and, 621–622
    organizational communication research and, 1207–1208
    origins of term, 188
    paraliterature and literary hierarchies and, 1114–1115
    speculative fiction and, 1112–1113
        genealogy of, 1117–1120
        paraliterature and literary hierarchies, 1114–1115
        paraliterature to fuzzy sets, 1115–1117
        representation and, 1122–1127
    theoretical alignments of, 1243–1246
Queer/Tongzhi China (anthology), 976
Queer Tracks, 1083–1084
queer translations and translators, 127–128
queer TV studies, 810–813
    crypto-normativity and, 817–819
    market conditions and, 815–817
    outsider outlook and, 813–815
    PSBs and, 821–823
    queerness for television in Western Europe, 823–825
    for Western Europe, 819–821
Queer Universes (Pearson, W. G., et al.), 1121–1122
queer utopia, 86–87, 162, 1033
    worldmaking and, 693–694
queer violence, 393–394
queer visibility, 36–37
    diverse, lack of, 118–120
    heteronormativity and, 154
queer worldmaking
    academia as site for, 696–698
    anti-social approaches and, 693–694
    in communication studies, 690–691
    defining, 688–690
    limitations and future directions for research on, 700–701
    memories, monuments, and archives, 698–700
    origins of, 686–688
    worlds and themes in, 691–700
Queer Youth Cultures (Driver), 910
Queer Zine Archive Project, 991–992
Queer Zine Library, 991–992
Quesada, Abel, 67
Quevedo y Zubieta, Salvador, 66
Quick, Tyler, 489–490

Rabid Puppies, 1126–1127
race
    in coming out narratives, 370
    cross-dressing, transvestism, and, 1091–1094
    dating websites and hookup apps and, 487–489
    gay pornography and, 860
    homonormativity and, 158–160
    queer safer sex communication and, 282–283
    RuPaul's Drag Race and, 1101–1102
    sexual scripts and, 759
Race Chaser (podcast), 1104
RaceFail, 1126–1127
racialized fetishization, 1250
racially situated knowledges, 1247
racial minority stress, 617–618
racism, 1115–1116
    dating websites and hookup apps and, 487–489
    homonormativity and, 158–160
    patterns of, 70–71
    in queer digital cultures, 70–71
Radi, Blas, 708–709
Radical Doula Guide (Pérez, M. Z.), 705–706
Radical History Review (journal), 1224–1225, 1237
radical tenderness, 510
Rafferty, Terrence, 802
RAI, 822–823
rainbow filters, 775
Rainbow Love, 36, 40–41
Rainer, Jamie, 921–922
Rainey, Ma, 1078
Rainha Diaba (film), 14
"Ramble-Ations" (performance), 693, 695
Ramos, Fernão Pessoa, 7
Ramos, Guiomar, 13–14
Ramos, Regner, 493
Rand, Erin, 584, 939
Ranma 1/2, 1119
rape myths, 955
Rapid, Johnny, 856
rapid-onset gender dysphoria, 907–908
Rapisardi, Flavio, 83
Rasmussen, Mary, 342
Raun, Tobias, 491–492
ravesti, 511
Rawson, K. J., 180–181, 1226–1227
La Raza Caucus, 407–408
RDT. *See* relational dialectics theory
"(Re)reading Queerly" (Hollinger), 1121–1122
Real ID Act, 443–444
reality television, 1095
Reality TV World (website), 831
The Real World (television series), 687–688

Reconstructionist, 1152
Record of a Spaceborn Few (Chambers), 1130
recovery work, 175
redemocratização, 15–17
Reed, Christopher, 171, 1029–1030
Reed, Lou, 1079
Reel in the Closet (documentary), 1036
Rees, Dee, 798–799, 807
Reflections in a Golden Eye (film), 387
reflexivity, queering, 1216
refugees, 123, 895
    digital media platforms and, 68–69
    gay, 68
Reichelt, Lisa, 487
Reid, Frances, 802
Reiff, Mary Jo, 1012
Reincarnation (nightclub), 139
Reitsamer, Rosa, 1078
rejection, familial, 662–664
    context and, 662–663
    forms of, 663–664
    outcomes, 664
Rela, 29
relational dialectics, 736
relational dialectics theory (RDT), 633–634
relational dynamics, 737–739
relationalities
    queer, 694–696
    Queer Asia and, 53–56
Relational Maintenance Behavior Measure (RMBM), 735
relational maintenance behaviors, 328–329
    CNM and, 557–560
Relational Maintenance Strategies Measure (RMSM), 735
relational outcomes, 736
relational performance, 695–696
relational resilience, 741
relational termination, 599–600
    experiences of, 604–605
    future research directions, 606–608
    gender composition and, 600–601
    minority stress and, 603–604
    relational arrangements and, 601–602
    relationships after, 605–606
    resources and, 602–603
    terminology and scope, 600
relationship dissolution
    experiences of, 604–605
    relationships after, 605–606
    risk factors for, 600
relationship education programs, 330–331

relationship maintenance, 744–745
  communication and, 734–735
  minority stress and, 736–737
  monogamy and, 742–744
  positive relationship functioning and, 735–736
  same-sex marriage and, 742
  social support and, 741
relationship maintenance behaviors (RMBs), 734–736
  HIV status and, 740
  in same-sex couples, 739–741
relationship-related perceptions, LGBTQ+ marriage and, 526
relationships
  coparenting, 606
  as dynamic interpersonal systems, 1171–1173
  experiences, within LGBTQ+ marriage and, 526–529
  extradyadic, 552–554
  LGBTQ+ marriage and, 525–530
  marriage impact on, 529
  minority stress and, 613–614
    calls for change, 618–619
    future research directions, 621–622
    limitations of research, 619
    relationship quality and, 615–617
  open, 554
  polyamory, 554–556
  polyfidelitious, 555
  queering notions of, 622
  after romantic relationship dissolution, 605–606
  sexual satisfaction in, 756–757
  SMGD, studying, 1162–1164
  studying, 1162–1164
    AA and EMA, 1173–1174
    between-person heterogeneity and, 1164–1165
    dyadic analysis in, 1167
    emerging techniques for intensive longitudinal data, 1174–1177
    indistinguishable dyadic analysis in, 1167–1171
    longitudinal and dynamic dyadic analysis, 1170–1171
    MLM and, 1165–1167
  swinging, 553–554
relationship satisfaction, 760
Remembering the AIDS Quilt (Morris, C.), 172, 175
remixed material, 1070
reparative reading, 934n.5, 1117
representation
  comedic, 832–835
  QAS and, 650–651
  self, 920–921
  speculative fiction and, 1122–1127
    health and disease discourses, 1124–1125

  intersectionality and, 1125–1127
  Stonewall changes in, 832
representational anxieties, 489–490
reproduction
  queer kinship and, 1128–1130
  in speculative fiction, 1127–1132
reproductive futurism, 211–212, 1127–1132
reproductive justice (RJ), 716–717
  framework for, 706–709
  queer family formation and, 709–714
  queering, 705–706
    kinship and family, 713–717
reproductive labor, 574
Republic (Plato), 1118–1119
rescue script, 880–881
resignification, 400–401
resistance
  cultural, 1245
  disidentification as mode of, 140–144
  identity and, 192
  as opposition, 1244–1245
  as subversion, 1244–1245
  as transformation, 1245
"Response to Haters" (video), 925–926
"Rethinking Conquergood" (Moreman), 407
"Rethinking Homonationalism" (Puar), 876
retomada, 15–17, 25n.27
retroactivism, 1235
Revisitation (Keegan), 214
Revista Cinearte (journal), 5
Revolutionary War (U.S.), 724
Revry, 805–806
Reyes, Yosimar, 419–420
R.G. & G.R. Harris Funeral Homes Inc. v. Equal Employment Opportunity Commission, 428
rhetorical studies
  evidence of situations, 938–941
  of queer temporalities, 215–219
  queer worldmaking and, 698
  visual, 991–992
Rhetoric & Public Affairs (journal), 175
Rhetorics of Fantasy (Mendelsohn), 1114
Rhimes, Shonda, 807
Rhue, Sylvia, 802
Ribeiro, Rita, 18
Rice, Anne, 1121
rice queen, 484, 1250
Rich, Adrienne, 1017
Rich, B. Ruby, 188, 792–793, 796–798
Richardson, Matt, 173
Ridinger, Robert B., 180
Rieder, John, 1114

Riff, Alice, 19
Riggs, Marlon, 174–175, 188, 793–798, 801–802, 840
right to have children, 709–713
right-wing populist movements, 923
do Rio, João, 4
Rio Nu (magazine), 4
Riot Acts (documentary), 1083
Riot Grrrl scene, 1045, 1075–1078, 1080–1081
risk compensation, 286
ritualized relations of kinship, 459
Rivera, Gabby, 992
Rivera, Ignacio, 502
Rivera, Sylvia, 502, 1192–1193, 1229
Rivera-Servera, Ramón H., 87
RJ. *See* reproductive justice
RMBM. *See* Relational Maintenance Behavior Measure
RMBs. *See* relationship maintenance behaviors
RMSM. *See* Relational Maintenance Strategies Measure
RMSM-R, 735
Roberts, Dorothy, 711–712
Roberts, Myra N., 693
Robinson, Angela, 796, 804, 807
Robinson, Frank, 942
Robinson, Russell, 488
Rocha, Glauber, 12–13
Rochester, Anna, 940–941
Rocío Nasser, Michelle, 67
Rock, Bretman, 492
"Rock and Sexuality" (Frith and McRobbie), 1044–1045
Rocketman (film), 800
Rockwell, Norman, 698
Rodriguez, Christopher, 806
Rodríguez, Juana María, 1076
Rofel, Lisa, 33–34
Rofes, E., 391–392
Roger, Mary, 215–216
Rogers, Robbie, 698
Röhm, Ernst, 375–376
Román, David, 403, 1225–1226
Romance (film), 15
romantic love, 52
romantic relational formation, 210–211
romantic relational goals, 360
romantic relationships, 734
  as dynamic interpersonal systems, 1171–1173
  studying
    AA and EMA, 1173–1174
    between-person heterogeneity and, 1164–1165
    dyadic analysis in, 1167
    emerging techniques for intensive longitudinal data, 1174–1177
    indistinguishable dyadic analysis in, 1167–1171

    longitudinal and dynamic dyadic analysis, 1170–1171
    MLM and, 1165–1167
  study of, 1163
Romesburg, Don, 715–716
Ronson, Mick, 1079
Room 222 (television series), 832–833
Roosevelt, Eleanor, 172–173, 175, 936–937
Roosevelt, Franklin D., 937
Rope (film), 10–11
Roque Ramírez, Horacio N., 403
Ross, Angelica, 502
Ross, Chase, 922–923
Ross, Loretta, 707
Ross, Marlon, 343–344
Rossman, Megan, 1035
Rothmann, Jacques, 864
Round Trip Ticket (television series), 844
Rowling, J. K., 1141n.11
Royster, Jacqueline Jones, 940
RTÉ, 821–823, 1066–1067
Rubin, Gayle, 188, 572–573, 587
The Runaways, 1079
RuPaul's Drag Race (television series), 1094–1105
  authenticity, consumption, and competition, 1095–1096
  global audiences, fandom, and participation and, 1096–1098
  hetero- and homonormativity and, 1099–1101
  race, nationality, language, and body and, 1101–1102
  subjectivity, transformation, and queer pedagogy and, 1098–1099
  transgender subjectivity and, 1102–1105
RuPaul's Drag Race All Stars (television series), 1104
rural-to-urban movements, 68
Rushdie, Salman, 1117
Russ, Joanna, 1121
Russell, Camisha, 712
Russell, Harold, 232–233
Russia, 883–884
Russo, Vito, 7, 10, 20, 386–390, 798–799
Rustin, Bayard, 795
Rycenga, Jennifer, 1046–1047
Ryman, Geoff, 1117, 1124–1125

Sacco, Joe, 994, 998–999
Sackville-West, Vita, 945–946
"Sad and Rabid Puppies" (Oleszczuk), 1126–1127
sadomasochism, 571–572
Sad Puppies, 1126–1127
safer sex communication
  conceptual and definitional issues and, 277–281
  operationalizations of, 279

safe spaces
  COVID-19 pandemic and, 681
  defining, 674–676
  Jotería Studies and, 404
  media and, 679
  offline contexts, 677
  pink market exploitation of, 34–36
Sagat, François, 860
Sahagún, Bernardino de, 64
Said, Edward, 641, 1244
Salcedo, Bamby, 419–420
Salessi, Jorge, 66, 81
Salgado, Julio, 419–420
Salih, Sara, 187–188
Salt Fish Girl (Lai), 1128–1129
Samek, Alyssa, 697
"Same Love" (song), 698
same-sex civil unions, 325
  in Brazil, 23n.5
same-sex couples, 734
  androgynous, 738
  maintenance and monogamy in, 742–744
  minority stress and, 736–737
  relational dynamics of, 737–739
  RMBs in, 739–741
  roles in, 738
  validation of, 737
same-sex family rights, 28
same-sex marriage, 28, 40, 325, 530–531, 1142n.18.
    See also LGBTQ+ marriage
  Australia and, 779
  Japan and, 48–49
  maintenance and, 742
  stigma and, 737
  support for, 771
same-sex relationship social support, 741
same-sex sexuality, 647–648
Samois, 571–572
Sampio, Adélia, 15
Samson, JD, 1081
sandbagging, 239
Sanders, Bernie, 147
Sandman (Gaiman), 1116
Sandoval, Chela, 136
Sanford Arms (television series), 832–833, 841–842
São Paulo, Symphony of a Metropolis
    (documentary), 18
SAPPRFT, 981
Sarkissian, Raffi, 815–816
Sarney, José, 14
Sassoi, 637–638, 647–648
The Satanic Verses (Rushdie), 1117

Saturday Night Live (television program), 837–838, 840,
    1093–1094
Saturday Night Thriller (Campuzano), 87
Savage, Dan, 216–217, 913
Save Me (film), 1068
"Save Our Children" campaign, 1127
"Save the Children" campaign, 385–386
Saving Face (film), 978–979
#sayhername campaign, 473–474
scavenger methodology, 1147–1148
Schiappa, Edward, 196–197
Schön, Donald A., 853
Schulman, Sarah, 1234–1235
Schvarzman, Sheila, 7
science fiction, 1113, 1126
  mundane, 1117
  transnational nature of, 1119
Science Fiction and the Mass Cultural Genre System
    (Rieder), 1114
Science Fiction Studies (journal), 1121–1122
Scientific-Humanitarian Committee, 65
"Scientific Racism and the Emergence of the
    Homosexual Body" (Somerville), 1115–1116
Scott, Joan, 589
Scream Club, 1081
Screening Queer Memory (Horvat), 1029–1031, 1037
screens
  queer activist memory and, 1033–1035
  queer memory and, 1028–1032
Scrolling Beyond Binaries, 906–907
Scruff (app), 487
Sean Cody (film), 856
secrecy *versus* revelation binary, 343
A Secret Love (documentary), 1036
Sedgwick, Eve Kosofsky, 7, 367–368, 375, 380, 857–858,
    974, 1079, 1112, 1121–1122, 1134–1135
  on closet, 344
  performativity theory and, 1188
  on reading and genre, 1117
Sedimentos/Sediments (film), 101–102
self-destructive behavior, 391–392
self-disclosure, 300
self-engineering, 909–910
self-esteem, relationship quality and, 616
self-oriented goals, 360
self-presentation, 1049–1050
self-publishing, 909, 992–994
self-representation, 920–921
  in comics, 998–1002
self-transformation, 1098–1099
SEM. *See* structural equation modeling
Semana de Arte Moderna (event), 8

Sense8 (television series), 650
sense-making, 664–668
The Sense of Brown (Muñoz), 460
sensibilities, 1090
Senyonjo, Christopher, 1157–1158
September 11, 2001 terrorist attacks, 160, 892
Serafemme, 1081–1082
Serano, Julia, 511
The Sergeant (film), 387
serodisclosure, 752
serosorting, 245, 280–281
serostatus, 752
Set It Off (film), 797–798
settler colonialism
　homonationalism and, 897–900
　paternalism and, 577
settler nations, 1251–1252
sex, defining, 277–278, 757
Sex and the City (television series), 957–958
sexile, 84–85
Sexing the Groove (Whiteley), 1045
"Sex in Public" (Warner, Mark, and Berlant), 687–689
The Sex Is Out of This World (Ginn, Cornelis, and Palumbo), 1122
sex law, 572–573
sex-positive feminism, 573
Sex Role Inventory, 738
sex roles, 738–739
"Sextext" (Corey and Nakayama), 171, 220, 589, 696
sex tourism, 53–54
sex trafficking, 569, 577–578
sexual and gender minority (SGM), 321–322
　AA and EMA, 1173–1174
　longitudinal and dynamic dyadic analysis, 1170–1171
　relationships as dynamic interpersonal systems, 1171–1173
sexual attitudes
　defining, 953
　focus of mediated depictions and, 956–959
　humor and conveyance of, 960–961
　media depictions of, 952–953
　　abuse *versus* consent, 958–959
　　consequences and, 959
　　emotions and, 959–960
　　focus in, 956–959
　　humor in, 960–961
　　mainstream, 956
　　sexual health depictions, 957–958
　　stereotypes in, 961–963
　　theoretical perspectives on effects of, 954
　　worldview cultivation and, 954
　teaching of, 955–956

sexual behaviors
　medical education assumptions and, 260–261
　teaching of, 955–956
sexual citizenship, 28, 878–880
sexual communication, 750, 752–754
　defining, 751
　future research directions, 754
　heterosexual partner studies, 752–753
　queer partner studies, 751–752
sexual dissidence, 65–66, 83–84
sexual diversity, 66–67
　medical education and, 261
sexual essentialism, 587
sexual exceptionalism, 160, 875, 878, 891
Sexual Futures (Rodríguez, J. M.), 1076
sexual health, media depiction of attitudes toward, 957–958
sexual identity
　discrimination in healthcare and, 263–264
　medical education and, 260
sexual initiation scripts, 960
Sexualities (journal), 977
sexuality
　in Brazil, 4
　communicating, 343
　　at work, 438–440
　cultural constructs about, 106
　defining, 105–106
　geographies of, 677
　intercultural communication and, 471–473
　prison, 155–156
　progressive, 891
　televisual, 832–835
　transnational and diasporic, 108–109
　work and, 1208–1210
　youth cultures and, 907–908
sexuality-related stressors, 767
sexuality studies, 582–583
sexual liberty, 262
sexually transmitted diseases (STDs), 278
sexually transmitted infections (STIs), 262, 277, 283–284
　HIV research and, 269–272
　transgender individuals and, 297
sexual minority and gender diverse (SMGD), 1162–1164
　between-person heterogeneity in individuals, 1164–1165
　　MLM and, 1165–1167
　dyadic analysis in relationships, 1167
　indistinguishable dyadic analysis in relationships, 1167–1171
sexual nationalism, 881
sexual normativity, 152–153

sexual orientation
    coming out conversation types, 309
    definitions for, 295–300
    disclosure in medical context, 295
    disclosure of, 303–304
    patient-provider disclosure and, 300–310
    sexual satisfaction and, 761–762
sexual othering, 876
sexual partner communication, 751–753
sexual pleasure
    communication studies and, 582–584
    normative public discourses and, 586–589
    performative writing and authoethnographies of, 589–591
    representations of, 584–586
sexual politics, 908–909
    neoliberal, 875
sexual racism, 70–71
sexual revolution, 847
sexual satisfaction, 756–757
    communication and, 761
    defining, 757–760
    future research directions for, 762–763
    individual difference variables and, 761–762
    internalized homonegativity and, 760
    relationship satisfaction and, 760
    relationship types and arrangements and, 760–761
    sexual orientation and, 761–762
sexual scripts, 759
    creation of, 954
sexual surveillance and regulation, resistance to, 345–346
"Sexual Trauma/Queer Memory" (Cvetkovich), 171
sexual violence, media depictions of attitudes toward, 958–959
sex wars, 570–573, 850, 862–863
sex work, 445
    class struggle and, 575
    in communication studies, 568–570
    consensual, 570
    decriminalization and legalization, 577–580
    economic justice and, 569
    labor and, 573–576
    laws and, 570
    monetary behavior in, 575
    neoliberalism and, 576–577
    nonconsensual, 569
sex workers, 53
Sganzerla, Rogério, 13–14
SGM. *See* sexual and gender minority
shadowbanning, 908–909
Shakespeare, 1118–1119
Shankman, Adam, 1090

shared tasks, 735
Shaw, Gareth, 981
Shaw, Lisa, 9
Shaw, Peggy, 222
Shawl, Nisi, 1134
Shelley, Mary, 1118, 1127
Shepard, Matthew, 171, 174, 178, 196, 390–391
Shinjuku Ni-chome, 54–55
Shi Tou, 1035
Shock, Suzy, 502
Shome, Raka, 1249
Shonkwiler, Alison, 715
Sierra Madero, Abel, 67
Sigal, Pete, 64
signification, 193–194
The Silence of the Lambs (film), 1091–1092
Silvera, Richard, 851–852
Silvério Trevisan, João, 4
Silvestre, Adrián, 101–102
Simpson, Monica, 708–709
Singapore, 47–48
    media and popular culture and, 56
Sistahfest, 1081
Sister Act (film), 1224
Sisters of Perpetual Indulgence, 1224
SisterSong Women of Color Reproductive Health Collective, 707–709
sitcoms, Black gay characters in
    Black-cast, 835–839
    white-/multicultural-cast, 835–839
sites of memory, 1027–1028
Six Feet Under (television series), 815–816, 844
16 and Pregnant (television show), 957
Sjunnesson, Jan, 881
Skam (television series), 819–820
sketch comedy, Black gayness in, 839–841
skinheads, 376
The Skinny (film), 798
slander, 64
slash videos, 1069
slavery, 577
SLAY TV, 1068
SLDN. *See* OutServe-Service Members Legal Defense Network
Sleater-Kinney, 1081
Slimani, Leila, 645–646
slippage, 477–478
slipstream, 1113, 1116–1117
Sloop, John, 171, 174, 584, 698, 939
smartphones, 66–67, 72, 483
    geolocative technologies and, 67
    hookup apps and, 487

SMGD. *See* sexual minority and gender diverse
Smith, Andrea, 146
Smith, Barbara, 420
Smith, Bessie, 799
Smith, Clarissa, 847
Smith, Donald, 589
Smith, Jesus, 71
Smith, Paul Julian, 93
SMZ Tomboy Crew, 56
Snapchat, 906–907
  presentation of self on, 910–911
Snorton, Riley, 343–346, 502–503, 585–586
SNS. *See* social networking sites
Snuff (film), 571
Soap (television series), 833–834
Sochi Winter Olympics of 2014, 884
social awareness, 12
social behaviors, teaching of, 955–956
social capital, 769
social cognitive theory, 281, 955
social contagion, 907–908
social distancing, 680
social documentary, 544
social exchange theory, 734–736
social factors, in marriage decisions, 527
social identity, 619–620, 665
social identity theory, cross-generational experiences and, 395
social inclusion, LGBTQ+ marriage and, 523
social integration, 769
social learning process, 955
social media, 58, 64, 66–67, 483, 489–490
  activism and, 236, 925
  affective well-being and, 908
  algorithms and, 1050–1051
  anti-trans sentiment on, 923
  civic engagement and, 925
  coming out and, 917–921
  early Internet precursors to, 911–912
  emancipatory potential of, 909–910
  gay male beauty influencers, 492
  geolocative turn and, 67
  hate and, 925–926
  identity work on, 914–923
  LGBTQ youth cultures and, 906–907
  mental health and, 907–908
  music and, 1049–1050
  performativity and, 1098–1099
  platform affordances and, 912, 914–915
  plurality of, 910–912
  political coalitions and, 232
  predigital periodicals as, 65–66
  Queer African diasporic connections on, 650–651
  queer practices on, 1051–1053
  rethinking risk and, 907–909
  self-expression and community formation and, 909–910
  self-publishing on, 909
  social support and, 768–769, 775, 924
  trans men and, 490–492
  trans youth cultures, 921–923
social model of disability, 232
social movements, 620
  reproductive justice and, 706
social negotiation, virtual platforms and, 681
social networking sites (SNS), 909, 915–916
  connectivity emphasized in, 910–911
social networks, 735, 769
social roles, 11
Social Security Administration (SSA), 443–444
The Social Shaping of Technology (MacKenzie and Wajcman), 1048
social support, 741, 767–768
  acceptance and, 771
  community climate, 774
  community connectedness and support, 773–774
  contextualizing, 776–780
  defining, 768–769
  factors in effectiveness of, 770
  formal, 780
  global trends in acceptance of LGBTQ+, 770–771
  intimate relationships and, 778
  life course approaches to, 777–780
  major life events and, 769
  measuring, 771–776
  older adults and, 778–779
  parenting and, 778–779
  perception of, 772
  primary groups and, 769
  secondary groups and, 769
  social media and, 924
  stress and communication of, 767–768
  times of elevated anti-gay rhetoric and, 779–780
  understanding meanings of, 775
social support behaviors scale, 772
Social Support Network measure, 773
Social Support to the Couple measure, 773
socioeconomic marginalization, 713
Sokel, Brian, 806
Solanas, Valerie, 586
Solberg, Helena, 12–13, 18–19
Solinger, Rickie, 711–712
Solomon, River, 1125–1126
Some of My Best Friends (television series), 834
Somerville, Siobhan, 1115–1116

Somewhere Over the Rainbow (song), 1079
Sonique, 1103, 1105
Sontag, Susan, 1079, 1090
The Sopranos (television series), 390
Sotomayor, Sonia, 237
Souline, Evguenia, 945–946
Sound Moves (Bull), 1056
Sousanis, Nick, 994
South Korea, gay men in, 50–51
sovereign identity, 665
sovereign power, necropolitics and, 893
space. *See also* safe space
    affinity, 906–907, 924
    cocreation of, 678
    cultural understandings of, disidentification and, 147–148
    gay pornography and, 862–863
    pedagogical, 678
space off, 217–218
Spade, Dean, 508, 1248–1249
Spain, 490
    during Franco dictatorship, 92
    LGBTQ+ cinema in, 93–103
        dictatorship and censorship, 94–95
        diverse representation in 2000s, 99–100
        explicit representation in 2020s, 100–103
        increasing visibility in 1990s, 98–100
        trailblazers, 96–99
        transition and, 95–97
    LGBTQ+ histories in, 91–93
    trans rights in, 91–92
spatialities
    comics and, 1002–1003
    Queer Asia and, 53–56
Spectra (journal), 589
speculative fiction
    AIDS and, 1124–1125
    critical investigations of queer, 1120–1122
    defining, 1113–1117
    queer genealogy of, 1117–1120
        global genealogies and indigenous interventions, 1119–1120
    queering chrononormativity and, 1132–1134
    queer kinship and, 1128–1130
    queer theory and, 1112–1113
        paraliterature and literary hierarchies and, 1114–1115
        paraliterature to fuzzy sets, 1115–1117
    representation and, 1122–1127
        health and disease discourses, 1124–1125
        intersectionality and, 1125–1127
    reproduction in, 1127–1132
speech acts, 193–194

Speed, Joshua, 936
Spencer, Leland, 818
Spiegelman, Art, 993, 1116
Spielberg, Steven, 797, 800
Spieldenner, Andrew, 472–473
Spillers, Hortense, 498–499
Spin City (television series), 835–837
Spit-Ball Sadie (film), 1091
Spivak, Gayatri Chakravorty, 418, 880–881
Spoon, Rae, 1157
sports, homophobia and, 374
Spotify, 1055–1057
Spotify Teardown (Eriksson et al.), 1055
Squires, Catherine, 687, 836–837
SSA. *See* Social Security Administration
Ssempe, Martin, 646
SSSR. *See* Strengthening Same-Sex Relationship
Stacey, Judith, 712, 714–715
staged performance, 221
Stam, Robert, 7
standpoint feminism, 1207
Star, Jeffree, 492
Starrr, Patrick, 492
Star Trek (television series), 1069, 1125
Star Trek: Voyager (television series), 1210
state paternalism, 576–577
state-space grids, 1174–1175
state violence, 713–714
STDs. *See* sexually transmitted diseases
stealthing, 855–856
Stefano, Joey, 861–862
Stein, Gertrude, 945–946
Stephens, Aimee, 428
Sterling, Bruce, 1116–1117
Stewart, Potter, 277–278
sticky rice, 475–476
stigma, 767
    concealable identity and, 301–304
    disclosure and, 301–303
    discreditable, 301–302
    fat, 1101–1102
    on gender identity, 246–247
    HIV-related, 246–247
    minority stress and, 736–737
    same-sex marriage and, 737
stigma fat, 1101–1102
Still Black (documentary), 802
STIs. *See* sexually transmitted infections
Stockton, Kathryn Bond, 907–908, 1131
Stoltenberg, John, 864
Stone, Lucy, 946
Stonewall (film), 1031

Stonewall (organization), 912–913
Stonewall Riots, 403–404, 832, 1192–1193, 1230–1231
　archival identifications and, 1229
　homonormative narratives of, 1229
　media representation after, 832
　public contestations over origins and significance of, 1225
storytelling
　CNSM and, 630–631
　participatory, 918–919
　in queer melodrama, 1016–1017
straight archives, 180
straight temporality, 215
straight time, 213–214
strategic organizational communication, 434–435
stratified reproduction, 706
Strawberry and Chocolate (film), 1031–1032
streaming and video-on-demand (SVOD), 804–805
streaming platforms, 1050
streaming services, 103
Street Transvestite Action Revolutionaries, 502
Strengthening Same-Sex Relationship (SSSR), 330
stress. *See also* minority stress
　communication of social support and, 767–768
　distal-proximal nature of, 614
　experiencing and coping with minority, 321–323
　factors in exposure to, 767
　as interpersonal, dyad-level construct, 327–328
　LGBTQ+ partners coping with, 328–330
　in LGBTQ+ relationships, 326
　models for, in LGBTQ+ relationships, 326–327
stress crossover, 327–328
stress spillover, 327–328
Strong Families Network, 716–717
Strong Island (documentary), 807
Strub, Whitney, 862–863
structural equation modeling (SEM), 1169–1171
　measurement invariance and, 1170–1171
Structural Transformation of the Public Sphere (Habermas), 686–688
Stryker, Jeff, 856–857, 859
Stryker, Susan, 504–505, 1118
studio photography, 552n.14
Studio Responsibility Report (GLAAD), 800
Studying Popular Music (Middleton), 1044
Sturgeon, Theodore, 1120–1121
Sturken, Marita, 1027–1028
Stychin, Carl F., 852
Subaltern Studies Group, 1244–1245
subcultural studies, queering musicology with, 1077–1078
subculture, Jotería as, 401

subject formation, disidentification and, 135, 145–147
subjectivities
　embodied translation and, 477–478
　mestizaje, 458–459
　RuPaul's Drag Race and, 1098–1099
　transgender, 1102–1105
subjects, signification and, 193–194
subversion
　disidentification as mode of, 140–144
　resistance as, 1244–1245
subversive refusal, 1244–1245
Sueños de exterminio (Giorgi), 81
suicide, 391–392
Sullivan, Nikki, 504–505
Summer Storm (film), 368–369, 372–375
"super crip" narratives, 237
Super Voice Girl (television program), 973–974
surrogacy, 712, 715
survival, disidentification as mode of, 139–140
Sutherland, Juan Pablo, 66–67
Suzi Quatro (band), 1079
SVOD. *See* streaming and video-on-demand
Sweden, 881
swinging relationships, 553–554, 560
symbolic annihilation, 835–836

Tacit Subjects (Decena), 84
Tacloban Pride 1016, 69
Tagg, Philip, 1043–1044
Taiwan, 55–56
　lesbian publications in, 418–420
　martial rule in, 32
　T bars in, 35
　tongzhi subject formation in, 31–32
　xianshen and, 347–348
The Talented Mr. Ripley (film), 1070
"The Tale of Plagues and Carnivals" (Delany), 1124–1125
The Tale of the Five (Duane), 1129–1130
Tales of the Arabian Nights, 1118–1119
Talley, Andre Leon, 803
Tamale, Sylvia, 642, 649, 651–652
Tambellini, Flavio, 11
Tan, Shaun, 992
Tangerine (film), 799
task goals, 361
TaSP. *See* treatment as prevention
T.A.T. Communications, 833–834
tattoos, 537
Taylor, Breonna, 620, 622
Taylor, Jodie, 1047, 1077
T bars, 35
teaching stories, 1113

Team Dresch, 1080
El Teatro Campesino, 461–462
technicity, 504–505
Technologies of Gender (de Lauretis), 212
Teena, Brandon, 171, 174
television
    cross-dressing on, 1092–1093
    gay-themed programming in, 1063
television comedy
    Black gay men in, 831–832
    televisual sexualities in, 832–835
television studies
    crypto-normativity and, 817–819
    market conditions and, 815–817
    outsider outlook and, 813–815
    queer, 810–813
        queerness for television in Western Europe, 823–825
        for Western Europe, 819–821
televisual sexualities, 832–835
temporal covariation, 1174
temporal displacement, 220–221
temporality. *See also* queer temporalities
    AIDS crisis impact and, 211
    comics and, 1002–1003
    generational connections and, 222–224
    queer, 209–211
    queer memory and, 179
    straight, 215
temporal synchrony, 1174–1176
Tendencies (Sedgwick), 974
"Teoria Queer" (Louro), 5
TERF. *See* trans-exclusionary radical feminist
Terrorist Assemblages (Puar), 874–877, 889, 892–893
The Testaments (Atwood), 1113
testimonios, 408–410
Testo Junkie (Preciado), 535
Text and Performance Quarterly (journal), 417–418, 464–465, 696
TGRC. *See* Transgender Resource Center of New Mexico
Thailand, 53–54
Thais-Williams, Jewel, 803
theories in the flesh, 410–411, 475
thick(er) intersectionalities, 120
thick intersectional theory (TI), 427, 444–445, 474–475
"Thinking Sex" (Rubin), 572–573
Third World Feminism, 410
13 Reasons Why (television series), 956
This Bridge Called My Back (Anzaldúa and Moraga), 410
Thoits, Peggy, 768–769
Thomas, Marquita, 1081
Thompson, Julie, 174–175

Thompson, Kenan, 1093–1094
Thorfinnsdottir, Dia, 820
Thornton, S., 1045
thought bubbles, 996–997
334 (Disch), 1121
Three Dollar Cinema, 1068
"Throw That Boy Pussy" (song), 693
Thuis (television series), 378–379
TI. *See* thick intersectional theory
The Tiger Flu (Lai), 1128–1129
Le Tigre, 1081
TikTok, 72, 906–907, 909, 1051
    algorithms of, 914–915
    coming-out videos on, 919–920
    #OkBoomer hashtag, 915
    presentation of self on, 910–911
    shadowbanning and, 908–909
time
    norms of, 210–211
    politics of, 209–211
    straight, 213–214
Time Binds (Freeman), 212–213
time-lagged interdependence, 1176
Time of Out Joint, 643–644
The Time Traveler's Wife (Niffenegger), 1133
Tinkuy (character), 65
TLA Releasing, 806
Tobias, Herbert, 546–547
Toklas, Alice B., 945–946
Toledo, Sérgio, 15
tolerance, 769
Tom of Finland (documentary), 1035–1036
"Tomorrow Belongs to Me" (song), 218–219
"Tomorrow Be-longs to Us" (song), 218–219
Tongues Untied (film), 793–794
tongzhi, 25–27, 971–976
    class-based visibility and, 36–37
    coming home and, 348–349
    masking tactic, 347
    safe space needs, pink market exploitation of, 34–36
    subject formation
        in emerging PRC market economy, 28–30
        Hong Kong and pink economy importance of, 30–31
        Taiwan and pink economy centrality to, 31–32
    transcultural media and activism, 973
Too Wong Foo Thanks for Everything! Julie Newmar (film), 389–390
Tortorici, Zeb, 64
"Towards a Politics of Sexuality" (conference), 572–573
"Towards a Queer Homeland" (conference), 404
tranifestation, 501

Trans* (Halberstam), 235
trans activism, 502–504
trans aging, 392–393
Transamerica (film), 1021
Transangelic Exodus (album), 1083–1084
Trans Buddy Program, 313
transcultural *tongzhi* media and activism, 973
Trans Empowerment Group, 1188
"Trans Entities" (documentary), 509
trans-exclusionary radical feminist (TERF), 504, 923, 1123
transfeminisms, 496–498, 512
    intersectionality and, 499–501
    necropolitics and activism, 502–504
    ontology and, 501–502
    refusing neoliberal capitalist logics of nation-statehood, 507–510
    shared corporeal quandaries of Blackness and transness, 501–504
transformation
    Jotería Studies and, 422
    resistance as, 1245
    RuPaul's Drag Race and, 1098–1099
Transgender Day of Visibility, 902
Transgender Dysphoria Blues (album), 1083–1084
transgender healthcare, 268
Transgender Nation, 188
transgender people
    closet at work and, 1215
    disclosure at work and, 436
    familial rejection of, 663–664
    family adjustment and, 665
    homonormativity and, 154–155
    in India, 47
    medical education and, 261
    in military, 725
    organizational research and, 1209
    parental reactions to coming out, 627–628, 667
    queer and, 1192
    RDT and, 633
    reproduction and, 710
    sexual communication research and, 751
    in Singapore, 47–48
    social media and, 907–908
Transgender Resource Center of New Mexico (TGRC), 448–449
transgender studies, Black feminisms and, 498–501
Transgender Studies Quarterly (journal), 1224–1225
transgender subjectivity, 1102–1105
transing, 695
    intersectionality and, 478
    linguistic practices in, 511
    music culture, 1083–1084

TransLatin@ Coalition, 419–420
translation, embodied, 477–478
Translocas (La Fountain-Stokes), 87
trans men, social media and, 490–492
trans* movements, 504–507
transnational and diasporic queer families, 112
    blurring first/third world binary and, 112–113
    futures and, 113
transnational and diasporic sexualities, 108–109
    heteronormativity and Western hegemony and, 110–112
    themes in, 109–113
transnational communication, 122–124
transnational homonormativity, 160–162
transnational identities, 122–124
transnationalism, 106
transnational queer, 124–126
    coming out discourse critique and, 344
transnational queer identities, 122–124
transnational queer networks
    decisions and paths to migration, 67–69
    media and
        geolocative turn, 67
        history of, 64–67
        online transition, 66–67
    predigital media and, 65–66
    settling in after migration and, 69–71
transnational queer translations, 117–118
    cultural identity formations and, 120–122
    queer diverse visibility and, 118–120
transnational women's rights organizing, 708
transness, subversive grammars of, 511–512
Transparent (television series), 218, 814
transphobia, 424–425
    terminology of, 431
transphobic violence, 713–714
Trans Queer Pueblo, 1192–1193
Transsexual Menace, 188
TransTech, 502
transvestism, 1091–1094
trauma archives, 1233
travesti community, 1097
Travis, John, 859
Travolta, John, 16, 1090
Treasure (documentary), 803
Treasure Island Media, 855
treatment as prevention (TaSP), 248
Treichler, Paula, 188
Trevisan, João Silvério, 12–15
triads, 555
Tribe 8, 1080
triple invisibility, 392
triple jeopardy effect, 328

Triton (Delaney), 1121
Tropiano, Stephen, 833, 836–837, 842
Tropicana, Carmelita, 419–420
troubles talk, 770
True Blood (television series), 814
True History (Lucian of Samosata), 1118–1119
Trump, Donald, 412–413, 577–578, 725
    anti-LGBTQ+ marriage legislation and, 524
    EEOC and, 427–428
    Muslim Band, 892
    protests against, 620
    transgender policies and, 923
Truth, Sojourner, 505
Truvada, 285–286
Tubman, Harriet, 1129
Tuck, Eve, 1253–1254
Tumblr, 314, 909–910, 915–916, 925
    online community and, 924–925
    tagging function, 914–915
    trans youth cultures and, 921
Tune in, Log on (Baym), 1054
Tupinambás, 4
twinks, 859
Twitter, 66–67, 229–230, 232, 236, 650–651, 725, 924–925, 1049
    performativity and, 1098–1099
two-faced racism, 71
Tyburczy, Jennifer, 585
Tziallas, Evangelos, 487

Ubiquitous Listening (Kassabian), 1056
Uganda, 645–646, 882–883, 1157–1158
    anti-LGBT laws in, 638–639
Los últimos homosexuales (Meccia), 82
Um Cinema Brasileiro Antropofágico (Ramos, G.), 13–14
UN. *See* United Nations
UNAIDS. *See* Joint United Nations Program on AIDS
The Unbreakable Kimmy Schmidt (television series), 835, 837–839
underground economy work, 445
    sex work as, 578
Undocuqueer movement, 422, 446
UndocuQueers, 147–148
Undoing Gender (Butler, J.), 212
Unflattening (Sousanis), 994
U.N. Fourth World Conference on Women, 648
ungendering, 499
United in Anger (documentary), 1234–1235
United Lesbians of African Heritage, 1081
United Nations (UN), 249, 254, 287
    Committee on the Elimination of Racial Discrimination, 708

United States
    Christian right movements, 641–642
    conservative evangelicals and, 641
    homonationalism and, 892, 897–899, 901–902
    LGBT history in military of, 723–725
    LGBTQ+ marriage in, 522
United States-Mexico border, 403–404
United States Transgender Survey (USTS), 296–298, 429, 438
United States v. Windsor, 522, 724–725
universal homosexuality, 158–159
An Unkindness of Ghosts (Solomon), 1125–1126
Unlimited Intimacy (Dean), 854
Uranian Worlds (Garber and Paleo), 1120
U.S. citizenship
    disidentification and resisting and subverting, 142–144
    DREAMers and, 147
U.S. Civil War, memory boom and, 170
U.S. Conservative Evangelical Churches, 641
U.S. exceptionalism, 160
U.S. television production, 812
    queer scholarship and, 813–815
USTS. *See* United States Transgender Survey
U.S. Women of Color Coalition for Reproductive Rights, 708

Vagina Monologues (Ensler), 505, 585
Valencia, Sayak, 503–504
Valeri, Robin, 376
Valkenburg, Patti M., 864
Vampyros Lesbos/Lesbian Vampires (film), 94–95
Van Dijck, J., 1049
Van Gilder, Bobbi, 474–475
VanHaitsma, Pamela, 175, 180, 700, 940
    on letters, 945–946
Vanlee, Florian, 1063, 1071
VAR. *See* vector autoregressive model
Variation (bar), 35, 39–40
Vats, Anjali, 698
vaudeville, 1078
vector autoregressive model (VAR), 1176
Velvet Goldmine (film), 1032
Venkatesh, Vinodh, 86
Venus Plus X (Sturgeon), 1120–1121
Vera (film), 15
Verbotene Liebe (television series), 819–820
vernacular culture, 547
vernacularization, 546–548
Verne, Jules, 1118–1119
V for Vendetta (Moore), 1116
VH1, 139–140, 1094–1095

VHS revolution, 862–863
Via Appia (film), 15
Viacom, 1067–1068
Viajes Virales (Meruane), 5–6
videographic essays, 1070
Vilela, Rosario Sánchez, 1020
de Villiers, Nicolas, 862
Vinagre, Gustavo, 19
"The Violence of Heteronormativity" (Yep), 153–154, 690
Violence on the Land, Violence on Our Bodies, 1252–1253
violent rejection, 663–664
Violetas de España (film), 94–95
virginity loss, 960
Virtual English (Enteen), 1053
Virtual Intimacies (McGlotten), 488
virtual platforms, 681
virtual spaces, 485–486
Visage, Michelle, 1102
visibility
  economies of, 40–41
  heteronormativity and, 154
  lack of diverse queer, 118–120
  politics of, 40–41
  queer representations and, 196
visual culture
  online, 486
  pain in, 546–547
visual rhetoric, 991–992
Viteri, María Amelia, 84–85
vlogging, 491–492, 919, 921–922
La volonté de savoir (*The Will to Knowledge*) (Foucault), 191–192
Von Praunheim, Rosa, 821–822
Vox, 91
V relationships, 555
VRT, 821–822, 1066–1067
VSA model. *See* vulnerability-stress-adaptation model
vulnerability-stress-adaptation model (VSA model), 326–327

Wagadu (journal), 422
Wajcman, J., 1048
Walden, Tillie, 1116
Walker, Alice, 410, 417–418, 797, 1246
Walters, Suzanna Danuta, 816–817, 834–837
Walton, Jo, 1132–1133
Wandel, Rich, 833
WAP. *See* Women Against Pornography
Ward, Jane, 856

Warner, Mark, 367, 687–688
  queer worldmaking and, 689–690, 697
Warner, Michael, 188–190, 585
  racialization and, 1249–1250
Warner, Sara, 586
war on terror, 875, 889, 892
Warren, Calvin, 501–502
Was (Ryman), 1124
The Watermelon Woman (film), 795
Waters, John, 16, 687–688, 1090
Watts, Eric King, 178
Waugh, Thomas, 484, 850, 852
WAVAW. *See* Women Against Violence Against Women
WAVMP. *See* Women Against Violence in Pornography and Media
Wayans, Damon, 837–838
Wayfarer series (Chambers), 1130
WDR, 821–822
We are here (documentary), 1035
"We are not Trayvon Martin" blog, 141–144
Web 2.0, 66–67
webcam modeling, 568, 575–576
websites, 483
  commercial, 486
  dating, race and racism and, 487–489
The Wedding Banquet (film), 56–57, 422
Wei, John, 919–920
Weissman, David, 1031
Wei Wei, 343
Wells, H. G., 1118–1119
Wergeland, Agnes, 170
"We Speak for Ourselves" (conference), 404
West, Cornell, 795
West, Isaac, 583, 698
West, Thomas J., 1032
Westcott, Clare N., 860
Western hegemony, 110–112
Western mythos, 174
Western queer formations, 46–49
We were here (documentary), 1031
WhatsApp, 923–924
What's the Tee? (podcast), 1102
What to Expect When You're Expecting, 1153
wheelchair rugby, 239
When Health Isn't Caring survey, 296–297
"When You're Invisible in Pop Culture" (Xunise and Coffey, S.), 1000–1001
"White" Asians, 54
White gayness, 832–835
Whitehead, Joshua, 1120
white individualism, 159
Whiteley, Sheila, 1045–1047, 1076–1077

whiteness, 831
  disidentification and resisting and subverting, 142–144
  expansion of, 159
  homonationalism and, 891
  homonormative, 158–160
  organizational communication scholarship and, 450
White supremacists, 680
whitewashing, 1125–1126
WHO. *See* World Health Organization
Wiedlack, Katharina, 1077–1078
Wikström, P., 1055
Wilde, Oscar, 170, 174–175, 179, 934–935, 1079, 1131
Wilders, Geert, 880
Wildmon, Donald E., 793
The Wild Swans (Kerr), 1124–1125
Will & Grace (television show), 7, 196–197, 389–390, 818, 831, 834
Williams, Linda, 847, 849
Williams Institute, 296–298, 428–429
Willingness to Engage in Consensual Non-Monogamy Scale, 552–553
Willis, P., 1043
Wilz, Kelly, 584–585
The Wire (television series), 217–218, 815–816, 844
Wittgenstein, Ludwig, 168
The Wizard of Oz (film), 215–216, 792, 1124
WMLA. *See* Women's Liberation Music Archive
Wolfenden Report, 1120
WolfeOnDemand, 805–806
Wolfe Video, 805
A Woman (film), 1091
WomaNews (newspaper), 997
womanism, 410, 417–418
The Womanist Reader, 421
Woman on the Edge of Time (Piercy), 1128, 1133–1134
Women Against Pornography (WAP), 571
Women Against Violence Against Women (WAVAW), 571
Women Against Violence in Pornography and Media (WAVMP), 571
women's festivals, 1081
Women's Liberation Movement, 570–571
Women's Liberation Music Archive (WMLA), 1081
Women's March of 2017, 620
Women's Music Festivals, 1082
Women's Studies in Communication (journal), 649
Womongold, Marcia, 571
Wong, Andrew, 27, 978–979
Wood, Alexander, 174–175, 939–940
Wood, Julia T., 1188–1189
Wood, Robert D., 832–833
Woods, Carly, 172–173
Woolf, Virginia, 945–946
The Word is Out (documentary), 1035–1036
work
  cisheteronormativity structuring relationships in, 437–438
  closet and, 433
    queering, 1214–1216
  disclosure at, 432–437, 450
    navigating complexities of, 435–437
  heteronormativity at, 424
  interpersonal relationship navigation at, 437–440, 450–451
  intersectional experiences, 444–449
  intersectional organizing and, 447–449
  outing and, 434–435
  passing and, 433–434
  queering gender and sexuality at, 1208–1210
worker protection laws, 427–429
work-family policy, 437–438
working closet, 433
workplace
  coming out and, 356
  cultures in, 438
  hostile communication in, 438–439
  inclusive and exclusive policies, 440–444
  nondiscrimination policies and, 356
  policies in, microaggressions and, 426
  policy dissemination, 442–443
workplace discrimination, 425–432
  actions for change, 431–432
  material consequences of, 429–430
  microaggressions and, 425–427
  policies for counteracting, 441
  worker protection laws and, 427–429
World Health Organization (WHO), 287, 551n.8, 642
  definitions for sexual health and safer sex, 278
  PrEP and, 285–286
worldmaking
  disidentification and, 144–145, 692–693
  queer
    academia as site for, 698–700
    in communication studies, 690–691
    defining, 688–690
    limitations and future directions for research, 700–701
    memories, monuments, and archives, 698–700
    origins of, 686–688
    worlds and themes in, 691–700
  queer futurity and, 693–694
  queer utopia and, 693–694
World Pride, 93

World War I, memory boom and, 170
World War II, 537
"The World Well Lost" (Sturgeon), 1120–1121
Wright, Katherine Fairfax, 802–803
Wright, Paul J., 851–852
writing back, 1244–1245
Wynter, Sylvia, 506

Xavier, Ismail, 8
Xenogenesis trilogy (Butler, O.), 1132
xenophobia, homophobia and, 67
xianshen, 347–348
xochihua, 64
Xochipilli, 411–412
Xu, Yanrui, 981–982
Xunise, Bianca, 1000–1002

Yale Journal of Law and Feminism, 855
Yam, Sharon, 708
Yan Daudo, 637–638
Yang, K. Wayne, 1253–1254
Yang, Ling, 981–982
Yellow Fever (film), 56–57
Yep, Gust, 117–118, 120–121, 153–154, 223–224,
    444–445, 472, 474–476, 478–479, 646–647,
    651, 843–844
  on Anzaldúa, 1246–1247
  on embodied translation, 477
  on heteronormativity in communication studies, 690,
    694–695, 1186–1187
  queer worldmaking and, 690–691
Yew, Chay, 1225–1226
Yogyakarta Principles, 72
Yo la peor de todas (film), 85–86
Yoruba, 500

Youhua Haoshuo (television program), 973
Young Queers United for Empowerment, 404
Young Soul Rebels (film), 796
youth/adult logics, 223
youth cultures, sexuality and, 907–908
youthism, 390–391
YouTube, 66–67, 216–217, 491–492, 805–806, 906–913,
    924–925, 1051–1052
  coming-out videos on, 918–921
  It Gets Better campaign and, 913
  online community and, 924–925
  performativity and, 1098–1099
  trans community on, 911–912
  trans youth cultures and, 921–922
Yue, Audrey, 977–978
Yuran, Noam, 575

Zahara Benet, BeBe, 1101
Zamora, Pedro, 687–688
Zapata, Angie, 174, 178
Zapatistas, 507
Zenne Dancer (film), 880, 1016
Zerolo, Pedro, 91–92
Zero Patience (musical), 1124–1125
Zhang, Qing, 27
Zhang, Qingfei, 972
Zhang, Xiaoling, 981
Zhao Jing, 1035
Zheng, Xiqing, 981–982
Ziegler, Kortney Ryan, 802
zines, 991–994
Zinn, Howard, 994, 1224–1225
zi shu nu, 419
zoom bombing, 680
Zouhali-Worrall, Malika, 802–803